June 4–6, 2014
Kyoto, Japan

Association for
Computing Machinery

Advancing Computing as a Science & Profession

ASIA CCS'14

Proceedings of the 9th ACM Symposium on Information, Computer and Communications Security

Sponsored by:

ACM SIGSAC

Association for
Computing Machinery

Advancing Computing as a Science & Profession

The Association for Computing Machinery
2 Penn Plaza, Suite 701
New York, New York 10121-0701

ISBN: 978-1-4503-2800-5 (Digital)

ISBN: 978-1-4503-3081-7 (Print)

Additional copies may be ordered prepaid from:

ACM Order Department
PO Box 30777
New York, NY 10087-0777, USA

Phone: 1-800-342-6626 (USA and Canada)
+1-212-626-0500 (Global)
Fax: +1-212-944-1318
E-mail: acmhelp@acm.org
Hours of Operation: 8:30 am – 4:30 pm ET

Printed in the USA

Welcome to ASIACCS 2014!

It is our great pleasure to welcome you to the 9th ACM Symposium on Information, Computer and Communications Security – *ASIACCS '14*, which will be held in Kyoto, Japan, June 3-6, 2014. The inaugural ASIACCS was held in Taipei (2006). Since then ASIACCS have been held in Singapore (2007), Tokyo (2008), Sydney (2009), Beijing (2010), Hong Kong (2011), Seoul (2012), and Hangzhou (2013).

ASIACCS is a major international forum for information security researchers, practitioners, developers, and users to explore and exchange the newest cyber security ideas, breakthroughs, findings, techniques, tools, and experiences. We welcome submissions from academia, government, and industry presenting novel research on all theoretical and practical aspects of computer and network security.

The conference received a record of 255 paper submissions, and accepted 42 regular papers and 8 short papers for presentation at the conference. The final versions of the accepted papers, which the authors finalized on the basis of comments from the reviewers, were included in the proceedings. Each accepted paper was carefully reviewed by at least three program committee members on the basis of its significance, novelty, and technical quality. The reviewing process was double-blind. It was followed by a web-based discussion. Based on the comments and scores given by reviewers, the final decisions on acceptance were made.

This year we have an excellent and diverse conference agenda with sessions on software security, network security, cryptography, and various applications of cryptography, among others. Unique papers on various kinds of authentication methods are mixed with papers on new advances on important research problems, such as Android security. In addition, we also encourage attendees to attend the keynote:

- *Fighting malicious code - An eternal struggle,* Christopher Kruegel of UC Santa Barbara

Putting together *ASIACCS '14* was a team effort. We first thank the authors for providing the content of the program. We are grateful to the program committee, who worked very hard in reviewing papers and providing feedback for authors. Finally, we thank the National Institute of Information and Communications Technology (NICT), Kyushu University, and Ritsumeikan University, Japan, for hosting the conference.

Enjoy the conference!

Trent Jaeger
ASIACCS '14 PC Co-Chair
Penn State University, USA

Kouichi Sakurai
ASIACCS '14 PC Co-Chair
Kyushu University, Japan

Shiho Moriai
ASIACCS '14 General Chair
NICT, Japan

Table of Contents

Session 4: Applications 1

Session 5: Crypto

Session 6: Access Control and Flow Analysis

Session 7: Software and Systems Security

Session 11: Short 1 — Network

Session: 12: Short 1 — Software

9th ACM Symposium on Information, Computer and Communications Security (ASIACCS 2014)

Honorary Chair: Koji Nakao, *(NICT/KDDI, Japan)*

General Chair: Shiho Moriai *(NICT, Japan)*

Program Chairs: Trent Jaeger *(Penn State University, USA)*
Kouichi Sakurai *(Kyushu University, Japan)*

Workshop Chair: Vinod Ganapathy *(Rutgers University, USA)*

Poster Chair: Miyako Ohkubo *(NICT, Japan)*

Local organizing Chair: Tetsutaro Uehara *(Ritsumeikan University, Japan)*

Publicity Chair: Ryo Nojima *(NICT, Japan)*

Financial Chair: Sachiko Kanamori *(NICT, Japan)*

Steering Committee Chair: Robert Deng *(SMU, Singapore)*

Steering Committee: Shiuhpyng Shieh *(NCTU, Taiwan)*
Elisa Bertino *(Purdue University, USA)*
Mike Reiter *(University of North Carolina at Chapel Hill, USA)*
Ninghui Li *(Purdue University, USA)*
Li Gong *(Mozilla Online Ltd., USA)*
Vijay Varadharajan *(Macquarie University, Australia)*
Kouichi Sakurai *(Kyushu University, Japan)*
Elena Ferrari *(University of Insubria, Italy)*
Dieter Gollmann *(Hamburg University of Technology, Germany)*
Yi Mu *(University of Wollongong, Australia)*
Dong Hoon Lee *(Korea University, Korea)*
Duncan Wong *(City University of Hong Kong, Hong Kong)*
Dongdai Lin *(Institute of Information Engineering, Chinese Academy of Sciences, China)*
Giovanni Russello *(University of Auckland, New Zealand)*
Atsuko Miyaji *(Japan Advanced Institute of Science and Technology)*

Program Committee: Gail-Joon Ahn *(Arizona State University, USA)*
Joonsang Baek *(Khalifa University of ST&R, UAE)*
Elisa Bertino *(Purdue University, USA)*
Ioana Boureanu *(EPFL, Switzerland)*
Kevin Butler *(University of Oregon, USA)*
Justin Cappos *(NYU Polytechnic University, USA)*
Alvaro Cardenas *(UT Dallas, USA)*
Kefei Chen *(Shanghai Jiaotong University, China)*
Liqun Chen *(HP Labs, UK)*
Sherman S. M. Chow *(Chinese University of Hong Kong, China)*
Michael Clarkson *(George Washington University, USA)*
Matthew Fredrikson *(University of Wisconsin, Madison, USA)*
Debin Gao *(Singapore Management University, Singapore)*
Thomas Gross *(University of Newcastle, UK)*
Guofei Gu *(Texas A&M University, USA)*
Ragib Hasan *(University of Alabama, Birmingham, USA)*
Sushil Jajodia *(George Mason University, USA)*
Xuxian Jiang *(North Carolina State University, USA)*
Ruediger Kapitza *(TU Braunschweig, Germany)*
Stefan Katzenbeisser *(TU Darmstadt, Germany)*
Hiroaki Kikuchi *(Meiji University, Japan)*
Dong Seong Kim *(University of Canterbury, New Zealand)*
Engin Kirda *(Northeastern University, USA)*
Xuejia Lai *(Shanghai Jiaotong University, China)*
Ruby Lee *(Princeton University, USA)*
Chin-Laung Lei *(National Taiwan University, Taiwan)*
Jiangtao Li *(Intel Corporation, USA)*
Ninghui Li *(Purdue University, USA)*
Yingjiu Li *(Singapore Management University, Singapore)*
Zhichun Li *(NEC Labs, USA)*
Zhiwei Li *(UC Berkeley, USA)*
Zhenkai Liang *(National University, Singapore)*
Zhiqiang Lin *(UT Dallas, USA)*
Harsha Madhyastha *(UC Riverside, USA)*
Aziz Mohaisen *(Verisign Labs, USA)*
David Naccache *(Ecole Normale Suprieure, France)*
Daniela Oliveira *(Bowdoin College, USA)*
Xinming Ou *(Kansas State University, USA)*
Mathias Payer *(UC Berkeley, USA)*
Zachary Peterson *(Cal Poly SLO, USA)*
Michalis Polychronakis *(Columbia University, USA)*
Georgios Portokalidis *(Stevens Institute of Technology, USA)*
Christian Probst *(TU of Denmark, Denmark)*
Zhiyun Qian *(NEC Labs, USA)*
Kui Ren *(University of Buffalo, USA)*

Program Committee (continued):

Susmita Ruj *(University of Ottawa, Canada)*
Pierangela Samarati *(University of Milan, Italy)*
Nuno Santos *(MPI-SWS, Germany)*
Joshua Schiffman *(Advanced Micro Devices, USA)*
Micah Sherr *(Georgetown University, USA)*
Dongwan Shin *(New Mexico Tech University, USA)*
Christian Skalka *(University of Vermont, USA)*
Abhinav Srinistava *(AT&T Labs -- Research, USA)*
Angelos Stavrou *(George Mason University, USA)*
Willy Susilo *(University of Wollongong, Australia)*
Patrick Tague *(CMU Silicon Valley, USA)*
Gang Tan *(Lehigh University, USA)*
Mahesh Tripunitara *(University of Waterloo, Canada)*
Wen-Guey Tzeng *(National Chiao Tung University, Taiwan)*
Eugene Vasserman *(Kansas State University, USA)*
Hayawardh Vijayakumar *(Penn State University, USA)*
Huaxiong Wang *(Nanyang Technological University, Singapore)*
Rui Wang *(Microsoft Research, USA)*
Yuji Watanabe *(IBM Research, Japan)*
Guoliang Xue *(Arizona State University, USA)*
Danfeng Yao *(Virginia Tech University, USA)*
Moti Yung *(Google & Columbia University, USA)*
Fangguo Zhang *(Sun Yat-sen University, China)*
Jianying Zhou *(Institute for Infocomm Research, Singapore)*

Organizing Committee:

Lihua Wang *(NICT, Japan)*
Yoshinori Aono *(NICT, Japan)*
Naoyuki Shinohara *(NICT, Japan)*
Atsushi Waseda *(NICT, Japan)*
Le Trieu Phong *(NICT, Japan)*
Takashi Kurokawa *(NICT, Japan)*
Rie Yamagata *(NICT, Japan)*
Keita Emura *(NICT, Japan)*
Takuya Hayashi *(NICT, Japan)*

Sponsor: acm SIGSAC

Fighting Malicious Code – An Eternal Struggle

Christopher Kruegel
University of California, Santa Barbara
chris@cs.ucsb.edu

ABSTRACT

Despite many years of research and significant commercial investment, the malware problem is far from being solved (or even reasonably well contained). Every week, the main- stream press publishes articles that describe yet another in- cident where millions of credit cards were leaked, a large company discloses that adversaries had remote access to its corporate secrets for years, and we discover a new botnet with tens of thousands of compromised machines. Clearly, this situation is not acceptable, but why isn't it getting any better?

In this talk, I will discuss some of the reasons why the malware problem is fundamentally hard, and why existing defenses in industry are no longer working. I will then outline progress that researchers and industry have made over the last years, and highlight a few milestones in our struggle to keep malicious code off our computer systems. This part will not focus on advances related to the analysis of malicious code alone, but take a broader perspective. How can we prevent malicious code from getting onto our machines in the first place? How can we detect network communication between malware programs and remote control nodes? And how can we lower the benefits that attackers obtain from their compromised machines? Finally, I will point out a few areas in which I believe that we should make progress to have the most impact in our fight against malicious code.

ASIA CCS'14, June 4–6, 2014, Kyoto, Japan.
ACM 978-1-4503-2800-5/14/06.
http://dx.doi.org/10.1145/2590296.2590348

Categories and Subject Descriptors

D.4.6 [Security and Protection]: Invasive Software

Keywords

Intrusion/anomaly detection and malware mitigation

Speaker's Bio

Christopher Kruegel is a Professor in the Computer Science Dept. at the University of California, Santa Barbara. He is also a co-founder of Lastline, Inc., where he currently serves as the Chief Scientist. Christopher's research interests are computer and communications security, with an emphasis on malware analysis and detection, web security, and intrusion detection. He enjoys to build systems and to make security tools available to the public. Christopher has published more than 100 conference and journal papers. He is a recipient of the NSF CAREER Award, the MIT Technology Review TR35 Award for young innovators, an IBM Faculty Award, and several best paper awards.

Letting the Puss in Boots Sweat: Detecting Fake Access Points using Dependency of Clock Skews on Temperature

Fabian Lanze
University of Luxembourg
fabian.lanze@uni.lu

Andriy Panchenko
University of Luxembourg
andriy.panchenko@uni.lu

Benjamin Braatz
University of Luxembourg
benjamin.braatz@uni.lu

Thomas Engel
University of Luxembourg
thomas.engel@uni.lu

ABSTRACT

The only available IEEE 802.11 network identifiers (i. e., the network name and the MAC address) can be easily spoofed. Consequently, an attacker is able to fake a real hotspot and attract its traffic. By this means, the attacker can intercept, collect, or change users' traffic (often even if it is encrypted).

In this paper, we describe an efficient method for detecting the replacement of access points (APs) by passive remote physical device fingerprinting. The main feature of our fingerprinting approach is the clock skew—an unavoidable phenomenon that causes clocks to run at minuscule yet remotely observable different speeds—which is extracted from information contained in beacon frames. We are the first to achieve a high discriminability of devices by completely eliminating the fingerprinters' influence and considering the clock skew's dependency on temperature.

Finally, we develop a method for reliable detection of the presence of AP impostors that works without explicit temperature information. Compared to the best state-of-the-art approach, our method improves detection accuracy from about 30 % to 90 % without generating any traffic and requires less than one minute to collect a sufficient number of observations. Our approach yields a strong feature for passive remote physical device fingerprinting in wireless networks.

Categories and Subject Descriptors

C.2.0 [**COMPUTER-COMMUNICATION NETWORKS**]: General—*Security and protection*; C.2.3 [**COMPUTER-COMMUNICATION NETWORKS**]: Network Operations—*Public networks*

Keywords

Evil Twin Attack; Security; Wireless Access Point; Fake Access Point; 802.11; Device Fingerprinting; Clock Skew

ASIA CCS'14, June 4–6, 2014, Kyoto, Japan.
Copyright 2014 ACM 978-1-4503-2800-5/14/06 ...$15.00.
http://dx.doi.org/10.1145/2590296.2590333.

1. INTRODUCTION

In recent years, Internet usage shifted from fixed locations to mobile environments. Nowadays, people are used to being online all the time, independent of their location, using laptops, smartphones, or tablets. Wi-Fi access points (APs) offer fast and cost-effective Internet connectivity. They are available almost everywhere, in offices, on university campuses, and in public places such as cafés, shopping malls, hotels, or airports. Although mobile cellular networks (e. g., 3G) have gained an increasing influence, the importance of Wi-Fi networks remains crucial. Generally, they provide faster connectivity, offer service whenever mobile networks are unavailable, overloaded, or overpriced (e. g., in roaming). They are indispensable for devices that do not have hardware to access mobile cellular networks, e. g., laptops or many tablets.

The only identifiers provided by the IEEE 801.11 standard for a user to verify the authenticity of an AP are its SSID (i. e., the network name) and its BSSID (i. e., the MAC address). Since these can easily be spoofed, an attacker is able to fake an AP without the user being able to notice (in the literature/media, this attack is also know as *evil twin* [23, 9] and has gained recent attention[1]).

Once a user is connected to a faked AP, the attacker can mount various attacks, including interception, collection, or manipulation of transmitted data. This even remains possible if the user explicitly enables encryption, e. g., by using SSL. Since the attacker already established his AP as intermediary, he can easily act as man-in-the-middle. Nowadays, this does not require special skills as deployable tools such as SSLstrip[2] (which transparently removes SSL encryption) and BurpProxy[3] (which can create faked certificates on-the-fly) are freely available and easy to use. Since most users incautiously accept unsigned or wrongly-signed SSL certificates [26, 6], malicious access points are able to conduct man-in-the-middle attacks on encrypted traffic (i. e., can read and modify the data) and to hijack sessions.

The danger of the described attacks arises from their simplicity: All common mobile operating systems including Android and iOS are capable of creating a wireless AP. Hence, this process can be be performed directly from smartphones,

[1] `http://www.abc15.com/dpp/money/consumer/alerts/alert-thieves-create-fake-hotel-wi-fi-hot-spots-to-steal-your-information`
[2] `http://www.thoughtcrime.org/software/sslstrip/`
[3] `http://portswigger.net/burp/proxy.html`

without attracting the attention of anybody in the vicinity. Additionally, fully-automated tools are available that are capable of spoofing APs, e. g., *rfakeap*[4], *airsnarf*[5], *jasager*[6].

Hence, we focus on attackers who mount short-duration evil twin attacks by using off-the-shelf hardware. Scenarios where an attacker needs to extensively modify hardware components are therefore out of the scope of this work.

The methods described in the 802.11 Robust Secure Network Association (RSNA) specification propose to solve this problem with cryptographic primitives using an additional authentication server [14]. This requires careful setup and maintenance. Operators of open hotspots in particular have no incentive to deploy such a mechanism and, hence, the solution is rarely used. The usage of virtual private networks (VPNs) also does not provide a satisfactory solution to the problem as, besides similar certificate-based attacks like those on SSL, it is possible to kill the VPN session (e. g., by dropping management packets) so that the connection falls back to plain mode, typically without explicit notification.

Many public hotspots deploy a web-based authentication scheme which is additionally used for accounting of clients. Nevertheless, such a mechanism does not provide any security for the user at all. The attacker could simply clone the login page and accept any credentials. Furthermore the attacker learns the legitimate credentials provided by users for further misuse. If pre-shared key (PSK) based encryption (such as WPA) is applied and the attacker knows the PSK, he can still mount the attack. Note that for public hotspots the PSK must be distributed to clients by some means or another (e. g., on a receipt).

Therefore, there is a strong need to equip users with additional tools and methods for verification of the APs they connect to, in order to make sure that these are authentic and not traps operated by an attacker. In our targeted solution, a user has access to a trusted third party that verifies the fingerprint of an authentic hotspot. Consequently, there is a vital necessity for tools that enable remote device identification and can be applied to currently deployed networks without modifying standardized protocols and without requiring the AP operator to cooperate or modify the deployment.

In this paper, we focus on remote device fingerprinting based on *clock skews*. This is an unavoidable physical phenomenon that causes crystal oscillator based clocks to run with minuscule yet measurable deviations in speed. The frequencies of crystal oscillators are determined by their manufacturing properties (e. g., the cut angle) and the crystal type. Inevitable inaccuracies during the production process lead to slight variations of the frequency, even for crystals produced within the same series [11].

Clock skew is based purely on physical properties, which makes it an attractive feature for physical device fingerprinting. It is typically measured in *parts per million (ppm)*.

For measuring the clock skew of a remote clock, it is essential to have access to precise timestamps generated by that clock. In the Wi-Fi scenario we benefit from the fact that APs emit management frames (called *beacons*) at a high frequency. These frames contain a high-precision timestamp with microsecond resolution, which is used for the Timing Synchronization Function (TSF) to synchronize sending and receiving slots on the shared wireless medium in the IEEE 802.11 communication process. All stations in a basic service set (BSS), i. e., all clients associated with an AP, synchronize their local TSF timer to the time broadcasted in beacon frames. Beacon frames are usually sent every 100 ms. By specification, they are not subject to any delay before sending. Therefore, they serve as a reliable basis for clock skew estimation.

[4]`http://rfakeap.tuxfamily.org/`
[5]`http://airsnarf.shmoo.com/`
[6]`http://www.digininja.org/jasager/`

Contribution:

We present a novel approach to reliably detect a spoofed access point utilizing the fact that, in general, other APs are simultaneously reachable in the vicinity. In detail, our contributions are as follows:

- We are the first to intensively study the influence of changing room temperatures on APs' clock skews in the context of fingerprinting. As we will show, APs exhibit significantly different temperature dependency characteristics. By learning these, the discriminability of clock-skew-based fingerprints (in terms of recognition interval sizes) can be improved by more than 75 %.

- We completely eliminate the influence of the fingerprinter (both skew and its dependency on temperature) on the fingerprint. This allows comparison of fingerprints produced by arbitrary fingerprinters. We substantiate this claim mathematically.

- We develop a method for fake AP detection which exploits temperature dependency without the need for explicit temperature knowledge and which provides similar accuracy. Here, a manageably small number of around 50 training observations is sufficient.

- Finally, we are the first to propose a practical solution to detect faked APs with a high probability.

2. RELATED WORK

Due to the severity of the underlying problem, the field of *remote physical device fingerprinting* has attracted considerable research interest in recent years and several methods have been proposed. We distinguish between *active* and *passive* techniques.

Active techniques explicitly interact with the device that is fingerprinted, e. g., by sending regular or manipulated packets and evaluating the response. Inherently, such methods can be detected by the fingerprintee or even cause interference with the regular communication. Sieka [25] evaluates timing patterns in the authentication procedure of an AP using two different measuring devices for fingerprinting. Bratus et al. [3] propose a technique called active behavioral fingerprinting, which is based on malformed stimuli response, i. e., how devices react to non-standard and malformed 802.11 frames.

Passive methods, on the other hand, do not require any cooperation with other nodes as they merely observe passing traffic without interaction or modification. Hence, these methods are by design undetectable and do not interfere with the regular communication. Therefore, we direct our focus to passive techniques.

The accuracy of remote wireless device fingerprinting can be optimized to more than 99 % if dedicated hardware is applied. Using, e. g., *radio frequency fingerprinting (RFF)* [24, 10, 4] such techniques investigate physical properties of the radio signal with specialized measurement devices. However, these methods are not applicable in our context as we target methods that work on regular mobile clients, which are not equipped with such hardware.

Another class of passive approaches does not aim to identify unique devices (APs) but rather unique device types [8] or device driver types [7]. Those methods do not satisfy our requirement of differentiating between APs with the same hardware and firmware.

Bahl et al. [2] identify the presence of two APs with the same BSSID. The method uses sequence numbers in 802.11 frame headers but is not able to recognize which of the APs is faked and is only applicable if both APs are active simultaneously in a nearby location. Gonzales et al. [9] present two methods to protect against the evil twin attack. The first method (EAP-SWAT) requires modification of the deployed authentication protocols which, in general, is undesirable as all deployed APs would have to be adapted. The second method (context-leashing) aims to detect whether the set of simultaneously visible APs has significantly changed. It achieves a comparably high detection accuracy. Note that this method can only detect a specific variant of the attack, where the evil twin AP is set up at a different location than the legitimate AP. Neumann et al. [21] analyze fingerprints based on network parameters such as transmission time and frame inter-arrival time. The best recognition rates for wireless devices are 40%–60% in a laboratory setting and 20%–32% in real-world traces.

A more promising field of research for wireless fingerprinting utilizes the phenomenon called *clock skew*. Originating from the work of Moon et al. [20], Kohno et al. [17] introduce the concept of clock skew based remote device fingerprinting using the TCP Timestamps option in TCP headers [13] or ICMP packets, both having timing resolution in milliseconds. They estimate the clock skew with linear programming (LP). Clock skews are shown to be distinguishable among different physical machines yet stable over time. The approach requires support of the timestamp option and observing a TCP connection or ICMP packets over a longer period of time, while wireless APs cannot be directly accessed via TCP/ICMP in general.

In [27] clock-skew-based fingerprinting is applied to wireless sensor nodes (WSN). The results are not comparable to our work as the authors assume that the fingerprinter is always the same (sink node) and can be kept in a constant temperature environment. This does not hold true in our scenario. Yang et al. [30] analyze the impact of temperature on clock skew estimation to improve clock synchronization for WSNs and the authors observe that two clocks exhibit a stable relationship of clock skew w.r.t. temperature which is not necessarily linear. This complies with our findings regarding TSF clocks (see Section 6). However, unlike in our scenario, for WSNs there is no necessity to model this temperature dependency fingerprinter-independent.

Jana et al. [15] transfer the idea of Kohno et al. to the 802.11 scenario, estimating APs' clock skews from TSF timestamps in beacon frames. Instead of the LP method the authors use a least squares fit estimation (LSF), which is more efficient but also more sensitive to outliers, since fewer outliers compared to timestamps in TCP packets are to be expected. Moreover, the use of TSF data requires significantly smaller sample sizes due to higher clock resolution. To measure the receiving time of a beacon frame, a modified driver is used. The authors argue that it is not possible to fake the clock skew using software alone because of unpredictable sending delays due to Medium Access Control. In their work, fingerprints are not comparable between different fingerprinter machines (FPs) due to the influence of the fingerprinting device's own clock skew. Arackaparambil et al. [1] improve the accuracy by utilizing the FP's TSF timer as more precise clock source. However, their technique does not remove the skew of the fingerprinter card from the clock skew estimation and is only evaluated with two Wi-Fi chipsets of the same type. In our previous work [18], we presented a lightweight method for clock skew estimation based on TSF timestamps in beacon frames using an online version of the LSF estimation with high precision. Our tools do not rely on modified drivers or system components and therefore enable clock skew estimation for APs from arbitrary mobile clients. An NTP based method was presented to eliminate the influence of the fingerprinter's skew. However, clock skew variations of approx. ± 1ppm at different measuring times remained. Our survey of 388 APs shows roughly a normal distribution of clock skews within a range of -30 to 30 ppm. We concluded that the information content of clock skews alone is too limited and unique device fingerprinting using clock skews is not practically feasible for wireless access points due to its limited distinctiveness. Note, however that our evaluation did not consider the actual influence of environmental conditions such as temperature.

In general, no approach for wireless device fingerprinting has been able to identify 802.11 APs with acceptable detection ratios, while being performed from arbitrary mobile clients. We address this challenge and show that by including temperature information and applying state-of-the-art machine learning techniques, we are able to reliably detect the presence of faked APs. Moreover, we completely exclude the influence of the fingerprinter on the fingerprint. Our method successfully detects the replacement of an AP on a representative data set with an accuracy of 90%, thus, 60% better that the best approach known so far. This is done without actively generating any traffic and requires less than one minute to collect a sufficient number of observations.

3. CLOCK SKEW BACKGROUND

In this section, we describe physical and mathematical background of clock skews in time measuring hardware.

3.1 Quartz Oscillator Fundamentals

Common computer clocks (and thus the ones that operate the TSF timer in Wi-Fi chipsets) are based on crystal oscillators. The major component of a crystal oscillator is an anisotropic crystal formed from SiO_2 (quartz). Due to its piezoelectric properties a mechanical strain is produced in the crystal when exposed to an electric field. The resulting vibration enables the crystal to be used as resonator in an oscillator unit that can generate clock signals. Although other types of resonators exist, quartz has proven to be superior regarding the properties frequency stability, intrinsic loss, simplicity of production and cost. Hence, since many years, quartz oscillators have been the preferred medium satisfying the needs for precise frequency generation [16].

Crystal oscillator stability and accuracy is affected by physical and electrical factors, with temperature being one of the most significant. The dependency on temperature is primarily determined by the angle at which the crystal is cut with respect to the crystallographic axes during the manufacturing process [29]. Most common is the AT-cut. This crystal type exhibits a cubic dependency on temperature [31]. The turning point of this cubic function and the local extrema can be controlled by small variations of the cut angle. The inflection point is typically located at a temperature of 25 °C (77 °F) leading to highest stability at typical operating temperatures. More than 90% of all deployed crystal oscillators are based on an AT-cut crystal.

The described properties of crystal oscillators enable the vendors of Wi-Fi chipsets to select units that meet given specifications. For 802.11 devices, a frequency tolerance of ±25ppm is specified [12].

3.2 Mathematics of Clock Skews

We model (discretized) *true time* by the set $\mathbb{Z}$ of integers with an arbitrarily chosen zero point and measured in arbitrarily chosen units. A *clock* counts time steps from a (possibly different) zero point, i. e., it is a function $C\colon \mathbb{Z} \to \mathbb{Z}$, giving the mapping from true time t to the time $C(t)$ measured by the clock. Without loss of generality, we assume that all clocks have the same time step resolution as the unit chosen for true time—microseconds in our case[7].

For an ideal clock, the difference $C(t_2)-C(t_1)$ between two time measurements at points t_1 and t_2 in true time would always be $t_2 - t_1$. However, due to physical properties (see Section 3.1), clocks based on crystal oscillators exhibit a certain *offset*

$$\text{offset}_C(t_1, t_2) = [C(t_2) - C(t_1)] - [t_2 - t_1] \quad (1)$$

when measuring such time intervals (positive if the clock is too fast and negative if the clock is too slow). The *skew* s_C of a clock C between points t_1 and t_2 in true time is the slope of the offset between these points:

$$s_C(t_1, t_2) = \frac{\text{offset}_C(t_1, t_2)}{t_2 - t_1} = \frac{C(t_2) - C(t_1)}{t_2 - t_1} - 1 \quad (2)$$

Typically, it is not possible to measure the clock skew directly, since the fingerprinter's clock has its own non-negligible skew. Hence, there are two clocks: the clock C of the access point and the clock D of the fingerprinter. We observe both at points t_1 and t_2 in true time and compute a *subjective offset*

$$\text{offset}_{D,C}(t_1, t_2) = [C(t_2) - C(t_1)] - [D(t_2) - D(t_1)] \quad (3)$$

and a *subjective skew*:

$$s_{D,C}(t_1, t_2) = \frac{\text{offset}_{D,C}(t_1, t_2)}{D(t_2) - D(t_1)} = \frac{C(t_2) - C(t_1)}{D(t_2) - D(t_1)} - 1 \quad (4)$$

Figure 1 shows the offsets of two different access point clocks measured from two different fingerprinters at two different measuring times. The fingerprinters' skews lead to significantly different subjective skews for the same access point clocks. Moreover, we observe a small difference for the different measuring times.

[7]In fact, all clocks considered here, i. e., the TSF clock and the system clock, have this resolution.

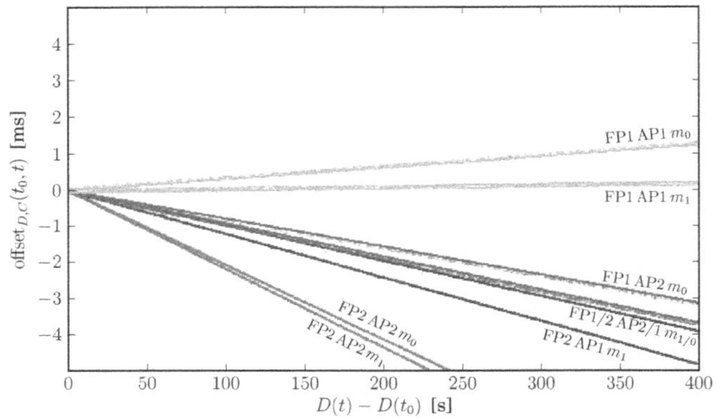

Figure 1: Subjective offsets of the clocks of two different access points (C = AP1 and C = AP2) measured from two different fingerprinters (D = FP1 and D = FP2) at two different measuring times ($t_0 = m_0$ and $t_0 = m_1$)

We can already see that (at least for short periods of time—in the range of several minutes) the offsets increase or decrease linearly. To overcome noise produced, e. g., by the communication hardware and the device drivers, we not only take the measurements at two border points (as in the mathematical formulae), but use all available measurements within a certain interval (several minutes for high precision). The skew is then approximated by the slope of a least squares fit (LSF) linear regression over these measurements. LSF has shown to be the superior method for the slope estimation in the described setting [18, 15].

The goal of the following sections is to eliminate the influence of the fingerprinters and model the influence of temperature on the access points in order to isolate the differences between access points and use them as a fingerprint. But first, we introduce our experimental setup and the resulting data set in the next section.

4. DATA SET

In this section, we describe our experimental setup. Our goal was to generate a representative data set containing APs from various vendors and a variety of fingerprinter machines. Therefore, we placed twelve different physical APs—2 AVM FritzBox 7050 (AP1–2), 1 LANCOM L-54G (AP3), 1 D-Link DAP-1360 (AP4), 2 Edimax EW-7228APn (AP5–6), 4 Linksys WRT54GL (AP7–10) and 2 Netgear WG602v4 (AP11–12)—in a dedicated room, all operating on the same channel (for simplicity of data collection). We induced different room temperatures by turning the heating off/on or opening/closing the windows from time to time. We measured the room temperature with a Voltcraft DL-181THP data logger. To measure the clock skew of the APs we used four different fingerprinter machines. All were customary laptops running Ubuntu 10.10. Beacons were sniffed using the modified scapy library proposed in [18].

The experiment was performed over about four weeks. The temperature conditions of our experimental environment are shown in Figure 2, and, as depicted cover all temperatures that are typically to be expected in non-airconditioned indoor settings, i. e., between 17–27 °C. We deliberately created periods where the temperature remained

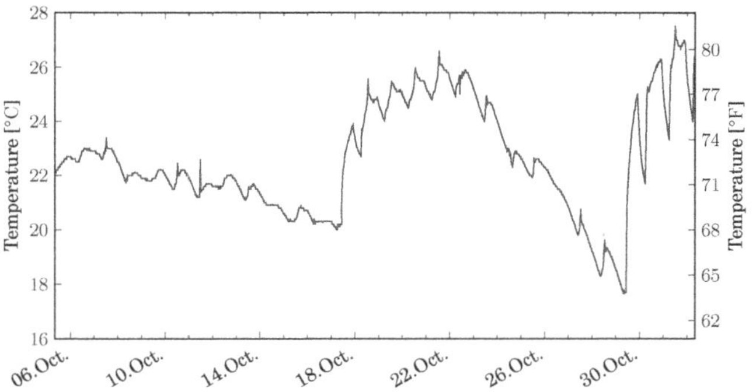

Figure 2: Temperature variation over time

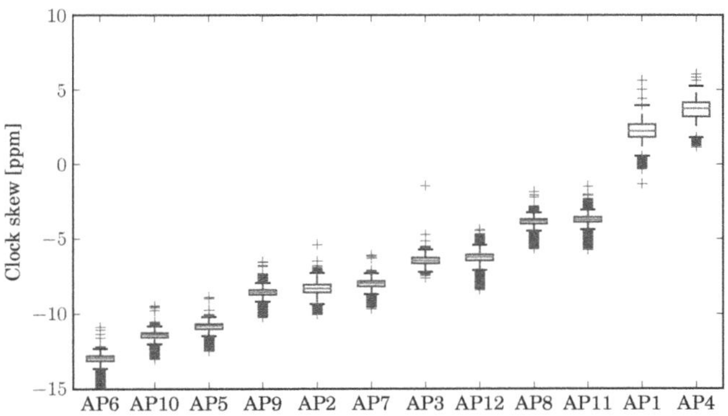

Figure 3: Clock skews (NTP corrected) of the access points in our data set

relatively stable over several days (e. g., weeks 1–2) as well as others with multiple sudden temperature fluctuations (e. g., week 4).

We estimated the clock skew of the twelve APs from the four FP machines for all consecutive intervals with a duration of ten minutes each using LSF linear regression. Note that in practice much shorter intervals are feasible to obtain precise clock skew approximations. With the online algorithm for LSF proposed in [18], 30–80 seconds of beacon sniffing would be enough to obtain a sufficiently small margin of error for the skew approximation. However, we refrain from applying this method to achieve a very high accuracy.

The data logger measured the temperature with a specified accuracy of ±0.1 °C once per minute and we took the mean of the ten measurements as the room temperature for one estimation interval.

The distribution of the APs' clock skews in our sample is shown in the box plots of Figure 3. Here, we eliminated the FP's influence on the measurement using the NTP method (described in more detail in the following section). As we can see, most APs belong to groups of similar clock skews (e. g., AP9, AP2, and AP7 or AP8 and AP11). Hence, even in such a small sample of APs, there is already significant confusion between the APs based on their clock skews. In the following, we will show how to radically improve the uniqueness of clock skew based fingerprints and, hence, the discriminability of APs by considering the dependency of the clock skew on temperature. But before that, we describe how to eliminate the distortion caused by the fingerprinter.

5. FINGERPRINTER INFLUENCE

In this section, we briefly revisit the previously proposed and, up to now, only available method for eliminating the influence of the fingerprinters' own clock skews, i. e., the *NTP method* [18]. It relies on an *estimation of the fingerprinters' skews* from a Network Time Protocol (NTP) service running on the fingerprinters. We show why this approach is insufficient for examining the dependency of clock skews on temperature. We then introduce a novel approach, the *2AP method*, which is based on the observation that the fingerprinters' skews are cancelled when calculating *clock skew differences* between two measured access points. Hence, this method eliminates the fingerprinter influence by design.

The NTP method is based on the observation that, after rewriting equation (2) for the (objective) skews of access point and fingerprinter to

$$C(t_2) - C(t_1) = [1 + s_C(t_1, t_2)] \cdot (t_2 - t_1) \quad (5)$$
$$D(t_2) - D(t_1) = [1 + s_D(t_1, t_2)] \cdot (t_2 - t_1) \quad (6)$$

and employing this substitution in the equation for subjective skew (4), we obtain:

$$s_{D,C}(t_1, t_2) = \frac{s_C(t_1, t_2) - s_D(t_1, t_2)}{1 + s_D(t_1, t_2)} \approx s_C(t_1, t_2) - s_D(t_1, t_2) \quad (7)$$

The last approximation holds since $s_D(t_1, t_2)$ is in the range ±30 ppm and, hence, division by $1+s_D(t_1, t_2)$ will maximally be relevant in the fifth significant digit.

We can rewrite this equation again to

$$s_C(t_1, t_2) \approx s_{D,C}(t_1, t_2) + s_D(t_1, t_2) \quad (8)$$

and, thereby, have an expression of the (objective) skew of C in terms of the subjective skew of C as seen by D and (an approximation of) the (objective) skew of D. The latter is obtained from an NTP service running for 48 hours on each FP. In the following, we will call all skew approximations obtained according to this method *NTP corrected clock skews*.

If we apply this correction of subjective skews to the example from Figure 1, we obtain the situation shown in Figure 4. We can see that the influence of the FPs' clock skew is significantly reduced, while the APs' clock skew still diverges substantially at different measuring times. The remaining inaccuracies of the fingerprinter skew approximations (especially visible in the slightly different slopes at measuring time m_1) are due to the fact that the results are only corrected by the *average* skew of the fingerprinters. This imprecision is enough to render the NTP method inappropriate for examining temperature dependency, as will be shown below.

Our proposal to overcome this inaccuracy is to calculate the difference between the subjective clock skews of two access points measured at the same time. We utilize the fact that Wi-Fi hotspots are rarely alone in their coverage area. By performing the 2AP method, we completely remove the influence of the fingerprinter. The difference between the subjective skews of AP clocks C and C' as measured by FP clock D is equal to the difference of the corresponding (objective) clock skews (except for practically irrelevant de-

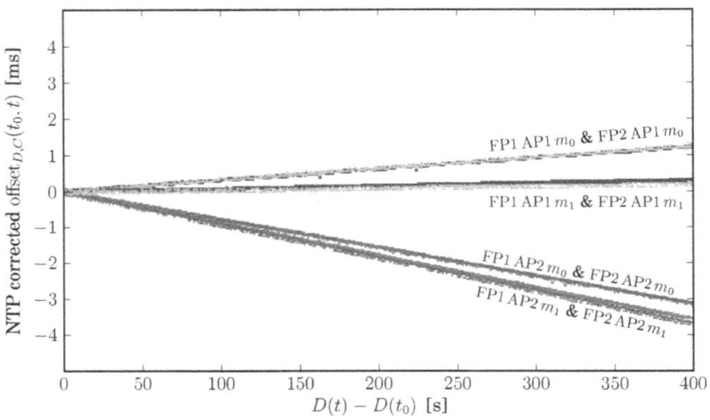

Figure 4: Subjective offsets from Figure 1 corrected by NTP method

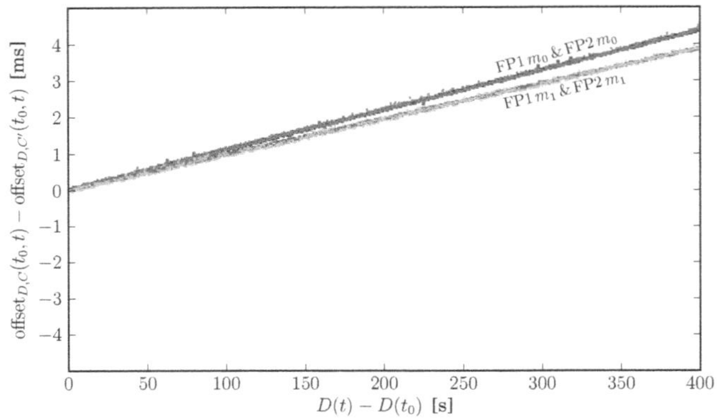

Figure 5: Offset differences of 2AP method (between C = AP1 and C' = AP2) for subjective offsets from Figure 1

viations), similarly to (7):

$$\begin{aligned} s_{D,C}(t_1,t_2) - s_{D,C'}(t_1,t_2) &= \frac{s_C(t_1,t_2) - s_{C'}(t_1,t_2)}{1 + s_D(t_1,t_2)} \\ &\approx s_C(t_1,t_2) - s_{C'}(t_1,t_2). \end{aligned} \tag{9}$$

Again, the last approximation holds since s_D is in the range ± 30 ppm and, hence, changes due to multiplication or division by $1 + s_D$ can be neglected.[8] In the following, we call all data obtained according to this method *2AP clock skew differences*, where we will without loss of generality always subtract the subjective skew of the AP with the lexicographically greater MAC address from that of the other.

In Figure 5, the offset differences of the clocks from Figure 1 are shown. We observe that taking these differences completely removes the influence of the fingerprinters' *current* skews and, hence, leads to values that are—in contrast to the NTP corrected skew approximations—*fully* comparable between different fingerprinters. The difference between the different measuring times is still visible and our main claim is that it is, to a large extent, due to the temperature dependency of the access points' clocks.

Using the 2AP method, we get meaningful values only for *pairs* of access points. Hence, it is at first ambiguous which of the two APs is responsible for a possible mismatch. Still, the information provided is essential. If more than two access points are visible then several or all possible pairs can be examined and a faked access point should lead to mismatches in significantly more of its pairs than the others. Moreover, the sole presence of a faked access point might be enough to render a whole environment untrustworthy or at least suspicious.

In Figure 6, we show samples of clock skew measurements as a function of temperature for two APs with the NTP method and the corresponding pair for the 2AP method, i.e., the approximate skews and skew differences in parts per million (ppm) of our ten minute measuring intervals are plotted over the average temperatures in these intervals. Apparently, the FPs have very distinct dependencies on temperature leading to different distributions of the data for the NTP method. These dependencies are intrinsic and cannot be modeled independently of the fingerprinter. Besides the variations caused by the FPs, the intrinsic temperature dependency characteristics of the APs are also clearly visible. As described above, for the 2AP method, only the APs' dependency on temperature remains, while the FPs' dependency is completely eliminated. Therefore, the 2AP method yields a fully fingerprinter-independent estimation of the clock skew differences and can be used to further examine the temperature dependency of the APs' clocks.

Accordingly, in the following section, we show how to model the temperature dependency for the 2AP method in order to drastically increase the fingerprinting accuracy. Finally, we will analyze the fake AP detection efficiency of our methods.

[8] Observe that this is, by equation (7), also approximately equal to the subjective skew $s_{C',C}(t_1,t_2)$ of access point C as seen by *access point* C'. Similar observations concerning clock skew arithmetic have been already made by Arackaparambil et al. [1], but not applied to eliminate fingerprinter influence.

6. TEMPERATURE DEPENDENCY

Theoretically, common crystal oscillators should exhibit a cubic dependency on temperature (see Section 3.1). However, our practical observations do not confirm this assumption. There are several possible reasons: Firstly, the cubic dependency is to be expected for crystal oscillators against the temperature of the crystal, while we measure the dependency of TSF clock skews on room temperatures. The dependency between room temperature and crystal temperature may be non-trivial, e. g., due to different (passive) cooling behavior of the AP. Besides, the regarded temperatures might cover only a small section of that cubic function. Secondly, there might be other physical influences that correlate with temperature and change the frequency and, hence, the skew. Thirdly, the crystals used in certain APs might not be AT-cut crystals that exhibit this cubic dependency (or suboptimal quality of the cuts might lead to a deviation from the theoretical properties).

Therefore, we use *Gaussian process regression (GPR)* [22], a method that does not make any assumptions about the underlying function and thus is suitable as a generic approach for modeling the dependency. The goal of our model is to predict values $f(x_*)$ of the clock skew difference of two APs that is to be expected at a given room temperature x_*. In general, a Gaussian process can represent $f(x)$ indirectly by considering the observed data. Each observation

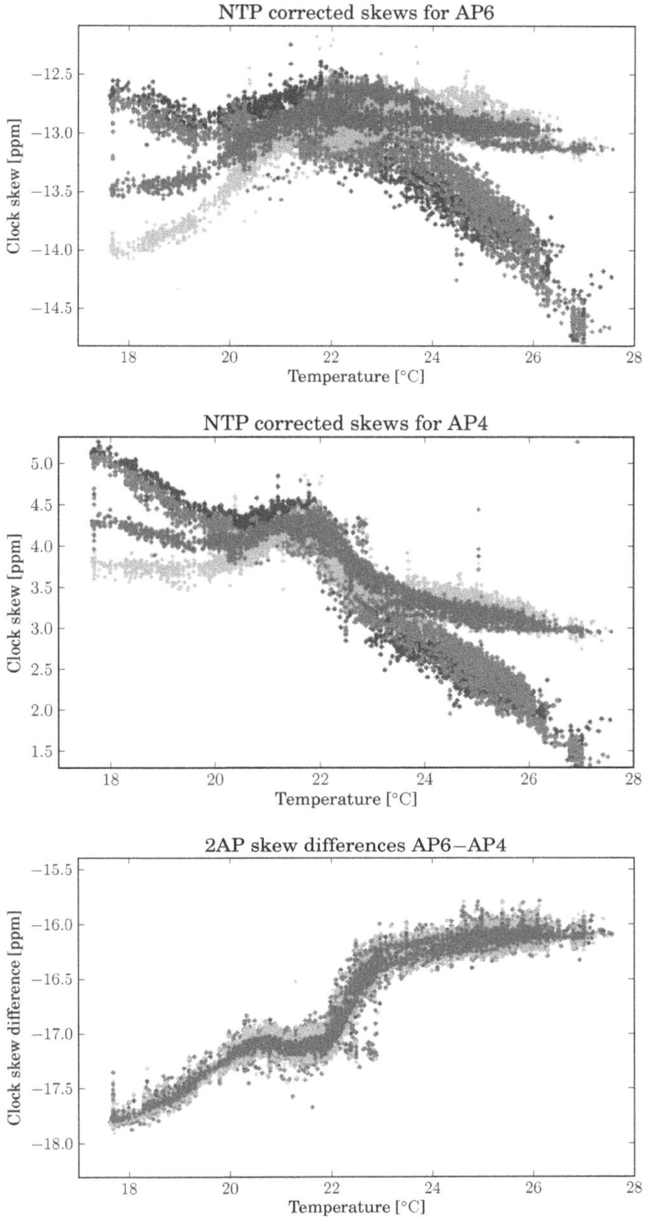

Figure 6: NTP-corrected clock skews and 2AP clock skew differences in relation to room temperature measured by four FPs (different colors)

$y_i \in \{y_1, ..., y_n\}$ for an input x_i is assumed to be a single point sampled from a multivariate Gaussian distribution, given by $y_i = f(x_i) + \varepsilon$, where $\varepsilon \sim \mathrm{N}(0, \sigma_n^2)$ is the additive noise term. A Gaussian process, specified by its mean function $m(x)$ (usually assumed to be zero) and the covariance function $k(x_p, x_q)$ can be used to define a prior over possible functions, $f \sim \mathrm{GP}(m(x), k(x_p, x_q))$. For the posterior distribution, the prior is restricted to contain only functions that meet the observed data. This is done by computing for each test input x_* a predictive mean $f(x_*)$, which is a linear combination of *all* training inputs and outputs built according to the covariance function, and a predictive variance $\mathbb{V}[f(x_*)]$, which only depends on the training inputs. GPR is designed to interpolate predictions for unobserved inputs. In practice, we have precomputed and stored the predictive mean and predictive variance for all temperatures needed in our evaluation with a granularity of 0.1 °C.

In our model, we use the *squared-exponential covariance function*

$$k(x_p, x_q) = \sigma_f^2 \exp\left(-\frac{1}{2\ell^2}(x_p - x_q)^2\right) + \sigma_n^2 \delta_{pq}$$

as it meets our requirements well: values whose inputs are close get a higher influence on the prediction, while distant observations have negligible effect; it is also infinitely differentiable, leading to smoothness of the generated predictions. It is parameterized by *hyperparameters* $\theta = (\sigma_f^2, \ell, \sigma_n^2)$, where σ_f^2 is the variance of the signal itself, ℓ is the length-scale and σ_n^2 is the expected variance of measurement noise. We estimate these hyperparameters by optimizing the marginal likelihood on our training data. For a detailed description we refer to Rasmussen and Williams [22].

Figure 7 shows examples for GPR applied to our data. We can see that the predicted mean functions perfectly fit our observed data. We verified that comparable predictions can be obtained using much smaller samples of about 100 observations.

When using clock skews (or clock skew differences) as fingerprints, suitable intervals for recognition (as shown in Figure 7) have to be defined due to the volatile nature of these measures. In the following section, we provide a formal definition of such recognition intervals.

7. EVALUATION OF PREDICTION

In this section, we first define recognition methods based on the results described above. We then evaluate the accuracy of these methods regarding fake AP detection. Finally, we provide an information theoretical perspective on temperature dependency as a feature for fingerprinting.

7.1 Recognition Intervals

In order to provide recognition methods for APs, we specify appropriate acceptance intervals of observed data for all considered methods. Regardless of the method, we classify 5% of our training data as outliers.

Therefore, we define this interval for the corrected skews of the NTP method and for the skew differences of the 2AP method as $\mu \pm 2\sigma$, where μ is the mean and σ the standard deviation of a normal distribution fitted to the training data. The NTP method directly allows the recognition of an AP, while the 2AP method needs at least one additional AP for comparison (as described in Section 5).

To apply temperature dependent skew difference predictions, we derive a new method, called *2AP-T*, that employs Gaussian process regression (as described in the previous section). Here, the recognition interval is specified by $f(x_*) \pm 2\sqrt{\mathbb{V}[f(x_*)]}$, where $f(x_*)$ is the predicted mean and $\mathbb{V}[f(x_*)]$ the predicted variance of the corresponding GPR, given the current room temperature x_*.

The properties of normal distribution and GPR ensure that the recognition intervals comprise about 95% of the training data.

To evaluate the discriminability of fingerprints generated by these three methods, we calculated their average recog-

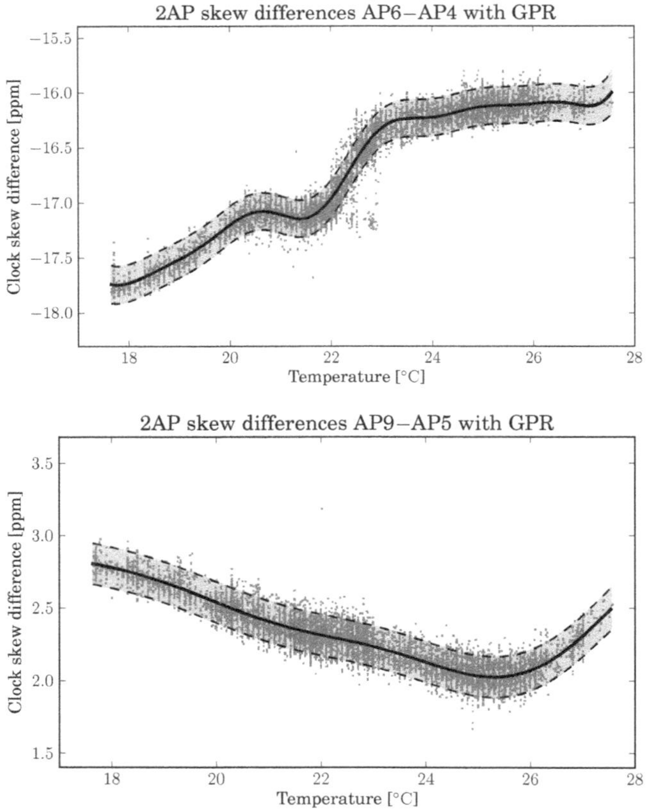

Figure 7: Two examples for GPR: pointwise mean prediction $f(x)$ ($\pm 2\sqrt{\mathbb{V}[f(x)]}$, corresponding to the 95 %-confidence region)

nition interval size. We obtained 1.73 ppm for the NTP method, 1.56 ppm for the 2AP method and 0.41 ppm for the 2AP-T method. The results reveal that the temperature-dependent prediction of the 2AP-T method improves fingerprinting discriminability by more than 75% on average compared to NTP. In the following, we examine how the three methods perform in detecting whether an AP has been replaced by an attacker.

7.2 Detection of Fake APs

We consider two attacker types: The *naïve attacker* has no information on the original AP's clock skew. He randomly selects an available AP for the attack. Practically, we model this attacker by replacing a considered AP with every other AP in our data set and taking the mean success rate. The *intelligent attacker* knows about the clock skews and the detection method used. Thus, he is able to select the AP with the clock skew closest to the original AP's clock skew in our data set as the replacement. Recall that we do not consider attackers who perform extensive hardware modifications to control the clock skew.

We divided our data into training and testing as follows: all data was separated into four equally long time periods (corresponding to approximately one week each). Training was performed by three (out of four) fingerprinters on the data of three (out of four) weeks and tested by the remaining fingerprinter on the data from the remaining week. To get a representative result, we performed 16-fold cross validation for all possible combinations. The separation of data was deliberately not random but followed a logical distinction. This guaranteed that the testing FP was never used for training and samples in the testing period had a significant temporal distance from those in the training period. This corresponds to a scenario where several users created fingerprints over time and a new user compares his current fingerpint against these at some different point in time, as exploited in our proposed architecture (Section 9).

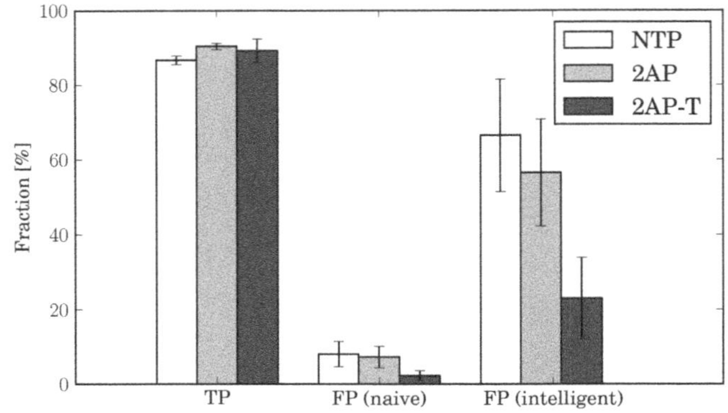

Figure 8: True positive (TP) and false positive (FP) rates for different attacker models; error bars show variation (95% confidence) over different original APs

Our evaluation focuses on two measures: whether an original AP is recognized (true positive) and whether a faked AP succeeds in spoofing the identity (false positive). Figure 8 shows the result. The true positive rate (TP) for 2AP-based methods is marginally better than for NTP and all rates are around 90%. This is slightly less than the targeted 95%, as the acceptance intervals are generated on disjoint training data. More interesting are the results for false positives (FP). A naïve attacker has hardly a chance of succeeding: All of our methods detect the impostor in more than 90% of all cases. The best results are obtained with the 2AP-T method (FP rate 2.23%).

The effectiveness of our method is particularly impressive when dealing with an intelligent attacker. While with the NTP method the attacker succeeds in 67% of all cases, the 2AP method decreases his success rate to 56% and the 2AP-T method to 22%. Regardless of the attacker type, the 2AP-T method is able to improve the spoof detection rate by a factor of three. Since the false positive rates for the intelligent attacker exhibit considerable variations for different original APs (indicated by error bars in Figure 8), we show the separated false positive rates per orginal AP and method in Figure 9. As we can see, in general the 2AP method outperforms NTP. However, the 2AP-T method is always significantly better than both the NTP and the 2AP methods. The error bars for the 2AP and 2AP-T methods indicate the variance over the different comparison APs. The 2AP method is prone to large variations caused by the different temperature dependency characteristics of the comparison APs. This effect is drastically reduced by 2AP-T, which explicitly considers the current temperature. We further see, that even for APs with similar attacker success rates against NTP and 2AP (e. g., AP5/7 or AP2/8), the success rate against the 2AP-T method differs notably. 2AP-T per-

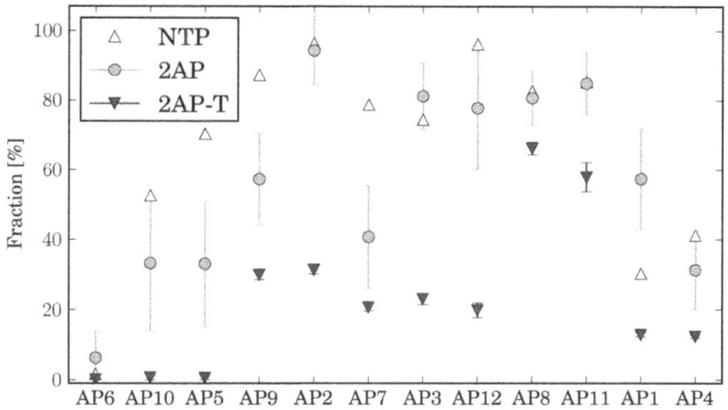

Figure 9: FP rate for intelligent attacker per AP; error bars show variation over comparison APs for 2AP and 2AP-T (95% confidence)

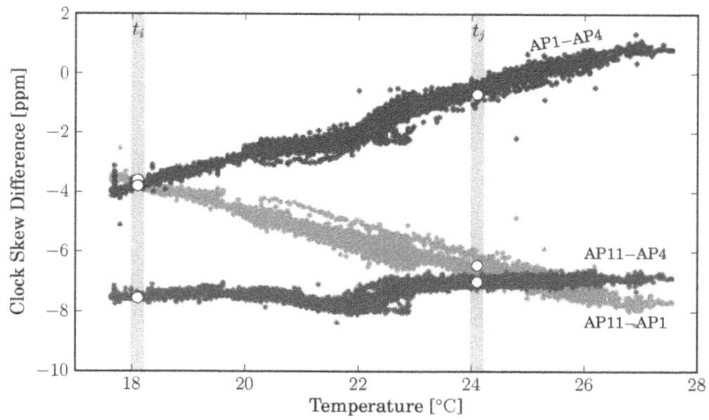

Figure 10: Exemplary input for the SVM

forms best for cases where temperature dependency is very pronounced.

We now present an information theoretical perspective on how much information the temperature contributes to the classification of the APs in our sample.

7.3 Information Theory

From an information theoretical point of view, we are interested in how much information is contained in the temperature dependency, which we use as additional feature for the 2AP-T recognition/fake detection method. A common evaluation measure is the *mutual information (MI)*, defined for two random variables X and Y as $I(X;Y) = \sum_{y \in Y} \sum_{x \in X} p(x,y) \log \frac{p(x,y)}{p(x)\,p(y)}$. In our case, Y represents the considered AP pair, while X denotes the classification feature, i. e., clock skew difference for the 2AP method and the combination of clock skew difference and temperature for the 2AP-T method.

The concept of MI is closely related to entropy and results are expressed as bits. For feature selection, MI measures how much information the presence of a feature contributes to making the correct classification decision. In the case of our methods, it measures how much additional information is provided by the temperature dependency (2AP-T) compared to observing only the clock skew difference (2AP). For details about the calculation we refer to [19]. For our data set, we obtain an MI for 2AP of 4.12 bits and for 2AP-T of 5.16 bits. Note that for our data, the MI is upper bounded by 6.04 bits (as we are classifying 66 different pairs). Therefore, the (information theoretically) perfect feature for classification cannot contribute more than 6.04 bits of information. We conclude that the knowledge of temperature dependency contains more than half of the remaining uncertainty of access point identification when combined with 2AP clock skew differences.

8. METHOD WITHOUT EXPLICIT KNOWLEDGE OF TEMPERATURE

Although our approach provides reliable detection of replaced APs, it depends on information that is not always available in measuring devices: the temperature that APs are exposed to. The question we address in this section is how, if at all, we can perform the detection of impostors if no explicit temperature information is available.

We assume that there are at least three APs transmitting in the environment to be evaluated (say, these are AP1, AP4, and AP11). For every time instance, the fingerprinter is able to derive three 2AP clock skew differences: AP1−AP4, AP11−AP4, AP11−A1. The key idea of our approach is to learn legitimate combinations of simultaneously occurring differences. Figure 10 shows an example of two time instances, time t_i with clock skew differences $(-3.797, -3.607, -7.552)$ and time t_j with $(-0.704, -6.451, -7.013)$. We use such triples of simultaneously measured clock skew differences as vectors to train a machine learning technique. Three APs is the minimum number required because from two APs only one difference could be derived. Note that when using only two APs the machine learning approach is equivalent to the 2AP method and does not learn legitimate combinations but rather single differences. The proposed method only detects whether one of the three APs is faked and not which one. This is similar to the 2AP and 2AP-T methods only detecting whether one out of two APs is potentially spoofed. As described in Section 5, a greater number of reachable APs can be used to identify the actual fake AP.

We apply support vector machines (SVMs), state-of-the-art classification methods used in machine learning, which are well-known for their high performance in terms of classification accuracy. The technique dates back to the work of Vapnik and Chervonenkis [28] in 1974. The focal idea is the interpretation of instances as vectors in a vector space. Based on training data, the classifier tries to fit a hyperplane into the vector space which separates the instances that belong to different classes. In our case (one class SVM) the plane is fitted in such a way that the training data is separated from the origin whereby a fraction of at most ν (which is a SVM parameter) training points are allowed to be outside the estimated region.

The plane is fitted such that the accumulated distance between the closest instances (support vectors) and the plane is maximized to ensure a clear distinction between the classes. In cases where the vectors are not linearly separable, the vector space is transformed into a higher dimensional space where the linear separation is possible (the *kernel trick*). An interested reader is pointed to [5] for thorough information about SVMs.

Sample Size [% / #]	TP [%] avg/mdn	FP [%] avg/mdn
100 / 3520	87.26 / 96.88	12.18 / 0.00
0.05 / 300–400	85.95 / 96.34	11.07 / 0.00
0.015 / 130–160	84.53 / 94.81	10.96 / 0.00
0.005 / 40–50	80.48 / 90.13	10.54 / 0.00

Table 1: True and false positive rate without explicit temperature knowledge

We divided our data into training and testing in the same way as in previous sections. The parameter ν defines an upper bound on the fraction of outliers and, at the same time, a lower bound on the fraction of support vectors (i. e., the generalizability of the model). We set $\nu = 0.05$; hence, at most 5% of training data may be assigned to false negatives by the model. Table 1 (first row) shows the results of the evaluation. We choose the intelligent attacker model described above (i. e., he replaces the original AP with a fake AP that best matches the original clock skew). We skipped the cases when the best fake AP is already included in the triple. As our evaluation shows, on average more than 87% of trustworthy environments are recognized as such (true positive). The median reaches almost 97%. The intelligent attacker is successful in only about 12% of all cases (false positive).

The result is at first glance superior to the 2AP-T method. However, the two methods cannot be directly compared as they consider different numbers of simultaneously reachable APs.

Nevertheless, the results without explicit knowledge of temperature provide surprisingly high accuracy. This is achieved even without tuning SVM parameters. We assume that by optimizing them, one would get even better results (but we omit this due to the high accuracy classification even with the default parameters).

Recall that all our observations were collected in an environment where all APs shared the same temperature exposure. In practical applications, this might not hold true. However, we expect our method to still provide significant detection accuracy as long as the different temperatures are correlated, e. g., due to outdoor temperature or time of day.

For practical relevance, it is important to know how many observations (training data) are needed to achieve good classification accuracy. To determine this number, we performed our evaluation by randomly selecting only 0.05%, 0.015%, and 0.005% of all available training data. This corresponds to roughly 350, 150, and 50 samples. The results are shown in Table 1 in rows two to four. As expected, less training data leads to lower classification accuracy. However, the accuracy degradation is very slight: using only 50 training samples, on average the accuracy is as high as 80% for true positives and 10% for false positives. These results underline the practical relevance of our method as only a few dozen observations without any temperature information are sufficient to learn the parameters of a trustworthy environment.

9. ARCHITECTURE

To exploit the results described above, we propose an architecture based on a crowdsourcing approach (Figure 11). The core of this system is a *trusted service* (TS) that collects fingerprints, performs the necessary calculations and provides feedback to users. Assume a user who wants to connect to a (potentially untrustworthy) access point (UAP) and wants to ensure its trustworthiness. A client application (*app*) first extracts timing information from beacon frames of all receivable APs, calculates the respective clock skews and, if available, measures the current temperature. The pairs of MAC address and clock skew with the optional temperature information represent the *fingerprints*. A secured channel to the TS can be established in two possible ways: 1. If the UAP provides free access to the Internet, using its connectivity, 2. If not possible (e. g., because access is bound to providing credit card information before enabled) via a side channel, e. g., 3G. Encryption and authenticity can be ensured by using well-known certificate-based standards such as SSL. Note that a man-in-the-middle attack on this channel by the UAP can be mitigated by hard-coding the certificate into the app. The client then sends the fingerprint via the secured channel to the TS. The TS decides, depending on the information provided by the client, which of the different proposed methods for verification (SVM/2AP-T/2AP) to use and calculates its decision about the trustworthiness (the *verdict*)—either binary or score-based. The verdict is sent back to the client, enabling the user to decide whether to use the UAP or not. All fingerprints queried for verification are stored and integrated by the TS into its assessment. The more users use the system, the broader is the base for this assessment and, therefore, its precision. Thereby, APs establish a reputation.

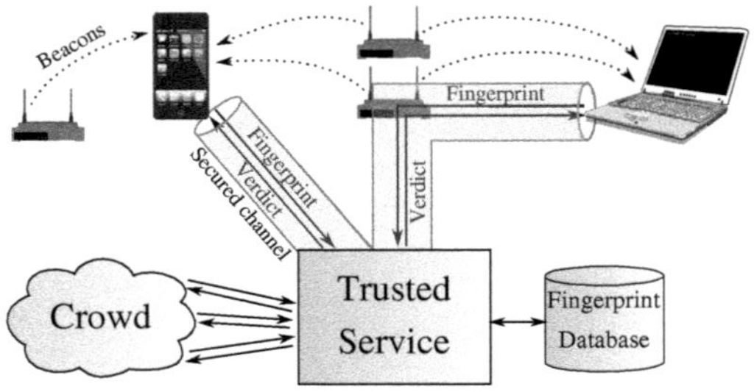

Figure 11: The architecture

A legitimate replacement of an AP by the operator will not cause any confusion: the new device will have a different MAC address and, hence, will be recognized as new AP in that environment. Therefore, our crowdsourced approach will automatically integrate this AP and begin to build its reputation. Note that an attacker would also be able to integrate his AP in this way. However, this would require him to provide reliable long-term service to gain sufficient reputation. The described approach could be implemented without changing any standardized protocols and without requiring the cooperation of network operators—instead, the incentive for using this system is shifted to users who care about their security. In future work we plan to implement this architecture and test its effectiveness in a real-world scenario.

Finally, it would also be possible to store the trained models of the SVM for a favored set of APs in the app itself, as the verification of an environment against a trained SVM model requires only low computational resources and the models need only small storage capacities (the trained models in our experiments are around 2–32KB in size).

10. CONCLUSION

In this paper, we provide a practical solution to reliably detect faked access points. This is done by passively estimating the clock skew from information contained in management frames. We show a way to significantly increase its information content by considering its dependency on temperature. Additionally, our method completely eliminates the influence of the measuring device on the fingerprint. Hence, measurements performed by different clients become comparable. Interestingly, our method works even without explicit access to temperature information and protects even against an attacker who selects a fake AP with a similar average clock skew.

Our method exploits an intrinsic physical property that provides the highest discriminability known so far of APs using standard client hardware. The effort for simulating this property is much more complex than adjusting the average clock skew, even if hardware is modified. This renders the attack practically infeasible.

Our approach yields a strong feature for passive remote physical device fingerprinting in wireless networks. Using only 50 observations for training, our approach detects faked access points in 90% of all cases.

No currently deployed protection mechanism for public hotspots (e. g., web-based authentication) provides any security against the described threat. With our proposed architecture it is possible to mitigate the danger without changing deployed systems or the standard protocols used.

Acknowledgements

The authors would like to thank Andreas Zinnen for valuable discussions about machine learning techniques.

This work has been supported by the National Research Fund of Luxembourg (FNR), the FNR CORE project MOVE, and the EU FP7 PPP project CONFINE.

11. REFERENCES

[1] C. Arackaparambil, S. Bratus, A. Shubina, and D. Kotz. On the reliability of wireless fingerprinting using clock skews. In *3rd ACM Conference on Wireless Network Security (WiSec '10)*, pages 169–174. ACM, 2010. `http://dx.doi.org/10.1145/1741866.1741894`.

[2] P. Bahl, R. Chandra, J. Padhye, L. Ravindranath, M. Singh, A. Wolman, and B. Zill. Enhancing the security of corporate wi-fi networks using DAIR. In *4th International Conference on Mobile Systems, Applications and Services (MobiSys '06)*, pages 1–14. ACM, 2006. `http://dx.doi.org/10.1145/1134680.1134682`.

[3] S. Bratus, C. Cornelius, D. Kotz, and D. Peebles. Active behavioral fingerprinting of wireless devices. In *1st ACM Conference on Wireless Network Security (WiSec '08)*, pages 56–61. ACM, 2008. `http://dx.doi.org/10.1145/1352533.1352543`.

[4] V. Brik, S. Banerjee, M. Gruteser, and S. Oh. Wireless device identification with radiometric signatures. In *14th ACM International Conference on Mobile Computing and Networking (MobiCom '08)*, pages 116–127. ACM, 2008. `http://dx.doi.org/10.1145/1409944.1409959`.

[5] N. Cristianini and J. Shawe-Taylor. *An Introduction to Support Vector Machines and Other Kernel-based Learning Methods*. Cambridge University Press, 2000. `http://www.support-vector.net/`.

[6] R. Dhamija, J. D. Tygar, and M. Hearst. Why phishing works. In *SIGCHI Conference on Human Factors in Computing Systems (CHI '06)*, pages 581–590. ACM, 2006. `http://dx.doi.org/10.1145/1124772.1124861`.

[7] J. Franklin, D. McCoy, P. Tabriz, V. Neagoe, J. Van Randwyk, and D. Sicker. Passive data link layer 802.11 wireless device driver fingerprinting. In *15th USENIX Security Symposium (SSYM '06)*, pages 167–178. USENIX Association, 2006. `https://www.usenix.org/legacy/events/sec06/tech/full_papers/franklin/franklin.pdf`.

[8] K. Gao, C. Corbett, and R. Beyah. A passive approach to wireless device fingerprinting. In *2010 IEEE/IFIP International Conference on Dependable Systems and Networks (DSN '10)*, pages 383–392. IEEE Computer Society, 2010. `http://dx.doi.org/10.1109/DSN.2010.5544294`.

[9] H. Gonzales, K. Bauer, J. Lindqvist, D. McCoy, and D. Sicker. Practical Defenses for Evil Twin Attacks in 802.11. In *IEEE Globecom Communications and Information Security Symposium (Globecom 2010)*, Miami, FL, December 2010.

[10] J. Hall, M. Barbeau, and E. Kranakis. Detection of transient in radio frequency fingerprinting using signal phase. In *3rd IASTED International Conference on Wireless and Optical Communications (WOC '03)*, pages 13–18. ACTA Press, 2003. `http://people.scs.carleton.ca/~kranakis/Papers/RFFPaper3.pdf`.

[11] IEEE Computer Society. *Standard 1193-2003: IEEE Guide for Measurement of Environmental Sensitivities of Standard Frequency Generators.* `http://standards.ieee.org/findstds/standard/1193-2003.html`.

[12] IEEE Computer Society. *Standard 802.11-2012: IEEE Standard for Information technology – Telecommunications and information exchange between systems, Local and metropolitan area networks – Specific requirements Part 11: Wireless LAN Medium Access Control (MAC) and Physical Layer (PHY) Specifications.* `http://standards.ieee.org/findstds/standard/802.11-2012.html`.

[13] IETF. *RFC 1323: TCP Extensions for High Performance*, May 1992. `http://www.rfc-editor.org/rfc/rfc1323.txt`.

[14] IETF. *RFC 2865: Remote Authentication Dial In User Service (RADIUS)*, June 2000. `http://www.rfc-editor.org/rfc/rfc2865.txt`.

[15] S. Jana and S. K. Kasera. On fast and accurate detection of unauthorized wireless access points using clock skews. In *14th ACM International Conference on Mobile Computing and Networking (MobiCom '08)*, pages 104–115. ACM, 2008. `http://dx.doi.org/10.1145/1409944.1409958`.

[16] Jauch Quartz GmbH. *Quartz Crystal Theory*, 2007. `http://www.jauch.de/ablage/med_00000619_1193753698_Quartz%20Crystal%20Theory%202007.pdf`.

[17] T. Kohno, A. Broido, and K. Claffy. Remote physical device fingerprinting. *IEEE Transactions on*

Dependable and Secure Computing, 2(2):93–108, 2005. http://dx.doi.org/10.1109/TDSC.2005.26.

[18] F. Lanze, A. Panchenko, B. Braatz, and A. Zinnen. Clock skew based remote device fingerprinting demystified. In *2012 IEEE Global Telecommunications Conference (GLOBECOM '12)*, pages 813–819. IEEE Computer Society, 2012. http://dx.doi.org/10.1109/GLOCOM.2012.6503213.

[19] C. D. Manning, P. Raghavan, and H. Schütze. *Introduction to Information Retrieval*. Cambridge University Press, 2008. http://nlp.stanford.edu/IR-book/.

[20] S. B. Moon, P. Skelly, and D. F. Towsley. Estimation and removal of clock skew from network delay measurements. In *18th Annual Joint Conference of the IEEE Computer and Communications Societies (INFOCOM '99)*, pages 227–234. IEEE Computer Society, 1999. http://dx.doi.org/10.1109/INFCOM.1999.749287.

[21] C. Neumann, O. Heen, and S. Onno. An empirical study of passive 802.11 device fingerprinting. In *32nd International Conference on Distributed Computing Systems Workshops (ICDCSW '12), Workshop on Network Forensics, Security and Privacy (NFSP)*, pages 593–602. IEEE Computer Society, 2012. http://dx.doi.org/10.1109/ICDCSW.2012.8.

[22] C. E. Rasmussen and C. K. I. Williams. *Gaussian Processes for Machine Learning*. MIT Press, 2006. http://www.gaussianprocess.org/gpml/.

[23] V. Roth, W. Polak, E. Rieffel, and T. Turner. Simple and effective defense against evil twin access points. In *1st ACM Conference on Wireless Network Security (WiSec '08)*, pages 220–235. ACM, 2008. http://dx.doi.org/10.1145/1352533.1352569.

[24] D. Shaw and W. Kinsner. Multifractal modelling of radio transmitter transients for classification. In *Communications, Power and Computing (WESCANEX '97)*, pages 306–312. IEEE Computer Society, 1997. http://dx.doi.org/10.1109/WESCAN.1997.627159.

[25] B. Sieka. Active fingerprinting of 802.11 devices by timing analysis. In *3rd IEEE Consumer Communications and Networking Conference (CCNC '06)*, pages 15–19. IEEE Computer Society, 2006. http://dx.doi.org/10.1109/CCNC.2006.1592979.

[26] J. Sunshine, S. Egelman, H. Almuhimedi, N. Atri, and L. F. Cranor. Crying wolf: An empirical study of SSL warning effectiveness. In *18th USENIX Security Symposium (SSYM '09)*, pages 399–416. USENIX Association, 2009. https://www.usenix.org/legacy/event/sec09/tech/full_papers/sunshine.pdf.

[27] M. B. Uddin and C. Castelluccia. Toward clock skew based wireless sensor node services. In *5th Annual ICST Wireless Internet Conference (WICON '10)*, pages 1–9. IEEE Computer Society, 2010. http://ieeexplore.ieee.org/xpl/articleDetails.jsp?arnumber=5452689.

[28] V. N. Vapnik and A. J. Červonenkis. *Theory of Pattern Recognition [in Russian]*. Nauka, 1974. (German Translation: Theorie der Zeichenerkennung, Akademie-Verlag, 1979).

[29] J. R. Vig. Introduction to quartz frequency standards. Research and Development Technical Report SLCET-TR-92-1, U.S. Army Electronics and Devices Laboratory, March 1992. http://www.dtic.mil/cgi-bin/GetTRDoc?AD=ADA248503.

[30] Z. Yang, L. Cai, Y. Liu, and J. Pan. Environment-aware clock skew estimation and synchronization for wireless sensor networks. In A. G. Greenberg and K. Sohraby, editors, *INFOCOM 2012*, pages 1017–1025. IEEE, 2012.

[31] H. Zhou, C. Nicholls, T. Kunz, and H. Schwartz. Frequency accuracy & stability dependencies of crystal oscillators. Technical Report SCE-08-12, Department of Systems and Computer Engineering, Carleton University, Ottawa, Ontario, Canada, November 2008. http://kunz-pc.sce.carleton.ca/thesis/CrystalOscillators.pdf.

Covert Ephemeral Communication in Named Data Networking

Moreno Ambrosin, Mauro Conti*
University of Padua, Italy
{ambrosin,conti}@math.unipd.it

Paolo Gasti†
New York Inst. of Technology
pgasti@nyit.edu

Gene Tsudik†
University of California, Irvine
gts@ics.uci.edu

ABSTRACT

In recent years, the growing belief that the current IP-based Internet is becoming obsolete prompted several research efforts that aim to design potential next-generation Internet architectures. Named Data Networking (NDN), an instantiation of the content-centric approach, is one such effort. In contrast with their IP counterparts, NDN routers maintain a significant amount of state information. In this paper, we investigate the use of this feature for covert ephemeral communication (CEC). CEC allows two or more parties to covertly exchange ephemeral messages, i.e., messages that become unavailable after a certain amount of time. Our techniques rely only on network-layer services. This makes our protocols robust, and stealthy communication – difficult to detect. We show that users can build high-bandwidth CEC channels by exploiting features unique to NDN: in-network caches, routers' forwarding state and name matching rules. We assess feasibility and performance of identified CEC channels using a local setup and the official NDN testbed.

Categories and Subject Descriptors

C.2 [**Computer-Communication Networks**]: Security and protection

Keywords

Ephemeral Communication, Covert Communication, Named Data Networking, CCN, NDN

---

*Mauro Conti was supported by a Marie Curie Fellowship, funded by the European Commission for the PRISM-CODE project (PCIG11-GA-2012-321980), and by the University of Padua Researchers' Mobility grant 2013. This work has been partially supported by the TENACE PRIN Project (20103P34XC) funded by the Italian MIUR.

†Paolo Gasti and Gene Tsudik were supported by the NSF under award CNS-1040802 – "FIA: Collaborative Research: Named Data Networking (NDN)".

ASIA CCS'14, June 4–6, 2014, Kyoto, Japan.

http://dx.doi.org/10.1145/2590296.2590306 .

1. INTRODUCTION

The current IP-based Internet architecture represents an unprecedented success story, having by far exceeded its designers' expectations in terms of flexibility, robustness, longevity and scalability. Part of IP's success is due to its light-weight design: virtually all state used for communication is maintained at the endpoints, rather than within the network. For this reason, IP-based networks are quite robust against random failures. However, lack of in-network state is the reason for some of IP's shortcomings, including poor support for efficient large-scale content distribution.

Content distribution currently accounts for most Internet traffic [28]. Since IP is not well-suited for this, most major content providers [32, 18, 12, 16] have been – for performance, cost and reliability reasons [3] – relying on Content Distribution Networks (CDNs): large, complex, geographically distributed overlays implemented at transport and higher layers of the protocol stack. This state of affairs motivated research into new networking architectures that can better serve today's content-dominated Internet traffic. Named Data Networking (NDN) [21] is one such architecture.

NDN is an example of Content-Centric Networking (CCN), sometimes also referred to as Information-Centric Networking (ICN). In NDN, location-independent content is directly addressable by an arbitrarily long human-readable name, regardless of who publishes it. This allows routers to cache a copy of forwarded content in order to efficiently satisfy subsequent requests. Content is requested using a special packet type, called an *interest*. Interests are routed similarly to IP packets; however, content is forwarded along the reverse path traversed by the corresponding interest. Routers keep state of outstanding interests in a data structure called Pending Interest Table (PIT).

User-driven state in routers facilitates efficient content distribution at the network layer. However, availability of this state within the network creates a new set of problems. In particular, NDN prompts new security [13, 2, 9, 29, 10, 31] and privacy [1, 11] issues. In this paper, we investigate how NDN router state can be used for covert ephemeral communication. We show that two or more parties can communicate secretly, without directly exchanging any packets, and without injecting new content into the network (i.e., without publishing new content). This is a significant departure from what can be done with IP, where lack of user-driven network state forces users to rely on the application layer for implementing covert channels.

We believe that this work is both timely and important. The former – because of a recent surge of interest in content-centric networking, and in NDN in particular. The latter, because, to the best of our knowledge, it represents the first attempt to identify and address covert ephemeral communication (CEC) in a CCN architecture. We believe that CEC is relevant in some realistic scenarios, e.g.:

1. In tightly-controlled environments, where mandatory access control is in place (e.g., in the military), CEC can be used to exfiltrate sensitive information, possibly collected by malware. Ephemeral nature of published content makes subsequent forensic analysis difficult.
2. In countries with oppressive governments, civil rights activists can covertly communicate to coordinate and exchange information. CEC offers plausible deniability.

Exploring CEC is an important step towards understanding the consequences and features of NDN, regardless of whether it sees limited deployment (e.g., as an overlay on top of IP) or widespread adoption (i.e., as a replacement for IP). Furthermore, while existing covert channels rely on state on the end-nodes, usually held by a specific applications (e.g., Skype) [19], this paper shows how to construct covert channels at the *network architecture level*, i.e., independently of any particular application.

With this motivation in mind, we design several protocols for exchanging covert ephemeral messages (CEMs) between a single sender and one or more receivers. We perform extensive evaluation of our techniques on a LAN and on a geographically distributed NDN testbed. Our experiments confirm that CEC is indeed possible, and show that our techniques provide high bandwidth and low error rate.

Organization. We begin with the overview of NDN in Section 2. Then, Section 3 introduces our system model. Delay-based CEC mechanisms in Section 4 and common-prefix-based CEC techniques are presented in Section 5. Section 6 discusses sources of error and error handling. Experimental results are described in Section 7. Next, security analysis is discussed in Section 8. Section 9 reviews related work and the paper concludes with Section 10.

2. NDN OVERVIEW

This overviews NDN; readers familiar with NDN may skip this section without loss of continuity.

NDN is a networking architecture based on named content. Content is requested via *interests*, and delivered in *content packets* [8]. Content packets include a name, a payload and a digital signature computed by the content producer.[1] A name has one or more components that have a hierarchical structure. In NDN notation, "/" separates name components, e.g., `/cnn/politics/frontpage`. Content is delivered to consumers only upon an explicit request, which reflects either the full name of a particular content or a prefix thereof, e.g., `/cnn/politics` is a prefix of `/cnn/politics/frontpage`. In case of multiple content packets under a given name (or prefix), optional control information can be carried within the interest to restrict desired content. If no additional information is provided, producers and routers return arbitrary content packets matching the request (preferably, from a local cache).

[1]Content packets also carry other fields not relevant to this paper, which we omit.

Upon receiving an interest, if no local copy of desired content is available, an NDN router forwards the interest towards the content producer responsible for the requested name, using name prefixes (instead of today's IP address prefixes) for routing. Each NDN router maintains a Pending Interest Table (PIT) – a lookup table containing outstanding [*interest, arrival-interfaces*] entries. When an NDN router receives an interest for content not in its cache, it looks up its PIT to determine whether another interest for the same name is currently outstanding. There are three possible outcomes: (1) If the same name is already in the router's PIT and the arrival interface of the present interest is already in the set of *arrival-interfaces* of the corresponding PIT entry, the interest is discarded. (2) If a PIT entry for the same name exists, yet the arrival interface is new, the router updates the PIT entry by adding a new interface to the set. The interest is not forwarded further. (3) Otherwise, the router creates a new PIT entry and forwards the present interest. We refer to (1) and (2) as PIT hit, and to (3) as PIT miss.

Upon receipt of the interest, the producer injects a matching content packet into the network, thus *satisfying* the interest. The requested content is then forwarded towards the consumer, traversing – in reverse – the path of the preceding interest. Each router on this path deletes the PIT entry corresponding to the satisfied interest. In addition, each router caches a copy of forwarded content in its local cache.

Unlike their IP counterparts, NDN routers can forward interests out on multiple interfaces simultaneously. This is done in order to maximize the chances of quickly retrieving requested content. A router that receives an interest for already-cached content does not forward the interest further; it simply returns cached content and retains no state about the interest.

Not all interests result in content being returned. If an interest encounters either a router that cannot forward it further, or a content producer that has no such content, no error packets are generated. PIT entries for unsatisfied interests in intervening routers are removed after a predefined *expiration* time. The consumer can choose whether to resend the same interest after a timeout.

3. SYSTEM MODEL

A CEC system involves a sender (Snd) and one or more receivers (Rcv). Snd wants to covertly publish a *time-bounded* (ephemeral) message M, while Rcv wants to retrieve it. A time-bounded message can only be read for a given period of time [5], after which it becomes unavailable, i.e., it *expires*. Depending on the scenario, the action of retrieving a CEM either makes it expire immediately, or "refreshes" it, hence deferring its expiration.

Snd and Rcv are not allowed to communicate directly. For example, the Internet provider of Snd and Rcv might monitor all activity between its users. Moreover, Snd and Rcv are not allowed to use services (such as email or on-line forums) to exchange content indirectly. Snd and Rcv have access to a producer (Pr), which is unaware of Snd and Rcv's intent to communicate, and only hosts content that can not be modified by consumers. All packets to and from Pr are routed through an NDN router (Rt), that caches all content packets it forwards. At first we will assume that Rt is Snd and Rcv's first-hop router. We later relax this assumption, allowing Rt to be an arbitrary number of hops away from both. Figure 1 depicts our model.

We assume that Snd and Rcv have tightly synchronized clocks.[2] We believe that this assumption is realistic: two parties can use NTP servers or GPS devices to synchronize their clocks accurately, i.e., within 500 ns to a few ms, depending on the protocol [27]. Our experiments, detailed in Section 7, confirm that tight synchronization can be achieved via NTP. Similar to [26], we also assume that Rcv knows when Snd starts to send a new message.

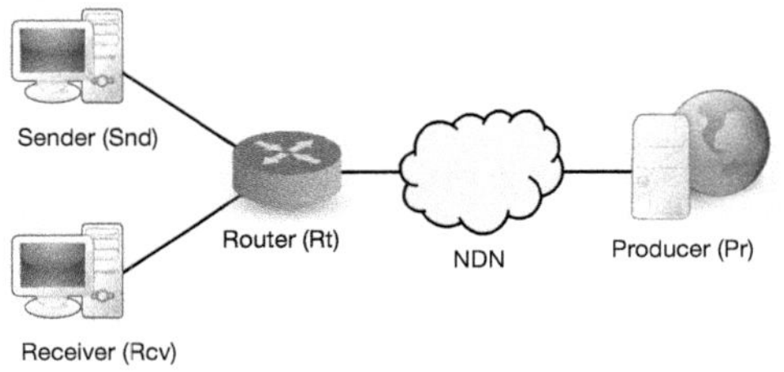

Figure 1: System model.

The adversary (Adv) has three goals: (1) detecting CEMs; (2) preventing Snd and Rcv from communicating; and (3) accessing CEMs after they expire. Adv can monitor and modify traffic between users. Following the definition of *retroactive privacy* in [5], we say that a CEC system is **secure** if any efficient Adv can win the following game with probability at most negligibly over 1/2:

1. Adv selects two same-length message M_0 and M_1, and sends them to Snd.
2. Snd selects a random bit a and publishes M_a.
3. After M_a is expired, Adv tries to retrieve M_a.
4. Adv outputs its guess a' for a; Adv wins if $a' = a$.

In all CECs discussed below, after Snd has sent a CEM, it deletes this CEM locally. Similarly, Rcv deletes all CEMs soon after receiving them, i.e., before they expire. We assume that all parties can effectively delete data.

4. DELAY-BASED COVERT COMMUNICATION

Delay-based communication relies on Rcv's ability to differentiate between a cache (or PIT) hit, and a cache (PIT) miss. Snd can exploit this by selecting a set of content for which it issues interests, therefore causing cache/PIT hits for Rcv. To start, we show how timing information can be used to covertly transmit a single-bit CEM from Snd to Rcv. Then, we describe how to extend this to CEMs of arbitrary length. To simplify the notation, we refer to the time elapsed between issuance of an interest and the arrival of the corresponding content as "content RTT".

4.1 Single-Bit Transmission via Cache

Suppose that Snd has a single bit $b \in \{0,1\}$ to communicate to Rcv. If $b = 1$, Snd requests a content packet C. Otherwise, it does nothing. Rcv determines b by requesting the same content packet C. If content RTT of C is below expected RTT for non-cached content packets, Rcv sets $b' = 1$. Otherwise, $b' = 0$. This mechanism is reliable, i.e., $b' = b$ with overwhelming probability, if the following conditions are met:

1. Snd and Rcv pre-agree on the name of content C and the time when Snd will send b.
2. Content C must not be popular, i.e., it must not be present in Rt's cache prior to Snd's request.
3. There must be a clear distinction between RTTs associated with cache hits and cache misses, and Rcv must have a good estimate for at least one of them with respect to C.
4. Rt must cache content packets for a non-negligible duration.

We believe that (1) and (2) can be easily satisfied in practice. With respect to (3), in order to distinguish a cache hit from a miss, Rcv must determine an appropriate threshold value t_{thresh}: iff RTT of C is below t_{thresh}, then Rcv considers C as originating from a nearby cache. t_{thresh} can be estimated by requesting (more than once) a large number of non- popular content packets from the same producer that publishes C. The first interest for each content packet will be satisfied by the producer itself. All subsequent (closely spaced) requests for the same content packet will come from a nearby cache. Regardless of the network topology, there is usually a clear distinction between cache hits and cache misses[3] Therefore, it is easy to set an appropriate value for t_{thresh}.

Rcv can determine if (4) holds by issuing multiple interests for content packets distributed by multiple producers, and measuring effects (if any) of content caching. If 4 does not hold, a different mechanism – such as the one based on PIT – is more appropriate.

We say that a CEM exchanged by Snd and Rcv is expired if C has been removed from all caches, or once it has been retrieved by Rcv.

Timing Constraints. In order to receive b reliably, Rcv must observe a set of timing constraints. In particular, Rcv's interest for C must be processed by Rt after C is cached (and made available to consumers), yet before C expires from the same cache. (Without loss of generality, in the rest of the paper we assume that content in Rt's cache is available as soon as it is received by the router.) Let I indicate an interest for C, and $[I : A \to B]$, $[C : A \to B]$ – the time required for I and C to travel from A to B. Let t_0 be the time when Snd writes b, either by issuing I ($b = 1$) or by doing nothing ($b = 0$). Let $t_C = [I : \mathsf{Snd} \to \mathsf{Pr}] + [C : \mathsf{Pr} \to \mathsf{Rt}]$. C is available from Rt's cache at $t_0 + t_C$. Therefore, Rcv can "read" b starting at $t_b = t_0 + t_C - [I : \mathsf{Rcv} \to \mathsf{Rt}]$. When $[I : \mathsf{Snd} \to \mathsf{Rt}] \approx [I : \mathsf{Rcv} \to \mathsf{Rt}]$, $t_b \approx t_0 + \mathrm{RTT}_{\mathsf{Rt} \to \mathsf{Pr}}$ where $\mathrm{RTT}_{\mathsf{Rt} \to \mathsf{Pr}}$ represents the RTT for C between Rt and Pr. Rcv must retrieve b before $t_b + Exp_{\mathsf{Rt}}$, where Exp_{Rt} represents the freshness field of C, or the time after which C is evicted from Rt's cache, whichever comes first. Figure 2a summarizes these observations.

Time to read a single bit depends on the RTT associated with a cache hit, from Rcv's point of view. Let $\mathrm{RTT}_{\mathsf{hit}}$ and $\mathrm{RTT}_{\mathsf{miss}}$ indicate the average RTT for a cache hit and cache miss relative to C, as observed by Rcv. Rcv sets $b = 1$ iff the RTT of C is below $\mathrm{RTT}_{\mathsf{hit}} + \Delta < \mathrm{RTT}_{\mathsf{miss}}$, where Δ is a small constant used to account for variance in C's RTT. Rt can therefore determine b within $\mathrm{RTT}_{\mathsf{hit}} + \Delta$.

[2]This assumption is common in the covert-channel literature, e.g., [4]. Moreover, this is required only for our PIT-based protocols.

[3]See Section 7, figures 3a and 3b.

Covert messages distributed with this technique are ephemeral, i.e., they become unavailable after a certain amount of time without any further action from Snd or Rcv. Because Rt caches forwarded traffic, C will be eventually flushed from Rt's cache. We claim that C is always a good candidate for deletion: since C is not popular, both Least Frequently Used (LFU) and Least Recently Used (LRU) cache replacement policies will consider it a good candidate for removal.

Once Rcv requests it, C will be cached regardless of the original value of b. Therefore, after being retrieved, b will be set to 1 until C is flushed from Rt's cache.

Our experiments, reported in Section 7, show that this technique provides high bandwidth, with a low error rate. Moreover, it is relatively easy to implement, since it does not require strict time synchronization.

4.2 Single-Bit Transmission via PIT

In some circumstances, cache-based CEC is not applicable:

1. Despite its emphasis on in-network caching, NDN does not mandate router cache size. In fact, a some routers might have no cache at all, e.g., small, low-cost and/or low-power embedded routers.
2. Rt's entire cache may be overwritten before Rcv issues I. This can happen if Rt's cache is very small, and the router forwards a large amount of traffic.
3. To prevent cache pollution attacks [10, 31], Rt might not cache content packets that are forwarded only once. This behavior would force Snd to issue I multiple times before C is cached by Rt, thus negatively affecting both bandwidth and detectability.
4. Rt may implement cache privacy techniques that involve delaying serving C when it is retrieved from the cache [1].

To overcome the above limitations, we construct a technique based exclusively upon PIT state. It requires strict time synchronization between Snd and Rcv. It is based on PIT hits (see Section 2): when Rt receives interest $I' = I$, while I is still in Rt's PIT, the two interests are "collapsed" within the same PIT entry. Rt adds the incoming interface of I' to the PIT entry of I, and does not propagate I' any further. Once C is received by Rt, it is forwarded to the interfaces on which I and I' were received.

This feature of NDN can be used by Snd and Rcv to covertly exchange one bit as follows. If $b = 1$, Snd issues I, otherwise it does nothing. To receive b, Rcv issues $I' = I$ while an entry corresponding to I is still in Rt's PIT. If I is in the PIT, Rcv's interest is satisfied faster than otherwise. This is because, by the time I' arrives at Rt, either: (1) the original I has been already processed and is being forwarded by subsequent upstream routers, or (2) C is already on its way back to Snd but has not yet reached Rt. In either case, I' is collapsed by Rt and is not forwarded further. If Rcv can correctly measure the corresponding difference in RTT, it can reliably determine b. (As discussed earlier, Rcv can easily measure the RTT for retrieving content directly from the same producer that originated C.)

In the context of this technique, we say that a CEM has expired if I has been removed from Rt's PIT *and* from all caches, or it has been retrieved by Rcv.

Timing Constraints. While PIT-based CEC works regardless of Rt's cache behavior (or even cache availability), it imposes much stricter timing requirements on Rcv. Specifically, I' must be received by Rt after I (if issued) is added to Rt's PIT. Also, I' must be received before C is received and forwarded by Rt. This gives Rcv a time window of $RTT_{Rt \rightarrow Pr}$. We note, however, that the unwitting producer of C can be easily chosen by Snd and Rcv to be sufficiently remote, so as to maximize this window.

As in the cache-based technique, messages exchanged via PIT are ephemeral: if I is not issued on time, the corresponding PIT entry is removed once C is forwarded to Snd. Also, after Rcv issues I', any attempt to retrieve b by issuing further interests for C (while the PIT entry still exists) will result in those interests being collapsed (therefore setting $b = 1$), regardless of the original value of b. Figure 2b depicts these constraints.

4.3 Tandem Data Packets

Assuming wide-scale deployment of NDN, when Rt is far from Rcv, RTT-s associated with cache hits and misses may fluctuate significantly over time. In order to reduce the probability of erroneously detecting cache hits/misses, we introduce a technique called Tandem Data Packets (TDP) that uses two content packets to covertly receive a single bit. To transmit b, Snd and Rcv pre-agree on content packets C_0 and C_1, which are assumed not to be in any router's cache. First, Snd requests C_b. Then, Rcv issue two consecutive interests: one for C_0 and one for C_1. If RTT of C_0 is less than that of C_1, Rcv sets $b' = 0$, otherwise $b' = 1$. CEM is exchanged correctly if $b' = b$.

This technique does not require Rcv to make any *a priori* assumption on the exact RTT associated with cache hits and misses, except that RTT of C_b is less than that of $C_{\neg b}$. As our experiments confirm, this reduces receiver error, since RTT for both hits and misses is continuously updated according to network conditions. After Rcv determines it, b becomes inaccessible. Since both C_0 and C_1 will be in Rt's cache, any difference in RTTs for C_0 and C_1 will not depend on b. Therefore, b essentially expires once it is retrieved by Rcv or removed from Rt's cache.

Timing Constraints. Identical to those in Section 4.1.

4.4 Transmitting Multi-Bit Messages

Naturally, Snd and Rcv may want to exchange multi-bit messages. We discuss how to determine Snd's and Rcv's speeds separately, since the two could send and receive at different rates.

Let $M = b_1, \ldots, b_n$ be an n-bit string. Suppose that Snd and Rcv agree on n different content packets $C_1, ..., C_n$. Instead of waiting for the full RTT of C, Snd can send new I_i for C_i before C_{i-1} has been received. Snd selects an interval t; two consecutive interests I_i, I_{i+1} are sent at t_i and t_{i+1}, where $t_{i+1} = t_i + t$. The minimum value for t is denoted as t_{min}; it corresponds to sending an uninterrupted burst of interests. Similarly, Rcv selects t which is used to determine how subsequent interests are spaced. Snd and Rcv can select t independently, as long as the timing constraints associated with the protocol are not violated. We evaluate how this technique affects transmission errors as a function of t and report our findings in Section 7.

Transmitting Multiple Bits with a Single Interest. For efficiency reasons, Snd can use a generalized TDP technique to send multiple bits using a single interest. Two parties agree a priori on a set of content packets, which we

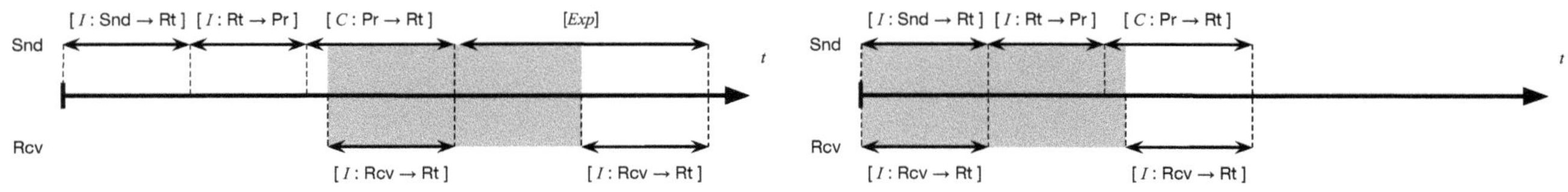

(a) Cache (b) PIT

Figure 2: Time constrains for retrieving a CEM published using Rt's cache (top) and PIT (bottom). The colored area delimits the interval in which Rcv can retrieve b.

represent as a matrix:

$$Y = \begin{bmatrix} C_{(1,1)} & \cdots & C_{(1,2^m)} \\ \vdots & & \\ C_{(\ell,1)} & & C_{(\ell,2^m)} \end{bmatrix}$$

where m is the number of bits transmitted using one interest, and $\ell = \lceil n/m \rceil$. In order to publish M, Snd splits it in words $W_1, \ldots, W_\ell$ of m bits each (i.e., $W_1 = (b_1, \ldots, b_m)$, $W_2 = (b_{m+1}, \ldots, b_{2m})$, etc.). Rcv then issues interests for $C_{(1,W_1)}, C_{(2,W_2)}, \ldots, C_{(\ell,W_\ell)}$, where W_i is used as integer representation of the corresponding bit string. Thus, Snd can publish an n-bit message using $\lceil n/m \rceil$ interests.

To retrieve M, Rcv issues interests for all content packets in Y. Let $C_{i,j}$ be the content packet on the i-th row of Y such that the RTT of $C_{i,j}$ is the smallest across all $C_{i,1}, \ldots, C_{i,2^m}$. Rcv sets $W_i = j$, and $M = W_1 | \ldots | W_\ell$. The cost of retrieving M for Rcv is therefore exponential in m. In practice, reasonable values for m are between 1 and 5. (Note that when $m = 1$, this technique corresponds to TDP.)

5. COMMON-PREFIX-BASED COVERT COMMUNICATION

Using previous techniques, a covert message can be retrieved only by a single receiver. Message is automatically "deleted" after it is "read" by Rcv. This is desirable when a CEM has only one intended recipient. However, when the CEM has multiple recipients, Snd must create a separate "instance" of the message for each. In this section, we propose a technique – called Common-Prefix-Based Covert Communication (CPC) – that allows Snd to publish a message once, and have multiple parties to retrieve it. Similarly to previous techniques, CEMs published using CPC are ephemeral.

CPC relies on NDN's longest prefix matching feature, instead of RTT measurements. This makes it robust against cache privacy techniques [1], which could defeat CEC techniques introduced in Section 4.

Communication via CPC works as follows. Snd and Rcv agree on two content packets C_0, C_1 which share a common name prefix, e.g., `/common/prefix/C0`, and `/common/prefix/C1`. [4] The common namespace is selected such that content packets published under it are not popular, i.e., not in Rt's cache. In order to transmit a single bit, Snd simply requests C_b. To receive b, Rcv issues an interest for `/common/prefix/`. Both C_0 and C_1 match Rcv's interest. Therefore, Rt will return one content packet among C_0 and C_1 that is still in its cache – or in its PIT, if Snd and Rcv's interests are closely spaced (see timing constraints below). This communicates b to Rcv.

This technique is very robust against changing network conditions. In particular, since timing is not used to either set or determine b, transient changes in RTT do not introduce communication errors: Rcv receives only C_b, regardless of how long it waits. Moreover, in contrast with previous techniques, when Rcv's interest is dropped (or, similarly C_b in response to Rcv's interest is dropped) Rcv can re-issue its interest, since this process does not affect C_b.

Common-prefix-based covert channels are suitable for distributing a single message to a (possibly large) set of receivers. Each interest for `/common/prefix/` issued by a recipient has the side-effect of "refreshing" C_b in Rt's cache, making b available longer. After recipients stop retrieving C_b, it "fades away" from all involved routers' caches, effectively erasing b. As an alternative, Snd or one of the recipients can request $C_{\neg b}$ which achieves a similar result.

A message exchanged using CPC expires when it is removed from all caches.

Timing Constraints. In order to successfully retrieve b, Rcv must issue an interest for `/common/prefix/` such that the interest is received by Rt after the interest for C_b from Snd. If the interest from Rcv is received before C_b is returned to Rcv, communication between Snd and Rcv is implemented through Rt's PIT. Otherwise, Rt's cache is used to exchange b. Snd's interest must also be received by Rt before C_b is removed from the cache.

5.1 Multiple-Bit Transmission

Since this technique is less susceptible to RTT fluctuations and packet loss, using it for sending and receiving multiple bits in bursts does not introduce significant errors. This is confirmed by our experiments, in Section 7.

Transmitting Multiple Bits with a Single Interest. Snd and Rcv can agree on content packets in matrix Y with the additional requirements that for $i \in [1, \ell]$, content packets in row i share the same common prefix $pref_i$. Snd splits M in $W_1, \ldots, W_\ell$, and – for each i – issues one interest for C_{i,W_i}.

Rcv needs to issue only *one* interest per word (i.e., per matrix row), requesting a content packet from $pref_i$. For this reason, Snd and Rcv can exchange an n-bit message using $\lceil n/m \rceil$ interests/content packets each. In practice, m is limited only by availability of un-popular namespaces containing a sufficient number of content packets.

[4]Common prefix can be followed by different children namespaces, e.g., `/common/prefix/foo/C0` and `/common/prefix/yet /another/prefix/C1`.

6. ERRORS AND ERROR HANDLING

Bit errors may be introduced by both Snd (write errors) and Rcv (read errors). Depending on the technique used to communicate, errors may be injected in M for different reasons and may be detected and dealt with in different ways. A write error occurs when a content packet requested by Snd is not added to Rt's cache or PIT. A read errors occurs as a result of an incorrect retrieval of a message bit after it has been correctly written, and before it is expired.

Delay-Based: Cache. We consider the following two issues as common causes for write errors:

1. Packet loss (either interests or content packets). Interests from Snd may be dropped along their way to Pr. Similarly, content packets from Pr may be dropped before they reach Rt. In both cases, no content packets added to Rt's cache, and therefore the send operation fails. This, however, can be detected by Snd, who simply re-issues interests for which it does not receive content packets.
2. Forwarded content packets not added to Rt's cache. This can be caused, for example, by meta-cache algorithms on Rt. Snd can detect this only by re-requesting all bits set to 1 in its messages and, for each comparing the RTT of the first request with the RTT of the second.

We identify the following causes for read errors:

1. RTT fluctuations. Since retrieving a message relies on correctly identifying cache hits and misses, any overlap in the RTT between Rcv and Rt and between Rcv and Pr could cause a read error. These errors are not detectable, and cannot be addressed by simply re-sending interests.
2. Interests from other consumers. Some consumers may request a content packet that correspond to a bit in the message set to 0, and have it added to Rt's cache. We assume that this happens with negligible probability, since Snd and Rcv exchange messages using a set of content packets that are not popular.
3. Packet loss (content packets). If a content packet is dropped on the path from Pr to Rt, it can be safely be re-requested by Rcv without altering the original message. However, if it is dropped on its way from Rt to Rcv, the corresponding message bit will be set to 1 regardless of its original value. Rcv can only distinguish between the two cases – and determine the correct value of the corresponding message bit b – when b is read as 0.
4. Packet loss (interests). When interests are dropped on their way from Rcv to Rt (if the corresponding content packet is in Rt's cache) or to Pr (if it is not), Rcv cannot retrieve the corresponding bit. In this case, Rcv can re-issue the same interest without altering the original message, since no content packets have been added to Rt's cache. However, since loss of interest cannot be distinguished from loss of content packet, Rcv may not be able to recover from this error.
5. Rt is rebooted. This causes all content packets in Rt's cache to be deleted, hence "erasing" all messages from Snd. This can be detected if Rcv knows that $M \neq 0^n$.

Rcv can reduce errors induced by RTT fluctuations using the "scope" field in interests, when Rt is its first-hop router. This field works similarly to the IP TTL field. When scope is set to 2, interests are forwarded for up to one hop. (Values higher than 2 are not allowed [7]). If the Rcv's first hop cannot satisfy the interests, it simply drops it. This way, Rcv does not need to measure any difference in the delay of cache hits and misses, since only cache hits will result in returned content. Moreover, this would allow interest retransmission in case of packet loss, since setting scope to 2 would prevent Rcv's interests from adding any new content into the cache. We argue that, however, setting the scope field would make Rcv's activity easier to detect.

Delay-Based: PIT. As in to the previous technique, write errors correspond to interests sent by Snd and are not added to Rt's PIT. The main cause for write errors is loss of the interest from Snd to Rt. This cannot be detected on time by Snd, since the same interest must be issued by Rcv before the corresponding content packet is received by Snd.

On the receiver side, errors may have the following causes:

1. RTT fluctuations. Similarly to the previous technique, significant fluctuations of RTT can introduce read errors.
2. Packet loss (either interests or content packets). In case of packet loss, Rcv will learn no information about the corresponding bit in the covert message. Moreover, re-transmitting an interest may provide no useful information, since by then the PIT entry corresponding to the original interest from Snd, if any, will be either expired or removed.
3. Interests from other consumers. Other consumers may issue the same interests that Snd and Rcv are using to covertly exchange information. However, this happens with negligible probability, because: (1) content packets used to covertly publish messages are non-popular, and (2) interests from other consumers must be issues a few milliseconds before Rcv issues its interests.
4. Lack of synchronization between Snd and Rcv. Depending on the topology, Snd and Rcv must be tightly synchronized, i.e., roughly within half RTT between Snd and Pr. Lack of synchronization may lead to a high rate of read errors.
5. Message expiration. Even though this technically is not a read error, it may happen that Rcv cannot retrieve part of the message on time due to the strict timing requirements.

As before, the scope field can be set in Rcv's interest to reduce error rate.

TDP. Write errors have the same causes, as well as detectability, as the write errors in delay-based cache technique.

Similarly, read errors have the same causes as with delay-based, single-bit cache. However, content packet-pairs provide more robustness against RTT fluctuations and packet loss. Since two subsequent RTTs – one corresponding to a cache hit, and one for a cache miss – are measured for each message bit, the probability of error associated with random RTT fluctuations is greatly reduced. With respect to packet loss, at least one of the content packets corresponding to a single message bit will be returned with relatively high probability. The associated RTT will still allow Rcv to estimate whether it is coming from Rt's cache – although less accurately.

Common-prefix-based Covert Communication. Using this technique, write errors may be introduced by the same events that trigger packet loss in delay-based, single bit cache. With respect to read errors, this technique is significantly more robust than the previous ones because: (1) it does not rely on timing measurements, and is therefore immune to RTT fluctuations; and (2) in case of packet loss (affecting either interests or data packets), Rcv can simply re-issue its interest, without affecting the covert message. Read errors can, however, be introduced by interests from other consumers, when they request content from the namespaces used by Snd and Rcv.

6.1 Error Correction

To address potential read/write errors, Snd can use error-correction codes with CEM. For example, Reed-Solomon error correction codes [24] could be used. We do not investigate this any further, since the goal of this paper is to assess feasibility of the channel and the corresponding error rate.

7. EVALUATION

We implemented a prototype CEC system to evaluate our protocols. In this section we present the results of our experiments. The prototype is based on CCNx [6], an open-source implementation of NDN which runs as an overlay on top of IP. We performed experiments on the two topologies:

- LAN, composed of Snd, Rcv, Rt and Pr within the same broadcast domain. Each party runs a separate instance of CCNx.
- NDN testbed [22], where Snd and Rcv (located in Europe) are connected to the UCLA NDN hub (which acts as Rt), and Pr is connected to the testbed through the UCI hub. UCLA and UCI hubs are one NDN hop apart (ten hops over IP).

Snd and Rcv exchange 1,000-bit messages. Each message is a fresh random bit string. This is representative of the distribution of encrypted messages.

Naturally, our protocols generate communication overhead. We used 41-byte interests and 377-byte content packets (on average). With single-bit transmission (either using PIT and cache), each message bit set to 1 requires Snd to exchange 418 bytes. Regardless of message content, Rcv needs to send/receive 418 bytes per message bit. With the TDP protocol, each message bit costs 418 bytes to Snd and 836 bytes to Rcv. When transmitting multiple bits with a single interest, m message bits cost Snd 418 bytes, and $2^m \cdot 418$ bytes to Rcv. Finally, with CPC both Snd and Rcv exchange 418 bytes for each m-bit word.

In our experiments, Snd can send messages at a rate different from the rate at which Rcv receives them. This is possible due to the state in routers (i.e., cache or PIT, depending on the technique used).

7.1 Evaluation of Delay-Based Cache Techniques

In order to assess feasibility of cache-based techniques, we compared RTT associated with cache hits and cache misses in both LAN and testbed scenarios.

Figure 3 summarizes our findings and represents average values over 100,000 content packets. While there is virtually no overlap between RTT of cache hits and misses in a controlled (LAN) environment, RTT fluctuations on the testbed do not always allow us to distinguish a cache hit from a cache miss. However, the overlap is still relatively small and, as confirmed by further experiments, it is possible to implement a reliable CEC on the testbed.

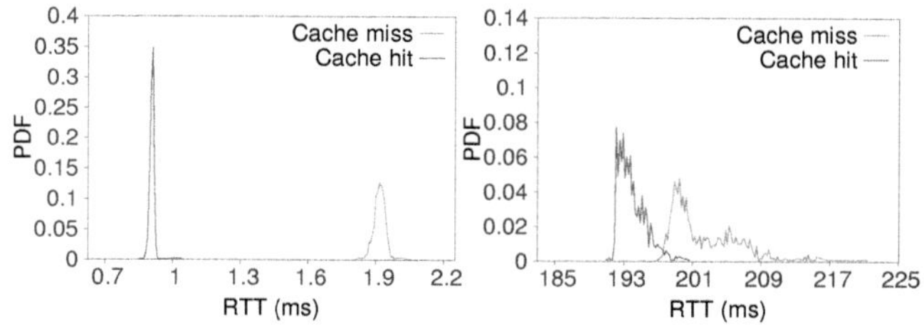

(a) LAN (b) Testbed

Figure 3: PDF for cache hit and cache miss.

We then looked into how interest sending rate affects RTT. We selected values for t varying from $t_{min} = 0.3$ μs to $t = 5$ ms (see Section 4.4). We performed several experiments, each using 100,000 content packets. Before each experiment, we restarted Rt in order to remove all cache entries. Results are reported in Figure 4.

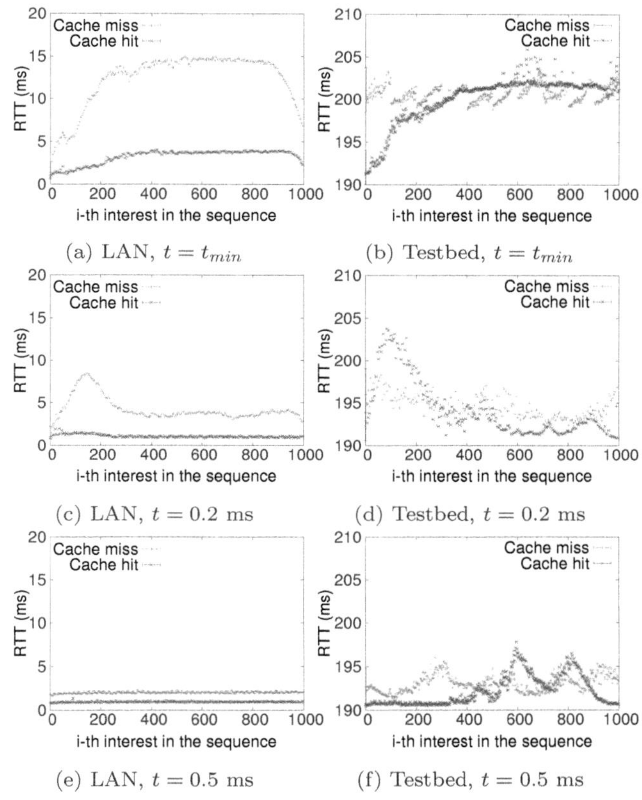

Figure 4: RTT for content packets, varying request rate.

In LAN (figures 4a, 4c, and 4e), RTTs of cache hits and cache misses are clearly separated, regardless of t. On the testbed (figures 4b, 4d, and 4f), for small values of t, cache hits and misses significantly overlap for messages longer than 200 bits. This suggests that short busts, separated by short pauses, provide lower error rates.

For cache-based CEC, we evaluated read and write errors separately, while varying t and t_{thresh}. To evaluate write errors, Snd published of 100,000 covert bits for each value

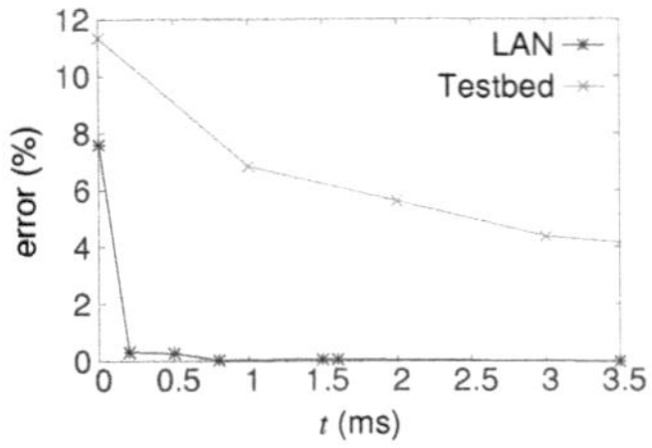

Figure 5: Cache-hit-based protocol: write error, varying t.

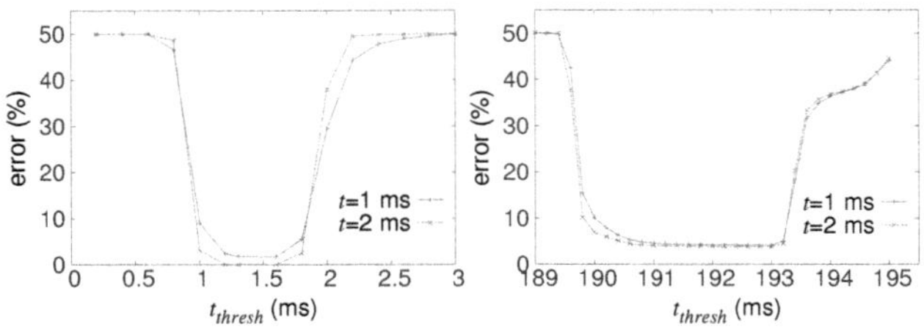

(a) LAN (b) Testbed

Figure 6: Cache-hit-based protocol: read error varying t_{thresh} and t.

of t. Covert bits were subsequently requested at a low rate ($t = 100$ ms) by Rcv. We then estimated how many content packets were not retrieved from cache. Figure 5 summarizes our findings. In this experiment, Rcv introduces a small measurement error. We estimate to be negligible in LAN, and below 1.5% on the testbed. With cache-based CEC, write errors can be completely eliminated if Snd re-issues interests for content that it did not receive; although, writing time increases.

To measure read errors, Snd published 100,000 covert bits, separated in groups of 1,000-bit CEMs, for each value of t and t_{thresh}. Results of this experiment are shown in Figure 6. Due to the clear separation between RTTs associated with cache hits and misses in LAN, read errors were very low for a wide range of parameters (e.g., for t_{thresh} between 1 and 1.5 ms). On the testbed, error was typically between 3% and 5% for t_{thresh} between 191 and 193 ms.

7.2 Evaluation of Delay-Based PIT Techniques

We requested the same content packet from both Snd and Rcv at very close intervals (i.e., 0.5 and 1 ms in LAN and 2 ms on testbed), in order to trigger interest collapsing on Rt, and, therefore, a PIT hit. Snd and Rcv were synchronized using a local NTP server; we estimated the time difference between the two hosts to be below 0.2 ms. Our experiments show that is possible to distinguish PIT hits from misses using appropriate intervals between interests from Snd and Rcv. Results of this experiment are shown in Figure 7. However, the separation is less clear than with cache, as shown in the same figure. Moreover, this channel requires much tighter synchronization between Snd and Rcv (i.e., sub-millisecond in LAN, and within 2 ms on testbed). For these reasons, PIT-based CEC are significantly more difficult to implement.

Since Snd and Rcv must operate synchronously and with the same t, we measured read and write errors jointly. For

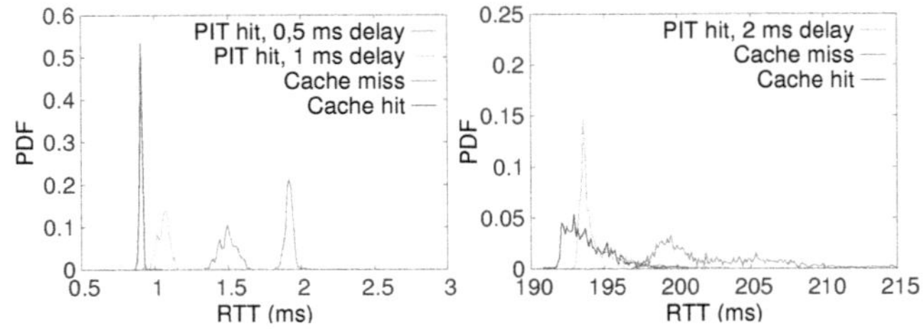

(a) LAN (b) Testbed

Figure 7: RTT for content packets causing PIT collisions.

this experiment, the delay between interests from Snd and Rcv is 0.8 ms in LAN, and 8 ms on the testbed. Results are shown in Figure 8. With appropriate choice of the threshold parameter, errors in LAN are negligible, and below 7.5% in the testbed.

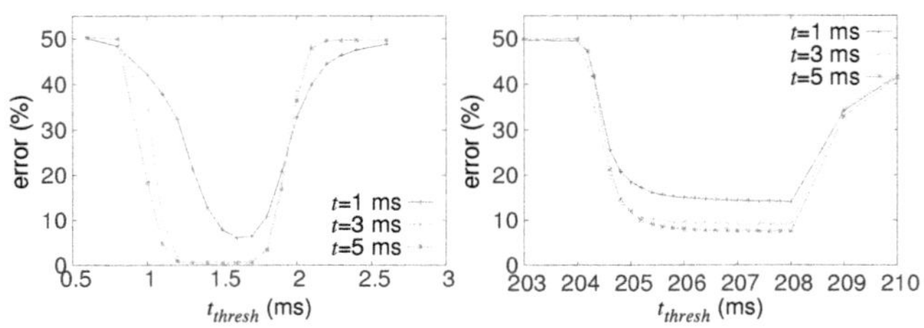

(a) LAN (b) Testbed

Figure 8: PIT hit-based protocol: joint write and read error varying t_{thresh} and t.

7.3 TDP Evaluation

We measured the error rate varying write and read speeds separately for Snd and Rcv. Figures 9a and 9b summarize our findings. On the receiver side, this technique performs better than the cache-hit-based one. For example, for $t = 1.5$ ms in the testbed, the error for TPD is less than 2% (see Figure 9b),while for $t = 3$ (i.e., the same effective bit rate relative to the CEM) in the cache-hit-based technique the error for is more than 4% (Figure 5).

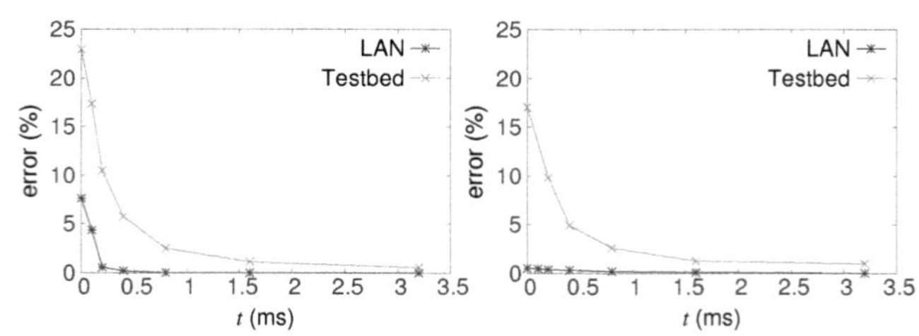

(a) Write error variation. (b) Read error variation.

Figure 9: TDP protocol: write and read error, varying, respectively, Snd's t and Rcv's t.

7.4 Evaluation of Common-Prefix-Based Technique

We set $m = 1$ (i.e., each content packet encodes one bit), in order to encode 1,000-bit CEM using 1,000 content packets. We run separate experiments to evaluate Snd and Rcv errors. As mentioned in Section 6, both parties can avoid packet-loss-induced errors using interest retransmission. For a fair comparison with previous protocols, we test how the common-prefix-based technique performs *without* retransmissions.

Results on write errors, both in our LAN and on the testbed, are identical to those in Figure 9a. Snd performs the same actions to send a CEM. Read errors on the testbed are reported in Figure 10. We omit the plot corresponding to read errors in LAN, since for all tested values of t error rate was below 0.03%. Errors for both Snd and Rcv are due to packet loss.

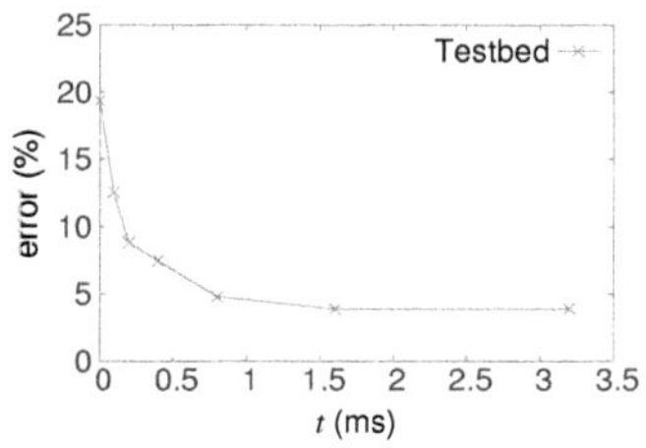

Figure 10: Common-prefix-based protocol: read error varying t.

7.5 Bit Rate and Error Comparison

To simplify comparison of techniques introduced in this paper, we combine effective bit rate and corresponding error for all our protocols in Figure 11. Note that, for TDP, Snd's effective bit rate can be *multiplied* by an arbitrary m, while Rcv's bit rate should be *divided* by 2^m. Analogously, the bit rate for both Snd and Rcv in the common-prefix protocol should be multiplied by m as discussed in Section 5.

8. SECURITY ANALYSIS

We now analyze security of CEC techniques. We start by showing that proposed protocols are retroactively private and secure against message recovery attack. We then conclude with an informal discussion on the detectability and robustness of our approaches.

8.1 Retroactive Privacy

Adv has non-negligible advantage over 1/2 in the retroactive privacy game (see Section 3) only if it can infer information about a from interaction with Snd, Rcv and Rt *after* the message M_a has expired. That is, Adv can only interact with protocol participants after content packets used to encode M_a have been removed from Rt's PIT and from all caches.

Since Snd and Rcv delete M_a as soon as they (respectively) send and receive it, Adv cannot acquire information about M_a by compromising the two parties. Similarly, NDN routers do not keep track of content packets once they disappear from both PIT and cache. Therefore, after M_a expires, Rt carries no information about the message. As a result, there is simply no information about M_a within the network after the message expires.

8.2 Security Against Message-Recovery Attacks

In order to reconstruct a CEM, Adv can probe all NDN routers, and try to identify content packets used for covert communication. However, this approach has two problems: (1) there is no content packet in routers caches for a bit set to 0; therefore, Adv cannot learn information about these bits by simply observing routers caches. (2) even for a relatively small NDN deployment, the number of routers and the size of their caches makes this attack infeasible.

Another adversarial strategy consists in infiltration of the routing infrastructure: Adv could mount a Sybil attack [30], deploying a large number of malicious NDN routers. We believe that this approach is not feasible, since: (1) Adv cannot deploy an arbitrary number of NDN routers. Even if NDN is implemented as an overlay, routers are identified by their unique IP address. This would force Adv to obtain a very large number of public IP address. (2) Even if the adversary succeeds deploying a large number of routers, it must log all content packets forwarded by all controlled routers. This may not be feasible. (3) Similarly, even if Adv can compromise arbitrary routers, maintaining logs for all forwarded content packets would not be viable.

8.3 Detectability

In order to exchange a message through our protocols, Snd and Rcv do not need to communicate directly, nor they need to be connected through the same NDN router. Moreover, they only interact with the network as prescribed by NDN specifications.

A single-bit message $b = 0$ sent using single-bit transmission via cache or PIT cannot be detected, since Snd performs no action. When $b = 1$, Snd retrieves a non-popular content packet. We believe that, in practice, by flagging all single interests for non-popular content packets as "suspicious", Adv would incur in an overwhelmingly large number of false alarms. Similarly, a single interest issued by Rcv to retrieve b would be easily hidden by the existing traffic.

When Snd and Rcv exchange messages longer than a single bit, however, their actions become more detectable. In particular, the longer the message, the more likely it is for Adv to correctly identify a CEM between two or more parties. While a single interest for non-popular content packets may not raise any suspect, a long streak of interests for non-popular content packets may be easy to notice. For this reason, Snd and Rcv should limit the size of the exchanged messages to reduce detectability.

Finally, with namespace-based covert communication detectability mostly depends on m and on the size of the covert. In particular, a higher value for m implies lower detectability: less content packets have to be requested to write and read a covert message.

8.4 Robustness

When Rt introduces arbitrary delays to conceal cache hits, our techniques based on measuring time difference between these two events do not work. However, techniques based on PIT and on common prefixes are not affected by cache hit delays, since they either do not rely on cache or do not consider RTT.

Similarly, when the network introduces unpredictable delays on packets (e.g., when traffic intensity has sudden wide fluctuations), common-prefix-based technique may be more appropriate since it does not rely on timing measurements.

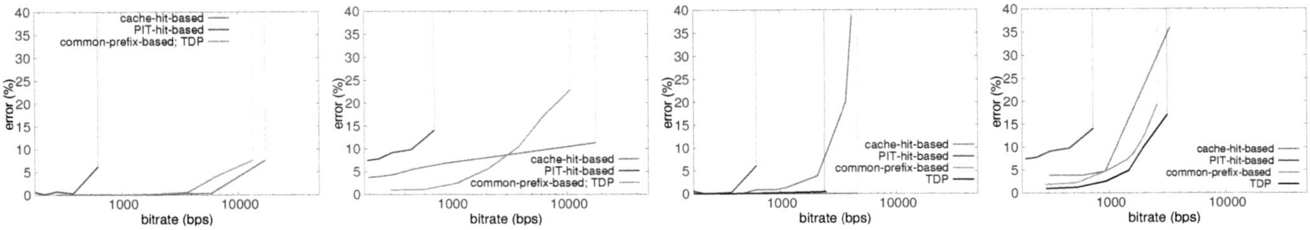

(a) LAN (Snd) (b) Testbed (Snd) (c) LAN (Rcv) (d) Testbed (Rcv)

Figure 11: Performance comparison.

9. RELATED WORK

We divide relevant related work in two classes: *covert communication* and *ephemeral communication*.

Covert Communication. The goal of a covert channel is to conceal the very existence of a covert message by communicating it through legitimate channels [17].

In [26], Shah et al. present Jitterbug, a hardware device and a communication protocol that covertly transmit content by perturbing the timing of keyboard events. In particular, the authors design and implement a small hardware *pass-through* device that introduces small – although, measurable – variations in the times at which keyboard events are delivered to the host. When the user runs an interactive communication protocol (e.g., SSH, instant messaging), a receiver monitoring the host's network traffic can recover the leaked content. According to the experimental results reported in [26], the bandwidth offered by Jitterbug is roughly 500 bps over 14 network hops, with 8.9% error rate. In contrast, our technique provide a bit rate of about 15,000 bps in a similar scenario with analogous error rate. Another difference is that with Jitterbug the receiver must be able to intercept network traffic, while our approach can be used by any unprivileged user.

CoCo, introduced in [17] by Houmansadr et al., is a framework for establishing covert channels via inter-packet delays. The sender generates a traffic flow directed to the receiver, then manipulates the flow according to the covert message and a key, shared between the two parties. The coding algorithm used in CoCo ensures robustness of the covert message to perturbations. The authors show statistical evidence on the undetectability of the communication channel. We emphasize that CoCo would not satisfy our requirements because sender and receiver must communicate directly.

Murdoch et al. [20] investigate covert channel implemented by embedding information in random-looking TCP fields. They show that naïve approaches – such as embedding ciphertext in the initial sequence number (ISN) field – can be easily detected. Then, they discuss how to implement networking stack-specific covert channel, which are provably undetectable. Similarly to CoCo, the main difference between our work and the work of Murdoch et al. is that sender and receiver must exchange packets directly.

Ephemeral Communication. Geambasu et al. introduced the Vanish system [15], which allows users to publish ephemeral messages. Users encrypt their messages using a random symmetric key. Then, they publish shares of the key (computed using Shamir secret sharing [25]) in random indices in a large, pre-existing distributed hash table (DHT). A DHT is a distributed data structure that holds key-value pairs. Since data on DHTs is automatically deleted over time, shares of the key automatically "disappear". Once enough shares have been deleted, the key – and therefore the encrypted message – is effectively erased.

Wolchok et al. [30] showed that Vanish can be defeated using low-cost Sybil attacks on the DHT. In particular, they exploited one of the design flaws of Vanish, namely the assumption that DHTs are resistant to crawling. This is in contrast with our approach, where monitoring all routers' caches is clearly infeasible. Although the authors of Vanish have since proposed countermeasures [14], these techniques only slightly raise the bar against existing attacks [5].

Castelluccia et al. [5] introduced EphPub, a DNS-based ephemeral communication technique. A publishers encrypts and distributes a message. Then, it distributes the decryption key as follows: for each key bit set to 1, the publisher picks a DNS resolver and uses it to answer a recursive DNS queries for a specific domain. Since DNS resolvers cache responses for a pre-determined amount of time, one or more receivers can subsequently issue *non-recursive* queries to the same resolver. These queries will be answered only if the corresponding domain-IP pair is in cache. Once enough cache entries expire (or get overwritten), the decryption key – and therefore the published message – disappears.

There are several differences between EphPub and our techniques. First, while EphPub relies on an application-layer service (DNS resolver) to publish an ephemeral piece of data, our techniques leverage routers' PITs and caches, which are part of the routing architecture. Moreover, while EphPub can be blocked by forcing users to use a local DNS server with no cache (e.g., by filtering out DNS queries at the network gateway), our PIT-based technique allows two parties to exchange CEMs even if routers do not provide content caching. Moreover, if EphPub sees wide adoption, there are several concerns (raised also by Castelluccia et al. in [5]) that would impose excessive load on DNS servers, which would then be forced to stop acting as "open" resolvers. In contrast, with our approach, communicating parties do not impose higher-than-usual load on routers: consumers simply use their allocated bandwidth for content retrieval. Furthermore, routers cannot determine the source of data requests (interests do not carry a source address), and therefore always operate similarly to open resolvers. Finally, EphPub does not provides covert communication, since the behavior of two users who communicate via EphPub is difficult to conceal. In fact, "regular" users rarely query multiple remote DNS servers in short bursts. With our techniques, instead, Snd and Rcv do not perform any easily identifiable activity.

Perlman [23] proposed Ephemerizer, a centralized approach to secure data deletion. The goal of Ephemerizer is to find a balance between data availability and the ability to properly delete data. Users encrypt their data using a symmetric encryption scheme. Then they delegate key storage to a trusted third party. This third party destroys cryptographic keys when they "expire", effectively making the original data unaccessible. Compared to [15], [5], as well as to our approach, Ephemerizer requires an always on-line, trusted third party.

10. CONCLUSIONS

In this paper, we have presented the first evaluation of covert ephemeral communication in NDN. Our techniques do not require Snd and Rcv to exchange any packet directly. Rather, they rely on user-driven state on routers to publish and retrieve covert messages. Messages published with our approach are ephemeral, i.e., they are automatically deleted from the network after a certain amount of time, without requiring any action from Snd or Rcv. Also, our delay-based techniques, messages *expire* immediately after being retrieved.

Our techniques are based on fundamental components on NDN, and do not require "abuse" of application-layer protocols. In practice Snd and Rcv only need access to non-popular content.

We performed experiments on a prototype implementation of our protocols. In particular, we measured the the bandwidth and robustness of our approaches on a local (LAN) setup and in a geographically distributed environment – the official NDN testbed. Our experiments confirm that the techniques proposed in this paper provide high bandwidth and low error rate.

11. ACKNOWLEDGEMENTS

We would like to thank Christos Papadopoulos, Steve DiBenedetto, Jeff Burke and Alex Horn for providing access to the NDN routers hosted at their respective institutions.

12. REFERENCES

[1] G. Acs, M. Conti, P. Gasti, C. Ghali, and G. Tsudik. Cache privacy in named-data networking. In *the 33rd International Conference on Distributed Computing Systems (ICDCS)*, pages 41–51, 2013.

[2] A. Afanasyev, P. Mahadevan, I. Moiseenko, E. Uzun, and L. Zhang. Interest flooding attack and countermeasures in Named Data Networking. In *IFIP Networking*, pages 1–9, 2013.

[3] Akamai. `http://www.akamai.com`.

[4] S. Cabuk, C. E. Brodley, and C. Shields. Ip covert timing channels: Design and detection. In *the 11th ACM Conference on Computer and Communications Security (CCS)*, pages 178–187, 2004.

[5] C. Castelluccia, E. D. Cristofaro, A. Francillon, and M. A. Kâafar. Ephpub: Toward robust ephemeral publishing. In *the IEEE International Conference on Network Protocols (ICNP)*, pages 165–175, 2011.

[6] Content centric networking (CCNx) project. `http://www.ccnx.org`.

[7] CCNx Interest Message. `http://www.ccnx.org/releases/latest/doc/technical/InterestMessage.html`.

[8] CCNx Node Model. `http://www.ccnx.org/releases/latest/doc/technical/CCNxProtocol.html`.

[9] A. Compagno, M. Conti, P. Gasti, and G. Tsudik. Poseidon: Mitigating interest flooding DDoS attacks in Named Data Networking. In *the IEEE Conference on Local Computer Networks (LCN)*, 2013.

[10] M. Conti, P. Gasti, and M. Teoli. A lightweight mechanism for detection of cache pollution attacks in Named Data Networking. *Computer Networks: The International Journal of Computer and Telecommunications Networking*, 57(16):3178–3191, Nov. 2013.

[11] S. DiBenedetto, P. Gasti, G. Tsudik, and E. Uzun. Andana: Anonymous named data networking application. In *the Network and Distributed System Security Symposium (NDSS)*, 2012.

[12] Facebook. `http://www.facebook.com`.

[13] P. Gasti, G. Tsudik, E. Uzun, and L. Zhang. DoS & DDoS in named-data networking. In *the International Conference on Computer Communications and Networks (ICCCN)*, pages 1–7, 2013.

[14] R. Geambasu, J. Falkner, P. Gardner, T. Kohno, and K. Krishnamurthy. Experiences building security applications on DHTs. Technical report, UW-CSE-09-09-01, University of Washington, 2009.

[15] R. Geambasu, T. Kohno, A. A. Levy, and H. M. Levy. Vanish: Increasing data privacy with self-destructing data. In *USENIX Security Symposium*, pages 299–316, 2009.

[16] Google global cache. `https://peering.google.com/about/ggc.html`.

[17] A. Houmansadr and N. Borisov. CoCo: Coding-Based Covert Timing Channels for Network Flows. In *the 13th Information Hiding Conference (IH)*, pages 314–328, 2011.

[18] Apple itunes. `http://itunes.apple.com`.

[19] W. Mazurczyk, K. Szczypiorski, and J. Lubacz. Four ways to smuggle messages through internet services. *Spectrum, IEEE*, 50(11):42–45, 2013.

[20] S. J. Murdoch and S. Lewis. Embedding covert channels into tcp/ip. In *Information Hiding: 7th International Workshop*, pages 247–261, 2005.

[21] Named Data Networking project (NDN). `http://named-data.org`.

[22] NDN Testbed. `http://www.named-data.net/testbed.html`.

[23] R. Perlman and R. Perlman. The ephemerizer: Making data disappear. *Journal of Information System Security*, 1:51–68, 2005.

[24] I. S. Reed and G. Solomon. Polynomial codes over certain finite fields. *Journal of the Society for Industrial and Applied Mathematics*, 8:300–304, 1960.

[25] R. L. Rivest, A. Shamir, and Y. Tauman. How to share a secret. *Communications of the ACM*, 22(22):612–613, 1979.

[26] G. Shah, A. Molina, and M. Blaze. Keyboards and covert channels. In *USENIX Security Symposium*, pages 59–75, 2006.

[27] Gps clock synchronization. `http://www.spectracomcorp.com/Solutions/Applications/GPSClockSynchronization/tabid/100/Default.aspx`.

[28] Google serves 25 percent of North American Internet traffic. http://www.wired.com/wiredenterprise/2013/07/google-internet-traffic/.

[29] M. Wählisch, T. C. Schmidt, and M. Vahlenkamp. Backscatter from the data plane - threats to stability and security in information-centric networking. *Computer Networks:The International Journal of Computer and Telecommunications Networking*, 57(16):3192–3206, Nov. 2013.

[30] S. Wolchok, O. S. Hofmann, N. Heninger, E. W. Felten, J. A. Halderman, C. J. Rossbach, B. Waters, and E. Witchel. Defeating vanish with low-cost sybil attacks against large DHTs. In *the Network and Distributed System Security Symposium (NDSS)*, 2010.

[31] M. Xie, I. Widjaja, and H. Wang. Enhancing cache robustness for content-centric networks. In *the IEEE International Conference on Computer Communications (INFOCOM)*, pages 2426–2434, 2012.

[32] Youtube. http://www.youtube.com.

Scanner Hunter: Understanding HTTP Scanning Traffic

Guowu Xie, Huy Hang
Department of Computer Science
University of California, Riverside
Riverside, California, United States
{xieg, hangh}@cs.ucr.edu

Michalis Faloutsos
Department of Computer Science
University of New Mexico, Albuquerque
Albuquerque, New Mexico, United States
michalis@cs.unm.edu

ABSTRACT

This paper focuses on detecting and studying HTTP scanners, which are malicious entities that explore a website selectively for "opportunities" that can potentially be used for subsequent intrusion attempts. Interestingly, there is practically no prior work on the detection of these entities, which are different from web crawlers or machines performing network-level reconnaissance activities such as port scanning. Detecting HTTP scanners is challenging as they are stealthy and often only probe a few key places on a website, so finding them is a needle-in-the-haystack problem. At the same time, they pose serious risk because they perform the first, exploratory step to provide the seed information that may allow hackers to compromise a website. Our work makes two main contributions. First, we propose Scanner Hunter, arguably the first method to detect HTTP scanners efficiently. The novelty and success of the method lies in the use of community structure, in an appropriately constructed bipartite graph, in order to expose groups of HTTP scanners. The rationale is that the aggregated behavior makes identifying groups of scanners easier than attempting to profile and label IP addresses individually. Scanner Hunter achieves an impressive 96.5% detection precision, which is roughly twice as high as the precision of the Machine Learning-based methods that we use as reference. Second, we provide an extensive study of HTTP scanners in an effort to understand: (a) their spatial and temporal properties, (b) the techniques and tools used by the scanners, and (c) the types of resources they are looking for, which can provides hints as to what the subsequent penetration attempt may target. We use six months worth of web traffic logs collected in 2012 from a University campus, the websites hosted by which received over 1.9 billion requests from 12.8 million IPs. We found that the number of HTTP scanners is non-trivial with roughly 4,000 IPs engaging in this type of activity per week. Our work will hopefully raise the awareness of the community regarding this problem while at the same time provide a promising detection technique that can provide the basis for mitigating the risk posed by HTTP scanners.

ASIA CCS'14, June 4–6, 2014, Kyoto, Japan.

ACM 978-1-4503-2800-5/14/06 ...$15.00.
http://dx.doi.org/10.1145/2590296.2590297.

Categories and Subject Descriptors

J.0 [**Computer Applications**]: General

Keywords

HTTP scanning, HTTP scanner, scanning traffic, web security, detection, vulnerability

1. INTRODUCTION

HTTP scanning is a fascinating and lesser known activity with which hackers aim to discover the security weaknesses of websites as a precursor to an actual penetration attempt. Specifically, in HTTP scanning, malicious entities probe a website for particular resources that seem promising for exploits or contain sensitive information that could reveal its structure and its underlying technology. These resources can be files with security-sensitive information, files containing passwords, zipped archives of the entire websites, or web interfaces for authorized users such as *phpmyadmin.php*.

The amount of requests sent by scanners is small compared to the traffic the websites received because they only probe for very specific files. At the same time, the risk that scanners pose is high. For example, an intrusion attempt that seems to have been enabled by HTTP scanning was carried out by the hacktivist group NullCrew [1]. The group broke into a Department of Homeland Security website after identifying files that should have been invisible to the general public.

The motivation for our work is the little attention that the problem has received so far and the ever-increasing importance of website security. First, there is currently no existing solution for this problem. Second, scanning is a first exploratory step towards compromising a website. Third, having a clear understanding of scanning behaviors could help administrators secure their websites and provide assistance during forensics analysis. Fourth, understanding what scanners are looking for can reveal what are the preferred vulnerabilities. Finally, understanding the spatiotemporal dynamics of these scanners can provide insights into the ecosystem that enables them.

The focus of this work is on the problem of HTTP scanning and our goal is to detect and understand the behavior of HTTP scanners. Ideally, a solution to this problem takes in as input web traffic logs that record all HTTP requests sent by external IPs and produces as the desired output a list of IPs that potentially engaged in HTTP scanning activities. For such a solution to be useful, it should be able to accomplish its task with minimal false alarms. This is a challenging problem for the following reasons: (a) scanners usually generate few requests, (b) it is not easy to distinguish between a scanner and a legitimate web user, and (c) the number of scanners is significantly smaller than the number of legitimate users, leading to a needle-in-the-haystack problem. We substantiate and quantify all these claims in later sections.

Surprisingly, this problem has attracted very little attention from the research community. In fact, ours is arguably the first work focusing on this problem, as we discuss in section 5. At the same time, it is equally important to clarify what we are **not doing**. Detecting HTTP scanners is different from identifying: (a) web crawlers, which collect information from the entire website for intelligence purposes (for instance, a retailer may want to know about the pricing offered by a competitor to adjust the prices of its own products), (b) network-level scanners such as IP or port scanners that try to discover vulnerable services running on specific ports of machines in the network, and (c) web application penetration attempts, which is the step following a successful HTTP scan, In section 5, we present related work in these areas, and discuss how the problems they aim to solve are different from the one we focus on.

As our main contribution, we present Scanner Hunter, arguably the most effective method to detect HTTP scanners, and study scanners and their behaviors over six months. The key novelty of Scanner Hunter is that it is a graph-based approach that detects HTTP scanners by focusing on the collective actions of scanners, who search for similar resources. In addition, we provide an extensive study of HTTP scanning activities over a six-month period to understand their scanning patterns and their spatiotemporal behavior. We use real web-logs collected from a University campus from March 2012 to September 2012 with over 1.9 billion HTTP requests from 12.8 million external IPs.

Note that, to enable further research in this novel direction, we will share with the research community the access logs from the HTTP scanners we have detected (with the IP addresses appropriately anonymized). Interested researchers may contact us for more information.

1. Scanner Hunter detects scanners with 96.5% precision. Our approach identifies malicious communities of IPs in an appropriately constructed bipartite graph that captures the interactions between two sets of entities: the IPs that generate HTTP requests and the resources[1] they have requested. Using a soft co-clustering technique, our approach identifies groups of IPs with similar requests. It then uses a labeling step that separates groups that engage in scanning from those of benign users. The use of clustering techniques on the graph makes the detection more accurate: scanning behaviors are easier to recognize for a group of IPs than for individual ones, especially since scanners are often stealthy. As a proof of concept, we conducted experiments with simple heuristics and standard Machine Learning techniques and observe that they only achieved 19.1% and 54.3% precision respectively, compared to 96.5% for Scanner Hunter. Even though a false positive rate of 3-4% may seem high, we want to stress that detecting scanners from millions of users at such a high precision is not trivial. We provide more details about the experiments in section 3

2. HTTP scanning is widespread: about 4,000 scanners per week for a medium-sized University network. We conducted an extensive study on scanning activities for a period of six months to understand: (a) their spatial and temporal properties, (b) their mechanisms and the effort to evade detection, and (c) what they are looking for. We highlight the most interesting observations.

a. Intensity: Roughly 4,000 unique IPs scan at least one website hosted by the University every week. At the same time, 80% of the IPs that appear every week have never been seen before.

b. Spatial distribution: Scanners are widely distributed across the IP space, which suggests that the IP prefix-based blocking of scanning activities would require a large and fine-grained filter set.

c. Complacency: Scanners do not seem afraid of getting caught, as they appear complacent and sloppy. For example, more than one third of the scanners used an unusual User-Agent in their requests and this User-Agent is `mozilla/4.0`, which, as we will show in section 4, is not a legitimate User-Agent.

d. Categories of scanners: We identify four major categories of scanners based on the resources they look for: (i) user registration and login pages, (ii) website management interfaces, (iii) pages with potential vulnerabilities that may allow activities like remote code execution, and (iv) compressed web archives such as `wwwroot.zip`, which are the products of website backup activities and should not be publicly visible.

Scope and intended use. Scanner Hunter is not meant to be: (i) a tool that can perform the same duties of an Intrusion Detection System, or (ii) a real-time solution for scanner detection.

Regarding (i), Scanner Hunter is an intelligence-gathering and advisory tool that can give the administrator a view into the malicious entities that are scoping out the website and the kinds of vulnerabilities that they are looking for. This knowledge can guide the administrator to take protective measures, as we discuss at the end of section 4.3.

Regarding (ii), real-time detection of scanners is inherently difficult. On the one hand, the labeling of an individual IP, especially one with few HTTP requests, is not easy given the wide variations in the behaviors of scanners as well as in the behaviors of legitimate users themselves. On the other hand, if we resort to traffic aggregation to obtain a more complete picture of behavior, like our approach does, we end up having to collect data over a sufficiently long window of observation. We discuss and substantiate this issue throughout the paper.

2. METHODOLOGY

In this section, we first provide some definitions and background and then present our method, Scanner Hunter.

2.1 Definitions and background

There are several types of **HTTP requests**, as one request can be a `POST`, a `GET`, a `HEAD`, or others. In this work, we are only interested in `POST`s and `GET`s for simplicity. A `POST` request sends information to the target website (e.g. filling an online form) and a `GET` request retrieves informa-

[1]A resource in this context is a file of any type and the full path leading to it. For example, `/phpmyadmin/scripts/inc.php`.

tion from the website. When a remote web server receives a HTTP request, the server will process it and return a response along with a response code that indicates whether the request succeeded.

A failed HTTP request is indicated by response code `40X`, where `X` is a single-digit number. For instance, the response code `404` indicates that the resource does not exist and `403` says that the server is refusing to return the requested resource [2]. Here, we refer to requests that trigger a response with code `40X` as failed HTTP requests, and the others, successful HTTP requests.

A User-Agent is a string contained in the `User-Agent` field of an HTTP request that provides some description about the application that generates the request. A typical value is the name of a web browser with version information.

The resource requested by an HTTP request (`example.com/inc/login.php?user=admin`) usually has four separate components: a domain name (`example.com`), a directory name (`/inc/`) that contains the file sought by an HTTP request, the name of the file (`login.php`), and a set of parameters (`user=admin`) that may alter the server's response. We define a **Re-Path**, which stands for Resource-Path, to be the portion of an URL that contains both the directory path and the name of the file. For example, the Re-Path in the example is `/inc/login.php`.

Although we have already defined HTTP scanners, here we want to highlight some interesting behaviors that we will exploit in detecting them. Note that these behaviors on their own are not sufficient without the additional techniques of our method, as we will show in section 3. Recall that scanners explore a website in a targeted fashion and their probing is a preparation for a subsequent exploitation. The behavior of scanners exhibits the following characteristics:

- Because scanners blindly look for resources of interest, many of their HTTP requests will fail.
- They do not request or even download embedded objects that are unlikely to lead to exploits like JPEG images.

Benign crawlers are automated programs chiefly used by search engines to index the Web. They are different from HTTP scanners in that they follow existing links instead of searching for resources that may not exist, b) they state what they are in the User-Agent field (e.g. Googlebot, Yahoo! Slurp, etc), c) the IP of the machine running the crawler program is usually registered by the company it belongs to, and d) they would (optionally) request the `robots.txt` file from the website that contains instructions as to where they're allowed to crawl.

A **stealthy crawler** is similar to a benign crawler in behavior except that it customizes its User-Agent field to make it look like their HTTP requests come from a regular web browser. There already exists work devoted to the detection of stealthy crawlers [3], and it is not a focus for our work.

2.2 Methodology

To identify HTTP scanners, there are four main steps, which Scanner Hunter executes as follows.

1. **Preprocessing**: Scanner Hunter processes the web traffic logs to filter out requests unlikely to be from HTTP scanners.
2. **Bipartite graph construction**: Scanner Hunter captures the suspicious HTTP requests in a bipartite graph where one set of vertices correspond to IPs and the other to the Re-Paths they requested.
3. **Co-clustering**: Scanner Hunter uses a soft co-clustering algorithm to group the IPs into communities where IPs in the same community have similar behaviors.
4. **Community labeling**: Scanner Hunter inspects each community output from previous step and label each of them as a community of users or scanners.

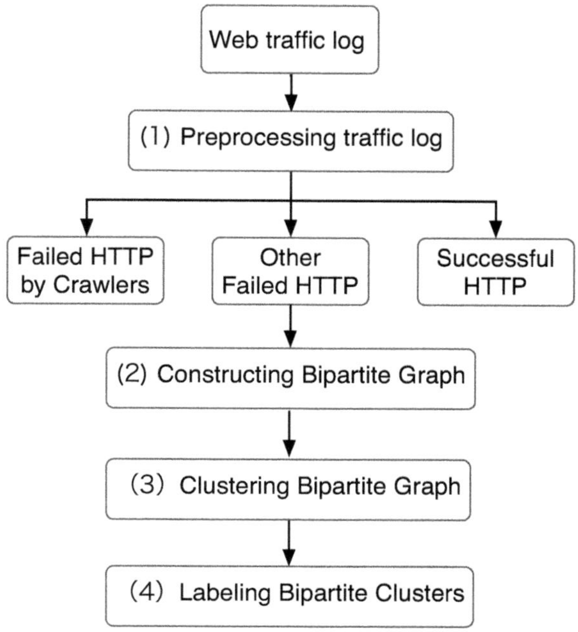

Figure 1: Scanner Hunter's main operations.

We now describe the operation and rationale of each step in detail. At the end, we will also explain why each step is necessary for achieving high precision in identifying scanners.

1. Preprocessing: Given web traffic logs as inputs, which may be collected by passively monitoring HTTP traffic or collected from web server logs (like Apache log files), Scanner Hunter reads in all HTTP requests from the logs and separate them into three different categories: successful HTTP requests, failed HTTP requests generated by web crawlers, and other failed HTTP requests. As their names suggest, the first category contains only successful HTTP requests, the second failed HTTP requests generated by known and benign web crawlers, and the third all other failed HTTP requests.

There are several reasons for including this step. First, popular websites receive an extremely high number of HTTP requests each day and processing all of them would consume a lot of time and resources. Second, we have seen from manual inspection that most scanners produce a large number of failed requests, which contain enough information for Scanner Hunter to identify the scanners.

In addition, we filter out requests that were followed by server-side errors and failed requests that may come from benign crawlers because they may generate them in the process of following all possible links whether they may be broken or not. The same crawlers may frequently re-check the web pages they have indexed before even after those same web pages have been removed. This means that crawlers exhibit similar behaviors to those of scanners and by removing the requests generated by legitimate crawlers, Scanner Hunter avoids mistaking the activities of benign crawlers for those of scanners and achieves higher accuracy. To this end, we first attempt to detect the presence of well known and benign web crawlers in the data according to the properties we mentioned in Section 2.1. Although there exist methods to detect web crawlers, as it is a well-studied problem [3], here we find it sufficient to label an IP as a benign crawler if two conditions are met:

C1: The User-Agent fields of its requests indicate that the application that generated the requests is a benign crawler (Googlebot, Yahoo! Slurp, etc.) and the IP has requested the file `robots.txt`.

C2: The information collected from reverse-DNS lookup of the IP indicates that the IP belongs to the organizations that User-Agent claims it is.

2. Bipartite graph construction: In this step, Scanner Hunter constructs a weighted undirected bipartite graph $G = \langle I, P, E\rangle$ where I is the set of IPs that produced the failed HTTP requests, P the set of Re-Paths that the IPs requested unsuccessfully, and E the set of edges. An edge $e \in E$ between IP $i \in I$ and Re-Path $p \in P$ if and only if IP i requested the Re-Path p but failed to access it during the monitoring interval. We assigned a uniform weight of 1 to all edges in the graph. Note that we did experiment with several other weight-assigning schemes (such as one where the weight of an edge is the number of times the IP requested the Re-Path) but we observed that the uniform weight allows Scanner Hunter to achieve the highest accuracy.

3. Co-clustering: Given the bipartite graph G generated in the previous step, Scanner Hunter uses a soft clustering algorithm[2] to partition G into a set of communities $C = \{c_1, c_2, \ldots c_n\}$. We adapted and used an algorithm inspired by Phantom [4], which we tailored to our problem. Each community c_i is a bipartite subgraph of the original G. Therefore, $c_i = \langle I_i, P_i, E_i\rangle$ where I_i is the set of all IPs in c_i, P_i the set of all Re-Paths in c_i, and E_i the set of all edges exclusively between I_i and P_i. We expect the output communities (used interchangeably with bipartite subgraphs from now on) from the soft clustering algorithm to have the following properties:

- The IPs (I_i) in each community are well-connected to each other through the Re-Paths (P_i) they requested.
- The soft-clustering approach may put an IP in more than one community because the IP may request many different Re-Paths.

The input to our adapted co-clustering algorithm is the bipartite graph G, represented by a weighted adjacency matrix M. In the beginning, the algorithm considers the graph as a single community that consists of all of the IPs and Re-Paths. For each community c:

1) The algorithm leverages a Singular Value Decomposition (SVD) technique to figure out how to best "cut" c into two child communities c_a and c_b so that a vertex in c_a will be more strongly connected to the other vertices in c_a than with those in c_b.

2) The algorithm computes the **cohesiveness** value of each of the two child communities. The cohesiveness of a child community indicates how well separated it is from its sibling.

Given a child community c_a and its sibling c_b, let $\gamma(c_a)$ and $\gamma(c_b)$ be the cohesiveness of c_a and c_b respectively, and they are calculated as follows. If E_c is the set of edges contained in the initial community c and E_{c_a} the set of all edges contained in c_a, $\gamma(c_a) = |E_{c_a}|/|E_c|$

3) Let T_γ be a predefined threshold for the cohesiveness value that dictates when Scanner Hunter would stop dividing communities. More specifically, if $\gamma(c_a) \geq T_\gamma$ and $\gamma(c_b) \geq T_\gamma$, the algorithm will retain both c_a and c_b and proceed to check if each of them can be divided further into smaller communities. Otherwise, the community c will not be divided further.

4) The algorithm stops when there is no community that can be subdivided.

The inquisitive reader can consult [4, 5] for details.

4. Community labeling: Even legitimate users may form communities in a bipartite graph because some popular web pages or embedded objects may become unavailable by accident. For this reason, in this step, Scanner Hunter inspects each community individually and employs a heuristic to determine whether the community consists of benign IPs or HTTP scanners. To this end, we carefully studied the scanners' activities to find potentially useful metrics. After many experiments, we narrowed down to two metrics that gave high precision: *average HTTP failure ratio* and *average embedded objects ratio*. The two metrics in combination capture the behavior of the scanners sufficiently for our algorithm to achieve high precision. Even though legitimate users may produce failed requests, their failure ratio is usually low. Moreover, scanners tend to not download embedded objects such as images or video and instead focus more on resources like `php`, `asp`, and `mdb` (database) files, which are more likely to be exploited.

We now define the average failure ratio and average embedded object ratio of a community c to capture the difference between communities of scanners and legitimate users.

- For IP address i, let T_i be its number of requests, F_i its number of failed requests, and N_i be the number of requests that IP i made for non-HTML document type resources (for example, images, javascript objects, etc.), i's **failure ratio** and **embedded-object ratio** are respectively: $FR(i) = F_i/T_i$, $ER(i) = N_i/T_i$
- The average failure ratio and the average embedded-object ratio of all IPs in a community c are respectively:
  $FR(c) = \frac{1}{|c|}\sum_{i\in c} FR(i)$, $ER(c) = \frac{1}{|c|}\sum_{i\in c} ER(i)$

If there exists a community c where $FR(c) > T_{FR}$ and $ER(c) < T_{ER}$, Scanner Hunter will label c as a community of HTTP scanners. All IPs in these community are considered as HTTP scanners. This heuristic is very useful because it allows Scanner Hunter to avoid mislabeling communities that may be formed by benign IPs requesting misplaced/temporarily unavailable resources. We will discuss the effectiveness of this heuristic in the following section.

We also would like to stress that both co-clustering and labeling are integral to the performance of Scanner Hunter because: i) inspecting individual IPs and relying on the IPs' failed requests alone will generate a high amount of False Positives (which we will show in section 3 and ii) blindly labeling each community after co-clustering will also lead to

[2] A soft clustering algorithm is one that allows a single node in the graph to be in more than one communities.

mislabeling benign IPs as scanners, as we have explained in Step 4 of Scanner Hunter.

3. PERFORMANCE EVALUATION

In this section, we present the dataset used in our study (3.1), how we select values for the parameters of Scanner Hunter (3.2), and how we evaluate the performance of Scanner Hunter (3.4).

3.1 Dataset and evaluation method

Our real-world dataset consists of 28 weeks of Web traffic collected from a University campus network.

Our data collection tool was deployed at the only edge gateway router connecting the University to the Internet, which all incoming and outgoing Web traffic passes through. At this gateway router, we captured the full payload of all packets arriving at TCP ports 80, 8000, and 8080 of the University's servers. Afterwards, we performed Deep-Packet Inspection (DPI) on each packet to extract all of the HTTP requests sent toward the websites internal to the University as well as the associated HTTP responses. The important fields that we logged from each HTTP request and response are: timestamp, URL, server IP, client IP, content-type, content-length, response code, referrer, and User-Agent.

On a average, we recorded 70.6M requests a week from 929.6K external IPs, 409.8K of which generated a total of 7.5M failed requests. We presented these weekly averages because we apply Scanner Hunter on the weekly partitions rather than the full dataset. We will discuss the motivation for partitioning data into weeks in the next section.

Metrics: We use two metrics to measure Scanner Hunter's performance: **Precision (P)** and the total number of labeled scanners. Given the numbers of **True Positive (TP)**, **False Positive (FP)**, the Precision, which is the fraction of IPs we label as scanners that are in fact scanners, is calculated as: $P = \text{TP}/(\text{TP} + \text{FP})$

Validation. Given that we do not have the ground-truth in our dataset, we did not evaluate the recall for Scanner Hunter. Instead, we focus on assessing the accuracy of identification, which we try to achieve through sampling and manual verification. We manually assess if each IP is an HTTP scanner or not based on all its HTTP transactions during the monitoring interval. Specifically, we consider its User-Agent, the Re-Paths it asked for, its failure ratio, its embedded-object ratio, the referrers for each of its requests, and the HTTP response codes that it received when the requests themselves failed. We are very conservative in our manual verification and only label those IPs with very obvious scanning activities as scanners.

To evaluate the precision, we randomly select 300 IPs from labeled scanners by Scanner Hunter, then manually verify them as described before, and label an IP as a True Positive, if it clearly exhibited the characteristics of an HTTP scanner. Otherwise, we count it as a False Positive.

3.2 Parameter selection

a. Cohesiveness threshold T_γ: The soft co-clustering algorithm has the cohesiveness threshold T_γ as its sole parameter. To recap, the cohesiveness threshold determines when the algorithm should stop subdividing a community. As Figure 2(a) shows, the lower the value of cohesiveness, the co-clustering algorithm creates more smaller but more strongly connected non-trivial communities. A non-trivial community is one in which there is more than one IP and one Re-Path. Essentially, lower cohesiveness value leads to the creation of communities in which the IPs are more similar in behaviors because they have requested similar resources.

To determine the right threshold value, we conducted an experiment where we varied T_γ and tried to assess the performance of Scanner Hunter on the training partion d. For each value of T_γ shown in Figure 2(b), we can see that when we set the value of T_γ to 0.975, we achieve a good balance between precision and the total number of labeled scanners. This is the value that we use in the rest of this paper.

b. Embedded and failure ratios: Once we have the communities, Scanner Hunter performs its labeling step. To recap, given a community $\mathbf{c_i}$ in the set of all communities $\mathbf{C}$, the community's failure ratio is $\mathbf{FR(c_i)}$ and $\mathbf{ER(c_i)}$ its embedded-object ratio. Let T_{FR} and T_{ER} be thresholds such that if $FR(c_i) > T_{FR}$ and $ER(c_i) < T_{ER}$, we label c as a community of HTTP scanners and c_i as a community of users otherwise. We will show below the process that helps us decide the values for T_{ER} and T_{FR}.

We first picked one weekly partition of our data as a training dataset, henceforth referred to as d, and ran Scanner Hunter's clustering step on d with a cohesiveness value of 0.975. Given the set of communities $C = \{c_1, c_2, ..., c_n\}$ produced by this step, we represent each c_i as a pair of coordinates (x_i, y_i) where $x_i = FR(c_i)$ and $y_i = ER(c_i)$ and plot the set C as a heat map as shown in Figure 2(c).

Recall that an HTTP scanner tends to have a higher failure ratio and a lower embedded-object ratio than a legitimate user because the scanner does not know exactly where the vulnerable resources reside and does not want to waste bandwidth downloading objects it does not need. This observation, in turns, implies that the communities located in the lower right quadrant of the heat map in Figure 2(c) would be the most suspicious.

Selecting threshold values for T_{FR} and T_{ER}. We begin with the community with the highest failure ratio and the lowest embedded-object ratio and set T_{FR} and T_{ER} to this community's values, in essence defining a rectangular area limited by the lines $y = T_{ER}$, $x = T_{FR}$, $x = 1.0$, and $y = 0$. We then manually inspected each community inside this area to judge whether each IP in that community is an HTTP scanner before we expanded the area by increasing T_{ER} and decreasing T_{FR}. What we observed in this process is that when we vary the values of T_{ER} and T_{FR} within the range of [0.25, 0.6], Scanner Hunter achieved a reasonable balance between the number of correctly identified scanners and the number of mislabeled legitimate users. We also repeated the same process with different values of cohesiveness and came to the same conclusion each time: with [0.25, 0.6] as a range of candidate values for T_{ER} and T_{FR}, Scanner Hunter achieves a high level of accuracy.

In conclusion, our study showed that the performance of our approach is quite robust to the values of the thresholds in the range [0.25, 0.6]. In the rest of this paper, we report results using $T_{ER} = 0.5$ and $T_{FR} = 0.5$.

3.3 Understanding False Positives

We want to further investigate why our approach misclassifies some IPs as HTTP scanners. An added benefit of using a manual verification process is that it provided us with a first-hand knowledge of falsely labeled IP addresses. We find two basic groups among the False Positive cases:

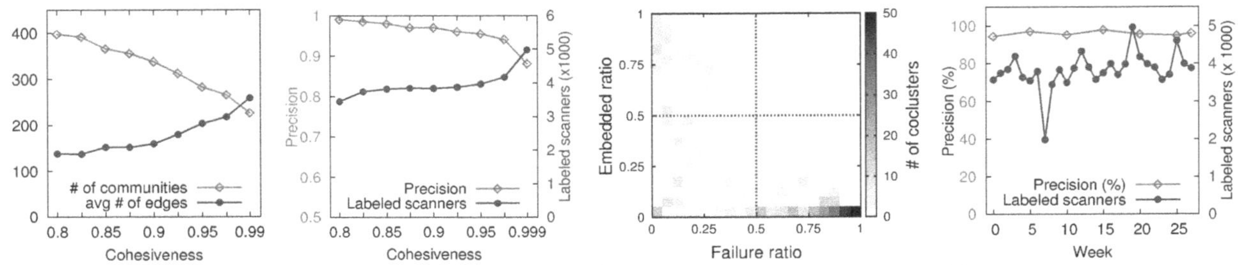

(a) # and avg. size of communities as a function of cohesiveness

(b) Precision and # of IPs labeled as scanners with varied cohesiveness

(c) T_{FR} and T_{ER} of communities generated by cohesiveness value 0.975

(d) # of IP prefixes of scanners and users

Figure 2: Parameter selection. In 2(b), the values for T_{ER} and T_{FR} are respectively 0.5 and 0.5

Benign web crawlers: 89% of all misclassified IPs belong to stealthy crawlers masquerading as regular users, as we determined in our manual inspection. These IPs downloaded very few embedded objects and they crawled a small number of pages, some of which happened to be unavailable due to broken links. The resulting high failure ratio and low embedded-object ratio confused our algorithm.

Legitimate web users: The remaining 11% of the False positives are legitimate users. Let's say that there exists a web page w_1 at the URL `abc.com/index.html` and there is an embedded object o on w that is hosted by website w_2 at the URL `xyz.com/tmp.php`, where our monitoring tool is placed. In the case that w_1 is very popular and o is suddenly unavailable, all of the requests intended for o will consequently fail.

Because our monitoring point is at w_2, it would appear as if a large number of users are requesting a non-existing resource because our monitoring tool is not aware of w_1. As a result, Scanner Hunter will group the IPs requesting o into a community in which the failure ratio and embedded-object ratio exceed the predefined thresholds. All of the IPs in this community will then be labeled as HTTP scanners. This is the reason why Scanner Hunter mislabeled that very small percentage of benign IPs in our dataset.

3.4 Evaluating Scanner Hunter

a. Precision is stable over time. We used one week's data to establish the values of the three parameters of our Scanner Hunter, namely cohesiveness threshold T_γ, embedded-object ratio threshold T_{ER}, and failure ratio T_{FR}.

We assess the performance of our approach on five other weekly data partitions in Figure 2(d) (top flat red line). On average, the precision of Scanner Hunter is 96.5%. This is a success, given that there are nearly one million external IPs in each weekly data partition. We validated these Precision rates in through sampling and manual inspection, using the same process as in the training set.

Figure 2(d) (lower jagged blue line) shows the total number of IPs labeled as scanners by Scanner Hunter for each of the weekly partitions. Note that the sharp drop in identified scanners on the 8th weekly partition is an artifact of the data collection: for three days out of seven of the 8th week, there were issues with the monitor device and the collection was incomplete.

b. Comparing Scanner Hunter with our baseline approaches. Here, we introduce two baseline approaches as reference points in evaluating the performance of our approach. We consider two fundamental approaches: a simple heuristic and a group of machine-learning algorithms. Both of these methods develop profiles and compare IPs in isolation, in contrast to our graph-based approach. We show the results for these two baseline approaches to provide some insight into the complexity of the problem of detecting HTTP scanners. Ultimately, this comparison demonstrates that the graph-based technique used by Scanner Hunter is crucial for obtaining high precision and recall rates.

First, the simple heuristic decides if an IP is a scanner only based on its failure and embedded-object ratios, as we explain below. Second, the machine-learning (ML) approach develops a profile of how a HTTP scanner behaves, and uses that to determine if an IP is a scanner or not. We used the WEKA machine learning software tool, and considered multiple ML algorithms and did significant fine-tuning and parameter optimization.

We introduce both approaches in order to provide some insight into the difficulty of the problem Scanner Hunter was designed to solve. Overall, both the simple heuristic and the ML approach perform poorly (19.1% and 54.3% respectively), compared to the 96.5% precision of Scanner Hunter. We attribute this to the use of communities that helps reveal the similar behaviors of scanners as they are viewed in terms of groups while looking at each IP in isolation does not provide enough information to identify scanners.

1. Simple heuristic: The simple heuristic determines if an IP i is an HTTP scanner or not based on the two metrics: $FR(i)$ and $ER(i)$. Specifically, if $FR(i) > T_{FR}$ and $ER(i) < T_{ER}$, then IP i is labeled as a scanner. Recall that Scanner Hunter determines whether a community is one of HTTP scanners based on the community's failure ratio FR and embedded-object ratio ER.

For evaluating the simple heuristic, we randomly selected a weekly data partition D_i and applied the heuristic on it. We varied the values for T_{ER} and T_{FR} and chose the ones that produced the **highest** Precision rates, which we obtained in the same way that we described in Section 2.

2. Machine-learning algorithms: From the machine leaning software collection WEKA [6], we selected three commonly used algorithms: Support Vector Machine (SVM), K-Nearest Neighbors (K = 1, 3, 5), and Decision Trees. We created our training data from HTTP scanners identified by Scanner Hunter, since we are not aware of any other method to obtain a large training set. We considered using only manually verified scanners, but the training set would have been to small.

Feature selection. For each algorithm, we consider a total of 15 features: failure ratio, embedded-object ratio, suspicious referrer ratio, the number of and the ratio of requested non-existing Re-Path, the maximum, average, and minimum size of connected component in the referrer graph, the maximum number of consecutive failed HTTP requests, the Inter-Arrival Time (IAT) between two consecutive failed requests, and the number of retries after a failure. Using WEKA's feature elimination capability, we narrowed the set of 15 features down to a total of 9: failure ratio, embedded-object ratio, suspicious referrer ratio (a referrer value is suspicious if it is the empty string or it is exactly the same value as the URL of the website), the ratio of requested non-existing Re-Paths, the size of the largest connected component in referrer graph, the maximum number of consecutive failed HTTP requests, the IAT between two consecutive failed requests, and the number of retries after a failure.

Training the ML algorithms. We picked two consecutive weekly data partitions D_i and D_{i+1}, the former for training and the latter for testing. We first applied Scanner Hunter on D_i to obtain a list of n potential scanners and selected also n IPs determined to be benign by Scanner Hunter; we call this first set M and the second B. We then used the HTTP requests produced by each IP in both sets to train the ML algorithms, which were then used to classify the IPs in the data partition D_{i+1}.

Note that the IPs in set M do not include all of the IPs labeled as scanners by Scanner Hunter in D_i. We have to exclude some IPs from Scanner Hunter's results because the ML algorithms require that there are enough HTTP requests produced by each IP (in this case, at least 5) to be effective. Each of the IPs in M then had at least 5 HTTP requests associated with them.

From our experiments, the three ML algorithms exhibited comparable performances. The Decision Tree algorithms (more specifically "Adtree") achieved slightly higher precision in a few of our experiments. As a result, we selected Decision Trees as the representative from the ML-based approach, and we use the term "ML learning algorithm" to refer to Decision Trees for the remaining of this paper.

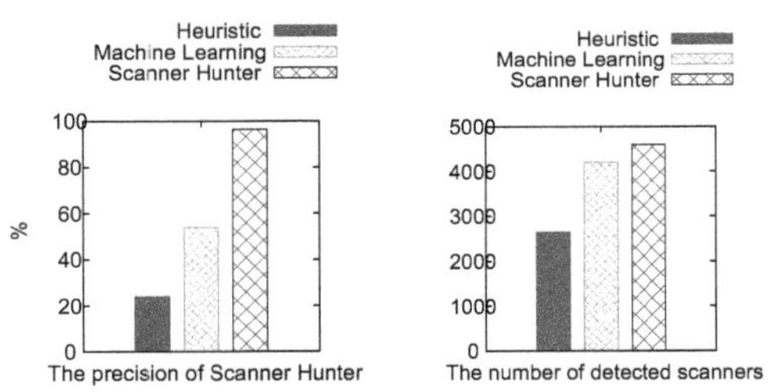

Figure 3: Performances of Scanner Hunter and baselines

Comparison: the precision of Scanner Hunter is close to twice that of the ML algorithm. We can see from Figure 3 (top) that the precision for the simple heuristic and ML approaches are only 19.1% and 54.3%, respectively. It must be stressed that for the heuristic approach, we varied the parameters and provided the **highest** precision it could achieve. For the ML approach, we picked the algorithm that gave the best performance with respect to precision. The fact that both approaches performed poorly underscores an important observation: scanners and users exhibit a wide range and often similar behaviors that classifying individual IPs is a difficult problem. This suggests that there is a need to aggregate the behavior and classify groups instead, which forms the basis of our graph-based approach.

Comparison: Scanner Hunter identifies more scanners more accurately. Not only is the precision of Scanner Hunter higher, it also identifies more scanners than the two baseline methods. In Figure 3 (bottom), we plot the number of scanners that each method identified. Although the difference between the numbers of detected scanners for Scanner Hunter and the ML algorithm is not large, the fact is that Scanner Hunter enjoys a much higher precision and therefore is capable of capturing more scanners while having much fewer false alarms.

3.5 Discussion

Here, we discuss various practical deployment tips, how adversaries may evade Scanner Hunter, and the effect of NAT and dynamic IP allocation.

Selecting the right window of observation. Throughout the paper, we used a week as the time interval units and partitioned our data accordingly. We experimented with daily web logs, but we observed that the amount of scanner traffic in each partition was too small. As a result, there was limited information available to the co-clustering step, which is a critical component of Scanner Hunter. Specifically, with an insufficient number of HTTP requests from scanners, cohesive communities would not be formed and scanners would eventually be isolated into their own trivial communities. When we applied Scanner Hunter on multiple daily data partitions, we observed that Scanner Hunter still exhibited high precision, but the amount of detected scanners dropped significantly.

As a practical tip, if a network administrator wants to use Scanner Hunter, we would recommend them to tune the monitoring interval according to the size of their network, as one that is large enough may attract sufficient requests from scanners to enable a finer-grained partitioning of data.

Evading detection. At a high level, the scanner should have to (a) visit available web pages that are unrelated to its purposes, (b) download embedded objects such as pictures and video, and (c) send HTTP requests from as many different IPs as possible, ideally, one HTTP request per IP. However, these efforts would increase the cost of scanning in terms of time, download bandwidth, or the number of IP addresses under the malicious entity's control. Furthermore, this would force the scanner to stand out from the targeted website's point of view, as the scanner would have no choice but produce much more traffic toward the website.

How dynamic IP allocation and NAT affect Scanner Hunter. Because Scanner Hunter captures the behaviors of HTTP scanners, the dynamic allocation of IPs with moderate dynamic behavior would not impair Scanner Hunter's performance. Scanner Hunter does not use any information that can be retrieved from the IP address for the purpose of detection. In fact, the use of a group-based method will likely circumvent the issue as the same scanner behind many different dynamic IPs would search for similar non-existent resources and be put into the same community.

It is possible that in the case where there are many machines sharing the same public IP due to the effect of Network Address Translation (NAT), the amount of failed requests produced by a malicious scanner may become "diluted" by of many more legitimate requests from the other machines with an identical IP. However, in practice the effect of NATs will depend on: (a) how popular the targeted website is, and (b) the number of real IPs behind the NAT.

Both factors determine the probability that a non-scanning IP behind the NAT will contact the same website that the scanner behind the NAT is probing. Finally, if NATs become a significant concern, we can modify the way in which Scanner Hunter operates: instead of grouping requests by the IP addresses can group the requests by the tuple ⟨IP, User-Agent⟩. We believe this would be a good solution as it has been shown in [7] that when a User-Agent is combined with an IP address, they can become a fingerprint that can effectively distinguishes remote browsers.

Using Scanner Hunter to assist in creating honeypots. Once Scanner Hunter has been run, the network administrator can certainly gather the nonexistent URLs requested by the scanners to create a set of fake webpages not linked to by any other legitimate pages. They then can monitor these fake pages and observe the IPs trying to access them.

4. PROFILING SCANNERS IN THE WILD

In this section, we present the results of the extensive study we conducted on the behaviors of HTTP scanners in the wild. These are the highlights from this study: 1) scanners are widely dispersed across IP space; 2) more than 90% of the returning scanners look for new resources and at least half of the Re-Paths that they request are new; 3) scanners spent little attention on disguising themselves to avoid detection, as seen by their complacent use of User-Agent and referrer fields in the requests; 4) there are four categories of vulnerabilities that the scanners in our dataset are interested in.

4.1 Spatiotemporal properties of scanners

One of the more obvious questions that comes to mind is whether a network administrator can prevent scanning activities by blocking HTTP requests from certain IP prefixes. The answer is that such a solution will not be very practical or efficient because of two conclusions that we made once we have studied more closely the spatial and temporal properties of scanners: 1) the filter set will have to be large enough to cover all of the diverse IP prefixes, 2) the filters would have short life-span and will be of limited use because most (80%) HTTP scanners, as we will show, are seen only once and never come back.

Figure 4(a) demonstrates the reason why we conclude that the IP addresses black list keep track of for the purpose of blocking scanning IPs will have to be large. In this figure, we show the percentage of distinct prefixes that remain each time we remove the least octet from the IP address. We can see that, for example, the number of distinct /16 IP prefixes accounts for at least 60% of the total number of original IPs. Furthermore, because HTTP scanners are as diversely distributed across the IP space as users, it follows that an extremely large and fine-grained filter set would be needed to block the scanners.

Figure 4(b) demonstrates the reason why the aforementioned filters will have limited life spans and usefulness. In this figure, we show the result of the experiment in which we kept track of each scanner labeled by Scanner Hunter and count how many daily visits they paid to the monitored websites during one week and during the entire six-month period. Interesting enough, no more than 20% of the scanners return to the websites hosted by the University campus in either periods. In fact, less than **5%** of them came back for a third time. This clearly indicates that no IP prefix-based, static blacklists can keep up with the scanning activities.

What we would like to know then, given that some (20%) scanners do return to the same websites, is whether scanners look for the same resources or different ones during subsequent visits. To find out, we performed an experiment on the entire six-month-long dataset as follows. Let the set S be scanner IPs that visited the monitored websites more than twice on different days. For each $s \in S$ we calculated the Average Ratio of new resources that s looks for using the following formula:

$$AR(s) = \frac{1}{n-1} \sum_{i=2}^{n} \frac{|W_i \setminus \bigcup_{j=1}^{i-1} W_j|}{|W_i|}$$

n is the total number of daily visits that s paid to the monitored websites, W_i is the set of Re-Paths sought by s on the ith visit in the dataset, and $\bigcup_{j=1}^{i-1} W_j$ represents the accumulative set of every resource that s has requested up to the $(i-1)^{th}$ visit. The $(i-1)^{th}$ and i^{th} visits do not have to be on consecutive days.

What we discovered from the experiment is shown in Figure 4(c): for more than 90% of the returning scanners, half of what they look for each time is new. This indicates that the scanners that do come back tend to probe for resources that they did not request before.

4.2 The tools used for HTTP scanning

Not only are we interested in identifying HTTP scanners, we also would like to know about the existing tools that allow them to carry out the act. As it turns out, the values of the User-Agent fields in the HTTP requests can give us an insight into the types of applications the scanners use. In Appendix A we show the values and statistics for the top 10 most popular User-Agents used by the HTTP scanners identified by Scanner Hunter so the more inquisitive reader can take a look. Although most of them are simpler than User-Agent strings produced by major browsers, there are three that deserve the most scrutiny:

- `mozilla/4.0`: Even though the User-Agent string mentions mozilla, the requests with this User-Agent string were not generated by the popular Firefox browser because it has no information on the system on which the browser runs or the information about the plugins within the browser. An example of a legitimate User-Agent string is: `Mozilla/5.0 (Macintosh; Intel Mac OS X 10_8_4) AppleWebKit/537.36 (KHTML, like Gecko) Chrome/ 28.0.1500.71 Safari/537.36`
- `<empty>`: This means the User-Agent field is empty. By default, none of the major web browsers generate requests with empty User-Agent field.
- `ineturl:/1.0`: This User-Agent string can be found by a number of HTTP-based applications that use a specific library. In this case, it may be possible that a number of malicious entities used the library to implement their scanning tools.

At the same time, we were also interested in the distribution of the number of User-Agents per scanning IP address. From Figure 4(d), we can clearly see that each IP in the 90% of the IPs labeled as scanners by Scanner Hunter produced requests with exactly one User-Agent string. We take this to suggest that most scanners use only one scanning application.

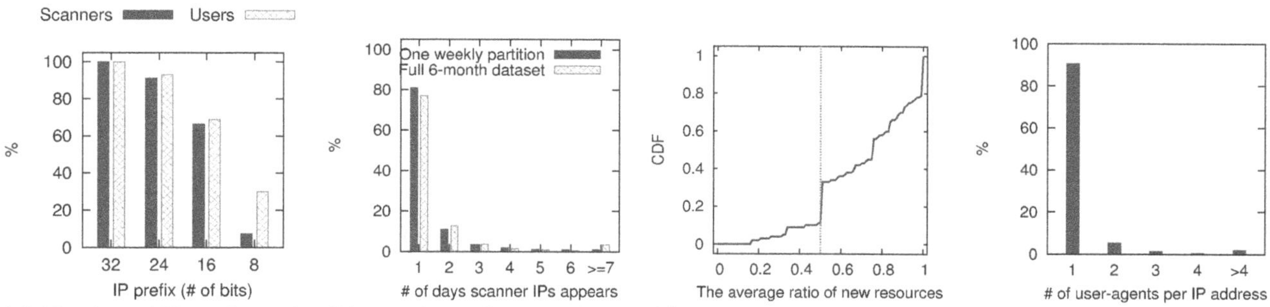

(a) Number of IP prefixes of scanners and users

(b) Number of IP prefixes of scanners and users

(c) Scanners look for new things when coming back

(d) Scanners tend to not have empty User-Agents.

Figure 4: Spatio-temporal behaviors of scanners in the wild

There are IPs associated with more than one User-Agent string, as seen in the same Figure. When we manually looked into the HTTP requests produced by those IPs, we observed that a) different User-Agents showed up at different times during the day, and b) different User-Agents requested different Re-Paths. Therefore we believed that most of them were different scanners that happened to fall under the same IPs due to the effect of Network Address Translation (NAT).

Interestingly, however, there is a reason for us to believe that there were also scanners that used more than one application at a time. For example, there are four IPs located inside the Autonomous System number `50543` that are suspicious because:

- Each IP appeared on multiple blacklists [8].
- Each IP is associated with the same two User-Agents.
- Their behaviors are similar. For example, suspicious IP s_1 sent two set of requests, each with a different User-Agent. The requests are close in time and the two User-Agents almost always appeared in a specific order.

Given the above facts, we came to the conclusion that there is a strong likelihood each of those IPs used two applications for malicious purposes: one application to probe for the existence of vulnerable resources and the other to analyze the resources that the first application actually discovered. Even more interesting is the fact that the same two User-Agents could be seen with each of the 4 IPs: `xpymep.exe` and `mozilla /4.0 (compatible; msie 6.0; windows 98; win 9x 4.90)`. According to [9], `xpymep.exe` is the name of a binary that is considered unsafe to download.

One natural question that can be asked is whether a network administrator can block scanning activities using the values of the User-Agent fields in the HTTP requests. The answer is no because of two reasons: 1) the False Positive rate would be high, and 2) even though such a solution may mitigate scanning activities in the short term, it would not be effective in the long run due to how trivial it is to change the value of the User-Agent field. After all, scanners leave their User-Agent strings as-is possibly because of the little attention the problem has received. Once the scanners realize that the User-Agent strings may be a liability, we believe they would spend more effort on disguising the User-Agent more carefully.

4.3 What resources scanners look for

We present our findings regarding the resources that a scanner may be most interested in because armed with this knowledge, network administrators can gain a better understanding of the scanners' motivations and better secure their networks. For this purpose, we collected all the Re-Paths requested by the IPs labeled as scanners by Scanner Hunter for the entire 6-month duration of our full dataset, extract their file types, and ranked them according to their popularity.

There are three types of files that dominate the list and account for 97% of the requests: **php** (43%), **asp/aspx** (26%), and **rar/zip/7z** (24%). The most probable explanation would be that **php** and **asp/aspx** scripts are the least secured with respect to access permissions or more likely to contain exploitable vulnerabilities. The **rar/zip/7z** are compressed archives that, in the context of web server management, tend to be files used for backup or storing outdated data and, if left unsecured, would provide information that could enable future exploitations.

Identifying groups of resources systematically. We wanted to obtain a deeper understanding as to the intention of the scanners beyond the file types they are looking for. For that, we tried to identify categories of scanners based on the targeted Re-Paths. More precisely, we performed the following actions on each of the communities labeled as scanners by Scanner Hunter:

(a) We extract all Re-Paths from the community and remove all non-alphanumeric characters from them.
(b) We convert each processed Re-Path into **trigrams**, which are sequences of three consecutive characters. Once the trigrams are extracted, the community is represented by the set of unique trigrams.

Given the set of communities $C = \{c_i\}$, $1 \leq i \leq |C|$, let t_i be the trigram set representation for each c_i. We then compute the Jaccard similarity measurement between every possible pair: $J(c_i, c_j) = |t_i \cap t_j|/|t_i \cup t_j|$

We then identify groups of similar communities of scanners as follows:

(a) We pick the pair of communities with the largest similarity value and, if this similarity exceeds a threshold T_J, we merge them to form a new community.
(b) We calculate the similarity measurement between the new community with all old ones.
(c) We repeat the above two steps until the largest similarity between any two communities is less than T_J.

We experimented with different values for the Jaccard similarity threshold T_J and found out $T_J = 0.3$ works reasonably well. Table 1 shows the top 10 largest groups (out of 42) that remain once the merging concludes. The first column contains the ranks of the groups according to the number of unique IPs, the second the number of scanning IPs in each

#	#IPs	#Re-Paths	File types	URL patterns	Description
1	913	337	asp(58.3%) php (36.7%)	reg.asp, user_reg.aspx bbs/reg.php, login.asp	User registration and login pages
2	664	1143	asp (91.2%)	*member/index_do.php	Unclear
3	569	11273	rar/zip/7z (94.7%)	*wwwroot.zip	Backup files
4	433	9098	php (87.1%)	{include | data | plus}/*.php	Unclear
5	203	4836	asp (99.8%)	wp-{admin | login | comments | trackback}*.php	wordpress-related vulnerabilities
6	126	689	php (94.7%)	wp-content/*/[tim]thumb.php	Vulnerabilities that may allow remote code execution
7	112	401	php (100.0%)	*/demo/index.php	Demo versions of web services. May be more vulnerable than actual services
8	88	638	asp (88.3%)	*admin*	Admin-related pages
9	59	123	asp/aspx (87.2%)	*/{fckeditor | ewebeditor | htmledit}/*	Some websites let users change contents through various editor interfaces, which the scanners searched for
10	58	139	php (90.6%)	*{phpmyadmin | sql}*	Control panels for backend databases

Table 1: The 10 largest groups of HTTP scanners and their targets. "*" indicates any sequence of characters.

group, the third the number of unique Re-Paths found in each group, the fourth the most dominant file types as well as the percentage of the Re-Paths with these file types, the fifth a brief description for the observed patterns in each group's Re-Paths, and the final column some explanations regarding the vulnerabilities the scanners were aiming for.

Note that there are many ways to do the above grouping, but we adopted this approach because it is simple and the groups it produces exhibit similar scanning behavior as we discuss below.

The following are the key take-aways from our close inspection of the final groups.

1. Individual groups are homogenous in terms of User-Agents and file types even though we only merged communities based on the trigrams in their Re-Paths. In fact, for each group, the most dominant User-Agent often accounts for at least 90% of the scanner IPs and the most popular file type appears in at least 87% of the Re-Paths except for Group number 1.

This observed homogeneity within groups shows our grouping scheme works well for the purpose of discovering popular categories of vulnerabilities the scanners are interested in.

2. There are four major categories of resources the scanners want to find on the websites hosted by the University campus. They are as follows.

(a) **Public login and registration pages** for regular users. Related group(s): 1.

(b) **Control panels exclusive to administrators**. For example, web interfaces for website management and interactions with backend databases. Related group(s): 5, 8, 9, 10.

(c) **Vulnerable pages**, which may allow intrusion through remote code execution, cross-site scripting, or SQL injection [10]. Related group(s): 6.

(d) **Backup files** that may contain sensitive information for exploits. Related group(s): 3.

The resources found in these categories are quite sensitive for security purposes. If the scanning entities successfully exploit them, they can seriously compromise the security of the websites. For example, the scanners in Group number 6 were primarily concerned with exploiting a known vulnerability in Wordpress [10] that would allow remote execution of malicious code.

There are groups whose intents are unclear (groups 2, 4, and 7), so we did not list them in the above categories.

3. Backup files are a major target of scanners. It is surprising how aggressive (11,273 Re-Paths for 569 IPs) they are in Group number 3 of the table in the way they tend to have more unique Re-Paths per IP than other groups.

4. Toward a systematic categorization of scanner intention. This grouping scheme helps us uncover the top 10 major vulnerability categories from the web traffic of the University campus. This represents another significant use of our approach. Using Scanner Hunter and the grouping scheme, network administrators would be well-informed about the most sought-after vulnerabilities, and thus be able to proactively secure vulnerable resources.

4.4 The complacency of Scanners

We have seen that scanners do not attempt to disguising their User-Agents. Further inspection shows a continuation of this complacency, where they do not try to make the values of the referrer field in the requests to look similar to those of legitimate users: **90%** of the times, the referrer field of a scanner's request is empty versus **10%** for a user.

Recall that a request usually has empty referrer field when a user types the URL directly into the URL bar of their browser or clicks on a bookmark. However, there are many embedded objects on a web page, so the referrer field in every request to an embedded object will be the URL of the original page. This is why only a small percentage of legitimate requests have empty referrer fields.

This is not the case with scanners because: a) the pages they requested do not exist most of the times and therefore there were no subsequent requests for embedded objects b) even if the pages existed, the scanners tend to only request the pages without downloading the embedded objects. Also noteworthy is the fact that in about 5% of the HTTP requests generated by scanners, the referrer field and the URL field are identical.

5. RELATED WORK

To the best of our knowledge, there exists no work on the specific problem of HTTP scanners. There are, as noted before, many studies that focus on the problem of detecting crawlers [3, 11, 12].

Much work has also been done on detecting port scanners [13, 14]. Port scanning is different from HTTP scanning in that port scanners check for open ports, which are limited and well-defined, to determine which applications are running. HTTP scanners explore a much wider field where they do not know where a file of interest (e.g. `myadmin.php`) may be on a remote server or even whether the name of the file has been changed. Moreover, the existing work may not translate to solutions in the case of HTTP scanner. For instance, solutions like [13] relies on the assumption that users rarely initiate failed connections while port scanners rarely make successful ones. This assumption doesn't hold with

HTTP scanners, which often locate an existing web directory (eliciting a successful HTTP response), then search for files under it. Even users can make failed HTTP requests in succession when a website goes down. Other solutions such as [14] work on port scanners because the port range is limited and fixed, which is not the case with HTTP scanners.

The use of honeypots [15, 16] may detect some scanning activities, but we see these efforts as a complementary effort to ours. We focus on the question of "who are the HTTP scanners exploring *my* network", which may benefit from learning about scanners who are targeting other networks. However, the entities operating the scanners may be clever enough to simply target already established websites.

There is also a body of work on developing applications for security professional to test the security of specific applications [17, 18, 19] and there have been some efforts invested in detecting covert, malicious web traffic [20]. [21, 22] are two works in the literature that confirms our observation that the behaviors of web users are diverse, which is why it is difficult to automatically look at an IP in isolation and decide whether the IP is engaging in scanning activities.

6. CONCLUSION

In this work, we identify and study the problem of HTTP scanners, which is by far not trivial and has received little attention to date.

Our main contribution is Scanner Hunter, an effective method to detect HTTP scanners that achieves a 96.5% detection precision. The key novelty of Scanner Hunter the use of a graph-based approach that detects HTTP scanners by comparing the group behavior of scanners versus that of legitimate users. The precision of Scanner Hunter is more than double of that of baseline solutions, while detecting more scanners at the same time.

As our second contribution, we provide an extensive study of HTTP scanning over a six-month period to understand: (a) what they are looking for and (b) their spatial and temporal behaviors. It is clear that the problem is acute, with roughly 4,000 unique IPs scanning a medium-sized University network every week and 80% new IPs every week.

Finally, we provide an initial effort towards systematically inferring the intention and targets of scanning. We identify four major categories based on the targeted resources: (i) user registration and login pages, (ii) website management interfaces, (iii) pages with potential vulnerabilities, and (iv) compressed web archives (e.g `wwwroot.zip`), the products of website backup activities and should not be publicly visible.

The ultimate goal of our work is to: (a) raise the awareness to this problem and (b) provide an initial but promising detection technique to mitigate the risk posed by HTTP scanners. Our goal is to provide one more complementary layer of defense to website security, at the early stage, when hackers are scoping out potential targets.

7. ACKNOWLEDGEMENTS

The authors would like to thank the reviewers for their helpful comments and suggestions regarding browser fingerprints and using Scanner Hunter to create effective honeypots.

8. REFERENCES

[1] P. Ducklin, "DHS website falls victim to hacktivist intrusion," http://nakedsecurity.sophos.com/2013/01/07/dhs-website-falls-victim-to-hacktivist-intrusion/, 2013.

[2] R. Fielding, J. Gettys, J. Mogul, H. Frystyk, L. Masinter, P. Leach, and T. Berners-Lee, "Hypertext transfer protocol–http/1.1," 1999.

[3] G. Jacob, E. Kirda, C. Kruegel, and G. a. Vigna, "Pubcrawl: protecting users and businesses from crawlers," in *Proceedings of the 21st USENIX conference on Security symposium.* USENIX Association, 2012, pp. 25–25.

[4] R. Keralapura, A. Nucci, Z.-L. Zhang, and L. Gao, "Profiling users in a 3g network using hourglass co-clustering," in *Proceedings of the sixteenth annual international conference on Mobile computing and networking.* ACM, 2010, pp. 341–352.

[5] I. S. Dhillon, "Co-clustering documents and words using bipartite spectral graph partitioning," in *Proceedings of the seventh ACM SIGKDD international conference on Knowledge discovery and data mining.* ACM, 2001, pp. 269–274.

[6] I. H. Witten, E. Frank, L. E. Trigg, M. A. Hall, G. Holmes, and S. J. Cunningham, "Weka: Practical machine learning tools and techniques with java implementations," 1999.

[7] P. Eckersley, "How unique is your web browser?" in *Privacy Enhancing Technologies.* Springer, 2010, pp. 1–18.

[8] "HE BGP Toolkit," http://bgp.he.net/.

[9] "http://f.virscan.org/xpymep.exe.html," http://f.virscan.org/xpymep.exe.html.

[10] "Wordpress timthumb plugin - remote code execution," http://www.exploit-db.com/exploits/17602/.

[11] A. Stassopoulou and M. D. Dikaiakos, "Crawler detection: A bayesian approach," in *Internet Surveillance and Protection, 2006. ICISP'06. International Conference on.* IEEE, 2006, pp. 16–16.

[12] A. Lourenço and O. Belo, "Applying clickstream data mining to real-time web crawler detection and containment using clicktips platform," in *Advances in Data Analysis.* Springer, 2007, pp. 351–358.

[13] J. Jung, V. Paxson, A. W. Berger, and H. Balakrishnan, "Fast portscan detection using sequential hypothesis testing," in *Security and Privacy, 2004. Proceedings. 2004 IEEE Symposium on.* IEEE, 2004, pp. 211–225.

[14] C. Gates, "Coordinated scans detection," in *Proceedings of the Network and Distributed System Security Symposium, NDSS 2009.* The Internet Society, 2009.

[15] N. Provos, "A virtual honeypot framework." in *USENIX Security Symposium*, vol. 173, 2004.

[16] B. Borisaniya, A. Patel, D. R. Patel, and H. Patel, "Incorporating honeypot for intrusion detection in cloud infrastructure," in *Trust Management VI.* Springer, 2012, pp. 84–96.

[17] A. Doupé, L. Cavedon, C. Kruegel, and G. Vigna, "Enemy of the state: a state-aware black-box web vulnerability scanner," in *Proceedings of the 21st*

USENIX conference on Security symposium. USENIX Association, 2012, pp. 26–26.

[18] T. Jensen, H. Pedersen, M. C. Olesen, and R. R. Hansen, "Thaps: automated vulnerability scanning of php applications," in *Secure IT Systems.* Springer, 2012, pp. 31–46.

[19] S. Kals, E. Kirda, C. Kruegel, and N. Jovanovic, "Secubat: a web vulnerability scanner," in *Proceedings of the 15th international conference on World Wide Web.* ACM, 2006, pp. 247–256.

[20] K. Borders and A. Prakash, "Web tap: detecting covert web traffic," in *Proceedings of the 11th ACM conference on Computer and communications security.* ACM, 2004, pp. 110–120.

[21] G. Xie, M. Iliofotou, T. Karagiannis, M. Faloutsos, and Y. Jin, "Resurf: Reconstructing web-surfing activity from network traffic," in *IFIP Networking Conference, 2013.* IEEE, 2013, pp. 1–9.

[22] M. Meiss, F. Menczer, and A. Vespignani, "On the lack of typical behavior in the global web traffic network," in *Proceedings of the 14th international conference on World Wide Web.* ACM, 2005, pp. 510–518.

APPENDIX

A. SUSPICIOUS USER-AGENTS

User-Agent	% requests
mozilla/4.0	31.2%
mozilla/3.0 (compatible; indy library)	14.5%
mozilla/4.0 (compatible; msie 6.0; windows nt 5.1; sv1)	6.0%
mozilla/4.0 (compatible; msie 6.0; windows nt 5.1; sv1;)	3.8%
<empty>	2.5%
mozilla/5.0 (windows; u; windows nt 5.1; en-us; rv:1.9.2) gecko/20100115 firefox/3.6	0.8%
mozilla/4.0 (compatible; msie 6.0; windows nt 5.1)	0.8%
mozilla/5.0 (compatible; msie 9.0; windows nt 6.1; trident/5.0)	0.8%
ineturl:/1.0	0.5%
mozilla/4.0 (compatible; msie 6.0; windows nt 5.1; sv1; .net clr 2.0.50727)	0.5%
	61.4%

Table 2: The 10 most popular User-Agents in our dataset.

In the table above we show the top ten most popular HTTP scanners User-Agents that we observed in our dataset. As mentioned in section 4, the scanner User-Agents are suspicious because they tend to be too short and do not contain information about specific browser plug-ins.

B. TIPS ON ENHANCING Scanner Hunter's PERFORMANCE

1. Opportunistically improving the accuracy of detection via customization. Here, we present several potential methods for improving the detection accuracy, if additional information or the assistance of the network administrator is provided. Note that these methods are **not used** in our current implementation of Scanner Hunter. We did not implemented these ideas due to two reasons: (a) we wanted to assess the performance of the algorithm in its own merit and in its generality, as customization and the necessary additional information may not be available at some deployment sites and (b) we did not have the necessary information for our dataset for some of the proposed improvements.

- **Using an IP whitelist.** The network administrator could over time identify web crawlers, either by considering external sources of information or by observing crawling behavior on their website. We expect this to have a considerably positive impact on precision since we saw in section 3.3 that 89% of the False Positives were stealthy crawlers.
- **Take into account the web resources that become unavailable.** The idea here is to explicitly consider web sources, such as pages or files, that become unavailable either temporarily or permanently, and exclude the failed requests for those resources from the bipartite graph. This would require a collaboration between the website administrator and the network administrator, which may not be the same person in large institutions. The addition of this technique could be particularly helpful for websites that undergo significant restructuring, which for many many is not that often.
- **Focus on requests for particular file types.** Scanners seem to be interested in particular resources and file types, such as `php`, `asp`, and `zip` as we will discuss further in section 4. Our algorithm could be configured to consider only those files or give them more weight during: (a) the creation of the bipartite graph, (b) creating the communities, or (c) labeling a community.

2. Handling non-standard HTTP failure messages. Some websites do not use the standard HTTP failure messages, but Scanner Hunter can easily consider such non-standard messages. In fact, our algorithm will be deployed by the network administrator who manages the website, or at least with their collaboration. Therefore, if the website responds with non-standard failure messages, it is trivial to specify those so that they algorithm can detect them properly. Note that the website in our dataset was using conforming, `40X` HTTP failure responses, so we had no reason to make this trivial extra step. In addition, most websites respond with a `40X` code when a request fails for one reason or another. Non-conforming failure responses is often accompanied by a customized web page containing a message that states the reason of the failure. Scanner Hunter will still work as expected as long as failed requests are properly specified by the network administrator or via observation. Scanner Hunter then would take into account this information when it preprocesses the log files.

Detection of Stealthy Malware Activities with Traffic Causality and Scalable Triggering Relation Discovery

Hao Zhang, Danfeng (Daphne) Yao, and Naren Ramakrishnan
Department of Computer Science, Virginia Tech
Blacksburg, VA, USA
{haozhang, danfeng, naren}@cs.vt.edu

ABSTRACT

Studies show that a significant portion of networked computers are infected with stealthy malware. Infection allows remote attackers to control, utilize, or spy on victim machines. Conventional signature-scan or counting-based techniques are limited, as they are unable to stop new zero-day exploits. We describe a traffic analysis method that can effectively detect malware activities on a host. Our new approach efficiently discovers the underlying triggering relations of a massive amount of network events. We use these triggering relations to reason the occurrences of network events and to pinpoint stealthy malware activities. We define a new problem of triggering relation discovery of network events. Our solution is based on domain-knowledge guided advanced learning algorithms. Our extensive experimental evaluation involving 6+ GB traffic of various types shows promising results on the accuracy of our triggering relation discovery.

Keywords

Network Security, Stealthy Malware, Anomaly Detection

1. INTRODUCTION

Stealthy malicious software poses serious threats to the security of networked computers and data. A recent study showed that a significant portion ($> 25\%$) of computers worldwide are infected with malware conducting clandestine activities [33]. Malware may spy on the victim user (e.g., stealing passwords such as in the newly discovered Pony botnet [34], tracking the user's activities, data exfiltration), abuse the computer for conducting bot activities (e.g., command-and-control, launching attacks from it).

Determining whether or not networked hosts are infected with stealthy malware is technically challenging. Virtually all malware activities require sending outbound network traffic from the infected machine. However, because of the low traffic volume of stealthy malware, frequency-based statistical anomaly detection is not effective. HTTP and DNS have been widely observed as the protocols for malware and botnet communications, as they are rarely blocked by firewalls.

The initial infection vector of most malware is usually through exploiting vulnerabilities of common networked software, e.g., heap overflow vulnerability in web browser or its plug-ins [13]. Once the infection is successful (e.g., zero-day exploits), network requests from advanced malware may not exhibit distinct communication patterns. Because of this lack of signatures, pattern-based scanning is ineffective.

Compared to independently inspecting individual network requests, a more effective network security approach is to discover characteristic behavioral patterns in network event attributes, e.g., [14, 18, 24]. For example, BINDER [14] detects anomalous network activities on personal computers through analyzing the correlation in traffic events by the temporal and process information. BotMiner [18] showed the effectiveness of correlation analysis across multiple hosts of a network in detecting similarly infected bots. King *et al.* constructed directed graphs from logs to show network connections for dissecting attack sequences [24]. However, none of these above solutions is designed for detecting general stealthy malware activities. Thus, they cannot be directly applied to solve the problem.

Stealthy malware can cause data exfiltration, spy on victim machines, and botnet command and control traffic on a host. We refer *stealthy malware activities* as the network traffic sending out from a host without user's intention.

We develop a new traffic analysis tool that detects network activities of stealthy malware through reasoning the causality among network events. Higher-level information such as the underlying relations or semantics of events is useful for human experts' cognition, reasoning, and decision making in cyber security [17]. Thus, analyzing relations among network events may provide important insights for identifying network anomalies.

There have not been systematic studies on network-request-level causal analysis for malware detection. Existing dependency analysis work (e.g., [9,31,43]) is on network service level and is not designed for malware detection. For example, Orion [9] and NSDMiner [31] addressed the problem of network application/service dependency for network stability and automatic manageability. Rippler [43] is proposed to actively perturb or delay traffic to understand the dependencies between service and devices. We aim to achieve the request-level causality structure in network traffic. This finer granularity (request vs. flow) requires different relation semantics and more scalable analysis methods. The existing

ASIA CCS'14, June 4–6, 2014, Kyoto, Japan.

http://dx.doi.org/10.1145/2590296.2590309.

binary classification solutions designed for JavaScript analysis [29] and malware detection [11] cannot be directly applied to our triggering relation discovery problem.

Triggering relations of events provide contextual interpretations for the behaviors of systems and networks, illustrating why sequences of events occur and how they relate to each other. Because of the transitivity, the problem of discovering triggering relations among a set of events may be transformed into discovering the triggering relations of pairs of events, which is defined as the *pairwise* triggering relation.

In this work, we introduce the problem of triggering relation discovery in network traffic and describe its application in solving challenging network security problems, such as stealthy malware detection. We present a scalable learning-based technique to compute the triggering relations among network events. We use the discovered triggering relations to reason about the legitimacy of observed network activities. Our analysis method successfully detects several types of anomalies including spyware activities, and botnet command-and-control traffic, as well as compromised web servers and web server misconfiguration. The accuracy and scalability of our triggering relation discovery method are evaluated with 6+ GB real-world network traffic, including HTTP, DNS, and TCP traffic. Experimental results show that our method efficiently predicts pairwise triggering relations with high accuracy in all metrics. With our tool, we discover and report the detected malicious HTTP and DNS activities due to various tracking malware and malware-hosting servers.

Our analysis using machine learning is scalable, capable of rapidly processing a large amount of traffic. We extract around 10 pairwise features from each type of network requests, based on timestamp, process ID, destination IP, domain name, etc.[1] Using machine learning algorithms eliminates the need for manually deriving classification rules and thus simplifies the detection. In addition, it achieves very high classification accuracy.

Our work demonstrates that triggering relations among cyberspace events at all levels can provide structural evidences for system and network assurance. The causality provides the logical interpretation to the vast amount of otherwise structureless and contextless network events. Comparing to link prediction problem in social networks [5, 16, 28], our work on triggering relation discovery has two major differences: *i)* Conceptually, link prediction problems focus on finding the similarity among nodes, while our work is on discovering triggering relations among network-related events. These two problems have different setups and requirements. *ii)* Our method includes the TRG construction operation and root-trigger security analysis, which are unique and beyond the link prediction type of inference problem.

2. MODEL AND OVERVIEW

In this section, we define the problem of *triggering relation discovery* and present the security applications.

2.1 TRG Definitions and Properties

Triggering relationship between event e_i and event e_j describes the temporal relation and causal relation between them, specifically e_i precedes e_j and e_i is one of the reasons that directly or indirectly causes e_j to occur. The specific semantics of triggering relation depend on the type of events and environment. An event may be defined at any relevant type or granularity, including user actions (e.g., keyboard stroke, mouse click), machine behaviors (e.g., network request, function call, system call, file system access), and higher-level operations and missions (e.g., database access, obtaining Kerberos authorization, distributing video to select users).

Triggering relations of events may be represented in a directed graph – referred to by us as *triggering relation graph* (TRG), where each event is a node and a directed edge ($e_i \rightarrow e_j$) from e_i and to e_j represents the triggering relation. We also refer the triggering relation ($e_i \rightarrow e_j$) as the *parent-child* relation, where e_i is the parent trigger or parent and e_j is the child. One can construct the TRG by incrementally inserting new events to the current graph.

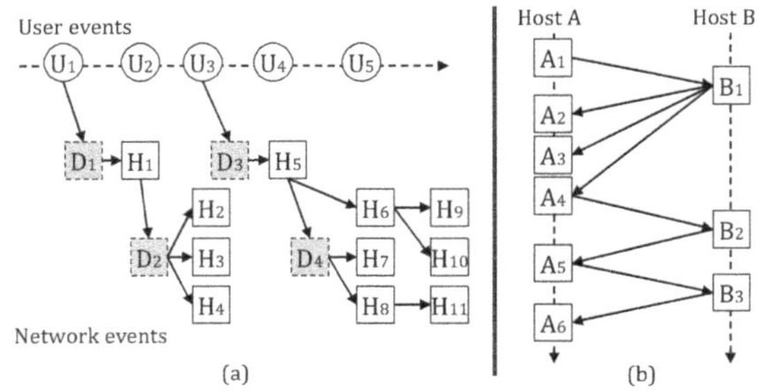

Figure 1: Schematic drawings of triggering relation graphs for outbound traffic from a host (a) and traffic between two hosts (b). In (a), the user events (e.g., U_3) such as entering a URL into the browser address bar are root triggers, which are followed by DNS queries (e.g., D_3) for translating the requested domain names. Then, one or multiple HTTP requests (e.g., H_5) are sent to the servers, and additional HTTP requests (e.g., H_6) may be triggered to fetch embedded objects. In (b), triggering relations in a TCP type of sessions are shown.

We illustrate two TRG examples in Figure 1. For specific types of network traffic, such a TRG may manifest unique topology and properties. For example, for outbound HTTP and DNS traffic from a host, the TRG forms a forest of trees, rooted by user inputs. The user input events are root triggers. Because of the temporal property of events, triggering relation graphs are free of cycles. This acyclic property differs the TRGs from social network graphs in link prediction problems. In a valid TRG, a node has at most one parent, thus, at most one root trigger. As confirmed by our experiments, a network triggering relation graph is usually sparse, i.e., the number of neighbors of a node compared to the total numbers of nodes is small. This sparsity is similar to what is observed in social network graphs [21].

The problem of triggering relation discovery is that given a set of events, to construct the complete triggering relation graph corresponding to the events. On the graph mode, the discovery problem is given a set of event nodes, to determine the existence of edges between pairs of the nodes and the directions of the edges. The *pairwise* triggering relation discovery is a simpler problem, which is to determine whether a triggering relation exists in two events. Given the pairwise triggering relations, we construct the complete the trigger-

[1]Examples of features are shown in Table 9 in the Appendix.

ing relation graph(s). We illustrate the TRG construction operation in Figure 2. A TRG provides a structural representation of triggering relations of observed events.

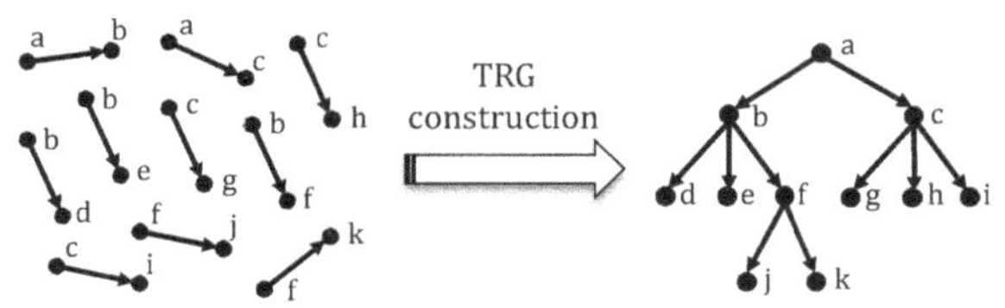

Figure 2: The triggering relation graph (TRG) on the right can be constructed from the pairwise triggering relations on the left.

Our definition of event-level causal relation relates to, but differs from the service dependency definition in existing service dependency research, such as network service dependency [31] and active delay injection [43]. Service dependency refers to that one service relies on another to function, e.g., web service depends on DNS name resolution. Our event-level causal relation refers to that one event triggers or causes the other event, e.g., the transmission of one network packet triggers the transmission of the other packet.

The TRG is defined differently from the parental dependency graph (PDG) in WebProphet [27] in terms of graph semantics and security applications. The PDG in WebProphet predicts the performance impact of webpage objects. Therefore it contains the timing information only, without capturing the causality among requests or objects. We rely on the semantic information (such as domain name, request string, etc.) of each request to build TRG, thus enabling the TRG to detect anomalous network events.

2.2 Security Applications of TRG

In our security model, network requests on TRG without valid root triggers are referred to as *vagabond* requests. They are anomalous events without legitimate causal relations, and likely due to stealthy malware activities.

The definition of root triggers may vary. For user-intention based triggering model, root triggers are user-input actions. The analysis pinpoints network activities that are not intended by users. Blocking these outbound malware network activities effectively isolates the malware, including

- websites collecting and reporting sensitive user data, affecting user privacy,
- spyware exfiltrating sensitive information through outbound network traffic from the monitored host,
- bots' command-and-control traffic, and attack activities (e.g., spam or DoS traffic) originated from the monitored host.

We describe a scenario for using our tool to detect stealthy outbound malware activities on a host. DNS tunneling has been abused by botnets for command and control communications [40]. These abnormal outbound DNS queries are automatically generated by malware on the host, typically with botnet-related payload. These surreptitious DNS activities are difficult to detect, because of their format resemblance to regular DNS queries. Our analysis tool reasons about the legitimacy of observed DNS traffic on a possibly infected host. Legitimate DNS queries are usually issued by an application (e.g., browser) upon receiving certain user inputs (e.g., entering a URL into the address bar). The application then issues additional DNS or other requests (e.g., HTTP, FTP). Botnet DNS queries lack of any matching user triggers. Our tool detects these vagabond events and reports them.

Data integrity We consider application-level malicious events, so the kernel-level system data (e.g., keyboard and mouse events) are assumed to be trustworthy. To prevent the forgery of user events, advanced keystroke and system integrity solutions such as [3, 19, 36, 41] can be incorporated in our work to further improve system-data assurance.

3. TRIGGERING RELATION DISCOVERY

The methods described in this section infer the triggering relation among network requests and construct triggering relation graphs. The automatic analysis pinpoints the occurrences of anomalous network requests from the voluminous traffic data, through reasoning triggering relations.

Given two network requests P and Q with P occurring before Q, one needs to decide whether P triggers Q, i.e., $P \rightarrow Q$. A straightforward approach for triggering relation discovery is the rule-based classification. One can define one or more rules summarizing the attribute properties of two parent-child requests, e.g., as shown in Example 3.1 below. Attribute names used in the example are described in Table 1.

EXAMPLE 3.1. *If* $P.time \leq Q.time \wedge P.PID = Q.PID \wedge P.host = Q.referrer$, *then* P *is the parent trigger of* Q, *i. e.,* $P \rightarrow Q$.

However, the rule-based approach has several drawbacks that hinder its scalability and accuracy. It requires manual rule specification, which is time consuming. The rigid rule structures are not flexible enough to recognize complex traffic scenarios, resulting in low classification accuracy and false alarms.

Our approach utilizes probabilistic machine learning algorithms and achieves high scalability and detection accuracy. We introduce a scalable feature extraction method referred to as *Pairing*. This operation converts individual network events into event pairs with comparable pairwise attributes. We show how binary classification algorithms can be used for triggering relation discovery.

3.1 Overview of Our Approach

The main operations in our analysis are DATA COLLECTION, PAIRING, DATA LABELING, TRAINING, CLASSIFICATION, TRG CONSTRUCTION, and REPORT. The DATA LABELING, TRAINING and CLASSIFICATION operations are standard for machine learning based methods. The new operations are PAIRING and TRG CONSTRUCTION.

- DATA COLLECTION is to record and store the events to be analyzed. Each event e has one or more attributes $(A_1, \ldots, A_m)$ describing its properties.
- PAIRING is a new operation that we design for extracting pairwise comparison results (i.e., features) of events' attributes. Its inputs are two events $e = (A_1, \ldots, A_m)$ and $e' = (A'_1, \ldots, A'_m)$. The output is the event pair (e, e') with m pairwise attribute values $(B_1, \ldots, B_m)$, where a pairwise attribute $B_i (i \in [1, m])$ represents the comparison result of attributes A_i and A'_i. That is, $B_i = f_i(A_i, A'_i)$, where $f_i()$ is a comparison function for the type of the i-th attribute in the

ID	Time	PID	DestAddr	Request (Q)	Host	Referrer (R)	Q Type	R Type	ParentID
...									
4	22.723	2724	64.30.224.103:80	/	www.cnet.com	N/A	website	NULL	0
5	22.733	2724	198.82.164.40:80	.../combined.js	i.i.com.com	www.cnet.com/	javascript	website	4
6	22.973	2724	198.82.164.40:80	.../matrix.css	i.i.com.com	www.cnet.com/	css	website	4
...									
14	25.307	2724	198.82.164.40:80	.../bgBody.gif	i.i.com.com	.../matrix.css	multimedia	css	6
...									

Table 1: Original network events observed. Time, Q Type, R Type, and ParentID stands for timestamp, request type, referrer type, and the ID of its parent event. The source IP of network events in this example is the same, while the source ports may differ (not shown).

(ID1,ID2)	TimeDiff	PIDDiff	AddrDiff	RequestSim	HostSim	ReferrerSim	Q1	R2	Relation
(4,5)	0.00	1	1111000001	1	0.5	0	website	website	1
(4,6)	0.25	1	1111000001	1	0.5	0	website	website	1
(4,14)	2.584	1	1111000001	0.1667	0.5	0	website	css	0
(5,6)	0.24	1	1111111111	0.1356	1	1	javascript	website	0
(5,14)	2.574	1	1111111111	0.5593	1	0.5	javascript	css	0
(6,14)	2.334	1	1111111111	1	1	0.5	css	css	1

Table 2: Examples of pairwise attributes as outputs of the Pairing operation. Q1 and R2 stand for the first event's request type and the second event's referrer type, respectively.

events. The comparison function $f_i()$ (e.g., `isEqual`, `isGreaterThan`, `isWithinThreshold`, `isSubstring`, etc.) is chosen based on the type of attribute. The feature construction can be extended to comparing different traffic types. Pairing is performed on every two events that may have the parent-child triggering relation. Moreover, we demonstrate an efficient pairing algorithm to reduce the cost of pairing without compromising the analysis accuracy in Section 3.3. The pairwise features are used as inputs to the subsequent learning algorithms.

- DATA LABELING is the operation that produces the correct triggering relations for the event pairs in a (small) training dataset. A binary label (1 or 0) indicates the existence or non-existence of any triggering relation in an event pair, e.g., $<(e, e'), 1>$ represents that event e triggers e'. Data labeling is based on pairwise attributes (e.g., $B_1, \ldots, B_m$) and may require manual efforts.
- TRAINING is the operation that produces a machine learning model with labeled training data.
- CLASSIFICATION is the operation to use the trained machine learning model to predict triggering relations on new event pairs $\mathbb{P} = \{(e_i, e_j)\}$. E.g., the outputs of binary prediction results are in the form of $\{<(e_i, e_j), l_{ij}>\}$, where the binary classification result $l_{ij} \in \{0, 1\}$ represents whether event e_i triggers e_j in $\mathbb{P}$.
- TRG CONSTRUCTION is the operation to construct the complete triggering relation graph based on pairwise classification results. If event e_i triggers e_j in the event pairs $\mathbb{P}$, then e_i is the parent of e_j in the TRG.
- REPORT is the operation to apply security definitions to the triggering relation graph and report anomalous events. A user-intention based security definition for TRG analysis is presented in Section 3.5.

We describe details of our new PAIRING operation in the next two sections. This feature extraction operation is unique in that the features enable the use of binary classification for pairwise directional relation discovery.

3.2 Pairing Operation

The PAIRING operation extracts features of event pairs. Pairwise attributes $(B_1, \ldots, B_m)$ are computed by comparing the attribute values $(A_1, \ldots, A_m)$ and $(A'_1, \ldots, A'_m)$ of two individual events e and e'. A comparison function $f_i(A_i, A'_i)$ for $i \in [1, m]$ is selected based on the type of attributes A_i and A'_i. An event attribute is of the numeric, nominal, string/text, or composite type. After the pairwise feature extraction, binary classification algorithms is used for classification. The classification requires labeled pairs for training, where triggering relations among events (i.e., labels) are known. For test data, triggering relations are unknown and need to be predicted.

Without loss of generality, we illustrate a basic pairing procedure with outbound HTTP network events as an example. The approach can be generalized to other event types. In Table 1 we show examples of some HTTP events. The triggering relations, if known, are shown in the last column (under ParentID). The features in Table 1 are derived from the header of HTTP requests. As the header contains operating parameters of an application layer transaction, the casual/semantic relation can be measured by the features of the requests. These features are previously used to understand the behavioral model of web traffic [10], while our work further leverages them to build the trigger relations of network traffic for security purpose. The pairwise attributes are formed by aligning the same event features and comparing the relevant ones (e.g., the request type and the referrer type). Six event pairs are generated and their new pairwise attributes are shown in Table 2. For example, the HostSim, ReferrerSim and RequestSim give the similarity of two events in Host, Referrer and Request attributes, respectively, according to certain similarity measures. Each pair has a binary representation of the existence of a triggering relation (under Relation in Table 2). The *pairing* details are illustrated as follows.

- Numeric attributes (e.g., timestamps) are compared by computing their difference, e.g., the interval TimeDiff between the timestamps of two network events. That is, $B_i = A_i - A'_i$.

- A nominal attribute (e.g., file type, protocol type) categorizes the property of an event. Comparing nominal attributes usually involves string comparison, e.g., substring or equality tests.
- For the string type of attributes, we compute the similarity of the attribute values as the pairing attribute value. That is, $B_i = f_s(A_i, A_i')$, where function f_s is a similarity measure, e.g., normalized edit distance. Take HTTP request as an example, we compute pair attributes HostSim and ReferrerSim by measuring the string similarities between two host fields and two referrer fields, respectively.
- A composite attribute is converted to primitive types, e.g., a destination address containing four octets for the IP address and an integer for the port. The comparison of two composite attribute values is made by comparing the sub-attribute values separately.

Given a list of n network events, the total number of event-pair candidates is bounded by $O(n^2)$. To reduce the computational cost, one may pair up the events that occur within a certain time frame τ, assuming that events occurring far apart are unlikely to have triggering relations. We design a more sophisticated pairing heuristic in the next section.

3.3 Efficient Pairing Algorithm

Our pairing algorithm pre-screens attributes to quickly eliminate unqualified pair candidates. The pseudocode of our algorithm is shown below. It takes a list of chronologically sorted network requests as the input and outputs a set of pairs of events.

Algorithm 1 Efficient Pairing Algorithm (EPA)

Input: a list of chronological sorted events, $\mathbb{L} = \{e_i\}$
Output: a set of event pairs, $\mathbb{P} = \{(e_i, e_j)\}$, $1 \leq i < j$

define a set $\mathbb{P}$ to store the compared pairs $\{(e_i, e_j)\}$
define a dictionary $D = (d, \{e\})$, where d is the domain of event and $\{e\}$ is a set of events whose domain is d.
for each event $e_j \in \mathbb{L}$ **do**
  $d \leftarrow$ the domain of e_j's Host
  if e_j's Referrer is not NULL **then**
    $dom \leftarrow$ the domain of e_j's Referrer
  else
    $dom \leftarrow d$
  end if
  if dom in D's keyset **then**
    for each event e_i in $D[dom]$ **do**
      if pass the $Screening(e_i, e_j)$ **then**
        $\mathbb{P} \leftarrow \mathbb{P} \cup Pairing(e_i, e_j)$
      end if
    end for
    calculate the expire time and update $D[d]$
    add e_j in $D[d]$
  else
    add new entry $(d, \{e_j\})$ in D
  end if
end for
return $\mathbb{P}$

Algorithm 1 uses a dictionary $D = \{(\text{key}, \text{value})\}$ to store the current network events. These events may be the parent triggers of future events. The key of the dictionary is the domain attribute of an event. The value is a set of requests, whose domain attribute is same as the key. Events with unmatched key values are filtered out (in *Screening* function of Algorithm 1), and not stored or paired, reducing both storage and computation overheads. As a result, a much longer time can be used to retire a domain, providing a more comprehensive coverage on pairs.

3.4 Feature Selection and Classification

Feature selection is to find an optimal set of representative features can greatly improve the effectiveness of machine learning classifiers. In our experiments, we use two different feature selection algorithms, namely *Information Gain* and *Gain Ratio*. Once a set of features is chosen, we train and classify the data using three common supervised machine-learning classifiers – Naive Bayes, a Bayesian network [20], and a support vector machine (SVM) [12].

Cost Sensitive Classifiers Because of the sparsity of triggering relations, we define customized cost matrices [15] to penalize missed relations during the training. The cost matrix can be defined to weigh the false positive (FP) and false negative (FN) differently. A false negative refers to the failure to discover a triggering relation. A false positive means finding triggering relation in a non-related pair.

Shown in Table 3, our cost matrix for classifying triggering relations is labeled by two categories: *with triggering relation* and *without triggering relation*. The values in the matrix are the weights for penalizing classification mistakes. We set positive values in the cells for FN and FP. The cost sensitive classification takes a cost matrix as an input. The trained model aims at minimizing the total penalty in imbalance data sets. For simplicity, we show the values and omit the labels of the cost matrix. For example, $\left[\begin{smallmatrix}0,1\\1,0\end{smallmatrix}\right]$ is a cost matrix that has no bias on FPs and FNs; $\left[\begin{smallmatrix}0,1\\10,0\end{smallmatrix}\right]$ penalizes the FNs 10 times more than FPs for a classifier. In Section 4, we thoroughly evaluate how cost matrices improve our analysis accuracy.

		Classified As	
		W/O TR	With TR
Ground Truth	W/O TR	TN: No penalty.	FP: penalty for finding triggering relations in non-related pairs.
	With TR	FN: penalty for failure to discover triggering relations.	TP: No penalty.

Table 3: Semantics of values in a cost matrix. TR stands for triggering relation.

3.5 TRG Construction and Root-Trigger Security

A list of pairwise triggering relations in network events can be used to construct the complete triggering relation graph (TRG). The resulting TRG then serves as a source for locating anomalous network activities. The security model, which defines legitimate and abnormal events, comes in many forms when used for analyzing TRGs.

Under the *root-trigger security* model, one determines the legitimacy of a network event e based on the legitimacy of e's root trigger, i.e., whether or not e has a legitimate root trigger. According to this definition, anomalous events are the events that do not have a valid root trigger. These events may be due to malware activities or host/server misconfiguration.

A specific root-trigger security definition is based on *user intention* [44], where a valid root trigger should be related to a user activity (e.g., a function call to retrieve user inputs, mouse clicks, or keyboard inputs). Other definitions for valid root triggers may be made according to the specific applications. We refer to the events that do not have any valid root triggers as the *vagabond* events.

In order to enforce the root-trigger security, the TRG CONSTRUCTION operation is used to calculate the discovered root triggers of all the events. To find the root of each event by traversal in TRG is equivalent to the transitive reduction of a directed graph. We design the root finding procedure (Algorithm 2) to return the root of an event, given all the pairwise triggering relations.

Algorithm 2 Root Finding Algorithm (RFA)

Input: an event e_k and $\mathbb{P}^* = \{(e_i \rightarrow e_j)\}$.
Output: a set $\mathbb{R}$, where each in $\mathbb{R}$ is a root of e_k.

define a set $\mathbb{R}$ to store the results
define a queue Q and enqueue e_k onto Q
while $Q \neq \emptyset$ **do**
    event $n \leftarrow$ dequeue Q
    set $\mathbb{T} \leftarrow$ find n's parent(s) based on $\mathbb{P}^*$
    for each event $e \in \mathbb{T}$ **do**
        if e is of type root **then**
            $\mathbb{R} \leftarrow \mathbb{R} \cup \{e\}$
        else if $e \notin Q$ **then**
            enqueue e onto Q
        end if
    end for
end while
return $\mathbb{R}$

The inputs of Algorithm 2 are an event e_k and a set $\mathbb{P}^*$ containing all the pairwise triggering relations $\{(e_i \rightarrow e_j)\}$. The output is a set containing all the roots of e_k. In order to compute the transitive reduction of a directed graph, we use a queue Q to perform breadth-first traversal of TRG. In each iteration, we obtain the parent(s) $\mathbb{T}$ of a dequeued event n. For each event e in the set $\mathbb{T}$, the algorithm checks if it is a root-type event. If yes, then e is added to the return set $\mathbb{R}$. Otherwise (i.e., e is an intermediate node on the path from e_k's root to e_k), the algorithm enqueues e onto Q for further iteration. This analysis returns root triggers for the network requests. Network requests without valid root triggers are labeled as vagabond events. They are flagged and alerted to the administrator for further inspection.

We demonstrate the use of our method for detecting three types of common malware in Section 4, including

- spyware as a browser extension,
- data-exfiltrating malware as a stand-alone process,
- a DNS-based botnet command and control channel.

4. EVALUATION AND RESULTS

Our prototype implements all parts of the TRG discovery system. The questions we seek to answer through our experiments are: *i)* How accurate is the prediction for pairwise triggering relations? *ii)* How accurate is the prediction for root triggers of events? *iii)* Can the method detect outbound network activities caused by stealthy malware? *iv)* Can the method detect network connections to suspicious servers? *v)* Can the methods analyze different traffic types?

4.1 Experimental Overview

We have conducted extensive tests on our proposed traffic-causality-analysis solution and obtained positive results. In this section, we describe the setup of our experimental evaluation. Then, our evaluation results are presented in the next few sections.

4.1.1 Accuracy and Security Metrics

- The *pairwise accuracy rate* of classification is the percentage of pairwise triggering relations that are predicted correctly. The pairwise accuracy is with respect to the ground truth obtained through rule-based analysis and manual classification. An rule example is shown in Example 3.1.
- The conventional *precision and recall* measures [6] evaluate the classification accuracy of the positives (i.e., the existence of triggering relations). In the equations below, TP, FP, and FN stand for true positives, false positives, and false negatives, respectively.

$$Precision = \frac{TP}{TP + FP}, \quad Recall = \frac{TP}{TP + FN}. \quad (1)$$

- The *root-trigger correctness rate* is computed based on the root of a node. It is the percentage of events whose roots in the constructed the triggering relation graph are correct with respect to the ground truth.

4.1.2 Datasets

Our evaluation is mainly focused on HTTP and DNS traffic, because they are very commonly used communication protocol both by legitimate users and attackers. Many botnets use HTTP or DNS as their communication protocol, because most firewalls allow them [40]. We collect and analyze outbound HTTP and DNS requests from hosts, aiming to detect suspicious activities by stealthy malware installed on the hosts. In addition, we also evaluate our algorithms with a much larger TCP dataset collected from a sever.

A summary of the experimental data is shown in Table 4. We define $\eta \in [0, 1]$ as the reduction percentage in Equation 2), where $EPA(n)$ is the number of event pairs after using the efficient pairing algorithm (in Section 3.3), and n is the total number of events.

$$\eta = 1 - \frac{EPA(n)}{n \times (n-1)/2} \quad (2)$$

- *Dataset I, HTTP.* We collected the user events and outbound HTTP traffic in a user study with 20 participants. Each participant was asked actively surf the web for 30 minutes on a computer equipped with our data collection program.
- *Dataset II, DNS and HTTP.* We used `tcpdump` to continuously collect the outbound DNS queries and HTTP requests on an active user's workstation for 19 days. We collected types `A/AAAA` DNS queries and the outbound HTTP requests that contain `GET`, `HEAD`, or `POST` information in their headers.
- *Dataset III, server TCP traffic.* We collected TCP packets on an active Linux server in a research lab. The inbound and outbound TCP packet headers were collected for 42 days using `tcpdump`.

4.1.3 Data Labels

Training data is labeled manually, with the use of simple rules such as in Example 3.1. The labeling process is

Data	Type	# of Events	η	# of Pairs	# of Feature	Size (MB)
I	Host-based HTTP	HTTP: 45,988; User: 899	94.7%	3,436,635	10	229.5
II	Host-based DNS and HTTP	DNS: 35,882; HTTP: 85,223	98.8%	953,916	9	55.1
III	TCP Traffic of a Server	TCP: 3,010,821	99.6%	119,372,631	9	6697.1

Table 4: An overview of datasets in the experiments. Number of events is the number of raw requests that have been collected. η is the reduction percentage after using our Efficient Pairing Algorithm. For Dataset I, the number of user events are also given in column 3.

Data	# of Pairs in Test Sets	Cost Matrix	Naive Bayes			Bayesian Network			SVM		
			Pairwise A.	Prec.	Recall	Pairwise A.	Prec.	Recall	Pairwise A.	Prec.	Recall
I	3,318,328	$\begin{bmatrix}0,1\\10,0\end{bmatrix}$	99.75%	0.954	0.996	99.75%	0.956	0.996	99.70%	0.958	0.997
II	693,903	$\begin{bmatrix}0,1\\1,0\end{bmatrix}$	99.82%	0.959	0.998	100.00%	1.000	1.000	100.00%	1.000	1.000
III	1,191,926,877	$\begin{bmatrix}0,1\\3,0\end{bmatrix}$	98.92%	0.995	0.986	99.72%	0.997	0.998	99.82%	0.998	0.999
Mean	–	–	99.50%	0.969	0.993	99.82%	0.984	0.998	99.84%	0.985	0.999

Table 5: Pairwise classification results of train-n-test for three datasets. The numbers are rounded before reporting. Pairwise A. and Prec. stands for pairwise classification accuracy and precision, respectively.

time consuming, and requires nontrivial human efforts. The labeling of DNS traffic requires the integral analysis of user-HTTP dependency and DNS-HTTP dependency, details of which are omitted. User events are labeled as root triggers, which are generated by leveraging `Tlogger` [2]. As a browser extension, `Tlogger` captures user inputs and tab events during the web browsing. By combining the data recorded on the kernel level, we generate the root-triggers used in TRG Construction for Dataset I and II.

4.1.4 *Classification Setup*

Three common classification techniques are compared: naive Bayes classifier, a Bayesian network, and a support vector machine (SVM).[2] Due to the sparsity of triggering relations in network traffic, we define a cost matrix that penalizes classifying false negatives more than classifying the false positives. CLASSIFICATION and TRG CONSTRUCTION operations are implemented in Java using the Weka library. We perform both 10-fold cross validation and train-n-test types of evaluation. The two evaluation methodologies yield similar classification results. We report the train-n-test results, unless otherwise specified.

4.2 Causality Analysis of Dataset I

Based on our two feature selection algorithms, 10 features out of a total of 12 are chosen for HTTP data. Selected features include three similarity indexes (RequestSim, ReferrerSim, HostSim), two nominal values to identify the file type (RequestType, ReferrerType), the nominal values to compare between particular attributes (PIDDiff, AddrDiff, TypeMatch, IndexOfSameRequest), and time difference (TimeDiff).

4.2.1 *Accuracy of Pairwise Triggering Relations*

The results in Table 5 show very good prediction accuracy for pairwise triggering relations. All classifiers give high precision and recall values, as well as the pairwise classification accuracy. These results indicate the effectiveness of our binary classification approach.

We vary the cost matrix used during the training and compute the pairwise accuracy results of the three classifiers for Dataset I. The results are shown in Figure 3 (a). The pairwise accuracy is consistently high for naive Bayes classifier with all cost matrices. Bayesian Network and SVM respond differently to the changes of penalty values in cost matrices. In Table 5, we report the accuracy results under the cost matrix of $\begin{bmatrix}0,1\\10,0\end{bmatrix}$. This matrix gives 10 units of penalty to a false negative and 1 unit of penalty to a false positive for the pairwise classification.

[2]SVM has a polynomial kernel function with a degree of 2.

4.2.2 *Correctness of Root Triggers*

The purpose of this analysis is to identify reasons for wrong predictions of triggering relations. Running the root finding algorithm (in Section 3.5) on the pairwise triggering relations, we identify the root triggers of all events and compare them to the ground truth values.

Figure 3 (b) shows the relationship between the cost matrix values and the accuracy of root-trigger analysis. The naive Bayes and Bayesian network yield nearly 100% accuracy of finding the root-triggers, both of which are not very sensitive to the cost matrices. In contrast, the accuracy of SVM increases significantly with increased false negative penalty in the cost matrix. In Table 6, we summarize the results of root trigger correctness for Dataset I. Our prediction of events' root triggers is accurate. It has a very small error rate, as low as 0.06%. These errors in finding root triggers generate false alerts. Wrong root triggers are mostly because of missing attributes in the original data or late-arriving requests. We further analyze false alerts later.

	Naive Bayes	Bayesian Network	SVM
Cost Matrix	$\begin{bmatrix}0,1\\10,0\end{bmatrix}$	$\begin{bmatrix}0,1\\10,0\end{bmatrix}$	$\begin{bmatrix}0,1\\100,0\end{bmatrix}$
Correct (case a-c)	99.94%	99.94%	99.37%
Wrong (case d-f)	0.00%	0.00%	0.28%
Wrong (case g)	0.06%	0.06%	0.35%

Table 6: Correctness of root triggers in Dataset I. Cases (a-g) refer to the various predicted root-trigger outcomes in Figure 4 in the Appendix.

4.3 Abnormal Traffic in Datasets I

4.3.1 *Malicious Browser Extension*

We wrote a proof-of-concept malicious Firefox extension, which is a piece of password-stealing spyware. The mal-

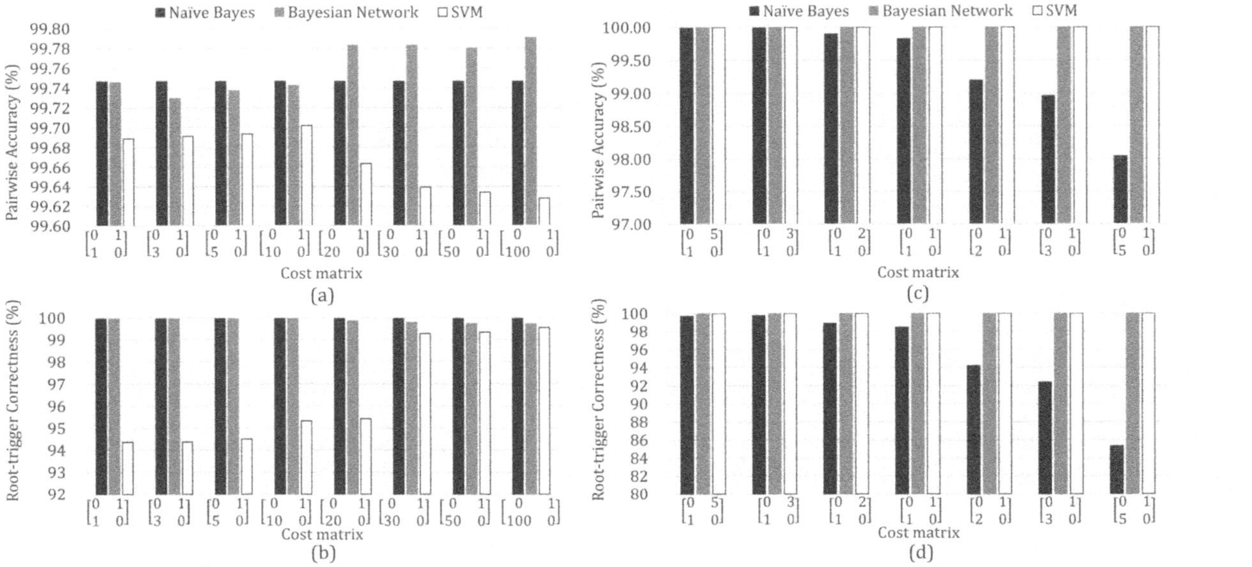

Figure 3: Accuracy and correctness results under various cost matrix conditions for Dataset I (pairwise classification accuracy in (a) and root-trigger correctness in (b)) and Dataset II (pairwise classification accuracy in (c) and root-trigger correctness in (d)).

ware sends the username and password when a user clicks on the `Submit` button in the browser. This spyware is similar to the existing spyware such as `FormSpy` and `FFsniff`. A victim user clicks the `Submit` to log on to various email services and Internet forums. The spyware requests, which contain the username and password in the `HTTP request` (`/query?id=user_id&ps=password`), are sent to its destination host. With our causality analysis tool, all malicious HTTP requests are detected by all three classifiers, without triggering any FPs and FNs.

4.3.2 *Data Exfiltrating Malware*

We write another proof-of-concept data-exfiltrating malware. This malware runs as a stand-alone process, similar to Pony bot. It sends out the `HTTP GET/POST requests` with system information to remote servers. The malware is programmed to transmit its payload right after the occurrence of a user event on the host, attempting to hide its communication among legitimate outbound traffic. The malicious communication may be a single request or a series of HTTP requests. Our method successfully detects the network activities of the malware in that the outbound malicious requests do not have valid triggering relations, i.e., the requests lack of any user event as the root-trigger.

4.3.3 *Detection of Malicious Traffic in Dataset I*

As defined in Section 3.5, vagabond events are those that do not have any valid user events as their root triggers. There are total 1.2% vagabond HTTP requests in Dataset I. Some of them are malicious traffic to known blacklisted websites. Our analysis finds in Dataset I that among these vagabond events, there are 169 suspicious requests sent to 36 distinct domains. Manual inspection reveals that these requests are to tracking sites, malware-hosting or blacklisted sites, and aggressive adware. They are partly due to users visiting compromised web sites. For example, some requests track the user's cookies and send back to remote hosts with known blacklisted sites (e.g., `2o7.net`, `imrworldwide.com`, `mediaplex.com`). We analyze the geographic locations of the malicious servers based on their IP addresses. All of them locate in the US, except one IP located in Netherlands. Some of the vagabond requests are false alerts (described in Section 4.3.4).

4.3.4 *False Alerts*

In our model, false alerts refer to the network requests that are vagabond requests (i.e., requests without proper triggers), but are legitimate (benign). False alerts in Dataset I are due to four main reasons:

- Automatic and periodic system and application updates that occur without user triggers. In Dataset I there are 157 update requests that are sent to 13 well-known legitimate domains. Whitelisting can be used to eliminate these alerts.
- Missing or incomplete attributes in the original data due to server configuration, e.g., redirection without properly setting the referrer field. There are 244 misconfigured requests that are sent to 38 different domains, usually image/video hosting websites.
- Unconventional attribute values, e.g., requests to `googlesyndication.com` (for Google Map) usually have long referrers that our prototype does not expect.
- Requests sent out much later than their parent request trigger, e.g., requests for favorites or bookmark icons.

Reducing false alerts can be achieved through more sophisticated inference methods under incomplete information, which will be investigated in our future work.

4.4 Causality Analysis of Datasets II

For dataset II, the goal of the experiment is to find the triggering relation in traffic with mixed types, such as DNS and HTTP requests. Features used for classification are given in Table 9 in the Appendix.

4.4.1 *Pairwise Classification Accuracy*

The pairwise classification results on dataset II are presented in Table 5. All three methods give high pairwise classification accuracy, confirming our method's ability of discovering triggering relations in mixed traffic types. Bayesian network and SVM yield better results than naive Bayes classifier, indicating that there are dependencies among attributes.

The pairwise classification accuracy under various cost matrices is shown in Figure 3 (c). Bayesian network and SVM consistently give high classification accuracy. In contrast, the performance of naive Bayes classifier decreases, as the cost matrix penalizes FNs more than FPs. We highlight the pairwise classification accuracy results under the cost matrix $\begin{bmatrix}0,1\\1,0\end{bmatrix}$ in Table 5.

4.4.2 *Correctness of Root Triggers*

We analyze the root-trigger accuracy for Dataset II, and show the results in Figure 3 (d). The root-trigger accuracy is high when using all three classifiers, with Bayesian network and SVM outperform the naive Bayes. We highlight the root-trigger accuracy results under the cost matrix of $\begin{bmatrix}0,1\\1,0\end{bmatrix}$ in Table 7.

	Naive Bayes	Bayesian Network	SVM
Cost Matrix	$\begin{bmatrix}0,1\\1,0\end{bmatrix}$	$\begin{bmatrix}0,1\\1,0\end{bmatrix}$	$\begin{bmatrix}0,1\\1,0\end{bmatrix}$
Correct (case a-c)	98.44%	100.00%	100.00%
Wrong (case d-f)	1.37%	0.00%	0.00%
Wrong (case g)	0.19%	0.00%	0.00%

Table 7: Root-trigger results on Dataset II. Cases (a-g) refer to the various predicted root-trigger outcomes in Figure 4 in the Appendix.

4.5 DNS Bot Detection

Botnet command and control channel using DNS tunneling [1] is extremely stealthy and difficult to detect [40]. We write a proof-of-concept bot that communicates with its bot master by tunneling command and control messages in DNS traffic. The bot generates carefully crafted outbound DNS queries whose payload contains encoded data e.g., `NBSWY3DPFQQHO33SNRSA000.domain.com`, `d1js21szq85hyn.cloudfront.net`. These bot queries are mixed with a 2-hour DNS-HTTP traffic dataset, which is then analyzed by our causality tool. Our evaluation confirms that our method successfully recognizes all the bot DNS queries as anomalies. These DNS queries do not have the valid user-event root triggers.

4.6 Causality Analysis of Datasets III

For Dataset III, the goal of the experiment is to find the triggering relation between inbound and outbound TCP packets by using our machine learning method. The accuracy results of pairwise triggering relation are in Table 5. All three classifications yield high values for the pairwise classification accuracy, with Bayesian network and SVM outperforming naive Bayes classifier. The features used for classification are shown in Table 10 in the Appendix.

4.7 Precision and Recall

Our methods result in high precision and recall for all data sets. In addition, the methods produce high pairwise classification accuracy and root-trigger correctness. Of particular significance are Bayesian Network and SVM, which yield the precision and recall of 1.0, a 100% pairwise classification accuracy, and a 100% root-trigger correctness for Dataset II.

Precision values are slightly lower than recall values in general, indicating more false positives than false negatives in the classification results. (False positive means finding triggering relations in non-related pairs. False negative is the failure to discover triggering relations.) The reason for slightly lower precision values is partly due to the customized penalty weights in the cost matrix.

4.8 Performance

Runtime results are obtained on a machine with Intel Duo Processor E8400, 3GB RAM and 250GB HDD. For each data set, we report the runtime of pairing, training, classification, and find-root operations. The means reported in Table 8 are averaged from five runs. Standard deviations are negligible and not shown.

Data	Pair	Train			Classify			Find
		NB	BN	SVM	NB	BN	SVM	Root
I	1848	0.5	1.2	79.9	22.7	16.8	14.2	1.7
II	622	0.8	2.1	13.4	4.0	2.2	2.1	0.6
III	14686	2.6	7.9	546	431	411	446	–

Table 8: Averaged performance (in seconds) of Pairing, Train, Classification, and Find-root operations. NB and BN stand for Naive Bayes and Bayesian Network classifiers, respectively. Pairing time includes feature extraction.

According to Table 8, the train, classification, and root-finding operations are fast. The PAIRING operation is the most time-consuming task in our method. For example, it can take as long as 4 hours to generate the pairs from 3 million TCP messages (42 days of a server's TCP data). Our experiments have determined that on a single day, at most 200MB of pairwise data can be generated from a server's TCP packet headers. As for the processing time, generating the daily pairwise data takes only 6 minutes on average, indicating that our method is efficient enough for practical use.

4.9 Summary

We summarize our experimental findings below.

- Bayesian network gives the best analysis accuracy for all datasets. The naive Bayes classifier gives the lowest accuracy, indicating the existence of dependencies in pairwise features. The accuracy can be improved by strategically defining the cost matrix.
- Precision and recall metrics are more sensitive to the quality of the classification results than the pairwise accuracy metric. The fundamental reason for this difference is the sparsity of the triggering relations, which results in different sizes of the denominators in these metrics.
- Our causality analysis successfully reveals all the outbound traffic to 36 malicious domains, i.e., with zero false negative rate. Our tool also detects the stealthy

network activities from our proof-of-concept browser spyware, DNS bot, and stand-alone data-exfiltrating malware.

- *Limitations* In our optimized prototype, PAIRING operation (for extracting pairwise features) has high computational overhead. This overhead is due to the quadratic complexity in pairing. Heuristics for improving the pairing efficiency may result in decreased analysis accuracy. We will investigate this tradeoff in our future work.
  Our current feature extraction method does not handle well HTTP requests involving incomplete or unconventional attributes. The failure of recognizing the causality in these requests results in false alerts. Advanced inference techniques are required to improve this recognition.

5. RELATED WORK

The classification and discovery of application or service dependencies for management and reliability purposes have been recently reported [7,9,22,23,31,43]. These existing service dependency analysis solutions differ from our triggering relation discovery work in two aspects.

- The semantics of relations to be discovered are different, as the dependency in those papers refers to the reliance on services provided by others, not the triggering relation.
- The granularity of analysis differs, requiring completely different techniques; our request-level triggering relations is more fine-grained than service- or application-level dependencies.

Machine learning approaches have been widely adopted in the security literature, since the work by Lee, Stolfo, and Mok [26]. The solutions described in [13, 29] use machine learning techniques to capture characteristics of Javascript code and identify malicious Javascript code. Xie *et al.* [39] proposed to use Bayesian network on justifying the important types of uncertainty in real time security analysis. However, their work is not designed for analyzing request-level network traffic. EXPOSURE [8] is designed to detect domains involved in malicious activities by conducting large-scale and passive DNS analysis at network level. Authors extracted 15 features of DNS traffic and used J48 classifier to find the malicious domains. EXPOSURE classifies the DNS request on an individual basis, while we use the machine learning tools on the pairwise relations. Besides, our method can be adopted to various types of network traffic.

Nguyen and Armitage surveyed on Internet traffic classification using machine learning methods in [32]. Williams *et al.* [38] did an empirical study on summarizing the features from payload-independent features. Their work classifies IP traffic flows. Besides computer traffic classification, learning-based security research includes database intrusion detection [35], identifying botnet traffic [30], and SMS/social network spam detection [37,42]. Compared to these aforementioned learning-based security solutions, the uniqueness of our triggering relation discovery model and technique is the ability to automatically extract and recognize directional relations and structures. Our problem is beyond the conventional binary classification problem.

Our triggering relation discovery problem may bear superficial similar to the link prediction problem in the context of mining social network data [5, 16, 21, 28]. Liben-Nowel and Kleinbergz [28] formalized the link prediction problem and surveyed an array of methods on measuring the proximity of nodes in a network. Follow-up works applied advanced machine learning methods to social network data. These advanced methods include logistic regression, decision tree, and naive Bayesian [21] as well as supervised random walks [5]. Besides the obvious semantic differences in the two problems, our work differs from social network link prediction.

- Links in social networks connect nodes that are considered equivalent by a given logical relationship. While, in our model, links are triggered by a hierarchical relationship between nodes. This conceptual difference makes it possible for our model to create pairwise features for finding the semantic relations, rather than analyzing the similarity of the nodes, or the link strength in a network.
- Our TRG construction operation and root-trigger security analysis are unique and beyond the link prediction type of inference problem.

Malware analysis studies build similar dependency graphs to generalize the malware behaviors [4, 25]. Kolbitsch *et al.* [25] analyzed malware programs and extract the dependency between the system calls. Besides the research domain, differences between their work and ours are significant. We adopted the machine learning tools to draw the TRG, while they used specification construction algorithm to generate the behavior graphs. In addition, we use the *vagabonds* in the TRG to identify the malicious network requests, while they use malicious behavior graphs to match the behavior of unknown programs. Similarly, Babic *et al.* [4] continued that line of research and built data-flow dependency graph based on their inference algorithm. Therefore, the construction mechanism and application of the dependency graphs in our work differ from those in the aforementioned approaches.

6. CONCLUSIONS AND FUTURE WORK

We presented a new traffic-reasoning technique for detecting the network activities of stealthy malware. The analysis approach exploring request-level traffic structures and semantic triggering relations is new. We demonstrated the use of triggering relation discovery as a useful security analysis approach, and showed its effectiveness against browser spyware, DNS bot, and data exfiltrating malware. Our evaluation showed high accuracy of the triggering relation prediction. Our analysis identified several types of network anomalies caused by traffic to malicious or misconfigured servers. For future work, we plan to design more complex security definitions and models for utilizing the triggering relation graphs to detect stealthy malware activities. We also plan to investigate the model retraining for practical deployment.

7. ACKNOWLEDGMENTS

We are grateful to the anonymous reviews for their insightful comments. This work has been supported in part by NSF grant CAREER CNS-0953638.

8. REFERENCES

[1] DNScat. A tool to tunnel traffic through DNS servers. `http://tadek.pietraszek.org/projects/DNScat/`.

[2] Tlogger. An Firefox extension. `http://dubroy.com/tlogger/`.

[3] H. Almohri, D. Yao, and D. Kafura. Process authentication for high system assurance. *IEEE Transaction on Dependable and Secure Computing (TDSC)*, 2014.

[4] D. Babić, D. Reynaud, and D. Song. Malware analysis with tree automata inference. In *Computer Aided Verification*, pages 116–131. Springer, 2011.

[5] L. Backstrom and J. Leskovec. Supervised random walks: predicting and recommending links in social networks. In *Proceedings of the fourth ACM international conference on Web search and data mining*, pages 635–644. ACM, 2011.

[6] R. Baeza-Yates, B. Ribeiro-Neto, et al. *Modern information retrieval*, volume 463. ACM press New York, 1999.

[7] P. V. Bahl, R. Chandra, A. Greenberg, S. Kandula, D. Maltz, and M. Zhang. Towards highly reliable enterprise network services via inference of multi-level dependencies. In *Proceedings of ACM SIGCOMM*, August 2007.

[8] L. Bilge, E. Kirda, C. Kruegel, and M. Balduzzi. EXPOSURE: Finding malicious domains using passive DNS analysis. In *Proceedings of the 18th Annual Network and Distributed System Security Symposium (NDSS)*, February 2011.

[9] X. Chen, M. Zhang, Z. M. Mao, and P. Bahl. Automating network application dependency discovery: Experiences, limitations, and new solutions. In *Proceedings of OSDI*, pages 117–130, 2008. USENIX Association.

[10] H.-K. Choi and J. O. Limb. A behavioral model of web traffic. In *Network Protocols, 1999.(ICNP'99) Proceedings. Seventh International Conference on*, pages 327–334.

[11] M. Christodorescu, S. Jha, and C. Kruegel. Mining specifications of malicious behavior. In *ISEC*, pages 5–14, 2008.

[12] C. Cortes and V. Vapnik. Support-vector networks. *Machine learning*, 20(3):273–297, 1995.

[13] M. Cova, C. Kruegel, and G. Vigna. Detection and analysis of drive-by-download attacks and malicious JavaScript code. In *Proceedings of 19th International World Wide Web Conference*, 2010.

[14] W. Cui, Y. H. Katz, and W. tian Tan. BINDER: An Extrusion-based Break-In Detector for Personal Computers. In *Proceedings: USENIX Annual Technical Conference*, page 4, 2005.

[15] C. Elkan. The foundations of cost-sensitive learning. In *International joint conference on artificial intelligence*, volume 17, pages 973–978, 2001.

[16] L. Getoor and C. P. Diehl. Link mining: a survey. *SIGKDD Explor. Newsl.*, 7(2):3–12, Dec. 2005.

[17] T. M. Green, W. Ribarsky, and B. Fisher. Visual analytics for complex concepts using a human cognition model. In *Visual Analytics Science and Technology, 2008. VAST'08. IEEE Symposium on*, pages 91–98. IEEE, 2008.

[18] G. Gu, R. Perdisci, J. Zhang, and W. Lee. BotMiner: Clustering analysis of network traffic for protocol- and structure-independent botnet detection. In *Proceedings of the 17th USENIX Security Symposium*, 2008.

[19] R. Gummadi, H. Balakrishnan, P. Maniatis, and S. Ratnasamy. Not-a-Bot: Improving service availability in the face of botnet attacks. In *Proceedings of the 6th USENIX Symposium on Networked Systems Design and Implementation (NDSI)*, 2009.

[20] G. John and P. Langley. Estimating continuous distributions in Bayesian classifiers. In *Proceedings of the Eleventh Conference on Uncertainty in Artificial Intelligence*, pages 338–345. Morgan Kaufmann, 1995.

[21] I. Kahanda and J. Neville. Using transactional information to predict link strength in online social networks. In *Proceedings of the Third International Conference on Weblogs and Social Media (ICWSM)*, 2009.

[22] S. Kandula, R. Chandra, and D. Katabi. What's going on? Learning communication rules in edge networks. In *Proceedings of ACM SIGCOMM*, August 2008.

[23] A. Keller, U. Blumenthal, and G. Kar. Classification and computation of dependencies for distributed management. In *Proceedings of International Symposium on Computers and Communications*, pages 78–83, 2000.

[24] S. T. King, Z. M. Mao, D. G. Lucchetti, and P. M. Chen. Enriching intrusion alerts through multi-host causality. In *Proceedings of Network and Distributed System Security (NDSS)*, 2005.

[25] C. Kolbitsch, P. M. Comparetti, C. Kruegel, E. Kirda, X.-y. Zhou, and X. Wang. Effective and efficient malware detection at the end host. In *USENIX Security Symposium*, pages 351–366, 2009.

[26] W. Lee, S. J. Stolfo, and K. W. Mok. A data mining framework for building intrusion detection models. In *Security and Privacy, 1999. Proceedings of the 1999 IEEE Symposium on*, pages 120–132. IEEE, 1999.

[27] Z. Li, M. Zhang, Z. Zhu, Y. Chen, A. G. Greenberg, and Y.-M. Wang. WebProphet: Automating performance prediction for web services. In *NSDI*, volume 10, 2010.

[28] D. Liben-Nowell and J. Kleinberg. The link-prediction problem for social networks. *Journal of the American society for information science and technology*, 58(7):1019–1031, 2007.

[29] P. Likarish, E. E. Jung, and I. Jo. Obfuscated malicious JavaScript detection using classification techniques. In *Proceedings of 4th International Conference on Malicious and Unwanted Software*, 2009.

[30] C. Livadas, R. Walsh, D. Lapsley, and W. T. Strayer. Using machine learning techniques to identify botnet traffic. In *2nd IEEE LCN Workshop on Network Security (WoNS) 2006*, pages 967–974, 2006.

[31] A. Natarajan, P. Ning, Y. Liu, S. Jajodia, and S. E. Hutchinson. NSDMiner: Automated discovery of network service dependencies. In *INFOCOM*, pages 2507–2515, 2012.

[32] T. T. T. Nguyen and G. J. Armitage. A survey of techniques for internet traffic classification using machine learning. *IEEE Communications Surveys and Tutorials*, 10(1-4):56–76, 2008.

[33] Panda Security Report. 2013. `http://press.pandasecurity.com/press-room/reports/`.

[34] Botnet Pony 1.9 Malware. `http://laboratoriomalware.blogspot.com/2013/01/botnet-pony-19-malware.html`.

[35] A. Srivastava, S. Sural, and A. Majumdar. Database intrusion detection using weighted sequence mining. *Journal of Computers*, 1(4):8–17, 2006.

[36] D. Stefan, C. Wu, D. Yao, and G. Xu. Cryptographic provenance verification for the integrity of keystrokes and outbound network traffic. In *Proceedings of the 8th International Conference on Applied Cryptography and Network Security (ACNS)*, June 2010.

[37] H. Tan, N. Goharian, and M. Sherr. $100,000 prize jackpot. Call now!: Identifying the pertinent features of SMS spam. In *Proceedings of the 35th international ACM SIGIR conference on Research and development in information retrieval*, pages 1175–1176. ACM, 2012.

[38] N. Williams, S. Zander, and G. Armitage. A preliminary performance comparison of five machine learning algorithms for practical IP traffic flow classification. *SIGCOMM Comput. Commun. Rev.*, 36(5):5–16, Oct. 2006.

[39] P. Xie, J. H. Li, X. Ou, P. Liu, and R. Levy. Using Bayesian networks for cyber security analysis. In *Dependable Systems and Networks (DSN), 2010 IEEE/IFIP International Conference on*, pages 211–220. IEEE, 2010.

[40] K. Xu, P. Butler, S. Saha, and D. Yao. DNS for massive-scale command and control. *IEEE Trans. Dependable Sec. Comput.*, 10(3):143–153, 2013.

[41] K. Xu, H. Xiong, C. Wu, D. Stefan, and D. Yao. Data-provenance verification for secure hosts. *IEEE Trans. Dependable Sec. Comput.*, 9(2):173–183, 2012.

[42] C. Yang, R. C. Harkreader, and G. Gu. Die free or live hard? Empirical evaluation and new design for fighting evolving twitter spammers. In *Recent Advances in Intrusion Detection*, pages 318–337. Springer, 2011.

[43] A. Zand, G. Vigna, R. Kemmerer, and C. Kruegel. Rippler: Delay injection for service dependency detection. Technical report, UCSB, 2013.

[44] H. Zhang, W. Banick, D. Yao, and N. Ramakrishnan. User intention-based traffic dependence analysis for anomaly detection. In *Security and Privacy Workshops (SPW), 2012 IEEE Symposium on*, pages 104–112. IEEE, 2012.

APPENDIX

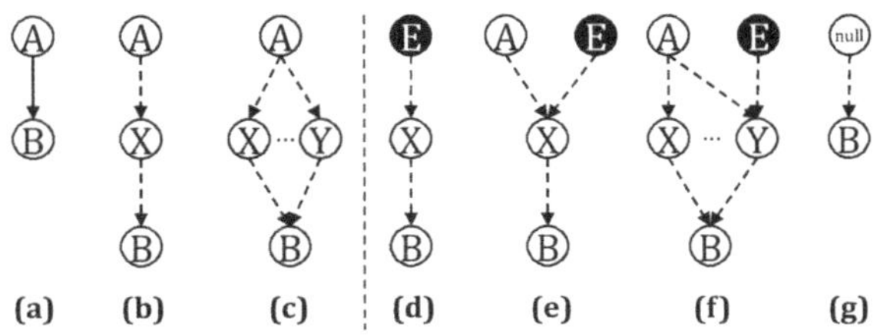

Figure 4: The illustration of various cases where B's predicted root trigger is correct (a-c) or wrong (d-g) on the triggering relation graph constructed from pairwise triggering relations. Let the ground truth of B's root trigger be A. Case (a) is where B's parent is also B's root. Cases (b) and (c) are where there is one or more paths from the single root A to B, respectively. Cases (d), (e), and (f) are where the predicted root of B is or includes a node other than A (e.g., E). Case (g) is where the predicted root of B is null, i.e., no root trigger.

By the definition of triggering relation graph (TRG) in Section 2, each node on a valid TRG should have at most one parent and thus at most one root trigger. In reality, we relax the definition in that this property may not hold in the TRGs constructed from pairwise classification results, e.g., a node may have multiple paths leading to the same root, or multiple paths leading to different roots. Therefore, our TRG construction algorithm needs to find *all* the root triggers of a network event, which makes the problem equivalent to compute the transitive reduction of a direct graph.

We illustrate the various cases where an event's predicted root trigger is correct (a-c) or wrong (d-g) on the triggering relation graph constructed from pairwise triggering relations in Figure 4. Our root-trigger definition allows the existence of multiple intermediate parents for a node, as long as the root trigger is correct, e.g., Figure 4 (c).

Feature	Rank IG	Rank GR	Brief Definition
HTTPRank	1	1	Rank of B in HTTP.
QueryHostSim	2	2	$Sim(A.query, B.host)$.
QueryDomainSim	3	3	$Sim(A.query, Dom(B.host))$.
TimeDiff	4	4	Time difference (ms).
QueryRefSim	5	7	$Sim(A.query, Dom(B.ref))$.
MissingRef	6	5	If $B.ref$ is null.
HTTPType	7	6	If B is IPv4 or IPv6.
DuplicatedDNS	8	8	# of same DNS after A.
PIDDiff	9	9	If both PIDs are equal.

Table 9: Feature ranking by InfoGain (IG) and GainRatio (GR) Selection on dataset II. Denote DNS and HTTP requests as A and B, and define $Dom(URL)$ to get the domain of a URL.

Feature	Rank IG	Rank GR	Brief Definition
DiffAck2Seq1	1	2	Calculate $B.ack - A.seq$.
ExpectedAck	2	1	If $B.ack = A.seq + A.len$.
TimeDiff	3	7	Time difference (ms).
Flag1	4	3	Control bits in A.
Len1Zero	5	5	If $A.len$ is 0.
Len1Large	6	4	If $A.len \geq$ MSS.
MatchAck1Seq2	7	8	If $A.ack = B.seq$.
Flag2	8	9	Control bits in B.
MissingAck1	9	6	If $A.ack$ is null.

Table 10: Feature ranking by InfoGain (IG) and GainRatio (GR) Selection on dataset III. Two TCP packets are A and B, which B follows A.

Towards Automated Protocol Reverse Engineering Using Semantic Information

Georges Bossert*† Frédéric Guihéry* Guillaume Hiet†

*AMOSSYS
R&D Security Lab
Rennes, France
first.last@amossys.fr

†Supelec/Inria
IRISA (UMR 6074)
Cesson-Sévigné, France
first.last@supelec.fr

ABSTRACT

Network security products, such as NIDS or application firewalls, tend to focus on application level communication flows. However, adding support for new proprietary and often undocumented protocols, implies the reverse engineering of these protocols. Currently, this task is performed manually. Considering the difficulty and time needed for manual reverse engineering of protocols, one can easily understand the importance of automating this task. This is even given more significance in today's cybersecurity context where reaction time and automated adaptation become a priority.

Several studies were carried out to infer protocol's specifications from traces. As shown in this article, they do not provide accurate results on complex protocols and are often not applicable in an operational context to provide parsers or traffic generators, some key indicators of the quality of obtained specifications. In addition, too few previous works have resulted in the publication of tools that would allow the scientific community to experimentally validate and compare the different approaches.

In this paper, we infer the specifications out of complex protocols by means of an automated approach and novel techniques. Based on communication traces, we reverse the vocabulary of a protocol by considering embedded contextual information. We also use this information to improve message clustering and to enhance the identification of fields boundaries. We then show the viability of our approach through a comparative study including our reimplementation of three other state-of-the-art approaches (ASAP, Discoverer and ScriptGen).

Categories and Subject Descriptors

C.2.2 [**Computer-Communication Networks**]: Network Protocols; D.2.7 [**Software Engineering**]: Distribution, Maintenance, and Enhancement—*Restructuring, reverse engineering, and reengineering*

ASIA CCS'14, June 4–6, 2014, Kyoto, Japan.

http://dx.doi.org/10.1145/2590296.2590346.

Keywords

Protocol Reverse Engineering; Contextual Clustering; Semantic Sequence Alignment

1. INTRODUCTION

Reverse engineering (RE) of communication protocols is used in many security contexts to retrieve the specification of undocumented protocols. Indeed, security products such as IDSes, application firewalls or honeypots often need to parse application level protocols to perform their analysis. As a matter of fact, reverse engineering of protocols can be a key aspect in the development of these security products to cover a wider range of protocols.

In addition, prior knowledge of protocol specification is highly useful to evaluate both the compliance and robustness of security products. To perform such evaluation, security auditors need to generate realistic traffic that contains legitimate and malicious patterns. Tools used to simulate this network activity should therefore precisely implement the targeted protocols. For example, vulnerability analysis and fuzzing tools can leverage protocol specifications to introduce invalid and unexpected patterns (*e.g.* integer or buffer overflows, wrong state transitions, *etc.*) in messages sent to a targeted application. This approach, also called *smart-fuzzing*, requires an accurate understanding of the message format and protocol state machine in order to obtain useful results. Protocol RE is also highly valuable in the context of malware analysis. Indeed, in order to identify leaked information and third party controllers (*e.g.* C&C botnet servers), and in the aim of taking down the latest without getting detected, malware analysts have to understand protocol internals and behaviour.

For all these needs, *i.e.* parser generation, compliance and robustness audit of network security products and malware analysis, our work aims at enhancing automated protocol RE. More precisely, in this article, we improve the reverse engineering of undocumented protocols relying on protocol traces. Unlike previous work, we use contextual information and its semantic definition as a key parameter in both the processes of message clustering and field partitioning. We also detect complex linear and nonlinear relationships between fields value, size and offset using correlation-based filtering. Besides, our multi-step pre-clustering phase reduces the required computation time of the main clustering phase. Furthermore, the experiments we conducted demonstrate that our solution is effective even with few samples.

We have implemented our approach in Netzob[1] an open-source protocol RE framework we made available. We successfully applied our approach on a representative set of different text and binary protocols traces. We compared the results obtained using our approach with those of three state-of-the-art tools in the field of trace-based protocol inference: ASAP [13], ScriptGen [16] and Discoverer [6]. We conducted experiments on well-known protocols such as FTP and SAMBA. We also compared the effectiveness of these different approaches on two unknown protocols: 1) the P2P protocol used by the ZeroAccess botnet and 2) the protocol used in a publicly available VoIP Commercial product. In summary, this paper makes the following contributions:

- We propose a new trace-based approach to infer protocol vocabulary. It relies on different pre-computing steps that enhance format inference and message clustering.
- We extend the Needleman & Wunsch [19] sequence alignment algorithm to leverage message semantic definition.
- We propose a correlation-based approach to automatically infer relationships between message fields.
- We present the results of an experimental comparative study. We compared our work with three other state-of-the-art solutions.

The remainder is structured as follows: we detail our problem scope and the related work in section 2 and our approach as well as novel techniques for the extraction of protocols specifications in section 3. Section 4 is dedicated to our comparative study. Finally, section 5 concludes this paper.

2. PROBLEM SCOPE & RELATED WORK

A communication protocol defines the rules allowing one or more entities (or actors) to communicate [11]. Its specification are mostly made of 1) the vocabulary, *i.e.* the set of messages and their format; 2) the grammar, which defines all the rules of procedure that represent the valid sequences of messages, usually modelled as state machines. Subsequently, inferring a protocol requires learning both its vocabulary and its grammar. The RE framework we developed covers these two aspects of protocol inference. However, we focus in this article on the first problem, *i.e.* improving the message format reverse engineering.

Previous works on message format reverse engineering fall into two families depending on whether they analyse an implementation of the protocol [3, 4, 5] or rather some communication samples [16, 2, 6, 13, 27, 26, 12]. The first approach infers message format by monitoring a given implementation to analyse how it parses and generates these messages. This requires to instrument or debug the software implementation. This solution cannot be easily automated, mostly due to its intrinsic complexity. Besides, such automation seems hardly possible if counter-measures such as obfuscation, code compression, anti-debugging or anti-instrumentation solutions are used. We thus focus on the second approach, *i.e.* trace-based approach. However, we do not consider these two families as completely orthogonal and foresee to combine our approach with dynamic binary analysis.

Proprietary protocols, and more specifically malware protocols, can use cryptography to protect message exchanges. Such mechanisms may limit the capabilities of protocol inference algorithms. Some solutions exist to bypass existing cryptographic methods by extracting clear text before encryption [14, 28]. However, the difficulty appears when proprietary protocols use strong or custom encryption. We believe this problem is relevant to the cryptanalysis field and cannot be resolved automatically. Indeed, even with access to the process memory, and thus to clear-text buffers, understanding the cryptographic algorithms is still mandatory for traffic simulation and fuzzing. Therefore, we developed our approach for unencrypted communications and let the relevant decryption work for cryptanalysts.

As mentioned in section 1, inferring message format is usually achieved in two main steps: message clustering and fields partitioning. Regarding the first step, previous works tend to split messages in tokens using n-grams [13, 27], delimiters [6] or sequence alignment algorithms [16]. A syntactic message clustering is then performed by comparing the type (binary or ASCII) and/or the value of each token. Message clustering uses the result of this comparison to find similar messages. However, this type of algorithm tends to have a high computational complexity. Pre-clustering steps can reduce the size of input data and thus the execution time. It can also improve the quality of the whole clustering process.

Once similar messages are identified, an alignment algorithm is often used as part of the fields partitioning step. However, current algorithms [6, 13, 16, 27] only rely on syntactic, *i.e.* value and type (ASCII or binary) comparisons, to delimit the static and dynamic parts of the common format of two messages. Following this approach, we cannot dissociate two consecutive static (or dynamic) fields, which have different semantics but share the same type. For instance, in DHCP messages, the Server IP Address (`SIAddr`) and the Gateway IP Address (`GIAddr`) are stored in consecutive dynamic fields that have the same type (binary) but different meanings. Consequently, these two fields must be separated, which is not possible using syntactic approaches.

Moreover, some information of a given semantic, such as an IP address, may be split over different fields by syntactic approaches. For example, if the prefix of observed IP addresses is always the same, *e.g.* addresses belonging to the same network, these approaches split this information into two consecutive fields: the first denoting the network part and the second the machine address in the network. In the worst case, information of different semantics could be associated to the same fields provided they share the same type. For example, a size field can be aligned with an IP address.

To address these issues, inherent to syntactic approaches, we propose an inference algorithm that takes into account the semantic associated with message parts. In particular, our approach does not limit the semantic definition of a message part neither to its data type (ASCII or binary) [6] nor to its appearance probability [26] but instead leverages contextual and environmental information to improve both message clustering and message format inference.

Message format RE must also infer relationships between fields, as they are common in protocols and participate in fields definition. These relationships can be simple as for

[1] Netzob: `http://www.netzob.org`

the HTTP "content-length" field or more complicated as for the DNS "number of questions" attribute that represents the number of field blocks in the message. Due to computational complexity, existing solutions only consider equality relationships [6, 16]. However, to detect simple and complex relationships, an inference algorithm should consider both linear and nonlinear relationships between fields. Indeed, these relationships are also elements of semantic and thus must be considered during sequence alignment and message clustering. Compared to previous works, that do not take into consideration such semantic information while computing the message format, our approach provides more accurate clusters.

Besides, previous works often include an evaluation of their solution but they do not make some experimental comparison of their own contributions against others. Such comparative study is very useful to improve existing solutions by allowing researchers to clearly identify the limitations of each approach. However, such study is difficult to conduct due to the lack of public datasets and because tools used in previous work are not often available. To the best of our knowledge, no previous work has attempted to perform such an experimental comparative study of existing trace-based message format inference approaches.

3. OUR APPROACH

The intuition behind our approach is that message classification and format inference are more effective if they also rely on the semantic definition of messages rather than only on their syntax, *i.e.* the sequence of static and dynamic fields. In our approach, we identify the semantic associated to a given part of a message. We then take this information into account both to identify fields boundaries and to cluster messages.

3.1 The Big Picture

As illustrated in figure 1, we take as inputs some traces containing application sessions and use them to infer the protocol specifications. The idea is to consider the semantic definition at every steps of message clustering and partitioning. Thus, our approach relies on several sub-steps participating in pre-clustering steps (*cf.* blocks 1, 2 and 3 in figure 1), the main clustering step (*cf.* blocks 4 and 5), the merging step (*cf.* block 6) and the inter-symbols relationships inference step (*cf.* block 7). The different pre-clustering steps aim at computing homogeneous clusters, which is mandatory to obtain good results during the sequence alignment. However, this approach can generate to many similar clusters. Thus, the goal of the merging step is to combine clusters that share the same format.

3.2 Collecting Semantic Information

Our approach not only requires messages belonging to different application sessions but also semantic information associated to these sessions. By semantic information, we refer to 1) the definition of actions performed by the implementation during the capture, each denoting the execution of a specific feature of the protocol, *e.g.* "List Directory", "Read File", "Write File" in an FTP session and 2) the contextual data accessed by the implementation while executing these actions. We use actions in the Sessions Slicing step detailed in section 3.3.1 while we leverage contextual data in our Contextual Clustering step detailed in section 3.3.3. To collect these semantic information, we use three different solutions, depending on the control we have on the collection process.

The first solution applies when we have access to an implementation of the protocol that exposes either a graphical or a command line interface. In that case, we first identify the different input parameters offered by the interface. Based on this, we establish various scenarios each implying different actions to perform with arbitrary predefined parameters. We then capture the communications resulting from the automatic execution of these scenarios either achieved with scripts or with the use of graphical interface testers such as Sikuli [29]. This solution is the most effective to collect both the actions performed by the implementation and the contextual data.

We use the second solution when we have no control over the implementation of the protocol but we can monitor its execution. This situation arises when reversing protocols used by malware. This solution relies on the instrumentation of the OS on which the implementation is executed. In practice, we use sandboxes, such as Cuckoo [10], to capture network traffic in parallel with any useful contextual information related to the application, such as names of accessed files, network parameters or system calls. To retrieve the actions associated to the generated traffic, we identify the different actions based on captured system calls. Indeed, we believe that a signature of successive system and function calls can distinctly represents a specific program action on a system. For example, we have successfully instrumented the Android Dalvik Virtual Machine with the Substrate Framework [8] to intercept and collect, at runtime, any environmental information accessed by an application, such as Android version number, phone contacts or SMS providers. We also monitor specific API calls denoting the execution of actions, *e.g.* the creation of activities, the activation of GPS or the reading and writing of personal user information.

If we have no access to the implementation, *e.g.* when traces are provided by third parties, we have to manually specify contextual information. In addition, environmental information is also automatically extracted from files metadata, such as IP addresses, hostnames and TCP/UDP port numbers.

3.3 Semantic-based Message Clustering

In this section, we describe the whole process of message clustering and we detail the different steps of clustering. The goal is to compute a common abstraction model, *i.e.* a symbol, for similar messages.

3.3.1 Session Slicing (Step 1)

This first step in our clustering process consists in slicing sessions into frames denoting different actions. We call these frames *action frames*. This step is based on the two following heuristics. At first, we believe that initiators, *i.e.* actors sending the first message, and non-initiators of a communication can use two different subsets of the vocabulary. Secondly, we observe that most of the different messages are linked to specific actions. Hence, identifying these action frames allows us to find and pre-cluster messages implied in the same action but captured in different application sessions or at different times in the same session.

To perform this step, message timestamps are compared against the start time of each action. Messages with a timestamp superior or equal to the start time of "action `N`" and

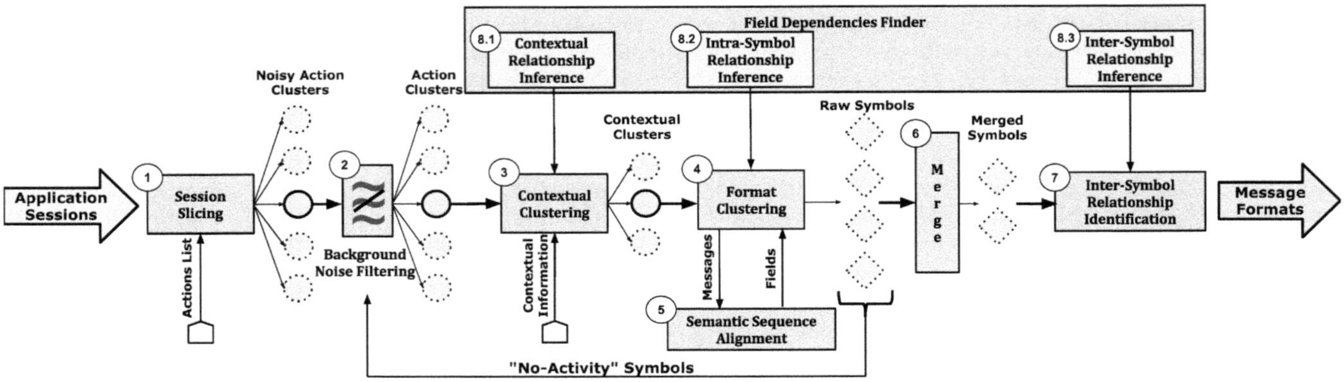

Figure 1: System overview

inferior to the start time of "action N+1" are clustered together.

When no information is available regarding the underlying actions performed by the application, we rely on a statistical analysis to detect action frames. We approximate action frame boundaries following the modifications of the inter-arrival time. Originally developed by U. Gargi [9] to cluster collections of pictures following their timestamps, this approach follows the following heuristics: 1) a long interval with no information usually marks the end of an action; and 2) a sharp upward change in the frequency of information inter-arrival time usually marks the beginning of a new action.

Finally, this step produces different *action clusters* for each type of action and for each type of actor (initiator or not). We compute an additional cluster for messages generated during a no-activity period. This cluster corresponds to an application session explicitly identified. We use this cluster to filter background noise as described in the following section.

3.3.2 Background Noise Filtering (Step 2)

Some messages are not correlated to a particular action and can occur at any time, for example the PING/PONG messages used in IRC protocol. These messages correspond to background noise. As they have their own format, which is generally different from the format of messages generated by user actions, we need to filter them from *action clusters*. To do so, we rely on sent and received messages during a period of no activity.

Filtering background noise is achieved in two steps. First we execute the contextual clustering (step 3) and format clustering (step 4) on messages belonging to the no activity cluster. As detailed in the following sections, these algorithms create a symbol for each type of messages belonging to background noise. In a second step, we filter each *action cluster* using these symbols. If a message can successfully be parsed with a noise symbol, we remove it from the *action cluster*.

3.3.3 Contextual Clustering (Step 3)

Action clusters can still suffer from imprecision, as a single action frame can contain messages of different formats. For instance, a single user action such as the connection to an SMB share directory generates sixteen different messages with smbclient[2].

The contextual clustering step refines *action clusters*. The main idea is to regroup messages that embed the same contextual data, such as host addresses, timestamps or usernames. To achieve this, we rely on contextual data collected during the capture or extracted from the capture files metadata. We search occurrences of these data in every messages of a given action frame. We finally subdivide action clusters by grouping messages that share the same sequence of contextual data occurrences.

This contextual information is searched in messages using different encoding (*e.g.* little-endian, big-endian, ASCII or UTF-16) and common transformations (*e.g.* CRC, Gzip or Base64). This step corresponds to the contextual relationship inference (*c.f.* block 8.1 in figure 1) which produces, for each message, a contextual signature, *i.e.* an ordered sequence of contextual information. For example, given two contextual data: an observed hostname "target.org" and the IP address of the implementation "192.168.0.103", it finds two occurrences in message: "1034.attack192.168.000.103443 target.org".

Sometimes, some part of a given message can correspond to different contextual data. This situation is more frequent with short contextual data. For example, if the contextual data "1034" that denotes the ID of the message is also collected, our contextual relationship inference wrongly identifies it at two different places in the previous message: 1) at the beginning of the message and 2) at both the end of the IP address and the beginning of the port number.

To address this situation, we use two resolutions scenario. The first applies when one contextual data is entirely embedded in the other. In that case, we give priority to the longest one. The second applies when the occurrences of two contextual data partially overlap. In that case, we use a disjunction in the contextual signature. For example, the contextual signature of the previous message is "ID;IP or ID;HOSTNAME".

We then use a greedy approach to cluster messages together if they share compatible contextual signatures, *i.e.* two signatures are said compatible if they are equal or if one is a possible realisation of the other. For example, the following message "2342.attack192.168.100.101443example.org"

[2]smbclient is a "client to access SMB/CIFS resources on servers" and is developed by the Samba Team.

which semantic signature is "ID;IP;HOSTNAME" is a valid realisation of the previous signature.

Finally, we compute the most precise common signature of each resulting cluster and iterate over its messages to tag their half-bytes. This last step consists in identifying each half-byte that corresponds to each part of the contextual signature. In our first example message, we tag the eight first half-bytes with the tag "ID", half-bytes between the 26th and the 60th half-bytes with both tags "ID" and "IP" while the last half-bytes are tagged with "HOSTNAME". These tags are used by the format clustering to promote a semantic alignment between messages.

3.3.4 Format Clustering (Step 4)

Contextual clusters should be refined for two reasons: 1) to manage messages carrying no contextual information; and 2) to dissociate messages that include the same contextual information but have a different format. The format clustering step corresponds to the final stage of classification and is applied on each *contextual cluster*. Unlike the two previous steps, this clustering compares the alignment quality between messages to compute clusters.

We propose to extend both the Needleman and Wunsch (NW) [19] sequence alignment algorithm and the UPGMA [24] hierarchical clustering algorithm. Our modifications take into account the semantic in both the alignment and the clustering phase. In the remainder, we give some details about these modifications.

We first propose an extension of the NW algorithm to produce a semantic-aware common alignment between messages. In fact, NW can be applied on a symbol, which represents the common alignment of a set of messages. In the following, we use the term of message to both refer to messages and symbols. In the original version of NW, the alignment of two messages m_1 and m_2 is performed in two steps. First, a matrix F including a column for each half-byte of m_1 and a row for each half-byte of m_2, is initiated. We denote $m[x]$ the half-byte of index x in message m. This matrix is then filled accordingly to the principle of optimality described by formula (1). It uses a gap penalty d and a similarity function S.

$$F_{i,j} = max(F_{i-1,j-1} + S(m_1[i], m_2[j]), F_{i,j-1} + d, F_{i-1,j} + d) \tag{1}$$

In previous works [2, 6, 16], the similarity function S is reduced to a simple function $v(a,b)$ returning a match or mismatch coefficient, respectively e and f:

$$S(a,b) = v(a,b) = \begin{cases} e, & \text{if } a = b \\ f, & \text{otherwise} \end{cases} \tag{2}$$

We propose to extend this syntactic comparison with the comparison of the semantic definition attached to each half-byte. Hence our function compares the value but also the semantic tags of each half-byte and preserves common semantic information if available. These semantic tags are computed and attached to half-bytes during the contextual clustering and every time an intra-symbol relationship is found.

We denote $\psi(a) = \langle T, \phi_a \rangle$, the multiset [25] of semantic tags attached to an half-byte a, with T the set of all semantic types and $\phi_a : T \to \mathbb{N}$, a function returning the multiplicity of a semantic tag in a. For example, $\psi(b) = \{\{IP, IP, Username\}\}$ means that IP and $Username$ semantic tags are attached to half-byte b. In this example the multiplicity of IP is two, *i.e.* $\phi(IP) = 2$. This situation may arise when the same semantic tag corresponds to different types of relationship. For example, an half-byte could correspond to both environmental and application information.

Now, suppose $\psi(a)$ and $\psi(b)$ respectively the multiset of semantic tags attached to half-byte a and b, we denote one includes the other with the relation:

$$\psi(a) \sqsubset \psi(b) \Leftrightarrow \forall e \in T, \phi_a(e) < \phi_b(e) \tag{3}$$

and we define a size function the following way:

$$\overline{\psi(a)} = \sum_{e \in T} \phi_a(e) \tag{4}$$

We compute the similarity between half-bytes a and b by comparing their values and their semantic tags. For the value comparison we keep the original $v(a,b)$ definition while for the semantic comparison we introduce two new semantic match and mismatch parameters: h and g.

Our experimentation has shown best results with the following parameter values: $d = 0$, $e = 5$, $f = -5$ $g = 6 \times e$ and $h = 6 \times f$.

Hence, as described in table 1, our similarity function returns a high score if the semantic tags match but the values differ and on the contrary, returns a low score if the values match but not the semantic tags.

$\psi(a) \cap \psi(b) = \oslash$	$S(a,b) = v(a,b) + h \times \overline{\psi(a)} + h \times \overline{\psi(b)}$
$\psi(a) = \psi(b)$	$S(a,b) = v(a,b) + g \times \overline{\psi(a)}$
$\psi(a) \sqsubset \psi(b)$	$S(a,b) = v(a,b) + g \times \overline{\psi(a)} + h \times \overline{\psi(b) \setminus \psi(a)}$
$\psi(a) \sqsupset \psi(b)$	$S(a,b) = v(a,b) + g \times \overline{\psi(b)} + h \times \overline{\psi(a) \setminus \psi(b)}$

Table 1: Similarity function $S(a,b)$.

Once the matrix F is computed using our new similarity function and following formula 1, a traceback is performed from the maximal score located in entry $F_{|m_1|+1,|m_2|+1}$ until $F_{1,1}$ is reached[3]. A diagonal traceback describes a perfect alignment between the two messages, while a vertical or an horizontal motion implies the addition of gaps in one of the two messages. Such traceback produces two messages m_1' and m_2' containing the necessary gaps to align messages m_1 and m_2 under the constraints introduced by their inner syntactic and semantic similarities.

We then execute a pairwise comparison to compute the symbol that corresponds to the common alignment between m_1' and m_2'. If the two half-bytes are equal we create a static field in the common alignment, if not a gap. We also consider the semantic tags of m_1' and m_2' and only propagate the common ones in the newly created field. Finally, we merge consecutive half-bytes that share the same characteristic (type and semantic) to delimit fields.

As illustrated in figure 2, our semantic based sequence alignment preserves the semantic definition while computing field boundaries. In this example, without our solution, email addresses get split among multiple fields and first-names definition is lost in a bigger dynamic field.

We use this extension of NW in our modification of the UPGMA algorithm. UPGMA is a heuristic clustering algorithm that recursively joins the two nearest clusters. It relies on a matrix, denoting the pairwise similarity of clusters.

[3] $|m|$ denotes the number of half-bytes in a message m.

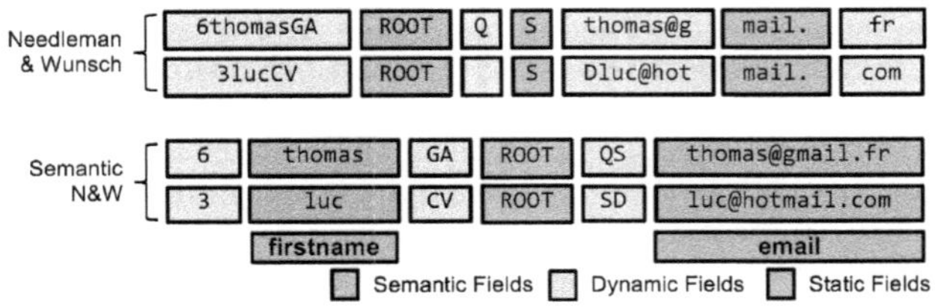

Figure 2: Examples of alignments computed by Needleman & Wunsch and our modified version of this algorithm.

In the nth iteration of the algorithm, we try to align each pair of symbols resulting from the $(n-1)^{th}$ iteration using our modified NW algorithm. We also compute a new symbol for each pair of messages and search for intra-symbol relationships. A semantic tag labeled with the type of the relationship is attached to each corresponding half-byte. More details on the relationship inference are provided in the next section. After that, we compute the quality score of each possible merge using a dedicated function H. We finally merge the two symbols that maximize H into the new corresponding symbol provided by our modified NW algorithm. We stop this iterative merging process when the highest score falls below a specific threshold.

Originally, after each merge, the UPGMA matrix is recomputed using an equation which estimates the similarity of the new clusters based on previous ones. However, because we wanted to keep track of the semantic definition when merging clusters, we modified this original behaviour. In our work, after each round we realign messages participating in the new clusters and recompute a symbol to represent it. We then compute its quality score. It allows us to detect that a semantic field will disappear if we merge two messages.

Hence, our UPGMA algorithm relies on $H(m_1, m_2)$. This function returns the quality score of s_{m_1,m_2}, a symbol representing the alignment of m_1 and m_2. This H function computes the euclidean norm of a vector composed of two measures, $Q(m_1, m_2)$ and $P(m_1, m_2)$:

$$H(m_1, m_2) = \|Q(m_1, m_2), P(m_1, m_2)\| \quad (5)$$

The first measure $Q(m_1, m_2)$ represents the syntactic and semantic similarity of the two messages and its value is extracted from the NW matrix F:

$$Q(m_1, m_2) = F_{|m_1|+1,|m_2|+1} \quad (6)$$

The second measure, denoted $P(m_1, m_2)$, evaluates the proportion of static half-bytes over the number dynamic fields in the symbol resulting from the NW alignment of m_1 and m_2.

3.3.5 *Merging Step and Inter-Symbol Relationship Identification (Steps 4 & 5)*

Format clustering produces *raw symbols*, each denoting a possible message format. However, this approach tends to produce a lot of redundant *raw symbols* corresponding to the same message format. To address this issue, we added a simple merging step that compares all the computed *raw symbols* and merges duplicate ones.

Finally, the last step of our approach consists in identifying inter-symbol relationships. As detailed in section 3.4, it searches for relationships between consecutive messages using a generic relationship inference. The same approach is also used during previous step to find contextual and intra-symbol relationships inside each message. Thus we can identify fields such as sequence ID or cookies. This last step in our approach returns symbols representing different message format, including the definition of their fields.

3.4 Fields Relationships Identification

In this section we present our approach to identify intra-symbol relationships (*i.e.* between fields that pertain to the same symbol) and inter-symbol relationships (*i.e.* between fields that pertain to two consecutive symbols). We consider three steps. At first, we generate a dataset that contains all combinations of field attribute couples. Then, we quickly eliminate bad candidates by means of a correlation approach and finally try to qualify the potential relationship that exists between the remaining field couples.

During the first step we generate a dataset with the following attributes for each field: its value, its size and its offset in current message. We then compute each possible combination of attributes couples as, for example, (field1.size, field3.value).

Then, we look in the dataset for correlations by leveraging the Maximal Information Coefficient (MIC) [21]. This coefficient retrieves many types of dependencies, including nonlinear ones. Moreover, it supports noisy datasets. This characteristic is useful as the clustering steps may have erroneously grouped messages of different formats together, thus preventing us to find dependencies when looking for exact relationships. In order to differentiate linear from nonlinear dependencies (*e.g.* a size field from a CRC32 field), we combine the MIC score with r, the Pearson product-moment correlation coefficient. As demonstrated in [21], a value of $MIC - r^2$ close to zero indicates a linear dependency, whereas a score close to one tends to point out a nonlinear dependency.

The qualification step takes as input the best couple candidates considering their $MIC - r^2$ scores. We experimentally established that we obtain good results if we select couples between 0.8 and 1 for linear relationships and between 0 and 0.2 for non linear relationships. We do not consider scores between 0.2 and 0.8 as they generally lead to weak results in terms of relationships. We then evaluate each potential field couple under a set of specific relationships, in order to retrieve one that exactly applies, *i.e.* that is valid for the entire set of messages.

In order to support the wide variety of encoding that exists in real protocols, we take into account different possible encoding and we try different combinations of endianness, signed number representation and byte interpretation (ASCII, decimal, hexadecimal and octal). In the current implementation, we consider the following basic relationships: size field, offset field, cookies and sequence number. We also consider the following complex relationships: SHA-1, CRC32 and the size of a repetition of a particular field or group of fields. The later can be found for example in the P2P ZeroAccess protocol, where a size field specifies the number of peer's IP address fields concatenated in a message.

4. COMPARATIVE STUDY

We evaluate our approach on various protocols and compare our contributions against state-of-the-art approaches.

We conducted two different types of experiments: 1) on well-known protocols to compare inferred message formats with their published specifications and 2) on unknown protocols to evaluate the effectiveness of the different approaches on more operational use cases.

For the first set of experiments, we selected a text protocol, *i.e.* FTP and a binary protocol, *i.e.* SAMBA, both often used in previous experiments [7, 3, 5, 6]. The second set includes two typical use cases of protocol reverse engineering to cover more operational contexts: the P2P protocol used by a recent botnet known as ZeroAccess [23] and a proprietary and undocumented VoIP protocol, Ventrilo[4].

In the remainder, we first give some key insights over the compared tools and then present the datasets, the metrics and the implementations we used in the study. We then conclude with a discussion on obtained results.

4.1 Choice of Compared Tools

Few works have been proposed to reverse protocols using trace-based approaches. Among them, only ASAP provides a publicly available implementation. As implementing these tools is time-consuming, we decided to retain the most representative ones while still covering the different types of approach. Thus, Discoverer uses a syntactic alignment approach, ScriptGen uses an inferred automaton and ASAP relies on statistics over message bytes. We consider that other works use the same types of approaches and are less advanced or outdated by the tools we selected. Moreover, the selected tools are often cited in scientific articles of the domain. Though ASAP is less popular, the tool is publicly available and other works that follow the same type of approach are very similar and not more popular.

Among works we excluded from our comparative studies are Roleplayer [7], Veritas [27] and PRISMA [12]. Roleplayer uses the same approach than Discoverer to find dynamic fields in a message. Veritas [27] is another work that we consider similar to ASAP, *i.e.* it uses a statistical analysis to infer protocols. Another work we did not consider in our comparative study is PRISMA [12]. In this extension of ASAP, authors consider the grammar of the protocol in the vocabulary inference process, which is similar to ScriptGen approach. In the following, we give more details about the retained tools.

ASAP, published by T. Krueger *et al.* in [13], focuses on message clustering. ASAP splits messages in tokens and searches for the most representative ones. To do so, they filter out keywords that have extreme (high and low) frequency of appearance. A Non-Negative Matrix Factorisation [15] is then performed to cluster similar messages. Finally, a template is extracted from each cluster to represent the message format associated with each cluster. However, the template is coarse-grained and not precise enough, especially to parse messages.

ScriptGen, developed by C. Leita *et al.* [16], includes features related to the vocabulary and the grammatical inference. It was initially designed to generate honeypot scripts[5]. ScriptGen differs from others because it uses the protocol automaton to identify similar messages. It passively builds an FSM by replaying the various sessions provided in traces. Messages that appear in the same state of the FSM are clustered together. Clusters are then subdivided following two main heuristics: 1) the number of bytes sent in response to a message; and 2) the result of Region Analysis algorithm execution. This algorithm is applied in two steps, first it clusters messages following a UPGMA execution coupled with a sequence alignment algorithm, then it subdivides obtained clusters following messages values.

Discoverer, by W. Cui *et al.* [6] tries to reverse unknown protocols following three main steps: tokenization, recursive clustering and merging. The tokenization process splits messages in ASCII and binary tokens to cluster messages that have the same token structure, *i.e.* the same sequence of token types. Then, the recursive clustering divides obtained clusters by identifying "format distinguisher" fields among them. To mitigate over-classification problems, the last step merges similar message formats by using a type-based sequence alignment.

[4]Ventrilo is a VoIP software: `http://www.ventrilo.com/`
[5]See Honeyd project: `http://www.honeyd.org/`

4.2 Datasets

Our comparative study relies on six datasets: two of them (① and ②) correspond to a well-known text protocol (FTP), two of them (③ and ④) to the well-known SAMBA binary protocol (SMB), one to a P2P botnet protocol (⑤) and one to a typical commercial proprietary product (⑥). Table 2 summarises the different dataset characteristics.

#	Protocol	Source	# Msg	# True Format
①	FTP	Generated	1717	40
②		LBNL	2328	46
③	SMB	Generated	2650	32
④		Company	937	22
⑤	ZAccess	Public	883	4
⑥	Commercial	Laboratory	482	15

Table 2: Summary of datasets used in our comparative study. The first column denotes the dataset identifier. Last columns denote the number of true formats and the number of messages in the dataset.

To compare the best results of each tool, we use two kind of datasets for each known protocol (FTP and SMB): a calibration dataset to empirically compute the optimal parameters of each tool and an evaluation dataset to compare them.

To create the calibration datasets ① and ③, we used the first solution detailed in section 3.2 and wrote client scripts executing various actions with predefined parameters on a server. For instance, the FTP script executes more than 10 different actions, including a connection attempt with a bad password, some directory listing and downloading multiple files. Each calibration dataset includes 20 application sessions containing the same actions but with different contextual parameters, *ie.* usernames, filenames, IP addresses, hostnames. Thus, we annotated the captured pcaps with the executed actions and contextual data used to generate them.

To create the evaluation datasets, we used traces captured in both academic and professional environments. The realistic FTP dataset (②) is a subset of traces published by LBNL [20], collected in an university network. We arbitrary considered the first 1000 packets in three different days of capture (days 10, 11 and 12) to produce a dataset of reasonable size. The second realistic dataset (④) comes from a full day of SMB traffic captured in a company network. Users agreed to participate and behaved in a normal way. We selected the first 1000 packets. Obtained dataset is composed of 937 SMB packets covering 22 different true formats. By true format, we hereby refer to the format detailed in protocol specifications.

For anonymity reasons, the LBNL dataset only includes pcap files without a precise definition of the context in which it was captured. Thus, we should have used the last solution proposed in section 3.2 to obtain necessary semantic information. In that case, parameters used on the evaluation datasets would not reflect the same quality as those used on calibration datasets. Returned results would therefore be difficult to interpret as various factors would have influenced them. Thus, to ensure consistency between parameters used for calibration and evaluation, we extracted from evaluation network traces the same types of contextual data than the one we used for calibration. We followed the same approach on the SMB datasets.

Finally, we applied the four approaches on more realistic reverse engineering situations: i) the P2P communication protocol used by ZeroAccess [23] botnet and ii) a subset of the protocol used by a commercial VoIP product. To create the dataset of ZeroAccess traces (⑤), we used the second version of the malware, provided by K. McNamee [18]. We deployed this malware in a confined and controlled network infrastructure. We then allowed our sample to connect with other botnet members through its P2P protocol (used to retrieve the P2P directory). To capture the traffic, we used a network probe implementing the deobfuscation algorithm previously detailed by K. McNamee [18]. The obtained dataset includes 883 messages for four true formats. Regarding contextual data, we used the last solution detailed in section 3.2 and used pcaps meta-data. Even though it does no bring a lot of contextual data, it still provides good results as messages generated by this P2P protocol often denotes network related information, such as the IP addresses of its peers. For the last dataset (⑥), we considered the protocol of a typical VoIP commercial product. To obtain traces of this protocol, we relied on a freely available implementation of this protocol and automatised its execution. In accordance with the solution we detailed in section 3.2, we selected a subset of the application features and established a scenario of 10 different actions, such as sending text messages, configuring personal data, disconnecting from or connecting to the server. We also arbitrary defined the values of each action parameters and stored them as contextual data. We then played this scenario three times and captured the generated traffic to create a dataset of 482 messages.

To ensure the reproducibility of these experiments, we stored and archived these datasets, but only some of them are made public. Generated datasets (① ③), FTP realistic dataset (②) and ZeroAccess dataset (⑤) are available for download. However, the realistic dataset of SMB packets captured from a company network cannot be published due to embedded sensitive information, and the one extracted from the commercial product cannot be published due to intellectual property restrictions. We also archived all the identified contextual information for each protocol that we summarised in table 5a.

4.3 Metrics

To measure and compare the effectiveness of message formats inference algorithms we need to define metrics. We reviewed all the metrics used in previous works experiments but no consensus emerged. For instance, some works report similar metrics but with different names (*i.e.* [6] and [5]), some compute their own measures [27, 1] and others only use qualitative metrics in their experiments [4]. We select two metrics and propose a new one to cover our needs in the evaluation of message clustering and field partitioning: the correctness, the conciseness and the precision. Correctness and conciseness are both used in [6] and are closed to the metrics used in [17, 5]. Figure 3 illustrates the three metrics we use.

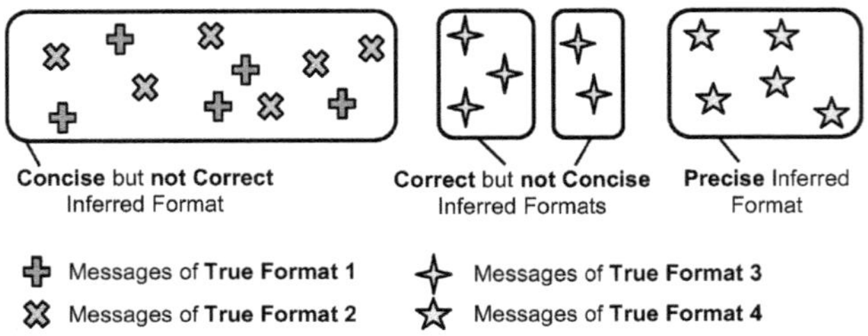

Figure 3: Illustration of our three metrics: conciseness, correctness and precision.

To define the conciseness and the correctness of a clustering algorithm we consider M the set of messages, F_{inf} the set of inferred formats and F_{true} the set of true formats. We also denote the function $I : M \rightarrow F_{inf}$, which defines the inferred format of a message and the function $T : M \rightarrow F_{true}$, which defines the true format of a message. We finally define two functions, $N_{con} : F_{true} \rightarrow \mathbb{N}$ and $N_{cor} : F_{inferred} \rightarrow \mathbb{N}$:

$$N_{con}(f) = |\{I(m)\ \forall m \in M \text{ such that } T(m) = f\}| \quad (7)$$

$$N_{cor}(f) = |\{T(m)\ \forall m \in M \text{ such that } I(m) = f\}| \quad (8)$$

Those two metrics are related to the mapping between true formats and inferred formats. Intuitively, the clustering is correct if it computes homogeneous clusters. It means that every cluster, *i.e.* inferred format, must contain only messages that share the same true format. In this case $N_{cor}(f) = 1$. Heterogeneous clusters decrease the correctness and in this case $N_{cor}(f) > 1$. Conversely, the clustering is concise if each true format is described by at most one inferred format. When messages corresponding to the same true format are clustered into different inferred formats, conciseness decrease and $N_{con}(f) > 1$. The clustering is correct if $N_{cor}(f)$ remains low (ideally equal to one) for a large number of true formats. It is concise if $N_{con}(f)$ remains low (ideally equal to one) for a large number of inferred formats. We thus define Conciseness (respectively Correctness) as the Cumulative Distributed Function of N_{con} (respectively N_{corr}): $Con(n) = P(N_{con} <= n)$ and $Cor(n) = P(N_{cor} <= n)$.

The overall shape of such CDF curves characterises the correctness or the conciseness of a given clustering approach. However, two points of such curves are of particular interests. The first one corresponds to $Cor(1) = p(N_{cor} = 1)$, *i.e.* the proportion of homogeneous clusters and the second one to $Con(1) = p(N_{con} = 1)$, *i.e.* the proportion of true format that correspond to at most one inferred format. We thus expect such values to be high.

Correctness and conciseness must be analysed together to understand the quality of the alignment. For example, an inference algorithm that classifies every messages into different clusters will be described as very accurate but unconcise. For this reason, we also use ROC curves to compare the different tools, by taking into account $Corr(1)$ and $Con(1)$.

We use an additional metric to evaluate the quality of the classification: the precision. To measure it, we compute the number of inferred formats that perfectly match a true format. We call them precise formats or precise clusters.

To use these metrics, we need to known the true format associated with each message. To identify the true format of well-known protocols, such as FTP and SMB, we used the results of Wireshark. More precisely, we extract the needed information out of a PDML file generated by Wireshark. This file includes the description of all the fields in captured messages. We then use a protocol-specific PDML parser that returns the value of some key fields. We assume that all the messages that share the same key values correspond to the same true format. To select these key fields we refer to the official specifications of the protocols and only select important fields. For instance, for the SMB protocol we consider the value of the "SMB Command" field, the value of optional "subCommands" fields and the value of the "status" field. Unlike previous work [6], we believe optional fields do not participate in the definition of a true format. For the two other protocols, we manually create specific parsers based on previous works published by other researchers that reversed such proprietary protocols.

4.4 Implementations

In this section, we describe the different implementations we developed for the experimentation phase.

Our open source framework for reverse engineering of communication protocols[6] is licensed under GPLv3. Freely available, its sources can be downloaded from a git repository and some packages for Linux platforms are provided. At the time of writing (December 2013), the source code of the framework comprises more than 50,000 lines of code, mostly in Python, some specific parts being implemented in C for performance purpose. It offers data models and basic algorithms to build, edit, visualise and simulate a communication protocol. We therefore implemented our approach and the others as plugins to reduce duplicated code and to simplify their comparisons.

The implementation of our work corresponds to only 500 lines of python since most of the computation codes are provided by our framework. We refer to it as Netzob in the following.

ASAP authors provide a publicly available implementation in R[7]. Thanks to the help of the authors, we developed a wrapper to execute ASAP implementation as a clustering plugin in our framework. This allows us to use the original ASAP code without inserting flaws. As recommended by authors, we uses Sally [22] to tokenize messages. Output clusters returned by ASAP are then transformed into symbols as presented in their article [13].

Unfortunately, implementing ScriptGen and Discoverer was much more difficult since neither source code nor implementation are publicly available, even for the scientific community. Among the two, Discoverer was the most difficult to re-implement as documentations and articles give too few details on some specific points such as on their merging strategy used in last step. In addition, both the authors of Discoverer and ScripGen did not publish the dataset they used to evaluate the effectiveness of their tools. Without publicly available datasets, it is thus difficult to validate our implementation of these approaches. However, we try to be as accurate as possible and check carefully our implementations of these approaches. Moreover, the results we obtained are similar to those described in the authors articles.

Each approach exposes parameters to the user that can highly impact the overall quality of their results when applied on a certain type of protocol. Thus, to ensure a fair comparison, we use the calibration datasets to compute the best parameters value and use them on their respective evaluation datasets. To identify these parameters, listed in figure 5b in appendix, we first established a large variation range for each of them and then compared the ROC curve of results brought by all possible combinations. For realistic datasets with no calibration, we only retained the best results given all the possible combination of parameter values.

4.5 Experimental Results

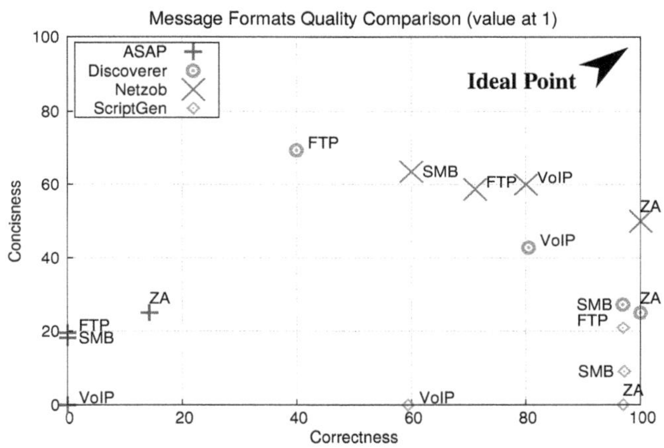

Figure 4: ROC Curve used to compare the quality of the inferred message clusters of ASAP, ScriptGen, Discoverer and Netzob. Best results are close to the top right corner.

In this section, we present the conclusions of our experimental comparative study of ASAP, ScriptGen, Discoverer and Netzob.

We expect results to be both concise and correct. This means that the ideal point of our ROC curves is the upper right corner of the graph, as illustrated in figure 4. It is also important that the tools balance concision with correctness. Indeed, incorrect clustering makes the tool useless as the user has to manually cluster the different messages. Conversely, a lost in conciseness entails an important problem: it generates too many symbols, which make the results difficult to interpret. Moreover, these symbols can be used to infer the grammar of the protocol and then to develop protocol generators. The size of the inferred protocol grammar automaton depends on the number of inferred symbols. A lost in conciseness will thus result in inefficient protocol generators. Concerning the ROC curve, this means that good results should be as close as possible to the upper right cor-

[6]Netzob- Reverse Engineering Communication Protocols: `http://www.netzob.org`

[7]ASAP sources: `https://github.com/tammok/PRISMA/`

ner, *i.e.* the "Ideal Point" on figure 4, and near the diagonal that goes from origin to that upper right corner.

First of all, general results depicted in figure 4 show that the compared approaches fall into two categories. On one hand, ASAP and ScriptGen obtained poor results and always suffer from the overfitting problem. Moreover, ASAP correctness is quite low meaning that most of its inferred message formats denotes multiple true formats. On the other hand, Discoverer and Netzob show better results with a clear advantage for Netzob which results are always nearer the ideal point.

The precision of the clustering is also another revealing measure of this distinction. Indeed, only Discoverer and Netzob infer precise clusters, *i.e.* inferred clusters that perfectly match true formats. Despite the use of calibration datasets to optimize their parameters value, ScriptGen and Discover inferred clusters never matched a true format. Indeed, none of their inferred message formats is accurate enough to support the automatic generation of a protocol parser.

We also observe in figure 4 that ASAP, Netzob and ScriptGen tend to be stable as they provide similar results for the different datasets. However, Discoverer is quite unstable. On SMB and ZA datasets, it suffers from the overfitting problem whereas on the FTP dataset it obtains a good conciseness but lower correctness (about 40%).

Our comparative study shows that ASAP does not return good results on the datasets we used. For instance, applied on the FTP realistic dataset (②), only 20% of the true formats match a unique inferred format (*c.f.* figure 4). We believe ASAP is not appropriate to infer precise specifications of a protocol. An approach solely based on a statistical analysis of keyword or n-grams in messages, does not appear sufficient to cluster them.

Another interesting point in our comparative study results is that ScriptGen creates far too much clusters. For instance, on the SMB realistic dataset (④) made of 937 messages for 22 true formats, ScriptGen infers 906 different message formats. Indeed, most of the computed clusters contain a single message. Figure 6(c) depicts this low conciseness problem when applied on SMB dataset: it needs more than 100 inferred formats to cover 100% of the true formats. The reason why ScriptGen over-classifies is that it clusters messages according to their position in a session. This is not efficient, because in realistic datasets users often behave differently in each session which brings different message formats at similar position in sessions. Besides, when a classification error occurs at the beginning of the session, it affects the classification quality of the all following messages.

Obtained results confirm that ScriptGen was not designed to achieve a complete reverse engineering of a protocol. Indeed, it seems more appropriate for the inference of the very first exchanges of a communication. As stated by its authors, ScriptGen is more adapted to build an agnostic honeypot.

As illustrated in figure 4, our comparative study shows that among all the tools, Netzob always infers the best message formats. Indeed, it always computes message formats with a minimum correctness of 60% and a minimum conciseness of 50%. Whereas Discoverer lack of conciseness on binary protocols produces hundred of inferred message formats for a single true format.

In addition to its stability, Netzob also computes the highest rate of precise clusters. Table 3 shows that Netzob always infers at least (and often more) precise clusters than Discoverer. From our point of view, inferring precise clusters is important for an algorithm. Not only that precise clusters represents perfectly inferred format but they can also help the expert to correct the other inferred message formats. That is because in most of the protocols, the different messages shares common aspects such as encoding functions or delimiters. The expert can apply this information on other inferred format to improve them.

Precision	FTP (②)	SMB (④)	ZA (⑤)	VoIP (⑥)
Discoverer	4.34%	22.72%	25%	6.66%
Netzob	**34.78%**	22.72%	**50%**	**26.6%**

Table 3: Number of precise clusters identified by Discoverer and Netzob.

5. CONCLUSION

In this paper, we proposed a complete and automated approach for trace-based message formats reverse engineering. Our approach relies on novel techniques that leverage contextual information and correlation means to enhance message clustering as well as field boundaries and relationship identification. We implemented our approach in a publicly available framework, and demonstrated its efficiency against both standard and unknown protocols. Moreover, we compared our approach against three other state-of-the-art approaches (Discoverer, ASAP and ScriptGen). The experimentation shows that it provides better overall results, in addition to extracting fields semantic.

Based on these results, network security products editors can rely on an approach that automates the creation of protocol parsers, thus providing fast and reactive response adapted to today's cybersecurity context. Same goes with the field of malware analysis, in the aim of speeding up, for example, the take down of botnets.

6. REFERENCES

[1] J. Antunes, N. Neves, and P. Verissimo. Reverse engineering of protocols from network traces. In *Proceedings of WCRE*, 2011.

[2] M. A. Beddoe. Network protocol analysis using bioinformatics algorithms. In *Toorcon*, 2004.

[3] J. Caballero, P. Poosankam, C. Kreibich, and D. Song. Dispatcher: enabling active botnet infiltration using automatic protocol reverse-engineering. In *Proceedings of CCS*, 2009.

[4] J. Caballero, H. Yin, Z. Liang, and D. Song. Polyglot: Automatic extraction of protocol format using dynamic binary analysis. In *Proceedings of CCS*, 2007.

[5] P. M. Comparetti, G. Wondracek, C. Kruegel, and E. Kirda. Prospex: Protocol specification extraction. In *Proceedings of SSP*, 2009.

[6] W. Cui. Discoverer: Automatic protocol reverse engineering from network traces. In *Proceedings of USENIX Security Symposium*, 2007.

[7] W. Cui, V. Paxson, N. C. Weaver, and Y. H. Katz. Protocol-independent adaptive replay of application dialog. In *Proceedings of NDSS*, 2006.

[8] J. Freeman. Hacking a closed ecosystem. In *O'Reilly Android Open Conference*, 2011.

[9] U. Gargi. Consumer media capture: Time-based analysis and event clustering. Technical report, HP Laboratories Palo Alto, aug 2003.

[10] C. Guarnieri, M. Schloesser, J. Bremer, and A. Tanasi. Cuckoo sandbox - open source automated malware analysis. In *Black Hat USA*, 2013.

[11] G. J. Holzmann. *Design and validation of computer protocols*. Prentice-Hall, Inc., 1991.

[12] T. Krueger, H. Gascon, N. Krämer, and K. Rieck. Learning stateful models for network honeypots. In *Proceedings of the 5th ACM workshop on Security and artificial intelligence*, 2012.

[13] T. Krueger, N. Kramer, and K. Rieck. Asap: automatic semantics-aware analysis of network payloads. In *Proceedings of ECML/PKDD*, 2011.

[14] F. Leder and P. Martini. Ngbpa next generation botnet protocol analysis. In *Emerging Challenges for Security, Privacy and Trust*, volume 297 of *IFIP Advances in Information and Communication Technology*. Springer Berlin Heidelberg, 2009.

[15] D. D. Lee and H. S. Seung. Algorithms for non-negative matrix factorization. In *NIPS*. MIT Press, 2000.

[16] C. Leita, K. Mermoud, and M. Dacier. Scriptgen: an automated script generation tool for honeyd. In *Proceedings of ACSAC*, 2005.

[17] Z. Lin, X. Jiang, D. Xu, and X. Zhang. Automatic protocol format reverse engineering through context-aware monitored execution. In *Procedings of NDSS*, 2008.

[18] K. McNamee. Malware analysis report - new c&c protocol for zeroacess/siref. Technical report, Kindsight Security Lab, 2012.

[19] S. B. Needleman and C. D. Wunsch. A general method applicable to the search for similarities in the amino acid sequence of two proteins. *Journal of Molecular Biology*, 48, 1970.

[20] R. Pang and V. Paxson. A high-level programming environment for packet trace anonymization and transformation. In *Proceedings of SIGCOMM*, 2003.

[21] D. N. Reshef, Y. A. Reshef, H. K. Finucane, S. R. Grossman, G. McVean, P. J. Turnbaugh, E. S. Lander, M. Mitzenmacher, and P. C. Sabeti. Detecting novel associations in large data sets. *Science*, 334, 2011.

[22] K. Rieck, C. Wressnegger, and A. Bikadorov. Sally: A tool for embedding strings in vector spaces. *Journal of Machine Learning Research*, 2012.

[23] J. Shearer. Trojan.zeroaccess threat report. Technical report, Symantec, 2011.

[24] R. R. Sokal and C. D. Michener. A statistical method for evaluating systematic relationships. *University of Kansas Scientific Bulletin*, 1958.

[25] A. Syropoulos. Mathematics of multisets. In *Proceedings of the Workshop on Multiset Processing: Multiset Processing, Mathematical, Computer Science, and Molecular Computing Points of View*, 2001.

[26] Y. Wang, X. Yun, M. Z. Shafiq, L. Wang, A. X. Liu, Z. Zhang, D. Yao, Y. Zhang, and L. Guo. A semantics aware approach to automated reverse engineering unknown protocols. In *Proceedings of ICNP*, 2012.

[27] Y. Wang, Z. Zhang, D. D. Yao, B. Qu, and L. Guo. Inferring protocol state machine from network traces: a probabilistic approach. In *Proceedings of ACNS*, 2011.

[28] C. Willems, T. Holz, and F. Freiling. Toward automated dynamic malware analysis using cwsandbox. *IEEE Security and Privacy*, 5(2):32–39, mar 2007.

[29] T. Yeh, T.-H. Chang, and R. C. Miller. Sikuli: Using gui screenshots for search and automation. In *Proceedings of the 22Nd Annual ACM Symposium on User Interface Software and Technology*, UIST '09, pages 183–192, New York, NY, USA, 2009. ACM.

APPENDIX

A. EXPERIMENTAL PARAMETERS

Protocols	Identified Actions	Identified Contextual Information
FTP	Connect with a bad password, successful connection, list current directory, invalid move directory, valid move directory, download file, upload a file, close connection	Client username, client password, server hostname, current directory, downloaded filename, uploaded filename, moving directory name, invalid directory name, directory listed.
SMB	Connect with a bad password, successful connection, list available shares, invalid move in a directory, list a directory, download file, upload a file, close connection	Client username, client password, server hostname, downloaded filename, uploaded filename, moving directory name, listed filenames, server domain name, server os, server version, server shares.
ZAccess	Receive a new peer address, propagate peer list.	IP addresses and UDP ports found in the pcap.
Commercial VoIP	Client 1 connects, client 2 connects, client 1 sends a message to client2, client 2 sends a message to client 1, client 1 changes its configuration, client 2 changes its configuration, client 1 disconnects, client 2 disconnects.	Server IP, server hostname, client IP, client phonetic names, client description, client comment message, client comment url, client messages.

(a) Identified Semantics

Tools	*Parameters*	FTP ①②	SMB ③④	ZAccess ⑤	Commercial VoIP ⑥
ASAP	Ngram Length	1	2	1	1
	Ngram Type	Text	Bin	Bin	Bin
	Ngram Delimiters	Extended	x	x	x
Discoverer	Min. Text Segments	2	2	2	2
	Min. Cluster Size	20	60	10	12
	Max. Distinct Values	10	5	20	350
ScriptGen	Macro-Clustering	0.9	0.7	0.6	0.6
	Micro-Clustering	0.5	0.5	0.4	0.4
Netzob	Similarity	0.9	0.6	0.5	0.8
	Matrix	10	10	10	-1

(b) Parameters used to configure each approach

Figure 5: Parameters used in our experimentation

B. EXPERIMENTAL DETAILED RESULTS

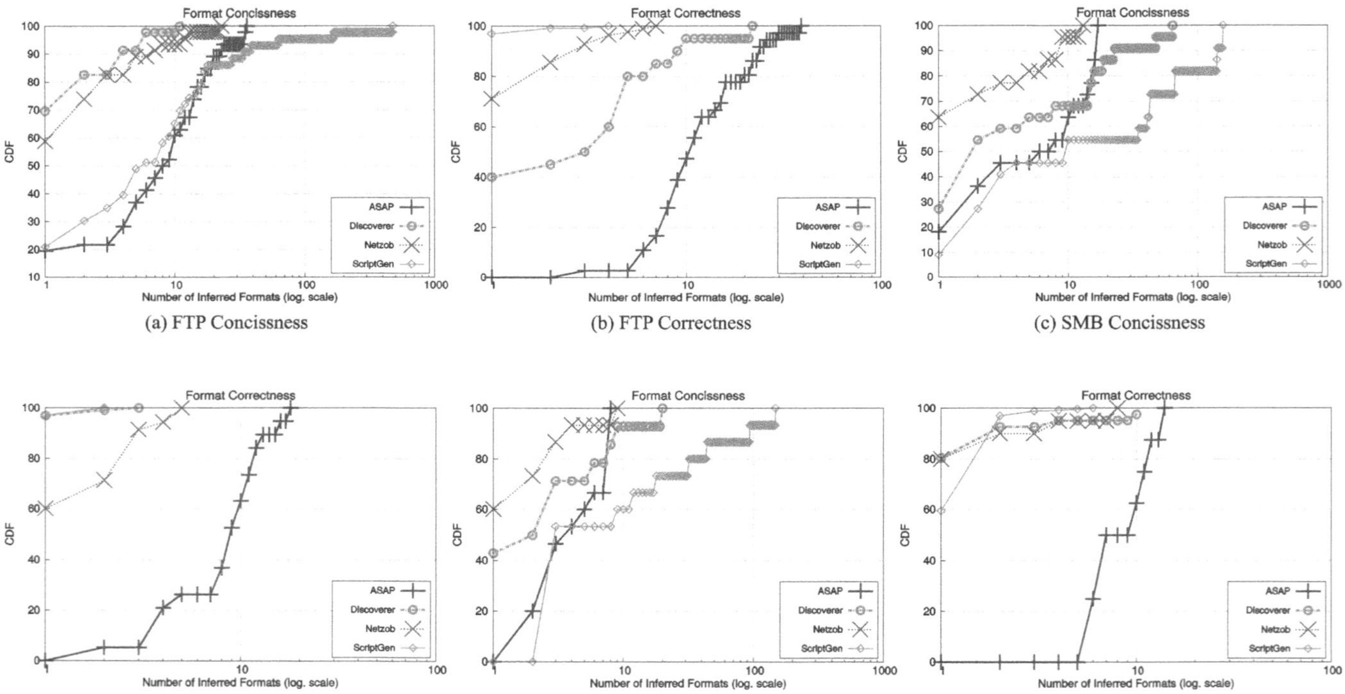

(a) FTP Concissness (b) FTP Correctness (c) SMB Concissness

(d) SMB Correctness (e) Commercial VoIP Concissness (f) Commercial VoIP Correctness

Figure 6: Detailed Experimental Results

Re^3: Relay Reliability Reputation for Anonymity Systems

Anupam Das, Nikita Borisov
University of Illinois at Urbana-Champaign
{das17,nikita}@illinois.edu

Prateek Mittal
Princeton University
pmittal@princeton.edu

Matthew Caesar
University of Illinois at Urbana-Champaign
caesar@illinois.edu

ABSTRACT

To conceal user identities, Tor, a popular anonymity system, forwards traffic through multiple relays. These relays, however, are often unreliable, leading to a degraded user experience. Worse yet, malicious relays may strategically introduce deliberate failures to increase their chance of compromising anonymity. In this paper we propose a reputation system that profiles the reliability of relays in an anonymity system based on users' past experience. A particular challenge is that an observed failure in an anonymous communication cannot be uniquely attributed to a single relay. This enables an attack where malicious relays can target a set of honest relays in order to drive down their reputation. Our system defends against this attack in two ways. Firstly, we use an adaptive exponentially-weighted moving average (EWMA) that ensures malicious relays adopting time-varying strategic behavior obtain low reputation scores over time. Secondly, we propose a filtering scheme based on the evaluated reputation score that can effectively discard relays involved in such attacks.

We use probabilistic analysis, simulations, and real-world experiments to validate our reputation system. We show that the dominant strategy for an attacker is to not perform deliberate failures, but rather maintain a high quality of service. Our reputation system also significantly improves the reliability of path construction even in the absence of attacks. Finally, we show that the benefits of our reputation system can be realized with a moderate number of observations, making it feasible for individual clients to perform their own profiling, rather than relying on an external entity.

Categories and Subject Descriptors

C.2.0 [**Computer-Communication Networks**]: General—Security and protection

General Terms

Security, Measurement

Keywords

Anonymity; Reputation Systems; Tor Network; Denial of Service

http://dx.doi.org/10.1145/2590296.2590338.

1. INTRODUCTION

Anonymous communication systems play a vital role in protecting users from network surveillance and traffic analysis. The widely-used Tor network [22] has approximately 5 000 relays and serves an estimated 300 000 unique users in a day, as of March 2014.[1] The effectiveness of Tor depends on the reliability of these relays. Unreliable relays can both degrade the user experience and impair the anonymity guarantees provided by Tor. Due to the unreliablity of Tor relays certain users will decide to abandon the system, thus decreasing the anonymity set, while the remaining users will end up retransmitting messages, presenting further opportunities for observation. This latter problem can be exploited by malicious relays where they can strategically affect the reliability of anonymous communications to increase their odds of compromising user anonymity [15, 16]. Given previous instances of active attacks on Tor [2, 10, 11], as well as recent governmental endeavors [24, 26] to deanonymize Tor users, it is important to identify active attackers in anonymity systems.

We propose a new reputation model, $\boldsymbol{Re^3}$, that can be used to detect and penalize relays involved in active attacks like selective DoS. The main challenge in building our model is that it is hard to pinpoint the single relay responsible for an observed failure. This enables an attack where malicious relays can target a set of honest relays in order to drive down their reputation. Moreover, malicious relays can oscillate between good and bad behavior in order to evade detection. To address these challenges we propose using an exponentially-weighted moving average (EWMA) that can dynamically adjust its weighting coefficient to capture the dynamic behavioral trend of a given Tor relay. $\boldsymbol{Re^3}$ ensures that a malicious relay that oscillates between reliable and unreliable state obtains a low reputation score over time. We then propose a filtering protocol based on relays' reputation score that can effectively discard relays mounting active attacks.

We analyze the security of our filtering protocol both probabilistically and through a prototype deployment in the live Tor network. We find that attackers gain no advantage through active attacks like selective DoS with $\boldsymbol{Re^3}$ deployed. We also show that our filtering scheme is not vulnerable to strategic attacks like the *targeted attack* and a particularly serious form of targeted attack known as the "*creeping death attack*" [23]. Furthermore, we study adaptive attackers who tailor their strategy specifically against our detection scheme, performing active dropping only if their reputation is above a chosen threshold. We conclude that with $\boldsymbol{Re^3}$ deployed the dominant strategy for such attackers is to not perform any circuit dropping. Finally, we show that our reputation model provides benefits even outside the context of active attacks, and is able to substantially increase the reliability of circuit construction in Tor.

[1] https://metrics.torproject.org

Contributions. We offer the following contributions:

- We present a reputation system that assigns quantitative scores to relays based on their provided reliability during anonymous communications. Our system captures dynamic behavioral change and penalizes relays exhibiting behavioral oscillation. (§3)
- We probabilistically analyze the security of our filtering protocol against the selective DoS attack, including its randomized variants. We also study strategic attacks against our reputation model such as the targeted attack and creeping-death attack. (§5)
- We perform simulation and experiments on the live Tor network to demonstrate that our reputation model can effectively filter out compromised relays. (§6)
- We demonstrate the benefits of our approach even outside the context of active attacks. Using real world experiments on the Tor network, we find that our filtering protocol is able to significantly improve the reliability of circuit construction. (§6.2.2)
- We present two strategies to incorporate our reputation model into Tor. One way is to run it locally at individual clients and the other is to run it at shared directory authority (DA) servers. (§7)

2. BACKGROUND

In this paper we take Tor as a case study to profile its participating relays. Hence, we present a brief overview of the Tor network, and then discuss how active attacks can lower anonymity in Tor. We also briefly discuss different types of reputation systems.

2.1 Tor: A Low-latency Anonymity Network

To anonymize TCP connections, a Tor user constructs a *circuit* comprised of several Tor *relays* (also known as routers). The relays form a pipeline through which traffic is forwarded back and forth between the user and destination. Circuits typically involve three relays: the *entry*, *middle*, and *exit*. Tor protects the contents of the traffic by using a layered encryption scheme [35], where each relay decrypts a layer while forwarding. As a result, any individual router cannot reconstruct the whole circuit and link the source to the destination. The relays in a circuit are chosen using specific constraints [21]. Each user selects the *entry* relay from a small, fixed number of relays that are flagged as "fast" and "stable". These relays are called *guard relays* [41]; their use is designed to defend from the predecessor attack [42]. To choose the exit relay, the user picks from among those relays that have an exit policy compatible with the desired destination. After these constraints, the relays for each position are chosen randomly, weighted by their bandwidth.[2]

Tor aims to provide low-latency traffic forwarding for its users. As a result, as traffic is forwarded along the path of a circuit, timing patterns remain observable, and an attacker who observes two different relays can use timing analysis to determine whether they are participating in the same circuit [30, 37, 39, 45]. Thus, to compromise anonymity it suffices to observe the entry and the exit relays for a circuit. Standard security analysis of Tor [22, 39] shows that if c is the fraction of relays that are observed, an adversary can violate anonymity on c^2 of all of the circuits. Due to bandwidth-weighted path selection in Tor, c is best thought of as the fraction of total Tor *bandwidth* that belongs to relays under observation.[3]

[2] This is a simplified description of the path selection; a detailed specification can be found at [21]. The omitted details do not significantly impact our analysis, and we use the full specification in our experiments.

[3] To be more precise, the correct fraction would be $c_g \cdot c_e$, where c_g and c_e are the fractions of the guard and exit bandwidth under observation, respectively. For simplicity of presentation, we will assume $c_g = c_e = c_m = c$ in the rest of the paper.

The security of Tor, therefore, relies on the assumption that a typical adversary will not be able to observe a significant fraction of Tor relays. For most adversaries, the easiest way to observe relay traffic is to run their own relays. It should be noted that other forms of adversaries do exist, such as ISP- and Internet exchange-level adversaries [25, 27, 33], but these adversaries are typically assumed to be passive and are thus not the focus of this paper.

2.2 Active Attack: Selective DoS in Tor

An adversary who controls a Tor relay can perform a number of active attacks to increase the odds of compromise [15, 16]. One approach is selective denial-of-service (DoS) [16]. A compromised relay that participates in a circuit can easily check whether both the entry and exit relays are under observation. If this is not the case, the relay can "break" the circuit by refusing to forward any traffic. This will cause a user to reformulate a circuit for the connection, giving the adversary another chance to compromise the circuit. A simple analysis shows that this increases the overall fraction of compromised circuits to: $\frac{c^2}{c^2+(1-c)^3} > c^2$, because only circuits with compromised entry and exit relays (c^2) or circuits with no compromised relays ($(1-c)^3$) will be functional, and out of those c^2 will be compromised. For example, if 20% of the bandwidth is controlled by an adversary (i.e., $c = 0.2$) then the selective DoS attack nearly doubles the overall fraction of compromised circuits from 4% to 7.2%.

The use of guard relays changes the analysis somewhat. If none of a user's guards are compromised, then the user is effectively immune from the selective DoS attack, since the user will never use a compromised entry regardless of the attack. If, on the other hand, one or more of the guards are malicious then the user is significantly impacted, as the dishonest guard(s) chosen for a significant fraction of all circuits will break any circuit that does not use a compromised exit. For $c = 0.2$, if one of the guards is compromised then the selective DoS attack increases the overall fraction of compromised circuits from 6.7% to 13.5% and for two compromised guards this value increases from 13.3% to 38.5%. Therefore, guard relays mitigate the selective DoS attack in that it will affect fewer users if they choose honest guards, but can adversly affect users who are unlucky enough to choose dishonest guards.

2.3 Reputation Models

A reputation model [36] collects, aggregates, and distributes feedback about participants' past behavior. Reputation models help users decide whom to trust, encourage trustworthy behavior, and discourage participation by users who are dishonest. Reputation models can be classified as either *local* or *global*, based on the way information is aggregated [32]. In a local reputation model, feedback is derived only from direct encounters (first-hand experience) whereas in a global reputation model feedback is also derived indirectly (second-hand evidence) from other users. Hence, in the case of a global reputation model [28, 43, 44], a user aggregates feedback from all users who have ever interacted with a given participant, thus enabling it to quickly converge to a better decision. However, global reputation models are much more complex to manage than local approaches as malicious users have the opportunity to provide false feedback. Our focus is on building a local reputation model that accumulates only first-hand experience with Tor relays.

3. Re^3: OUR REPUTATION MODEL

Our goal is to construct a local reputation model that can be used by a Tor user to filter out less reliable Tor relays. This section discusses the different components of our model.

3.1 Reputation Score

To evaluate the reputation of a given Tor relay, a user keeps track of its own local experience with the relay through a modified form of exponentially-weighted moving average (EWMA). EWMA combines both recent and historical evaluations of a chosen feature which enables it to compute a representative evaluation of the feature under question. However, a conventional EWMA assigns fixed weights to recent and historical evaluations, and as a result it fails to capture any oscillating behavior. In our system we consider strategic relays, capable of altering their behavior in a way that may benefit them. Aringhieri et al. [13] proposed dynamically modifying the weighting co-efficient of EWMA to obtain a better evaluation, but they do not consider strategic oscillations where malicious users oscillate between building and milking their reputation. Srivatsa et al. [38] proposed a PID controller-based reputation framework which can handle strategic behavior by malicious users. We adopt a similar approach where we dynamically change the weighting coefficient of our adaptive EWMA in such a way that it penalizes any relay exhibiting frequent behavioral oscillation. Figure 1 shows an overview of how we compute a relay's reputation score.

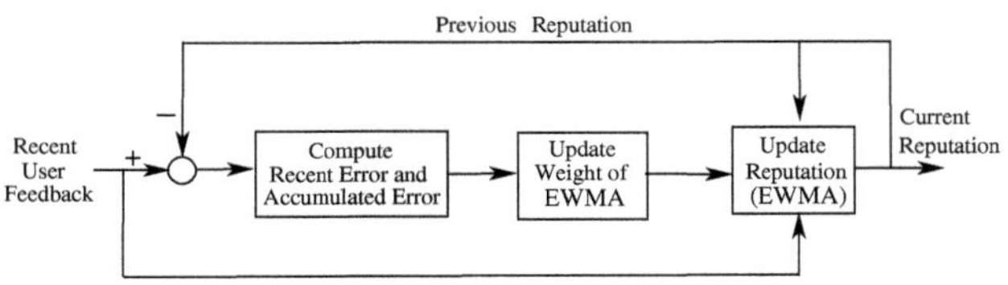

Figure 1: Block diagram of our reputation model. A feedback loop is used to model the dynamic behavior of a Tor relay. We dynamically adjust the weighting coefficient of our EWMA based on a relay's behavior.

Let $R_n(x)$ represent the local reputation of relay x after n interactions (where $R_n \in [-1, 1]$). The local reputation update function is defined as follows:

$$R_n(x) = \alpha_n(x) \cdot R_c + [1 - \alpha_n(x)] \cdot R_{n-1}(x) \quad (1)$$

with $R_0(x) = 1$; i.e., all relays are initially assumed to be good because we want all relays to be initially usable. Here, R_c represents the rating of the most recent experience. For simplicity we have used a binary rating system where a user rates a relay based on whether the circuit built through that relay was usable or not.

$$R_c = \begin{cases} -1, & \text{if circuit failed} \\ 1, & \text{otherwise} \end{cases} \quad (2)$$

The weighting coefficient $\alpha_n(x)$ determines the degree to which we want to discount older observations. To penalize relays oscillating between good and bad behavior, we keep track of accumulated deviation $\xi_n(x)$ from recent error $\delta_n(x)$, and lower reputation proportionally (with proportional constant, K_p). The update function of $\alpha_n(x)$ is given as follows:

$$\alpha_n(x) = K_p \cdot \frac{\delta_n(x)}{1 + \xi_n(x)} \quad (3)$$

$$\delta_n(x) = \begin{cases} \frac{R_c(x) - R_{n-1}(x)}{\mu}, & \text{if } R_c(x) \geq R_{n-1}(x) \\ \frac{R_{n-1}(x) - R_c(x)}{\nu}, & \text{if } R_c(x) < R_{n-1}(x) \end{cases} \quad (4)$$

$$\xi_n(x) = \xi_{n-1}(x) + \delta_n(x) \quad (5)$$

Here proportional constant, $K_p (0 \leq K_p \leq 1)$ controls to what extent we want to react to recent error ($\delta_n(x)$) compared to accumulated deviation ($\xi_n(x)$). We set $K_p = 0.5$ after performing a sensitivity analysis (see Appendix B for more details).

As stated earlier we want our reputation function to penalize oscillating behavior and to achieve that we update the error function $\delta_n(x)$ using a reward and punishment strategy where we reward relays for successful communication and punish them for unsuccessful communication. Incorporating such a strategy enforces relays to behave faithfully. In equation (4), μ and ν represent the reward and punishment factor respectively. Both $\mu, \nu \in \Re$, but we must ensure that $\mu > \nu$ because the impact of punishment should be greater than that of reward. In other words, $\delta_n(x)$ should increase more for unsuccessful communication than successful communication, because that would in turn increase $\alpha_n(x)$, giving higher significance to the recent bad evaluation.

To get a better understanding of how Re^3 reacts to different scenarios like random network failures or strategic oscillating behavior, we evaluate the reputation score of a relay dropping circuits at different rates. Figure 2 shows the evaluated reputation score for different characteristics. We see that any form of circuit dropping results in lowering reputation. Even strategic oscillating behavior (i.e., strategically building and milking reputation) is punished *severely* and this is evident from the lower reputation score for the same drop rate. For example, oscillating at 50% drop rate results in a lower reputation score compared to 50% random drop rate. Hence, for a relay to achieve good reputation, it will have to provide good service consistently (more results available in Section 6.1.3). In Appendix B we describe how different parametric choices affect our reputation metric. We also analyze the stability of our reputation model in Appendix A.

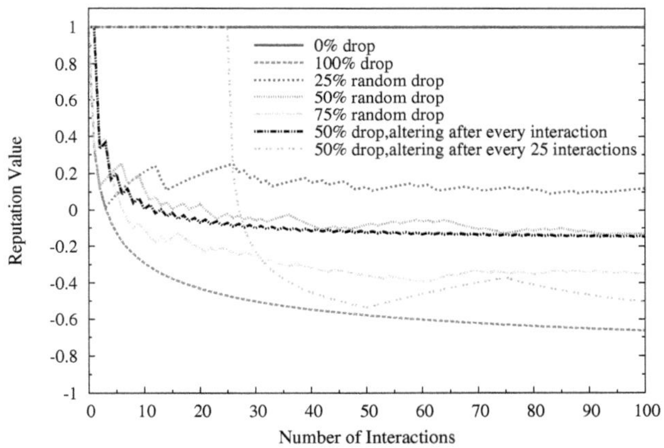

Figure 2: Reaction of our reputation metric to different combinations of cooperative and malicious behavior. We can see that different dropping characteristics result in lowering reputation.

3.2 Confidence Factor

We follow the principle that the more you interact with a relay, the more confident you become about its behavior, and associate a confidence factor with our local reputation score. In other words, if a user A performs n_1 and n_2 (where $n_1 > n_2$) interactions with relays B and C respectively, then the reputation score reported for relay B is more close to its stable score than that reported for C. We, therefore, formulate the confidence factor as a monotonically increasing function of the number of interactions with a given relay. We use the following confidence metric:

$$C_n(x) = \beta^{\frac{1}{n}} \quad (6)$$

where n represents the number of times a user has communicated through relay x. Here, β ($0 < \beta < 1$) is a user defined variable which determines how quickly the user becomes confident about his/her rating (sensitivity analysis is provided in Appendix B).

3.3 Ranking Score

The ranking score reflects how well a given relay has been performing so far. To obtain a high ranking score a relay will have to persistently exhibit good behavior for a long period of time. We formulate the final ranking score of a relay by multiplying the reputation score with the confidence value:

$$Rank_n(x) = R_n(x) \cdot C_n(x) \quad (7)$$

This ensures that the ranking score of a relay is high only when both its reputation score and confidence value is high. A relay with a high reputation score but a low confidence value will result in an overall low ranking score. This hinders whitewashing attacks.

4. FILTERING PARTICIPANTS IN TOR

In this section we describe how Re^3 can be used to filter out potentially compromised relays. As mentioned above, Re^3 matures as the user gathers more experience and by assuming that only a small fraction of all relays are compromised, we can probabilistically show that the average reputation of honest relays will be higher than that of compromised ones. So to filter out potentially compromised relays, we only need to find outliers in terms of ranking score. Our filtering protocol assumes γ fraction of the relays are potentially outliers (ideally γ is equivalent to the fraction of compromised relays in the system). Now, to filter outliers a client takes the following steps:

- First, the client computes the average (μ) ranking score and standard deviation (σ) in ranking score of the top $1 - \gamma$ fraction of the relays he/she has interacted with.
- Filters out any relay x with $|Rank(x) - \mu| > k\sigma$ as outlier. Here, k represents to what degree of deviation we are willing to tolerate from the expected ranking score. We filter outliers in both directions because when a large fraction of the guards are compromised, compromised exits tend to obtain a higher ranking score (as majority of the circuits have a compromised guard in such scenario) compared to the other honest relays.[4]

From a security perspective, we are interested in cases when clients have some compromised guards. In such cases, we can adopt the following two strategies with respect to selecting guards:

- **Strategy 1**: Consider all guards that are not outliers.
- **Strategy 2**: Consider only the highest ranked guard.

The reason behind using strategy 2 is that if 1 or 2 of the guards are compromised then their reputation score should be lower than that of the honest ones, so strategy 2 helps to filter out potentially compromised guard relays. We evaluate both strategies later in Section 6. We want to point out that clients consider the filtered list of Tor relays (after profiling a large set of Tor relays) for future circuit construction following Tor's conventional bandwidth-proportional path construction protocol.

5. PROBABILISTIC ANALYSIS

In this section we probabilistically analyze the effectiveness of Re^3 in filtering out compromised relays under four adversarial strategies. Filtering is done based on the ranking score of relays, which in turn is computed based on the fraction of time a relay receives positive (+ve) and negative (-ve) feedback from a user (see equation (2)). Hence, we conduct our analysis by computing the probability of receiving positive and negative feedback for different types of relays. First, we analyze the selective DoS attack scenario. Next, we analyze the impact of targeted attack against Re^3; followed by an analysis of creeping-death attack. Finally, we analyze random drop strategy where the adversary randomly drops non-compromised circuits to masquerade its true nature. To carry out our probabilistic analysis we consider the following parameters:

- g: fraction of guard relays per user that are compromised (by default each user has 3 guard relays).
- g': fraction of guard relays per user that are targeted (used for targeted attack analysis only).
- c: fraction of other relays in the network that are compromised.

Our probabilistic computation assumes that different types of relays can appear only in the middle and exit position of a Tor circuit, as guard relays are preselected by users and they are changed only after a period of 30 to 60 days (uniformly chosen). For the following analyses we give more emphasis to scenarios where $g = 1/3, 2/3$, as $g = 0, 1$ are trivial scenarios.

5.1 Analysis of Selective DoS Attack

We start by computing the fraction of positive and negative feedback that a given Tor relay will obtain when compromised relays are carrying out selective DoS attack. For example, a compromised exit relay will only allow a given circuit to continue if the guard relay is also compromised. So, the probability of receiving positive feedback is at most g for a compromised exit relay. We can similarly calculate the other probabilities. Table 1 summarizes the different probabilities.

Now our filtering protocol can successfully filter compromised relays only if they are outliers in the reputation spectrum. We can approximate reputation scores as the difference between the fraction of positive and negative feedback. For $g = 1/3$, we see that the reputation of compromised relays is less than that of honest relays for any value of $c < 0.75$. But for $g = 2/3$ we see that the reputation score of compromised relays is higher than that of honest relays, however, if we assume compromised relays as minorities then they become outliers compared to honest relays making it possible for Re^3 to filter them. More analysis is in Section 6.1.2.

Table 1: Probabilities under selective DoS attack

Relay	Probability of Positive (+ve) Feedback	Probability of Negative (-ve) Feedback
Honest	$\frac{1}{2}gc + (1-g)(1-c)$	$1 - \frac{1}{2}gc - (1-g)(1-c)$
Compromised	$\frac{1}{2}(gc + g)$	$1 - \frac{1}{2}(gc + g)$

Table 2: Probabilities under targeted attack strategy

Relay	Positive Feedback(+ve)	Negative Feedback(-ve)
Target	$\frac{1}{2}[(1-c)(2-g) - gt]$	$1 - \frac{1}{2}[(1-c)(2-g) - gt]$
Compromised	$\frac{1}{2}[(1-t)(2-g') - g'c]$	$1 - \frac{1}{2}[(1-t)(2-g') - g'c]$
Other	$\frac{1}{2}[2 - g'c - gt]$	$\frac{1}{2}[g'c + gt]$

5.2 Analysis of Targeted Attack

In this section we analyze the impact of targeted attack against Re^3. Here we assume that the set of compromised relays target a set of honest relays (preferably high bandwidth relays) and try to frame them as compromised. The attack strategy is defined as follows: *"Whenever a compromised relay discovers that a targeted relay lies on the circuit, it kills the circuit forcing the user to lower the reputation score of the targeted relay"*. Now lets assume c fraction of the compromised Tor relays target t fraction of the honest relays. Intuitively, this scheme will work only if $c > t$, otherwise both the compromised and targeted set of relays will have similar low reputation scores causing them to be filtered out. Table 2 summarizes the probabilities of receiving positive and negative feed-

[4]Under our assumption a high ranking score does not always imply a trustworthy relay, rather a ranking score in the vicinity of the expected ranking score implies a trustworthy relay.

back for the different types of relays (e.g., if a compromised relay is in the middle position of a Tor circuit then it will let the circuit continue only if the adjacent relays are not in the targeted set, this corresponds to $\frac{1}{2}(1-g')(1-t)$, one of the terms in the table).[5]

Now we want to check if our filtering protocol can identify relays mounting targeted attacks. To do so we need to ensure that the reputation score of compromised relays is outside the acceptable region, i.e., outside $(\mu - k\sigma, \mu + k\sigma)$. First, we approximate the reputation score of the different types of relays. Next, we compute the average (μ) and standard deviation (σ) of the top $(1-\gamma)$ fraction of the relays. Finally, we determine the value of k for which the reputation score of compromised relays is outside $(\mu - k\sigma, \mu + k\sigma)$.

Lets first approximate the average reputation score of different types of relays. Since we use a binary rating system (see equation (2)), we can approximate the average reputation score of different types of relays using the following equations:

$$R_T = \Pr(+ve_{fb})_{target} - \Pr(-ve_{fd})_{target}$$
$$R_C = \Pr(+ve_{fb})_{compromised} - \Pr(-ve_{fd})_{compromised}$$
$$R_O = \Pr(+ve_{fb})_{other} - \Pr(-ve_{fd})_{other}$$

Here the probabilities represent the fraction of the feedbacks that are positive and negative. R_T, R_C and R_O refers to the reputation score of relays belonging to the targeted, compromised and non-targeted honest set respectively. From Table 2, we see that for $c > t$, the reputation score of a compromised relay is greater than that of a targeted relay. But both of their reputation score are much lower than that of a non-targeted honest relay, i.e., $R_O > R_C > R_T$. If we assume that c is still a minority group, we can use this discrepancy to filter out the malicious relays from the selection.

A client starts by ignoring a fraction γ of the relays with the lowest reputation and then computes the average and standard deviation of the remaining reputation scores. If $c < \gamma < c+t$, then this computation will exclude all of the targeted relays but include a fraction of the malicious relays:

$$\mu = \frac{(1-t-c)\cdot R_O + (c+t-\gamma)\cdot R_C}{1-\gamma}$$

$$\sigma = \sqrt{\frac{(1-t-c)(\mu - R_O)^2 + (c+t-\gamma)(\mu - R_C)^2}{1-\gamma}}$$

The client only keeps the relays whose reputation score lies within k standard deviations from the mean, i.e., in the interval $(\mu - k\sigma, \mu + k\sigma)$. Some calculations show that if we set $\gamma = 0.2$ and $k < \sqrt{3}$, then R_C will fall outside this interval. This is true for all value of g and g' taken from the set $\{1/3, 2/3\}$.

Figure 3(a) highlights the average reputation score of the different relays along with the acceptable upper and lower bound when $c = 0.2$. Now, let us assume that the compromised relays perform targeted attack first, and once the targeted relays are blacklisted they start performing selective DoS attack to increase their chance of being selected. Figure 3(b) shows the probability of selecting a compromised circuit for different values of k with different fractions of honest relays being targeted. From Figure 3(b) we can see that with the proper setting of $k < \sqrt{3}$, we can effectively filter compromised relays even when they launch targeted attacks on a small set of honest relays.

Thus, we can see that compromised relays do lower the reputation score of the targeted set (as evident from Figure 3(a)). However, this in turn increases the reputation score of the remaining

[5] Our analyses are approximations where we are assuming replacement of relays after selection, however, with a large number of relays this introduces negligible error.

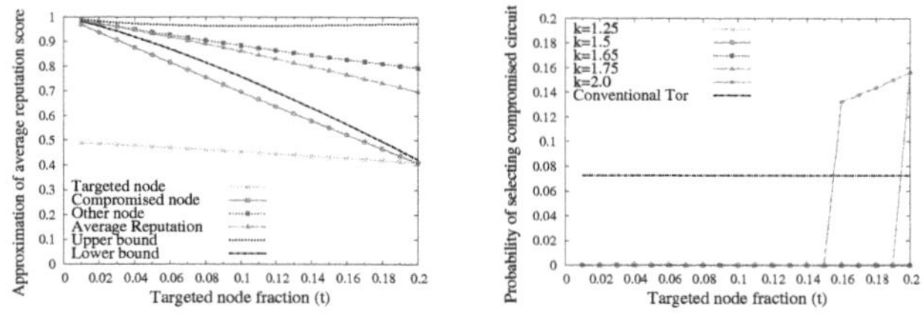

(a) (b)

Figure 3: For the targeted attack scenario: (a) Average ranking score of different types of relays along with the acceptable upper and lower bounds. We see that the reputation score for both the targeted and compromised relays lie outside the acceptable bounds. (b) Probability of selecting a compromised circuit once filtering has been done. As we increase the acceptable range of reputation (by increasing k) the probability of selecting a compromised circuit increases.

relays (i.e., relays that are neither in the compromised or targeted set) because under this attack strategy the target set is much smaller compared to the vanilla selective DoS scenario where all honest relays are included in the targeted set. And since we use the average and standard deviation of the top $(1-\gamma)$ fraction of the relays, this raises the bar of acceptance, making it harder for compromised relays to be accepted. If adversaries adopt the strategy to change the target set then relays in the previous target set will eventually be reconsidered for usage due to their honest nature. Thus, shifting the target set does not affect the system as compromised relays will also have to wait until they buildup a good reputation.

5.3 Analysis of the Creeping Death Attack

Dingledine et al. defined the "*creeping death attack*" [23] as follows: "*Whenever a compromised relay discovers that majority of the relays on the circuit are honest, it kills the circuit forcing the user to lower the reputation score of the honest relays*". In Tor, circuits contain three relays, so a honest relay will succeed only if the other two participating relays are honest or compromised (with probability $(1-g)(1-c)+gc$). Table 3 summarizes the probabilities for different types of relays. Again we see that for $g = 1/3$ the reputation score of honest relays is higher than that of compromised relays, but for $g = 2/3$ it is reverse. But assuming compromised relays as minorities we can successfully filter them by setting $k < \sqrt{3}$.

Table 3: Probabilities of under the creeping death attack strategy

Relay	Positive Feedback(+ve)	Negative Feedback(-ve)
Honest	$(1-g)(1-c)+gc$	$1-(1-g)(1-c)-gc$
Compromised	$g+c-gc$	$1-g-c+gc$

Table 4: Probabilities under the random drop attack strategy

Relay	Positive Feedback (+ve)	Negative Feedback (-ve)
Honest	$(1-g-c+\frac{3}{2}gc)+[g+c-\frac{3}{2}gc](1-d)$	$[g+c-\frac{3}{2}gc]d$
Compromised	$\frac{1}{2}(gc+g)+[1-\frac{1}{2}(gc+g)](1-d)$	$[1-\frac{1}{2}(gc+g)]d$

5.4 Analysis of the Random Drop Attack

Next we analyze the impact of random dropping strategy, a variant of selective DoS. In this scenario, compromised relays randomly drop circuits that they cannot compromise instead of always dropping non-compromised circuits. The objective behind randomly dropping some fraction of the non-compromised circuits is to masquerade their circuit dropping characteristic as a simple network/reliability failure.

Now, let us compute the probabilities of receiving positive and negative feedback for different types of relays with Re^3 deployed. Table 4 summarizes the different probabilities. For $c = 0.2$, we verify that any form of dropping results in reducing reputation, but compared to honest relays compromised relays suffer greatly for $g = 1/3$. For $g = 2/3$, the reputation score of compromised relays is greater than that of honest relays, but that makes them outliers which in turn helps our filtering scheme to easily filter them. Thus, random circuit dropping (i.e., $d > 0$) becomes a losing proposal with Re^3 deployed.

6. EXPERIMENTAL EVALUATION

In this section, we present a series of simulation and real-world experimental results, all of which highlight the effectiveness of Re^3 in filtering unreliable/compromised relays under real-world settings. We first look at the false positive and false negative errors of our filtering scheme. Next, we evaluate the probability of selecting a compromised circuit. Finally, we run experiments over the live Tor network and find that there is significant difference in the application and network level reliability of individual Tor relays. All these findings help us conclude that Re^3 can assist users in selecting more reliable and well-behaved Tor relays.

6.1 Simulation Results

6.1.1 Simulation Setup

We implemented a simulator that emulates the basic functionality of Tor circuit construction and active circuit dropping. We collected actual relay information (such as IP address, advertised bandwidth and probability of the relay being selected for entry, middle and exit position) from the Tor compass project [4] and randomly tagged 20% of the bandwidth to be controlled by an adversary; i.e., in our threat model we assume $c = 0.2$. For our experimental setup we consider 3 guards, 23 middle relays and 23 exits where all relays belong to a distinct /16 IP subnet. The reason behind using 23 middle and exit relays is that we assume a user uses Tor for three hours continuously[6] and since a given circuit is alive for only 10 minutes, a user would need 18 circuits in a 3 hour period, i.e., at most 18 different middle and exit relays. Since we assume 20% of the available bandwidth is controlled by a malicious entity, on average we need $18/0.8 \approx 23$ relays to build 18 non-compromised circuits.[7] We create a total of $3 \times 23 \times 23 = 1587$ circuits (each tested exactly once) to determine the reputation score of the selected relays.

Table 5 summarizes the parametric settings for our simulation. We vary two environmental parameters (g, d) to analyze the robustness and effectiveness of Re^3 against active circuit dropping attacks. Here, 100% drop rate refers to selective DoS and 0% drop means no dropping at all. In the following evaluations we again give more emphasis to results for $g = 1/3, 2/3$, as $g = 0, 1$ are trivial scenarios. Regarding guard selection strategy, our default strategy is to use all guards that are not outliers (i.e., strategy 1 as described in Section 4). To approximate the circuit failure rate present in the current Tor network we use scripts from the TorFlow project [8]. The TorFlow project measures the performance of Tor network by creating Tor circuits and recording their failure rate. We run TorFlow's *buildtime.py* [8] python-script to generate 10 000 Tor circuits and record their failure rate. We found the average failure rate over 10 runs to be approximately 21%. Thus, we set the circuit failure rate, f to 0.21 in all our simulations. All simulation results are averaged over 100 000 runs with 95% confidence intervals shown on all graphs (though they are sometimes too small to see).

[6] Tor users download the Tor consensus data every three hours so it would make sense to refresh the relay list every three hours.

[7] Due to uneven bandwidth allocation, the actual number of honest relays could be significantly different.

6.1.2 Filtering Compromised Relays

To compare the ranking score of honest relays with that of compromised relays, we set $d = 1$ and compute the ranking score of all the relays by varying g. Figure 4 shows the ranking score of both honest and compromised relays for different numbers of compromised guards. As discussed in Section 4, we set cutoffs based on the average ranking score of the top 80% ($= 1 - c$) ranked relays. To filter outliers we exclude relays that are further than $\sqrt{3}$ standard deviations away from the average (i.e., $k = \sqrt{3}$; we analyze the sensitivity of k in Appendix C). The dotted/dashed lines in the figure represent the boundaries for acceptable region $(\mu - k\sigma, \mu + k\sigma)$. Figure 4 shows that as the number of compromised guards increases the distinction between honest and compromised relay shrinks. This is understandable because as the number of compromised guards increase, the ranking score for compromised relays also start to increase because more and more circuits with compromised guards are created. However, since honest relays dominate the total population, the average reputation score of the system lies close to the average reputation score of the honest relays. As a result, even with $g = 2/3$ we can successfully filter out a significant portion of the compromised relays.

Table 5: Simulation Parameters

	Parameter	Description	Value/Range
Computation Setting	K_p	Proportional gain	0.5
	μ	Rewarding factor	2
	ν	Punishment factor	1
	β	Confidence co-efficient	0.5
Environment Setting	g	Fraction of compromised guards	$\{0, 1/3, 2/3, 1\}$
	d	Drop rate for compromised relays	$0 \leq d \leq 1$
	f	Transient network failure	0.21

6.1.3 Evaluating Robustness

In this section we present results that show the robustness of our reputation model in the presence of compromised relays. First, we look at false positive and false negative errors of our filtering protocol, and then we evaluate the probability of constructing a compromised circuit under different strategic scenarios.

False errors of our filtering scheme: We define false negative (FN) and false positive (FP) error as follows:

- **FN:** Fraction of compromised relays in the accepted list.
- **FP:** Fraction of honest relays in the discarded list.

Figure 5 highlights the calculated FN and FP errors. Ideally you want both false errors to be low but since compromised relays are a minority and honest relays are plentiful, lowering FN is *more important* than lowering FP. Figure 5 shows that as the drop rate d increases, FN decreases (except for $g = 1$, which is not interesting to look at as all the guards are compromised). We see a similar trend for FP, where the FP error decreases as the drop rate d increases. This is expected because as the drop rate increases the distinction between compromised and honest relays becomes more clearer. So, whether honest relays are heavily penalized (for $g \geq 2/3$) or rewarded (for $g \leq 1/3$), the average ranking score of the relays in the system shifts towards the ranking score of honest relays as the majority of the relays are assumed to be honest. That is why we see FP error reduce to almost 5%. These results indicate that carrying out active attacks like selective DoS is a losing proposition for an attacker.

Probability of constructing compromised circuits: Next, we evaluate the probability of constructing a compromised circuit once outliers have been discarded. The probability of such an event is:

$$\frac{g_f c_f}{g_f c_f + (1-g_f)(1-c_f)^2 + (1-d)\big(1 - g_f c_f - (1-g_f)(1-c_f)^2\big)} \quad (8)$$

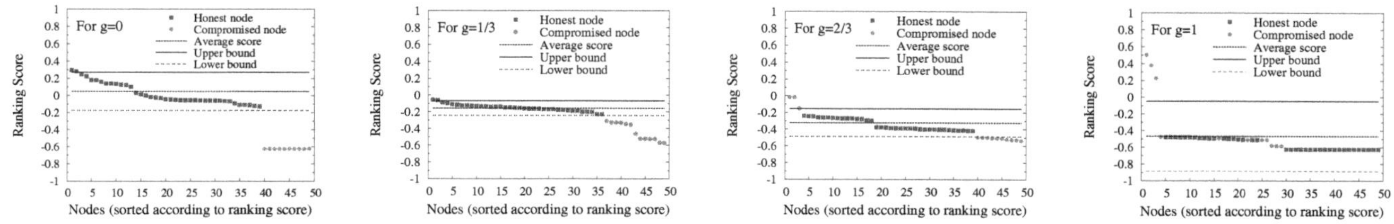

Figure 4: Ranking score of honest and compromised relays for various fractions of compromised guards. relays that are $k = \sqrt{3}$ standard deviations away from the mean are considered outliers. We can see that even with $g = 2/3$ a client can successfully filter out a significant portion of the compromised relays.

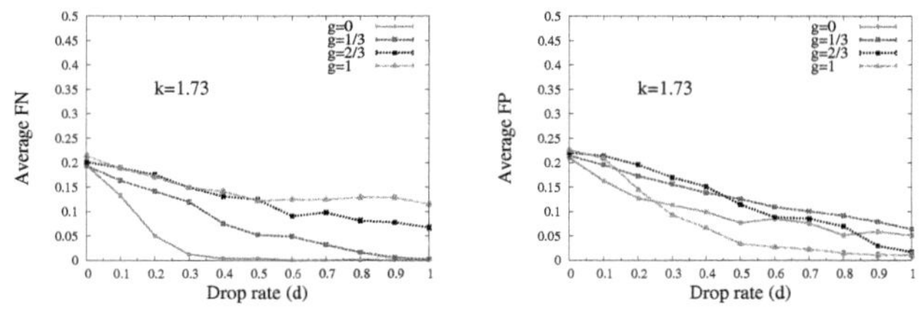

Figure 5: Average FN and FP with 95% confidence interval against drop rate d. Both FN and FP decrease as drop rate increases.

where $g_f c_f$ refers to the fraction of circuits with a compromised guard and exit, while $(1 - g_f)(1 - c_f)^2$ refers to the fraction of circuits with all honest relays at each position in the circuit (g_f and c_f represent the fraction of compromised guards and other relays in the accepted list, respectively). Now we evaluate this probability under both guard selection strategies as outlined in Section 4. Figure 6 shows the probability of constructing a compromised circuit against drop rate d, under both strategies. For $g \leq 1/3$, we see that this probability quickly decreases to almost zero as the drop rate increases, which is significantly better than what conventional Tor guarantees (indicated by the dashed lines). Even for $g = 2/3$, we see a significant improvement but compared to strategy 1, strategy 2 performs much better. The main reason behind this is that with two guards out of the three being compromised we could potentially lower the probability of constructing a compromised circuit by considering only the honest available guard. This is what strategy 2 does, as it considers only the top ranked guard relay while discarding the remaining two guards during actual usage. For $g = 1$, we do not see much improvement, however, $g = 1$ is a hopeless case as all the guards are already compromised. Thus, for $g < 1$ the dominant attack strategy is to perform *no* dropping.

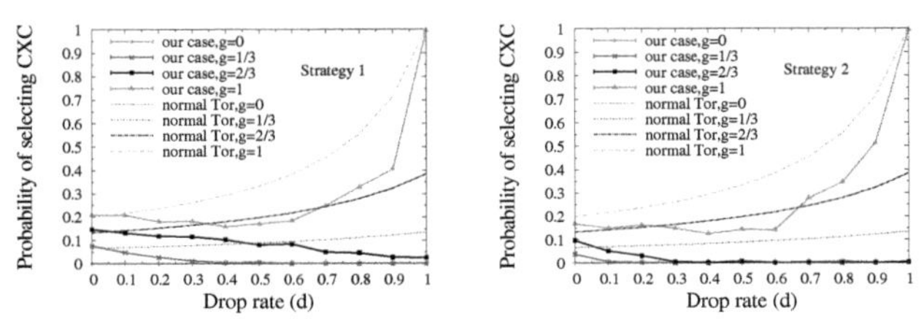

Figure 6: Probability of constructing a compromised (CXC) circuit after filtering outliers using strategy 1 and 2. We see that our approach outperforms conventional Tor as drop rate increases.

Finally, we test our reputation model against an adversary who tries to oscillate between building and milking its reputation. The adversary adopts the following strategy—*"Drop circuit only if its reputation is above a chosen threshold"*. Under this scenario we assume the adversary mimics a normal user in the system and keeps track of the reputation score of its relays, so that it can optimally decide whether to drop a circuit or not. We vary the reputation threshold chosen by the adversary from -1 to +1 in increments of 0.1. In all the simulations we compute the drop rate carried out by the adversary along with the probability of constructing a compromised circuit by clients. Figure 7 shows that as the reputation threshold increases the drop rate declines to zero. In other words, to obtain a positive reputation score the adversary cannot afford to to drop too many circuits. The probability of constructing a compromised circuit ($Pr(CXC)$) rises to a stable value as drop rate declines to zero. This happens because with no dropping, the reputation score of each relay remains unaffected. We, therefore, conclude that Re^3 discourages active circuit dropping by compromised relays.

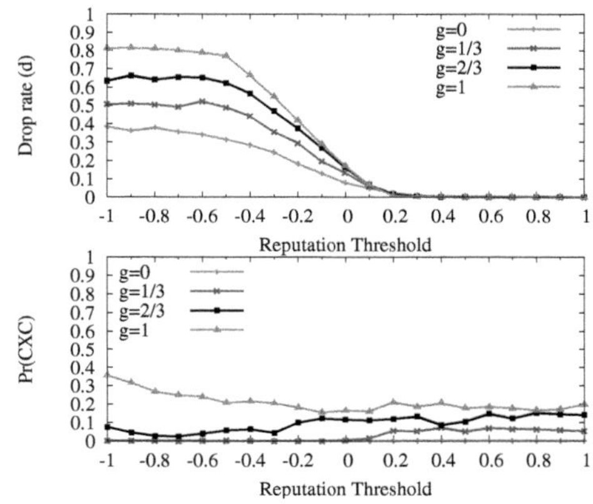

Figure 7: Evaluating drop rate and probability of constructing a compromised circuit for various reputation threshold. In this scenario compromised relays drop circuits only if its reputation is above the chosen threshold. We see that to retain positive reputation compromised relays cannot afford to drop too many circuits.

6.2 Real World Experiments

In this section we perform a series of live experiments on the Tor network to show the effectiveness of our reputation system. First of all, we show that clients from different geographic regions successfully filter compromised relays. Next, we determine what kind of benefit our reputation system provides in terms of reliability.

6.2.1 Filtering Compromised relays

We carried out our experiment by introducing our own relays into the Tor network, all of which acted as compromised relays. For this purpose we used 11 Emulab [1] machines, 10 of which were configured to act as Tor relays with a minimum bandwidth capacity of 20KBps. Note that all our relays belonged to the same /16 subnet, meaning that no user would (by default) choose two of our relays in the same circuit. Moreover, to prevent other users from using our relays as exit relays, we configured our relays with a fixed exit policy (allowing connection to only specific web sites). All these steps were taken to respect user privacy. To emulate real clients we used 10 PlanetLab [3] machines from 5 different continents and had them create circuits through the Tor network.

To implement selective DoS we take an approach similar to the one described by Bauer et al. [15]. Here, out of the 11 machines, we run Tor protocol (version *tor-0.2.2.35*) on 10 of them, and used the remaining machine as a server for gathering timing information about which relay is communicating with whom at what time. The sever performs timing analysis and informs the other 10 machines when to drop communication to carry out selective DoS. We implemented our reputation model in the client side in Python (we used the open source Python library of the Tor Controller [6]).

In our experiments we first query the Tor directory server to retrieve a list of all available Tor routers and then filter this list by considering only those routers which are flagged as *running*, *stable* and *valid*, because we want our routers to be alive and running during our experiments. We selected 39 Tor relays (3 guards, 18 exits and 18 middle relays) at random with probability proportional to their bandwidth and added our own 10 relays to this set to get a total of 49 relays (for the same reasons as described in Section 6.1.1). This choice results in about 20% of the relays being compromised.[8] To emulate user traffic, we retrieve a random web file of 300 KB in size. Each client investigates a total of $3 \times 23^2 = 1587$ circuits and builds its own reputation score for those relays.[9] Clients first filter outliers and then compute FN and FP errors.

Table 6 summarizes our findings. Real world results are quite similar to what we found in our simulation. However, some of the false positive errors are somewhat higher than what we found in our simulation. One plausible reason is that some of the relays were down during our experiment, which is understandable because Tor consensus is updated every 1 hour. Also, since not all the PlanetLab machines were of the same configuration, the total time required to complete all the probing varied from machine to machine. However, similar to our simulation results, we see that as the number of compromised guards increases, FN also increases. For $g \leq 2/3$ FN is almost zero. Another observation is that clients, though geographically distant, observe a similar ranking of Tor relays. Thus, Re^3 succeeds in capturing the selective dropping characteristics of our deployed Tor relays.

Table 6: Experimental results from the live Tor network (all values are in %)

Continent	Country (State)	g=0		g=1/3		g=2/3		g=1	
		FN	FP	FN	FP	FN	FP	FN	FP
North America	US(Illinois)	0	10.3	0	10.3	0	17.9	15.2	0
	US(California)	0	7.69	0	10.3	0	15.4	11.4	0
South America	Argentina	0	5.13	0	10.3	0	17.9	11.4	0
	Brazil	0	7.69	0	5.13	0	10.3	15.2	0
Europe	UK	0	7.69	0	7.69	0	12.8	15.2	0
	Russia	0	7.69	0	10.3	2.9	15.4	11.3	0
Asia	India	0	7.69	0	10.3	2.8	10.3	11.4	0
	Singapore	0	7.69	0	10.3	0	15.9	9.3	0
Australia	Australia	0	5.13	0	12.8	0	17.9	9.3	0
	NewZealand	0	17.9	0	17.9	0	20.5	15.2	0

6.2.2 *Reliability*

In addition to protecting Tor against maliciousness, our reputation model can also improve Tor's resilience to poorly performing relays. To motivate this, we first show that there is a high degree of variance in reliability across Tor relays. For this experiment we build Tor circuits using our own entry and exit relay pairs while using existing Tor relays as the middle relay of a Tor circuit. We then record statistics of circuit construction success rate for each Tor relay. We use the *nmap* command to scan the Tor-port (OR-port) of all the available Tor relays to cross-check whether they are actually online. The whole experiment was rerun every 30 minutes for a period of one full day. Figure 8 shows the difference between application level and network level reliability. We see that a certain fraction of the Tor relays drop circuits more often than others even though they are reachable. Figure 8 also shows the ratio of the total number of relays that failed to the total number of relays that succeed in building our customized circuit over different time intervals. Again we see a significant deviation in the application and network level reliability across the full day inspection and it is not the case that the deviation alters significantly across the time axis. We also highlight the distribution of these failures against the Tor relay's observed and advertised bandwidth. We computed the correlation between the advertised bandwidth and reliability. We found the correlation coefficient to be less than 10^{-8} in magnitude. So, we can say bandwidth is not an indicator of reliability in Tor network. We also verified that *past performance is an indication of future results*. For this we compute the "**Pearson Correlation**" between past observed failure probability and next observed outcome; we found the correlation co-efficient to be 0.72 which suggests that monitoring the reliability of relays is helpful for predicting their future performance.

From this, we can see that a client potentially benefits by keeping track of the reliability of the Tor relays he/she uses. To demonstrate this we run experiments on the live Tor network where a client creates circuits from a small set of Tor relays (3 guards, 23 middle relays and 23 exits). In one setting the client first generates a ranking of the Tor relays by probing each possible circuit once and then filters out potentially unreliable ones. The client then creates 100 circuits from the filtered list of relays. In the other setting the client just simply creates 100 circuits randomly from the full set of 49 non-filtered Tor relays. In both cases we record the percentage of circuits failing at different hops (we take the avg. of 10 runs). Table 7 shows the obtained results and we can see that Re^3 assists users to choose more reliable Tor relays for anonymous communications.

Table 7: Reliability result from the live Tor network

Measurements	Our Model			Conventional Tor		
	1st hop (%)	2nd hop (%)	3rd hop (%)	1st hop (%)	2nd hop (%)	3rd hop (%)
Mean	0.00	0.00	2.55	0.00	4.00	9.73
SD	0.00	0.00	2.21	0.00	3.01	8.01
Max	0.00	0.00	6.00	0.00	9.00	22.00
Min	0.00	0.00	0.00	0.00	0.00	0.00

7. DEPLOYMENT CONSIDERATIONS

In this section we discuss the following two ways of deploying Re^3 into the live Tor network.

- Localized: Individual clients run Re^3
- Centralized: Re^3 is run by directory authorities (DA servers).

We also study the convergence of Re^3 as this is important for any practical deployment.

7.1 Localized Approach

The easiest way to incorporate our reputation model is to have it run in the client side. Each client can accumulate his/her experience to compute the reputation of Tor relays. Such a local approach does not require cooperation from any other relays in the system. However, this approach requires some incubation time to mature. That being said, clients can speedup the bootstrapping process by randomly browsing a small number of nonsensitive web sites or replaying some nonsensitive browsing history. The client could probe circuits periodically if needed and can also share reputation score

[8] Alternatively, we could set the bandwidth of our relays such that they make up 20% of the total bandwidth

[9] Without considering the same relay at different position, because guards and exits can be middle relays, too.

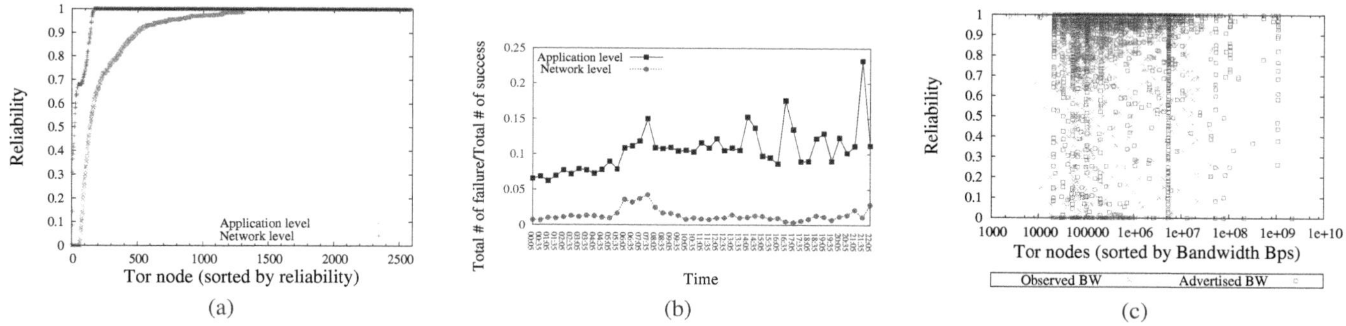

Figure 8: (a) Comparison of application and network level reliability of Tor relays. (b) Distribution of the ratio of total failure to success across different time intervals (c) Distribution of reliability against both observed and advertised bandwidth. We see that there is a significant difference between application level and network level availability.

with friends that they trust to speedup the convergence. Additionally, a client can initially concentrate on profiling higher bandwidth Tor relays before profiling other relays. For example, about 500 relays provide 80% of the available bandwidth in Tor [9].

7.2 Centralized Approach

In this approach the reputation model is run by the Tor directory authorities (DA servers). Tor authority servers already gather statistics of Tor relays (mainly observed bandwidth) to build a consensus database [5]. Each DA server can probe Tor circuits periodically and build its own reputation table. DAs can then include this information when they participate in the consensus protocol. The benefit of this approach is that it requires very few modifications to the existing protocol and the overhead of this approach is minimal. However, centralized probes need to be indistinguishable from real user traffic, otherwise malicious relays may alter their behavior during periods when they are probed. Randomizing both the entry relay of a probe and the time at which probes are made can make it harder for compromised relays to distinguish probes from actual user traffic.

7.3 Convergence of Re^3

For any system to be practically deployable it must converge quickly to its stable state. In this section we investigate how the number of interactions affect the accuracy of Re^3. For this purpose, we run our simulator where a client iteratively creates circuits following the default Tor path selection algorithm and then applies our filtering scheme. We then compute the probability of selecting a compromised circuit after every 10 interactions. We vary drop rate d $(0 \leq d \leq 1)$ and consider the maximum probability that an adversary can achieve. Results are averaged over 100 000 runs.

Figure 9 shows the probability of selecting compromised circuits after every 10 interactions. We can see that as the number of interactions increases this probability dies down. This is expected because the more a client interacts with relays the more he/she becomes confident about those relays' reliability. However, we see that this probability quickly descends to a stable value after $\approx$200 interactions. We also look at the distribution of the number of unique relays against different number of interactions. Figure 10 shows that after 1000 interactions a client can roughly profile around 600 Tor relays (or 60% of Tor's bandwidth). Alternatively, clients can profile higher bandwidth relays first. We conclude that a user does not need to accumulate too much experience to obtain a consistent view of the reliability of the Tor relays. Therfore, it is feasible for individual clients to perform their own profiling, rather than relying on an external entity.

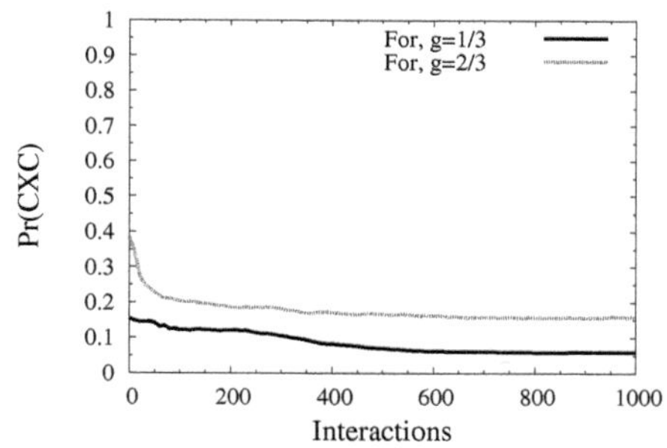

Figure 9: Probability of constructing compromised circuits after various number of interactions. This probability quickly converges to a stable value after only 200 interactions.

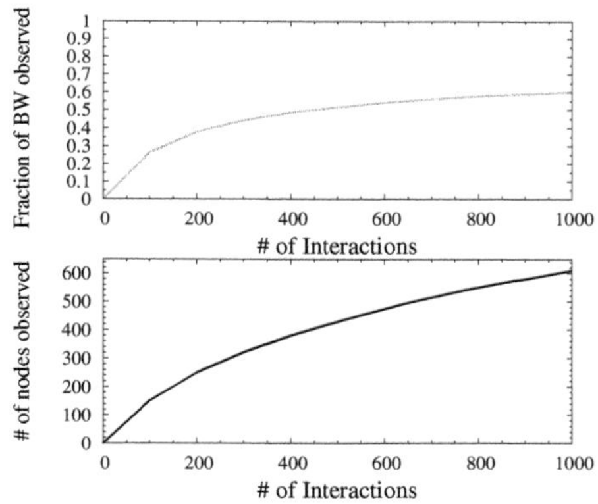

Figure 10: Average fraction of Tor bandwidth and Tor relays observed for different number of interactions.

8. RELATED WORK

Securing anonymity systems against active attacks is relatively a new research topic. Borisov et al. [16] first showed that a selective DoS attack can have devastating consequences for both high and low-latency anonymity systems.

More recently, Danner et al. [19] proposed a detection algorithm for selective DoS attack in Tor. Their algorithm probes each individual Tor relay in the network and requires $O(n)$ probes to detect all compromised relays for a network comprising of n participants. However, to handle transient network failures they proposed repeating each probe r number of times, so their approach requires $O(nr)$ probes. So, at best their approach seems suitable for a centralized deployment. However, their algorithm assumes that compromised relays exhibit fixed characteristic of always dropping non-compromised circuits. They do not consider complex attack strategies where compromised relays may perform random dropping. Such dynamic malicious behavior could potentially increase the number of probes required to successfully identify compromised relays.

Mike Perry proposed a client-side accounting mechanism that tracks the circuit failure rate for each of the client's guards [7]. The goal is to avoid malicious guard relays that deliberately fail circuits extending to non-colluding exit relays. However, profiling only guards is not enough because it is less likely that an attacker will launch selective DoS at guard position, only to sacrifice the cost of obtaining a guard status (guards fulfill strong commitments like minimum bandwidth and minimum uptime). Rather deploying a moderate number of cheap middle-only relays can boost the effect of selective DoS attack [14].

Researchers have also leveraged incentive schemes [12, 40] to encourage good behavior from Tor relays. All incentive schemes basically encourage participants to be cooperative by providing the cooperating participants with something that they care about; however, incentive schemes do not enforce malicious participants to behave properly.

There are reputation based routing protocols for wireless adhoc networks [17, 31, 34] that try to identify selfish/malicious routers with the objective of avoiding them during forward path setup. While these protocols have similar goal as ours there are different challenges in directly using them for anonymity systems. For example, in all of these protocols routers maintain reputation information about their neighbors which they share with other routers in the network. This information sharing could potentially introduce new attack vectors where an adversary could figure out which relays certain users are using. Moreover, to the best of our knowledge none of these protocols handle strategic malicious behavior.

There are many papers on reputation systems for P2P networks [28,43,44]. TrustGuard [38] proposes a reputation framework which is capable of handling strategic malicious behavior. But TrustGuard is vulnerable to whitewashing attack, we introduce a confidence metric to hinder whitewashing attack. Moreover, most models focus on building distributed reputation systems, rather than worrying about privacy and anonymity as described br Resnick et al. [36]. Dingledine et al. [20] described a reputation system for MIX-net environment [18]. But their approach relies on trusted witnesses which are hard to find in Tor network. Later on Dingledine et al. [23] restructured their initially proposed reputation system [20] to avoid trusted witnesses and proofs in favor of self-rating groups of remailers. However, their approach does not reduce or prevent the creeping death attack. They only propose to randomize the choice of node selection hoping that compromised nodes occupying the top positions in the reputation spectrum are not selected. In our case we propose a filtering scheme based on reputation score to discard such compromised relays, where the reputation metric itself can handle strategic oscialltions.

9. LIMITATIONS

Our work has a few limitations. First, in the absence of attacks, a small fraction of honest relays are classified as outliers due to random network failures. For anonymity systems, it is much more critical to blacklist malicious relays than to ensure that all honest relays are included. Moreover, these discarded honest relays should reflect either low performing or highly congested relays in absence of attack. Thus, discarding them might actually help in shuffling the overall network load. Second, for the local deployment approach, our model does not defend against the scenario where all of a user's guard relays are malicious. We note that for 20% of malicious relays, the probability of all three of a user's guard relays being malicious is less than 1%. Finally, new users benefit from our reputation model only after a certain amount of usage.

10. CONCLUSION

Anonymity systems are vulnerable to active attacks like selective denial-of-service. Such attacks, however, can be detected by profiling relay behavior. We proposed a generic reputation model that profiles relays based on their historical behavior. Our model takes adaptive malicious behavior into consideration and penalizes any participant exhibiting such behavior. We theoretically analyze our system under different attack scenarios, including probabilistic variants of selective DoS, targeted framing attack and the creeping-death attack. Our simulation and experimental results on the live Tor network suggest that our reputation model can effectively filter compromised relays mounting active attacks. We also show that our reputation model provides benefits even outside the context of active attacks; Tor clients using our model experienced significant improvement in the reliability of circuit construction.

Our reputation model has broad applicability, and can be used in domains such as P2P and recommendation systems, where users would benefit from profiling participants with dynamic behavior.

Acknowledgement

We would like to thank all the anonymous reviewers who have reviewed our work and have provided us with valuable feedback. This paper reports on work that was supported in part by NSF CNS 0953655 as well as an International Fulbright S&T Fellowship.

11. REFERENCES

[1] Emulab. https://www.emulab.net.
[2] Known bad relays in Tor. https://trac.torproject.org/projects/tor/wiki/doc/badRelays.
[3] PlanetLab. http://www.planet-lab.org/.
[4] Tor Compass. https://compass.torproject.org/.
[5] Tor Consensus. https://metrics.torproject.org/consensus-health.html.
[6] Tor controller. https://svn.torproject.org/svn/blossom/trunk/TorCtl.py.
[7] Tor Proposal 209. https://gitweb.torproject.org/user/mikeperry/torspec.git/blob/path-bias-tuning:/proposals/209-path-bias-tuning.txt.
[8] TorFlow Project. https://gitweb.torproject.org/torflow.git.
[9] TorStatus. http://torstatus.blutmagie.de/index.php.
[10] Trotsky IP addresses. https://trac.torproject.org/projects/tor/wiki/doc/badRelays/trotskyIps.
[11] Tor directory authorities compromised., 2010. https://blog.torproject.org/blog/tor-project-infrastructure-updates.
[12] E. Androulaki, M. Raykova, S. Srivatsan, A. Stavrou, and S. Bellovin. PAR: Payment for Anonymous Routing. In *Proceedings of the 8th Symposium on Privacy Enhancing Technologies*, PETS'08, pages 219–236. Springer Berlin Heidelberg, 2008.
[13] R. Aringhieri, E. Damiani, S. D. C. Di Vimercati, S. Paraboschi, and P. Samarati. Fuzzy Techniques for Trust and Reputation Management in Anonymous Peer-to-peer Systems. *J. Am. Soc. Inf. Sci. Technol.*, 57(4):528–537, 2006.
[14] K. Bauer, J. Juen, N. Borisov, D. Grunwald, D. Sicker, and D. Mccoy. On the Optimal Path Length for Tor, 2010. http://petsymposium.org/2010/papers/hotpets10-Bauer.pdf.
[15] K. Bauer, D. McCoy, D. Grunwald, T. Kohno, and D. Sicker. Low-resource Routing Attacks Against Tor. In *Proceedings of the 6th ACM Workshop on Privacy in the Electronic Society*, WPES '07, pages 11–20. ACM, 2007.

[16] N. Borisov, G. Danezis, P. Mittal, and P. Tabriz. Denial of Service or Denial of Security? In *Proceedings of the 14th ACM Conference on Computer and Communications Security*, CCS '07, pages 92–102. ACM, 2007.

[17] S. Buchegger and J. Y. Le Boudec. A Robust Reputation System for P2P and Mobile Ad-hoc Networks. In *Proceedings of the 2nd Workshop on the Economics of Peer-to-Peer Systems (P2PEcon)*, 2004.

[18] D. L. Chaum. Untraceable online mail, return addresses, and digital pseudonyms. *Commun. ACM*, 24(2):84–90, 1981.

[19] N. Danner, D. Krizanc, and M. Liberatore. Detecting Denial of Service Attacks in Tor. In *Proceedings of the 13th International Conference on Financial Cryptography and Data Security*, FC '09, pages 273–284. Springer Berlin Heidelberg, 2009.

[20] R. Dingledine, M. Freedman, D. Hopwood, and D. Molnar. A Reputation System to Increase MIX-Net Reliability. In *Proceedings of the 4th International Workshop on Information Hiding*, pages 126–141. Springer Berlin Heidelberg, 2001.

[21] R. Dingledine and N. Mathewson. Tor path specification. https://gitweb.torproject.org/torspec.git?a=blob_plain;hb=HEAD;f=path-spec.txt.

[22] R. Dingledine, N. Mathewson, and P. Syverson. Tor: The Second-generation Onion Router. In *Proceedings of the 13th USENIX Security Symposium*, SSYM'04. USENIX Association, 2004.

[23] R. Dingledine and P. Syverson. Reliable MIX Cascade Networks Through Reputation. In *Proceedings of the 6th International Conference on Financial Cryptography*, FC'03, pages 253–268. Springer-Verlag, 2003.

[24] P. Eckersley, E. Galperin, and K. Rodriguez. Dutch government proposes cyberattacks against... everyone., 2012. https://www.eff.org/deeplinks/2012/10/dutch-government-proposes-cyberattacks-against-everyone.

[25] M. Edman and P. Syverson. AS-awareness in Tor Path Selection. In *Proceedings of the 16th ACM Conference on Computer and Communications Security*, CCS '09, pages 380–389. ACM, 2009.

[26] A. C. Estes. NSA attacks Tor. http://gizmodo.com/the-nsas-been-trying-to-hack-into-tors-anonymous-inte-1441153819.

[27] N. Feamster and R. Dingledine. Location diversity in anonymity networks. In *Proceedings of the 2004 ACM Workshop on Privacy in the Electronic Society*, WPES '04, pages 66–76, New York, NY, USA, 2004. ACM.

[28] S. D. Kamvar, M. T. Schlosser, and H. Garcia-Molina. The Eigentrust Algorithm for Reputation Management in P2P Networks. In *Proceedings of the 12th International Conference on World Wide Web*, WWW '03, pages 640–651. ACM, 2003.

[29] H. Kwakernaak. *Linear Optimal Control Systems*. John Wiley & Sons, Inc., New York, NY, USA, 1972.

[30] B. Levine, M. Reiter, C. Wang, and M. Wright. Timing Attacks in Low-Latency Mix Systems. In *Proceedings of the 8th International Conference on Financial Cryptography*, pages 251–265. Springer Berlin Heidelberg, 2004.

[31] P. Michiardi and R. Molva. Core: A Collaborative Reputation Mechanism to Enforce Node Cooperation in Mobile Ad Hoc Networks. In *Proceedings of the 6th IFIP TC6/TC11 Joint Working Conference on Communications and Multimedia Security*, pages 107–121. Springer US, 2002.

[32] L. Mui, M. Mohtashemi, and A. Halberstadt. A computational model of trust and reputation for e-businesses. In *Proceedings of the 35th Annual Hawaii International Conference on System Sciences*, HICSS '02, Washington, DC, USA, 2002. IEEE Computer Society.

[33] S. J. Murdoch and P. Zieliński. Sampled Traffic Analysis by Internet-exchange-level Adversaries. In *Proceedings of the 7th Symposium on Privacy Enhancing Technologies*, PETS'07, pages 167–183. Springer-Verlag, 2007.

[34] F. Oliviero and S. Romano. A Reputation-Based Metric for Secure Routing in Wireless Mesh Networks. In *Proceedings of the 27th IEEE Global Telecommunications Conference*, IEEE GLOBECOM '08, pages 1–5, 2008.

[35] M. Reed, P. Syverson, and D. Goldschlag. Anonymous connections and onion routing. *IEEE Journal on Selected Areas in Communications*, 16(4):482–494, May 1998.

[36] P. Resnick, K. Kuwabara, R. Zeckhauser, and E. Friedman. Reputation systems. *Commun. ACM*, 43(12):45–48, 2000.

[37] V. Shmatikov and M.-H. Wang. Timing Analysis in Low-Latency Mix Networks: Attacks and Defenses. In *Proceedings of the 11th European Symposium On Research In Computer Security*, ESORICS'06, pages 18–33. Springer Berlin Heidelberg, 2006.

[38] M. Srivatsa, L. Xiong, and L. Liu. TrustGuard: Countering Vulnerabilities in Reputation Management for Decentralized Overlay Networks. In *Proceedings of the 14th International Conference on World Wide Web*, WWW '05, pages 422–431. ACM, 2005.

[39] P. Syverson, G. Tsudik, M. Reed, and C. Landwehr. Towards an Analysis of Onion Routing Security. In *Proceedings of International Workshop on Designing Privacy Enhancing Technologies: Design Issues in Anonymity and Unobservability*, pages 96–114. Springer Berlin Heidelberg, 2001.

[40] Tsuen-Wan, R. Dingledine, and D. Wallach. Building Incentives into Tor. In *Proceedings of the 14th International Conference on Financial Cryptography and Data Security*, FC'10, pages 238–256. Springer Berlin Heidelberg, 2010.

[41] M. Wright, M. Adler, B. Levine, and C. Shields. Defending anonymous communications against passive logging attacks. In *Proceedings of the 2003 IEEE Symposium on Security and Privacy*, SP '03, pages 28–41, 2003.

[42] M. K. Wright, M. Adler, B. N. Levine, and C. Shields. An Analysis of the Degradation of Anonymous Protocols. In *Proceedings of the 9th Network and Distributed System Security Symposium*, NDSS '02, 2002.

[43] L. Xiong and L. Liu. PeerTrust: supporting reputation-based trust for peer-to-peer online communities. *IEEE Transactions on Knowledge and Data Engineering*, 16(7):843–857, 2004.

[44] R. Zhou and K. Hwang. PowerTrust: A Robust and Scalable Reputation System for Trusted Peer-to-Peer Computing. *IEEE Transactions on Parallel and Distributed Systems*, 18(4):460–473, April 2007.

[45] Y. Zhu, X. Fu, B. Graham, R. Bettati, and W. Zhao. On Flow Correlation Attacks and Countermeasures in Mix Networks. In *Proceedings of the 4th International Workshop on Privacy Enhancing Technologies*, PET'04, pages 207–225. Springer Berlin Heidelberg, 2005.

APPENDIX

A. STABILITY ANALYSIS

From control theory we know that for a discrete-time linear system to be stable all of the poles of its *transfer function* must lie inside the unit circle [29]. To determine this we first need to take the *Z-transform* of the transfer function and then determine its poles. We first rewrite equation (1) as the following first order discrete-time linear system.

$$y(n) = \alpha x(n) + (1 - \alpha)y(n - 1) \tag{9}$$

where $y(n)$ and $x(n)$ denotes the n-th output and input of the system respectively (i.e., $y(n)$ refers to newly generated reputation value R_n of a relay while $x(n)$ refers to the reference value R_c). Taking the *Z-transform* of equation (9) yields:

$$Y(z) = \alpha X(z) + (1 - \alpha)z^{-1}Y(z) \tag{10}$$

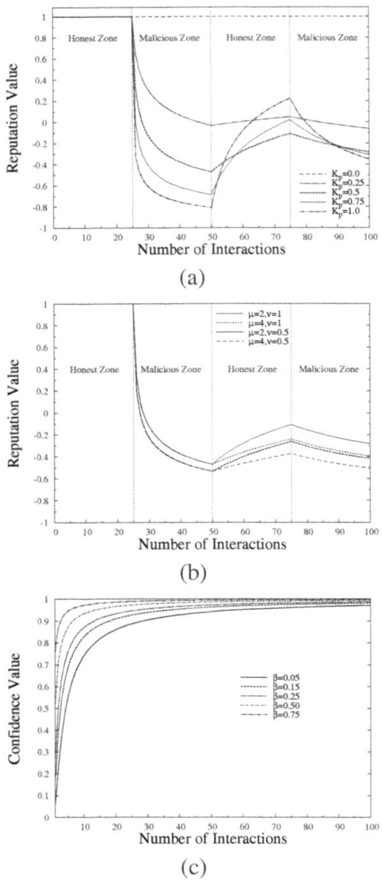

Figure 11: Sensitivity analysis of (a) controller gain K_p (b) reward μ and punishment ν factor (c) confidence factor β.

From equation (10) we can compute the transfer function as:

$$H(z) = \frac{Y(z)}{X(z)} = \frac{\alpha z}{z - (1 - \alpha)} \tag{11}$$

So the transfer function $H(z)$ has a pole at $z = 1 - \alpha$. From equation (3) we know that $0 < \alpha < 1$, so the pole will always lies inside the unit circle. Thus, our closed-loop reputation system guarantees stability.

B. TUNING MODEL PARAMETERS

In this section we look at how the parameters related to Re^3 affect the reputation score of compromised relays. As shown in Table 5, Re^3 has a total of four parameters. We will study each of their impact on reputation score. In the following study, we mainly want to see how our model reacts to dynamic behavioral change. For this purpose we assume that a compromised relay, with all the other relays being honest, participates in a total 100 circuits oscillating between honest and malicious nature every 25 interactions.

B.1 Proportional constant (K_p)

The proportional constant, K_p, determines to what degree we want to react to the deviation between the reference value (R_c) and current system output (R_{n-1}). This should not be set either too high (near 1) or too low (near 0). If it is set too high it will oscillate too much and if it is set too low then it will discount most of the deviation and result in slow convergence. Figure 11(a) highlights what we have just discussed. As we can see from the figure for $K_p = 1$ it oscillates heavily and for $K_p = 0$, it totally discards the difference between the reference value and system output. We, therefore, conservatively set K_p to 0.5, so that the model becomes neither too sensitive nor too insensitive to sudden deviation.

B.2 Reward (μ) and Punishment (ν) Factor

We now investigate how our reputation model responds to a series of failures and successes. We want the degree of punishment to be greater than that of reward. So whenever the model receives a negative feedback (in our case a rating of -1) we want our EWMA function (equation (3)) to give higher weight to the current feedback (i.e., consider a larger value of α). As α in dependent of δ (see equation (5)), we need to increase δ more for failure than success. So under our setting we require $\mu > 1$ and $\nu \leq 1$. Figure 11(b) highlights how reputation score reacts to different combinations of (μ, ν). As long as $\mu > 1$ and $\nu \leq 1$ our model can effectively discourage selective DoS.

B.3 Confidence Factor (β)

Now, we look at our confidence factor β. The confidence factor determines how confident a user is about the reputation score of a particular relay. As the number of experience with a particular relay increases, a user becomes more confident about his/her computed reputation score. β controls how quickly we become confident about a reputation score. Figure 11(c) highlights how confidence factor increases as the number of interaction increases. It should be mentioned that any monotonically increasing function of the number of interactions can be used as a confidence metric.

C. TUNING CUTOFFS FOR OUTLIERS

In filtering outliers we previously chose a deviation interval of $\sqrt{3}$ times the standard deviation from the average (see Section 6). Here, we investigate what kind of impact other deviation intervals would have on the performance of Re^3. A tradeoff exists between the value of k and false errors — FN and FP. As we increase k more relays become acceptable, so FP goes down but FN rises. We tested for $k = 1.3, 2.0$. Figure 12 illustrates the FN and FP errors for different values of k. From the figure we see that as we increase the allowed deviation from average, more and more relays become acceptable and as a result FP decreases while FN increases.

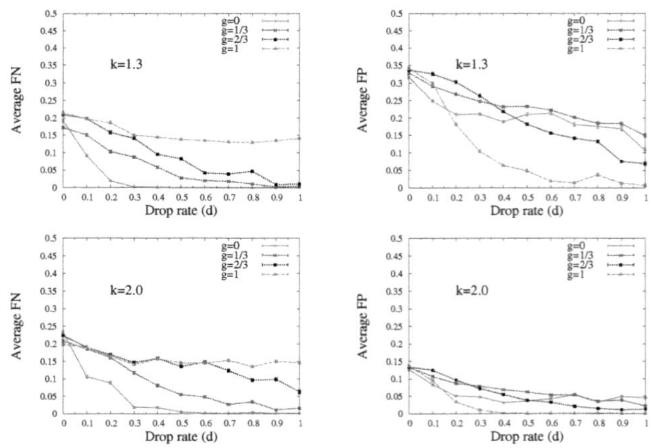

Figure 12: False Negative (FN) and False positive (FP) errors for different values of k. As k increases FN tends to rise and FP tends to fall.

Design and Evaluation of Persea, a Sybil-Resistant DHT

Mahdi Nasrullah Al-Ameen
The University of Texas at Arlington
Arlington, TX, USA
mahdi.al-ameen@mavs.uta.edu

Matthew Wright
The University of Texas at Arlington
Arlington, TX, USA
mwright@cse.uta.edu

ABSTRACT

P2P systems are inherently vulnerable to Sybil attacks, in which an attacker creates a large number of identities and uses them to control a substantial fraction of the system. We propose Persea, a novel P2P system that derives its Sybil resistance by assigning IDs through a bootstrap tree, the graph of how nodes have joined the system through invitations. Unlike prior Sybil-resistant P2P systems based on social networks, Persea does not rely on two key assumptions: (1) that the social network is fast mixing and (2) that there is a small ratio of attack edges to honest nodes. Both assumptions have been shown to be unreliable in real social networks. A node joins Persea when it gets an invitation from an existing node in the system. The inviting node assigns a node ID to the joining node and gives it a chunk of node IDs for further distribution. For each chunk of ID space, the attacker needs to socially engineer a connection to another node already in the system. The hierarchical distribution of node IDs confines a large attacker botnet to a considerably smaller region of the ID space than in a normal P2P system. We then build upon this hierarchical ID space to make a distributed hash table (DHT) based on the Kad network. The Persea DHT uses a replication mechanism in which each (key, value) pair is stored in nodes that are evenly spaced over the network. Thus, even if a given region is occupied by attackers, the desired (key, value) pair can be retrieved from other regions. We evaluate Persea in analysis and in simulations with social network datasets and show that it provides better lookup success rates than prior work with modest overheads.

Categories and Subject Descriptors

C.2.4 [**Communication Networks**]: Distributed Systems-Distributed applications

Keywords

Sybil attack; security; social DHT

1. INTRODUCTION

Peer-to-peer (P2P) systems are highly susceptible to Sybil attacks, in which an attacker creates a large number of pseudonymous entities and uses them to gain a disproportionately large influence over the system [6, 7, 9, 13]. A malicious node may present multiple identities to a P2P system that appear and function as distinct nodes. By becoming part of the P2P system, the Sybil attackers can then collude to launch further attacks to subvert the system's operation, such as taking over resources and disrupting connectivity. Researchers have documented this vulnerability in real-world systems, including the Maze P2P file-sharing system [14, 34] and the Vanish data storage system [33].

Many P2P systems employ a distributed hash table (DHT), which provides a lookup service similar to a hash table: (key, value) pairs are stored in a DHT, and any participating node can efficiently retrieve the value associated with a given key. Well-known DHT-based systems, or simply DHTs, include Chord [27], CAN [22], Pastry [23], and Kademlia [17]. Kademlia was the basis for both the Kad network and Vuze, DHTs used in the popular BitTorrent file-sharing P2P system with millions of users each.

Recent research has focused on leveraging information from social networks to make the system robust against Sybil attackers, resulting in a number of decentralized *community-based* schemes [11, 12, 19, 28, 31, 36, 37]. The key to these approaches is the idea that honest and malicious nodes can be effectively partitioned into two subgraphs in the social network. The link between an honest node and a malicious peer is called an *attack edge*, which represents an act of social engineering to convince the honest node to add the link.

These mechanisms are based on two key assumptions:

- Online social networks are *fast mixing*, meaning that a random walk in the honest part of the network approaches the uniform distribution in a small number of steps.
- The number of attack edges are rather limited in an online social network, as benign users are unlikely to accept friend requests from strangers.

Recent studies [3, 20, 30, 35], however, show that the above assumptions do not hold in real-world social networks. Thus, the effectiveness of these schemes are left as an open question. In particular, Mohaisen et. al. [20] show that in social graphs where edges correspond to strong real-world trust (e.g., Epinions, Physics co-authorship, DBLP, etc.), the mixing-time is not as fast as the community-based schemes assume. Thus, the schemes do not perform well on "trusted" social graphs. Further, Viswanath et al. have shown that a number of Sybil defenses are ineffective for slower-mixing, highly *modular* social networks [30].

At the same time, recent work shows that the probability with which fake identities are accepted as friends is much higher than anticipated [25], with studies reporting that users accept $40 - 80\%$ of friendship requests from strangers [3, 5]. This implies that that number of attack edges may not be small, even as a fraction of

ASIA CCS'14, June 4–6, 2014, Kyoto, Japan.
Copyright 2014 ACM 978-1-4503-2800-5/14/06 ...$15.00.
http://dx.doi.org/10.1145/2590296.2590326.

the number of honest nodes. As the assumption of few attack edges breaks down, prior schemes do not work well. The Whānau scheme, for example, requires 10-100 times the overhead to get successful lookups when there is one attack edge per honest node.

Contributions. These findings about online social networks mean that it remains an open research problem to design an effective Sybil defense that does not rely on the assumptions of a fast-mixing social network and a small number of attack edges. In this paper, we propose a Persea, a new Sybil-resistant DHT that addresses these problems.

In Persea, existing nodes invite new peers to join the system. When a node joins the DHT it also creates a link with the inviting node. This creates a *bootstrap tree*, linking nodes together through invitation relationships. We then leverage the social relationships among honest nodes for building a robust DHT. We develop a mechanism to distribute hierarchical node IDs based on the bootstrap tree. In this mechanism, when a node joins the system after getting an invitation, the inviting node assigns a node ID to the joining node and gives it a chunk of node IDs for further distribution.[1] ID and chunk assignment are certified in a chain from the root of the bootstrap tree. The use of a bootstrap tree relies heavily on the root nodes in the early stages of system deployment, but by careful design of how IDs are certified, the reliance on these nodes can be minimized. Based on this ID distribution method, we then design a DHT routing table and lookup protocol based on the Kademlia design [17], with modest modifications to enhance robustness.

The Persea approach offers a number of important advantages over existing schemes:

- Persea does not depend on assuming that there are few attack edges compared to the benign nodes. Let g denote the number of attack edges and n be the honest nodes. Our simulation results show that even for $g/n = 1.0$—i.e. one attack edge for every honest node—95.6% of lookups still succeed.
- Although Persea may work better for fast-mixing social networks, our system is also dependable for slow-mixing social networks. For the slowest-mixing social network we evaluated on and $g/n = 0.5$, Persea lookups succeed 96.2% of the time.
- The hierarchical distribution of node IDs limits the attackers to isolated regions in the ID space. Even for $g/n = 1.0$, only 0.7% of the total ID space is occupied by attackers.
- Building a bootstrap tree is more realistic than assuming that the clients have access to authenticated lists of social network connections or activity levels from a system like Facebook; such lists may also bear little resemblence to social connections inside the P2P system.

Additionally, Persea has several other important features:

- Although we test Persea with a DHT routing table design similar to Kademlia [17], which is widely used, it can be adapted to other DHTs.
- IDs are certified, making attacks based on ID forging impossible outside of attacker-controlled ID ranges.
- Varying the number of attackers per attack edge does not significantly affect the lookup success rate in Persea.
- Sybil-resilient system design is inherently probabilistic [28], and thus our system provides resilience against further attacks, including *denial of service*, *node ID hijacking*, and *node insertion*, that may be launched by the existing Sybil nodes in the system.

[1] The name Persea comes from a tree in ancient Egyptian mythology (also called the ished tree) upon whose leaves the Gods wrote the names of the pharaohs (see `http://www.touregypt.net/featurestories/treegoddess.htm`).

2. RELATED WORK

Due to the power and generality of the Sybil attack, a large number of defenses have been proposed [1, 13]. In this section, we examine the use of social networks for Sybil defense.

Random walks over social networks. A number of works have proposed Sybil detection techniques or Sybil resistance based on random walks over a social network [8, 11, 12, 19, 28, 31, 36, 37]. The basic idea is that we can divide the social network into a Sybil region and an honest region connected via a small number of attack edges (a *small cut*). Random walks starting from the honest region have a low probability of ending in the Sybil region. This can be leveraged in a variety of ways, leading to detection mechanisms [8, 30, 31, 36, 37], admission control mechanisms [28], and Sybil-resistant P2P designs [11, 12, 19].

These mechanisms require the absence of small cuts within the honest region in the underlying social network. Equivalently, the honest region should be fast-mixing. Mohaisen et al., however, show that the mixing time of many real social networks is slower than the mixing times assumed by these works [20]. Additionally, many real-world social networks fail to satisfy the other requirements of the systems, either because a significant fraction of nodes are sparsely connected or the users are organized in small tightly-knit communities, which are sparsely interconnected [29]. Finally, even perfect community-based defenses would fail against existing Sybil attacks due to the lack of a Sybil community structure [1,35].

DHTs Built on Social Networks. Three key related works are the Sybil-resistant DHT, Whānau, and X-Vine, and we compare these with Persea in Table 1.

Danezis et al. propose a Sybil-resistant DHT routing protocol [7] that makes use of latent social information that is present in the bootstrap graph of the network. While they pioneered the bootstrap graph model that inspires our work, we note two major shortcomings of their approach. First, the DHT layer is built on top of the bootstrap graph, creating a second overlay layer. This means that one hop in the DHT layer corresponds to a number of hops in the bootstrap graph, each of which is itself an Internet connection. This adds substantial delay and overhead beyond the DHT. Second, the scheme provides diversity in the bootstrap graph at the expense of following the DHT lookup graph. This further extends the lookup delay and overhead. When there is one attack edge per honest node, a lookup in a network of just 100 honest nodes requires over 50 requests to succeed.

Lesniewski-Laas proposed Whānau [11, 12], in which a node constructs its routing table through independent random walks and recording the final node in each walk as the finger in its routing table. Whānau requires significant routing table state on the order of $O(\sqrt{m}\log m)$, where m is the number of objects stored in the DHT. Mittal et al. point out that the network overhead for maintaining this state can be substantial (e.g. 800 KBps per node) [19]. Further, Whānau overheads increase further if large numbers of attack edges grows, such that for $g/n = 1.0$, either routing table sizes grow by 10-100 times or lookup redundancy must grow to 50 or more compared to the regular protocol [12].

X-Vine [19] is a DHT built by communicating only over social network edges. Honest peers rate-limit the number of paths that are allowed to be built over their adjacent edges, which helps to limit the number of Sybil nodes that can join the system. X-Vine, however, relies on the fast-mixing assumption and was only evaluated with a small number of attack edges (one for every ten honest nodes). Rate-limiting only works when there are few attack edges,

Table 1: Comparison of Sybil-resistant DHTs. Grey squares indicate limitations of the system. [($\star$): varies from less than 20 to over 50 depending on the network and routing table sizes, ($\dagger$): based on limited results [7]]

	Whānau	X-Vine	Sybil-resistant	**Persea**
Reliance on fast mixing	Yes	Yes	No	**No**
Requires that users provide a full social network	Yes	Yes	No	**No**
Lookups succeed at $g/n = 1.0$	Yes	Not tested	Yes	**Yes**
Total messages for a lookup at $g/n = 1.0$	$O(1)\star$	Unknown	$\sim 0.53 \times n\dagger$	$\mathbf{O(\log(n))}$
Total messages for a lookup at $g/n = 0.1$	$O(1)$	$O(\log(n))$	$\sim 0.44 \times n\dagger$	$\mathbf{O(\log(n))}$
Routing table size	$\Omega(\sqrt{n})$	$O(\log(n))$	$O(\log(n))$	$\mathbf{O(\log(n))}$

as an attacker with one attack edge per honest node should have the same rate of paths as the honest nodes in the system. Thus, very high levels of redundancy may be required for successful lookups when the number of attack edges is high.

We note that both Whānau and X-Vine use public keys to provide important security properties.

3. GOALS AND ASSUMPTIONS

In this section, we describe our system design goals and our system and attacker models.

3.1 Design Goals

In designing Persea, we have the following *Design Goals*:

1. Sybil-resistent lookups. The system should maintain high success rates for lookups in the presence of Sybil attackers seeking to undermine the system's operations, even if the number of attack edges grows to high levels (e.g. $g/n = 1.0$). Prior work does not handle large numbers of attack edges.

2. Works on a range of social networks. The system should work well for any reasonable structure in the underlying social network, even if the social network is not fast mixing. Most existing systems rely on the fast-mixing property.

3. Builds its own social network. The system should build its own social network to defeat Sybil attacks and not rely on users or online social networks (OSNs).

4. Moderate overhead. System overheads, such as routing table size, the number of overlay hops to perform a lookup, and the number of redundant lookups, should be kept to reasonable levels.

Regarding *Design Goal #3*, we find that most existing Sybil defenses require a social network without specifying where the network information comes from. One possible source would be from user input, but it is unclear how to motivate users to provide more than a minimal amount of information. Note that the fast-mixing property needed by many systems is particularly hard to obtain from a limited subset of edges. Another possible source would be to get the data from an OSN, but this has many issues. First, a few users may not even have accounts on the selected OSN, while others may not want to share their OSN network with the P2P system for privacy reasons. Also, relationships between users in the P2P system may be vastly different than those in the OSN, as even a popular P2P system would likely have only a fraction of all OSN members. Finally, an OSN like Facebook may attempt to block the P2P system from mining its network information, which is generally protected due to its value for advertising. This is especially true for mining enough information to formulate *interaction graphs* that only include edges between active communication partners and are thus more reliable than friendship graphs for use in Sybil defense [3,4,10,32].

3.2 System Model

The key assumptions about our system involve how we model users and social links. Participating in Persea requires an invitation from an existing user, and new users can request invitations from an existing user if they have her out-of-band contact information, such as an email address. The P2P client UI can integrate a request in the system with a code sent to the email address for verification. We assume that honest users generally accept invitation requests from people they know in real life. Thus, the links created from the set of accepted invitations form a subgraph of the social network known as a *bootstrap graph*. The structure of this network may vary and it is beyond the scope of this paper to identify requirements for either the bootstrap graph or the underlying social network. We instead evaluate our system with a variety of social networks with different properties to show that Persea is effective for a broad range of networks.

The bootstrap graph starts with a small set of *bootstrap nodes*. We make the following assumptions about the early stages of building the system: (1) bootstrap nodes are honest and (2) bootstrap nodes trust each other. The creation of a bootstrap graph starting from a trusted set of nodes allows us to obviate the use of OSN data and thus achieve *Design Goal #3*. The assumptions are reasonable, since the bootstrap nodes together take the initiative to start building the system. As the system passes the initial stage of growth and reaches a modest population size, we can gradually relax these requirements. In particular, the bootstrap nodes no longer need to be honest or trust each other for the system to work well.

As with the prior works on leveraging social networks for Sybil-resistent DHTs [12,19] (see §2), Persea uses public keys to certify IDs. Also like X-Vine [19], we suggest to ensure the integrity of content or services by using self-certifying identifiers on returned lookup results [2,18].

3.3 Attacker Model

We assume that the attacker is a single entity, or a small and highly coordinated group, with access to substantial computational and network resources. For example, the attacker can control a botnet. The attacker's goal is to disrupt the operations of the P2P network, and the lookup operation in particular, as lookups are the mechanism for distribution of information and resources in a DHT. To do this, the attacker seeks to add malicious nodes to the system and then have them disrupt the system's activities.

Adding malicious nodes. The attacker can first attempt to find users of the P2P system and socially engineer them into giving up an invitation. Such an invitation is called an *attack edge* in the social network. We note that targeting specific users may be desirable when attacking Persea, but this is difficult without external information about exactly who the key users are and how to contact

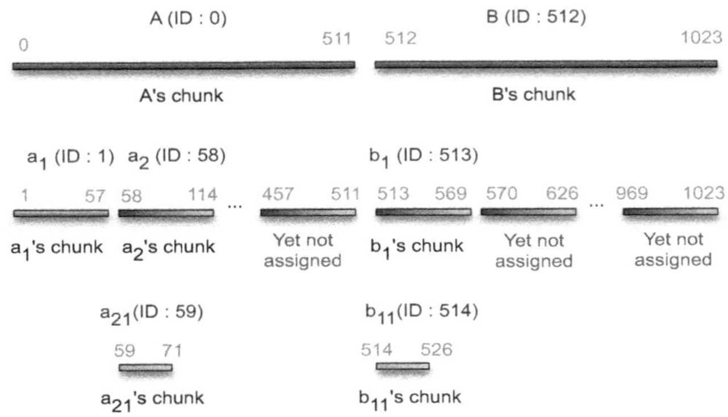

Figure 1: Hierarchical Distribution of Node IDs

them. This information is not meant to be publicly available. Instead, the attacker gathers invitations from anyone using the system who he can identify and trick. We model this as getting invitations via uniform selection from the set of honest users. We have not evaluated Persea for the case that targeted attacks are feasible.

In our evaluations, we limit the number of attack edges that an attacker can get via social engineering to a ratio of at most one per honest node on average. We note that prior schemes face very high overheads at such ratios, which are realistic given studies showing that OSN users accept fake and duplicate accounts at a rate of $40-80\%$ [3,4]. Unlike most OSNs, we attempt to limit attack edges via three methods: (i) Invitation requests should require that a code be sent through an out-of-band channel; (ii) When using such a code to issue an invitation, the client UI can warn users to not invite strangers; and (iii) Each user has a limited number of invitations (the amount used would be shown to users) due to our system design (see §4). Thus, there is an incentive for users to not be overly promiscuous with invitations and to only invite peers based on actual social connections.

Once an invitation is accepted, the attacker may proceed to invite an arbitrary number of malicious peers. This is unlike X-Vine and detection approaches like SybilLimit that use rate limits to effectively keep the attacker to a small number of Sybil nodes per attack edge [19,36]. In such approaches, an attacker can use a large number of attack edges (e.g. one per honest node) to overcome the rate limits and overwhelm the system.

The attacker does not invite honest nodes, as this provides him with no advantage in our system. An attacker node could leave the system and join again under a different identity, but doing so provides no advantages, as we do not employ detection or reputation mechanisms. Further, the attacker might lose an attack edge, and so we do not model attacker churn in our evaluation.

Attacking lookups. An attacker with a large number of malicious peers then proceeds to attack the system. Rather than simply dropping lookup requests, the attacker nodes respond with the closest other attacker nodes to the requested keys. This gives the attacker nodes the best chance to appear later in the lookup path and thus manipulate the final lookup results. If, at the end of the lookup, an attacker node is finally asked for the requested information, it will then drop the request.

We also assume that the attacker attempts to manipulate DHT routing tables. The routing tables in our system, which is based on Kad, are opportunistically modified based on intermediate query results, so the attacker's strategy of returning other attacker nodes benefits him in this way as well. We assume that the attacker does not make any lookups.

4. SYSTEM DESIGN

We now describe the Persea design. Persea consists of two layers: a social network layer (the *bootstrap graph*) and a DHT layer. In this paper, an *edge* refers to a link between two nodes in the DHT layer. The social network and DHT are simultaneously built starting with a set of bootstrap nodes. The bootstrap nodes assign IDs to themselves such that they are evenly spaced over the circular ID space. Thus, the ID space of the DHT is divided into one region for each bootstrap node.

A new peer must join the Persea system through an invitation from an existing node in the network. In general, it is expected that a node that is invited is socially known to the inviting peer. Thus, inviting a new node is a feature of the social network layer of Persea. More specifically, when a node is invited, it becomes a child of the inviting peer in the bootstrap graph. The inviting peer also gives it an ID and a *chunk* of IDs that it can use to invite more nodes to join the network.

The number of nodes that a peer can invite is limited by the number of IDs in its chunk. Thus, there is an incentive for peers to only invite other peers based on actual social connections so that it does not run out of IDs.

The DHT layer of Persea is based largely on Kademlia [17], a DHT that is widely adopted for the BitTorrent P2P file-sharing system. In particular, we use Kademlia's XOR distance metric to perform routing and k-buckets to store contacts. The main difference in Persea is that IDs are replicated evenly around the ID space for greater resiliency given our ID distribution scheme.

4.1 Hierarchical ID Space

We now describe how IDs are distributed in Persea. Each bootstrap node has a contiguous range of IDs called a *chunk*, which includes the bootstrap node's ID. A bootstrap node divides its chunk of IDs into sub-chunks based on the *chunk-factor*, a system parameter.

When a bootstrap node invites a peer to join the system, it assigns the new node an ID from one of its sub-chunks and gives it control over the rest of the sub-chunk. The newly joined node becomes the authority for distributing IDs from the given sub-chunk and uses this to invite more nodes to join the system. Based on the invitation-relationship among peers, a *bootstrap tree* is formed, in which an inviter node is the parent of its invited peers. If we have more than one bootstrap node, then we would have a forest of trees, where each bootstrap node is the root of a tree. The chunk-factor and size of the ID space define the maximum possible height and width of the trees.

This hierarchical ID distribution mechanism features the advantage that even if the attacker compromises a node in the system, and through it a large number of malicious nodes join the network, they will still be confined to a particular region of the ID space.

We briefly explain the mechanism with an example illustrated in Fig. 1. Let A and B be two bootstrap nodes that initiate the system. If we consider a b-bit ID space, then the total number of IDs in the DHT n_{max} would be 2^b. In this toy example, we consider a 10-bit ID space, so $n_{max} = 2^{10}$. If Z is the number of bootstrap nodes, each bootstrap nodes has $\lfloor \frac{n_{max}}{Z} \rfloor$ IDs in its chunk. To simplify the discussion, we ignore issues of uneven division of IDs. In this example, both node A and node B have 512 IDs. The lowest ID in a chunk is assigned to the bootstrap node itself and the remaining IDs are for further distribution to new nodes. In this example, node A's ID is 0 and the interval $[1, 511]$ is its chunk of IDs for further distribution.

Input: S_c: An integer, denoting the number of sub-chunks
Output: B[ ]: The integer array of size S_c
Variables: i, p, q: Integers
Operations: a=0
for $i = 1$ *to* S_c **do**
  if $i == 2^a$ **then**
    a=a+1 B[i]=*floor*($S_c/2^a$)
  end
  else
    B[i] = B[$i-1$] +*floor*($S_c/2^{a-1}$)
  end
end

Algorithm 1: Computing the balanced ordering of sub-chunks for distribution

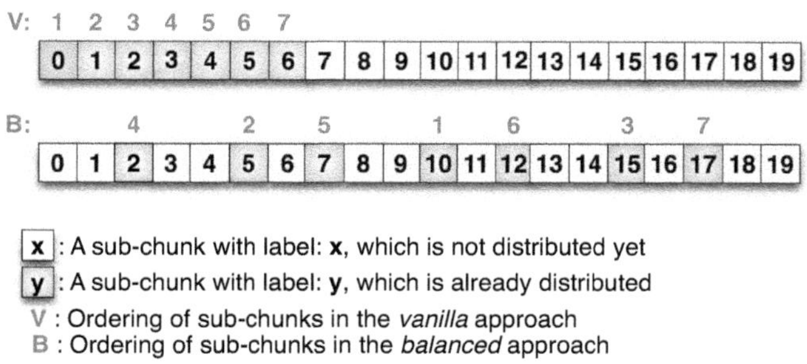

Figure 2: Ordering of sub-chunks for distribution

Each node divides its chunk into sub-chunks based on the chunk-factor. Let n_c be the number of IDs in a chunk and n_s represent the number of IDs in each of its sub-chunks. In a chunk, the lowest ID is assigned to the owner node and the remaining IDs are for further distribution. Thus $n_c - 1$ represents the number of IDs in a chunk available for distribution by the owner node. If the chunk factor is c_f $(0 \leq c_f \leq 1)$ then n_s would be $\lfloor (n_c - 1)^{c_f} \rfloor$. The number of sub-chunks (S_c) that can be created from a chunk is $\lfloor \frac{n_c - 1}{n_s} \rfloor + 1$. This also represents the maximum number of nodes that can be invited by a node having chunk of size n_c.

Let $c_f = 0.65$ in this example. Node A divides its chunk into nine sub-chunks where each sub-chunk has 57 IDs (the last sub-chunk has 55 IDs). Node a_1 joins the network after getting an invitation from node A and A assigns a sub-chunk to a_1. The lowest ID in this sub-chunk is 1, which is assigned as a_1's ID, and the interval $[2, 57]$ represents the remaining IDs of the sub-chunk that are for further distribution by a_1. Another node a_2 joins the network through an invitation from A. Using $c_f = 0.65$, both a_1 and a_2 divide their chunks into five sub-chunks, where each sub-chunk has 13 IDs (the last one has four). Node a_{21} joins the network through the invitation from node a_2, which assigns it the ID 59. Nodes b_1 and b_{11} join the network through the invitations from nodes B and b_1, respectively.

We assume that each node knows the value of Z, b, and c_f. Thus, if a node assigns an ID from its chunk to a joining node, the joining node can easily verify it, because any node in Persea can calculate the chunk distribution.

Balanced ordering of sub-chunks. As shown at the top of Fig. 2, if chunks are assigned in consecutive order, the distribution of ID space will be uneven. To maintain reasonable load distribution, we instead space out the chunk distribution as shown in the lower part of Fig. 2.

More specifically, a node doles out each sub-chunk so as to divide its chunk's ID space into the most balanced distribution possible at each moment. Using Fig. 2, in which there are 20 sub-chunks, the node will first allocate sub-chunk 10, which divides its ID space in half between itself and its first child. Further allocations will be to cut the total ID space into quarters (chunks 5 and 15), eighths (chunks 2, 7, 12, and 17), and so on. More formally, a node issues its chunks according to Algorithm 1.

4.2 Certification of IDs and Chunk Allocations

Persea employs a simple public key infrastructure to protect the advantages of hierarchical ID distribution from fraudulent ID and chunk ownership claims. In Persea, each node has a certificate, signed by its parent in the bootstrap tree, containing its ID, its public key, the parent's ID, and the last ID of its chunk. The ID of the node itself is the first ID of its chunk, and thus the chunk ranges from the node's ID to the last ID. The information in the certificate helps to prevent attacks based on fraudulent node creation. We discuss the resilience of Persea to such attacks in §5.

To ensure that its certificate can be found, each node takes the hash of its ID to get a target ID and publishes the certificate to the Persea DHT, using replication (see §4.3). When node P contacts node Q in the DHT, it validates Q's ID as follows. First, it uses the DHT to find Q's certificate, which is signed by Q's parent Q_1. Q_1's certificate is also obtained from the DHT, and the public key it contains is used to verify Q's certificate. Each replica that stores Q's certificate will also look up Q_1's certificate in the DHT to prevent an attacker from storing fake certificates. Note that Q_1's certificates have already been verified, and so on logically up to the bootstrap node. The bootstrap node certificates themselves can be distributed along with the P2P software or during the invitation process.

Note that the Persea lookup for Q_1's certificate obtains all R replicas. If there are any discrepancies between the replicas, P can continue to look up additional ancestors in the bootstrap tree up to the bootstrap node itself, if necessary. This provides resilience in the face of content poisoning attacks. If such attacks are widespread as an annoyance, the lookups for ancestors can be made probabilistic to avoid excessive overhead while still ensuring that fraudulent ID claims are detected quickly.

By placing certificates in the DHT, we avoid relying too much on the bootstrap nodes. When the system is first deployed, the bootstrap nodes are highly trusted as being in charge of large chunks of the ID space. After a number of peers have joined, however, much of the ID space is allocated. If a bootstrap or other node is compromised, it may attempt to issue certificates for malicious peers in space that has already been allocated. To prevent this, we propose the following mechanism: Nodes who store a certificate for a peer will not allow this certificate to be replaced by another node's information. We expect that this rule can be made more flexible by establishing consensus that a node has left the system or should be expelled, but protocols for doing so are beyond the scope of this paper.

4.3 Replication Mechanism

In this section, we describe our replication mechanism, which is the key difference between the Persea DHT layer and Kademlia.

As with other DHTs, we calculate the key for a given (key, value) pair by taking the consistent hash (e.g. SHA-1) of a search key, such as a file name. The node with the closest ID to the key in terms of the XOR of the key and the ID, interpreted as an integer, is deemed to be the owner of the key and should store the (key, value) pair. A lookup for the key should return this owner. In Persea, we replicate each (key, value) pair over R owners that are evenly

Table 2: Topologies [MT: mixing time]

Network	Abbrv.	Nodes	Edges	MT
advogato	**adv**	6551	51332	2.3
hamsterster	**ham**	2426	16631	3.0
youtube	**ytub**	15088	5574249	3.0
ca-AstroPh	**astro**	18772	396160	8.0
flickr	**flic**	80513	5899882	11.5
catster	**cat**	149700	5449275	8.0

spaced over the circular ID space. Thus, even if a region is occupied by the malicious peers, the redundant lookup operations can retrieve the desired (key, value) pair from owners in other regions of the network.

More specifically, when the initiator intends to store or retrieve a (key, value) pair in Persea, it calculates the ID of the target nodes as follows. Assume a b-bit ID space, such that $n_{max} = 2^b$. We virtually divide the ID space into R regions where each region (except the last one) accommodates at most $D = \lfloor \frac{n_{max}}{R} \rfloor$ IDs, and the last region has $n_{max} - D \times (R-1)$ IDs. The interval $[D \times r, D \times (r+1) - 1]$ for $0 \leq r < R-1$ represents the IDs that are in the rth region; the last region spans $[D \times (R-1), n_{max} - 1]$. A node ID i is replicated to each other region by taking $(i + D \times r)$ mod n for $1 \leq r < R$.

4.4 Routing Table Organization and Lookup

Our routing table organization and lookup mechanism follow closely to the model of Kademlia [17], though we note that other models could be followed. Here, we briefly describe the mechanisms for completeness.

Routing table organization. In the DHT layer, each node maintains a routing table consisting of b node lists for a b-bit ID space. Each list, or *k-bucket*, contains up to k entries, each of which contains the IP address, port, ID, and public key of another node. The ID of a node in the bth k-bucket of a node with ID i should share the first $b-1$ bits of i and have a different b^{th} bit from i.

Lookup mechanism. To initiate a **lookup**(key) request, the querying node contacts the α nodes in its k-buckets that are the closest ones to the desired key. Each of the α nodes sends the initiator β IDs from its k-bucket closest to the target node. If any of the β nodes is found not alive, the next closest node to the desired key, which is alive, is returned to the initiator. From the set of returned IDs, the initiator selects α nodes for the next iteration. This process is iterated until the target is found or no nodes are returned that are closer than the previous best results.

In Persea, the initiator performs R such independent parallel lookup operations and calculates the ID of the target nodes according to the mechanism described in §4.3. When an owner is found from any of R independent lookups, the initiator sends the owner a message for either the store (**put**($key, value$)) or retrieval (**get**(key)) operation.

5. SECURITY ANALYSIS

In this section, we examine the possible avenues of attack against Persea. We focus primarily on examining the resilience of Persea against attacks on ID control.

5.1 Attacks on ID Control

An attacker could attempt to undermine Persea's restrictions on ID space. We now discuss these attacks and how Perseea is resilient to them.

Note that our arguments for security against these attacks are inductive: Starting from a small base of honest nodes, in which lookups will succeed, additional nodes can be added according to the rules of protocol without substantial risk that lookups will be subverted as long as the ratio of attack edges to nodes remains moderate (i.e. $g/n \leq 1.0$) at all times. This assumption would only be violated if the early adopters were particularly vulnerable to social engineering.

Node insertion. In a node insertion attack, the attacker responds to a **lookup**(key) request by pretending that there is a malicious node with an ID that matches very closely to the key currently being searched for and returning this node's information. The attacker creates a certificate with this ID and signs it with a plausible key for a parent.

The certificate checks in Persea will cause this attack to fail. In particular, the node that initiated the **lookup**(key) request will also perform a lookup for the certificate of the returned node. The attacker will not be able to store the certificate in the DHT, as the replicas for the given ID will look up the parent's certificate. Note that the parent's certificate similarly cannot be stored in the DHT by the attacker. Additionally, the node ID must fit the fixed values determined by Z, b, and c_f (see §4.1). Each node can very simply calculate whether a returned node ID fits these system-wide values. Thus, the attacker's certificate will fail to validate and the user can use the other returned lookup results.

Node ID hijacking. In this attack, the malicious peer M falsely claims to have the node ID of an existing honest peer H and sends a request to a victim node V to insert this node ID into its k-bucket. If effective, this attack would allow widespread poisoning of k-buckets.

Persea is also resilient against this attack. A node cannot falsely claim a node ID in Persea because of the certification mechanism (§4.2). When node P requests node Q to add it to Q's k-bucket, node P has to show its certificate, which shows the actual node ID.

5.2 Other Attacks on DHTs

P2P systems, and DHTs in particular, are subject to a wide range of attacks. As most of these are orthogonal to our approach, we limit our discussion to the most salient issues.

Persea, being based on Kad, is subject to the *eclipse attack*, in which routing tables are filled the attacker [26]. Any P2P system must address this attack, but it is orthogonal to our design and can be solved using existing techniques, such as the approach of Singh et al. [24].

Index poisoning attacks, in which the attacker adds a large volume of invalid information into the DHT [15], are no more problematic in Persea than other DHTs, and can also be addressed with existing approaches [16].

Denial of service (DoS) is another possible attack on DHTs. DoS has minimal additional impact on our system beyond the impact on other DHTs. Notably, DoS on bootstrap nodes does not prevent nodes from joining, except through the targeted nodes, and does not stop nodes from verifying any certificates, as these are stored in a replicated manner in the DHT.

6. SIMULATION AND RESULTS

To evaluate Persea, we built a custom simulation of the protocol, including building the bootstrap tree and filling the ID space, adding malicious peers via attack edges, and performing lookups over the modified Kad overlay. In this section, we describe the design of our simulation and present the results of our experiments.

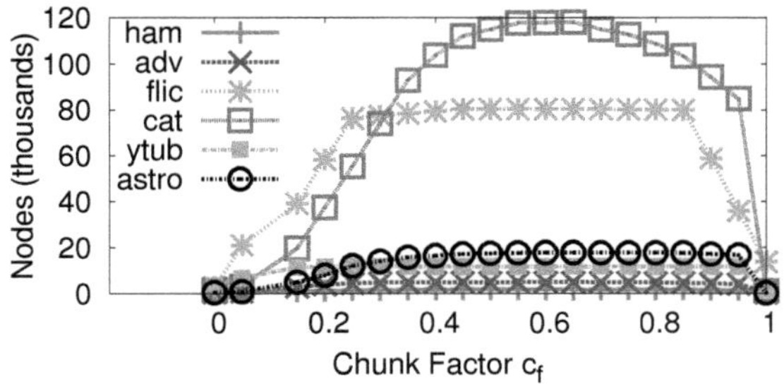

Figure 3: Effect of parameter c_f on the number of nodes in the system

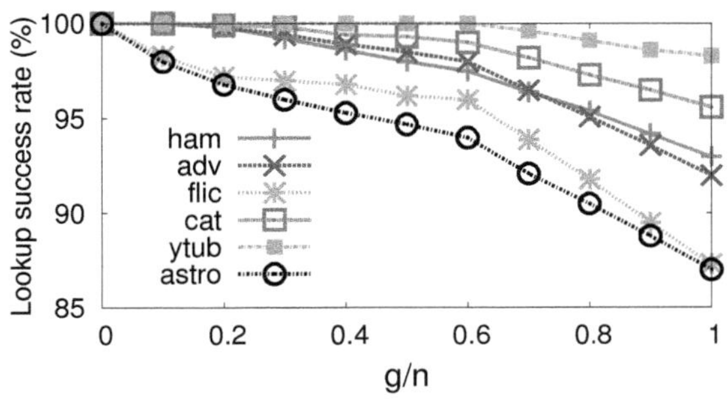

Figure 4: Lookup success rate for varying attack ratio g/n]

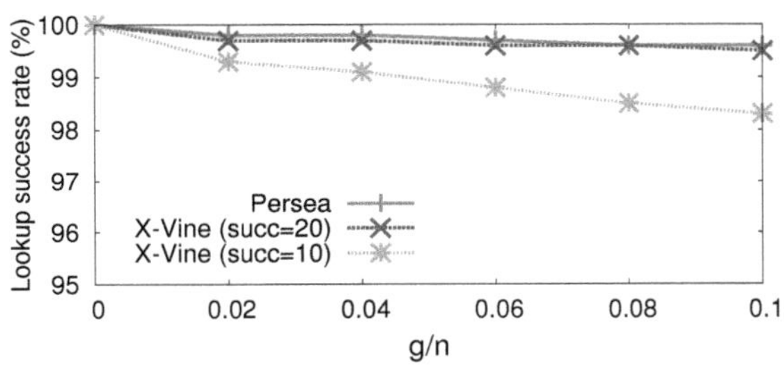

Figure 5: Comparison with X-Vine for $R = 5$

In all of our experiments, we simulate for a 31-bit ID space. Unless otherwise specified, we use default system values of chunk-factor $c_f = 0.65$, redundancy $R = 7$, and Kad parameters $\alpha = 5$, $\beta = 7$, and bucket size $k = 7$. Although the redundancy parameters (R, α, and β) may seem high, we show in Section 6.2.4 that the overheads for lookups are quite reasonable.

6.1 Building the Network and Joining of Attackers

To build the bootstrap tree, we emulate the process of nodes joining via existing connections in a social network graph. Although Persea does not rely on the structure of the social graph for its security properties, we use real social network graphs to provide a realistic basis for the choices that nodes make in building the tree.

To show that Persea will work for a variety of underlying social networks, we evaluate over six different social networks[2] with a range of mixing times. We evaluate Persea in simulations for five social network datasets: advogato (**adv**), hamsterster (**ham**), youtube (**ytub**), flickr (**flic**), and catster (**cat**), and one collaboration network: ca-AstroPh (**astro**). **ham**, **flic**, **ytub**, and **cat** are social networks drawn from users on the Hamsterster.com, Flickr.com, Youtube.com, and Catster.com Websites, respectively. Table 2 shows the sizes and mixing times of the network datasets. We measure the mixing times of these networks by using the code and procedures from Mohaisen et al. [20]; details are in the Appendix. Larger values show slower mixing times.

As we construct the initial boostrap graph, the nodes in these datasets are considered to be honest. We build our system starting with seven bootstrap nodes. In deployment, bootstrap nodes would be the users who take initiative to build the system. In our experiments, we choose seven highly connected nodes from the social network to start building the network. We then use breadth-first-search over the social graph to add other nodes. A link between node P and node Q in the dataset is interpreted as an invitation from node P to node Q. Thus, P becomes Q's parent in the boostrap graph. Also, P and Q add each other to their k-buckets.

After adding all of the honest nodes, we add Sybil nodes by creating attack edges to randomly selected honest peers. An attack edge represents an invitation from the honest node, providing the attacker with a certified ID and chunk of ID space through which it could invite more Sybil nodes. An attack edge can be created with a benign peer from any level of the hierarhcial ID space.

One may think that the attacker is at a disadvantage by being added after honest nodes build a bootstrap tree. This is not the case. The attackers have an equal chance to get attack edges at all levels of the tree, and there are always chunks to be given out at the highest levels of the tree. To demonstrate this, we examined the ratio of attack edges to honest nodes (g/n) in our simulations for all levels of the ID space (see Table 3 for the results for $g/n = 1.0$ overall). The ratios are roughly equal across the levels. We note that the ratios are actually greater than the overall ratio at the top level for the two networks (**cat** and **ytub**) for which Persea has the best lookup performance.

Maximizing the number of nodes. As the bootstrap graph is built, Persea should allow any new node to join through any existing node who is a real social connection. This means that both the number of IDs in each node's chunk and the depth of the tree should be large to prevent significant limitations on legitimate invitations. These two numbers are balanced by the chunk factor c_f—a larger c_f means larger chunks for each node, while a smaller c_f means a larger maximum tree depth. In Figure 3, we show this trade-off for our ID space and our social network graphs in terms of the maximum number of nodes in the system. Based on these results, we use $c_f = 0.65$ in our simulations to maximize the size of the experiment.

Table 3: g/n in each level of hierarchical ID space [overall $g/n = 1.0$]

Level	ham	adv	flic	cat	ytub	astro
1	0.91	0.95	1.17	1.10	1.15	0.95
2	0.96	1.10	0.96	0.97	0.93	0.98
3	1.01	1.03	0.97	0.97	0.97	0.99
4	0.98	1.04	0.95	0.97	0.95	1.03
5	1.00	0.93	0.97	0.97	1.00	1.03
6	1.16	0.95	0.98	0.98	–	1.04
7	0.94	–	–	0.98	–	1.05
8	1.04	–	–	1.11	–	0.93

[2] http://snap.stanford.edu/data, http://konect.uni-koblenz.de, http://socialcomputing.asu.edu/pages/datasets

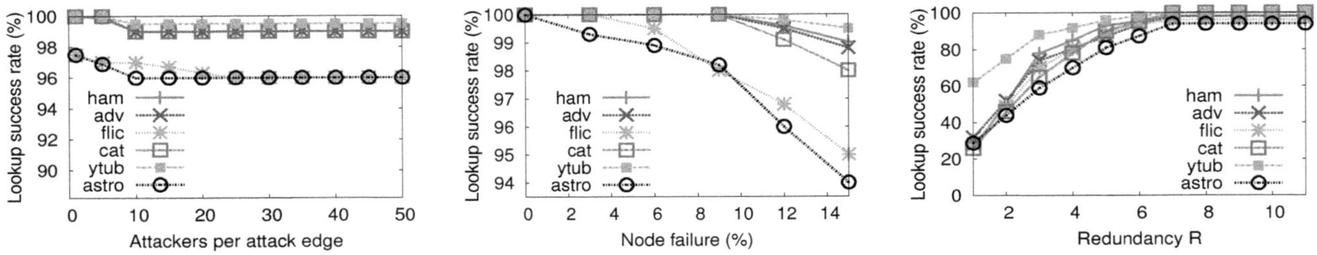

(a) Varying attackers per attack edge ($g/n = 0.10$)

(b) Varying percentage of node failure

(c) Varying R ($g/n = 0.50$)

Figure 6: Lookup success rates in Persea. Note the different y-axis ranges.

6.2 Results

In this section, we justify our claims through the results of simulation. We also analyze the effects of changing parameters and report the results for overhead.

6.2.1 *Justification of claims*

In this paper, we make the following claims about Persea:

- **Claim I:** Persea provides a high lookup success rate, even when the ratio of attack edges to honest nodes is not small.
- **Claim II:** Persea works well for both fast- and slow-mixing social networks.
- **Claim III:** The hierarchical node ID distribution confines the attackers in considerably smaller regions of ID space.
- **Claim IV:** The lookup success rate in Persea is not significantly affected by varying the number of attackers per attack edge.
- **Claim V:** Even when a significant fraction of nodes fail simultaneously, lookups should still succeed.

Claims I and III-V all speak to *Design Goal #1* of offering Sybil-resistent lookups. Claim II concerns *Design Goal #2* of not depending on the structure of the underlying social network. We justify our claims through our simulation experiments.

Claim I. In Persea, we get a 100% lookup success rate for up to $g/n = 0.45$ in a network of $149,700$ honest nodes (Figure 4). When $g/n = 1.0$ in the largest network in our evaluation, Persea's lookup success rate is 95.6%. In comparison, X-Vine only shows results for g/n up to 0.1, where the success rate is already below 100% [19]. We directly compare Persea with X-Vine in Figure 5, which is limited to at most $g/n = 0.07$ using results from Mittal et al. [19]. See the Appendix for details. Persea performs similarly to X-Vine using 20 successors per node. Whānau has significantly lower success rates for $g/n \geq 0.15$ [11] and can be expanded to improve success rates at the cost of greatly increased overheads [12].

Persea's DHT is based on Kad, which originally did not have any protections against the Sybil attack. Cholez et al. report that recent versions of Kad clients (aMule and eMule) attempt to protect against Sybil attacks by restricting IP addresses from appearing more than once in a node's k-buckets [6]. This does not affect our attacker, who we assume to have a large number of IP addresses, e.g. by running a botnet. We evaluated Kad in our experiments as well. For $g/n = 0.1$, the lookup success rate in Kad is 30% in **cat** and 40% in **flic**, both much worse than Persea.

Claim II. For these experiments, we select six networks with mixing times varying from 2.3 steps (fast-mixing) to 11.5 steps (slow-mixing) (Table 2). Using the lookup results when $g/n = 1.0$, we do find an inverse correlation between mixing time and lookup success ($r(4) = 0.60, p = 0.1$). Though it is not statistically significant, we do note that Persea performed the worst on two of the slowest mixing graphs (**flic** and **astro**). It is possible that faster mixing leads to better distribution of ID space among honest nodes, though we have not investigated this in detail. Nevertheless, the lookup results remain reasonable for these social networks. When $g/n = 0.5$, Persea has a success rate of 96.2% on **flic**, the slowest mixing graph, and 94.7% on **astro**.

In tables showing lookup overhead (Table 5, 6, and 7) and the amount of attacker-controlled ID space (Table 4), we show the mixing time in parentheses after the network name. Slower mixing networks also have higher overheads, though all overheads are quite reasonable for all six networks. The amount of attacker-controlled ID space does not seem to be correlated with mixing time.

Claim III. In Persea, the hierarchical node ID distribution limits the attacker nodes to a small fraction of the ID space, even for a significant number of attack edges. Table 4 shows the fraction of ID space controlled by the attacker. Even for $g/n = 1.0$, no more than 0.9% of the ID space is controlled by attacker nodes.

Claim IV. When an attacker joins the system, it can invite more malicious nodes. However, the lookup success rate in Persea should not be significantly affected by increasing the number of attackers per attack edge, since the hierarchical node ID distribution limits the attackers to isolated regions in the ID space. To test this, we increase the number of attackers per attack edge from one to fifty, which makes the number of attackers become 60% of total nodes in the network. We keep $g/n = 0.10$ fixed. For example, the lookup success rate is 99.5% in **ytub** and 99% in **ham** and **cat** when the number of attackers per attack edge is 50 (Figure 6(a)). We see no drops in performance in any network when the number of attackers per attack edges grows above 25.

Claim V. We evaluate the performance of Persea under node failure. We are interested in the static resilience of our system, i.e., the lookup success rate after a percentage of nodes in the system fail simultaneously. This is a worst-case version of a system with churn

Table 4: Fraction of ID space occupied by the attackers for varying g/n

g/n	0.10	0.50	0.80	1.0
adv (2.3)	0.0004	0.001	0.002	0.003
ham (3.0)	0.0005	0.0006	0.001	0.002
ytub (3.0)	0.001	0.004	0.006	0.007
astro (8.0)	0.0003	0.001	0.002	0.003
flic (11.5)	0.001	0.005	0.007	0.009
cat (8.0)	0.0007	0.003	0.006	0.007

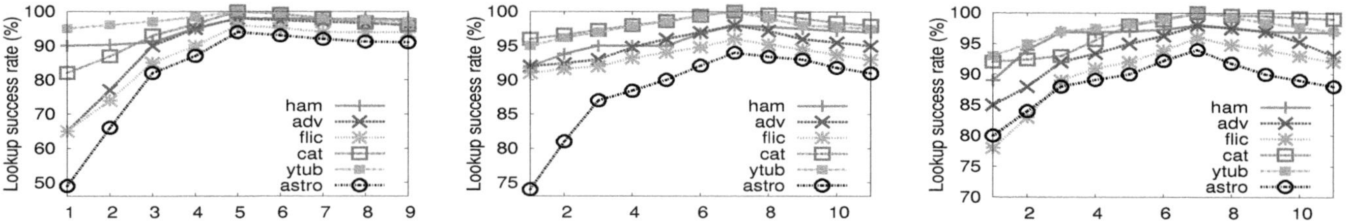

(a) Nodes queried α (b) Nodes returned β (c) k-bucket size

Figure 7: Lookup success rate for varying Kad-based system parameters $[g/n = 0.50]$

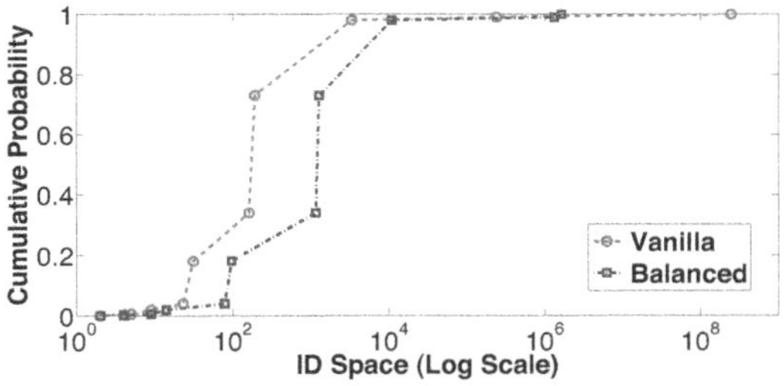

Figure 8: Empirical CDF of ID ownership in the catster network

in which the nodes fail and routing updates have not yet propagated to any peers. Figure 6(b) depicts the lookup success rate as a function of the percentage of nodes that fail simultaneously, averaged over 10,000 lookups. The results show that the lookup success rate remains 100% in the largest network of our evaluation, even when 10% of nodes fail. We do not add any malicious peers during this experiment. In Figure 9 (in the Appendix), we present the results of an experiment in which we vary the percentage of node failure and have attackers, with $g/n = 0.1$.

6.2.2 *Varying system parameters*

We now examine the effect of changing the key system parameters. When we increase redundancy R, nodes will store each (key, value) pair in more nodes and consequently lookup the key in more nodes. Thus, a larger value of R will result in better lookup performance at the cost of greater overheads. In Figure 6(c), we see that success rates appear to level off at $R = 7$. When β is increased, more nodes are returned to the source by each of α nodes in an iteration. We get the maximum lookup success rates for $\alpha = 5$ (Figure 7(a)) and $\beta = 7$ (Figure 7(b)). For a large number of attackers, higher values of α and β may increase the probability of selecting more malicious nodes in each iteration. We also examine settings for the bucket size k. We get seven as the optimal value for k with these settings (Figure 7(c)). The lookup success rate may decrease for higher values of k, since it means that routing tables can hold more attackers.

Table 5: Lookup Overhead $[g/n = 1.0]$

Network	Msgs (R lookups)	hop count (1 lookup)
adv (2.3)	21.65	3.09
ham (3.0)	18.87	2.69
ytub (3.0)	19.27	2.75
astro (8.0)	26.63	3.80
flic (11.5)	25.90	3.70
cat (8.0)	24.36	3.48

6.2.3 *ID ownership distribution*

We now examine the distribution of IDs across nodes. Figure 8 shows the distribution of IDs when using **cat**, the largest network on which we tested. In *vanilla Persea*, with in-order ID distribution, some nodes own 11.4% of the ID space. With our balanced approach, however, no node owns more than 0.077% of the ID space. The balanced approach provides much more even distribution of IDs to the peers.

6.2.4 *Overheads*

We now discuss how our system meets *Design Goal #4* of having moderate overheads. One overhead in DHTs is maintaining routing tables due to churn, e.g. by using *heartbeat messages*. Mittal et al. report that Whānau has an average routing table size of 20,000 in a network of 100,000 nodes, leading to very high maintenance costs [19]. In our experiments, however, Persea systems had between 10.1 and 68.1 routing table entries per node for different networks. This suggests moderate maintenance costs and is in line with other DHTs, including X-Vine.

Another overhead is in lookup costs, as measured by the *number of messages* and the *hop count*, the number of nodes required to reach a lookup target. In Persea, the certificate of a peer is stored in R nodes in the DHT, and the source retrieves them for validation by using the lookup mechanism (§4.4). Thus, the lookup overhead shown in Table 5 also includes the overhead for the retrieval of the certificates of a node. The number of messages is quite reasonable at less than 27 in all cases. As for hop count, Table 5 shows that the average hop count in Persea is low, e.g., 3.48 for $g/n = 1.0$ in the 149,700-node **cat** network. In contrast, for topologies with 100,000 nodes, X-Vine requires 10-15 hops for routing [19]. Whānau has a fixed hop count of two.

Increasing the rate of node failure does not greatly increase the average hop count and messages during lookup in Persea. Results (shown in Table 6 in the Appendix) show that for 15% node failure in the largest network in our evaluation, the average hop count per lookup increases by only 0.31. Finally, we find that increasing the number of attackers per attack edge has a small impact on the lookup overhead in Persea, as shown in Table 7 (in the Appendix).

7. CONCLUSION

Persea leverages the social relationships among honest peers to build a Sybil-resistant DHT that does not depend on the assumptions of a fast-mixing social network and a small number of attack edges. Persea also provides resilience against attacks (denial of service, node ID hijacking, and node insertion) launched by attacker nodes.

We see Persea as a first step in exploring mechanisms for using one's social network as an identifier and leveraging that for security. It is well known that social network information is strongly identifying [21], but it is non-obvious as to how we can convert this information into a usable identifier. The bootstrap tree is one approach to this, and the effectiveness of Persea suggests to us that this broader idea has significant potential and should be further explored.

8. ACKNOWLEDGMENTS

We thank our shepherd Aziz Mohaisen and the anonymous reviewers for their detailed comments and feedback. We also thank Aziz Mohaisen for providing code and assistance for measuring mixing times of social networks. This material is based upon work supported by the National Science Foundation under Grant No. CNS-1117866 and CAREER award number CNS-0954133.

9. REFERENCES

[1] L. Alvisi, A. Clement, A. Epasto, S. Lattanzi, and A. Panconesi. SoK: The evolution of Sybil defense via social networks. In *IEEE S&P*, 2013.

[2] D. G. Andersen, H. Balakrishnan, N. Feamster, T. Koponen, D. Moon, and S. Shenker. Accountable Internet Protocol (AIP). *ACM SIGCOMM Computer Communication Review*, 38(4):339–350, 2008.

[3] L. Bilge, T. Strufe, D. Balzarotti, and E. Kirda. All your contacts are belong to us: Automated identity theft attacks on social networks. In *WWW*, 2009.

[4] Y. Boshmaf, I. Muslukhov, K. Beznosov, and M. Ripeanu. The socialbot network: when bots socialize for fame and money. In *ACSAC*, 2011.

[5] Y. Boshmaf, I. Muslukhov, K. Beznosov, and M. Ripeanu. Design and analysis of a social botnet. *Computer Networks*, 57(2):556–578, 2013.

[6] T. Cholez, I. Chrisment, and O. Festor. Evaluation of Sybil attacks protection schemes in KAD. In *AIMS*, 2009.

[7] G. Danezis, C. Lesniewski-Laas, M. F. Kaashoek, and R. Anderson. Sybil-resistant DHT routing. In *ESORICS*, 2005.

[8] G. Danezis and P. Mittal. SybilInfer: Detecting Sybil nodes using social networks. In *NDSS*, 2009.

[9] J. R. Douceur. The Sybil attack. In *IPTPS*, 2002.

[10] D. Irani, M. Balduzzi, D. Balzarotti, E. Kirda, and C. Pu. Reverse social engineering attacks in online social networks. In *DIMVA*, 2011.

[11] C. Lesniewski-Laas. A Sybil-proof one-hop DHT. In *Workshop on Social Network Systems*, 2008.

[12] C. Lesniewski-Laas and M. F. Kaashoek. Whānau: A Sybil-proof distributed hash table. In *USENIX NSDI*, 2010.

[13] B. Levine, C. Shields, and N. Margolin. A survey of solutions to the Sybil attack. Technical Report 2006-052, University of Massachusetts Amherst, 2006.

[14] Q. Lian, Z. Zhang, M. Yang, B. Y. Zhao, Y. Dai, and X. Li. An empirical study of collusion behavior in the Maze P2P file-sharing system. In *IEEE ICDCS*, 2007.

[15] J. Liang, N. Naoumov, and K. W. Ross. The index poisoning attack in P2P file sharing systems. In *INFOCOM*, pages 1–12, 2006.

[16] X. Lou and K. Hwang. Prevention of index-poisoning DDoS attacks in peer-to-peer file-sharing networks. Technical Report TR-2006-5, USC Internet and Grid Computing Lab, November 2006.

[17] P. Maymounkov and D. Mazieres. Kademlia: A peer-to-peer information sytem based on the XOR metric. In *IPTPS*, 2002.

[18] D. Mazieres, M. Kaminsky, M. F. Kaashoek, and E. Witchel. Separating key management from file system security. *ACM SIGOPS Operating Systems Review*, 33(5):124–139, 1999.

[19] P. Mittal, M. Caesar, and N. Borisov. X-Vine: Secure and pseudonymous routing in DHTs using social networks. In *NDSS*, 2012.

[20] A. Mohaisen, A. Yun, and Y. Kim. Measuring the mixing time of social graphs. In *ACM IMC*, 2010.

[21] A. Narayanan and V. Shmatikov. De-anonymizing social networks. In *IEEE S&P*, 2009.

[22] S. Ratnasamy, P. Francis, M. Handley, R. M. Karp, and S. Shenker. A scalable content-addressable network. In *ACM SIGCOMM*, 2001.

[23] A. Rowstron and P. Druschel. Pastry: Scalable, decentralized object location, and routing for large-scale peer-to-peer systems. In *Middleware*, 2001.

[24] A. Singh, M. Castro, P. Druschel, and A. Rowstron. Defending against eclipse attacks on overlay networks. In *ACM SIGOPS European Workshop*, page 21. ACM, 2004.

[25] M. Sirivianos, X. Yang, and T. Pregueiro. Aiding the detection of fake accounts in large scale social online services. In *USENIX NSDI*, 2012.

[26] M. Steiner, T. En-Najjary, and E. W. Biersack. Exploiting kad: possible uses and misuses. *ACM SIGCOMM Computer Communication Review*, 37(5):65–70, 2007.

[27] I. Stoica, R. Morris, D. Karger, F. Kaashoek, and H. Balakrishnan. Chord: A scalable peer-to-peer lookup service for internet applications. In *ACM SIGCOMM*, 2001.

[28] N. Tran, J. Li, L. Subramanian, and S. S. Chow. Optimal Sybil-resilient node admission control. In *IEEE INFOCOM*, 2011.

[29] B. Viswanath, M. Mondal, A. Clement, P. Druschel, K. P. Gummadi, A. Mislove, and A. Post. Exploring the design space of social network-based Sybil defenses. In *COMSNETS*, 2012.

[30] B. Viswanath, A. Post, K. P. Gummadi, and A. Mislove. An analysis of social network-based Sybil defenses. In *ACM SIGCOMM*, 2010.

[31] W. Wei, F. Xu, C. C. Tan, and Q. Li. SybilDefender: Defend against Sybil attacks in large social networks. In *IEEE INFOCOM*, 2012.

[32] C. Wilson, B. Boe, A. Sala, K. P. Puttaswamy, and B. Y. Zhao. User interactions in social networks and their implications. In *Eurosys*, 2009.

[33] S. Wolchoky, O. S. Hofmanny, N. Heninger, E. W. Felten, J. A. Halderman, C. J. Rossbach, B. Waters, and E. Witchel. Defeating Vanish with low-cost Sybil attacks against large DHTs. In *NDSS*, 2010.

[34] M. Yang, Z. Zhang, X. Li, and Y. Dai. An empirical study of free-riding behavior in the Maze P2P file-sharing system. In *IPTPS*, 2005.

[35] Z. Yang, C. Wilson, X. Wang, T. Gao, B. Y. Zhao, and Y. Dai. Uncovering social network Sybils in the wild. In *ACM IMC*, 2011.

[36] H. Yu, P. B. Gibbons, M. Kaminsky, and F. Xiao. SybilLimit: A near-optimal social network defense against Sybil attacks. In *IEEE S&P*, 2008.

[37] H. Yu, M. Kaminsky, P. B. Gibbons, and A. Flaxman. SybilGuard: Defending against Sybil attacks via social networks. In *ACM SIGCOMM*, 2006.

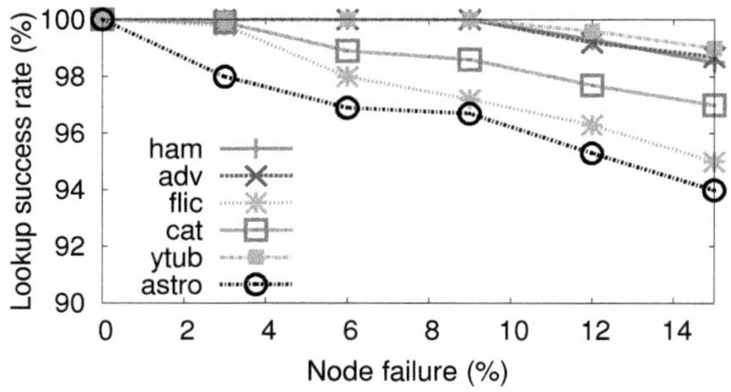

Figure 9: Lookup success rate for varying percentage of node failure [$g/n = 0.10$]

APPENDIX

A. ADDITIONAL RESULTS

Measuring Mixing time. Mixing time represents the number of steps required by a random walk to approach the uniform distribution [20]. We measure the mixing time of networks used in our simulation by using the codes and methodology provided by the authors of [20], where the walk length at total variation distance 0.1 represents the lower bound of the mixing time of a network. To measure the mixing time for large networks (e.g., **flic** and **cat**), we adopt the sampling technique described in [20] to get $25,000$ nodes for each network. For other networks, we use the largest connected component to measure mixing time. Our results (see Table 2) show that **flic**, **cat**, and **astro** are relatively slow-mixing compared to **ham**, **adv**, and **ytub** networks.

Results for node failure ($g/n = 0.1$). We evaluate for varying percentage of node-failure having $g/n = 0.1$, where n represents the number of total benign peers (alive+failed). For this experiment, we consider that only benign peers fail in the system. Figure 9 illustrates the results. We find that 99% lookups still succeed in Persea, when 10% fail in a network of $149,700$ nodes.

Results for the distribution of g/n**.** For $g/n = 1.0$ in the whole network, Table 3 shows the distribution of this ratio over different levels of hierarchical ID space. Here, **flic** has six levels and other networks have eight levels in their hierarhcial ID space (see §6 for a detailed explanation).

Additional overhead results. Table 6 compares the amount of overhead for a Persea system with no failures and one with 15% node failures, which should be considered high. We show both total messages and hop count. The number of messages increases in the high failure rate scenario by an average of 2.8 for $R = 7$ redundant lookups across our social networks. The hop count increases by an average of 0.41.

Table 7 compares the amount of overhead for a Persea system with one attacker per attack edge and 10 attackers per attack edge. When averaged across our social networks, the total number of messages increases by 1.4 for $R = 7$ redundant lookups and the hop count increases by 0.2.

Comparison with X-Vine. We compare Persea and X-Vine in terms of lookup success rate and overhead, where the results for X-Vine are taken from [19] and then we perform simulation on Persea for the same dataset (New Orleans Facebook Friendship Graph) and parameter ($R = 5$). The number of nodes and edges in this interaction graph are 63731 and 1545686, respectively. However, in X-Vine [19] the number of nodes and edges are reduced to 50150 and 661850, respectively through pre-processing. So, while comparing Persea and X-Vine (see Figure 5), for each value of g/n the number of attack edges are different for the two systems. In our comparison, for X-Vine we consider two values (10 and 20) as the number of successors.

The results for lookup success rate are shown in Figure 5 (see §6.2), where we find that Persea performs very similarly to X-Vine for the given parameters. The mean lookup path length in Persea is found less than that in X-Vine, where for $R = 5$ the mean lookup path lengths for X-Vine are 13.7 (succ=10) and 10.7 (succ=20), and for Persea the mean lookup path length is 4.4.

Table 6: Overhead for Node Failure

Overhead	Avg. Messages in R Lookups		Avg. Hop-Count in each of R Lookups	
Failure (%)	No Failure	15%	No Failure	15%
adv (2.3)	18.61	20.78	2.65	2.96
ham (3.0)	15.32	20.83	2.19	2.98
ytub (3.0)	17.43	18.25	2.49	2.61
cat (8.0)	22.54	24.71	3.22	3.53
astro (8.0)	23.65	26.55	3.37	3.79
flic (11.5)	23.2	25.04	3.31	3.57

Table 7: Overhead for Varying Attackers per Attack Edge [$g/n = 0.10$]

Overhead	Avg. Messages in R Lookups		Avg. Hop-Count in each of R Lookups	
Attackers per attack edge	1	10	1	10
adv (2.3)	18.72	19.95	2.67	2.85
ham (3.0)	15.41	17.04	2.20	2.43
ytub (3.0)	18.25	18.40	2.60	2.63
astro (8.0)	23.73	26.02	3.39	3.71
flic (11.5)	23.3	25.29	3.32	3.61
cat (8.0)	22.66	23.87	3.23	3.41

OTIT: Towards Secure Provenance Modeling for Location Proofs

Rasib Khan, Shams Zawoad, Md Munirul Haque, Ragib Hasan
SECRETLab, Department of Computer and Information Sciences
University of Alabama at Birmingham, AL, USA
{rasib, zawoad, mhaque, ragib}@cis.uab.edu

ABSTRACT

Personal mobile devices and location based services are gaining popularity every day. Since the location based services are often customized based on the location information, it is important to securely generate, preserve, and validate the claim of presence at a given location at a given time as well as location provenance – the history of locations for a mobile device user over a given time period. Location provenance needs to imply secure and chronological ordering of location proofs, which can be successfully verified at a later time. Otherwise, the location based services can be easily spoofed by falsified location history. In this paper, we present OTIT – a model for designing secure location provenance. We formalized the features and characteristics for the domain of secure location provenance schemes, using formal propositional logic and logical proofs. We also present several schemes, which can be used in various modes to provide secure location provenance services. Based on the characteristics defined in OTIT, we have analyzed different schemes to show their adherence to the desired features of secure location provenance. Furthermore, we present experimental results on the performance of the various schemes, in terms of time and storage, to show a comparative applicability analysis. We posit that OTIT will serve as a comprehensive benchmark framework to evaluate the models for secure location provenance.

Categories and Subject Descriptors

K.6.m [**MANAGEMENT OF COMPUTING AND INFORMATION SYSTEMS**]: Security and Protection: Security

Keywords

History Preservation, Location Provenance, Security, OTIT

1. INTRODUCTION

Smartphones and other mobile devices have removed the barriers for network oriented services. Fixed physical locations for network attachment are no longer a concern when it comes to deploying distributed systems. Users are no longer confined to a particular geographic location and can now be moving around locations to access various services. Location based services have therefore gained popularity as an application of mobility in networking. Location based services are targeted to provide customization of services based on the current physical location of the users. Service providers perform authentication, authorization, access control, accounting, and similar critical actions for the users in association with the geographical locations of the mobile devices [22].

Validity of location information and the process of validation is always a critical task. High-stake applications require the trustworthiness of location information and related proofs. Motives behind manipulation of such information may vary from trivial personal gains, such as, in social-games like FourSquare [26], to national security issues, as that of spoofing Drones with false location data [19]. Hence, location history and preservation of the corresponding records can be considered very important in various aspects.

History is not preserved by itself [1]. The source of data is important to validate the authenticity of information. Provenance is important for tracing the authenticity of an item back to its source [23]. Securing data and information provenance requires a single stamp from the issuing authority, which can be validated by any requester at a later time [15]. History of locations, or location provenance, is the history of locations traveled by a user. The provenance of location is a crucial requirement in path critical scenarios. A valid claim of travel path needs to be validated only in terms of the location provenance of the travel. The integrity of a product may be highly justified by the supply chain and the intermediate locations which a product travels, as it is transported from the manufacturer to the hands of the final consumer [16]. Location presence and generating proof of presence require the information to be valid and unmodified at a later time, such that it can be used as a secure token of evidence. However, provenance for location is a continuous process. The provenance records require location provenance to be preserved, as the user travels around collecting location proofs. Moreover, unlike the general data items, the sequence, in which the locations are traveled, needs to be preserved in chronological order within the provenance. As a result, provenance for location proofs portrays a greater challenge than that for general data items.

In this paper, we present OTIT[2], a model for secure provenance for chronological preservation of location proofs. OTIT presents a formal model for generating and maintaining a secure and order-preserving chronological chain of the location proofs. We model location provenance as a combination of propositional logic, and their corresponding required properties. Based on our model, we present different approaches for such provenance recording protocol. The paper includes formal proofs for each approach, experi-

ASIA CCS'14, June 4–6, 2014, Kyoto, Japan.

http://dx.doi.org/10.1145/2590296.2590339.

[1]"History is the version of past events that people have decided to agree upon." – *Napoléon Bonaparte*

[2]OTIT (\'o-θi:θ\) is the Bengali word for 'past' or 'history'.

mental evaluation, and comparative applicability analysis for each of the approaches.

Contributions: Our contributions in this paper are as follows:

- We present OTIT, a novel and formal model for chronological order-preserving location proofs in provenance chains. To the best of our knowledge, this is the first work done on secure and order preserving location provenance records.
- We present different approaches, which can be used to design chronological location provenance. Each of the approaches are proved formally using our propositional model for OTIT.
- We provide experimental results to analyze the performance of each of the approaches for preserving chronological location provenance. Our comparative analysis based OTIT can help users in choosing the schemes based on their preferences and priorities.

The rest of the paper is organized as follows. We discuss the desired features of any provenance model and a summary of possible provenance schemes in Section 2. Section 3 presents the security analysis of the schemes based on the selected features. Performance analysis of different provenance models has been presented in Section 4. Section 5 shows a comparative analysis among different models. Related work is presented in Section 6 followed by conclusion in Section 7.

2. SECURE LOCATION PROVENANCE

Securing provenance records can be accomplished in a number of ways. In this section, we first present the threat model for secure location provenance. Subsequently, we present the requirements for any secure and chronological location provenance scheme. We also lay out the different approaches for secure preservation of location provenance, the legacy ones as well as the ones which we have modified for our purpose.

2.1 Threat Model

One of the assets in our model for secure location provenance is the chronological ordering of location proofs. An attacker will always try to alter the sequence of proofs in the provenance chain, and present the tampered provenance record to validate a false timeline for his travel path. We consider that the provenance chain resides with the user at all time. Additionally, it is assumed that an attacker has complete access to all storage and computation resources on his personal device on which he stores the proofs and the corresponding location provenance chain. Therefore, an attacker is able to modify the order of the proofs in the chain at any later time, when presenting the records to a provenance auditing authority. In addition to modifying the provenance chain, the attacker can also tamper with the location provenance record chain or the individual proofs within the provenance records.

Given that a valid provenance chain is presented by a user to an auditing authority, the auditor may look at the information from the proofs for which the user has not intended. Thus, a breach of privacy for the user's information occurs as the auditor verifies the provenance of location proofs. Moreover, given that the location provenance is a chain of records, the user is unable to protect himself from exposing a subset of proofs from within the chain.

In an alternative scenario, a malicious user may want to hide an intermediate point in a sequence of location proofs. Even though the source and destination locations are the same, and in order, the attacker is able to hide a temporary off-track movement from the claimed provenance of locations. Therefore, the auditor, validating the claim of chronological location proofs, will be oblivious to the fact that the malicious user is hiding a rerouted path between two given locations. Finally, an attacker may want to daunt a verifying auditor with a huge task of validation in terms of data overload.

2.2 Requirements for Location Provenance

Here, we formalize and present the features and requirements for OTIT, which are necessary for designing any secure location provenance scheme.

Chronological: The location proof records should be ordered according to the sequence of their visits. It is required that, the order in which the location proofs are obtained by the user, should be entered into the location provenance chain in that order. The chronology of the proofs ensures that a malicious user is not able to create false provenance chains for the order of visits. Given that a user visited locations A, B and C in the sequence $A \rightarrow B$ and $B \rightarrow C$, the provenance record chain should hold the corresponding proofs in the given chronology of visits. Considering a location provenance chain, ... + Proof(A) + Proof(B) + Proof(C) + ... should be the order in the given sub-sequence.

Order Preserving: Given the chronology of the location proofs in the provenance chain, the provenance chain of location proofs should preserve the order in which the proofs were entered into the chain. As we assume location provenance in a completely user-centric environment, a user has complete access to the provenance records stored on his personal device. As a result, it is required that the order of proofs, with which the provenance chain is created, is preserved at any point of time. This means that at a later time $(t_i + \delta t_i)$, where t_i is the time at which any proof i has been entered in the provenance chain, the order of the proofs should be unaltered.

Verifiable: The proofs in the provenance and the order of the proof items should be verifiable by a trusted auditor. Users possess location provenance chains and use the chain of records to prove a given sequence of travel. Hence, when an auditor is presented with a provenance chain by the user, the auditor should be able to verify the claim by the user of visiting locations A, B, and C in the order $A \rightarrow B$ and $B \rightarrow C$. A successful verification would validate the claim by the user, and would have to be a false claim otherwise.

Tamper Evident: The information within the location provenance chain should be tamper evident. In contrast to ensuring tamper proof information, we emphasize that the provenance records should reside with the user. We assume that the location provenance is a user-centric scheme. Thus, the user has the flexibility of tampering with the information within the provenance chain. Given a tampered item, the verifying auditor should be able to detect that the provenance chain has been modified by an unauthorized party.

Privacy Preserved: Given that a location provenance chain is presented to an auditor, it should not reveal any additional information, which is not intended by the user to be revealed. Even though we model location provenance preservation as a user-centric design, the user needs to present the proofs to the verifying auditor for validating the claimed provenance. For the proofs, which are being presented for verifying the provenance chain, it is required that the user has a control on the level of privacy exposure. The overall expectation is, when the provenance chain is verified for specific location proofs, the privacy is preserved for the other location proofs within the chain.

Selective In-Sequence Privacy: A provenance scheme is required to support sub-set verification in terms of privacy and convenience. Location provenance generation is a continuous process and evolves with time. The provenance chain adds the collected proofs in chronological order and builds itself. At any given moment, it is highly likely that the user will want to prove only a sub-set from the current location provenance chain. Therefore, given a sequence of

	HC	BC	BF	SH	MH	RC
Chronological	✓	✓	✓	✓	✓	✓
Order Preserving	✓	✓	✓	✓	✓	✓
Verifiable	✓	✓	✓	✓	✓	✓
Tamper Evident	✓	✓	✓	✓	✓	✓
Privacy Preserved	✗	✗	✗	✓	✗	✓
Selective In-Sequence Privacy	✗	✗	✓	✗	✗	✗
Privacy Protected Chronology	✗	✗	✗	✗	✗	✓
Convenience and Derivability	✗	✓	✓	✗	✓	✗

Table 1: Comparison of Location Proof Provenance Approaches: Hash Chains (HC), Block-Hash Chains (BC), Bloom Filter (BF), Shadow Hash Chain (SH), Multi-Link Hashing (MH), and RSA Chaining (RC)

proofs ... + Proof(A) + Proof(B) + Proof(C) + ..., a user may wish not to reveal the information regarding Proof(*B*), such that the auditor verifying the information should not be able to view the information within the particular proof or a selective subset of in-sequence proofs.

Privacy Protected Chronology: As it highly likely that a user will only desire to prove a sub-set of the location provenance chain, the provenance scheme should also ensure that the user does not hide away important information from the items within the subset of the provenance chain. Given that the sequence of proofs is ... + Proof(A) + Proof(B) + Proof(C) + ..., the user may selectively hide *Proof(B)*. However, the auditor must be able to view the chronology of the sub-sequence. This is because, in case of privacy protected provenance validation, ... + Proof(A) + Proof(C) + ... is an invalid claim, as it shows the user went from location A $\rightarrow$ C. However, ... + Proof(A) + Proof(?) + Proof(C) + ... is a valid claim with one privacy preserved subset of in-sequence proofs, as it shows the user traveled from location A $\rightarrow$ (?) $\rightarrow$ C, where Proof(?) is a hidden proof.

Convenience and Derivability: As we consider the process of collection of location proofs is a continually evolving process, the provenance chain will go on increasing in length with time. Thus, given that an auditor requires verifying a provenance claim, the process of verification should be convenient. The provenance scheme should ensure that the user does not burden the verifying auditor with a huge load of data. We specify space complexity as a measure of convenience for both the user and the auditor. Therefore, the location provenance should ensure minimal number of items, which are required to be presented by the user to the auditor for verification. A naïve approach requires a sequential access along the whole chain to allow the auditor to derive and verify a subsequence A $\rightarrow$ B $\rightarrow$ C. However, an ideal scheme should allow derivation and verification of sub-sequences in a convenient manner.

2.3 Provenance Approaches

Next, we discuss the approaches that we have considered for secure preservation of location provenance using our model - OTIT. We describe each of the schemes and also present a summarized comparison of the schemes in Table 1.

Hash Chain: Hashing refers to the most primitive form of integrity preservation techniques. Hash chains are an extension of the basic hashing scheme to preserve the order of hashed values. We use the hash of the ith proof and append it to proof $(i+1)$ to create the $(i+1)^{th}$ hash element [15]. For the first proof, hash of element 0 uses an initialization vector to begin the chain creation process.

Block Hash Chain: In our block hash chains, we create sub-segments or blocks of hash chains, each starting with a unique initialization vector. Therefore, for every k^{th} proof, we terminate the chain block, and begin the next chain block using another unique initialization vector. Additionally, we also store a hash chain of the unique initialization vectors for each block, which ensures that the blocks of hash chain cannot be altered in sequence. The user is required to store a total of n/k initialization vectors, where n is the total number of proofs.

Bloom Filter: The Bloom filter is an accumulator based data structure, with a probabilistic membership verification [5]. Our Bloom filter based approach uses individual fixed length Bloom filter for each proof. The individual Bloom filters accumulate the hash values for the proofs and are used to prove implicit chronology of location proofs. For the given Bloom filter for proof i, all the proofs from 0 to i are hashed individually and included in the Bloom filter. Therefore the Bloom filter for proof $(i+1)$ holds the set bits for all the hashes of the proofs from 0 to $(i+1)$.

Shadow Hash Chain: We introduce the concept of a shadow hash chain, which refers to two hash chains together being generated in the same way as for a single hash chain. We generate the first chain by forming the hashes from the plain text proofs. However, another corresponding hash entry is made into the second hash chain, which is a hash generated from encrypting proof $(i+1)$ and padding the hash for encrypted proof i. In this context, the second hash chain is referred to as the shadow hash. The shadow hash chain is useful in proving a sequence of location proofs $(i-1)$, i, and $(i+1)$, without revealing the plain text contents of proof i.

Multi-Link Hash Chain: In multi-linked hashing, each proof entry i in the hash chain is padded with the hash of k other proofs, where k is a subset of of proofs such that $k_m \in [0..(i-1)]$, and $m \ll n$, where n is the total number of proofs, and $|k| = m$.

RSA Chaining: An RSA chain is formed using the concepts of an RSA accumulator [2, 3, 7]. An RSA accumulator is a cryptographic one-way data structure, similar to Bloom filter. The accumulator is based on RSA assumption and provides the functionality of checking the membership of an element in a set. Unlike Bloom filters, RSA accumulators works with zero false negative and false positive probability. In this case, we create a cryptographic accumulator using the hash of the previous proof in the provenance chain and a secret number. The RSA chain helps to prove location provenance without requiring the user to expose any proofs, unless intended.

3. SECURITY ANALYSIS

In this section, we present the security analysis for the aforementioned provenance schemes for location proofs. Our proofs are based on the required properties for location provenance.

Lemma 1: *A location proof is a securely generated data item for user U, which validly verifies the presence of user U at location L_i, where i $\in$ {1, 2, ..., n}.*

Lemma 2: *A location provenance chain C is a record of location proofs for locations L_i, where i $\in$ {1, 2, .., n }, and presence at each location L is verified using a location proof Proof(L) for that location.*

Therefore, using **Lemma 1** and **Lemma 2**, we can say that if a user U presents a provenance chain C, which has Proof(*L*) as one of the elements, this securely verifies the claim that the user U was present at location L.

3.1 Security Propositions

Using the above lemmas, we put forward the following security propositions for location provenance.

Proposition 1 - Chronological (P1):
If user U visited locations (L_{i-1}), (L_i), *and* (L_{i+1}) *in order* $(L_{i-1}) \rightarrow (L_i) \rightarrow (L_{i+1})$, *the provenance chain C enters the location proofs as Proof(*L_{i-1}*) + Proof(*L_i*) + Proof(*L_{i+1}*), which is the order in which they were received by user U.*

Proposition 2 - Order Preserving (P2):
If user U visited locations (L_{i-1}), (L_i), *and* (L_{i+1}) *in order* $(L_{i-1}) \rightarrow (L_i) \rightarrow (L_{i+1})$, *given that Proposition 1 holds true at time t, the provenance chain C preserves the order at time* $(t + \delta t)$*, where* δt *is a positive value.*

Proposition 3 - Verifiable (P3):
If user U presents an auditor A the location provenance chain C with Proof(L_{i-1}*) + Proof(*L_i*) + Proof(*L_{i+1}*), and individual proofs - Proof(*L_{i-1}*), Proof(*L_i*), and Proof(*L_{i+1}*), the auditor can successfully verify the claimed order of visits* $(L_{i-1}) \rightarrow (L_i) \rightarrow (L_{i+1})$ *for user U.*

Proposition 4 - Tamper Evident (P4):
If user U presents a tampered location provenance chain C_T *and/or tampered individual proofs to the auditor A, the auditor can successfully detect the tampering and the falsely claimed order of visits for user U.*

Proposition 5 - Privacy Preserved (P5):
If user U wants to validate his location provenance to an auditor A, no information intended to be hidden is visible to the auditor A.

Proposition 6 - Selective In-Sequence Privacy (P6):
If user U presents the location provenance chain C which is currently holding Proof(L_{i-1}*) + Proof(*L_i*) + Proof(*L_{i+1}*), the user is able to prove Proof(*L_{i-1}*), Proof(*L_{i+1}*), without revealing Proof(*L_i*)* to the auditor A.

Proposition 7 - Privacy Protected Chronology (P7):
If a user U presents to an auditor A the location provenance chain C containing Proof(L_{i-1}*) + Proof(*L_i*) + Proof(*L_{i+1}*), and hides Proof(*L_i*), the auditor A is able to validate the provenance chain for the sequence of visits as* $(L_{i-1}) \rightarrow (?) \rightarrow (L_{i+1})$.

Proposition 8 - Convenience and Derivability (P8):
If a user U has a provenance chain C with n number of proofs, and wants to prove m number of proofs from the provenance chain C to an auditor A, with the maximum range of proofs as r, the complexity of computation for verification is less than O(r), and greater or equal to O(m).

Given the above propositions (P1 - P8), next we will show the proofs for the different location provenance approaches discussed in Section 2.

3.2 Provenance Proofs

Here we prove/disprove all 8 propositions for each of the schemes mentioned in Section 2.

3.2.1 Hash Chain

For including Proof(L_i) in the provenance chain C, where $i = 0$, we use an initialization vector V, and a hash function *hf(x)*, and $x = Proof(L_O) + V$.

For including Proof(L_i), where $(i > 0) \wedge (i \in \Re)$, we use the hash function *hf(x)*, and $x = Proof(L_i) + hf(Proof(L_{i-1}))$.

Therefore, the order in which user U had received Proof(L_{i-1}), Proof(L_i), and Proof(L_{i+1}), is maintained in order within the location provenance chain C.

$\therefore$ **Proposition *P1* is true.**

Given *P1* is true, if Proof(L_i) is entered in the provenance chain C at time t_i, it implies that Proof(L_{i-1}) was already present in the chain, which was entered at time t_{i-1}. A trusted provenance authority generating the provenance chain for the user ensures the order preservation before the current proof is entered into the chain. Therefore, $t_{i-1} < t_i$, that is, $t_{i-1} + \delta t = t_i$.

$\therefore$ **Proposition *P2* is true.**

A user U intends on proving the location proof provenance $(L_i) \rightarrow (L_{i+m})$, where $m \geq 1$. The user U presents the following items to the auditor: (i) the proofs Proof(L_x), where $i \leq x \leq i+m$, and (ii) the hash value $hf(Proof(L_{i-1}))$.

The auditor A calculates *hf(x)* for Proof(L_x), where $i \leq x \leq i + m$. Once it reaches Proof(L_{i+m}), the auditor compares the calculated value with the value in the hash chain C to be true.

$\therefore$ **Proposition *P3* is true.**

The user U possess the provenance chain C at time *t*. At time $t + \delta t$, tampered location provenance chain C_T is presented to the auditor A. However, the auditor calculates the whole sub-chain of the hashes and then compares the calculated value with the value in the hash chain C to be true. Additionally, the hash values used in the location provenance chain C bears a trusted signature from a provenance authority.

$\therefore$ **Proposition *P4* is true.**

For verification, the user U presents all plain text proofs, without any information hiding schemes applied. Proofs which are not intended to be exposed are enforced to be presented as well. As a result hash chain does not preserve the privacy related propositions.

$\therefore$ **Propositions *P5, P6, P7* are false.**

Additionally, all proofs are required by the auditor A to be able to derive the final hash value contradicting the convenience and derivability issue.

$\therefore$ **Proposition *P8* is false.**

Proof 1: ***Hash Chain*** *holds the following truth values for the propositions* $P1, P2, P3, P4, \neg P5, \neg P6, \neg P7, \neg P8$.

3.2.2 Block Hash Chain

For including Proof(L_i) in the provenance chain C, where $i\%b = 0$ and b is our block size, we use an initialization vector (V_j), and a hash function *hf(x)*, and $x = Proof(L_i) + V_j$, where j ∈ {1, 2, .., n/b }.

For including Proof(L_i), where $(i\%b \neq 0) \wedge (i \in \Re)$, we use the hash function *hf(x)*, and $x = Proof(L_i) + hf(Proof(L_{i-1}))$.

For maintaining chronology of initialization vectors (V_j), we maintain a hash chain C_V of initialization vectors, where j ∈ {1, 2, .., n/b }. We use the hash function *hf(x)*, and $x = V_j + hf(V_{j-1})$.

Therefore, the order in which user U had received Proof(L_{i-1}), Proof(L_i), and Proof(L_{i+1}), is maintained within the location provenance chain C within each block b_i. The order of the blocks are maintained using hash chain C_V. Provenance proof for hash chains is already proved true in Proof 1.

$\therefore$ **Proposition *P1* is true.**

The chronological order preservation of location proofs in the provenance chain functions in a similar manner as to that in hash chains.

Proposition *P2* is true, $\because$ already true in Proof 1.

A user U intends on proving the location proof provenance $(L_i) \rightarrow (L_{i+m})$, where $m \geq 1$.

In the first case, (L_i) and (L_{i+m}) are within the same block. In this scenario, the verification proceeds the same way as in Proof 1.

In the second case, (L_i) and (L_{i+m}) are in two separate blocks *j* and *k*, where each block is of size *b*, and $j < k$. The user U presents the following items to the auditor: (i) the jth block of the provenance chain C, where the jth block holds (L_i), (ii) the proofs Proof(L_x), where $j * b \leq x \leq i$, (iii) the kth block of the provenance chain C, where the kth block holds (L_{i+m}), (iv) the proofs

Proof(L_y), where $k * b \leq y \leq i + m$, (v) the block initialization vectors V_z, where $j \leq z \leq k$, and (vi) the hash value $hf(V_{j-1})$.

The auditor A calculates *hf(x)* for Proof(L_x), where $j * b \leq x \leq i$, till it reaches Proof(L_i). The auditor A then calculates *hf(x)* for Proof(L_y), where $k * b \leq x \leq i + m$, till it reaches Proof(L_{i+m}). The auditor compares the calculated values with the value in the hash chain C to be true.

The auditor A then verifies the initialization vector hash chain C_V, using $hf(V_{j-1})$, and initialization vectors V_j to V_k. The auditor compares the value with the presented hash chain C_V to be true.

∴ **Proposition *P3* is true, given *P3* is true in Proof 1.**

Proposition *P4* is true, ∵ already true in Proof 1.

Similar to hash chains, the block hash chain does not incorporate any information encapsulation. Although the block hash chain does not require all items within Proof(L_x) and Proof(L_y), where $x < y$, it does not allow selectively hiding proofs. Neither does it allow in-sequence privacy, as it does not allow the user U to choose the item for which to preserve the privacy in chronology.

∴ **Propositions *P5, P6, P7* are false**.

As shown above, in the worst case, the user U only presents a sub-set of the proofs between Proof(L_x) and Proof(L_y).

∴ **Proposition *P8* is true**.

Proof 2: ***Block Hash Chain*** *holds the following truth values for the propositions* $P1, P2, P3, P4, \neg P5, \neg P6, \neg P7, P8$.

3.2.3 Bloom Filters

We use Bloom filters for implicitly maintaining location proof entries in the provenance chain C. For every location proof Proof(L_i), there is a corresponding Bloom filter BF_i. The Bloom filter accumulator BF_i inserts the signed location proofs as a function *FuncBEnt()*, such that $BF_i = \forall_x FuncBEnt[Proof(L_x)]$, where $x \in \{0 \ldots i\}$. Therefore, by induction, BF_{i+1} for Proof(L_{i+1}) is created such that, $BF_{i+1} = \forall_x FuncBEnt[Proof(L_x)]$, where $x \in \{0 \ldots i+1\}$.

∴ **Proposition *P1* is true**.

Given *P1* is true, if the provenance Bloom filter BF_i is created for Proof(L_i) at time t_i, it implies that BF_{i-1} which existed for Proof(L_{i-1}) was created at time t_{i-1}. Therefore, $t_{i-1} < t_i$, that is, $t_{i-1} + \delta t = t_i$.

∴ **Proposition *P2* is true**.

A user U intends on proving the location proof provenance (L_i) $\rightarrow$ (L_{i+m}), where $m \geq 1$. The user U presents the following items to the auditor: (i) the proofs Proof(L_i) and Proof(L_{i+m}), and (ii) the corresponding Bloom filters BF_i and BF_{i+m}.

The auditor A performs a membership check on the Bloom filter, using function *FuncBChk()*, which returns either *True* or *False*. Membership check for Proof(L_i) in both BF_i and BF_{i+m} using *FuncBChk()* should return *True*. Membership check for Proof(L_{i+m}) in both BF_i and BF_{i+m} using *FuncBChk()* should return *False* and *True* respectively. Therefore, it is verified that $BF_i \subset BF_{i+m}$, and (L_i) $\rightarrow$ (L_{i+m}).

∴ **Proposition *P3* is true**.

At time *t*, the user U possesses the Bloom filters BF_k, where $0 \leq k \leq t$. At time $t + \delta t$, tampered Bloom filters BF_i^T and BF_j^T are presented to the auditor A in correspondence with Proof(L_i) and Proof(L_j), where $i < j$. However, the auditor uses both the proofs and the Bloom filters with the membership check function *FuncBChk()* to verify $BF_i \subset BF_{i+m}$. Additionally, the proofs used for creating the Bloom filters for function *FuncBEnt()* are signed by a trusted provenance authority.

∴ **Proposition *P4* is true**.

Our Bloom filter approach does not include any encryption for the proofs. As a result, the user U does not have any option for information hiding within the location proofs.

∴ **Proposition *P5* is false**.

User U wants to prove (L_{i-1}) $\rightarrow$ (L_{i+1}) without revealing (L_i). Therefore, the user U presents Proof(L_{i-1}), Proof(L_{i+1}), and the corresponding Bloom filters BF_{i-1} and BF_{i+1} to the auditor A. As already shown above, $BF_{i-1} \subset BF_{i+1}$. Therefore, the auditor A can verify the claim by user U.

∴ **Proposition *P6* is true**.

User U wants to prove (L_{i-1}) $\rightarrow$ (?) $\rightarrow$ (L_{i+1}). Therefore, the auditor checks only BF_{i-1} and BF_{i+1}, and verifies $BF_{i-1} \subset BF_{i+1}$, without the knowledge that there is another location in between (L_{i-1}) and (L_{i+1}).

∴ **Proposition *P7* is false**.

As shown above, given that there are n proofs and Bloom filters in the provenance chain C, the user U only presents m proofs and Bloom filters. Here, m is number of locations for which user U wants to receive validation from the auditor A and $m << n$.

∴ **Proposition *P8* is true**.

Proof 3: ***Bloom Filter*** *holds the following truth values for the propositions* $P1, P2, P3, P4, \neg P5, P6, \neg P7, P8$.

3.2.4 Shadow Hash Chain

A shadow hash chain works in the same way for hash chains. However, in addition to the chain of hash values for Proof(L_i), where $(i \neq 0) \wedge (i \in \Re)$, there is a secondary chain of encrypted hash values of the proofs Enc[K_i, Proof(L_i)], where *Enc()* is an encryption function, and K_i is the unique encryption key for Proof(L_i).

Proposition *P1, P2, P3, P4* is true, ∵ already true in Proof 1.

The user U wants to prove (L_i) $\rightarrow$ (L_{i+1}) to auditor A, without revealing the information within Proof(L_{i+1}). Therefore, along with the segment of the hash chain, the user U presents the unique key K_i, Enc[K_i, Proof(L_i)], and Enc[K_i, Proof(L_{i+1})]. The auditor A thus calculates the encrypted proof hash chain in the same way as before, without Proof(L_{i+1}) being visible. Verification by preserving sub-chain privacy can also be executed by presenting three sub-chains: (i) (L_i) $\rightarrow$ (L_{i+j-1}) from the regular hash chain, (ii) (L_{i+j}) $\rightarrow$ (L_{i+k-1}) from the encrypted shadow hash chain, and (iii) (L_{i+k}) $\rightarrow$ (L_{i+m}), where $0 \leq i < j < k < m \leq n$.

∴ **Proposition *P5* is true**.

The auditor A requires the shadow hash chain to be generated sequentially, and does not allow the user U to selectively hide any proof from within a sequence. The chain requires all the proofs or the encrypted proofs to be presented to the auditor A.

∴ **Propositions *P6, P7* are false**.

Given that *P1* is true, and *P6, P7* are false, the user U proving (L_i) $\rightarrow$ (L_{i+r}) requires to present r items for verification.

∴ **Proposition *P8* is false.**

As an extension to shadow hash chains, we can apply the block based approach to the shadow hash chain scheme, as shown in block hash chains. In this case, we will use the initialization vector V_k for each block k of the hash chain, as well as the encrypted hash chain. Therefore, we are able to achieve the complexity of computation less than *O(n)*.

Proposition *P8* is true for blocks, ∵ already true in Proof 2.

Proof 4a: ***Shadow Hash Chain*** *holds the following truth values for the propositions* $P1, P2, P3, P4, P5, \neg P6, \neg P7, \neg P8$.

Proof 4b: ***Block Shadow Hash Chain*** *holds the following truth values for the propositions* $P1, P2, P3, P4, P5, \neg P6, \neg P7, P8$.

3.2.5 Multi-Link Hash Chain

In our scheme for multi-link hash chains, we use two-link (or more) hashing for each proof in the provenance chain C.

For including Proof(L_i) in the hash chain, we use the hash function *hf(x)*, and $x = Proof(L_i) + V_i + V_{i+s-1}$, where $0 \leq i \leq s-1$, and s is the link size. For including Proof(L_i), where $s \leq i \leq n$, we use the hash function *hf(x)*, and $x = Proof(L_i) + hf(Proof(L_{i-1})) + hf(Proof(L_{i-s}))$. The other properties and operations are the same as hash chains.

Proposition *P1, P2* is true, ∵ already true in Proof 1.

If user U wants to prove $(L_i) \rightarrow (L_{i+m})$ to auditor A, where $m \leq s$, the convenience and derivability remains the same as in hash chains. When $m \leq s$, user U presents the following to the auditor A: (i) Proof(L_i) and Proof(L_{i+m}), (ii) immediately preceding hash values $hf(Proof(L_{i-1}))$, $hf(Proof(L_{i+m-1}))$, (iii) the linker hash value for i^{th} position $hf(Proof(L_{i-s}))$, and (iv) the linker hash values for $(i+m)^{th}$ position $hf(Proof(L_{(q*r)-s}))$, and the proofs Proof(L_{q*r})), where $q = ((i+m)\%s)$, and *r* is the number of leaps of size s, from $i \rightarrow (i+m)$.

Example: *User U wants to prove* $(L_6) \rightarrow (L_{13})$ *to an auditor A.*

For proving $(L_6) \rightarrow (L_{13})$, let us assume that the user U maintains a multi-link hash chain, with link length $s = 5$, and presents the following items to the auditor for verification of the claim:

Proofs: Proof(L_6), Proof(L_7), Proof(L_8), and Proof(L_{13}).

Hash values:$hf(Proof(L_1)), hf(Proof(L_2)), hf(Proof(L_3)), hf(Proof(L_5))$, and $hf(Proof(L_{12}))$.

For verification, the auditor A calculates $hf(Proof(L_6))$ using Proof(L_6), $hf(Proof(L_5))$, and $hf(Proof(L_1))$. The auditor then calculates $hf(Proof(L_7))$ using Proof(L_7), $hf(Proof(L_2))$, and the previously calculated $hf(Proof(L_6))$. Next, the hash $hf(Proof(L_8))$ is calculated using Proof(L_8), $hf(Proof(L_3))$, and the previously calculated $hf(Proof(L_7))$. Finally, the auditor calculates $hf(Proof(L_{13}))$ using Proof(L_{13}), $hf(Proof(L_{12}))$, and the previously calculated $hf(Proof(L_8))$.

∴ **Proposition *P3* is true.**

Proposition *P4* is true, ∵ already true in Proof 1.

Propositions *P5, P6, P7* are false, ∵ already false in Proof 2.

As shown in the example, for proving $(L_i) \rightarrow (L_{i+m})$, the user U presents a subset of the proofs from the range $i \rightarrow (i+m)$.

∴ **Proposition *P8* is true.**

Proof 5: ***Multi-Link Hash Chain*** *holds the following truth values for the propositions* $P1, P2, P3, P4, \neg P5, \neg P6, \neg P7, P8$.

3.2.6 RSA Chaining

We use RSA accumulators to design our RSA chains for location provenance. For every RSA provenance chain, we require private values P and Q, which are large prime numbers. The first public value is N, where N = P*Q, and the second public value is a large random number which is the initial seed R.

An accumulator C_i for the RSA chain is created using the function *FuncRSACreate()*, such that $C_i \in \forall_i$*FuncRSACreate(x)*. Here, *x*=[$R^{hf(Proof(L_i))}$ % N], for i=0; and *x*=[$C_{i-1}^{H(Proof(L_i))}$ % N], for $(i \in \Re) \wedge (i > 0)$, and $hf(Proof(L_i))$ is the numerical hash value for Proof(L_i).

∴ **Proposition *P1* is true.**

Given *P1* is true, C_i is created for the Proof(L_i) at time t_i. Therefore, it implies that either it is the first location proof, for which we have the initial public seed R, which is the trivial case. Otherwise, we know that C_{i-1} was created at t_{i-1}, in which case $t_{i-1} < t_i$, that is $t_{i-1} + \delta t = t$.

∴ **Proposition *P2* is true.**

The user U wants to prove the location provenance $L_i \rightarrow L_{i+m}$. He presents the auditor A the following items: (i) the RSA chain accumulators C_i and C_{i+m}, (ii) the hash values $hf(Proof(L_r))$, where $(i-1) \leq r \leq (i+m)$, (iii) the proofs Proof(L_i) and Proof(L_{i+m}), and (iv) the public value N. The auditor A uses the presented items to create C_{i+m} from C_i, and compares the validity with the one presented by the user U.

∴ **Proposition *P3* is true.**

At time *t*, user U possesses the RSA chain accumulators C_k, where $0 \leq k \leq t$. The tampered accumulators C_i^T and C_j^T are presented to the auditor A by the user U, which correspond to the locations L_i and L_j, and $i < j$. However, the auditor only accepts the claim of location provenance if and only if the sequential derivation of the accumulator from C_i^T to C_j^T is successful. Additionally, the hash values for $hf(Proof(L_r))$, where $(i-1) \leq r \leq (j)$, are signed by the trusted provenance authority, need to be validated as well.

∴ **Proposition *P4* is true.**

The auditor A verifies the location provenance using the hash values for all proofs, the RSA chain accumulators, and the visible proofs for only the intended items. The user U never presents anything which is not intended to be revealed to the auditor A.

∴ **Proposition *P5* is true.**

User U intends on proving the location provenance $L_{i-1} \rightarrow L_i \rightarrow L_{i+1}$, without revealing location L_i. He presents the hashes $hf(Proof(L_{i-1}))$, $hf(Proof(L_i))$, and $hf(Proof(L_{i+1}))$, and the plain text proofs Proof(L_{i-1}) and Proof(L_{i+1}).

∴ **Proposition *P6* is false.**

However, no information apart from the hash regarding L_i is exposed, which is a one-way function, and does not effect the privacy. As a result, the user U is able to prove $L_{i-1} \rightarrow (?) \rightarrow L_{i+1}$.

∴ **Proposition *P7* is true.**

For verifying $L_i \rightarrow L_{i+m}$, the auditor A requires all the hash values of proofs $hf(Proof(L_r))$, where $(i-1) \leq r \leq (i+m)$.

∴ **Proposition *P8* is false.**

Proof 6: ***Multi-Link Hash Chain*** *holds the following truth values for the propositions* $P1, P2, P3, P4, P5, P6, P7, \neg P8$.

4. EVALUATION

In this section, we present the performance analysis of the proposed schemes based on storage and time requirement for different operations on provenance chain.

4.1 Experimental Setup

Location proof database: Since we have not found any database containing location proofs directly, we have modified the Foursquare database [12] for our purpose. Foursquare database contains 2073740 check-ins of 18107 users from March 2010 to January 2013. Each entry of this database contains user ID, latitude, longitude, time, and location ID. We concatenate all the fields and hash the concatenation using MD5 hash algorithm generating a 32 byte string, which we use as a location proof entry.

Criteria: We have evaluated the performance of each of the schemes based on the following common operations done on location proofs.

- *Provenance generation time:* This refers to the time required to generate provenance information from the location proofs and insert them in the provenance chain. To evaluate the performance of the schemes, we generate provenance for different number of proofs e.g. 500, 1000, etc. and measure their respective timing requirement.

- *Sequential chain verification time:* This is the time required to verify all the location proofs in the provenance chain in sequential manner.

- *Sparse chain verification time:* This is the time required to verify the sequence (who comes first) of any two randomly selected location proofs of the provenance chain. We have termed the first proof as the source proof and the second proof as the destination proof in the rest of the paper. It should be noted that, the sparse verification time increases with the increase of the gap between these randomly selected proofs. This issue creates a problem since for one scheme, the gap between random selections might be too small compared to other schemes and thus creating drastic difference in the performance. In order to handle this scenario, we have always picked proofs with fixed gap size for all the schemes. For example, we have measured the sparse verification time for the 1st and 100th proof, 1st and 200th proof and so on for all the schemes.

System configuration: We implemented the schemes on a Dell laptop, running Debian 3.2.46-1 on Intel Core 2 Duo CPU (6MB Cache, 2.66GHz) with 4GB of RAM. All of the schemes are developed on OpenJDK (version:1.6.0_27). We used SHA-2 (SHA-256) hash function for hashing and RSA (1024 bit) for encryption.

4.2 Block Hash Chain

Figure 1 presents the performance analysis of block hash chain scheme for different block sizes.

Provenance Generation Time: From Figure 1a, we notice that the provenance generation time increases linearly with the increase in number of proofs, and performance increases with the increase in block size. For smaller block size, we will have more number of blocks, i.e., we need to maintain a longer chain of initialization vectors (V) for smaller block size. Hence, for bigger block size, we get better performance for provenance generation.

Sequential Verification Time: Figure 1b shows the time requirement for sequential chain verification. We notice that, the verification time increases linearly with the number of proofs irrespective of the block size. Moreover, the graph shows that the timing requirements vary a little with the increased block size. For sequential verification, we need to verify the provenance of each proof in relation with its previous proof inside the same block. The provenance information of the first element of a block is verified using the initialization vector of that block. Hence, for the first element of a block, we do not need to retrieve the hash chain of its previous element. Retrieving initialization vector of a block is slightly faster than retrieving the hash chain of the previous element. For this reason, we get slightly better performance for smaller blocks.

Sparse Verification Time: Figure 1c presents the performance analysis of verifying two provenance entries, where the location proofs are separated by varying distances. In block hash chain scheme, first we need to verify the presence of the selected proofs in their respective blocks. Once the blocks are identified, we need to check whether the initialization vector of the source proof (V_s) comes before that of the destination proof (V_d). In order to do so, we traverse through the provenance chain of the initialization vectors starting with V_s and try to reach V_d. We get better performance for larger block size since it ensures shorter length for the provenance chain of initialization vectors.

Space Requirement: Provenance information is stored as a signature of location authority on the hash. Hence, for each provenance information, we require 128 bytes (for RSA 1024). As we are maintaining two provenance chains (location proofs and initialization vectors), *N* number of proofs require N*128 + (N/Block Size)*128 bytes. The space requirement is for one proof is therefore:

$$128 * (1 + 1/BlockSize) \qquad (1)$$

According to equation 1, space requirement for block size 5, 25, and 50 are 153.6, 133.12, and 130.56 bytes respectively.

4.3 Bloom Filter

Figure 2 presents the performance analysis of Bloom filter based scheme for two different filter sizes: 1000 and 2000 byte.

Provenance Generation Time: From Figure 2a, we notice that the provenance generation time increases linearly with the increase in number of proofs. We can generate approximately 12 provenance entries per second using 1000 byte Bloom filter. Whereas, using 2000 byte Bloom filter, we can generate roughly 3 provenance entries per second. However, the smaller sized Bloom filter suffers from higher false positive probability. For example, 1000 byte Bloom filter generates 2% false positive results considering 1000 proofs. Whereas, using 2000 byte Bloom filter, we can reduce the false positive probability to 0.04% for the same number of proofs [5].

Sequential Verification Time: Figure 2b shows the time requirement for sequential chain verification. We notice that, for both the Bloom filters, time increases linearly with the number of proofs. Using 1000 byte Bloom filter, we can verify a provenance chain of length ≈ 3758 in one second and for the 2000 byte Bloom, the corresponding chain length is approximately 2685. The difference in sequential verification timing requirement, for the different sized Bloom filters, is significantly less compared to that of provenance generation.

Sparse Verification Time: Figure 2c presents the performance analysis of sparse verification for two different sized Bloom filters. Both the Bloom filters take nearly constant time for this verification. The reason is that, we always need to run only one subset checking operation for the two provenance entries. Because of the larger bit array, we get slightly higher time for the larger Bloom filter.

Space Requirement: As location authority will sign the Bloom filter and we preserve only the signature, Bloom Filter scheme requires 128 bytes (for RSA 1024) to preserve the provenance of one proof. Noticeably, the storage requirement does not change with the size of the Bloom filter.

4.4 Multi-Link Hash Chain

Figure 3 presents the performance analysis of multi-link hash chain scheme for different link sizes.

Provenance Generation Time: From Figure 3a, we notice that the provenance generation time increases linearly with the increase in number of proofs for each of the link sizes. We did not get much variation in time for different sized links. we get the best performance for the link with highest size. As we need lesser linking operations for larger link size, the provenance generation time decreases with the increase in link size.

Sequential Verification Time: Figure 3b shows the time requirement for sequential chain verification. For each of the link sizes, time increases linearly with the number of proofs, and the required times are very close for different link sizes. For sequential verification, we need to verify the provenance of each proof with its previous proof and the proof with whom it is linked. As larger link size requires lesser number of links, number of operations that check the provenance with the linked proof will be reduced. Hence, higher link size gives better performance.

Sparse Verification Time: Figure 1c presents the performance analysis of sparse verification for different size of links. As we can quickly reach from the source proof to the destination proof using larger links, we observe better performance with increased link

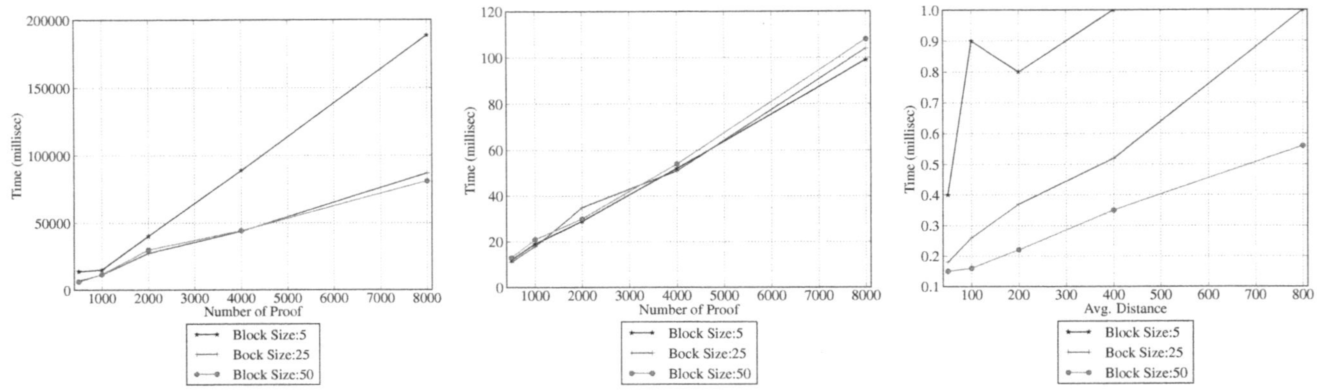

(a) Provenance Generation (b) Sequential Verification (c) Sparse Verification

Figure 1: Time Required in Different Operations for Block Hash Chain

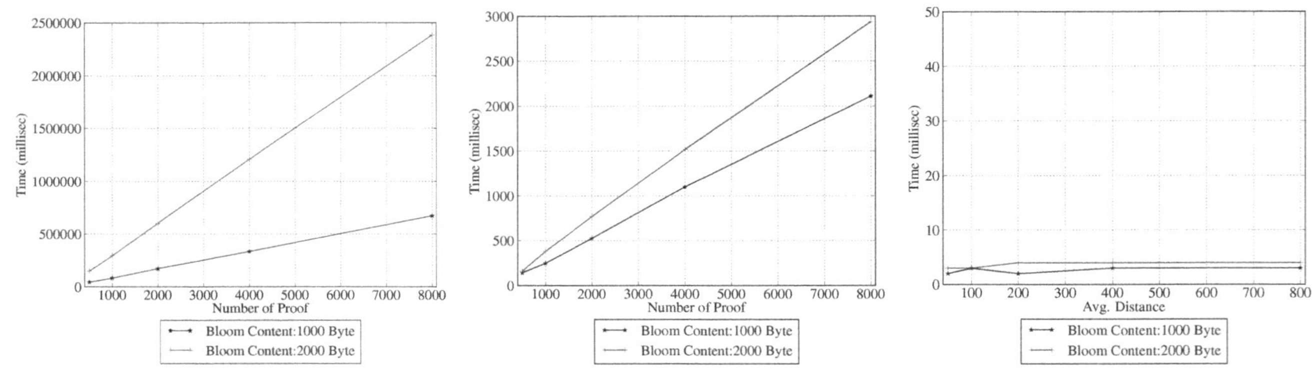

(a) Provenance Generation (b) Sequential Verification (c) Sparse Verification

Figure 2: Time Required in Different Operations for Bloom Filter

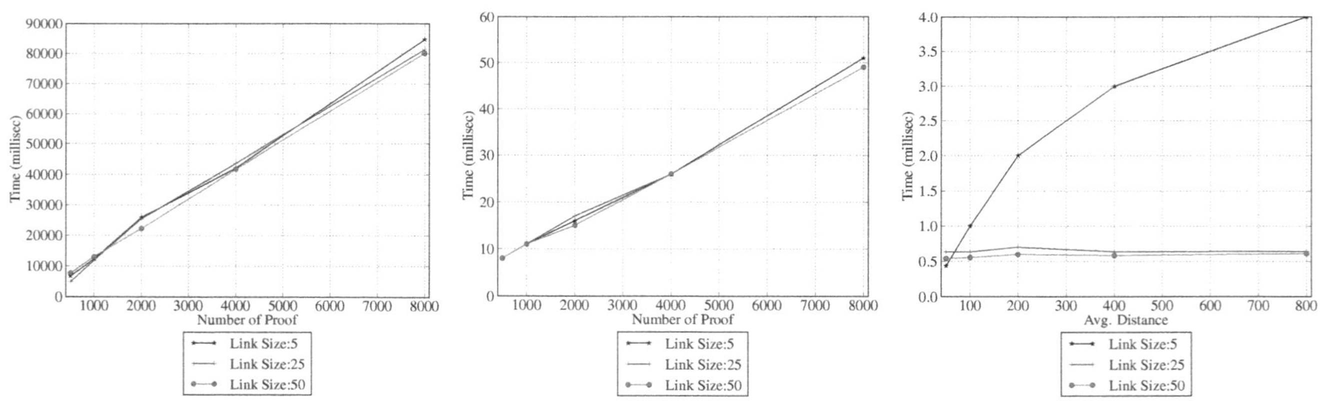

(a) Provenance Generation (b) Sequential Verification (c) Sparse Verification

Figure 3: Time Required in Different Operations for Multi-link Chain

size. However, if the distance between the source and destination proof is less than the link size, we cannot utilize the benefit of using multi-link chain. Hence, we get better performance using smaller sized links, where the distance between the source and destination proof is smaller.

Space Requirement: Space requirement does not vary with link size for this scheme, as we do not need any extra storage for the links. Location authority signs the hash value and preserves only the signature. Hence, multi-link hash chain scheme requires 128 bytes (for RSA 1024) to preserve the provenance of one proof.

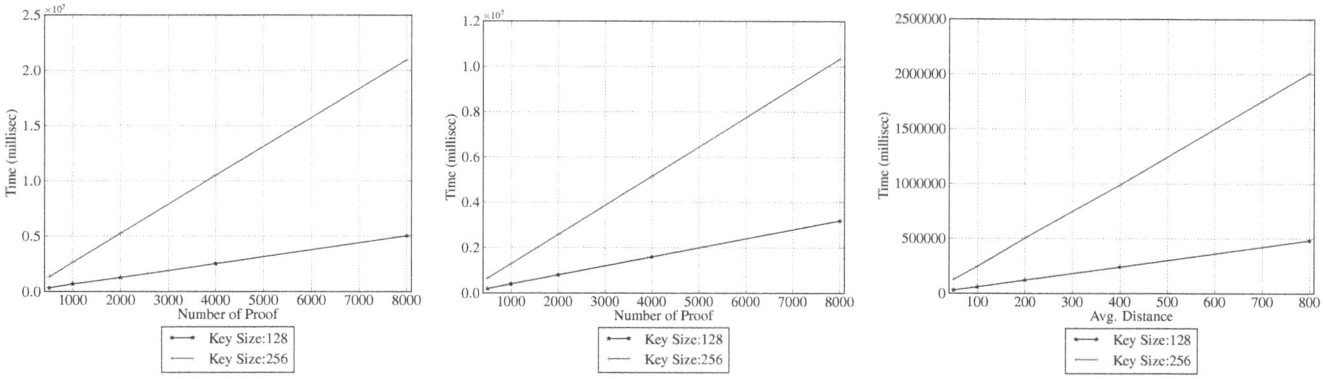

(a) Provenance Generation (b) Sequential Verification (c) Sparse Verification

Figure 4: Time Required in Different Operations for RSA Chaining

4.5 RSA Chaining

Figure 3 presents the performance analysis of RSA chaining scheme for two different sized private keys: 128 and 256 bits.

Provenance Generation Time: From Figure 4a, we notice that the provenance generation time increases linearly with the increase in number of proofs for both of the key sizes. For larger key size, the performance decreases significantly. Time to generate one provenance entry using 128 bits key is approximately 628 milliseconds. Whereas, using the 256 bits key, time required to generate one proof is about 2620 milliseconds. However, the larger the key size, the higher the security against chosen cypher-text attack.

Sequential Verification Time: Figure 4b shows the time requirement for sequential chain verification using RSA chaining scheme. For each of the key sizes, time increases linearly with the number of proofs. Time required to verify the provenance of two consecutive proofs using 128 bits key is approximately 398 milliseconds, and using 256 bits key, it is around 1290 milliseconds.

Sparse Verification Time: Figure 4c presents the performance analysis of sparse verification for different key sizes. In RSA chaining scheme, we need to traverse the whole provenance chain from the source proof to the destination proof. Hence, for RSA chaining scheme, sparse verification time increases linearly with the distance between source and destination proofs.

Space Requirement: For RSA chaining scheme, space requirement to preserve the provenance of one proof is constant. The accumulator value is signed by the location authority and stored as the provenance entry. Hence, the space requirement for RSA chaining scheme is 128 bytes (for RSA 1024).

4.6 Hash Chain and Shadow Hash Chain

As we used a fixed hash algorithm for all the schemes, there is no criteria for hash chain and shadow hash chain which can be varied to compare the performance of these schemes. Moreover, the performance of hash chain and shadow hash chain should be similar, as we actually just use two hash chains: one using regular proof, and the other using encrypted proof.

However, the space requirement is higher in shadow hash chain compared to hash chain. In hash chain, we require 128 bytes (for RSA 1024) for the provenance entry of one proof. In a shadow hash chain, we make two entries of the proof in the two separate chains. Therefore, in the shadow hash chain scheme, we require (2*128 + Key Size) bytes for the provenance entry of one proof.

5. DISCUSSION

To compare the performance of different schemes, we select the best performing criteria of each scheme. As discussed in Section 4, we get the best performance for block hash chain with block size 50, multi-link hash chain with link size 50, Bloom filter with filter size 1000 byte, and RSA chaining with key size 128. As the performance of shadow hash chain is similar to that of hash chain scheme, we have just included hash chain in the comparison.

However, when we tried to compare the required time for all three operations (insertion, sequential verification, and sparse verification) by all the schemes, we found that the gap between the required time by the best and worst scheme is too big to be appropriately represented in graphs. Since RSA chaining requires the highest time for each of the three operations, we chose the required time of RSA chaining as 100% and represented the time required by other schemes as a percentage of the time required by RSA chaining. For better visualization, we represented the data as the Log_{10} of the percentage of time in Figure 5. However, for sequential verification and sparse verification, the time required by other schemes is too small compared to that of RSA chaining and thus resulting in negative values as shown in Figure 5b and 5c. For sparse verification, we have randomly picked two proofs, which are apart by a distance of 136. According to four square database [12], on an average each user traverses 136 locations in one year. Hence, for duration of one year, average distance between the source and destination proof can be safely assumed to be 136.

Figure 5a presents the comparison of provenance entry generation time for one location proof by different schemes. We observe that for provenance generation, multi-link hash chain provides the best performance. Hash-chain and block hash chain provides nearly the similar performance compared to multi-link. Figure 5b compares the time to sequentially verify a provenance chain containing 136 entries. For both sequential and sparse verification, block hash chain scheme provides the best performance as shown in Figure 5b and Figure 5c. Considering the three operations, we can say that block hash chain scheme performs better than all other schemes and RSA chain requires the highest time for all the cases.

However, computational performance is not always the selection criteria for choosing a provenance scheme. We have presented the requirements of any provenance scheme in Section 2, and have proved the security propositions for the given provenance schemes in Section 3. RSA chain complies with maximum number of criteria as mentioned in Table 1. On the other hand, block hash chain

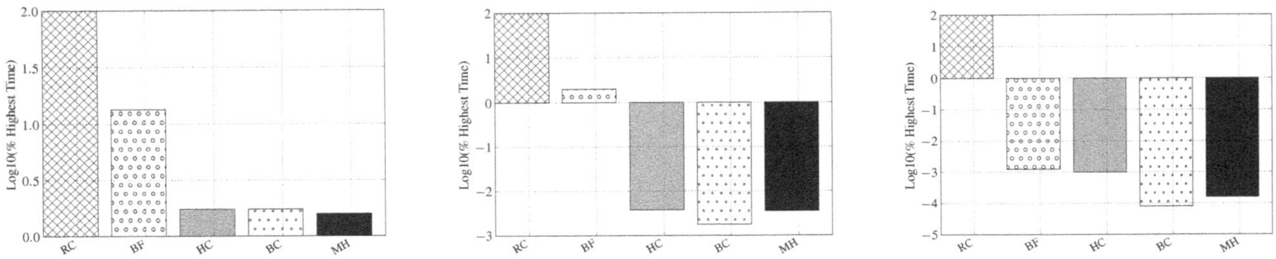

(a) Provenance Generation (b) Sequential Verification (c) Sparse Verification

Figure 5: Comparison among Different Schemes

does not comply with any privacy requirement. Hence, for sensitive applications, where users' privacy is critical, we can employ the RSA chain scheme, which gives a reasonable performance with highest privacy protection.

6. RELATED WORK

All location tracking and reporting mechanisms require a reliable and tamper proof architecture to preserve the integrity of the location data. Traditional Global Positioning Systems (GPS) [10] are effective in general purpose location reporting. However, it is not a suitable option in terms of security and indoor tracking. Recent papers have proposed a combination of GPS signals with other mechanisms, such as, cellular tower triangulations and identification of the access network channel. Gabber *et al.* [11] utilized multi-channel information to verify the location. They used the Caller-ID feature, GPS, cellular telephony, and satellite ranging, in a combined approach to determine the movement and location of user devices. Unfortunately, malicious entities can bypass such combinatorial schemes [18, 22]. Additionally, GPS signatures [9] are not useful since they are open to spoofing attacks [18]. Secure and unforgeable location proof was discussed by Waters *et al.* [28], which introduced the idea of collecting location proofs from a location manager. A secure geo-tagging service has been proposed by Lenders *et al.* [17], which allowed the verification of the location and timestamp for user-generated content. Zhu *et al.* proposed APPLAUS, a collusion resistant location proof updating system [30]. The collusion resistance is ensured using betweenness ranking-based and correlation clustering-based approaches. Wang *et al.* proposed STAMP, a similar approach for providing spatial-temporal provenance assurance for mobile users [27]. But none of these schemes consider preserving secure location provenance. Without secure location history, discrete location proofs cannot be used in real-life scenario.

However, provenance has been explored in diverse areas of computer science. Provenance has been proposed for file system [21], database system [4, 6, 29], grid and distributed system [8, 24, 25]. Hasan et al. first introduced secure data provenance [14] and later they proposed a solution to ensure secure data provenance [15]. However, these schemes do not provide solution for secure location provenance.

Ananthanarayanan et al. discussed a framework for collecting and storing sequence of user locations [1]. In their StarTrack system, sequence of a user's location and time entries are stored in tracks which can later be shared, compared, clustered, and queried. While tracks are similar to location provenance chains, security issues are not considered here making tracks vulnerable to attacks by malicious users. Zugenmaier et al. introduced the notion of location stamps [31] for cell phones. The stamps provide proof about the location of the user at a certain time. Based on this idea, Gonzalez-Tablas et al. developed the notion of Path-stamps [13], where the location history of the user is considered. Here, a sequence of location stamps, i.e., location proofs, is combined by creating a hash chain. The Path-stamps protocol requires each user to possess a specialized hardware that is used to authenticate the user. This requirement makes the system difficult and expensive to deploy. Path-stamps protocol does not support publication of partial path. Therefore, users must reveal their entire path to auditors even when they are proving a subset of their path. In contrast, some of our proposed schemes allow users to have privacy by enabling them to prove any arbitrary subset of their location history. Finally, Interaction-based missed connection services have been described by Manweiler et al. [20]. Here, two mutual strangers can use the SMILE protocol to establish shared knowledge, which can later be used to prove that they have met before. However, none of these works define the criteria for secure location provenance scheme or measure the performance based on the required characteristics. In our work, we provide a complete guideline for generating secure location provenance, analyzed the performance of current schemes, and discuss their applicability.

7. CONCLUSION

As location based services become popular, collecting and securely maintaining location provenance also becomes very important. Secure generation of location proofs and their applications have the promise to revolutionize many domains, such as, in supply chains and digital forensics. In this paper, we presented OTIT, a model for formalizing the characteristics of location provenance under a single domain and map the current models based on these formal propositions. Simulated results give a clear idea about the performance of different schemes created using our model. We believe that our proposed framework can serve as a benchmarking tool for designing any secure location proof generation scheme. Currently we are working on building further schemes and a generic framework for secure and automated provenance generation. Our future work includes designing an off-the-shelf model for creating secure location provenance under a domain specific language driven definition of any arbitrary location proof generation scheme.

Acknowledgement

This research was supported by a Google Faculty Research Award and the Department of Homeland Security Grant #FA8750-12-2-0254.

References

[1] G. Ananthanarayanan, M. Haridasan, I. Mohomed, D. Terry, and C. A. Thekkath. Startrack: a framework for enabling track-based applications. In *Proceedings of the 7th international conference on Mobile systems, applications, and services*, pages 207–220. ACM, 2009.

[2] N. Barić and B. Pfitzmann. Collision-free accumulators and fail-stop signature schemes without trees. In W. Fumy, editor, *Advances in Cryptology - EUROCRYPT 1997*, volume 1233 of *Lecture Notes in Computer Science*, pages 480–494. Springer Berlin Heidelberg, 1997.

[3] J. Benaloh and M. Mare. One-way accumulators: A decentralized alternative to digital signatures. In T. Helleseth, editor, *Advances in Cryptology - EUROCRYPT 1993*, volume 765 of *Lecture Notes in Computer Science*, pages 274–285. Springer Berlin Heidelberg, 1994.

[4] D. Bhagwat, L. Chiticariu, W.-C. Tan, and G. Vijayvargiya. An annotation management system for relational databases. *The VLDB Journal*, 14:373–396, 2005.

[5] B. H. Bloom. Space/time trade-offs in hash coding with allowable errors. *Communication of the ACM*, 13(7):422–426, 1970.

[6] P. Buneman, S. Khanna, and T. Wang-Chiew. Why and where: A characterization of data provenance. In J. Bussche and V. Vianu, editors, *Database Theory ? ICDT 2001*, volume 1973 of *Lecture Notes in Computer Science*, pages 316–330. Springer Berlin Heidelberg, 2001.

[7] J. Camenisch and A. Lysyanskaya. Dynamic accumulators and application to efficient revocation of anonymous credentials. In M. Yung, editor, *Advances in Cryptology - CRYPTO 2002*, volume 2442 of *Lecture Notes in Computer Science*, pages 61–76. Springer Berlin Heidelberg, 2002.

[8] D. Crawl and I. Altintas. A provenance-based fault tolerance mechanism for scientific workflows. In J. Freire, D. Koop, and L. Moreau, editors, *Provenance and Annotation of Data and Processes*, volume 5272 of *Lecture Notes in Computer Science*, pages 152–159. Springer Berlin Heidelberg, 2008.

[9] D. E. Denning and P. F. MacDoran. Location-based authentication: Grounding cyberspace for better security. *Computer Fraud & Security*, 1996(2):12–16, 1996.

[10] P. Enge and P. Misra. Special issue on global positioning system. *Proceedings of the IEEE*, 87(1):3 –15, jan. 1999.

[11] E. Gabber and A. Wool. How to prove where you are: tracking the location of customer equipment. In *Proceedings of the 5th ACM conference on Computer and communications security (CCS)*, pages 142–149. ACM, 1998.

[12] H. Gao, J. Tang, and H. Liu. Exploring social-historical ties on location-based social networks. In *Proceedings of the 6th International AAAI Conference on Weblogs and Social Media*, 2012.

[13] A. I. González-Tablas, B. Ramos, and A. Ribagorda. Path-stamps: A proposal for enhancing security of location tracking applications. In *Ubiquitous Mobile Information and Collaboration Systems Workshop*. Citeseer, 2003.

[14] R. Hasan, R. Sion, and M. Winslett. Introducing secure provenance: problems and challenges. In *Proceedings of ACM StorageSS*, pages 13–18, 2007.

[15] R. Hasan, R. Sion, and M. Winslett. The case of the fake Picasso: Preventing history forgery with secure provenance. In *Proceedings of the 7th USENIX Conference on File and Storage Technologies (FASTŠ09)*, pages 1–12. USENIX Association, 2009.

[16] R. Khan, M. M. Haque, and R. Hasan. A secure location proof generation scheme for supply chain integrity preservation. In *Proceedings of The 2013 IEEE International Conference on Technologies for Homeland Security*, HST '13, pages 446–450, Waltham, MA, USA, 2013.

[17] V. Lenders, E. Koukoumidis, P. Zhang, and M. Martonosi. Location-based trust for mobile user-generated content: applications, challenges and implementations. In *Proceedings of HotMobile*, pages 60–64. ACM, 2008.

[18] W. Luo and U. Hengartner. Proving your location without giving up your privacy. In *Proceedings of HotMobile*, pages 7–12, 2010.

[19] I. Maduako. Wanna hack a drone? possible with geo-location spoofing! Online at `http://geoawesomeness.com/?p=893`, 26th July 2012.

[20] J. Manweiler, R. Scudellari, and L. P. Cox. SMILE: encounter-based trust for mobile social services. In *CCS '09: Proceedings of the 16th ACM conference on Computer and communications security*, pages 246–255. ACM, 2009.

[21] K. Muniswamy-Reddy, D. Holland, U. Braun, and M. Seltzer. Provenance-aware storage systems. In *Proceedings of the 2006 USENIX Annual Technical Conference*, pages 43–56, 2006.

[22] S. Saroiu and A. Wolman. Enabling new mobile applications with location proofs. In *Proceedings of HotMobile*, pages 1–6, 2009.

[23] Y. L. Simmhan, B. Plale, and D. Gannon. A survey of data provenance in e-science. *SIGMOD Rec.*, 34(3):31–36, September 2005.

[24] I. Souilah, A. Francalanza, and V. Sassone. A formal model of provenance in distributed systems. *TAPP*, 9:1–11, 2009.

[25] P. Townend, P. Groth, and J. Xu. A provenance-aware weighted fault tolerance scheme for service-based applications. In *Object-Oriented Real-Time Distributed Computing, 2005. ISORC 2005. Eighth IEEE International Symposium on*, pages 258 – 266, may 2005.

[26] J. VanGrove. Foursquare cracks down on cheaters. Online at `http://mashable.com/2010/04/07/foursquare-cheaters/`, April 2010.

[27] X. Wang, J. Zhu, A. Pande, A. Raghuramu, P. Mohapatra, T. Abdelzaher, and R. Ganti. STAMP: Ad Hoc Spatial-Temporal Provenance Assurance for Mobile Users. In *Proceedings of The 21st IEEE International Conference on Network Protocols*, ICNP '13, Gottingen, Germany, October 2013.

[28] B. R. Waters and E. W. Felten. Secure, private proofs of location. Technical report TR-667-03, Princeton University, January 2003.

[29] J. Widom. Trio: A system for integrated management of data, accuracy, and lineage. Technical Report 2004-40, Stanford InfoLab, August 2004.

[30] Z. Zhu and G. Cao. Toward privacy preserving and collusion resistance in a location proof updating system. *IEEE Transactions on Mobile Computing*, 12(1):51–64, 2013.

[31] A. Zugenmaier, M. Kreutzer, and M. Kabatnik. Enhancing applications with approved location stamps. In *Proceedings of IEEE Intelligent Network Workshop, 2001*, page 140. IEEE, 2001.

Privacy-Preserving Distance Computation and Proximity Testing on Earth, Done Right

Jaroslav Šeděnka*
Dept. of Mathematics and Statistics
Masaryk University
Kotlářská 2, 61137 Brno, Czech Republic
sedenka@mail.muni.cz

Paolo Gasti
School of Engineering and Computing Sciences
New York Institute of Technology
1855 Broadway, New York, NY 10023, USA
pgasti@nyit.edu

ABSTRACT

In recent years, the availability of GPS-enabled smartphones have made location-based services extremely popular. A multitude of applications rely on location information to provide a wide range of services. Location information is, however, extremely sensitive and can be easily abused. In this paper, we introduce the first protocols for secure *computation of distance* and for *proximity testing* over a sphere. Our *secure distance* protocols allow two parties, Alice and Bob, to determine their mutual distance without disclosing any additional information about their location. Through our *secure proximity testing* protocols, Alice only learns if Bob is in close proximity, i.e., within some arbitrary distance.

Our techniques rely on three different representations of Earth, which provide different trade-offs between accuracy and performance. We show, via experiments on a prototype implementation, that our protocols are practical on resource-constrained smartphone devices. Our distance computation protocols runs, in fact, in 54 to 78 ms on a commodity Android smartphone. Similarly, our proximity tests require between 1.2 s and 2.8 s on the same platform. The imprecision introduced by our protocols is very small, i.e., between 0.1% and 3% on average, depending on the distance.

Categories and Subject Descriptors

K.4.1 [COMPUTERS AND SOCIETY]: Public Policy Issues—*Privacy*; E.3 [DATA ENCRYPTION]

1. INTRODUCTION

Since the introduction of the first popular GPS-enabled smartphones, location-aware services have been growing in popularity. Users have now access to a wide array of location-based applications, including social networks [21], directories of restaurants and hotels [49, 44], taxi pick-up schedulers [5], on-line publishing of geo-tagged photos and videos [11], local deals [17], lost/stolen phone locators [20], and "friend finders" [16, 1, 4, 34].

These services often raise severe privacy concerns. By disclosing location data to third parties (e.g., application developers, cellphone manufacturers, friends), user can be easily tracked, usually against their will. Although most users might be comfortable with (or unaware of) being tracked by cellphone carriers, they may be more reluctant to share location information with third parties of unknown reputation. The dangers of incautious location sharing have been shown to be very real with documented cases of location data being actively used by stalkers [47]. Privacy is not only an issue for the party disclosing its location: service providers may, in fact, be unwilling to learn the whereabouts of their users, for fear of bad press and lawsuits [46].

As of today, revealing location information is, in practice, an all-or-nothing proposition. Mobile devices usually implement coarse-grained "privacy settings", that allow users to turn off location services for specific applications – often preventing location-based applications from working at all.

In recent years, researchers have investigated a suitable middle ground between *full disclosure* and *no disclosure* of location information. This effort has resulted in the introduction of various techniques such as location cloaking [30], noisy distance computation [18], and privacy-preserving distance [36] and proximity protocols [50]. However, existing approaches either provide privacy at the expense of accuracy, or rely on assumptions that restricts their usefulness. In particular, cloaking and noisy techniques introduce artificial "measurement errors" in the original location, perturbing the result of the distance computation. Existing protocols for computing distances in the encrypted domain, on the other hand, offer accurate results only over small distances, since they work on either coarse approximations of Earth, or on small projections of Earth on Euclidean planes. When multiple small projections are used, parties must privately determine if their respective coordinates fall within the same projection. If they do not, and the protocols do not account for it, distance computation will return meaningless results. Finally, existing work does not address the problem of defining a suitable projection for distance computation. This makes comparison of accuracy between existing techniques difficult, since the choice of the projection affects the performance of the protocols.

Contributions. In this paper we introduce novel privacy-preserving protocols for reliably computing distances and

*Part of this work was done while visiting the New York Institute of Technology

ASIA CCS'14, June 4–6, 2014, Kyoto, Japan.
Copyright 2014 ACM 978-1-4503-2800-5/14/06 ...$15.00.
http://dx.doi.org/10.1145/2590296.2590307.

proximity between two arbitrary points on Earth. With our protocols, the two parties – henceforth, "Alice" and "Bob" – are not required to disclose their location. However, at the end of our distance protocols, Alice learns how far she is located from Bob, while Bob learns nothing.

Using our *secure proximity testing* protocols, Alice only learns whether Bob is within a certain distance. Moreover, Bob can return an *unconditional positive* (i.e., the distance between Alice and Bob always appear to be smaller than the threshold) or *unconditional negative* (the distance between Alice and Bob is always larger than the threshold) response to proximity queries from Alice, in order to provide him with an extra layer of privacy.

An important difference between two of our protocols and the current state of the art is the ability of our protocols to accurately compute distance between two parties located in arbitrary locations on earth. To achieve this, the two protocols do not make use of projections of small parts of Earth's surface.

Our Protocols. The first protocol, **PP-UTM**, is a concrete instantiation of Euclidean distance over a projection of Earth. The projection we use, called UTM, maps Earth over set of planes. As discussed in Section 3, this technique provides accurate results if the two parties are located within the same UTM zone. For this reason, we consider this protocol as a *baseline* for assessing the performance of our contribution. To the best of our knowledge, this is the first instantiation of an Euclidean-distance-based privacy-preserving protocol that considers a real projection. This, in turn, allows us to evaluate, for the first time, the real-world error introduced by a privacy-preserving distance computation protocol and secure proximity testing protocol.

The second protocol, **PP-ECEF**, allows Alice to calculate distances in the Earth-Centered, Earth-Fixed (ECEF, also known as Earth Centered Rotational, or ECR) coordinate system. This protocol provides very accurate results (less than 0.1% error) when the two parties are within 14,000 km (roughly 8,700 miles), and reasonably accurate results (less than 1% error) for greater distances.

Our third protocol, **PP-HS**, is based on the haversine formula [42], which is a trigonometric formula used to compute distances on a sphere. Although slightly less efficient than the previous two protocols, PP-HS is very accurate regardless of the position of Alice and Bob. The protocol introduces very small error (below 0.1%) when the two parties are more than 14,000 km apart.

Organization. The rest of the paper is organized as follows. In Section 2 we review the related literature. Section 3 discusses several techniques for computing distances on various approximations of Earth. In Section 4 we introduce our security model and the cryptographic tools used in our protocols. Section 5 presents our protocols for privacy-preserving distance computation. We provide a security analysis of the protocols in Section 6, and evaluate accuracy and performance in Section 7. We conclude in Section 8.

2. RELATED WORK

Related work on location privacy can be divided in three classes: (1) work that aims at quantifying location privacy (or lack thereof); (2) techniques that anonymize user location information, and possibly add location obfuscation; and (3) privacy-preserving protocols based on secure multiparty computation (SMC).

Quantifying Location Privacy. In [40] Shokri et al. develop a formal framework for the analysis of location-privacy protection mechanisms. This framework captures adversary's prior information, and models various attacks. They introduce metrics for attacker's performance, such as *accuracy*, *certainty* and *success*.

Shokri et al. [41] classify location exposure into *continuous* (i.e., the adversary can track users over time and space) and *sporadic* (the adversary's focus is on localizing users data specific point in time). Their work addresses the case of sporadic location exposure, formalizing location privacy. In their framework, the authors also perform localization attacks using Bayesian inference for Hidden Markov Processes on anonymized traces.

Location Anonymization and Obfuscation. Gruteser et al. [18] design a middleware architecture, used by a location broker service to anonymize user locations and still allow them to receive the intended service. This technique provide a median resolution of 125 meters, and does not protect users' privacy against the location broker. Several papers have followed the work of Grueteser et al. (see, e.g., [2, 24, 32, 39]).

Duckham et at. [9] introduced a formal model for location obfuscation techniques. The authors argue that location inaccuracy (lack of correspondence between information and reality), imprecision (lack of specificity of information), and vagueness (existence of boundary cases in information) provide an feasible way for implementing location privacy. In particular, they argue that their model provides a generic mechanism for balancing quality of information with privacy.

Krumm's work [30] shows that spatial cloaking, Gaussian noise and reduced location resolution can degrade the identification success of the adversary. Gruteser et al. [18] use k-anonymity, implemented via spatial and temporal cloaking, to increase the adversary's uncertainty.

In general, techniques belonging to this class provide only limited accuracy. Moreover, as has been shown by Golle et at. [15], Beresford et al. [2], Hoh et al. [19] and many others, the highly identifying nature of location information often makes proper anonymization difficult, if not impossible. This makes location anonymization not suitable for a large array of location-based services, including social networks.

Privacy-Preserving Protocols. More related to our work, there has been a large amount of research on SMC protocols for privacy-preserving proximity testing and privacy-preserving distance computation between two points or a point and a curve.

Zhong et al. [50] introduced Louis, Lester and Pierre, three privacy-preserving protocols for proximity testing. The Louis protocol requires a semi-trusted third party that does not learn any location information. Lester, the second protocol, does not require a third party, but one of the participants might learn the location of the other even if they are no longer close. Finally, the Pierre protocol provides better security, at the cost of reduced accuracy.

Narayanan et al. [36] show how to reduce proximity testing to equality testing. Their approach is based on dividing the Euclidean space into a grid system; the position of each user is defined as a set of adjacent triangles on the grid. If two users are within a certain range, they must share at least one grid component. Proximity is therefore computed through a simple and efficient privacy-preserving protocol. The authors extend the protocol to work on Earth by slicing it into thin one-degree strips. This instantiation of their technique introduces three classes of error: (1) even though the strips are relatively thin, the curvature of Earth still leads to errors for points at different latitudes; (2) grids from different strips do not align at the strip boundary, and therefore the parties must belong to the same strip for best accuracy; and (3) since the basic unit for the tessellation is a triangle, the perimeter of an area which represent the user location is not a circle, and therefore there may be false positives or false negatives across the boundaries of a user's zone. Classes (1) and (2) limit the applicability of this approach to relatively small distances.

Mascetti et al. [33] present *Longitude*, a privacy-aware centralized technique for determining the distance of two points. The proposed protocol implements Euclidean distance, and the result is obliviously compared with a threshold. This way, one of the parties only learns whether the other protocol participant's input is within a certain distance.

Li et al. [26] design a suite of privacy-preserving protocols that allows two parties to share information about their location with fine-grained access control. Users can specify a condition and match all users that satisfy such condition. Alternatively, their protocols rely on attribute-based encryption and homomorphic encryption.

To the best of our knowledge, [36] is the only work that addresses distances in a non-Euclidean space. However, the authors do not discuss how mapping a grid on a curved surfaces affects the accuracy of the protocol.

3. DISTANCE COMPUTATION BETWEEN TWO POINTS ON EARTH

Although Earth is usually considered a sphere, its shape is closer to an *oblate spheroid*, or *ellipsoid* [43]. The exact shape, called *geoid*, is defined as the global mean sea level. However, for simplicity and efficiency, geodetic computations are usually performed over an approximation of Earth's shape – a sphere or one of the various standard ellipsoids. In this paper, we consider the spherical approximation with radius 6,371 km (which is the radius for a sphere with the same surface area as the Earth's ellipsoid) and the World Geodetic System 84 (WGS84).

The WGS84 geoid is used in the Global Positioning System (GPS), and is thus a major source of coordinates available today. As this paper focuses mainly on location privacy, and not on geodesy, we refer the reader to [43] for proper treatment of this topic and introduce only the required notion below.

The position of any point on Earth can be described as *geodesic data* based on different reference system. A datum in WGS84 consists of two angles, expressed in degrees, denoted *latitude* and *longitude*. Latitude describes the north-south position of a point as the angle between the equatorial plane (i.e., the plane that intersects Earth through the equator) and the line between the point and Earth's center. The value of latitude is between $-90°$ (South pole) and $90°$ (North pole). Longitude describes the east-west position of a point as the angle between the plane containing the Prime Meridian and the line between the point and the Earth's center. The Prime

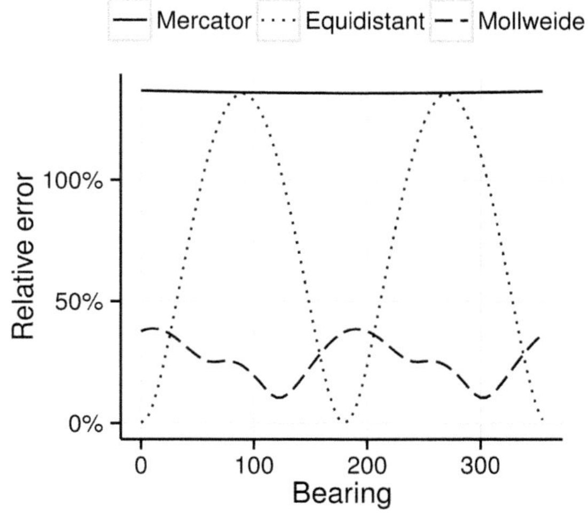

Figure 1: Average distance measurement error over the Mercator, Equidistant Cylindrical and Mollweide projections. One party is located at a random location with latitude 65°, while the other is 10 km away, at different bearings.

Meridian has longitude $0°$, the values range from $-180°$ to $180°$ with negative values to the west of Prime Meridian.

The shortest path between two points on a sphere or an ellipsoid is along the *great circle*, i.e., the intersection between a sphere and a plane which passes through the center of the sphere. When viewed on a projection, the shortest distance may appear as a curve – this is why the airplanes trajectories usually appear as arcs on in-flight maps. Distance between two points on the Earth ellipsoid can be computed using Vincenty's formula [45], or Karney's algorithm [27]. The error introduced be these techniques is less than 1 mm [45] and 15 nm [27] respectively.

Faster – although less accurate – methods for distance computation exist. We describe three of these methods next.

3.1 Distances over UTM Projection

A straightforward approach to computing distances on Earth is to transform the problem into computing distances on a plane. This is done by selecting a projection (e.g., a map) of Earth's surface, or part of it. Two points are then mapped to the projection, where Euclidean distance can be computed. Although simple, this approach has at least two important drawbacks. First, two parties willing to measure their distance must agree on the same projection in order to properly map their locations. Second, and more importantly, it introduces errors.

Different projections (and projection sizes) have different properties, and lead to different distance measurement errors. Figure 1 illustrates measurement errors on the Mercator, Equidistant Cylindrical and Mollweide whole Earth projections, compared to the "exact" distance, computed over the WGS84 ellipsoid using Vincenty's formula. All three whole Earth projections introduce very high average error on the measured distance. To limit this problem, projections are usually computed from small slices of Earth, instead of the whole surface. Universal Transversal Mercator (UTM) [8] is one such projections.

UTM divides Earth's surface in 60 longitudinal areas, called *zones*. The width of each zone is 6°, with no zone covering the polar regions. Position of a point is given by the zone number and its (*northing, easting*) coordinate pair, expressed in meters. Northing of a point is the distance on the projection of the point from the equator, while easting is the distance of the point from the zone's central meridian. For navigational purposes, negative coordinates are avoided by adding large constants to northing and easting. These constants are called "false northing" (which corresponds to 10,000 km) and "false easting" (500 km). Negative values do not pose any problem for distance computation, so we ignore false northing and false easting in the rest of the paper.

Once two points $C_A = (x_A, y_A)$, $C_B = (x_B, y_B)$ have been mapped to the same UTM zone, their distance can be computed as:

$$\mathsf{D}_{\mathrm{UTM}}(C_A, C_B) = \sqrt{(x_A - x_B)^2 + (y_A - y_B)^2}$$

This approach can only be used if both points lay in the same zone. Therefore, as mentioned in Section 1, UTM distance should be considered as a baseline for accuracy and performance.

3.2 Distances over ECEF Coordinate System

The Earth-Centered Earth-Fixed coordinate system uses cartesian coordinates to describe the position of any point on Earth. Each location is described using a triplet (x, y, z), where $(0, 0, 0)$ is the center of Earth's mass (hence, Earth-Centered). All coordinates are expressed in meters.

The x, y axes lay on the plane going through the Equator, with the x axis "pointing" towards the Prime Meridian and the y axis is oriented to make the system right-handed. The z axis is oriented towards North Pole. In order to prevent coordinates on Earth to change with time, the x and y axes (and thus the whole coordinate system) rotate together with Earth (hence, Earth-Fixed). Spherical (lat, lon) coordinates from WGS84, or any other coordinate system, can be easily converted to ECEF coordinates.

Distance $\mathsf{D}_{\mathrm{ECEF}}(C_A, C_B)$ between two points $C_A = (x_A, y_A, z_A)$ and $C_B = (x_B, y_B, z_B)$ on the great circle can be computed as:

$$\begin{aligned} a &= \frac{(x_A - x_B)^2 + (y_A - y_B)^2 + (z_A - z_B)^2}{4R^2} \\ c &= 2\,\mathrm{atan}\left(\sqrt{a/(1-a)}\right) \\ d &= Rc \end{aligned}$$

where $\mathsf{D}_{\mathrm{ECEF}}(C_A, C_B) = d$.

Value a is the squared Euclidean distance between points C_A and C_B (divided by a constant) in three-dimensional space, i.e., the distance between C_A and C_B over a straight line that cuts through Earth. Therefore, in order to compute the distance on the surface, we derive the central angle c between C_A, Earth's center, and C_B. Finally, the length of the arc between the two points, represented as d, corresponds to the distance over the surface. For the angle and arc length computation, we use a spherical approximation of Earth with radius R.

3.3 Distances on a Sphere Using Haversine

According to [42], angular distance between two points (represented as (*latitude, longitude*) pairs) on a sphere has been traditionally expressed using the cosine formula. Let $C_A = (lat_A, lon_A)$ and $C_B = (lat_B, lon_B)$ denote the spherical coordinates of Alice and Bob, respectively. Distance between C_A and C_B is computed using the cosine formula as:

$$\begin{aligned} c = \cos^{-1}&(\sin(lat_A)\sin(lat_B) \\ &+ \cos(lat_A)\cos(lat_B)\cos(lon_A - lon_B)) \end{aligned}$$

where c is central angle between C_A and C_B. When used in conjunction with limited precision arithmetics (e.g., in privacy-preserving protocols, where precision affects performance), the cosine formula may introduce significant measurement error when two points are in close proximity. As an example, when Alice and Bob are one kilometer apart, both on the equator, $lon_A - lon_B \approx 0.083°$, and $\cos(lon_A - lon_B) \approx 0.9999999894$. Approximating $\cos(\alpha)$ to 8 significant digits, the resulting distance between Alice and Bob is zero.

The haversine formula [42] is often used as a replacement for the cosine formula in order to reduce measurement errors introduced by cosine of small angles. Haversine, i.e., *half the versed sine*, is defined as $\mathrm{hav}(\theta) = (1 - \cos(\theta))/2$.

Let R be the radius of Earth. The haversine formula allows us to compute the distance $\mathsf{D}_{\mathrm{HS}}(C_A, C_B)$ as follows:

$$\begin{aligned} a =& \mathrm{hav}(lat_A - lat_B) \\ &+ \cos(lat_A)\cos(lat_B)\mathrm{hav}(lon_A - lon_B) \\ c =& 2\,\mathrm{atan}\left(\sqrt{a/(1-a)}\right) \\ d =& Rc \end{aligned}$$

where $\mathsf{D}_{\mathrm{HS}}(C_A, C_B) = d$. (The meaning of a, c and d is the same as that in the ECEF formula from Section 3.2.)

Given the trigonometric identity $\mathrm{hav}(\theta) = \sin^2(\theta/2)$, we can rewrite the haversine formula in such a way that $lat_A - lat_B$ and $lon_A - lon_B$ are not used as arguments for cosine:

$$\begin{aligned} a =& \sin^2((lat_A - lat_B)/2) \\ &+ \cos(lat_A)\cos(lat_B)\sin^2((lon_A - lon_B)/2) \\ c =& 2\,\mathrm{atan}\left(\sqrt{a/(1-a)}\right) \\ d =& Rc \end{aligned}$$

Therefore, although the cosine and haversine formulas are *mathematically* identical, the latter provides better accuracy with limited machine precision when Alice and Bob are separated by a small angle.

In the rest of the paper, we use WGS84 as a reference system for (*latitude, longitude*) coordinates.

3.4 Proximity Testing

Alice may be interested in determining only if Bob is in close proximity, i.e., within an arbitrary distance ε. Clearly, Alice could compute the distance between her and Bob along Earth's surface, and then check if it is greater than ε.

For ECEF and haversine distance, however, Alice can use a simple shortcut; she can convert ε to a_ε as follows:

$$a_\epsilon = \frac{(\tan\frac{\epsilon}{2R})^2}{1 + (\tan\frac{\epsilon}{2R})^2}$$

This way, a_ε represents the threshold expressed as straight-through-Earth distance in the three-dimensional space. Since the distance between Alice and Bob is a monotonically increasing function of a, we have that $a < a_\epsilon \iff d < \varepsilon$.

4. CRYPTOGRAPHIC PRELIMINARIES

We use the term *adversary* to refer to insiders, i.e., Alice and Bob. This includes the case when one of the two parties is compromised. Outside adversaries, e.g., those who can eavesdrop on the communication channel, are not considered since their actions can be mitigated via standard network security techniques.

Our protocols are secure in the presence of semi-honest (also known as honest-but-curious or passive) participants. In this model, while participants follow prescribed protocol behavior, they might try to learn additional information beyond that obtained during normal protocol execution. Formally [13]:

DEFINITION 1. *Let P_1 and P_2 participate in protocol π that computes function $f(\mathsf{in}_1, \mathsf{in}_2) = (\mathsf{out}_1, \mathsf{out}_2)$, where in_i and out_i denote P_i's input and output, respectively. Let $\mathrm{VIEW}_\pi(P_i)$ denote the view of participant P_i during the execution of protocol π. More precisely, P_i's view is formed by its input, internal random coin tosses r_i, and messages $m_1, \ldots, m_t$ passed between the parties during protocol execution: $\mathrm{VIEW}_\pi(P_i) = (\mathsf{in}_i, r_i, m_1, \ldots, m_t)$.*

We say that protocol π is secure against semi-honest adversaries if for each party P_i there exists a probabilistic polynomial time simulator S_i such that:

$$\{S_i(\mathsf{in}_i, f_i(\mathsf{in}_1, \mathsf{in}_2))\} \stackrel{c}{\equiv} \{\mathrm{VIEW}_\pi(P_i), \mathsf{out}_i\}$$

where $\stackrel{c}{\equiv}$ denotes computationally indistinguishability.

Homomorphic Encryption. Our constructions use a semantically secure (public key) additively homomorphic encryption scheme. Let $[\![m]\!]$ indicate the encryption of message m using a homomorphic encryption scheme. (To keep notation simple, we omit specifying the public key used for encryption. All encryptions in our protocols are performed under Alice's public key.)

In an additively homomorphic encryption scheme, $[\![m_1]\!] \cdot [\![m_2]\!] = [\![m_1 + m_2]\!]$, which also implies that $[\![m]\!]^a = [\![m \cdot a]\!]$. While any encryption scheme with the above properties (such as the well known Paillier encryption scheme [37]) suffices for the purposes of this work, the construction due to Damgård et al. [7, 6] (DGK hereafter) is of particular interest here because it is fast and it produces small ciphertexts. In DGK a public key consists of (1) a (small, possibly prime) integer u that defines the plaintext space; (2) k-bit RSA modulus $N = p \cdot q$ such that p and q are $k/2$-bit primes, v_p and v_q are t-bit primes, and $uv_p|(p-1)$ and $uv_q|(q-1)$; and (3) elements $g, h \in \mathbb{Z}_N^*$ such that g has order uv_pv_q and h has order v_pv_q. Given a message $m \in \mathbb{Z}_u$, encryption is performed as $[\![m]\!] = g^m h^r \bmod N$, where $r \leftarrow \{0,1\}^{2.5t}$. We refer the reader to [7, 6] for any additional information.

Garbled circuit evaluation. Originated in Yao's work [48], garbled circuit evaluation allows two parties to securely evaluate any function represented as a boolean circuit. The basic idea is that, given a circuit composed of gates, Bob creates a garbled circuit by assigning to each wire two randomly chosen keys. Bob also encodes gate information in a way that given keys corresponding to the input wires (encoding specific inputs), the key corresponding to the output of the gate on those inputs can be recovered. Alice then evaluates the circuit using keys corresponding to inputs of both Alice and Bob (without learning anything in the process). At the end, the result of the computation can be recovered by linking the output keys to the bits which they encode.

Recent literature provides optimizations that reduce computation and communication overhead associated with circuit construction and evaluation. Kolesnikov and Schneider [29] describe an optimization that permits XOR gates to be evaluated *for free*, i.e., there is no communication overhead associated with such gates and their evaluation does no involve cryptographic functions. Pinkas et al. [38] additionally give a mechanism for reducing communication complexity of binary gates by 25%: now each gate can be specified by encoding only three outcomes of the gate instead of all four. Finally, Kolesnikov et al. [28] improve the complexity of certain commonly used operations such as addition, multiplication, comparison, etc. by reducing the number of non-XOR gates: adding two n-bit integers requires $5n$ gates, n of which are non-XOR gates; comparing two n-bit integers requires $4n$ gates, n of which are non-XOR gates; and computing the minimum of t n-bit integers (without the location of the minimum value) requires $7n(t-1)$ gates, $2n(t-1)$ of which are non-XOR gates.

With the above techniques, evaluating a non-XOR gates involves one invocation of the hash function. During garbled circuit evaluation, Alice directly obtains keys corresponding to the Bob's inputs from the Bob, and engages in the oblivious transfer (OT) protocol to obtain keys corresponding to its own input.

Oblivious Transfer. In 1-out-of-2 Oblivious Transfer, OT_1^2, one party, the sender, has as its input two strings m_0, m_1 and another party, the receiver, has as its input a bit b. At the end of the protocol, the receiver learns m_b and the sender learns nothing. Similarly, in 1-out-of-N OT the receiver obtains one of the N strings held by the sender. There is a rich body of research literature on OT, and in this chapter we use its efficient implementation from [35] as well as techniques from [22] that reduce a large number of OT protocol executions to κ of them, where κ is the security parameter.

Discretization. Because our privacy-preserving protocols are designed to work on integer values, we map each real-valued protocol input to integers according to the following formula: $\mathsf{discretize}_e(x) = \lfloor 10^e \cdot x + 0.5 \rfloor$. The e parameter controls the shift of the decimal point (the choice of appropriate values for e is discussed in Section 7). Therefore, the higher the e, the more digits after the decimal point are preserved.

5. OUR PROTOCOLS

In this section, we present our PP-UTM, PP-ECEF and PP-HS protocols. These protocols privately compute the distance between two points in the UTM, ECEF and WGS84 coordinate systems, respectively.

5.1 PP-UTM Protocol

Our PP-UTM protocol computes Euclidean distance between two points laying on the same UTM zone. (Due to this limitation, and as mentioned earlier, we consider this protocol

Input: Alice: her position, expressed as coordinates $C_A = (x_A, y_A)$ with respect to a specific UTM zone; her public/private keypair. Bob: his position, expressed as coordinates $C_B = (x_B, y_B)$ in the same zone as Alice; Alice's public key pk_A.
Output: Alice learns $\mathsf{D}_{\mathrm{UTM}}(C_A, C_B)$, defined as the Euclidean distance between C_A and C_B.
Protocol steps:
1. Alice computes $[\![x_A^2 + y_A^2]\!], [\![-2x_A]\!], [\![-2y_A]\!]$ and sends these ciphertexts to Bob.
2. Bob computes:
$$[\![a]\!] = [\![x_A^2 + y_A^2]\!] \cdot [\![-2x_A]\!]^{x_B} \cdot [\![-2y_A]\!]^{y_B} \cdot [\![x_B^2 + y_B^2]\!]$$
$$= [\![(x_A^2 + x_B^2 - 2x_A x_B) + (y_A^2 + y_B^2 - 2y_A y_B)]\!]$$
$$= [\![\mathsf{D}_{\mathrm{UTM}}(C_A, C_B)^2]\!]$$
and sends $[\![a]\!]$ back to Alice.
3. Alice decrypts $[\![a]\!]$ and outputs $\mathsf{D}_{\mathrm{UTM}}(C_A, C_B)$ as $\sqrt{a}$.

Figure 2: PP-UTM Protocol

Input: Alice: her position, expressed as coordinates $C_A = (x_A, y_A, z_A)$ in the ECEF coordinate system; her public/private keypair. Bob: his position, expressed as coordinates $C_B = (x_B, y_B, z_B)$ in the same coordinate system; Alice's public key pk_A.
Output: Alice learns $\mathsf{D}_{\mathrm{ECEF}}(C_A, C_B)$, defined as the Euclidean distance between C_A and C_B.
Protocol steps:
1. Alice computes $[\![x_A^2 + y_A^2 + z_A^2]\!], [\![-2x_A]\!], [\![-2y_A]\!], [\![-2z_A]\!]$ and sends these ciphertexts to Bob.
2. Bob computes:
$$[\![a']\!] = [\![x_A^2 + y_A^2 + z_A^2]\!] \cdot [\![-2x_A]\!]^{x_B} \cdot [\![-2y_A]\!]^{y_B} \cdot [\![x_B^2 + y_B^2 + z_B^2]\!] \cdot [\![-2z_A]\!]^{z_B}$$
$$= [\![(x_A^2 + x_B^2 - 2x_A x_B) + (y_A^2 + y_B^2 - 2y_A y_B) + (z_A^2 + z_B^2 - 2z_A z_B)]\!]$$
and sends $[\![a']\!]$ back to Alice.
3. Alice decrypts $[\![a']\!]$, computes $a = a'/4R^2$ and outputs $\mathsf{D}_{\mathrm{ECEF}}(C_A, C_B)$ as $2R\,\mathrm{atan}\left(\sqrt{a/(1-a)}\right)$.

Figure 3: PP-ECEF Protocol

as a baseline for evaluating both accuracy and performance of our PP-ECEF and PP-HS protocols.)

Alice and Bob must determine whether their coordinates lay on the same zone, prior to running the PP-UTM protocol. To do so, they can assign a unique identifier to each zone, and then compare their respective identifiers using any protocol that implements private equality test. As an example, they can use the following simple algorithm:

> Let z_A represent Alice's zone, and z_B – Bob's zone. Alice sends $[\![z_A]\!]$ to Bob, who computes $[\![d]\!] = ([\![z_A]\!] \cdot [\![-z_B]\!])^r = [\![r \cdot (z_A - z_B)]\!]$, where r is a random value uniformly chosen from the message space. $[\![d]\!]$ is sent back to Alice, who decrypts it. If Alice and Bob belong to the same zone (i.e., $z_A = z_B$), then $d = 0$. Otherwise, d is uniformly distributed in the message space, and does not reveal any additional information about z_B.

Even if Alice and Bob are not in the same zone, Alice may still participate in the UTM protocol – although the result of the computation will be unrelated to their correct distance. This will prevent Bob from learning the output of the private equality test.

Alice and Bob discretize their coordinates, as discussed in Section 4, prior to using them in the protocol. The PP-UTM protocol is shown in Figure 2.

5.2 PP-ECEF Protocol

Our PP-ECEF protocol computes the distance between Alice and Bob in the ECEF coordinate system. Computation of distance is divided in two phases:

1. Alice and Bob interact to privately compute the straight-line (Euclidean) distance between their respective inputs; only Alice learns the results (i.e., variable a in Section 3.2).
2. Then Alice converts this straight-line distance to the corresponding distance on Earth's surface (i.e., variable d in Section 3.2).

Since Earth is represented as a sphere, step 2. is independent from the absolute locations of Alice and Bob, and therefore does not require any private input from the parties.

Similarly to the PP-UTM protocol, Alice and Bob's coordinates are discretized as discussed in Section 4. The PP-ECEF is detailed in Figure 3.

5.3 PP-HS Protocol

The PP-HS protocol involves private computation of haversine formula over Alice and Bob's private input. However, if the formula is used *as is* for the construction of a privacy-preserving protocol, it requires Alice and Bob to interactively compute $\sin^2((lat_A - lat_B)/2)$ and $\sin^2((lon_A - lon_B)/2)$. While both *can* be computed within a privacy-preserving framework (e.g., by implementing Taylor series expansion as shown in [31]), the cost of the resulting protocol would be prohibitive, especially on resource-constrained devices such as smartphones and tablets.

However, this can be avoided by simply using the following well-known trigonometric identity:

$$\sin(\varphi - \psi) = \sin(\varphi)\cos(\psi) - \cos(\varphi)\sin(\psi).$$

After we apply this identity to the haversine formula from Section 3.3, we can rewrite a as:

$$\begin{aligned} a =& (\sin(lat_A/2)\cos(lat_B/2) - \cos(lat_A/2)\sin(lat_B/2))^2 \\ &+ \cos(lat_A)\cos(lat_B) \\ &\cdot (\sin(lon_A/2)\cos(lon_B/2) - \cos(lon_A/2)\sin(lon_B/2))^2 \end{aligned}$$

Input: Alice: her position, expressed as coordinates $C_A = (lat_A, lon_A)$ as defined in Section 3 and her public/private keypair; Bob: his position, expressed as coordinates $C_B = (lat_B, lon_B)$ and Alice's public key.
Output: Alice learns $\mathsf{D}_{\mathrm{HS}}(C_A, C_B)$ as defined in Section 3.
Protocol steps:

1. Let $\alpha, \ldots, \mu$ defined as in Section 3. Alice computes:
$$[\![\alpha^2]\!], [\![-2\alpha\gamma]\!], [\![\gamma^2]\!], [\![\zeta\eta\theta^2\lambda^2]\!], [\![-2\zeta\eta\theta\lambda]\!], [\![\zeta\eta]\!]$$
and sends the ciphertexts to Bob.
2. Bob computes:
$$\begin{aligned}[\![a]\!] &= [\![\alpha^2]\!]^{\beta^2} \cdot [\![-2\alpha\gamma]\!]^{\beta\delta} \cdot [\![\gamma^2]\!]^{\delta^2} \cdot [\![\zeta\eta\theta^2\lambda^2]\!] \cdot [\![-2\zeta\eta\theta\lambda]\!]^{\mu\nu} \cdot [\![\zeta\eta]\!]^{\mu^2\nu^2} \\ &= [\![\alpha^2\beta^2 - 2\alpha\beta\gamma\delta + \gamma^2\delta^2 + \zeta\eta\theta^2\lambda^2 - 2\zeta\eta\theta\lambda\mu\nu + \zeta\eta\mu^2\nu^2]\!]\end{aligned}$$
3. Bob sends $[\![a]\!]$ to Alice, which decrypts it and outputs $\mathsf{D}_{\mathrm{HS}}(C_A, C_B)$ as $2R\,\mathrm{atan}\left(\sqrt{a/(1-a)}\right)$.

Figure 4: PP-HS Protocol

Let us denote the cosine/sine values with greek letters, for more concise notation, as:

$$\begin{aligned} \alpha &= \cos(lat_A/2) & \eta &= \cos(lat_B) \\ \beta &= \sin(lat_B/2) & \theta &= \sin(lon_A/2) \\ \gamma &= \sin(lat_A/2) & \lambda &= \cos(lon_B/2) \\ \delta &= \cos(lat_B/2) & \mu &= \cos(lon_A/2) \\ \zeta &= \cos(lat_A) & \nu &= \sin(lon_B/2) \end{aligned}$$

We can then rewrite and expand a as:

$$a = \alpha^2\beta^2 - 2\alpha\beta\gamma\delta + \gamma^2\delta^2 + \zeta\eta\theta^2\lambda^2 - 2\zeta\eta\theta\lambda\mu\nu + \zeta\eta\mu^2\nu^2$$

With this formulation, computing a does not involve joint evaluation of any trigonometric function on private input. In fact, each party can separately compute their share of the formula, and combine their shares using only operations over encrypted data.

Similarly to the PP-ECEF protocol, computing the distance between Alice and Bob given a does not require any private input from either party. (Moreover, a can be easily reconstructed from the distance between the protocol participants.) For this reason, our PP-HS protocol allows Alice to learn a, and to subsequently convert it to the actual distance on Earth's surface – in the unencrypted domain.

Instead of discretizing their coordinates, Alice and Bob discretize values $\alpha, \ldots, \nu$. The protocol is illustrated in Figure 4.

5.4 Privacy-Preserving Proximity Testing with Unconditional Response

We extend the protocols presented in sections 5.1-5.3 to perform privacy-preserving proximity testing (PPPT). PPPT reveals a single bit of information to Alice, which represents:

$$\mathrm{PPPT}_{\mathsf{D}(\cdot,\cdot)}(C_A, C_B, \varepsilon) \triangleq \left(\mathsf{D}(C_A, C_B) \overset{?}{<} \varepsilon\right)$$

where $\mathsf{D}(\cdot,\cdot)$ is a distance function (in our case, D is either $\mathsf{D}_{\mathrm{UTM}}(\cdot,\cdot)$, $\mathsf{D}_{\mathrm{ECEF}}(\cdot,\cdot)$, or $\mathsf{D}_{\mathrm{HS}}(\cdot,\cdot)$), C_A and C_B are Alice's and Bob's coordinates, and ε is an arbitrary distance below which Alice and Bob are considered to be in close proximity.

Additionally, Bob can decide whether to faithfully participate in the PPPT protocol, allowing Alice to compute the correct results, or to defect, forcing Alice to compute a bit of his choice. This may be preferable to Bob than simply opting out of the protocol. In fact, by not interacting with Alice, Bob may reveal information about his location.

In order to provide different performance tradeoffs, we implemented PPPT using two different privacy-preserving comparison techniques: (1) the privacy-preserving homomorphic comparison protocol of Erkin et al. [10], and (2) the garbled circuits of Kolesnikov et al. [28].

Homomorphic Comparison of [10]. This protocol is based on the observation that $a < a_\varepsilon$ is true iff the $l+1$-th bit of $w = 2^l + a - a_\varepsilon$, denoted w_l from now on, is 0 (for $2^l > a - a_\varepsilon$). Given $[\![a]\!]$, $[\![a_\varepsilon]\!]$, encryption of w is computed by Bob as $[\![w]\!] = [\![2^l]\!] \cdot [\![a]\!] \cdot [\![a_\varepsilon]\!]^{-1}$. Encryption of the l-th bit of w is then computed as $[\![w_l]\!] = [\![2^{-l} \cdot (w - (w \bmod 2^l))]\!]$. Value w is available to Bob only in encrypted form, and computing $w \bmod 2^l$ in the encrypted domain requires interaction between Alice and Bob: Bob "masks" $[\![w]\!]$ by selecting a random value r and computing $[\![w']\!] = [\![w]\!] \cdot [\![r]\!]$. Then, Bob sends $[\![w']\!]$ to Alice, who decrypts it and returns the encryption of $c = w' \bmod 2^l$ to Alice. Next, Bob "unmasks" $[\![c]\!]$ by computing $[\![c]\!] \cdot [\![r]\!]^{-1} = [\![w \bmod 2^l]\!]$. We refer the reader to [10] for additional details.

After Bob computes $[\![a]\!]$ in our distance protocols ($[\![a']\!]$ for PP-ECEF), he does not return it to Alice. Instead, he computes – with Alice's help – value $[\![w - (w \bmod 2^l)]\!]$, which is 0 if and only if $\mathsf{D}(C_A, C_B) < \varepsilon$. This value is then sent to Alice, who decrypts it and outputs the corresponding plaintext. Since Bob operates on both a and a_ε in encrypted form, Alice can choose not to reveal the threshold to Bob during the protocol.

Comparison Based on [28]. In order to reduce the cost of the integer comparison circuit, Kolesnikov et al. [28] minimize the use of non-XOR gates. The result is a circuit that uses $4n$ gates, out of which n are non-XOR, to compare two unsigned n-bit integers: the comparison circuit contains n 1-bit comparators with carry, which use three XOR gates and one AND gate (see figures 5 and 6 of [28]). The advantage of this technique is that a significant part of the computation can be performed offline by Alice and Bob, resulting in faster on-line computation.

After Bob computes $[\![a]\!]$ ($[\![a']\!]$ for PP-ECEF) using our distance protocols, he selects a random value $s \leftarrow \{0,1\}^{\kappa+l}$ where κ is the security parameter and l is the number of bits used to represent location information. Bob then *blinds* a as $[\![\bar{a}]\!] = [\![a + s]\!]$ and returns $[\![\bar{a}]\!]$ to Alice. s is uniformly selected from $\{0,1\}^{\kappa+l}$ instead of the message space of DGK for efficiency reasons. This allows us to achieve statistical hiding for a, instead of unconditional hiding, since the blinding value is κ bits longer that the value it protects [3].

Alice and Bob then perform circuit evaluation, where Alice's input is $\overline{a}$ and Bob's input is $a_\varepsilon + s$. At the end of the circuit evaluation, Alice learns the correct result, since $a < a_\varepsilon \iff \overline{a} < a_\varepsilon + s$.

Unconditional Response. In order to return an *unconditional positive* to Alice, when using homomorphic comparison Bob discards $[\![a]\!]$ and $[\![a_\varepsilon]\!]$ and replaces them with $[\![\overline{a}]\!]$ and $[\![\overline{a_\varepsilon}]\!]$, for two arbitrary values $\overline{a}$ and $\overline{a_\varepsilon}$ such that $\overline{a} < \overline{a_\varepsilon}$. Analogously, an *unconditional negative* can be returned by selecting $\overline{a} > \overline{a_\varepsilon}$.

When using the garbled circuit for comparison, Bob's input to the circuit is 0 for unconditional negative ($0 < \overline{a}$ holds with overwhelming probability), and $s + a_{max} + 1$ for unconditional positive, where a_{max} is the largest value that a (a' for PP-ECEF) can assume. ($s + a_{max} + 1 > \overline{a}$ always holds.)

The security of the comparison protocols guarantees that Alice cannot distinguish between a correct result and an unconditional response.

6. SECURITY ANALYSIS

Security of our protocols relies on the security of the underlying building blocks. In particular, we need to assume that the underlying homomorphic encryption scheme is semantically secure.

We instantiate $[\![\cdot]\!]$ using the DGK encryption scheme, which has been shown to be semantically secure under a hardness assumption that uses subgroups of an RSA modulus [7, 6]. The privacy-preserving comparison protocol of Erkin et al. was shown to be secure in [10], and therefore we do not include it in our analysis.

To show the security of the protocols, we informally sketch how to simulate the view of each party using its inputs and outputs alone. If such simulation is indistinguishable from the real execution of the protocol, for semi-honest parties this implies that the protocols do not reveal any unintended information to the participants (i.e., they learn only the output and what can be deduced from their respective inputs and outputs).

Security of PP-UTM. Alice's view of the protocols consists of the encryption and decryption keys for $[\![\cdot]\!]$, and ciphertext $[\![a]\!]$ from Bob. Alice's output is $\sqrt{a}$. Simulator S_A provides Alice with decryption key for $[\![\cdot]\!]$ as input. It then encrypts the protocol output as $[\![(\sqrt{a})^2]\!] = [\![a]\!]$ and sends it to Alice. Since $[\![a]\!]$ is properly distributed, Alice cannot distinguish between the simulation and a real execution of the protocol. Therefore, the protocol is secure against a curious Alice.

Bob's view of the protocol consists in Alice's public key, and three ciphertexts from Alice, namely $[\![x_A^2 + y_A^2]\!]$, $[\![-2x_A]\!]$, $[\![-2y_A]\!]$. Bob has no output. Simulator S_B selects a random pair $(\bar{x}_A, \bar{y}_A)$ and sends $[\![\bar{x}_A^2 + \bar{y}_A^2]\!]$, $[\![-2\bar{x}_A]\!]$ and $[\![-2\bar{y}_A]\!]$ to Bob. The semantic security of $[\![\cdot]\!]$ prevents Bob from determining that $\bar{x}_A^2 + \bar{y}_A^2$, $-2\bar{x}_A$ and $-2\bar{y}_A$ are not distributed properly. Therefore, no PPT algorithm can distinguish $[\![\bar{x}_A^2 + \bar{y}_A^2]\!]$, $[\![-2\bar{x}_A]\!]$ and $[\![-2\bar{y}_A]\!]$ from the encryption of properly distributed values. For this reason, Bob cannot distinguish between interaction with the S_B and with a honest Alice. Hence the protocol is secure against a curious Bob.

Security of PP-ECEF. Alice's view of the protocols consists of the encryption and decryption keys for $[\![\cdot]\!]$, and ciphertext $[\![a]\!]$ from Bob. Alice's output is $2R\,\mathrm{atan}(\sqrt{a/(1-a)})$. Simulator S_A provides Alice with decryption key for $[\![\cdot]\!]$ as input. It then computes a from the protocol output and sends $[\![a]\!]$ to Alice. Since $[\![a]\!]$ is properly distributed, Alice cannot distinguish between the simulation and a real execution of the protocol. Therefore, the protocol is secure against a curious Alice.

Bob's view of the protocol consists in Alice's public key, and four ciphertexts from Alice, namely $[\![x_A^2 + y_A^2 + z_A^2]\!]$, $[\![-2x_A]\!]$, $[\![-2y_A]\!]$, and $[\![-2z_A]\!]$. Bob has no output. Simulator S_B selects a random set of coordinates $(\bar{x}_A, \bar{y}_A, \bar{z}_A)$ and sends $[\![\bar{x}_A^2 + \bar{y}_A^2 + \bar{z}_A^2]\!], [\![-2\bar{x}_A]\!], [\![-2\bar{y}_A]\!], [\![-2\bar{z}_A]\!]$ to Bob. The semantic security of $[\![\cdot]\!]$ prevents Bob from determining that $\bar{x}_A^2 + \bar{y}_A^2 + \bar{z}_A^2$, $-2\bar{x}_A$, $-2\bar{y}_A$ and $-2\bar{z}_A$ are not distributed properly. Therefore, no PPT algorithm can distinguish $[\![\bar{x}_A^2 + \bar{y}_A^2 + \bar{z}_A^2]\!]$, $[\![-2\bar{x}_A]\!]$, $[\![-2\bar{y}_A]\!]$ and $[\![-2\bar{z}_A]\!]$ from the encryption of properly distributed values. For this reason, Bob cannot distinguish between interaction with the S_B and with a honest Alice. Hence the protocol is secure against a curious Bob.

Security of PP-HS. Alice's view of the protocols consists of the encryption and decryption keys for $[\![\cdot]\!]$, and ciphertext $[\![a]\!]$ from Bob. Alice's output is $2R\,\mathrm{atan}(\sqrt{a/(1-a)})$. Simulator S_A provides Alice with decryption key for $[\![\cdot]\!]$ as input. It then computes a from the protocol output, encrypts it as $[\![a]\!]$, and sends it to Alice. Since $[\![a]\!]$ is properly distributed, Alice cannot distinguish between the simulation and a real execution of the protocol. Therefore, the protocol is secure against a curious Alice.

Bob's view of the protocol consists in Alice's public key, and six ciphertexts from Alice, namely $[\![\alpha^2]\!]$, $[\![-2\alpha\gamma]\!]$, $[\![\gamma^2]\!]$, $[\![\zeta\eta\theta^2\lambda^2]\!]$, $[\![-2\zeta\eta\theta\lambda]\!]$ and $[\![\zeta\eta]\!]$. Bob has no output. Simulator S_B selects six random values $s_1, \ldots, s_6$ from the message space of $[\![\cdot]\!]$, encrypts them and sends $[\![s_1]\!], \ldots, [\![s_6]\!]$ to Bob. The semantic security of $[\![\cdot]\!]$ prevents Bob from distinguishing $[\![s_1]\!], \ldots, [\![s_6]\!]$ from the encryption of properly distributed values. For this reason, Bob cannot distinguish between interaction with the S_B and with a honest Alice. Hence the protocol is secure against a curious Bob.

Security of Comparison with Garbled Circuit of [28]. It is well known that Garbled Circuits can be used to implement secure two party computation in the honest but curious model [14, 28]. When using it as a building block, we have to show that combining our distance protocol with the comparison circuit of [28] does not affect security.

Before the circuit execution, Bob reveals $[\![\overline{a}]\!] = [\![a + s]\!]$ to Alice, where $a \in \{0,1\}^l$ is a representation of the distance between the two parties and $s \leftarrow \{0,1\}^{\kappa+l}$ is chosen uniformly at random. We argue that a computationally-bound adversary does not learn information about a from $\overline{a}$, since s provides statistical hiding. (Unconditional hiding can be obtained selecting s from $s \leftarrow \{0,1\}^l$ and performing modulo subtraction within the circuit. However, this could negatively affect performance since it would add complexity to the comparison circuit.) More specifically, the success probability of the adversary decreases exponentially in κ.

Bob's view does not include any unencrypted values, so the security of the combined protocol simply relies on the security of its building blocks.

Remark on Location Triangulation. A potential security weakness inherent in distance computation is the ability of a set of three or more colluding parties, acting as Alice, to

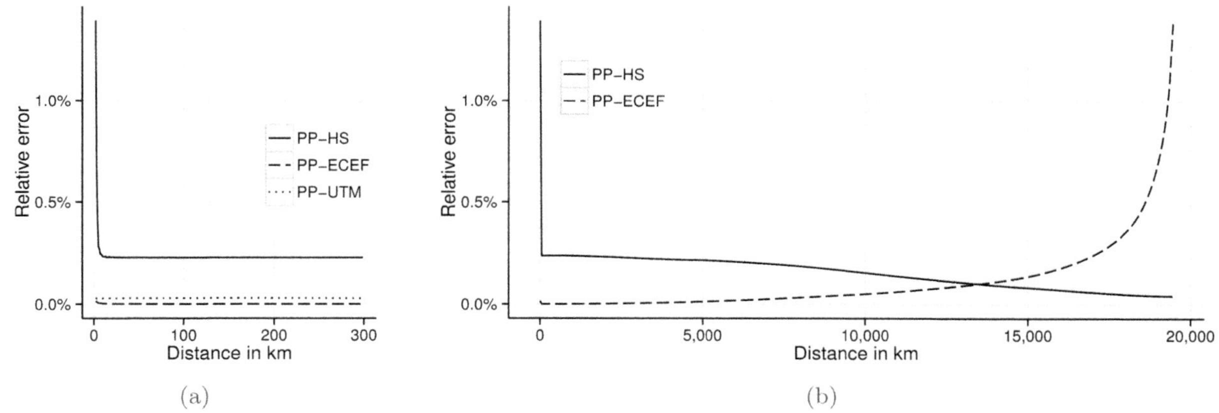

Figure 5: Comparison of PP-UTM, PP-ECEF and PP-HS accuracy for short (a) and long (b) distances. Discretization is performed with 1-meter accuracy for PP-UTM and PP-ECEF and roughly equivalent accuracy (9 digits) for PP-HS. Relative error is plotted from the 2 km distance.

precisely determine the location of Bob through triangulation. This is not an issue specific to our protocol, but rather to the functionality that our protocol implements. Any protocol implementing the same functionality has the same issue. Similarly, proximity testing allows multiple colluding parties to determine Bob's exact location – although with significantly higher cost. We do not discuss this issue any further, since this is a limitation of the underlying functionality rather than of our protocols.

7. EVALUATION

We now present our protocol evaluation. We assess the proposed protocols in terms of accuracy and performance. For accuracy, we compare the exact distance with the output of the specific distance function (i.e., haversine formula, ECEF arc, Euclidean distance on UTM), after performing input discretization. To assess performance, we measure protocol execution time and bandwidth requirements. For garbled circuits, the time is divided into the *precomputation*, which can be done before knowing the input of either party, and *execution*. Both precomputation and execution require interaction between the protocol participants.

Our tests are performed on a prototype implementation, detailed below. For generality's sake, all tests were run on both a regular desktop computer and on a commodity Android device.

7.1 Accuracy

To evaluate the accuracy of our protocols, we use WGS84 as the reference shape of Earth. We select random pairs of coordinates and compute the reference distance on WGS84. This distance is then compared with the output of the protocols on the same coordinates. We report errors as a fraction of the WGS84 distance.

There are two main sources of imprecision in our protocols: (1) the distance computation methods we consider are inherently inaccurate, as they use a spherical approximation or a projection instead of the actual shape of Earth; (2) computation in the encrypted domain is performed on discretized values, i.e., over the integers; for efficiency reasons, the number of digits used for discretization is limited – this introduce approximation errors.

The effect of coordinate discretization on PP-UTM and PP-ECEF is that all points are mapped on a grid with fixed-size cells. Additions and subtractions of discretized values performed in the encrypted domain do not introduce further errors. Square root and trigonometric functions are computed in the unencrypted domain, and can therefore be performed with arbitrary precision. In our tests, we used 64-bit IEEE 754 floating point variables (i.e., `double` in Java). We evaluated cells of size 1 m and 100 m (i.e., $\mathsf{discretize}_e(\cdot)$ with $e = 0$ and $e = -2$ respectively). Let u denote the cell size. Errors introduced in the encrypted domain are bounded by $\sqrt{2} \cdot u$ for PP-UTM and approximately $\sqrt{3} \cdot u$ for PP-ECEF.

This does not apply to PP-HS. In fact, the discretization is performed on the output of trigonometric functions computed over Alice and Bob's coordinates. As the number of digits increases, the error caused by discretization decreases exponentially. In all our experiments, we used $e = 9$, that is, 9 significant decimal digits. This value showed, in fact, a reasonable trade-off between cost and accuracy. Moreover, by further increasing e the impact on accuracy was negligible.

The *relative* error of our protocols is shown in figures 5(a) and 5(b), for short and long distances respectively. The error on UTM projection is shown in Figure 5(a) only, since it is not meaningful to compare distances between coordinates laying on different zones (any two random points separated by over 300 km would likely fall in different zones).

PP-ECEF is better suited when the distance between the two parties is below 12,000 km. As a generic distance function (i.e., when there is no a-priory knowledge of the range of distances involved), both PP-HS and PP-ECEF provide accurate results. We compare the PP-ECEF protocol with existing protocols in Table 1.

Our prototype relies on the Java Geodesy Library [12] to compute distances on WGS84. The JScience library [25] is used to project WGS84 coordinates to UTM and ECEF, while the Java Map Projection Library [23] – to project spherical coordinates to the Mercator, Equidistant Cylindrical and Mollweide projections.

	PP-ECEF	Narayanan et. al. [36]	Louis [50]	Lester [50]	Pierre [50]
Suitable for proximity testing	yes	yes	yes	yes	yes
Suitable for distance computation	yes	no	w/ small changes	w/ small changes	no
Location resolution independent of threshold	yes	no	yes	yes	no
Error characterization	linear with resolution	linear with threshold/resolution	linear with resolution	linear with resolution	linear with threshold/resolution
Max. error for threshold $\varepsilon < 100$ km	≈ 3 m (with 1 m resolution)	$> 135\%$ of ε	≈ 2 m (with 1 m resolution)	≈ 2 m (with 1 m resolution)	$> 180\%$ of ε
Requires third party	no	no	yes	yes	no

Table 1: Comparison of our PP-ECEF protocol to related work. For protocols that allow independent choice of resolution, 1m resolution was chosen for the 100m proximity test.

7.2 Performance

Protocol performance was evaluated on a desktop computer (Intel Xeon E5420 2.5 GHz CPU, 16GB RAM) and on an Android smartphone (LG Nexus 4, Quad-core 1.5 GHz Krait CPU, 2 GB RAM). Both the distance computation protocol and the protocol for proximity testing were implemented in Java using the `BigInteger` API. For simplicity, the prototype implementation was single-threaded.

In this section we report time measurements only for computation; communication overhead is instead expressed in terms of amount of data exchanged between the parties during protocol execution. We ignore additional overhead necessary for establishing a secure channel between the Alice and Bob (e.g., via TLS).

In our experiments, we use 1024-bit modulus, 160-bit subgroup size for DGK cryptosystem. Plaintext space for the distance computation protocols and proximity testing based on homomorphic comparison was 48 bits for PP-UTM, 65 bits for PP-HS, PP-ECEF, and 165 bits for proximity testing with garbled circuits. The security parameter κ for garbled circuits was set to 80 in all of our experiments. Average execution time and bandwidth usage for distance computation is reported in Table 2, for proximity testing in Table 3.

Our experiments show that all protocols are practical on both our desktop setup and on a regular smartphone. Distance computation, regardless of the protocol, requires up to 41 ms on the desktop computer, and 78 ms on the smartphone. Small amount of computation, in conjunction with negligible bandwidth usage (below 1 kB) make our protocols suitable for resource-constrained devices. For distance computation, discretization parameters have no impact on bandwidth usage and negligible effects on computation time. Therefore, we show results for 1-meter discretization for PP-UTM and PP-ECEF, and roughly equivalent accuracy for PP-HS.

While PP-UTM is the fastest of our protocols, both PP-HS and PP-ECEF offer better accuracy for longer and shorter distances, respectively. Moreover, the cost increase over PP-UTM is small.

Proximity testing is significantly slower (and requires higher bandwidth) than simple distance computation. We perform tests using different discretization parameters, which impact computation and communication cost for both the homomorphic comparison protocol and garbled circuits.

On the desktop, comparison with garbled circuits takes 0.5 to 0.6 seconds, compared to 0.7 to 1.7 seconds with Erkin's protocol. The time and bandwidth for precomputation and protocol execution are listed separately in Table 3. On the other hand, bandwidth requirements for garbled circuits is between 37.5 and 41.0 kB, more than twice as much as the 7 to 14 kB required for Erkin's protocol.

Unlike the Erkin's comparison protocol, garbled circuits allow part of the computation to be done without providing any user input. This precomputation can be done in advance (e.g., while charging the smartphone or during extended periods of inactivity), but still requires communication between protocol participants. Without precomputation, comparison using garbled circuits takes 2.4 to 2.8 s, while the Erkin's protocol is faster with 1.2 to 2.8 seconds, depending on discretization and distance function. With precomputation, however, protocol execution time and bandwidth usage is reduced to 1.2-1.6 s.

	Time	Communication
Desktop		
PP-HS	41.3 ms	896 B
PP-ECEF	34.9 ms	640 B
PP-UTM	26.5 ms	512 B
Smartphone		
PP-HS	78.0 ms	896 B
PP-ECEF	66.7 ms	640 B
PP-UTM	53.5 ms	512 B

Table 2: Cost of our privacy-preserving distance measurement protocols. Discretization is performed with 1-meter accuracy for PP-UTM and PP-ECEF and roughly equivalent accuracy (9 digits) for PP-HS.

8. CONCLUSION

In this paper we introduced PP-UTM, PP-ECEF and PP-HS, three privacy-preserving protocols for secure distance computation and secure proximity testing. In contrast with previous work, our PP-ECEF and PP-HS protocols compute distances over a spherical surface instead of a plane. This allows us to provide significantly more accurate results over long distances, while incurring in very small overhead.

We rely on different techniques for distance computation – namely, Euclidean distance on a plane (which we use as a baseline) and distance on the surface of a sphere – in order to offer different trade-offs between accuracy and cost.

To the best of our knowledge, this is the first work that provides a thorough characterization of the geometrical error and the approximation introduced by input discretization on distances computed using privacy-preserving protocols.

We evaluated the cost of our protocols on a commodity Android device and on a desktop computer via a prototype implementation. Our analysis shows that our protocols are

Proximity testing	With Homomorphic Comparison Time	Comm.	With Garbled Circuit Precomp.	Comm.	Exec.	Comm.
Desktop						
PP-HS (9 decimal digits)	1.7 s	17 kB	409 ms	22.1 kB	124 ms	18.9 kB
PP-ECEF (1 m discretization)	1.3 s	14 kB	404 ms	22.1 kB	109 ms	17.7 kB
PP-ECEF (100 m discretization)	1.0 s	10 kB	404 ms	22.1 kB	105 ms	16.6 kB
PP-UTM (1 m discretization)	1.1 s	10 kB	401 ms	22.1 kB	102 ms	16.6 kB
PP-UTM (100 m discretization)	0.7 s	7 kB	401 ms	22.1 kB	104 ms	15.4 kB
Smartphone						
PP-HS (9 decimal digits)	2.8 s	17 kB	1.2 s	18.1 kB	1.6 s	16.4 kB
PP-ECEF (1 m discretization)	2.2 s	14 kB	1.2 s	18.1 kB	1.4 s	15.2 kB
PP-ECEF (100 m discretization)	1.6 s	10 kB	1.2 s	18.1 kB	1.3 s	14.1 kB
PP-UTM (1 m discretization)	1.8 s	10 kB	1.2 s	18.1 kB	1.3 s	14.1 kB
PP-UTM (100 m discretization)	1.2 s	7 kB	1.2 s	18.1 kB	1.2 s	12.9 kB

Table 3: Cost of proximity testing protocols with Homomorphic Comparison and Garbled Circuits.

practical and can be run efficiently on standard smartphones. Finally, we analyzed the security of our protocols under standard assumptions.

9. ACKNOWLEDGEMENTS

Jaroslav Šeděnka kindly acknowledges the support by the ESF Project CZ.1.07/2.3.00/20.0051 Algebraic Methods in Quantum Logic of the Masaryk University. Supported by

european social fund in the czech republic
EUROPEAN UNION
MINISTRY OF EDUCATION, YOUTH AND SPORTS
OP Education for Competitiveness
INVESTMENTS IN EDUCATION DEVELOPMENT

10. REFERENCES

[1] Find my Friends. `http://www.apple.com/icloud/features/find-my-friends.html`.

[2] A. Beresford and F. Stajano. Location Privacy in Pervasive Computing. *Pervasive*, 2(1), 2003.

[3] M. Blanton and P. Gasti. Secure and efficient protocols for iris and fingerprint identification. In *ESORICS*, 2011.

[4] Boost Mobile Loopt. `http://www.boostmobile.com/boostloopt/how.html`.

[5] Cab4me. `http://www.cab4me.com`.

[6] I. Damgård, M. Geisler, and M. Krøigård. A correction to efficient and secure comparison for on-line auctions. Cryptology ePrint Archive, Report 2008/321, 2008.

[7] I. Damgård, M. Geisler, and M. Krøigård. Homomorphic encryption and secure comparison. *IJACT*, 2008.

[8] Defense Mapping Agency, Hydrographic/Topographic Center. The universal grids: Universal transverse mercator (UTM) and universal polar stereographic (UPS). Technical Report TM8358.2, 1989.

[9] M. Duckham and L. Kulik. A formal model of obfuscation and negotiation for location privacy. In *Pervasive*, 2005.

[10] Z. Erkin, M. Franz, J. Guajardo, S. Katzenbeisser, I. Lagendijk, and T. Toft. Privacy-preserving face recognition. In *PETS*, 2009.

[11] Flickr. `http://www.flickr.com`.

[12] Java geodesy library. `http://www.gavaghan.org/blog/free-source-code/geodesy-library-vincentys-formula-java/`.

[13] O. Goldreich. *Foundations of Cryptography: Volume 2, Basic Applications*. Cambridge University Press, 2004.

[14] O. Goldreich, S. Micali, and A. Wigderson. How to play any mental game or a completeness theorem for protocols with honest majority. In *ACM Symposium on Theory of Computing (STOC)*, pages 218–229, 1987.

[15] P. Golle and K. Partridge. On the anonymity of home/work location pairs. In *Pervasive*, 2009.

[16] Google Latitude. `http://www.google.com/latitude`.

[17] Groupon Local. `http://www.groupon.com`.

[18] M. Gruteser and D. Grunwald. Anonymous usage of location-based services through spatial and temporal cloaking. In *MobiSys*, 2003.

[19] B. Hoh, T. Iwuchukwu, Q. Jacobson, D. Work, A. Bayen, R. Herring, J. Herrera, M. Gruteser, M. Annavaram, and J. Ban. Enhancing privacy and accuracy in probe vehicle-based traffic monitoring via virtual trip lines. *TMC*, 11(5), 2012.

[20] Find my iPhone - iCloud. `http://www.icloud.com`.

[21] Instagram. `http://instagram.com`.

[22] Y. Ishai, J. Kilian, K. Nissim, and E. Petrank. Extending oblivious tranfers efficiently. In *Advances in Cryptology – CRYPTO*, 2003.

[23] Java map projection library. `http://www.jhlabs.com/java/maps/proj/`.

[24] T. Jiang, H. Wang, and Y.-C. Hu. Preserving location privacy in wireless lans. In *MobiSys*, 2007.

[25] Jscience library. `http://jscience.org/`.

[26] T. Jung and X.-Y. Li. Search me if you can: Privacy-preserving location query service. *CoRR*, abs/1208.0107, 2012.

[27] C. Karney. Algorithms for geodesics. *Journal of Geodesy*, 87(1), Jan. 2013.

[28] V. Kolesnikov, A.-R. Sadeghi, and T. Schneider. Improved garbled circuit building blocks and applications to auctions and computing minima. In *Cryptology and Network Security (CANS)*, 2009.

[29] V. Kolesnikov and T. Schneider. Improved garbled circuit: Free XOR gates and applications. In *International Colloquium on Automata, Languages and Programming (ICALP)*, 2008.

[30] J. Krumm. Inference attacks on location tracks. In *Pervasive*, 2007.

[31] P. Lory. Enhancing the efficiency in privacy preserving learning of decision trees in partitioned databases. In *PSD*, 2012.

[32] J. Manweiler, R. Scudellari, Z. Cancio, and L. Cox. We saw each other on the subway: secure, anonymous proximity-based missed connections. In *HotMobile*, 2009.

[33] S. Mascetti, C. Bettini, and D. Freni. Longitude: Centralized privacy-preserving computation of users' proximity. In *SDM*, 2009.

[34] MIT iFIND Project. `http://web.mit.edu/newsoffice/2006/ifind.html`.

[35] M. Naor and B. Pinkas. Efficient oblivious transfer protocols. In *ACM-SIAM Symposium On Discrete Algorithms (SODA)*, 2001.

[36] A. Narayanan, N. Thiagarajan, M. Lakhani, M. Hamburg, and D. Boneh. Location privacy via private proximity testing. In *NDSS*, 2011.

[37] P. Paillier. Public-key cryptosystems based on composite degree residuosity classes. In *EUROCRYPT*, 1999.

[38] B. Pinkas, T. Schneider, N. Smart, and S. Williams. Secure two-party computation is practical. In *Advances in Cryptology – ASIACRYPT*, volume 5912 of *LNCS*, 2009.

[39] P. Shankar, V. Ganapathy, and L. Iftode. Privately querying location-based services with sybilquery. In *UbiComp*, 2009.

[40] R. Shokri, G. Theodorakopoulos, J. Boudec, and J. Hubaux. Quantifying location privacy. In *SP*, 2011.

[41] R. Shokri, G. Theodorakopoulos, G. Danezis, J.-P. Hubaux, and J.-Y. Boudec. Quantifying location privacy: The case of sporadic location exposure. In *PETS*, 2011.

[42] R. Sinnott. Virtues of the haversine. *Sky and Telescope*, 68(2), 1984.

[43] W. Torge. *Geodesy*. De Gruyter, 2001.

[44] TripAdvisor. `http://www.tripadvisor.com`.

[45] T. Vincenty. Direct and inverse solutions of geodesics on the ellipsoid with application of nested equations. *Survey Review*, 22(176), 1975.

[46] Apple Pays Out $946 in Locationgate Settlement. `http://www.wired.com/gadgetlab/2011/07/apple-locationgate-settlement/`.

[47] Stalkers Exploit Cellphone GPS. `http://online.wsj.com/article/SB10001424052748703467304575383522318244234.html`.

[48] A. Yao. How to generate and exchange secrets. In *FOCS*, 1986.

[49] Yelp. `http://www.yelp.com`.

[50] G. Zhong, I. Goldberg, and U. Hengartner. Louis, Lester and Pierre: Three protocols for location privacy. In *PET*, 2007.

Maple: Scalable Multi-Dimensional Range Search over Encrypted Cloud Data with Tree-based Index

Boyang Wang*
Dept. of Computer Science
Utah State University
Logan, UT, 84322
xd.bywang@gmail.com

Yantian Hou
Dept. of Computer Science
Utah State University
Logan, UT, 84322
houyantian@gmail.com

Ming Li
Dept. of Computer Science
Utah State University
Logan, UT, 84322
ming.li@usu.edu

Haitao Wang
Dept. of Computer Science
Utah State University
Logan, UT, 84322
haitao.wang@usu.edu

Hui Li
State Key Laboratory of ISN
Xidian University
Xi'an, Shaanxi, 710071, China
lihui@mail.xidian.edu.cn

ABSTRACT

Cloud computing promises users massive scale outsourced data storage services with much lower costs than traditional methods. However, privacy concerns compel sensitive data to be stored on the cloud server in an encrypted form. This posts a great challenge for effectively utilizing cloud data, such as executing common SQL queries. A variety of searchable encryption techniques have been proposed to solve this issue; yet efficiency and scalability are still the two main obstacles for their adoptions in real-world datasets, which are multi-dimensional in general. In this paper, we propose a tree-based public-key Multi-Dimensional Range Searchable Encryption (MDRSE) to overcome the above limitations. Specifically, we first formally define the leakage function and security of a tree-based MDRSE. Then, by leveraging an existing predicate encryption in a novel way, our tree-based MDRSE efficiently indexes and searches over encrypted cloud data with multi-dimensional tree structures (i.e., R-trees). Moreover, our scheme is able to protect single-dimensional privacy while previous efficient solutions fail to achieve. Our scheme is selectively secure, and through extensive experimental evaluation on a large-scale real-world dataset, we show the efficiency and scalability of our scheme.

Categories and Subject Descriptors

E.3 [**Data Encryption**]: Public Key Cryptosystems; H.3 [**Information Search and Retrieval**]: Information Search and Retrieval

*Boyang Wang is also a member of State Key Laboratory of ISN, Xidian University.

ASIA CCS'14, June 4–6, 2014, Kyoto, Japan.

http://dx.doi.org/10.1145/2590296.2590305.

Keywords

Multiple dimension; Range search; Encrypted cloud data; Tree structures

1. INTRODUCTION

With the adoption of cloud computing, data owners can reap huge economic benefits by outsourcing their data to the cloud instead of storing their data locally. Due to the serious privacy concerns in the cloud, sensitive data, such as financial or medical records, should be encrypted before being outsourced to the cloud server [2]. As a result, the cloud server is not allowed to reveal the content of outsourced data unless it possesses proper decryption keys. Unfortunately, the encryption on outsourced data inevitably introduces new challenges to data utilization. Specifically, how to enable users to effectively search over encrypted data as they generally perform in the plaintext domain, is one of the most significant issues needed to be solved in the cloud.

To enable different search functions over encrypted data, many Searchable Encryption (SE) schemes have been proposed. However, most of the existing SE schemes [4,7,12,14, 15,19,20,24,29,30,32,33,35] are only able to handle rather simple queries, such as keyword search or single-dimensional range queries, which are not able to well support *multi-dimensional range queries* over encrypted data. Considering real-world datasets are often multi-dimensional while common SQL queries (such as equality and comparison) can all be flexibly expressed as range queries [28], we believe designing an efficient Multi-Dimensional Range Searchable Encryption (MDRSE) will be an important step forward to make searchable encryption practical and scalable on large datasets in a real-world cloud setting.

Boneh and Waters [9] proposed a predicate encryption, named Hidden Vector Encryption, which can be utilized to support multi-dimensional range queries over encrypted data. Meanwhile, Shi et al. [28] designed an encryption scheme to handle multi-dimensional range queries as well. These two schemes are both public-key approaches. Unfortunately, the straightforward applications of these two schemes can only achieve linear search time with regard to the total number of data records. Since the number of data records in a real-world dataset is generally very large (e.g.

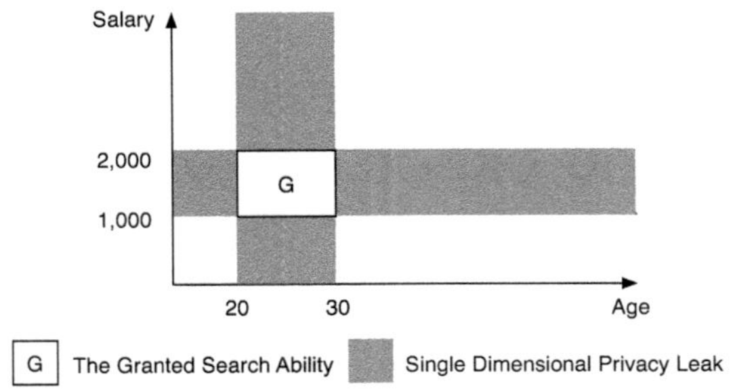

Figure 1: An example of privacy leak in LSED$^+$ [25].

in the order of millions or larger), the straightforward applications of these two schemes are clearly not practical.

Moving a step forward, Lu [25] designed a symmetric-key single dimensional range search scheme (named LSED) on encrypted data within *logarithmic* search time, and mentioned a direct extension of it (denoted as LSED$^+$) in the multi-dimension by achieving *sublinear* search time. However, this direct extension, which decomposes each multi-dimensional search token into independent ones in each single dimension, will result in significant privacy leak in every single dimension [25]. For instance, as described in Fig. 1, given the search token of a two-dimensional range query $Q = (age \in [20, 30]) \wedge (salary \in [1,000, 2,000])$ in LSED$^+$, the cloud server is able to independently search the corresponding results to a single dimensional range query $Q^x = (age \in [20, 30])$ on X-dimension or $Q^y = (salary \in [1,000, 2,000])$ on Y-dimension, which clearly reveals more private information to the cloud server than it is allowed to. Such type of leakage is referred to as *single-dimensional privacy* in this paper.

The recent work [34] proposed by Wang et al. also has privacy leakage in single dimensions for the same reason as LSED$^+$, although its efficiency is faster than linear search as well. Cash et al. [13] recently designed a sublinear SE scheme supporting conjunctive keyword search, which can protect privacy in single dimensions. However, how to extend this work to efficiently support multi-dimensional range queries is still unknown. Therefore, how to design an efficient and single-dimensionally private MDRSE remains open.

In this paper, we endeavor to solve the above problem by proposing Maple, a *tree-based* public-key MDRSE. By utilizing multi-dimensional tree structures (specifically, R-trees [17]) to index data records, we can achieve faster-than-linear search efficiency with respect to the number of data records[1]. Obviously, this goal is easy to achieve in the plaintext domain utilizing various multi-dimensional tree structures [5, 6, 17]. However, when data records and index are all encrypted, the main design challenge is how to preserve faster-than-linear search complexity while not sacrificing too much privacy (including single-dimensional privacy), which is not achieved by recent solutions [25, 34]. A high-level comparison among our scheme and previous solutions is presented in Table 1. Our main contributions are:

(1) We formally define the privacy leakage function, selective security and single-dimensional privacy of a tree-based public-key MDRSE in this paper. Particularly, we are among the first to distinguish *path pattern* from traditional access pattern and include path pattern in the privacy

[1]R-trees do not guarantee a good *worst-case* performance [17, 18], but they generally perform well with real-world data. Therefore, in the rest of this paper, when we mention R-trees achieve faster-than-linear search, we mean it is under an *empirical* sense.

	Faster than Linear Search?	Single-Dimensional Privacy
Shi et al. [28]	×	√
Boneh et al. [9]	×	√
LSED$^+$ [25]	√	×
Wang et al. [34]	√	×
Our Scheme	√	√

Table 1: Comparison among Different Solutions.

leakage function of a tree-based searchable encryption; we also introduce the necessary requirement of *isomorphic* tree structures in the security of a tree-based searchable encryption.

(2) By leveraging Hidden Vector Encryption [9] in a novel way, we can test geometric relations (including whether a point is inside a hyper-rectangle or two hyper-rectangles intersect) over encrypted data. By doing this, we can design a tree-based public-key MDRSE, which is able to efficiently support multi-dimensional range queries. Since our scheme is able to exactly follow the search algorithm of an R-tree in the plaintext domain while all the nodes of the tree are encrypted, our scheme can achieve the same search complexity (i.e., faster-than-linear search with regard to the number of data records) as a traditional R-tree in the plaintext domain. Moreover, the security analyses show that our scheme is selectively secure and single-dimensionally private.

(3) We observe that, in order to achieve single-dimensional privacy during the design of a tree-based MDRSE, we should be very careful about not only what type of tree structure is leveraged, but also which kind of predicate encryption is used. That is why the recent work in [34] is also based on R-trees as ours, but it cannot achieve single-dimensional privacy. On the other hand, some tree structures, such as kd-trees [5] and range trees [6], are faster-than-linear search as well. However, these trees cannot achieve single-dimensional privacy due to the nature of their tree structures (explainations about this observation are presented in Sec. 5).

2. PROBLEM DEFINITION

System Model. As shown in Fig. 2, the system model of our scheme includes two entities: a data owner and the cloud server. The data owner wants to outsource its database (i.e., a sets of data records) to the cloud server in order to reduce the storage cost on its local device. For example, $(25, 170, 2000)$ is one of the data records described in Fig. 2. Besides outsourcing storage, the data owner also wants to use its own data correctly. Specifically, the data owner should be able to retrieve the correct results from the outsourced data records by submitting a range query (e.g., $Q = [30, 40] \wedge [160, 185] \wedge [3000, 7000]$).

As in previous works [13, 15, 19, 20], the cloud server is assumed to be an *honest-but-curious* party. It means the cloud server can provide reliable data storage (will ensure the integrity of data [3]) and search services (will return the correct search results by following the protocols), but it is curious about the content of data records that are outsourced by the data owner.

Definition of MDRSE. Since we focus on handle multi-dimensional data in this paper, we first present some basic definitions in the multi-dimension, including lattices, points, and hyper-rectangles [28]:

Lattice. *Let $\Delta = (T_1, ..., T_w)$, where T_i is the upper bound in the i-th dimension and $1 \leq i \leq w$. A lattice $\mathbb{L}_\Delta$ is defined as $\mathbb{L}_\Delta = [T_1] \times \cdots \times [T_w]$, where $[T_i] = \{1, ..., T_i\}$.*

Point. *A point $\mathbf{X}$ in $\mathbb{L}_\Delta$ is defined as $\mathbf{X} = (x_1, ..., x_w)$, where $x_i \in [T_i]$, $\forall i \in [1, w]$.*

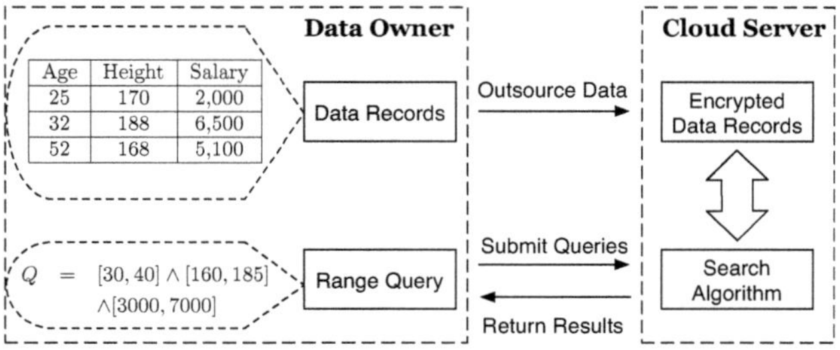

Figure 2: The system model includes a data owner and the cloud server.

Hyper-Rectangle. *A hyper-rectangle* $\mathbf{HR}$ *in* $\mathbb{L}_\Delta$ *is defined as* $\mathbf{HR} = (\mathbf{R}_1, ..., \mathbf{R}_w)$*, where* $\mathbf{R}_i$ *is a range in the i-th dimension,* $\mathbf{R}_i \subseteq [1, T_i]$*,* $\forall i \in [1, w]$*.*

It is easy to see that, in the aforementioned system model, a data record is essentially a point and a range query is actually a hyper-rectangle. Next, we introduce the definition of public-key MDRSE. Since we intend to improve search efficiency, we introduce a multi-dimensional tree structure Γ in the following definition to index data.

Definition 1. **(Multi-Dimensional Range Searchable Encryption).** *A tree-based public-key MDRSE scheme is a tuple of five polynomial-time algorithms* Π = (`GenKey`, `BuildTree`, `Enc`, `GenToken`, `Search`) *such that:*

- $(\mathtt{PK}, \mathtt{SK}) \leftarrow \mathtt{GenKey}(1^\lambda, \Delta)$: *is a probabilistic key generation algorithm that is run by the data owner to setup the scheme. It takes as input a security parameter* λ *and* $\Delta = (T_1, ..., T_w)$*, and outputs a public key* PK *and a secret key* SK.
- $\Gamma \leftarrow \mathtt{BuildTree}(\mathbf{D})$: *is a deterministic algorithm run by the data owner to build a multi-dimensional tree structure to index data records. It takes as input n data records* $\mathbf{D} = \{D_1, ..., D_n\}$*, where each data record* $D_i = (d_{i,1}, ..., d_{i,w})$ *is essentially a point in* $\mathbb{L}_\Delta$*, and outputs a multi-dimensional tree structure* Γ.
- $(\Gamma^*, \mathbf{C}) \leftarrow \mathtt{Enc}(\mathtt{PK}, \Gamma, \mathbf{M})$: *is a probabilistic algorithm run by the data owner to encrypt a multi-dimensional tree structure and messages. It takes as input a public key* PK*, multi-dimensional tree structure* Γ *and n messages* $\mathbf{M} = \{M_1, ..., M_n\}$*, where message* $M_i \in \mathcal{M}$ *is for each data record* D_i *and* $\mathcal{M}$ *is the message space, and outputs an encrypted multidimensional tree structure* Γ^* *and n ciphertexts* $\mathbf{C} = \{C_1, ..., C_n\}$.
- $\mathtt{TK}_Q \leftarrow \mathtt{GenToken}(\mathtt{SK}, Q)$: *is a probabilistic algorithm run by the data owner to generate a search token for a given range query. It takes as input a secret key* SK *and a range query (i.e., a hyper-rectangle) Q, and outputs a search token* $\mathtt{TK}_Q$.
- $\mathbf{I}_Q \leftarrow \mathtt{Search}(\Gamma^*, \mathbf{C}, \mathtt{TK}_Q)$: *is a deterministic algorithm run by the server to search over an encrypted multi-dimensional tree structure and ciphertexts. It takes as input an encrypted multi-dimensional data structure* Γ^**, n ciphertexts* $\mathbf{C} = \{C_1, ..., C_n\}$ *and a search token* $\mathtt{TK}_Q$*, and outputs a set* $\mathbf{I}_Q$ *of identifiers, where* I_i *is the identifier (e.g., a memory location in the cloud server) of data record* D_i*, and* $I_i \in \mathbf{I}_Q$ *if the corresponding data record* $D_i \in Q$.

Correctness. *We say that the above tree-based public-key MDRSE scheme is correct if for all* $\lambda \in \mathbb{N}$*, all* (PK, SK) *output by* $\mathtt{GenKey}(1^\lambda, \Delta)$*, all* $D_i \in \mathbb{L}_\Delta$*, all* Γ *output by* $\mathtt{Buildtree}(\mathbf{D})$*, for all* $M_i \in \mathcal{M}$*, all* $(\Gamma^*, \mathbf{C})$ *output by* $\mathtt{Enc}(\mathtt{PK}, \Gamma, \mathbf{M})$*, all* $Q \subseteq \mathbb{L}_\Delta$*, all* $\mathtt{TK}_Q$ *output by* $\mathtt{GenToken}(\mathtt{SK}, Q)$*, for any* $i \in [1, n]$

- *If* $D_i \in Q$: $\mathtt{Search}(\Gamma^*, \mathbf{C}, \mathtt{TK}_Q) = \mathbf{I}_Q$*, where* $I_i \in \mathbf{I}$*;*
- *If* $D_i \notin Q$: $\Pr[\mathtt{Search}(\Gamma^*, \mathbf{C}, \mathtt{TK}_Q) = \mathbf{I}_Q$*, where* $I_i \notin \mathbf{I}] \geq 1 - \mathtt{negl}(\lambda)$*;*

where $\mathtt{negl}(\lambda)$ *denotes a negligible function in* λ.

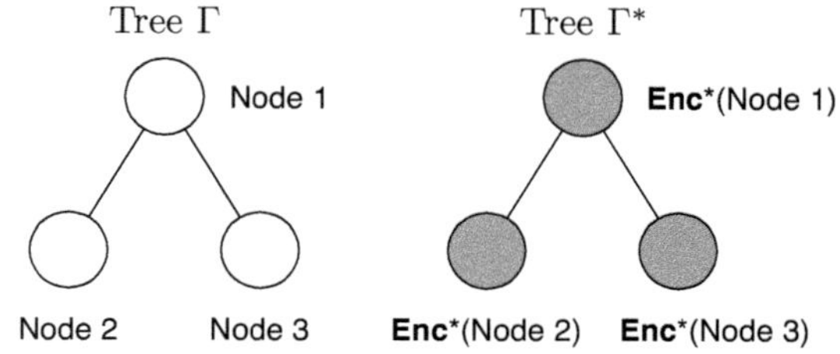

Figure 3: An example of Γ and Γ^*, where $\Gamma \simeq \Gamma^*$ and $\mathtt{Enc}^*$ is assumed as a probabilistic encryption algorithm performed on each node.

In the above scheme, the tree structures of Γ and its encrypted version Γ^* are *isomorphic* (denoted as $\Gamma \simeq \Gamma^*$). The main difference is that all the nodes (including non-leaf nodes and leaf nodes) in Γ^* are encrypted compared to the nodes in Γ. An example of Γ and Γ^* is shown in Fig. 3.

As pointed out by [10], since the main objective of a searchable encryption is to test whether a data record D_i is satisfying a query Q (i.e., $D_i \in Q$ in this paper) without revealing D_i, the message space $\mathcal{M}$ can be set to a singleton, such as $\mathcal{M} = \{\mathtt{Flag}\}$. Then, in $\mathtt{Search}(\Gamma^*, \mathbf{C}, \mathtt{TK}_Q)$, the algorithm will reveal a string `Flag` for each ciphertext C_i if data record $D_i \in Q$, and return the identifier I_i of this data record D_i. A larger message space of $\mathcal{M}$ can be used if more information need to be unlocked when $D_i \in Q$ [9].

Moreover, as emphasized in [10], there is no need for a searchable encryption to explicitly provide an extra algorithm for decrypting the content of search results (e.g., data records) returned by the cloud server. It is because the data owner can always independently encrypt and decrypt each data record by leveraging a standard public-key (or symmetric-key) encryption.

3. SECURITY DEFINITION

Informally, the security objective of a searchable encryption is to reveal as less information as possible to the honest-but-curious cloud server while successfully searching the data records for a given query. As the descriptions of other searchable encryption schemes, before we introduce the security definition of our tree-based MRDSE, let us first define what kinds of information will be leaked to the cloud server.

Privacy Leakage. First, since the data owner stores all the data records in the cloud server and submits queries to the cloud server for search, the basic size information of data records and queries, such as the total number of data records (n), the number of dimensions (w), the size of each dimension ($|T_i|$), and the number of queries submitted (t), are inevitably leaked to the cloud server.

Definition 2. **(Size Pattern).** *Given n data records* $\mathbf{D} = \{D_1, ..., D_n\}$*, the size pattern of* $\mathbf{D}$ *induced by a number of t query* $\mathbf{Q} = \{Q_1, ..., Q_t\}$ *is a tuple* $\alpha(\mathbf{D}, \mathbf{Q}) = (n, w, |T_1|, ..., |T_w|, t)$*.*

In addition, as previous searchable encryption schemes [15, 19, 20], our tree-based MDRSE scheme will not be able to preserve *access pattern* or *search pattern*. Specifically, revealing access pattern means the cloud server can learn the identifiers (e.g., memory locations in the server) of data records that satisfied for each query; leaking search pattern indicates the cloud server can distinguish whether a same data record is returned for two different queries. The definitions of access pattern and search pattern are presented as below by following [15,19,20].

Definition 3. **(Access Pattern).** *Given n data records* $\mathbf{D} = \{D_1, ..., D_n\}$, *the access pattern of* $\mathbf{D}$ *induced by a number of t query* $\mathbf{Q} = \{Q_1, ..., Q_t\}$, *is a tuple* $\beta(\mathbf{D}, \mathbf{Q}) = (\mathbf{I}_{Q_1}, ..., \mathbf{I}_{Q_t})$, *where* $\mathbf{I}_{Q_i}$ *is the set of identifiers of data records that returned by query* Q_i, *for* $1 \le i \le t$.

Definition 4. **(Search Pattern).** *Given n data records* $\mathbf{D} = \{D_1, ..., D_n\}$, *the search pattern of* $\mathbf{D}$ *induced by a number of t query* $\mathbf{Q} = \{Q_1, ..., Q_t\}$, *is an* $n \times t$ *binary matrix* $\gamma(\mathbf{D}, \mathbf{Q})$ *such that for* $1 \le i \le n$, *and* $1 \le j \le t$, *the element in the i-th row and j-th column is* 1, *if an identifier* I_i *is returned by a query* Q_j.

Theoretically speaking, access pattern and search pattern can be protected by using Oblivious RAM [13,31], but the efficiency of Oblivious RAM is still a huge concern for real applications. How to protect access pattern and search pattern for multi-dimensional range queries is out of the scope of this paper.

Besides access pattern and search pattern mentioned in previous works, another privacy leakage we would like to particularly capture for a tree-based searchable encryption is *path pattern*. Specifically, revealing path pattern means the cloud server learns the paths from the root node to several leaf nodes in a tree structure for a given query (i.e., the identifiers of all the non-leaf nodes and all the leaf nodes that a query reaches while searching in a tree structure).

Definition 5. **(Path Pattern).** *Given n data records* $\mathbf{D} = \{D_1, ..., D_n\}$ *and the corresponding tree structure* $\Gamma = \texttt{BuildTree}(\mathbf{D})$, *the path pattern of* $(\mathbf{D}, \Gamma)$ *induced by a number of t query* $\mathbf{Q} = \{Q_1, ..., Q_t\}$, *is a tuple* $\delta(\mathbf{D}, \Gamma, \mathbf{Q}) = (\mathbf{P}_{Q_1}, ..., \mathbf{P}_{Q_t})$, *where* $\mathbf{P}_{Q_i}$ *is the set of identifiers of nodes in* Γ *that reached by query* Q_i, *for* $1 \le i \le t$.

Path pattern not only exists in the multi-dimensional tree structures we utilized in this paper, but also lives in general tree structures in the single dimension, such as binary trees. Essentially, we can also think path pattern as "access pattern" revealed in a tree structure for a given query.

One of the main motivations for us to capture this new pattern in a searchable encryption while the access pattern (defined in Def. 3) have already been included in the privacy leakage is that, given the same access pattern for two queries, the path pattern of these two queries in our later design may not be the same. A simple example of this case is illustrated in Fig. 4, where the search decision at each non-leaf node in tree Γ is made by testing whether a query intersects with the range represented that non-leaf node. Here tree Γ can be imaged as a simple case of an R-tree with only one dimension (further introduction of R-trees will be presented in Sec. 4).

To the best of our knowledge, our work is among the first to distinguish path pattern from the traditional access pattern and capture path pattern in the privacy leakage of a tree-based searchable encryption. Note that the recent solution [19] for keyword search based on the keyword red-black (KRB) tree does not need to particularly capture path pattern in its privacy leakage. It is because if the access pattern

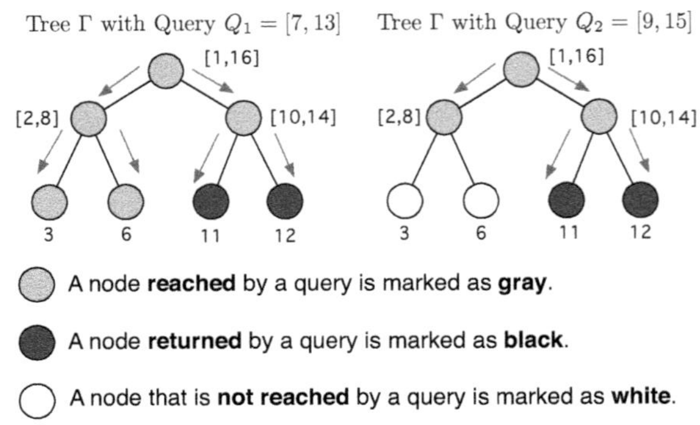

Figure 4: An example of query Q_1 and Q_2 on tree Γ, where Q_1 and Q_2 return the same node (the access pattern defined by Def. 3 are the same) but these two queries do not have the same search paths in the tree (the path pattern are different).

are the same in KRB-trees, the path pattern are also the same [19]. Further details of KRB-trees can found in [19].

Another leakage of our scheme is that, it will also reveal the values of each query to the cloud server (i.e., the cloud server learns which particular range the data owner is searching for a given query), which is referred to as *query privacy*. The query privacy induced by a number of t query $\mathbf{Q} = \{Q_1, ..., Q_t\}$ can be defined as a tuple $\eta(\mathbf{Q}) = (\mathbf{V}_{Q_1}, ..., \mathbf{V}_{Q_t})$, where $\mathbf{V}_{Q_i}$ is the set of values revealed by query Q_i. We will discuss the essential reason about why our scheme fails to protect query privacy, and how to *mitigate* the leakage of query privacy in practice in Sec. 5.

Now we define a *leakage function* [19,20] to capture all the information leakage we mentioned above in a tree-based public-key MDRSE scheme.

Definition 6. **(Leakage Function).** *Given n data records* $\mathbf{D} = \{D_1, ..., D_n\}$, *the corresponding tree structure* $\Gamma = \texttt{BuildTree}(\mathbf{D})$, *the leakage function of* $(\mathbf{D}, \Gamma)$ *induced by a number of t query* $\mathbf{Q} = \{Q_1, ..., Q_t\}$, *is a sequence*

$$\mathcal{L}(\mathbf{D}, \Gamma, \mathbf{Q}) = \{\alpha(\mathbf{D}, \mathbf{Q}), \beta(\mathbf{D}, \mathbf{Q}), \gamma(\mathbf{D}, \mathbf{Q}), \delta(\mathbf{D}, \Gamma, \mathbf{Q}), \eta(\mathbf{Q})\},$$

comprised of size pattern, access pattern, search pattern, path pattern, and content of queries.

Selective Security. By understanding the preceding leakage function, we discuss the selective security of a tree-based public-key MDRSE scheme. Informally speaking, *selective security* means by submitting two sets $\mathbf{D}_0$, $\mathbf{D}_1$ of data records with the same length and isomorphic tree structure (i.e., $\Gamma_0 \simeq \Gamma_1$), a computationally bounded adversary, who has obtained search tokens for t queries $\mathbf{Q} = \{Q_1, ..., Q_t\}$ (*the selection of each query is restricted by* $\mathbf{D}_0$, $\mathbf{D}_1$ *and leakage function* $\mathcal{L}$), is not able to distinguish the two sets of data records.

Definition 7. **(Selective Security).** *Let* $\Pi = ($`GenKey`, `BuildTree`, `Enc`, `GenToken`, `Search`$)$ *be a tree-based public-key MDRSE scheme over lattice* $\mathbb{L}_\Delta$, $\lambda \in \mathbb{N}$ *be the security parameter, the selective security game between an adversary and the challenger in* Π *is described as below*

- **Init:** *The adversary submits two sets* $\mathbf{D}_0$ *and* $\mathbf{D}_1$ *of data records with the same length and isomorphic tree structure* $\Gamma_0 \simeq \Gamma_1$, *where* $\mathbf{D}_0 = \{D_{0,1}, ..., D_{0,n}\}$, $\mathbf{D}_1 = \{D_{1,1}, ..., D_{1,n}\}$, $D_{0,i}$, $D_{1,i} \in \mathbb{L}_\Delta$, *for* $1 \le i \le n$, $\Gamma_0 = \texttt{BuildTree}(\mathbf{D}_0)$ *and* $\Gamma_1 = \texttt{BuildTree}(\mathbf{D}_1)$.

- **Setup:** *The challenger runs* $\texttt{GenKey}(1^\lambda, \Delta)$ *to generate a public key* PK *and a secret key* SK. *It gives* PK *to the adversary, and keeps* SK *private.*

- **Phase 1:** *The adversary adaptively requests search tokens for a number of* t' *range queries* $\mathbf{Q}' = \{Q_1, ..., Q_{t'}\}$ *with the following two restrictions:*

  1. *For* $1 \le j \le t'$, $\mathcal{L}(\mathbf{D}_0, \Gamma_0, Q_j) = \mathcal{L}(\mathbf{D}_1, \Gamma_1, Q_j)$;
  2. *For* $1 \le j \le t'$ *and for* $1 \le i \le n$, *either* $(D_{0,i} \in Q_j) \wedge (D_{1,i} \in Q_j)$, *or* $(D_{0,i} \notin Q_j) \wedge (D_{1,i} \notin Q_j)$,

  The challenger responses each query Q_j, *for* $1 \le j \le t'$, *by running* $\texttt{GenToken}(\texttt{SK}, Q_j)$.

- **Challenge:** *The adversary submits two message sets* $\mathbf{M}_0 = \{M_{0,1}, ..., M_{0,n}\}$ *and* $\mathbf{M}_1 = \{M_{1,1}, ..., M_{1,n}\}$, *where for* $1 \le i \le n$, $M_{0,i}$ *and* $M_{1,i}$ *have the equal length and are subjected to the following restrictions:*

  1. *If there exist some* $j \in [1, t']$ *such that* $(D_{0,i} \in Q_j) \wedge (D_{1,i} \in Q_j)$, *then* $M_{0,i} = M_{1,i}$;
  2. *Otherwise, if for every* $j \in [1, t']$, $(D_{0,i} \notin Q_j) \wedge (D_{1,i} \notin Q_j)$, *then* $M_{0,i} \ne M_{1,i}$.

  Then, the challenger flips a coin $b \in \{0, 1\}$, *and returns* $(\Gamma_b^*, \mathbf{C}_b) \leftarrow \texttt{Enc}(\texttt{PK}, \Gamma_b, \mathbf{M}_b)$ *to the adversary.*

- **Phase 2:** *The adversary continues to adaptively request search tokens for a number of* t *range queries* $\mathbf{Q}_t = (Q_{t'+1}, ..., Q_{t'+t})$, *which are still subjected to the same restrictions in Phase 1 and Challenge.*

- **Guess:** *The adversary takes a guess* b' *of* b.

The advantage of an adversary $\mathcal{A}$ *in the above selective security game is defined as* $\mathbf{Adv}^{SS}_{\Pi,\mathcal{A}}(1^\lambda, \Delta)$. *We say that a tree-based public-key MDRSE scheme* Π *is selectively secure, if for all polynomial time adversaries have at most negligible advantage in the above game:*

$$\mathbf{Adv}^{SS}_{\Pi,\mathcal{A}}(1^\lambda, \Delta) = |\Pr[b' = b] - 1/2| \le \texttt{negl}(\lambda).$$

where $\texttt{negl}(\lambda)$ *denotes a negligible function in* λ.

For the ease of understanding, we can also say that, for $\mathbf{D}_0$ and $\mathbf{D}_1$, as long as the information leakage induced by $\mathbf{Q}$ are the same under leakage function $\mathcal{L}$, $\mathbf{D}_0$ and $\mathbf{D}_1$ are computationally indistinguishable to the adversary.

Note that the requirement of the *isomorphic* tree structure for the two sets of data records in the above security game is necessary, which is similar as the requirement of the *same length* for two messages in the security game of a traditional encryption (e.g., AES). Otherwise, two sets of data records can be easily distinguished via two different tree structures.

Single-Dimensional Privacy. As we mentioned in previous sections, protecting *single-dimensional privacy* is one of the major objectives in this paper. Informally, single-dimensional privacy indicates that, given a search token generated by a multi-dimensional query Q, the cloud server should not be able to obtain the exact search results for any single-dimensional query of Q. In the rest of this paper, we use Q^k to describe the single-dimensional query of Q in the k-th dimension. For instance, given a multi-dimensional query $Q = ([20, 30] \wedge [600, 800])$, the single-dimensional queries of Q in the first and second dimension are presented as $Q^1 = ([20, 30])$ and $Q^2 = ([600, 800])$, respectively. It is easy to see that, if $D \in Q$, then $D \in Q^k$ is true, for every $k \in [1, w]$. However, on the other hand, given $D \in Q^k$, for some $k \in [1, w]$, we cannot sure whether $D \in Q$ is true.

In order to rigorously capture single-dimensional privacy in a tree-based public-key MDRSE scheme, we would like to define a single-dimensional privacy game as follows:

Definition 8. **(Single-Dimensional Privacy).** *Let* $\Pi = (\texttt{GenKey}, \texttt{BuildTree}, \texttt{Enc}, \texttt{GenToken}, \texttt{Search})$ *be a tree-based public-key MDRSE scheme over lattice* $\mathbb{L}_\Delta$, $\lambda \in \mathbb{N}$ *be the security parameter, the single-dimensional privacy game between an adversary and the challenger in* Π *is described as below*

- **Init:** *is same as* **Init** *in* Def. 7.

- **Setup:** *is same as* **Setup** *in* Def. 7.

- **Phase 1:** *The adversary adaptively requests search tokens for a number of* t' *range queries* $\mathbf{Q}' = \{Q_1, ..., Q_{t'}\}$ *with the following three restrictions:*

  1. *For* $1 \le j \le t'$, $\mathcal{L}(\mathbf{D}_0, \Gamma_0, Q_j) = \mathcal{L}(\mathbf{D}_1, \Gamma_1, Q_j)$;
  2. *For* $1 \le j \le t'$ *and for* $1 \le i \le n$, *either* $(D_{0,i} \in Q_j) \wedge (D_{1,i} \in Q_j)$, *or* $(D_{0,i} \notin Q_j) \wedge (D_{1,i} \notin Q_j)$.
  3. *If* $(D_{0,i} \notin Q_j) \wedge (D_{1,i} \notin Q_j)$, *for some* $i \in [1, n]$ *and some* $j \in [1, t']$, *there exists some* $k \in [1, w]$, *such that* $(D_{0,i} \in Q_j^k) \wedge (D_{1,i} \notin Q_j^k)$ *or* $(D_{0,i} \notin Q_j^k) \wedge (D_{1,i} \in Q_j^k)$

  The challenger responses each query Q_j, *for* $1 \le j \le t'$, *by running* $\texttt{GenToken}(\texttt{SK}, Q_j)$.

- **Challenge:** *is same as* **Challenge** *in* Def. 7.

- **Phase 2:** *is same as* **Phase 2** *in* Def. 7.

- **Guess:** *The adversary takes a guess* b' *of* b.

The advantage of an adversary $\mathcal{A}$ *in the above single-dimensional privacy game is defined as* $\mathbf{Adv}^{SDP}_{\Pi,\mathcal{A}}(1^\lambda, \Delta)$. *We say that a tree-based public-key MDRSE scheme* Π *is single-dimensionally private, if for all polynomial time adversaries have at most negligible advantage in the above game:*

$$\mathbf{Adv}^{SDP}_{\Pi,\mathcal{A}}(1^\lambda, \Delta) = |\Pr[b' = b] - 1/2| \le \texttt{negl}(\lambda).$$

where $\texttt{negl}(\lambda)$ *denotes a negligible function in* λ.

Note that if we compare the two games in Def. 7 and Def. 8, the main difference is that Def. 8 has an additional **third** restriction in Phase 1. It is easy to see that if a tree-based public-key MDRSE scheme is selectively secure defined in Def. 7, then it is also single-dimensionally private presented in Def. 8.

4. PRELIMINARIES

Hidden Vector Encryption. Hidden Vector Encryption (HVE) [9], which is a type of predicate encryption proposed by Boneh and Waters, can be utilized to search whether a value is inside a range (e.g., whether $x \in [a, b]$) without revealing this value. Specifically, the encryptor encrypts a pair (x, x), and then the predicate tests $(x \ge a) \wedge (x \le b)$ over the ciphertext of x [9]. Besides, this advanced search is single-dimensionally private (i.e., the predicate will not reveal whether $x \ge a$ or $x \le b$ independently). Details of security analyses and how to initialize this advanced search based on HVE can be found in [9].

According to [9,28], the above method can be further extended to test whether a point is inside a hyper-rectangle

(PK, SK)←**Setup** (1^λ, Δ): Given a security parameter λ and $\Delta = (T_1, \cdots, T_w)$, output a public key PK and a secret key SK.

C ←**Enc** (PK, D, M): Given a public key PK, a point D, a message M, where $M \in \mathcal{M}$ and $\mathcal{M} = \{\texttt{Flag}\}$, output a ciphertext C.

$\texttt{TK}_Q$ ←**GenToken** (SK, Q): Given a secret key SK and a hyper-rectangle Q, output a token $\texttt{TK}_Q$.

$\{M, \perp\}$ ←**Query** ($\texttt{TK}_Q$, C): Given a token $\texttt{TK}_Q$ and a ciphertext C, output M, if $D \in Q$ (the decryption of C is $M = \texttt{Flag}$), and output $\perp$ otherwise.

Correctness: PPE is correct, if for all $D \in \mathbb{L}_\Delta$, all $Q \subseteq \mathbb{L}_\Delta$, all $M \in \mathcal{M}$, all (PK, SK)←**Setup** (1^λ, Δ), all C ←**Enc** (PK, D, M), all $\texttt{TK}_Q$ ←**GenToken** (SK, Q),

- $\texttt{Query}(\texttt{TK}_Q, C) = M$, if $D \in Q$;
- $\Pr[\texttt{Query}(\texttt{TK}_Q, C) = \perp] \geq 1 - \texttt{negl}(\lambda)$, if $D \notin Q$;

where $\texttt{negl}(\lambda)$ is a negligible function in λ.

Figure 5: A Brief Description of PPE.

(e.g., $(x, y) \in [a, b] \wedge [c, d]$) without revealing the point. More concretely, the encryptor can encrypt a tuple (x, x, y, y), and then the predicate tests $(x \geq a) \wedge (x \leq b) \wedge (y \geq c) \wedge (y \leq d)$ over encrypted data. We simply denote this extended approach, which is essentially based on HVE as well, as Point Predicate Encryption (PPE) in this paper. A brief description of PPE is presented in Fig. 5. The security of PPE can be easily conducted based on the security of HVE [9, 28]. We will leverage PPE as a building block in our design to encrypt every node in a tree structure.

R-trees. The R-tree, proposed by Guttman [17], is a type of multi-dimensional data structure, which can be used in many applications, such as range search. The basic idea of an R-tree is to group nearby objects (e.g., points or hyper-rectangles) and represent them with a *bounding box* in the next higher level of the tree. Each leaf node in the tree represents a point (i.e., a data record), and each non-leaf node represents a bounding box (i.e., a hyper-rectangle). An example of an R-tree with four points in the two-dimension are described in Fig. 6.

Clearly, in an R-tree, if a range query does not intersect a bounding box, it also cannot intersect with any objects inside this box. Based on this principle, the search algorithm can efficiently filter most of the unmatched points out of the results while traversing an R-tree, which essentially improves the search efficiency of range queries. A detailed description of the search algorithm in an R-tree is illustrated in Algorithm 1. We can observe that **whether a point lies in a hyper-rectangle** (line 2) and **whether two hyper-rectangles intersect** (line 4) are the two basic factors to make decisions in the search algorithm of an R-tree.

Algorithm 1: SearchR-Tree(v,Q)

Input: The root (or a node) v of an R-tree, and a range query (i.e., a hyper-rectangle) Q.
Output: All points at leaves below v that lie in Q.

```
1 if v is a leaf then
2     Report the point stored at v if it lies in Q.
3 else if v is a non-leaf then
4     if The hyper-rectangle stored at v intersects Q then
5         SearchR-Tree(ChildNode(v), Q).
```

Note that there are other similar multi-dimensional tree structures, such as kd-trees [5], range trees [6] and etc., which can also provide a better search efficiency than linear search with regard to the number of data records. Besides the consideration of improving efficiency, another major reason for us to leverage R-trees is that the designs with R-trees have the potential to achieve single-dimensional privacy. While other multi-dimensional tree structures, like kd-trees or range trees, cannot satisfy single-dimensional privacy no matter what kind of encryption primitive is used on each node. Further discussions about this issue will be presented in the next section.

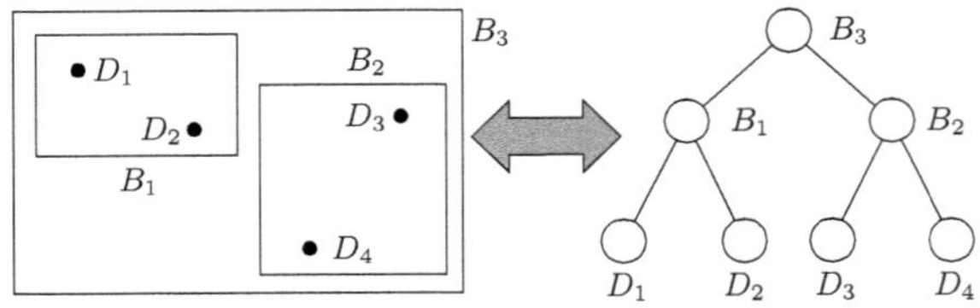

Figure 6: An example of an R-tree with four points.

5. TREE-BASED PUBLIC-KEY MDRSE

In this section, we will first show how to design a basic solution, which is based on PPE without any tree structure but only achieves linear search time regarding to the number of data records. Then, taking this basic solution as a stepping stone, we will describe how to build Maple, a tree-based public-key MDRSE scheme, which is able to not only improve the search efficiency (i.e., faster-than-linear complexity with regard to the number of data records) but also protect the privacy of data records.

Basic Solution. By directly using PPE without any tree structure, we can build a basic solution of public-key MDRSE. Specifically, the data owner can encrypt every data record with PPE, and outsource all the encrypted data to the cloud server. Then, the cloud server can perform search on all the encrypted data records **one by one** based on a token submitted by the data owner. Clearly, the search complexity of this basic solution is **linearly** increasing with the number of data records stored in the cloud server. Considering the databases outsourced to the cloud generally contain a huge number of records, this basic solution is clearly not practical. In fact, this basic solution is essentially the direct implementation of HVE [9] for multi-dimensional range queries. Although it is not efficient, this basic solution can still be included in the formal definition of a public-key MDRSE presented in Sec. 2 by setting tree structure Γ as `null`.

Our Design: Overview and Challenge. In order to improve the search efficiency, we would like to exploit multi-dimensional tree structures (specifically, R-trees) to index all the data records and handle range queries by exactly following the search algorithm of the tree structures. Obviously, it is easy to implement with traditional techniques if the data records are in plaintext. However, it is not simple to exactly follow the search algorithm of the R-tree while all the nodes in the tree are encrypted. More importantly, we need to protect single-dimensional privacy as well, which previous efficient solutions [25, 34] fail to achieve.

Specifically, we can still directly leverage PPE to encrypt every leaf node (i.e., a data record) in an R-tree in order to decide whether a point lies in a hyper-rectangle (line 2 in Algorithm 1) when a range query is submitted; besides, we also need to find a method to encrypt every non-leaf node, so that we can verify whether two hyper-rectangles intersect (line 4 in Algorithm 1) in the ciphertext domain given a range query. Interestingly, by continuing to use PPE in a novel way, we can find a solution to decide whether two hyper-rectangles intersect over encrypted data. More importantly, we can still protect single-dimensional privacy.

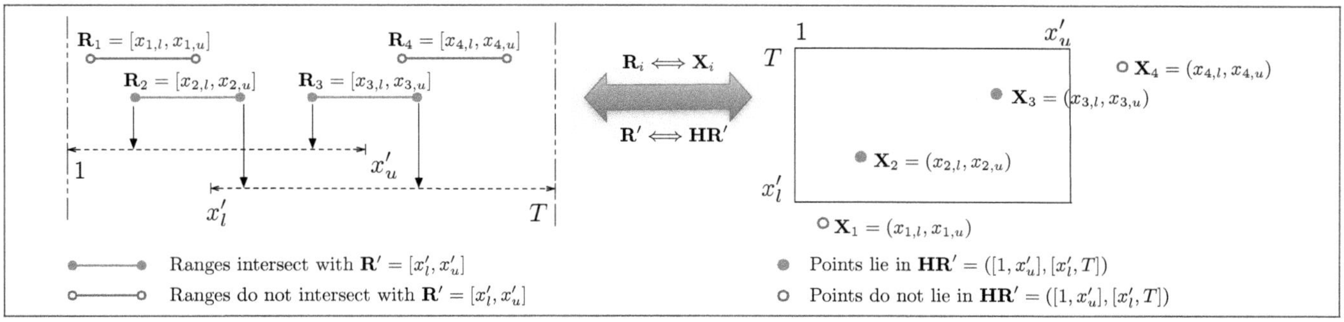

Figure 7: Examples of whether two ranges intersect, and the equivalent relation between a 2-dimensional point and a rectangle.

Using predicate encryption to test other types of geometric relations over encrypted data, such as whether a point is on a line, can be found in [36].

Hyper-Rectangle Intersection. We now explain how to use PPE to verify whether two hyper-rectangles intersect in the ciphertext domain without revealing single-dimensional privacy. For the ease of description, we first start with testing whether two ranges intersect in a single dimension, and then we extend this method into the multi-dimension for verifying the intersection of two hyper-rectangles. The essential idea of our method here is to first transform the geometric relation of two ranges into an **equivalent** geometric relation between a 2-dimensional point and a rectangle, and then encrypt this 2-dimensional point with PPE.

Specifically, given two ranges $\mathbf{R}$ and $\mathbf{R}'$ in a single dimension, we treat the first range $\mathbf{R} = [x_l, x_u]$ as a 2-dimensional point as $\mathbf{X} = (x_l, x_u)$, and transform the second range $\mathbf{R}' = [x'_l, x'_u]$ into a rectangle as $\mathbf{HR}' = ([1, x'_u], [x'_l, T])$. Then, we can decide whether the two original ranges $\mathbf{R}$, $\mathbf{R}'$ intersect by checking whether the point $\mathbf{X}$ lies in the rectangle $\mathbf{HR}'$. If the point is indeed in the rectangle, then the two ranges intersect with each other. Otherwise, they do not intersect. The reason is that these two geometric relations are equivalent, which is proved in the following lemma. Some examples of the intersections of two ranges and the equivalent geometric relation between a point and a rectangle are described in Fig. 7.

Lemma 1. *For two ranges $\mathbf{R} = [x_l, x_u]$ and $\mathbf{R}' = [x'_l, x'_u]$, we have a point $\mathbf{X} = (x_1, x_2) = (x_l, x_u)$ based on range $\mathbf{R}$ and a rectangle $\mathbf{HR}' = (\mathbf{R}'_1, \mathbf{R}'_2)$ based on range $\mathbf{R}'$, where $\mathbf{R}'_1 = [1, x'_u]$ and $\mathbf{R}'_2 = [x'_l, T]$. If $\mathbf{X} \in \mathbf{HR}'$, then $\mathbf{R} \cap \mathbf{R}' \neq \varnothing$; otherwise, $\mathbf{X} \notin \mathbf{HR}'$, then $\mathbf{R} \cap \mathbf{R}' = \varnothing$.*

The correctness of this lemma can be explained as below

$$\mathbf{R} \cap \mathbf{R}' \neq \varnothing \Leftrightarrow \begin{cases} x_l \leq x'_u \\ x_u \geq x'_l \end{cases} \Leftrightarrow \begin{cases} x_l \in [1, x'_u] \\ x_u \in [x'_l, T] \end{cases} \Leftrightarrow \mathbf{X} \in \mathbf{HR}'.$$

Based on this equivalent geometric relation, we can actually encrypt a special message (e.g., `Flag`) with this 2-dimensional point (transformed from $\mathbf{R}$) using PPE, then the decryption result of the ciphertext with a token generated by a rectangle (transformed from $\mathbf{R}'$) will be the special message `Flag`, if the two ranges intersect (i.e., $\mathbf{R} \cap \mathbf{R}' \neq \varnothing$). In this way, we can decide the intersection of two ranges over ciphertexts.

Why Do We Transfer It to An Equivalent Geometric Relation? Readers may wonder why do we have to transfer the geometric relation of two ranges to an equivalent relation between a 2-dimensional point and a rectangle before encryption. How about we directly verify whether the two ranges (i.e., $\mathbf{R} = [x_l, x_u]$ and $\mathbf{R}' = [x'_l, x'_u]$) intersect by checking whether $x_l \in [1, x'_u]$ and $x_u \in [x'_l, T]$ respectively? Is this simpler?

In fact, we have no doubt that the method mentioned in the previous paragraph is simpler than ours, and it is indeed able to correctly verify whether the two ranges intersect. However, the problem about this method is that if we verify the two values (i.e., x_l and x_u) separately, it will inevitably compromise single-dimensional privacy as the same as the limitation introduced in LSED$^+$ [25] and the example we explained in Fig. 1.

Now, by extending our method in Lemma 1, we can decide whether the intersection of two hyper-rectangles is null in the multi-dimension.

Lemma 2. *For two hyper-rectangles $\mathbf{HR} = (\mathbf{R}_1, ..., \mathbf{R}_w)$ and $\mathbf{HR}' = (\mathbf{R}'_1, ..., \mathbf{R}'_w)$, where $\mathbf{R}_i = [x_{i,l}, x_{i,u}]$ and $\mathbf{R}'_i = [x'_{i,l}, x'_{i,u}]$, for $i \in [1, w]$, we have a point $\mathbf{X} = (x_1, ..., x_{2w}) = (x_{1,l}, x_{1,u}, ..., x_{w,l}, x_{w,u})$ and a hyper-rectangle $\mathbf{HR}'' = (\mathbf{R}''_1, ..., \mathbf{R}''_{2w})$, where $\mathbf{R}''_{2i-1} = [1, x'_{i,u}]$ and $\mathbf{R}''_{2i} = [x'_{i,l}, T]$, for $1 \leq i \leq w$. If $\mathbf{X} \in \mathbf{HR}''$, then $\mathbf{HR} \cap \mathbf{HR}' \neq \varnothing$; otherwise, $\mathbf{X} \notin \mathbf{HR}''$, then $\mathbf{HR} \cap \mathbf{HR}' = \varnothing$.*

The correctness of this lemma can be proved using the similar approach in Lemma 1. Similarly, we can encrypt a special message `Flag` with this $2w$-dimensional point (transformed from $\mathbf{HR}$) using PPE, and the result of the decryption of the ciphertext with a token generated by a $2w$-dimensional hyper-rectangle (transformed from $\mathbf{HR}'$) is `Flag`, if $\mathbf{HR} \cap \mathbf{HR}' \neq \varnothing$.

Maple: Scheme Details. With the approach we explained above, we now introduce Maple, a tree-based public-key MDRSE scheme by following the definition presented in Sec. 2. Details of Maple are illustrated in Fig. 8. Specifically, the data owner first generates a public key and a secret key in `GenKey`, and builds an R-tree Γ based on a set $\mathbf{D}$ of data records in `BuildTree`. In `Enc`, the data owner encrypts every node in Γ, and outputs an encrypted R-tree Γ^* and a set of ciphertexts, where Γ^* has the isomorphic tree structure as Γ. Each leaf node (i.e., a point) is directly encrypted with PPE; while each non-leaf node (i.e., a hyper-rectangle) is first transformed into a $2w$-dimensional point, and then encrypted with PPE.

The data owner is able to generate a search token based on a range query in `GenToken`, and submit it to the cloud server to operate `Search`, which starts from the root node of the encrypted R-tree Γ^*. As presented in Fig. 8, at a non-leaf node, if the decryption of a ciphertext is `Flag` (means the hyper-rectangle represented this non-leaf node intersects with the hyper-rectangle represented the range query), then the cloud server continues to search all the child nodes of this non-leaf node; otherwise, the cloud server stops searching its

GenKey(1^λ, Δ): Given a security parameter λ and $\Delta = (T_1, ..., T_w)$, the data owner defines 2Δ as $2\Delta = (T_1, T_1, ..., T_w, T_w)$, and computes

$$(\mathtt{PK}_1, \mathtt{SK}_1) \leftarrow \mathtt{PPE.Setup}(1^\lambda, \Delta),$$
$$(\mathtt{PK}_2, \mathtt{SK}_2) \leftarrow \mathtt{PPE.Setup}(1^\lambda, 2\Delta);$$

and outputs a public key $\mathbf{PK} = \{\mathtt{PK}_1, \mathtt{PK}_2\}$ and a secret key $\mathbf{SK} = \{\mathtt{SK}_1, \mathtt{SK}_2\}$.

BuildTree($\mathbf{D}$): Given a set of data records $\mathbf{D} = (D_1, ..., D_w)$, where $D_i = (d_{i,1}, ..., d_{i,w})$, for $1 \leq i \leq w$, the data owner builds an R-tree Γ.

Enc($\mathbf{PK}$, Γ, $\mathbf{M}$): Given a public key $\mathbf{PK}$, an R-tree Γ and a set of messages $\mathbf{M} = (M_1, ..., M_n)$, the data owner encrypts each node in R-tree Γ as follows:

- If it is a non-leaf node, let $\mathbf{HR}$ be the hyper-rectangle that represents this node, transform $\mathbf{HR} = (\mathbf{R}_1, ..., \mathbf{R}_w)$, where $\mathbf{R}_i = [x_{i,l}, x_{i,u}]$, into a point $\mathbf{X} = (x_1, ..., x_{2w}) = (x_{1,l}, x_{1,u}, ..., x_{w,l}, x_{w,u})$, and compute

$$C \leftarrow \mathtt{PPE.Enc}(\mathtt{PK}_2, \mathbf{X}, \mathtt{Flag}),$$

- If it is a leaf node, it can be represented as a data record $D_i = (d_{i,1}, ..., d_{i,w})$. Let $\mathbf{X}$ be the point that represents this node, set $\mathbf{X} = (x_1, ..., x_w) = (d_{i,1}, ..., d_{i,w})$, and compute

$$C_i \leftarrow \mathtt{PPE.Enc}(\mathtt{PK}_1, \mathbf{X}, M_i),$$

  where $M_i \in \mathcal{M}$ and $\mathcal{M} = \{\mathtt{Flag}\}$.

Eventually, the data owner outputs an encrypted R-tree Γ^* and a set of ciphertext $\mathbf{C} = (C_1, ..., C_n)$.

GenToken($\mathbf{SK}$, Q): Given a secret key $\mathbf{SK}$ and a range query $Q = [x_{1,l}, x_{1,u}] \wedge \cdots \wedge [x_{w,l}, x_{w,u}]$, the data owner represents Q as a hyper-rectangle $\mathbf{HR} = (\mathbf{R}_1, ..., \mathbf{R}_w)$, where $\mathbf{R}_i = [x_{i,l}, x_{i,u}]$ and $1 \leq i \leq w$; generates another hyper-rectangle $\mathbf{HR}' = (\mathbf{R}'_1, ..., \mathbf{R}'_{2w})$, where $\mathbf{R}'_{2i-1} = [1, x_{i,u}]$ and $\mathbf{R}'_{2i} = [x_{i,l}, T_i]$, for $1 \leq i \leq w$; computes

$$\mathtt{TK}_1 \leftarrow \mathtt{PPE.GenToken}(\mathtt{SK}_1, \mathbf{HR}),$$
$$\mathtt{TK}_2 \leftarrow \mathtt{PPE.GenToken}(\mathtt{SK}_2, \mathbf{HR}');$$

and outputs $\mathbf{TK}_Q = \{\mathtt{TK}_1, \mathtt{TK}_2\}$.

Search(Γ^*, $\mathbf{C}$, $\mathbf{TK}_Q$): Given an encrypted R-tree Γ^*, a set of ciphertexts $\mathbf{C} = \{C_1, ..., C_n\}$, a search token $\mathbf{TK}_Q$, the cloud server searches from the root node of Γ^* and performs as follows:

- If it is a non-leaf node represented with a ciphertext C, then if

$$\mathtt{Flag} = \mathtt{PPE.Query}(\mathtt{TK}_2, C);$$

  continue to search its child nodes; otherwise stop searching its child nodes.

- If it is a leaf node represented with a ciphertext C_i, then if

$$M_i = \mathtt{PPE.Query}(\mathtt{TK}_1, C_i);$$

  where $M_i \in \mathcal{M}$ and $\mathcal{M} = \{\mathtt{Flag}\}$, indicate $D_i \in Q$ and return I_i; otherwise, do not return I_i.

Eventually, the cloud server returns a set of identifiers $\mathbf{I}_Q$, where $I_i \in \mathbf{I}_Q$, if $D_i \in Q$.

Figure 8: Details of Maple.

child nodes. At a leaf node, if the decryption of a ciphertext is $M_i \in \mathcal{M}$ (indicates the point represented this leaf node lies in the hyper-rectangle represented the range query), the cloud server returns the identifier (e.g., memory location) of the corresponding data record stored on this leaf node. Eventually, the cloud server returns all the identifiers of the data records that satisfy the submitted range query.

Correctness. Since every node in an encrypted R-tree Γ^* is essentially encrypted with an instance of PPE, the correctness of Maple can be easily explained based on the correctness of PPE. Details are presented in Appendix.

Efficiency. Compared to the search algorithm (described in Sec. 4) of an R-tree in the plaintext domain, the search algorithm in Maple **exactly** follows the same search rules in an R-tree not only at every non-leaf node but also at every leaf node, which enables Maple to achieve the same search complexity as an R-tree with regard to the number of data records. Therefore, our scheme is able to achieve a better efficiency (faster-than-linear complexity regarding to the number of data records) compared to the basic solution.

According to the analyses in [9, 28], an instance of PPE on each node in the tree introduces $O(wT)$ encryption time, ciphertext size and public key size, and $O(w)$ token size and search time, where w denotes the number of dimensions and T denotes the size of each dimension.

Security Analysis. We now discuss the security of Maple.

Theorem 1. *(Selective Security). Maple is selectively secure, if HVE is selectively secure.*

Proof. In our scheme, the encryption of an R-tree Γ is essentially to encrypt all the nodes in Γ one by one. Every node can be *directly or indirectly* encrypted with an instance of PPE, which is essentially an instance of HVE. Briefly speaking, since HVE is selectively secure, Maple – the multiple instances of HVE – is also selectively secure, which is based on the claims about the security of multiple encryption from the textbook [21]. Detailed analyses of Maple by following the selective security game defined in Sec. 2 are presented in Appendix. □

Theorem 2. *(Single-Dimensional Privacy). Maple is single-dimensionally private, if it is selectively secure.*

Proof. According to Def. 7 and Def. 8, if Maple is selectively secure under Def. 7, then it is single-dimensionally private under Def 8. See details in Appendix. □

Note that in Maple, the search token $\mathbf{TK}_Q$ contains two sub-tokens $\{\mathtt{TK}_1, \mathtt{TK}_2\}$, which can be separately used to test different geometric relations during range search in an R-tree (described in Fig. 8). Since each sub-token is generated based on all the w dimensions using PPE, the separate use of these sub-tokens does not compromise single-dimensional privacy of Maple.

About Query Privacy. As we defined in the leakage function $\mathcal{L}$, our scheme does not protect query privacy. It is because the HVE [9] we essentially leveraged in Maple is a public-key approach. While public-key approaches inherently fail to protect query privacy as pointed out by [27].

Based on the current design, one practical approach for us to *mitigate* query privacy leakage in real applications is to add redundancy for each range query. Specifically, for each range query, the data owner can slightly and randomly enlarge the range query to a redundant one. Then, it will first retrieve redundant encrypted results from the cloud server, decrypt them, and calculate the exact results on local devices. In this way, the cloud server will not directly learn the actual range query that the data owner is searching for. As a necessary trade-off, the data owner needs to spend additional overheads to retrieve the redundant encrypted results from the cloud server, and consume extra overheads to calculate the exact results on its local devices as well.

Design with Other Trees. With the same designing methodology (i.e., leveraging HVE to verify geometric relations), we can also build tree-based MDRSE schemes with

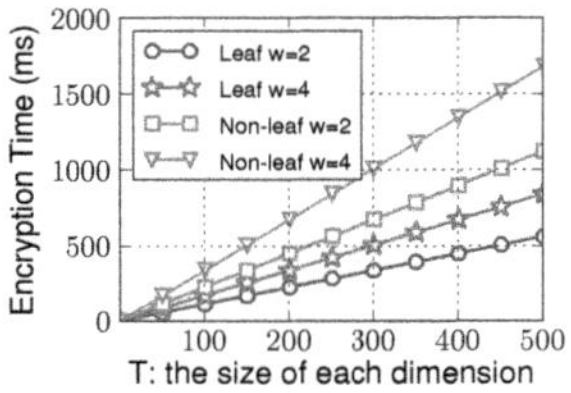

Figure 9: Impact of T on encryption time (millisecond) per node.

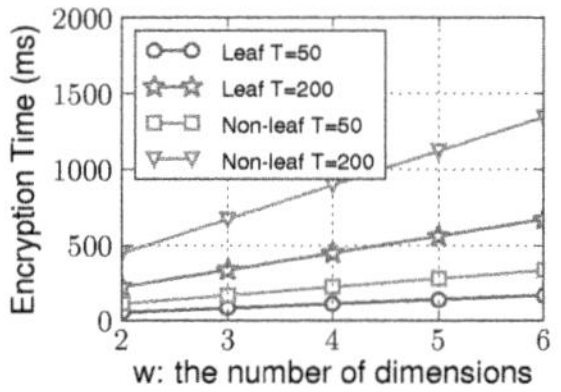

Figure 10: Impact of w on encryption time (millisecond) per node.

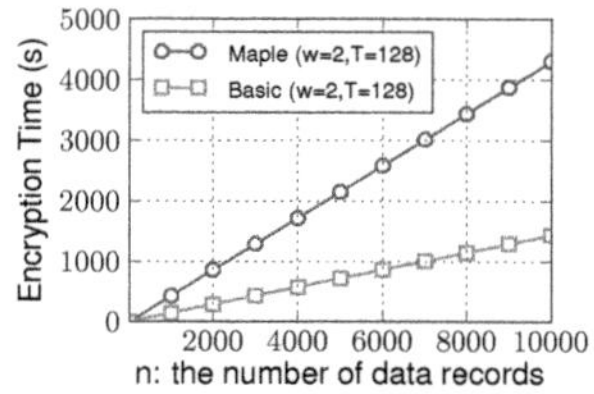

Figure 11: Impact of n on the total encryption time (second).

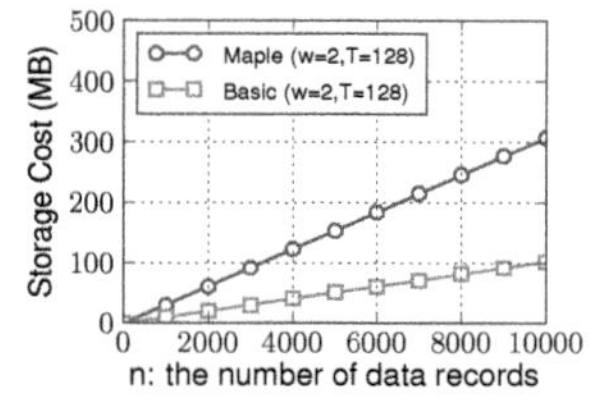

Figure 12: Impact of n on the total storage cost (MB).

different trees, such as kd-trees [5] and range trees [6]. Because the search algorithms of these trees also depend on the geometric relations of hyper-rectangles. However, due to the different nature of tree structures, the design with these two tree structures cannot achieve single-dimensional privacy, even through the use of HVE itself can protect the privacy in single dimensions.

The reason is that, in these trees, the search decision (i.e., the test of the geometric relation) from one node to its child nodes only depends on a single dimension. For instance, the search algorithm of a range tree is to first search all the results in X-dimension, and then based on these results, it will continue to search in Y-dimension. As a result, while searching from one node to its child nodes in X-dimension, the search algorithm does not need to consider the predicate of a multi-dimensional range query in other dimensions. In this case, the cloud server can stop the algorithm right after the search in X-dimension, which easily compromise the single-dimensional privacy in X-dimension. The privacy of Y-dimension can be compromised as well by searching all the data records only in Y-dimension (by skipping X-dimension). The privacy of each particular single dimension in kd-trees can be compromised in a similar way by skipping irrelevant dimensions. Due to the space limitation, we omit the further details in this paper.

Informally, with these trees and HVE, we could still achieve selective security, but only with *tighter* restrictions:

- *For* $1 \leq j \leq t'$, $\mathcal{L}(\mathbf{D}_0, \Gamma_0, Q_j) = \mathcal{L}(\mathbf{D}_1, \Gamma_1, Q_j)$;
- *For* $1 \leq j \leq t'$, *for* $1 \leq i \leq n$ *and for* $1 \leq k \leq w$, *either* $(D_{0,i} \in Q_j^k) \wedge (D_{1,i} \in Q_j^k)$, *or* $(D_{0,i} \notin Q_j^k) \wedge (D_{1,i} \notin Q_j^k)$.

If we compare the restrictions of the single-dimensional privacy game presented in Def. 8, it is easy to see that the above restrictions fail to protect single-dimensional privacy.

R-trees do not have such type of limitations, because the search decision of R-trees from one node to its child nodes depends on all the dimensions. It is worth to notice that, the recent work in [34] is also based on R-trees, however, it is not able to protect single-dimensional privacy. The reason is that the encryption primitive they used at each node requires to divide each search token of a multi-dimensional query into the independent ones in single dimensions just like the limitation introduced in [25]. Therefore, according to our observation, in order to design a faster-than-linear and single-dimensionally private tree-based MDRSE scheme, we need to be careful about not only what type of tree structures will be leveraged, but also what kind of encryption primitive at each node will be used.

6. PERFORMANCE

In this section, we evaluate the performance of our scheme in experiments based on a large-scale real-world dataset. All the experiments are tested in Ubuntu with Intel Core i5 3.30 GHz Processor and 4 GB Memory. We leverage Pairing-Based Library (PBC[2]) to simulate the cost of cryptographic operations. More specifically, the cost of a pairing operation, which is the dominating operation in the search of Maple, is around 6.33 milliseconds (tested on super-singular curve $y^2 = x^3 + x$). We use a part of a large-scale real world data set with millions of records (U.S. census data 1990[3]) to evaluate the search performance of our scheme and the basic solution. In the following experiments, the number of dimensions is denoted as w; the number of data records is denoted as n; and we assume the size of each dimension T.

Encryption Overhead. As shown in Fig. 9 and 10, the encryption time of a non-leaf node and a leaf node are linearly increasing with the number of dimensions and the size of each dimension respectively. For Maple, the total encryption time for all the data records is less efficient than the one in the basic solution as illustrated in Fig. 11. It is because Maple needs to spend additional time to encrypt all the non-leaf nodes in the tree compared to the basic solution. In addition, Maple also requires additional overhead in terms of the storage cost compared to the basic solution. These extra overheads in encryption time and storage cost are necessary trade-offs for improving search efficiency. It is because the essential idea of using tree structures (even in the plaintext domain) is to reduce search time by spending more cost in terms of indexing and storage.

Token Generation Time. In Fig. 13, we describe and compare the generation time of a search token in Maple and the basic solution. Maple requires more time in this process because Maple needs to essentially generate two sub-tokens, one for verifying whether one point lies in a hyper-rectangle and one for deciding whether two hyper-rectangles intersect. While in the basic solution, it only needs to compute one token to test whether a point lies in a hyper-rectangle.

Search Efficiency. We can see from Fig. 14 that the search time per node in Maple is linearly increasing with the number of dimensions. Meanwhile, we can also observe that the search time for each leaf node and the one for each non-leaf node in our scheme are different. The reason is that for each non-leaf node, Maple verifies the geometric relation (whether two hyper-rectangle intersect) with a PPE instance of $2w$ dimensions; while for each leaf node, deciding the geometric relation (whether a point lies in a hyper-rectangle) is performed with a PPE instance of w dimensions.

Next, we compare the efficiency of Maple and the basic solution with 20 random range queries for each case. In order to simulate the search efficiency of Maple, we run the search code of R-trees in the plaintext domain, but add additional time of computing cryptographic operations for testing the geometric relation at each node during the search process.

[2] crypto.stanford.edu/pbc/
[3] http://archive.ics.uci.edu/ml/datasets.html

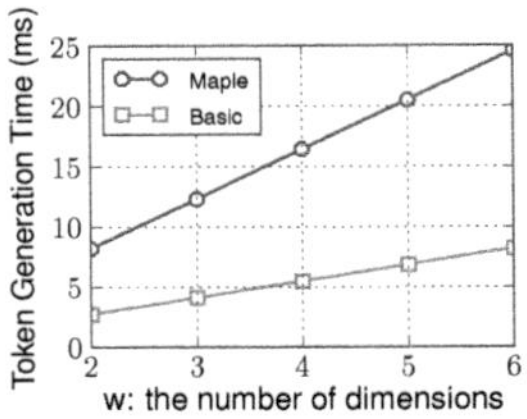

Figure 13: Impact of w on generation time (millisecond) per token.

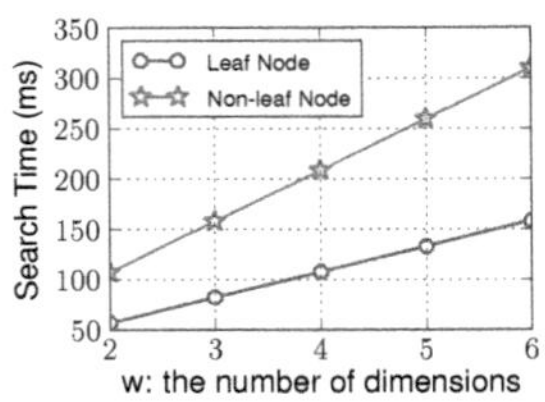

Figure 14: Impact of w on search time (millisecond) per node.

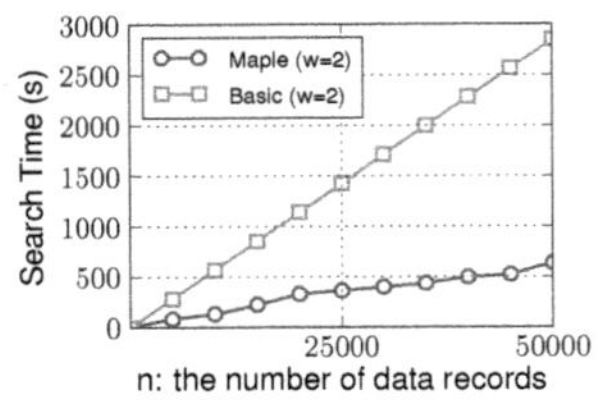

Figure 15: Impact of n on search time (second) with $w = 2$.

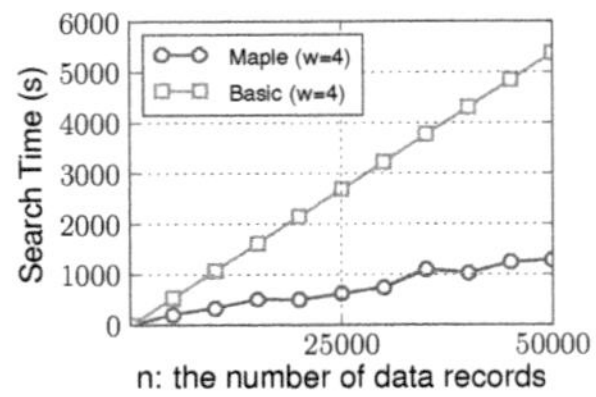

Figure 16: Impact of n on search time (second) with $w = 4$.

As presented in Fig. 15 and 16, the total search time of the basic solution is linearly increasing with the number of data records while the search time can be significantly reduced with the use of Maple.

In Table 2, we compare the search performance of Maple and the basic solution under different scales of data records. We can observe that Maple has a better scalability for large datasets. Specifically, when $n = 100,000$ and $w = 2$, the basic solution requires an average of $5,700$ seconds on each range query while Maple only costs about 928 seconds for operating each range query. Since the dominating cryptographic operations during search is pairing operations [9], we can reduce the computation time for each pairing operation by taking the advantage of special hardware (such as Elliptic Semiconductor CLP-17[4]), which can essentially further improve the search efficiency of Maple in practice.

Table 2: Average Search Time (second) when $w = 2$.

The number of data records	Basic	Maple
1,000	57.02	18.16
10,000	570.18	133.33
100,000	5,700.80	928.42

7. RELATED WORK

Searchable Encryption. SE schemes can be divided into two categories, symmetric-key-based and public-key-based. The first practical symmetric-key keyword search for encrypted text documents was proposed by Song et al. [29], which has *linear* complexity with regard to the document length. Since then, the quest for higher efficiency and better functionality has never stopped. Various schemes have been proposed to improve the efficiency of keyword search by creating an encrypted searchable index such like an inverted index [14,15,33,35]. However, the above works can only support single keyword search functionalities. Recently Cao et al. [11] proposed a multi-keyword ranked search scheme over encrypted cloud data. Kamara et al. focused on enabling privacy-preserving dynamic updates for SSE [20]. However, the search complexity is still *linear* with the number of documents. Moreover, the above works mostly focus on document search and do not apply very well to multi-dimensional range search considered in this paper.

On the other hand, the first public-key keyword searchable encryption was proposed by Boneh et al. [7]. To support more complex queries, conjunctive keyword search solutions over encrypted data have been proposed [16], where the search needs to touch every data record. Bellare et al. [4] proposed an efficient deterministic searchable public-key encryption scheme. Logarithmic search complexity can be achieved with this scheme; however, it only allows equality test. Li et al. [24] proposed a public-key scheme by introducing an additional trusted proxy that keeps a secret proxy key. Unfortunately, it lacks support for efficient arbitrary range queries. Recently, Lai et al. proposed a public-key scheme to support expressive keyword search [23].

Predicate Encryption. Predicate Encryption (or Functional Encryption) is a promising approach to achieve more flexible search functionalities [8, 26]. In general, given a ciphertext encrypted under an attribute A and a predicate function $f()$, the encryption enables a user who holds the corresponding token to $f()$ to test whether $f(A) = 1$ without decrypting ciphertexts.

The primitives designed in [9, 28] are both predicate encryption schemes. According to our discussion in Sec. 1, the straightforward applications of these two schemes can only achieve linear complexity. Katz et al. [22] proposed another public-key predicate encryption scheme that supports inner products. Theoretically, equality, subset, conjunctive, disjunctive predicates can all be expressed in the form of inner-products. However, this scheme incurs an exponential blowup for handling range queries. A good summary about the security definitions of Functional Encryption (FE) and some recent positive results about FE can be found in [1].

8. CONCLUSION

In this paper, we design a tree-based public-key MDRSE for supporting multi-dimensional range queries on encrypted cloud data. We formally define the leakage function and security game of a tree-based public-key MDRSE. By using non-trivial combination of R-trees and HVE, our proposed scheme is able to improve search efficiency and protect single-dimensional privacy simultaneously, while previous solutions fail to achieve. Through rigorous analyses and experiments with real-world datasets, we demonstrate the security and efficiency of our scheme. Our future works include 1) enhancing query privacy while keeping all the good properties in the current design; 2) studying other types of tree structures to improve efficiency and privacy as well.

9. ACKNOWLEDGMENTS

We would like to thank the anonymous reviewers for providing useful suggestions and pointing out the insecurity of our preliminary version based on kd-trees. This work was supported in part by the US National Science Foundation under grant CNS-1218085, NSF of China 61272457, National Project 2012ZX03002003-002, 863 Project 2012AA013102, 111 Project B08038, IRT 1078, FRF K50511010001 and NSF of China 61170251.

10. REFERENCES

[1] S. Agrawal, S. Agrawal, S. Badrinarayanan, A. Kumarasubramanian, M. Prabhakaran, and A. Sahai. Function Private Functional Encryption and Property Preserving Encryption: New Definitions and Positive Resuslts. https://eprint.iacr.org/2013/744.

[4] http://www.elliptictech.com

[2] M. Armbrust, A. Fox, R. Griffith, A. D. Joseph, R. H. Katz, A. Konwinski, G. Lee, D. A. Patterson, A. Rabkin, I. Stoica, and M. Zaharia. A View of Cloud Computing. *Communications of the ACM*, 53(4):50–58, Apirl 2010.

[3] G. Ateniese, R. Burns, R. Curtmola, J. Herring, L. Kissner, Z. Peterson, and D. Song. Provable Data Possession at Untrusted Stores. In *Proc. of ACM CCS'07*, pages 598–610, 2007.

[4] M. Bellare, A. Boldyreva, and A. O'Neill. Deterministic and Efficiently Searchable Encryption. In *Proc. of CRYPTO'07*, pages 535–552, 2007.

[5] J. L. Bentley. Multidimensional Binary Search Trees Used for Associative Searching. *Communications of the ACM*, 18(9):509–517, 1975.

[6] J. L. Bentley. Decomposable Searching Problems. *Information Processing Letters*, 8(5):201–244, 1979.

[7] D. Boneh, G. D. Crescenzo, R. Ostrovsky, and G. Persiano. Public Key Encryption with Keyword Search. In *Proc. of EUROCRYP'04*, pages 506–522, 2004.

[8] D. Boneh, A. Sahai, and B. Waters. Functional Encryption: A New Vision for Public Key Cryptography. *Communications of the ACM*, 55(11):56–64, 2012.

[9] D. Boneh and B. Waters. Conjunctive, Subset, and Range Queries on Encrypted Data. In *Proc. of TCC'07*, pages 535–554, 2007.

[10] X. Boyen and B. Waters. Anonymous Hierarchical Identity-Based Encryption (Without Random Oracles). In *Proc. of CRYPTO'06*, pages 290–307, 2006.

[11] N. Cao, C. Wang, M. Li, K. Ren, and W. Lou. Privacy-Preserving Multi-keyword Ranked Search over Encrypted Cloud Data. In *Proc. of IEEE INFOCOM'11*, pages 829–837, 2011.

[12] D. Cash, J. Jaeger, S. Jarecki, C. Jutla, H. Krawczyk, M.-C. Rosu, and M. Steiner. Dynamic Searchable Encryption in Very-Large Databases: Data Structures and Implementation. In *Proc. of NDSS'14*, 2014.

[13] D. Cash, S. Jarecki, C. Jutla, H. Krawczyk, M.-C. Rosu, and M. Steiner. Highly-Scalable Searchable Symmetric Encryption with Support for Boolean Queries . In *Proc. of CRYPTO'13*, pages 353–373, 2013.

[14] Y.-C. Chang and M. Mitzenmacher. Privacy Preserving Keyword Searches on Remote Encrypted Data. In *Proc. of ACNS'05*, pages 442–455, 2005.

[15] R. Curtmola, J. A. Garay, S. Kamara, and R. Ostrovsky. Searchable Symmetric Encryption: Improved Definitions and Efficient Constructions. In *Proc. of ACM CCS'06*, pages 79–88, 2006.

[16] P. Golle, J. Staddon, and B. Waters. Secure Conjunctive Keyword Search over Encrypted Data. In *Proc. of ACNS'04*, pages 31–45, 2004.

[17] A. Guttman. R-Trees: A Dynamic Index Structure for Spatial Searching. In *Proc. of ACM SIGMOD'84*, pages 47–57, 1984.

[18] S. Hwang, K. Kwon, S. Cha, and B. Lee. Performance Evaluation of Main-Memory R-tree Variants. In *Advances in Spatial and Temporal Databases*, 2003.

[19] S. Kamara and C. Papamanthou. Parallel and Dynamic Searchable Symmetric Encryption. In *Proc. of FC*, pages 258–274, 2013.

[20] S. Kamara, C. Papamanthou, and T. Roeder. Dynamic Searchable Symmetric Encryption. In *Proc. of ACM CCS'12*, pages 965–976, 2012.

[21] J. Katz and Y. Lindell. *Introduction to Modern Cryptography*. CRC Press, 2007.

[22] J. Katz, A. Sahai, and B. Waters. Predicate Encryption Supporting Disjunctions, Polynomial Equations, and Inner Products. In *Proc. of EUROCRYPT'08*, pages 146–162, 2008.

[23] J. Lai, X. Zhou, R. H. Deng, Y. Li, and K. Chen. Expressive Search on Encrypted Data. In *Proc. of ACM ASIACCS'13*, pages 243–251, 2013.

[24] M. Li, S. Yu, N. Cao, and W. Lou. Authorized Private Keyword Search over Encrypted Data in Cloud Computing. In *Proc. of IEEE ICDCS'11*, pages 383–392, 2011.

[25] Y. Lu. Privacy-Preserving Logarithmic-time Search on Encrypted Data in Cloud. In *Proc. of NDSS'12*, 2012.

[26] T. Okamoto and K. Takashima. Hierarchical Predicate Encryption for Inner-Products. In *Proc. of ASIACRYPT'09*, pages 214–231, 2009.

[27] E. Shen, E. Shi, and B. Waters. Predicate Privacy in Encryption Systems. In *Proc. of TCC'09*, pages 457–473, 2009.

[28] E. Shi, J. Bethencourt, T.-H. H. Chan, D. Song, and A. Perrig. Multi-Dimensional Range Query over Encrypted Data. In *Proc. of IEEE S&P'07*, pages 350–364, 2007.

[29] D. Song, D. Wagner, and A. Perrig. Practical Techniques for Searches on Encrypted Data. In *Proc. of IEEE S&P'00*, pages 44–55, 2000.

[30] E. Stefanov, C. Papamanthou, and E. Shi. Practical Dynamic Searchable Encryption with Small Leakage. In *Proc. of NDSS'14*, 2014.

[31] E. Stefanov, M. van Dijk, E. Shi, C. Fletcher, L. Ren, X. Yu, and S. Devadas. Path ORAM: An Extremely Simple Oblivious RAM Protocol. In *Proc. of ACM CCS'13*, pages 299–310, 2013.

[32] W. Sun, B. Wang, N. Cao, M. Li, W. Lou, Y. T. Hou, and H. Li. Privacy-Preserving Multi-keyword Text Search in the Cloud Supporting Similarity-based Ranking. In *Proc. of ACM AISACCS'13*, pages 71–82, 2013.

[33] C. Wang, N. Cao, J. Li, K. Ren, and W. Lou. Secure Ranked Keyword Search over Encrypted Cloud Data. In *Proc. of ICDCS'10*, pages 253–262, 2010.

[34] P. Wang and C. V. Ravishankar. Secure and Efficient Range Queries on Outsourced Databases Using R-trees. In *Proc. of IEEE ICDE'13*, pages 314–325, 2013.

[35] Z. Yang, S. Zhong, and R. N. Wright. Privacy-Preserving Queries on Encrypted Data. In *Proc. of ESORICS'06*, pages 479–495, 2006.

[36] M. Zhang and T. Takagi. GeoEnc: geometric are based keys and policies in functional encrytion systems. In *Proc. of ACISP'11*, pages 241–258, 2011.

APPENDIX

Proof of Correctness. *We say Maple is correct if for all* $\lambda \in \mathbb{N}$*, all* $(\mathbf{PK}, \mathbf{SK})$ *output by* $\texttt{GenKey}(1^\lambda, \Delta)$*, all* $D_i \in \mathbb{L}_\Delta$*, all* Γ *output by* $\texttt{BuildTree}(\mathbf{D})$*, for all* $M_i \in \mathcal{M}$*, all* $(\Gamma^*, \mathbf{C})$ *output by* $\texttt{Enc}(\mathbf{PK}, \Gamma, \mathbf{M})$*, all* $Q \subseteq \mathbb{L}_\Delta$*, all* $\mathbf{TK}_Q$ *output by* $\texttt{GenToken}(\mathbf{SK}, Q)$*, for any* $i \in [1, n]$*:*

- *If* $D_i \in Q$, $\texttt{Search}(\Gamma^*, \mathbf{C}, \mathbf{TK}_Q) = \mathbf{I}_Q$, *where* $I_i \in \mathbf{I}_Q$.
- *If* $D_i \notin Q$: $\Pr[\texttt{Search}(\Gamma^*, \mathbf{C}, \mathbf{TK}_Q) = \mathbf{I}_Q,$ *where* $I_i \notin \mathbf{I}] \geq 1 - \texttt{negl}(\lambda)$;

where $\texttt{negl}(\lambda)$ *is a negligible function in* λ. It is because if $D_i \in Q$,

$$\begin{aligned} & \Pr[\texttt{Search}(\Gamma^*, \mathbf{C}, \mathbf{TK}_Q) = \mathbf{I}_Q, \ \textit{where } I_i \in \mathbf{I}_Q] \\ = \ & \Pr[\texttt{PPE.Query}(\texttt{TK}_1, C_i) = M_i, \ \textit{where } M_i \in \mathcal{M}] = 1. \end{aligned}$$

If $D_i \notin Q$,

$$\begin{aligned} & \Pr[\texttt{Search}(\Gamma^*, \mathbf{C}, \mathbf{TK}_Q) = \mathbf{I}_Q, \ \textit{where } I_i \notin \mathbf{I}_Q] \\ = \ & \Pr[\texttt{PPE.Query}(\texttt{TK}_1, C_i) = \perp] \geq 1 - \texttt{negl}(\lambda). \end{aligned}$$

Proof of Theorem 1. In **Init** of the selective security game of Maple, it is equivalent for the adversary to submit two sets of points $\{\mathbf{D}_0, \mathbf{B}_0\}$ and $\{\mathbf{D}_1, \mathbf{B}_1\}$ with $\Gamma_0 \simeq \Gamma_1$, $\Gamma_0 = \texttt{BuildTree}(\mathbf{D}_0)$ and $\Gamma_1 = \texttt{BuildTree}(\mathbf{D}_1)$, where

$$\begin{aligned} \{\mathbf{D}_0, \mathbf{B}_0\} &= \{D_{0,1}, ..., D_{0,n}, B_{0,1}, ..., B_{0,m}\}, \\ \{\mathbf{D}_1, \mathbf{B}_1\} &= \{D_{1,1}, ..., D_{1,n}, B_{1,1}, ..., B_{1,m}\}. \end{aligned}$$

Here, each D denotes a leaf node, each B denotes a non-leaf node, n denotes the number of leaf nodes and m represents the number of non-leaf nodes. Since the two tree structures are isomorphic, without loss of generality, there should exist an isomorphic function f between these two sets, such that for $1 \leq i \leq n$ and $1 \leq k \leq m$, $f(D_{0,i}) = D_{1,i}$ and $f(B_{0,j}) = B_{1,j}$.

In the **Setup**, the challenger runs $\texttt{GenKey}(1^\lambda, \Delta)$ as

$$\begin{aligned} (\texttt{PK}_1, \texttt{SK}_1) &\leftarrow \texttt{PPE.Setup}(1^\lambda, \Delta), \\ (\texttt{PK}_2, \texttt{SK}_2) &\leftarrow \texttt{PPE.Setup}(1^\lambda, 2\Delta); \end{aligned}$$

to generate a public key $\mathbf{PK} = \{\texttt{PK}_1, \texttt{PK}_2\}$ and secret key $\mathbf{SK} = \{\texttt{SK}_1, \texttt{SK}_2\}$. It gives $\mathbf{PK}$ to the adversary, and keeps $\mathbf{SK}$ private.

In the **Phase 1**, The adversary adaptively issues search tokens for a number of t' range queries $\mathbf{Q}' = \{Q_1, ..., Q_{t'}\}$ with the following two restrictions:

1. For $1 \leq j \leq t'$, $\mathcal{L}(\mathbf{D}_0, \Gamma_0, Q_j) = \mathcal{L}(\mathbf{D}_1, \Gamma_1, Q_j)$;
2. For $1 \leq j \leq t'$ and for $1 \leq i \leq n$, either $(D_{0,i} \in Q_j) \wedge (D_{1,i} \in Q_j)$, or $(D_{0,i} \notin Q_j) \wedge (D_{1,i} \notin Q_j)$.

According to the definition of our leakage function, the first restriction indicates that each query Q_j has the same path pattern on Γ_0 and Γ_1. Specifically, it means at each non-leaf node $B_{0,k}$, each query Q_j makes the same search decision as the one at non-leaf node $B_{1,k}$ (e.g., if query Q_j continues to search the child nodes of node $B_{0,k}$, it will also continue to search the child nodes of node $B_{1,k}$). Since the search decision at each non-leaf node in an R-tree is made by verifying the intersection of two hyper-rectangles without any information on any single-dimension (described in Algorithm 1), the same path pattern based on leakage function $\mathcal{L}$ further indicates

- For $1 \leq j \leq t'$ and for $1 \leq k \leq m$, either $(B_{0,k} \in Q_j) \wedge (B_{1,k} \in Q_j)$, or $(B_{0,k} \notin Q_j) \wedge (B_{1,k} \notin Q_j)$.

For each query $Q_j \in \mathbf{Q}$, its search token $\mathbf{TK}_{Q_j} = (\texttt{TK}_{j,1}, \texttt{TK}_{j,2})$ is computed as

$$\begin{aligned} \texttt{TK}_{j,1} &\leftarrow \texttt{PPE.GenToken}(\texttt{SK}_1, \mathbf{HR}_j), \\ \texttt{TK}_{j,2} &\leftarrow \texttt{PPE.GenToken}(\texttt{SK}_2, \mathbf{HR}'_j); \end{aligned}$$

where $\mathbf{HR}_j$ and $\mathbf{HR}'_j$ are represented via Q_j by following the rules in $\texttt{GenToken}(\mathbf{SK}, Q_j)$.

In **Challenge**, The adversary submits two message sets $\mathbf{M}_0 = \{M_{0,1}, ..., M_{0,n}\}$ and $\mathbf{M}_1 = \{M_{1,1}, ..., M_{1,n}\}$, where for all $1 \leq i \leq n$, $M_{0,i}$ and $M_{1,i}$ have the equal length and are subjected to the following restrictions:

1. If there exist some $j \in [1, t']$ such that $(D_{0,i} \in Q_j) \wedge (D_{1,i} \in Q_j)$, then $M_{0,i} = M_{1,i}$;
2. Otherwise, if for every $j \in [1, t']$, $(D_{0,i} \notin Q_j) \wedge (D_{1,i} \notin Q_j)$, then $M_{0,i} \neq M_{1,i}$.

Then, the challenger flips a coin $b \in \{0, 1\}$, and returns

$$\begin{aligned} &\texttt{PPE.Enc}(\texttt{PK}_1, D_{b,i}, M_{b,i}), \ \textit{for } 1 \leq i \leq n, \\ &\texttt{PPE.Enc}(\texttt{PK}_2, B_{b,k}, \texttt{Flag}), \ \textit{for } 1 \leq k \leq m. \end{aligned}$$

Then, in **Phase 2**, the adversary continues to submit a number of t queries subjected to the same restrictions in **Phase 1** and **Challenge**. Finally, the adversary guesses the value of b in **Guess**.

Based on the security of HVE in [10], given two points X_0 and X_1, PPE is selectively secure under the following restriction:

- For $1 \leq j \leq t'$, either $(X_0 \in Q_j) \wedge (X_1 \in Q_j)$, or $(X_0 \notin Q_j) \wedge (X_1 \notin Q_j)$,

which means the advantage of an adversary $\mathcal{A}$ to distinguish this two points is negligible (i.e., $\mathbf{Adv}^{SS}_{\texttt{PPE},\mathcal{A}}(1^\lambda, \Delta) \leq \texttt{negl}(\lambda)$).

As we explained in the security game of Maple, for each pair of $D_{0,i}$ and $D_{1,i}$ (the second restriction in **Phase 1**) or each pair of $B_{0,k}$ and $B_{1,k}$ (the first restriction in **Phase 1**), it satisfies the restriction of the security game of PPE (essentially HVE [9]), then the advantage of an adversary to guess each $D_{b,i}$ or each $B_{b,k}$ is negligible. Since if the adversary can distinguish any pair of $(D_{0,i}, D_{1,i})$ or $(B_{0,k}, B_{1,k})$, it will be able to distinguish the two sets $\mathbf{D}_0$ and $\mathbf{D}_1$. Therefore, the total advantage of an adversary to guess the value of b in the security game of Maple can be calculated as

$$\begin{aligned} \mathbf{Adv}^{SS}_{\texttt{Maple},\mathcal{A}}(1^\lambda, \Delta) &\leq 1 - (1 - \mathbf{Adv}^{SS}_{\texttt{PPE},\mathcal{A}}(1^\lambda, \Delta))^{n+m} \\ &= 1 - (1 - \texttt{negl}(\lambda))^{n+m} \\ &= 1 - (1 - \texttt{negl}'(\lambda)) \\ &= \texttt{negl}'(\lambda), \end{aligned}$$

where $\texttt{negl}(\lambda)$ and $\texttt{negl}'(\lambda)$ are negligible functions in λ[5]. Therefore, Maple is selectively secure if HVE is selectively secure.

Proof of Theorem 2. Since we already have that for any two points $X_{0,i}$ and $X_{1,i}$ under the restriction of

- For $1 \leq j \leq t'$, either $(X_0 \in Q_j) \wedge (X_1 \in Q_j)$, or $(X_0 \notin Q_j) \wedge (X_1 \notin Q_j)$,

in the selective security game, the advantage of an adversary to distinguish these two points is negligible. Then, with an additional restriction in single-dimensional privacy game:

- And if $(X_{0,i} \notin Q_j) \wedge (X_{1,i} \notin Q_j)$, for some $i \in [1, n]$ and some $j \in [1, t']$, there exists some $k \in [1, w]$, such that $(X_{0,i} \in Q^k_j) \wedge (X_{1,i} \notin Q^k_j)$ or $(X_{0,i} \notin Q^k_j) \wedge (X_{1,i} \in Q^k_j)$,

it does not increase the advantage of the adversary. Therefore, we have

$$\mathbf{Adv}^{SDP}_{\texttt{Maple},\mathcal{A}}(1^\lambda, \Delta) = \mathbf{Adv}^{SS}_{\texttt{Maple},\mathcal{A}}(1^\lambda, \Delta) \leq \texttt{negl}'(\lambda),$$

where $\texttt{negl}'(\lambda)$ is a negligible function in λ. So, Maple is single-dimensionally private if it is selectively secure.

[5]According to the properties of negligible functions presented in Chapter 3 in the textbook [21], for a negligible function $\texttt{negl}(\lambda)$, it is easy to have $(1 - \texttt{negl}(\lambda))^n = 1 - \texttt{negl}(\lambda) \cdot F = 1 - \texttt{negl}'(\lambda)$, where F is a positive polynomial and $\texttt{negl}'(\lambda)$ is still a negligible function in λ.

Privacy of Outsourced k-Means Clustering*

Dongxi Liu
CSIRO Computational Informatics, Australia
dongxi.liu@csiro.au

Elisa Bertino
CS Department, Purdue University
bertino@purdue.edu

Xun Yi
College of Eng. and Sci., Victoria University, Australia
xun.yi@vu.edu.au

ABSTRACT

It is attractive for an organization to outsource its data analytics to a service provider who has powerful platforms and advanced analytics skills. However, the organization (data owner) may have concerns about the privacy of its data. In this paper, we present a method that allows the data owner to encrypt its data with a homomorphic encryption scheme and the service provider to perform k-means clustering directly over the encrypted data. However, since the ciphertexts resulting from homomorphic encryption do not preserve the order of distances between data objects and cluster centers, we propose an approach that enables the service provider to compare encrypted distances with the trapdoor information provided by the data owner. The efficiency of our method is validated by extensive experimental evaluation.

Categories and Subject Descriptors

E.3 [**Data**]: Data Encryption; C.2.4 [**Distributed Systems**]: Distributed applications

General Terms

Security;Algorithms

Keywords

k-Means Clustering; Outsourcing; Data Privacy; Homomorphic Encryption

1. INTRODUCTION

Organizations are collecting increasingly amounts data as knowledge mined from these data is a key enabler for improving decisions and productivity. However, an organization may not have expertise and resource in-house to correctly and efficiently analyze big data. To address this problem, an attractive business model is represented by data analytics service providers who have powerful platforms and advanced analytic skills. Organizations can then outsource their analytics tasks to such service providers.

However, when outsourcing data analytics, organizations (referred to as data owners) often have concerns on the privacy of their data. Such concerns might hamper the acceptance of advanced data analytics services, as in other data management services [1]. To protect the data privacy, the data owners might choose to perturb their data before sending data to the service provider, as often done in privacy-preserving data mining [4]. However, data perturbation may not protect privacy completely [15], and the analytics based on the purturbed data might not be accurate enough.

In this paper, we present a method for protecting the privacy of outsourced k-means clustering, which is a data mining algorithm that partitions a set of data objects into clusters. A data object is closest (e.g., it has the shortest Euclidean distance) to the center of cluster it is allocated into, compared with the centers of other clusters. In our method, the data owner encrypts its data with a homomorphic encryption scheme before sending the data to the service provider. Then, over the encrypted data, the service provider performs k-means clustering and reports clustering results back to the data owner. Under this approach, the privacy of data is protected from the service provider.

The homomorphic encryption scheme we use supports both addition and multiplication over ciphertexts. From the ciphertexts of a data object and a cluster center, this scheme allows the service provider to calculate the ciphertext of squared Euclidean distance between them. To allocate a data object into a cluster, the service provider needs to determine which cluster is closest by comparing the encrypted distances of the data object to all cluster centers.

However, the encrypted distances cannot be compared, since the homomorphic encryption scheme we use, like other modern encryption schemes, is probabilistic and even the same distances are usually encrypted into different ciphertexts. To address this problem, a straightforward approach is to send back to the data owner the encrypted distances for decryption and comparison. However, this approach may incur a huge computational cost at the data owner if there is a large number of data objects, thus negating the benefits of data analytics outsourcing.

In this work, we propose an approach that enables the service provider to compare encrypted distances with the trapdoor information that can be efficiently calculated by the data owner. In particular, the dynamic trapdoor information calculated during each iteration of k-means clustering is dependent only on updated cluster centers, not on any data objects. That is, regardless of the number of data objects, the data owner has only a small amount of constant computation load in each iteration of k-means clustering.

*The work reported in this paper has been partially supported by the US National Science Foundation under grants CNS-1111512 and CNS-1016722.

ASIA CCS'14, June 4–6, 2014, Kyoto, Japan.
Copyright 2014 ACM 978-1-4503-2800-5/14/06 ...$15.00.
http://dx.doi.org/10.1145/2590296.2590332 .

There are order-preserving encryption schemes, such as [6, 2, 18]. However, we cannot use these schemes to encrypt data objects for outsourced k-means clustering, since they are not homomorphic and cannot support the computation of comparable distances and new cluster centers from ciphertexts. Actually, in our method, we use the idea of order-preserving encryption to make ciphertexts from homomorphic encryption comparable with the assistance of trapdoor information.

Privacy-preserving distributed (or two-party) k-means clustering has been proposed [20, 13, 22]. However, distributed k-means clustering has a different goal from outsourced k-means clustering. In distributed k-means clustering, each party contributes part of data to cluster and carries out the computation tasks symmetrically over its own data. For outsourced k-means clustering, the data owner contributes all data and is expected to take as less computational load as possible, while the service provider is supposed to take computational load as much as possible.

The rest of this paper is organized as follows. In Section 2 and Section 3, we introduce the k-means clustering algorithm and the homomorphic encryption scheme we use. Then, in Section 4, we discuss why homomorphic encryption along is unable to support outsourced k-means clustering. Our method for comparing encrypted distances is described in Section 5 and its application to outsourced k-means clustering is given in Section 6. We evaluate our method in Section 7 and discuss the related works in Section 8. The paper is concluded in Section 9.

2. OVERVIEW OF K-MEANS CLUSTERING

In this section, we give a brief overview of the k-means clustering algorithm, which will be modified into a distributed algorithm to cluster homomorphically encrypted data in Section 6. The detailed description and analysis of the k-means clustering algorithm can be found in textbooks, such as [14].

Given a set of data objects, the k-means clustering algorithm partitions these objects into k disjoint subsets, each of which is called a cluster. Each cluster has a center, and each data object in a cluster has the shortest distance (or squared distance) to the center, compared with the distances (or squared distances) to other cluster centers. In our work, each data object is supposed to have multiple attributes (or dimensions), which have real numbers as values. The distances between data objects and cluster centers are defined as their Euclidean distances.

At the initial step, the clustering algorithm selects k initial cluster centers. There are different ways of selecting initial centers [20]. Our work is not related to how initial centers are selected. After determining the initial centers, the clustering algorithm is executed iteratively. In each clustering iteration, the squared distances between each data object and all cluster centers are calculated, and the data object is allocated into a cluster to which the squared distance is the shortest.

After all data objects are allocated, the center of each cluster needs to be updated. The new centers are calculated by averaging each attribute over all the objects allocated into the same clusters. With the new centers, the clustering algorithm starts a new iteration. The clustering algorithm terminates when the allocation of data objects does not change any more, or the specified number of iterations has reached. No allocation change is the termination condition used in our distributed clustering algorithm.

3. HOMOMORPHIC ENCRYPTION

In our approach, the outsourced data is encrypted homomorphically. The encryption scheme we use is defined in a patent specification [17]. To make this paper self-contained, this scheme is introduced below with examples and brief security analysis. Our contribution in this work is an efficient method of applying this scheme to protect the data privacy in outsourced k-means clustering, not the encryption scheme itself. Actually, this method can also be applied with other homomorphic encryption schemes, as discussed in Section 8.

3.1 Key, Encryption and Decryption

A key $K(m)$ is a list $[(k_1, s_1, t_1), ..., (k_m, s_m, t_m)]$, where k_i, s_i and t_i are real numbers ($i = 1, ..., m$). This scheme requires $m \geq 3$, $k_i \neq 0$ $(1 \leq i \leq m-1)$, $k_m + s_m + t_m \neq 0$, and only one i $(1 \leq i \leq m-1)$ such that $t_i \neq 0$. Given the key $K(m)$, the algorithm $\texttt{Enc}$ encrypts a real number v into the ciphertext $(e_1, ..., e_m)$, denoted by $\texttt{Enc}(K(m), v) = (e_1, ..., e_m)$, where e_i is called a subciphertext. The algorithm $\texttt{Enc}$ is defined by the following steps[1].

- Uniformly sample m random real numbers r_1,..., r_m, which can be arbitrarily large.
- Compute $e_1 = k_1 * t_1 * v + s_1 * r_m + k_1 * (r_1 - r_{m-1})$.
- Compute $e_i = k_i * t_i * v + s_i * r_m + k_i * (r_i - r_{i-1})$ for $2 \leq i \leq m-1$.
- Compute $e_m = (k_m + s_m + t_m) * r_m$.

Given a ciphertext $(e_1, ..., e_m)$ and the key $K(m)$, the decryption algorithm $\texttt{Dec}$ returns the plaintext v by the following steps. The decryption operation is denoted as $\texttt{Dec}(K(m), (e_1, ..., e_m)) = v$.

- $T = \sum_{i=1}^{m-1} t_i$.
- $S = e_m/(k_m + s_m + t_m)$.
- $v = (\sum_{i=1}^{m-1} (e_i - S * s_i)/k_i)/T$.

Here is an example for this scheme. Suppose a key $K(4)$ is the list $[(3.2, 2.7, 0), (9.1, 3.1, 1.5), (3.6, 7.9, 0), (2.1, 8.8, 7.9)]$, and the value to be encrypted is 34.7. Suppose that the following four random numbers are generated for the encryption: 5689.23, 375623145.2, −8523.87 and 24231.47. Then, the four subciphertexts are generated as follows.

- $e_1 = 3.2 * 0 * 34.7 + 2.7 * 24231.47 + 3.2 * (5689.23 - (-8523.87)) = 110906.889$.
- $e_2 = 9.1*1.5*34.7+3.1*24231.47+9.1*(375623145.2 - 5689.23) = 3418194440.539$.
- $e_3 = 3.6 * 0 * 34.7 + 7.9 * 24231.47 + 3.6 * (-8523.87 - 375623145.2) = -1352082580.039$.
- $e_4 = (2.1 + 8.8 + 7.9) * 24231.47 = 455551.636$.

For decryption, we first calculate $T = 0+1.5+0 = 1.5$ and $S = 455551.636/(2.1+8.8+7.9) = 24231.47$. Then, we evaluate the expression $((e_1 - 2.7 * S)/3.2 + (e_2 - 3.1 * S)/9.1 + (e_3 - 7.9 * S)/3.6)/T$, obtaining the correct plaintext 34.7.

This scheme is semantically secure when the size of plaintexts is bounded (i.e., not allowing arbitrarily large plaintexts). Here we briefly discuss its security. Let e be a ciphertext which encrypts v or

[1]In [17], this scheme is more secure by allowing a more flexible key structure, which may have multiple s components in a key element (i.e., a key element can be $(k_i, s_{i1}, s_{i2}, ..., t_i)$ in[17]) and accordingly a subciphertext may include multiple such terms as s_{ij} multiplying by a random.

v'. The semantic security requires that the adversary cannot distinguish whether e encrypts v or v' with a probability non-negligibly higher than $\frac{1}{2}$ [16]. Intuitively, since the plaintexts are bounded and the random numbers in this scheme can be arbitrarily large, the value of cipherext e is dominated by the value of random numbers. Hence, the advantage of distinguishing whether e encrypts v or v' is asymptotically equal to distinguishing the value of random numbers used in e. Suppose each random number has p decimal digits. Then, the probability of distinguishing a particular value of random numbers is $O(\frac{1}{10^p})$ due to uniformly sampling. The function $\frac{1}{10^p}$ is negligible with respect to the variable p, because it is the inverse of the exponential function 10^p.

3.2 Homomorphism

This encryption scheme supports both addition and multiplication over ciphertexts. Suppose two plaintext values v and v' are encrypted with the key $K(m)$: $\texttt{Enc}(K(m), v) = (e_1, ..., e_m)$, and $\texttt{Enc}(K(m), v') = (e'_1, ..., e'_m)$. Then, this scheme is additively homomorphic and thus ensures that $\texttt{Dec}(K(m), (e_1 + e'_1, ..., e_m + e'_m)) = v + v'$.

For the multiplicative homomorphism, there are two cases for this scheme. The first one is that given a real number b we have $\texttt{Dec}(K(m), (b*e_1, ..., b*e_m)) = b*v$. Combined with the additive homomorphism, we have $\texttt{Dec}(K(m), (e_1 + b * e'_1, ..., e_m + b * e'_m)) = v + b * v'$. When $b = -1$, we can calculate $v - v'$ from the two ciphertexts. The calculation of $v - v'$ is needed when calculating the Euclidean distance in k-means clustering.

The second case of multiplicative homomorphism is about calculating $v * v'$ from their ciphertexts. In this case, the two ciphertexts need to be multiplied as their outer product $(e_1 * e'_1, ..., e_1 * e'_m, ..., e_m * e'_1, ..., e_m * e'_m)$. Then, $v * v'$ is obtained by decrypting this ciphertext in two steps: 1) for $1 \leq i \leq m$, by performing the operation $\texttt{Dec}(K(m), (e_i * e'_1, ..., e_i * e'_m) = e_i * v'$, and then 2) by performing the operation $\texttt{Dec}(K(m), (e_1 * v', ..., e_m * v') = v * v'$.

Based on the additive and multiplicative homomorphism, this encryption scheme supports the calculation of multivariate polynomials over encrypted data, as explained by the following example. Suppose six real numbers v_i $(1 \leq i \leq 6)$ are encrypted as the ciphertexts $\texttt{Enc}(K(m), v_i)$, and from these ciphertexts, we want to calculate $v_1 + v_2 * v_3 + v_4 * v_5 * v_6$. Then, this can be done by using the expression:

$$(\texttt{Enc}(K(m), v_1) \otimes \texttt{Enc}(K(m), 1) \otimes \texttt{Enc}(K(m), 1)) \oplus$$
$$(\texttt{Enc}(K(m), v_2) \otimes \texttt{Enc}(K(m), v_3) \otimes \texttt{Enc}(K(m), 1)) \oplus$$
$$(\texttt{Enc}(K(m), v_4) \otimes \texttt{Enc}(K(m), v_5) \otimes \texttt{Enc}(K(m), v_6))$$

where $\otimes$ represents the operation of calculating the outer product of two ciphertexts, and $\oplus$ the operation of adding two ciphertexts. The encryption of one, $\texttt{Enc}(K(m), 1))$, is used to ensure the three ciphertexts resulted for calculating $v_1 * 1 * 1$, $v_2 * v_3 * 1$ and $v_4 * v_5 * v_6$ have the same number of subciphertexts, so that they can be added to produce the ciphertext for $v_1 * 1 * 1 + v_2 * v_3 * 1 + v_4 * v_5 * v_6$.

Our method for securely outsourcing k-means clustering can also be applied with other homomorphic encryption schemes, such as [8]. However, the homomorphism of this scheme makes it more suitable to encrypt data for k-means clustering, as explained by the following two reasons.

First, other schemes allow only integer or bit operations over ciphertexts. The integer or bit operations are not suitable for calculating new cluster centers, since averaging each attribute of data objects in a cluster involves real numbers (i.e., the inverse of the number of data objects in a cluster) [10]. For example, if a cluster includes 3 data objects, then the new center for this cluster is obtained by multiplying the sum of each attribute of these 3 data objects by 0.33 (i.e., $\frac{1}{3}$).

Second, other schemes usually bound the results of homomorphic operations (e.g., the squared distances between data objects and cluster centers) by the modulus used in decryption; that is, if the results are larger than the modulus, the decrypted results will not be correct [19]. On the contrary, the homomorphic encryption scheme introduced in this section does not bound the squared distances or the sums of data objects in the same cluster, since it does not rely on modulus operations in decryption.

4. THE PROBLEM OF CLUSTERING ENCRYPTED DATA

In this section, we discuss the problem of clustering homomorphically encrypted data. To make the discussion easier, we assume that the data objects have only one dimension (i.e., we assume that each data object is a real number). Let v be a data object, and c and c' be two cluster centers. These values are encrypted, as shown below, with a key $K(m)$, which is known only by the data owner.

$$\texttt{Enc}(K(m), v) = (ve_1, ..., ve_m)$$
$$\texttt{Enc}(K(m), c) = (ce_1, ..., ce_m)$$
$$\texttt{Enc}(K(m), c') = (ce'_1, ..., ce'_m)$$

The encrypted data are then outsourced to the service provider for clustering. The privacy of these data is kept, since the service provider does not know the encryption key.

A step of the k-means clustering algorithm is to calculate the Euclidean distances between data objects and cluster centers. From the above three ciphertexts, the service provider can calculate the squared Euclidean distances between the data object v and two clusters c and c', respectively. Let $VC_i = ve_i - ce_i$ and $VC'_i = ve_i - ce'_i$ $(1 \leq i \leq m)$. Then, the squared distance between v and c calculated by the service provider is the following ciphertext (i.e., the ciphertext of $(v - c) * (v - c)$).

$$(VC_1 * VC_1, ..., VC_1 * VC_m, ..., VC_m * VC_1, ..., VC_m * VC_m)$$

Similarly, the squared distance between v and c is the following ciphertext (i.e., the ciphertext of $(v - c') * (v - c')$).

$$(VC'_1 * VC'_1, ..., VC'_1 * VC'_m, ..., VC'_m * VC'_1, ..., VC'_m * VC'_m)$$

After calculating the distance, the k-means clustering algorithm will assign the data object v into the cluster with respect to which v has the shortest distance. However, since the encryption scheme is probabilistic and not order preserving [3], the service provider cannot compare the above encrypted distances to determine which cluster has a smaller distance to v. Moreover, to the best of our knowledge, there is no homomorphic encryption scheme that is also homomorphically order-preserving.

A simple approach might be to send the above encrypted distances back to the data owner, who has the key to decrypt the distances to get $(v - c) * (v - c)$ and $(v - c') * (v - c')$, which can then be compared. However, this approach is not practical and negates the advantages of outsourcing data analytics, since the number of encrypted distances, equal to the number of data objects times the number of clusters, might be very large and decrypting those encrypted distances places too much computational load on the data owner.

5. COMPARING ENCRYPTED DISTANCES

In this section, we describe a method that can securely derive order information from the encrypted distances, such that the service provider can compare the encrypted distances directly.

5.1 Order-Preserving Indexing

We start with introducing an order-preserving indexing scheme [18]. Given an indexing key k and a value v, the expression $OPI(k, v)$ produces an index of v. For two values v_1 and v_2, if $v_1 > v_2$, the order-preserving indexing scheme ensures that $OPI(k, v_1) > OPI(k, v_2)$. This indexing scheme does not support the recovery of value v from an index $OPI(k, v)$, even if k is known. However, this indexing scheme is acceptable for us, since we observe that k-means clustering does not really need the decrypted distances, instead only their order.

The definition of $OPI(k, v)$ needs the sensitivity of plaintext values, which is a positive real number reflecting the minimum gap between two different plaintext values. The sensitivity can be determined by the scale of plaintext values (i.e., the number of digits to the right of the decimal point in plaintext values). For example, if the plaintext values have the format $XXX.XX$, where X is a decimal digit, then their sensitivity is 0.01. That is, if plaintext values have the scale s, then their sensitivity is 10^{-s}.

The indexing key k in [18] is defined as a pair of real numbers (a, b), where $a > 0$ and $sens$ is the sensitivity of plaintexts, and $OPI(k, v) = a*v+b+r$, where r is a random number uniformly sampled from $[0, a * sens)$. Suppose $v_1 > v_2$, $OPI(k, v) = a * v_1+b+r_1$ and $OPI(k, v_2) = a*v_2+b+r_2$. Then, $OPI(k, v_1) - OPI(k, v_2) = a*(v_1-v_2)+r_1-r_2$. Since $a*(v_1-v_2) \geq a*sens$ and $-a*sens < r_1-r_2 < a*sens$, we have the order-preserving property $OPI(k, v_1) - OPI(k, v_2) > 0$.

5.2 The Method for Comparing Ciphertexts

Our method for comparing ciphertexts is to convert a cipherext into an order-preserving index. We use this method to compare encrypted distances in k-means clustering. However, it can also be applied to compare ciphertexts in other applications. Hence, for generality, we represent a ciphertext in the form $a*f(V)+g(V, R)$, where a belongs to the encryption key, V a set of plaintext values, R a set of random numbers, f and g two functions defined with addition or multiplication operations (i.e., reflecting the operations over ciphertexts in a fully homomorphic encryption scheme).

Our method needs the sensitivity of $f(V)$, which specifies the minimum gap between $f(V_1)$ and $f(V_2)$ for two different sets of plaintext values V_1 and V_2. The sensitivity of $f(V)$ is determined by its maximum scale. If its maximum scale is s, then its sensitivity is 10^{-s}. The scale of $f(V)$ can be derived from the scales of values in V by the following rules. Suppose $v_1 \in V$ and $v_2 \in V$ have the scales s_1 and s_2, respectively. Then, the scale of $v_1 + v_2$ is the bigger one in s_1 and s_2, and the scale of $v_1 * v_2$ is $s_1 + s_2$.

Suppose $f(V)$ has sensitivity $sens_f$. Given a ciphertext $a * f(V) + g(V, R)$, our method converts it into the order-preserving index $a * f(V) + b + r$, where the pair (a, b) is the indexing key and r is a random number uniformly sampled from $[0, a * sens_f)$. Hence, according to the above order-preserving indexing scheme, if $f(V_1) > f(V_2)$, we have $a*f(V_1)+b+r_1 > a*f(V_2)+b+r_2$.

To allow a service provider to convert a ciphertext into an order-preserving index, the data owner needs to provide the trapdoor information $-g(V, R)+b+r$. By adding the trapdoor information to the ciphertext, the service provider gets the order-preserving index $a*f(V)+b+r$. Note that the trapdoor information $-g(V, R)+b+r$ is randomised with r, so it is secure for the data owner to provide such information to the service provider. Moreover, in our application of k-means clustering, $f(V)$ will be the squared distances between data objects and cluster centers, so the conversion of $f(V)$ to order-preserving indexes does not reduce the security of homomorphically encrypted data objects.

In the following, we apply this method to compare encrypted distances in the k-means clustering algorithm. For this application, we define an approach that allows the data owner to use only the updated cluster centers to compute the trapdoor information in each k-means clustering iteration. Since the number of clusters is usually small, the approach makes it possible for the data owner to efficiently compute the trapdoor information.

5.3 Encrypted Distances

Suppose that there are $n > 1$ data objects and k clusters, and that O_i $(1 \leq i \leq n)$ is the ith data object and C_t $(1 \leq t \leq k)$ is the tth cluster center. The data object O_i and the cluster center C_t are supposed to have d dimensions. The values of the jth dimension of O_i and C_t are represented by v_{ij} and c_{tj}, respectively. That is, $O_i = (v_{i1}, ..., v_{id})$ and $C_t = (c_{t1}, ..., c_{td})$. Then, the squared distance between O_i and C_t is $\sum_{j=1}^{d}(v_{ij} - c_{tj})^2$, denoted by $D^2(O_i, C_j)$. In the following, we compute the encrypted distance from the ciphertexts of O_i and C_t. This computation can be done by the service provider.

Let $K(m)$ be the key used to encrypt each attribute in all data objects and cluster centers. With this key, the encryption of v_{ij} is $\texttt{Enc}(K(m), v_{ij}) = (e_{ij1}, ..., e_{ijm})$ and the encryption of c_{tj} is $\texttt{Enc}(K(m), c_{tj}) = (e'_{tj1}, ..., e'_{tjm})$. Recall that the key $K(m)$ is a list $[(k_1, s_1, t_1), ..., (k_m, s_m, t_m)]$ and there is only one i $(1 \leq i \leq m-1)$ such that $t_i \neq 0$. For simplicity, we assume $t_1 \neq 0$. Hence, only the subciphertext e_{ij1} contains the information of v_{ij}, and the subciphertext e'_{tj1} contains the information of c_{tj}. We use e_{ij1} and e'_{tj1} to compute the encrypted distance between O_i and C_t. The other subciphertexts e_{ij2},...,e_{ijm} of v_{ij} will be needed when calculating new cluster centers, while the subciphertexts e'_{tj2},...,e'_{tjm} of c_{tj} are not needed.

According to the encryption scheme, we have $e_{ij1} = k_1 * t_1 * v_{ij}+s_1*r_{ijm}+k_1*(r_{ij1}-r_{ij(m-1)})$ and $e'_{tj1} = k_1*t_1*c_{tj}+s_1*r'_{tjm} + k_1 * (r'_{tj1} - r'_{tj(m-1)})$, where the random numbers r_{ij1}, $r_{ij(m-1)}$, r_{ijm} are generated for the encryption of v_{ij}, and r'_{tj1}, $r'_{tj(m-1)}$, and r'_{tjm} are for the encryption of c_{tj}. By using e_{ij1} and e'_{tj1}, the service provider can calculate $ED^2(O_i, C_t)$, which encrypts $D^2(O_i, C_t)$.

$$
\begin{aligned}
ED^2(O_i, C_t) &= \textstyle\sum_{j=1}^{d}(e_{ij1} - e'_{tj1})^2 \\
&= \textstyle\sum_{j=1}^{d}(k_1 * t_1 * (v_{ij} - c_{tj}) + (NV_{ij} - NC_{tj}))^2 \\
&= (k_1 * t_1)^2 * \textstyle\sum_{j=1}^{d}(v_{ij} - c_{tj})^2 \\
&\quad +2 * k_1 * t_1 * \textstyle\sum_{j=1}^{d}(v_{ij} - c_{tj}) * (NV_{ij} - NC_{tj}) \\
&\quad +\textstyle\sum_{j=1}^{d}(NV_{ij} - NC_{tj})^2 \\
&= (k_1 * t_1)^2 * D^2(O_i, C_t) \\
&\quad +2 * k_1 * t_1 * \textstyle\sum_{j=1}^{d}(v_{ij} - c_{tj}) * (NV_{ij} - NC_{tj}) \\
&\quad +\textstyle\sum_{j=1}^{d}(NV_{ij} - NC_{tj})^2 \\
\text{where} \quad NV_{ij} &= s_1 * r_{ijm} + k_1 * (r_{ij1} - r_{ij(m-1)}) \\
NC_{tj} &= s_1 * r'_{tjm} + k_1 * (r'_{tj1} - r'_{tj(m-1)})
\end{aligned}
$$

To convert $ED^2(O_i, C_t)$ into an order-preserving index, we need to express it in the format $a * f(V) + g(V, R_{it})$. This can be achieved by defining a, $f(V)$ and $g(V, R_{it})$ as follows, where $V = \{O_i, C_t\}$ and $R_{it} = \{r_{ij1}, r_{ij(m-1)}, r_{ijm}, r'_{tj1}, r'_{tj(m-1)}, r'_{tjm} | 1 \leq j \leq d\}$.

$$
\begin{aligned}
a &= (k_1 * t_1)^2 \\
f(V) &= D^2(O_i, C_t) = \textstyle\sum_{j=1}^{d}(v_{ij} - c_{tj})^2 \\
g(V, R_{it}) &= 2 * k_1 * t_1 * \textstyle\sum_{j=1}^{d}(v_{ij} - c_{tj}) * (NV_{ij} - NC_{tj}) \\
&\quad +\textstyle\sum_{j=1}^{d}(NV_{ij} - NC_{tj})^2
\end{aligned}
$$

As discussed above, if the data owner can provide the trapdoor information $-g(V, R_{it}) + b + r$ to the service provider, then the order-preserving index $a * f(V) + b + r$ can be obtained for the the service provider to compare the squared distance $ED^2(O_i, C_j)$. The sampling range of r needs the sensitivity of $D^2(O_i, C_t)$ for all $1 \le i \le n$ and $1 \le t \le k$. As discussed before, the sensitivity can be determined from the scale of $D^2(O_i, C_t)$. If the bigger scale of v_{ij} and c_{tj} is s, then the scale $D^2(O_i, C_t)$ is $s + s = 2 * s$ and hence the sensitivity of $D^2(O_i, C_t)$ is 10^{-2*s}.

5.4 Efficient Computation of Trapdoor Information

In the trapdoor information for $ED^2(O_i, C_t)$, the term $g(V, R)$ is dependent on the data object O_i and the cluster center C_t. Then, in an iteration of the k-means clustering algorithm, the data owner needs to compute the trapdoor information $n * k$ times for each combination of data objects and cluster centers. Since n might be large, it is still not efficient for the data owner to compute so many times of trapdoor information in each iteration. In the following, we present an efficient method to compute trapdoor information.

5.4.1 *Refining Trapdoor Information*

Our idea is to refine the trapdoor information for the encrypted distance $ED^2(O_i, C_t)$ into static trapdoor information and dynamic trapdoor information. The static trapdoor information is fixed after the data objects and initial cluster centers have been encrypted. In other words, the static trapdoor information will not change after being generated; hence, it can be reused by all k-means clustering iterations. On the contrary, the dynamic trapdoor information needs to be recomputed for new cluster centers in each iteration. However, the dynamic trapdoor information is computed only from the cluster centers, which are usually few.

In the previous section, the trapdoor information for $ED^2(O_i, C_t)$ is defined as $-g(\{O_i, C_t\}, R_{it}) + b + r$, where R_{it} contains the random numbers generated during the encryptions of O_i and C_t, b is a secret key, and r is a random number sampled from $[0, (k_1 * t_1)^2 * sens)$ with $sens$ being the sensitivity of $ED^2(O_i, C_t)$. To compute this trapdoor information efficiently, we refine it into the following expression:

$$\mathtt{STrap}_{it}(O_i, R_{it}) + \sum_{j=1}^{d} \mathtt{DTrap}_{tj}(c_{tj}) * \mathtt{STrap}_{itj}(R_{it}) + \mathtt{DTrap}_{t}(C_t, b)$$

where the terms $\mathtt{STrap}_{it}(O_i, R_{it})$ and $\mathtt{STrap}_{itj}(R_{it})$ contain the static trapdoor information, while $\mathtt{DTrap}_{tj}(c_{tj})$ and $\mathtt{DTrap}_{t}(C_t, b)$ contain the dynamic trapdoor information. The subscripts i, t or j in a term (e.g., $\mathtt{STrap}_{it}(O_i, R_{it})$) indicate that the term contains the static or dynamic trapdoor information for the ith data object, the tth cluster or the jth dimensional value. Since these terms will be separately generated and stored, the subscripts i, t and j are used to correlate them.

In the following, we give the definitions of these terms, with their correctness proved in the next section. From the definitions below, we can see that $\mathtt{STrap}_{it}(O_i, R_{it})$ and $\mathtt{STrap}_{itj}(R_{it})$ are not dependent on the cluster center C_t, so even if C_t is updated in a new clustering iteration, $\mathtt{STrap}_{it}(O_i, R_{it})$ and $\mathtt{STrap}_{itj}(R_{it})$ do not need to be recomputed. On the other hand, $\mathtt{DTrap}_{tj}(c_{tj})$ and $\mathtt{DTrap}_{t}(C_t, b)$ are not dependent on the data object O_i. Hence, the computation or recomputation of $\mathtt{DTrap}_{tj}(c_{tj})$ and $\mathtt{DTrap}_{t}(C_t, b)$ does not involve the large number of data objects.

- $\mathtt{STrap}_{it}(O_i, R_{it})$ is defined by the following expression, where NV_{ij} and NC_{tj} are the same as in the definition of $ED^2(O_i, C_t)$.

$$-2 * k_1 * t_1 * \sum_{j=1}^{d} v_{ij} * (NV_{ij} - NC_{tj}) - \sum_{j=1}^{d} (NV_{ij} - NC_{tj})^2$$

In $\mathtt{STrap}_{it}(O_i, R_{it})$, the values v_{ij} in O_i are aggregated and randomized with the random numbers in NV_{ij} and NC_{tj}. Thus, it is secure to pass $\mathtt{STrap}_{it}(O_i, R_{it})$ to the service provider.

- $\mathtt{STrap}_{itj}(R_{it})$ is defined as $NV_{ij} - NC_{tj} + NS_{tj}$, where NS_{tj} is a new random number, ensuring $NV_{ij} - NC_{tj} + NS_{tj} > 0$. By incorporating the new random number, $NV_{ij} - NC_{tj}$ is protected in $\mathtt{STrap}_{it}(R_{it})$, without being directly exposed to the service provider.

For the jth dimension of the tth cluster, we need the maximal and minimal values of $\mathtt{STrap}_{itj}(R_{it})$ over all data objects, denoted by $\mathtt{max}_{tj}$ and $\mathtt{min}_{tj}$, respectively. That is, for n data objects, $\mathtt{max}_{tj}$ and $\mathtt{min}_{tj}$ denote the maximum and minimum values in the set $\{\mathtt{STrap}_{itj}(R_{it}) | 1 \le i \le n\}$, respectively. Since $NV_{ij} - NC_{tj} + NS_{tj} > 0$, we have $\mathtt{max}_{tj} > 0$ and $\mathtt{min}_{tj} > 0$. The values $\mathtt{max}_{tj}$ and $\mathtt{min}_{tj}$ will be used below when determining the ranges of new random numbers in $\mathtt{DTrap}_{t}(C_t, b)$ and $\mathtt{DTrap}_{tj}(c_{tj})$.

- $\mathtt{DTrap}_{t}(C_t, b)$ is defined as the following expression.

$$b - \sum_{j=1}^{d} (2 * k_1 * t_1 * c_{tj} * NS_{tj} + NB_{tj})$$

where NB_{tj} $(1 \le j \le d)$ are d new random numbers, which randomize $\mathtt{DTrap}_{t}(C_t, b)$ in each iteration. Each NB_{tj} is required to satisfy

$$0 < NB_{tj} < \frac{\mathtt{min}_{tj} * (k_1 * t_1)^2 * sens/d}{\mathtt{max}_{tj} - \mathtt{min}_{tj}}$$

where $sens$ is the sensitivity of $D^2(O_i, C_t)$ as described above. Note that we have $\frac{\mathtt{min}_{tj} * (k_1 * t_1)^2 * sens/d}{\mathtt{max}_{tj} - \mathtt{min}_{tj}} > 0$, since $sens > 0$, $d > 0$, $\mathtt{min}_{tj} > 0$ and $\mathtt{max}_{tj} \ge \mathtt{min}_{tj}$. NB_j is used below to determine the range of the new random number in $\mathtt{DTrap}_{tj}(c_{tj})$.

- $\mathtt{DTrap}_{tj}(c_{tj})$ is defined as $2 * k_1 * t_1 * c_{tj} + NR_{tj}$, where NR_{tj} is a new random number generated in each iteration. It should satisfy the following condition.

$$0 \le NR_{tj} * r_{tj} - NB_{tj} < (k_1 * t_1)^2 * sens/d$$

where $\mathtt{min}_{tj} \le r_{tj} \le \mathtt{max}_{tj}$, and $sens$ is the sensitivity of $D^2(O_i, C_t)$ as described above. This condition is used to prove the correctness of these trapdoor information terms. In the following, we show that there exists NR_{tj} that can satisfy this condition. For this purpose, the condition is rewritten into the following one.

$$NB_{tj} < NR_{tj} * r_{tj} \le NB_{tj} + (k_1 * t_1)^2 * sens/d$$

Since $\mathtt{min}_{tj} \le r_{tj} \le \mathtt{max}_{tj}$ and $\mathtt{min}_{tj} > 0$, we can replace r_{tj} in the condition with $\mathtt{max}_{tj}$ and $\mathtt{max}_{tj}$, obtaining the following range for NR_{tj}.

$$\frac{NB_{tj}}{\mathtt{min}_{tj}} < NR_{tj} \le \frac{NB_{tj} + (k_1 * t_1)^2 * sens/d}{\mathtt{max}_{tj}}$$

This range is valid, that is,

$$\frac{NB_{tj}}{\mathtt{min}_{tj}} < \frac{NB_{tj} + (k_1 * t_1)^2 * sens/d}{\mathtt{max}_{tj}}$$

due to the condition on NB_{tj}.

5.4.2 Correctness

We prove that the trapdoor information for $ED^2(O_i, C_t)$ can be correctly constructed by the following expression with the static and dynamic trapdoor information defined above.

$$\mathtt{STrap}_{it}(O_i, R_{it})+\sum_{j=1}^{d}\mathtt{DTrap}_{tj}(c_{tj})*\mathtt{STrap}_{itj}(R_{it})+\mathtt{DTrap}_t(C_t, b)$$

The following are the steps for the correctness proof.

1. By replacing each term with its definition, the above expression is re-written into:
$$-2*k_1*t_1*\sum_{j=1}^{d} v_{ij}*(NV_{ij}-NC_{tj})$$
$$-\sum_{j=1}^{d}(NV_{ij}-NC_{tj})^2$$
$$+\sum_{j=1}^{d}(2*k_1*t_1*c_{tj}+NR_{tj})*(NV_{ij}-NC_{tj}+NS_{tj})$$
$$+b-\sum_{j=1}^{d}(2*k_1*t_1*c_{tj}*NS_{tj}+NB_{tj})$$

2. By rewriting $\sum_{j=1}^{d}(2*k_1*t_1*c_{tj}+NR_{tj})*(NV_{ij}-NC_{tj}+NS_{tj})$ and $\sum_{j=1}^{d}(2*k_1*t_1*c_{tj}*NS_{tj}+NB_{tj})$, we obtain:
$$-2*k_1*t_1*\sum_{j=1}^{d} v_{ij}*(NV_{ij}-NC_{tj})$$
$$-\sum_{j=1}^{d}(NV_{ij}-NC_{tj})^2$$
$$+\sum_{j=1}^{d}(2*k_1*t_1*c_{tj})*(NV_{ij}-NC_{tj})$$
$$+\sum_{j=1}^{d}(2*k_1*t_1*c_{tj})*(NS_{tj})$$
$$+\sum_{j=1}^{d}(NR_{tj})*(NV_{ij}-NC_{tj}+NS_{tj})$$
$$+b-\sum_{j=1}^{d}(2*k_1*t_1*c_{tj}*NS_{tj})-\sum_{j=1}^{d} NB_{tj}$$

3. Since $\sum_{j=1}^{d}(2*k_1*t_1*c_{tj})*(NS_{tj})$ and $-\sum_{j=1}^{d}(2*k_1*t_1*c_{tj}*NS_{tj})$ cancel each other, the above expression is reduced to:
$$-2*k_1*t_1*\sum_{j=1}^{d} v_{ij}*(NV_{ij}-NC_{tj})$$
$$-\sum_{j=1}^{d}(NV_{ij}-NC_{tj})^2$$
$$+\sum_{j=1}^{d}(2*k_1*t_1*c_{tj})*(NV_{ij}-NC_{tj})$$
$$+\sum_{j=1}^{d}(NR_{tj})*(NV_{ij}-NC_{tj}+NS_{tj})$$
$$+b-\sum_{j=1}^{d} NB_{tj}$$

4. After combining like terms, the following expression is produced.
$$-2*k_1*t_1*\sum_{j=1}^{d}(v_{ij}-c_{tj})*(NV_{ij}-NC_{tj})$$
$$-\sum_{j=1}^{d}(NV_{ij}-NC_{tj})^2$$
$$+\sum_{j=1}^{d}(NR_{tj}*(NV_{ij}-NC_{tj}+NS_{tj})-NB_{tj})$$
$$+b$$

5. Based on the definition of $g(V, R_{it})$ in Section 5.3, the above expression can be represented as:
$$-g(\{O_i, C_t\}, R_{it})+b+r$$
where $r=\sum_{j=1}^{d}(NR_{tj}*(NV_{ij}-NC_{tj}+NS_{tj})-NB_{tj})$. In order to obtain correct trapdoor information, the random number r must be in the range $[0,(k_1*t_1)^2*sens)$, as required in Section 5.3. Since $\mathtt{min}_{tj}\le NV_{ij}-NC_{tj}+NS_{tj}\le\mathtt{max}_{tj}$, the following inequation holds due to the condition on NR_{tj}.
$$0\le NR_{tj}*(NV_{ij}-NC_{tj}+NS_{tj})-NB_{tj}<(k_1*t_1)^2*sens/d$$
Hence, we have $0\le r<(k_1*t_1)^2*sens$. That is, r is in the range $[0,(k_1*t_1)^2*sens)$.

6. CLUSTERING HOMOMORPHICALLY ENCRYPTED DATA

By using our proposed method for comparing encrypted distances, we propose a distributed algorithm for clustering homomorphically encrypted data. There are two stages for this approach: preparation and clustering, which are explained below. In addition, the data objects might need to be updated after being outsourced. We also discuss how to manage the changes to the outsourced data objects and clusters.

6.1 Preparation Stage

Suppose the data owner has n data objects O_i $(1\le i\le n)$, which are to be clustered into k clusters. By using some method of its choice, the data owner determines k initial cluster centers C_t $(1\le t\le k)$. Each data object and cluster center is supposed to have d attributes. Let $O_i=(v_{i1},...,v_{id})$ and $C_t=(c_{t1},...,c_{td})$. The values of n, k and d need to be sent to the service provider.

To protect his data, the data owner generates the homomorphic encryption key $K(m)=[(k_1,s_1,t_1),...,(k_m,s_m,t_m)]$, in which we assume $t_1\ne 0$. Using the key $K(m)$, the data owner can encrypt data objects and cluster centers, and then produce the static trapdoor information.

However, the memory usage is different depending on whether data objects or cluster centers are encrypted first. This is because the calculation of $\mathtt{STrap}_{it}(O_i, R_{it})$ and $\mathtt{STrap}_{itj}(R_{it})$ needs the random numbers from all combinations of encrypted data objects and cluster centers. Suppose the data object O_i is encrypted before all cluster centers. Then, the random numbers used in encrypting O_i must be kept until all cluster centers are encrypted, so that $\mathtt{STrap}_{it}(O_i, R_{it})$ and $\mathtt{STrap}_{itj}(R_{it})$ can be calculated. Since the number of data objects is usually big, the memory space needed for storing the used random numbers is also big. Hence, we choose to encrypt the initial cluster centers before encrypting the data objects.

6.1.1 Encryption of Cluster Centers

For $1\le t\le k$ and $1\le j\le d$, the value c_{tj} in C_t is encrypted by performing $\mathtt{Enc}(K(m), c_{tj})=(e'_{tj1},...,e'_{tjm})$. For each ciphertext $(e'_{tj1},...,e'_{tjm})$, our method for comparing encrypted distances only needs the first subciphertext e'_{tj1}. Thus, the other subciphertexts $e'_{tj2},...,e'_{tjm}$ can be discarded.

For the first subciphertext e'_{tj1}, the data owner will send it to the service provider without keeping it. But the random numbers r'_{tj1}, $r'_{tj(m-1)}$ and r'_{tjm} used in e'_{tj1} needs to be kept and will be used in each clustering iteration. Let RC_t denote the set of random numbers to be kept for C_t, that is, $RC_t=\{r'_{tj1}, r'_{tj(m-1)}, r'_{tjm}|1\le j\le d\}$. RC_t will be used to calculate the static trapdoor information and also be used during iterations of k-means clustering.

6.1.2 Encryption of Data Objects

Each value v_{ij} in an object O_i is encrypted as $\mathtt{Enc}(K(m), v_{ij})=(e_{ij1},...,e_{ijm})$ for $1\le i\le k$ and $1\le j\le d$. Let $RV_i=\{r_{ij1}, r_{ij(m-1)}, r_{ijm}|1\le j\le d\}$ be the set of random numbers used in e_{ij1} for $1\le j\le d$.

Using RV_i, the data owner can calculate the static trapdoor information terms $\mathtt{STrap}_{it}(O_i, RV_i\cup RC_t)$ and $\mathtt{STrap}_{itj}(RV_i\cup RC_t)$, with respect to each RC_t. During the calculation of $\mathtt{STrap}_{itj}(RV_i\cup RC_t)$, $k*d$ random numbers NS_{tj} are generated and they need to be kept for calculating the dynamic trapdoor information. Then, the ciphertext $(e_{ij1},...,e_{ijm})$, the terms $\mathtt{STrap}_{it}(O_i, RV_i\cup RC_t)$ and $\mathtt{STrap}_{itj}(RV_i\cup RC_t)$ are sent to the service provider without being kept by the data owner.

After the above processing, the original data object O_i is not needed any more by the clustering algorithm. If the service provider has a long-term storage service, the data object O_i can be securely stored there as the ciphertext $(e_{ij1}, ..., e_{ijm})$ and the data owner can discard O_i on his local machine.

6.1.3 *Maximum and Minimum of* $\mathtt{STrap}_{itj}(RV_i \cup RC_t)$

Recall that for calculating the dynamic trapdoor information, our method needs the maximum value $\mathtt{max}_{tj}$ and minimum value $\mathtt{min}_{tj}$ in the set $\{\mathtt{STrap}_{itj}(RV_i \cup RC_t) | 1 \leq i \leq n\}$. The static trapdoor information $\mathtt{STrap}_{itj}(RV_i \cup RC_t)$ will not change after the preparation stage, nor do the values $\mathtt{max}_{tj}$ and $\mathtt{min}_{tj}$.

For $\mathtt{max}_{tj}$ and $\mathtt{min}_{tj}$, we let the service provider to calculate them and the result is sent back to the data owner. This choice reduces the computation burden of the data owner.

6.2 Clustering

After the preparation stage, the service provider starts clustering encrypted data with the assistance of dynamic trapdoor information provided by the data owner.

6.2.1 *Service Provider's Clustering Algorithm*

The clustering algorithm carried out by the service provider is shown in Figure 1. Before explaining this algorithm, we should mention that this algorithm intends to be a specification for correctness. A service provider should consider the high performance implementation of this specification based on the features of its platform.

In the clustering algorithm for the service provider, an iteration of k-means clustering starts from the label `StartIterations`. Before the clustering iterations, an arrays of n integers, `allo[n]`, is declared to record the allocation for each data object. This array is initialized to 0 for each element. The array `allo[n]` is shared among iterations, so that the new allocation for a data object can be detected.

In an iteration, the algorithm first allocates each data object into one of clusters. For this purpose, the algorithm calculates the encrypted distances $\mathtt{ED}^2(\mathtt{O}_i, \mathtt{C}_t)$ between each data object i and each cluster t. Note that $\mathtt{ED}^2(\mathtt{O}_i, \mathtt{C}_t)$ is used as a variable name, so as to reuse the notations from the last section. The value of this variable is determined by the expression $\sum_{j=1}^{d}(e_{ij1} - e'_{tj1})^2$. Similarly, $\mathtt{STrap}_{it}(O_i, R_{it})$, $\mathtt{STrap}_{itj}(R_{it})$, $\mathtt{DTrap}_t(C_t, b)$, $\mathtt{DTrap}_{tj}(c_{tj})$ and $\mathtt{OED}^2(\mathtt{O}_i, \mathtt{C}_t)$ are all variable names, with their values coming from the preparation stage, the network channel (indicated by the `receive` keyword), or the corresponding right-hand side expression.

From $\mathtt{ED}^2(\mathtt{O}_i, \mathtt{C}_t)$, the algorithm produces the order-preserving encrypted distances $\mathtt{OED}^2(\mathtt{O}_i, \mathtt{C}_t)$ by adding it up with the trapdoor information $\mathtt{Trap}_{it}$. The calculation of $\mathtt{Trap}_{it}$ requests the dynamic trapdoor information $\mathtt{DTrap}_t(C_t, b)$ and $\mathtt{DTrap}_{tj}(c_{tj})$ for each t and j $((1 \leq j \leq d))$ from the data owner. Then, a data object is allocated into a cluster with the minimum distance $\mathtt{OED}^2(\mathtt{O}_i, \mathtt{C}_t)$ for $1 \leq t \leq k$.

If an iteration does not change the allocation of any data object, indicated by the boolean variable `newAllo`, the clustering stage is completed and the service provider sends the **END** message to the data owner. Otherwise, the service provider will proceed to calculate the centers of new clusters and ask the data owner to reencrypt these new centers, as described below.

Since the data objects are homomorphically encrypted, the new cluster centers can be obtained by adding up the corresponding encrypted attributes of all data objects in the same cluster and then dividing the sum by the number of data object in this cluster. Note that each attribute of a data object is encrypted into a vector of subciphertexts, and the operations of adding two ciphertexts and divid-

```
let allo[n] be an array of integers
for i from 1 to n do {
  allo[i]=0
}
StartIterations:
newAllo=false
//allocate each data object
for i from 1 to n do {
  minD=0 //the minimum distance
  cNum=0 //the nearest cluster
  for t from 1 to k do {
    ED^2(O_i,C_t)=Σ_{j=1}^{d}(e_{ij1} − e'_{tj1})^2
    //get dynamic trapdoor information
    receive DTrap_t(C_t,b)
    receive DTrap_{tj}(c_{tj}) for 1≤j≤d
    Trap_{it}=STrap_{it}(O_i, R_{it})
             +Σ_{j=1}^{d} DTrap_{tj}(c_{tj}) * STrap_{itj}(R_{it})
             +DTrap_t(C_t,b)
    //the order-preserving distance
    OED^2(O_i,C_t)=ED^2(O_i,C_t)+Trap_{it}
    if t=1 or OED^2(O_i,C_t) < minD then
      cNum=t; minD=OED^2(O_i,C_t)
  }
  if allo[i]!=cNum then
    newAllo=true; allo[i]=cNum
}
if newAllo = false then
   send END
else
  //calculate the new cluster centers
  let newcc[k][d] be an array of ciphertexts
  let cnt[k] be an array of integers
  for t from 1 to k do {
    for j from 1 to d do {
      newcc[t][j]=null
    }
    cnt[t]=0
  }
  for i from 1 to n do {
    let t=allo[i]
    for j from 1 to d do {
      let EC_{ij}=(e_{ij1},...,e_{ijm})
      if newcc[t][j]=null then
       newcc[t][j]=EC_{ij}
      else
       newcc[t][j]=newcc[t][j]+EC_{ij}
    }
    cnt[t]= cnt[t]+1
  }
  //send back new cluster centers
  for t from 1 to k do {
    for j from 1 to d do {
      newcc[t][j]=newcc[t][j]/cnt[t]
      send newcc[t][j]
    }
  }
  for t from 1 to k do {
   receive e'_{tj1} for 1≤j≤d
  }
  go to StartIterations
```

Figure 1: Service Provider's Clustering Algorithm

ing a ciphertext by a constant (or multiplying the ciphertext by the inverse of the constant) correspond to vector addition or multiplication, respectively.

After new cluster centers are computed, the algorithm sends them back to the data owner, and waits to receive the reencrypted cluster centers. The new cluster centers are reencrypted by the data owner with the same random numbers as used in the encryption of initial cluster centers, such that the static trapdoor information is still valid.

6.2.2 Data Owner's Processing Steps

During the clustering stage, the data data owner needs to provide dynamic trapdoor information. For each cluster center C_t, which is an initial cluster center or an updated cluster center decrypted from the ciphertext, the calculation of $\mathtt{DTrap}_t(C_t, b)$ and $\mathtt{DTrap}_{tj}(c_{tj})$ $(1 \leq j \leq d)$, where b is a random number for each iteration, just follows their definitions.

Recall that the ciphertext in `newcc[t][j]` is sent back by the service provider for reencryption. The data owner first decrypts this ciphertext into c_{tj} (i.e., the value of jth dimension of cluster C_t) and then encrypts c_{tj} into $e'_{tj1} = k_1 * t_1 * c_{tj} + s_1 * r'_{tjm} + k_1 * (r'_{tj1} - r'_{tj(m-1)})$, where $r'_{tj1}, r'_{tj(m-1)}$ and r'_{tjm} are the random numbers kept at the preparation stage. That is, the random numbers $r'_{tj1}, r'_{tj(m-1)}$ and r'_{tjm} are reused to encrypt c_{tj} in every iteration. The reuse of these random numbers ensures the validity of static trapdoor information for all clustering iterations. The security effect of reusing these random numbers is discussed below.

Let x be the ciphertext e'_{tj1} from one iteration, and y be the corresponding ciphertext from another iteration. Thus, they are encrypted with the same random numbers $r'_{tj1}, r'_{tj(m-1)}$ and r'_{tjm}. Since the service provider can access both x and y, he is able to know the product $k_1 * t_1 * z$, where z is the difference of c_{tj} from the two iterations. Suppose that in the worst case $k_1 * t_1$ is guessed correctly by the service provider. However, for a value v_{ij} in a data object, its first subciphertext $e_{tj1} = k_1 * t_1 * c_{tj} + s_1 * r_{tjm} + k_1 * (r_{tj1} - r_{tj(m-1)})$ is still secure, because s_1 and the random numbers $r_{tj1}, r_{tj(m-1)}$ and r_{tjm} are still secret and these random numbers can be arbitrarily large. That is, e_{tj1} is still dominated by the secret part $s_1 * r_{tjm} + k_1 * (r_{tj1} - r_{tj(m-1)})$ even after $k_1 * t_1$ is known. The other subciphertexts of v_{ij} are not dependent on k_1 and t_1, hence not affected.

After a clustering task is finished, the data owner can then get back the clustering result (i.e., the allocation of data objects and the final cluster centers). We skip the steps of how to communicate clustering results between the data owner and the service provider.

6.3 Change Management

A data owner may store its encrypted data on the platform of the service provider for a long period of time. During this period, the data owner may need to add new data objects, delete old data objects, change the initial clusters and the number of clusters. In the following, we discuss how to manage these changes.

Changes to data objects are straightforward to handle. To add a new data object, the data owner processes it as described in the preparation stage, that is, by encrypting the object and producing the corresponding static trapdoor information. To delete the data object indexed by i, the data owner sends a request to delete all ciphertexts together with the terms of static trapdoor information indexed by i, that is, $(e_{ij1}, ..., e_{ijm})$, $\mathtt{STrap}_{it}$ and $\mathtt{STrap}_{itj}$ for $1 \leq j \leq d$ and $1 \leq t \leq k$.

A change to the initial cluster centers is handled by encrypting the new initial cluster with the same random numbers as used in the encryption of old initial cluster centers. Those random numbers are kept at the preparation stage when encrypting the old initial cluster centers. With the same random numbers used, the static trapdoor information does not need to be changed.

A change to the number of clusters might be more problematic. Let k be the original cluster number and k' be the new cluster number. If $k' < k$, the change can be simply handled by notifying the new cluster number k' to the service provider. If $k' > k$, the change is not easy to handle because there is no corresponding static trapdoor information $\mathtt{STrap}_{it}$ and $\mathtt{STrap}_{itj}$ for $1 \leq i \leq n, 1 \leq j \leq d$ and $k < t \leq k'$. Since the number of data objects n might be big, it is not efficient to generate the missing static trapdoor information with respect to each data object. Our solution to this problem is that if the data objects will be clustered for different numbers of clusters, the data owner takes a big enough cluster number to prepare static trapdoor information at the preparation stage. Thus, there will be no problem for a smaller cluster number.

7. PERFORMANCE EVALUATION

We have implemented our method for securing outsourced k-means clustering with Java in a prototype. In this section, we evaluate the performance of our method by comparing the computation costs for the client and the service provider.

7.1 Configuration

The homomorphic encryption scheme is configured to produce eight subciphertexts for a plaintext (i.e., a key is $K(8)$). The number of subciphertexts affects the size of key space and hence the security level of homomorphic encryption. Together with the following configuration on key components, eight subciphertexts for a plaintext can produce sufficiently large key space.

The key components k_i $(1 \leq i \leq 8)$ are randomly generated with the form of $d_1d_2d_3d_4.d_5$, where d_i is a digit, t_i $(1 \leq i \leq 8)$ with the form of $d_1d_2d_3.d_4$, and s_i are random numbers having the form of $d_1d_2d_3.d_4d_5$. Based on this configuration, for $1 \leq i \leq 7$, there is at least 10^4 possibilities of the only one non-zero t_i, and 10^5 possibilities of both k_i and s_i. Conservatively, we do not take account the 10^5 possibilities of $k_8+s_8+t_8$ into the key space, since the information of $k_8 + s_8 + t_8$ might be leaked by factoring the last ciphertext. Hence, the key space provided by this configuration is at least $10^4 * 10^{5*7} * 10^{5*7} = 10^{74}$, which is bigger than 2^{192}, the key space of AES-192.

A data object in our experiment consists of attribute values of the form $d_1d_2d_3d_4.d_5$, and the random numbers r_i used in encryption have the form $d_1d_2d_3d_4d_5d_6.d_7d_8d_9d_{10}$. That is, the size of random numbers is much bigger in a ciphertext. Ciphertexts are represented in our implementation by the Java BigDecimal class, which supports arbitrary-precision decimal numbers and their operations.

We test the prototype in two machines. One is Dell Ultrabook XPS 13, running Windows 7, used by the data owner to encrypt data objects and generate trapdoor information, and the other is a Virtual Server, with one CPU and 4G RAM, running Windows Server 2008, used by the service provider to run our clustering algorithm over encrypted data. The Java implementation programs are run within Java development environment Eclipse on both machines.

In the test, we change the number of data objects from 5000 to 30000, and each data object has 50 attributes (i.e., a data object is a 50-dimensional vector). These objects will be initially allocated into 10 clusters. We produced 30000 data objects randomly and choose 10 of them as the initial cluster centers, and they are used through the test.

Data Objects	Encryption (s)	Static Trapdoor (s)
5000	2.12	1.85
10000	3.93	2.91
15000	6.07	4.68
20000	8.64	5.94
25000	10.26	7.39
30000	12.01	10.68

Table 1: Preparation Time by Data Owner

Data Objects	Iterations	Owner (s)	Provider (s)
5000	50	1.19	44.79
10000	126	2.85	250.16
15000	251	5.59	774.90
20000	194	4.38	759.20
25000	206	4.95	1225.87
30000	315	7.78	2427.29

Table 2: Clustering Time and Iterations

Data Objects	Encrypted Data (s)	STrap (s)	DTrap (s)
5000	5.48	6.66	0.06
10000	12.07	12.27	0.03
15000	17.35	16.65	0.05
20000	21.25	29.26	0.05
25000	28.29	38.17	0.08
30000	41.71	43.49	0.19

Table 3: Communication Times

Data Objects	Iterations	Owner (s)
5000	50	22.82
10000	126	107.69
15000	251	322.69
20000	194	324.98
25000	206	435.34
30000	315	787.55

Table 4: Time Of Using Original Clustering Algorithm

7.2 Evaluation

Recall that our clustering algorithm consists of two stages: preparation and clustering. The preparation stage is mainly performed by the data owner. Table 1 shows the time in seconds the data owner takes to encrypt data objects and compute static trapdoor information, with respect to different number of data objects. The time for encrypting the initial cluster centers is ignored and not shown in the table, because it is very small (0 milliseconds in our test). With the increase in the number of data objects, we can see an increase in preparation time. However, the preparation stage is performed only once; if these data objects are clustered multiple times or also the server is used as the storage platform, the cost of preparation stage can be amortized.

At the clustering stage, the service provider clusters the data objects with the dynamic trapdoor information interactively provided by the data owner. Table 2 shows the processing time for both the data owner and the service provider and the number of iterations, with respect to the number of data objects. From this table, we can see at the clustering stage the service provider spends much more time than the data owner. This table also shows that the increase of data objects does not mean more iterations needed by k-means clustering.

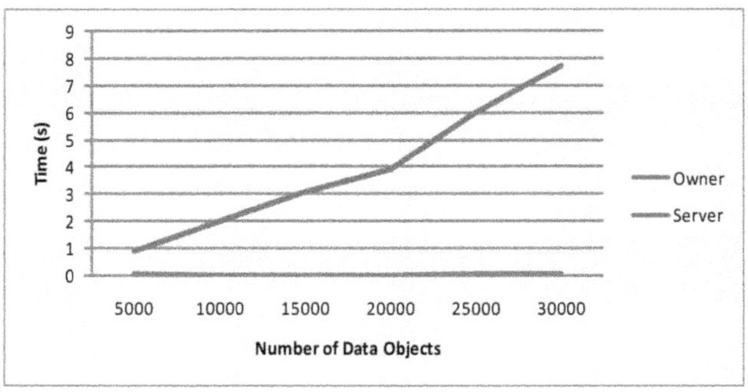

Figure 2: Clustering Time per Iteration

To understand the relation between the clustering time and the number of data objects in each clustering iteration, we divide the clustering time in Table 2 by the corresponding number of iterations. Figure 2 shows the clustering time per iteration spent by the data owner and the service provider. It shows that, with the increase of data objects number, the clustering time per iteration for the data owner does not increase, while the time for the service provider does.

In our clustering method, the data owner needs to communicate with the service provider. Table 3 shows the communication time for the data owner to send encrypted data objects, the static and dynamic trapdoor information. We should mention that the communication time is sensitive to the network status and how to communicate efficiently is orthogonal to our clustering method. However, Table 3 tells us that the time for communicating dynamic trapdoor information is much smaller than the time for communicating encrypted data objects and static trapdoor information, and does not increase with the number of data objects. For encrypted data objects and static trapdoor information, they are communicated only once and their communication time can be amortised like the time of calculating them. The data owner still spends much less time than the service provider even if the communication time in Table 3 is taken into account.

In addition, we also implemented the original clustering algorithm described in Section 2 with the values represented by the Java BigDecimal class and run it on the same data objects with the same initial centers. By comparing the clustering results of two implementations, we can check the correctness of clustering results using our method. Table 4 gives the number of iterations and the clustering time when running the original clustering algorithm on Dell Ultrabook XPS 13 (the data owner's machine). The numbers of iterations in Table 2 and Table 4 with respect to the same set of data objects are the same (also the same for the final cluster centers and allocations, which are not shown here), indicating the correct clustering results of our method. On the other hand, for the data owner, the time spent by the original clustering algorithm is higher than the time spent in our clustering method (i.e., the sum of the preparation time, the time of calculating dynamic trapdoor information, and the communication time in Table 3), and much higher with the increase of the number of data objects.

We also take a test by clustering the data objects into 20 clusters. For the preparation stage, the increase of clusters does not affect the time of encrypting data objects, while the time of calculating static trapdoor information is increased proportionally. For example, the time of calculating static trapdoor information increases from 2.91s to 6.76s for 10000 data objects, and from 5.94s to 13.23s for 20000 data objects. For the clustering stage, the time spent by the data owner is not affected too much, while the time for the provider is affected a lot. For example, there are 131 loops when clustering 10000 data objects and 140 loops when clustering 20000 data objects, with 4.61s and 4.90s spent by the data owner,and 465.68s and 1188.73 spent by the provider.

8. RELATED WORKS

The most related is the work on privacy-preserving distributed (or two-party) k-means clustering, such as [13, 22, 10]. The difference between distributed k-means clustering and outsourced k-means clustering has been discussed in the introduction. Since these two clustering methods have different goals, they can be complementary to each other. If a data owner in a distributed k-means clustering does not have the capability to complete its task, then this owner can outsource the task to a service provider. The combination of these two k-means clustering methods can be a future work.

In [9, 5], a diagnostic program or a linear branching program provided by a service provider is applied to data from the data owner. The service provider wants to protect the privacy of the program, while the data owner wants to ensure the privacy of data. Similarly, in our work, the k-means clustering program, which might be implemented for instance in a novel way that the service provider wants to protect, is run by the service provider itself, hence the privacy of the clustering program is protected. On the other hand, in [9, 5], the conditional comparison of two values, one from the data owner and the other from the service provider (i.e., the input data and the parameters in the programs), is implemented by using the garbled circuit [21]. Since this comparison method needs to convert a comparison operation into a software circuit, encrypt each bit in the compared values and run the oblivious transfer protocol, this method might not scale to a large volume of data like in k-means data clustering. On the contrary, our method compares ciphertexts by just comparing ordinary real numbers, with the assistance of trapdoor information.

In functional encryption [7], there are restricted secret keys and the key holder can learn the output of a program over the encrypted input data without learning anything else about the data. Similarly, our method allows the service provider to run the clustering program over homomorphically encrypted data. In our work, the static and dynamic trapdoor information can be regarded as secret keys in functional encryption held by the service provider. The functional encryption schemes, such as [11, 12], usually represent a function as a Turing machine or software circuits with circuit depth restriction. These schemes have not been applied in practical applications.

Our method can also be applied to comparing encrypted distances generated by using other homomorphic encryption schemes, such as [19]. For the homomorphic encryption scheme described in [19], a message m is encrypted into a pair of subciphertexts $(a_0 * r_0 + t * r_1 + m, a_1 * r_0 + t * r_2)$, where a_0 and a_1 are two constants used as public keys, t a constant used as the modulus, and r_i $(1 \leq i \leq 3)$ three random numbers. Then, using this scheme, the first subciphertexts of v_{ij} and c_{tj} (the jth attributes of data object O_i and the cluster center C_t) are $a_0 * r_{ij0} + t * r_{ij1} + v_{ij}$ and $a_0 * r'_{tj0} + t * r'_{tj1} + c_{tj}$, respectively. Let $k_1 * t_1 = 1$, $NV_{ij} = a_0 * r_{ij0} + t * r_{ij1}$ and $NC_{tj} = a_0 * r'_{tj0} + t * r'_{tj1}$. Then, the encrypted distance $ED^2(O_i, C_t)$, and the static and trapdoor information can be calculated according to their definitions in Section 5. However, if data objects are encrypted with the scheme in [19], the order-preserving indexes of squared distances between data objects and cluster centers may not be randomized well, since the noises used in the indexes can only be sampled from the small range $[0, 1 * sens)$, where $sens$ is the sensitivity of the squared distances.

9. CONCLUSION

In this paper, we described a method that allows the k-means clustering algorithm to run over data encrypted with a homomorphic encryption scheme. This method can mitigate the privacy concern of data owners when they outsource their data to a service provider for analytics. The homomorphic encryption schemes are usually probabilistic, and hence the ciphertexts of homomorphic encryption cannot be compared by using the usual comparison operations. In our method, we proposed an efficient approach to comparing ciphertexts with the trapdoor information provided the key holder or the data owner. We have implemented our method in a prototype and evaluated its performance. The future work is to combine outsourced k-means clustering with the existing distributed k-means clustering, or apply our method to securely outsource other data analytics algorithms.

10. REFERENCES

[1] D. Agrawal, A. E. Abbadi, F. Emekçi, and A. Metwally. Database management as a service: Challenges and opportunities. In *Proceedings of the 25th International Conference on Data Engineering*, pages 1709–1716, 2009.

[2] R. Agrawal, J. Kiernan, R. Srikant, and Y. Xu. Order preserving encryption for numeric data. In *Proceedings of the 2004 ACM SIGMOD international conference on Management of data*, SIGMOD '04, pages 563–574, 2004.

[3] R. Agrawal, J. Kiernan, R. Srikant, and Y. Xu. Order preserving encryption for numeric data. In *Proceedings of the 2004 ACM SIGMOD international conference on Management of data*, SIGMOD '04, pages 563–574, New York, NY, USA, 2004. ACM.

[4] R. Agrawal and R. Srikant. Privacy-preserving data mining. In *Proceedings of the 2000 ACM SIGMOD international conference on Management of data*, pages 439–450, 2000.

[5] M. Barni, P. Failla, V. Kolesnikov, R. Lazzeretti, A.-R. Sadeghi, and T. Schneider. Secure evaluation of private linear branching programs with medical applications. In M. Backes and P. Ning, editors, *ESORICS*, volume 5789 of *Lecture Notes in Computer Science*, pages 424–439. Springer, 2009.

[6] A. Boldyreva, N. Chenette, Y. Lee, and A. O'Neill. Order-preserving symmetric encryption. In *Proceedings of the 28th Annual International Conference on Advances in Cryptology*, EUROCRYPT '09, pages 224–241, 2009.

[7] D. Boneh, A. Sahai, and B. Waters. Functional encryption: Definitions and challenges. In *Proceedings of the 8th Conference on Theory of Cryptography*, TCC'11, pages 253–273, Berlin, Heidelberg, 2011. Springer-Verlag.

[8] Z. Brakerski and V. Vaikuntanathan. Fully homomorphic encryption from ring-lwe and security for key dependent messages. In P. Rogaway, editor, *CRYPTO*, volume 6841 of *Lecture Notes in Computer Science*, pages 505–524. Springer, 2011.

[9] J. Brickell, D. E. Porter, V. Shmatikov, and E. Witchel. Privacy-preserving remote diagnostics. In *Proceedings of the*

14th ACM Conference on Computer and Communications Security, CCS '07, pages 498–507, New York, NY, USA, 2007. ACM.

[10] P. Bunn and R. Ostrovsky. Secure two-party k-means clustering. In *Proceedings of the 14th ACM conference on Computer and communications security*, CCS '07, pages 486–497, New York, NY, USA, 2007. ACM.

[11] S. Goldwasser, Y. Kalai, R. A. Popa, V. Vaikuntanathan, and N. Zeldovich. Reusable garbled circuits and succinct functional encryption. In *Proceedings of the 45th Annual ACM Symposium on Symposium on Theory of Computing*, STOC '13, pages 555–564, New York, NY, USA, 2013. ACM.

[12] S. Goldwasser, Y. T. Kalai, R. A. Popa, V. Vaikuntanathan, and N. Zeldovich. How to run turing machines on encrypted data. In R. Canetti and J. A. Garay, editors, *CRYPTO (2)*, volume 8043 of *Lecture Notes in Computer Science*, pages 536–553. Springer, 2013.

[13] G. Jagannathan and R. N. Wright. Privacy-preserving distributed k-means clustering over arbitrarily partitioned data. In *Proceedings of the 11th ACM SIGKDD international conference on Knowledge discovery in data mining*, 2005.

[14] M. K. Jiawei Han and J. Pei. *Data Mining: Concepts and Techniques, 3rd ed.* Morgan Kaufmann Publishers, 2011.

[15] H. Kargupta, S. Datta, Q. Wang, and K. Sivakumar. On the privacy preserving properties of random data perturbation techniques. In *Proceedings of the Third IEEE International Conference on Data Mining*, ICDM '03, pages 99–, Washington, DC, USA, 2003. IEEE Computer Society.

[16] J. Katz and Y. Lindell. *Introduction to Modern Cryptography (Chapman & Hall/Crc Cryptography and Network Security Series)*. Chapman & Hall/CRC, 2007.

[17] D. Liu. Homomorphic encryption for database querying. Inernational Patent Application No.: PCT/AU2013/000674 (Accessible via http://patentscope.wipo.int/search/en/WO2013188929), 2013.

[18] D. Liu and S. Wang. Programmable order preserving secure index for encrypted database query. In *Proceedings of the 5th IEEE International Conference on Cloud Computing*, 2012.

[19] M. Naehrig, K. Lauter, and V. Vaikuntanathan. Can homomorphic encryption be practical? In *Proceedings of the 3rd ACM workshop on Cloud computing security workshop*, CCSW '11, pages 113–124, 2011.

[20] R. Ostrovsky, Y. Rabani, L. J. Schulman, and C. Swamy. The effectiveness of lloyd-type methods for the k-means problem. In *Proceedings of the 47th Annual IEEE Symposium on Foundations of Computer Science*, pages 165–176, 2006.

[21] A. C.-C. Yao. How to generate and exchange secrets. In *Proceedings of the 27th Annual Symposium on Foundations of Computer Science*, SFCS '86, pages 162–167, Washington, DC, USA, 1986. IEEE Computer Society.

[22] X. Yi and Y. Zhang. Equally contributory privacy-preserving k-means clustering over vertically partitioned data. *Inf. Syst.*, 38(1):97–107, 2013.

PIDGIN: Privacy-Preserving Interest and Content Sharing in Opportunistic Networks

Muhammad Rizwan Asghar*
CREATE-NET
Trento, Italy
asghar@create-net.org

Ashish Gehani
SRI International
Menlo Park, California, USA
ashish.gehani@sri.com

Bruno Crispo
University of Trento
Trento, Italy
crispo@disi.unitn.it

Giovanni Russello
University of Auckland
Auckland, New Zealand
g.russello@auckland.ac.nz

ABSTRACT

Opportunistic networks have recently received considerable attention from both industry and researchers. These networks can be used for many applications without the need for a dedicated IT infrastructure. In the context of opportunistic networks, content sharing in particular has attracted significant attention. To support content sharing, opportunistic networks often implement a publish-subscribe system in which users may publish their own content and indicate interest in other content through subscriptions. Using a smartphone, any user can act as a broker by opportunistically forwarding both published content and interests within the network.

Unfortunately, opportunistic networks are faced with serious privacy and security issues. Untrusted brokers can not only compromise the privacy of subscribers by learning their interests but also can gain unauthorised access to the disseminated content. This paper addresses the research challenges inherent to the exchange of content and interests without: (i) compromising the privacy of subscribers, and (ii) providing unauthorised access to untrusted brokers. Specifically, this paper presents an interest and content sharing solution that addresses these security challenges and preserves privacy in opportunistic networks. We demonstrate the feasibility and efficiency of the solution by implementing a prototype and analysing its performance on smart phones.

Categories and Subject Descriptors

D.4.6 [**Security and Protection**]: Access control; E.3 [**Data**]: Data Encryption

*Most of this research was carried out while visiting SRI International as an International Fellow.

ASIA CCS'14, June 4–6, 2014, Kyoto, Japan.
Copyright is held by the owner/author(s). Publication rights licensed to ACM.
ACM 978-1-4503-2800-5/14/06 ...$15.00.
http://dx.doi.org/10.1145/2590296.2590303.

Keywords

Secure Opportunistic Networks; Privacy-preserving Content Sharing; Sensitive Policy Enforcement; Encrypted CP-ABE Policies; Secure Haggle

1. INTRODUCTION

Over the last few years, the use of smartphones has grown dramatically and is predicted to increase even more in the coming years [7]. Considering the pervasive nature of smartphones, mobile opportunistic networks can be leveraged to share information. Several of the concepts behind opportunistic networks originate from Delay Tolerant Networks (DTNs) that offer flexible content sharing without requiring a dedicated IT infrastructure [18].

Haggle [1], an example of such a network architecture, allows smartphones to opportunistically share content via short-range communication [17]. To share content, opportunistic networks, such as Haggle, implement a publish-subscribe system in which nodes can publish their own content and subscribe to other content by indicating their interests. Any node can also act as a broker (also called a relay) that opportunistically receives content and interest, matches them, and possibly delivers that content to other nodes.

Opportunistic networks can be used to exchange information in a wide range of domains from social media to military applications. However, such networks also present serious privacy and security issues, particularly the need for an approach to exchange content and interests that neither (i) compromises the privacy of subscribers nor (ii) provides unauthorised access to untrusted brokers.

Cryptographic approaches such as Attribute-Based Encryption (ABE), which include Ciphertext-Policy ABE (CP-ABE) [4] and Key-Policy ABE (KP-ABE) [9], offer fine-grained control over content but leak information about the policies and attributes that protect that content, respectively. To protect the access policies, state-of-the-art solutions exist to enforce sensitive policies in outsourced environments [2,3,12]. However, such solutions assume that the outsourced server does not collude with any client. Thus, these solutions cannot be applied in opportunistic network settings in which nodes communicate in a peer-to-peer fashion – that is, serving as both a client and a server.

This paper presents PIDGIN, an interest and content sharing scheme that preserves privacy, in which:

- brokers match subscribers' interests against content access policies associated without compromising the subscribers' privacy (by learning content attributes or node interests).
- unauthorised nodes do not gain access to content, and authorised nodes gain access only if they satisfy fine-grained policies specified by the publishers.
- the system provides scalable key management in which loosely-coupled nodes communicate with each other without any prior contact.

As a proof-of-concept, we have developed and analysed the performance of a prototype running on real smartphones in order to show the feasibility of our approach.

The rest of this paper is organised into the following sections. Section 2 provides a brief overview of opportunistic networks, describes a motivating scenario, and lists some of the major research challenges for interest and content sharing in opportunistic networks with privacy-preserving guarantees. In Section 3, we describe the system model. Next, we explain the proposed scheme in Section 4. Section 5 elaborates on PIDGIN. In Section 6, we provide the concrete construction. Section 7 reports on our security and performance analysis. Related work is reviewed in Section 8. Finally, we conclude in Section 9 and highlight some directions for future work.

2. OPPORTUNISTIC NETWORKS

In this section, we provide a brief overview of opportunistic networks, a motivating scenario, and the major research challenges that we address.

2.1 Overview

Conceptually, opportunistic networks originate from DTNs that enable content exchange between nodes in a publish-subscribe fashion, generally via short-range communication. In a typical opportunistic network, such as Haggle, a subscriber node specifies its interests while a publisher node shares content with its neighbouring nodes [17]. These neighbouring nodes are intermediate nodes, known as brokers, that epidemically disseminate interests and content within the network. A resolution takes place when a broker node finds a match between the interests of a subscriber and the tags associated with published content. As a result of resolution, a broker forwards content to the subscriber.

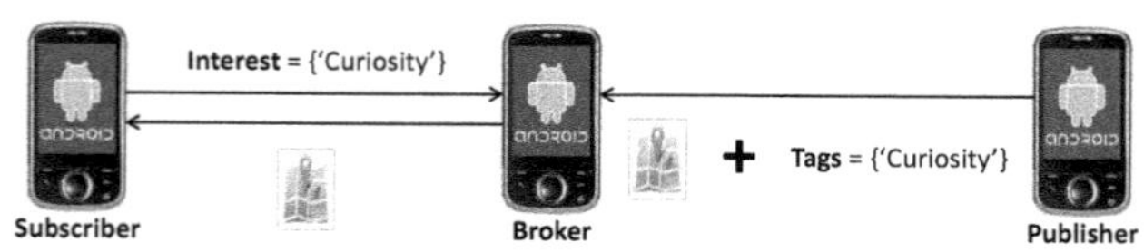

Figure 1: An example of content sharing in an opportunistic network.

2.2 Motivating Scenario

Curiosity - A Military Mission: Let us consider a battlefield scenario for a mission called *Curiosity* in which soldiers are equipped with smartphones. During the mission, a scout collects some sensitive information about the enemy (for instance, an image of the enemy's position) using her smartphone camera. After acquiring this sensitive information, a scout desires to share it with other soldiers. For this reason, she may tag the image with the mission name, i.e., *Curiosity*. Unfortunately, there is no Internet connectivity on the battlefield and the only way to share is to use the short-range communication offered by smartphones. Therefore, the scout would like to share the image with other soldiers using their smartphones. We assume that the soldiers are interested in getting information about the mission and subscribe using their smartphones.

Haggle: A Possible Solution: To exchange information in such scenarios, we can leverage opportunistic networks, such as Haggle. Using Haggle, the scout publishes the image with *Curiosity* as a tag. Any soldier can express interest in *Curiosity* by subscribing to it, as illustrated in Figure 1. Here we assume that someone acting as a broker receives both the interest and the tagged image. Whenever that happens, the broker checks whether the interests of a subscriber matches any tags associated with the image. If so, the broker forwards the image to the subscriber(s).

Privacy and Confidentiality Issues: First of all, to preserve confidentiality, the information about the *Curiosity* mission should be shared only within a particular group of soldiers. Each content item is associated with an access policy that indicates who should have access to it. For example, information about the *Curiosity* mission might have a policy (P) that content is shared with either a *Major* or a *Soldier* from the *Infantry* unit. Even if the content (i.e., image) is encrypted, the policy itself could reveal sensitive information. An enemy may infer useful information from the fact that some contents are sent to a *Major* or a *Soldier* from the *Infantry* unit. Outsiders (i.e., enemies) and insiders (i.e., soldiers) serving as brokers may gain unauthorised access to contents. Furthermore, the interests of subscribers and the tags associated with the content may also reveal sensitive information. Therefore, in addition to the content itself, its associated tags, policies, and subscription information (i.e., interests) should also be protected.

This scenario motivates the need to tackle the security and privacy issues that we generally face in opportunistic networks. In the following section, we list some major research challenges inherent to these issues that we address in this paper.

2.3 Research Challenges

To guarantee the preservation of privacy for interest and content sharing in opportunistic networks, the following research challenges related to both (i) privacy and confidentiality (i.e., *C1-C3*) and (ii) functionality (i.e., *C4-C5*) need to be addressed:

C1 In the presence of unauthorised brokers, how do we regulate access to disseminated content and preserve confidentiality?

C2 In the presence of curious brokers, how does the network exchange content without compromising the privacy of its subscribers?

C3 How can a subscriber obtain content without exposing her interests to untrusted brokers?

C4 In order to minimise the flood of unnecessary traffic through the communication network, how do we ensure that a subscriber receives content if and only if authorised to decrypt?

C5 Assuming the loose coupling of the publish- subscribe model, how do we address the challenges above (i.e., *C1-C4*) without sharing keys between publishers and subscribers?

3. SYSTEM MODEL

Before presenting our threat model and assumptions, we identify the entities involved in the system:

Publishers are nodes that originate content.

Subscribers are nodes that express interests.

Brokers are nodes that may receive and disseminate both content and interests. They evaluate whether available content matches known node interests. On successful evaluation, they forward content to subscribers.

Trusted Key Management Authority (TKMA) is an offline entity that distributes cryptographic key material (including private keys and public parameters) to all nodes. This is done out-of-band (usually once in the lifetime of a node, typically when the node is initialised).

Threat Model. We assume that brokers are *honest-but-curious*, i.e., they honestly follow the protocol, but remain curious to learn about content and interest. Also, we assume that brokers may collude. Further, we consider the TKMA to be fully trusted and assume that it only plays a role at the time of system initialisation. Last but not least, we assume only passive adversaries and do not consider active adversaries that can manipulate the information being exchanged.

4. APPROACH

In this section, we describe the proposed scheme for preserving privacy during interest and content sharing in opportunistic networks. As a starting point, we consider some basic schemes that partially address the research challenges listed in Section 2.3. Next, we incrementally address each of the research challenges. Finally, we describe the proposed scheme.

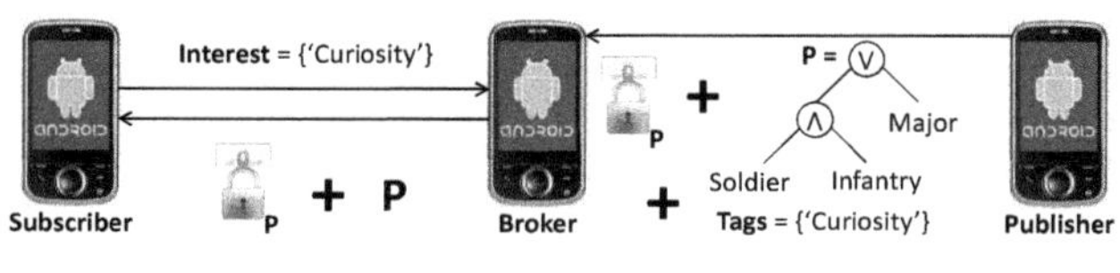

Figure 2: Regulation of access to content using CP-ABE policies.

Scheme I: Regulate Access to Content

To preserve the confidentiality of content, a publisher can specify who should have access. One possible approach for the publisher to regulate access to content is by employing an ABE scheme, such as CP-ABE [4] or KP-ABE [9]. ABE supports fine-grained policies for limiting content access. In this work, we consider CP-ABE because it allows a publisher to exert control over access to content, as described in the use case scenario. In contrast, with the use of KP-ABE, a key generation authority controls who can access content.

Figure 2 illustrates the scheme where the image is encrypted according to this policy: *either a Major or a Solider from the Infantry can gain access.* The policy is expressed as a tree whose leaf nodes represent the attributes; non-leaf nodes denote the AND, OR and threshold gates. In this scheme, a broker forwards content to subscribers if their interests match the content's tags.

This approach preserves the confidentiality of the disseminated contents without providing access to unauthorised brokers. This scheme, however, has a drawback. A broker might send content to subscribers who might not be able to decrypt it. In fact, a broker's role is merely to match the interest of subscribers against tags associated with content (without checking whether a subscriber has access authorisation). For instance, consider a subscriber who is a soldier but neither a *Major* nor a member of the *Infantry* unit.

In summary, this scheme resolves the access control problem *(C1)* while raising the problem of a communication network flooded with unnecessary traffic *(C4)*.

Scheme II: Refined Authorisation Checks

This scheme extends Scheme I and resolves the flooding problem *C4*. In this scheme, a subscriber may send attributes and interests to brokers so that a broker can perform an authorisation check prior to forwarding the content. To perform the authorisation check, a broker matches leaf nodes in the policy tree with the subscriber's attributes. If there is a match, a leaf node will be marked as satisfied. After evaluating leaf nodes, a broker evaluates intermediate nodes (including AND, OR and threshold) in the policy. A broker will forward encrypted content to a subscriber if and only if (i) the root node of the policy is marked as satisfied and (ii) the interests match the tags.

This scheme targets both the access control problem *(C1)* and the flooding problem *(C4)*. However, it still has some privacy issues. First, both the cleartext attributes of subscribers and the cleartext CP-ABE policies can compromise the privacy of subscribers, i.e., *C2*. For example, the enemy may learn from the access policies that there is information intended for a *Major*. Second, the cleartext interests of a subscriber may also leak information, i.e., *C3*. For instance, the enemy may learn that the content or interests concern the *Curiosity* mission.

Scheme III: Hashing Private Information

In order to partially overcome the issue of subscriber privacy *(C2)*, a subscriber and a publisher may hash attributes and leaf nodes in the policy tree, respectively. Similarly, a subscriber's interests could be protected by calculating the hash values of interest items and content tags. In this scheme, a broker forwards encrypted content to subscribers if and only

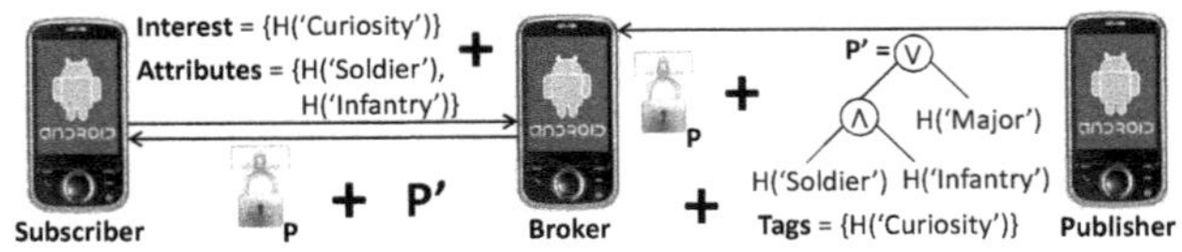

Figure 3: Private information is hidden through replacement of leaf nodes in the CP-ABE policy (that are tags, attributes, or interests) with their corresponding hashes.

if (i) the hashed values of the interests match the hashed values of the tags (i.e., h('Curiosity')) and (ii) hashed values of attributes (i.e., {h('Soldier'), h('Infantry')}) satisfy the policy P' whose leaf nodes are also hashed, as shown in Figure 3.

Unfortunately, this scheme is vulnerable to a pre-computed dictionary attack. The enemy may pre-calculate a list of hashes for possible attributes (and leaf nodes in the policy tree) and a list of hashes for potential interest items and content tags). The pre-calculated list of hashes may reveal the original attributes, leaf nodes in the policy tree, interests, and tags.

Scheme IV: Countering Dictionary Attacks

To harden the system against pre-computed dictionary attacks, a publisher can replace each leaf node in the policy with the hash of a concatenated pair of a tag and an attribute. Similarly, a user may subscribe using the hash of a concatenated pair of an interest item and an attribute (i.e., {H('Curiosity' || 'Soldier'), H('Curiosity' || 'Infantry')}) as illustrated in Figure 4. In this scheme, a broker just needs to check whether the items in a subscription satisfy the hashed policy P'. Upon successful evaluation, the broker will forward the content to subscribers.

The advantage of this scheme is that it not only hardens the system against pre-computed dictionary attacks but also decreases the number of comparisons performed by the broker when compared to Scheme III. This is because a broker performs integrated checks that cover both authorisation and interest matching simultaneously in contrast to Scheme III in which a broker must perform two separate checks: one to check the authorisation and one to match the interest. Though this significantly expands the range of elements that must be computed in a dictionary attack, the scheme is still vulnerable to adversaries with sufficient storage.

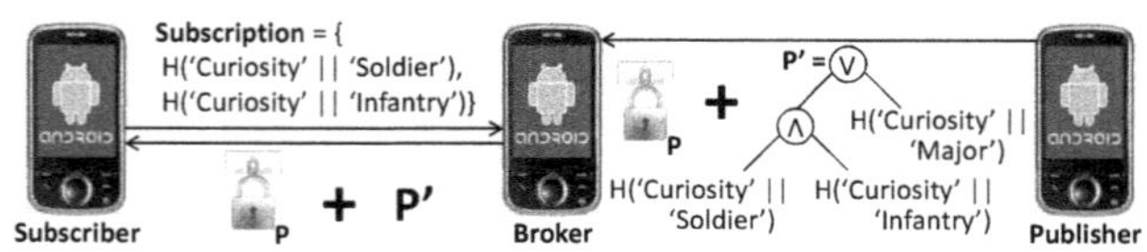

Figure 4: Hardening against a pre-computed dictionary attack through concatenating (i) each content tag with a leaf node in the CP-ABE policy, and (ii) each interest item with an attribute, then calculating the hash of each concatenated string.

PIDGIN: The New Scheme

Our proposed scheme, PIDGIN, aims to address all the research challenges (i.e., *C1-C5*) listed in Section 2.3. The main idea behind PIDGIN is regulation of access to content using CP-ABE and extension of cleartext CP-ABE policies with the Public-key Encryption with Keyword Search (PEKS) scheme [5] to protect attributes, interests, tags, and leaf nodes in the policy tree.

The PEKS scheme consists of four basic functions – **Keygen**, **Etag**[1], **Trapdoor** and **Test**. For each attribute, we run **Keygen** to calculate a key pair consisting of both public (i.e., $h_{Soldier}$) and private (i.e., $x_{Soldier}$) keys corresponding to the given attribute (i.e., *Soldier*). To protect policies and tags, a publisher can replace each leaf node in the policy tree with the output of the **Etag** function of the PEKS scheme, which takes as input a tag (i.e., *Curiosity*) and the public key of the attribute, as shown in Figure 5. A subscriber protects attributes and interests by replacing each interest item in the subscription list with the output of a **Trapdoor** function that takes as input an interest item (i.e., *Curiosity*) and the private key (generated by the PEKS scheme) corresponding to the attribute.

A broker performs matching under encryption between transformed policies and subscriptions. It runs the **Test** function, a building block that matches a trapdoor to an encrypted tag. If an encrypted tag in the policy tree P' matches with any encrypted trapdoor in the subscription list, the tree node is marked as satisfied. The broker evaluates all nodes in the policy tree starting from the leaf nodes, and progresses to the root. If the root is satisfied, the broker will forward the content along with the encrypted policy to the subscribers.

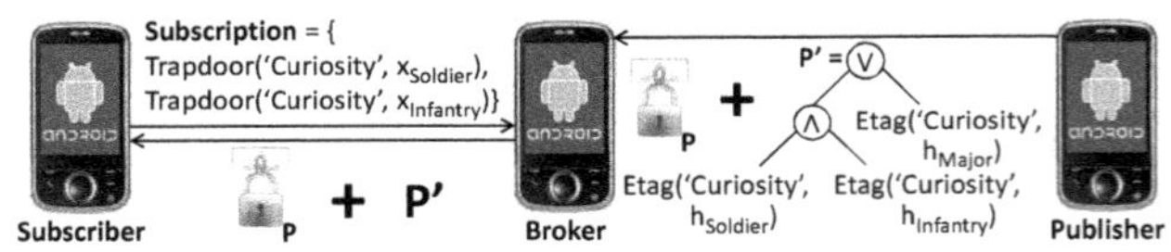

Figure 5: PIDGIN protects the content, the policy, the tags associated with content, and the subscriber's interest and attributes.

5. DESIGN

Setup and Key Generation

During the initialisation phase, the system sets up both the CP-ABE and PEKS primitives. The PIDGIN TKMA generates and distributes keys. It also generates a private set of attributes (i.e., CP-ABE private keys) and sends these securely to the subscriber via out-of-band communication. The TKMA broadcasts the public part of attributes (i.e., CP-ABE public keys). Since the attributes are protected using the PEKS scheme, the TKMA also generates a pair of keys corresponding to each attribute. Similar to CP-ABE key distribution, the TKMA sends the private and public parts of the PEKS key pairs to the subscribers and publishers, respectively. The major difference between the CP-ABE private key set and the PEKS private key set is that the former is unique for each user, while the latter is not.

[1]The Etag function is called PEKS in the original paper [5].

Publisher's Encryption

To protect the content and preserve the privacy of subscribers, a publisher encrypts content with CP-ABE policies and then protects the policies. The content is encrypted with a symmetric cipher, such as the Advanced Encryption Standard (AES), as a performance optimization. The symmetric key is encrypted with the CP-ABE policy. Since the CP-ABE policies may compromise the privacy of subscribers, the policies are encrypted using PEKS. While encrypting CP-ABE policies using PEKS, PIDGIN also incorporates tags that are associated with the published content.

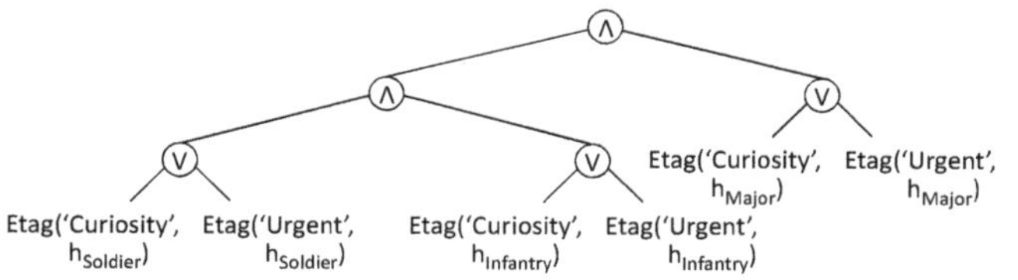

Figure 6: An extended CP-ABE policy with two tags, i.e., 'Curiosity' and 'Urgent'.

To extend CP-ABE policies for PEKS, a publisher considers each leaf node in the policy tree as well as the tags that are associated with the content. If there is just a single tag then the publisher replaces the leaf node with the **Etag** function's output, as was illustrated in Figure 5. The **Etag** function takes a tag keyword to be encrypted and the public key corresponding to the leaf node under consideration. After running the **Etag** function, a publisher gets an encrypted tag. The **Etag** function does not leak information about the tags or leaf nodes in the policy tree. In the case that there is more than one tag, the publisher runs the **Etag** function for each tag item and encrypts it with the public key corresponding to the leaf node under consideration. Finally, the leaf node attribute is replaced with the subtree that is the disjunction (i.e. OR) of the newly generated encrypted tags. Figure 6 illustrates an example of a policy with two tags, i.e., 'Curiosity' and 'Urgent'.

Subscriber's Encryption Phase

In order to protect the privacy of the interests and attributes of a subscriber, each interest item is encrypted using the subscriber's private key (generated by the PEKS scheme) that corresponds to the attribute. PIDGIN considers the possibility that a subscriber might have multiple attributes and interests. Each interest item is encrypted with each private key (generated by the PEKS scheme) that corresponds to an attribute. Figure 5 describes the case in which a subscriber has two attributes and subscribes with a single interest item. Let us assume that a subscriber instead has two interest items, say 'Curiosity' and 'Urgent', while holding attributes Solider and Infantry. The subscription list would contain four items including **Trapdoor**('Curiosity', $x_{Soldier}$), **Trapdoor**('Curiosity', $x_{Infantry}$), **Trapdoor**('Urgent', $x_{Soldier}$) and **Trapdoor**('Urgent', $x_{Infantry}$). The trapdoor representation does not leak information about the interest item or the attribute.

Broker's Matching Phase

A broker opportunistically exchanges both content and subscriptions. Once a broker receives both the encrypted subscription and the encrypted content along with the encrypted policy, it evaluates whether they match. For this, the broker runs a function that recursively evaluates the encrypted policy tree. The **Test** function checks each encrypted leaf node in the policy against the encrypted interest item in the subscription.

The **Test** function returns either *TRUE* or *FALSE*, indicating only whether the trapdoor matched the encrypted tag or not, respectively. By running the **Test** function, a broker does not learn the tag or the interest item because both are encrypted and the matching only occurs under encryption. If an encrypted tag in the policy tree matches with any trapdoor in the subscription list, that node is marked as satisfied. After evaluating the leaf nodes, a broker can evaluate intermediate AND, OR and threshold nodes in the policy tree to finally identify whether the root node of the policy tree is satisfied or not. If the root node is satisfied, the broker will forward content along with the encrypted policy to the subscriber.

Subscriber's Decryption Phase

Once a subscriber receives a piece of encrypted content along with its encrypted policy, they must first recover the original CP-ABE policy. Each leaf node (with a single tag, as in Figure 2) or subtree of tags (if more than one tag is used, as in Figure 6) is replaced with the corresponding attribute. Before sharing their encrypted interests, a subscriber checks a lookup table that associates attributes with corresponding trapdoors. If a trapdoor matches any encrypted tag in the leaf node of the policy, the lookup table will used to find the corresponding attribute. Next, each leaf node (in the case of a single tag) or subtree of tags (if multiple tags are used) will be replaced with the attribute that was found. If no match was found, a dummy attribute will be inserted. This recovers the original CP-ABE policy (i.e., one shown in Figure 2) that can be used by the CP-ABE decryption function to get the symmetric key needed to decrypt the content.

6. CONSTRUCTION

In this section, we provide some definitions and details of core functions used in different phases of the PIDGIN lifecycle.

6.1 Definitions

Policy Structure. We assume a policy tree P that represents an access structure. Each non-leaf node represents an AND, an OR or a threshold gate. Let us consider that num_x denotes number of children of a node x and k_x represents the threshold value. For OR and AND gates, k_x is 1 and num_x, respectively. For the threshold gate, the value of k_x is: $0 < k_x \leq num_x$. Let us consider that $\mathbf{parent}(x)$ represents the parent of a node x, $\mathbf{att}(x)$ denotes the attributes associated with leaf node x, and $\mathbf{index}(x)$ returns the number associated with a node x, with nodes numbered from 1 to num.

Bilinear Maps. Let $\mathbb{G}_1$ and $\mathbb{G}_2$ be two multiplicative cyclic groups of prime order p. Let g be a generator of $\mathbb{G}_1$ and

$e : \mathbb{G}_1 \times \mathbb{G}_1 \rightarrow \mathbb{G}_2$ be a bilinear map. The bilinear map e satisfies the following properties:

- Computability: given $g, h \in \mathbb{G}_1$, there is a polynomial time algorithm to compute $e(g, h) \in \mathbb{G}_2$.
- Bilinearity: $\forall u, v \in \mathbb{G}_1$ and $a, b \in \mathbb{Z}_p$, we have $e(u^a, v^b) = e(u, v)^{ab}$.
- Non-degeneracy: if g is a generator of $\mathbb{G}_1$ then $e(g, g)$ is a generator of $\mathbb{G}_2$, where $e(g, g) \neq 1$.

Notice that the bilinear map e is symmetric since $e(g^a, g^b) = e(g, g)^{ab} = e(g^b, g^a)$.

Hash Functions. We consider the hash functions:

$$H_1 : \{0,1\}^* \rightarrow \mathbb{G}_1$$
$$H_2 : \mathbb{G}_2 \rightarrow \{0,1\}^{\log p}$$

Lagrange Coefficient. We define the Lagrange coefficient $\Delta_{i,A}$ for $i \in \mathbb{Z}_p$ and a set A of elements in $\mathbb{Z}_p$:

$$\Delta_{i,A}(x) = \prod_{j \in A, j \neq i} \frac{x - j}{i - j}$$

6.2 Primitives

Init(1^K). The init algorithm takes as input the security parameter k that determines the size of p. It randomly picks two exponents $\alpha,\beta \in \mathbb{Z}_p$ and outputs the public key $PK = (\mathbb{G}_1, g, h = g^\beta, e(g,g)^\alpha)$ and the master key $MK = (\beta, g^\alpha)$. The public key PK is published while the master key MK is kept securely by the TKMA. Moreover, two stores, the Search Key Secret Store ($SKSS$) and the Search Key Public Store ($SKPS$), which are managed by the TKMA, are initialised as:

$$SKSS \leftarrow \phi$$
$$SKPS \leftarrow \phi$$

KeyGen(MK, A). The key generation algorithm is run by the TKMA. It takes as input a list of attributes A and outputs a CP-ABE decryption key and a set of search key pairs. To generate the decryption key, it first chooses a random $r \in \mathbb{Z}_p$ and then a random $r_j \in \mathbb{Z}_p$ for each attribute $j \in A$. Next, it computes the decryption key as:

$$DK = (D = g^{(\alpha+r)/\beta},$$
$$\forall \in A : D_j = g^r \cdot H_1(j)^{r_j}, D'_j = g^{r_j})$$

Before the generation of a search key pair for an attribute $j \in A$, a search key store (either $SKSS$ or $SKPS$) can be looked up. If the search key pair already exists, then the public and private keys will be collected from $SKPS$ or $SKSS$, respectively. Otherwise, the algorithm chooses a random $x_j \in \mathbb{Z}_p^*$, calculates $h_j = g^{x_j}$, and updates both private and public key stores as:

$$SKSS \leftarrow SKSS \cup (j, x_j)$$
$$SKPS \leftarrow SKPS \cup (j, h_j)$$

Next, it computes the search key secret as: $SKS = (\forall \in A : x_j)$. Finally, the $SKPS$ is publicised while the decryption key DK and the search key secret SKS are securely transmitted to the subscriber.

Etag(PK, h_i, t). The **Etag** algorithm encrypts a given tag t with h_i. It chooses a random $r \in \mathbb{Z}_p^*$ and computes $z = e(H_1(t), h^r)$. Next, it computes $A = g^r$ and $B = H_2(z)$ and outputs the encrypted tag as: $ET = (A, B)$.

Pub-Enc$(PK, SKPS, C, P, T)$. The publisher encryption algorithm encrypts content C under the access policy P with a list of tags T. It also encrypts P. In reality, it randomly generates a symmetric key K and encrypts C as $\{C\}_K$ and then encrypts K under P. To encrypt K under P, it chooses a polynomial q_x for each node x in a top-down manner, starting from the root R, such that it sets degree d_x one less than the threshold value k_x, i.e., $d_x = k_x - 1$. Starting from the root R, it chooses a random $s \in \mathbb{Z}_p$, sets $q_R(0) = s$ and chooses other d_R points randomly. For any other non-root node x, it sets $q_R(0) = q_{parent(x)}(index(x))$ and chooses other d_x points randomly. Let Y be the set of leaf nodes in P. The ciphertext is computed as:

$$CT = (\tilde{E} = Ke(g,g)^{\alpha s}, E = h^s,$$
$$\forall y \in Y : E_y = g^{q_y(0)}, E'_y = H_1(att(y))^{q_y(0)})$$

Next, the policy P is encrypted as follows. For each leaf node i, it looks up the corresponding private secret key h_i from the $SKPS$. Then, it runs **Etag**(h_i, t) for each tag $t \in T$ and combines all encrypted tags corresponding to an attribute to form an OR subtree. The original leaf node attribute is replaced with this OR subtree. If only one tag exists in T, the original attribute is replaced with the output of the **Etag** function. This basically generates the encrypted policy P'. Finally, this algorithm returns $PE = (P', CT, \{C\}_K)$.

Trapdoor(x_i, t). The **Trapdoor** algorithm encrypts interest item t using x_i. It returns the encrypted interest item $TD = H_1(t)^{x_i}$.

Sub-Enc(I, SKS). The subscriber encryption algorithm encrypts interest I using the attributes SKS. For each interest item $t \in I$, it runs **Trapdoor**(x_i, t) using search key secret x_i corresponding to each attribute $i \in SKS$. A subscriber also maintains a history of subscription HS to keep track of all trapdoors belonging to a subscription. HS is initialised as $HS \leftarrow \phi$ and updated as:

$$\forall i \in SKS : HS \leftarrow HS \cup (i, TD_i)$$

HS maintains each trapdoor with its corresponding attribute. Finally, this algorithm publicises $SE = (TD_1, TD_2, \ldots, TD_{|I|.|SKS|})$ and keeps HS securely.

Test(ET, TD). The **Test** algorithm takes the encrypted tag and trapdoor and returns $TRUE$ if $H_2(e(TD, A)) \stackrel{?}{=} B$ is $TRUE$ and $FALSE$ otherwise.

Bro-Match(P', SE). This algorithm takes the publisher encrypted policy P' and the subscriber encrypted interest SE and returns $TRUE$ if they match and $FALSE$ otherwise. To perform the match, a broker runs **Test**(ET_i, TD_j) for each leaf node i in P' and trapdoor $TD_j \in SE$. If an encrypted leaf node matches with any trapdoor, it is marked as satisfied (i.e., $TRUE$). After evaluating leaf nodes, the algorithm evaluates intermediate nodes (AND, OR and threshold). After this evaluation, if the root node of the encrypted policy P' is satisfied, that is, $TRUE$, then this algorithm returns $TRUE$ and $FALSE$ otherwise.

Sub-Dec(PE, HS, DK) This algorithm decrypts the policy P' and then decrypts the encrypted contents PE. First, it matches encrypted leaf nodes with a trapdoor in HS by running **Test**. If a match is found, the corresponding attribute is selected from HS. The leaf node (if a single tag) or a subtree of encrypted tags conjuncted with OR (if more tags) will be replaced with the selected attribute. If no match is found, then a dummy attribute will be placed. This recovers the original policy, which will be used to decrypt the symmetric key: if node x is a leaf node then we assume $i = att(x)$ and run the following function if $i \in A$:

$$\begin{aligned} DecryptNode(CT, DK, x) &= \frac{e(D_i, E_x)}{e(D'_i, E'_x)} \\ &= \frac{e(g^r.H(i)^{r_i}, g^{q_x(0)})}{e(g^{r_i}, H(i)^{q_x(0)})} \\ &= e(g,g)^{rq_x(0)} \end{aligned}$$

If $i \notin A$ then $DecryptNode(CT, DK, x) = \perp$. For a non-leaf node x, the algorithm runs $DecryptNode(CT, DK, z)$ for each child z of x and stores output as F_z. Let A_x be an arbitrary k_x-sized set of child nodes z such that $F_z \neq \perp$. If no such set exists then the node was not satisfied and the function returns $\perp$. Otherwise, it computes:

$$F_x = \prod_{z \in A_x} F_z^{\Delta_{i,A'_x}(0)}$$

(where $i = index(z)$ and $A'_x = index(z) : z \in A_x$)

$$\begin{aligned} &= \prod_{z \in A_x} (e(g,g)^{r.q_z(0)})^{\Delta_{i,S'_x}(0)} \\ &= \prod_{z \in A_x} (e(g,g)^{r.q_{parent(z)}(index(z))})^{\Delta_{i,A'_x}(0)} \end{aligned}$$

(by construction)

$$\begin{aligned} &= \prod_{z \in A_x} (e(g,g)^{r.q_x(0)})^{\Delta_{i,A'_x}(0)} \\ &= (e(g,g)^{r.q_x(0)} \end{aligned}$$

(using polynomial interpolation)

If the tree is satisfied by A, we set

$$\begin{aligned} G &= DecryptNode(CT, DK, R) \\ &= e(g,g)^{rq_R(0)} \\ &= e(g,g)^{rs} \end{aligned}$$

The symmetric key is decrypted by computing:
$\tilde{E}/(e(E,D)/G) = \tilde{E}/(e(h^s, g^{(\alpha+r)/\beta})/e(g,g)^{rs}) = K$.

Finally, K is used to decrypt $\{C\}_K$ in order to access contents C.

7. EVALUATION

PIDGIN is designed to optimize performance by encrypting content with a symmetric key. This keys is then encrypted with the CP-ABE policy. The leaf nodes in the policy tree are protected using the PEKS **Etag** primitive described by Boneh *et al.* [5]. PEKS is semantically secure against a chosen keyword attack in the random oracle model, assuming that the Bilinear Diffie-Hellman (BDH) problem is hard (as proved by Theorem 3.1 of the PEKS paper [5]). However, the CP-ABE policy structure is not protected and leaks information about the number of attributes or tags used. This leak could partially be tackled by the inclusion of dummy attributes at the cost of increased complexity. PIDGIN addresses the case where brokers collude but must still not gain access to content, policies, or subscriptions. If a broker colludes with a subscriber, together they learn no more information than is already available to the subscriber alone. In the case that two subscribers collude to receive content that each of them alone cannot get otherwise, PIDGIN remains safe due to the randomness embedded in each subscriber's (CP-ABE) decryption key.

Platform

As a proof of concept, we developed a prototype of PIDGIN. It is based on an extension of the open source *libfenc*[2] library that is written in C. The library includes an implementation of CP-ABE. Since we proposed to extend CP-ABE with PEKS, we have implemented PEKS in C using the PBC[3] library. (PBC also used by libfenc.) PBC is based on Elliptic Curve Cryptography (ECC). The curve we use in our experimentation is of type A.

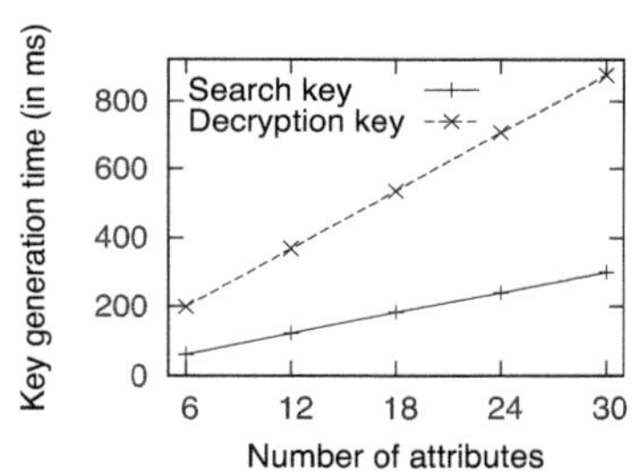

Figure 7: Effect of attributes on key generation time.

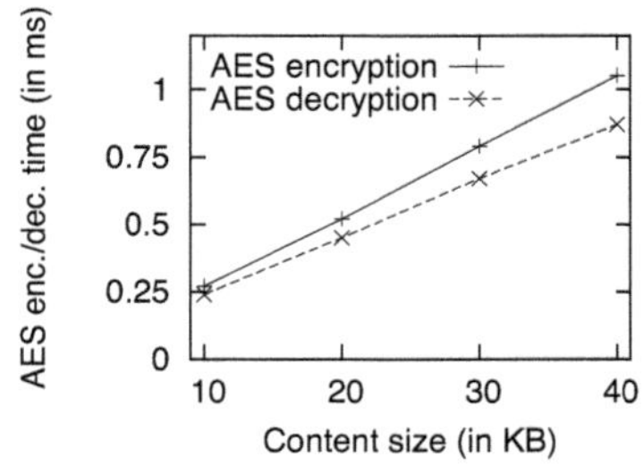

Figure 8: Effect of content size on AES encryption and decryption time.

[2]`https://code.google.com/p/libfenc/`
[3]`http://crypto.stanford.edu/pbc/`

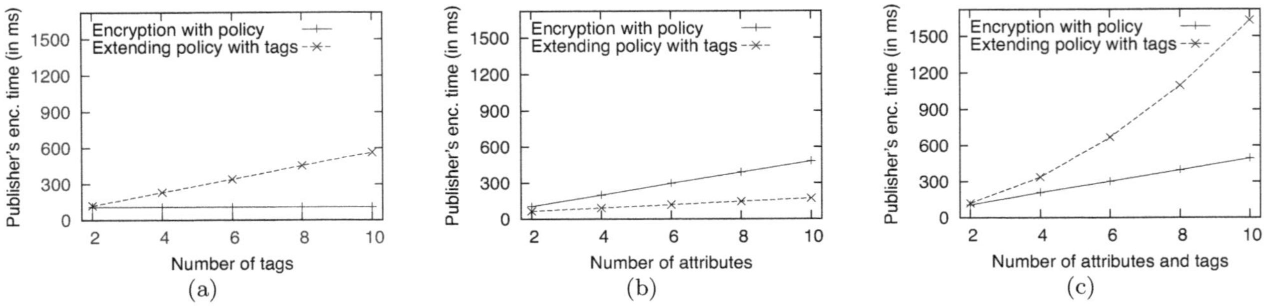

Figure 9: Effect of (a) tags, (b) attributes, and (c) both tags and attributes on publisher's encryption time.

After extending CP-ABE with PEKS (on the x86 architecture), we cross-compiled it for the ARM architecture. This allowed us to test the prototype on a Samsung Galaxy SIII smartphone (running Android version 4.1.2 with kernel version 3.0.31, and using 1 GB RAM and 1.4 GHz processor). To use the prototype, we cross-compiled both GMP[4] (the GNU Multiple Precision arithmetic library required by PBC) and PBC for the ARM architecture. These were all installed on the smartphone. We present results that are averaged over 20 runs.

Our analysis does not consider battery consumption since the prototype does not implement energy-related optimizations (that could be deployed without compromising private information). For instance, adding Time-To-Live (TTL) tags to content and subscriptions can bound the quantity of matching operations performed by brokers. Similarly, subscriptions could specify bounds on the freshness of content.

Setup and Key Generation

During the initialisation phase, system-wide key material is generated. In the key generation phase, both search and decryption keys are generated for a given set of attributes. Both phases can be run on a computer since the keys are distributed out-of-band. However, we have considered running both phases on a smartphone (with the specifications described above), should these need to occur in the field. The initialisation phase takes 108.5 milliseconds (ms). The time for generating search keys grows linearly with an increase in the number of attributes, as illustrated in Figure 7 (where 30 search keys take 300 ms – i.e., an average of 10 ms per attribute). Similarly, the key generation time for decryption keys also grows linearly with an increase in the number of attributes – 30 decryption keys take approximately 877 ms (i.e., an average of 29.25 ms per attribute). Asymptotically, the complexity of the key generation is$\Theta(\ |A|)$, where $|A|$ indicates number of attributes in list A.

Publisher's Encryption

A publisher encrypts content with a randomly generated symmetric key. Our prototype uses AES for the symmetric cipher. The symmetric key is encrypted with the CP-ABE policy for the content. The CP-ABE policy is extended with tags that are also encrypted. Figure 8 shows the time to perform symmetric encryption, which is seen to grow linearly with the content size (C). Encryption of a piece of content of size 40 kilobytes (KB) takes 0.105 ms (at an average of 0.026 ms per KB). To measure the performance overhead of the encryption time, we varied the numbers of tags and attributes (A_P^*), as shown in Figure 9.

Figure 9(a) and Figure 9(b) show the effect of the number of tags and attributes on the publisher's encryption time, respectively. Figure 9(a) shows the effect of tags (ranging from 2 to 10) while keeping the number of attributes constant (i.e., 2 attributes - the minimum attributes required to create a policy with an AND or an OR operation). As expected, the time to extend a policy with tags grows linearly with the number of tags. Figure 9(b) reports the effect of varying the number of attributes (from 2 to 10) in a policy while using a single tag. The time for encryption of the symmetric key with the policy grows linearly with the number of attributes. As the number of attributes increases, the time to extend a policy with a set of tags grows linearly.

Figure 9(c) reports the most complex case, where we increase both attributes and tags simultaneously. The growth of the time needed to extend a policy with tags is quadratic, depending on both the number of attributes and the number of tags. We ran experiments with the same number of tags and attributes to analyze this case. Extension of a policy with 2 attributes, using 2 tags for each, takes approximately 120 ms, while extension of a policy with 10 attributes, using 10 tags for each, takes 1632 ms. More generally, the asymptotic complexity of the publisher's encryption phase is$\Theta(\ |A_P^*| \cdot |T| + |C|)$.

Subscriber's Encryption

Figure 10 shows the performance overhead incurred during the encryption (in Figure 10(a)) and decryption phases (in Figure 10(b) and Figure 10(c)). The subscriber's encryption phase complexity depends on the number of interest items (I) and attributes (A_S^*).

We first examined the effect on the subscription time that resulted from varying the number of attributes and interests independently. We increased the attributes from 2 to 10 while keeping the number of interest items constant (i.e., 1 interest item). Generation of trapdoors for 10 attributes with a single interest item each took 106 ms. Next, we observed the effect of varying the number of interest items from 2 to 10 while keeping number of attributes constant (i.e., 2 attributes combined with either an AND or OR operation). It took approximately 284 ms to encrypt an interest containing 10 items. As illustrated in Figure 10(a), varying only the number of attributes or interest items affects the subscriber's encryption time linearly.

[4] `http://gmplib.org/`

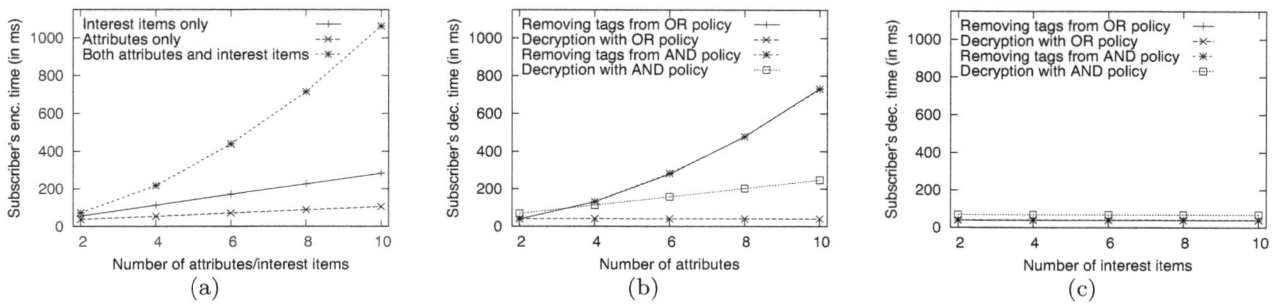

Figure 10: Effect of (a) attributes and interest items on subscriber's encryption time. Effect of (b) attributes and (c) tags on subscriber's decryption time.

We also considered the case where both the number of attributes and interest items varied. For this experiment, we assumed that the number of attributes and interest items are the same – that is, if there are two attributes, it means there are two interest items per attribute as well. Similarly, 10 attributes were used with 10 interest items for each. This took 1063 ms. The combined effect of attributes and interest items causes quadratic growth in the subscriber's encryption time, as shown in Figure 10(a). The asymptotic complexity is:$\Theta(\ |A^*_S| \cdot |I|)$.

As explained above, the curve we used in our experiment is of type A. Using this curve, the storage required for an encrypted tag and a trapdoor are 256 and 128 bytes, respectively.

Broker's Matching

This is the most important step in PIDGIN. During this phase, a broker attempts to match an encrypted subscription with an encrypted policy associated with encrypted content. We first examined the effect of varying the numbers of tags and interest items independently, while keeping the number of attributes constant (i.e., 2 attributes, the minimum necessary to have a policy with an AND or OR operation). We also consider both the cases where the policy contains AND and OR operations, as well as the worst case when no match occurs.

Figure 11 shows the performance analysis of this phase. Figure 11(a) illustrates the effect of the number of tags on the matching time while keeping the number of interest items constant, i.e., 1. As the graph shows, the matching time increases linearly with the number of tags. Similarly, we measured the effect of the number of interest items on the matching time while keeping the number of tags constant, i.e., 1. Figure 11(b) shows that the matching time grows linearly with the number of interest items. In both Figure 11(a) and Figure 11(b), the OR policy takes less time as compared to that of the AND policy, when a match occurs. This is because both OR and AND operations use short circuit evaluation to halt further policy analysis once it is known to be true or false.

Finally, we consider the most complex case where the number of tags and interest items are increased together. Similar to the cases examined in Figure 11(a) and Figure 11(b), it takes less time to evaluate an OR policy when compared to an AND policy. We considered the worst case in which there are 5 tags and 5 interest items with a 2-attribute policy combined with an OR. Since there are 2 attributes in the policy tree with 5 tags each, there are a total of 10 leaf nodes in the encrypted policy. The 2 attributes with 5 interest items each will require 10 trapdoors in the subscription.

The broker checks whether any encrypted leaf node in the policy matches any trapdoor in the subscription. In this worst case, the broker runs the **Test** function 100 times, taking approximately 1324 ms. In addition to this experiment, we measured the overhead of running the **Test** function and discovered that it takes 13.28 ms. We can infer that the primary overhead is from the **Test** function, which is implemented with a bilinear pairing operation. Hence, the matching operation heavily depends on the efficiency of the bilinear pairing primitives. The best and worst case complexities of this phase areΩ (1) and $O(|A^*_P| \cdot |T| \cdot |A^*_S| \cdot |I|)$, respectively.

Subscriber's Decryption

A subscriber receives a piece of encrypted content (along with the corresponding encrypted policy) from the broker if its encrypted interests matched. During the decryption phase, a subscriber first removes the tags from the policy. If they are successful, they can then perform decryption with the policy to recover the symmetric key, which is finally used to decrypt the content.

Figure 10(b) and Figure 10(c) show the effect of the number of attributes and interest items, respectively, on the subscriber's decryption time. In Figure 10(b), we increase the number of attributes from 2 to 10 while keeping the number of interest items constant i.e., 1. we consider both AND and OR policies to see the effect of attributes on tag removal. The performance overhead for the decryption that recovers the symmetric key is also shown.

Figure 10(c) reports on the case where the number of interest items are increased from 2 to 10 (but the attribute count is kept constant i.e., 2). The publisher and subscriber use the same tags and interest items, respectively, to ensure that the matching succeeds. The overhead does not increase with the number of interest items. This is due to our implementation of short circuit evaluation of policies with AND and OR operations. The trapdoor in the subscription matches interest items against tags in the policy. This allows the policy evaluation to proceed without further matching.

In the final step, a symmetric key is recovered if the CP-ABE decryption succeeds. This symmetric key is used to decrypt the content. Figure 8 shows the time required for content decryption using AES. Decrypting a 40 LB piece of

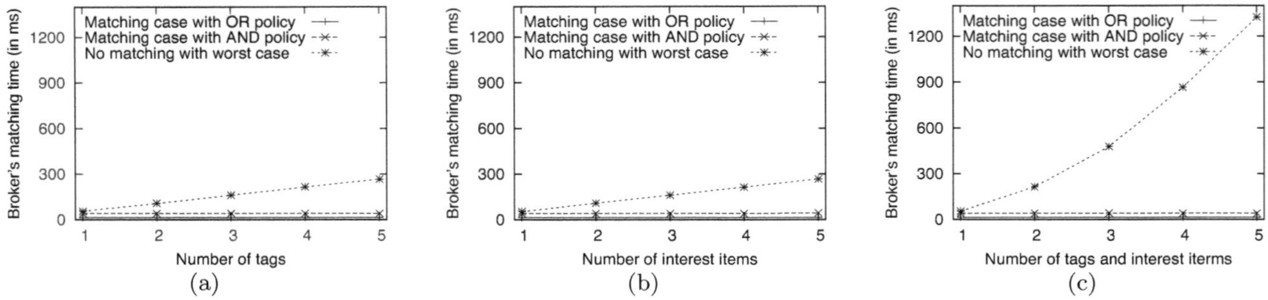

Figure 11: Effect of (a) tags, (b) interest items, and (c) both tags and interest items, on broker's time to perform matching under encryption.

Table 1: Description of symbols used.

Symbol	Description
A	List of attributes
A^*_P	Llist of attributes used to encrypt content
A^*_S	List of attributes used to encrypt interests
C	Content
I	List of keywords a subscriber is interested in
T	List of search tags associated with content

Table 2: Complexity of each phase of PIDGIN.

Phase	Best Case	Worst Case
Key generation	$\Theta(\lvert A\rvert)$	
Publisher encryption	$\Theta(\lvert A^*_P\rvert \cdot \lvert T\rvert + \lvert C\rvert)$	
Subscriber encryption	$\Theta(\lvert A^*_S\rvert \cdot \lvert I\rvert)$	
Broker matching	$\Omega(1)$	$O(\lvert A^*_P\rvert \cdot \lvert T\rvert \cdot \lvert A^*_S\rvert \cdot \lvert I\rvert)$
Subscriber decryption	$\Omega(\lvert C\rvert)$	$O(\lvert A^*_P\rvert \cdot \lvert T\rvert \cdot \lvert A^*_S\rvert \cdot \lvert I\rvert + \lvert C\rvert)$

content takes 0.87 ms (i.e., an average of 0.22 ms per KB). The complexity of subscriber's decryption is: $O(|A^*_P| \cdot |T| \cdot |A^*_S| \cdot |I| + |C|)$ in the worst case and $\Omega\ (|C|)$ in the best case.

Table 2 summarises the complexity of each phase of PIDGIN. The symbols used are described in Table 1.

8. RELATED WORK

The problem of encrypted matching in opportunistic networks is an instance of the larger problem of search over encrypted data. Song *et al.* [22] propose a search scheme over encrypted data based on symmetric keys. The symmetric nature of the scheme rules out its applicability when mobile nodes communicate with each other without any prior contact. The PEKS scheme [5] supports search of encrypted data in the public key setting. PIDGIN uses the PEKS scheme as a building block; moreover, its usage in isolation does not solve privacy and confidentiality issues in opportunistic networks because it lacks the ability to regulate access to content while providing collusion-resistant decryption keys.

ABE schemes can regulate access to content while guaranteeing collusion resistance. However, both the CP-ABE [4] and KP-ABE [9] variants do not protect the policies and attributes associated with content, respectively. PIDGIN uses CP-ABE [4] as a building block after we protect the policies (since the original CP-ABE scheme does not protect them). The complimentary KP-ABE [9] scheme does not protect attributes. While Goyal *et al.* leave the problem of encrypted attributes as an open question [9], this challenging issue is addressed in this paper.

ESPOON [2] can protect security policies in outsourced environments. Asghar *et al.* [3] propose ESPOON$_{ERBAC}$ to extend ESPOON with Encrypted Role-Based Access Control (ERBAC) in outsourced environments. However, these solutions [2, 3, 12] assume that there is no collusion between a user and a server. Thus, none of these solutions [2, 3, 12] are applicable to opportunistic networks where each node can serve in all three roles – that is, publisher, broker, and subscriber.

There are schemes that protect policies [13, 14, 16, 20] by assuming that the policy is evaluated at the receiver's end. Furthermore, schemes offering hidden credentials [11] and hidden policies [8] assume direct interaction between the sender and the receiving parties. Unfortunately, such schemes cannot work in opportunistic networks where policy enforcement is delegated to untrusted brokers.

Shikfa *et al.* [21] propose a method that provides privacy and confidentiality in the content-based forwarding setting. However, their method is orthogonal to our work. Their proposed scheme disseminates information in one direction – i.e., from publishers, without taking into account whether a subscriber is interested or not. In other words, it does not provide the opportunity for a node to subscribe. Moreover, our proposed scheme regulates access to content while offering more expressive and fine-grained policies when compared to theirs [21]. Similarly, schemes [14, 16] hiding CP-ABE policies assume end-to-end communication while we address the case where brokers in the middle must make access decisions before forwarding content in the network.

Nabeel *et al.* [15] provide a solution for preserving privacy in content-based publish-subscribe systems. In their approach, brokers in outsourced environments make routing decisions without knowing the content. However, they assume that subscribers register with publishers prior to any communication and that publishers share symmetric keys with subscribers. This solution cannot work in opportunistic network settings where loosely-coupled publishers and subscribers may not have a chance to pre-arrange key sharing with each other.

In the context of publish-subscribe systems, there are many solutions that address privacy and security issues [6, 19, 23]. However, the state-of-the-art techniques are mainly based on centralised solutions that cannot be applied to opportunistic networks, where each node may serve as publisher, broker, and subscriber.

9. CONCLUSION

This paper presents PIDGIN, a privacy-preserving interest and content sharing scheme for opportunistic networks that does not leak information to untrusted parties. To show the feasibility of our approach, we implemented PIDGIN and evaluated its performance by measuring the overhead incurred for cryptographic operations on a smartphone.

As evident from the performance evaluation, the real bottleneck is the overhead incurred by pairing operations at the brokers. In fact, an efficient pairing implementation would drastically improve the performance of the system. Future work could investigate possible optimisations and the use of more efficient pairing implementations [10].

10. ACKNOWLEDGEMENTS

The authors would like to thank Daniele Miorandi for providing his valuable feedback on the initial draft, as well as the anonymous reviewers for their comments and suggestions to improve the quality of this work. The work of the first and third authors has been partially supported by EIT ICT Labs and the TENACE PRIN project (Grant no. 20103P34XC) funded by the Italian MIUR, respectively.

11. REFERENCES

[1] Haggle: An EU funded project. `http://www.haggleproject.org/`, June 2010. Last accessed: August 7, 2013.

[2] M. R. Asghar, M. Ion, G. Russello, and B. Crispo. ESPOON: Enforcing Encrypted Security Policies in Outsourced Environments. In *The Sixth International Conference on Availability, Reliability and Security*, ARES'11, pages 99–108. IEEE Computer Society, August 2011.

[3] M. R. Asghar, M. Ion, G. Russello, and B. Crispo. $ESPOON_{ERBAC}$: Enforcing security policies in outsourced environments. *Elsevier Computers & Security (COSE)*, 35:2–24, 2013. Special Issue of the International Conference on Availability, Reliability and Security (ARES).

[4] J. Bethencourt, A. Sahai, and B. Waters. Ciphertext-policy attribute-based encryption. In *Security and Privacy, 2007. SP '07. IEEE Symposium on*, pages 321 –334, may 2007.

[5] D. Boneh, G. Crescenzo, R. Ostrovsky, and G. Persiano. Public key encryption with keyword search. In C. Cachin and J. Camenisch, editors, *Advances in Cryptology - EUROCRYPT 2004*, volume 3027 of *Lecture Notes in Computer Science*, pages 506–522. Springer Berlin Heidelberg, 2004.

[6] S. Choi, G. Ghinita, and E. Bertino. A privacy-enhancing content-based publish/subscribe system using scalar product preserving transformations. In P. G. Bringas, A. Hameurlain, and G. Quirchmayr, editors, *Database and Expert Systems Applications*, volume 6261 of *Lecture Notes in Computer Science*, pages 368–384. Springer Berlin Heidelberg, 2010.

[7] Emarketer. Smartphones, tablets drive faster growth in ecommerce sales - mobile will take a greater percentage of total ecommerce retail sales. http://goo.gl/48Mbp, April 2013. Last accessed: August 7, 2013.

[8] K. Frikken, M. Atallah, and J. Li. Attribute-based access control with hidden policies and hidden credentials. *Computers, IEEE Transactions on*, 55(10):1259–1270, 2006.

[9] V. Goyal, O. Pandey, A. Sahai, and B. Waters. Attribute-based encryption for fine-grained access control of encrypted data. In *Proceedings of the 13th ACM conference on Computer and communications security*, CCS '06, pages 89–98, New York, NY, USA, 2006. ACM.

[10] G. Grewal, R. Azarderakhsh, P. Longa, S. Hu, and D. Jao. Efficient implementation of bilinear pairings on ARM processors. In L. Knudsen and H. Wu, editors, *Selected Areas in Cryptography*, volume 7707 of *Lecture Notes in Computer Science*, pages 149–165. Springer Berlin Heidelberg, 2013.

[11] J. E. Holt, R. W. Bradshaw, K. E. Seamons, and H. Orman. Hidden credentials. In *Proceedings of the 2003 ACM workshop on Privacy in the electronic society*, WPES '03, pages 1–8, New York, NY, USA, 2003. ACM.

[12] A. Kapadia, P. P. Tsang, and S. W. Smith. Attribute-based publishing with hidden credentials and hidden policies. In *NDSS*. The Internet Society, 2007.

[13] J. Katz, A. Sahai, and B. Waters. Predicate encryption supporting disjunctions, polynomial equations, and inner products. In N. Smart, editor, *Advances in Cryptology EUROCRYPT 2008*, volume 4965 of *Lecture Notes in Computer Science*, pages 146–162. Springer Berlin Heidelberg, 2008.

[14] J. Lai, R. Deng, and Y. Li. Fully secure cipertext-policy hiding CP-ABE. In F. Bao and J. Weng, editors, *Information Security Practice and Experience*, volume 6672 of *Lecture Notes in Computer Science*, pages 24–39. Springer Berlin Heidelberg, 2011.

[15] M. Nabeel, N. Shang, and E. Bertino. Efficient privacy preserving content based publish subscribe systems. In *Proceedings of the 17th ACM symposium on Access Control Models and Technologies*, SACMAT '12, pages 133–144, New York, NY, USA, 2012. ACM.

[16] T. Nishide, K. Yoneyama, and K. Ohta. Attribute-based encryption with partially hidden encryptor-specified access structures. In S. Bellovin, R. Gennaro, A. Keromytis, and M. Yung, editors, *Applied Cryptography and Network Security*, volume 5037 of *Lecture Notes in Computer Science*, pages 111–129. Springer Berlin Heidelberg, 2008.

[17] E. Nordström, P. Gunningberg, and C. Rohner. A search-based network architecture for mobile devices. Technical report, Department of Information Technology, Uppsala University, 2009.

[18] L. Pelusi, A. Passarella, and M. Conti. Opportunistic networking: data forwarding in disconnected mobile ad hoc networks. *Communications Magazine, IEEE*, 44(11):134–141, 2006.

[19] N. Shang, M. Nabeel, F. Paci, and E. Bertino. A privacy-preserving approach to policy-based content dissemination. In *Data Engineering (ICDE), 2010 IEEE 26th International Conference on*, pages 944–955, 2010.

[20] E. Shen, E. Shi, and B. Waters. Predicate privacy in encryption systems. In O. Reingold, editor, *Theory of Cryptography*, volume 5444 of *Lecture Notes in Computer Science*, pages 457–473. Springer Berlin Heidelberg, 2009.

[21] A. Shikfa, M. Önen, and R. Molva. Privacy and confidentiality in context-based and epidemic forwarding. *Computer Communications*, 33(13):1493 – 1504, 2010.

[22] D. X. Song, D. Wagner, and A. Perrig. Practical techniques for searches on encrypted data. In *IEEE Symposium on Security and Privacy*, pages 44–55. IEEE Computer Society, 2000.

[23] M. Srivatsa and L. Liu. Secure event dissemination in publish-subscribe networks. In *Distributed Computing Systems, 2007. ICDCS '07. 27th International Conference on*, pages 22–22, 2007.

S-ORAM: A Segmentation-based Oblivious RAM

Jinsheng Zhang
Department of Computer Science
Iowa State University
Ames, IA, USA
alexzjs@iastate.edu

Wensheng Zhang
Department of Computer Science
Iowa State University
Ames, Iowa, USA
wzhang@iastate.edu

Daji Qiao
Department of Electrical and Computer Engineering
Iowa State University
Ames, Iowa, USA
daji@iastate.edu

ABSTRACT

As outsourcing data to remote storage servers gets popular, protecting user's pattern in accessing these data has become a big concern. ORAM constructions are promising solutions to this issue, but their application in practice has been impeded by the high communication and storage overheads incurred. Towards addressing this challenge, this paper proposes a segmentation-based ORAM (S-ORAM). It adopts two segment-based techniques, namely, *piece-wise shuffling* and *segment-based query*, to improve the performance of shuffling and query by factoring block size into design. Extensive security analysis proves that S-ORAM is a highly secure solution with a negligible failure probability of $O(N^{-\log N})$. In terms of communication and storage overheads, S-ORAM outperforms the Balanced ORAM (B-ORAM) and the Path ORAM (P-ORAM), which are the state-of-the-art hash and index based ORAMs respectively, in both practical and theoretical evaluations. Particularly under practical settings, the communication overhead of S-ORAM is 12 to 23 times less than B-ORAM when they have the same constant-size user-side storage, and S-ORAM consumes 80% less server-side storage and around 60% to 72% less bandwidth than P-ORAM when they have the similar logarithmic-size user-side storage.

Categories and Subject Descriptors

D.0 [**Software**]: General; E.3 [**Data**]: Data Encryption

Keywords

Data outsourcing; Access pattern; Privacy; Oblivious RAM

1. INTRODUCTION

Along with the increasing popularity of outsourcing data services to remote storage servers, arise also security and privacy concerns. Although encrypting data content has been a common practice for data protection, it does not fully eliminate the concerns, because users' data access pattern is not preserved and researchers have found that a wide range of private information could be revealed by observing the data access pattern [12].

ASIA CCS'14, June 4–6, 2014, Kyoto, Japan.

http://dx.doi.org/10.1145/2590296.2590323.

To address this issue, more and more efficient constructions have been developed to implement oblivious RAM (ORAM) [6], which was originally proposed for software protection but also is a provable solution to data access pattern preservation. Among these efforts, hash based ORAMs [6,8–11,13,15,20] utilize hash functions (including ordinary hash functions, cuckoo hash functions, bloom filters, etc.) to distribute data blocks to storage locations when data is stored or shuffled and to look up intended data blocks when data is queried. In comparison, index based ORAMs [16–19] maintain index structures to record the mapping between data blocks and locations and facilitate data lookup at the query time.

Though a large variety of techniques has been proposed and adopted, most existing ORAM constructions are still not applicable in practice because of the high communication and/or storage overheads incurred. Particularly, hash based ORAMs require a large extra storage space at the server side to deal with hash collisions; hence, access pattern privacy usually has to be preserved via heavy data retrievals and complicated data shuffling. Index based ORAMs rely on index structures to avoid the above problems. However, they fail to provide an efficient solution with which the index structures can be stored in a space-efficient manner and meanwhile can be searched and updated in a time-efficient manner. This limitation has also impeded their applications in practice.

We propose a novel ORAM scheme, called *segmentation-based oblivious RAM (S-ORAM)*, aiming to bring theoretical ORAM constructions one step closer to practical applications. Our proposal is motivated by the observation that a large-scale storage system (e.g., a cloud storage system such as Amazon S3 [2]) usually stores data in blocks and such a block typically has a large size [18], but most existing ORAM constructions treat data blocks as atomic units for query and shuffling, and do not factor block size into their designs. S-ORAM is designed to make better use of the large block size by introducing two *segment-based* techniques, namely, *piece-wise shuffling* and *segment-based query*, to improve the efficiency in data shuffling and query. With piece-wise shuffling, data can be perturbed across a larger range of blocks in a limited user-side storage; this way, the shuffling efficiency can be improved, and the improvement gets more significant as the block size increases. With segment-based query, S-ORAM organizes the data storage at the server side as a hierarchy of single-segment and multi-segment layers, and an encrypted index block is introduced to each segment. With these two techniques at the core, together with a few supplementary algorithms for distributing blocks to segments, S-ORAM can accomplish efficient query with only $O(\log N)$ communication overhead and a constant user-side storage, while existing ORAM constructions have to use a larger user-side storage to achieve the same level of communication efficiency in query.

Extensive security analysis has been conducted to verify the security of the proposed S-ORAM. Particularly, S-ORAM has been shown to be a provably highly secure solution that has a negligible failure probability of $O(N^{-\log N})$, which is no higher than that of existing ORAM constructions.

In terms of communication and storage overheads, S-ORAM outperforms the Balanced ORAM (B-ORAM) [13] and the Path ORAM (P-ORAM) [19], which are the best known theoretical hash-based and practical index-based ORAMs under small local storage assumption, respectively. Particularly, under practical settings [18] where the number of data blocks N ranges from 2^{20} to 2^{36} and the block size is 32 KB to 256 KB, (i) the communication overhead of S-ORAM is 12 to 23 times less than B-ORAM when they have the same constant-size user-side storage; (ii) S-ORAM consumes 80% less server-side storage and around 60% to 72% less bandwidth than P-ORAM when they have the similar logarithmic-size user-side storage.

The rest of the paper is organized as follows. Section 2 briefly reviews existing ORAM constructions. In Section 3, the basic system model and threat model are described, and a formal security definition is provided. Our proposed S-ORAM is described in detail in Section 4. The subsequent Section 5 provides the security and overhead analysis as well as the comparisons between S-ORAM and two representative existing ORAM constructions. Finally, Section 6 concludes the paper.

2. RELATED WORK

In the past decades, there are numerous ORAM schemes proposed to hide user's pattern of access to remote data storage. We roughly classify them into two categories based on the data lookup technique used. From each category, one representative ORAM with the best performance among its peers is chosen to be compared with S-ORAM in Section 5.3.

- Hash based ORAMs: A number of ORAMs [6, 8–11, 13, 15, 20] belong to this category. With hash functions used for data lookup, these ORAMs require facilities such as buckets and stashes to deal with hash collisions. To the best of our knowledege, the Balanced ORAM (B-ORAM) [13] proposed by Kushilevitz et. al. achieves the best asymptotical communication efficiency among hash based ORAMs.

- Index based ORAMs: For ORAMs [16–19] belonging to this category, an index structure is used for data lookup. Therefore, it requires that the user-side storage stores the index, which is feasible only if the number of data blocks is not quite large. When the user-side storage cannot afford to store the index, it can outsource the index to the server in a way similar to storing real data blocks at the cost of increased communication overhead. The Path ORAM (P-ORAM) [19] proposed by Stefanov et. al. is a representative scheme in this category.

2.1 B-ORAM

In B-ORAM, the server-side storage is organized as a hybrid hierarchy with a total of $\frac{\log N}{\log\log N}$ layers, where each layer consists of $\log N$ equal-size sublayers. For the top $O(\log\log N)$ layers, the bucket-hash structure [6] proposed by Goldreich and Ostrovsky is deployed and the remaining layers are cuckoo-hash structures with a shared stash [8]. Since each layer is extended to multiple sublayers, the shuffling frequency is reduced while the query overhead is increased; a balance is struck between the query and shuffling overheads. The randomized shellsort [7] is selected as the underlying oblivious sorting algorithm for the shuffling process. In theory, the amortized communication overhead of B-ORAM is $O\left(\frac{\log^2 N}{\log\log N}\right)$ blocks per query. In practice, however, the overhead is on the magnitude of $\log^3 N$ due to a large constant ignored in the above big-O notation; particularly, querying one data block may require the user to access at least 1000 data blocks, which may not be acceptable in many practical applications.

2.2 P-ORAM

In P-ORAM, the server-side storage is organized as a binary tree in which each node contains a constant-size bucket for storing data blocks. Initially, data are randomly stored at leaf nodes, and an index structure is maintained to record the mapping between the IDs of data blocks and the IDs of the leaf nodes storing the blocks. Based on the index, a data query process retrieves all blocks on the path that contains the query target block and then moves the target block to the root node. In addition, a background eviction process is performed after each query process, to gradually evict blocks from the root node to nodes of lower-height so as to avoid or reduce node overflowing. The index can also be outsourced to the server and stored in a similar binary tree. Besides, to keep bucket size constant at each node, a user-side storage whose size is a logarithmic function of the number of data blocks is needed to form a stash. P-ORAM achieves a communication overhead of $O\left(\frac{\log^2 N}{\log(Z/\log N)}\right)\cdot\omega(1)$ blocks per query, where Z is data block size and $\omega(1)$ is a security parameter. Though the communication overhead is considered to be acceptable in practice [19], the overhead of server-side storage, which is about $32N$ blocks, may pose as a big cost to the user.

Note that, other ORAM constructions such as the partition based ORAM [18], PrivateFS [21], and the single-round ORAM [22], either are based on different user-side storage assumptions than ours or focus on aspects other than bandwidth and storage efficiency, which is the main focus of our work. Due to these prominent differences, we do not compare them with our proposed S-ORAM.

3. PROBLEM STATEMENT

3.1 System Model

Similar to existing ORAM constructions [6, 8–11, 13, 15, 20], we consider a system composed of a user and a remote storage server. The user exports a large amount of data to store at the server, and wishes to hide from the server the pattern of his/her accesses to the data. Data are assumed to be stored and accessed in the unit of blocks, and the typical size of a block ranges from 32 KB to 256 KB [18]. Let N denote the total number of data blocks exported by the user. For simplicity, we assume $\log N$ is an even number.

Each data request from the user, which the user wishes to keep private, can be one of the following types:

- read a data block D of unique ID i from the storage, denoted as a 3-tuple $(read, i, D)$; or

- write/modify a data block D of unique ID i to the storage, denoted as a 3-tuple $(write, i, D)$.

To accomplish a data request, the user may need to access the remote storage multiple times. Each access to the remote storage, which is observable by the server, can be one of the following types:

- retrieve (read) a data block D from a location l at the remote storage, denoted as a 3-tuple $(read, l, D)$; or

- upload (write) a data block D to a location l at the remote storage, denoted as a 3-tuple $(write, l, D)$.

3.2 Threat Model

We assume the user is trusted but the remote server is not. Particularly, the server is assumed to be honest but curious; that is, it behaves correctly in storing data and serving users' data accesses, but it may attempt to figure out the user's access pattern. The network connection between the user and the server is assumed to be secure; in practice, this can be achieved using well-known techniques such as SSL [4].

We inherit the standard security definition of ORAMs [6, 18, 19] to define the security of our proposed ORAM. Intuitively, an ORAM system is considered secure if the server learns nothing about the user's data access pattern. More precisely, it is defined as follows:

Definition Let $\vec{x} = \langle (op_1, i_1, D_1), (op_2, i_2, D_2), \cdots \rangle$ denote a private sequence of the user's intended data requests, where each op is either a $read$ or $write$ operation. Let $A(\vec{x}) = \langle (op'_1, l_1, D'_1), (op'_2, l_2, D'_2), \cdots \rangle$ denote the sequence of the user's accesses to the remote storage (observed by the server), in order to accomplish the user's intended data requests. An ORAM system is said to be secure if (i) for any two equal-length private sequences $\vec{x}$ and $\vec{y}$ of the intended data requests, their corresponding observable access sequences $A(\vec{x})$ and $A(\vec{y})$ are computationally indistinguishable; and (ii) the probability that the ORAM system fails to operate is negligibly small, i.e., $O(N^{-\log N})$.

4. SCHEME

4.1 Overview

The design of S-ORAM is motivated by the observation that a large-scale storage system usually stores data in blocks and such a block typically has a large size. To the best of our knowledge, most existing ORAM constructions treat data blocks as atomic units for query and shuffling, and do not factor block size into their designs. The recently proposed index-based ORAM constructions [5, 16–19] have used large-size blocks to store indices to improve index search efficiency; still, more opportunities wait to be explored to fully utilize this feature.

S-ORAM is designed to make better use of the large block size to improve the efficiency in data shuffling and query, which are two critical operations in an ORAM system. Specifically, we propose the following two *segment-based* techniques:

- *Piece-wise Shuffling.* In S-ORAM, each data block is segmented into smaller *pieces*, and in a shuffling process, data is shuffled in the unit of pieces rather than blocks. As we know, data shuffling has to be performed at the user-side storage in order to achieve obliviousness. With the same size of user-side storage, shuffling data in pieces rather than blocks enables data perturbation across a larger range of blocks. This way, the shuffling efficiency can be improved, and the improvement gets more significant as the block size increases.

- *Segment-based Query.* In order to improve query efficiency, S-ORAM organizes the data storage at the server side as a hierarchy of single-segment and multi-segment layers. In each segment, an encrypted index block (with the same size as a data block) is introduced to maintain the mapping between data block IDs and their locations within the segment. This way, when a user needs to access a block in a segment, he/she only needs to access two blocks - the index block and the intended block. By adopting this technique together with supplementary algorithms for distributing blocks to segments, S-ORAM can accomplish efficient query with only $O(\log N)$ communication overhead and a constant user-side storage, while existing ORAM constructions have to use a larger user-side storage to achieve the same level of communication efficiency in query.

The following sections elaborate the details of the proposed S-ORAM construction, emphasizing on the above two techniques.

4.2 Storage Organization and Initialization

4.2.1 Data Block Format

Similar to existing ORAMs, S-ORAM stores data in blocks, and a data block is the basic unit for read/write operations by the user. A plain-text data block can be split into *pieces* and each piece is $z = \log N$ bits long, where N is the total number of data blocks. The first piece contains the ID of the data block, say i, which is also denoted as $d_{i,1}$. The remaining pieces store the content of the data block, denoted as $d_{i,2}, d_{i,3}, \cdots, d_{i,P-1}$. Before being exported to the remote storage server, the plain-text data block is encrypted piece by piece with a secret key k, as shown in Figure 1:

$$\begin{aligned} c_{i,0} &= E_k(r_i), \text{ where } r_i \text{ is a random number;} \\ c_{i,1} &= E_k(r_i \oplus d_{i,1}); \\ c_{i,2} &= E_k(c_{i,1} \oplus d_{i,2}); \\ &\cdots, \\ c_{i,P-1} &= E_k(c_{i,P-2} \oplus d_{i,P-1}). \end{aligned} \quad (1)$$

Thus, the encrypted data block (denoted as D_i and hereafter called data block for brevity) has the following format:

$$D_i = (c_{i,0}, c_{i,1}, c_{i,2}, \cdots, c_{i,P-1}). \quad (2)$$

It contains P pieces and has $Z = z \cdot P$ bits.

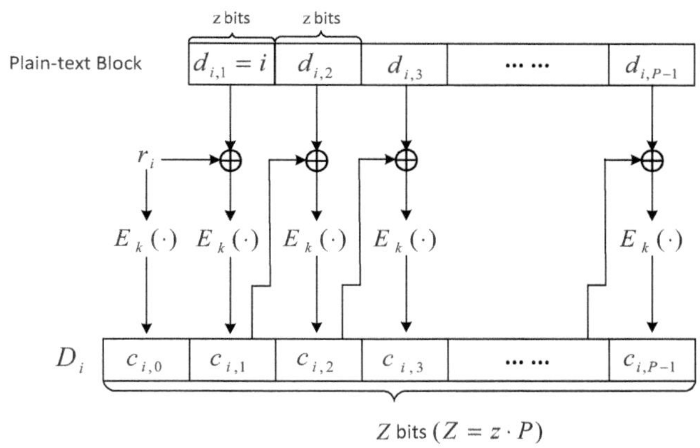

Figure 1: Format of a data block in S-ORAM.

4.2.2 Server-side Storage

S-ORAM stores data at the remote server in a pyramid-like structure as shown in Figure 2. The top layer, called *layer 1*, is an array containing at most four data blocks. The rest of the layers are divided into two groups as follows.

T1 (Tier 1) Layers: Single-Segment Layers. T1-layers refer to those between (inclusive) layer 2 and layer $L_1 = \lfloor 2 \log \log N \rfloor$. As illustrated in Figure 3, each T1-layer consists of a single segment, which includes an encrypted index block I_l and 2^{l+1} data blocks. Among the data blocks, at most half of them are real data blocks as formatted in Figure 1, while the rest are dummy blocks each

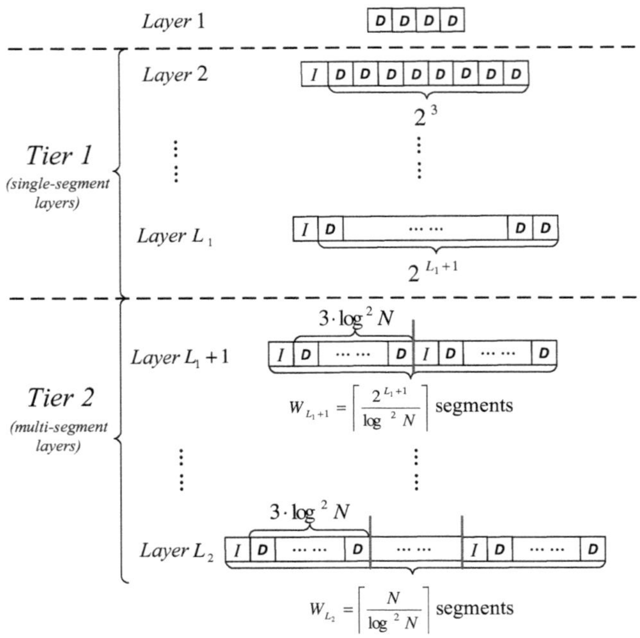

Figure 2: Organization of the server-side storage.

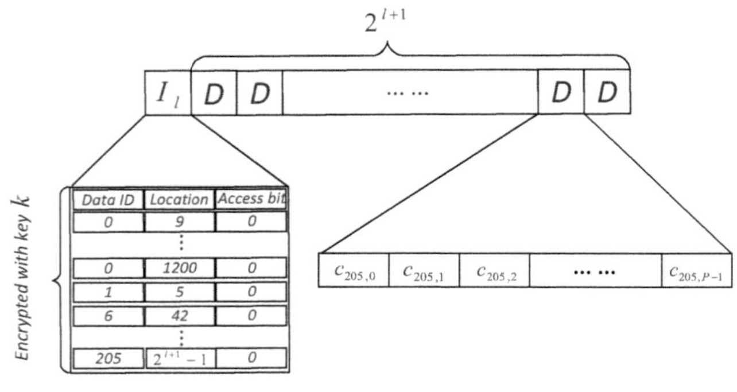

Figure 3: Structure of a T1-layer.

with ID 0 and randomly-stuffed content. The index block has 2^{l+1} entries; each entry corresponds to a data block in the segment which consists of three fields: *ID of the data block*, *location of the data block in the segment*, and *access bit* indicating whether the block has been accessed since it was placed to the location.

T2 (Tier 2) Layers: Multi-Segment Layers. T2-layers refer to those between (inclusive) layer $L_1 + 1$ and layer L_2, where $L_2 = \log N$. Each T2-layer consists of $W_l = \lceil \frac{2^l}{\log^2 N} \rceil$ segments, and each T2-layer segment has the same format as a T1-layer segment except that a T2-layer segment contains $3 \log^2 N$ data blocks.

Note that, in the above storage structure, a segment (regardless whether at a T1-layer or T2-layer) contains at most $3 \log^2 N$ data blocks. Therefore, the index block of a segment has at most $3 \log^2 N$ entries. As each entry contains three fields: *ID of the data block* (needing $\log N$ bits), *location of the data block in the segment* (needing $\log(3 \log^2 N)$ bits), and *access bit*, an index block needs at most $3 \log^2 N[\log N + \log(3 \log^2 N) + 1]$ bits. In practice, with $N \leq 2^{36}$ which is considered large enough to accommodate most practical applications, the size of an index block is less than 32 KB, which can fit into a typical data block assumed in the existing studies of practical ORAM schemes [18].

4.2.3 User-side Storage

The user organizes its local storage into two parts: *cache (temporary storage)* and *permanent storage*. Cache is used to buffer and process (including encrypt and decrypt) data blocks downloaded from the server. We assume that the size of the cache is αZ bits where α is a constant. In the S-ORAM design presented in this section, we set $\alpha = 2$. This design can be conveniently adapted to other configurations of cache size, as will be discussed in Section 5.3.

Permanent storage stores the user's secret information, including (i) a query counter keeping track of the number of queries that have been issued, (ii) a secret key k, and (iii) a one-way hash function $H_l(\cdot)$ for each T2-layer l, which maps a data block to one of the segments belonging to the layer. Note that, the size of permanent storage is much smaller than that of the cache, since only several hundreds of bits are needed to store the query counter, secret key, and hash functions.

4.2.4 Storage Initialization

The user initializes the S-ORAM system as follows:

- It randomly selects a secret key k and a one-way hash function $H_{L_2}(\cdot)$ of layer L_2, i.e., the bottom layer.
- N plain-text data blocks are encrypted into blocks D_i where $i = 1, \cdots, N$ with the secret key k in the format illustrated by Figure 1. In addition, $2N$ dummy blocks are randomly generated and encrypted also with key k.
- N real data blocks and $2N$ dummy blocks are uploaded to layer L_2 of the server storage in a delicate manner to ensure that (i) each real data block D_i of unique ID i is distributed to segment $H_{L_2}(i)$ at layer L_2, (ii) each segment is assigned with exactly $3 \log^2 N$ data blocks, and (iii) data blocks distributed to the same segment are randomly placed within the segment. Note that, a process like *data shuffling* elaborated in Section 4.4.4 can be adopted to distribute and place the data blocks to satisfy the above properties.

Besides, the user upload a dummy block D to the server and let the server know it is a dummy block.

4.3 Data Query

As formally described in Algorithm 1, the process for querying a data block D_t of ID t consists of the following four phases.

In Phase I, the user retrieves and decrypts all data blocks stored at layer 1, attempting to find D_t in the layer.

In Phase II, each non-empty T1-layer l is accessed sequentially. Specifically, the index block I_l of the layer is first retrieved and decrypted, and then one of the following two operations is performed:

- If D_t has not been found at any layer prior to layer l and I_l indicates that D_t is at layer l, record the location where D_t resides, set the access bit of the location to 1, and re-encrypt and upload I_l to save cache space. Then, retrieve D_t. Meanwhile, the server makes a copy of user uploaded dummy block D to the location where D_t was retrieved.
- Otherwise, the location of a dummy block $D_{t'}$ whose access bit in I_l is 0 (i.e., it has not been accessed since last time it was distributed to its current location) is randomly picked and recorded. After the block's access bit is set to 1 in I_l, I_l is re-encrypted and uploaded. Then, $D_{t'}$ is retrieved and discarded. The server also makes a copy of dummy block D to fill in this location.

Algorithm 1 Query data block D_t of ID t.

$found \leftarrow false$
/* *Phase I: access layer 1* */
Retrieve & decrypt blocks in layer 1
if D_t is found in layer 1 **then** $found \leftarrow true$
/* *Phase II: access T1-layers* */
for each non-empty layer $l \in \{2, \cdots, L_1\}$ **do**
  Retrieve & decrypt I_l – index block of the layer
  if $(found = false \wedge t \in I_l)$ **then**
    Set the access bit of D_t to 1 in I_l
    Re-encrypt & upload I_l
    Retrieve & decrypt D_t
    $found \leftarrow true$
  else
    Randomly pick a dummy $D_{t'}$ with access bit 0
    Set the access bit of $D_{t'}$ to 1 in I_l
    Re-encrypt & upload I_l
    Retrieve & discard $D_{t'}$
  end if
end for
/* *Phase III: access T2-layers* */
for each non-empty layer $l \in \{L_1 + 1, \cdots, L_2\}$ **do**
  if $(found = false)$ **then**
    $s \leftarrow H_l(t)$
  else
    s is randomly picked from $\{0, \cdots, W_l - 1\}$
  end if
  Retrieve & decrypt I_l^s – index block of segment s
  if $(found = false \wedge t \in I_l^s)$ **then**
    Set the access bit of D_t to 1 in I_l^s
    Re-encrypt & upload I_l^s
    Retrieve & decrypt D_t
    $found \leftarrow true$
  else
    Randomly find a dummy $D_{t'}$ with access bit 0
    Set the access bit of $D_{t'}$ to 1 in I_l^s
    Re-encrypt & upload I_l^s
    Retrieve & discard $D_{t'}$
  end if
end for
/* *Phase IV: wrap up* */
if (D_t is found in layer 1) **then**
  Encrypt an extra dummy D in local storage
else
  Re-encrypt D_t in local storage
end if
Upload all blocks in local storage back to layer 1

In Phase III, each non-empty T2-layer l is accessed sequentially as follows.

- If D_t has not been found at any layer prior to layer l, segment $s = H_l(t)$ of layer l is picked to access. The index block I_l^s of the segment is first retrieved and decrypted to check whether D_t is at this segment. If so, the access bit of D_t is set to 1 in I_l^s before I_l^s is encrypted and uploaded; then, D_t is retrieved, server fill up D_t's original location with a copy of dummy block D. Else, the user randomly selects a dummy block $D_{t'}$ in this segment whose access bit in I_l^s is 0; after the access bit of $D_{t'}$ is set to 1, I_l^s is re-encrypted and uploaded; then, $D_{t'}$ is retrieved and discarded, while a copy of dummy block D is filled in $D_{t'}$'s original location.
- If D_t has already been found at a layer prior to layer l, a segment is randomly selected from layer l and the user randomly selects a dummy block $D_{t'}$ in this segment whose access bit in I_l^s is 0. After the access bit of $D_{t'}$ is set to 1, I_l^s is re-encrypted and uploaded. Then, $D_{t'}$ is retrieved, discarded, and a copy of dummy block D is filled in $D_{t'}$'s original location.

Finally in Phase IV, the user wraps up the query process to ensure that D_t is at layer 1, i.e., the top layer. To achieve this, the user first checks whether D_t has been found at layer 1. If so, add a dummy block D to local storage, re-encrypt all blocks in local storage (including D_t and all blocks fetched from layer 1), and upload them back to layer 1; otherwise, the user directly re-encrypts all blocks in local storage and uploads them back to layer 1.

4.4 Data Shuffling

A critical step in S-ORAM is *data shuffling* which is used to perturb data block locations. It may occur at all layers of the storage hierarchy. Specifically, data shuffling at layer l ($l = 2, \cdots, L_2 - 1$) is triggered when the total number of queries that have been processed is an odd multiple of 2^l (i.e., a multiple of 2^l but not a multiple of 2^{l+1}). At this moment, layer l is empty because: (i) it was empty immediately after data shuffling for some layer l', where $l' > l$, has completed; (ii) since then, only 2^l queries have been processed, and during this course no data block has been added to this layer. During data shuffling at layer l, all data blocks in layers $\{1, \cdots, l-1\}$ are re-distributed randomly to layer l, and dummy blocks may be introduced to make layer l full. Data shuffling at layer L_2, i.e., the bottom layer, however, is triggered when the total number of processed queries is any multiple of 2^{L_2}; it re-distributes all real data blocks and selected dummy blocks in the entire hierarchy to fully occupy the bottom layer.

4.4.1 *Preliminary: A Segment-Shuffling Algorithm*

Compared to existing ORAM schemes, S-ORAM utilizes the user cache space more efficiently to speed up data shuffling. Specifically, the user cache is divided into four parts:

- π, which is a buffer to store a *permutation* of up to $2m^2$ inputs and thus needs $2m^2 \log(2m^2)$ bits, where m is a system parameter.
- B_0, B_1, and B_2, which are three buffers and each may temporarily store up to $2m^2$ data pieces.

Recall that the size of a data piece is z bits and the size of user cache is αZ. Therefore, the following relation shall hold between m, z, α, and Z:

$$2m^2 \cdot [\log(2m^2) + 3z] \leq \alpha Z. \quad (3)$$

Data shuffling in S-ORAM is based on a *segment-shuffling algorithm* (as shown in Algorithm 2). It is able to shuffle n ($\leq 3\log^2 N$) data blocks with a communication cost of $O(n)$ data blocks, by setting the system parameter m to $\sqrt{1.5}\log N$, under the following practical assumptions: (1) $N \leq 2^{36}$ which is considered large enough to accommodate most practical applications [18]; (2) the size of Z is between 32 KB and 256 KB which is typically assumed in practical ORAM schemes [18]; and (3) $\alpha = 2$ meaning that a small local cache of two data blocks is assumed. It is easy to verify that, under these assumptions, Equation (3) holds. Moreover, as $n \leq 3\log^2 N = 2m^2$, π is large enough to store a permutation of the IDs of n data blocks, and B_0, B_1, and B_2 are large enough to store n data pieces, which are required in the algorithm.

The segment-shuffling algorithm has two phases. Phase I processes the first two data pieces of all n blocks as follows. After the first two pieces of all n blocks are retrieved, IDs of the blocks are obtained and permuted according to a newly picked permutation function, and then re-encrypted using the key and newly-picked random numbers. After that, the new random numbers are uploaded after being encrypted, which is followed by the uploading of the shuffled and re-encrypted block IDs.

In Phase II, the remaining pieces of all n blocks are retrieved, shuffled according to the new permutation function (newly picked in Phase I), re-encrypted, and then uploaded back to the server. This phase runs iteratively and the $(v+1)$-st pieces are retrieved and processed at the v-th ($v = 1, \cdots, P-2$) iteration. Particularly, when the $(v+1)$-st pieces are retrieved, two encrypted versions of the v-th pieces are present in the user cache. Using the key and the older version of the v-th pieces, the plain-text embedded in the $(v+1)$-st pieces are obtained; then, the pieces are permuted, and re-encrypted using the same key and the newer version of the v-th pieces, before being uploaded back to the server. At the end of the iteration, two encrypted versions of the $(v+1)$-st pieces are left in the user cache, which will be used in the processing of the $(v+2)$-nd pieces in the next iteration.

4.4.2 *Shuffling a T1-layer* l $(2 \leq l \leq L_1)$

When a T1-layer l is to be shuffled, all the blocks belonging to the layers above shall be shuffled and distributed to layer l, which has $4 + 2^{2+1} + \cdots + 2^l = 2^{l+1} - 4$ blocks in total. The server first makes 4 copies of dummy block D such that the total number of blocks to be shuffled is 2^{l+1}. Then, the segment-shuffling algorithm is invoked to shuffle these blocks to layer l.

Algorithm 2 Segment-Shuffling of Blocks $(D_{i_1}, \cdots, D_{i_n})$.

/* *Phase I: shuffling first two pieces of all blocks* */
Retrieve $(c_{i_1,0}, \cdots, c_{i_n,0})$ to B_0
Decrypt B_0 to $(r_{i_1,0}, \cdots, r_{i_n,0})$ using k
Retrieve $(c_{i_1,1}, \cdots, c_{i_n,1})$ to B_1
Decrypt B_1 to $(i_1, \cdots, i_n)$ using k and B_0
Store $(i_1, \cdots, i_n)$ in B_2
Pick & store a random permutation in π
Permute B_2 to $(i'_1, \cdots, i'_n)$ according to π
Generate, re-encrypt & upload entries of a new index block based on B_2 and π
for each i'_j in B_2 **do**
    Randomly picks $r'_{i'_j}$
    Encrypt $r'_{i'_j}$ to $c'_{i'_j,0}$ using k, and upload it
    Encrypt i'_j to $c'_{i'_j,1}$ using k and $c'_{i'_j,0}$
end for
Upload B_2 to designated locations
/* *Phase II: shuffling remaining pieces of all blocks* */
for each $v \in \{2, \cdots, P-1\}$ **do**
    Retrieve $(c_{i_1,v}, \cdots, c_{i_n,v})$ to B_0
    for each $j \in \{1, \cdots, n\}$ **do**
        Decrypt $c_{i_j,v}$ to $d_{i_j,v}$ using k and $c_{i_j,v-1}$ in B_1
        Replace $c_{i_j,v-1}$ in B_1 by $c_{i_j,v}$ from B_0
        Replace $c_{i_j,v}$ by $d_{i_j,v}$ in B_0
    end for
    Permute B_0 to $(d_{i'_1,v}, \cdots, d_{i'_n,v})$ according to π
    Encrypt $(d_{i'_1,v}, \cdots, d_{i'_n,v})$ in B_0 using k and B_2
    Replace B_2 by B_0
    Upload B_2 to designated locations
end for

4.4.3 *Shuffling a T2-layer* l $(L_1 < l < L_2)$

Similar to a T1-layer, when a T2-layer l (excluding the bottom layer L_2) is to be shuffled, all the blocks belonging to the layers above shall be shuffled and distributed to layer l. The total number of these blocks is $w = 4 + 2^{2+1} + \cdots + 2^{L_1+1} + 3 \cdot 2^{L_1+1} + \cdots + 3 \cdot 2^{l-1}$ which is less than $3 \cdot 2^l$. Note that, among these blocks, the number of real data blocks is at most 2^l as data shuffling is triggered every 2^l queries.

Before shuffling, the user updates the hash function $H_l(\cdot)$ used for layer l. Then, it uploads a dummy block to the server, and requests the server to make $4 \cdot 2^l - w$ copies of the dummy block to be temporarily stored at layer l. This way, the total number of data blocks to be shuffled becomes $4 \cdot 2^l$, among which there are at most 2^l real data blocks.

Data shuffling at layer l consists of the following three rounds of scanning and two rounds of oblivious sorting.

Round I: Scanning. Blocks are retrieved, labeled, re-encrypted, and then uploaded. Labeling obeys the following rules: (i) Each block is labeled with a tuple of two tags; (ii) Each real data block of ID i has $H_l(i)$ as its first-tag and its second-tag is 0; (iii) Dummy blocks are labeled in such a way that exactly $3 \log^2 N$ dummy blocks have j as their first-tag for each $j \in \{1, \cdots, \lceil \frac{2^l}{\log^2 N} \rceil\}$ while all other dummy blocks have ∞ as their first-tag. All dummy blocks have ∞ as the second-tag.

Round II: Oblivious Sorting. All the labeled blocks are sorted obliviously (using the *oblivious data sorting* scheme presented in Section 4.4.5 and the Appendix) in the non-descending order based on the tag-tuple. Particularly, a block with a smaller first-tag should precede ones with larger first-tags; blocks with the same first-tag are sorted in the non-descending order based on the second-tag. This way, real data blocks are sorted to precede dummy blocks.

Round III: Scanning. The sorted sequence of blocks is scanned and divided into segments each containing $3 \log^2 N$ blocks. A counter is used to facilitate the process. Specifically, the following rule is applied when a block is scanned:

- If the block is the very first one or it has a different first-tag from its immediate predecessor, it becomes the first one of a new segment, and the counter is reset to 1.
- Otherwise: If the counter is less than $3 \log^2 N$, the counter is incremented by 1. If the counter reaches $3 \log^2 N$, the block is considered redundant and hence its first-tag is relabeled as ∞, which means this block is a redundant dummy blocks.

Round IV: Oblivious Sorting. This round sorts all the redundant blocks (i.e., those with ∞ as the first-tag) to the end of the sequence. Similar to Round II, this is achieved by obliviously sorting the blocks in the non-decreasing order based on the tag-tuple. Then, the redundant blocks are removed.

Round V: Scanning. This round is to rebuild an index block for each segment. For each segment formed in the previous round, the segment-shuffling algorithm is applied to distribute the $3 \log^2 N$ data blocks back to the server.

4.4.4 *Shuffling the Bottom Layer* L_2

Every time when the number of queries is a multiple of $2^{L_2} = N$, layer L_2 needs to be shuffled, which means the entire storage shall be shuffled and all blocks from every layer shall participate in data shuffling. Hence, the total number of blocks to be shuffled is $w' = 4 + 2^{2+1} + \cdots + 2^{L_1+1} + 3 \cdot 2^{L_1+1} + \cdots + 3 \cdot 2^{L_2-1} + 3 \cdot 2^{L_2} < 6N$.

Similar to the shuffling of other T2-layers, there are also three rounds of scanning and two rounds of oblivious sorting to accomplish layer L_2 shuffling. To be more specific, Round I scanning and Round II oblivious sorting are performed on $w' < 6N$ blocks instead of $4 \cdot 2^l$ blocks in T2-layer shuffling. After Round II oblivious sorting, only the first $4N$ blocks participate in Rounds III, IV, and V; therefore, they are identical to the ones in T2-layer shuffling.

4.4.5 *Oblivious Data Sorting*

Existing oblivious sorting techniques for ORAMs with constant local storage either incurs high asymptotical overhead (for example, Batcher's sorting network [3] incurs $O(n \log^2 n)$ communication overhead) or large hidden constant behind the big-O notations (e.g., AKS sorting network [1] incurs $c \cdot n \log n$ communication overhead with $c \geq 10^3$ and randomized shellsort [7] incurs $> 24 \cdot n \log n$ overhead), which significantly impede their practical efficiency. Hence, a more practically efficient sorting method is needed.

In S-ORAM, we develop an m-way oblivious sorting scheme based on the m-way sorting algorithm in [14]. It sorts data in pieces rather than blocks, which exploits the user cache space more efficiently and thus achieves a better performance than the aforementioned algorithms, particularly when the block size is relatively large (which is common in practice [18]). Modifications have also been made to the original m-way sorting algorithm to ensure the obliviousness of data sorting. Details of the proposed m-way oblivious sorting scheme are omitted due to space limitation. Please refer to the Appendix for a complete description.

5. ANALYSIS

5.1 Security Analysis

To prove the security of S-ORAM, we describe three lemmas before presenting the main theorem.

LEMMA 1. *When shuffling a T2-layer l, the probability that more than $1.5 \log^2 N$ real data blocks are distributed to any given segment is $O(N^{-\log N})$.*

PROOF. When shuffling a T2-layer l as in Section 4.4.3, up to 2^l real data blocks are mapped (by a hash function) to $\lceil \frac{2^l}{\log^2 N} \rceil$ segments uniformly at random. In the following proof, we first assume the number of real data blocks is 2^l and compute the probability that there exists a segment with at least $1.5 \log^2 N$ real blocks.

Let us consider a particular segment, and define $X_1, \cdots, X_{2^l}$ as random variables such that

$$X_i = \begin{cases} 1 & \text{the } i^{\text{th}} \text{real block mapped to the segment,} \\ 0 & \text{otherwise.} \end{cases} \tag{4}$$

Note that, $X_1, \cdots, X_{2^l}$ are independent of each other, and hence for each X_i, $\textbf{Pr}[X_i = 1] = \frac{1}{2^l/\log^2 N} = \frac{\log^2 N}{2^l}$. Let $X = \sum_{i=1}^{2^l} X_i$. The expectation of X is

$$E[X] = E\left[\sum_{i=1}^{2^l} X_i\right] = \sum_{i=1}^{2^l} E[X_i] = 2^l \cdot \frac{\log^2 N}{2^l} = \log^2 N. \tag{5}$$

According to the multiplicative form of Chernoff bound, for any $j \geq E[X] = \log^2 N$, it holds that

$$\textbf{Pr}[\text{at least } j \text{ real data blocks in this particular segment}]$$
$$= \textbf{Pr}[X \geq j] < \left(\frac{e^{\delta-1}}{\delta^{\delta}}\right)^{\log^2 N}, \tag{6}$$

where $\delta = \frac{j}{\log^2 N}$. By applying the union bound, we can obtain

$$\textbf{Pr}[\ \exists \text{ a segment with at least } j \text{ real data blocks}]$$
$$< \frac{2^l}{\log^2 N} \cdot \left(\frac{e^{\delta-1}}{\delta^{\delta}}\right)^{\log^2 N}. \tag{7}$$

Further considering that $2^l \leq N$, it follows that

$$\textbf{Pr}[\ \exists \text{ a segment with at least } 1.5 \log^2 N \text{ real data blocks}]$$
$$< \frac{N}{\log^2 N} \cdot \left(\frac{e^{0.5}}{1.5^{1.5}}\right)^{\log^2 N} = O(N^{-\log N}). \tag{8}$$

When the number of real blocks is less than 2^l, obviously, the above probability is also $O(N^{-\log N})$. Therefore, the lemma is proved. □

LEMMA 2. *(Failure probability of S-ORAM). The probability that the S-ORAM construction fails is $O(N^{-\log N})$. Particularly, a data query or shuffling process will never fail on any T1-layer; a data query or shuffling process on a T2-layer may fail with probability $O(N^{-\log N})$.*

PROOF. The S-ORAM construction fails if a query or shuffling process fails.

A data query process fails only if: (Q1) the process fails to find the target data block; or (Q2) the process fails to find a non-accessed dummy block on a layer when it needs to retrieve one according to the query algorithm. As the storage server is assumed to be honest, case (Q1) will not occur. Case (Q2) will not occur when the query process is accessing a T1-layer, due to the following reasons: Each layer l contains 2^{l+1} blocks, among which the number of dummy blocks is at least 2^l; since the data blocks in the layer are shuffled once every 2^l queries, there must exist at least one non-accessed dummy block for each of the 2^l queries.

A data shuffling process for layer l fails only if: (S1) layer overflow occurs, i.e., the process tries to store more data blocks to the layer than its capacity; or (S2) segment overflow occurs when layer l is a T2-layer, i.e., the process tries to store more than $3 \log^2 N$ real data blocks to a segment. As discussed in Sections 4.4.2, case (S1) will not occur when shuffling a T1-layer l because the total number of blocks to be shuffled is 2^{l+1}, which is the capacity of the layer. According to Section 4.4.3, case (S1) will not occur when shuffling a T2-layer l, because Round IV of the shuffling algorithm marks and removes redundant blocks to make the total number of blocks less than the capacity of the layer.

Hence, we only need to study the probability for cases (Q2) and (S2) to occur on a T2-layer.

Case (Q2) occurring on a T2-layer l means that a query process fails to find a non-accessed dummy block on a segment of the layer. This can only happen in one of the following two scenarios: (i) more than $1.5 \log^2 N$ real data blocks are distributed to this segment, or (ii) more than $1.5 \log^2 N$ dummy data blocks are accessed from this segment since last time the blocks were shuffled. According to Lemma 1, scenario (i) occurs with probability $O(N^{-\log N})$. As the selections of dummy blocks during the query processes are also randomly distributed among all segments of the layer, which is the same as the distribution of real data blocks to the segments during the shuffling process, the probability for scenario (ii) to occur is also $O(N^{-\log N})$. Hence, the probability for case (Q2) to occur is $O(N^{-\log N})$.

When case (S2) occurs on a T2-layer, there must be at least one segment of the layer distributed with more than $3 \log^2 N$ blocks. The probability that this case occurs is smaller than the probability that at least one segment of the layer is distributed with at least

$1.5 \log^2 N$ blocks, which is $O(N^{-\log N})$. Hence, the probability for case (S2) to occur is also $O(N^{-\log N})$.

To summarize, the probability that the S-ORAM construction fails is $O(N^{-\log N})$. □

LEMMA 3. *(Random and non-repeated location access in S-ORAM). In S-ORAM, a query process accesses locations from each non-empty layer l ($l > 1$) in a random and non-repeated manner. Here, the non-repeatedness means that, a data block is accessed for at most once between two consecutive shuffling processes that involve the block.*

PROOF. When layer l is a T1-layer, there are two cases. *Case 1.1.* If the query target data block D_t has not been found at any layer prior to layer l, and layer l contains D_t, D_t is accessed. Due to the randomness of the hash function $H_l(\cdot)$ used to distribute data blocks to locations, the location of D_t is randomly distributed among all the locations of layer l. Hence, the access is random. Also, D_t must not have been accessed since last time it was involved in data shuffling; otherwise, the block must have been a query target of an earlier query and then moved to layer 1 already. Hence, the access is also non-repeated. *Case 1.2.* Otherwise, a non-access dummy block is randomly selected to access, which makes the access to be random and non-repeated.

When layer l is a T2-layer, there are following cases. *Case 2.1.* If the query target D_t has not been found at any layer prior to layer l, a segment $s = H_l(t)$ of layer l is picked to access. Due to the randomness of the hash function $H_l(\cdot)$, the selection of s is random. Then:

- If D_t is in segment s, the block is accessed. As the shuffling process randomly permutes blocks within the same segment, the access of D_t within segment s is random. The access is also non-repeated due to the same reasoning as in *Case 1.1*.
- If D_t is not in segment s, a non-accessed dummy block is randomly picked to access in the segment. Hence, the access is random and non-repeated.

Case 2.2. If the query target D_t has already been found above layer l, segment s is randomly selected and a non-accessed dummy block is randomly picked and accessed in the selected segment. Hence, the access is random and non-repeated. □

THEOREM 1. *S-ORAM is secure under the security definition in Section 3.2.*

PROOF. Given any two equal-length sequence $\vec{x}$ and $\vec{y}$ of data requests, their corresponding observable access sequences $A(\vec{x})$ and $A(\vec{y})$ are computationally indistinguishable, because of the following reasons:

- Firstly, according to the query algorithm, sequences $A(\vec{x})$ and $A(\vec{y})$ should have the same format; that is, they contain the same number of accesses, and each pair of corresponding accesses have the same format.
- Secondly, all blocks in the storage of S-ORAM are randomized encrypted and each block is re-encrypted after each access. Hence, the two sequences could not be distinguished based on the appearance of blocks.
- Thirdly, according to the query algorithm, the j-th accesses ($j = 1, \cdots, |A(\vec{x})|$) of the $A(\vec{x})$ and $A(\vec{y})$ are from the same non-empty layer of the storage; and according to Lemma 3, the locations accessed from the layer are random and non-repeated in both sequences.

Also, according to Lemma 2, the S-ORAM construction fails with probability $O(N^{-\log N})$, which is considered negligible and no larger than the failure probability of existing ORAMs [6, 8–11, 13, 15–20]. □

5.2 Overhead Analysis

We analyze the overhead of S-ORAM including bandwidth consumption (i.e., communication overhead), user-side storage overhead, and server-side storage overhead.

The server-side storage in S-ORAM is no more than $6N \cdot Z$ bits at any time. Note that a storage of at most $6N \cdot Z$ bits is needed only when shuffling layer L_2, i.e., the bottom layer; for all other layers, a storage of at most $3N \cdot Z$ bits is needed. The user-side storage is constant; specifically, it is $2 \cdot Z$ bits.

The bandwidth consumption consists of two parts: query overhead $Q(N)$ and shuffling overhead $S(N)$, which are analyzed next.

The query overhead includes the retrieval and uploading of up to four data blocks for layer 1 and one data block (i.e., the index block) for each non-empty layer. Hence, the maximum communication cost $Q(N)$ is the retrieval and uploading of $1.5 \log N + 2$ blocks per query.

When shuffling a T1-layer l of 2^{l+1} data blocks, each data block is processed once in the user cache. Hence, the communication cost is the retrieval and uploading of 2^{l+1} blocks.

When shuffling a T2-layer l of $n = 4 \cdot 2^l$ data blocks or the bottom layer L_2 of $n < 6N$ data blocks, the shuffling process includes three rounds of scanning and two rounds of oblivious sorting. The scanning rounds can be integrated into the oblivious sorting rounds. Specifically, Round I (scanning round) can be performed side-by-side with the segment-sorting (line 2 of Algorithm 3) of Round II (oblivious sorting round). Round III (scanning round) can be performed concurrently with the last step of merging (line 19 of Algorithm 5) in Round II. Similarly, Round V (the third scanning round) can also be performed concurrently with the last step of merging in Round IV (oblivious sorting round). This way, the shuffling cost becomes the cost for two rounds of oblivious sorting.

Next, we compute the cost of m-way obliviously sorting n data blocks. With Algorithm 3, n blocks are divided into $\frac{n}{2m^2}$ subsets of equal size. These subsets are sorted at the user cache and then recursively merged into a large sorted set by Algorithm 5. During each merging phase, every m smaller sorted subsets are merged into one larger sorted subset. Thus, there is a total of $\log_m \frac{n}{2} - 1$ merging phases needed to form the final sorted set. Let $G(m, s)$ denote the number of times that each block is retrieved and then uploaded during a merging phase, where m smaller sorted subsets are merged into one larger sorted subset and each smaller subset contains s data blocks.

We have the following recursive relation:

$$G(m, s) = G\left(m, \frac{s}{m}\right) + 2. \tag{9}$$

This is because, during the merging phase, each block should (i) perform another phase of merging in which smaller subsets each containing s/m blocks are merged into subsets of s blocks (line 10 in Algorithm 5), incurring $G(m, \frac{s}{m})$ times of retrieval and uploading for each block, and then (ii) perform steps 13-20 in Algorithm 5, incurring 2 times of retrieval and uploading of each block. Hence, each data block should be retrieved and uploaded for

$$T(n) = \sum_{i=1}^{\log_m \frac{n}{2} - 1} G(m, 2m^{i+1}) = \left(\log_m \frac{n}{2} - 1\right)^2 \tag{10}$$

times during the entire shuffling process.

As shuffling is performed periodically at layers, the amortized shuffling overhead consists of the following:

- Each T1-layer l ($2 \le l \le L_1$) is shuffled once every time when an odd multiple of 2^l queries have been made, and each of the 2^l data blocks at T1-layer l is scanned once for every shuffling. Hence, the amortized overhead is $S_l(N) = \frac{2^{l+1}}{2^{l+1}} = 1$ block scanning per query.
- Each T2-layer l ($L_1 < l < L_2$), except the bottom layer L_2, is shuffled also once every time when an odd multiple of 2^l queries have been made, and two rounds of oblivious sorting are performed on $4 \cdot 2^l$ data blocks. Hence, the amortized overhead is $S_l(N) = \frac{2 \cdot 4 \cdot 2^l \cdot T(4 \cdot 2^l)}{2^{l+1}} = 4 \cdot T(4 \cdot 2^l)$ block scannings per query.
- The bottom layer L_2 is shuffled every time when a multiple of N queries have been made, and two rounds of oblivious sorting are performed. The first oblivious sorting is performed on $w < 6N$ blocks and second one is performed on $4N$. Hence, the amortized overhead is at most $S_{L_2}(N) = \frac{6N \cdot T(6N)}{N} + \frac{4N \cdot T(4N)}{N} = 6 \cdot T(6N) + 4 \cdot T(4N)$ block scannings per query.

Therefore, amortized shuffling overhead $S(N)$ is:

$$S(N) = \sum_{l=2}^{L_1} S_l(N) + \sum_{l=L_1+1}^{L_2-1} S_l(N) + S_{L_2}(N) = O\left(\frac{\log^3 N}{\log^2 m}\right).$$

To summarize, the bandwidth consumption for S-ORAM is

$$Q(N) + S(N) = O\left(\frac{\log^3 N}{\log^2 m}\right). \quad (11)$$

5.3 Overhead Comparison

We now compare the performance of S-ORAM with that of B-ORAM and P-ORAM from both theoretical and practical aspects. The theoretical results of bandwidth, user-side storage and server-side storage overheads are denoted as T_b, T_c, and T_s, and the practical results as P_b, P_c, and P_s, respectively. The practical settings used here are as follows: the number of data blocks N ranges from 2^{20} to 2^{36} and the block size ranges from 32 KB to 256 KB, which are similar to the practical settings adopted in [18]. In the comparisons, system parameter α in S-ORAM may be set to a value other than 2. If $\alpha \neq 2$, the scheme presented in Section 4 can be modified to accommodate this by simply setting parameter m to the largest integer satisfying Equation (3).

	S-ORAM	B-ORAM
T_b	$O(\frac{\log^3 N}{\log^2(Z/\log N)} \cdot Z)$	$O(\frac{\log^2 N}{\log\log N} \cdot Z)$
T_c	$O(Z)$	$O(Z)$
T_s	$O(N \cdot Z)$	$O(N \cdot Z)$
P_b	$c \log^2 N \cdot Z (0.599 \le c \le 0.978)$	$> \frac{60 \log^2 N}{\log\log N} \cdot Z$
P_c	512 KB	512 KB
P_s	$\le 6N \cdot Z$	$\ge 8N \cdot Z$

Table 1: Performance Comparison: S-ORAM vs. B-ORAM

5.3.1 S-ORAM vs. B-ORAM

In order to compare S-ORAM with B-ORAM, the user cache size is set to 512 KB in both constructions.

	S-ORAM	P-ORAM
T_b	$O(\frac{\log^3 N}{\log^2(Z/\log N)} \cdot Z)$	$O(\frac{\log^2 N}{\log(Z/\log N)} \cdot Z) \cdot \omega(1)$
T_c	$O(Z)$	$O(\log N \cdot Z) \cdot \omega(1)$
T_s	$O(N \cdot Z)$	$O(N \cdot Z)$

Table 2: Theoretical Performances: S-ORAM vs. P-ORAM

As shown in Table 1, the bandwidth consumption of S-ORAM is 12 to 23 times less than that of B-ORAM under practical settings, while the server-side storage overhead of S-ORAM is about 75% of that of B-ORAM. The improvement in bandwidth efficiency is attributed to two factors: (i) the query overhead of S-ORAM is only $2 \log N$ blocks while the overhead of B-ORAM is $\frac{2 \log^2 N}{\log\log N}$; and (ii) the shuffling algorithm of S-ORAM is more efficient than that of B-ORAM. In addition, the failure probability S-ORAM is $O(N^{-\log N})$, which is asymptotically lower than that of B-ORAM which is $O(N^{-\log\log N})$ [13].

5.3.2 S-ORAM vs. P-ORAM

To fairly compare the performance of S-ORAM and P-ORAM, their user-side storage sizes are both set to around $\log^2 N$ blocks and their failure probabilities are set to the same level, which are both $O(N^{-\log N})$. For this purpose, the security parameter $\omega(1)$ of P-ORAM has to be set to $\frac{\log^2 N}{\log(Z/\log N)}$, and the user-side storage size of P-ORAM is set to $\frac{\log^3 N}{\log(Z/\log N)} \cdot Z$ bits; the user-side storage size of S-ORAM is expanded to $\log^2 N \cdot Z$ bits. Note that, $\frac{\log^3 N}{\log(Z/\log N)} \cdot Z \ge \log^2 N \cdot Z$ as long as $Z \le N$ (which is usually true in practice).

Table 2 shows the theoretical performances of both S-ORAM and P-ORAM and Table 3 is the practical performance comparison of these two ORAMs.

In Table 3, it can be seen that S-ORAM outperforms P-ORAM in both bandwidth efficiency and server-side storage efficiency. It requires 80% less server-side storage and consumes around 60% to 72% less bandwidth than P-ORAM.

6. CONCLUSION AND FUTURE WORK

In this paper, we propose a segmentation-based Oblivious RAM (S-ORAM). S-ORAM adopts two segment-based techniques, i.e., piece-wise shuffling and segment-based query, to improve the performance of shuffling and query by factoring block size into design. Extensive security analysis proves that S-ORAM is a highly secure solution with a negligible failure probability of $O(N^{-\log N})$. In terms of communication and storage overheads, S-ORAM outperforms the Balanced ORAM (B-ORAM) and the Path ORAM (P-ORAM), which are two state-of-the-art hash and index based ORAMs respectively, in both practical and theoretical evaluations.

In the future, we plan to study the de-amortization of S-ORAM, and completely implement the S-ORAM design.

Acknowledgments

This work is supported partly by the ONR under grant N00014-09-1-0748 and by the NSF under grant EECS-1128312.

7. REFERENCES

[1] M. Ajtai, J. Komlos, and E. Szemeredi. An $O(n \log n)$ sorting network. In *Proc. STOC*, 1983.

[2] Amazon. http://aws.amazon.com/s3/. In *Amazon S3*, 2006.

	$N = 2^{20}$		$N = 2^{36}$	
	S-ORAM	P-ORAM	S-ORAM	P-ORAM
$P_b(Z = 32\text{ KB})$	$0.394\log^2 N \cdot Z$	$1.170\log^2 N \cdot Z$	$0.456\log^2 N \cdot Z$	$1.247\log^2 N \cdot Z$
$P_b(Z = 64\text{ KB})$	$0.334\log^2 N \cdot Z$	$1.090\log^2 N \cdot Z$	$0.456\log^2 N \cdot Z$	$1.157\log^2 N \cdot Z$
$P_b(Z = 128\text{ KB})$	$0.334\log^2 N \cdot Z$	$1.021\log^2 N \cdot Z$	$0.392\log^2 N \cdot Z$	$1.079\log^2 N \cdot Z$
$P_b(Z = 256\text{ KB})$	$0.259\log^2 N \cdot Z$	$0.959\log^2 N \cdot Z$	$0.392\log^2 N \cdot Z$	$1.011\log^2 N \cdot Z$
P_c	$\log^2 N \cdot Z$	$\frac{\log^3 N}{\log(Z/\log N)} \cdot Z$	$\log^2 N \cdot Z$	$\frac{\log^3 N}{\log(Z/\log N)} \cdot Z$
P_s	$< 6N \cdot Z$	$32N \cdot Z$	$< 6N \cdot Z$	$32N \cdot Z$

Table 3: Practical Performances: S-ORAM vs. P-ORAM

[3] K. E.Batcher. Sorting networks and their applications. In *Proc. AFIPS*, 1968.

[4] A. O. Freier, P. Karlton, and P. C. Kocher. The secure sockets layer (SSL) protocol version 3.0. In *RFC 6101*, 2011.

[5] C. Gentry, K. Goldman, S. Halevi, C. Julta, M. Raykova, and D. Wichs. Optimizing ORAM and using it efficiently for secure computation. In *Proc. PETS*, 2013.

[6] O. Goldreich and R. Ostrovsky. Software protection and simulation on oblivious RAM. *Journal of the ACM*, 43(3), May 1996.

[7] M. T. Goodrich. Randomized shellsort: a simple oblivious sorting algorithm. In *Proc. SODA*, 2010.

[8] M. T. Goodrich and M. Mitzenmacher. Mapreduce parallel cuckoo hashing and oblivious RAM simulations. In *Proc. CoRR*, 2010.

[9] M. T. Goodrich and M. Mitzenmacher. Privacy-preserving access of outsourced data via oblivious RAM simulation. In *Proc. ICALP*, 2011.

[10] M. T. Goodrich, M. Mitzenmacher, O. Ohrimenko, and R. Tamassia. Oblivious RAM simulation with efficient worst-case access overhead. In *Proc. CCSW*, 2011.

[11] M. T. Goodrich, M. Mitzenmacher, O. Ohrimenko, and R. Tamassia. Privacy-preserving group data access via stateless oblivious RAM simulation. In *Proc. SODA*, 2012.

[12] M. Islam, M. Kuzu, and M. Kantarcioglu. Access pattern disclosure on searchable encryption: ramification, attack and mitigation. In *Proc. NDSS*, 2012.

[13] E. Kushilevitz, S. Lu, and R. Ostrovsky. On the (in)security of hash-based oblivious RAM and a new balancing scheme. In *Proc. SODA*, 2012.

[14] D.-L. Lee and K. E. Batcher. A multiway merge sorting network. *IEEE Transactions on Parallel and Distributed Systems*, 6(2), February 1995.

[15] B. Pinkas and T. Reinman. Oblivious RAM revisited. In *Proc. CRYPTO*, 2010.

[16] E. Shi, T.-H. H. Chan, E. Stefanov, and M. Li. Oblivious RAM with $O((\log N)^3)$ worst-case cost. In *Proc. ASIACRYPT*, 2011.

[17] E. Stefanov and E. Shi. ObliviStore: high performance oblivious cloud storage. In *Proc. S&P*, 2013.

[18] E. Stefanov, E. Shi, and D. Song. Towards practical oblivious RAM. In *Proc. NDSS*, 2011.

[19] E. Stefanov, M. van Dijk, E. Shi, C. Fletcher, L. Ren, X. Yu, and S. Devadas. Path ORAM: an extremely simple oblivious RAM protocol. In *Proc. CCS*, 2013.

[20] P. Williams and R. Sion. Building castles out of mud: practical access pattern privacy and correctness on untrusted storage. In *Proc. CCS*, 2008.

[21] P. Williams, R. Sion, and A. Tomescu. PrivateFS: a parallel oblivious file system. In *Proc. CCS*, 2012.

[22] P. Williams, R. Sion, and A. Tomescu. Single round access privacy on outsourced storage. In *Proc. CCS*, 2012.

Appendix

We present the details of the proposed m-way oblivious sorting algorithm in this Appendix.

As shown in Algorithm 3, to sort a set $\mathcal{D}$ of n blocks, the m-way oblivious sorting algorithm works recursively as follows: if $n \leq 2m^2$, a *segment-sorting algorithm* similar to the segment-shuffling algorithm is applied to sort the n blocks at the communication cost of $O(n)$ blocks; otherwise, the n blocks are split into m subsets each of $\frac{n}{m}$ blocks, the m-way oblivious sorting algorithm is applied to sort each of the subsets, and finally a *merging algorithm* is used to merge the sorted subsets into a sorted set of n blocks.

Next, we describe the segment-sorting algorithm (Algorithm 4) and the merging algorithm (Algorithm 5) The segment-sorting algorithm is based on the segment-shuffling algorithm (Algorithm 2) with the following revisions: (1) The segment-sorting algorithm sorts blocks that are labeled with tags. The format of a labeled block is slightly different from the one shown in Figure 1; particularly, the encrypted tag is inserted as an extra piece before the encrypted block ID. (2) While the segment-shuffling algorithm can randomly pick a permutation function to shuffle pieces and blocks, the segment-sorting algorithm must permute pieces and blocks according to the non-decreasing order of tags. (3) The segment-sorting algorithm does not need to re-construct index blocks.

Finally, Algorithm 5 formally presents the merging algorithm.

Algorithm 3 m-way Oblivious Sorting ($\mathcal{D}$: a set of data blocks)

if ($|\mathcal{D}| \leq 2m^2$) **then**
    Apply Algorithm 4 to sort $\mathcal{D}$
else
    Split $\mathcal{D}$ into m equal-size subsets of blocks $\mathcal{D}_0, \cdots, \mathcal{D}_{m-1}$
    for each i ($0 \leq i \leq m-1$) **do**
        Apply Algorithm 3 to sort $\mathcal{D}_i$
    end for
    Apply Algorithm 5 to merge $\mathcal{D}_0, \cdots, \mathcal{D}_{m-1}$
end if

Algorithm 4 Segment-Sorting of Blocks $(D_{i_1}, \cdots, D_{i_n})$.

1-5: the same as in Algorithm 2
6: Construct a permutation function that sorts B_2 in the non-decreasing order
7: the same as in Algorithm 2
8: blank
9-14: the same as in Algorithm 2
15: **for** each $v \in \{2, \cdots, P\}$ **do**
16-26: the same as in Algorithm 2

Algorithm 5 Merging Sorted-subsets of Blocks $(\mathcal{D}_0, \cdots, \mathcal{D}_{m-1})$

/ Regroup blocks */*
$s = |\mathcal{D}_0|$
for each i ($0 \leq i \leq m-1$) **do**
    for each j ($0 \leq j \leq m-1$) **do**
        Add $\mathcal{D}_i[j], \mathcal{D}_i[m+j] \cdots, \mathcal{D}_i[s-m+j]$ to $\mathcal{D}'_j$
    end for
end for
/ Recursively merge regrouped blocks */*
for each j ($0 \leq j \leq m-1$) **do**
    if $|\mathcal{D}'_j| \leq 2m^2$ **then**
        Apply Algorithm 4 to sort $\mathcal{D}'_j$
    else
        Apply Algorithm 5 to merge sort $\mathcal{D}'_j$
    end if
end for
/ Merge sorted blocks */*
for each i ($0 \leq i \leq \frac{s}{m} - 2$) **do**
    for each j ($0 \leq j \leq m-1$) **do**
        Add $\mathcal{D}'_j[im], \mathcal{D}'_j[im+1], \cdots, \mathcal{D}'_j[im+2m-1]$ to $\mathcal{D}''_i$
    end for
end for
for each i ($0 \leq i \leq \frac{s}{m} - 1$) **do**
    Apply Algorithm 4 to sort $\mathcal{D}''_i$
end for

Differential Privacy with δ-Neighbourhood for Spatial and Dynamic Datasets*

Chengfang Fang
Huawei International
fang.chengfang@huawei.com

Ee-Chien Chang
School of Computing
National University of Singapore
changec@comp.nus.edu.sg

ABSTRACT

Differential privacy provides a strong guarantee in protecting privacy of individuals who contributed to a published dataset. In this paper, we focus on spatial datasets and dynamic datasets, and attempt to exploit the intuition that farther-apart entities should have lesser influences to each other, and thus more privacy budget should be invested to protect close-by entities. To capture such intuition, we propose embedding the underlying spatial or temporal distance function into the notion of dataset neighbourhood. We called the proposed neighbourhood *δ-neighbourhood*, and discuss its implications in both spatial and dynamic datasets. For dynamic datasets, while there are known negative results on the standard differential privacy, it is possible to continuously and indefinitely publish under δ-neighbourhood by reusing the privacy budgets. Although known mechanisms, by definition, are also differentially private under δ-neighbourhood, they are not designed to exploit the relaxed notion for better utility. For spatial datasets, we propose an approach on 2D spatial points that re-allocates more budgets to nearby entities and thus obtains significantly higher utility. In addition, we give mechanisms that achieve "sustainable privacy" on dynamic datasets under both online and offline setting.

Categories and Subject Descriptors

H.2.8 [**Database management**]: Database Administration—*Security, integrity, and protection*; K.4.1 [**Computers and Society**]: Privacy

Keywords

Differential Privacy, Bounded Neighbourhood, Spatial and Temporal Datasets

1. INTRODUCTION

Many datasets contain useful statistical information for public usage. To publish such information while preserving privacy of each contributor is challenging. The recent notion of differential privacy provides a strong form of assurance in protecting individual contributors.

A probabilistic publishing mechanism $\mathcal{A}$ is ϵ-differentially private if the published data is sufficiently noisy, so that it is difficult to distinguish the membership of an entity in a group. More specifically, the following bound holds for any $R \subseteq \text{range}(\mathcal{A})$:

$$Pr(\mathcal{A}(D_1) \in R) \leq \exp(\epsilon) \cdot Pr(\mathcal{A}(D_2) \in R), \quad (1)$$

for any two *neighbouring datasets* D_1 and D_2 that differ on at most one entity. A useful property of the formulation is that, for two datasets D_1 and D_2 that differ in more than one entity, there is still protection but with a weaker bound $\exp(c\epsilon)$, where c is the "distance" between D_1 and D_2.

In this paper, we focus on spatial datasets and dynamic datasets, and attempt to exploit the intuition that farther-apart entities should have lesser influence to each other, and thus more budget should be invested to protect close-by entities. To capture the notion of spatial and temporal distance, we adopt a alternative definition of neighbourhood. Under the original neighbourhood (let us call it the standard neighbourhood), two neighbouring datasets D_1 and D_2 differ by one entity, in the sense that $D_1 = D_2 - \{x\}$, or $D_1 = D_2 - \{y\} + \{z\}$ for some x, y, z. In other words, D_1 and D_2 are neighbours if one can be obtained from another by either adding a new entity x or replacing an entity y by z.[1] We propose an alternative form of neighbourhood: instead of having arbitrary entity x and z, they have to meet some spatial conditions. The new x must be near to some "sources" and the replacement z must near to y within a threshold δ. Such neighbourhood naturally arises from spatial datasets, for example locations of Twitter users [12] where the distance between two entities is the geographical distance between them. We call this variant *δ-neighbourhood*, where δ is the threshold.

Similar definitions of dataset neighbourhood have been considered before. For example, Kifer et al. [14] considered the *attribute differential privacy*, where two datasets are considered neighbours iff they differ at one attribute in one record. Konstantinos et al. [2] consider broadening the neighbourhood relationship with arbitrary metrics. Our no-

*This work is supported by the Singapore NRF under its IRC@SG Funding Initiative and administered by the IDMPO.

ASIA CCS'14, June 4–6, 2014, Kyoto, Japan.
Copyright 2014 ACM 978-1-4503-2800-5/14/06 ...$15.00.
http://dx.doi.org/10.1145/2590296.2590320.

[1] There are a few versions of standard neighbourhood, for example, unbounded differential privacy [11, 25], and bounded differential privacy [24, 14].

tion of δ-neighbourhood can be viewed as a variant that stresses on spatial and temporal locality.

There are a few ways to view the assurance provided by the proposed neighbourhood. In some applications, the data are subject to some constraints and thus not all possible datasets are valid. For example, Blocki et al. [1] consider social network graphs where the degree of any node is bounded, instead of all possible graphs. When such constraints are captured by δ-neighbourhood, the guarantee provided by both notions are equivalent.

Viewing from another perspective, if the domain (where the entities of the datasets are drawn from) is connected and bounded w.r.t. the underlying metric, then a mechanism that is differentially private under δ-neighbourhood is also differentially private under the standard neighbourhood. However, the guaranteed bound (as in inequality (1)) is stronger when the entities are close-by. Hence, the proposed δ-neighbourhood can be viewed as a "redistribution" of assurance, instead of a relaxation of assurance when compares to the standard neighbourhood. Illustrating examples will be discussed in Section 4 and 6.

In addition, the δ-neighbourhood can also be adopted for dynamic datasets where entities are added and removed over time. One example is the scenario considered by Dwork et al. [7], where aggregated information on users' health conditions in a region or building (say airport) is to be monitored over time. Under the standard neighbourhood, due to the fixed budget, it is impossible to publish the dataset repeatedly with high utility. However, there are scenarios where entities do not stay in the dataset for long and thus, intuitively, the effect of information published earlier would diminish over time, and hence we should be able to continuously publish with high utility. We can define a δ-neighbourhood that captures the above intuition, so as to achieve *sustainable privacy* on dynamic datasets.

Existing differential private mechanisms designed for the standard neighbourhood are, by definition, also differentially private under the δ-neighbourhood. However, these mechanisms may not fully exploit the δ-neighbourhood for better utility. For example, publishing equi-width histogram of 1D datasets induces the same amount of sensitivity under both standard and δ-neighbourhood, and thus following the well-known method of adding Laplace noise proportional to the sensitivity would not achieve higher utility. We propose an optimization approach and give a mechanism for 2D spatial points that achieve significantly higher utility. Whereas for dynamic dataset, we investigate how to allocate the privacy budget to sustain the publishing process over time, so as to minimize the expected total amount of noise in both offline and online settings. On the other hand, some mechanisms can be naturally extended to δ-neighbourhood, such as publishing sorted 1D points, and median publishing as described in Section 5.5.

The rest of the paper is organized as follow: Section 2 introduces the background on differential privacy, followed by the proposed notion of δ-neighbourhood in Section 3. The motivating examples on spatial datasets are given in section 4, and the mechanisms catered for δ-neighbourhood are given in Section 5. Section 6 and 7 are devoted to dynamic datasets. We discuss the related works in Section 8 and conclude our work in Section 9.

2. BACKGROUND

In this section, we briefly describe the notion of differential privacy.

2.1 Neighbourhood and Differential Privacy

A dataset is a multiset (i.e. a set with possibly repeating elements) of entities from the domain $\mathcal{M}$, and let us denote the collection of all datasets as $\mathbf{D}$.

Definition (**ϵ-differential privacy [4]**) A mechanism $\mathcal{A}$ satisfies ϵ-differential privacy if for all $R \subseteq \text{range}(\mathcal{A})$, and any pair of neighbours (D_1, D_2), we have:

$$Pr(\mathcal{A}(D_1) \in R) \leq \exp(\epsilon) \cdot Pr(\mathcal{A}(D_2) \in R). \quad (2)$$

In the above definition, two datasets D_1 and D_2 are neighbours if they "differ on one entity". There are a few interpretations of the above statement: some interpret it as $D_1 = D_2 \cup \{x\}$ or $D_2 = D_1 \cup \{x\}$, i.e. one dataset is a proper subset of the other with one less in size [11][25]; and in some literatures [24][14], it is interpreted as $D_1 - \{x\} = D_2 - \{y\}$ for some x, y. The former interpretation is also known as the *unbounded differential privacy*, whereas the latter as *bounded differential privacy*. In this paper, we consider both, i.e. D_1 and D_2 are neighbours iff $D_1 = D_2 \cup \{x\}$ or $D_1 - \{x\} = D_2 - \{y\}$ for some $x, y \in \mathcal{M}$, and call this the *standard* neighbourhood. Such definition of neighbourhood is also considered by Roth et al. [19].

A consequence of the bound provided by differential privacy is that, when two datasets D_1 and D_2 differ by c entities, then if a mechanism $\mathcal{A}$ is ϵ-differentially private, we have:

$$Pr(\mathcal{A}(D_1) \in R) \leq \exp(c\epsilon) \cdot Pr(\mathcal{A}(D_2) \in R), \quad (3)$$

for all possible $R \subseteq \text{range}(\mathcal{A})$. In other words, although the definition only explicitly dictates the relationship among neighbours, there are still protections on datasets that are far apart, but with a weaker bound.

2.2 Sensitivity and Laplace Mechanism

It is shown [6] that given a function $f : \mathbf{D} \to \mathbb{R}^k$ for some $k \geq 1$, the probabilistic mechanism $\mathcal{A}$ that outputs:

$$f(D) + (Lap(\triangle_f/\epsilon))^k,$$

achieves ϵ-differential privacy, where $(Lap(\triangle_f/\epsilon))^k$ is a vector of k independently and randomly chosen values from the Laplace distribution, and $\triangle_f$ is the *sensitivity* of the function f. The sensitivity of f is defined as the least upper bound on the ℓ_1 difference of all possible neighbours:

$$\triangle_f := \sup \|f(D_1) - f(D_2)\|_1,$$

where the supremum is taken over pairs of neighbours D_1 and D_2. Here, $Lap(b)$ denotes the zero mean distribution with variance $2b^2$, and a probability density function:

$$\ell(x) = \frac{1}{2b} e^{-|x|/b}.$$

3. δ-NEIGHBOURHOOD

We assume that there is a distance function $d : \mathcal{M} \times \mathcal{M} \to \mathbb{R}$ on the domain that captures the distance between a pair of entities, and there is a set of *sources* $S \subseteq \mathcal{M}$. With this distance function and sources, for a threshold δ, we say that two datasets D_1, D_2 are δ-neighbours if, and only if the following holds:

1. there exists x_1 and $x_2 \in \mathcal{M}$, such that $d(x_1, x_2) \leq \delta$, and $D_1 - \{x_1\} = D_2 - \{x_2\}$, or
2. there exists an x_3 and $s \in S$ s.t. $d(x_3, s) \leq \delta$, and $D_1 - \{x_3\} = D_2$ or $D_2 - \{x_3\} = D_1$.

In other words, either D_1 can be obtained from D_2 by replacing an entity x_2 with a nearby entity x_1, or by adding a new entity x_3 emerged near a source s. Note that if S is empty, then the size of D_1 and D_2 must be the same.

Given two datasets $D_1, D_2 \in \mathbf{D}$, we say that D_1 and D_2 are *connected* if there exists a finite sequence $E_0, E_1, E_2, \ldots, E_m$ with $E_0 = D_1$ and $E_m = D_2$ s.t. for any i, the consecutive E_i and E_{i+1} are δ-neighbours, and call the smallest such m the distance between D_1 and D_2. If any two datasets in $\mathbf{D}$ are connected, we say that $\mathbf{D}$ is connected, and call the least upper bound on the distance, if it exists, the *diameter* of $\mathbf{D}$.

3.1 Differential Privacy under δ-Neighbourhood

We say that a mechanism $\mathcal{A}$ is ϵ-differential privacy under δ-neighbourhood if for all $R \subseteq \text{range}(\mathcal{A})$ and any pair of δ-neighbours (D_1, D_2):

$$Pr(\mathcal{A}(D_1) \in R) \leq \exp(\epsilon) \cdot Pr(\mathcal{A}(D_2) \in R). \quad (4)$$

Similar to standard neighbourhood, we can define the sensitivity of a function f: $\mathbf{D} \to \mathbb{R}$ with respect to the δ-neighbourhood, which is

$$\sup \|f(D_1) - f(D_2)\|_1,$$

where the supremum is taken over all pairs (D_1, D_2) of δ-neighbours.

3.2 Properties

Since δ-neighbours are also neighbours under the standard neighbourhood, thus an ϵ-differentially private mechanism under standard neighbourhood is also ϵ-differential private mechanism under δ-neighbourhood. The converse also holds but with a weaker bound, as stated in the following lemma(proof omitted):

Lemma 1 *If a mechanism $\mathcal{A}$ is ϵ-differential private under the δ-neighbourhood and the diameter of $\mathbf{D}$ is d, then it is $(d\epsilon)$-differential private under the standard neighbourhood.*

Sequential composition: The composition of two differentially private mechanisms is also differentially private. It is easy to show that this property also holds under δ-neighbourhood: given a sequence of k mechanisms, $\mathcal{A}_1, \mathcal{A}_2, \ldots \mathcal{A}_k$, where $\mathcal{A}_i$ is ϵ_i-differentially private under δ-neighbourhood, then the mechanism

$$\mathcal{A}^*(D) = \mathcal{A}_1(D, \mathcal{A}_2(D, \ldots))$$

is $(\sum_{i=1}^{k} \epsilon_i)$-differentially private under δ-neighbourhood.

4. SPATIAL DATASETS

The δ-neighbourhood can be naturally defined on spatial points, say $\mathcal{M} = [0,1]^k$ for some $k \geq 1$. The underlying distance function $d(\cdot, \cdot)$ can be the Euclidean distance and the sources can be the boundary of $\mathcal{M}$, which implies that entities enter through the boundary, or simply none, corresponding to the bounded differential privacy. Let us investigate a few scenarios where the proposed notion is meaningful.

4.1 Example 1

Consider a situation where the dataset is constrained, in the sense that not all multisets of entities from $\mathcal{M}$ are in $\mathbf{D}$ (recall that $\mathbf{D}$ is the set of all possible datasets). Let us call the multisets that are not in $\mathbf{D}$ *invalid datasets*. If those invalid datasets are excluded by the restriction on δ-neighbourhood, then essentially the two assurances, either under standard neighbourhood or δ-neighbourhood, are equivalent. For instance, consider a D that contains the locations of a vehicle sampled at periodic intervals, say at time $1, 2, \ldots, n$, and is represented as a set of tuples where each tuple (t, x) indicates that the vehicle is at location x on time t. Suppose D is to be published by a mechanism $\mathcal{A}$ that is ϵ-differentially private under the standard neighbourhood, then for any possible output r, any D, (t, x) and (t, y), we have

$$Pr(\mathcal{A}(D + \{(t, x)\}) = r) \leq exp(\epsilon) Pr(\mathcal{A}(D + \{(t, y)\}) = r).$$

Since D essentially represents a sequence, the two tuples in the above inequality must have the same t.

We can take a step further. Due to speed limit of the vehicles (which is public knowledge), some datasets are invalid. For example, if D_1 is a valid dataset, a location y that is far from x will lead to an invalid dataset. Since the bound is not required to hold for the invalid datasets, thus, with an appropriate metric and a sufficiently large δ, the assurance provided under δ-neighbourhood is equivalent to the assurance provided under the standard neighbourhood. Similar examples are considered by Blocki et al. [1]. They consider social networks where the maximum degree of any node is likely to be bounded by a number k that is much smaller than the network size n. In such situations, an interesting question is whether the utility can be improved by exploiting the constraints. To illustrate, it is not clear how to improve the well-known histogram-based mechanisms on the constrained datasets, since the sensitivity incurred under the standard and δ-neighbourhood is the same.

4.2 Example 2

In this example, we want to publish a dataset D which contains locations of n entities drawn from the domain $\mathcal{M}$. Consider in an extreme case, where an adversary knows the locations of n-1 entities in D (let us denote this D'). The adversary wants to guess whether x is in D, in other words, whether the unknown entity is x. Under the standard neighbourhood, differential privacy guarantees that the published data does not help the adversary in guessing whether x or y is in D, where y is another location the adversary does not know, by bounding the distance of the two probabilities $P(A(D' + \{x\}) \in R)$ and $P(A(D' + \{y\}) \in R)$. Hence, from the perspective of any contributor Bob, if Bob accepts the assumption that there is at least one entity of whom the adversary does not have background information, he is comfortable in contributing his location.

Under δ-neighbourhood, the same guarantee holds when x and y are close-by. From the perspective of Bob, if he accepts the assumption that there is at least one entity y near Bob, say within δ =40km, of whom the adversary has no background knowledge, then differential privacy with δ-neighbourhood suffices for Bob to contribute.

Now let us consider another more resourceful adversary who has more accurate background information on region near Bob. With respect to this background information, the indistinguishable entities similar to Bob can be 40 to 80 km away. In this case, when D is published by an ϵ-differential private mechanism under 40 km-neighbourhood, Bob's privacy is still protected but with a weaker assurance similar to a 2ϵ-differential privacy. Thus, compared to the standard neighbourhood, δ-neighbourhood "redistributes" the assurance by placing more emphasis on close-by entities, with the value of δ determines the rate the assurance decreases over distance. Hence, we can view the δ-neighbourhood not as a relaxation of the standard neighbourhood, but as a redistribution of assurance, where δ is a parameter controlling the rate of redistribution.

5. PUBLISHING SPATIAL DATASET

Although an ϵ-differentially private mechanism under the standard neighbourhood is also ϵ-differentially private under δ-neighbourhood, it may not achieve our intention of investing more budget on nearby entities. In this section, we consider publishing histogram of 2D spatial points to be used for subsequent range queries. Essentially, we want to determine an "optimal" linearly transformed histogram similar to the work by Li et al. [15], but with a different sensitivity function derived from the δ-neighbourhood. We observe that the sensitivity function in 2D leads to an interesting combinatoric structure in the design of the linear transformation, and propose a few constructions. We also note that for 1D spatial points, a known technique under standard neighbourhood [9] can be easily modified to achieve high utility under δ-neighbourhood, as shown in Section 5.5.

5.1 Illustration

Let us demonstrate how to capitalize the notion of δ-neighbourhood with the following simple example in 1D. Consider a dataset containing (possibly with repetitions) 4 possible values: $\{\frac{1}{4}, \frac{2}{4}, \frac{3}{4}, 1\}$. Let c_i be the number of points with value $i/4$. Table 1 gives a 1-differentially private mechanism under the standard neighbourhood that publishes the counts (c_1, c_2, c_3, c_4).

Let us compare the case under 0.25-neighbourhood, and with a source of $\{0\}$, i.e. points are added/removed within distance of 0.25 from 0. The mechanism in Table 1 is also 1-differentially private under 0.25-neighbourhood.

Now let us publish the counts as shown in Table 2, where a linear transformation is applied before adding noise. Our main observation is that, the sensitivity of publishing the values (a_1, a_2, a_3, a_4) is 1 with respect to the 0.25-neighbourhood: changing a single entity by a distance of 0.25, or adding an entity within 0.25 to the source affects only one a_i for some i. Hence, a Laplace noise of $Lap(1)$ is sufficient to guarantee 1-differential privacy under 0.25-neighbourhood. However, under the standard neighbourhood, an entity changing from value $\frac{1}{4}$ to 1 will decrease each a_1, a_2, a_3 by 1, leading to a sensitivity of 3.

By publishing the a_i''s in Table 2, we can answer range queries with higher accuracy through linear combination of the a_i's. For example, when a query asks for the frequency counts in the range $[0.4, 0.6]$, reporting the value c_2' leads to an unbiased estimator with variance 8, which is the variance of $Lap(2)$. On the other hand, from Table 2, it can be estimated by $a_1' - a_2'$ giving an unbiased estimator with a smaller variance of 4, which is the variance of the sum of two independent Laplace noises, $Lap(1) + Lap(1)$. Such difference is more significant for larger query range. The comparisons are shown in Table 3: row i of the table shows the noise variances when the query range covers exactly i number of the counts c_i's.

Table 1: Publishing c_i's directly.

Actual Values	Published values
c_1	$c_1' = c_1 + Lap(2)$
c_2	$c_2' = c_2 + Lap(2)$
c_3	$c_3' = c_3 + Lap(2)$
c_4	$c_4' = c_4 + Lap(2)$

Table 2: Publishing a linearly transformed histogram.

Actual values	Published values
$a_1 = c_1 + c_2 + c_3 + c_4$	$a_1' = a_1 + Lap(1)$
$a_2 = c_2 + c_3 + c_4$	$a_2' = a_2 + Lap(1)$
$a_3 = c_3 + c_4$	$a_3' = a_3 + Lap(1)$
$a_4 = c_4$	$a_4' = a_4 + Lap(1)$

Table 3: Variance of the estimator for different range size.

Number of c_i's covered	number of queries	Derived from Table 1	Derived from Table 2
1	4	8	4
2	3	16	4
3	2	24	4
4	1	32	2

By exhaustive checking, it can be verified that, in terms of minimizing the total variance of all possible range queries, i.e. the weighted sum of the variance in the rightmost column with the weights in the second column in Table 3, the construction in Table 2 is optimal among all linear combinations of c_1, c_2, c_3 and c_4 where the coefficients are binary, i.e. either 0 or 1.

Note that the above methods estimate the query results using linear combinations of the published values. One could enforce the constraints that all c_i's are non-negative, leading to a non-linear estimator. Although this may create bias, it further lowers the variance of the estimation.

5.2 Generalization

Let us generalize the illustrating example. The method shown in Table 1 corresponds to the direct method of adding noise to the frequency counts of an equi-width histogram, whereas Table 2 corresponds to a method that applies a linear transformation before adding noise. Li et al. [15] studied such general form of publishing under the standard neighbourhood. In this section, we extend it to δ-neighbourhood. As illustrated in the example, the key difference of our method is the lower sensitivity incurred under δ-neighbourhood.

Formally, a histogram $\mathcal{H}_B(D)$ for a partition of the domain $B = \{b_1, \ldots, b_k\}$ on D gives a column vector of frequency counts $\mathbf{c} = (c_1, \ldots, c_k)^t$ where $c_i = |D \cap b_i|$. We call each set in the partition B a bin. In particular, an equi-width histogram corresponds to a partition whose bins are of the same size. Since all the bins do not overlap, the effect of replacing an entity in D affects frequency counts in at most two bins, and thus the sensitivity of $\mathcal{H}_B(\cdot)$ is 2 under the standard neighbourhood. Hence the mechanism of publishing $\mathbf{c} + Lap(2/\epsilon)^k$ is ϵ-differential private under the standard neighbourhood.

We consider queries whose answers are linear combination of counts in $\mathbf{c}$, and can be expressed as $\mathbf{qc}$ where $\mathbf{q}$ is a row vector. For example, a range query can be a summation of counts in some bins. For a sequence of m queries, let us express it as an m by k matrix $\mathbf{Q}$ and hence the answer to the queries are the coefficients in $\mathbf{Qc}$. As proposed by Li et al., to answer the query $\mathbf{Q}$, one may employ a *strategy* $\mathbf{A}$, which is represented as a k by n matrix for some n, and publish

$$\widetilde{\mathbf{c}} = \mathbf{Ac} + Lap(\triangle_{\mathbf{A}}/\epsilon)^n,$$

where $\triangle_{\mathbf{A}}$ is the sensitivity of the function that on input D, returns $\mathbf{Ac}$. From the published $\widetilde{\mathbf{c}}$, we want to estimate the query results. It can be shown [21] that the following estimate is unbiased:

$$\mathbf{A}^{+}\widetilde{\mathbf{c}},$$

where $\mathbf{A}^{+} = (\mathbf{A}^t\mathbf{A})^{-1}\mathbf{A}^t$ is the pseudo-inverse of $\mathbf{A}$, and the variance of the estimator is

$$(\triangle_{\mathbf{A}})^2 trace(\mathbf{Q}(\mathbf{A}^t\mathbf{A})^{-1}\mathbf{Q}^t). \quad (5)$$

Now, given $\mathbf{Q}$, we want to find the $\mathbf{A}$ s.t. the variance is minimized. In the illustrating example, $\mathbf{Q}$ is a 10 by 4 matrix where each row corresponds to a range queries, and

$$\mathbf{A} = \begin{bmatrix} 1 & 1 & 1 & 1 \\ 0 & 1 & 1 & 1 \\ 0 & 0 & 1 & 1 \\ 0 & 0 & 0 & 1 \end{bmatrix} \quad (6)$$

Now let us look at the problem in the context of δ-neighbourhood. The sensitivity of $\mathbf{A}$ under δ-neighbourhood leads to an interesting combinatoric structure that is not present in the standard neighbourhood. Under the standard neighbourhood, the sensitivity of $\mathbf{A}$ is

$$\max_{i,j \in \mathbb{Z}_n} \{ \ \|\mathbf{a}_i - \mathbf{a}_j\|_1 \ \}, \quad (7)$$

where each $\mathbf{a}_i$'s is a column vector in $\mathbf{A}$, that is, $\mathbf{A} = [\mathbf{a}_1, \mathbf{a}_2, \ldots, \mathbf{a}_n]$. To understand the above expression, note that $\|\mathbf{a}_i - \mathbf{a}_j\|_1$ is the sum of L_1 difference when an entity change between bin i and bin j. Since the sensitivity is the least upper bound on all possible pairs of neighbouring datasets, we have the above expression.

Under the δ-neighbourhood, the sensitivity of $\mathbf{A}$ is

$$\max_{(i,j) \in N} \{ \ \|\mathbf{a}_i - \mathbf{a}_j\|_1 \ \},$$

where N is a set induced from the requirement on δ-neighbourhood,

$$N = \{(i,j) \mid \exists\ x \in b_i, y \in b_j,\ s.t.\ d(x,y) \leq \delta\}.$$

Compare to the expression in (7), the maximum is taken over a smaller set N and thus could be smaller.

For the matrix $\mathbf{A}$ in the illustrating example, we have $N = \{(1,2),(2,3),(3,4)\}$ under 0.25-neighbourhood, and thus the sensitivity of $\mathbf{A}$ is 1; whereas the sensitivity under the standard neighbourhood is 3, as $\|\mathbf{a}_1 - \mathbf{a}_4\|_1 = 3$.

Solving the optimization problem in general is difficult for standard neighbourhood, partly due to the fact that the sensitivity $\triangle_{\mathbf{A}}$ as a function of $\mathbf{A}$, is non-differentiable. Likewise it is difficult for δ-neighbourhood. We will show in the next section how we can improve $\mathbf{A}$ for range queries by exploiting the combinatoric structure.

5.3 Proposed Algorithm

The main idea of our proposed algorithm can be illustrated with a graphical representation of the bins when the entries in $\mathbf{A}$ are binary, i.e. either 0 or 1. Let us treat each bin as a vertex in the graph. Hence there are k vertices $v_1, v_2, \ldots, v_k$. There is an edge between two vertices v_i and v_j iff $(i,j) \in N$.

For a matrix $\mathbf{A}$, since the entries are binary, each row corresponds to a subset of bins. Hence, $\mathbf{A}$ can be viewed as a collection of sets $\{\mathbf{a}_1, \mathbf{a}_2, \ldots, \mathbf{a}_n\}$ where each set in $\mathbf{A}$ is a set of bins. For an edge (v_i, v_j), we say it is being *cut* by a set $\mathbf{a}$ iff

$$(v_i \in \mathbf{a} \wedge v_j \notin \mathbf{a}) \ \vee \ (v_i \notin \mathbf{a} \wedge v_j \in \mathbf{a}).$$

For each edge e, let us call the number of sets in $\mathbf{A}$ that cut the edge e the number of cuts on e, denoted as $C(e)$. Now, the sensitivity of $\mathbf{A}$ is the maximum number of cuts over all edges, i.e. $\max_e C(e)$.

Note that given a particular $\mathbf{A}$, it may be possible to insert a set into $\mathbf{A}$ without increasing its sensitivity. That is, it may be possible to find a subset that only cuts edges that have not been cut by subsets in $\mathbf{A}$. Since sensitivity is not increased, it would not hurt to add this set into $\mathbf{A}$ which in turn publishes this extra information[2]. This observation leads to a simple greedy algorithm that improves a strategy: simply add rows to $\mathbf{A}$ until it is not possible to do so without increasing the sensitivity.

For instance, consider a 2D histogram with bins $\{b_{i,j} \mid i,j \in \mathbb{Z}_n\}$, with neighbourhood $N = \{((i,j),(i',j')) \mid |i-i'| + |j-j'| \leq 1\}$ as shown in Figure 1 where each bin is a bullet(blue), and the neighbours are connected by a dotted(red) line. Consider the set $\mathbf{A}$ that contains $\mathbf{a}_{i,j} = \{b_{2i-1,2j-1}, b_{2i-1,2j}, b_{2i,2j-1}, b_{2i,2j}\}$, for $i,j = 1,2,\ldots\frac{n}{2}$, that is, each $a_{i,j}$ is a solid(blue) square that contains four blue vertices. Note that the solid(blue) squares do not "cut" all the neighbouring edges, and therefore, if we add $\mathbf{a}'_{i,j} = \{b_{2i,2j}, b_{2i,2j+1}, b_{2i+1,2j}, b_{2i+1,2j+1}\}$ to $\mathbf{A}$, for $i,j = 1,2,\ldots\frac{n}{2}-1$, (i.e. the dash(black) squares containing 4 vertices each), the sensitivity remains the same.

On the other hand, for some $\mathbf{A}$, inserting any additional $\mathbf{a}'$ into $\mathbf{A}$ will increase the sensitivity of $\mathbf{A}$. Therefore, the key question lies on whether the noise reduced by the additional $\mathbf{a}'$s is more significant than the noise introduced by the increment of sensitivity. Such comparison is application dependent, i.e. it depends on the queries $\mathbf{Q}$.

For 2D spatial data, we consider random range queries and propose publishing a series of equi-width histograms, similar to the construction illustrated in Figure 1. We consider datasets whose elements are in the normalized domain $[0,1)^2$. Our construction is build on publishing equi-width histograms. An equi-width histogram in 2D corresponds to the partition $B = \{b_{1,1}, b_{1,2}, \ldots, b_{k,k}\}$, where each bin $b_{i,j}$ is a square region $[\frac{i-1}{k}, \frac{i}{k}) \times [\frac{j-1}{k}, \frac{j}{k})$.

[2]One may see this from expression (5), where adding a row to $\mathbf{A}$ without increasing $\triangle_{\mathbf{A}}$ will not increase the variance.

We propose publishing a series of overlapping histograms where each histogram is shifted by an offset δ from the previous histogram in the series. Specifically, let $B_0, B_1 \dots B_{m-1}$ be a sequence of partitions, where $m = \lceil \frac{1}{k\delta} \rceil$ and B_x is a partition $\{b^x_{1,1}, b^x_{1,2}, \dots, b^x_{k+1,k+1}\}$ with each $b^x_{i,j}$ is a square region $[\frac{i-2}{k} + x\delta, \frac{i-1}{k} + x\delta) \times [\frac{j-2}{k} + \delta, y + \frac{j-1}{k} + x\delta)$.

Note that the sensitivity of $\mathbf{A}$ constructed in this way is 4, instead of 2 as demonstrated in Figure 1. This is because in 2D spatial data, there are edges connected the vertices $b_{i,j}$ and $b_{i+1,j+1}$. However, we will show in the next section that, when δ is relatively small, the insertion of additional $\mathbf{a}'$ can overcome the increment of the sensitivity.

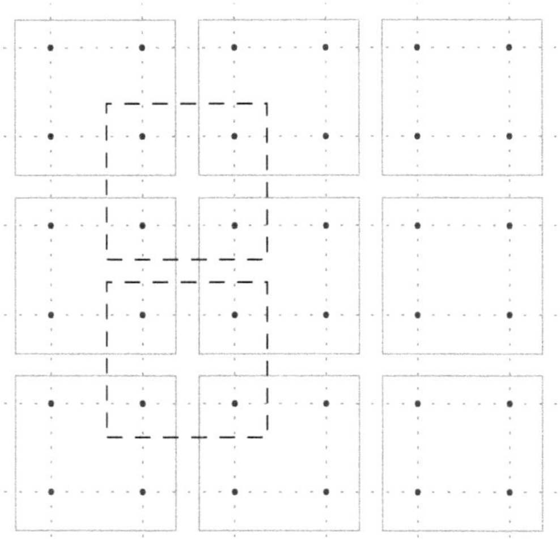

Figure 1: Demonstration of adding a' to A without increasing sensitivity.

5.4 Evaluation

5.4.1 1D range query

The earlier example described in Section 5.1 can be generalized to publish linear transformation of histograms with n bins. The transformation $\mathbf{A}$ is a lower triangular matrix of size $n \times n$ and the entries on and below diagonal are 1. Essentially, row i of $\mathbf{A}$ cumulates the counts for bin 1 to bin i. Let us call this strategy C_n. The answer to a range query that covers bin i to j can be obtained by subtracting the j-th row and $(i-1)$-th row. We are interested in how accurate C_n performs in answering 1D range queries, i.e. in answering the set of all range queries, $\mathbf{Q}$.

Li et al. [15] consider the maximum error and total error of three strategies: H_n which queries a series of equi-width histograms [11], Y_n which is a Haar wavelet transformation matrix [24] and the identity matrix I_n. Figure 2 shows H_4, Y_4, I_4 and C_4. The maximum error refers to the maximum variance among all row vectors of $\mathbf{Q}$, and total error refers to the sum of the variance. The asymptotic bounds on the errors of H_n, Y_n and I_n are as shown in Table 4. The constructions do not exploit δ-neighbourhood, and the errors of H_n, Y_n and I_n are the same under either standard neighbourhood or δ-neighbourhood.

C_n benefits from δ-neighbourhood, in the sense that the sensitivity $\triangle_{C_n}$ is lower for smaller δ. The corresponding maximum error and total error of $C_{n,\delta}$ is also shown in Table

$$\underset{H_4}{\begin{bmatrix} 1 & 0 & 0 & 0 \\ 0 & 1 & 0 & 0 \\ 0 & 0 & 1 & 0 \\ 0 & 0 & 0 & 1 \\ 1 & 1 & 0 & 0 \\ 0 & 0 & 1 & 1 \\ 1 & 1 & 1 & 1 \end{bmatrix}} \quad \underset{Y_4}{\begin{bmatrix} 0 & 0 & 1 & -1 \\ 1 & -1 & 0 & 0 \\ 1 & 1 & -1 & -1 \\ 1 & 1 & 1 & 1 \end{bmatrix}} \quad \underset{I_4}{\begin{bmatrix} 1 & 0 & 0 & 0 \\ 0 & 1 & 0 & 0 \\ 0 & 0 & 1 & 0 \\ 0 & 0 & 0 & 1 \end{bmatrix}} \quad \underset{C_4}{\begin{bmatrix} 1 & 1 & 1 & 1 \\ 0 & 1 & 1 & 1 \\ 0 & 0 & 1 & 1 \\ 0 & 0 & 0 & 1 \end{bmatrix}}$$

Figure 2: Strategy H_4, Y_4, I_4 and C_4.

4. When $\delta = n$, it performs similar to identity matrix, but when δ is small, we can reduce the errors by exploiting the δ-neighbours.

Table 4: Max and total errors.

	H_n	Y_n	I_n	$C_{n,\delta}$
max error	$\Theta(\frac{log^3 n}{\epsilon^2})$	$\Theta(\frac{log^3 n}{\epsilon^2})$	$\Theta(\frac{n}{\epsilon^2})$	$\Theta(\frac{\delta}{\epsilon^2})$
total error	$\Theta(\frac{n^2 log^3 n}{\epsilon^2})$	$\Theta(\frac{n^2 log^3 n}{\epsilon^2})$	$\Theta(\frac{n^3}{\epsilon^2})$	$\Theta(\frac{n^2 \delta}{\epsilon^2})$

5.4.2 2D range query

We consider mechanisms that answer 2D range queries with fixed range size in $[0,1)^2$. A 2D range query of size s asks for the number of points in the region $[x - \frac{s}{2}, x + \frac{s}{2}) \times [y - \frac{s}{2}, y + \frac{s}{2})$. We compare the algorithm described in Section 5.3 with the equi-width histogram method as a baseline.

Recall that an equi-width histogram is the partition $B = \{b_{1,1}, b_{1,2}, \dots, b_{k,k}\}$. Let $\widetilde{c_x}$ be the published frequency counts in bin b_x.

Given a range query q, we estimate the answer to q as:

$$\sum_{b_x \in B} \left(\frac{|b_x \cap q|}{|b_x|} c_x \right). \tag{8}$$

where $|b_x|$ is the area of b_x. Note that if the query partially intersects with a bin, that bin contributes proportionally to the answer. Our proposed method answers a range query in a similar way, but using the average of the series of equi-width histograms.

We conduct experiments on three 2D datasets. Dataset 1 contains locations of Twitter users in the world [12]. The dataset contains over 193,841 Twitter users' data from the period of March 2006 to March 2010. Dataset 2 contains the locations of users in dataset 1 cropped at the North American region. It contains locations of 183,072 users. Dataset 3 [13] contains 164,860 tuples collected from tags that continuously record the location information of 5 individuals. The data points are normalized to the space $\mathcal{M} = [0,1]^2$, and Figure 3(a), 3(b) and 3(c) illustrate the distributions of the data points for dataset 1, 2, and 3 respectively. To avoid clogging, only 5% of the points (randomly selected) are plotted for each dataset.

For the first two datasets, we consider two cases where $\delta = 0.001$ and $\delta = 0.0001$, which translate to a bound of approximately 40 and 4 kilometers for dataset 1, and 5 and 0.5 kilometers for dataset 2 respectively. For dataset 3, we consider $\delta = 0.01$ and $\delta = 0.001$, which translate to 500 and 50 meters. We evaluate the construction described in

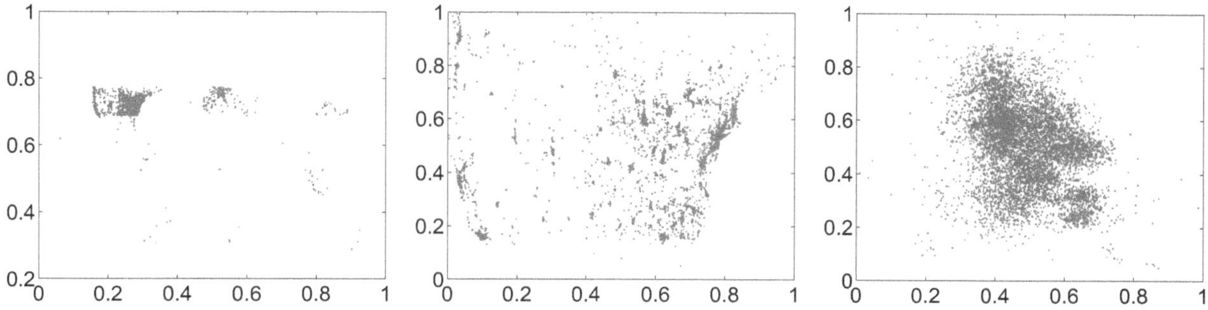

(a) Randomly selected 5% of points from Dataset 1. (b) Randomly selected 5% of points from Dataset 2. (c) Randomly selected 5% of points from Dataset 3.

Figure 3: The 2D location datasets.

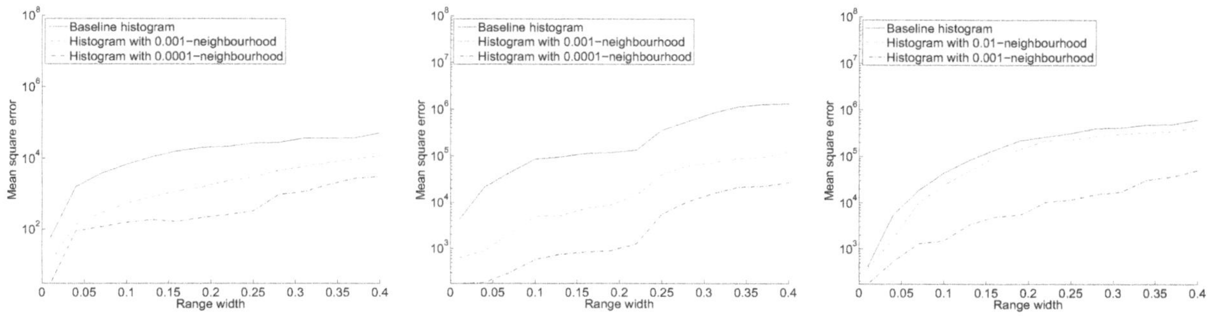

(a) Dataset 1. (b) Dataset 2. (c) Dataset 3.

Figure 4: The mean square error of range queries in linear-logarithmic scale.

Table 5: Query range and corresponding best bin-width for the Dataset 1.

	Query range	Mean Square Error			
		$k = 0.005$	$k = 0.01$	$k = 0.015$	$k = 0.02$
Dataset 1	0.01	62.01	86.16	94.12	100.69
	0.1	13218	9895.7	6726	8901.6
	0.2	72161	40301	24952	20381
Dataset 2	0.01	4112.7	6166.4	8227.1	13105
	0.1	232689	82449	86034	175203
	0.2	249344	186891	115664	103929

Section 5.3, and compare its accuracy with a baseline histogram method. For comparison purpose, we empirically choose the optimal bin width for the histogram method[3]. That is, for each query range, we computer the mean square error for $k = 0.0025$ to 0.04 with a step of 0.0025, and choose the smallest error among them. Part of the errors are shown in Table 5. Figure 4 shows the details of the experiment result. For example, when the queries is of size 0.1, the mean square error of the baseline method is 6726, where as with the construction under 0.001-neighbourhood is 543, and with 0.0001-neighbourhood is 109. By exploiting δ-neighbourhood, we can achieve significantly higher utility. For example, in dataset 1, the utility improves by a factor of 100 with 4km-neighbourhood, while many existing mechanisms can only improve the result by a factor of 2 [25, 3]. Note that our notion is orthogonal to existing techniques, and thus potentially could be combined to attain higher utility.

[3]The step of revealing the optimal bin width could reveal more information and thus the whole process may not be differentially private. Nevertheless, it can serve as a baseline to compare the performance of the purposed mechanisms.

5.5 Other Publishing Mechanisms

For some mechanisms, it is easier to apply the notion of δ-neighbourhood. In this Section we analyze their performance under δ-neighbourhood.

5.5.1 Publishing Sorted 1D Points

Fang et al. [9] propose a method of publishing 1D histogram by directly publishing the sorted point. The sensitivity of this mechanism depends on the size of the domain, say m.

Under δ-neighbourhood, the sensitivity of the publishing method is reduced to δm and therefore the Laplace noise required to achieve ϵ-differential privacy is reduced from $Lap(m/\epsilon)$ to $Lap(m\delta/\epsilon)$. Thus, there is significant improvement when applying the publishing method as it is. Figure 5 shows the improvement for expected mean square error for range query of 10,000 runs for each range size.

Although the error is significantly decreased (the factor of improvement on mean square error is approximately $(1/\delta^2)$

for δ-neighbourhood), it is not clear how to generalize the construction to higher dimensions. The method of using locality preserving transformation as described by Fang et al. [9] would not help since here we are required to preserve locality in the "difficult" direction.

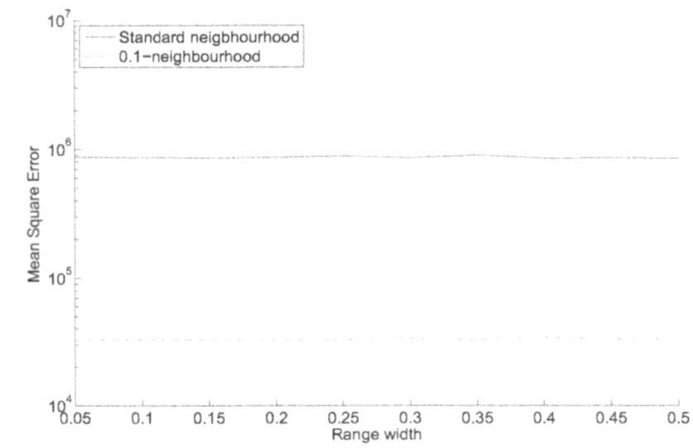

Figure 5: Average error for range query.

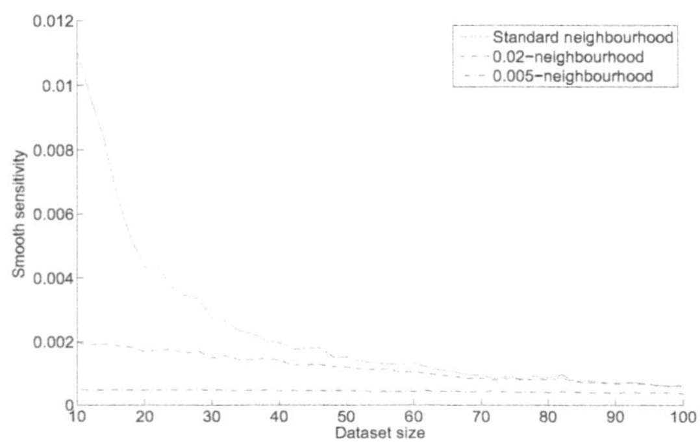

Figure 6: Average error for median.

5.5.2 *Publishing Median*

Publishing median differentially privately is technically challenging. To publish the median of a set of 1D points in $[0, m]$, a noise of $Lap(m/\epsilon)$ is required, although for most database instances, the "local sensitivity" is low, i.e. changing any element in that particular database instance will not significantly change the value of the median. Nissim et al. [18] proposed a method that adds noise proportional to the "smooth sensitivity" (a smooth bound of the local sensitivity) of a database instance. He showed that this mechanism has high accuracy when the smooth sensitivity is low.

The δ-neighbourhood can further reduce the noise requirement when "local sensitivity" can be still large. With δ-neighbourhood, we can reduce the global sensitivity, and thus bound the smooth sensitivity for some worst case s-cenarios. Figure 6 shows the noise required to publish the median of a synthesized dataset with random 1D points generated under the exponential distribution and then scaled to $[0, 1]$. For each size of the dataset, we repeat the process 300 times and the average smooth sensitivity is recorded under different neighbourhood definitions.

6. DYNAMIC DATASETS

We now investigate dynamic datasets. Consider situations where information on entities are collected periodically over time, say at discrete time $1, 2 \ldots$. Occasionally, statistics are to be published. Intuitively, with limited budget, it is impossible to continuously publish meaningful information indefinitely, in fact, Dwork et al. [7] showed a negative result under a setting that captures this intuition. However, in some scenarios, the entities are not required to contribute at all collection times, and are likely to leave within a short period. With such restriction, it should be now possible to continuously publish with low noise indefinitely, as effect of information contributed earlier would diminish in time.

6.1 Example 1

One situation where publishing dynamic dataset can benefit from δ-neighbourhood is when sensitive information only last for a short period. Consider a regional flu response organization who wants to continuously collect daily information on the health conditions of visitors, and release the information occasionally. Alice wants to infer whether Bob has been to the region based on the released information. If the publishing mechanism $\mathcal{A}$ is ϵ-differential privacy, then Alice's inference is bounded by:

$$Pr(\mathcal{A}(D_0 + \{\mathbf{x}\}) \in R) \leq exp(2\epsilon) Pr(\mathcal{A}(D_0) \in R),$$

where $\mathbf{x}$ is Bob's information. If all visitors must leave within 14 days, then $\mathbf{x}$ must be near the source, i.e. $d(\mathbf{x}, \perp) < 14$ days, otherwise the dataset is invalid. Hence, under this constraint on the datasets, the guarantee under the standard neighbourhood and δ-neighbourhood are equivalent.

6.2 Example 2

Let us revisit Example 1. Suppose the authority allows some visitors to stay for a longer period, say 28 days, even if the dataset is published under 14-neighbourhood, there is still protection. If Bob indeed stayed for 28 days, the bound is relaxed to $exp(2\epsilon)$. Hence, similar to the spatial datasets, the protection is being redistributed with more protection to entities with shorter stay.

6.3 Formulation

Let a sequence $x_1, x_2, \ldots$ be the data contributed by an entity, where each $x_i \in \mathbf{U} + \{\perp\}$ is the data contributed at time i, with $\mathbf{U}$ being the domain of the contributed data, and $\perp$ being a special symbol indicating that the entity is not contributing at that time. Let us call a sequence containing only the symbol $\perp$ a *null sequence*. A dataset D is a set of the aforementioned sequences. We assume that every entity in D has contributed a data in $\mathbf{U}$ at some time, and thus D does not contain null sequence. The prefix of a sequence x contains data contributed by the entity up to time n, denoted $x_{[1..n]}$, where n is the length of the prefix. Let us denote $D_{[1..n]}$ the set of such prefixes in D that are not null sequence. In addition, denote D_n the set of all n-th elements of the sequences in D that is not $\perp$, that is, D_n contains all data contributed at time n.

At certain time, say time t, some information on D_t is to be published. We assume that information is published at any time i, and let $\mathcal{A}_i$ be the publishing mechanism employed at time i. Hence, the data published are $\mathcal{A}_1(D_1)$, $\mathcal{A}_2(D_2), \ldots$. Combining all the data published before time

$n+1$, we can treat the "effects" of mechanisms $\mathcal{A}_1, \mathcal{A}_2, \ldots, \mathcal{A}_n$ as a single mechanism $\mathcal{A}_n^*$ that operates on $D_{[1..n]}$.

6.4 δ-Neighbour on Dynamic Dataset

Given two datasets, D and D', under the standard neighbourhood, they are neighbours if, and only if they differ by one entity. That is, there is a sequence x and y s.t. $D+\{x\} = D'$, or $D+\{x\} = D'+\{y\}$. This is essentially the same notion of neighbourhood for *user-level privacy* studied by Dwork et al. [7][8].

For two sequences $\mathbf{x} = \langle x_1, x_2, \ldots \rangle$ and $\mathbf{y} = \langle y_1, y_2, \ldots \rangle$, let us define $d(\mathbf{x}, \mathbf{y})$ to be the value $i_s - i_t$ where i_s is the smallest index s.t. $x_{i_s} \neq y_{i_s}$ and i_t is the largest index s.t. $x_{i_t} \neq y_{i_t}$. That is, it is the length of the smallest consecutive subsequence that contains all the differences. We take the null sequence as the source. Hence, D and D' are δ-neighbourhood if, and only if $D + \{\mathbf{x}\} = D'$, or $D + \{\mathbf{y}\} = D' + \{\mathbf{z}\}$, for some $\mathbf{y}, \mathbf{z}$ s.t. $d(\mathbf{y}, \mathbf{z}) \leq \delta$, or some $\mathbf{x}$ s.t. $d(\mathbf{x}, \hat{\perp}) \leq \delta$ where $\hat{\perp}$ denotes the null sequence. When $\delta = 1$, then providing differential privacy under δ-neighbourhood is same as the *event-level privacy* studied by Dwork et al. [7].

6.5 Sustainable Differential Privacy

If each mechanism $\mathcal{A}_i$ is ϵ-differentially private under either notions of neighbourhood, then the mechanism $\mathcal{A}_n^*$ is $(n\epsilon)$-differentially private under the respective neighbourhood. However, for δ-neighbourhood, we should be able to "reuse" the budget spent on much earlier published data. This observation is formulated in the following theorem:

Theorem 2 *Let D be a dynamic dataset with the mechanism $\mathcal{A}_n^*$, $\mathcal{A}_1, \mathcal{A}_2, \ldots \mathcal{A}_n$ as defined above in Section 6.3. If mechanism $\mathcal{A}_i$ is ϵ_i-differentially private under the standard neighbourhood for each $i \in \{1, \ldots, n\}$, and*

$$\sum_{i=1}^{\delta} \epsilon_{k+i} \leq \epsilon, \quad \textit{for } k \in \{0, 1, \ldots, (n-\delta)\},$$

then $\mathcal{A}_n^*$ is ϵ-differentially private under δ-neighbourhood.

PROOF. Consider two datasets D and D', where $D' + \{\mathbf{y}\} = D + \{\mathbf{x}\}$ and $d(\mathbf{x}, \mathbf{y}) \leq \delta$. Let i_s be the smallest index at which $\mathbf{x}$ and $\mathbf{y}$ differ. Consider an output $\mathbf{a} = \langle a_1, a_2 \ldots a_n \rangle$ of $\mathcal{A}_n^*(D)$, we have the probability that $\mathcal{A}_n^*$ gives the same output on dataset D' as:

$$
\begin{aligned}
Pr(\mathcal{A}_n^*(D') = r) &= \prod_{i=1}^{n} Pr(\mathcal{A}_i(D_i') = a_i) \\
&\leq \left(\prod_{i=i_s}^{i_s+\delta-1} exp(\epsilon_i) \right) \cdot \left(\prod_{i=1}^{n} Pr(\mathcal{A}_i(D_i) = a_i) \right) \\
&\leq exp(\epsilon) Pr(\mathcal{A}_n^*(D) = r)
\end{aligned}
$$

Similarly argument holds for any pair D and D' where $D' = D + \{x\}$ and x is near the source. Therefore, $\mathcal{A}_n^*$ is ϵ-differentially private under δ-neighbourhood. □

For instance, if $\epsilon_i = \delta^{-1}$ for all i, under standard neighbourhood, $\mathcal{A}_n^*$ is a n/δ-differentially private, but it is a 1-differentially private mechanism under δ-neighbourhood. Note that the assurance is independent of n, and thus it is possible to continue publishing indefinitely and yet achieve ϵ-differential privacy. In general, we say that a mechanism achieves *sustainable differential privacy* when the factor in the assurance is bounded by a constant independent of n.

7. PUBLISHING DYNAMIC DATASET: ALLOCATING BUDGET

The privacy requirement ϵ is often called the privacy budget as it can be divided between and allocated to a group of mechanisms. As shown in section 6.5, sustainable ϵ-differential privacy can be achieved by ensuring budget spent in any sliding window is bounded by ϵ (Theorem 2). There are many ways to allocate the budget over the time window and yet achieving sustainable privacy. An interesting question is on how to allocate the budget ϵ_i to the mechanism A_i at each time i, so as to minimize the "total error".

We consider total error of the form $\sum_1^n (w_i \mathcal{E}rr_i(\epsilon_i))$, where $\mathcal{E}rr(\cdot)$ is a non-negative function quantifying the error incurred by the mechanism A_i in term of the budget, and the non-negative weight w_i gives the weightage of the query at time i. A zero weight at time i, i.e. $w_i = 0$, corresponds to the event that no publishing is required at time i. Now, given a weightage $w = \langle w_1, \ldots, w_n \rangle$ and the privacy requirement, we want to find an allocation of the budget ϵ_i so as to minimize the total error.

We consider two settings. Under the *offline* setting, the publisher knows all the weights at time 0, and hence the publisher can determine the allocation before publishing. This setting could be unrealistic in scenarios where the publisher does not know the queries in advance. Under the *online* setting, the value of w_i is only known at time i and the budget ϵ_i has to be committed before time $t+1$.

7.1 Offline Allocation

The offline budget allocation problem can be formulated as the following optimization problem:

Problem 1 Offline Budget Allocation

Given:	$\delta \in \mathbb{Z}_n, \epsilon, \mathbf{w} = \langle w_1 \ldots w_n \rangle \in \mathbb{R}_{\geq 0}^n$
Find:	$\langle \epsilon_1, \epsilon_2, \ldots, \epsilon_n \rangle$
Minimize:	$\sum_{i=1}^{n} w_i \mathcal{E}rr_i(\epsilon_i)$
Subject to:	$\sum_{i=1}^{\delta} \epsilon_{k+i} \leq \epsilon$, for $k = 1, 2, \ldots, (n-\delta)$.

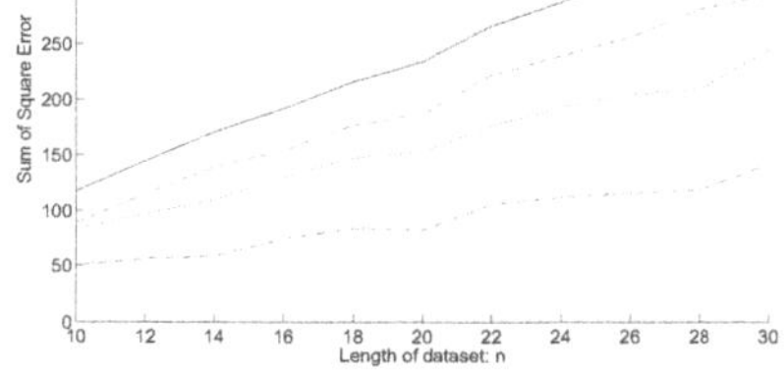

Figure 7: Improvement of offline version for $\delta = 4$.

In general, solving the above optimization problem is difficult. However, when the objective function is quadratic, it is a convex optimization problem whose solution can be found using existing optimization solvers, for example, a SDPT3 solver [22][23]. In this section, we study error function of the form $\mathcal{E}rr_i(\epsilon) = c_i\epsilon^{-2}$ for some constant c_i. This form of error function corresponds to mechanisms such as the Laplace mechanism, whereby the variance of the error is a quadratic function w.r.t. ϵ_i^{-1}. Since the constant c_i can be captured by the weight vector $\mathbf{w}$, Without loss of generality, we assume $c_i = 1$ for all i.

Let $\mathbf{e}_I = \langle \frac{\epsilon}{\delta}, \ldots, \frac{\epsilon}{\delta} \rangle$, which corresponds to an allocation that divides the budget equally across time; and let $\mathbf{e}_O$ to be the optimal allocation. Note that $\mathbf{e}_I$ is in the feasible region of the problem and could be a good initial solution for a solver.

Figure 7 shows the comparison of errors between $\mathbf{e}_I$ and the optimal budget allocation $\mathbf{e}_O$, where $\mathbf{w}$ is a binary vector and each $w_i \in \{0, 1\}$ is independently randomly chosen to be 1 with probability $p = 0.5$ and $p = 0.75$, respectively.

7.2 Online Allocation

Under online setting, only $w_1, \ldots, w_i$ are available at time i, and the allocating algorithm has to commit the budget for e_i which may later turn out to be sub-optimal. Indeed, it is easy to construct a counter example to show that for any deterministic algorithm, in the worst case, there is an instance where the error incurred is twice as large than the offline optimal. In this section, we focus on average case performance where the $\mathbf{w}$ is drawn from some distribution known to the publisher.

We propose an online algorithm as follow. At time i, given the committed budget allocation $e_1, \ldots, e_{i-1}$ and $w_1, \ldots, w_i$, the following steps are carried out:

1. N (in our experiment, N =1,000) samples of weights $\mathbf{w}_1, \ldots, \mathbf{w}_N$ are drawn from the distribution on condition that the first i values are $w_1, \ldots, w_i$.
2. For each candidate of e_i (in our experiment, we try $0.01, 0.02, \ldots, 1$) and each $\mathbf{w}$ among the N weight samples, compute the "optimal" error by solving the constrained offline allocation problem given below (Problem 2). After the errors by the N samples are obtained, the average error is computed.
3. The candidate that attains the smallest average error is committed to be the budget of e_i.

Problem 2 Constrained Offline Allocation

Given: $\delta \in \mathbb{Z}_n, \epsilon, \mathbf{e}' = \langle \epsilon_1', \epsilon_2', \ldots, \epsilon_m' \rangle \in \mathbb{R}^m_{\geq 0}$, $\mathbf{w} = \langle w_1 \ldots w_n \rangle \in \mathbb{R}^n_{\geq 0}$

Find: $\langle \epsilon_1, \epsilon_2, \ldots, \epsilon_n \rangle$

Minimize: $\displaystyle\sum_{i=1}^{n} w_i \mathcal{E}rr_i(\epsilon_i)$

Subject to: $\displaystyle\sum_{i=1}^{\delta} \epsilon_{k+i} \leq \epsilon$, for $k = 1, 2, \ldots, (n-\delta)$;

$\epsilon_k = \epsilon_k'$, for $k = 1, 2, \ldots, m$.

7.3 Evaluations

We evaluate the performance of the online algorithm, comparing to the offline optimal solution and $\mathbf{e}_I$. We consider $\epsilon = 1$, and $\delta = 4$ or 7. For each setting, we repeat the experiment for 1,000 times and record the average error of the three solutions.

We consider a $\mathbf{w}$ where each $w_i \in \{0, 1\}$ is taken to be 1 with probability $p = 0.5$. Figure 8(a) shows the errors of $\mathbf{e}_O$, $\mathbf{e}_X$ and $\mathbf{e}_I$ for $\delta = 4$, and Figure 8(b) shows errors when $\delta = 7$. Figure 8(c) consider a $\mathbf{w}$ where each $w_i \in \{0, 1\}$ is taken to be 1 with probability $p = 0.75$.

8. RELATED WORK

There are extensive works on privacy-preserving data publishing. The recent survey by Fung et al. [10] gives a comprehensive overview on various notions, for example, k-anonymity [20], ℓ-diversity [16], and differential privacy [4].

In practice, ϵ-differential privacy can be too strong to be achieved in some scenarios. Many relaxations capture alternative notions of "indistinguishability", in particular, on how the two conditional probabilities in the bound are compared. For example, (ϵ, δ)-differential privacy [5] relaxes the bound with an additive factor δ, and (ϵ, τ)-probabilistic differential privacy [17] allows the bound to be violated with a probability τ. Similar to our work, Konstantinos et al.[2] proposed broadening the differential privacy definition by considering different underlying metrics.

Alternative relaxations include attribute differential privacy and bit differential privacy considered by Kifer et al. [14], where two datasets are neighbours if they differ at only one attribute value or one bit. Blocki et al. [1] consider differentially private graph algorithms, with restriction that the maximum degree of any node in a social network graph is bounded. They consider the restricted datasets and show that such restricted sensitivity can be significantly lower than the smooth sensitivity for subgraph counting queries and local profile queries.

There are many mechanisms designed for histogram publishing. Xiao et al. [24] proposed a mechanism of adding Laplace noise to the coefficients of a wavelet transformation of an equi-width histogram, whereby range query can be answer with different combination of the published transformation. Hay et al. [11] proposed a method that a series of equi-width histograms for different bin-widths is to be published, and a range query can then be decomposed and answered from the histograms series different scales. Li et al. [15] gave an analysis on linear transformations to answer to a query workload. Machanavajjhala et al. [17] proposed a 2D dataset publishing method that can handle the sparse data in 2D equi-width histogram. However, it is not clear how to adapt the above-mentioned mechanisms to exploit δ-neighbourhood. One exception is the method by Fang et al. [9] as demonstrated in Section 5.5.

Dwork et al. [7] consider applications that involve repeated computations on dynamic datasets, such as monitoring data or searching thread. They gave a general transformation that converts mechanisms on static dataset to mechanisms under dynamic dataset. The idea of processing dynamic datasets also lead to a concept of pan-privacy [8], which require each datum to be discarded immediately after processing, and therefore guarantee that the internal state be differentially private as well.

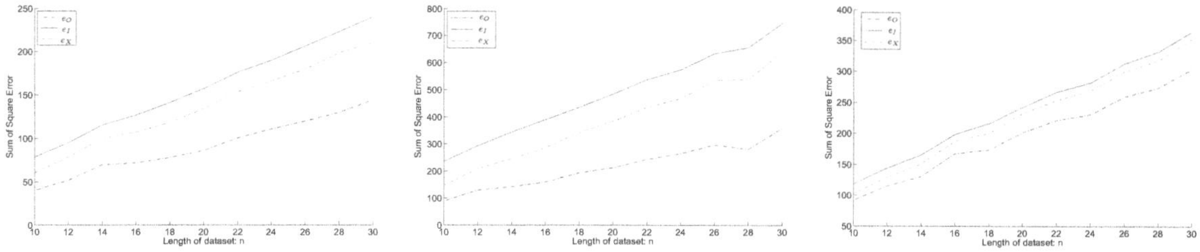

(a) $\delta = 4$, $p = 0.5$. (b) $\delta = 7$, $p = 0.5$. (c) $\delta = 4$, $p = 0.75$.

Figure 8: Comparison of offline and online algorithms.

9. CONCLUSION

In this paper, we propose to relax differential privacy by adopting an alternative definition of neighbourhood which "redistributes" the assurances based on the underlying distance of the entities. Although the idea is simple, for some applications, it is not clear how to exploit the relaxation to achieve higher utility. We consider two types of datasets, spatial datasets and dynamic datasets, and show that the noise level can be further reduced by constructions that exploit the δ-neighbourhood. We give a few scenarios where δ-neighbourhood would be more appropriate, and we believe the notion provides a good trade-off for better utility.

10. REFERENCES

[1] J. Blocki, A. Blum, A. Datta, and O. Sheffet. Differentially private data analysis of social networks via restricted sensitivity. In *Proceedings of the 4th conference on Innovations in Theoretical Computer Science*, pages 87–96, 2013.

[2] K. Chatzikokolakis, M. E. Andrés, N. E. Bordenabe, and C. Palamidessi. Broadening the scope of differential privacy using metrics. In *Privacy Enhancing Technologies*, pages 82–102, 2013.

[3] G. Cormode, C. Procopiuc, D. Srivastava, E. Shen, and T. Yu. Differentially private spatial decompositions. In *ICDE*, pages 20–31, 2012.

[4] C. Dwork. Differential privacy. *Automata, languages and programming*, pages 1–12, 2006.

[5] C. Dwork, K. Kenthapadi, F. McSherry, I. Mironov, and M. Naor. Our data, ourselves: Privacy via distributed noise generation. *Advances in Cryptology-EUROCRYPT*, pages 486–503, 2006.

[6] C. Dwork, F. McSherry, K. Nissim, and A. Smith. Calibrating noise to sensitivity in private data analysis. *Theory of Cryptography*, pages 265–284, 2006.

[7] C. Dwork, M. Naor, T. Pitassi, and G. Rothblum. Differential privacy under continual observation. *Proceedings of the 42nd ACM symposium on Theory of computing*, pages 715–724, 2010.

[8] C. Dwork, M. Naor, T. Pitassi, G. Rothblum, and S. Yekhanin. Pan-private streaming algorithms. *In Proceedings of ICS*, 2010.

[9] C. Fang and E. C. Chang. Adaptive differentially private histogram of low-dimensional data. *Privacy Enhancing Technologies*, pages 160–179, 2012.

[10] B. Fung, K. Wang, R. Chen, and P. Yu. Privacy-preserving data publishing: A survey of recent developments. *ACM Computing Surveys*, pages 14–57, 2010.

[11] M. Hay, V. Rastogi, G. Miklau, and D. Suciu. Boosting the accuracy of differentially private histograms through consistency. *VLDB Endowment*, pages 1021–1032, 2010.

[12] Infochimps. Twitter census: Twitter users by location [online]. http://www.infochimps.com/datasets/twitter-census-twitter-users-by-location.

[13] B. Kaluža, V. Mirchevska, E. Dovgan, M. Luštrek, and M. Gams. An agent-based approach to care in independent living. *Ambient Intelligence*, pages 177–186, 2010.

[14] D. Kifer and A. Machanavajjhala. No free lunch in data privacy. *Proceedings of the 2011 international conference on Management of data*, pages 193–204, 2011.

[15] C. Li, M. Hay, V. Rastogi, G. Miklau, and A. McGregor. Optimizing linear counting queries under differential privacy. *ACM symposium on Principles of database systems of data*, pages 123–134, 2010.

[16] A. Machanavajjhala, J. Gehrke, D. Kifer, and M. Venkitasubramaniam. ℓ-diversity: Privacy beyond k-anonymity. *International Conference on Data Engineering*, pages 24–36, 2006.

[17] A. Machanavajjhala, D. Kifer, J. Abowd, J. Gehrke, and L. Vilhuber. Privacy: Theory meets practice on the map. *International Conference on Data Engineering*, pages 277–286, 2008.

[18] K. Nissim, S. Raskhodnikova, and A. Smith. Smooth sensitivity and sampling in private data analysis. *ACM Symposium on Theory of Computing*, pages 75–84, 2007.

[19] A. Roth and T. Roughgarden. Interactive privacy via the median mechanism. *ACM Symposium on Theory of Computing*, pages 765–774, 2010.

[20] P. Samarati. Protecting respondents identities in microdata release. *Knowledge and Data Engineering*, pages 1010–1027, 2001.

[21] S. Silvey. *Statistical inference*, volume 7. Chapman & Hall/CRC, 1975.

[22] K. Toh, M. Todd, and R. Tütüncü. Sdpt3ąla matlab software package for semidefinite programming, version 1.3. *Optimization Methods and Software*, pages 545–581, 1999.

[23] R. Tütüncü, K. Toh, and M. Todd. Solving semidefinite-quadratic-linear programs using sdpt3. *Mathematical programming*, pages 189–217, 2003.

[24] X. Xiao, G. Wang, and J. Gehrke. Differential privacy via wavelet transforms. *IEEE Transactions on Knowledge and Data Engineering*, pages 1200–1214, 2010.

[25] J. Xu, Z. Zhang, X. Xiao, Y. Yang, and G. Yu. Differentially private histogram publication. *International Conference on Data Engineering*, pages 32–43, 2012.

On the Effectiveness of Risk Prediction Based on Users Browsing Behavior

Davide Canali
EURECOM, France
canali@eurecom.fr

Leyla Bilge
Symantec Research Labs, France
leylya_yumer@symantec.com

Davide Balzarotti
EURECOM, France
balzarotti@eurecom.fr

ABSTRACT

Users are typically the final target of web attacks: criminals are interested in stealing their money, their personal information, or in infecting their machines with malicious code. However, while many aspects of web attacks have been carefully studied by researchers and security companies, the reasons that make certain users more "at risk" than others are still unknown. Why do certain users never encounter malicious pages while others seem to end up on them on a daily basis?

To answer this question, in this paper we present a comprehensive study on the effectiveness of risk prediction based only on the web browsing behavior of users. Our analysis is based on a telemetry dataset collected by a major AntiVirus vendor, comprising millions of URLs visited by more than 100,000 users during a period of three months. For each user, we extract detailed usage statistics, and distill this information in 74 unique features that model different aspects of the user's behavior.

After the features are extracted, we perform a correlation analysis to see if any of them is correlated with the probability of visiting malicious web pages. Afterwards, we leverage machine learning techniques to provide a prediction model that can be used to estimate the risk class of a given user. The results of our experiments show that it is possible to predict with a reasonable accuracy (up to 87%) the users that are more likely to be the victims of web attacks, only by analyzing their browsing history.

Categories and Subject Descriptors

K.6.m [**Management of Computing and Information Systems**]: Miscellaneous—*Insurance, Security*

Keywords

risk prediction, profiling, web browsing

ASIA CCS'14, June 4–6, 2014, Kyoto, Japan.

http://dx.doi.org/10.1145/2590296.2590347.

1. INTRODUCTION

The World Wide Web is one of the main vectors used by cyber criminals to reach their victims. Malicious or compromised web pages are routinely used to infect user machines, spread malware, steal user credentials, and perform other phishing and scamming operations.

A large amount of research has been conducted on the tools and techniques adopted by attackers, to automatically identify and mitigate software vulnerabilities, or to protect web browsers from exploitation. Despite this effort, the percentage of web pages that are either malicious or that have been compromised to serve malicious content is steadily increasing [11, 29, 34]. Even though this is certainly an alarming phenomenon, these global figures are computed on the entire Internet population, and therefore fail to express what is the real risk for a single user to encounter a malicious page on her daily activity. The increasing number of dangerous sites does not necessarily affect everyone in the same way. For instance, it is possible that the majority of users only navigate in "safe neighborhoods" where malicious pages are still extremely rare. In this case, it should be possible to associate to each user, based on her usual online behavior, a certain *risk* profile. In other words, there should be a correlation between the *browsing habits* of a user and the probability she has to visit potentially harmful pages. This scenario is particularly attractive in the area of cyber-insurance [6], in which user profiling is an important step toward an accurate risk evaluation. In the physical world, insurance rates are normally computed based on a risk classification. For example, car insurances are more expensive in large cities or for inexperienced drivers – because this conditions are known to be positively correlated to the probability of car accidents. Unfortunately, an equivalent measurement of risk factors in the virtual world is still missing.

While the hypothesis of a correlation between the risk and the browsing behavior is reasonable, when dealing with the analysis of user browsing behaviors, there are also other factors that one has to take into account. For instance, independently from their daily activity, users are often socially engineered to click on links sent to them over email. As a consequence, it is possible that other attributes such as the user experience in computer science, as discussed by Onarlioglu et al. [22] could be more important to determine the risk factor of a user than her browsing habits.

Unfortunately, few works have tried to answer this question and understand if there are certain behaviors or certain characteristics that may influence the probability of users to visit malicious web pages. As discussed in Section 7, some works have tried to answer similar questions by performing field studies on the computer usage of a limited number of subjects [13]. Others have speculated whether certain behaviors may be related to higher chances of being compromised, such as the relation between browsing porn sites and being subject to infections [35]. However, no study has so far been general enough to build user profiles and analyze this information in order to assess if there is any relation between specific user habits and the probability of visiting malicious web pages.

In this paper, we conduct the first comprehensive study in this area by using the telemetry data collected by Symantec. In particular, we analyzed the webpages visited by 160,229 users over a period of 3 months (92 days). Using anonymized information, we first identified two classes of users: the *safe* ones who never visited malicious webpages during our experiments, and the ones *at risk* who visited several malicious sites in the same timespan. Our goal was to determine what kind of behavior can be used to differentiates the two classes. For this reason, we identified and extracted 74 attributes that can be used to summarize the user browsing behavior, and we correlated each of them with the users' class. It is important to note that correlation does not necessarily imply the presence of a causality relationship. In our study we only analyzed the *voluntary* browsing activity performed within a browser, and we did not include any URL that did not originate from user actions (such as the ones visited automatically by malware to contact the Command and Control infrastructures). Therefore, the fact of being already infected could not affect the data we collected.

Our experiments confirm that the volume of user activity is one of the best indicators for the level of risk. The more pages a person browses everyday, and the more diverse is the set of pages, the more likely she would be to come across a malicious website. We also show that malicious pages are more likely to be encountered during the weekend and that people in the risk class are more active during the night than users who belong to the safe class. Looking at the website categories, we found that some of them – such as adult content and shortened URLs – are positively correlated to the probability of being at risk. Finally, the results of the experiments we performed indicate that it is possible to combine all this information and train a classifier to predict whether a user is at risk of infection, just by analyzing her browsing profile.

The rest of the paper is structured as follows: In Section 2, we present the dataset we used for our experiments and how we labeled it. In Section 3, we provide a discussion about time and geographical trends adopted by different user categories. In Section 4, we explain features we employ to define user profiles. In Section 5, we analyzed the correlations between the features and being at risk and, present how we predict each category of users using the 74 features. We then discuss our findings in Section 6, summarize related work in Section 7, and briefly conclude the paper in Section 8.

2. DATASET AND EXPERIMENTS SETUP

We performed our analysis using a telemetry dataset collected by Symantec. This data is obtained from clients that voluntarily opt-in to let their computers share information on usage statistics and encountered threats. AntiVirus (AV) vendors typically employ this kind of client feedback with the purpose of identifying new threats and improve their products and services.

The dataset we used in our experiments consists of a 3-month snapshot of the web browsing history of a subset of clients that had opted in to allow the company collect information on their browsing activity. The dataset covered all the web requests issued by approximately 160,000 distinct client machines in a three-month period, from August 1st, 2013 to October 31st, 2013. This consisted in a total of 202,306,687 URL visits, covering a total of 37,797,151 distinct URLs. The data collected by Symantec included only URLs of websites visited through the HTTP protocol. All information was provided in an anonymized form, and no private client information was available to us, with the exception of the client's country. It is important to note that customers who agreed in sharing their browsing history are aware that the company stores this information in anonymized form, and that client identifiers are anonymized too. This means it is not possible for the AV company to link back the collected data to the client from which the requests originated. The specific fields we have analyzed in our study include only the unique client identifier, the timestamp of the visit, and the URL of the web site. Moreover, to further improve the privacy of the users, we anonymize each URL by removing the path and eventual URL parameters – limiting our analysis to the fully qualified domain name.

Since our main goal is to perform a statistical analysis of the dataset, we focused our study on those clients who visited at least 100 web pages during our timeframe. This prevents clients whose information has low statistical significance to pollute, or bias, our measurements. We believe the threshold of 100 pages over 3 months to be conservative enough to include almost all regular user behavior, while excluding those machines that are only sporadically used to browse the Web. Visiting less than 100 web pages over three months means, in average, around one URL per day: it would be very difficult to build a user profile based on such a limited browsing history.

2.1 Data Labeling

To be able to estimate if there is a correlation between risk and user behavior, we first need to define what the definition of *risk* is for our study. As explained in Section 3, we define the risk categories by setting an experimentally chosen threshold for the number of times a user visits distinct malicious URLs or domain names during the experiment period.

We constructed our labeled set of malicious URLs from URLs detected to be malicious either by the Norton SafeWeb service [30] or by Google SafeBrowsing [27]. We further collected malicious domain names from several public services that provide a list of domains involved in various malicious activities, such as drive-by-download, phishing, and scam web sites. In particular, we built the list by merging information collected by malware domain list [15], abuse.ch [3] and malc0de [18].

All this information allowed us to label each URL in our dataset as either *Benign*, *Malicious*, or hosted in a *Blacklisted* domain. We decided to keep this last class separated from the malicious URLs because domains have a larger granularity and therefore provides a less accurate classification. Please note that the labeling phase was performed in an automated way on Symantec's servers, thus prior to discarding the full URL path. Once the matching was completed, the rest of the analysis only operated, in an aggregated form, on the anonymized URLs.

2.2 Risk Categories

One of the goals of this paper is to answer the question of whether it is feasible to identify a category of people that, while surfing the Internet, incurs in a higher chance of visiting malicious web pages, when compared to other users. To be able achieve this goal, we first need to separate users in different risk categories.

Following a classical insurance approach, we separate users based on their past experience. With a good approximation, users that never ended up visiting a malicious page during our three-month observation period can be considered *safe* users. We noticed, however, that the contrary is not necessarily true. Indeed, given the high number of factors contributing to the maliciousness of a website and the delay in updating popular blacklists, misclassifications are not too rare. For example, it happens even to trusted websites to serve malicious ads or to become victims of DNS hijacking attacks [33]. Thus, when looking at our classification scores, a certain noise margin has to be taken into account. To handle this problem, we define a user to be *at risk* if she visited at least two distinct malicious URLs, or at least three blacklisted domains over the 3-month period. Again, the reason to use different thresholds for URLs and Domains is that the latter have a lower granularity and thus a higher probability of misclassification.

We put users who do not belong to the previous two categories into an *uncertain* middle category. For instance, the fact that a person visits a single dangerous URL over three months (with multiple visits to the same URL counting as one) may be just due to an error in classifying the URL. This is not sufficient for us to conclude that the user has a risky browsing behavior.

Table 1 shows the average number of different types of URLs visited by each category of users. Users who are "not at risk" appear to browse over five times less malicious URLs than *at risk* users. This means that typically, as the table shows, users in the *uncertain* category end up on malicious websites less frequently than *at risk* ones. Another clear difference is that *at risk* users typically visit more pages than other categories of users, and this factor may be related to the chance of ending up on malicious websites (we will discuss this hypothesis in more detail in Section 5). This is also valid in relation to the "variety" of visited websites, since for *at risk* users the average number of *distinct* URLs, and *distinct* URLs per day are about twice as much as the same values for the *uncertain* group. Finally, the table highlights that roughly one user out of five in our dataset belongs to the *at risk* category. If we consider the total number of users who are exposed at least once to malicious websites, then, this ratio increases to half of the entire user population. This is more than what found by a recent study on Australian customers by one major AV company [12], that observed that one customer every eight was exposed to web threats.

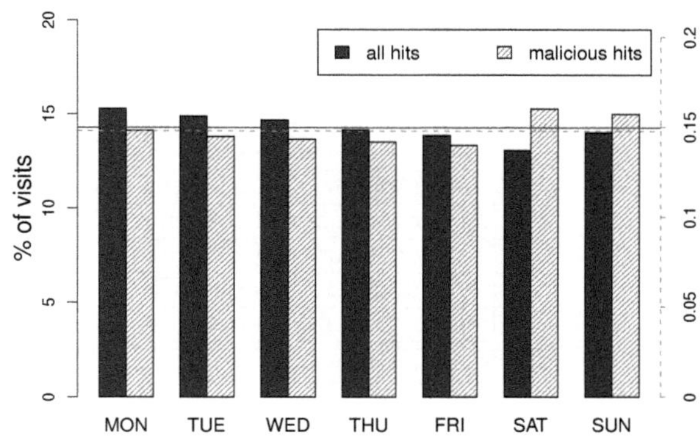

Figure 1: Global daily distribution of URL hits. The percentage of malicious hits is expressed as a fraction of the total hits on the same day.

3. GEOGRAPHICAL AND TIME-BASED ANALYSIS

This section describes the preliminary analysis we have conducted on our dataset, providing details about time and geographical trends.

3.1 Daily and Weekly Trends

We start our analysis of users' browsing behavior by looking at the weekly and hourly trends emerging from our dataset. First of all, Figure 1 shows that, as we expected, people surf less during the weekend. This trend is valid, with slight variations, all over the world, and country-wise daily trends do not differ much between each other. One can notice that there is a slight but significant increase in the percentage of malicious URLs visited during the weekend, compared to the trend of malicious hits during the rest of the week. This amounts approximately to a 10% increase in the chance of incurring in a malicious URL during the weekend, compared to the risk of doing so between Monday and Friday. The average *p-value* when comparing the two distributions is 6.44×10^{-7}, which shows the difference is indeed significant (as often found in literature [28], we consider to be statistically significant those differences showing computed *p-values* of less than 0.05).

Figure 2 shows instead the hourly trends for website visits, split between the two categories of users. As the hourly trends show, browsing trends for the *safe*, and *at risk* users do not differ much, even though *at risk* users are slightly more active during the night and less active in the morning. The statistical significance of these variations if confirmed by means of the Wilcoxon Signed Rank Test, that returned *p-values* significantly lower than the typical 0.05 significance level (e.g., the *p-value* of the test between 1 and 2am was of only 2.2×10^{-16}). However, the fact that users in the *at risk* category spend more time on the Internet at night does not imply that it is more risky to browse after midnight. Therefore, in Figure 3, we look at the same hourly trends, but from the point of view of the URLs instead of

Value	Risk Category		
	safe	*uncertain*	*at risk*
Total number of visited URLs	743	1386	2411
Distinct URLs visited	231.3	452.4	873.7
Average number of URLs visited per day	16.8	23.8	36.6
Distinct URLs visited per day	5.8	8.5	14.0
Total number of malicious URLs visited	0	0.78	8.4
Total number of blacklisted domains visited	0	2.44	8.5
Distinct number of malicious URLs visited	0	0.5	4.0
Distinct number of blacklisted domains visited	0	0.9	2.8
Percentage of malicious URLs	-	0.14%	0.71%
Percentage of blacklisted domains	-	0.32%	0.4%
Number of users	80128 (50%)	49127 (31%)	30974 (19%)

Table 1: **Average** values of different indicators, for users in the three risk categories.

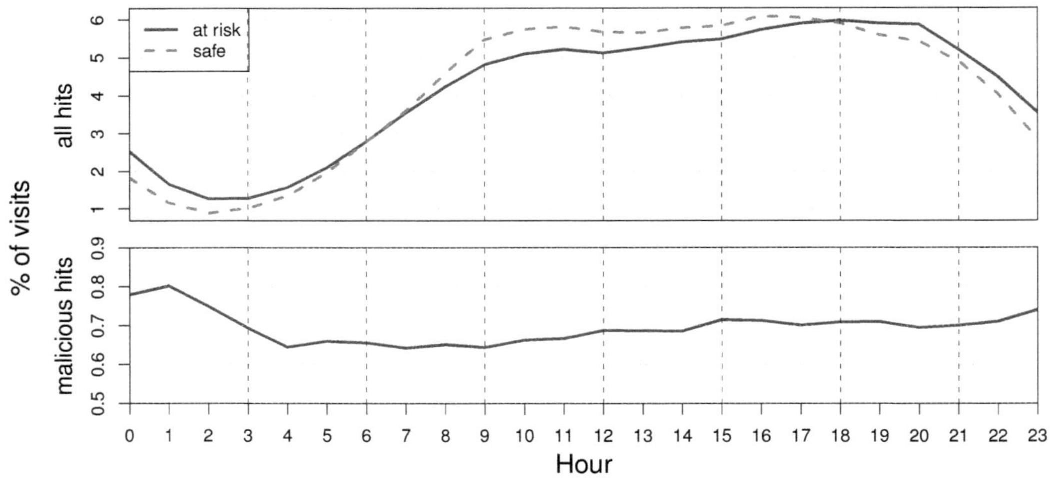

Figure 2: Hourly trends for, respectively, all the hits (upper) and malicious hits (lower) in our dataset. Malicious hits are expressed as percentage of the total hits for the same category of users, in the given hour.

users. In this case, the graph shows that hits on blacklisted domains are higher than other malicious hits between 9pm and 2am, and lower than others during business hours. Hits on malicious URLs seem instead to be prevalent in the afternoon, between 3pm and 8pm. Again, the signed rank test confirmed the differences in these distributions to be statistically significant.

Overall, these results confirm what found by a recent report on the Australian customers of a known security firm [12]. Indeed, as the mentioned study shows, also our analysis of time trends shows an increase in the percentage of malicious hits during nights and weekends. We are thus able to confirm that trends that have been reported on Australian users still hold when observing browsing statistics of users from all around the world.

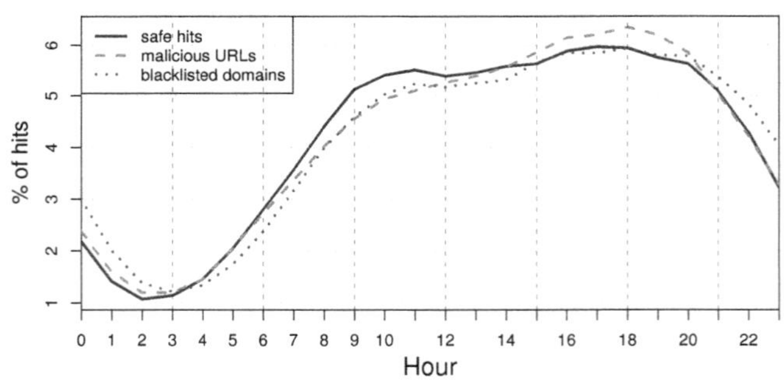

Figure 3: Hourly global trends for all hits and malicious hits in our dataset, showing also trends for the two separate sources of malicious hits

3.2 Geographical Trends

Our dataset contains information about clients located in 167 different countries. Table 2 summarizes some general statistics for those countries for which we have at least 1000 users. Simply by looking at the outliers (emphasized in bold in the table), one can notice several interesting trends.

For instance, Japan appears to have by far the lowest per-user ratio of malicious hits, and the lowest percentage of users at risk. However, the absolute value of malicious pages visited by Japanese users is in line with the ones of other countries. Percentages are just lower because average users

Country	Users	% users *at risk*	Average hits on		Visited Pages			# languages
			malicious URLs	blacklisted domains	total	distinct	domains	
US	67967	20.8	2.2 (0.22%)	2.0 (0.15%)	1250	422	194	3.6
UK	26204	17.8	1.5 (0.16%)	2.0 (0.16%)	1097	379	183	4.2
JP	16556	**10.0**	1.1 (**0.05%**)	3.1 (0.14%)	**1989**	**641**	205	3.8
CA	6798	20.9	2.0 (0.22%)	2.4 (0.17%)	1214	387	186	3.8
AU	6107	16.4	1.5 (0.17%)	1.5 (0.15%)	1007	343	173	3.7
DE	5606	22.3	2.0 (0.20%)	2.6 (0.23%)	1042	366	192	4.9
FR	4566	**29.1**	2.8 (0.27%)	3.3 (0.27%)	1127	390	209	4.5
NL	3415	15.9	1.1 (0.12%)	2.3 (0.21%)	1009	361	195	5.2
ES	1842	**28.3**	2.4 (0.23%)	3.9 (**0.33%**)	1121	391	200	**5.7**
SE	1755	15.3	1.9 (0.17%)	1.9 (0.14%)	1049	327	167	6.4
IT	1665	**27.4**	1.8 (0.18%)	**7.0** (**0.69%**)	1097	350	186	5.4
BE	1454	21.3	2.2 (0.21%)	2.5 (0.20%)	1126	396	208	5.5
NO	1208	**11.8**	1.1 (**0.10%**)	2.5 (0.11%)	1219	341	166	**6.1**

Table 2: **Average** values of several indicators, for users in the top 13 countries appearing in our dataset.

in Japan browse twice as many pages as their counterparts in other countries. At the other end of the scale, we have several Mediterranean countries (notably France, Spain, and Italy) that share similar high values of several risk indicators. These countries have a percentage of *at* risk users ranging between 27% and 29%, three times higher than Japan, and approximately twice as much as other top countries.

Finally, the last column of the table shows the average number of languages of web pages visited by users in each country. As it can be expected, users from English speaking countries appear to visit pages in a limited number of languages compared to those visited by users in non-english speaking countries. In average, over the 3-months period, users in English speaking countries appeared to browse pages written in less than 4 different languages, while users from other countries visited pages in an average of 5.3 different languages. This fact seems however not to have any clear relation with the percentage of *at* risk users in each country.

4. FEATURE EXTRACTION FOR USER PROFILING

After looking at time patterns and geographical trends, we decided to focus in more detail on the behavior of users. The basic idea motivating this work is that we expect users that belong to the risky category (i.e., those that regularly visit malicious web pages) to behave differently, when browsing the Internet, than users who are safe. We thus define a user profile as a sort of a multi-dimensional template such that we can characterize the behavior of each user group. In particular, we model each user profile by using a combination of 74 unique variables, or *features*, designed to precisely capture many aspects of a user's browsing habit.

Due to space limitations we cannot discuss each individual feature. Instead, in the following paragraphs we will describe the different categories that compose our features set, based on which aspect of the user behavior they are meant to represent.

How Much a User Surfs the Web.

The first set of features are designed to capture the volume of user activity. The rationale behind this is that, as common sense suggests, the more time a person spends browsing the Web, the more likely she would be to encounter a malicious web site. For instance, this category of features includes the number of total (*hits*) and unique (*distinct_urls*) hits over the three month period, the average number of hours (*hours_per_day*) and web pages (*hits_per_day*) visited in a day, and the percentage of days in which the client was active during the period of the experiment (*days_active_perc*).

In Which Period of the Day a User is More Active.

When looking at time trends (see Section 3.1), we noticed that the distribution of malicious URLs is proportionally higher during the night and in the weekend. Therefore, we added a set of features to capture this difference. In particular, we introduced the percentage of the client's hits issued, respectively, during night time (*hits_night_perc*), business hours (*hits_bh_perc*), and the evening (*hits_evening_perc*). We consider midnight to 6 am as night, 6 am to 7 pm as business hours, and 7pm-midnight as evening. These time windows were chosen in order to be as conservative as possible in the evaluation of business hours, as these differ significantly between countries in the world, and thus we may otherwise wrongly categorize this value.

How Diversified is the Set of Websites Visited by a User.

Another possible root cause for being at risk when browsing could be related to browsing a very broad and diversified class of web sites as this might increase the likelihood of landing on a malicious page. We model this aspect by counting the number of visited hostnames (*hostnames*), domain names (*domains*), and the number of visited unique top level domains (TLDs) (*tlds*).

Among these features we also consider the percentage of distinct URLs calculated over the total number of hits for the given user (*distinct_urls_perc*) and the percentages of unique hostnames and of unique domain names over the total number of hits (*distinct_hostnames_perc*, *distinct_domains_perc*). The purpose of these features is to estimate if the user tends to revisit the same set of URLs or websites, or instead appears to browse a more diversified set of web sites.

Finally, we measured the number of languages of the web pages visited by a certain user (*n_languages*). The language of websites was obtained from the same service we used to obtain the category of web pages, as explained in the following paragraph.

Which Website Categories the User is Mostly Interested in.

One of the main characteristics of a user profile is the categories of the visited web pages. To label each URL with the corresponding category, we used an internal website categorization system from Symantec. This service was designed to apply a set of heuristics to extract categories and languages from the URLs visited by the AV customers. Unfortunately, website categorization being based on heuristics, in some cases the categorization engine was able to retrieve only the main language used in the web page, but failed to properly capture the category, or vice versa. Therefore, we complemented the company database by using a number of publicly available website categorization services such as Alexa [1] and Open Directory Project [24], and a number of lists of known URL shorteners, bittorrent web sites, one-click hosting providers and porn websites [16,31,32,36]. We employed these lists to complement the heuristic service provided by Symantec, as it is common belief that visiting websites from these categories yields to higher chances of being infected by malicious web code. As a result, we were able to cover 76% of the web sites in our dataset (96% for the Alexa top 10,000 domains). The language coverage was instead 77% overall, and 70% for domains in the Alexa top 10,000.

Once the website categorization phase was completed, we extracted a number of features extracted from the category information in the user profile. For example, we reported the percentage of activity in each of the following 8 categories: business websites, adult websites, communications and information search, general interest, hacking, entertainment and leisure, multimedia and downloading, uncategorized (sites for which we were not able to obtain a category).

Computer Type.

The main aspect we want to capture with this class of features is the difference between office and personal computers. The assumption we make to identify office computers is that computers that do not show any activity during the weekends are very likely to be office computers. We label all computers that are silent during the weekend as office and the others as personal computers (*work_pc*). In addition, for personal computers, we also compute the percentage of activity during the weekend (*hits_we_perc*).

The remaining features that are extracted to characterize the computer type are computed using properties of the anonymized IP addresses of the devices. Note that we do not have access to the absolute value of the IP addresses and to the name of the Internet Service Providers (ISP) they belong to. The AV company keeps the hashed values of IP addresses and their corresponding ISPs such that it is possible to calculate their distinct numbers (*n_ips* and *n_isps*). The final feature in this category is the number of countries from which the user appeared to be surfing the web from (*n_countries_user*). By using features, we aim at representing the user's mobility, and helping to assess whether a person is browsing the Internet from a static IP address or a dynamic one.

How Popular are the Websites Visited by the User.

This set of features are computed to model how common the websites visited by a user are, under the assumption that malicious pages are more commonly found in less popular sites.

The first indicator we look at is the percentage of `.com`, `.net` and `.org` top level domain (TLD) hits that appear in each user's browsing history (*hits_comnetorg_perc*), and the number of visited URLs that belong to other TLDs (*no_comnetorg_tlds*). We also extracted a number of features related to the Alexa ranking of domains [2], namely the total number of hits and distinct websites visited in the Alexa top 500 (*n_hits_top500*, and *n_dist_sites_top500*), the total number of hits and of distinct websites visited in Alexa's top one million (*n_hits_top1M*, and *n_dist_sites_top1M*) and the number of hits and of distinct websites visited out of Alexa's top one million list (*n_hits_noAlexa*, *n_dist_sites_noAlexa*). All these features are computed both as absolute numbers and as percentage among all web sites visited by the user.

How Stable is the Set of Visited Pages.

To conclude our features set, we modeled the variability of a user's browsing activity. The rationale in this case is that users who always visit the same set of pages may be less at risk than users who change their targets very often. In particular, it is possible that users are mostly exposed to malicious pages when they deviate from their usual interests and temporarily browse web sites they do not know very well. In order to obtain these features, we performed a one week training over the web browsing history of each client in our dataset. We thus recorded, for each client machine, the set of web sites visited during its first 7 days of activity (*training set*). For every other day, we recorded the set of visited websites and their intersection and difference with the *traning set*. We averaged these values, and obtained the average percentage of common web sites between the daily browsing session and the initial 7-day training period (*inters_day_host*), as well as the percentage of new web sites – not visited during the 7-day training window – browsed in average every day (*delta_day_host*). We also recorded, for each client machine, the whole set of web sites visited during all its browsing activity, and calculate its intersection with the *training set*. The size of this intersection is then scaled by the size of the training set to obtain the percentage (*inters_host*) of hosts visited after the training period that cover the initial *training set*. Finally, we also computed a measure of the increment in the number of web sites visited by the client during its entire browsing history, compared to the number of web sites in the initial *training set* (*inc_host*).

5. EVALUATION

In this section, we present the results of our analysis. We first evaluate if any of the 74 features we have presented in the previous section are correlated to the fact that a user belongs or not to the *at risk* category. Afterwards, we build on top of these results to see if it is possible to use these features in a classifier, to predict the risk class of a user given her behavior.

Feature	At Risk	Safe	Percent Difference
hits	2411	742	106%
distinct_urls	873	231	116%
domains	331	88	116%
hostnames	388	108	113%
TLDs	17.5	7.9	76%
no_comnetorg_tlds	14.6	5.2	94%
n_languages	5.4	3.4	45%
days_active_perc	0.66	0.46	36%
hits_night_perc	0.09	0.07	27%
n_dist_sites_top500_perc	0.12	0.18	38%
hits_per_day	36.5	16.8	74%
hours_per_day	4.7	3.1	41%
hits_shorteners_perc	0.0034	0.0017	67%
hits_och_perc	0.0030	0.0018	50%
hits_porn_perc	0.0282	0.0112	86%
hits_downloading_perc	0.051	0.033	42%
hits_hacking_perc	0.0002	0.0000	113%
hits_business_perc	0.147	0.220	39%
hits_adult_perc	0.144	0.042	109%
inters_day_host	0.125	0.190	41%
inc_host	11.7	8.0	38%

Table 3: Comparison of the **average** values of certain features for *safe* and *at risk* users. Only features having a percentage difference greater than 25% are shown.

5.1 Feature Correlations

In the first part of our experiments, we extracted the feature values for all the users in our dataset and we used them to perform a correlation analysis with the risk class.

To start with, we compared the average values of each feature computed on *safe* and *at risk* users. While for the majority of them the difference was relatively small, in 22 features there was a difference of more than 25%. Those features, and the respective average values, are summarized in Table 3. The fact that several features clearly show up to a threefold increase between the activity of *safe* users and users *at risk*, suggested us to look at the correlation of these variables in more detail.

The correlation analysis we have adopted is based on the value of the Spearman's correlation coefficient [10]. Spearman's correlation is a statistical measure of the strength of a monotonic relationship between paired data. This coefficient by design is constrained between -1 and 1. While -1 indicates very strong negative correlation and +1 very strong positive correlation, the values close to 0 denote the absence of a monotonic relation between variables. We chose to employ the Spearman's rank correlation because, unlike the Pearson's correlation coefficient, it does not require a normal distribution in the dataset.

After calculating the Spearman's correlation coefficient, we tested the confidence of the obtained results by performing a standard significance test. As already discussed in Section 3.1, we consider that the correlation value of a feature is statistically significant if the computed *p-value* (i.e, significance level) is less than 0.05. A set of selected features for which the *p-value* was under this threshold is summarized in Figure 4.

Note that in the literature [10], a Spearman's coefficient value below 0.20 is normally considered an indication of a *very weak* correlation. Similarly, values between 0.2 and 0.4 are considered *weak*, between 0.4 and 0.6 *moderate*, between 0.6 and 0.8 *strong*, and above 0.8 *very strong* indication of a correlation between the variables. As it can be clearly seen in Figure 4, most of the features we have extracted have weak or no correlation with the fact that a user is at risk.

In the weakly correlated category we find features related to the amount of daily web activity (hits and hours per day), the number of porn and adult websites visited by a user, the number of languages, and an inverse correlation with the percentage of visited websites falling in the top Alexa 500. In the moderate correlation interval we find again some absolute measures of the amount of URLs, domains, and hostnames visited by a user. Moreover, and more interestingly, we also find a correlation between being at risk and the number of web pages with a TLD different from `.org`, `.com`, and `.net`.

Not surprisingly, these results indicate that the more a user surfs the Internet, the more she might be exposed to the risk of encountering a malicious page. The category does not seem to matter much, with very little correlation found with the percentage of usage of URL shorteners, downloading, and hacking websites – and a small negative correlation with the percentage of business sites. The only exception, as discussed in more detail in Section 6, is the higher correlation with adult and porn categories.

5.2 Predictive Analysis

The results we obtained from the correlation analysis show that some of the features we examined, although not very strongly, have some mild correlation with the fact that a user is *at risk*. Therefore, the same information might be helpful as well to predict whether a user is at risk or not. Motivated by this assumption, we have generated a number of prediction models leveraging state-of-the art machine learning techniques. Before opting for Logistic Regression [5], we experimented with many other machine learning approaches including decision trees [14,25], support vector machines [7], and Bayesian classifiers [37]. In our tests, logistic regression achieved the best results in terms of accuracy and false positive rates.

Logistic regression is a probabilistic statistical classification model that aims at predicting a category from features presenting either continuous or discrete values [5]. Compared to other classification methods, one of its advantages is that it does not explicitly require features that are not correlated with each other. Moreover, when new data is available, logistic regression can efficiently update the models with the new input.

The Receiver Operating Characteristic (ROC) curve summarizing the true and false positive rates of our classifier, applied to the entire dataset, is shown in Figure 5. The curve has an area of 0.919. For instance, if used to detect *at risk* users, the system can be tuned to have a detection rate of 74% (i.e., users *at risk* properly classified as *at risk*) with 8% false positives (i.e., users not at risk misclassified as being *at risk*). These results, both in terms of the best classifier algorithm and of the area under the ROC curve, are in line with what has been measured in previous studies about the precision of classification algorithms for financial risk prediction [23].

Since, as explained in Section 3.2, the distribution and behaviors of users' risk classes are different in different countries, we decided to retrain our classifier on each country in isolation. The results are quite similar to the overall results,

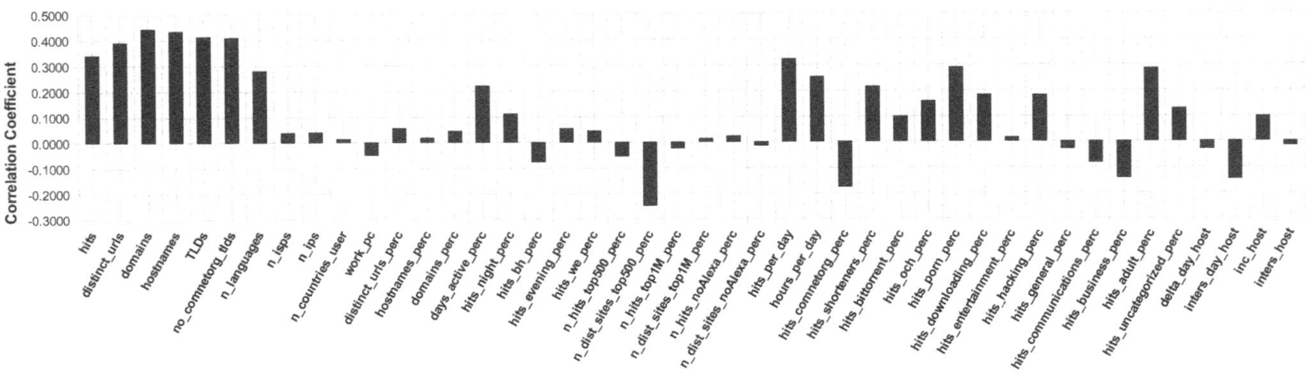

Figure 4: Spearman's Correlation Coefficient between user profile features and being *at risk*.

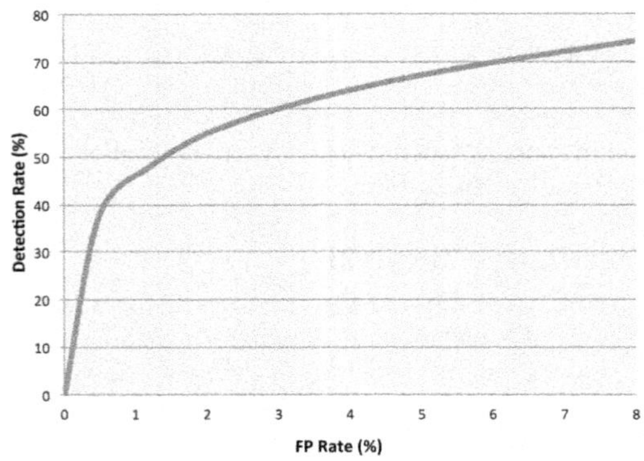

Figure 5: ROC Curve of the risk class classifier applied to the entire dataset

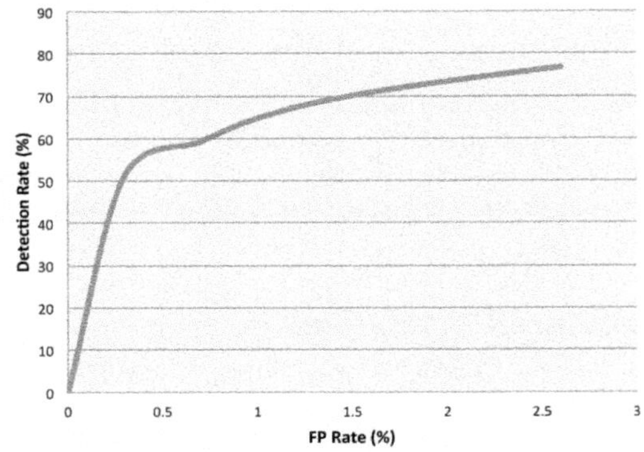

Figure 6: ROC Curve of the risk class classifier applied to the Japanese users only

with the only exception of Japan, for which the system was more precise – achieving 73% detection with 1.9% false positives, and an area under the ROC curve of 0.958, as shown in Figure 6.

6. DISCUSSION AND LESSONS LEARNED

Our experiments confirm the finding of a recent study by Levesque et al. [13] regarding the fact that the more websites a user visits the higher is her exposure to threats. However, we reach a different conclusion regarding the correlation of browsing adult content. Levesque et al. found that the amount of sport or Internet infrastructure websites visited by a user are more related to the fact of being infected than the number of porn websites [13]. However, while the absolute number of porn website may not be a good indicator, the percentage of time spent browsing porn seems to be a better feature. In fact, even though browsing adult web pages may not be a risky activity per se, from our results it looks like people who browse (in proportion) more porn and adult websites are more likely to also visit malicious pages in their daily activity. To better investigate this phenomenon, in Figure 7 we plotted the percentage of users at risk for different ranges (using a decile split) of the *hits_adult_perc* feature. The graph clearly shows that the percentage of safe users decreases as the ratio of adult hits increase.

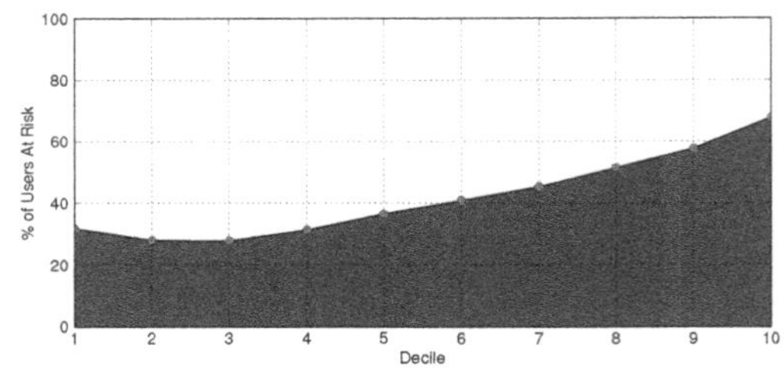

Figure 7: Decile plot for *at risk* users with respect to the percentage of hits on adult web sites.

Similar trends can be plotted also for the other variables. For instance, Figure 8 presents an even clearer picture of the relationship between the number of unique top level domains and the steep increase in the percentage of users at risk. While the large majority of safe users lie in the first half of the decile plot (more than 50% of the total number of safe users actually lie in the 1st decile – visiting less than 8 TLDs in the 3-month period), their percentage drops to less than 20% in the last three deciles of the plot, corresponding to users that visit at least 21 different TLDs. This is yet another confirmation that the variety, and not just the number, of the pages visited by a user is a strong indicator for its risk factor.

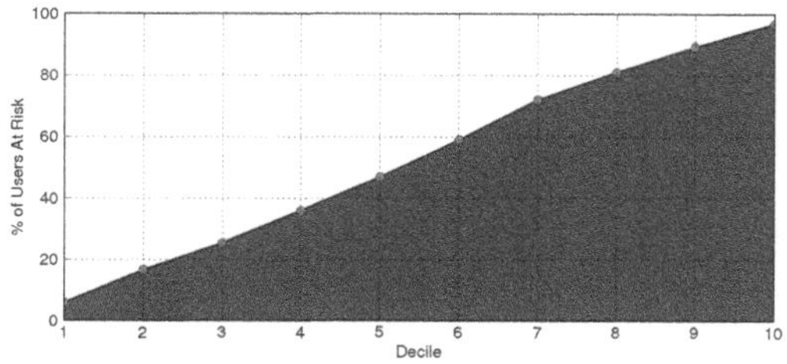

Figure 8: Decile plot for *at risk* users with respect to the number of different TLDs visited.

As mentioned in Section 3.2, also the geographical location of a user is very important. Citizens of certain countries (such as Norway and Japan) seem to be more careful in their browsing habits compared to their peers located, for example, in Italy or Spain.

While some of the features we used in our experiments were already discussed in previous works, the main finding of our study is the fact that by extracting and combining a much larger number of features from the URLs visited by a user in a certain period of time, it is possible to train a classifier to predict the risk class a user belongs to. This is a very interesting finding from several points of views. First, our results can be obtained by looking only at HTTP requests, without any access to the end-user devices. This allows companies (or even ISPs) to silently profile their users and even combine their risk class into an aggregated risk factor at a company or network level. Second, while still far from perfect, the accuracy of the extracted models is sufficient to be used in a risk prediction scenario. Comparable models are used everyday to compute the risk associated to financial operations [23], such as when processing credit card requests. This opens the door to a simple yet effective way to implement a cyber-insurance mechanism that rewards users who show a safe browsing profile.

7. RELATED WORK

Web-based attacks are one of the main vectors for cybercriminals to compromise Internet users. Therefore, there has been a considerable amount of work aimed at building defense mechanisms for web attacks [4, 9, 26]. However, due to lack of data about people's web browsing habits and experiences, the number of studies that tried to understand if there is any relation between users' behaviors or characteristics and their probability of visiting malicious web pages is still very limited. Moreover, most of the existing studies have been built upon the observation of very limited customer bases, or on clinical-style case studies based on data collection and surveys on tens or hundreds of users in a monitored environment [13].

7.1 User-based Risk Analysis

One of the first studies that sought to understand the risk factors behind user infections was carried out by researchers at the École Polytechnique de Montréal and Carleton University [13]. This study, which has a similar nature to works that evaluate medical interventions, examined the interactions among three important players: the users, the AV software and the malicious software detected on the system. The authors provided 50 users that accepted to join the experiment with a laptop that was configured to constantly monitor possible malware infections and collect information about how the users behaved in such cases. The results of the experiment show that user behavior is significantly related to infections, but that demographic factors such as age, sex, and education cannot be significantly related to risk. Furthermore, innocuous categories of websites such as sports and Internet infrastructure are associated with a higher rate of infection when compared to other categories, such as porn and illegal content sites, that common sense traditionally associates with higher risk. Similarly, and surprisingly, computer expertise seems to be one of the factors positively related to higher risk of infection.

Onarlioglu et al. [22] studied the behavior of users when they are faced with concrete Internet attack scenarios. The authors built an online experimental platform that was used to evaluate the behavior of 164 users with different backgrounds. Their findings confirm that non-technical users tend to fail in spotting sophisticated attacks, and that they are easily deceived by tricky advertising banners. On the other hand, they are able to protect themselves as effectively as technical users when dealing with simple threats.

Maier et al. [17] conducted a study of the security hygiene of approximately 50K users from four diverse environments: a large US research institute, a European ISP, a community network in rural India, and a set of dormitory users of a large US university. The paper analyzes anonymized network traces, which were collected from each observed environment for a period that ranges between 4 and 14 days, containing only the first bytes of each connection. The results of the analysis indicate that having a good security hygiene (i.e., following antivirus and OS software updates) has little correlation with being at risk. However, on the other hand, risky behaviors such as accessing blacklisted URLs double the likelihood of becoming infected with malware. Unlike our work, this paper has the advantage of being able to monitor all the Internet activity of the users, and thus is not limited to the analysis of web browsing traffic. However, it considers only malicious behaviors that overtly manifest themselves at a network level, e.g., sending spam emails, performing address scans or communications with botnet C&C servers. For this reason, attacks that produce little traffic, or install themselves on victim's machines and remain latent for long periods of time, may have been missed.

Finally, a recent report by TrendMicro and the Deakin University provided an analysis on the Australian web threat landscape [12]. The report states that, in average, 0.14% of the web browsing hits collected by the AV company are malicious in nature. One interesting finding is that Australians seem to incur in a higher percentage of daily malicious hits during holidays and weekends, when compared to weekdays. Moreover, the percentage of malicious hits rises during night time, with a peak around 4 am. As explained in Section 3.1, these findings are also confirmed as a worldwide trend by our experiments. Finally, the reported statistics show that one out of eight Australian IP addresses are exposed to web threats, on a typical day. In our study, instead, we find a higher risk of exposure to web threats for users in our dataset (19% of *at risk* users, overall).

Our work is fairly different from these studies in many respects. Compared to the majority of previous works, we perform our analysis on a much larger dataset (i.e. three months of data generated by 160K distinct users). Moreover, our analysis does not rely on personal information about the users such as their educational background, sex and age. We significantly extend the study of the Australian threat landscape by conducting similar analysis on a *worldwide* basis. In addition, we performed a more precise and deeper analysis by building user profiles based on over 70 features, and we tried to understand if different risk categories have different probabilities to end up in malicious web sites.

7.2 User Profiling

Olejnik et al. [21] presented a study in which they evaluated the possibility of fingerprinting users given their past web browsing history. The methodology the authors adopt to fingerprint users was able to profile 42% out of approximately 380,000 users involved in the study. From the experiment they performed with only 50 web pages, they conclude that categorization information of visited websites could be a useful parameter to build more accurate user profiles. The results of our study confirm that categorization information could be used for user profiling.

The problem of user profiling has been largely studied within recommender systems [8, 19, 20], to help users find topics that are in their interest, while hiding those topics that are unattractive to them. Therefore, the goals of user profiling in recommender systems' research are completely different from ours.

8. CONCLUSIONS

In this work, we have presented a first step towards the prediction of users' risk when browsing the Internet. Our in-depth analysis of a large telemetry dataset collected by one of the major AV companies allowed us to gain a number of insights on the relation between users' browsing habits and their chances of visiting malicious web pages on the Internet. For example, we have been able to confirm some known trends, such as the fact that browsing the web late at night and during weekends is typically correlated with higher chances of ending up on malicious web sites. Another general trend confirmed by our work is that, in general, the more a user surfs the Internet, the more her chances are of ending up in some "unsafe neighborhood".

We have also been able to shed some light on whether profiling can be effectively used as a basis for predicting the risk for a user to end up on malicious web sites. By employing machine learning, we showed that user profiling could actually be employed, at least to some extent, in predicting the class of risk for a user on the web, similarly to what is currently done in the field of insurances and financial risk prediction.

In order to provide even more complete insights on human risk factors linked to visiting malicious web pages, it would be interesting to have access to users' "social" features, such as their sex, age, profession and personal interests. This would improve the completeness of users profiles we build, and could be the object of some future work.

9. ACKNOWLEDGEMENTS

The research leading to these results has received funding from the European Union Seventh Framework Programme (FP7/2007-2013) under grant agreement n.257007.

10. REFERENCES

[1] Alexa. Alexa Browse by Category. http://www.alexa.com/topsites/category/Top, 2013.

[2] Alexa. Alexa Top Websites. http://www.alexa.com/topsites, 2013.

[3] amada.abuse.ch. Malware Database (AMaDa) :: AMaDa Blocklist. http://amada.abuse.ch/blocklist.php?download=domainblocklist, 2013.

[4] A. Barth, C. Jackson, and J. C. Mitchell. Robust defenses for cross-site request forgery. In *15th ACM Conference on Computer and Communications Security (CCS 2008)*, 2008.

[5] C. M. Bishop. nformation Science and Statistics. In *Pattern Recognition and Machine Learning*. Springer, 2006.

[6] R. Böhme and G. Schwartz. Modeling cyber-insurance: Towards a unifying framework. In *Ninth Workshop on the Economics of Information Security (WEIS)*, 2010.

[7] N. Cristianini and J. Shawe-Taylor. An introduction to support vector machines and other kernel-based learning methods. In *Cambridge University Press*, 2000.

[8] J. Delgado and R. Davidson. Knowledge bases and user profiling in travel and hospitality recommender systems. In *Proceedings of the ENTER 2002 Conference*, pages 1–16. Citeseer, 2002.

[9] M. Egele, P. Wurzinger, C. Kruegel, and E. Kirda. Defending browsers against drive-by downloads: Mitigating heap-spraying code injection attacks. In *Detection of Intrusions and Malware, and Vulnerability Assessment*, pages 88–106. Springer, 2009.

[10] Y. G.U. and K. M.G. *An Introduction to the Theory of Statistics (14th ed.)*. .Charles Griffin & Co., 1968.

[11] Kaspersky. Kaspersky Security Bulletin 2012. http://www.securelist.com/en/analysis/204792255/Kaspersky_Security_Bulletin_2012_The_overall_statistics_for_2012, 2012.

[12] C. Ke, J. Oliver, and Y. Xiang. Analysis of the Australian Web Threat Landscape. http://www.trendmicro.com.au/cloud-content/au/pdfs/security-intelligence/white-papers/australian_web_threat_landscape_-v7.pdf, May 2013.

[13] F. L. Lévesque, J. Nsiempba, J. M. Fernandez, S. Chiasson, and A. Somayaji. A Clinical Study of Risk Factors Related to Malware Infections. In *Proceedings of the ACM Conference on Computer and Communications Security (CCS)*, Nov. 2013.

[14] A. Liaw and M. Wiener. Classification and regression by randomforest. In *R News*, volume 2/3, page 18, 2002.

[15] M. D. List. Malware Domains List. http://www.malwaredomainlist.com/, 2013.

[16] URL Shortening Services - A List of URL Shorteners. http://longurl.org/services, 2013.

[17] G. Maier, A. Feldmann, V. Paxson, R. Sommer, and M. Vallentin. An assessment of overt malicious activity manifest in residential networks. In *Detection*

of Intrusions and Malware, and Vulnerability Assessment, pages 144–163. Springer, 2011.

[18] Malcode. Malcode. http://malc0de.com/bl/BOOT, 2013.

[19] D. W. McDonald and M. S. Ackerman. Expertise recommender: a flexible recommendation system and architecture. In *Proceedings of the 2000 ACM conference on Computer supported cooperative work*, pages 231–240. ACM, 2000.

[20] S. E. Middleton, N. R. Shadbolt, and D. C. De Roure. Ontological user profiling in recommender systems. *ACM Transactions on Information Systems (TOIS)*, 22(1):54–88, 2004.

[21] L. Olejnik, C. Castelluccia, and A. Janc. Why Johnny Can't Browse in Peace: On the Uniqueness of Web Browsing History Patterns. In *5th Workshop on Hot Topics in Privacy Enhancing Technologies (HotPETs 2012)*, Vigo, Espagne, July 2012.

[22] K. Onarlioglu, U. O. Yilmaz, D. Balzarotti, and E. Kirda. Insights into user behavior in dealing with internet attacks. In *19th Annual Network and Distributed System Security Symposium (NDSS)*, NDSS 12, January 2012.

[23] Y. Peng, G. Wang, G. Kou, and Y. Shi. An empirical study of classification algorithm evaluation for financial risk prediction. *Applied Soft Computing*, 11(2):2906 – 2915, 2011. <ce:title>The Impact of Soft Computing for the Progress of Artificial Intelligence</ce:title>.

[24] O. D. Project. DMOZ Open Directory Project. http://www.dmoz.org/, 2013.

[25] J. Quinlan. C4.5: Programs for machine learning. In *Morgan Kaufmann Publishers*, 1993.

[26] P. Ratanaworabhan, B. Livshits, B., and Zorn. Nozzle: a defense against heap-spraying code injection attacks. In *Proceedings of the USENIX Security Symposium*, 2009.

[27] Google Safe Browsing API. http://code.google.com/apis/safebrowsing/, 2008.

[28] S. Stigler. Fisher and the 5*CHANCE*, 21(4):12–12, 2008.

[29] Symantec. 2013 Internet Security Threat Report. http://www.symantec.com/security_response/publications/threatreport.jsp, 2013.

[30] Symantec. Norton Safe Web. https://safeweb.norton.com/, 2013.

[31] TBLOP - The Big List of Porn. http://www.tblop.com/, 2013.

[32] Torrent Sites. http://www.torrentresource.com/, 2013.

[33] S. J. Vaughan-Nichols. How the Syrian Electronic Army took out the New York Times and Twitter sites. http://www.zdnet.com/how-the-syrian-electronic-army-took-out-the-new-york-times-and-twitter-sites-7000019989/, August 2013.

[34] Websense. Websense 2013 Threat Report. http://www.websense.com/content/websense-2013-threat-report.aspx?cmpid=prnr2.13.13, 2013.

[35] G. Wondracek, T. Holz, C. Platzer, E. Kirda, and C. Kruegel. Is the internet for porn? an insight into the online adult industry. In *Ninth Workshop on the Economics of Information Security (WEIS)*, 2010.

[36] List of File Hosting and Sharing Websites. http://xboxpirate.eu/forums/topic/280-list-of-file-hosting-and-sharing-websites-137-entries/, 2013.

[37] H. Zhang. The Optimality of Naive Bayes. In *FLAIRS2004 conference*, 2004.

Protecting Users Against XSS-based Password Manager Abuse

Ben Stock
FAU Erlangen-Nuremberg
ben.stock@cs.fau.de

Martin Johns
SAP AG
martin.johns@sap.com

Abstract

To ease the burden of repeated password authentication on multiple sites, modern Web browsers provide password managers, which offer to automatically complete password fields on Web pages, after the password has been stored once. Unfortunately, these managers operate by simply inserting the clear-text password into the document's DOM, where it is accessible by JavaScript. Thus, a successful Cross-site Scripting attack can be leveraged by the attacker to read and leak password data which has been provided by the password manager. In this paper, we assess this potential threat through a thorough survey of the current password manager generation and observable characteristics of password fields in popular Web sites. Furthermore, we propose an alternative password manager design, which robustly prevents the identified attacks, while maintaining compatibility with the established functionality of the existing approaches.

Categories and Subject Descriptors

K.6.5 [**Security and Protection**]: Unauthorized access; H.4.3 [**Communications Applications**]: Information browsers

Keywords

Cross-site Scripting, XSS, Passwords, Password Managers, Countermeasure, Web Security

1. INTRODUCTION

In this section, we present the motivation behind our work and give a short outlook on the remainder of the paper.

1.1 Motivation

Passwords are the primary authentication method of the Web. With the growing set of Web applications that enter our life, the number of utilized passwords rises continuously. Security's best practices dictate, that each password should be sufficiently hard to guess and unique for the respective site, to limit dangers that arise from password reuse and guessing attacks. However, due to the traits of human nature, our capacities for remembering large sets of good passwords are limited, which in turn evidently leads to violation of the aforementioned password discipline [18, 13].

To provide assistance in this matter, password managers were introduced, that store passwords for the user and offer to (semi)automatically enter them into the matching password dialogues. Nowadays, all popular Web browser provide built-in password managers. Unfortunately, these managers operate by simply inserting the clear-text password into the document's DOM, where it is accessible by JavaScript. Thus, a successful Cross-site Scripting (XSS) attack can be leveraged by the attacker to read and leak password data which has been provided by the program.

Cross-Site Scripting is one of the most common security issues on the Web. The Open Web Application Security Project (OWASP) regularly lists XSS as one of the top three security vulnerability problems on the Web [24] and in its yearly analysis report [27], Whitehat Security lists XSS vulnerabilities documents that 43% of all discovered serious vulnerabilities can be accounted to XSS.

Thus, XSS-driven, automated password stealing attacks appear to be a realistic threat. In this paper, we assess the susceptibility of the current password (manager) landscape and propose a lightweight countermeasure, that robustly prevents the identified attacks, while maintaining compatibility with the established functionality of the existing approaches.

1.2 Contribution and Paper Outline

After providing the required technical background (Sec. 2), we make the following contributions:

- We give a comprehensive overview on potential XSS-based attack patterns on browser-provided password managers (Sec. 3) and explore potential mitigation strategies, that can be realized with the currently available technology (Sec. 4).
- We present two systematic studies: For one, we examine the current generation of existing password managers and show their susceptibility to the outlined attacks. Furthermore, we report on a large-scale study on the Alexa Top 4000 site, in which we studied how password fields are used by popular Web sites (Sec. 5).
- Motivated by the gained insights, that the vast majority of password scenarios are indeed vulnerable to the

ASIA CCS'14, June 4–6, 2014, Kyoto, Japan.

ACM 978-1-4503-2800-5/13/06...$15.00.
http://dx.doi.org/10.1145/2590296.2590336 .

identified attacks, and that the currently available mitigation strategies are insufficient, we propose a client-side countermeasure, which robustly protects against XSS-based password theft without changing the general interaction scheme between user, Web page and password manager. Using a prototypical implementation as a Firefox extension, we practically evaluate our solution's security and functionality characteristics (Sec. 6).

We end the paper with a discussion of related work (Sec. 7) and a conclusion (Sec. 8).

2. TECHNICAL BACKGROUND

In the following, we give a brief technical background on password managers and the concepts of Cross-Site Scripting.

2.1 Password Managers

As studies [18, 13] have shown, users tend to choose bad passwords and/or reuse passwords over multiple sites, therefore undermining the security of their login credentials. To support users in employing a more secure password strategy, browser vendors as well as third party programmers have implemented password managers capable of storing these secret credentials for the users. This allows users to choose more complex and possibly random passwords by lifting the burden of remembering numerous complicated passwords. Hence, password managers can be beneficial for supporting better security practices in password handling.

Current implementations of password managers in browsers all work in a similar manner. Just before a form is submitted, the form is checked for password fields. If any such field exists, the username and password fields are determined and their values are subsequently extracted. These extracted credentials are then – along with the domain they were entered into – passed to the password manager. The password manager's database is subsequently checked for a matching entry, whereas no action is taken if the extracted credentials already match the stored ones. If, however, no matching entry is found, the user is prompted to approve storing of the password data. Analogously to that, if an entry for the same username but different password is found, the user is prompted to consent to updating the stored data. This process only works with forms that are submitted, either by the user clicking a submit button or by JavaScript invocation of the `submit()` method of that form. According to Mozilla [6], storing passwords which are sent using JavaScript XMLHttpRequests is not supported since no actual submission of the form takes place.

For each page containing a username and password field, the password manager is queried for entries matching the URL (or domain, depending on the implementation). If an entry is found, the fields on that page are automatically filled with the previously persisted credentials. Hence, the user then only has to submit the form to log into the application.

2.2 Cross-site Scripting

In the Web, access from a document to another document's content is governed by the Same-Origin Policy [2]. This policy makes sure that interaction between two documents may only occur if their origins match. An origin in this sense is the combination of protocol, domain and port of the interacting resources. Hence, an attacker, hosting his code on his own page, cannot directly access the content of, e.g., Google Mail even if the visitor of the page is logged in to that service. In the Web context, the term Cross-Site Scripting (*XSS*) is used for a class of attacks that allow an attacker to inject HTML or script code into a vulnerable Web application. This code is then executed in the context and, thus in the origin of the vulnerable application. In our example, this would mean that the code would be executed in the origin of Google Mail, thus allowing it to read arbitrary content from the site. Hence, Cross-Site Scripting can be seen as a way of circumventing the Same-Origin Policy. Cross-Site Scripting attacks are typically classified into three categories, namely *persistent*, *reflected* and *DOM-based* XSS. The first term adheres to the fact that the attackers code is persistently stored in an application's database, where in the second case, data provided to the application – e.g. via the URL – is reflected back into the response, allowing for malicious code to be executed. The third kind, which was first described by Amit Klein [15] in 2005 and – in contrast to the previously outlined attacks – abuses client-side code vulnerabilities. Although it was first discussed in 2005, DOM-based XSS still appears to be a major threat as Lekies et al. [16] recently showed by finding DOM-based XSS vulnerabilities on 9.6% of the Alexa top 5000 sites.

3. ATTACKS

In this section, we discuss the general attack pattern usable for stealing passwords via Cross-Site Scripting vulnerabilities and follow up with means of leveraging password managers to automate these kinds of pattacks. Afterwards, we give an overview of specific attack scenarios aiming to extract credentials from password managers and conclude the section with a related, active network-based attacker model.

3.1 Stealing passwords with XSS

Cross-Site Scripting gives an attacker ample opportunity to steal secret data from his victim. Typically, login forms for Web applications are realized using two input fields, which the user fills with his username and password, respectively. By design, JavaScript may interact with the document and thus is also capable of accessing the username and password field. This feature is often used by applications to verify that certain criteria are met – such as checking for e-mail addresses. However, this functionality also allows an attacker to retrieve the credentials utilizing Cross-Site Scripting. If the attacker can successfully inject his own JavaScript code into the login page, that code can extract the credentials entered by the user and subsequently leak them back to the attacker. This kind of vulnerability obviously only works if the user is not yet logged in when clicking on the crafted link. However, this is where password managers come to the aid of the attacker, as we will discuss in the following.

3.2 Leveraging Password Managers to Automate Attacks

Password managers provide a convenient way for users to automate parts of logins into Web applications. To make the login as simple and comfortable as possible, they automatically pre-fill forms for which the user stored the password beforehand. This feature can be exploited by a Cross-Site Scripting attacker. If a site is susceptible to XSS attacks, the adversary can inject his own code into the application's login form in a similar manner as described earlier.

However, the attacker no longer needs to wait for the form filled by the user, since the password manager auto-fills the required fields. The attacker's code can then automatically retrieve the information and leak it back to the attacker. The biggest advantage in comparison to the aforementioned attack is the fact that the user does not need to be involved at all. This process can – depending on the browser – be fully automated in a hidden frame while the user is looking at a seemingly innocent page.

Figure 1 shows this process. First, when the login page is initially loaded, the fields are both empty. In the next step, the password manager automatically fills in the username and password, which can be subsequently retrieved by the code the attacker injected. The password is then automatically leaked back to the attacker as depicted in the lower part of the figure.

3.3 Specific Attack Patterns

In terms of Cross-Site Scripting, an attack targeting password managers specifically aims at extracting the stored user credentials in an automated way. The attacker therefore tries to embed a form into a vulnerable application which is then filled in by the password manager. This form can afterwards be read by the attacker's JavaScript code to retrieve the data that was inserted by the victim's browser and eventually leak the information back to the attacker.

In our study of current password manager implementation, which we will discuss in further detail in Section 5.1, we found that their behavior could be distinguished in four dimensions. In the following, we will discuss the discriminating factors and the attack patterns associated with them.

Matching requirements for the URL and form.

The first factor we examined was the way in which password managers react to changes both to the URL and the form itself. Password managers often fill passwords regardless of the context, as long as the domain matches, and, potentially, other easily fabricated indicators such as field names and types or form action are present.

When a password manager does not explicitly store the complete form the credentials were stored for, but rather only the origin, an attacker can easily extract the credentials. To achieve this, he can abuse a Cross-Site Scripting vulnerability on an arbitrary part of the application to inject his form and corresponding JavaScript code. This form is then filled by the password manager and the stolen data can be sent to the attacker. In cases where a password manager also does not store the names of the fields the data was stored from, the attack is even easier since an attacker does not need to craft a form specifically mimicking the login page of the target application, but may use a generic form. This allows him to automate the attack for multiple vulnerable pages in a very simple and almost effortless manner.

Viewports.

If a password manager explicitly checks the URL rather than the origin, the attacker has to force the victim's browser to load the original login page to make the password manager fill out all the relevant fields. Hence, the second criterion we found is the difference in handling viewports. In our notion, a viewport can either be a top frame, a sub frame or a popup window. With respect to that, the interesting question is whether a password manager still fills out forms if they are not located in the top frame of a page.

If login field data is inserted regardless of the viewport, an adversary can place a hidden frame pointing to the login page on the vulnerable page. As enforced by the Same-Origin Policy, any page may only access another document's content and resources if the protocol, the domain and the port of both involved documents match. As we assume the attacker has control over some page inside the vulnerable Web application, he can therefore access the aforementioned frame's content, thus enabling extraction of the credentials that were filled in by the password manager. If a password manager does not automatically fill in the values of interest to the attacker, or the application itself forces not to be framed using the `X-Frame-Options` header [19], the login page can be opened in a popup window. Still operating under the assumption that vulnerable and login page are of the same origin, the attacker's code can retrieve the data from the opened popup.

User interaction.

As a third distinguishing feature of the examined password managers, we identified user interaction – i.e. whether the user has to somehow interact with the password manager before it fills out the forms, e.g., via clicking or typing into the password field. If a given password manager requires such interaction, fully automated XSS password stealing attacks are not feasible.

However, in such cases, an attacker can attempt to conduct a ClickJacking [26] attack. ClickJacking attacks work by tricking the user to interact with a security sensitive Web UI without his knowledge. In the general attack case, the adversary loads the document which contains the security sensitive UI into an iframe and hides the frame from the user's eyes via CSS properties, such as `opacity`. Subsequently, he overlays the targeted (and now invisible) UI elements with unsuspicious elements and motivates the user to click them, for instance in the context of a game or a competition. If the user falls for the adversary's bait, he involuntary interacts with the hidden UI.

Using this attack, the adversary can trick the victim to interact with the password field in the required fashion, thus, causing the password manager to fill the field with the stored value.

Adherence to the autocomplete attribute.

The fourth and last dimension we found was the adherence to the `autocomplete` attribute for fields. According to the W3C standard [12], a browser must not store data that is inserted into input fields which have `autocomplete` set to `off`.

From the attacker's point of view, this feature is very interesting. If a password manager does not respect the `autocomplete` value when *storing* the credentials but only when later *filling out* the input fields, it is still susceptible to attacks. In order to extract password data from clients, the adversary can simply add a second form with the same names and input types to the document, this time without the `autocomplete` attribute, which is then filled with the persisted credentials.

Figure 1: Process of leveraging the password manager to steal stored credentials

In Section 5, we will discuss in detail how the browsers that we examined behaved with respect to the aforementioned four dimensions.

3.4 Network-based attacks

In concurrent and independent work, Gonzalez et al. [9] discovered a related attack. However, in contrast to our attacker model, their attacker is located in the network and can thus introduce content into every site of his choosing. They developed a tool called Lupin which automatically injects iframes for each site they want to steal credentials from and then extracts the inserted data. However, if we assume that the attacker cannot produce a valid TLS certificate for any domain he wants to extract data from, this attacker can only steal login data from sites that do not use HTTPS to serve their login form. Thus, this attack scenario can be thwarted if all pages use strict HTTPS for both the login form and the URL the data is then sent to. Although this attacker model is not the focus of our work, we evaluate the suspecibility of current Web applications to these attacks in Section 5.

4. MITIGATION STRATEGIES

Before presenting our solution approach in Section 6, we briefly discuss existing remedies and potential techniques, which could be applied by application providers and end users.

4.1 Server-side Mitigation

Several approaches exist, which could be adopted by Web application providers to protect their users against the presented attacks. However, as we will discuss, each of these techniques comes with certain drawbacks.

Switching to alternative authentication methods.

Instead of relying on form-based authentication, which is susceptible to XSS attacks due to the fact that injected JavaScript can access the value of the password field, Web application providers could switch to authentication processes that utilize credentials which are out of the adversary's reach:

- *HTTP authentication:* HTML forms are not the only available user interface component for password entry offered by Web browsers. If a Web application's server side requires HTTP authentication, signaled through a 401 HTTP response [7], the user is presented with a dedicated authentication dialog, which is realized with UI components that are outside of the current document's DOM, and hence, out of reach for a JavaScript attacker. Unfortunately, HTTP authentication is cumbersome to integrate the general workflow of Web applications: Form data is *pushed* by the browser to the server on form submit, while HTTP authentication is *pulled*, after the server notices an attempt to access restricted information. Mixing the two paradigms potentially leads to incoherent and confusing end user interfaces.
- *Client-side SSL authentication:* Instead of using passwords, the application could switch to public key authentication. Authenticating via client-side SSL certificates [5] is well supported by the browser's SSL/TLS implementation. However, such certificates have significant disadvantages over passwords in respect to deployment (the application needs to outfit all users with valid certificates), usability (handling browser-based certificates is well out of the expertise of the average Web end user), and portability (the certificates are enrolled in the browser, switching browsers or computers requires certificate migration).

Moving password forms to a dedicated sub domain.

Furthermore, to mitigate the outlined threat, sites could leverage the Same-Origin Policy's protection capabilities. If all password handling forms, and only these forms, are hosted on a dedicated (sub)domain, XSS vulnerabilities of the main application won't compromise the password's security. The injected JavaScript is executed under an origin that differs from the origin of the password-hosting document, hence, the JavaScript has no access to the field. Furthermore, the password manager stores the password for the domain value of the dedicated (sub)domain, thus, injecting further password fields into the document of the injected JavaScript has no effect, as no password has been stored for this document's origin in the first place. For apparent reasons, choosing this path comes with the price of elevated setup, deployment, and maintenance costs for the application provider (e.g., valid SSL certificates for the subdomain need to be acquired).

Disabling the password manager.

As covered earlier, using the HTML attribute `autocomplete="off"` [12], a Web application can prevent the browser from storing the password in the first place. The reasoning behind this is that the data, which is entered into fields which have this attribute set to `off`, is particularly sensitive and should therefore neither be stored nor inserted later. While being secure against the outlined attacks, this technique causes the loss of the usability advantage of the password manager, which in turn (see Sec. 2.1) could lead to situations in which end users potentially choose less secure passwords.

4.2 End-user Protection

Currently, end-users have two options to protect themselves against XSS password theft:

For one, they can simply turn their browser's password manager off through switching the corresponding setting in the browser's configuration [21]. While this is certainly the safest choice, the user looses both the functionality gain and the potential security advantage (see Sec. 2.1) of using a password manager.

The second option is to switch to a third-party password manager that requires explicit user interaction. If explicit user interaction, such as clicking a button, is a prerequisite for the system to fill the password value, fully automatic XSS-driven attacks are thwarted. Please note: It is crucial to mention, that the UI component which triggers the required user interaction is positioned outside of the DOM of the attacked page. Otherwise, the adversary can resort to the ClickJacking attack variant (see Sec. 3.3) and undermine the provided mitigation.

The primary focus of most third-party password managers is on security and not on ease-of-use or transparency. For instance, in it's default configuration, 1Password[1] requires the pressing of a predefined key combination, followed with the entry of the tool's master password. Hence, they might be not a viable option for end users that utilize password managers foremost as a convenience feature.

5. EXPLORING THE PASSWORD (MANAGER) LANDSCAPE

As explained above, several potential XSS attack patterns on password managers exist. To examine the degree to which these theoretic attacks are applicable with the currently deployed password managers and Web sites, we conducted two comprehensive studies. For one, we systematically examined the built-in password managers of the current browser generation (see Sec. 5.1). Furthermore, we conducted a large scale study on how password fields are used by existing applications (see Sec. 5.2).

5.1 Password managers

In this section we present the results of our experiments on the behavior of different modern browsers. Our tests were aimed in the four different dimensions previously discussed in Section 3.3.

To ensure a broad coverage of internet users, we opted to examine Google Chrome (version 31), Mozilla Firefox (version 25), Opera (version 18), Safari (version 7), Internet Explorer (version 11) and the Maxthon Cloud Browser (version 3). Although the latter one might not be as well-known as the other candidates, it is one of the options that is shown to users installing the latest Windows versions. Hence, we looked at the behavior of this browser along with the previously named.

Before investigating the behavioral changes when tampering with the form or the URLs the form was located in, we first analyzed the general fill-in behavior of our test subjects according to the specific attacks discussed in Section 3.3.

[1] 1Password: `https://agilebits.com/onepassword`

Filling only in the top frame.

To assess whether password managers would fill out forms only in top frames, we created a page that framed the original, unchanged login page we had initially stored our credentials for. Apart from Internet Explorer, which refused to insert any data, all browsers filled in the username and password field.

Explicit user interaction.

Next, we investigated whether a browser would actually need any form of interaction from the user to fill in passwords. Again, Internet Explorer was the (albeit positive) outlier, being the only browsing engine that required any form of interaction. In Internet Explorer, the user has to manually put the focus to the username field and is then presented with a dropdown menu allowing him to select which credentials he wants to insert. The user then has explicitly click on an entry to trigger the browsers fill-in action. Also, this is done properly outside of the DOM, thus the ClickJacking attacker discussed in Section 3.3 can also not force the filling of password fields.

URL matching.

We assume that the attacker wants to steal the credentials from his victim in a stealthy manner. We consider the following example: an application hosts its login at `/login`. The attacker has found a XSS vulnerability at `/otherpage` which he wants to abuse to steal the stored credentials. Hence, if a password manager only supplies the password to the exact URL it stored the passwords for, the attacker would have to open a popup window or embed a frame to the login page to steal the secret data. However, opening a popup window is very suspicious and therefore not desirable. Also, framing the login page in an invisible frame might not work due to `X-Frame-Options` headers. In our study, which we discuss in Section 6.3, we found that only 8.9% of login pages make use of this header to ensure that they are not framed. Thus, in our work, we wanted to determine how easy it was to make password managers fill in the stored credentials into forms if the URL did not match the one the password was originally stored for. To examine the browsers' behaviours, we created a simple Web application with a login form. We visited this login and let the password manager under investigation save the credentials that we entered. We then created multiple other pages running under different protocol (HTTP vs. HTTPS), different ports, different (sub-)domains as well as changing paths to determine what the implemented matching criteria were for all our test subjects. In the following, we discuss the results of the analysis of the aforementioned browsers.

- *Google Chrome:* Our tests showed that changing the protocol, sub domain or port lead to the password to not be filled in anymore. In contrast, when visiting a form running under a different path, Chrome still inserted the stored credentials. This leads us to reason that Chrome stores the password alongside their origin in the sense of the Same-Origin Policy, namely the triple protocol, domain and port.
- Our second candidate was *Firefox*. Similar to the behaviour Chrome exhibited, Firefox also refused to fill out login fields if either protocol, (sub-)domain or port were changed. It also behaved in a similar manner to

Chrome with respect to a change in the path – still automatically setting the username and password fields to the stored values.

- Both, *Opera and Safari* behaved in a similar manner. With changed origins, they refused to fill out forms, whereas the path was not taken into consideration in the decision whether to insert the stored credentials or not.

- *Internet Explorer:* In contrast to all the aforementioned, Microsoft's Internet Explorer apparently stores the complete URL of the form it saved the password data for. In our tests, it showed to be the only browser that did not insert stored credentials even if only the path changed.

- *Maxthon Cloud Browser:* Alongside all the well-known browsers we examined thus far, we also looked at the password manager of the Maxthon Cloud Browser. Most interestingly, the passwords were apparently only stored coupled with the second-level domain they stemmed from. In our tests, the browser would still fill in password fields even if the protocol, sub domain, port or path changed.

Summarizing, our tests showed that out of the most commonly used browsers on the Web, all but Internet Explorer gladly fill forms on any part of the same Web application, whereas the application borders are determined by the Same-Origin Policy. The Maxthon Cloud Browser even fills in credentials if only the same second-level domain is visited – ignoring both the protocol and the port of resource – making it even easier for an attacker to extract the passwords from its storage.

Form matching.

After having examined how browsers treat changes in the URL with respect to their password managers, we analyzed what kind of information on the actual form browsers would store. To gain insight into this, we built another set of test pages – this time with different modifications to the login form itself. Our test pages were different from the original form in different aspects, which we discuss briefly in the following.

For the first test case, we removed the action and the method of the form. Our second modification was the removal of the names of all fields in the form, whereas the third change was to only change the names of all fields rather than removing them. For the next part of our analysis, we removed the types from all fields, essentially resetting them all to `type=text`. We then derived a minimal form as shown in Listing 1, only consisting of two input fields with random names, no action or method as well as no additional submit buttons. After these changes to the form fields, we build a final testing page, setting the `autocomplete` attribute for the *password* field to off. According to the W3C specification [12], this value indicates the browser should neither store the data inserted into that field nor automatically fill it in later.

Utilizing these, we now discuss the matching criteria with respect to the structure of the form presented to the password manager.

- *Google Chrome:* We observed that neither action nor method of the form were criteria in the decision, whereas the same held true for changes to the names of the fields we provided. However, if we presented Chrome with fields without any name, it would not provide the credentials to the form. Chrome did not strictly adhere to the autocomplete setting of the password field, prompting the user to save the password nonetheless. It did however adhere to the setting when inserting the password into the form – nevertheless, we could extract secret data by adding a second form, as described in Section 3.3. Since the matching is done on a structural basis, the minimal form shown in Listing 1 was sufficient for this attack.

- *Firefox* also only performed matching against a form's structure, not the content itself. In contrast to what we had seen with Chrome, Firefox did however also insert credentials into forms that only contained input fields without names. Also unlike Chrome, Firefox adhered to the `autocomplete` attribute – if either field had this set to off, Firefox would not store any data. Due to these factors, injecting the minimal form would still trigger the auto-fill functionality of Firefox's password manager.

- *Opera and Safari* again behaved alike, filling in passwords into the minimal form but not into forms containing only input fields without names. On our test machine, a Macbook running OS X Mavericks, we discovered that both Opera and Safari also use the OS X keychain to store their passwords. Thus, after having stored a password in Opera, Safari automatically filled out our fields although we had not previously stored a password in its database. While Opera – similar to Chrome – also offered to store passwords if at least one of the posted fields did not have `autocomplete` set to off, Safari behaved like Firefox and did not save any data in that case. Again, the test subjects only performed structural rather than content matching, leading to both of them also auto-filling the minimal form. Contrary to Firefox, both browsers would not fill input fields without names.

- *Internet Explorer:* As explained in Section 5.1, Internet Explorer was the only browser that required any form of user interaction to fill in the passwords. To nevertheless check the functionality, we manually interacted with the browser to ensure that it would fill in the username and password. In that, we discovered that Internet Explorer applies matching criteria in the same manner as Firefox, namely inserting passwords even into forms containing only input fields without any name. In terms of adhering to the autocomplete attribute, Internet Explorer did respect the value by not saving any information if either field had the autocomplete value set to off.

- *Maxthon Cloud Browser:* Not unlike the insecure behaviour it showed regarding matching the URL, the Maxthon Cloud Browser was not at all strict in matching the form, even filling in input fields that had no name and – most notably – that had autocomplete set to off.

To sum up: Most browsers are very relaxed in terms of matching criteria. All but Internet Explorer would still fill in passwords if only the origins matched, whereas the Maxthon Cloud Browser even only took the second-level domain into consideration for its decision. Similar to that, matching against a form was mostly performed on a structural level, i.e. meaning that any two fields were filled out if the latter was a password. According to Mozilla[6], this is done by design as a convenience feature. Looking at the results, the tests with different forms showed that the attacker only has to create a minimal form as shown in Listing 1 to trick the browser's password managers into providing the stored passwords from any site that uses two input fields for its login dialogue.

All the previously discussed results are depicted in Table 1, whereas *'Yes'* denotes that the criterion must match. For the minimal form, *'Yes'* denotes that the minimal form was sufficient, whereas *'Yes'* for autocomplete means that the browsers would not save passwords if the autocomplete attribute was set to off.

Listing 1: Minimal HTML form used in our tests

```
<form>
<input name="random1">
<input name="random2" type="password">
</form>
```

5.2 Password fields

To obtain a realistic picture on how password fields are currently used in practice and to which degree real-world password dialogs are susceptible to the attacks discussed in Section 3, we conducted a survey on the password fields of the top ranked Web sites according to the Alexa index [1].

5.2.1 *Methodology*

To locate and analyze password fields in real-world Web sites, we conducted a lightweight crawl of the top 4000 Alexa sites. As many modern sites rely on client-side markup creation and DOM manipulation via JavaScript, we chose a full fledged browser engine as the technical foundation of our crawling infrastructure: We implemented an extension for the Chrome browser, that pulls starting URLs from a backend component, which are subsequently visited by the browser. This way, we not only can examine the same final DOM structure that is also presented to the browser, it also gives us the opportunity to observe client-side actions after a password has been entered (more on this below). Our Chrome extension consists of the following JavaScript components [10]:

- A single *background script*, which is able to monitor network traffic and distribute the crawling process over multiple browser tabs,
- and multiple *content script* instances, one for each Web document that is rendered by the browser. A content script is instantiated as soon as a new document is created by the browser engine. This script has direct access to this document's DOM tree. However, the script's execution context is strictly isolated from the scripts running in the document.
- Thus, the content script injects a *user script* directly into the documents' DOM. Unlike the content script, which is cleanly separated from the document's script environment, the user script runs directly in the same global context as the document's own script content. This in turn grants us the ability to wrap and intercept native JavaScript functions [17], such as `XMLHttpRequest` or getter/setter properties of HTML objects.

Criteria	# Sites	% rel.	% abs.
Password found	2143	100 %	53,6 %
PW on HTTPS page	821	38,31 %	20,5 %
Secure action[1]	1197	55,9 %	29,9 %
Autocomplete off	293	13,6 %	7,3 %
X-Frame-Options	189	8,9 %	4,7 %
JavaScript access	325	15,1 %	8,1 %

[1]: Password form submitted to an HTTPS URL

Table 2: Recorded characteristics of the Alex Top 4K password fields

Using this infrastructure, our extension conducted the following steps:

The homepage URL of the next examination candidate is pulled from the backend and loaded into one of the browsers tabs. After the rendering process has terminated, the DOM tree is traversed to find password fields. However, most sites do not immediately contain the login dialog (if they have one at all) on their homepages. Instead, it is usually contained in a dedicated subpage, linked from the homepage. Hence, in case no password field could be found on the homepage, all hyperlinks on this page are examined, if they contain indicators that the linked subpage leads to the site's login functionality. This is done via a list of indicative keywords, consisting of e.g., "sign in", "login", or "logon". If such a link was found, the browser tab is directed to the corresponding URL and this document is examined for password fields. While this methodology is apparently incomplete, e.g., due to the keyword list only containing terms derived from the English language, turned out to be sufficient to find a representative number of password fields (see Sec. 5.2).

If a password field was found, important characteristics of the document were recorded, including the hosting document's URL, the corresponding HTML form's `action` attribute, as well as the presence of `autocomplete` attributes and `X-Frame-Option` headers.

Furthermore, to observe potential client-side processing after a password has been entered, we instrumented the `get`-property of the password field using JavaScript's `Object.defineProperty` API [22], after the page's rendering process has terminated, but before the page's own scripts executed.

Subsequently, after the page's scripts have been run, the user script simulates user interaction with the password field to potentially activate JavaScripts that access the password value legitimately. More precisely, our script triggers JavaScript events, that would occur if a user clicks into the field, changes its values, and leaves the password field, i.e., moves the focus to a different field. Finally, the script submits the form, in order to activate any JavaScript that is tied to the `onsubmit` event.

5.2.2 *Results*

During our crawl, we could successfully detect a login form on 2,143 of the 4,000 domains. In the following, we will

	Port	Path	sub domain	any name req.	name match	input type match	min form	autocomp.
Chrome 31	Yes	No	Yes	Yes	No	Yes	Yes	No
Internet Expl. 11	Yes	Yes	Yes	No	No	Yes	Yes	Yes
Firefox 25	Yes	No	Yes	No	No	Yes	Yes	Yes
Opera 18	Yes	No	Yes	Yes	No	Yes	Yes	No
Safari 7	Yes	No	Yes	Yes	No	Yes	Yes	Yes
Maxthon 3	No	No	No	No	No	Yes	Yes	No

Table 1: Overview of tested browsers and their matching criteria

outline the analysis of the data we gathered from these fields with respect to different, security-relevant questions.

As discussed in Section 4.1, the use of the `autocomplete` attribute on input fields allows an application to ensure that no data is persisted into the password manager's storage. We therefore investigated how often this was explicitly set to `off`, essentially instructing the browser to neither store login data nor auto-filling these forms. Out of the 2,143 domains we examined, a total of 293 domains prohibited password managers from storing the credentials this way.

In respect to the ClickJacking attack on a password manager that requires user interaction (see Sec 3.3), the applicable remedy is the usage of the HTTP's `X-Frame-Options` response header [26]. By using this header an application can explicitly tell the browser that a page may not be rendered inside a frame. However, this only helps against the discussed attacks if the header is set to `DENY`, since we must assume that the XSS attacker is capable of positioning an iframe containing the login form on a page located in the same application, thus running under the same origin. In our investigation, we found that only 189 domains set the header to `DENY`, while another 173 had set it to the `SAMEORIGIN`, which is useless in the context of the discussed attacks.

Furthermore, to gain insight on the extent of legitimate client-side functionality that uses JavaScript to read password fields, we instrumented the password field, such that we were able to record read access (see above). For a total of 325 password fields, we were able to witness read operations via JavaScript.

Finally, we examined to which degree the sites were potentially susceptible to network attackers. To do so, we checked how many forms containing password fields are delivered via plain HTTP rather than HTTPS. In the attacks scenario described by Gonzalez et al. [9], enabling HTTPS effectively blocks their attacker. In our study, we found that only 821 domains utilize HTTPS when transmitting the password field itself. The remaining 1,289 domains are hence susceptible to the network-based attacker who directly inserts JavaScript into the server's response to retrieve the password data from the victim.

Additionally, a network-based attacker may also retrieve passwords from users once they log in to an application if the credentials are sent to the server using HTTP and not HTTPS. Investigating how many applications send out secret login data in an unencrypted manner, we found that in total, 1197 sites used HTTPS to send the password data to the server, leaving 946 sites with unencrypted communication.

5.3 Assessment

As shown in Section 5.1, most browsers only store the origin of a password and not the complete URL of the form it was initially stored from. Thus, placing a form on an arbitrary page with the same origin as the login form is sufficient to extract credentials from the victim.

The Cross-Site Scripting attacker, which we discussed in the previous sections, is capable of injecting his malicious payload into applications that are delivered via HTTP as well as over HTTPS. Thus, the only line of defense in this case is the `autocomplete` feature. As discussed earlier, this is only used in 293 login pages, thus resulting in a total number of 1,850 out of 2,143 domains which are potentially vulnerable to password stealing by an XSS attacker. This amounts to a total of 86.3% of analyzed pages which are susceptible to the attack scenario we outlined. Apart from Microsoft's Internet Explorer, the built-in password managers of all browsers we examined automatically filled out forms presented to them and would also behave in the same manner if the login page was put into a frame. In order to successfully conduct an attack on Internet Explorer, the attacker would have to have found a vulnerability on the exact login page and would also have to rely on the victim actively selecting the credentials to insert.

The network-based attacker, who is only capable of injecting his malicious payload into login pages which are not served using HTTPS, can only successfully attack 1,029 different domains, summing up to 48% of all applications we analyzed.

These observations lead us to the conclusion that the current implementation of browsers' password managers is highly vulnerable with respect to password stealing – both by a network and a XSS attacker. Also, the server-side measures we discussed in Section 4.1 are not employed in prevailing web applications in a satisfactory manner. Therefore, in the following section, we will discuss a new approach to the concept and implementation of a password manager capable of tackling these issues.

6. CLIENT-SIDE PROTECTION

Our analysis has shown that popular browsers implement password managers in a way that is susceptible to Cross-Site Scripting attacks. We have shown that most of the browsers neither save information on the URL the password was initially stored for nor do they require user interaction to fill out forms. This allows the attacker to retrieve passwords in the presence of an XSS vulnerability. In the following, we propose a simple yet effective solution to counter these types of attacks on password managers.

6.1 Concept

The common enabling factor of the documented attack types (see Sec. 3) is the fact that the secret data is directly inserted into the forms when the page is loaded, and can subsequently be retrieved by JavaScript.

The underlying problem is that concept and implementation of password managers are not aligned. Abstracting what a password manager's task is, we see that it should aid users in the login process to Web applications. This process can be seen as the credentials being sent to the login page. The implementation of that paradigm however aims at filling out forms before the actual, clear-text login data is required. A XSS attacker aims specifically at this conceptual flaw, extracting the credentials from the auto-filled form. In our notion, a password manager should ensure that only once the login data is sent to the server, the plain-text password is contained in the request. Hence, in the following, the propose an enhanced password manager which tackles this conceptual flaw.

Our proposal is that a password manager should only insert placeholding nonces into a form. Once the user then submits the form towards the application, the password manager replaces the nonce with the original, clear-text password. Thus, if an attacker can extract the content of this form utilizing a XSS vulnerability, he is nevertheless unable to retrieve the real password of the targeted user.

Furthermore, our mechanism requires strict matching of the password field `name` attribute and the corresponding POST value. For better understanding of the rationale behind this, consider the following scenario: The attacker is able to inject a new field called `query` into the form. Once the password manager has filled in the placeholder into the `password` field, the attacker's code copies the value of that field into the newly added `query` field. He then changes the action of the form to the application's search functionality. If the password manager now replaced all occurrences of the placeholder in the request, the `query` parameter would also contain the clear-text password. Under the assumption that a search page will in some manner reflect the search term back to the user, the attacker could then extract the password from this response. Therefore, making sure that the password manager only exchanges the correct field is essential.

6.2 Implementation

To investigate the soundness of our proposal, we implemented a proof-of-concept password manager. Since completely changing the implementation of one of the built-in password managers in the modern browsers would have been to complex, we opted to instead build an extension for Firefox. The extension is built upon the original, built-in password manager which is used to only store the placeholder values. The clear-text passwords in turn are stored in a separate storage located inside the extension. For our prototype, we did not implement any form of encryption for these values, since securely storing the passwords inside the browser is out of scope for this work.

Figure 2 shows how our approach works when a new username and password combination is saved. First, the user is prompted to have the login manager remember the recently sent password. In the second step, once the user has agreed to do so, the login manager stores the username and password combination. Firefox provides all plugins with a means of being notified when credentials are stored in the password manager [20]. The notification message contains – along with the recently stored username and password – the origin of the site the password was posted to as well as the names for both the username and password field in the submitted form. Our extension saves all this information in its own storage and replaces the password in the built-

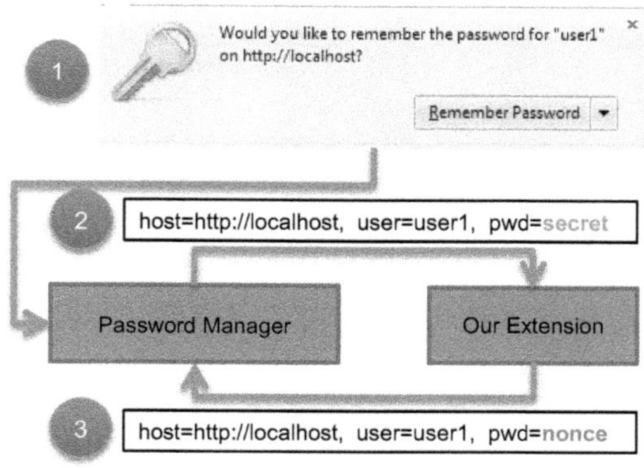

Figure 2: Initial login and credential storing

in storage with a random placeholder value (nonce). This placeholder value is subsequently also stored inside the extension's database alongside the previously persisted data to ensure that the matching credentials can be extracted later on.

Figure 3 outlines how the placeholder is later restored in a normal login. When opening the login page, the built-in password manager inserts the username and the placeholder into the form. Similar to the internal password manager, the extension is notified of a password form being submitted. [6] Subsequently, the next outgoing POST request is scanned by our extension for the easily discernible placeholder value. If the nonce is found, the extension searches its own database for the corresponding entry. Next, the entry's origin is checked against the origin of the page the data is being sent to. If the origins match, the placeholder is replaced with the actual passwords adhering to the aforementioned constraint that only the password field (whose name is stored in the extension's data storage) should be changed. On the lower half of the figure, this is shown. Although the nonce is contained in the HTTP request, it is not replaced with the actual secret data since the name of the POST parameter does not match. Thus, the attacker cannot utilize the search functionality to extract the secret password data from our password manager.

We also evaluated the option of exchanging GET parameters in a request. In our empirical study we found that none of the sites use a form in combination with a GET request. An attacker could however easily exchange the method of a form from POST to GET. If our proposed password manager would then exchange the nonce with the secret password, the adversary could easily read the complete URL of the newly loaded page and thus retrieve the password. Therefore, we explicitly disable the replacement of our nonces in GET parameters and only exchange them for the real credentials in POST requests.

6.3 Evaluation

In this section, we discuss both the security and the functional evaluation of our approach, showing that it adds security while not causing incompatibility with existing applications.

6.3.1 Security Evaluation

After the password value has initially been stored by the password manager, it is never again inserted into Web docu-

Figure 3: Replacement of login credentials by our enhanced password manager

ments. Hence, it is kept out of reach of potentially malicious JavaScript.

Furthermore, our implementation enforces strict matching constraints, before the replacement process executes: Only password nonces for which the combination of *target origin* and *password parameter name* matches the recorded values are substituted with the actual password value in the outgoing request. This requirement effectively thwarts attack attempts in which the adversary tries to leak the password via tampering with the password field's form element in the timespan between the autofill process and the form submission. Thus, our proposed implementation of a secure password manager effectively hinders an attacker who utilizes XSS attacks against his victim.

However, the attacker model discussed by Gonzalez et al. [9] – positioned at the network layer – could still be successful if password data is transmitted in clear-text to the server. In our study of the Alexa Top 4000 sites, we found that 44,1% of the examined sites utilize HTTP instead of HTTPS to transmit the credentials to the server. In these cases, the network-based attacker could wait for the form to be submitted and subsequently retrieve the secret login data from the traffic capture. Nevertheless, this kind of attack does not specifically target password managers and can therefore not be fully prevented by a secure password manager in any case.

6.3.2 *Functional Evaluation*

From the user's point of view, nothing changes compared to the behavior of the current generation of deployed password managers: After page load, the password field is automatically filled with characters, which are presented to the user with masquerading asterisks. After form submit, the browser exchanges the password nonce with the actual values, before it is sent to the server.

Our approach aims at only putting the real password of a user in the outgoing request to the server and not into the password field. This however leads to potential problems with Web applications that do some transformation on the original field's value before submitting it. For instance, an application might derive the hash sum of the user-provided password on the client-side before submitting it.

In the evaluation of the top 4000 Alexa sites, we detected 325 JavaScript accesses to password data (see Sec. 5.2). We then manually analyzed the snippets responsible for these accesses and detected that a total 96 domains used client-side functionality such as XmlHttpRequests to transmit the password data to the server. Out of these 96 cases, 24 pages transformed the provided password before forwarding it to the server, whereas 23 employed hashing functions like MD5 and SHA1 and the remaining case encoded the password as Base64. Of the remaining 72 pages that did not post the form directly to server, only 6 pages employed HTTP GET requests to transmit the credentials, whereas the rest used HTTP POST in their XmlHttpRequests. Our proposed approach would obviously not work in these 30 cases, since our extension neither exchanges passwords directly in the input field nor does it modify HTTP GET requests. However, the current implementations of the password managers do not support storing passwords that are not sent via submitting HTML forms – thus our approach is in no way inferior to the currently deployed concepts [6]. Also, if the built-in password manager stored these credentials, there is no way of detecting whether access to a given password field is done by the legitimate page or is a Cross-Site Scripting attack. Hence, we deliberately fail in the aforementioned scenario by not replacing the nonce in the input field with the real password. Therefore, our approach is secure by default and can also not be undermined by an unknowing user.

The purpose of the remaining 229 scripts was verify was that certain criteria had been met in filling the user and password field, e.g. the username being an e-mail address or the password consisting of at least a certain amount of chars.

7. RELATED WORK

Most research in the area of password managers focussed mainly on three different aspects: generating pseudo-random and unique passwords for each single Web application based one some master secret [11, 25, 4], storing passwords in a secure manner [31, 3, 14, 8] and protecting users from phishing attacks [29, 30].

The problem of weak password manager implementations with respect to their vulnerability towards Cross-Site Scripting attacks has been discussed by browser vendors since 2006 [23]. However, researchers did not re-evaluate possibilities in terms of adopting new concepts to protect users from these kinds of attacks. In a recent blog post, Ben Toews again brought up the issue of password managers that were prone to XSS attacks [28]. However, the question on how to improve the security of password managers remained unanswered.

Furthermore, in 2013, Gonzalez et al. [9] discovered a related attack. They described a network-based attacker that can inject code of his own choosing into any unencrypted HTTP connection. To leverage this, they injected multiple invisible frames into pages loaded by the victim and iterated through the login pages of different domains. They automated their attack using a self-developed tool called Lupin and were able to extract 1000 passwords in 35 seconds from a victim's machine. They propose a first set of countermeasures, which are either in line with the mitigation strategies covered in Sec. 4, and thus, share the same drawbacks, or are targeted at strict network layer security, which is not applicable to our XSS attacker.

8. CONCLUSION

In this paper, we have demonstrated that current implementations of built-in password managers in browsers are vulnerable to XSS attacks targeting the stored passwords. We have identified the root cause of these problems, namely the fact that password managers automatically fill out password fields with the clear-text password which are subsequently accessibly by client-side code.

Our approach thwarts this class of attacks through keeping the actual password value out of the reach of potentially malicious JavaScript. It works by filling the password fields with placeholder values which are only replaced later, once the request is sent to the server. For robust protection, our prototype enforces strict integrity constraint in respect to the password form's context and only exchanges the placeholder for the credentials if the origins and names of both login URL and saved password match.

Our solution robustly protects auto-saved passwords from XSS-based theft attempts, and, in the majority of the examined cases, mitigates related, network-level attacks uncovered by Gonzalez et al [9], while maintaining a high degree of compatibility with the currently established behavior of password managers and real-world practices in handling password fields.

Acknowledgements

The authors would like to thank Eric Schmall and Armin Stock for their work pertaining to the implementational parts of this work as well as the anonymous reviewers for their helpful comments. Martin Johns' work was partially funded by the EU projects WebSand (FP7-256964, `http://websand.eu`) and STREWS (FP7-318097, `http://strews.eu`). The support is gratefully acknowledged.

9. REFERENCES

[1] Alexa Internet, Inc. Alexa Top 500 Global Sites. Website, `http://www.alexa.com/`, accessed in March 2010.

[2] Barth, A. The web origin concept, November 2009.

[3] Bojinov, H., Bursztein, E., Boyen, X., and Boneh, D. Kamouflage: Loss-resistant password management. In *Computer Security–ESORICS 2010*. Springer, 2010, pp. 286–302.

[4] Chiasson, S., van Oorschot, P. C., and Biddle, R. A usability study and critique of two password managers. In *15th USENIX Security Symposium* (2006), pp. 1–16.

[5] Dierks, T., and Allen, C. The TLS Protocol Version 1.0. RFC 2246, `http://www.ietf.org/rfc/rfc2246.txt`, January 1999.

[6] Dolske, J. On firefox's password manager. [online] `https://blog.mozilla.org/dolske/2013/08/20/on-firefoxs-password-manager/`, August 2013.

[7] Franks, J., Hallam-Baker, P., Hostetler, J., Lawrence, S., Leach, P., Luotonen, A., and Stewart, L. HTTP Authentication: Basic and Digest Access Authentication. RFC 2617, `http://www.ietf.org/rfc/rfc2617.txt`, June 1999.

[8] Gasti, P., and Rasmussen, K. B. On the security of password manager database formats. In *Computer Security–ESORICS 2012*. Springer, 2012, pp. 770–787.

[9] Gonzalez, R., Chen, E. Y., and Jackson, C. Automated password extraction attack on modern password managers. *arXiv preprint arXiv:1309.1416* (2013).

[10] Google Developers. Chrome Extensions - Developer's Guide. [online], `http://developer.chrome.com/extensions/devguide.html`, last access 06/05/13, 2012.

[11] Halderman, J. A., Waters, B., and Felten, E. W. A convenient method for securely managing passwords. In *Proceedings of the 14th international conference on World Wide Web* (2005), ACM, pp. 471–479.

[12] Hickson, I. Web forms 2.0, Apri 2005.

[13] Ives, B., Walsh, K. R., and Schneider, H. The domino effect of password reuse. *Communications of the ACM 47*, 4 (2004), 75–78.

[14] Karole, A., Saxena, N., and Christin, N. A comparative usability evaluation of traditional password managers. In *Information Security and Cryptology-ICISC 2010*. Springer, 2011, pp. 233–251.

[15] Klein, A. Dom based cross site scripting or xss of the third kind. *Web Application Security Consortium, Articles 4* (2005).

[16] Lekies, S., Stock, B., and Johns, M. 25 million flows later: large-scale detection of dom-based xss. In *Proceedings of the 2013 ACM SIGSAC conference on Computer & communications security* (2013), ACM, pp. 1193–1204.

[17] Magazinius, J., Phung, P. H., and Sands, D. Safe wrappers and sane policies for self protecting JavaScript. In *The 15th Nordic Conference in Secure IT Systems* (October 2010), T. Aura, Ed., LNCS, Springer Verlag. (Selected papers from AppSec 2010).

[18] Mazurek, M. L., Komanduri, S., Vidas, T., Bauer, L., Christin, N., Cranor, L. F., Kelley, P. G., Shay, R., and Ur, B. Measuring password guessability for an entire university. In *Proceedings of the 2013 ACM SIGSAC conference on Computer & communications security* (2013), ACM, pp. 173–186.

[19] Microsoft. Ie8 security part vii: Clickjacking defenses, 2009.

[20] Mozilla. *Firefox Add-On SDK - Passwords.*

[21] Mozilla Developer Network. How to Turn Off Form Autocompletion. [online], `https://developer.mozilla.org/en-US/docs/Mozilla/How_to_Turn_Off_Form_Autocompletion`, May 2013.

[22] Mozilla Developer Network. Object.defineProperty(). [online], `https://developer.mozilla.org/en-US/docs/Web/JavaScript/Reference/Global_Objects/Object/defineProperty`, November 2013.

[23] O'Shannessy, P. Bug 359675 - provide an option to manually fill forms and log in.

[24] OWASP. Cross-site scripting (xss), September 2013.

[25] Ross, B., Jackson, C., Miyake, N., Boneh, D., and Mitchell, J. C. Stronger password

authentication using browser extensions. In *Proceedings of the 14th Usenix Security Symposium* (2005), vol. 1998.

[26] Rydstedt, G., Bursztein, E., Boneh, D., and Jackson, C. Busting Frame Busting: a Study of Clickjacking Vulnerabilities on Popular Sites. In *Web 2.0 Security and Privacy (W2SP 2010)* (2010).

[27] Security, W. Website security statistics report, May 2013.

[28] Toews, B. Abusing password managers with xss. online, 04 2012.

[29] Wu, M., Miller, R. C., and Little, G. Web wallet: preventing phishing attacks by revealing user intentions. In *Proceedings of the second symposium on Usable privacy and security* (2006), ACM, pp. 102–113.

[30] Ye, Z. E., Smith, S., and Anthony, D. Trusted paths for browsers. *ACM Transactions on Information and System Security (TISSEC) 8*, 2 (2005), 153–186.

[31] Zhao, R., and Yue, C. All your browser-saved passwords could belong to us: A security analysis and a cloud-based new design. In *Proceedings of the third ACM conference on Data and application security and privacy* (2013), ACM, pp. 333–340.

A Three-Way Investigation of a Game-CAPTCHA: Automated Attacks, Relay Attacks and Usability

Manar Mohamed[1] Niharika Sachdeva[2*] Michael Georgescu[1] Song Gao[1]
Nitesh Saxena[1†] Chengcui Zhang[1] Ponnurangam Kumaraguru[2]
Paul C. van Oorschot[3] Wei-Bang Chen[4]

[1] Computer and Information Sciences, University of Alabama at Birmingham, USA
[2] Indraprastha Institute of Information Technology, India
[3] Computer Science, Carleton University, Canada
[4] Math and Computer Science, Virginia State University, USA

ABSTRACT

Existing captcha solutions on the Internet are a major source of user frustration. Game captchas are an interesting and, to date, little-studied approach claiming to make captcha solving a fun activity for the users. One broad form of such captchas – called *Dynamic Cognitive Game (DCG) captchas* – challenge the user to perform a game-like cognitive task interacting with a series of dynamic images. We pursue a comprehensive analysis of a representative category of DCG captchas. We formalize, design and implement such captchas, and dissect them across: (1) fully automated attacks, (2) human-solver relay attacks, and (3) usability. Our results suggest that the studied DCG captchas exhibit high usability and, unlike other known captchas, offer some resistance to relay attacks, but they are also vulnerable to our novel dictionary-based automated attack.

1. INTRODUCTION

The abuse of the resources of online services using automated means, such as denial-of-service or password dictionary attacks, is a common security problem. To prevent such abuse, a primary defense mechanism is CAPTCHA [2] (denoted "captcha"), a tool aimed to distinguish a human user from a computer based on a task that is easier for the former but much harder for the latter.

The most commonly encountered captchas today take the form of a garbled string of words or characters, but many other variants have also been proposed (we refer the reader to [30], [7], [17] which provide excellent review of different captcha categories). Unfortunately, existing captchas suffer from several problems. *First*, successful automated attacks have been developed against many existing schemes. For example, algorithms have been designed that can achieve character segmentation with a 90% success rate [18]. Real world attacks have also been launched against captchas employed by Internet giants [15, 19, 27].

*Part of the work done while visiting UAB

†Contact author: saxena@cis.uab.edu

ASIA CCS'14, June 4–6, 2014, Kyoto, Japan.

http://dx.doi.org/10.1145/2590296.2590298.

Second, low-cost attacks have been conceived whereby challenges are relayed to, and solved by, users on different web sites or paid human-solvers in the crowd [10, 13, 16]. In fact, it has been shown that [23] such relay attacks are much more viable in practice than automated attacks due to their simplicity and low economical costs.

Third, the same distortions that are used to hide the underlying content of a captcha puzzle from computers can also severely degrade human usability [9, 31]. More alarmingly, such usability degradation can be so severe on many occasions that users get frustrated and give up using the services that deploy captchas. Consequently, companies lose customers and suffer economic losses [25].

Given these problems, there is an urgent need to consider alternatives that place the *human user at the center of the captcha design*. *Game captchas* offer a promising approach by attempting to make captcha solving a fun activity for the users. These are challenges that are built using games that might be enjoyable and easy to play for humans, but hard for computers.

In this paper, we focus on a broad form of game captchas, called *Dynamic Cognitive Game (DCG)* captchas. This captcha challenges a user to perform a *game*-like *cognitive* task interacting with a series of *dynamic* images. Specifically, we consider a representative DCG captcha category which involves objects floating around within the images, and the user's task is to match the objects with their respective target(s) and drag/drop them to the target location(s). A startup called "are you a human" [4, 26] has recently been offering such DCG captchas.

Besides promising to significantly improve user experience, DCG captchas are an appealing platform for touch screen enabled mobile devices (such as smartphones). Traditional captchas are known to be quite difficult on such devices due to their small displays and key/touch pads, while touch screen games are much easier and already popular. Motivated by these unique and compelling advantages of DCG captchas, we set out to investigate their security and usability. Specifically, we pursue a comprehensive study of DCG captchas, analyzing them from three broad yet intersecting dimensions: (1) *usability*, (2) *fully automated attacks*, and (3) *human-solver relay attacks*. Our main contributions are as follows:

1. We formalize, design and implement four instances of a representative category of DCG captchas. *(Sections 2 and 3)*
2. We conduct a usability study of these instances, evaluating them in terms of time-to-completion, error rates and perceived usability. Our results indicate the overall usability to be very good. *(Section 4)*
3. We develop a novel, fully automated framework to attack these DCG captcha instances based on image processing techniques and principles of unsupervised learning. The attack is compu-

tationally efficient and highly accurate, but requires building a dictionary to be effective. (*Section 5*)

4. We explore different variants of human-solver relay attacks against DCG captchas. Specifically, we show that the most simplistic form of relay attack (in line with traditional captcha relay attack) reduces to a *reaction time task* for the solver, and conduct a user study to evaluate the performance of this attack. In general, our results indicate that DCG captchas with mobile answer objects offer some level of resistance to relay attacks, differentiating them from other captchas. Our user study may also be of independent interest in other human-centered computing domains. (*Section 6*)

2. BACKGROUND

We use the term Dynamic Cognitive Game (DCG) captcha to define the broad captcha schemes that form the focus of our work. We characterize a DCG captcha as having the following features: (1) *dynamic* because it involves objects moving around in image frames; (2) either *cognitive* because it is a form of a puzzle that relates to the semantics of the images or *image recognition* because it involves visual recognition; and (3) a *game* because it aims to make captcha solving task a fun activity for the user. In this section, we discuss the security model and design choices for DCG captcha, and present the DCG captcha category and associated instances studied in this paper.

2.1 Security Model and Design Choices

The DCG captcha design objective is the same as that of captcha: a bot (automated computer program) must only be able to solve captcha challenges with no better than a negligible probability (but a human should be able to solve with a sufficiently high probability).[1]

A pre-requisite for the security of a DCG captcha implementation (or any captcha for that matter) is that the responses to the challenge must not be provided to the client machine in clear text. For example, in a character recognition captcha, the characters embedded within the images should not be leaked out to the client. To avoid such leakage in the context of DCG captchas, it is important to provide a suitable underlying game platform for run-time support of the implemented captcha. Web-based games are commonly developed using Flash and HTML5 in conjunction with JavaScript. However, both these platforms operate by downloading the game code to the client machine and executing it locally. Thus, if these game platforms were directly used to implement DCG captchas, the client machine will know the correct objects and the positions of their corresponding target region(s), which can be used by the bot to construct the responses to the server challenges relatively easily. This will undermine the security of DCG captchas.

The above problem can be addressed by employing encryption and obfuscation of the game code which will make it difficult for the attacker (bot) on the client machine to extract the game code and thus the correct responses. Commercial tools, such as SWF Encrypt [3], exist which can be used to achieve this functionality. This approach works under a security model in which it is assumed that the bot does not have the capability to learn the keys used to decrypt the code and to deobfuscate the code. A similar model where the attacker has only partial control over the client machine has also been employed in prior work [28].

In our model, we assume that the implementation provides continuous feedback to the user as to whether the objects dragged and dropped to specific target region(s) correspond to correct answers or not. The server also indicates when the game successfully finishes, or times out. This feedback mechanism is essential from the usability perspective otherwise the users may get confused during the solving process. The attacker is free to utilize all of this feedback in attempting to solve the challenges, but within the time-out. We also assume that it is possible for the server to preclude brute force attacks, such as when the attacker tries to drag and drop the regions within the image exhaustively/repeatedly so as to complete the game successfully. Such a detection is possible by simply capping the number of drag/drop attempts per moving object.[2]

In addition to automated attacks, the security model for DCG captchas (and any other captcha) must also consider human-solver relay attacks [10, 23]. In fact, it has been shown that such relay attacks are much more appealing to the attackers than automated attacks currently due to their simplicity and low cost [23]. In a relay attack, the bot forwards the captcha challenges to a human user elsewhere on the Internet (either a payed solver or an unsuspecting user accessing a web-site [14]); the user solves the challenges and sends the responses back to the bot; and the bot simply relays these responses to the server. Unfortunately, most, if not all, existing captcha solutions are insecure under such a relay attack model. For example, character recognition captchas are routinely broken via such relay attacks [23]. For DCG captchas to offer better security than existing captchas, they should provide some resistance to such human-solver relay attacks (this is indeed the case as we demonstrate in Section 6).

2.2 Game Instances and Parameters

Many forms of DCG captchas are possible. For example, they may be based on visual matching or semantic matching of objects, may consist of multiple target objects or none at all, and may involve static or moving targets. In this paper, we focus on one representative category, and four associated instances, of DCG captcha with static target(s) (see Figure 1). Specifically, our studied DCG captcha instances involve:

1. *single target object*, such as place the ship in the sea (the Ships game).
2. *two target objects*, such as match the shapes (the Shapes game).
3. *three target objects*, such as feed the animals (the Animals game).
4. *no target objects*, such as park the boat (the Parking game), where the target area does not consist of any objects.

The Shapes game is based on visual matching whereas the other games involve semantic matching.

For each of these 4 instances, different parameterizations affect security and usability. These include: (1) the number of foreground moving objects, including answer objects and other "noisy" objects; and (2) the speed with which the objects move. The larger the number of objects and higher the speed, the more difficult and time consuming it might be for the human user to identify the objects and drag/drop them, which may degrade usability. However, increasing the number and speed of objects may also make it harder for a computer program to play the games successfully, which may improve security. Thus, for our analysis of the DCG captcha, we will evaluate the effect of these parameters for captcha usability and captcha security (against automated as well as relay attacks).

[1]For example, target thresholds might limit bot success rates below 0.6% [32], and human user success rates above 90% [11].

[2]The "are you a human" DCG captcha implementation claims to adopt a sophisticated (proprietary) mechanism, based on mouse events, to differentiate human game playing activity from an automated activity. We did not implement such a human-vs-bot behavioral analysis component because our paper's goal is to examine the underlying captcha scheme only. A behavioral component can be added to other captchas also and represents a topic orthogonal to our work. Besides, it is not clear if behavioral analysis would add security; it may instead degrade usability by increasing false negatives.

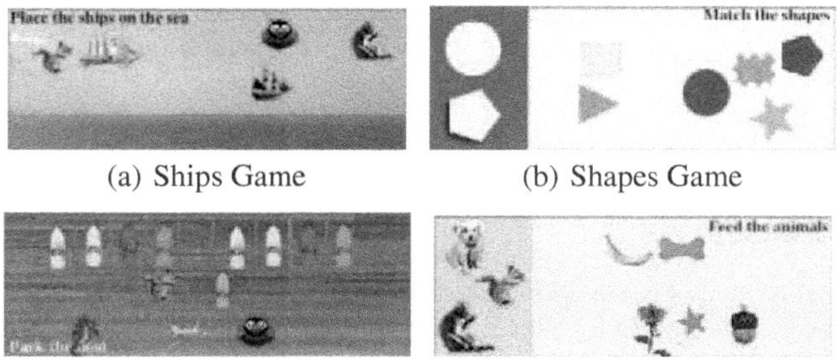

(a) Ships Game (b) Shapes Game

(c) Parking Game (d) Animals Game

Figure 1: Static snapshots of 4 game instances of a representative DCG captcha analyzed in this paper (targets are static; objects are mobile)

3. DESIGN AND IMPLEMENTATION

Due to legal considerations, we did not resort to directly evaluate an existing DCG captcha implementation (e.g., "are you a human" DCG captchas). In particular, developing automated attacks against these captchas directly violates the company's asserted terms and conditions [5]. Instead, we designed and implemented our own equivalent and generalized versions of DCG captchas from scratch, and analyzed these versions. Developing our own versions also allowed us to freely vary the game parameters, such as the number and speed of objects, and investigate the DCG captcha security and usability with respect to these parameters.[3]

We created four instances of games as specified in Section 2.2 using Adobe Flash.

The game image/frame size is 360 x 130 pixels, which can easily fit onto a web page such as in a web form. Each game starts by placing the objects in certain pre-specified locations on the image. Then, each object picks a random direction in which it will move. A total of 8 directions were used, namely, N, S, E, W, NE, NW, SE and SW. If the chosen direction is one of E, W, S, or N, the object will move (across X or Y axis) by 1 pixel per frame in that direction. Otherwise, the object will move $\sqrt{2} = 1.414$ pixels per frame along the hypotenuse, corresponding to 1 pixel across both X and Y axes. This means that on an average the object moves 1.207 $[= (1 * 4 + 1.414 * 4)/8]$ pixels per frame. The object continues in the current direction until colliding with another object or the game border, whereupon it moves in a new random direction.

The game starts when the user presses a "Start" button on the screen center. Each game briefly explains to users their task, e.g., "Place the ships on the sea." The game ends when the user clicks/drags all the correct objects onto their corresponding target(s), in which case a "Game Complete" message is provided. To successfully match an object with its target, the user clicks inside the bounding box across the shape of the object, drags the object and drops it by releasing it inside the bounding box across the respective target. The game must be successfully completed within a fixed time (we allow 60s); the user gets feedback on the correctness of every drag-drop, by a star on success and a cross on failure (Figure 6, Appendix A).

For each of the 4 games, we set 5 parameterizations, choosing object speed (low, medium, high) as (10, 20, 40) frames per second (FPS), and number of moving objects as (4, 5, 6). (These frame rates translate into average object speeds of 12.07, 24.14 and 48.28 pixels/second, resp., given the objects move 1.207 pixels/frame.) For each game, we used 5 combinations of speed and number of objects: (10 FPS, 4 objects); (20 FPS, 4 objects); (20 FPS, 5 objects); (20 FPS, 6 objects); and (40 FPS, 4 objects). This resulted in a total of 20 games in our corpus.

[3]Although our implementation and analyses does not directly involve the "are you a human" captchas, it is generalized enough for our results to be applicable to these captchas also (i.e., the ones that fall under the categories evaluated in our work).

4. USABILITY

In this section, we report on a usability study of our representative DCG captcha category.

4.1 Study Design, Goals, and Process

Our study involved **40 participants** who were primarily students from various backgrounds. (For demographics, see Appendix A, Table 9). The study was *web-based* and comprised of three phases. The *pre-study phase* involved registering and briefly explaining the participants about the protocols of the study. In particular, the participants were shown "consent information," which they had to agree before proceeding with the study. This was followed by collecting participant demographics and then the participants playing the different DCG captcha games. This *actual study phase* attempted to mimic a realistic captcha scenario which typically involves filling out a form followed by solving captcha. To avoid explicit priming, however, we did not mention that the study is about captcha or security, but rather indicated that it is about assessing the usability of a web interface. In the *post-study phase*, participants answered questions about their experience with the tested DCG captchas. This comprised the standard SUS (Simple Usability Scale) questions [8], a standard 10-item 5-point Likert scale ('1' represents "Strong disagreement" and '5' represents "Strong agreement"). SUS polls satisfaction with respect to computer systems [6], in order to assess their usability. Additionally, we asked several other questions related to the games' usability.

In the actual study phase, each participant played 20 instances as discussed in Section 3, aimed at understanding how different parameterizations impact users' solving capabilities. The order of games presented to different participants involved a standard 20x20 Latin Square design to counter-balance learning effects. Via our study, our goal was to assess the following aspects of the DCG captchas:

1. *Efficiency*: time taken to complete each game.
2. *Robustness*: likelihood of not completing the game, and of incorrect drag and drop attempts.
3. *Effect of Game Parameters*: the effect of the object speed and number on completion time and error rates.
4. *User Experience*: participants' SUS ratings and qualitative feedback about their experience with the games.

For each tested game, completion times, and errors were automatically logged by our web-interface software.

4.2 Study Results

We now provide the results from our usability study, including time to completion and error rates, as well as perceived qualitative aspects of the methods based on user ratings.

Completion Time: Table 1 shows the completion time per game type. Clearly, all games turned out to be quite fast, lasting for less than 10s on an average. Users took longest to solve the Animals game with an average time of 9.10s, whereas the other games took almost half of this time. This might have been due to increased semantic load on the users in the Animals game to identify three target objects and then match them with the corresponding answer objects. Moreover, we noticed a decrease in the solving time (equal to 3.84s) when the target objects were decreased to 2 (i.e., in the Shapes game), and this time was comparable to games which had 1 target object in the challenge (Ships and Parking). A one-way repeated-measures ANOVA test showed significant difference (at 95% confidence) in the mean timings of all 4 types of games ($p < 0.0001$, $F = 79.98$). Aalyzing further using pairwise paired t-tests with Bonferroni correction, we found significant difference between the mean times of following pairs: Animals and Parking ($p < 0.001$), Ships and Shapes ($p < 0.0005$), Animals and Ships ($p < 0.001$), Animals and Shapes ($p < 0.001$), and Parking and Shapes ($p = 0.0024$).

Table 1: Error rates per click and completion time per game type

Game Type	Completion Time (s) *mean (std dev)*	Error Rate Per Click *mean*
Ships	4.51 (1.00)	0.04
Animals	9.10 (0.96)	0.05
Parking	4.37 (0.90)	0.09
Shapes	5.26 (0.59)	0.03

Error Rates: An important result is that all the tested games yielded 100% accuracy (*overall error rate of 0%*). In other words, none of the participant failed to complete any of the games within the time out. This suggests our DCG captchas instances are quite robust to human errors.

Next, we calculated the likelihood of incorrect drag and drop attempts (*error rate per click*). For example, in the Animals game, an incorrect attempt would be to feed the monkey with a flower instead of a banana. We define the error rate per click as the number of incorrect objects (from the pool of all foreground objects) dragged to the target area *divided by* the total number of objects dragged and dropped. The results are depicted in Table 1. We observe that the Shape game yields the smallest average per click error rate of 3%. This suggests that the visual matching task (as in the Shapes game) is less error prone compared to the semantic matching task (as in the other games). The game challenge which seemed most difficult for participants was the Parking game (average per click error rate 9%). Since objects in this game are relatively small, participants may have had some difficulty to identify them.

Effect of Object Speed and Number: Table 2 shows the performance of the game captchas in terms of per click error rates and completion time as per different object speeds. We can see that the maximum number of per click errors were committed at 10 FPS speed. Looking at the average timings, we find that it took longest to complete the games when the objects move at the fastest speed of 40 FPS, while 20 FPS yielded fastest completion time followed by 10 FPS. ANOVA test revealed statistical difference among the mean completion time corresponding to three speeds ($p = 0.0045$, $F = 5.65$). Further analyzing using the t-test with Bonferroni correction, we found statistical difference between the mean timing corresponding to the following pair of speeds only: 10 FPS and 20 FPS ($p = 0.0001$).

Table 2: Error rates per click and completion time per object speeds

Object Speed	Completion Time (s) *mean (std dev)*	Error Rate Per Click *mean*
10 FPS	5.74 (2.11)	0.06
20 FPS	4.90 (2.22)	0.05
40 FPS	6.53 (2.87)	0.04

Another aspect of the usability analysis included testing the effect of increase in the number of objects (including noisy answer objects) on the overall game performance. Table 3 summarizes the per click error rates and completion time against different number of objects. Here, we can see a clear pattern of increase, albeit very minor, in average completion time and average rate with increase in the number of objects. This is intuitive because increasing the number of objects increases the cognitive load on the users which may slow down the game play and introduce chances of errors. ANOVA test did not indicate this difference to be significant, however.

User Experience: Now, we analyze the data collected from the participants during the post-study phase. The average SUS score came out to be 73.88 (standard deviation = 6.94). Considering that the average SUS scores for user-friendly industrial software tends to hover in the 60–70 range [21], the usability of our DCG game captcha instances can be rated as high.

Table 3: Error rates per click & completion time per # of objects

# of Objects	Completion Time (s) *mean (std dev)*	Error Rate Per Click *mean*
6	6.58 (1.69)	0.06
5	5.30 (2.28)	0.05
4	4.90 (2.22)	0.04

In addition to SUS, we asked the participants a few 5-point Likert scale questions about the usability of the games ('1' means "Strong Disagreement"). Specifically, we asked if the games were "visually attractive" and "pleasurable," and whether they would like to use them in "practice." Table 4, shows the corresponding average Likert scores. We found that 47% percent participants felt that the games were visually attractive and 45% said that it was pleasurable to play the games. These numbers indicate the promising usability exhibited by the games. We further inquired users if they noticed change in speed or number of objects in the games. 27.5% noticed no change (increase and/or decrease) in speed of objects, whereas only 22.5% noticed no change in number of objects (see Table 5). Thus, the change in the number of objects and speed (within the limits we tested) was noticeable by a large fraction of participants.

Table 4: User feedback on game attributes

Attribute	Likert Score *mean (std dev)*
Visually Attractive	3.18 (0.94)
Pleasurable	3.33 (0.96)

Table 5: % of users noticing change in speed and number of objects

Object Speed	(%)
Moved faster	30
Moved slower	5
No change	27.5
Both slower and faster	37.5
Number of objects	(%)
Increased	47.5
Decreased	2.5
No change	22.5
Both increase and decrease	27.5

Summary of Usability Analysis: Our results suggest that the DCG captcha representatives tested in this work offer very good usability, resulting in short completion times (less than 10s), very low error rates (0% per game completion, and less than 10% per drag and drop attempt),[4] and good user ratings. We found that increasing the object speed and number is likely to degrade the game performance, but up to 6 objects and up to 40 FPS speed yield a good level of usability. Although our study was conducted with a relatively young participant pool, given the simplcity of the games (involving easy matching and clicking tasks), the game performance would generally be in line with these results, as shown by our parallel study with Mechanical Turk participants [22].

5. AUTOMATED ATTACKS

Having validated, via our usability study, that it is quite easy for the human users to play our DCG captcha instances, we next proceeded to determine how difficult these games might be for the computer programs. In this section, we present and evaluate the performance of a fully automated framework that can solve DCG captcha

[4]When contrasted with many traditional captchas [9], these timings are comparable but the accuracies are better.

challenges based on image processing techniques and principles of unsupervised learning. We start by considering random guessing attacks and then demonstrate that our framework performs orders of magnitude better than the former.

5.1 Random Guessing Attack

An attacker given a DCG captcha challenge can always attempt to perform a random guessing attack. Let us assume that the attacker knows which game he is being challenged with as well as the location of the target area (e.g., the blue region containing the target circle and pentagon in the Shapes game) and the moving object area (e.g., the white region in the Shapes game within which the objects move). Although determining the latter in a fully automated fashion is a non-trivial problem (see our attack framework below), an attacker can obtain this knowledge with the help of a human solver.

However, the attacker (bot) still requires knowledge of: (1) the foreground objects (i.e., all the objects in the moving object area) and (2) the target objects (i.e., the objects contained within the target area). A randomized strategy that the attacker could adopt is to pick a random location on the moving object area and drag/drop it to a random location on the target area. More precisely, the attacker can divide the moving object area and the target area into grids of reasonable sizes so as to cover the sizes of foreground moving objects and target objects. For example, the moving object area can be divided into a 10 pixel x 10 pixel grid and target region can be divided into a 3 pixel x 3 pixel grid (given that the target area size is roughly 3 times the object area size). If there are a total of r target objects, the total number of possibilities in which the cells (possibly containing the answer objects) on the object area can be dragged and dropped to the cells on the target area are given by $t = C(100, r) * P(9, r)$. This is equivalent to choosing r cells in the object area out of a total of 100 cells, and then rearranging them on to 9 cells in the target area. Thus, the probability of attacker success in solving the challenge in a single attempt is $1/t$. For the DCG captcha instances targeted in this paper, r is 3, 2 and 1, resulting in the respective success probabilities of 0.00000123%, 0.000281% and 0.1%. Each attempt corresponds to r drag-and-drop events. Even if the attacker is allowed a limited (3-4) number of attempts to solve the captcha, these probabilities are still much lower than the target probabilities for a real-world captcha system security (e.g., 0.6% as suggested by Zhu et al. [32]).

While this analysis suggests that such DCG captchas are not vulnerable to naive guessing attacks, the next step is to subject them to more sophisticated, fully automated attacks, as we pursue below.

5.2 Our Automated Attack and Results

Our attack framework involves the following phases:

1. Learning the background image of the challenge and identifying the foreground moving objects. A background is the canvas on which the foreground objects are rendered. The foreground objects, for example, in the Ships game, as shown in Figure 1(a), are bird, ship, monkey, and squirrel.
2. Identifying the target area and the target area center(s). For example, the sea in the Ships game, and the animals in the Animals game.
3. Identifying and learning the correct answer objects. For example, the ships in the Ships game.
4. Building a dictionary of answer objects and corresponding targets, the background image, the target area and their visual features, and later using this knowledge base to attack the new challenges of the same game.
5. Continuously learning from new challenges containing previously unseen objects.

Next, we elaborate upon our design and matlab-based implementation per each attack phase as well as our experimental results. We note that, on a web forum [1], the author claims to have developed an attack against the "are you a human" captcha. However, *unlike our generalized framework*, this method is perfected for *only one simple game* that has one single target area and a fixed set of answer objects. It is not known whether or how easily this method can be adapted to handle different games, games with multiple instances that carry different sets of answer objects, and those with multiple target objects. Since only one game is cracked, one needs to keep refreshing the game page, if allowed, until that specific game appears. Since no technical details are provided in [1], we can only doubt if any background learning or object extraction is implemented by observing the short time it takes to finish the attack.

(1) Background & Foreground Object Extraction: To extract the static background of a DCG challenge, the intuitive way is to superimpose some sampling frames that cross a valid period (e.g., 40 frames captured at a fixed time interval (0.2s)), then select the most frequent color value (dominant color) from each pixel as the background color for that pixel. This is based on the assumption that the background image is static and the foreground objects are constantly moving, such that the true background color almost always appears as the most frequent (or consistent) color observed for a pixel. By subtracting the background image from a video frame, the foreground moving objects become readily extractable. To further reduce the computational cost, a 6-bit color code[5], rather than a 24-bit or 3-byte representation of a color value, is used to code the video frame, the learned background image, and the learned foreground objects.

However, one drawback of this preliminary method is that if the moving speed of the foreground objects is too slow, especially when some foreground objects hover over a small area, the dominant color values of most pixels in that area will be contributed by the foreground objects instead of by the background. A shadow of foreground objects may appear as pseudo patches in the background image as shown in Figure 2(b) for the Shapes game of Figure 2(a), indicated by the dashed rectangle. Using more sampling frames for initial background learning could alleviate this problem, but resulting in a time-consuming learning procedure. Our preliminary experiment indicates that an average 30.9s, generated by running the above learning method 15 times per game challenge, is needed for learning a game background completely.

In our new method, we overcome the conflict between the number of sampling frames and the pseudo patch effect by actively changing the location of one moving object per sampling frame. In the first step, a few frames N_1 (e.g., 10 frames captured in 0.3s interval) are collected to generate the initial background that is used to extract the foreground object (through background subtraction) in the next step. Because the number of sampling frames is very limited, pseudo patches may exist. The second step, called active learning, is to actively drag-and-drop each moving object to a specified destination, which aims to speed up the object movement in order to reduce the pseudo patch effect. Then, N_2 ($N_2 > N_1$) sampling frames are re-collected whenever a moving object is actively dragged to a new location. Because of the high efficiency of the moving object detection and the latter mouse operations, enough sampling frames (e.g., $N_2 = (30, 50)$) without/with minor hovering effect could be collected within a short period. The new background is detected again based on the dominant color of the collected frames. Figure 2(c) and 2(d) show the detected background with non-trivial pseudo patches and with a minor patch, resp., by applying the 1st and 2nd steps of the new active learning method on the Shapes game of Figure 2(a). Minor patches could affect the detection of a complete object, but since the affected area is minor, partial matching could still be used in the latter identification of the answer object.

[5] http://en.wikipedia.org/wiki/Color_code

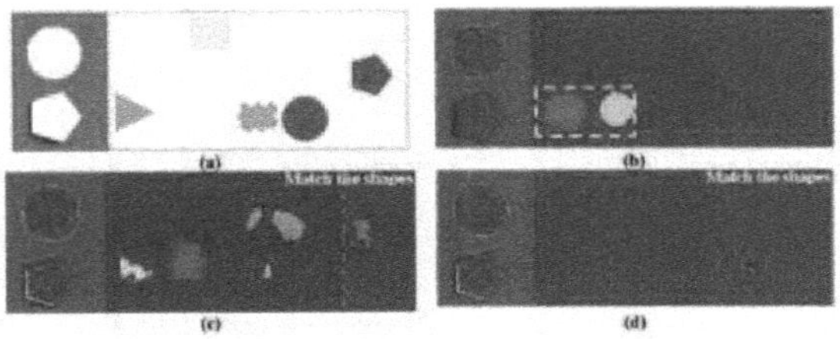

Figure 2: Detected backgrounds. (a) original frame image; (b) detected background with pseudo patches by using preliminary method; (c) detected background with pseudo patches after performing the 1st step of the proposed method; (d) detected background with a minor patch after performing the 2nd step of the proposed method.

Each learned background image is saved in the database. After removing the extracted background from 5-8 equally distant frames from the collected frames, the objects in each of the selected frame are extracted. The objects below a certain size threshold were discarded as noise. The frame with the maximum number of objects was then selected to extract various objects. Using multiple frames for object extraction also helped us discard the frames in which the objects overlapped each other and were hence detected as a single object instead of distinct individual objects.

According to our experimental results, the likelihood of observing such pseudo patches is sufficiently low ($< 7\%$). However, pseudo patches may not pose a big issue. Even though the existence of pseudo patches may result in over-segmented foreground objects when they overlap each other, a partially detected object can still be used to extract visual features and later to locate an object that matches the visual features at the time of attacking.

As the final step as part of this phase, the visual features, coded as color code histograms (a visual feature commonly used to describe the color distribution in an image), of the foreground objects and the background image, are stored in the database, together with some other meta-data such as the object size and dimensions.

(2) Target Area Detection: Identifying the target area requires analysis of the background extracted in the previous phase. For this purpose, we implemented two alternative approaches, namely the *Minimum Bounding Rectangle (MBR)* [12] method and the *Edge-based method*, and compared and contrasted them with regard to detection accuracy and time efficiency.

The MBR-based method is based on the observation that the activity/moving area of foreground objects has no or very little overlap with the target area. Therefore, by detecting and removing the foreground moving area from the background image, a reasonable estimate of the target area can be obtained. As the first step of this approach, the selected 5-8 frames and their foreground object masks from the previous phase are used to identify the foreground moving area mask. More specifically, the foreground mask is generated by identifying those pixels that have a different color code value than that of the corresponding pixels in the background image. Then, a Minimum Bounding Rectangle (MBR) is generated that bounds the area where the foreground objects are detected in the current frame (Figure 3). The final estimate of the foreground moving area, denoted as MBR_{final}, is the superimposition of all the MBRs extracted from the sample frames, also represented as a minimum bounding rectangle (see Figure 3(c)).

After the removal of the entire area bounded by MBR_{final} from the background image, the remaining background is divided into eight sub-areas as shown in Figure 4. The sub-area with the largest area (e.g., sub-area #2 in Figure 4) is identified as the target area, and its centroid is the target center. It is worth noting that the computational cost of this method is very low ($O(MN)$, where N is the number of pixels in a game scene, M is the number of sample frames, and $M \ll N$) since the foreground object masks are readily available as part of the output from the previous phase. In other words, the most time consuming part, which is the extraction of foreground objects ($O(MN^2)$) from sample frames, has been covered in the previous phase.[6]

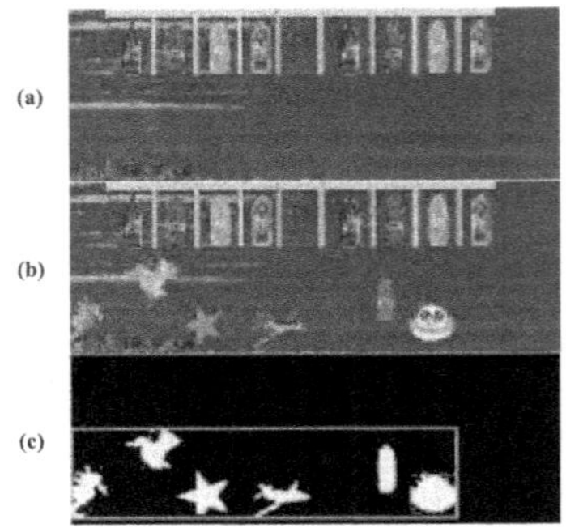

Figure 3: Target Detection. (a) The detected background for the Parking challenge; (b) One sample frame represented in color code; (c) Detected foreground objects from (b) and their MBR.

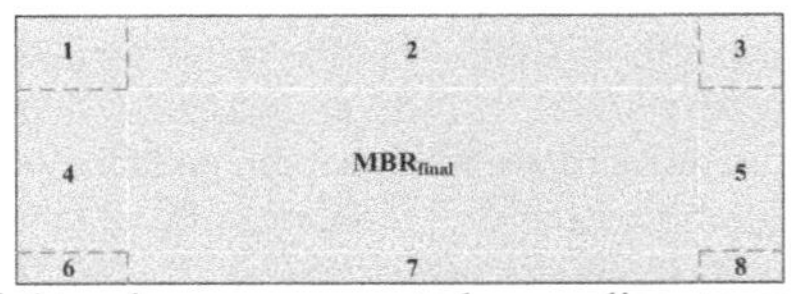

Figure 4: Eight sub-areas generated according to moving area of foreground objects

The Edge-based method employs a different design principle than MBR-based method. It is based on the hypothesis that there are strong edges in the target area because of the likely presence of objects in the target area, such as the dog and the squirrel in the Animals game. The steps involved in the edge-based method are listed below:

1. Collect a sequence of frames and learn the background image as in the MBR-based method.
2. Detect edge pixels on the background image. Group connected edge pixels into edge segments.
3. Remove trivial edge segments that have too few pixels by a user-input threshold.
4. The mean of all the centroids of remaining segments is used as the target area center.

The comparison results of the MBR-based and Edge-based methods are shown in Figure 5. The solid square dot in each game scene in Figure 5(a) is the MBR-detected target area center for that challenge. Also displayed in Figure 5(a) are the detected foreground object moving areas, namely MBR_{final}, displayed as a black rectangle in each game scene. According to our experimental results, MBR-based method was able to detect the correct target area center in all the challenges. In contrast, for the edge-based method, it is difficult to find a global threshold that works for all the challenges. Rather, we need to adjust the threshold for a specific game in order to achieve "reasonably good" results, and this method is also sensitive to the existence of texts in the background. Figure 5(b) shows the "optimal" edge detection result for each challenge with a manually tuned threshold which is different for each challenge. As shown

[6]We also implemented an alternative design, called the *exclusion method* (see Appendix B), which detects the target area by simply removing foreground object pixels accumulated from all the sample frames. However, while this method is slightly faster than the MBR-based method, it is less robust.

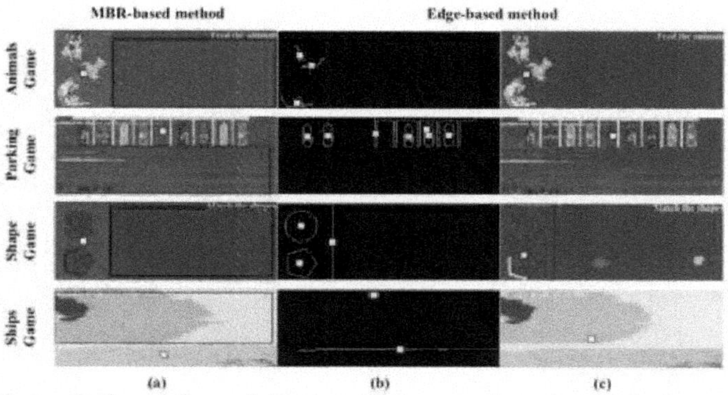

Figure 5: Comparison of the target area center detection results between the MBR-based and the edge-based methods. (a) Results from MBR-based method (solid square dot represents the target area center and black rectangle represents the object moving area); (b) centroids of non-trivial edges from the edge-based method; and (c) final target area centers from the edge-based method.

in Figure 5(c), some target area centers are incorrectly detected because some edge segments belong to the texts that are part of the background but not of the target area. This means that the accuracy of the edge-based method could be significantly undermined by the presence of strong edges in the background that are not part of the target area (e.g., presence of texts) and the absence of objects in the target area (e.g., the absence of objects in the target area of the Ships Game). As for efficiency, the MBR-based method has a time complexity of $O(MN)$ where M is a constant in the range of 5-8, while the time complexity of the edge-based method is $O(NL+N^2)$ where L is a constant in the range of 3-8 estimated based on the typical time complexity of a non-combining edge detection method [29]. Overall, this shows that the MBR method outperforms the Edge method on several aspects.

(3) Answer Object & Target Location Detection: Once the target area is identified, the next step is to identify the correct answer objects and their respective matching sub-target areas. Since a game can not have too many sub-target areas (otherwise, usability will be compromised), we divide the entire probable target area into 9 equal-sized blocks, each represented by its area centroid, drag each foreground object to each of the 9 centroids, and stop and record the knowledge learned whenever there is a "match." A match occurs when an answer object is dragged to its corresponding sub-target area (e.g., a "bone" dragged onto a "dog"). This is detected by monitoring the change of the area summation of all the foreground objects, since an answer object, once dragged to its correct target location, will stay in the target area and therefore result in a reduction of the foreground area. In our experiments, this method has proven 100% effective when applied to all four games. As for efficiency, while the worst case upper bound is $O(N)$, where N is the total number of foreground objects, in practice, much less number of drags are required. Our experimental results show that, with 5 foreground objects for each game (the maximum setting) and 15 training runs for each game, the average number of drags needed for a game is 9, i.e., less than 2 drags per each object on average. In case the server imposes a strict limit on drag/drop attempts, this process can be repeated over mutiple runs.

(4) Knowledge Database Building and Attacking: The background, target area, and learned answer objects as well as their corresponding sub-target areas together constitute the knowledge database for a game. After learning about sufficient number of games, whenever a new game challenge is presented, the knowledge base is checked for the challenge. The target area of the currently presented challenge is matched with the target areas present in the database to identify the challenge. If a match is found, the extraction of objects from the foreground follows. The visual features such as the color code histogram of the currently extracted objects are matched with that of the answer objects in the database for that challenge. The extracted objects identified as correct answer objects are then dragged to their corresponding sub-target areas. To measure the performance of our approach, we ran this attacking module 100 times for each game instance, and the average successful attacking time is 6.9s with the number of foreground objects ranging from 4 to 6. The maximum successful attacking time is 9.3s, observed for an instance of the Animal game with 6 foreground objects. These timings are in line with those exhibited by honest users in our usability study, which will make it impossible for the captcha server to time-out our attack.

(5) Continuous Learning: During attacking, if a challenge matches a game in our database but contains previously unseen answer object(s) (e.g., a new ship object in a Ships game instance), the attack will not terminate successfully. Whenever such a situation arises, an answer object learning module that is similar to the aforementioned module is activated, but differs from the latter in that it only needs to drag a potential answer object to each of the previously learned sub-target areas that have matching answer objects in the database. The newly learned answer objects and their corresponding sub-target area centroids are then added to the knowledge base for that game.

5.3 Discussion and Summary

There are two benefits in the background learning. First, the learned background can be used to quickly extract foreground moving objects. Second, the learned background can be used to locate the target area where foreground answer objects need to be dragged to. The proposed active learning is tested on all 36 game challenges (i.e., 3 (speeds), 3 (# of objects), 4 (game prototypes)). N_1 is set to be 10. The shape objects in the Shape Game have larger size than objects in other games, which easily result in pseudo patch effect when 6 moving objects exist in the game window with limited size. Therefore, N_2 is set to be 50 for the Shape Game challenges with 6 objects while 30 frames is used for all the other game challenges. In total, a complete background can be extracted in average 9.04s that is about three times faster than the preliminary method mentioned earlier (i.e., 30.9s).

The adoption of a large image database for each answer object could pose a challenge to our approach since it allows for the creation of many different foreground answer object configurations for the same game. In the worst case, a challenge may contain none of the previously learned answer objects for that particular game. Continuous learning will be activated in such cases and can also be used as a way for auto attacking in the run time. Such cases fall into the category of "known foreground answer objects and known target objects," and the success rate can be estimated using the number of foreground objects (o), number of answer objects (t), and number of drag and drop attempts allowed for each object (a). For example, if $o = 5$, $t = 3$ and $a = 2$, the success rate is approximately $\frac{2^3}{C(5,3)3!} = 13\%$. Though as low as it seems, the rate itself is not affected by the image database size.

During attacking, there is a time lapse between selecting a foreground object and verifying whether it is an answer object. Both feature extraction and database lookup (through feature matching) take time. In our implementation, we chose to click and hold a selected object until a match with an answer object in the database is registered. In doing so, we guarantee that an answer object, once verified, can be readily dragged and dropped, thus to avoid dealing with the issue of constantly moving objects. However, this approach may fail if a constraint is added by the captcha implementation that limits the amount of time one can hold an object from moving. A less invasive attacking method would be to utilize parallel processing, in which one thread is created to perform feature extraction and comparison, and another parallel thread is used to track and predict the movement of the object currently under verification.

Summary of Automated Attack Analysis: Our attack represents a novel approach to breaking a representative DCG captcha category. Attacking captcha challenges, for which the knowledge already exists in the dictionary, is 100% accurate and has solving times in line with that of human users. However, building the dictionary itself is a relatively slow process. Although this process can be sped-up as we discussed, it may still pose a challenge as the automated attack may need to repeatedly scan the different captcha challenges from the server to continuously build an up-to-date dictionary. The defense strategies for the DCG captcha designers may thus include: (1) incorporating a large game database as well as large object image databases for each game; and (2) setting a lower game time-out (such as 20-30s) within which human users can finish the games but background learning does not fully complete. Since our attack relies on the assumption that the background is static, another viable defense would be to incorporate a dynamically changing background (although this may significantly hurt usability). It is also important to note that, as per the findings reported in [23], the use of fully automated solving services represent economical hurdles for captcha attackers. This applies to traditional captchas as well as DCG captchas. Eventually, this may make automated attacks themselves less viable in practice [23], and further motivates the attacker, similar to other captchas, to switch to human-solver attacks against DCG captchas.

6. RELAY ATTACKS

Human-solver relay attacks are a significant problem facing the captcha community, and most, if not all, existing captchas are completely vulnerable to these attacks routinely executed in the wild [23]. In this section, we assess DCG captchas w.r.t. such attacks.

6.1 Difficulty of Relaying DCG captchas

The attacker's sole motivation behind a captcha relay attack is to completely avoid the computational overhead and complexity involved in breaking the captcha via automated attacks. A pure form of a relay attack, as the name suggests, only requires the attacker to relay the captcha challenge and its response back and forth between the server and a human-solver. For example, relaying a textual captcha simply requires the bot to (asynchronously) send the image containing the captcha challenge to a human-solver and forward the corresponding response from the solver back to the server.

Similarly, even video-based character recognition captchas [24, 30] can be broken via a relay attack by taking enough snapshots of the video to cover the captcha challenge (i.e., the distorted text within the video) which can be solved by remotely located humans. They can also be broken by simply taking a video of the incoming frames and relaying this video to the human-solver.

In contrast, DCG captchas offer some level of resistance to relay attacks, as we argue in the rest of this section. In making this argument, we re-emphasize that the primary motivating factors for a human-solver relay attacker are simplicity, low economical cost and practicality. As such, a relay attack that requires sophistication (e.g., special software, complexity and overhead), is likely not viable in practice [23].

There appears to be a few mechanisms using which DCG captchas could potentially be subject to a relay attack. First, if the server sends the game code to the client (bot), the bot may simply ship the code off to the human-solver, who can complete the game as an honest user would. However, in the DCG captcha security model (Section 2.1), the game code is obfuscated and can be enforced to be executable only in a specific domain/host (e.g., only the client machine challenged with the captcha) authorized by the server using existing tools[7], which will make this attack difficult, if not impossible.

The second possibility, called *Stream Relay*, is for the bot to employ a streaming approach, in which the bot can synchronously relay the incoming game stream from the server over to the solver, and then relay back the corresponding clicks made by the solver to the server. Although the *Stream Relay* attack might work and its possibility can not be completely ruled out, it presents one main obstacle for the attacker. Streaming a large number of game frames over a (usually) slow connection between the bot (e.g., based in the US) and the solver's machine (e.g., based in China) may degrade the game performance (similar to video streaming over slow connections), reducing solving accuracy and increasing response time. Such differences from an average honest user game play session may further be used to detect the attack with high accuracies, as shown in our recent work [22].

These challenges associated with the above relay attack approaches motivate us to consider another much simpler and more economical relay attack approach called *Static Relay*. Here, the bot asynchronously relays a *static snapshot* of the game to a human-solver and uses the responses (locations of answer objects and that of the target objects) from the solver to break the captcha (i.e., drag and drop the object locations provided by the solver to the target object locations provided by the solver).

The Static Relay attack approach is very simple and in line with a traditional captcha attack (and thus represents a viable and economical relay attack). However, it is expected to have poor success rates. The intuitive reason behind this is a natural *loss of synchronization* between the bot and the solver, due to the dynamic nature of DCG captchas (moving objects). In other words, by the time the solver provides the locations of target object and the answer objects within a challenge image (let us call this the nth frame), the objects themselves would have moved in the subsequent, k^{th}, frame ($k > n$), making the prior responses from the solver of no use for the bot corresponding to the kth frame. Recall that the objects move in random directions and often collide with other objects and game border, and therefore it would not be possible for the bot to predict the location of an object in the kth frame given the locations of that object in the nth frame ($n < k$). Such a loss of synchronization will occur due to: (1) communication delay between the bot and human solver's machine, and (2) the manual delay introduced by the solver him/herself in responding to the received challenge.

A determined Static Relay attacker (bot) against the DCG captcha can, however, attempt to maximize the level of synchronization with the solver. Although it may not possible for the attacker to minimize (ideally, eliminate) the communication delays (especially for bots potentially thousand of miles away from human solvers), it may be possible to minimize the manual delay via the introduction of carefully crafted tasks for the human-solver. In the rest of this section, we report on an experiment and the results of an underlying user study in order to evaluate the feasibility of Static Relay attack against our DCG captcha instances. This novel experiment takes the form of a *reaction time* or *reflex action* task for the human-solver. A reaction time task involves performing some operation as soon as a stimulus is provided. A common example is an athlete starting a race as quickly as a pistol is shot. The subject of reaction time has been extensively studied by psychologists (see Kosinski's survey [20]).

6.2 Reaction Time Static Relay Experiment

Our hypothesis is that DCG captchas will be resistant to the *Static Relay* attack, and so we give the attacker a strong power in the following sense: our tests eliminate the communication delay between the bot and the human solver, by putting them on the same machine.

[7] http://www.kindi.com/swf-encryption.php

The focus of the experiment then shifts towards motivating human-solvers to perform at their best by employing meaningful interfaces and by framing the underlying task in a way that is amenable to these solvers. In particular, since attacker's goal is to minimize the delay incurred by the human solver in responding to the challenges, we model human-solver attack as a reaction time [20] task described below. Our Section 6.3 study further facilitates the attacker with human solvers having low response times and quick reflex actions, such as youths in their 20s [20].

Experimental Steps: The reaction time Static Relay attack experiment consists of the following steps:

1. A snapshot of the game challenge is extracted by the bot (B), and the human solver (H) is asked to identify/mark a target object for that game challenge (e.g., the dog in the Shapes game).
2. For each target object identified above, H is asked to identify one answer object in the snapshot specific to the game challenge (e.g., bone for the dog in the Shapes game). However, since B wants to minimize the delay between the time the challenge snapshot is given and the response is received from H, a stimulus will be associated with the snapshot. We make use of a combination of (1) a visual stimulus (the border across the game window flashes in Red) and (2) an audio stimulus (a beeping sound). The task for H is to identify an answer object in the image *as soon as* the stimuli are provided.
3. B will emulate the dragging and dropping of the objects based on the response of H (simply use the pixel values provided by H as the coordinates of the objects and respective targets).
4. Steps 2-3 are repeated until all answer objects for a given target object are identified by H and dragged/dropped by B.
5. Step 1 is repeated until all target objects have been covered.

The experiment succeeds if the captcha game completes successfully, i.e., if all answer objects are dragged to their respective targets by B per input from H.

Experimental Implementation: Our implementation of the above experiment consists of a user interface (UI) developed in Java that interacts with the human solver and a bot. The core of this implementation is designed using an algorithm following which the screen captures are updated and displayed on the screen as well as an algorithm used to make the mouse drag and drop of the objects.

The game starts by the bot capturing an image of the game challenge from the browser (i.e., the captcha challenge that the bot received from the server) and displays that image in the UI. The solver is then asked to click on a target object within that image. After selecting the target, the solver is instructed to click a "Next" button, wait for a flashing and a beep (our stimuli), followed by clicking the object that matches with that target. Once the solver has clicked on the object, the bot takes control of the mouse by clicking and dragging the object to the target in the flash game. The solver must be able to identify and choose the correct object before the object has moved too far in the flash game displayed in the browser. Whether the click is successful or not, a new screen capture is retrieved from the game on the browser. If the solver has chosen the object in time on the UI, then he/she can pick a new target if one exists by clicking on the "New Target" button. If the solver has missed clicking on the object fast enough (i.e., if the click was not successful), the solver will automatically get another attempt to choose the correct object followed by the flashing and the beep. Figure 7, Appendix A depicts the UI of our implementation.

6.3 Static Relay Attack User Study

We now report on a user study of the aforementioned reaction time relay attack experiment presented in Section 6.2.

6.3.1 *Study Design, Goals and Process*

In the relay attack study, users were given the task to play our 4 game instances through the UI (described above). The study comprised of **20 participants**, primarily Computer Science university students. This sample represents a near ideal scenario for an attacker, given that young people typically have fast reaction times [20], presumably optimizing the likelihood of the success of the relay attack. The demographics of the participants are shown in Appendix A, Table 10. The study design was similar to the one used in our usability study (Section 4). It comprised of three phases. The *pre-study phase* involved registering and briefly explaining the participants about the protocols of the study. This was followed by collecting participant demographics and then the participants playing the games via our interface. The participants were told to perform at their best in playing the games. The *post-study phase* required the participants to respond to a set of questions related to their experience with the games they played as part of the interface, including the SUS questions [8].

Each participant was asked to play the relay versions corresponding to each of the 20 variations of the 4 DCG captcha games as in Section 3; we used ordering based on Latin squares, as in the usability study. The specific goal of our study was to evaluate the reaction time experiment UI in terms of the following aspects:

1. *Efficiency*: time taken to complete the games (and succeeding at the relay attack).
2. *Robustness*: likelihood of not completing the game (relay attack failure), and incorrect drags/drops.
3. *User Experience*: quantitative SUS ratings and qualitative feedback from the participants.
4. *Reaction time*: Time delay between the presentation of the stimuli and the response from the participant. This is a fundamental metric for the feasibility of the attack. If reaction time is large, the likelihood of attack success will be low.

Another important goal of our user study was to compare its performance with that of the usability study. If the two differ significantly, the relay attack can be detected based on this difference.

For each tested game, completion times and errors were automatically logged by the our web-interface software. In addition, we maintained "local logs" of the clicks made by the participants on our game interface to measure the reaction timings.

6.3.2 *Study Results*

We present various mechanical data, i.e., time to completion and error rates as part of the relay attack study. We further analyze the local logs for the reaction time analysis.

Completion Time and Error Rates: Table 6 shows the time taken and error rates to play the games for each game type by different participants. Unlike our usability study, many game instances timed out, i.e., the participants were not able to always complete these game instances within the time out of 60s. In this light, we report two types of timings: (1) *successful time*, which is the time only corresponding to the games that the participants were able to complete successfully within the time out, and (2) *overall time*, which is the time corresponding to both the game instances completed successfully within the time out and those which timed out (in which case we consider the timing to be 60s). The overall time therefore will effectively be higher.

All games turned out to be quite slow, and much slower than that of the usability study where the games lasted for less than 10s on an average (Section 4). As in our usability study, we found that users took longest to solve the Animals (overall average: 46.51s), whereas the other games took slightly less time. This might have been due to the increased semantic load in the Animals game due to the presence of 3 target objects. We observed that the error rates were the highest for the Animals game (40%), and the least for the Shapes games (9%)

although the corresponding per click error rates were high (56%). The Ships and Parking games had comparable overall error rates between 20-30%. We analyzed and further compared the mean time for different game categories. Using the ANOVA test, the games showed statistically different behavior from each other ($F = 12.85$, $p < 0.0001$). On further analyzing the data, we found the following pairs of games to be statistically different from each other: Shapes and Ships ($p = 0.027$) and Animals and all other games ($p < 0.001$).

To analyze errors better, we investigated error rates per click, i.e. for each drag attempt whether the object being dragged was dropped at the correct position or not. The error rate per click was the least for the Ships game (17%), much lower compared to all other games (50-70%), the latter itself being much higher than observed during the usability study. This suggests that the server could prevent the relay attack against Animals, Parking and Shapes games by simply capping the number of drag/drop attempts.

Table 6: Error rates and completion time per game type

Game Type	**Overall Time (s)** *mean (std dev)*	**Successful time (s)** *mean (std dev)*	**Error Rate** *mean*	**Error Rate Per click** *mean*
Ships	30.92 (5.91)	22.25 (5.04)	0.26	0.17
Animals	46.51 (5.05)	37.93 (4.91)	0.40	0.65
Parking	28.16 (7.36)	20.45 (5.04)	0.22	0.66
Shapes	26.19 (1.59)	22.94 (1.74)	0.09	0.56

Reaction Time: We now analyze the reaction time corresponding to different games during the relay attack experiments. We consider two types of reaction times, one corresponding to all clicks made by the participants, and the other corresponding to only the correct clicks (i.e., those that resulted in a correct drag and drop). The averaged results for the two types of reaction times for each game type are summarized in Table 7. We can see that the average reaction time (all clicks) for all game categories was more than 2s and the least for the Shapes game (2.17s). The average reaction time (correct clicks) is slightly lower than reaction time (all clicks), but still higher than 1.5s and still lowest for the Shapes game (1.62s). Neither types of reaction times change significantly across different game categories. ANOVA test, however, did find significant difference between the mean reaction time (all clicks) of the four games ($F = 13.19$, $p < 0.01$). On further analyses using paired t-tests with Bonferroni correction, we found that there was a significant difference between the Animals and Parking games ($p < 0.01$). Similarly, using the ANOVA test, we found significant difference between the mean reaction time (correct clicks) ($F = 3.24$, $p < 0.027$). Further, we found a significant difference between the Shape and Ship games ($p < 0.005$) with respect to mean reaction time (correct clicks).

Table 7: Reaction times per game type

Game Type	**Reaction Time All Clicks (s)** *mean (std dev)*	**Reaction Time Correct Clicks (s)** *mean (std dev)*
Ships	2.27 (0.34)	2.06 (0.17)
Animals	2.58 (0.35)	1.85 (0.23)
Parking	2.50 (0.51)	2.00 (0.31)
Shapes	2.17 (0.2)	1.62 (0.11)

User Experience: We now consider the data collected via direct user responses during the post-study phase. The average SUS score from the study came out to be only 49.88 (std dev = 5.29). This is rather low given that average scores for commerical usable systems range from 60-70 [21], and suggests a poor usability of the system. This means that it would be difficult for human users to perform well at the relay attack task and implies that launching relay attacks against DCG captchas can be quite challenging for an attacker.

Table 8 shows the 5-point Likert scores ('1' is "Strong Disagreement"; '5' is "Strong Agreement") for the visual appeal and pleasurability of the games. Although the former average ratings are on the positive side (more that 3), the latter ratings are low, suggesting the participants did not find the games to be pleasurable. In our games, we made use of visual and audio stimuli to which the users had to respond. In order to understand what type of stimulus worked best for the participants, we asked them to what extent the audio, visual or both stimuli together was useful as an indicator to respond fastest to the game. These ratings are depicted in Table 8. The responses were on average in favor of the visual stimulus, followed by the two stimuli together, and finally the audio stimulus. 35% participants found audio stimulus and visual stimulus to be sufficient whereas 45% participants agreed or strongly agreed with the statement that both visual and audio stimulus are necessary to play the game. We further performed the ANOVA test for responses corresponding to the three – visual, audio and visual+audio – stimuli, but did not find a statistically significant difference. Finally, 80% of the participants felt that training will help them play the games better with an average score of 3.95. This suggests an attacker might improve success in relay attack through advance training of human solvers.

Table 8: Participant Feedback Summary

Features	**Likert Mean (std dev)**
Visually Attractive	3.20 (0.92)
Pleasurable	2.85 (0.99)
Visual Stimulus	3.20 (1.17)
Audio Stimulus	2.95 (0.93)
Both Audio and Visual	3.10 (1.25)
Need Training	3.95 (1.01)

Summary of Relay Attack Analysis: Our analysis suggests that subjecting the DCG captcha to relay attacks poses certain challenges in practice. Specifically, for the Static Relay attack to succeed, the human solvers have to perform a reaction time task (average reaction time is more than 2s). This task, except for the Shapes game, takes much longer (> about 30s on average), is significantly more error prone (error rates more than 20%; per click error rates more than 50%), and much harder for the users *when compared* to directly playing the games by honest users under a non-relay attack setting. In real life, where the communication delays between the bot and solver's machine will be non-zero and average solver population samples are used (unlike our attack set-up), the timings and error rates might be higher and launching a relay attack might be even more difficult. Although our experiments were conducted on our 4 DCG captcha instances, we believe that our analysis is generally applicable to other DCG captcha types involving moving answer objects.

7. CONCLUSIONS AND FUTURE WORK

This paper represents the first academic effort towards investigating the security and usability of game-oriented captchas in general and DCG captchas in particular. Our overall findings are mixed. On the positive side, our results suggest that DCG captchas, unlike other known captchas, offer *some* level of resistance to relay attacks. We believe this to be a primary advantage of these captchas, given that other captchas offer no relay attack resistance at all. Furthermore, the studied representative DCG captcha category demonstrated high usability. On the negative side, however, we have also shown this category to be vulnerable to a dictionary-based automated attack.

An immediate consequence from our study is that further research on DCG captchas could concentrate on making these captchas better resistant to automated attacks while maintaining a good level of usability.[8] Moreover, our paper focused on "pure automated" and "pure

[8]The modifications made to the original DCG captchas to resist automated attacks, such as a dynamic background, may further make relay attacks more difficult.

relay attacks" (in line with traditional captchas). However, hybrid attacks can also be envisioned, which combine the computing power and human knowledge. Future research is necessary to investigate how well hybrid attacks work, and how they alter the economics of captcha-solving (following up [23]). Finally, the results of our user study on reaction-time task performance may have general applications in human-centered computing (security and non-security) domains. For instance, these results may rule out the possibility of usable captcha schemes themselves based on reaction-time tests.

8. ACKNOWLEDGMENTS

We thank: the team of "are you a human" for creating the CAPTCHAs that inspired our work; John Grimes, John Sloan and Anthony Skjellum for guiding us regarding the ethical aspects of our work; Sonia Chiasson, Fabian Monrose and Gerardo Reynaga regarding early discussions; and various members of the SPIES group at UAB and PreCog group at IIITD for helpful suggestions throughout the study. The work of Mohamed, Georgescu, Gao and Saxena is partially supported by a grant on "Playful Security" from the National Science Foundation CNS-1255919. Van Oorschot holds the Canada Research Chair in Authentication and Computer Security and acknowledges NSERC for funding the chair and a Discovery Grant.

9. REFERENCES

[1] Cracking the areyouahuman captcha. http://spamtech.co.uk/software/bots/cracking-the-areyouhuman-captcha/.

[2] L. V. Ahn, M. Blum, N. J. Hopper, and J. Langford. Captcha: using hard ai problems for security. In *EUROCRYPT*, 2003.

[3] Amayeta. Swf encrypt: Encrypt, obfuscate & protect your flash swf actionscript & resources from decompilers. http://www.amayeta.com/software/swfencrypt/.

[4] Are You a Human. https://www.areyouahuman.com/.

[5] Are You a Human. Terms of service. Available at: http://portal.areyouahuman.com/termsofservice.

[6] A. Bangor, P. T. Kortum, and J. T. Miller. An empirical evaluation of the system usability scale. *International Journal of Human-Computer Interaction*, 24(6):574–594, 2008.

[7] A. Basso and F. Bergadano. Anti-bot strategies based on human interactive proofs. In *Handbook of Information and Communication Security*. 2010.

[8] J. Brooke. SUS: a "quick and dirty" usability scale. In P. W. Jordan, B. Thomas, B. A. Weerdmeester, and A. L. McClelland, editors, *Usability Evaluation in Industry*. Taylor and Francis, London, 1996.

[9] E. Bursztein, S. Bethard, C. Fabry, J. Mitchell, and D. Jurafsky. How Good Are Humans at Solving CAPTCHAs? A Large Scale Evaluation. In *IEEE Symposium on Security and Privacy*, 2010.

[10] C. Doctorow. Solving and Creating CAPTCHAs with Free Porn. In *Boing Boing*, Available at: http://www.boingboing.net/2004/01/27/solving_and_creating.html, 2004.

[11] K. Chellapilla, K. Larson, P. Simard, and M. Czerwinski. Designing human friendly human interaction proofs (hips). In *ACM CHI*, 2005.

[12] S. ching Chen, M. ling Shyu, C. Zhang, and R. L. Kashyap. Identifying overlapped objects for video indexing and modeling in multimedia database systems. In *Multimedia Database Systems, International Journal on Artificial Intelligence Tools*, 2001.

[13] Dancho Danchev. Inside indias captcha solving economy. Available at: http://blogs.zdnet.com/security/?p=1835.

[14] M. Egele, L. Bilge, E. Kirda, and C. Kruegel. Captcha smuggling: hijacking web browsing sessions to create captcha farms. In *Proceedings of the 2010 ACM Symposium on Applied Computing*, 2010.

[15] G. Keizer. Spammers' Bot Cracks Microsoft's CAPTCHA. In *Computer World*, Available at: http://www.computerworld.com/s/article/9061558/Spammers_bot_cracks_Microsoft_s_CAPTCHA_, 2008.

[16] C. Gentry, Z. Ramzan, and S. Stubblebine. Secure distributed human computation. In *Proceedings of the 6th ACM conference on Electronic commerce*, EUROCRYPT, 2005.

[17] J. M. G. Hidalgo and G. Alvarez. CAPTCHAs: An Artificial Intelligence Application to Web Security. *Advances in Computers, Volume 83 (editor: Marvin V. Zelkowitz)*, pages 110–181, 2011.

[18] Jeff Yan and Ahmad Salah El Ahmad. A Low-cost Attack on a Microsoft CAPTCHA. In *ACM CCS*, 2008.

[19] K. Kluever. Breaking the PayPal.com CAPTCHA. Available at: http://www.kloover.com/2008/05/12/breaking-the-paypalcom-captcha, 2008.

[20] R. Kosinski. A literature review on reaction time. Available at: http://biology.clemson.edu/bpc/bp/Lab/110/reaction.htm, 2012.

[21] J. Lewis and J. Sauro. The factor structure of the system usability scale. In *Human Computer Interaction International Conference (HCII)*, 2009.

[22] M. Mohamed, S. Gao, N. Saxena, and C. Zhang. Dynamic cognitive game captcha usability and detection of streaming-based farming. In *the Workshop on Usable Security (USEC), co-located with NDSS*, 2014.

[23] M. Motoyama, K. Levchenko, C. Kanich, D. McCoy, G. M. Voelker, and S. Savage. Re: Captchas-understanding captcha-solving services in an economic context. In *USENIX Security Symposium*, 2010.

[24] NuCaptcha. Nucaptcha: Adaptive captcha authentication. http://www.nucaptcha.com/.

[25] J. Ogden. Captcha can kill your conversion rate. Available at: http://www.evancarmichael.com/Marketing/6352/CAPTCHA-Can-Kill-Your-Conversion-Rate.html.

[26] PRNewsWire. Are you a human's user-friendly game-based security solution aims to replace distorted text captchas. Available at: http://www.prnewswire.com/news-releases/are-you-a-humans-user-friendly-game-based-security-solution-aims-to-replace-distorted-text-captchas-152266285.html.

[27] S. Prasad. Googles CAPTCHA Busted in Recent Spammer Tactics. Available at: http://securitylabs.websense.com/content/Blogs/2919.aspx, 2008.

[28] D. Stefan and D. Yao. Keystroke-dynamics authentication against synthetic forgeries. In *CollaborateCom*, pages 1–8, 2010.

[29] S. Wesolkowski. Stochastic nested aggregation for images and random fields. In *Ph.D. Thesis, University of Waterloo*, 2007.

[30] Y. Xu, G. Reynaga, S. Chiasson, J.-M. Frahm, F. Monrose, and P. C. van Oorschot. Security and usability challenges of moving-object captchas: Decoding codewords in motion. In *USENIX Security*, 2012.

[31] Yan, Jeff and El Ahmad, Ahmad Salah. Usability of CAPTCHAs Or usability issues in CAPTCHA design. In *SOUPS*, 2008.

[32] B. B. Zhu, J. Yan, Q. Li, C. Yang, J. Liu, N. Xu, M. Yi, and K. Cai. Attacks and design of image recognition captchas. In *ACM CCS*, 2010.

APPENDIX

A. ADDITIONAL FIGURES AND TABLES

(a) A star indicating correct object match

(b) A cross indicating incorrect object match

Figure 6: User Feedback per Game Interaction

B. TARGET AREA DETECTION USING THE EXCLUSION METHOD

A design alternative for target area detection, called the *exclusion method* is to detect the target area by simply removing foreground object pixels accumulated from all the sample frames. However, while this alternative is slightly faster but still at about the same time efficiency as the MBR-based method, it is less robust than the latter especially when the objects are moving slow such that the remaining area, i.e., the detected target area, may include too much of the foreground object moving area that has not had a chance to be covered by the footprints of foreground objects extracted from the limited set of sample frames. Figure 8 shows our experimental results for this design alternative applied to four different challenges, where the blue dots represent the detected target area centers. This alternative method failed to detect the correct target center in all four cases.

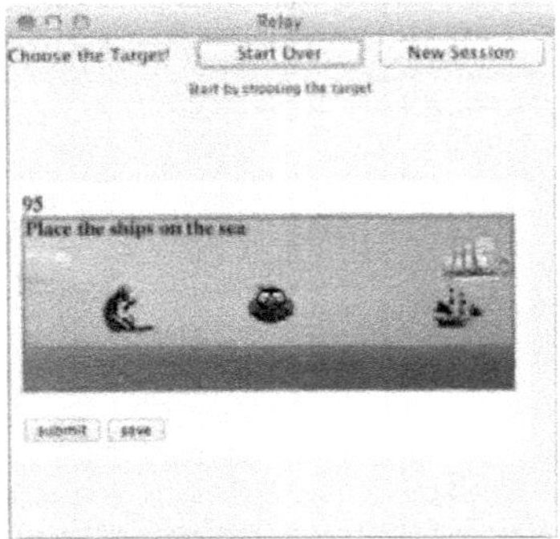

(a) The solver is asked to choose a target object

(b) The solver is asked to choose the next answer object, if any

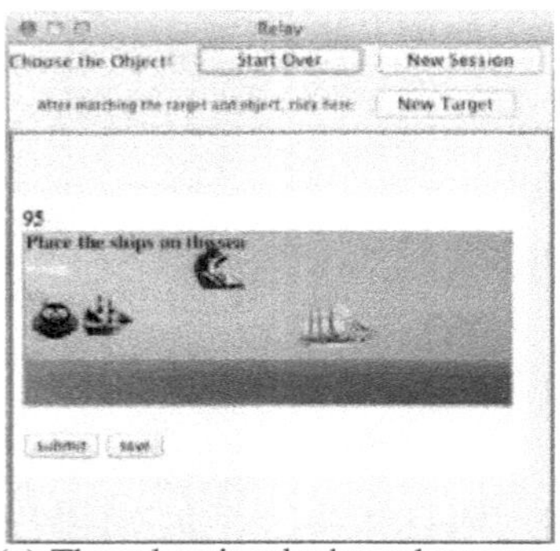

(c) The solver is asked to select a new target object, if any

Figure 7: User interface implementing the reaction time relay experiment (95 represents the User ID; the red rectangle in (c) represents our visual stimulus)

Table 9: Usability Study Participant Demographics

	N=40
Gender	(%)
Male	50
Female	50
Age	(%)
18 - 24	80
25 - 35	20
Education	(%)
Highschool	45
Bachelors	27.5
Masters	22.5
Ph. D.	5
Profession / field of study	(%)
Computer Science	60
Engineering	5
Science, Pharmaceuticals	10
Law	2.5
Journalism	2.5
Finance	2.5
Business	5
Others	12.5

Table 10: Relay Attck User Study Participant Demographics

	N=20
Gender	%
Male	70
Female	30
Age	%
18 - 24	35
25 - 35	60
35 - 50	5
Education	%
Highschool	25
Bachelors	45
Masters	30
Ph. D.	0
Profession / field of study	%
Computer Science	90
Engineering	5
Medicine	5

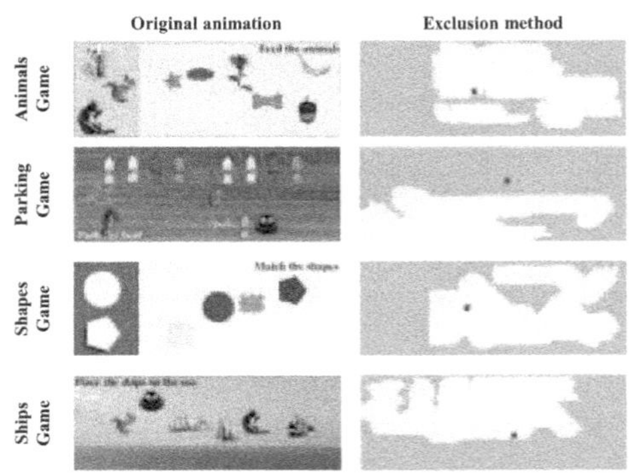

Figure 8: The target area centers (blue dots) detected by exclusion method

Modelling After-the-fact Leakage for Key Exchange

Janaka Alawatugoda[1], Douglas Stebila[1,2]
[1] Electrical Engineering and Computer Science
[2] Mathematical Sciences
Queensland University of Technology
Brisbane, Australia
{janaka.alawatugoda,stebila}@qut.edu.au

Colin Boyd
Department of Telematics
Norwegian University of Science and Technology
Trondheim, Norway
colin.boyd@item.ntnu.no

ABSTRACT

Security models for two-party authenticated key exchange (AKE) protocols have developed over time to prove the security of AKE protocols even when the adversary learns certain secret values. In this work, we address more granular leakage: *partial leakage* of long-term secrets of protocol principals, even after the session key is established. We introduce a generic key exchange security model, which can be instantiated allowing bounded or continuous leakage, even when the adversary learns certain ephemeral secrets or session keys. Our model is the strongest known partial-leakage-based security model for key exchange protocols. We propose a generic construction of a two-pass leakage-resilient key exchange protocol that is secure in the proposed model, by introducing a new concept: the leakage-resilient NAXOS trick. We identify a special property for public-key cryptosystems: *pair generation indistinguishability*, and show how to obtain the leakage-resilient NAXOS trick from a pair generation indistinguishable leakage-resilient public-key cryptosystem.

Categories and Subject Descriptors

C.2.2 [**Computer-Communication Networks**]: Key Exchange Protocols; E.3 [**Data Encryption**]: Public Key Cryptography

Keywords

key exchange protocols; side-channel attacks; security models; leakage-resilient; after-the-fact; NAXOS

1. INTRODUCTION

In order to capture leakage (side-channel) attacks in cryptography, the notion of leakage resilience has been developed. Examples of information which may leak and so allow side-channel attacks include timing information [5, 8, 23], electromagnetic radiation [19], and power consumption [27]. Leakage may reveal partial information about the secret parameters which have been used for computations in cryptosystems. To abstractly model leakage attacks, cryptographers have proposed the notion of *leakage-resilient* cryptography [1, 3, 7, 16, 17, 21, 20, 26], where the information that leaks is not fixed, but instead chosen adversarially. As key exchange protocols are among the most widely used cryptographic protocols, it is important to analyze their leakage resilience.

Earlier key exchange security models, such as the Bellare–Rogaway [4], Canetti–Krawczyk [9], and extended Canetti–Krawczyk (eCK) [25] models, aim to capture security against an adversary who can fully compromise some, but not all, secret values. This is not a very granular form of leakage, and thus is not suitable for modelling side-channel attacks enabled by partial leakage of secret keys. This motivates the development of leakage-resilient key exchange security models [3, 12, 29, 32].

Previous key exchange models including leakage have been limited in one or more ways. In most of the proposed models [3, 12, 29] the total amount of leakage allowed is bounded, which is troublesome because a protocol may reveal a limited amount of leakage each time it runs, and hence reveal "continuous" leakage. In addition, the adversary cannot obtain any leakage information after the session key is established for the session which the adversary targets for its attack. This is problematic because it does not address the security of one session, even if some leakage happens in subsequent sessions. A recent paper [32] uses a different leakage model with allows auxiliary input [13] but this cannot be directly compared with other leakage models. Although this model allows the adversary to make leakage queries on the complete secret, the values returned to the adversary are limited to those which are hard to invert and therefore are of limited use to the adversary. Our aim is to accommodate all the common leakage resistance models. We do not consider the auxiliary input model here.

In this paper, we construct a *generic leakage-security model* for key exchange protocols, which can be instantiated as a *bounded* leakage variant as well as a *continuous* leakage variant. In the bounded leakage variant, the total amount of leakage is bounded, whereas in the continuous leakage variant, a protocol execution may reveal a small amount of leakage each time. Further, the adversary is allowed to obtain the leakage even after the session key is established for the session, in which the adversary tries to distinguish the real session key from a random session key. We emphasize that the leakage functions are arbitrary polynomial time functions. Thus, our approach allows *after-the-fact leakage* in bounded or continuous leakage model. We now review the

ASIA CCS'14, June 4–6, 2014, Kyoto, Japan.

ACM 978-1-4503-2800-5/14/06 ...$15.00.
http://dx.doi.org/10.1145/2590296.2590317.

Security Model	Monolithic Leakage Queries			Partial Leakage Queries	
	Session Key	Long-term Key	Ephemeral Key	Leakage Model	After-the-fact
eCK [25]	Yes	Yes	Yes	None	No
MO [29]	Yes	Yes	Yes	Bounded	No
BAFL-eCK (Section 3.3)	Yes	Yes	Yes	Bounded	Yes
CAFL-eCK (Section 3.4)	Yes	Yes	Yes	Continuous	Yes

Table 1: Key exchange security models with reveal queries and leakage allowed

various approaches to modelling leakage, and then describe our contributions.

1.1 Leakage Models

Inspired by "cold boot" attacks, Akavia, Goldwasser and Vaikuntanathan [1] constructed a general framework to model memory attacks for public-key cryptosystems. With the knowledge of the public key, the adversary can choose an efficiently computable arbitrary leakage function, f and send it to the leakage oracle. The leakage oracle returns $f(sk)$ to the adversary where sk is the secret key. The only restriction here is that the sum of output length of all the leakage functions that an adversary can obtain is bounded by some parameter λ which is smaller than the size of sk.

In the work of Micali and Reyzin [28], a general framework was introduced to model the leakage that occurs during computation with secret parameters. This framework relies on the assumption that *only computation leaks information.* They mentioned that leakage only occurs from the secret memory portions which are actively involved in a computation. The adversary is allowed to obtain leakage from many computations, therefore the overall leakage amount is *unbounded* and in particular it can be larger than the size of the secret-key. Zvika et al. [7] proposed a continual memory leakage model in which it is not assumed that the information is only leaked from the secret memory portions involved in computations. Instead it is assumed that leakage happens from the entire secret memory but the amount of leakage is bounded per occurrence. This model allows the adversary to obtain arbitrarily large amounts of leakage information.

1.2 After-the-fact Leakage

Leakage which happens after the challenge is given to the adversary is considered as after-the-fact leakage. In security experiments for public-key cryptosystems, the challenge to the adversary is to distinguish the real plaintext corresponding to a particular ciphertext from a random plaintext. In key exchange security models, the challenge to the adversary is to identify the real session key of a chosen session from a random session key [4, 9, 25]. In leakage models for public-key cryptosystems, after-the-fact leakage is the leakage which happens after the challenge ciphertext is given whereas in leakage-resilient key exchange security models, after-the-fact leakage is the leakage which happens after the session key is established.

For leakage-resilient public-key encryption there are three properties which may be important differentiators for the different models. One is whether the model allows access to decryption of chosen ciphertexts before (CCA1) and after (CCA2) the challenge is known. The second is whether the leakage allowed to the adversary is *continuous* or *bounded.* The third is whether the leakage is allowed only before the challenge ciphertext is known or also after the fact. In earlier models, such as that of Naor and Segev [30], it was expected that although the adversary is given access to the decryption oracle (CCA2), the adversary cannot be allowed to obtain leakage after the challenge ciphertext is given. This is because the adversary can encode the decryption algorithm and challenge ciphertext with the leakage function and by revealing a few bits of the decrypted value of the challenge ciphertext trivially win the challenge. Subsequently, Halevi et al. [18] introduced after-the-fact leakage-resilient semantic security (CPLA2) on public-key cryptosystems. In their security experiment, the adversary is not allowed to access the decryption oracle. Dziembowski et al. [15] defined an adaptively chosen ciphertext after-the-fact leakage (CCLA2) in which the adversary is allowed to access the decryption oracle adaptively and obtain leakage information even after the challenge ciphertext is given. Furthermore, they allow continuous leakage, so the total leakage amount is unbounded.

Recall that in key exchange security models, the challenge to the adversary is to distinguish the real session key of a chosen session from a random session key. In the previous leakage-resilient key exchange security models [29, 3], the adversary is not allowed to obtain leakage after the session key is established, because if the adversary gets the ephemeral secret key of the owner by ephemeral key reveal query, the adversary can encode the specification of the key derivation function with the ephemeral secret key and other public keys into the leakage function. This reveals some information about the session key allowing the adversary to successfully answer the challenge. In the literature there are no key exchange protocols or security models available that allow leakage after the session key is established.

1.3 Our Contribution

We propose a *generic eCK-style security model,* which additionally allows partial leakage of long-term secret keys of protocol principals, even after the session key is established. We choose to build on the eCK model because it is a widely used security model capturing a wide variety of possible attacks such as key compromise impersonation attacks, weak forward secrecy, and unknown key share attacks. Our generic model can be instantiated in two different ways. The instantiations of the generic model differ in the extent to which the adversary can obtain the leakage of long-term keys in a *bounded* amount or obtain *continuous* leakage such that a protocol execution may reveal a small amount of leakage each time, and still expect security. Thus, we begin by presenting the *after-the-fact leakage eCK model* ((·)AFL-eCK model), where leakage is modelled using the output of a *tuple leakage function* $\mathbf{f}$ such that $\mathbf{f} = (f_1, f_2, \ldots, f_n)$. Introducing a tuple leakage function allows us to address the leakage of different protocol constructions, such as protocols constructed using stateful cryptographic primitives, or using more than one

Protocol	Initiator Cost	Responder Cost	Security Model	Partial Leakage Resilience	
				Leakage Model	After-the-fact
NAXOS [25]	4 **Exp**	4 **Exp**	eCK	None	None
MO [29]	8 **Exp**	8 **Exp**	MO	Bounded	No
π	12 **Exp**	12 **Exp**	BAFL-eCK	Bounded	Yes

Table 2: Security and efficiency comparison of key exchange protocols

cryptographic primitive, or both. Table 1 shows a clear picture of our contribution.

We introduce a new property for public-key cryptosystems, which states that any randomly chosen ciphertext should be decrypted without rejection. The new property is named *pair generation indistinguishability* (PG-IND) and is defined in Definition 7. We demonstrate the use of PG-IND property in *leakage-resilient NAXOS trick* computation, which we introduce as the key idea of constructing $(\cdot)$AFL-eCK-secure key exchange protocols. We then construct a *generic protocol* π, which can be proven secure in the generic $(\cdot)$AFL-eCK model. The protocol π is a key-agreement-style protocol which relies on two primitives: (1) a public-key cryptosystem that is PG-IND and after-the-fact leakage-resilient semantically secure (CPLA2); and (2) an unforgeable signature scheme against chosen message leakage attacks (UFCMLA). Whenever both of these two primitives are proven secure in either the bounded leakage model or the continuous leakage model, the instantiation of the protocol π is secure in the BAFL-eCK model or CAFL-eCK model respectively.

In Table 2, we compare an instantiation of the proposed generic protocol, π, with the NAXOS [25] and the Moriyama-Okamoto (MO) [29] protocols. The protocol π is instantiated using the CPLA2-secure, 0-PG-IND public-key cryptosystem of Halevi et al. [18], and UFCMLA-secure signature scheme of Katz et al. [20], in the bounded leakage model. The instantiation of the generic protocol π is BAFL-eCK-secure, and provides significant leakage resilience for practically achievable computation costs. We could not instantiate a CAFL-eCK-secure protocol π, because we do not have a CPLA2-secure, PG-IND public-key cryptosystem in the continuous leakage model. Halevi et al.[18] emphasized that adjusting their scheme to be CPLA2-secure in the continuous leakage model is an open problem. There are UFCMLA-secure signature schemes in the continuous leakage model [26, 12, 7]. So once CPLA2-secure, PG-IND public-key cryptosystem is available in the continuous leakage model, CAFL-eCK-secure π can be instantiated. Thus, the generic protocol π is a viable framework for $(\cdot)$AFL-eCK-secure protocols, and can achieve the leakage tolerance which the underlying schemes provide in the bounded or the continuous leakage model.

2. PRELIMINARIES

We review the formal security definitions of cryptographic primitives which will be used to construct the generic protocol.

2.1 UFCMLA-Secure Signature Schemes

We review the definition of UFCMLA security in the split-states-model, where the signing key sk is split into arbitrarily n parts such that $sk = (sk_1, \ldots, sk_n)$. The tuple leakage function $\mathbf{f} = (f_1, \ldots, f_n)$ is an adversary chosen efficiently computable adaptive tuple leakage function, which consists of n arbitrary number of leakage functions. Each leakage function f_i leaks $f_i(sk_i)$ from each sk_i split of the secret key individually. Following we consider bounded leakage from each split.

Definition 1. (Unforgeability Against Chosen Message Leakage Attacks (UFCMLA)). Let $k \in \mathbb{N}$ be the security parameter and $\boldsymbol{\lambda}$ be a vector of n elements. Let SIG = (KG, Sign, Vfy) be a signature scheme, we define $Adv_{\text{SIG}}^{\text{UFCMLA}}(\mathcal{E})$ as the advantage of any PPT adversary $\mathcal{E}$, winning the following game:

1. $(sk, vk) \xleftarrow{\$} \text{KG}(1^k)$
2. $(m^*, \sigma^*) \leftarrow \mathcal{E}^{\mathcal{O}(\cdot)}(vk)$
3. If $\text{Vfy}(vk, m^*, \sigma^*) =$ "true" and m^* is not been previously signed, then $\mathcal{E}$ wins.

Oracle $\mathcal{O}(m, \mathbf{f})$

- $\sigma \xleftarrow{\$} (sk, m)$
- for $i = 1, \ldots, n$, $\gamma_i \leftarrow f_i(sk_i)$
- If $\Sigma|\gamma_i| \leq \lambda_i$, then append γ_i to γ
- Return (σ, γ)

SIG is UFCMLA if $Adv_{\text{SIG}}^{\text{UFCMLA}}(\mathcal{E})$ is negligible in k.

Katz et al. [20] constructed an UFCMLA-secure signature scheme in bounded leakage model in which $n = 1$. It contains signing and verification operations based on NIZK proofs, where signature can be generated with cost of 2 **Exp**onentiations, and verified with cost of 4 **Exp**onentiations (with a simple NIZK proof).

2.2 CPLA2-Secure Public-Key Cryptosystems

We review the definition of CPLA2 security in the split-states-model, where the secret key s is split into arbitrarily n parts such that $s = (s_1, \ldots, s_n)$. The tuple leakage function $\mathbf{f} = (f_1, \ldots, f_n)$ is an adversary chosen efficiently computable adaptive tuple leakage function, which consists of n arbitrary leakage functions. Each leakage function f_i leaks $f_i(s_i)$ from each s_i split of the secret key individually. Following we consider bounded leakage from each split.

Definition 2. (After-the-fact Leakage-resilient Semantic Security (CPLA2)). Let $k \in \mathbb{N}$ be the security parameter and $\boldsymbol{\lambda} = (\boldsymbol{\lambda}_{pre}, \boldsymbol{\lambda}_{post})$ be a tuple of two vectors, where $\boldsymbol{\lambda}_{pre} = (\lambda_{pre_1}, \ldots, \lambda_{pre_n})$ is the leakage bound vector before the challenge ciphertext is issued, and $\boldsymbol{\lambda}_{post} = (\lambda_{post_1}, \ldots, \lambda_{post_n})$ is the leakage bound vector after the challenge ciphertext is issued. Let PKE = (KG, Enc, Dec) be a public-key cryptosystem, we define $Adv_{\text{PKE}}^{\text{CPLA2}}(\mathcal{D})$ as the advantage of any probabilistic polynomial time (PPT) adversary $\mathcal{D}$, winning the following game:

1. $(s, p) \xleftarrow{\$} \text{KeyGen}(1^k)$.
2. $(m_0, m_1) \leftarrow \mathcal{D}^{\text{Leak}(\mathbf{f})}(p)$ such that $|m_0| = |m_1|$, for $i = 1, \ldots, n$, $\text{Leak}(\mathbf{f})$ returns $f_i(s_i)$ if $\Sigma|f_i(s_i)| \leq \lambda_{pre_i}$.

3. $b \xleftarrow{\$} \{0,1\}$.
4. $C \xleftarrow{\$} \text{Enc}(pk, m_b)$.
5. $b' \leftarrow \mathcal{D}^{\text{Leak}(\mathbf{f})}(p, C)$ for $i = 1$ to $i = n$, Leak($\mathbf{f}$) returns $f_i(s_i)$ if $\Sigma|f_i(s_i)| \leq \lambda_{post_i}$.
6. $\mathcal{D}$ wins if $b' = b$.

PKE is CPLA2-secure, if $Adv_{\text{PKE}}^{\text{CPLA2}}(\mathcal{D})$ is negligible in k.

Halevi et al. [18] constructed a generic CPLA2-secure public-key cryptosystem which is secure against bounded leakage in the split-state model. It can be instantiated with the DDH-based leakage-resilient public-key cryptosystem of Naor et al. [30] with decryption cost of 4 **Exp**onentiations.

Remark 1. Both Definition 1 and 2 can be easily adjusted into their continuous leakage versions.

We use the definitions of key derivation functions proposed by Krawczyk [24]. Secure and efficient key derivation functions are available in the literature, for example based on HMAC [24].

3. THE GENERIC AFTER-THE-FACT LEAKAGE-eCK ((·)AFL-eCK) MODEL

The generic after-the-fact leakage eCK model can be instantiated in two different ways which leads to two security models. Namely, *bounded* after-the-fact leakage eCK (BAFL-eCK) model and *continuous* after-the-fact leakage eCK (CAFL-eCK) model. The BAFL-eCK model allows the adversary to obtain a bounded amount of leakage of the long-term secret keys of the protocol principals, as well as reveal session keys, long-term secret keys and ephemeral keys. Differently, the CAFL-eCK model allows the adversary to continuously obtain arbitrarily large amount of leakage of the long-term secret keys of the protocol principals, enforcing the restriction that the amount of leakage per observation is bounded.

In both instantiations of the generic (·)AFL-eCK model the partnering definition and the adversarial powers are same. The freshness conditions differ by means of the leakage allowed. So we can define the partnering and adversarial powers in the generic (·)AFL-eCK model and define the freshness separately in each BAFL-eCK and CAFL-eCK models.

Let $\mathcal{U} = \{U_1, ..., U_{N_P}\}$ be a set of n parties. We use the term *principal* to identify a party involved in a protocol instance. Each party U_i where $i \in [1, N_P]$ has a pair of long-term public and secret-keys, (pk_{U_i}, sk_{U_i}). The term *session* is used to identify a protocol instance at a principal. Each principal may have multiple sessions and they may run concurrently. The oracle $\Pi^s_{U,V}$ represents the sth session at the owner principal U, with intended partner principal V. The principal which sends the first protocol message of a session is the *initiator* of the session, and the principal which responds to the first protocol message is the *responder* of the session.

Definition 3. (Partner sessions in generic (·)AFL-eCK *model).* Two oracles $\Pi^s_{U,V}$ and $\Pi^{s'}_{U',V'}$ are said to be partners if all of the following hold:

1. both $\Pi^s_{U,V}$ and $\Pi^{s'}_{U',V'}$ have computed session keys;
2. messages sent from $\Pi^s_{U,V}$ and messages received by $\Pi^{s'}_{U',V'}$ are identical;
3. messages sent from $\Pi^{s'}_{U',V'}$ and messages received by $\Pi^s_{U,V}$ are identical;
4. $U' = V$ and $V' = U$;
5. Exactly one of U and V is the initiator and the other is the responder.

The protocol is said to be *correct* if two partner oracles compute identical session keys.

3.1 Modelling Leakage

Considering side-channel attacks which can be mounted against key exchange protocols, the most realistic way is to obtain the leakage information of secret keys from the protocol computations which use secret keys for computations. Following the premise "only computation leaks information", we have modeled the leakage in a place where a computation takes place on secret keys. After issuing a `Send` query, the adversary will get a protocol message which is computed according to the normal protocol computations. So sending an adversary-chosen adaptive leakage function with the `Send` query reflects the premise "only computation leaks information".

We introduce a tuple of n adaptively chosen efficiently computable leakage functions $\mathbf{f} = (f_1, f_2, \ldots, f_n)$; the size n of the tuple is *protocol-specific*. A key exchange protocol may use more than one cryptographic primitive and each primitive uses a distinct secret key. Hence, we need to address the leakage of secret keys from each of those primitives. Otherwise, some cryptographic primitives which have been used to construct a key exchange protocol may be stateful cryptographic primitives. The execution of a stateful cryptographic primitive is split into a number of sequential stages and each of these stages use one part of the secret key.

3.2 Adversarial Powers

The adversary $\mathcal{A}$ is a probabilistic polynomial time (PPT) algorithm that controls the whole network. $\mathcal{A}$ interacts with a set of oracles which represent protocol instances. The following query allows the adversary $\mathcal{A}$ to run the protocol.

- `Send`$(U, V, s, m, \mathbf{f})$ query: The oracle $\Pi^s_{U,V}$, computes the next protocol message according to the protocol specification and sends it to the adversary $\mathcal{A}$, along with the leakage $\mathbf{f}(sk_U)$. $\mathcal{A}$ can also use this query to activate a new protocol instance as an initiator with blank m and $\mathbf{f}$.

The following set of queries allow the adversary $\mathcal{A}$ to compromise certain session specific ephemeral secrets and long-term secrets from the protocol principals.

- `SessionKeyReveal`(U, V, s) query: $\mathcal{A}$ is given the session key of the oracle $\Pi^s_{U,V}$.
- `EphemeralKeyReveal`(U, V, s) query: $\mathcal{A}$ is given the ephemeral keys (per-session randomness) of the oracle $\Pi^s_{U,V}$.
- `Corrupt`(U) query: $\mathcal{A}$ is given the long-term secrets of the principal U. This query does not reveal any session keys or ephemeral keys to $\mathcal{A}$.

Once the oracle $\Pi^s_{U,V}$ has accepted a session key, asking the following query the adversary $\mathcal{A}$ attempt to distinguish it from a random session key. The `Test` query is used to formalize the notion of the semantic security of a key exchange protocol.

- `Test`(U, s) query: When $\mathcal{A}$ asks the `Test` query, the challenger first chooses a random bit $b \xleftarrow{\$} \{0,1\}$ and if $b = 1$ then the actual session key is returned to $\mathcal{A}$, otherwise a random string chosen from the same session key space is returned to $\mathcal{A}$. This query is only allowed to be asked once across all sessions.

Remark 2. (`Corrupt` *query vs Leakage queries).* By issuing a `Corrupt` query, the adversary gets the party's entire long-term secret key. Separately, by issuing leakage queries (using a tuple leakage function $\mathbf{f}$ embedded with the `Send` query) the adversary gets λ-bounded leakage information about the long-term secret key(s). It may seem paradoxical to consider `Corrupt` and Leakage queries at the same time. But there is a good reason to consider both.

The eCK model addresses KCI attacks, because the adversary is allowed to corrupt the owner of the test session before the activation of the test session. In the generic $(\cdot)$AFL-eCK model, we allow the adversary to obtain bounded amount of leakage from the partner of the test session, in addition to allowing the adversary to corrupt the owner of the test session.

Hence, the generic $(\cdot)$AFL-eCK model allows the adversary to obtain more information than eCK model. Moreover, none of the existing security models such as BR, CK, CK_{HMQV}, eCK allow a `Send` query with a tuple leakage function $\mathbf{f}$. Hence, we can see that $(\cdot)$AFL-eCK allows the adversary to obtain leakage information which none of the existing security models allow. Further, we emphasize that the technique of sending a tuple leakage function $\mathbf{f}$ with the `Send` query can be applied to any of the existing key exchange security models to obtain their leakage versions.

3.3 The Bounded After-the-fact Leakage eCK (BAFL-eCK) Model

In the BAFL-eCK model the total amount of leakage of each secret key of the underlying cryptographic primitives or each split of the secret key of the underlying stateful cryptographic primitives are bounded by leakage parameters. The leakage parameters are *primitive-specific*.

If the total leakage bound of the ith cryptographic primitive (or the total leakage bound of the ith state of the stateful cryptographic primitive) is λ_i and the leakage function f_i outputs leakage bits of the secret key of the ith cryptographic primitive (or leakage bits of the ith split of the secret key), then for leakage resilience of ith cryptographic primitive (or the stateful cryptographic primitive), we need that $\sum |f_i(sk_i)| \leq \lambda_i$.

Definition 4. ($\boldsymbol{\lambda}$-BAFL-eCK-*freshness).* Let $\boldsymbol{\lambda} = (\lambda_1, \ldots, \lambda_n)$ be a vector of n elements (same size as $\mathbf{f}$ in `Send` query). An oracle $\Pi^s_{U,V}$ is said to be $\boldsymbol{\lambda}$-BAFL-eCK-fresh if and only if:

1. The oracle $\Pi^s_{U,V}$ or its partner, $\Pi^{s'}_{V,U}$ (if it exists) has not been asked a `SessionKeyReveal`.
2. If the partner $\Pi^{s'}_{V,U}$ exists, none of the following combinations have been asked:
   (a) `Corrupt`(U) and `EphemeralKeyReveal`(U, V, s).
   (b) `Corrupt`(V) and `EphemeralKeyReveal`(V, U, s').
3. If the partner $\Pi^{s'}_{V,U}$ does not exist, none of the following combinations have been asked:
   (a) `Corrupt`(V).
   (b) `Corrupt`(U) and `EphemeralKeyReveal`(U, V, s).
4. For all `Send`$(\cdot, U, \cdot, \cdot, \mathbf{f})$ queries, $\sum |f_i(sk_{U\,i})| \leq \lambda_i$.
5. For all `Send`$(\cdot, V, \cdot, \cdot, \mathbf{f})$ queries, $\sum |f_i(sk_{V\,i})| \leq \lambda_i$.

3.4 The Continuous After-the-fact Leakage eCK (CAFL-eCK) Model

In the CAFL-eCK model, continuous leakage of each secret key of the underlying cryptographic primitives or each split of the secret key of the underlying stateful cryptographic primitives is allowed. The only restriction is, the amount of leakage per occurrence is bounded by leakage parameters. The leakage parameters are *primitive-specific*.

If the leakage bound of the ith cryptographic primitive is λ_i per leakage occurrence and the leakage function f_i outputs leakage bits of the secret key of the ith cryptographic primitive, then for leakage resilience of ith cryptographic primitive we need that $f_i(sk_i) \leq \lambda_i$, per leakage occurrence. If the leakage bound of the ith state of the stateful cryptographic primitive is λ_i per leakage occurrence and the leakage function f_i outputs leakage bits of the ith split of the secret key, then for leakage resilience of the stateful cryptographic primitive we need that $f_i(sk_i) \leq \lambda_i$, per leakage occurrence.

Definition 5. ($\boldsymbol{\lambda}$-CAFL-eCK-*freshness).* Let $\boldsymbol{\lambda} = (\lambda_1, \ldots, \lambda_n)$ be a vector of n elements (same size as $\mathbf{f}$ in `Send` query). An oracle $\Pi^s_{U,V}$ is said to be $\boldsymbol{\lambda}$-CAFL-eCK-fresh if and only if: Conditions (1)-(3) of Definition 4 hold, and

4. For each `Send`$(\cdot, U, \cdot, \cdot, \mathbf{f})$ query, size of the output of $f_i(sk_{U\,i}) \leq \lambda_i$.
5. For each `Send`$(\cdot, V, \cdot, \cdot, \mathbf{f})$ queries, size of the output of $f_i(sk_{V\,i}) \leq \lambda_i$.

3.5 Security Game and Security Definition

We introduce the security game of the generic $(\cdot)$AFL-eCK model. If we consider $\boldsymbol{\lambda}$-BAFL-eCK-freshness, the security game is BAFL-eCK, otherwise if we consider $\boldsymbol{\lambda}$-CAFL-eCK-freshness, it is CAFL-eCK security game.

Security of a key exchange protocol in the generic $(\cdot)$ AFL-eCK model is defined using the following security game, which is played by PPT adversary $\mathcal{A}$ against the protocol challenger.

- **Stage 1:** $\mathcal{A}$ may ask any of `Send`, `SessionKeyReveal`, `EphemeralKeyReveal` and `Corrupt` queries to any oracle at will.
- **Stage 2:** $\mathcal{A}$ chooses a $\boldsymbol{\lambda}$-$(\cdot)$AFL-eCK-fresh oracle and asks a `Test` query. The challenger chooses a random bit $b \xleftarrow{\$} \{0,1\}$, and if $b = 1$ then the actual session key is returned to $\mathcal{A}$, otherwise a random string chosen from the same session key space is returned to $\mathcal{A}$.
- **Stage 3:** $\mathcal{A}$ may continue asking `Send`, `Corrupt`, `SessionKeyReveal` and `EphemeralKeyReveal` queries. $\mathcal{A}$ may not ask a query that violates the $\boldsymbol{\lambda}$-$(\cdot)$AFL-eCK-freshness of the test session.

- **Stage 4:** At some point $\mathcal{A}$ outputs the bit $b' \leftarrow \{0,1\}$ which is its guess of the value b on the test session. $\mathcal{A}$ wins if $b' = b$.

$Succ_{\mathcal{A}}$ is the event that the adversary $\mathcal{A}$ wins the above security game.

Definition 6. *((·)AFL-eCK-security).* A protocol π is said to be (·)AFL-eCK-secure if there is no PPT algorithm $\mathcal{A}$ that can win the (·)AFL-eCK security game with non-negligible advantage. The advantage of an adversary $\mathcal{A}$ is defined as $Adv_{\pi}^{(\cdot)\text{AFL-eCK}}(\mathcal{A}) = |2\Pr(\text{Succ}_{\mathcal{A}}) - 1|$.

3.6 Practical Interpretation of Security of the Generic (·)AFL-eCK Model

We review the relationship between the generic (·)AFL-eCK model real world attack scenarios.

Active adversarial capabilities: Send queries address the powers of an active adversary who can control the message flow over the network.

Side-channel attacks: Leakage functions are embedded with the Send query. Thus, a wide variety of side-channel attacks based on **leakage of long-term secrets** are addressed, assuming that the leakage happens when computations take place in protocol principals. BAFL-eCK model addresses the situation where the adversary is only allowed to obtain a bounded amount of total leakage. CAFL-eCK model addresses a stronger situation, where the adversary is allowed to obtain continuous leakage, but the amount of leakage per invocation is bounded.

Cold-boot attacks: Corrupt queries address situations which reveal the long-term secret keys of protocol principals like in cold-boot attacks.

Malware attacks: EphemeralKeyReveal queries cover the malware attacks which steal stored ephemeral keys, given that the long-term keys may be securely stored separately from the ephemeral keys in places such as smart cards or hardware security modules. Separately, Corrupt queries address malware attacks which steal the long-term secret keys of protocol principals.

Weak random number generators: After knowing a previous set of randomly generated ephemeral values the adversary may be able to identify the statistical pattern of the random number generator and hence correctly guess the next value with a high probability. EphemeralKeyReveal query addresses situations where the adversary can get the ephemeral secrets.

Known key attacks: SessionKeyReveal query covers the attacks which can be mounted by knowing past session keys.

Key compromise impersonation attacks: In the generic (·)AFL-eCK model, freshness conditions allow the adversary to corrupt the owner of the test session before the activation of the test session. Hence, the generic (·)AFL-eCK model security protects against the key compromise impersonation attacks.

Weak forward secrecy: In the generic (·)AFL-eCK model, freshness conditions allow the adversary to corrupt both of the protocol principals, after the test session is activated. Hence, the generic (·)AFL-eCK model addresses weak forward secrecy.

eCK security: The generic (·)AFL-eCK model is a leakage version of the eCK model [25], hence, it captures all possible attacks from long-term and ephemeral key compromises. More precisely, in sessions where the adversary does not modify the communication between parties (passive sessions), the adversary is allowed to reveal both ephemeral secrets, both long-term secrets, or one of each from two different parties, whereas in sessions where the adversary may forge the communication of one of the parties (active sessions), the adversary is allowed to reveal the long-term or ephemeral key of the other party.

The main reason to introduce a generic security model, (·)AFL-eCK model, and then propose two instantiations (BAFL-eCK model and CAFL-eCK model) is to offer more flexibility to construct leakage-resilient key exchange protocols. The generic (·)AFL-eCK model gives a reasonable security framework for key exchange protocols capturing wide range of practical attacks including side-channel attacks. The only difference between the two instantiations is the leakage allowance (bounded or continuous). If we need to implement a key exchange protocol which captures all the properties mentioned in Section 3.6 in the bounded leakage model, we use the BAFL-eCK model as the security framework, whereas if we need security in the continuous leakage model, we use the CAFL-eCK model as the security framework.

4. CONSTRUCTING (·)AFL-eCK-SECURE KEY EXCHANGE PROTOCOLS

We investigate how to construct (·)AFL-eCK-secure key exchange protocols. The motivation of LaMacchia et al. [25] in designing the eCK model was that an adversary should have to compromise both the long-term and ephemeral secret keys of a party in order to recover the session key. In their NAXOS protocol, the main way this is accomplished is using what is now called the "NAXOS trick": a "psuedo" ephemeral key $\widetilde{esk}$ is computed as the hash of the long-term key lsk and the actual ephemeral key esk: $\widetilde{esk} \leftarrow H(esk, lsk)$. The value $\widetilde{esk}$ is never stored, and thus in the eCK model the adversary must learn both esk and lsk in order to be able to compute $\widetilde{esk}$. Note however, that in the NAXOS protocol, the initiator must compute $\widetilde{esk} = H(esk, lsk)$ twice: once when sending its Diffie–Hellman ephemeral public key $g^{\widetilde{esk}}$, and once when computing the Diffie–Hellman shared secrets from the received values. This is to avoid storing a single value that, when compromised, can be used to compute the session key.

4.1 Leakage-Resilient NAXOS Trick

Moving to the leakage-resilient setting requires rethinking the NAXOS trick. In the model "only computation leaks information", we must consider leakage at any place the long-term secret key is used. Thus, we need some kind of *leakage-resilient NAXOS trick*. As noted above, the initiator must not store the pseudo-ephemeral value, $\widetilde{esk}$, and instead must apply the NAXOS trick twice for each session. We replace the hash function H with a new leakage-resilient NAXOS trick to compute the pseudo-ephemeral value. The requirement is, given the long-term secret key and a particular ephemeral key, the NAXOS trick should always compute the same pseudo-ephemeral value, such that without knowing both the long-term and ephemeral keys the adversary is unable to compute the pseudo-ephemeral value. Moreover, the NAXOS trick computation should be resilient to the leakage of the long-term secret key, which happens even after the test session is activated.

A leakage-resilient NAXOS trick can be achieved by using the decryption function of a CPLA2-secure public-key cryptosystem [18]. Since decryption is deterministic, given the long-term secret key and a randomly chosen ciphertext, it will output the corresponding plaintext. So one can randomly choose an ephemeral key and use it as the ciphertext to the decryption function, and obtain the corresponding plaintext (output of the decryption function) as the pseudo-ephemeral value. Without knowing both the long-term and ephemeral keys, it is infeasible to compute the pesudo-ephemeral value. Thus, a leakage-resilient NAXOS trick can be achieved and the pseudo-ephemeral value can be computed. Further, bounded or continuous leakage-resilient key exchange protocol can be constructed, if the underlying public-key cryptosystem is bounded or continuous leakage-resilient.

4.2 Pair Generation Indistinguishability

Using a decryption algorithm of a CPLA2-secure public-key cryptosystem does not work for our requirement unless the public-key cryptosystem has a special property: any randomly chosen ciphertext should be decrypted without rejection. A randomly chosen ciphertext can be rejected with a significant probability if NIZK proofs have been used for CPLA2-secure public-key cryptosystems. In NIZK proofs, the party which creates a ciphertext should provide a proof of knowledge of the plaintext, and the party which decrypts the ciphertext first verifies the proof, then only if the proof is correct it decrypts the ciphertext, otherwise rejects. Use of a CPLA2-secure public-key cryptosystem without the special property would allow the adversary to break the protocol with a significant probability, whenever a randomly chosen ciphertext is rejected. We formally define the special property as *pair generation indistinguishability*.

Definition 7. (Pair Generation Indistinguishability). Let PKE $=$ (KeyGen, Enc, Dec) be a public-key cryptosystem. For $(p, s) \xleftarrow{\$} \mathrm{KeyGen}(1^k)$, let $D_1^{(p,s)}$, $D_2^{(p,s)}$ be two distributions such that $D_1^{(p,s)} = \{(m, c) : m \xleftarrow{\$} M, c \xleftarrow{\$} \mathrm{Enc}(p, m)\}$ and $D_2^{(p,s)} = \{(m, c) : c \xleftarrow{\$} \mathrm{C}, m \leftarrow \mathrm{Dec}(s, c)\}$ where M is the message space and C is the ciphertext space. For $\epsilon \geq 0$, the public-key cryptosystem PKE is *ϵ-pair-generation-indistinguishable* (ϵ-PG-IND) if for all $(p, s) \xleftarrow{\$} \mathrm{KeyGen}(1^k)$, $\mathrm{SD}(D_1^{(p,s)}, D_2^{(p,s)}) \leq \epsilon$.

Recall that the statistical distance, SD, between two distributions X and Y over a domain U is defined as $\mathrm{SD}(X, Y) = \frac{1}{2}\sum_{u \in U} \left|\Pr[X = u] - \Pr[Y = u]\right|$.

Now we show a 0-PG-IND public-key cryptosystem available in the literature. Naor et al. [30] described the framework of a hash proof system [10] as a key-encapsulation mechanism using the notion of Kiltz et al. [22]. Let K be the symmetric key space, C be the ciphertext space and M be the message space. Both K and C are the same size and elements of M are μ-bit strings. The leakage-resilient public-key cryptosystem of Naor et al. encrypts an arbitrary message $m \xleftarrow{\$} \mathrm{M}$ as $(\Psi, c, seed)$, where $c \xleftarrow{\$} \mathrm{C}$ with the corresponding witness ω, $seed \xleftarrow{\$} \{0, 1\}^t$ is a random seed and $\Psi = Ext(Pub(p, c, \omega), seed) \oplus m$. $Ext : \mathrm{K} \times \{0, 1\}^t \to \{0, 1\}^m$ is a public average-case strong extractor function [14], p is the public key and Pub is the deterministic public evaluation function of the underlying key-encapsulation mechanism. So whenever a random $(\Psi, c, seed)$ is sampled, the decryption, $m \leftarrow \Psi \oplus Ext(Priv_s(c), seed)$ corresponds to a random $m \in \mathrm{M}$. $Priv$ is a private evaluation algorithm of the underlying key-encapsulation mechanism, which is parametrized by the secret key s. Thus, the leakage-resilient public-key cryptosystem of Naor et al. is 0-PG-IND. The generic CPLA2-secure public-key cryptosystem of Halevi et al. [18] can be instantiated using the leakage-resilient public-key cryptosystem of Naor et al. Hence, the instantiation of the generic CPLA2-secure public-key cryptosystem of Halevi et al. is also 0-PG-IND.

Remark 3. In Table 3, let $\widehat{\mathrm{C}}$ be the ciphertext space: in a setting like Naor et al. [30] the random r. values are not just chosen from the C but from $\widehat{\mathrm{C}}$ which gives random r. in the form $(\Psi, c, seed)$.

4.3 Authenticating Protocol Messages

In this section we review how to provide authentication to the protocol messages. After computing the pseudo-ephemeral value by the NAXOS trick, a principal computes a Diffie-Hellman exponentiation and sends it to the other protocol principal. If that value is sent alone, the protocol is not secure because there is no authentication for the protocol messages, and hence an attacker can simply replace the original protocol message with its own value. In order to prevent this, we need to provide authenticity to the protocol messages. There are UFCMLA-secure signature schemes available in the literature [20, 17, 26, 7], which we can use to sign the protocol messages and provide authenticity. Further, the key exchange protocol is bounded or continuous leakage-resilient, if the underlying signature scheme is bounded or continuous leakage-resilient.

4.4 Protocol π

In Table 3, we show the construction of protocol π. KeyGen, Enc and Dec are the key generation, encryption and decryption algorithms of the underlying CPLA2-secure, ϵ-PG-IND-public-key cryptosystem PKE respectively. KG, Sign and Vfy are the key generation, signature generation and signature verification algorithms of the underlying leakage-resilient signature scheme SIG respectively. KDF is a secure key derivation function which generates the session key of length k. The protocol π is a Diffie-Hellman-type [11] key agreement protocol where $\mathbb{G}$ is a group of prime order q and generator g. We require that q is the size of the message space M. After exchanging the public values both principals compute a Diffie-Hellman-type shared secret value, and then compute the session key using the key derivation function KDF, with inputs identities of the two principals and the Diffie-Hellman-type shared secret. The computations which leak information are underlined.

4.5 Security Proof of the Protocol π

We prove the security of the generic protocol π in the $(\cdot)$AFL-eCK model. If the underlying primitives are secure in bounded or continuous leakage model, the protocol π is BAFL-eCK-secure or CAFL-eCK-secure respectively.

Theorem 1. Let $\mathcal{A}$ be any PPT adversary against the protocol π. Then the advantage of $\mathcal{A}$ against $(\cdot)$AFL-eCK-

A (Initiator)		B (Responder)
	Initial Setup	
$sk_A, vk_A \xleftarrow{\$} \mathrm{KG}(1^k)$		$sk_B, vk_B \xleftarrow{\$} \mathrm{KG}(1^k)$
$s_A, p_A \xleftarrow{\$} \mathrm{KeyGen}(1^k)$		$s_B, p_B \xleftarrow{\$} \mathrm{KeyGen}(1^k)$
	Protocol Execution	
$r_A \xleftarrow{\$} \widehat{\mathrm{C}}$		**If** $\mathrm{Vfy}(vk_A, X_A, \sigma_A) =$ "true" $\{$
$\widetilde{r_A} \leftarrow \underline{\mathrm{Dec}}(s_A, r_A)$		$r_B \xleftarrow{\$} \widehat{\mathrm{C}}$
$X_A \leftarrow g^{\widetilde{r_A}}$		$\widetilde{r_B} \leftarrow \underline{\mathrm{Dec}}(s_B, r_B)$
$\sigma_A \xleftarrow{\$} \underline{\mathrm{Sign}}(sk_A, (A, B, X_A))$	$\xrightarrow{A,B,X_A,\sigma_A}$	$X_B \leftarrow g^{\widetilde{r_B}}$
	$\xleftarrow{B,A,X_B,\sigma_B}$	$\sigma_B \xleftarrow{\$} \underline{\mathrm{Sign}}(sk_B, (B, A, X_B))$
If $\mathrm{Vfy}(vk_B, (B, A, X_B), \sigma_B) =$ "true" $\{$		
$\widetilde{r_A} \leftarrow \underline{\mathrm{Dec}}(s_A, r_A)$		
$K_{AB} \leftarrow \mathrm{KDF}(A, B, X_B^{\widetilde{r_A}})$		$K_{AB} \leftarrow \mathrm{KDF}(A, B, X_A^{\widetilde{r_B}})$
$\}$		$\}$

Table 3: Protocol π. Underline denotes operations to which leakage functions apply.

security of protocol π, $Adv_{\pi}^{(\cdot)\text{AFL-eCK}}$ is:

$$Adv_{\pi}^{(\cdot)\text{AFL-eCK}}(\mathcal{A}) \leq \max\Big[N_P Adv_{\text{SIG}}^{\text{UFCMLA}}(\mathcal{E}), N_P^2 {N_s}^2\big(\epsilon_{pg} + 2Adv_{\text{PKE}}^{\text{CPLA2}}(\mathcal{D}) + Adv_{q,g}^{\text{DDH}}(\mathcal{C}) + Adv_{\text{KDF}}(\mathcal{B})\big)\Big].$$

$\mathcal{B}, \mathcal{C}, \mathcal{D}, \mathcal{E}$ are efficient algorithms constructed using the adversary $\mathcal{A}$, against the underlying key derivation function, KDF, DDH problem, public-key cryptosystem, PKE and the signature scheme, SIG, respectively, where PKE is ϵ-PG-IND.

In order to formally prove the $(\cdot)$AFL-eCK-security of the protocol π, we use the game hopping technique [31]: define a sequence of games and relate the adversary's advantage of distinguishing each game from the previous game to the advantage of breaking one of the underlying cryptographic primitive. The proof structure is similar to Boyd et al. [6]. The proof sketch of Theorem 1 is available in Appendix A. The full proof is available in the full version of the paper [2].

5. REFERENCES

[1] A. Akavia, S. Goldwasser, and V. Vaikuntanathan. Simultaneous hardcore bits and cryptography against memory attacks. In *Theory of Cryptology Conference*, pages 474–495, 2009.

[2] J. Alawatugoda, D. Stebila, and C. Boyd. Modelling after-the-fact leakage for key exchange (full version). *IACR Cryptology ePrint Archive*, Report 2014/131.

[3] J. Alwen, Y. Dodis, and D. Wichs. Leakage-resilient public-key cryptography in the bounded-retrieval model. In *CRYPTO*, pages 36–54, 2009.

[4] M. Bellare and P. Rogaway. Entity authentication and key distribution. In *CRYPTO*, pages 232–249, 1993.

[5] D. J. Bernstein. Cache-timing attacks on AES. Technical report, 2005. http://cr.yp.to/antiforgery/cachetiming-20050414.pdf.

[6] C. Boyd, Y. Cliff, J. M. G. Nieto, and K. G. Paterson. One-round key exchange in the standard model. *International Journal of Advanced Computer Technology*, pages 181–199, 2009.

[7] Z. Brakerski, Y. T. Kalai, J. Katz, and V. Vaikuntanathan. Overcoming the hole in the bucket: Public-key cryptography resilient to continual memory leakage. *IACR Cryptology ePrint Archive*, Report 2010/278, 2010.

[8] D. Brumley and D. Boneh. Remote timing attacks are practical. In *USENIX Security Symposium*, pages 1–14, 2003.

[9] R. Canetti and H. Krawczyk. Analysis of key-exchange protocols and their use for building secure channels. In *EUROCRYPT*, pages 453–474, 2001.

[10] R. Cramer and V. Shoup. Universal hash proofs and a paradigm for adaptive chosen ciphertext secure public-key encryption. In *EUROCRYPT*, pages 45–64. Springer, 2002.

[11] W. Diffie and M. Hellman. New directions in cryptography. *IEEE Transactions on Information Theory*, pages 644 – 654, 1976.

[12] Y. Dodis, K. Haralambiev, A. López-Alt, and D. Wichs. Efficient public-key cryptography in the presence of key leakage. In *ASIACRYPT*, pages 613–631, 2010.

[13] Y. Dodis, Y. T. Kalai, and S. Lovett. On cryptography with auxiliary input. In *STOC*, pages 621–630, 2009.

[14] Y. Dodis, L. Reyzin, and A. Smith. Fuzzy extractors: How to generate strong keys from biometrics and other noisy data. In *EUROCRYPT*, pages 523–540, 2004.

[15] S. Dziembowski and S. Faust. Leakage-resilient cryptography from the inner-product extractor. In *ASIACRYPT*, pages 702–721, 2011.

[16] S. Dziembowski and K. Pietrzak. Leakage-resilient cryptography. In *IEEE Symposium on Foundations of Computer Science*, pages 293–302, 2008.

[17] S. Faust, E. Kiltz, K. Pietrzak, and G. N. Rothblum. Leakage-resilient signatures. *IACR Cryptology ePrint Archive*, Report 2009/282, 2009.

[18] S. Halevi and H. Lin. After-the-fact leakage in public-key encryption. In *Theory of Cryptology Conference*, pages 107–124, 2011.

[19] M. Hutter, S. Mangard, and M. Feldhofer. Power and EM attacks on passive 13.56MHz RFID devices. In *CHES*, pages 320–333, 2007.

[20] J. Katz and V. Vaikuntanathan. Signature schemes with bounded leakage resilience. In *ASIACRYPT*, pages 703–720, 2009.

[21] E. Kiltz and K. Pietrzak. Leakage resilient elgamal encryption. In *ASIACRYPT*, pages 595–612, 2010.

[22] E. Kiltz, K. Pietrzak, M. Stam, and M. Yung. A new randomness extraction paradigm for hybrid encryption. In *EUROCRYPT*, pages 590–609, 2009.

[23] P. C. Kocher. Timing attacks on implementations of Diffie-Hellman, RSA, DSS, and other systems. In *CRYPTO*, pages 104–113, 1996.

[24] H. Krawczyk. On extract-then-expand key derivation functions and an HMAC-based KDF. http://webee.technion.ac.il/ hugo/kdf/kdf.pdf, 2008.

[25] B. LaMacchia, K. Lauter, and A. Mityagin. Stronger security of authenticated key exchange. In *ProvSec*, pages 1–16, 2007.

[26] T. Malkin, I. Teranishi, Y. Vahlis, and M. Yung. Signatures resilient to continual leakage on memory and computation. In *Theory of Cryptology Conference*, pages 89–106, 2011.

[27] T. Messerges, E. Dabbish, and R. Sloan. Examining smart-card security under the threat of power analysis attacks. *IEEE Transactions on Computers*, pages 541–552, 2002.

[28] S. Micali and L. Reyzin. Physically observable cryptography (extended abstract). In *Theory of Cryptology Conference*, pages 278–296, 2004.

[29] D. Moriyama and T. Okamoto. Leakage resilient eCK-secure key exchange protocol without random oracles. In *ASIACCS*, pages 441–447, 2011.

[30] M. Naor and G. Segev. Public-key cryptosystems resilient to key leakage. In *CRYPTO*, pages 18–35. 2009.

[31] V. Shoup. Sequences of games: a tool for taming complexity in security proofs. *IACR Cryptology ePrint Archive*, Report 2004/332, 2004.

[32] G. Yang, Y. Mu, W. Susilo, and D. S. Wong. Leakage resilient authenticated key exchange secure in the auxiliary input model. In *ISPEC*, pages 204–217, 2013.

APPENDIX

A. PROOF SKETCH

A.1 A partner to the test session exists.

In this case, the adversary is allowed to corrupt both principals or reveal ephemeral keys from both oracles. We assume that the adversary $\mathcal{A}$ can win the $(\cdot)$AFL-eCK challenge against the protocol π with non-negligible advantage $Adv_\pi^{(\cdot)\text{AFL-eCK}}(\mathcal{A})$. We split this case into four sub cases as follows:

1. Adversary corrupts neither owner or nor partner principal to the test session.
2. Adversary corrupts both the owner and partner principals to the test session.
3. Adversary corrupts the owner to the test session, but does not corrupt the partner to the test session.
4. Adversary corrupts the partner to the test session, but does not corrupt the owner to the test session.

A.1.1 Adversary corrupts neither owner or nor partner principal to the test session.

Game 1: This game is the original game.

Game 2: Same as Game 1 with the following exception: before $\mathcal{A}$ begins, two distinct random principals $U^*, V^* \xleftarrow{\$} \{U_1, ..., U_{N_P}\}$ are chosen and two random numbers $s^*, t^* \xleftarrow{\$} \{1, ...N_s\}$ are chosen, where N_P is the number of protocol principals and N_S is the number of sessions on a principal. The oracle $\Pi_{U^*,V^*}^{s^*}$ is chosen as the target session and the oracle $\Pi_{V^*,U^*}^{t^*}$ is chosen as the partner to the target session. If the test session is not the oracle $\Pi_{U^*,V^*}^{s^*}$ or partner to the oracle is not $\Pi_{V^*,U^*}^{t^*}$, the Game 2 challenger aborts the game.

Game 3: Same as Game 2 with the following exception: the Game 3 challenger randomly chooses a pseudo-ephemeral value $\widetilde{r_{U^*}} \xleftarrow{\$} \mathbb{Z}_q^*$ and computes the ephemeral key $r_{U^*} \xleftarrow{\$} \text{Enc}(p_{U^*}, \widetilde{r_{U^*}})$. Then computes $K_{U^*V^*} \leftarrow \text{KDF}(U^*, V^*, X_{V^*}^{\widetilde{r_{U^*}}})$. When the adversary asks the $\texttt{Test}(U^*, V^*, s^*)$, Game 3 challenger will answer with K_{U^*,V^*}. Further, since a partner session to the test session exists, when the adversary asks $\texttt{Test}(V^*, U^*, t^*)$, Game 3 challenger will answer with K_{U^*,V^*}.

Game 4: Same as Game 3 with the following exception: the Game 4 challenger randomly chooses a pseudo-ephemeral value $\widetilde{r'_{U^*}} \xleftarrow{\$} \mathbb{Z}_q^*$. Then computes $K_{U^*V^*} \leftarrow \text{KDF}(U^*, V^*, X_{V^*}^{\widetilde{r'_{U^*}}})$ and sends it to the adversary $\mathcal{A}$ as the answer to the $\texttt{Test}(U^*, V^*, s^*)$ query or $\texttt{Test}(V^*, U^*, t^*)$ query.

Game 5: Same as Game 4 with the following exception: the Game 5 challenger randomly chooses a pseudo-ephemeral value $\widetilde{r'_{V^*}} \xleftarrow{\$} \mathbb{Z}_q^*$. Then computes $K_{U^*V^*} \leftarrow \text{KDF}(U^*, V^*, X_{U^*}^{\widetilde{r'_{V^*}}})$ and sends it to the adversary $\mathcal{A}$ as the answer to the $\texttt{Test}(U^*, V^*, s^*)$ query or $\texttt{Test}(V^*, U^*, t^*)$ query.

Game 6: Same as Game 5 with the following exception: the Game 6 challenger randomly chooses $z \xleftarrow{\$} \mathbb{Z}_q^*$ and computes $K_{U^*V^*} \leftarrow \text{KDF}(U^*, V^*, g^z)$. When the adversary asks the $\texttt{Test}(U^*, V^*, s^*)$ query, Game 3 challenger will answer with K_{U^*,V^*}. Further, since a partner session to the test session exists, when the adversary asks $\texttt{Test}(V^*, U^*, t^*)$ query, Game 3 challenger will answer with K_{U^*,V^*}.

Game 7: Same as Game 6 with the following exception: the Game 7 challenger randomly chooses $K \xleftarrow{\$} \{0,1\}^k$ and sends it to the adversary $\mathcal{A}$ as the answer to the $\texttt{Test}(U^*, V^*, s^*)$ query or $\texttt{Test}(V^*, U^*, t^*)$ query.

Differences between games: In this section the adversary's advantage of distinguishing each game from the previous game is investigated. $Succ_{\text{Game x}}(\mathcal{A})$ denotes the event that the adversary $\mathcal{A}$ wins Game x, $Adv_{\text{Game x}}(\mathcal{A})$ denotes the advantage of the adversary $\mathcal{A}$ of winning Game x. Game 1 is the original game. Hence,

$$Adv_{\text{Game 1}}(\mathcal{A}) = Adv_\pi^{(\cdot)\text{AFL-eCK}}(\mathcal{A}). \quad (1)$$

Game 1 and Game 2: The probability of Game 2 to be halted due to incorrect choice of the test session is $1 - \frac{1}{N_P^2 N_s^2}$. Unless the incorrect choice happens, Game 2 is identical to Game 1. Hence,

$$Adv_{\text{Game 2}}(\mathcal{A}) = \frac{1}{N_P{}^2 N_s^2} Adv_{\text{Game 1}}(\mathcal{A}). \quad (2)$$

Game 2 and Game 3: We introduce an algorithm $\mathcal{F}$ which is constructed using the adversary $\mathcal{A}$. If $\mathcal{A}$ can distinguish the difference between Game 2 and Game 3, then $\mathcal{F}$ can distinguish whether a message/cphertext pair (m, c) belongs to the distribution D_1 or D_2. $\mathcal{F}$ receives a pair $(r_{U^*}, \widetilde{r_{U^*}})$

such that $\widetilde{r_{U^*}} = \text{Dec}(s_{U^*}, r_{U^*})$. $\mathcal{F}$ uses r_{U^*} as the ephemeral key of U^* and $\widetilde{r_{U^*}}$ as the pseudo-ephemeral key of U^*. If a random ephemeral key $r_{U^*} \xleftarrow{\$} \mathbb{Z}_p^*$ is chosen first and the pseudo-ephemeral value $\widetilde{r_{U^*}} \leftarrow \text{Dec}(s_{U^*}, r_{U^*})$ is computed, then the simulation constructed by $\mathcal{F}$ is identical to Game 2. Otherwise if a random pseudo-ephemeral value $\widetilde{r_{U^*}} \xleftarrow{\$}$ $mathbbZ_p^*$ is chosen first and the ephemeral key $r_{U^*} \xleftarrow{\$}$ $\text{Enc}(p_{U^*}, \widetilde{r_{U^*}})$ is computed, then the simulation constructed by $\mathcal{F}$ is identical to Game 3. If $\mathcal{A}$ can distinguish whether a message/cphertext pair (m, c) belongs to the distribution D_1 or D_2. Hence,

$$|Adv_{\text{Game }2}(\mathcal{A}) - Adv_{\text{Game }3}(\mathcal{A})| \leq \epsilon. \quad (3)$$

Game 3 and Game 4: We introduce an algorithm $\mathcal{D}$ which is constructed using the adversary $\mathcal{A}$. If $\mathcal{A}$ can distinguish the difference between Game 3 and Game 4, then $\mathcal{D}$ can be used against a CPLA2 challenger. The algorithm $\mathcal{D}$ uses the public-key of the CPLA2 challenger as the public key of the protocol principal U^* and generates public/secret key pairs for all other protocol principals. $\mathcal{D}$ generates signing/verification key pairs for every protocol principal. $\mathcal{D}$ picks two random strings, $r_0, r_1 \xleftarrow{\$} \{0,1\}^k$ and passes them to the CPLA2 challenger. From the CPLA2 challenger, $\mathcal{D}$ receives a challenge ciphertexts C_1 such that $C_1 \xleftarrow{\$} \text{Enc}(pk_{U^*}, r_\theta)$ where $r_\theta = r_0$ or $r_\theta = r_1$. If $\theta = 1$, then r_1 is the decryption of C_1 and the simulation constructed by $\mathcal{D}$ is identical to Game 3 whereas if $\theta = 0$, then r_0 is the decryption of C_1 and the simulation constructed by $\mathcal{D}$ is identical to Game 4. Hence,

$$|Adv_{\text{Game }3}(\mathcal{A}) - Adv_{\text{Game }4}(\mathcal{A})| \leq Adv_{\text{PKE}}^{\text{CPLA2}}(\mathcal{D}). \quad (4)$$

Game 4 and Game 5: Similar to Game 3 and Game 4.

$$|Adv_{\text{Game }4}(\mathcal{A}) - Adv_{\text{Game }5}(\mathcal{A})| \leq Adv_{\text{PKE}}^{\text{CPLA2}}(\mathcal{D}). \quad (5)$$

Game 5 and Game 6: We get We construct an algorithm $\mathcal{C}$ against the DDH challenge, using the adversary $\mathcal{A}$. The DDH challenger sends values (g^x, g^y, g^z) such that either $z = xy$ or $z \xleftarrow{\$} \mathbb{Z}_q^*$, as the inputs to the algorithm $\mathcal{C}$. If $\mathcal{C}$'s input is a Diffie-Hellman triple, simulation constructed by $\mathcal{C}$ is identical to Game 5, otherwise it is identical to Game 6. If $\mathcal{A}$ can distinguish whether $g^z = g^{xy}$ or not, then $\mathcal{C}$ can answer the DDH challenge. Note that `EphemeralKeyReveal`(U^*, V^*, s^*) or `EphemeralKeyReveal`(V^*, U^*, t^*) is prohibited since the adversary is allowed to corrupt both the owner and the partner to the test session. Hence,

$$|Adv_{\text{Game }5}(\mathcal{A}) - Adv_{\text{Game }6}(\mathcal{A})| \leq Adv_{q,g}^{\text{DDH}}(\mathcal{C}). \quad (6)$$

Game 6 and Game 7: We construct an algorithm $\mathcal{B}$ against the security of the key derivation function KDF, using the adversary $\mathcal{A}$. $\mathcal{B}$ receives K such that K is computed using the KDF or randomly chosen from the session key space. If K is computed using the KDF, simulation constructed by $\mathcal{B}$ is identical to Game 6, otherwise it is identical to Game 7. If $\mathcal{A}$ can distinguish between Game 6 and Game 7, then $\mathcal{B}$ can distinguish whether the value K is computed using KDF or randomly chosen, and answer the security challenge on key derivation function. Hence,

$$|Adv_{\text{Game }6}(\mathcal{A}) - Adv_{\text{Game }7}(\mathcal{A})| \leq Adv_{\text{KDF}}(\mathcal{B}). \quad (7)$$

Semantic security of the session key in Game 7: Since the session key K of $\Pi_{U^*,V^*}^{s^*}$ is chosen randomly and independently from all other values, $\mathcal{A}$ does not have any advantage in Game 7. Hence,

$$Adv_{\text{Game }7}(\mathcal{A}) = 0 \quad (8)$$

Using equations (1)–(8) we find,

$$Adv_\pi^{(\cdot)\text{AFL-eCK}}(\mathcal{A}) \leq N_P^2 N_s^{\,2}\big(\epsilon + 2Adv_{\text{PKE}}^{\text{CPLA2}}(\mathcal{D}) + Adv_{q,g}^{\text{DDH}}(\mathcal{C}) + Adv_{\text{KDF}}(\mathcal{B})\big).$$

A.1.2 Adversary corrupts both the owner and partner principals to the test session.

Game 1: Same as Game 1 in Case A.1.1. Game 2: Same as Game 2 in Case A.1.1. Game 3: Same as Game 6 in Case A.1.1. Game 4: Same as Game 7 in Case A.1.1. Hence,

$$Adv_\pi^{(\cdot)\text{AFL-eCK}}(\mathcal{A}) \leq N_P^2 N_s^{\,2}\big(Adv_{q,g}^{\text{DDH}}(\mathcal{C}) + Adv_{\text{KDF}}(\mathcal{B})\big).$$

A.1.3 Adversary corrupts the partner, but not the owner to the test session.

Game 1: Same as Game 1 in Case A.1.1. Game 2: Same as Game 2 in Case A.1.1. Game 3: Same as Game 3 in Case A.1.1. Game 4: Same as Game 4 in Case A.1.1. Game 5: Same as Game 6 in Case A.1.1. Game 6: Same as Game 7 in Case A.1.1. In this case we find that,

$$Adv_\pi^{(\cdot)\text{AFL-eCK}}(\mathcal{A}) \leq N_P^2 N_s^{\,2}\big(\epsilon + Adv_{\text{PKE}}^{\text{CPLA2}}(\mathcal{D}) + Adv_{q,g}^{\text{DDH}}(\mathcal{C}) + Adv_{\text{KDF}}(\mathcal{B})\big).$$

A.1.4 Adversary corrupts the owner, but not the partner to the test session.

Game 1: Same as Game 1 in Case A.1.1. Game 2: Same as Game 2 in Case A.1.1. Game 3: Same as Game 3 in Case A.1.1. Game 4: Same as Game 5 in Case A.1.1. Game 5: Same as Game 6 in Case A.1.1. Game 6: Same as Game 7 in Case A.1.1. In this case we find that,

$$Adv_\pi^{(\cdot)\text{AFL-eCK}}(\mathcal{A}) \leq N_P^2 N_s^{\,2}\big(\epsilon + Adv_{\text{PKE}}^{\text{CPLA2}}(\mathcal{D}) + Adv_{q,g}^{\text{DDH}}(\mathcal{C}) + Adv_{\text{KDF}}(\mathcal{B})\big).$$

A.2 No partner exists to the test session.

When the partner session does not exist, the owner of the test session shares the session key with the active adversary. In this situation adversary is not allowed to corrupt the intended partner principal to the test session. Assume that the adversary $\mathcal{A}$ asks a Send query to some fresh oracle, such that it accepts, but the signature used in the query is not generated by a legitimate party.

Game 1: Same as Game 1 in Case A.1.1. Game 2: Same as Game 1 with the following exception: before $\mathcal{A}$ begins, the Game 2 challenger guesses the identity, V^*, of the partner principal to the test session and if the guess in incorrect it aborts the game. The probability of Game 2 to be aborted due to incorrect guess of the partner principal to the test session is $1 - \frac{1}{N_P^2}$. Unless the incorrect guess happens, Game 2 is identical to Game1. The owner principal accepts the message coming from the intended partner, because the owner computes $\text{Vfy}(vk_{V^*}, X_{V^*}, \sigma_{V^*})$ is "true". But the principal V^* is not corrupted and the message X_{V^*} is not signed by the principal V^*, because of no partner. Hence,

$$Adv_\pi^{(\cdot)\text{AFL-eCK}}(\mathcal{A}) = N_P Adv_{\text{SIG}}^{\text{UFCMLA}}(\mathcal{E}).$$

Combine Case A.1 and A.2 to obtain the relationship in Theorem 1.

Practical Secret Key Agreement for Full-Duplex Near Field Communications

Rong Jin
University of Michigan,
Dearborn , MI 48128
jinrong@umich.edu

Xianru Du
University of Michigan,
Dearborn , MI 48128
duxianru@umich.edu

Zi Deng
University of Michigan,
Dearborn, MI 48128
zdeng@umich.edu

Kai Zeng
University of Michigan,
Dearborn , MI 48128
kzeng@umich.edu

Jing Xu
Huazhong University of
Science and Technology
xujing@hust.edu.cn

ABSTRACT

Near Field Communication (NFC) is a promising short distance radio communication technology for many useful applications. Although its communication range is short, NFC alone does not guarantee secure communication and is subject to security attacks, such as eavesdropping attack. Generating a shared key and using symmetric key cryptography to secure the communication between NFC devices is a feasible solution to prevent various attacks. However, conventional Diffie-Hellman key agreement protocol is not preferable for resource constrained NFC devices due to its extensive computational overhead and energy consumption. In this paper, we propose a practical, fast and energy-efficient key agreement scheme, called RIWA (Random bIts transmission with Waveform shAking), for NFC devices by exploiting its full-duplex capability. In RIWA, two devices send random bits to each other simultaneously without strict synchronization or perfect match of amplitude and phase. On the contrary, RIWA randomly introduces synchronization offset and mismatch of amplitude and phase for each bit transmission in order to prevent a passive attacker from determining the generated key. A shared bit can be established when two devices send different bits. We conduct theoretical analysis on the correctness and security strength of RIWA, and extensive simulations to evaluate its effectiveness. We build a testbed based on USRP software defined radio and conduct proof-of-concept experiments to evaluate RIWA in a real-world environment. It shows that RIWA achieves a high key generation rate about 26kbps and is immune to eavesdropping attack even when the attacker is within several centimeters away from the legitimate devices. RIWA is a practical, fast, energy-efficient, and secure key agreement scheme for resource-constrained NFC devices.

ASIA CCS'14, June 4–6, 2014, Kyoto, Japan.

http://dx.doi.org/10.1145/2590296.2590327 .

Categories and Subject Descriptors

C.2.0 [**Computer-Communication Networks**]: General—*Security and protection*; D.2.0 [**Software Engineering**]: General—*Protection mechanisms*

General Terms

Theory,Design,Security

Keywords

near field communication, practical key agreement, energy efficient, USRP

1. INTRODUCTION

Near Field Communication (NFC) provides a convenient proximity radio communication technology for many useful applications [14, 3, 10, 18], including contactless payment [20], identification, data exchange, and simplified device pairing [2]. Although the communication range of NFC is short, NFC alone does not prevent data modification and eavesdropping [14, 13]. Unfortunately, ISO standard offers no security technique for NFC [1]. Applications may use higher-layer cryptographic mechanisms to deal with security threats.

Previous works show that using symmetric key cryptography to establish a secure channel between two NFC devices is a fesaible way to protect against various attacks [14]. A conventional mechanism used to generate a symmetric key between two devices is the Diffie-Hellman (D-H) key agreement protocol. However, since NFC devices are usually powered by battery with limited computation and communication capability, D-H key agreement protocol is not preferable for NFC devices due to its high computational overhead and energy consumption [15].

Recently, a low-cost key agreement scheme exploiting duplex capability of NFC devices has been proposed in [14, 3]. The basic idea is illustrated in Fig. 1 showing the baseband signal with Manchester encoding. Both NFC devices, say Alice and Bob, simultaneously send random bits of 0's or 1's. While sending, one (or both) of the devices can detect the receiving signal. When Alice and Bob send different bits (one sends 0 and the other sends 1), an eavesdropper only overhears the superposed signal as a flat voltage, so cannot figure out who sent the 0 or who sent 1. Since Alice and

Bob know what they have sent and received, they can use the bits sent at either side to establish a shared key.

Unfortunately, this scheme is impractical due to the strict requirements of perfect synchronization [14] and perfect match of signal amplitude and phase, which are very hard to be satisfied in practice due to the following reasons. First, it is well known that time synchronization for distributed devices is a difficult problem [16] and suffers from clock drift and skew. Second, at RF front-end, digital baseband signal is converted to analog, up-converted to the carrier frequency, scaled to the right power, and sent. Due to the impairment of the device, the RF signal being transmitted is in fact distorted relative to the digital baseband representation [6]. As a result, it is nearly impossible for a device to exactly control what it is transmitting and making perfect synchronization and absolute match of amplitude and phase.

Once there is a slight synchronization offset or mismatch of the amplitude or phase, the key can be broken. An intuitive way to break the key is shown in Fig. 2 under non-perfect synchronization. An eavesdropper can determine the bit sent by Alice and Bob by observing the peak or valley in the superposed RF signal. Suppose Bob is ahead of Alice. If eavesdropper detects a valley, he would know that Alice sends 0 and Bob sends 1 and vice versa.

In this paper, aiming at a practical key agreement scheme tackling imperfect synchronization and mismatch of signal amplitude and phase, we propose RIWA (Random bIts transmission with Waveform shAking), which uses a novel idea of waveform shaking shown in Fig. 3. Suppose there is a slight synchronization offset of ε between Alice and Bob. Rather than compensating ε, RIWA introduces another random synchronization offset γ by shifting the waveform. γ differs from ε in that it has a random value and can be positive or negative, corresponding to right or left shifting. γ disturbs the start moment of the bits and covers up ε. Attackers who use ε to distinguish the RF signals of Alice and Bob will make mistakes. For amplitude and phase mismatch, we propose similar ideas of adding randomness to cover it up.

Our main contributions are as follows:

- We propose a key agreement scheme, RIWA, for NFC devices by exploiting its duplex capability without strict requirement of perfect time synchronization or absolute match of signal amplitude and phase.
- We prove the correctness of RIWA analytically, and show its effectiveness by simulations.
- We build a testbed based on USRP software defined radio and conduct proof-of-concept experiments to evaluate the effectiveness and security strength of RIWA in a real-world environment.

We make the following findings:

- RIWA can generate a shared key between two NFC devices at a high rate about 26kbps.
- RIWA is immune to eavesdropping attacks even when the attacker is a few centimeters away from the legitimate users.

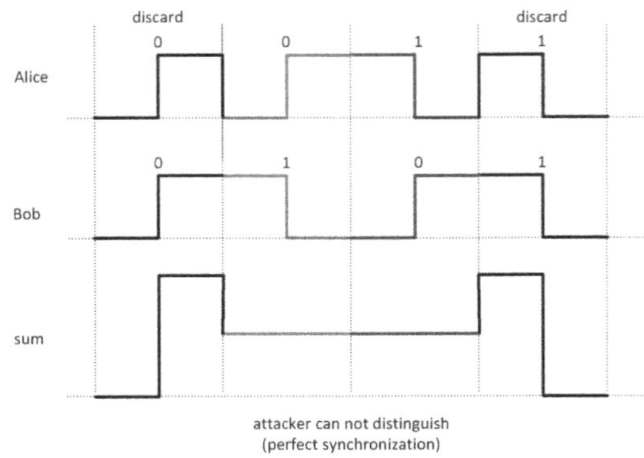

Figure 1: NFC specific key agreement assuming perfect synchronization

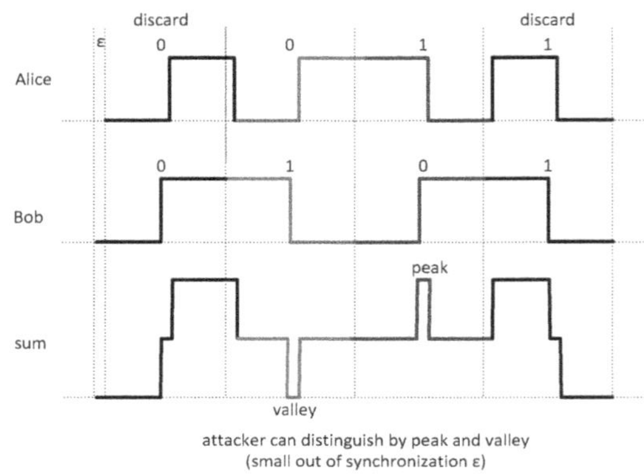

Figure 2: NFC specific key agreement considering out of synchronization

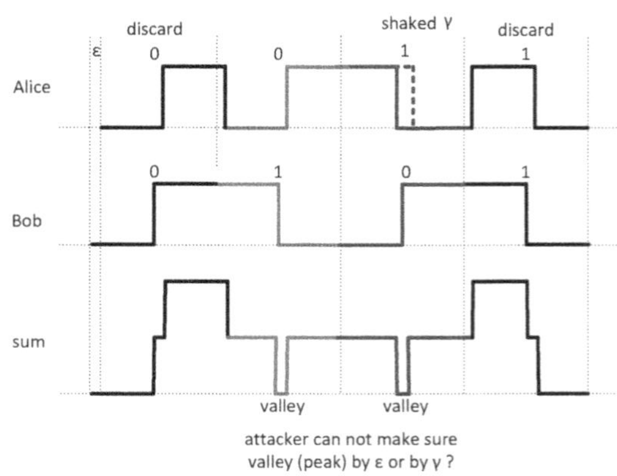

Figure 3: Proposed key agreement considering out of synchronization

2. SYSTEM MODEL

We consider two legitimate parties, say Alice and Bob, who want to extract a shared secret key via communication without any pre-shared secret. They are equipped with active NFC devices which are full duplex enabled. That is, they can transmit random signals to each other while detecting the received signal. As specified by the ISO standard, Alice and Bob use Manchester encoding and ASK modulation [1]. They are close to each other within several centimeters, and operate at 13.5MHz carrier frequency.

2.1 Attacker Model

We consider a powerful passive attacker, Eve, who tries to compromise the generated key by eavesdropping on the communication between Alice and Bob. Eve possesses a high quality wireless channel in eavesdropping. Eve may have multiple antennas, and may be in any location with respect to the legitimate NFC devices. She may use standard or custom-built hardware. She can capture baseband and RF signals with high sensitivity and sampling rate. In this case, she can sense slight out of synchronization and the mismatch of signal amplitude and phase. Eve also has powerful computational ability. She can store all the overheard signals and conduct sophisticated signal processing or data analysis.

2.2 Signal Model

We assume Alice and Bob send random bits of 0's and 1's to each other simultaneously. The bit streams sent by Alice and Bob are $\mathbf{C_a}$ and $\mathbf{C_b}$, respectively.

$$\begin{aligned}\mathbf{C_a} &= [C_a(1), C_a(2), \cdots C_a(N_a)] \\ \mathbf{C_b} &= [C_b(1), C_b(2), \cdots C_b(N_b)]\end{aligned} \tag{1}$$

where $C_a(i)$ and $C_b(i)$ $(1 \leq i \leq N)$ are the ith bit sent by Alice and Bob, respectively.

We give the representation of the signal received at Alice, Bob, and Eve as follows.

2.2.1 *Signal Model of Legitimate Users*

The RF signals transmitted by Alice and Bob are

$$\begin{aligned}x_a(t) &= h_a^t r^t(C_a) + n_a^t(t) \\ x_b(t) &= h_b^t r^t(C_b) + n_b^t(t)\end{aligned} \tag{2}$$

where $r^t(C_a)$ and $r^t(C_b)$ are base band representation of $\mathbf{C_a}$ and $\mathbf{C_b}$. $x_a(t)$ and $x_b(t)$ are the RF waveform at carrier frequency. h_a^t and h_b^t represent the modulated transmission at the RF front-end. $n_a^t(t)$ and $n_b^t(t)$ are channel noises. Fig. 4 shows an example of ideal $\mathbf{C}$, r^t and $x(t)$, where typical NFC modulation method of Manchester coding with 100% ASK [1, 10] is assumed.

Due to proximity, the RF signals received by Alice and Bob are inductive coupling of each other [10], and can be written as

$$\begin{aligned}y_a(t) &= h_a^s x_a(t) + \eta x_b(t) \\ y_b(t) &= h_b^s x_b(t) + \eta x_a(t)\end{aligned} \tag{3}$$

where η is coupling coefficient [4]. h_a^s and h_b^s are the channels of NFC devices' self interference [19].

At receiving end, RF Signals are down converted to baseband

$$\begin{aligned}r_a^r &= h_a^r y_a(t) + n_a^r(t) \\ r_b^r &= h_b^r y_b(t) + n_b^r(t)\end{aligned} \tag{4}$$

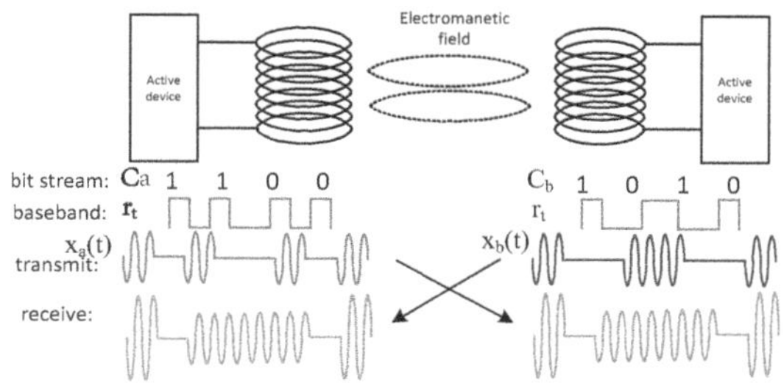

Figure 4: Proposed key agreement method working on two active NFC devices

where h_a^r and h_b^r represent down converted channels. $n_a^r(t)$ and $n_b^r(t)$ are channel noises.

2.2.2 *Signal Model of Attacker*

Similar to (3), the RF signals received by Eve can be written as

$$y_e(t) = \eta_{ea} x_a(t) + \eta_{eb} x_b(t) \tag{5}$$

where η_{ea} is the coupling coefficient between Eve and Alice. η_{eb} is the coupling coefficient between Eve and Bob. The baseband envelop is:

$$r_e^r = h_e^r y_e(t) + n_e^r(t) \tag{6}$$

where h_e^r is Eve's down converted channel. $n_e^r(t)$ is the channel noise.

3. BASIC SCHEME IS NOT SECURE IN PRACTICE

In order to motivate our solution, RIWA, we describe the basic key generation scheme proposed in [3] below, and show that it is not secure in practice under non-perfect synchronization and mismatch of signal amplitude and phase.

3.1 Basic Scheme

The basic scheme with baseband signal representation is illustrated in Fig. 1 assuming perfect synchronization and Manchester encoding. There are four possible cases when Alice and Bob send bits simultaneously:

- Case 1: Alice sends 0, Bob sends 1;
- Case 2: Alice sends 1, Bob sends 0;
- Case 3: both Alice and Bob send 1;
- Case 4: both Alice and Bob send 0.

For case 3, the superposed signal at Eve is the double of 1's. This does not help because Eve knows that both devices sent a 1. The same thing happens for case 4. Alice and Bob will discard the bits of these two cases.

It gets interesting for case 1 and case 2. Manchester coding has symmetric (flipped) waveform for 0 and 1. The superposed RF signals at Eve are exactly the same under case 1 and case 2; thus Eve cannot distinguish them. Alice and Bob can make use of the bits at either side as the shared bits to establish a key.

Unfortunately, the basic scheme is not secure in practice where there are inevitable inconsistency on time, amplitude, and phase between Alice and Bob's RF signals due to non identical devices, which gives Eve clues to distinguish case 1 and case 2.

The inconstancy exists in practice mainly due to the following two reasons:

1) Perfect transmission synchronization requires clock synchronization. It is well known that synchronization is a difficult problem for distributed devices [16] and suffers from clock drift and skew.

2) In fact, Alice or Bob *does not know exactly* what they are transmitting. What Alice or Bob does know is the clean digital representation of the signal in baseband $r^t(C_a)$ or $r^t(C_b)$. However, once the signal is converted to analog and up-converted to the carrier frequency and transmitted, the transmitted signal $x_a(t)$ or $x_b(t)$ will be distorted by the channel and noise randomly as modeled in Eq. (2). As a result, neither Alice nor Bob can make accurate compensation for inconsistency.

We identify three types of *inconsistency* between Alice and Bob that Eve can exploit to break the key.

1) Out of synchronization

$$x_a(t) = x_b(t + \varepsilon) \tag{7}$$

2) Amplitude mismatch

$$x_a(t) = \alpha x_b(t) \tag{8}$$

3) Phase mismatch

$$Hilbert[x_a(t)] = e^{j\theta} Hilbert[x_b(t)] \tag{9}$$

where Hilbert() represents Hilbert transform of a signal to present its analytic representation. NFC has a high bit rate of 106kbps. Since the bit duration is very small, ε, α and θ can be considered stable during the key generation [17]. Eve can use them to break the key.

3.2 Key Compromise Under Out of Synchronization

As illustrated in Fig. 2, we assume Bob is ahead of Alice. If Eve detects a valley in the middle of a bit, she would know that Alice sends 0 and Bob sends 1. If Eve detects a peak, she would know that Alice sends 1 and Bob sends 0.

3.3 Key Compromise Under Amplitude Mismatch

As illustrated in Fig. 5, we assume Bob's signal is stronger than Alice. If Eve detects a higher voltage at the first half bit and lower voltage at the second half bit, she would know that Alice sends 0 and Bob sends 1. If Eve detects a lower voltage at the first half bit and higher voltage at the second half bit, she would know that Alice sends 1 and Bob sends 0.

3.4 Key Compromise Under Phase Mismatch

As illustrated in Fig. 6, we assume Bob has postponed phase. If Eve detects a positive phase change in the middle of a bit, she would know that Alice sends 0 and Bob sends 1. If Eve detects a negative phase change, she would know that Alice sends 0 and Bob sends 1.

As a conclusion, the basic scheme is not secure in practice due to inevitable synchronization offset and mismatch of signal amplitude and phase. A more practical key agreement scheme is needed.

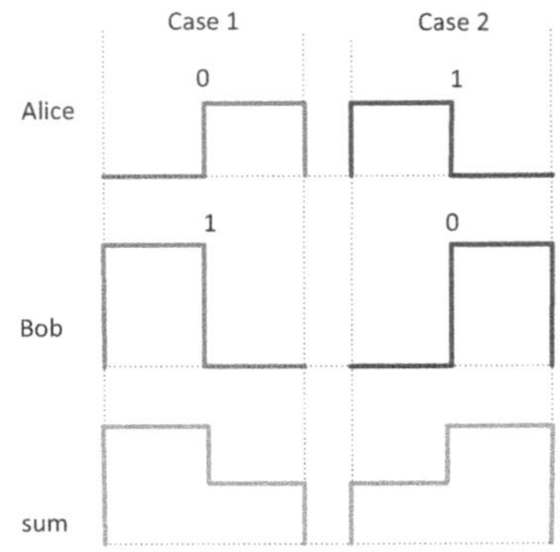

Figure 5: Superposed RF signal's envelop under non perfect amplitude match

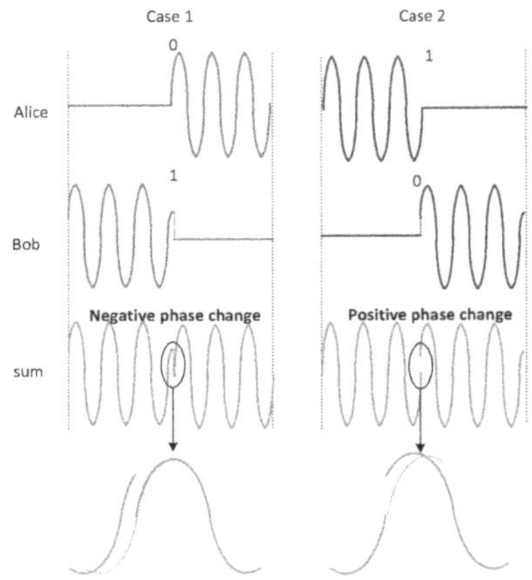

Figure 6: Superposed RF signal under non perfect phase match

4. RIWA

In this section, we propose RIWA to prevent an eavesdropper from breaking the key when there are inevitable non-perfect synchronization and mismatch of signal amplitude and phase. The basic idea of RIWA is to add randomness into Alice's and Bob's RF signal ($x_a(t)$ and $x_b(t)$) to make the signals received by Eve indistinguishable under case 1 and case 2. The randomness we introduce include 1) time shifting, 2) amplitude scaling, and 3) phase shifting, which are used to tackle out of synchronization, amplitude mismatch, and phase mismatch, respectively.

In the following subsections, we will describe these three types of waveform shaking methods and show their effectiveness.

In order to differentiate the shaken waveform from the original ones, we use $X_a(t)$ and $X_b(t)$ to denote shaken RF waveform. We also use $Y_e(t)$ to replace $y_e(t)$ in Eq. (5). We further use $Y_e^{c1}(t)$ and $Y_e^{c2}(t)$ to denote the superposed signal received by Eve under case 1 and case 2. Denote the set of all the possible $Y_e^{c1}(t)$ as S_{c1} and $Y_e^{c2}(t)$ as S_{c2}. If we can make S_{c1} and S_{c2} have a common set,

$$S_{c1} \cap S_{c2} \neq \phi \tag{10}$$

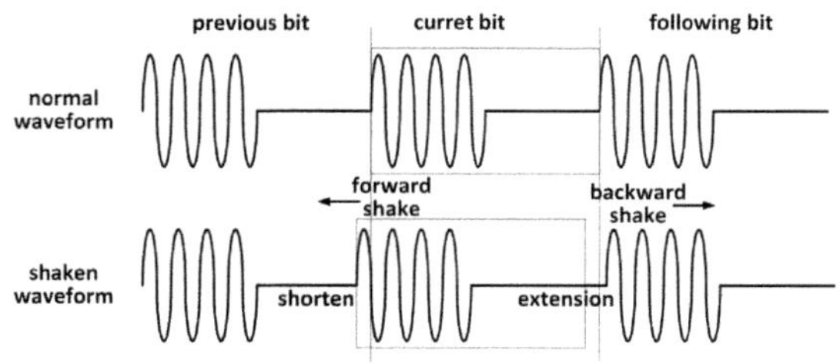

Figure 7: RF waveform shaking

Eve will not be able to distinguish case 1 and case 2 based on the received signal $z(t)$ if the following condition is satisfied

$$\exists\ Y_e^{c1}(t) = Y_e^{c2}(t) = z(t),\ z(t) \in S_{c1} \cap S_{c2} \tag{11}$$

That is, $z(t)$ could be an instance of $Y_e^{c1}(t)$ or an instance of $Y_e^{c2}(t)$. Therefore, as long as we can ensure (10), the effectiveness and security of RIWA can be ensured.

4.1 Random Time Shifting against Out of Synchronization

The random time shifting method against out of synchronization is shown in Fig. 7. For each bit, the waveform is shifted by γ in time, where γ is a random value that uniformly distributed in $[-\gamma_0, \gamma_0]$. The framework of the waveform is fixed. For forward shifting, the waveform of previous bit will be shorten by cutting off its last part. For backward shifting, the waveform of previous bit will be extended by prolonging its last part.

Now, we are going to prove that this shifting scheme provides security under the existence of out of synchronization. That is, (10) can be satisfied. We first prove a simple lemma

lemma 1: There are two cases: 1) Bob is υ ahead of Alice. The current bit that Alice sends is 1; the previous bit is 1; the following bit is 0. the current bit that Bob sends is 0; the previous bit is 1; the following bit is 0. 2) The same as 1) except that Alice is υ ahead of Bob; the current bit that Alice sends is 0; the current bit that Bob sends is 1. *During the period Alice and Bob transmitting the current bits, the two cases are identical to Eve.*

PROOF. Suppose the RF waveform of one bit without shifting has the length of T. The RF waveforms of current bits of Alice and Bob under case 1 has the total length of $T + \upsilon$, and can be written as

$$X_a^{c1}(t) = \begin{cases} 0 & \text{if } 0 < t \leq \upsilon \\ x_a(t) & \text{if } \upsilon < t \leq T + \upsilon \end{cases} \tag{12}$$

$$X_b^{c1}(t) = \begin{cases} x_b(t) & \text{if } 0 < t \leq T \\ 0 & \text{if } T < t \leq T + \upsilon \end{cases} \tag{13}$$

where $x_a(t) = x_b(t - \upsilon)$

Similarly, we can obtain the RF waveforms of Alice and Bob under case 2:

$$X_a^{c2}(t) = \begin{cases} x_a(t) & \text{if } 0 < t \leq T \\ 0 & \text{if } T < t \leq T + \upsilon \end{cases} \tag{14}$$

$$X_b^{c2}(t) = \begin{cases} 0 & \text{if } 0 < t \leq \upsilon \\ x_b(t) & \text{if } \upsilon < t \leq T + \upsilon \end{cases} \tag{15}$$

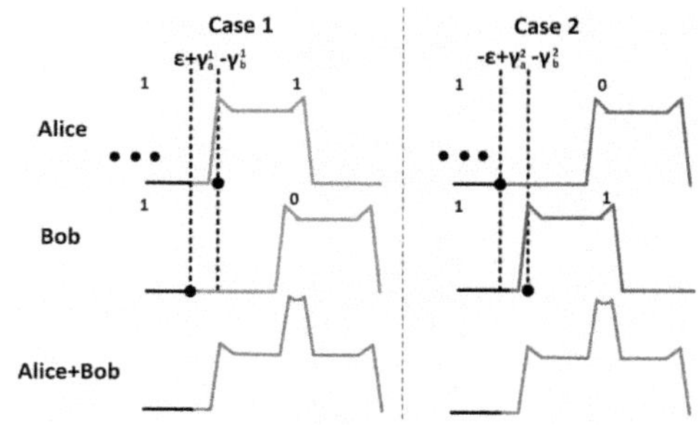

Figure 8: Superposed RF waveform (previous bits are both 1 for Alice and Bob)

where $x_b(t) = x_a(t - \upsilon)$

One can easily verify that $X_a^{c1}(t) = X_b^{c2}(t)$, and $X_b^{c1}(t) = X_a^{c2}(t)$. Thus $X_a^{c1}(t) + X_b^{c1}(t) = X_a^{c2}(t) + X_b^{c2}(t)$, which leads to $Y_e^{c1}(t) = Y_e^{c2}(t)$.

We use γ_a^1 to denote the shifting of Alice at case 1. For a small out of synchronization $\varepsilon \ll T$, as long as $\gamma_0 > \varepsilon/2$, we can easily find instances satisfying $2\varepsilon = \gamma_b^1 + \gamma_b^2 - \gamma_a^1 - \gamma_a^2$. So that

$$\upsilon = \varepsilon + \gamma_a^1 - \gamma_b^1 = -\varepsilon + \gamma_a^2 - \gamma_b^2 \tag{16}$$

We denote I_s as the set of instances. Using lemma 1 and (7), we can prove $I_s \subset S_{c1} \cap S_{c2} \neq \phi$. So that (10) is proved. □

Lemma 1 actually proves that for $C_a = [1X0]$, $C_b = [1X'0]$, where $X = 0, 1$, $X' = 1 - X$ are opposite bits. X can be used as a shared secret bit between Alice and Bob. Similarly, we can further prove the other 3 situations that can hide X from Eve.

lemma 2: $C_a = [0X0]$, $C_b = [0X'0]$
lemma 3: $C_a = [1X1]$, $C_b = [1X'1]$
lemma 4: $C_a = [0X1]$, $C_b = [0X'1]$

We conclude lemmas 1-4 to get lemma 5. Lemma 5: if the current bits of Alice and Bob are opposite, they are invisible to Eve under the condition that the previous bits of Alice and Bob are the same, as well as the following bits of Alice and Bob are the same.

Fig. 8 and Fig. 9 show the envelop of the superposed RF waveforms under case 1 and case 2, where the previous bits of Alice and Bob are the same. It can be seen that the superposed RF waveforms under two different cases are perfectly matched.

4.1.1 *Adding Guard Bits*

We must be cautious to design RIWA dealing with out of synchronization, because it is unable to prove the safety of current bits if previous bits of Alice and Bob are different. Fig. 10 shows such situation. It can be seen from the figure that, indeed there might be a small difference at $Y_e(t)$ between case 1 and case 2 due to the Gibbs phenomenon. A very powerful attacker may use it to crack some of the bits.

To avoid it, we add *guard bits*. The bits that Alice and Bob send are

$$\begin{aligned} \mathbf{C}_a &= [0, C_a(1), 0, C_a(2), 0 \cdots 0, C_a(N)] \\ \mathbf{C}_b &= [0, C_b(1), 0, C_b(2), 0 \cdots 0, C_b(N)] \end{aligned} \tag{17}$$

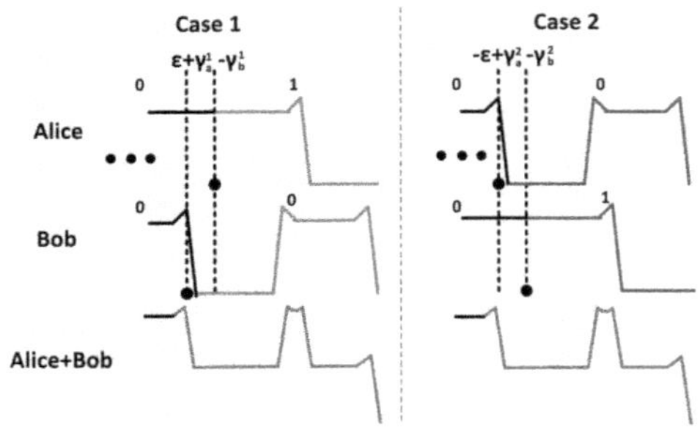

Figure 9: Superposed RF waveform (previous bits are both 0 for Alice and Bob)

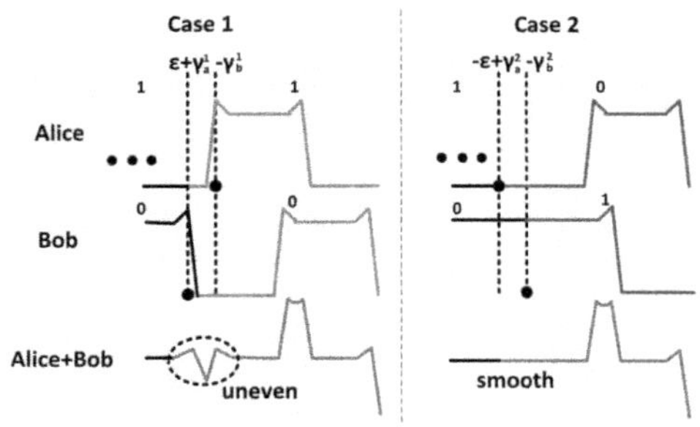

Figure 10: Superposed RF waveform (previous bits of Alice 1 and Bob 0)

where only $C_a(k)$ and $C_b(k)$ are random bits. In this way, the previous and following bits of $C_a(k)$ and $C_b(k)$ can be guaranteed identical. The key generation rate however reduces by 1/2. Considering 50% probability that a bit is effective, the key generation rate is about 1/4 of bit rate. For 106 kBaud rate, the key generation rate of RIWA is about 26kbps, which is fast enough in practice.

4.1.2 Discarding Bits that Eve may Discover

Another situation should be noticed is when the actual out of synchronization is larger than a threshold:

$$\upsilon > 2\gamma_0 - \varepsilon \tag{18}$$

Substituting (16) into (18), it can be seen that case 2 cannot cause such a large out of synchronization ($\gamma_a^2 - \gamma_b^2 > 2\gamma_0$). Eve will know that Alice sends 1 and Bob sends 0 (case 1).

A powerful attacker can crack some bits from the above situation. So in RIWA, we can choose to detect the actual out of synchronization. If it is larger than a threshold estimated by (18), we discard it in advance. Due to this discard, the bits left may have more zeros than ones at Alice side. Finally, randomness amplification is optional.

4.2 Random Amplitude Scaling against Amplitude Mismatch

Similar to out of synchronization, for amplitude mismatch, the amplitude of waveform is multiplied by a random coefficient β uniformly between $[1-\beta_0, 1+\beta_0]$ at each bit.

The RF waveforms of Alice and Bob under case 1 and case 2 are

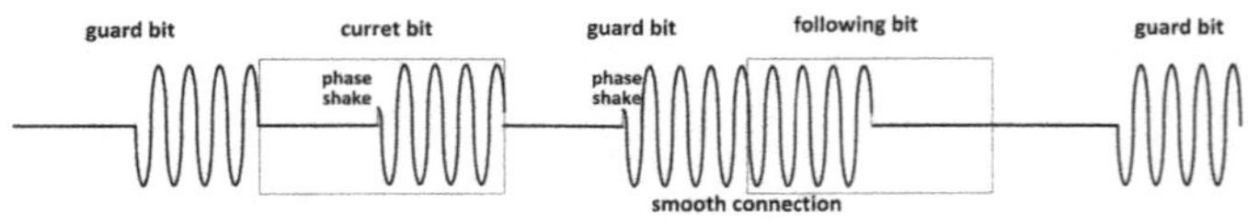

Figure 11: RF waveform phase shaking

$$\begin{aligned} X_a^{c1}(t) &= \beta_a^1 x_a^{c1}(t) \\ X_b^{c1}(t) &= \beta_b^1 x_b^{c1}(t) \\ X_a^{c2}(t) &= \beta_a^2 x_a^{c2}(t) \\ X_b^{c2}(t) &= \beta_b^2 x_b^{c2}(t) \end{aligned} \tag{19}$$

We need to get

$$\begin{aligned} X_a^{c1}(t) &= X_b^{c2}(t) \\ X_b^{c1}(t) &= x_a^{c2}(t) \end{aligned} \tag{20}$$

to make two cases equal, i.e., $X_a^{c1}(t) + X_b^{c1}(t) = X_a^{c2}(t) + X_b^{c2}(t)$. With the help of (8), (20) can be simplified as

$$\begin{aligned} \beta_a^1 \alpha &= \beta_b^2 \\ \beta_a^2 \alpha &= \beta_b^1 \end{aligned} \tag{21}$$

We can easily find instances satisfying (21) as long as $\beta_0 > (\alpha - 1)/(\alpha + 1)$. We denote I_a as the set of instances, $I_a \subset S_{c1} \cap S_{c2} \neq \phi$. Therefore (10) is proved.

We need to pay attention when actual amplitude mismatch is larger than a threshold

$$\alpha' > \frac{1+\beta_0}{\alpha(1-\beta_0)} \tag{22}$$

case 2 cannot cause such a big amplitude mismatch. So in RIWA, we can choose to detect the actual amplitude mismatch. If it is larger than a threshold estimated by (22) , we discard it in advance.

4.3 Random Phase Shifting against Phase Mismatch

We also add phase shaking φ uniformly distributed between $[-\varphi_0, \varphi_0]$ to deal with phase mismatch. In this case, we need to pay attention to the phase change between bits. It could be a clue for Eve to separate borderline of consecutive bits. Recall that we already add guard bits between consecutive random bits. It makes things easier to prevent phase change between bits. The shaking method is shown in Fig. 11. We use previous guard bit to make a smooth connection when transmitting a 1. In this way, the borderline of the envelop will not be exposed to Eve.

The RF waveforms of Alice and Bob under two cases are

$$\begin{aligned} Hilbert(X_a^{c1}(t)) &= e^{j\varphi_a^1} Hilbert(x_a^{c1}(t)) \\ Hilbert(X_b^{c1}(t)) &= e^{j\varphi_b^1} Hilbert(x_b^{c1}(t)) \\ Hilbert(X_a^{c2}(t)) &= e^{j\varphi_a^2} Hilbert(x_a^{c2}(t)) \\ Hilbert(X_b^{c2}(t)) &= e^{j\varphi_b^2} Hilbert(x_b^{c2}(t)) \end{aligned} \tag{23}$$

We need to get

$$\begin{aligned} X_a^{c1}(t) &= X_b^{c2}(t) \\ X_b^{c1}(t) &= X_a^{c2}(t) \end{aligned} \tag{24}$$

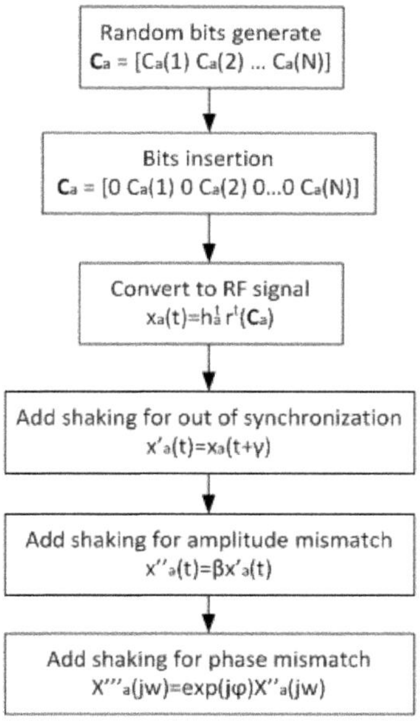

Figure 12: Steps to generate shaken RF signal for Alice

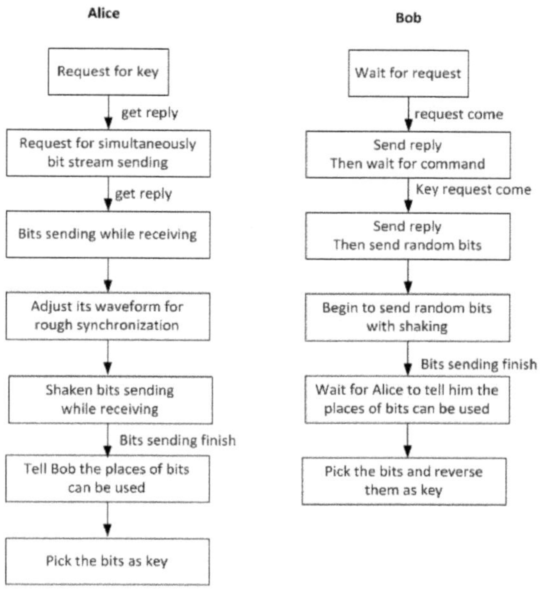

Figure 13: Steps to generate key on Alice and Bob side

to make two cases equal $X_a^{c1}(t) + X_b^{c1}(t) = X_a^{c2}(t) + X_b^{c2}(t)$. With the help of (9), (24) can be simplified as

$$\begin{aligned} \varphi_a^1 &= \varphi_b^2 - \theta \\ \varphi_a^2 &= \varphi_b^1 - \theta \end{aligned} \tag{25}$$

We can easily find instances satisfying (25) as long as $\varphi_0 > \theta/2$. We denote I_p as the set of instances, $I_p \subset S_{c1} \cap S_{c2} \neq \phi$. Therefore (10) is proved.

Finally, we show the whole steps to generate shaken RF signal in Fig. 12.

4.4 Key Agreement Procedure of RIWA

The key agreement procedure is shown in Fig. 13. After both sides agree for key generation, at Alice side, she sends a request for simultaneous random bit stream sending. Then she begins to send bit stream while listening. The bit stream has two parts. The first part is normal unshaken bit stream. It is aiming for Alice to make a rough synchronization and amplitude, and phase match. The second part is shaken bit stream. At Bob side, when he receives the request of bit sending, he begins to send bit stream. Same as Alice, first-part bits are normal bits, and the following bits are shaken bits.

After finishing bits sending, Alice tells Bob the positions of bits that can be used. Alice picks her bits as a key; Bob picks his bits and reverse them as a key. *Example*: Suppose Alice sends $\mathbf{C}_a[01000101]$, Bob sends $\mathbf{C}_a[00010100]$. Alice listens to the signal, so she knows the 2nd, 4th and 8th bits can be used. She picks the corresponding bits [101] and tells Bob the positions are $[2, 4, 8]$. Bob picks the corresponding bits on his side [010] and reverse them to get [101]. Eve who only sees superposed RF signal, cannot know the 2nd, 4th and 8th bits that Alice sends.

4.5 Discussion

We briefly compare RIWA with the Elliptic Curve Diffie-Hellman key exchange method(ECDH) [11].

4.5.1 *Energy Consumption*

For energy consumption, RIWA only needs simple computations of bit comparisons. The main energy consumption is bit transmissions. To generate 128 bit key, considering 50% probability that a bit is effective and the discard of guard bits, the number of bits transmitted is about 512. ECDH needs about 1 kbit transmission (both overheads of ECDH and RIWA are not considered), which is a little more than RIWA. More importantly, ECDH has high computational complexity; the energy consumed by computation of the cryptographic operations is at least one order of magnitude larger than transmissions [11].

4.5.2 *Time Consumption*

For time consumption, to generate 128 bit key, RIWA needs $512bit/106kbps = 4.8ms$ assuming 106 kBaud rate. For ECDH, computations alone cost $9.1s$ to $15.1s$ [11].

4.5.3 *How about MIMO Attacker*

For NFC, the operating distance is within 10cm, significantly smaller than half of a wavelength (11m). In this case, it is well known that MIMO techniques cannot separate their signals. Hence, the eavesdropper cannot exploit MIMO to decode the RFID's data [19] . We believe our method deals with major threats in NFC, and is generally applicable.

5. SIMULATIONS

In the following, we conduct numerical simulations to investigate our method. We set the baud rate to 106 kBaud. The modulation is Manchester coding with 100% ASK. We add random channel noises at Alice and Bob sides $n_a^t(t)$,

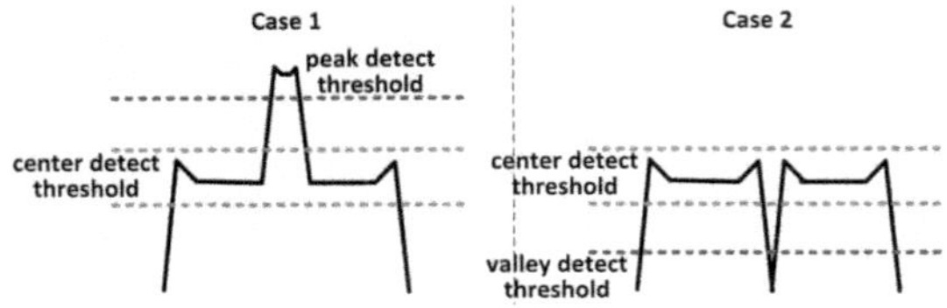

Figure 14: Attacker's method to break the key by out of synchronization

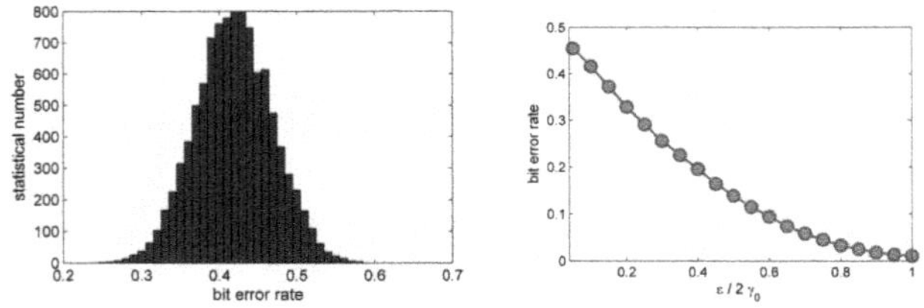

Figure 15: (left) BER at eavesdropper trying to break the key by out of synchronization(right) BER under different degrees of out of synchronizations

$n_b^t(t)$ with the SNR of 20dB. We assume antenna efficiency of Alice and Bob are $\eta_a = \eta_b = 1$.

5.1 RIWA's Performance against Out of Synchronization

In order to analyse RIWA's performance against out of synchronization, we generate a delay at Alice side, $\varepsilon = 0.1\mu s$. To deal with this delay, Alice and Bob both generate a waveform shaking of $\gamma_0 = 0.5\mu s$, (the amount of shaking is about 1/10 of one bit duration, which is too small to cause bit errors for Alice and Bob). For each simulation, Alice and Bob both send 200 random bits. The chance that one user send 1 and the other send 0 is 50%; so the number of effective bits is approximately 100. Alice and Bob discard ineffective bits and generate the key with effective bits using the method introduced in section 4.1.

At Eve's side, she uses the envelop of superposed RF waveform to guess the key. The scheme is shown in Fig. 14. She first detects whether the bit is an effective bit. If most of the sample points (70% in the simulation) is within the center part (upper and lower threshold in the simulation are 0.4 and 0.6 respectively). She takes it for an effective bit that one user sends 1, and the other sends 0. She then observe the middle part of the bit. If there is a peak (detect threshold in the simulation is 0.7) he takes it as case 1, where Alice sends 1, Bob sends 0. If there is a valley (detect threshold in the simulation is 0.3), she takes it as case 2, where Alice sends 0, Bob sends 1. If there is no peak or valley detected, she will make a random guess.

We did the simulation 10000 times. The BER histogram at Eve is shown in Fig. 15(left). Eve's BER is 42% on average, with a standard deviation of 6%. The result closes to a random guess where BER is 50%.

We also investigate the impact of different degrees of out of synchronization on BER. We vary ε from $0.1\mu s$ to $1\mu s$. It makes the ratio of out of synchronization to shaking, $\varepsilon/2\gamma_0$, vary from 10% to 100%. The result is shown in Fig.

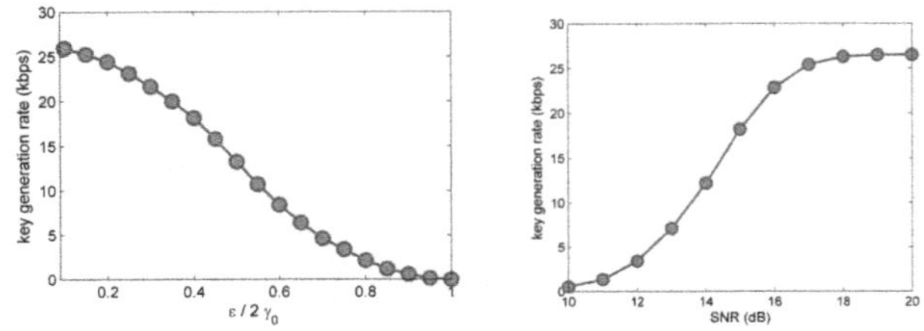

Figure 16: (left) Key generation rate under different degrees of out of synchronizations(right) Key generation rate under different SNR

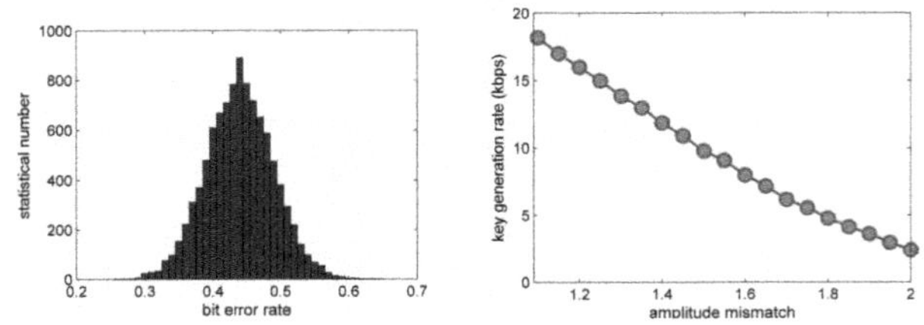

Figure 17: (left) BER at eavesdropper trying to break the key by amplitude mismatch (right) Key generation rate under different degrees of amplitude mismatch

15(right). It can be seen that as ε increases, the number of bits that Eve makes correct guess increases. When $\varepsilon = 2\gamma_0$, ε is too large that γ can not cover it. As a result, Eve can completely determine the bit. Section 4.1 also proposed a method to deal with large ε by discarding the bits that Eve may discover. However, this will cause a drop on key generation rate. Fig. 16(left) shows the key generation rate under different degrees of out of synchronizations. As expect, when ε increases, the key generation rate decreases. For $\varepsilon/2\gamma_0 < 0.3$, the key generation rate is larger than $20kbps$. Fig. 16(right) shows the impact of SNR to key generation rate. For SNR>16dB, the key generation rate is larger than $20kbps$.

5.2 RIWA's Performance against Amplitude Mismatch

In this simulation, we generate an amplitude mismatch $\alpha = 1.1$. To deal with it, Alice and Bob both generate an amplitude shaking of $\beta_0 = 0.4$. Manchester coding has half high voltage and half low voltage (0 for $100\%ASK$). At Eve's side, she will see half bit of Alice's high voltage and half bit of Bob's high voltage. She takes the higher one as Alice's high voltage and the other as Bob's high voltage.

We run the simulation for 10000 times. The BER histogram at Eve is shown in Fig. 17(left). Eve's BER is 44% on average, with a standard deviation of 6%. The result closes to a random guess where BER is 50%. As the degree of amplitude mismatch increases, the number of bits that Eve makes correct guess increases. In this case, we discard the bits that Eve may discover. As a result, the key generation rate decreases. Fig. 17(right) shows the key generation rate under different degrees of amplitude mismatch. For $\alpha < 1.2$, the key generation rate is larger than $15kbps$.

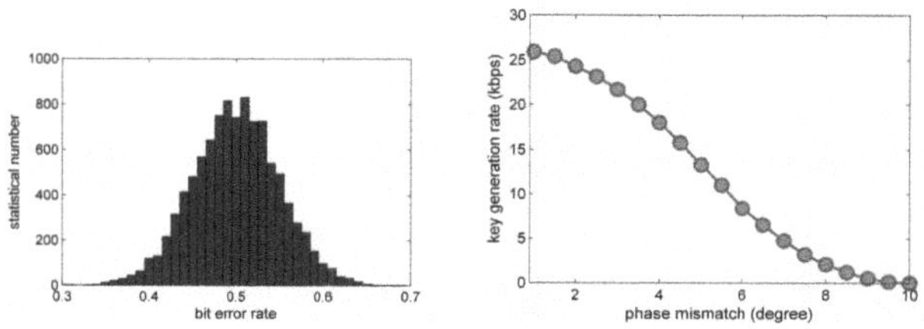

Figure 18: (left) BER at eavesdropper trying to break the key by phase mismatch (right) Key generation rate under different degrees of phase mismatch

5.3 RIWA's Performance against Phase Mismatch

In this simulation, we generate a phase mismatch at Bob's side $\theta = 1°$, where Alice's initial phase is $0°$, and Bob's initial phase is $1°$. To deal with it, Alice and Bob both generate a phase shaking with $\varphi_0 = 5°$. Eve will see two phases for one bit duration. She chooses the RF waveform with a larger initial phase as Bob's RF waveform.

We run the simulation 10000 times. The BER histogram at Eve is shown in Fig. 18(left). Eve's BER is 48% on average, with a standard deviation of 5%. The result closes to a random guess. As the degree of phase mismatch increases, the number of bits that Eve makes correct guess increases. In this case, we discard the bits that Eve may discover. As a result, the key generation rate decreases. Fig. 18(right) shows the Key generation rate under different degrees of phase mismatch. For $\theta < 3°$, the key generation rate is larger than $20kbps$.

6. EXPERIMENTS

We conduct experiments to prove the concept of RIWA. We use software defined radios, USRP n210 to simulate the channels of NFC devices. We use BasicTX and BasicRX Daughter board to send RF signals at 13.56MHz. We set the baud rate to 106 kBaud. The modulation is Manchester coding with 100% ASK. The sample rate is set to 2MHz, that is 20 sample points a bit. The antennas are the DLP-RFID-ANT antennas. We use a power splitter to implement full-duplex on single antenna. The trunk port is connected to antenna, and two branch ports are connected to TX and RX respectively.

In the experiment, we aim at showing the effectiveness of RIWA dealing with the existence of out of synchronization. The experiment set up is shown in Fig. 19. Eve's antenna is in the middle of Alice and Bob's, so she can hear clearly on the communication between Alice and Bob. For simplicity, we set the bit streams that Alice and Bob send as $[0, 1, 0, 1 \cdots]$ and $[1, 0, 1, 0 \cdots]$, respectively. According to the analysis in section 5.1, we add guard bits to the bit streams.

$$\begin{aligned} \mathbf{C}_a &= [0, 0, 0, 1, 0, 0, 0, 1, 0 \cdots] \\ \mathbf{C}_b &= [0, 1, 0, 0, 0, 1, 0, 0, 0 \cdots] \end{aligned} \tag{26}$$

Fig. 20 shows the RF envelop that Alice receives while Bob is sending. Blue line shows the waveform for normal bits; red line shows the waveform for shaken bits. Fig. 21 shows the RF envelop that Alice receives, while Alice and Bob are simultaneous sending (without synchronization). It

Figure 19: Experiment set up

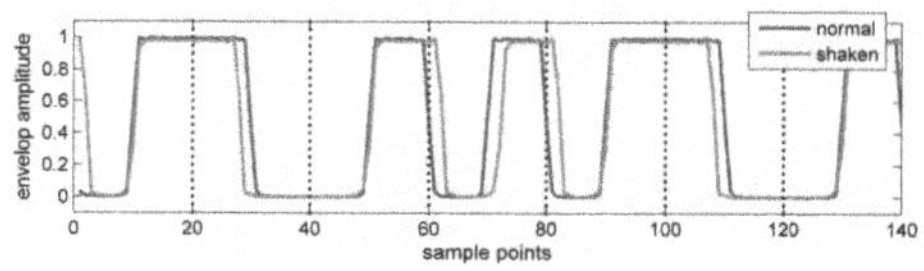

Figure 20: Normal waveform and shaken waveform

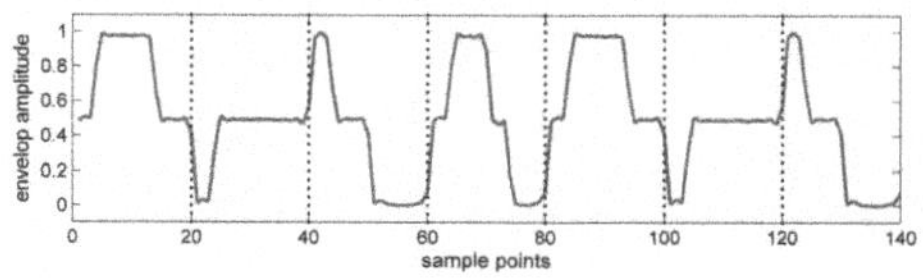

Figure 21: Superposed RF envelop at Alice's side

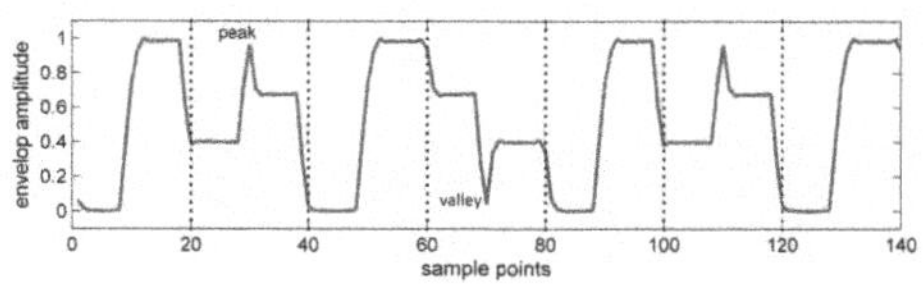

Figure 22: Superposed RF envelop at Eve with the existence of out of synchronization

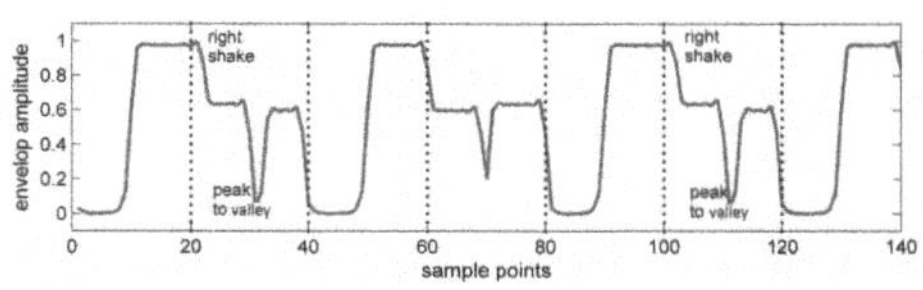

Figure 23: Superposed RF envelop at Eve after shaking

can be seen that, the waveform is approximately the superposed waveform of Alice and Bob.

We then make a rough synchronization for Alice and Bob (there exists a small out of synchronization of about $0.5\mu s$). Fig. 22 shows the received RF envelop at Eve. For convenience, we temporarily do not take amplitude mismatch into consideration. It can be seen from the figure that, due to out of synchronization, Eve can separate Alice from Bob. By assuming that Alice is ahead of Bob (opposite assumption leads to a mirror symmetric result). Eve can tell that when there is a peak in the middle of RF envelop, it is the case that Alice sends 0 and Bob sends 1. When there is a valley in the middle of RF envelop, it is the case that Alice sends 1 and Bob sends 0.

To cover up the out of synchronization, we add a random shaking ($-1\mu s$ to $1\mu s$ in the experiment) on both Alice and Bob. Fig. 23 shows a snapshot of the received RF envelop at Eve. It can be seen from the figure that, due to shaking, a peak is turned into a valley. If Eve still uses the above method to separate Alice and Bob, she will make a mistake.

7. RELATED WORK

Existing works [14, 3, 7, 12, 8] indicate that using symmetric key cryptography to secure the NFC is a practical solution to protect against many kinds of attacks. It is mentioned in [14] that due to the inherent protection of NFC against Man-in-the-Middle-Attacks, standard key agreement protocols like Diffie-Hellman based on RSA or Elliptic Curves could be applied to establish symmetric keys. Many works [5, 9] focus on finding the least expensive protocol for NFC and RFID. However, standard key agreement protocols intrinsically have extensive computational overhead and energy consumption. They are not preferable for resource constrained NFC devices.

The works in [3, 7] proposed specific key agreements. The idea is for both devices to send random bits at exactly the same time. For the case when two parties send different bits, the attacker will not be able to identity which device sent the 0 and which device sent the 1. However, this concept is difficult to be implemented in practice due to the strict requirement of perfect synchronization as well as amplitude and phase match. This issue has been discussed in detail in this paper.

The works in [12, 8] proposed Physical layer key generation methods by using the wireless channel measurements. By exploiting the reciprocal property of the wireless fading channel between two NFC devices, shared secret key can be generated. The methods have low computational overhead compared with standard key agreement protocols. However, the key generation rate is low. The time interval between two effective measurements of channel randomness is bounded by coherence time. Moreover, the methods have multiple steps including advantage distillation, information reconciliation and privacy amplification, which add computation and transmission overhead and time consumption.

RIWA overcomes major problems in NFC key generation. It is a practical, fast, energy-efficient, and secure key agreement scheme for resource constrained NFC devices.

8. CONCLUSION

We propose a practical and energy efficient key agreement method for duplex NFC. In the proposed method RIWA, two users, Alice and Bob simultaneously send random bits of 0 or 1. There are probabilities one of them sends 0 and the other sends 1. An attacker only sees the superposed RF signal cannot figure out which device sent the 0 and which device sent the 1. Alice and Bob themselves know what they have sent and can make use of the advantage to establish a secret key. RIWA also considers various inconsistency which attackers may use to break the method: out of synchronization, amplitude mismatch and phase mismatch. To deal with inconsistency, RIWA introduces random shaking on RF waveform and guard bits between consecutive random bits. The shaking acts like random noise to cover up the inconsistency. The guard bits prevent the attacker determining the bit from the previous one.

Numerical simulations show that, with the existence of out of synchronization, Eve's BER is 42% on average with $\varepsilon/2\gamma_0 = 10\%$. With the existence of amplitude mismatch, Eve's BER is 44% on average with $\alpha = 1.1$, $\beta_0 = 0.4$. With the existence of phase mismatch, Eve's BER is 48% on average with $\theta = 1^\circ$, $\varphi_0 = 5^\circ$. Since BERs are close to random guesses, the result confirms that Eve gains nearly no information about the bits. Concept-proof experiments based on software defined radio demonstrate that, the shaking added covers up the out of synchronization between Alice and Bob. Eve, trying to use out of synchronization to crack the key, will make mistakes. RIWA is a simple and convenient security method with low energy and time consumption applicable to low cost, resource-constrained NFC devices.

References

[1] Information technology - telecommunications and information exchange between systems 'near field communication' interface and protocol (nfcip-1). In *ISO/IEC 18092*, 2004.

[2] Bluetooth secure simple pairing using nfc. In *NFC Forum*, 2012.

[3] M. M. A. Allah. Strengths and weaknesses of near field communication (nfc) technology. In *Global Journal of Computer Science and Technology*, volume 3, pages 51–56, 2011.

[4] U. Azad, H. Jing, and Y. Wang. Link budget and capacity performance of inductively coupled resonant loops. In *Antennas and Propagation, IEEE Transactions on*, volume 60, pages 2453–2461, 2012.

[5] L. Batina, J. Guajardo, T. Kerins, N. Mentens, P. Tuyls, and I. Verbauwhede. Public-key cryptography for rfid-tags. In *Pervasive Computing and Communications Workshops, 2007. PerCom Workshops '07. Fifth Annual IEEE International Conference on*, pages 217–222, 2007.

[6] D. Bharadia, E. McMilin, and S. Katti. Full duplex radios. In *SIGCOMM Comput. Commun. Rev.*, volume 43, pages 375–386, New York, NY, USA, Aug. 2013. ACM.

[7] C. Castelluccia and G. Avoine. Noisy tags: A pretty good key exchange protocol for rfid tags. In

J. Domingo-Ferrer, J. Posegga, and D. Schreckling, editors, *Smart Card Research and Advanced Applications*, volume 3928 of *Lecture Notes in Computer Science*, pages 289–299. Springer Berlin Heidelberg, 2006.

[8] H. Chabanne and G. Fumaroli. Noisy cryptographic protocols for low-cost rfid tags. In *Information Theory, IEEE Transactions on*, volume 52, pages 3562–3566, 2006.

[9] H.-J. Chae, M. Salajegheh, D. Yeager, J. Smith, and K. Fu. Maximalist cryptography and computation on the wisp uhf rfid tag. In J. R. Smith, editor, *Wirelessly Powered Sensor Networks and Computational RFID*, pages 175–187. Springer New York, 2013.

[10] V. Coskun, K. Ok, and B. Ozdenizci. *Near Field Communication (NFC): From Theory to Practice.* Wiley, 2011.

[11] G. de Meulenaer, F. Gosset, O.-X. Standaert, and O. Pereira. On the energy cost of communication and cryptography in wireless sensor networks. In *Networking and Communications, 2008. WIMOB '08. IEEE International Conference on Wireless and Mobile Computing,*, pages 580–585, 2008.

[12] A. Elbagoury, A. Mohsen, M. Ramadan, and M. Youssef. Practical provably secure key sharing for near field communication devices. In *Computing, Networking and Communications (ICNC), 2013 International Conference on*, pages 750–755, 2013.

[13] G. Hancke. Eavesdropping attacks on high-frequency rfid tokens. In *Workshop on RFID Security – RFIDSec'08*, 2008.

[14] E. Haselsteiner and K. Breitfuß. Security in near field communication (nfc). In *Workshop on RFID Security RFIDSec*, 2006.

[15] A. Joux and V. Vitse. Elliptic curve discrete logarithm problem over small degree extension fields. In *Journal of Cryptology*, volume 26, pages 119–143. Springer-Verlag, 2013.

[16] L. Lamport. Time, clocks, and the ordering of events in a distributed system. In *Commun. ACM*, volume 21, pages 558–565, New York, NY, USA, July 1978. ACM.

[17] T. Rappaport. *Wireless Communications: Principles and Practice.* Prentice Hall PTR, Upper Saddle River, NJ, USA, 2nd edition, 2001.

[18] J. Riekki, I. Sanchez, and M. Pyykkonen. Nfc-based user interfaces. In *Near Field Communication (NFC), 2012 4th International Workshop on*, pages 3–9, 2012.

[19] J. Wang, H. Hassanieh, D. Katabi, and T. Kohno. Securing deployed rfids by randomizing the modulation and the channel. In *CSAIL Technical Reports*, 2013.

[20] S.-H. Wu and C. Yang. Promoting collaborative mobile payment by using nfc-micro sd technology. In *Services Computing (SCC), 2013 IEEE International Conference on*, pages 454–461, 2013.

Multi-recipient Encryption, Revisited*

Alexandre Pinto
Royal Holloway,
University of London
and
Instituto Universitário da Maia

Bertram Poettering
Royal Holloway,
University of London

Jacob C.N. Schuldt
Royal Holloway,
University of London

ABSTRACT

A variant of public key encryption that promises efficiency gains due to batch processing is multi-recipient public key encryption (MR-PKE). Precisely, in MR-PKE, a dedicated encryption routine takes a vector of messages and a vector of public keys and outputs a vector of ciphertexts, where the latter can be decrypted individually, as in regular PKE.

In this paper we revisit the established security notions of MR-PKE and the related primitive MR-KEM. We identify a subtle flaw in a security model by Bellare, Boldyreva, and Staddon, that also appears in later publications by different authors. We further observe that these security models rely on the knowledge-of-secret-key (KOSK) assumption—a requirement that is rarely met in practice. We resolve this situation by proposing strengthened security notions for MR-PKE and MR-KEMs, together with correspondingly secure yet highly efficient schemes. Importantly, our models abstain from restricting the set of considered adversaries in the way prior models did, and in particular do not require the KOSK setting. We prove our constructions secure assuming hardness of the static Diffie-Hellman problem, in the random oracle model.

1. INTRODUCTION

Standard public key encryption is concerned with two communicating parties, a sender and a receiver, and enables the sender to encrypt a confidential message for the receiver using the latter's public key. Should a sender want to encrypt the same or different messages for two or more receivers, the use of a standard public key encryption scheme would require the sender to encrypt the messages under the intended receivers' public keys independently of each other.

In contrast to this, a *multi-recipient multi-message public key encryption* scheme (MR-MM-PKE) enables a sender to simultaneously encrypt many messages for many receivers in a single operation. More specifically, an MR-MM-PKE scheme provides an encryption algorithm which, given a vector $(pk_1, \ldots, pk_n)$ consisting of the public keys of n receivers and a corresponding vector $(m_1, \ldots, m_n)$ of n messages, returns a vector $(c_1, \ldots, c_n)$ of n ciphertexts. It is required that these ciphertexts can be decrypted individually, i.e., each receiver i (holding the public/private key pair (pk_i, sk_i)) be able to decrypt c_i without knowledge of the public keys of the other recipients or the remaining ciphertexts c_j, $j \neq i$. Hence, syntactically, decryption is identical to that of an ordinary public key encryption scheme.

By simultaneously processing messages for multiple receivers, MR-MM-PKE schemes allow computational and, in some settings, bandwidth savings compared to the parallel use of standard public key encryption. This property is highly attractive in applications where batch processing of encryptions naturally occurs. For example, consider an online banking system which, following a regular schedule, sends encrypted bank account statements to all customers who have provided the bank with a corresponding public key. By employing an MR-MM-PKE scheme as opposed to an ordinary public key encryption scheme, the bank could considerably reduce the computational workload for providing this service.

1.1 The evolution of MR-MM-PKE

A promising approach towards the construction of efficient MR-MM-PKE schemes is to use an ordinary encryption scheme to encrypt the messages for their respective receivers, but to use the same randomness for all encryptions [13, 5, 4]. Depending on the structure of the encryption scheme, this can potentially provide a significant reduction in the computational requirements for the encryption process, but at the same time requires that the used encryption scheme remain secure under randomness re-use.

In [13], Kurosawa shows that both ElGamal encryption [11] and (a version of) Cramer-Shoup encryption [8] are secure in this setting. Furthermore, it is highlighted that the MR-MM-PKE schemes obtained by employing randomness re-use in combination with these encryption schemes provide a reduction of almost 50% in terms of computational cost, compared to individually encrypting the messages. However, the MR-MM-PKE security model used in [13] does not take into account malicious receivers: all public keys used in the (multi-recipient) encryption producing the challenge ciphertext need to be honestly generated, and the corresponding private keys need to remain unknown to the adversary. Hence, the security guarantees provided *in practice* are rather weak.

*The research of the second and third authors was supported by an EPSRC Leadership Fellowship, EP/H005455/1.

ASIA CCS'14, June 4–6, 2014, Kyoto, Japan.
Copyright 2014 ACM 978-1-4503-2800-5/14/06 ...$15.00.
http://dx.doi.org/10.1145/2590296.2590329.

This issue was identified and addressed by Bellare, Boldyreva, and Staddon [5] who introduced a strengthened variant of Kurosawa's security definition. The updated model explicitly considers insiders, i.e., malicious receivers, by allowing the adversary to provide some of the public keys used in the encryption generating the challenge ciphertext. However, for these keys the adversary also has to reveal the corresponding secret keys—a requirement generally known as the *knowledge-of-secret-key (KOSK)* assumption.

Commonly seen justifications for this quite strong assumption argue that in all practical systems, in order to be considered valid, public keys are registered with a Certificate Authority (CA), and that this CA will require zero-knowledge proofs of knowledge of the corresponding private keys. This, however, is rarely done in practice. In fact, we are not aware of any CA on the Internet which requires a user to provide a full proof of knowledge of her private key. It is important to note here that KOSK-based security arguments generally do not translate to more realistic settings. Indeed, as we discuss in Section 3.2, multi-recipient ElGamal encryption in the plain (i.e., non-KOSK) setting is trivially breakable, in strong contrast with the (KOSK-based) results from [5].

Besides the strengthened security model, Bellare *et al.* also introduce the notion of *reproducibility* for an encryption scheme and obtain the powerful result that all schemes fulfilling this additional requirement are amenable to a generic conversion to an MR-MM-PKE via randomness re-use. In particular, it is shown that ElGamal and Cramer-Shoup encryption are reproducible, and hence give rise to secure MR-MM-PKE in a generic way. Note that this re-establishes the results by Kurosawa, but in a stronger security model.

1.2 Our Contributions

We first revisit the (already strengthened) security notion for MR-MM-PKE as defined by Bellare *et al.* [5] and observe that it contains a subtle technical flaw. Specifically, we note that when the challenge ciphertext is produced, the used public keys are always prefixed by honest ones. This feature makes it possible to define an (admittedly artificial) MR-MM-PKE scheme which can be shown secure in the model of [5], but which is obviously insecure in any practical setting where the adversary can influence the order in which the encryption algorithm receives its public keys. Furthermore, we note that the security model of [5] does not allow repetition of (honest) public keys. Hence, security is not guaranteed should the sender encrypt more than one message for a given receiver. See Section 3.2 for a more detailed discussion of these issues.

We fix these issues by further strengthening the model of [5]. In the same step we also drop the KOSK assumption, i.e., the adversary is from now on allowed to introduce maliciously generated public keys for which he does not know the decryption keys. We argue that, to ensure security in practice, MR-MM-PKE schemes should achieve the level of security captured by this new model.

As discussed above, the schemes proposed in [5] might become insecure in the new setting, and some definitively do. Unfortunately, this seems to generally hold for all schemes obtained via the reproducibility-based transformation, as the latter inherently requires the KOSK assumption. Hence, in order to find stronger instantiations of MR-MM-PKE, we need to follow a different approach.

As a first step towards an MR-MM-PKE scheme that is secure in our new security model, we introduce the notion of *multi-recipient multi-key key encapsulation mechanism* (MR-MK-KEM). Following the well-known hybrid approach, by combining this KEM with an appropriate *data encapsulation mechanism* (DEM) we obtain an MR-MM-PKE scheme.

We then show that the 'hashed ElGamal' technique from [1] combined with randomness re-use gives rise to a secure MR-MK-KEM and, by consequence, to a secure MR-MM-PKE scheme. The latter is efficient and provides compact ciphertexts: when compared to the parallel use of the original hashed ElGamal scheme, the reduction in the ciphertext size and in the computational cost associated with encryption is approximately 50%. In addition, although providing much stronger security guarantees and not limiting the sender to encrypt the same message for all receivers, our scheme is as efficient as the best known MR-PKE scheme for *single* messages (see related work).

1.3 Related Work

Research on multi-recipient encryption was initiated by Kurosawa [13] who defined the first security model for MR-MM-PKE schemes and proposed randomness re-using constructions based on ElGamal and Cramer-Shoup encryption. The primary goal of [13] was to shorten ciphertexts, and computational advantages of the new primitive were considered only of subordinate importance. As pointed out above, Bellare *et al.* [5] improved upon this work by introducing a stronger security model and describing a general transformation from reproducible encryption schemes to MR-MM-PKE schemes.

The concept of multi-recipient key encapsulation (MR-KEM) was introduced by Smart in [15]. Intuitively, this primitive is closely related to MR-PKE due to the hybrid approach for obtaining public key encryption by generically combining key encapsulation (KEM) with data encapsulation (DEM). It is important to note, however, that Smart only considers single-key MR-KEMs, i.e., MR-KEMs that establish for all recipients the same session key. In combination with a DEM, such KEMs are helpful to construct *multi-recipient single-message public key encryption (MR-SM-PKE)* schemes which are restricted to applications where the same message is encrypted for all receivers. This is an often considered subclass of the more general MR-MM-PKE primitive. Note that the work of Smart does not consider insider attacks; indeed, it seems that in the single-key setting such a notion is inapplicable.

The work of Barbosa and Farshim [3] lifts the MR-KEM results by Smart to the identity-based setting, by correspondingly adapting the definitions from [15] and carefully taking into account the arising subtleties. By consequence, the paper restricts attention to the single-key setting and does not consider insider attacks.

In apparently independent work, Baek, Safavi-Naini, and Susilo [2] construct a single-key MR-KEM in the identity-based setting that computes the ciphertexts for an arbitrary number of recipients using a single pairing computation in total. While this is highly attractive from an efficiency-centric point of view, unfortunately the scheme is proven secure only in a 'selective-id' model.

Chatterjee and Sarkar [7] complement the results from [3, 2] by constructing two multi-recipient single-key identity-based KEMs that do not require the random oracle heuristic. Their constructions require a hierarchical IBE scheme (HIBE) with constant-size ciphertexts as a building block and are hence interesting more from a theoretical perspective.

Broadcast encryption [12, 14, 6] is closely related to MR-SM-PKE. More specifically, a broadcast encryption scheme allows a sender to encrypt a message for any subset of recipients belonging to a pre-defined universe of users. The latter is typically fixed at the time the scheme is initialized, but specific constructions, denoted *dynamic* broadcast encryption [10], allow users to be added as prospective recipients *after* scheme initialization. In contrast, MR-SM-PKE allows addressing any set of users on an ad-hoc basis, regardless of when their public/private keys were generated. Independently of that, broadcast encryption requires a central authority to generate a public key for the universe of users as well as a private decryption key for each individual. These private keys would then have to be delivered to the users through a confidential and authenticated channel. In contrast, MR-SM-PKE allows users to independently generate their own public/private keys and can hence be used in settings where a trusted third party is not available. Lastly, note that the more general MR-MM-PKE is not comparable to broadcast encryption as it supports encrypting different messages to the recipients.

2. PRELIMINARIES

2.1 Notation

We write $[n]$ for $\{1,\ldots,n\}$ and use arrow notation for vectors (e.g., $\vec{a} = (a_1,\ldots,a_n)$ if $n = |\vec{a}|$). If A is a finite set, we write $a \leftarrow_R A$ for sampling a uniformly from A. If A is an algorithm, we write $a \leftarrow_R A^{\mathcal{O}}(x)$ for assigning to a the outcome of an execution of A on input x with uniformly picked random coins and oracle access to $\mathcal{O}$. In experiments and algorithms we write "`Require` X" as a shortcut for "`Return` $\bot$ `unless` X".

2.2 Static Diffie-Hellman Assumption

We recall the cyclic group setting and the static Diffie-Hellman assumption.

Definition 1 (Group generator). *A* group generator *$\mathcal{G}$ is an efficient algorithm which, on input security parameter 1^λ, returns the description of an efficient prime-order group $\mathbb{G}$. We assume that the group order p and a distinguished generating element $g \in \mathbb{G}$ are part of this description. We will use the notation $(\mathbb{G},p,g) \leftarrow_R \mathcal{G}(1^\lambda)$ accordingly.*

Definition 2 (SDH assumption). *Let $\mathcal{G}$ be a group generator. The advantage of an algorithm $\mathcal{A}$ in solving the* static Diffie-Hellman problem *with respect to $\mathcal{G}$ is defined as*

$$\mathrm{Adv}^{\mathsf{SDH}}_{\mathcal{G},\mathcal{A}}(\lambda) = \Pr\Big[(\mathbb{G},p,g) \leftarrow_R \mathcal{G}(1^\lambda);\ u \leftarrow_R \mathbb{Z}_p;\ v \leftarrow_R \mathbb{Z}_p;\ Z \leftarrow_R \mathcal{A}^{\mathcal{O}_u,\mathcal{O}_v}(\mathbb{G},p,g,g^u,g^v) : Z = g^{uv}\Big],$$

where $\mathcal{O}_u(\cdot,\cdot)$ and $\mathcal{O}_v(\cdot,\cdot)$ are decisional oracles which on input $X, Y \in \mathbb{G}$ return 1 if and only if $X^u = Y$, and if and only if $X^v = Y$, respectively. The probability is taken over the random coins used to sample u and v and those consumed by $\mathcal{G}$ and $\mathcal{A}$. The static Diffie-Hellman assumption *holds with respect to $\mathcal{G}$ if for all efficient algorithms $\mathcal{A}$ the advantage function $\mathrm{Adv}^{\mathsf{SDH}}_{\mathcal{G},\mathcal{A}}(\lambda)$ is negligible in λ.*

2.3 Data Encapsulation Mechanisms

The concept of hybrid encryption and the related notion of data encapsulation was first introduced in [9]. We recall the definition and one of the possible security definitions.

Definition 3 (Data encapsulation mechanism). *A* data encapsulation mechanism (DEM) $D = (\mathcal{K}, \mathsf{DEM}, \mathsf{DEM}^{-1})$ *consists of a keyspace $\mathcal{K} = \{0,1\}^{l(\lambda)}$, for a polynomial l in the security parameter, and two efficient algorithms as follows:*

- $\mathsf{DEM}(K,m)$. *On input a key $K \in \mathcal{K}$ and a message $m \in \{0,1\}^*$, this algorithm returns a ciphertext c.*
- $\mathsf{DEM}^{-1}(K,c)$. *On input a key $K \in \mathcal{K}$ and a ciphertext c, this algorithm returns either a message m or the error symbol $\bot$.*

A DEM is correct *if for all $K \in \mathcal{K}$ and all $m \in \{0,1\}^*$ we have $\mathsf{DEM}^{-1}(K, \mathsf{DEM}(K,m)) = m$.*

Definition 4 (One-time CCA security). *A DEM $D = (\mathcal{K}, \mathsf{DEM}, \mathsf{DEM}^{-1})$ is said to be* indistinguishable against a one-time chosen ciphertext attack (IND-OT-CCA) *if for all efficient adversaries $\mathcal{A} = (\mathcal{A}_1, \mathcal{A}_2)$ interacting in the experiments $\mathrm{Expt}^{\mathsf{IND\text{-}OT\text{-}CCA},b}_{D,\mathcal{A}}$ from Figure 1 the following advantage function is negligible in λ,*

$$\mathrm{Adv}^{\mathsf{IND\text{-}OT\text{-}CCA}}_{D,\mathcal{A}}(\lambda) = \Big|\Pr\Big[\mathrm{Expt}^{\mathsf{IND\text{-}OT\text{-}CCA},1}_{D,\mathcal{A}}(1^\lambda) = 1\Big] - \Pr\Big[\mathrm{Expt}^{\mathsf{IND\text{-}OT\text{-}CCA},0}_{D,\mathcal{A}}(1^\lambda) = 1\Big]\Big|,$$

where the probabilities are taken over the random coins used in the experiment (including those consumed by $\mathcal{A}$).

$\mathrm{Expt}^{\mathsf{IND\text{-}OT\text{-}CCA},b}_{D,\mathcal{A}}(1^\lambda)$:

(a) $K \leftarrow_R \mathcal{K}$
(b) $(m^0, m^1, st) \leftarrow \mathcal{A}_1(1^\lambda)$
(c) `Require` $|m^0| = |m^1|$
(d) $c^* \leftarrow \mathsf{DEM}(K, m^b)$
(e) $d \leftarrow \mathcal{A}_2^{\mathcal{D}}(c^*, st)$
(f) `Return` d

Oracle $\mathcal{D}(c)$:

(a) `Require` $c \neq c^*$
(b) $m \leftarrow \mathsf{DEM}^{-1}(K,c)$
(c) `Return` m

Figure 1: IND-OT-CCA experiment for DEMs

3. MULTI-RECIPIENT PKE

In this section we expose the most important concepts of multi-recipient encryption. After motivating its purpose and specifying the syntax, we critically review the security models that appear so far in corresponding publications. Indeed, concerning the latter we identify a couple of shortcomings and show how to resolve them. We defer the construction of a multi-recipient encryption scheme that is secure in the new model to Sections 4.2 and 5.

3.1 Syntax of MR-MM-PKE

We recall the notion of multi-recipient encryption from [5]. In contrast to plain public key encryption this primitive allows batch processing, i.e., the execution of many encryption operations in one shot. The work of [5] restricts attention to the multi-message setting where for each specified recipient key an individual message is encrypted. An important property of multi-recipient encryption is that the decryption operation is oblivious of the other keys used for creating a given ciphertext. The main advantage of this primitive is the potential efficiency gain due to cost amortization in the encryption process where some computations might be used for the creation of several ciphertexts.

DEFINITION 5 (MR-MM-PKE). *A multi-recipient multi-message public key encryption scheme (MR-MM-PKE)* $E = (\mathsf{PGen}, \mathsf{KGen}, \mathsf{Enc}, \mathsf{Dec})$ *consists of four efficient algorithms as follows:*

- $\mathsf{PGen}(1^\lambda)$. *On input security parameter 1^λ, this algorithm outputs public parameters pp.*

  We will assume implicitly that the following algorithms are defined in respect to a single distinguished instance of pp.

- $\mathsf{KGen}(\,)$. *This probabilistic algorithm outputs a key pair* (sk, pk).

- $\mathsf{Enc}(\vec{pk}, \vec{m})$. *On input vectors $\vec{pk} = (pk_1, \ldots, pk_n)$ of public keys and $\vec{m} = (m_1, \ldots, m_n)$ of messages, this probabilistic algorithm outputs a vector $\vec{c} = (c_1, \ldots, c_n)$ of ciphertexts.*

- $\mathsf{Dec}(sk, c)$. *On input a secret key sk and a ciphertext c, this algorithm outputs either a message or the error symbol $\perp$.*

For fixed parameters pp and any $n \in \mathbb{N}$ let $(sk_j, pk_j) \leftarrow_R \mathsf{KGen}(\,)$ and $m_j \in \{0,1\}^*$ for all $j \in [n]$. The MR-MM-PKE is correct *if for all encryptions*

$$(c_1, \ldots, c_n) \leftarrow_R \mathsf{Enc}\left((pk_1, \ldots, pk_n), (m_1, \ldots, m_n)\right)$$

we have $\mathsf{Dec}\left(sk_j, c_j\right) = m_j$ for all $j \in [n]$.

Note that we obtain regular public key encryption as a special case of MR-MM-PKE by restricting the Enc algorithm to accept only single-element vectors $\vec{pk}$ and $\vec{m}$. Moreover, a canonic (but rather uninteresting) way to construct MR-MM-PKE from regular public key encryption is to create all ciphertexts independently of each other by invoking $c_j \leftarrow_R \mathsf{Enc}\left(pk_j, m_j\right)$ once for each $j \in [n]$.

3.2 Security of MR-MM-PKE

To model the security of MR-MM-PKE schemes, [5] proposes a generalization of the standard indistinguishability notion for public key encryption (in fact, the authors propose two notions: one corresponding to CPA security, the other to CCA security; here we focus on the CCA variant only). Briefly, in their game-based definition, the adversary is required to tell apart an encryption of one set of messages from an encryption of another set. However, after closely studying the formalizations from [5], we came to the conclusion that a couple of technical artifacts severely weaken the security guarantees provided by the model in practice. Before we elaborate on our findings and fix the model accordingly, let us first recall the definitions from [5] in more detail.

3.2.1 The security model by Bellare, Boldyreva, and Staddon [5]

In Figure 2 we reproduce details of the CCA security experiment from [5] (slightly adapting the notation towards our needs). The experiment simulates to the adversary an environment with k honest users by providing her, in line (c), with the corresponding public keys $\vec{pk} = (pk_1, \ldots, pk_k)$ and decryption oracles. Among others, the adversary outputs two vectors of messages, $\vec{m}^0$ and $\vec{m}^1$, where either the one or the other shall be encrypted for the keys in $\vec{pk}$ in challenge ciphertext $\vec{c}$. Also encrypted, but for the adversarially-generated keys in $\vec{pk}^*$, shall be the messages in vector $\vec{m}^*$. Finally, in $\vec{sk}^*$ the adversary is required to reveal the decryption keys corresponding to $\vec{pk}^*$ (see discussion below). The consistency of adversary's output is checked in lines (d)–(f). Challenge ciphertext $\vec{c}$ is created in line (g); observe here that in the recipient list the honest public keys come first, followed by the corrupt ones. The remaining part of the experiment is as expected, with the natural restrictions on the second-phase decryption oracle. According to [5], an MR-MM-PKE scheme E is secure if the return value d of the experiment is computationally independent of parameter b, for all efficient adversaries $\mathcal{A} = (\mathcal{A}_1, \mathcal{A}_2)$.

3.2.2 Shortcomings in the model from [5]

We next discuss a couple of properties of the experiment from Figure 2 that indicate that schemes proved secure in respect to the model might, in practice, not offer the intuitively expected level of security.

The first problem stems from the fact that in line (g) the vector of encryption keys is always prefixed by honestly chosen ones. To see that this is problematic, fix an arbitrary MR-MM-PKE scheme E that is secure in the model from [5] and, without loss of generality, assume that each ciphertext of E starts with prefix "0". Execute the KGen algorithm of E to create a distinguished key pair $(sk^\times, pk^\times)$. Consider now the scheme E' obtained from E by modifying the encryption algorithm such that, on input $\vec{pk} = (pk_1, \ldots, pk_n)$ and $\vec{m} = (m_1, \ldots, m_n)$, ciphertext vector $\vec{c}$ is computed as usual if $pk_1 \neq pk^\times$, but is set to $(\texttt{"1"} \,\|\, m_1, \ldots, \texttt{"1"} \,\|\, m_n)$ otherwise. Assume in addition that the decryption routine is adapted such that ciphertexts of the latter form are 'decrypted' correctly. It is not difficult to see that scheme E' is secure in the sense of [5]; indeed, as case $pk_1 = pk^\times$ occurs only with negligible probability in experiment $\mathrm{Expt}^{\mathsf{MR\text{-}PKE\text{-}IND\text{-}BBS}}$, security of E implies security of E'. However, intuitively, scheme E'

$\underline{\mathrm{Expt}_{E,\mathcal{A},k,n}^{\textsf{MR-PKE-IND-BBS},b}(1^\lambda)}$:

(a) $pp \leftarrow_R \mathsf{PGen}(1^\lambda)$

(b) $(\vec{sk}, \vec{pk}) \overset{k}{\leftarrow}_R \mathsf{KGen}()$

(c) $(\vec{m}^0, \vec{m}^1, \vec{m}^*, \vec{pk}^*, \vec{sk}^*, st) \leftarrow_R \mathcal{A}_1^{\mathcal{D}_1}(pp, \vec{pk})$

(d) $\texttt{Require}\ |\vec{m}^0| = |\vec{m}^1| = k \wedge \forall i \in [k] : |m_i^0| = |m_i^1|$

(e) $\texttt{Require}\ |\vec{m}^*| = |\vec{pk}^*| = |\vec{sk}^*| = n - k$

(f) $\texttt{Require}\ \forall j \in [n-k] : pk_j^*$ matches sk_j^*

(g) $\vec{c} \leftarrow_R \mathsf{Enc}(\vec{pk} \,\|\, \vec{pk}^*, \vec{m}^b \,\|\, \vec{m}^*)$

(h) $d \leftarrow_R \mathcal{A}_2^{\mathcal{D}_2}(\vec{c}, st)$

(i) $\texttt{Return}\ d$

$\underline{\text{Oracle } \mathcal{D}_1(i,c)}$:

(a) $\texttt{Require}\ i \in [k]$

(b) $m \leftarrow \mathsf{Dec}(sk_i, c)$

(c) $\texttt{Return}\ m$

$\underline{\text{Oracle } \mathcal{D}_2(i,c)}$:

(a) $\texttt{Require}\ i \in [k]$

(b) $\texttt{Require}\ c \neq c_i$

(c) $m \leftarrow \mathsf{Dec}(sk_i, c)$

(d) $\texttt{Return}\ m$

Figure 2: Security experiment for MR-MM-PKE from [5]

is weak: by claiming $(sk^\times, pk^\times)$ as her own key pair and by arranging $pk^\times$ to appear first in the input to an encryption operation, the confidentiality of all other ciphertext components is trivially broken.

As an independent (and possibly less far-fetched) problem we identify the fact that experiment $\mathrm{Expt}_{E,\mathcal{A},k,n}^{\textsf{MR-PKE-IND-BBS},b}$ does not allow the adversary to make the same honest public key appear multiple times on the input to the encryption routine. For instance, intuitively, an MR-MM-PKE scheme where the encryption routine consistently transforms inputs of the form $\vec{pk} = (pk, pk)$ and $\vec{m} = (m, m)$ into ciphertext pairs of the form $\vec{c} = (c, c)$ is weak: if messages m, m_0, m_1 are chosen such that $m = m_0 \neq m_1$, encryptions of (m, m_0) and (m, m_1) for (pk, pk) can trivially be distinguished from each other, since in exactly one of the cases the ciphertext vector has the form (c, c). However, in principle such a scheme can be secure in respect to the experiment from Figure 2, simply because the logic of the game will effectively prevent the special $\vec{pk} = (pk, pk)$ situation to occur (observe that if one of the copies of pk is part of $\vec{pk}^*$, then $\mathcal{A}$ will not be able to reveal the corresponding decryption key sk^*).

3.2.3 A criticism of the KOSK assumption

Recall that in line (c) of $\mathrm{Expt}_{E,\mathcal{A},k,n}^{\textsf{MR-PKE-IND-BBS},b}$ the adversary is expected to reveal the decryption keys $\vec{sk}^*$ corresponding to the potentially maliciously-chosen encryption keys $\vec{pk}^*$. This represents what is commonly known as the *knowledge-of-secret-key* (KOSK) assumption and shall provide some indication of well-formedness of the keys in $\vec{pk}^*$. We observe, however, that it is generally unclear how to verify that the adversary's outputs $\vec{pk}^*$ and $\vec{sk}^*$ are indeed consistent, i.e., how to accurately implement the corresponding test in line (f). Indeed, in a follow-up work by the authors of [5], this situation is formally clarified by restricting the adversary even further than it is in Figure 2: in [4], the adversary does not have to output $\vec{pk}^*$ and $\vec{sk}^*$ any more, but instead the random coins used to create them with KGen.

Generally speaking, security models assuming KOSK are obviously so strong that one might question their practical relevance. Authors typically argue in support of the KOSK assumption by claiming that in any practical setting public keys are certified by trusted authorities (CAs) anyway, and in the certification process the latter could require zero-knowledge proofs of knowledge of secret keys (or random coins). However, we are not aware of any CA on the Internet or elsewhere that would require such a proof (or would at least have corresponding infrastructure available).

The following simple example illustrates that the approach to obtain MR-MM-PKE from ElGamal encryption [11] by re-using the ephemeral randomness does not lead to a secure scheme. We stress that this holds even though the very same scheme was proved secure in [5] (under the KOSK assumption). In detail, in the DL setting, the scheme encrypts messages $m_1, m_2 \in \mathbb{G}$ for public keys $X_1, X_2 \in \mathbb{G}$ by picking a random exponent $r \in \mathbb{Z}_p$ and computing ciphertexts $c_1 = (g^r, X_1^r \cdot m_1)$ and $c_2 = (g^r, X_2^r \cdot m_2)$. Now, if X_1 is an honestly generated key and the adversary claims $X_2 = X_1^t$ as hers, for arbitrary $t \in \mathbb{Z}_p$, then from any (multi-)encryption

$$(c_1, c_2) = \Big((g^r, X_1^r \cdot m_1), (g^r, X_1^{tr} \cdot m_2)\Big)$$

of secret message m_1 and known message m_2 under keys (X_1, X_2), message m_1 can readily be recovered via $m_1 = (X_1^r \cdot m_1)/((X_1^{tr} \cdot m_2)/m_2)^{t^{-1}}$.

This clearly illustrates the danger of adopting MR-MM-PKE schemes shown secure under the KOSK assumption in practical systems where proofs of knowledge of private keys are not required. However, as we show in Sections 4 and 5, simultaneously efficient and secure MR-MM-PKE schemes can be achieved without requiring the KOSK assumption or any third-party certification of public keys.

3.2.4 Our strengthened security model for MR-MM-PKE

We proceed with the exposition of our new security model for multi-recipient encryption that tackles the issues discussed above. We particularly highlight that in the new model the adversary is allowed to specify arbitrary vectors of encryption keys to be challenged on (i.e., it may arrange the public keys in any order, and also repetitions are allowed); additionally, the KOSK assumption is not required any more. It is easy to see that our model is (strictly) stronger than the one from [5] as our experiment encompasses the one from Figure 2 as a special case.

Definition 6. (Indistinguishability of MR-MM-PKE)

An MR-MM-PKE scheme $E = (\mathsf{PGen}, \mathsf{KGen}, \mathsf{Enc}, \mathsf{Dec})$ *is indistinguishable* (MR-PKE-IND-secure) *if for all* k *and* n *polynomially dependent on the security parameter and all efficient adversaries* $\mathcal{A} = (\mathcal{A}_1, \mathcal{A}_2)$ *interacting in experiments*

$\mathrm{Expt}^{\text{MR-PKE-IND}}_{E,\mathcal{A},k,n}$ *from Figure 3 the following advantage function is negligible in* λ*, where the probabilities are taken over the random coins of the experiment (including over* $\mathcal{A}$*'s randomness):*

$$\mathrm{Adv}^{\text{MR-PKE-IND}}_{E,\mathcal{A},k,n}(\lambda) = \left| \Pr\left[\mathrm{Expt}^{\text{MR-PKE-IND},1}_{E,\mathcal{A},k,n}(1^\lambda) = 1\right] - \Pr\left[\mathrm{Expt}^{\text{MR-PKE-IND},0}_{E,\mathcal{A},k,n}(1^\lambda) = 1\right] \right| .$$

$\mathrm{Expt}^{\text{MR-PKE-IND}}_{E,\mathcal{A},k,n}(1^\lambda)$:

(a) $pp \leftarrow_R \mathsf{PGen}(1^\lambda)$

(b) $(\vec{sk}, \vec{pk}) \overset{k}{\leftarrow}_R \mathsf{KGen}(\,)$

(c) $(\vec{m}^0, \vec{m}^1, \vec{pk}^*, st) \leftarrow_R \mathcal{A}_1^{\mathcal{D}_1}(pp, \vec{pk})$

(d) $\texttt{Require}\ |\vec{m}^0| = |\vec{m}^1| = |\vec{pk}^*| = n$

(e) $\texttt{Require}\ \forall j \in [n] : pk_j^* \in \vec{pk} \Rightarrow |m_j^0| = |m_j^1|$

(f) $\texttt{Require}\ \forall j \in [n] : pk_j^* \notin \vec{pk} \Rightarrow m_j^0 = m_j^1$

(g) $\vec{c} \leftarrow_R \mathsf{Enc}(\vec{pk}^*, \vec{m}^b)$

(h) $d \leftarrow_R \mathcal{A}_2^{\mathcal{D}_2}(\vec{c}, st)$

(i) $\texttt{Return}\ d$

Oracle $\mathcal{D}_1(i, c)$:

(a) $\texttt{Require}\ i \in [k]$

(b) $m \leftarrow \mathsf{Dec}(sk_i, c)$

(c) $\texttt{Return}\ m$

Oracle $\mathcal{D}_2(i, c)$:

(a) $\texttt{Require}\ i \in [k]$

(b) $\texttt{Require}\ \nexists j \in [n] : pk_j^* = pk_i \wedge c_j = c$

(c) $m \leftarrow \mathsf{Dec}(sk_i, c)$

(d) $\texttt{Return}\ m$

Figure 3: Our strengthened security experiment for MR-MM-PKE

In experiment $\mathrm{Expt}^{\text{MR-PKE-IND}}_{E,\mathcal{A},k,n}$ the adversary first receives the public keys of k honest users and has access to corresponding decryption oracles. She then outputs two vectors of messages, $\vec{m}^0$ and $\vec{m}^1$, on which she wants to be challenged. She also outputs a vector $\vec{pk}^*$ of public keys which may contain honest and malicious keys in any configuration. The only (and natural) condition on $\vec{m}^0, \vec{m}^1, \vec{pk}^*$ is that the messages in $\vec{m}^0$ and $\vec{m}^1$ have the same length when targeting honest public keys, and that the messages are equal when targeting malicious keys (see lines (e) and (f), respectively). Note that the rules for the second-phase decryption oracle are also as liberal as they can possibly be.

4. MULTI-RECIPIENT MULTI-KEY KEY ENCAPSULATION

A natural building block for the construction of a multi-recipient encryption scheme seems to be a multi-recipient multi-key key encapsulation mechanism (MR-MK-KEM). In this section we formalize this primitive and specify its security properties. In addition, by showing that MR-MK-KEMs can be combined with appropriate DEMs to obtain secure MR-MM-PKE we provide evidence that our formalizations are indeed helpful and accurate.

4.1 Syntax and security of MR-MK-KEM

In an MR-MK-KEM, the encapsulation algorithm takes a number of public keys and creates vectors of ciphertexts and corresponding (symmetric) keys. Using the decapsulation algorithm, each such key can individually be recovered from the corresponding ciphertext component. Similarly to the MR-MM-PKE case, the functionality of multi-recipient KEMs is readily emulated by running appropriately-many instantiations of a regular KEM in parallel. Correspondingly, regular KEMs are obtained from MR-MK-KEMs by restricting the input of the encapsulation algorithm to a single element. We formalize the primitive as follows:

DEFINITION 7 (MR-MK-KEM). *A multi-recipient multi-key key encapsulation mechanism (MR-MK-KEM)* $M = (\mathsf{PGen}, \mathsf{KGen}, \mathsf{Encap}, \mathsf{Decap})$ *consists of four algorithms as follows:*

- $\mathsf{PGen}(1^\lambda)$. *On input security parameter* 1^λ*, this algorithm outputs public parameters* pp *and the description of a keyspace* $\mathcal{K}$.

  We will assume implicitly that the following algorithms are defined in respect to a single distinguished copy of $(pp, \mathcal{K})$.

- $\mathsf{KGen}(\,)$. *This probabilistic algorithm outputs a key pair* (sk, pk).

- $\mathsf{Encap}(\vec{pk})$. *On input a vector* $\vec{pk} = (pk_1, \ldots, pk_n)$ *of public keys, this probabilistic algorithm outputs vectors* $\vec{c} = (c_1, \ldots, c_n)$ *of ciphertexts and* $\vec{K} = (K_1, \ldots, K_n)$ *of keys from keyspace* $\mathcal{K}$.

- $\mathsf{Decap}(sk, c)$. *On input a secret key* sk *and a ciphertext* c*, this algorithm outputs either a key in* $\mathcal{K}$ *or* $\perp$.

For fixed parameters pp *and any* $n \in \mathbb{N}$ *let* $(sk_j, pk_j) \leftarrow_R \mathsf{KGen}(\,)$ *for all* $j \in [n]$*. The MR-MK-KEM is* correct *if for all encapsulations*

$$((c_1, \ldots, c_n), (K_1, \ldots, K_n)) \leftarrow_R \mathsf{Encap}(pk_1, \ldots, pk_n)$$

we have $\mathsf{Decap}(sk_j, c_j) = K_j$ *for all* $j \in [n]$.

We proceed with our security definition for MR-MK-KEMs. Similarly to Section 3 we assume particularly strong adversaries: the availability of decapsulation oracles ensures CCA security, arbitrary configurations are allowed for the challenge public key vector, and, importantly, we do not require the premises of the KOSK assumption.

DEFINITION 8. (INDISTINGUISHABILITY OF MR-MK-KEM) *An MR-MK-KEM scheme* $M = (\mathsf{PGen}, \mathsf{KGen}, \mathsf{Encap}, \mathsf{Decap})$ *is* indistinguishable (MR-KEM-IND-secure) *if for all* k *and* n *polynomially dependent on the security parameter and all efficient adversaries* $\mathcal{A} = (\mathcal{A}_1, \mathcal{A}_2)$ *interacting in experiments* $\mathrm{Expt}^{\text{MR-KEM-IND},b}_{M,\mathcal{A},k,n}$ *from Figure 4 the following advantage function is negligible in* λ*, where the probabilities are taken over the random coins of the experiment (including over* $\mathcal{A}$*'s randomness):*

$$\mathrm{Adv}^{\text{MR-KEM-IND}}_{M,\mathcal{A},k,n}(\lambda) = \left|\Pr\left[\mathrm{Expt}^{\text{MR-KEM-IND},1}_{M,\mathcal{A},k,n}(1^\lambda) = 1\right] - \Pr\left[\mathrm{Expt}^{\text{MR-KEM-IND},0}_{M,\mathcal{A},k,n}(1^\lambda) = 1\right]\right| .$$

$\mathrm{Expt}^{\text{MR-KEM-IND},b}_{M,\mathcal{A},k,n}(1^\lambda)$:

(a) $(pp, \mathcal{K}) \leftarrow_R \mathsf{PGen}(1^\lambda)$
(b) $(\vec{sk}, \vec{pk}) \overset{k}{\leftarrow}_R \mathsf{KGen}()$
(c) $(\vec{pk}^*, st) \leftarrow_R \mathcal{A}_1^{\mathcal{D}_1}(pp, \mathcal{K}, \vec{pk})$
(d) **Require** $|\vec{pk}^*| = n$
(e) $(\vec{c}, \vec{K}^1) \leftarrow_R \mathsf{Encap}(\vec{pk}^*)$
(f) $\forall j \in [n]$:
- **if** $pk_j^* \in \vec{pk}$ **then** $K_j^0 \leftarrow_R \mathcal{K}$
- **if** $pk_j^* \notin \vec{pk}$ **then** $K_j^0 \leftarrow K_j^1$

(g) $d \leftarrow_R \mathcal{A}_2^{\mathcal{D}_2}(\vec{c}, \vec{K}^b, st)$
(h) **Return** d

Oracle $\mathcal{D}_1\,(i, c)$:

(a) **Require** $i \in [k]$
(b) $K \leftarrow \mathsf{Decap}\,(sk_i, c)$
(c) **Return** K

Oracle $\mathcal{D}_2\,(i, c)$:

(a) **Require** $i \in [k]$
(b) **Require** $\nexists j \in [n] : pk_j^* = pk_i \wedge c_j = c$
(c) $K \leftarrow \mathsf{Decap}\,(sk_i, c)$
(d) **Return** K

Figure 4: Our security experiment for MR-MK-KEMs

4.2 Constructing MR-MM-PKE from MR-MK-KEMs

We formally verify that the composition of an MR-MK-KEM and a DEM yields a secure MR-MM-PKE scheme.

CONSTRUCTION 1. (MR-MM-PKE FROM MR-MK-KEM) *Let* $M = (\mathsf{PGen}, \mathsf{KGen}, \mathsf{Encap}, \mathsf{Decap})$ *be an MR-MK-KEM and* $D = (\mathcal{K}, \mathsf{DEM}, \mathsf{DEM}^{-1})$ *be a DEM such that the KEM's and DEM's keyspaces coincide. We build an MR-MM-PKE* $E = (\mathsf{PGen}, \mathsf{KGen}, \mathsf{Enc}, \mathsf{Dec})$ *by implementing its algorithms in the following way:*

- $E.\mathsf{PGen}(1^\lambda) = M.\mathsf{PGen}(1^\lambda)$
- $E.\mathsf{KGen}() = M.\mathsf{KGen}()$
- $E.\mathsf{Enc}(\vec{pk}, \vec{m})$. *Run* $(\vec{c^1}, \vec{K}) \leftarrow_R M.\mathsf{Encap}(\vec{pk})$ *and* $\forall j \in [n] : c_j^2 \leftarrow_R D.\mathsf{DEM}\left(K_j, m_j\right)$. *Return* $((c_j^1, c_j^2))_{j\in[n]}$.
- $E.\mathsf{Dec}\,(sk, c)$. *Parse* $(c^1, c^2) \leftarrow c$ *and compute* $K \leftarrow_R M.\mathsf{Decap}(sk, c^1)$. *Return* $\perp$ *if* $K = \perp$; *otherwise, return* $D.\mathsf{DEM}^{-1}(K, c^2)$.

THEOREM 1. *If M is an* MR-KEM-IND*-secure MR-MK-KEM and D is an* IND-OT-CCA*-secure DEM, then E defined according to Construction 1 is an* MR-PKE-IND*-secure MR-MM-PKE. Specifically, given* $k, n \in \mathbb{N}$ *and any efficient adversary* $\mathcal{A}$ *against E, we can build efficient adversaries* $\mathcal{B}$ *and* $\mathcal{C}$ *against M and D, respectively, such that*

$$\mathrm{Adv}^{\text{MR-PKE-IND}}_{E,\mathcal{A},k,n}(\lambda) \le 2 \cdot \mathrm{Adv}^{\text{MR-KEM-IND}}_{M,\mathcal{B},k,n}(\lambda) + n \cdot \mathrm{Adv}^{\text{IND-OT-CCA}}_{D,\mathcal{C}}(\lambda) .$$

We leave the proof for the appendix.

REMARK 1. *While Theorem 1 establishes that the security notions from Definitions 4 and 8 are sufficiently strong to obtain* MR-PKE-IND*-secure MR-MM-PKE schemes, conceivably also other combinations of KEM/DEM security notions will imply a secure hybrid. Indeed, if the requirements in Definition 8 are relaxed such that (some of) the keys K established for different occurrences of the same public key in an* Encap *invocation may coincide, security of the hybrid scheme is still provided if the requirements on the DEM are simultaneously strengthened from* IND-OT-CCA *to* IND-CCA *[9] (observe how, in this setting, the stronger DEM thwarts the second attack described in Section 3.2.2).*

5. CONSTRUCTING MULTI-RECIPIENT MULTI-KEY KEY ENCAPSULATION

Taking into account the results from Section 4.2, the missing building block on our way towards MR-MM-PKE is an MR-MK-KEM. We propose a construction that is indistinguishable in the sense of Definition 8 and in particular does not rely on the KOSK assumption.

CONSTRUCTION 2 (HASHED ELGAMAL KEM). *Let* $\mathcal{G}$ *be a group generator as in Definition 1 and let l be a polynomial. The algorithms of our MR-MK-KEM* HEK *are specified as follows:*

- $\mathsf{PGen}(1^\lambda)$. *Let* $(\mathbb{G}, p, g) \leftarrow_R \mathcal{G}(1^\lambda)$. *Fix keyspace* $\mathcal{K} = \{0,1\}^{l(\lambda)}$ *and choose a hash function* $H\colon \mathbb{G} \times \mathbb{G} \times \mathbb{N} \to \mathcal{K}$. *Return public parameters* $pp = (\mathbb{G}, p, g, H)$.
- $\mathsf{KGen}()$. *Sample* $x \leftarrow_R \mathbb{Z}_p$ *and return* $(sk, pk) = (x, g^x)$.
- $\mathsf{Encap}(\vec{pk})$. *Let* $\vec{pk} = (pk_1, \ldots, pk_n)$. *Sample* $r \leftarrow_R \mathbb{Z}_p$ *and compute* $\hat{c} \leftarrow g^r$. *For all* $j \in [n]$ *let* $c_j \leftarrow (\hat{c}, j)$ *and* $K_j \leftarrow H\left((pk_j)^r, pk_j, j\right)$. *Return* $(\vec{c}, \vec{K})$.
- $\mathsf{Decap}\left(sk, (\hat{c}, j)\right)$. *Return* $K = H(\hat{c}^{sk}, pk, j)$, *where* $pk = g^{sk}$.

THEOREM 2. *Our MR-MK-KEM* HEK *from Construction 2 is* MR-KEM-IND*-secure under the static Diffie-Hellman assumption, in the random oracle model. Specifically, given* $k, n \in \mathbb{N}$ *and any efficient adversary* $\mathcal{A}$ *against* HEK, *we can build an efficient adversary* $\mathcal{B}$ *solving the SDH problem in* $\mathbb{G}$ *such that*

$$\mathrm{Adv}^{\text{MR-KEM-IND}}_{\mathsf{HEK},\mathcal{A},k,n}(\lambda) \le \mathrm{Adv}^{\text{SDH}}_{\mathcal{G},\mathcal{B}}(\lambda) + \frac{q_{d1}}{p} + \frac{q_{h1}}{p} ,$$

where q_{d1} *and* q_{h1} *represent the number of queries* $\mathcal{A}_1$ *issues to the decapsulation and the hash oracles, respectively.*

$\mathcal{B}^{\mathcal{O}_u,\mathcal{O}_v}(\mathbb{G},p,g,U,V)$:

(a) $HL \leftarrow [\,],\ DL \leftarrow [\,]$

(b) $\mathsf{Bad}_1 \leftarrow 0,\ \mathsf{Bad}_2 \leftarrow 0$

(c) Fix keyspace $\mathcal{K} = \{0,1\}^{l(\lambda)}$

(d) $pp \leftarrow (\mathbb{G},p,g)$

(e) $\forall i \in [k]$: $w_i \leftarrow_R \mathbb{Z}_p$

(f) $\forall i \in [k]$: $pk_i \leftarrow V^{w_i}$

(g) $(\vec{pk}^*, st) \leftarrow_R \mathcal{A}_1^{\mathcal{D}_1,\mathcal{H}}(pp,\mathcal{K},\vec{pk})$

(h) $\texttt{Require}\ |\vec{pk}^*| = n$

(i) $\forall j \in [n]$
- $c_j \leftarrow (U,j)$
- $K_j^* \leftarrow_R \mathcal{K}$
- $\texttt{if}\ \exists i \in [k] : pk_j^* = pk_i$: $DL[i,U,j] \leftarrow K_j^*$

(j) $d \leftarrow_R \mathcal{A}_2^{\mathcal{D}_2,\mathcal{H}}(\vec{c},\vec{K}^*,st)$

(k) $\texttt{Halt with output}\ \bot$

Simulation of $\mathcal{D}_{phase}(i,\hat{c},j)$ oracle:

(a) $\texttt{Require}\ i \in [k]$

(b) $\texttt{if}\ phase = 1 \wedge \hat{c} = U$: $\mathsf{Bad}_1 \leftarrow 1$

(c) $\texttt{if}\ phase = 2$: $\texttt{Require}\ pk_j^* \neq pk_i \vee \hat{c} \neq U$

(d) $\texttt{if}\ \exists Z \in \mathbb{G}, t \in \mathcal{K}$: $HL[Z,pk_i,j] = t \wedge \mathcal{O}_v(\hat{c}^{w_i},Z) = 1$: $\texttt{Return}\ t$

(e) $\texttt{if}\ DL[i,\hat{c},j] \neq \varepsilon$: $\texttt{Return}\ DL[i,\hat{c},j]$

(f) $t \leftarrow_R \mathcal{K}$

(g) $DL[i,\hat{c},j] \leftarrow t$

(h) $\texttt{Return}\ t$

Simulation of $\mathcal{H}(Z,W,j)$ oracle:

(a) $\texttt{if}\ \exists i \in [k] : W = pk_i \wedge \mathcal{O}_v(U^{w_i},Z) = 1$: $\texttt{Halt with output}\ Z^{1/w_i}$

(b) $\texttt{if}\ phase = 1 \wedge \mathcal{O}_u(W,Z) = 1$ $\mathsf{Bad}_2 \leftarrow 1$

(c) $\texttt{if}\ phase = 2 \wedge j \in [n] \wedge W = pk_j^* \wedge \mathcal{O}_u(W,Z) = 1$: $\texttt{Return}\ K_j^*$

(d) $\texttt{if}\ \exists i \in [k], \hat{c} \in \mathbb{G}, t \in \mathcal{K}$: $W = pk_i \wedge DL[i,\hat{c},j] = t \wedge \mathcal{O}_v(\hat{c}^{w_i},Z) = 1$: $\texttt{Return}\ t$

(e) $\texttt{if}\ HL[Z,W,j] \neq \varepsilon$: $\texttt{Return}\ HL[Z,W,j]$

(f) $t \leftarrow_R \mathcal{K}$

(g) $HL[Z,W,j] \leftarrow t$

(h) $\texttt{Return}\ t$

Figure 5: The code for adversary $\mathcal{B}$, trying to break the SDH assumption

PROOF. Throughout the proof we will denote by DH the function $\mathbb{G} \times \mathbb{G} \rightarrow \mathbb{G}$ that maps pairs (g^x, g^y) to g^{xy} for all $x, y \in \mathbb{Z}_p$. The proof is in the random oracle model, i.e., hash function H is implemented as a random function.

Given fixed k, n and an MR-KEM-IND adversary $\mathcal{A}$ for these parameters, we build an SDH adversary $\mathcal{B}$ that receives a challenge $(\mathbb{G}, p, g, U = g^u, V = g^v)$ and has access to oracles $\mathcal{O}_u(\cdot,\cdot)$ and $\mathcal{O}_v(\cdot,\cdot)$, as defined in Definition 2, and aims at computing $\mathsf{DH}(U, V)$, by the help of $\mathcal{A}$. The description of $\mathcal{B}$ is given in Figure 5.

We argue that the environment that adversary $\mathcal{B}$ provides to $\mathcal{A}$ is (almost) indistinguishable from experiments $\mathrm{Expt}^{\mathsf{MR\text{-}KEM\text{-}IND},b}$, $b \in \{0,1\}$. Indeed, it is readily verified that the vector $\vec{pk}$ of public keys that $\mathcal{A}_1$ receives follows the right (uniform) distribution (cf. lines (e) and (f) of $\mathcal{B}$). In addition, the vector $\vec{K}^*$ of keys given in line (j) to $\mathcal{A}_2$ as a result of the challenge encapsulation is completely random, which is, due to the random oracle model, in agreement with both experiments $\mathrm{Expt}^{\mathsf{MR\text{-}KEM\text{-}IND},b}$, assuming specific hash queries are not submitted.

To ensure consistency, decapsulation and hash queries are taken care of by accurately designed oracles: precisely, line (c) of the $\mathcal{H}$ oracle ensures consistency between the hash function and the components of $\vec{K}^*$; observe that a corresponding condition in the $\mathcal{D}$ oracle is not required as challenge ciphertexts may not be queried for decapsulation. Lines (d) of $\mathcal{D}$ and (d) of $\mathcal{H}$ ensure consistency between the oracles for queries not related to the challenge. Line (b) in the $\mathcal{D}$ oracle and line (b) in the $\mathcal{H}$ oracle mark $\mathcal{A}_1$-queries related to the (yet unknown) challenge ciphertext as bad; we show that this happens only with negligible probability. Lines (e)–(h) of $\mathcal{D}$ and (e)–(h) of $\mathcal{H}$ are standard for implementing consistent random oracles. Note that line (c) of $\mathcal{D}$ is just a rewriting of condition (b) in the $\mathcal{D}_2$ oracle of Figure 4.

Hash function queries related to challenge encapsulations for honest keys are handled in line (a) of $\mathcal{H}$. These queries are of the form $(\mathsf{DH}(U, pk_i), pk_i, j)$. As mentioned above, if no such hash query is submitted by $\mathcal{A}$, its views in experiments $\mathrm{Expt}^{\mathsf{MR\text{-}KEM\text{-}IND},0}$ and $\mathrm{Expt}^{\mathsf{MR\text{-}KEM\text{-}IND},1}$ are identical. On the other hand, if $\mathcal{A}$ does make such a query, an event we denote E, this allows the extraction of the SDH solution g^{uv} by $\mathcal{B}$, as implemented in line (a).

We continue with the analysis of $\mathcal{B}$'s advantage, starting with bounding the probabilities that flags Bad_1 and Bad_2 are set, and that event E occurs. Observe that the two flags can be set only in the first phase of $\mathcal{B}$'s simulation, and that the corresponding conditions depend on $\mathcal{A}_1$ guessing the right value of U *before* obtaining any information about it. Since U is uniformly distributed, the probability that in any query $\mathcal{A}_1$ finds the right value is $1/|\mathbb{G}|$. That is, the probabilities of these flags being set are bounded by

$$\Pr[\mathsf{Bad}_1] \leq \frac{q_{d1}}{p} \quad \text{and} \quad \Pr[\mathsf{Bad}_2] \leq \frac{q_{h1}}{p} \ .$$

As highlighted above, if the event E occurs, $\mathcal{B}$ solves the SDH problem, i.e., $\Pr[E] = \mathrm{Adv}^{\mathsf{SDH}}_{\mathcal{G},\mathcal{B}}$.

Observe that $\mathcal{B}$ provides a perfect simulation of the experiments $\mathrm{Expt}^{\mathsf{MR\text{-}KEM\text{-}IND},b}_{\mathsf{HEK},\mathcal{A},k,n}$, $b \in \{0,1\}$, if the events Bad_1, Bad_2, and E do not occur. Denote by S_b the event that $\mathcal{A}_2$ outputs 1 at the end of $\mathrm{Expt}^{\mathsf{MR\text{-}KEM\text{-}IND},b}_{\mathsf{HEK},\mathcal{A},k,n}$. The above allows us to conclude

$$\Pr[S_0 \mid \neg E, \neg\mathsf{Bad}_1, \neg\mathsf{Bad}_2] = \Pr[S_1 \mid \neg E, \neg\mathsf{Bad}_1, \neg\mathsf{Bad}_2] \ ,$$

which implies

$$\mathrm{Adv}^{\mathsf{MR\text{-}KEM\text{-}IND}}_{\mathsf{HEK},\mathcal{A},k,n}(\lambda) = |\Pr[S_0] - \Pr[S_1]| \leq \Pr[E] + \Pr[\mathsf{Bad}_1] + \Pr[\mathsf{Bad}_2] \ .$$

Combining this with the above established bounds on $\Pr[E]$, $\Pr[\mathsf{Bad}_1]$, and $\Pr[\mathsf{Bad}_2]$, we have

$$\mathrm{Adv}^{\mathsf{MR\text{-}KEM\text{-}IND}}_{\mathsf{HEK},\mathcal{A},k,n}(\lambda) \leq \mathrm{Adv}^{\mathsf{SDH}}_{\mathcal{G},\mathcal{B}}(\lambda) + \frac{q_{d1}}{p} + \frac{q_{h1}}{p}.$$

□

REMARK 2. *It is instructive to trace how the various components of Construction 2 contribute to its security: Firstly, we exploit the power of the static Diffie-Hellman assumption, as opposed to standard CDH, for getting rid of the KOSK restriction required in [5]; more precisely, in the proof of Theorem 2 it is exactly the oracle from Definition 2 that allows a consistent simulation of the challenge encryption and the random oracle—even in the presence of maliciously chosen public keys. Secondly, by incorporating the counter i into the input of hash function H in the* Encap *routine we prevent the second attack described in Section 3.2.2 from working: intuitively, if the same public key appears more than once in $\vec{pk}$, the different values of i will ensure that all occurrences are treated independently of each other.*

Conclusion

We revisit the security notion for multi-recipient encryption introduced in [5] and point out a number of subtle yet serious technical flaws. We propose a strengthened security model that fixes the identified issues and also avoids the unrealistic knowledge-of-secret-key assumption. We proceed by lifting the hybrid KEM/DEM construction methodology for achieving public key encryption to the multi-recipient setting and formally prove the soundness of this approach. Finally, we propose a new multi-recipient KEM (and, hence, a multi-recipient PKE scheme) that we prove secure under the static Diffie-Hellman assumption, in the random oracle model. We leave the construction of a standard model multi-recipient PKE scheme that achieves the level of security implied by our definitions for future work.

6. REFERENCES

[1] M. Abdalla, M. Bellare, and P. Rogaway. The oracle Diffie-Hellman assumptions and an analysis of DHIES. In D. Naccache, editor, *CT-RSA 2001*, volume 2020 of *LNCS*, pages 143–158, San Francisco, CA, USA, Apr. 8–12, 2001. Springer, Berlin, Germany.

[2] J. Baek, R. Safavi-Naini, and W. Susilo. Efficient multi-receiver identity-based encryption and its application to broadcast encryption. In S. Vaudenay, editor, *PKC 2005*, volume 3386 of *LNCS*, pages 380–397, Les Diablerets, Switzerland, Jan. 23–26, 2005. Springer, Berlin, Germany.

[3] M. Barbosa and P. Farshim. Efficient identity-based key encapsulation to multiple parties. In N. P. Smart, editor, *10th IMA International Conference on Cryptography and Coding*, volume 3796 of *LNCS*, pages 428–441, Cirencester, UK, Dec. 19–21, 2005. Springer, Berlin, Germany.

[4] M. Bellare, A. Boldyreva, K. Kurosawa, and J. Staddon. Multirecipient encryption schemes: How to save on bandwidth and computation without sacrificing security. *IEEE Transactions on Information Theory*, 53(11):3927–3943, 2007.

[5] M. Bellare, A. Boldyreva, and J. Staddon. Randomness re-use in multi-recipient encryption schemes. In Y. Desmedt, editor, *PKC 2003*, volume 2567 of *LNCS*, pages 85–99, Miami, USA, Jan. 6–8, 2003. Springer, Berlin, Germany.

[6] D. Boneh, C. Gentry, and B. Waters. Collusion resistant broadcast encryption with short ciphertexts and private keys. In V. Shoup, editor, *CRYPTO 2005*, volume 3621 of *LNCS*, pages 258–275, Santa Barbara, CA, USA, Aug. 14–18, 2005. Springer, Berlin, Germany.

[7] S. Chatterjee and P. Sarkar. Multi-receiver identity-based key encapsulation with shortened ciphertext. In R. Barua and T. Lange, editors, *INDOCRYPT 2006*, volume 4329 of *LNCS*, pages 394–408, Kolkata, India, Dec. 11–13, 2006. Springer, Berlin, Germany.

[8] R. Cramer and V. Shoup. A practical public key cryptosystem provably secure against adaptive chosen ciphertext attack. In H. Krawczyk, editor, *CRYPTO'98*, volume 1462 of *LNCS*, pages 13–25, Santa Barbara, CA, USA, Aug. 23–27, 1998. Springer, Berlin, Germany.

[9] R. Cramer and V. Shoup. Design and analysis of practical public-key encryption schemes secure against adaptive chosen ciphertext attack. *SIAM J. Computing*, 33(1):167–226, 2003.

[10] C. Delerablée. Identity-based broadcast encryption with constant size ciphertexts and private keys. In K. Kurosawa, editor, *ASIACRYPT 2007*, volume 4833 of *LNCS*, pages 200–215, Kuching, Malaysia, Dec. 2–6, 2007. Springer, Berlin, Germany.

[11] T. ElGamal. A public key cryptosystem and a signature scheme based on discrete logarithms. In G. R. Blakley and D. Chaum, editors, *CRYPTO'84*, volume 196 of *LNCS*, pages 10–18, Santa Barbara, CA, USA, Aug. 19–23, 1984. Springer, Berlin, Germany.

[12] A. Fiat and M. Naor. Broadcast encryption. In D. R. Stinson, editor, *CRYPTO'93*, volume 773 of *LNCS*, pages 480–491, Santa Barbara, CA, USA, Aug. 22–26, 1993. Springer, Berlin, Germany.

[13] K. Kurosawa. Multi-recipient public-key encryption with shortened ciphertext. In D. Naccache and P. Paillier, editors, *PKC 2002*, volume 2274 of *LNCS*, pages 48–63, Paris, France, Feb. 12–14, 2002. Springer, Berlin, Germany.

[14] D. Naor, M. Naor, and J. Lotspiech. Revocation and tracing schemes for stateless receivers. In J. Kilian, editor, *CRYPTO 2001*, volume 2139 of *LNCS*, pages 41–62, Santa Barbara, CA, USA, Aug. 19–23, 2001. Springer, Berlin, Germany.

[15] N. P. Smart. Efficient key encapsulation to multiple parties. In C. Blundo and S. Cimato, editors, *SCN 04*, volume 3352 of *LNCS*, pages 208–219, Amalfi, Italy, Sept. 8–10, 2004. Springer, Berlin, Germany.

APPENDIX

Proof of Theorem 1

PROOF. Fix $k, n \in \mathbb{N}$ and an efficient adversary $\mathcal{A}$ against E. The proof proceeds by a series of game hops. Let

$$G^0 = \mathrm{Expt}_{E,\mathcal{A},k,n}^{\text{MR-PKE-IND},0}(1^\lambda) \quad G^1 = \mathrm{Expt}_{E,\mathcal{A},k,n}^{\text{MR-PKE-IND},1}(1^\lambda)$$

(see Figure 3).

Next, define two other games, H^0 and H^1. For $b \in \{0,1\}$, game H^b is equal to game G^b with the following exceptions:

- in games G^b, the challenge ciphertext is created by

$$(\vec{c^1}, \vec{K}^1) \leftarrow_R M.\mathsf{Encap}\left(\vec{pk}^*\right);$$
$$\vec{c^2} \leftarrow_R D.\mathsf{DEM}(\vec{K}^1, \vec{m}^b);$$
$$\vec{c} \leftarrow ((c_j^1, c_j^2))_{j\in[n]}.$$

  while in games H^b the challenge ciphertext is created by

$$(\vec{c^1}, \vec{K}^1) \leftarrow_R M.\mathsf{Encap}(\vec{pk}^*);$$
$$\vec{c^2} \leftarrow_R D.\mathsf{DEM}(\vec{K}^0, \vec{m}^b);$$
$$\vec{c} \leftarrow ((c_j^1, c_j^2))_{j\in[n]},$$

  where the components of $\vec{K}^0$ are defined like this

$$\begin{cases} K_j^0 \leftarrow_R \mathcal{K}, & pk_j^* \in \vec{pk} \\ K_j^0 \leftarrow K_j^1, & pk_j^* \notin \vec{pk} \end{cases}$$

  for $j \in [n]$.
- when handling decryption queries in games G^b, a DEM key is computed from the first component of the submitted ciphertext, and then used to decrypt the second component according to the scheme's specifications; in games H^b, the key vector $\vec{K}^0$ will be used in decryption queries involving the challenge encapsulations $\vec{c^1}$. That is, when the decryption oracle receives a query $(i, (\hat{c}^1, \hat{c}^2))$ for which $\exists j : pk_j^* = pk_i \wedge \hat{c}^1 = c_j^1$, decryption of $\hat{c}^2$ will be done using K_j^0. In all the other cases, it proceeds normally, first decapsulating $\hat{c}^1$ to obtain a DEM key, and then decrypting $\hat{c}^2$ with it.

We can write

$$\begin{aligned}\mathrm{Adv}_{E,\mathcal{A},k,n}^{\textsf{MR-PKE-IND}}(\lambda) = \left|\Pr[G^1 = 1] - \Pr[G^0 = 1]\right| &\le \\ \left|\Pr[G^1 = 1] - \Pr[H^1 = 1]\right| &+ \\ \left|\Pr[H^1 = 1] - \Pr[H^0 = 1]\right| &+ \\ \left|\Pr[H^0 = 1] - \Pr[G^0 = 1]\right| &.\end{aligned}$$

Note that the difference between games G^0 and H^0, and the difference between games G^1 and H^1, correspond to the difference between the KEM experiments $\mathrm{Expt}_{E,\mathcal{A},k,n}^{\textsf{MR-KEM-IND},b}(1^\lambda)$, $b \in \{0,1\}$. Hence, there exist KEM adversary $\mathcal{B}^0$ and $\mathcal{B}^1$ such that

$$\left|\Pr[G^l = 1] - \Pr[H^l = 1]\right| \le \mathrm{Adv}_{M,\mathcal{B}^l,k,n}^{\textsf{MR-KEM-IND}}$$

for $l \in \{0,1\}$.

Furthermore, the only difference in games H^0 and H^1 is in the challenge encryption: H^0 always encrypts $\vec{m}^0$ and H^1 always encrypts $\vec{m}^1$. To analyze the distance between these games, we proceed by a hybrid argument. Define a game E^j for $0 \le j \le n$ such that $E^0 = H^1$ and $E^n = H^0$: if $\vec{m}$ is the vector that is encrypted, then $m_k = m_k^0$ for all $1 \le k \le j$ and $m_k = m_k^1$ for all $j < k \le n$. That is, in two consecutive games, E^{j-1} and E^j, the only difference is in the component c_j^2 of the challenge ciphertext: in E^{j-1} it is the encryption of an element in $\vec{m}^1$ whereas in E^j it is the encryption of an element in $\vec{m}^0$ of the same length.

It easily follows that there exist adversaries $\mathcal{C}^j$ for $1 \le j \le n$, such that $\mathcal{C}^j$ interpolates between the games E^{j-1} and E^j, and

$$\mathrm{Adv}_{D,\mathcal{C}^j}^{\textsf{IND-OT-CCA}}(\lambda) = \left|\Pr[E^{j-1} = 1] - \Pr[E^j = 1]\right|.$$

Thus,

$$\begin{aligned}&\left|\Pr\left[H^1 = 1\right] - \Pr\left[H^0 = 1\right]\right| \\ &= \sum_{j=1}^{n} \left|\Pr[E^{j-1} = 1] - \Pr[E^j = 1]\right| \\ &= \sum_{j=1}^{n} \mathrm{Adv}_{D,\mathcal{C}^j}^{\textsf{IND-OT-CCA}}(\lambda)\end{aligned}$$

Hence, there exist adversaries $\mathcal{B}$ and $\mathcal{C}$ such that[1]

$$\begin{aligned}\mathrm{Adv}_{E,\mathcal{A},k,n}^{\textsf{MR-PKE-IND}}(\lambda) \le 2 \cdot \mathrm{Adv}_{M,\mathcal{B},k,n}^{\textsf{MR-KEM-IND}}(\lambda) &+ \\ n \cdot \mathrm{Adv}_{D,\mathcal{C}}^{\textsf{IND-OT-CCA}}(\lambda) &.\end{aligned}$$

□

[1] $\mathcal{B}$ and $\mathcal{C}$ can be constructed by randomly picking and running an adversary from $\{\mathcal{B}^b\}_{b\in\{0,1\}}$ and $\{\mathcal{C}^j\}_{j\in[n]}$, respectively, which will yield an advantage for $\mathcal{B}$ and $\mathcal{C}$ corresponding to the average advantage of their underlying adversaries.

Fully Secure Key-Policy Attribute-Based Encryption with Constant-Size Ciphertexts and Fast Decryption

Junzuo Lai
Dept. of Computer Science
Jinan University, China
The State Key Laboratory of Integrated Services Networks
Xidian University, China
laijunzuo@gmail.com

Robert H. Deng
School of Information Systems
Singapore Management University
Singapore 178902
robertdeng@smu.edu.sg

Yingjiu Li
School of Information Systems
Singapore Management University
Singapore 178902
yjli@smu.edu.sg

Jian Weng
Dept. of Computer Science
Jinan University
Guangzhou 510632, China
cryptjweng@gmail.com

ABSTRACT

Attribute-based encryption (ABE), introduced by Sahai and Waters, is a promising cryptographic primitive, which has been widely applied to implement fine-grained access control system for encrypted data. In its key-policy flavor, attribute sets are used to annotate ciphertexts and secret keys are associated with access structures that specify which ciphertexts a user is entitled to decrypt. In most existing key-policy attribute-based encryption (KP-ABE) constructions, the size of the ciphertext is proportional to the number of attributes associated with it and the decryption cost is proportional to the number of attributes used during decryption.

In this paper, we present a new construction of KP-ABE. Our proposed construction is the first KP-ABE scheme, which has the following features simultaneously: expressive (i.e., supporting arbitrary monotonic access structures); fully secure in the standard model; constant-size ciphertexts and fast decryption. The downside of our construction is that secret keys have quadratic size in the number of attributes.

Categories and Subject Descriptors

E.3 [**Data Encryption**]: Public Key Cryptosystems; D.4.6 [**Security and Protection**]: Access controls, Cryptographic controls

General Terms

Security, Design

ASIA CCS'14, June 4–6, 2014, Kyoto, Japan.

http://dx.doi.org/10.1145/2590296.2590334.

Keywords

Key-Policy Attribute-Based Encryption; Full Security; Constant-Size Ciphertexts; Fast Decryption

1. INTRODUCTION

In the traditional public key encryption or identity-based encryption schemes [35, 10], encrypted data is targeted for decryption by a single known user; hence, they lack the expressiveness needed for more advanced data sharing. Many distributed applications require complex access control mechanisms for encrypted data which is stored in untrusted servers, such as in the cloud. Sahai and Waters [34] addressed this issue by introducing the concept of attribute-based encryption (ABE). ABE enables public key one-to-many encryption and is envisioned as a promising cryptographic primitive for realizing scalable and fine-grained access control systems. There are two kinds of ABE: key-policy ABE (KP-ABE) [21] and ciphertext-policy ABE (CP-ABE) [7]. In this paper, our concern is on the former.

In a KP-ABE scheme [21], every ciphertext is associated with a set of attributes, and every user's secret key is associated with an access structure on attributes. A user will be able to decrypt a ciphertext only if the access structure associated with the user's secret key is satisfied by the set of attributes associated with the ciphertext. This access control functionality can be very powerful, but also costly. In most existing KP-ABE constructions, the size of the ciphertext is proportional to the number of attributes associated with it and the decryption cost is proportional to the number of attributes used during decryption. Specifically, it usually requires one pairing operation per attribute used during decryption. To the best of our knowledge, the schemes in [4, 23] are the only efforts to design KP-ABE schemes with constant-size ciphertexts[1] and/or fast decryption.

In [4], Attrapadung et al. first showed that a certain class of identity-based broadcast encryption (IBBE) schemes

[1]Constant-size ciphertexts mean that the size of a ciphertext only depends on the security parameter and not on the number of attributes associated with the ciphertext.

readily yields KP-ABE schemes with monotonic (though LSSS-realizable) access structures via a generic transformation. Then, they presented an IBBE scheme with constant-size ciphertexts, which can be seen as an instance of the function encryption for zero inner-product with constant-size ciphertexts proposed in [2, 3] and is implied by spatial encryption of [12], thus yielding a KP-ABE scheme with constant-size ciphertexts. Their scheme also reduces the number of pairing evaluations to a constant during decryption. However, the generic transformation proposed in [4] from a certain class of IBBE to KP-ABE only guarantees the resulting KP-ABE scheme to be selectively secure (i. e., the adversaries have to make up their mind about their target before seeing the public parameters), which is a weak security model analogous to the selective-ID model [8, 13] in IBE schemes. Moreover, the scheme proposed in [4] brought in an inner-product instance as a basic building block which fundamentally demands a bound on the maximum number of attributes that can appear in a ciphertext.

More recently, based on the KP-ABE scheme (denoted as GPSW scheme) by Goyal et al. [21], Hohenberger and Waters [23] presented a KP-ABE scheme in which a ciphertext can be decrypted with only 2 pairings by increasing the secret key size by a factor of $|\Lambda|$, where Λ is the set of distinct attributes that appear in the secret key. They also presented a generalized construction that allows each user to independently tune various efficiency tradeoffs to their liking on a spectrum where the extremes are GPSW scheme on one end and their very fast scheme on the other. Compared with the scheme proposed in [4], their schemes do not place a limit on the number of attributes used in a ciphertext and have shorter secret key size. However, the size of the ciphertext in [23] is proportional to the number of attributes associated with it. On the other hand, the base construction of KP-ABE scheme with fast decryption proposed in [23] only supports a small universe U of attributes, where $|U|$ is a polynomial in the security parameter. Hohenberger and Waters [23] described how to alter their base construction to accommodate a large universe $U = \{0,1\}^*$ of attributes, but relying on the random oracle (RO) model [6].

1.1 Our Contribution

We first observe that, each attribute can be divided into two parts: an attribute name and its value. In most cases, the total number of attribute names in a system is *polynomial*, and the possible number of values of an attribute name is *exponential*. We use the application scenario in [23] to illustrate this. In a KP-ABE system, an encrypted email can be tagged with a set of attributes, such as "from: Alice", "to: IACR board", "subject: voting", "date: October 1, 2013". The master authority for the system issues secret decryption keys associated with access structures to users, such as giving to Bob a decryption key that enables him to decrypt any ciphertexts that satisfy the following access structure,

"to: Bob" OR ("to: IACR board" AND
(January 1, 2013 $\leq$ "date" $\leq$ December 31, 2013)).

In this application scenario, there only exist several attribute names (i.e., "from", "to", "subject" and "date"), but the possible number of values of an attribute name, such as "date", could be exponential.

Based on the above observation, drawing on the hierarchical identity-based encryption (HIBE) scheme with constant-size ciphertexts by Boneh et al. [9] and the fully secure KP-ABE scheme by Lewko et al. [25], we present in this paper the first KP-ABE scheme which has the following features simultaneously: expressive (i.e., supporting arbitrary monotonic access structure); fully secure (cf. selectively secure) in the standard model; constant-size ciphertexts and fast decryption. The downside of our construction is that secret keys have quadratic size, which comprise $O(\ell \cdot n)$ elements, where n is the total number of attribute names in the system and ℓ is the number of leaf nodes in an access tree/structure. A comparison of our scheme to the schemes in [4, 23] focusing on designing KP-ABE schemes with constant-size ciphertexts and/or fast decryption is given in Table 1. Note that, we take the KP-ABE scheme for a small universe of attributes with the fastest decryption algorithm proposed by Hohenberger and Waters [23] for comparison, since their KP-ABE scheme for a large universe of attributes relies on the random oracle model.

1.2 Related Work

The notion of ABE was introduced by Sahai and Waters as an application of their fuzzy identity-based encryption (IBE) scheme [34], where both ciphertexts and secrete keys are associated with sets of attributes. The decryption of a ciphertext is enabled if and only if the set of attributes for the ciphertext and the set of attributes for the secret key overlap by at least a fixed threshold value d. Goyal et al. [21] formulated two complementary forms of ABE: KP-ABE and CP-ABE. In a KP-ABE scheme, decryption keys are associated with access structures and ciphertexts are associated with sets of attributes. In a CP-ABE scheme, the situation is reversed: decryption keys are associated with sets of attributes while ciphertexts are associated with access structures. There exists a general method to transform KP-ABE to CP-ABE [20].

In terms of the expressive power of access structures, Goyal et al. [21] presented the first KP-ABE supporting monotonic access structures. To enable more flexible access control policy, Ostrovsky et al. [32] presented a KP-ABE system that supports the expression of non-monotonic formulas in key policies. Lewko et al. [25] proposed the first fully secure KP-ABE scheme supporting arbitrary monotonic access formulas. Previous constructions of KP-ABE [21, 32] were only proven to be selectively secure. Lewko and Waters [28] proposed a KP-ABE scheme which is "unbounded" in the sense that the public parameters do not impose additional limitations on the functionality of the scheme. Rouselakis and Waters [33] improved the efficiency of the unbounded KP-ABE scheme proposed in [28]. Recently, with the distinct method, Garg et al. [18] and Gorbunov et al. [19] provided the constructions of KP-ABE for general circuits. The problem of building KP-ABE systems with multiple authorities was investigated in [14, 30, 15]. In virtually all existing KP-ABE schemes, the size of the ciphertext is proportional to the number of attributes associated with it, and the decryption cost is proportional to the number of attributes that have been used for decryption. In this paper, we focus on designing KP-ABE scheme with constant-size ciphertexts and fast decryption. To the best of our knowledge, besides the work of us, there only exist two efforts [4, 23] with the

Scheme	Public parameters size[2]	Private key size[2]	Ciphertext overhead[2]	Decryption cost PAIR.	EXP.	Security
ALP[3] [4]	$O(\bar{n})$	$O(\ell \cdot \bar{n})$	2	2	$O(\|I\| \cdot \|S\|)$	selective
HW [23]	$O(\|U\|)$	$O(\ell \cdot \|\Lambda\|)$	$O(\|S\|)$	2	$O(\|I\| \cdot \|\Delta\|)$	selective[4]
Our scheme	$O(n)$	$O(\ell \cdot n)$	2	2	$O(\|I\| \cdot n)$	full

Table 1: Comparison with other KP-ABE schemes having constant-size ciphertexts and/or fast decryption.

† $\bar{n}$ is the maximum number of attributes that can appear in a ciphertext. ℓ is the number of attributes in an access structure for a key. $|I|$ is the number of attributes used in decryption and $|S|$ denotes the number of attributes associated with the ciphertext. U is the universe of attributes in the system and $|U|$ denotes the number of attributes in U. $|\Lambda|$ denotes the number of distinct attributes that appear in the private key and $|\Delta|$ denotes the number of distinct attributes used in decryption. n is the total number of attribute names/categories in the system, which is normally a small number, as illustrated in the email example.

‡ PAIR. and EXP. denote the number of paring and exponentiation computation (in $\mathbb{G}$ or $\mathbb{G}_T$), respectively.

same concern. An overview comparing our work to their efforts [4, 23] is given in Table 1.

The first CP-ABE construction proposed by Bethencourt et al. [7] was proven secure under the generic group model. Later, Cheung and Newport [16] presented a CP-ABE scheme that is secure under the standard model; however, the access policies in that scheme are restricted to be in the form of a AND combination of different attributes. Recently, secure and more expressive CP-ABE schemes [36, 25, 29, 18, 19] were proposed. Rouselakis and Waters [33] proposed the first unbounded CP-ABE scheme where the public parameters do not impose additional limitations on the functionality of the scheme. Müller et al. [31] and Lewko et al. [27] led another line of research, considering CP-ABE schemes with multiple authorities, in an attempt to meet the need of a more general framework where data are shared according to policies defined over attributes or credentials issued across different trust domains and organizations. Similar to KP-ABE, in virtually all existing CP-ABE schemes, the size of a ciphertext is proportional to the size of its associated access policy, and the decryption cost is proportional to the number of attributes that have been used for decryption. Emura et al. [17] suggested a CP-ABE scheme with constant-size ciphertexts but policies are restricted to a single AND gate. Herranz et al. [22] described a CP-ABE scheme with constant-size ciphertexts, only supporting threshold access policies. Recently, Hohenberger and Waters [23] observed that if one is willing to consider "bounded" CP-ABE systems, where a value k_{max} can be set system-wide as the maximum number of times a single attribute can appear in a particular formula (or access structure), then one can achieve fast decryption without an increase in ciphertext size or encryption time.

Besides the two usual flavors of ABE, another kind of ABE schemes [1], called dual-policy ABE, mixes features from both KP-ABE and CP-ABE schemes.

[2]The measurement is in terms of $|\mathbb{G}|$.

[3]The scheme proposed by Attrapadung et al. [4] supports non-monotonic access structures. We take their KP-ABE construction supporting monotonic access structures for comparison.

[4]In [23], Hohenberger and Waters mentioned that one may modify their construction to achieve full security using dual encryption system [26].

1.3 Organization

The rest of this paper is organized as follows. Section 2 gives some preliminaries and formal definition of KP-ABE. Section 3 describes the proposed construction and its security proof. Section 4 concludes the paper.

2. PRELIMINARIES

If S is a set, then $|S|$ denotes its size and $s_1, \ldots, s_t \leftarrow S$ denotes the operation of picking elements $s_1, \ldots, s_t$ uniformly at random from S. Let $\mathbb{N}$ denote the set of natural numbers. If $n \in \mathbb{N}$ then $[n]$ denotes the set $\{1, \ldots, n\}$. If $\lambda \in \mathbb{N}$ then 1^λ denotes the string of λ ones. Let $z \leftarrow \mathsf{A}(x, y, \ldots)$ denote the operation of running an algorithm A with inputs $(x, y, \ldots)$ and output z. A function $f(\lambda)$ is *negligible* if for every $c > 0$ there exists a λ_c such that $f(\lambda) < 1/\lambda^c$ for all $\lambda > \lambda_c$.

2.1 Access Structures

Definition 1 (Access Structure [5]). *Let $\{P_1, \ldots, P_n\}$ be a set of parties. A collection $\mathbb{A} \subseteq 2^{\{P_1,\ldots,P_n\}}$ is monotone if $\forall B, C$: if $B \in \mathbb{A}$ and $B \subseteq C$, then $C \in \mathbb{A}$. An access structure (respectively, monotonic access structure) is a collection (respectively, monotone collection) $\mathbb{A}$ of non-empty subsets of $\{P_1, \ldots, P_n\}$, i.e., $\mathbb{A} \subseteq 2^{\{P_1,\ldots,P_n\}} \backslash \{\emptyset\}$. The sets in $\mathbb{A}$ are called authorized sets, and the sets not in $\mathbb{A}$ are called unauthorized sets.*

In our context, attributes play the role of parties and we restrict our attention to monotonic access structures. It is possible to (inefficiently) realize general access structures using our techniques by treating the negation of an attribute as a separate attribute.

2.2 Linear Secret Sharing Schemes

Our construction will employ linear secret-sharing schemes (LSSS). We use the definition adapted from [5]:

Definition 2 (Linear Secret-Sharing Schemes). *A secret sharing scheme Π over a set of parties $\mathcal{P}$ is called linear (over $\mathbb{Z}_p$) if*

1. *The shares for each party form a vector over $\mathbb{Z}_p$.*

2. *There exists a matrix $\mathbf{A}$ with ℓ rows and n columns called the share-generating matrix for Π. For all $i =$*

$1, \ldots, \ell$, *the* i^{th} *row of* $\mathbf{A}$ *is labeled by a party* $\rho(i)$ *(*ρ *is a function from* $\{1, \ldots, \ell\}$ *to* $\mathcal{P}$*). When we consider the column vector* $v = (s, r_2, \ldots, r_n)$*, where* $s \in \mathbb{Z}_p$ *is the secret to be shared, and* $r_2, \ldots, r_n \in \mathbb{Z}_p$ *are randomly chosen, then* $\mathbf{A}v$ *is the vector of* ℓ *shares of the secret* s *according to* Π*. The share* $(\mathbf{A}v)_i$ *belongs to party* $\rho(i)$*.*

It is shown in [5] that every linear secret-sharing scheme according to the above definition also enjoys the linear reconstruction property, defined as follows. Suppose that Π is an LSSS for the access structure $\mathbb{A}$. Let $S \in \mathbb{A}$ be any authorized set, and let $I \subset \{1, \ldots, \ell\}$ be defined as $I = \{i | \rho(i) \in S\}$. Then there exist constants $\{\omega_i \in \mathbb{Z}_p\}_{i \in I}$ such that, if $\{\lambda_i\}$ are valid shares of any secret s according to Π, then $\sum_{i \in I} \omega_i \lambda_i = s$. Let A_i denotes the i-th row of $\mathbf{A}$, we have $\sum_{i \in I} \omega_i A_i = (1, 0, \ldots, 0)$. These constants $\{\omega_i\}$ can be found in time polynomial in the size of the share-generation matrix $\mathbf{A}$ [5]. Note that, for unauthorized sets, no such constants $\{\omega_i\}$ exist.

Boolean Formulas Access structures might also be described in terms of monotonic boolean formulas. Using standard techniques [5] one can convert any monotonic boolean formula into an LSSS representation. We can represent the boolean formula as an access tree. An access tree of ℓ nodes will result in an LSSS matrix of ℓ rows. We refer the reader to the appendix of [27] for a discussion on how to perform this conversion.

2.3 Key-Policy Attribute-Based Encryption

A KP-ABE scheme consists of the following four algorithms:

$\mathsf{Setup}(1^\lambda)$ takes as input a security parameter λ. It outputs the public parameters PK and a master secret key MSK.

$\mathsf{KeyGen}(\mathsf{PK}, \mathsf{MSK}, \mathbb{A})$ takes as input the public parameters PK, the master secret key MSK and an access structure $\mathbb{A}$. It outputs a private key $\mathsf{SK}_{\mathbb{A}}$ corresponding to $\mathbb{A}$.

$\mathsf{Encrypt}(\mathsf{PK}, M, S)$ takes as input the public parameters PK, a message M and a set of attributes S. It outputs a ciphertext CT.

$\mathsf{Decrypt}(\mathsf{PK}, \mathsf{SK}_{\mathbb{A}}, CT)$ takes as input the public parameters PK, a private key $\mathsf{SK}_{\mathbb{A}}$, and a ciphertext CT associated with a set of attributes S. If the set S of attributes satisfies the access structure $\mathbb{A}$, then the algorithm will decrypt the ciphertext and return a message M.

We now give the full security definition for KP-ABE schemes. This is described by a seucirty game between a challenger and an adversary. The game proceeds as follows:

Setup The challenger runs Setup to obtain the public parameters PK and a master secret key MSK. It gives the public parameters PK to the adversary and keeps MSK to itself.

Query phase 1 The adversary adaptively queries the challenger for secret keys corresponding to sets of access structures $\mathbb{A}_1, \ldots, \mathbb{A}_q$. In response, the challenger runs $\mathsf{SK}_{\mathbb{A}_i} \leftarrow \mathsf{KeyGen}\ (\mathsf{PK}, \mathsf{MSK}, \mathbb{A}_i)$ and gives the secret key $\mathsf{SK}_{\mathbb{A}_i}$ to the adversary, for $1 \le i \le q$.

Challenge The adversary submits two (equal length) messages M_0, M_1 and a set of attributes S, subject to the restriction that S cannot satisfy any of the queried access structures in Query phase 1. The challenger selects a random bit $\beta \in \{0, 1\}$, sets $CT = \mathsf{Encrypt}(\mathsf{PK}, M_\beta, S)$ and sends CT to the adversary as the challenge ciphertext.

Query phase 2 The adversary continues to adaptively query the challenger for secret keys corresponding to access structures with the restriction that none of these can be satisfied by S.

Guess The adversary outputs its guess $\beta' \in \{0, 1\}$ for β.

The advantage of the adversary in this game is defined as $|\Pr[\beta = \beta'] - \frac{1}{2}|$ where the probability is taken over the random bits used by the challenger and the adversary.

DEFINITION 3. *A key-policy attribute-based encryption scheme is (fully) secure if all PPT adversaries have at most a negligible advantage in the above security game.*

2.4 Composite Order Bilinear Groups

We will construct our scheme in composite order bilinear groups whose order is the product of three distinct primes. Composite order bilinear groups were first introduced in [11].

Let $\mathcal{G}$ be an algorithm that takes as input a security parameter 1^λ and outputs a tuple $(p_1, p_2, p_3, \mathbb{G}, \mathbb{G}_T, e)$, where p_1, p_2, p_3 are distinct primes, $\mathbb{G}$ and $\mathbb{G}_T$ are cyclic groups of order $N = p_1 p_2 p_3$, and $e : \mathbb{G} \times \mathbb{G} \to \mathbb{G}_T$ is a map such that

1. (Bilinear) $\forall g, h \in \mathbb{G}, a, b \in \mathbb{Z}_N, e(g^a, h^b) = e(g, h)^{ab}$;
2. (Non-degenerate) $\exists g \in \mathbb{G}$ such that $e(g, g)$ has order N in $\mathbb{G}_T$.

We further require that multiplication in $\mathbb{G}$ and $\mathbb{G}_T$, as well as the bilinear map e, are computable in time polynomial in λ. We use $\mathbb{G}_{p_1}, \mathbb{G}_{p_2}, \mathbb{G}_{p_3}$ to denote the subgroups of $\mathbb{G}$ having order p_1, p_2, p_3, respectively. Observe that $\mathbb{G} = \mathbb{G}_{p_1} \times \mathbb{G}_{p_2} \times \mathbb{G}_{p_3}$. Note also that if $g_1 \in \mathbb{G}_{p_1}$ and $g_2 \in \mathbb{G}_{p_2}$ then $e(g_1, g_2) = 1$. The same rule holds whenever e is applied to elements in distinct subgroups.

We now state the complexity assumptions we use. Assumptions 1, 2 and 3 have already been used in [25, 26]. Utilizing the theorems proposed in [24], one can easily prove that the assumptions hold in the generic group model.

ASSUMPTION 1. *Let* $\mathcal{G}$ *be as above. We define the following distribution::*

$$(p_1, p_2, p_3, \mathbb{G}, \mathbb{G}_T, e) \leftarrow \mathcal{G}(1^\lambda),\ N = p_1 p_2 p_3,$$

$$g, X_1 \leftarrow \mathbb{G}_{p_1},\ X_2, Y_2 \leftarrow \mathbb{G}_{p_2},\ X_3, Y_3 \leftarrow \mathbb{G}_{p_3},$$

$$D = (\mathbb{G}, \mathbb{G}_T, N, e, g, X_1 X_2, Y_2 Y_3, X_3),$$

$$T_1 \leftarrow \mathbb{G}_{p_1} \times \mathbb{G}_{p_2} \times \mathbb{G}_{p_3},\ T_2 \leftarrow \mathbb{G}_{p_1} \times \mathbb{G}_{p_3}.$$

The advantage of an algorithm $\mathcal{A}$ *in breaking Assumption 1 is defined as*

$$Adv^1_{\mathcal{A}} = |\Pr[\mathcal{A}(D, T_1) = 1] - \Pr[\mathcal{A}(D, T_2) = 1]|.$$

DEFINITION 4. *We say* $\mathcal{G}$ *satisfies Assumption 1 if for any polynomial time algorithm* $\mathcal{A}$*,* $Adv^1_{\mathcal{A}}$ *is negligible.*

ASSUMPTION 2. *Let $\mathcal{G}$ be as above. We define the following distribution:*

$$(p_1, p_2, p_3, \mathbb{G}, \mathbb{G}_T, e) \leftarrow \mathcal{G}(1^\lambda), \ N = p_1p_2p_3,$$

$$g \leftarrow \mathbb{G}_{p_1}, \ X_3 \leftarrow \mathbb{G}_{p_3},$$

$$D = (\mathbb{G}, \mathbb{G}_T, N, e, g, X_3),$$

$$T_1 \leftarrow \mathbb{G}_{p_1} \times \mathbb{G}_{p_2}, \ T_2 \leftarrow \mathbb{G}_{p_1}.$$

The advantage of an algorithm $\mathcal{A}$ in breaking Assumption 2 is defined as

$$Adv^2_{\mathcal{A}} = |\Pr[\mathcal{A}(D, T_1) = 1] - \Pr[\mathcal{A}(D, T_2) = 1]|.$$

DEFINITION 5. *We say $\mathcal{G}$ satisfies Assumption 2 if for any polynomial time algorithm $\mathcal{A}$, $Adv^2_{\mathcal{A}}$ is negligible.*

ASSUMPTION 3. *Let $\mathcal{G}$ be as above. We define the following distribution:*

$$(p_1, p_2, p_3, \mathbb{G}, \mathbb{G}_T, e) \leftarrow \mathcal{G}(1^\lambda), \ N = p_1p_2p_3,$$

$$\alpha, s \leftarrow \mathbb{Z}_N, \ g \leftarrow \mathbb{G}_{p_1}, g_2, X_2, Y_2 \leftarrow \mathbb{G}_{p_2},$$

$$X_3 \stackrel{\$}{\leftarrow} \mathbb{G}_{p_3},$$

$$D = (\mathbb{G}, \mathbb{G}_T, N, e, g, g_2, g^\alpha X_2, g^s Y_2, X_3),$$

$$T_1 = e(g, g)^{\alpha s}, \ T_2 \leftarrow \mathbb{G}_T.$$

The advantage of an algorithm $\mathcal{A}$ in breaking Assumption 3 is defined as

$$Adv^3_{\mathcal{A}} = |\Pr[\mathcal{A}(D, T_1) = 1] - \Pr[\mathcal{A}(D, T_2) = 1]|.$$

DEFINITION 6. *We say $\mathcal{G}$ satisfies Assumption 3 if for any polynomial time algorithm $\mathcal{A}$, $Adv^3_{\mathcal{A}}$ is negligible.*

3. OUR PROPOSED CONSTRUCTION

In this section, drawing on the hierarchical identity-based encryption (HIBE) scheme with constant-size ciphertexts by Boneh et al. [9] and the KP-ABE scheme by Lewko et al. [25], we present a KP-ABE scheme with constant-size ciphertexts and fast decryption.

Our construction supports arbitrary monotonic access formulas. As in [25], we express access formulas by an LSSS over the attributes in the system, but with a significant difference. In our construction, each attribute includes two parts: attribute name and its value. Without loss of generality, we assume that there are n categories of attributes in the system, such as "from", "to", "subject" and "date" in the email example. For simplicity, we also make the following assumptions:

- We assume that the same value never appears in two distinct attribute categories. This requirement can be satisfied easily. For example, by prepending the values with the name of the attribute category they belonging to, the value H("from: Bob") belongs to the attribute category "from" and can not be confused with the value H("to: Bob") that belongs to the attribute category "to", where H is a collision-resistant hash function.
- We assume that each set of attributes associated with a ciphertext has n attributes exactly with each attribute belonging to a different category. In the email example, we may assign the value H("subject: NULL") in the attribute category "subject" to emails that have no subject.

For notational purposes, let i denote the attribute name of the ith attribute category. Each set of attributes S associated with a ciphertext can be parsed as $(z_1, \ldots, z_n)$, where $z_i \in \mathbb{Z}_N$ is the value of attribute name i. We express an access formula by $(\mathbf{A}, \rho, \mathcal{T})$, where $\mathbf{A}$ is $\ell \times m$ share-generating matrix, ρ is a map from each row of $\mathbf{A}$ to an attribute name (i.e., ρ is a function from $\{1, \ldots, \ell\}$ to $\{1, \ldots, n\}$), $\mathcal{T}$ can be parsed as $(t_{\rho(1)}, \ldots, t_{\rho(\ell)})$ and $t_{\rho(i)}$ is the value of attribute name $\rho(i)$ specified by the access formula.

Using our notations, a set of attributes $S = (z_1, \ldots, z_n)$ satisfies an access formula $(\mathbf{A}, \rho, \mathcal{T})$ if and only if there exist $\mathcal{I} \subseteq \{1, \ldots, \ell\}$ and constants $\{\omega_i\}_{i \in \mathcal{I}}$ such that

$$\sum_{i \in \mathcal{I}} \omega_i A_i = (1, 0, \ldots, 0) \text{ and } z_{\rho(i)} = t_{\rho(i)} \text{ for } \forall i \in \mathcal{I},$$

where A_i denotes the ith row of $\mathbf{A}$.

Similar to the KP-ABE scheme in [25], our proposed KP-ABE scheme has the restriction that each attribute name can only be used once in an access structure, which is called one-use KP-ABE. We can obtain a secure KP-ABE scheme where attribute names being used multiple times (up to a constant number of uses fixed at setup) from the one-use scheme by applying the generic transformation given in Lewko et al. [25]. The transformation does not affect the features of our proposed KP-ABE scheme, i.e., constant-size ciphertexts and fast decryption. On the other hand, utilizing the new proof methods proposed by Lewko and Waters [29] recently, it may allow our proposed KP-ABE scheme unrestricted use of attribute names.

Concretely, the proposed KP-ABE scheme consists of the following algorithms:

$\mathsf{Setup}(1^\lambda)$ The setup algorithm first runs $\mathcal{G}(1^\lambda)$ to obtain $(p_1, p_2, p_3, \mathbb{G}, \mathbb{G}_T, e)$ with $\mathbb{G} = \mathbb{G}_{p_1} \times \mathbb{G}_{p_2} \times \mathbb{G}_{p_3}$, where $\mathbb{G}$ and $\mathbb{G}_T$ are cyclic groups of order $N = p_1p_2p_3$. Next it chooses $g, h_0, h_1, \ldots, h_n \in \mathbb{G}_{p_1}$, $X_3 \in \mathbb{G}_{p_3}$ and $\alpha \in \mathbb{Z}_N$ uniformly at random. The public parameters are published as $\mathsf{PK} = (\mathbb{G}, \mathbb{G}_T, e, N, g, h_0, h_1, \ldots, h_n, e(g, g)^\alpha)$. The master secret key is $\mathsf{MSK} = (\alpha, X_3)$.

$\mathsf{KeyGen}(\mathsf{PK}, \mathsf{MSK}, \mathbb{A} = (\mathbf{A}, \rho, \mathcal{T}))$ $\mathbf{A}$ is an $\ell \times m$ matrix, ρ is a map from each row A_i of $\mathbf{A}$ to $\{1, \ldots, n\}$ and $\mathcal{T} = (t_{\rho(1)}, \ldots, t_{\rho(\ell)}) \in \mathbb{Z}_N^\ell$. The key generation algorithm chooses a random vector $v \in \mathbb{Z}_N^m$ such that $\mathbf{1} \cdot v = \alpha$. (Here, $\mathbf{1}$ denotes the vector with the first entry equal to 1 and the rest equal to 0). Let Q_i denote the set $[n] \backslash \{\rho(i)\}$ for each $i \in [\ell]$. For each row A_i of $\mathbf{A}$, it chooses a random $r_i \in \mathbb{Z}_N$ and random elements $R_i, R'_i, \{R_{i,j}\}_{j \in Q_i} \in \mathbb{G}_{p_3}$ (this is done by raising X_3 to a random power). The secret key $\mathsf{SK}_{\mathbb{A}} = ((\mathbf{A}, \rho, \mathcal{T}), \{D_i, D'_i, \{D_{i,j}\}_{j \in Q_i}\}_{i \in [\ell]})$ is computed as

$$D_i = g^{A_i \cdot v}(h_0 h_{\rho(i)}^{t_{\rho(i)}})^{r_i} R_i, \ D'_i = g^{r_i} R'_i, \ D_{i,j} = h_j^{r_i} R_{i,j}.$$

$\mathsf{Encrypt}(\mathsf{PK}, M \in \mathbb{G}_T, S = (z_1, \ldots, z_n) \in \mathbb{Z}_N^n)$ The encryption algorithm chooses $s \in \mathbb{Z}_N$ uniformly at random. The ciphertext $CT = (S, C, C_0, C_1)$ is computed as

$$C = M \cdot e(g,g)^{\alpha s},\ C_0 = g^s,\ C_1 = \left(h_0 \prod_{i=1}^{n} h_i^{z_i}\right)^s.$$

$\mathsf{Decrypt}(\mathsf{PK}, \mathsf{SK}_{\mathbb{A}}, CT)$ Let $CT = (S = (z_1, \ldots, z_n), C, C_0, C_1)$ and $\mathsf{SK}_{\mathbb{A}} = ((\mathbf{A}, \rho, \mathcal{T}),\ \{D_i,\ D_i', \{D_{i,j}\}_{j \in Q_i}\}_{i \in [\ell]})$, where $\mathbf{A}$ is an $\ell \times m$ matrix, ρ is a map from each row A_i of $\mathbf{A}$ to $\{1, \ldots, n\}$ and $\mathcal{T} = (t_{\rho(1)}, \ldots, t_{\rho(\ell)}) \in \mathbb{Z}_N^\ell$. If S satisfies $\mathbb{A}$, the decryption algorithm first finds $\mathcal{I} \subseteq [\ell]$ and constants $\{\omega_i\}_{i \in \mathcal{I}}$ such that

$$\sum_{i \in \mathcal{I}} \omega_i A_i = (1, 0, \ldots, 0) \text{ and } z_{\rho(i)} = t_{\rho(i)} \text{ for } \forall i \in \mathcal{I}.$$

Let Q_i denote the set $[n] \backslash \{\rho(i)\}$ for each $i \in \mathcal{I}$. Next, the decryption algorithm computes

$$\widetilde{D}_i = D_i \prod_{j \in Q_i} D_{i,j}^{z_j}, \text{ for each } i \in \mathcal{I}.$$

Note that, if $j \in Q_i$, then $j \neq \rho(i)$. Since for each $i \in \mathcal{I}$, $t_{\rho(i)} = z_{\rho(i)}$, then we have

$$\widetilde{D}_i = g^{A_i \cdot v} \left(h_0 \prod_{j=1}^{n} h_j^{z_j}\right)^{r_i} \cdot \widetilde{R}_i.$$

where $\widetilde{R}_i = R_i \prod_{j=1}^n R_{i,j}^{z_j}$.

It then computes:

$$e(C_0, \prod_{i \in \mathcal{I}} \widetilde{D}_i^{\omega_i}) / e(C_1, \prod_{i \in \mathcal{I}} D_i'^{\omega_i}) = e(g,g)^{\alpha s}.$$

The message can then be recovered as $C / e(g,g)^{\alpha s}$.

3.1 Security

We now state the security theorem of our KP-ABE scheme.

THEOREM 1. *If Assumptions 1, 2 and 3 hold, then the proposed KP-ABE scheme is secure.*

Proof. Following the approach by Lewko and Waters [26], we define two additional structures: *semi-functional* ciphertexts and *semi-functional* keys. These will not be used in the real system, but will be used in our proof.

Semi-functional Ciphertext Let g_2 denote a generator of the subgroup $\mathbb{G}_{p_2}$. A semi-functional ciphertext is created as follows. We first use the encryption algorithm to form a normal ciphertext $CT = (S, C, C_0, C_1)$. Then, we choose a random exponent $c \in \mathbb{Z}_N$. We also choose a random value $\eta \in \mathbb{Z}_N$. The semi-functional ciphertext CT' is set to be

$$(S, C,\ C_0 \cdot g_2^c,\ C_1 \cdot g_2^{c\eta}).$$

Semi-functional Key A semi-functional key for an access structure $\mathbb{A} = (\mathbf{A}, \rho, \mathcal{T})$, where $\mathbf{A}$ is an $\ell \times m$ matrix, ρ is a map from each row A_i of $\mathbf{A}$ to $\{1, \ldots, n\}$ and $\mathcal{T} = (t_{\rho(1)}, \ldots, t_{\rho(\ell)}) \in \mathbb{Z}_N^\ell$, will take on one of two forms. To create a semi-functional key, we first use the key generation algorithm to form a normal secret key $\mathsf{SK}_{\mathbb{A}} = ((\mathbf{A}, \rho, \mathcal{T}),\ \{D_i,\ D_i', \{D_{i,j}\}_{j \in Q_i}\}_{i \in [\ell]})$, where Q_i denote the set $[n] \backslash \{\rho(i)\}$. Then, we choose $\eta_0, \eta_1, \ldots, \eta_n$ uniformly at random, and random values $\gamma_i \in \mathbb{Z}_N$ associated with row i of $\mathbf{A}$. We also choose a random vector $w \in \mathbb{Z}_N^m$. The semi-functional key of type 1 is set as

$$((\mathbf{A}, \rho, \mathcal{T}),\ \{D_i \cdot g_2^{A_i \cdot w + \gamma_i(\eta_0 + \eta_{\rho(i)} t_{\rho(i)})},\ D_i' \cdot g_2^{\gamma_i},\ \{D_{i,j} \cdot g_2^{\gamma_i \eta_i}\}_{j \in Q_i}\}_{i \in [\ell]}).$$

A semi-functional key of type 2 is formed without the terms $g_2^{\gamma_i(\eta_0 + \eta_{\rho(i)} t_{\rho(i)})}, g_2^{\gamma_i}, g_2^{\gamma_i \eta_i}$ (one could also interpret this as setting $\gamma_i = 0$):

$$((\mathbf{A}, \rho, \mathcal{T}),\ \{D_i \cdot g_2^{A_i \cdot w},\ D_i',\ \{D_{i,j}\}_{j \in Q_i}\}_{i \in [\ell]}).$$

Let q denote the number of secret key queries made by the adversary. We will prove the security of our scheme based on Assumptions 1, 2 and 3 using a hybrid argument over a sequence of games.

$\mathsf{Game}_{\mathsf{real}}$ The real security game.

$\mathsf{Game}_{\mathsf{restricted}}$ Let $CT = (S, C, C_0, C_1)$ be the challenge ciphertext, where $S = (z_1, \ldots, z_n)$. This game is the same as $\mathsf{Game}_{\mathsf{real}}$ except that the challenger outputs reject and halts if event E_1 happens. Event E_1 is defined as: the adversary issues a key query $\langle \mathbb{A} = (\mathbf{A}, \rho, \mathcal{T}) \rangle$, where $\mathbf{A}$ is an $\ell \times m$ matrix, ρ is a map from each row A_i of $\mathbf{A}$ to $\{1, \ldots, n\}$ and $\mathcal{T} = (t_{\rho(1)}, \ldots, t_{\rho(\ell)}) \in \mathbb{Z}_N^\ell$, such that $\exists i \in [n], j \in [\ell]$,

$$z_i \not\equiv t_{\rho(j)} \mod N, \text{ and } z_i \equiv t_{\rho(j)} \mod p_2.$$

$\mathsf{Game}_{\mathsf{ch}}$ This game is the same as $\mathsf{Game}_{\mathsf{restricted}}$ except that the challenge ciphertext is replaced with a semi-functional ciphertext.

$\mathsf{Game}_{k,1} (1 \leq k \leq q)$ This game is like $\mathsf{Game}_{\mathsf{ch}}$ except for the way that the challenger answers the adversary's secret key queries. The first $k-1$ secret keys are semi-functional of type 2, the kth secret key is semi-functional of type 1, and the remaining secret keys are normal.

$\mathsf{Game}_{k,2} (0 \leq k \leq q)$ This game is like $\mathsf{Game}_{\mathsf{ch}}$ except for the way that the challenger answers the adversary's secret key queries. The first k secret keys are semi-functional of type 2, and the remaining secret keys are normal.

$\mathsf{Game}_{\mathsf{Final}}$ This game is like $\mathsf{Game}_{q,2}$ except that the challenge ciphertext is a semi-functional ciphertext of a random message chosen from $\mathbb{G}_T$.

We prove that these games are computationally indistinguishable in the following four lemmas. Note that $\mathsf{Game}_{\mathsf{ch}} = \mathsf{Game}_{0,2}$. In $\mathsf{Game}_{\mathsf{Final}}$, it is clear that the value of β is information-theoretically hidden from the adversary. Hence the adversary has no advantage in $\mathsf{Game}_{\mathsf{Final}}$. Therefore, we conclude that the advantage of the adversary in $\mathsf{Game}_{\mathsf{real}}$ (i.e., the real security game) is negligible. This completes the proof of Theorem 1.

LEMMA 1. *Suppose that $\mathcal{G}$ satisfies Assumption 1. Then $\mathsf{Game}_{\mathsf{real}}$ and $\mathsf{Game}_{\mathsf{restricted}}$ are computationally indistinguishable.*

Proof. Observe that, if event E_1, which is defined in the description of $\mathsf{Game}_{\mathsf{Restricted}}$, does not happen, $\mathsf{Game}_{\mathsf{Restricted}}$ is identical to $\mathsf{Game}_{\mathsf{Real}}$. All we have to do is to prove that E_1 happens with negligible probability.

If E_1 happens with non-negligible probability, we construct a PPT algorithm $\mathcal{B}$ that breaks Assumption 1 with non-negligible probability. Observe that, given $\mathbb{G}, \mathbb{G}_T, e, N, g, X_1X_2, Y_2Y_3, X_3, T$, algorithm $\mathcal{B}$ can perfectly simulate $\mathsf{Game}_{\mathsf{Real}}$.

Let $CT = (S, C, C_0, C_1)$ be the challenge ciphertext, where $S = (z_1, \ldots, z_n)$. During the simulation, for each key query $\langle \mathbb{A} = (\mathbf{A}, \rho, \mathcal{T})\rangle$ issued by the adversary, where $\mathbf{A}$ is an $\ell \times m$ matrix, ρ is a map from each row A_i of $\mathbf{A}$ to $\{1, \ldots, n\}$ and $\mathcal{T} = (t_{\rho(1)}, \ldots, t_{\rho(\ell)}) \in \mathbb{Z}_N^{\ell}$, if $z_i \not\equiv t_{\rho(j)} \mod N$ for $i \in [n]$ and $j \in [\ell]$, $\mathcal{B}$ computes $a = \gcd(z_i - t_{\rho(j)}, N)$. $\mathcal{B}$ identifies the occurrence of E_1 (i.e., p_2 divides a) with $e(X_1X_2, Y_2Y_3)^a = 1_{\mathbb{G}_T}$. Set $b = \frac{N}{a}$. We consider two cases: 1. p_1 divides b; 2. p_3 divides b.

$\mathcal{B}$ can determine if case 1 has occurred by testing if $e(X_1X_2, g)^b = 1_{\mathbb{G}_T}$. If this happens, $\mathcal{B}$ can then learn whether T has a $\mathbb{G}_{p_2}$ component or not by testing if $e(T, X_1X_2)^b = 1_{\mathbb{G}_T}$. If not, then T has a $\mathbb{G}_{p_2}$ component, i.e., $T \in \mathbb{G}_{p_1p_2p_3}$; otherwise, $T \in \mathbb{G}_{p_1p_3}$.

$\mathcal{B}$ can determine if case 2 has occurred by testing if $e(Y_2Y_3, X_3)^b = 1_{\mathbb{G}_T}$. If this happens, $\mathcal{B}$ can then learn whether T has a $\mathbb{G}_{p_2}$ component or not by testing if $e(T, Y_2Y_3)^b = 1_{\mathbb{G}_T}$. If not, then T has a $\mathbb{G}_{p_2}$ component, i.e., $T \in \mathbb{G}_{p_1p_2p_3}$; otherwise, $T \in \mathbb{G}_{p_1p_3}$.

LEMMA 2. *Suppose that $\mathcal{G}$ satisfies Assumption 2. Then $\mathsf{Game}_{\mathsf{restricted}}$ and $\mathsf{Game}_{\mathsf{ch}}$ are computationally indistinguishable.*

Proof. Suppose there exists an adversary $\mathcal{A}$ that distinguishes $\mathsf{Game}_{\mathsf{restricted}}$ and $\mathsf{Game}_{\mathsf{ch}}$. Then we can build an algorithm $\mathcal{B}$ with non-negligible advantage in breaking Assumption 2. $\mathcal{B}$ is given $\mathbb{G}, \mathbb{G}_T, e, N, g, X_3, T$ and will simulate $\mathsf{Game}_{\mathsf{restricted}}$ or $\mathsf{Game}_{\mathsf{ch}}$ with $\mathcal{A}$. $\mathcal{B}$ first chooses $\alpha, a_0, a_1, \ldots, a_n \in \mathbb{Z}_N$ uniformly at random. It then sets $h_0 = g^{a_0}, h_1 = g^{a_1}, \ldots, h_n = g^{a_n}$, and sends $\mathcal{A}$ the public parameters:

$$\mathsf{PK} = (\mathbb{G}, \mathbb{G}_T, e, N, g, h_0, h_1, \ldots, h_n, e(g, g)^{\alpha}).$$

$\mathcal{B}$ can generate normal secret keys in response to $\mathcal{A}$'s key requests by using the key generation algorithm KeyGen, since it knows the master secret key $\mathsf{MSK} = (\alpha, X_3)$ associated with PK. (Notice that, if the event E_1 which is described in $\mathsf{Game}_{\mathsf{restricted}}$ happens when $\mathcal{A}$ makes a key query, $\mathcal{B}$ responds as in $\mathsf{Game}_{\mathsf{restricted}}$.)

At some point, $\mathcal{A}$ sends $\mathcal{B}$ two (equal length) messages M_0, M_1 and a set of attributes S. $\mathcal{B}$ chooses $\beta \in \{0, 1\}$ randomly and does the following.

1. Parse S as $(z_1, \ldots, z_n)$. $\mathcal{B}$ computes

$$C = M_{\beta} \cdot e(g^{\alpha}, T),\ C_0 = T,\ C_1 = T^{a_0 + \sum_{i=1}^{n} a_i z_i}.$$

2. $\mathcal{B}$ sets the challenge ciphertext as $CT = (S, C, C_0, C_1)$ and sends it to $\mathcal{A}$.

If $T \leftarrow \mathbb{G}_{p_1} \times \mathbb{G}_{p_2}$, let $T = g^s g_2^c$, then

$$C = M_{\beta} \cdot e(g, g)^{\alpha s},$$
$$C_0 = g^s \cdot g_2^c,\ C_i = \left(h_0 \prod_{i=1}^{n} h_i^{z_i}\right)^s \cdot g_2^{c\eta}.$$

where $\eta = a_0 + \sum_{i=1}^{n} a_i z_i$. This is a semi-functional ciphertext and $\mathcal{B}$ simulates $\mathsf{Game}_{\mathsf{ch}}$. We note that the values of a_0, a_i, z_i modulo p_1 are uncorrelated from their values modulo p_2, so this is properly distributed. If $T \leftarrow \mathbb{G}_{p_1}$, it is easy to observe that this is a normal ciphertext and $\mathcal{B}$ simulates $\mathsf{Game}_{\mathsf{restricted}}$. Hence, $\mathcal{B}$ can use the output of $\mathcal{A}$ to distinguish between these possibilities for T.

LEMMA 3. *Suppose that $\mathcal{G}$ satisfies Assumption 1. Then for each $k \in [q]$, $\mathsf{Game}_{k-1,2}$ and $\mathsf{Game}_{k,1}$ are computationally indistinguishable.*

Proof. Suppose there exists an adversary $\mathcal{A}$ that distinguishes $\mathsf{Game}_{k-1,2}$ and $\mathsf{Game}_{k,1}$. Then we can build an algorithm $\mathcal{B}$ with non-negligible advantage in breaking Assumption 1. $\mathcal{B}$ is given $\mathbb{G}, \mathbb{G}_T, e, N, g, X_1X_2, Y_2Y_3, X_3, T$ and will simulate $\mathsf{Game}_{k-1,2}$ or $\mathsf{Game}_{k,1}$ with $\mathcal{A}$. $\mathcal{B}$ chooses $\alpha, a_0, a_1, \ldots, a_n \in \mathbb{Z}_N$ uniformly at random. It then sets $h_0 = g^{a_0}, h_1 = g^{a_1}, \ldots, h_n = g^{a_n}$, and sends $\mathcal{A}$ the public parameters:

$$\mathsf{PK} = (\mathbb{G}, \mathbb{G}_T, e, N, g, h_0, h_1, \ldots, h_n, e(g, g)^{\alpha}).$$

Note that $\mathcal{B}$ knows the master secret key $\mathsf{MSK} = (\alpha, X_3)$ associated with PK. Let us now explain how $\mathcal{B}$ answers the μ-th key query for an access structure $\mathbb{A} = (\mathbf{A}, \rho, \mathcal{T})$, where $\mathbf{A}$ is an $\ell \times m$ matrix, ρ is a map from each row A_i of $\mathbf{A}$ to $\{1, \ldots, n\}$ and $\mathcal{T} = (t_{\rho(1)}, \ldots, t_{\rho(\ell)}) \in \mathbb{Z}_N^{\ell}$. Let Q_i denote the set $[n] \backslash \{\rho(i)\}$ for each $i \in [\ell]$. (Notice that, if the event E_1 described in $\mathsf{Game}_{\mathsf{restricted}}$ happens when $\mathcal{A}$ makes a key query, $\mathcal{B}$ responds as in $\mathsf{Game}_{\mathsf{restricted}}$.)

For $\mu < k$, $\mathcal{B}$ creates a semi-functional key of type 2 by choosing a random vector v such that $\mathbf{1} \cdot v = \alpha$, a random vector $w' \in \mathbb{Z}_N^m$, random exponents $r_i \in \mathbb{Z}_N$, random elements $R_i, R_i', \{R_{i,j}\}_{j \in Q_i} \in \mathbb{G}_{p_3}$, and for each $i \in [\ell], j \in Q_i$ setting:

$$D_i = g^{A_i \cdot v}(h_0 h_{\rho(i)}^{t_{\rho(i)}})^{r_i} R_i (Y_2Y_3)^{A_i \cdot w'},\ D_i' = g^{r_i} R_i',$$
$$D_{i,j} = h_j^{r_i} R_{i,j},$$

We note that this is a properly distributed semi-functional key of type 2 because the value of $A_i \cdot w'$ modulo p_2 is uncorrelated to its value modulo p_3.

For $\mu > k$, $\mathcal{B}$ creates a normal secret key by running the key generation algorithm KeyGen since it knows the master secret key MSK.

To answer the k-th key quest for $(\mathbf{A}, \rho, \mathcal{T} = (t_{\rho(1)}, \ldots, t_{\rho(\ell)}))$, $\mathcal{B}$ chooses a random vector $v' \in \mathbb{Z}_N^m$ such that $v' \cdot \mathbf{1} = \alpha$, a random vector $w \in \mathbb{Z}_N^m$ such that $w \cdot \mathbf{1} = 0$, random exponents $\tilde{\gamma}_i \in \mathbb{Z}_N$, random elements $\tilde{R}_i, \tilde{R}_i', \{\tilde{R}_{i,j}\}_{j \in Q_i} \in \mathbb{G}_{p_3}$ and for each $i \in [\ell], j \in Q_i$ sets:

$$D_i = g^{A_i \cdot v'} T^{A_i \cdot w} T^{\tilde{\gamma}_i(a_0 + a_{\rho(i)} t_{\rho(i)})} \tilde{R}_i,$$
$$D_i' = T^{\tilde{\gamma}_i} \tilde{R}_i',\ D_{i,j} = T^{\tilde{\gamma}_i a_j} \tilde{R}_{i,j}.$$

We have the following observations. If $T \leftarrow \mathbb{G}_{p_1} \times \mathbb{G}_{p_2} \times \mathbb{G}_{p_3}$, then T can be written as $g^r g_2^d R$, and

$$D_i = g^{A_i \cdot v}(h_0 h_{\rho(i)}^{t_{\rho(i)}})^{r_i} R_i \cdot g_2^{\delta_i + \gamma_i(\eta_0 + \eta_{\rho(i)} t_{\rho(i)})},$$
$$D_i' = g^{r_i} R_i' \cdot g_2^{\gamma_i},\ D_{i,j} = h_j^{r_i} R_{i,j} \cdot g_2^{\gamma_i \eta_j}$$

where $v = v' + rw$, $r_i = r\tilde{\gamma}_i$, $\delta_i = dA_i w$, $\gamma_i = d\tilde{\gamma}_i$, $R_i = R^{A_i w + \tilde{\gamma}_i(a_0 + a_{\rho(i)} t_{\rho(i)})} \tilde{R}_i$, $R_i' = R^{\tilde{\gamma}_i} \tilde{R}_i'$, $R_{i,j} = R^{\tilde{\gamma}_i a_j} \tilde{R}_{i,j}$, $\{\eta_l = a_l\}_{l \in [n]}$. This is a semi-function key of type 1. Note that the values of $\tilde{\gamma}_i, a_0, a_i, t_{\rho(i)}$ modulo p_1 are uncorrelated from their values modulo p_2. If $T \leftarrow \mathbb{G}_{p_1} \times \mathbb{G}_{p_3}$, this is a properly distributed normal secret key.

At some point, $\mathcal{A}$ sends $\mathcal{B}$ two (equal length) messages M_0, M_1 and a set of attributes S. $\mathcal{B}$ chooses $\beta \in \{0, 1\}$ randomly and does the following.

1. Parse S as $(z_1,\ldots,z_n)$. $\mathcal{B}$ computes
$$C = M_\beta \cdot e(g^\alpha, X_1X_2),\ C_0 = X_1X_2,$$
$$C_1 = (X_1X_2)^{a_0+\sum_{i=1}^n a_i z_i},$$

2. $\mathcal{B}$ sets the challenge ciphertext as $CT = (S, C, C_0, C_1)$ and sends it to $\mathcal{A}$.

If we write X_1X_2 as $g^s g_2^c$, then
$$C = M_\beta \cdot e(g,g)^{\alpha s},\ C_0 = g^s \cdot g_2^c,$$
$$C_1 = \left(h_0 \prod_{i=1}^n h_i^{z_i}\right)^s \cdot g_2^{c\eta}.$$
where $\eta = a_0 + \sum_{i=1}^n a_i z_i$. This is a semi-functional ciphertext. Note that the values of a_0, a_i, z_i modulo p_1 are uncorrelated from their values modulo p_2.

Next, we show that the kth key and the challenge ciphertext are properly distributed. Observe that, if $T \leftarrow \mathbb{G}_{p_1} \times \mathbb{G}_{p_3}$, then the kth key is a properly distributed normal secret key and the challenge ciphertext is a properly distributed semi-functional ciphertext. If $T \leftarrow \mathbb{G}_{p_1} \times \mathbb{G}_{p_2} \times \mathbb{G}_{p_3}$, since the event E_1 happens with negligible probability which has been proven in Lemma 1, then with overwhelming probability, there exits $i \in [\ell]$ such that $t_{\rho(i)} \not\equiv z_{\rho(i)} \mod N$ and $t_{\rho(i)} \mod p_2$ is uniformly distributed[5]; thus similar to the analysis in the proof of Lewko *et al.* 's KP-ABE scheme [25], the kth key and the challenge ciphertext are properly distributed.

We can thus conclude that, if $T \leftarrow \mathbb{G}_{p_1} \times \mathbb{G}_{p_2} \times \mathbb{G}_{p_3}$, then $\mathcal{B}$ has properly simulated $\mathsf{Game}_{k,1}$. If $T \leftarrow \mathbb{G}_{p_1} \times \mathbb{G}_{p_3}$, then $\mathcal{B}$ has properly simulated $\mathsf{Game}_{k-1,2}$. Hence, $\mathcal{B}$ can use the output of $\mathcal{A}$ to distinguish between these possibilities for T.

LEMMA 4. *Suppose that $\mathcal{G}$ satisfies Assumption 1. Then for each $k \in [q]$, $\mathsf{Game}_{k,1}$ and $\mathsf{Game}_{k,2}$ are computationally indistinguishable.*

Proof. Suppose there exists an adversary $\mathcal{A}$ that distinguishes $\mathsf{Game}_{k,1}$ and $\mathsf{Game}_{k,2}$. Then we can build an algorithm $\mathcal{B}$ with non-negligible advantage in breaking Assumption 1. $\mathcal{B}$ is given $\mathbb{G}, \mathbb{G}_T, e, N, g, X_1X_2, Y_2Y_3, X_3, T$ and will simulate $\mathsf{Game}_{k,1}$ or $\mathsf{Game}_{k,2}$ with $\mathcal{A}$. $\mathcal{B}$ chooses $\alpha, a_0, a_1, \ldots, a_n \in \mathbb{Z}_N$ uniformly at random. It then sets $h_0 = g^{a_0}, h_1 = g^{a_1}, \ldots, h_n = g^{a_n}$, and sends $\mathcal{A}$ the public parameters:
$$\mathsf{PK} = (\mathbb{G}, \mathbb{G}_T, e, N, g, h_0, h_1, \ldots, h_n, e(g,g)^\alpha).$$
The responses to all key queries and challenge ciphertexts are the same as in Lemma 3, except that the k-th key query which is given below.

To answer the k-th key quest for $(\mathbf{A}, \rho, \mathcal{T} = (t_{\rho(1)}, \ldots, t_{\rho(\ell)}))$, $\mathcal{B}$ chooses a random vector $v \in \mathbb{Z}_N^m$ such that $v \cdot \mathbf{1} = \alpha$, a random vector $w \in \mathbb{Z}_N^m$, random exponents $\tilde{\gamma}_i \in \mathbb{Z}_N$, random elements $\tilde{R}_i, \tilde{R}'_i, \{\tilde{R}_{i,j}\}_{j \in Q_i} \in \mathbb{G}_{p_3}$ and for each $i \in [\ell], j \in Q_i$ sets:
$$D_i = g^{A_i \cdot v}(Y_2Y_3)^{A_i \cdot w} T^{\tilde{\gamma}_i(a_0 + a_{\rho(i)} t_{\rho(i)})} \tilde{R}_i,$$
$$D'_i = T^{\tilde{\gamma}_i} \tilde{R}'_i,\ D_{i,j} = T^{\tilde{\gamma}_i a_j} \tilde{R}_{i,j}.$$

[5]Notice that, We have already assumed that the same value never appears in two distinct attribute categories and each attribute name/category can only be used once in an access structure. That is, for each $i_1, i_2 \in [n]$ and $j_1, j_2 \in [\ell]$, if $i_1 \neq i_2, j_1 \neq j_2$, then $z_{i_1} \neq z_{i_2}$ and $t_{\rho(j_1)} \neq t_{\rho(j_2)}$.

We have the following observations. If $T \leftarrow \mathbb{G}_{p_1} \times \mathbb{G}_{p_2} \times \mathbb{G}_{p_3}$, then T can be written as $g^r g_2^d R$, and
$$D_i = g^{A_i \cdot v}(h_0 h_{\rho(i)}^{t_{\rho(i)}})^{r_i} R_i \cdot g_2^{\delta_i + \gamma_i(\eta_0 + \eta_{\rho(i)} t_{\rho(i)})},$$
$$D'_i = g^{r_i} R'_i \cdot g_2^{\gamma_i},\ D_{i,j} = h_j^{r_i} R_{i,j} \cdot g_2^{\gamma_i \eta_j},$$
where $r_i = r\tilde{\gamma}_i$, $\delta_i = \log_{g_2} Y_2 \cdot A_i w$, $\gamma_i = d\tilde{\gamma}_i$, $R_i = Y_3^{A_i \cdot w} \cdot R^{\tilde{\gamma}_i(a_0 + a_{\rho(i)} t_{\rho(i)})} \tilde{R}_i$, $R'_i = R^{\tilde{\gamma}_i} \tilde{R}'_i$, $R_{i,j} = R^{\tilde{\gamma}_i a_j} \tilde{R}_{i,j}$, $\{\eta_l = a_l\}_{l \in [n]}$. This is a semi-function key of type 1. Note that the values of $\tilde{\gamma}_i, a_0, a_i, t_{\rho(i)}$ modulo p_1 are uncorrelated from their values modulo p_2. If $T \leftarrow \mathbb{G}_{p_1} \times \mathbb{G}_{p_3}$, this is a properly distributed semi-functional key of type 2.

Similar to the above lemma, We can conclude that, if $T \leftarrow \mathbb{G}_{p_1} \times \mathbb{G}_{p_2} \times \mathbb{G}_{p_3}$, then $\mathcal{B}$ has properly simulated $\mathsf{Game}_{k,1}$. If $T \leftarrow \mathbb{G}_{p_1} \times \mathbb{G}_{p_3}$, then $\mathcal{B}$ has properly simulated $\mathsf{Game}_{k,2}$. Hence, $\mathcal{B}$ can use the output of $\mathcal{A}$ to distinguish between these possibilities for T.

LEMMA 5. *Suppose that $\mathcal{G}$ satisfies Assumption 3. Then $\mathsf{Game}_{q,2}$ and $\mathsf{Game}_{\mathsf{Final}}$ are computationally indistinguishable.*

Proof. Suppose there exists an adversary $\mathcal{A}$ that distinguishes $\mathsf{Game}_{q,2}$ and $\mathsf{Game}_{\mathsf{Final}}$. Then we can build an algorithm $\mathcal{B}$ with non-negligible advantage in breaking Assumption 3. $\mathcal{B}$ is given $(\mathbb{G}, \mathbb{G}_T, N, e, g, g_2, g^\alpha X_2, g^s Y_2, X_3, T)$ and will simulate $\mathsf{Game}_{q,2}$ or $\mathsf{Game}_{\mathsf{Final}}$ with $\mathcal{A}$. $\mathcal{B}$ chooses $a_0, a_1, \ldots, a_n \in \mathbb{Z}_N$ uniformly at random. It then sets $h_0 = g^{a_0}, h_1 = g^{a_1}, \ldots, h_n = g^{a_n}$, and sends $\mathcal{A}$ the public parameters:
$$\mathsf{PK} = (\mathbb{G}, \mathbb{G}_T, e, N, g, h_0, h_1, \ldots, h_n, e(g^\alpha X_2, g) = e(g,g)^\alpha).$$
Each time $\mathcal{B}$ is asked to provide a secret key for an access structure $\mathbb{A} = (\mathbf{A}, \rho, \mathcal{T})$, where $\mathbf{A}$ is an $\ell \times m$ matrix, ρ is a map from each row A_i of $\mathbf{A}$ to $\{1, \ldots, n\}$ and $\mathcal{T} = (t_{\rho(1)}, \ldots, t_{\rho(\ell)}) \in \mathbb{Z}_N^\ell$, $\mathcal{B}$ creates a semi-functional key of type 2 as follows.

1. $\mathcal{B}$ chooses $v_2, \ldots, v_m \in \mathbb{Z}_N$ randomly and implicity sets $v = (\alpha, v_2, \ldots, v_m) \in \mathbb{Z}_N^m$. Note that $\mathbf{1} \cdot v = \alpha$. $\mathcal{B}$ also chooses a random vector $w' \in \mathbb{Z}_N^m$

2. For each $i \in [\ell]$, $\mathcal{B}$ random exponents $r_i \in \mathbb{Z}_N$ and random elements $R_i, R'_i, \{R_{i,j}\}_{j \in Q_i} \in \mathbb{G}_{p_3}$, where Q_i denote the set $[n] \backslash \{\rho(i)\}$.

3. For each $i \in [\ell]$, let $A_i = (A_{i,1}, \ldots, A_{i,m}) \in \mathbb{Z}_N^m$, where A_i is the row i of $\mathbf{A}$. $\mathcal{B}$ sets the secret key $\mathsf{SK}_\mathbb{A}$ as $((\mathbf{A}, \rho, \mathcal{T}), \{D_i, D'_i, \{D_{i,j}\}_{j \in Q_i}\}_{i \in [\ell]})$ and sends it to $\mathcal{A}$, where
$$D_i = (g^\alpha X_2)^{A_{i,1}} g^{\sum_{l=2}^m A_{i,l} v_l} g_2^{A_i \cdot w'} \cdot (h_0 h_{\rho(i)}^{t_{\rho(i)}})^{r_i} R_i,$$
$$D'_i = g^{r_i} R'_i,\ D_{i,j} = h_j^{r_i} R_{i,j}.$$
Observe that, D_i can be written as
$$g^{A_i \cdot v}(h_0 h_{\rho(i)}^{t_{\rho(i)}})^{r_i} R_i \cdot g_2^{A_i \cdot w},$$
where $w = w'$ except with a $\log_{g_2} X_2$ added in the first coordinate; hence $\mathsf{SK}_\mathbb{A}$ is a properly distributed semi-functional key of type 2.

At some point, $\mathcal{A}$ sends $\mathcal{B}$ two (equal length) messages M_0, M_1 and a set of attributes S. $\mathcal{B}$ chooses $\beta \in \{0,1\}$ randomly and does the following.

1. Parse S as $(z_1, \ldots, z_n)$. $\mathcal{B}$ computes

$$C = M_\beta \cdot T,\ C_0 = g^s Y_2,\ C_1 = (g^s Y_2)^{a_0 + \sum_{i=1}^n a_i z_i}.$$

2. $\mathcal{B}$ sets the challenge ciphertext as $CT = (S, C, C_0, C_1)$ and sends it to $\mathcal{A}$.

Let $g^s Y_2 = g^s g_2^c$, then

$$C_0 = g^s \cdot g_2^c,\ C_1 = \left(h_0 \prod_{i=1}^n h_i^{z_i}\right)^s \cdot g_2^{c\eta},$$

where $\eta = a_0 + \sum_{i=1}^n a_i z_i$. Note that the values of a_0, a_i, z_i modulo p_1 are uncorrelated to their values modulo p_2. Hence, if $T = e(g,g)^{\alpha s}$, then CT is a properly distributed semi-functional ciphertext of M_β. On the other hand, if $T \leftarrow \mathbb{G}_T$, then CT is a properly distributed semi-functional ciphertext of a random message.

We can conclude that, if $T = e(g,g)^{\alpha s}$, then $\mathcal{B}$ has properly simulated $\mathsf{Game}_{q,2}$. If $T \leftarrow \mathbb{G}_T$, then $\mathcal{B}$ has properly simulated $\mathsf{Game}_{\mathsf{Final}}$. Hence, $\mathcal{B}$ can use the output of $\mathcal{A}$ to distinguish between these possibilities for T.

4. CONCLUSIONS

We presented the first KP-ABE scheme, which has the following features simultaneously: expressive (i.e., supporting arbitrary monotonic access structure); fully secure in the standard model; constant-size ciphertexts and fast decryption. In the future, it will be interesting to see if shorter secret keys can be obtained without affecting the other features of our proposed scheme. Another challenging problem is to design CP-ABE schemes with the similar features of our proposed KP-ABE scheme.

5. ACKNOWLEDGMENTS

We are grateful to the anonymous reviewers for their helpful comments. The work of Junzuo Lai was supported by the National Natural Science Foundation of China (Nos. 61300226, 61272534, 61272453), the Research Fund for the Doctoral Program of Higher Education of China (No. 20134401120017), the Guangdong Provincial Natural Science Foundation (No. S2013040014826), the Open Research Fund of State Key Lab. of Integrated Services Networks (No. ISN15-04), and the Fundamental Research Funds for the Central Universities. The work of Robert H. Deng was supported by the the research grant 13-C220-SMU-05 from the Office of Research, Singapore Management University. The work of Jian Weng was supported by the National Science Foundation of China (Nos. 61272413, 61373158, 61133014, 61272415), the Fok Ying Tung Education Foundation (No. 131066), the Program for New Century Excellent Talents in University (No. NCET-12-0680), and the Research Fund for the Doctoral Program of Higher Education of China (No. 20134401110011).

6. REFERENCES

[1] N. Attrapadung and H. Imai. Dual-policy attribute based encryption. In *ACNS*, pages 168–185, 2009.

[2] N. Attrapadung and B. Libert. Functional encryption for inner product: Achieving constant-size ciphertexts with adaptive security or support for negation. In *Public Key Cryptography*, pages 384–402, 2010.

[3] N. Attrapadung and B. Libert. Functional encryption for public-attribute inner products: Achieving constant-size ciphertexts with adaptive security or support for negation. *J. Mathematical Cryptology*, 5(2):115–158, 2012.

[4] N. Attrapadung, B. Libert, and E. de Panafieu. Expressive key-policy attribute-based encryption with constant-size ciphertexts. In *Public Key Cryptography*, pages 90–108, 2011.

[5] A. Beimel. *Secure Schemes for Secret Sharing and Key Distribution*. PhD thesis, Israel Institute of Technology, 1996.

[6] M. Bellare and P. Rogaway. Random oracles are practical: A paradigm for designing efficient protocols. In *ACM Conference on Computer and Communications Security*, pages 62–73, 1993.

[7] J. Bethencourt, A. Sahai, and B. Waters. Ciphertext-policy attribute-based encryption. In *IEEE Symposium on Security and Privacy*, pages 321–334, 2007.

[8] D. Boneh and X. Boyen. Efficient selective-id secure identity-based encryption without random oracles. In *EUROCRYPT*, pages 223–238, 2004.

[9] D. Boneh, X. Boyen, and E.-J. Goh. Hierarchical identity based encryption with constant size ciphertext. In *EUROCRYPT*, pages 440–456, 2005.

[10] D. Boneh and M. K. Franklin. Identity-based encryption from the weil pairing. *SIAM J. Comput.*, 32(3):586–615, 2003.

[11] D. Boneh, E.-J. Goh, and K. Nissim. Evaluating 2-dnf formulas on ciphertexts. In *TCC*, pages 325–341, 2005.

[12] D. Boneh and M. Hamburg. Generalized identity based and broadcast encryption schemes. In *ASIACRYPT*, pages 455–470, 2008.

[13] R. Canetti, S. Halevi, and J. Katz. A forward-secure public-key encryption scheme. In *EUROCRYPT*, pages 255–271, 2003.

[14] M. Chase. Multi-authority attribute based encryption. In *TCC*, pages 515–534, 2007.

[15] M. Chase and S. S. M. Chow. Improving privacy and security in multi-authority attribute-based encryption. In *ACM Conference on Computer and Communications Security*, pages 121–130, 2009.

[16] L. Cheung and C. C. Newport. Provably secure ciphertext policy ABE. In *ACM Conference on Computer and Communications Security*, pages 456–465, 2007.

[17] K. Emura, A. Miyaji, A. Nomura, K. Omote, and M. Soshi. A ciphertext-policy attribute-based encryption scheme with constant ciphertext length. In *ISPEC*, pages 13–23, 2009.

[18] S. Garg, C. Gentry, S. Halevi, A. Sahai, and B. Waters. Attribute-based encryption for circuits from multilinear maps. *IACR Cryptology ePrint Archive*, 2013:128, 2013.

[19] S. Gorbunov, V. Vaikuntanathan, and H. Wee. Attribute-based encryption for circuits. In *STOC*, pages 545–554, 2013.

[20] V. Goyal, A. Jain, O. Pandey, and A. Sahai. Bounded ciphertext policy attribute based encryption. In *ICALP (2)*, pages 579–591, 2008.

[21] V. Goyal, O. Pandey, A. Sahai, and B. Waters. Attribute-based encryption for fine-grained access control of encrypted data. In *ACM Conference on Computer and Communications Security*, pages 89–98, 2006.

[22] J. Herranz, F. Laguillaumie, and C. Ràfols. Constant size ciphertexts in threshold attribute-based encryption. In *Public Key Cryptography*, pages 19–34, 2010.

[23] S. Hohenberger and B. Waters. Attribute-based encryption with fast decryption. In *Public Key Cryptography*, pages 162–179, 2013.

[24] J. Katz, A. Sahai, and B. Waters. Predicate encryption supporting disjunctions, polynomial equations, and inner products. Cryptology ePrint Archive, Report 2007/404, 2007. `http://eprint.iacr.org/`.

[25] A. B. Lewko, T. Okamoto, A. Sahai, K. Takashima, and B. Waters. Fully secure functional encryption: Attribute-based encryption and (hierarchical) inner product encryption. In *EUROCRYPT*, pages 62–91, 2010.

[26] A. B. Lewko and B. Waters. New techniques for dual system encryption and fully secure HIBE with short ciphertexts. In *TCC*, pages 455–479, 2010.

[27] A. B. Lewko and B. Waters. Decentralizing attribute-based encryption. In *EUROCRYPT*, pages 568–588, 2011.

[28] A. B. Lewko and B. Waters. Unbounded hibe and attribute-based encryption. In *EUROCRYPT*, pages 547–567, 2011.

[29] A. B. Lewko and B. Waters. New proof methods for attribute-based encryption: Achieving full security through selective techniques. In *CRYPTO*, pages 180–198, 2012.

[30] H. Lin, Z. Cao, X. Liang, and J. Shao. Secure threshold multi authority attribute based encryption without a central authority. In *INDOCRYPT*, pages 426–436, 2008.

[31] S. Müller, S. Katzenbeisser, and C. Eckert. Distributed attribute-based encryption. In *ICISC*, pages 20–36, 2008.

[32] R. Ostrovsky, A. Sahai, and B. Waters. Attribute-based encryption with non-monotonic access structures. In *ACM Conference on Computer and Communications Security*, pages 195–203, 2007.

[33] Y. Rouselakis and B. Waters. New constructions and proof methods for large universe attribute-based encryption. *IACR Cryptology ePrint Archive*, 2012:583, 2012.

[34] A. Sahai and B. Waters. Fuzzy identity-based encryption. In *EUROCRYPT*, pages 457–473, 2005.

[35] A. Shamir. Identity-based cryptosystems and signature schemes. In *CRYPTO*, pages 47–53, 1984.

[36] B. Waters. Ciphertext-policy attribute-based encryption: An expressive, efficient, and provably secure realization. In *Public Key Cryptography*, pages 53–70, 2011.

Improved Anonymous Proxy Re-encryption with CCA Security

Qingji Zheng
Department of Computer Science
University of Texas at San Antonio, TX, USA
qingjizheng@gmail.com

Wei Zhu
Julymobile Tech Co., Ltd
Anhui, China
zhuweijm@sina.com

Jiafeng Zhu
Huawei Research Center
Santa Clara, CA, USA
edwardzhu95@gmail.com

Xinwen Zhang
Huawei Research Center
Santa Clara, CA, USA
xinwenzhang@gmail.com

ABSTRACT

Outsourcing private data and heavy computation tasks to the cloud may lead to privacy breach as attackers (e.g., malicious outsiders or cloud administrators) may correlate any relevant information to penetrate information of their interests. Therefore, how to preserve cloud users' privacy has been a top concern when adopting cloud solutions. In this paper, we investigate the identity privacy problem for the proxy re-encryption, which allows any third party (e.g., cloud) to re-encrypt ciphertexts in order to delegate the decryption right from one to another user. The relevant identity information, e.g., whose ciphertext was re-encrypted to the ciphertext under whose public key, may leak because re-encryption keys and ciphertexts (before and after re-encryption) are known to the third party. We review prior anonymity (identity privacy) notions, and find that these notions are either impractical or too weak. To address this problem thoroughly, we rigorously define the anonymity notion that not only embraces the prior anonymity notions but also captures the necessary anonymity requirement for practical applications. In addition, we propose a new and efficient proxy re-encryption scheme. The scheme satisfies the proposed anonymity notion under the Squared Decisional Bilinear Diffie-Hellman assumption and achieves security against chosen ciphertext attack under the Decisional Bilinear Diffie-Hellman assumption in the random oracle model. To the best of our knowledge, it is the *first* proxy re-encryption scheme attaining both chosen-ciphertext security and anonymity simultaneously. We implement a prototype based on the proposed proxy re-encryption scheme and the performance study shows that it is efficient.

ASIA CCS'14, June 4–6, 2014, Kyoto, Japan.
Copyright 2014 ACM 978-1-4503-2800-5/14/06 ...$15.00.
http://dx.doi.org/10.1145/2590296.2590322.

Categories and Subject Descriptors

E.3 [**Data Encryption**]: Public Key Cryptosystems; H.3.4 [**Information Storage and Retrieval**]: Distributed Systems

General Terms

Security

Keywords

proxy re-encryption, anonymity, chosen-ciphertext security, outsourced computation

1. INTRODUCTION

Cloud computing has become an increasingly popular computing paradigm as it offers numerous benefits, e.g., on-demand service, service elasticity and low maintenance cost. However, when outsourcing data and heavy computation tasks to the cloud, cloud users can enjoy these benefits only if they are willing to assume that the cloud is full trusted. This assumption is inevitably impractical because the cloud imposes great attack surface from the inside and outside attackers. Therefore, privacy concern might hinder cloud users deploying applications in the public cloud.

In this paper, we study the anonymity problem for Proxy Re-Encryption (PRE), which is to delegate the decryption right by re-encrypting ciphertexts decrypted by Alice to new ciphertexts that can be decrypted by Bob without revealing plaintexts. In order to understand the anonymity problem for PRE, consider the following application: Company A has an email gateway handling all incoming encrypted emails and forwarding them to appropriate recipients. Alice (an employee of Company A) can send a re-encryption request to the gateway in order to delegate the decryption right to Bob (another employee of Company A) when she is unable to manage her emails properly (e.g., when she is traveling or on vacation). Due to large amount of re-encryption requests and its own limited computation capability, the gateway will outsource those re-encryption operations to a public cloud. As re-encryption keys and corresponding ciphertexts need to be delivered to the cloud, it is expected that the re-encryption procedure does not reveal any participant's identity, which otherwise might leak important business information (e.g., schedule information).

To address this concern, the anonymity notion (or key-private) for PRE was introduced by Ateniese et al. [5] [1]. They pointed out that many prior proxy re-encryption schemes (before their paper) cannot satisfy the intuition of anonymity: an adversary cannot learn identities by observing sufficient ciphertexts (before or after re-encryption) and re-encryption keys, even it colludes with some corrupted users. That is, for any probabilistically polynomial time adversary, it cannot distinguish a valid re-encryption key for a pair of users, from a random one selected from the re-encryption key space, although it can access re-encryption key generation oracle and re-encryption oracle (perhaps decryption oracle additionally).

Why prior anonymity notions are insufficient? There are two anonymity notions in the literature. The first anonymity notion of PRE in [5] suffers from the limitation that it only allows one re-encryption key for any pair of users. As stated in [5], the proposed scheme cannot achieve the anonymity definition if someone could obtain multiple re-encryption keys per pair of users. That is, if the cloud possesses multiple re-encryption keys for the same pair of users, then it can derive the identities involved in these re-encryption keys. Let us take the above motivational application as an example: If the cloud received two re-encryption keys that were used to delegate the decryption right from Alice to Bob at different times, then it is able to infer that the re-encryption key corresponds to Alice and Bob. Consequently, the constraint of allowing only one re-encryption key per pair of users does not meet the requirement in practice, because in reality it likely happens that multiple re-encryption keys coexist for any pair of users.

Another anonymity notion was introduced by [19, 20]. While their notion allows multiple re-encryption keys coexisting for any pair of users, it achieves weak anonymity because the adversary is not allowed to access the re-encryption oracle (section 2.2.4 [19] and section 2.3.3 [20]) to obtain re-encrypted ciphertexts. Instead, the adversary has to query the re-encryption key generation oracle and applies the returned re-encryption key to compute re-encrypted ciphertexts. Intuitively, their notion fails to capture the following attack: If knowing the identity corresponding to the re-encrypted ciphertext, then the attack may be possible to infer the identities involved in the re-encryption key that is used to generate that re-encrypted ciphertext. To further understand this attack, let us look at the scenario of the motivational example: The cloud receives a re-encryption key to delegate the decryption right from Alice to Bob, then it re-encrypts the ciphertext and sends the re-encrypted ciphertext to the gateway. Since the cloud communicates with the gateway without private channel (all communication data is encrypted), an attacker can eavesdrop the channel to obtain the re-encrypted ciphertext and might learn the related identity without seeing the re-encryption key (perhaps via some side channels). As long as the attacker sees the re-encryption key, he might be able to infer the participants's identity because the corresponding re-encrypted ciphertexts leaks that information. Especially, this attack always happens when the re-encryption algorithm is deterministic. Indeed, this is the reason why the scheme in [19] satisfies their anonymity notion while still suffering from this attack. Therefore, disallowing the adversary directly accessing re-encryption oracle weakens its capability of distinguishing the difference between a valid re-encryption key and a random one from the re-encryption key space.

[1]The anonymity for PRE has two-fold: the anonymity of ciphertexts and the anonymity of re-encryption keys. The former has been investigated by Bellare et al [7] and the latter one is the additional target in the context of PRE, which is the focus of this paper.

Our contributions. As prior anonymity notions are incomplete, we rigorously define the anonymity notion which adequately fixes these insufficiencies. We propose the first PRE construction that not only achieves chosen-ciphertext security (CCA) in the random oracle model, but also attains the anonymity property. To be specific, our contribution can be characterized as follows:

- We rigorously define the anonymity notion with a well-defined anonymous game, which cannot be extended trivially from that in [19, 20] by simply providing access to the re-encryption oracle.
- We present a single-hop, unidirectional PRE scheme satisfies the proposed anonymity notion. Our construction is anonymous under the Squared Decisional Bilinear Diffie-Hellman assumption and CCA secure under the Decisional Bilinear Diffie-Hellman assumption in the random oracle model, which resolves one of the open problems stated in [5].
- Towards building a generic cloud-based re-encryption service, we have built a prototype that integrates the proposed scheme and the Amazon Web Services (AWS), where EC2 is for re-encryption computation and S3 for data storage. We defined general web services interfaces that can be easily integrated into existing applications to provide anonymous re-encryption function. As a case study, we have implemented an anonymous email forwarding service built upon our scheme. Our experimental evaluation demonstrates that the proposed anonymous PRE scheme is efficient.

Paper organization. Section 2 reviews the definitions of single-hop, unidirectional PRE and its CCA security, and then proposes a strong anonymity notion. Section 3 constructs an anonymous and CCA secure PRE and shows its security analysis. Section 4 presents the detail of our implementation and performance study. Section 5 summarizes related work and Section 6 concludes this paper.

2. PRE: DEFINITION AND SECURITY NOTIONS

Let $s \stackrel{R}{\leftarrow} S$ denote selecting element s from set S uniformly at random, $\perp$ denote an error message, and $||$ denote string concatenation. In the present paper we consider single-hop, unidirectional proxy re-encryption only, and name an original ciphertext as a *second level ciphertext* and the ciphertext after re-encryption as a *first level ciphertext* as in [6, 17]. Let $\mathbb{U}$ be the set of users, denoted by $\mathbb{U} = \{1, \cdots, n\}$. Denote the set of uncorrupted users by $\mathbb{U}_h$ and the set of corrupted users by $\mathbb{U}_e$, such that $\mathbb{U}_h \bigcup \mathbb{U}_e = \mathbb{U}$. The following PRE definition and the CCA notion are based on prior work [6, 5, 9].

DEFINITION 1. *A single-hop, unidirectional* PRE *consists of following algorithms:*

- $\mathsf{Param} \leftarrow \mathsf{Setup}(1^\ell)$*: Given a security parameter* 1^ℓ*, this algorithm is run by the trusted party to generate the public parameter* Param. *For brevity, we assume that the following algorithms implicitly take* Param *as parts of inputs.*

- $(\mathsf{pk}_i, \mathsf{sk}_i) \leftarrow \mathsf{KeyGen}(i)$*: This algorithm is run by the user* i *to generate public and private keys* $(\mathsf{pk}_i, \mathsf{sk}_i)$*.*

- $\mathsf{rk}_{i\to j} \leftarrow \mathsf{ReKeyGen}(\mathsf{sk}_i, \mathsf{pk}_j)$*: This algorithm is run by user* i *to output a re-encryption key* $\mathsf{rk}_{i\to j}$*, which can be used to re-encrypt second level ciphertexts decrypted by user* i *to first level ciphertexts decrypted by user* j*.*

- $\mathsf{C} \leftarrow \mathsf{Enc}(\mathsf{pk}_i, \mathsf{m})$*: This algorithm is run to encrypt message* m *to a second level ciphertext* C *which can be decrypted by user* i*.*

- $\mathsf{C}' \leftarrow \mathsf{ReEnc}(\mathsf{rk}_{i\to j}, \mathsf{C})$*: This algorithm is run to re-encrypt a second level ciphertext* C *to a first level ciphertext* C′ *which can be decrypted by user* j*.*

- $\{\mathsf{m}, \perp\} \leftarrow \mathsf{Dec}(\mathsf{sk}_i, \mathsf{C}(\mathsf{C}'))$*: This algorithm is run to decrypt a second level ciphertext* C *(or a first level ciphertext* C′*), which might output the message* m *or a error message* $\perp$*.*

Correctness: A single-hop, unidirectional PRE is correct if: given any m from the message space, (i) $\forall\, i \in \mathbb{U}, (\mathsf{pk}_i, \mathsf{sk}_i) \leftarrow \mathsf{KeyGen}(i)$, so that $\mathsf{Dec}(\mathsf{sk}_i, \mathsf{Enc}(\mathsf{pk}_i, \mathsf{m})) = \mathsf{m}$, and (ii) $\forall\, i, j \in \mathbb{U}, (\mathsf{pk}_i, \mathsf{sk}_i) \leftarrow \mathsf{KeyGen}(i), (\mathsf{pk}_j, \mathsf{sk}_j) \leftarrow \mathsf{KeyGen}(j)$, and $\mathsf{rk}_{i\to j} \leftarrow \mathsf{ReKeyGen}(\mathsf{sk}_i, \mathsf{pk}_j)$, so that $\mathsf{Dec}(\mathsf{sk}_j, \mathsf{ReEnc}(\mathsf{rk}_{i\to j}, \mathsf{Enc}(\mathsf{pk}_i, \mathsf{m}))) = \mathsf{m}$.

CCA Security: The CCA notion [9] can be formalized by the following CCA-security game between an adversary $\mathcal{A}$ and the challenger $\mathcal{C}$.
Phase 1: $\mathcal{C}$ runs $\mathsf{Setup}(1^\ell)$ to initialize the public parameter. $\mathcal{A}$ can access oracles below in polynomially many times. Note that before querying $\mathcal{O}_{\mathsf{ReKeyGen}}(\mathsf{pk}_i, \mathsf{pk}_j)$ and $\mathcal{O}_{\mathsf{ReEnc}}(\mathsf{pk}_i, \mathsf{pk}_j, \mathsf{C})$, $(\mathsf{pk}_i, \mathsf{sk}_i)$ and $(\mathsf{pk}_j, \mathsf{sk}_j)$ have been generated.

- key generation oracle $\mathcal{O}_{\mathsf{KeyGen}}(i)$: (i) If i has not been queried before, $\mathcal{C}$ runs KeyGen to obtain $(\mathsf{pk}_i, \mathsf{sk}_i)$ and records $(i, \mathsf{pk}_i, \mathsf{sk}_i)$. If i is a corrupted user, s.t. $i \in \mathbb{U}_e$, $\mathcal{C}$ returns $(\mathsf{pk}_i, \mathsf{sk}_i)$ to $\mathcal{A}$, and pk_i otherwise. (ii) Otherwise $\mathcal{C}$ retrieves $(\mathsf{pk}_i, \mathsf{sk}_i)$ and returns $(\mathsf{pk}_i, \mathsf{sk}_i)$ to $\mathcal{A}$ if $i \in \mathbb{U}_e$, and pk_i otherwise.

- Re-encryption key generation oracle $\mathcal{O}_{\mathsf{ReKeyGen}}(\mathsf{pk}_i, \mathsf{pk}_j)$: If $i \in \mathbb{U}_h$ and $j \in \mathbb{U}_e$, $\mathcal{C}$ outputs $\perp$; otherwise $\mathcal{C}$ runs ReKeyGen to obtain $\mathsf{rk}_{i\to j}$, and returns it to $\mathcal{A}$.

- Re-encryption oracle $\mathcal{O}_{\mathsf{ReEnc}}(\mathsf{pk}_i, \mathsf{pk}_j, C)$: $\mathcal{C}$ runs $\mathsf{rk}_{i\to j} \leftarrow \mathsf{ReKeyGen}(\mathsf{sk}_i, \mathsf{pk}_j)$, computes $\mathsf{C}' \leftarrow \mathsf{ReEnc}(\mathsf{rk}_{i\to j}, C)$, and returns C′ to $\mathcal{A}$.

- Decryption oracle $\mathcal{O}_{\mathsf{Dec}}(\mathsf{pk}_i, \mathsf{C})$: Given the ciphertext C (either a first level ciphertext or second level ciphertext), $\mathcal{C}$ runs $\{\mathsf{m}, \perp\} \leftarrow \mathsf{Dec}(\mathsf{sk}_i, \mathsf{C})$ and returns the result to $\mathcal{A}$.

Challenge: Once $\mathcal{A}$ decides that Phase 1 is finished, it outputs a public key pk^*, and two messages $\mathsf{m}_0, \mathsf{m}_1$ of equal length, and sends them to $\mathcal{C}$. $\mathcal{C}$ selects $\lambda \xleftarrow{R} \{0,1\}$, runs $\mathsf{C}^* \leftarrow \mathsf{Enc}(\mathsf{pk}^*, \mathsf{m}_\lambda)$, and returns C^* to $\mathcal{A}$. Here the user with respect to pk^* should be uncorrupted, namely belonging to $\mathbb{U}_h$.
Phase 2: $\mathcal{A}$ queries oracles in polynomially many times with these restrictions.

- $\mathcal{O}_{\mathsf{KeyGen}}(i)$ and $\mathcal{O}_{\mathsf{ReKeyGen}}(\mathsf{pk}_i, \mathsf{pk}_j)$: Work as in Phase 1.

- $\mathcal{O}_{\mathsf{ReEnc}}(\mathsf{pk}_i, \mathsf{pk}_j, \mathsf{C})$: If $i \in \mathbb{U}_h$ and $j \in \mathbb{U}_e$, output $\perp$, otherwise work as in Phase 1.

- $\mathcal{O}_{\mathsf{Dec}}(\mathsf{pk}_i, \mathsf{C})$: Work as in Phase 1, subject to the conditions that (i)$\mathcal{A}$ cannot query $\mathcal{O}_{\mathsf{Dec}}$ if $\mathsf{pk}_i = \mathsf{pk}^*$ and $\mathsf{C} = \mathsf{C}^*$, and (ii) $\mathcal{A}$ cannot query $\mathcal{O}_{\mathsf{Dec}}$ if C is the ciphertext computed with a re-encrypted key of pk^* and pk_i.

Guess: Finally, $\mathcal{A}$ outputs a guess $\lambda' \in \{0,1\}$. $\mathcal{A}$ wins the game if $\lambda' = \lambda$.

DEFINITION 2. *Given any polynomial time adversary* $\mathcal{A}$*, we say a single-hop, unidirectional* PRE *scheme is* CCA *secure for second level ciphertexts, if the probability of* $\mathcal{A}$ *winning* CCA*-security game is at most* $\frac{1}{2} + \epsilon(\ell)$*, where* ϵ *is negligible in security parameter* ℓ*.*

Definition 2 describes the CCA security for second level ciphertexts. We also can define a complementary definition of CCA security for first level ciphertexts. We skip this and refer readers to [17].

Anonymity notion: Now we define the anonymity notion for re-encryption keys, which is partially inspired by prior anonymity notions in [5, 19, 20]. The anonymity notion for second level ciphertexts can be referred to [7].

We simulate the following anonymous game between an adversary $\mathcal{A}$ and a challenger $\mathcal{C}$, where $\mathcal{C}$ maintains a re-encryption key list storing all $\mathsf{rk}_{i\to j}$ for users i and j with the form $(i \to j, \{(\mathsf{rk}_{i\to j}, query)\})$. $i \to j$ is the search key to identify each pair of users, and $\{(\mathsf{rk}_{i\to j}, query)\}$ is a set of re-encryption keys, each of which is associated with a boolean indicator *query*. If $\mathsf{rk}_{i\to j}$ has been queried via $\mathcal{O}_{\mathsf{ReKeyGen}}$, then $query = 1$; otherwise $query = 0$. Initially, $\{(\mathsf{rk}_{i\to j}, query)\}$ is empty for the search key (i, j). The anonymous game proceeds as follows, where $\mathcal{C}$ runs $\mathsf{Setup}(1^\ell)$ to set up the public parameter.

Phase 1: The adversary $\mathcal{A}$ queries oracles below in polynomially many times.

- $\mathcal{O}_{\mathsf{KeyGen}}(i)$: It works the same as $\mathcal{O}_{\mathsf{KeyGen}}(i)$ described in CCA-security game.

- $\mathcal{O}_{\mathsf{ReKeyGen}}(\mathsf{pk}_i, \mathsf{pk}_j)$: Given pk_i and pk_j, $\mathcal{C}$ fetches $(i \to j, \{(\mathsf{rk}_{i\to j}, query)\})$ and works as follows:

  1. If $\{(\mathsf{rk}_{i\to j}, query)\}$ is `null` or all $\mathsf{rk}_{i\to j}$ have been queried (i.e., all indicators $query = 1$), $\mathcal{C}$ runs $\mathsf{rk}_{i\to j} \leftarrow \mathsf{ReKeyGen}(\mathsf{sk}_i, \mathsf{pk}_j)$, adds $(\mathsf{rk}_{i\to j}, query = 1)$ to the set $\{(\mathsf{rk}_{i\to j}, query)\}$, and returns $\mathsf{rk}_{i\to j}$;
  2. Otherwise $\mathcal{C}$ selects $\mathsf{rk}_{i\to j}$ from $\{(\mathsf{rk}_{i\to j}, query = 0)\}$ uniformly at random, updates $query = 1$ for $\mathsf{rk}_{i\to j}$, and passes $\mathsf{rk}_{i\to j}$ to $\mathcal{A}$.

- $\mathcal{O}_{\mathsf{ReEnc}}(\mathsf{pk}_i, \mathsf{pk}_j, \mathsf{C})$: Given pk_i and pk_j, $\mathcal{C}$ fetches $(i \to j, \{(\mathsf{rk}_{i\to j}, query)\})$ and works as follows:
  1. If $\{(\mathsf{rk}_{i\to j}, query)\}$ is $\mathtt{null}$, $\mathcal{C}$ runs $\mathsf{rk}_{i\to j} \leftarrow \mathsf{ReKeyGen}(\mathsf{sk}_i, \mathsf{pk}_j)$ and adds $(\mathsf{rk}_{i\to j}, query = 0)$ to the set $\{(\mathsf{rk}_{i\to j}, query)\}$;
  2. Otherwise $\mathcal{C}$ randomly selects $\mathsf{rk}_{i\to j}$ from the set $\{(\mathsf{rk}_{i\to j}, query)\}$.

  Finally, $\mathcal{C}$ runs $\mathsf{C}' \leftarrow \mathsf{ReEnc}(\mathsf{rk}_{i\to j}, \mathsf{C})$ and returns C' to $\mathcal{A}$.
- $\mathcal{O}_{\mathsf{Dec}}(\mathsf{pk}_i, \mathsf{C})$: $\mathcal{C}$ executes $\{\mathsf{m}, \perp\} \leftarrow \mathsf{Dec}(\mathsf{sk}_i, \mathsf{C})$ and returns the result to $\mathcal{A}$. Note that C can be either a first level ciphertext or a second level ciphertext.

Challenge: Once $\mathcal{A}$ decides that Phase 1 is finished, it outputs a pair of users (i^*, j^*). $\mathcal{C}$ fetches $(i^* \to j^*, \{(\mathsf{rk}_{i^*\to j^*}, query)\})$ and works as follows:

- If $i^* \in \mathbb{U}_e$ or $j^* \in \mathbb{U}_e$, $\mathcal{C}$ aborts;
- If the set $\{(\mathsf{rk}_{i^*\to j^*}, query)\}$ is $\mathtt{null}$ or all $\mathsf{rk}_{i^*\to j^*}$ have been queried (i.e., all indicators $query = 1$), $\mathcal{C}$ runs $\mathsf{rk}_{i^*\to j^*} \leftarrow \mathsf{ReKeyGen}(\mathsf{sk}_{i^*}, \mathsf{pk}_{j^*})$, and adds $(\mathsf{rk}_{i^*\to j^*}, query = 1)$ to the set $\{(\mathsf{rk}_{i^*\to j^*}, query)\}$;
- Otherwise $\mathcal{C}$ selects a $\mathsf{rk}_{i^*\to j^*}$ from $\{(\mathsf{rk}_{i^*\to j^*}, query = 0)\}$ uniformly at random, and updates $query = 1$ for $\mathsf{rk}_{i^*\to j^*}$.

$\mathcal{C}$ selects $\lambda \xleftarrow{R} \{0,1\}$. If $\lambda = 0$, $\mathcal{C}$ delivers $\mathsf{rk}_{i^*\to j^*}$ to $\mathcal{A}$, otherwise returns a re-encrypted key selected from the re-encryption key space uniformly at random.

Phase 2: $\mathcal{A}$ can continually query the oracles in polynomially many times.

- $\mathcal{O}_{\mathsf{KeyGen}}(i)$, $\mathcal{O}_{\mathsf{ReKeyGen}}(\mathsf{pk}_i, \mathsf{pk}_j)$ and $\mathcal{O}_{\mathsf{ReEnc}}(\mathsf{pk}_i, \mathsf{pk}_j, \mathsf{C})$: Works as in Phase 1.
- $\mathcal{O}_{\mathsf{Dec}}(\mathsf{pk}_j, \mathsf{C})$: Work as in Phase 1 while being subject to the condition that $\mathcal{A}$ cannot query $\mathcal{O}_{\mathsf{Dec}}$, where $\mathsf{pk}_j = \mathsf{pk}_{j^*}$. [2]

Guess: Eventually, $\mathcal{A}$ outputs a guess $\lambda' \in \{0,1\}$ and wins the game if $\lambda' = \lambda$.

REMARK 1. *Let us consider the challenge phase. If $\lambda = 0$, then $\mathcal{C}$ returns the valid re-encryption key $\mathsf{rk}_{i^*\to j^*}$. Access to $\mathcal{O}_{\mathsf{ReEnc}}(\mathsf{pk}_i, \mathsf{pk}_j, \mathsf{C})$ enables $\mathcal{A}$ to obtain enough first level ciphertexts re-encrypted with $\mathsf{rk}_{i^*\to j^*}$. However, the anonymity notion [19, 20] cannot model this case, because $\mathcal{O}_{\mathsf{ReKeyGen}}(\mathsf{pk}_i, \mathsf{pk}_j)$ does not return this $\mathsf{rk}_{i^*\to j^*}$ to $\mathcal{A}$.*

DEFINITION 3. *We say a single hop, unidirectional* PRE *scheme is anonymous for re-encryption keys, if for any polynomial time adversary $\mathcal{A}$, the probability of $\mathcal{A}$ winning the* anonymous *game is at most $\frac{1}{2} + \epsilon(\ell)$, where ϵ is negligible in security parameter ℓ.*

Definition 3 characterizes the anonymity of the re-encrypted key and [5] has discussed that the anonymity of re-encryption keys implies the anonymity of first level ciphertexts.

[2]The reason is that it is hard for the challenger to distinguish whether C is a first level ciphertext computed by the challenge re-encrypted key or not. This problem also exists in [19, 20] in order to simulate the decryption oracle.

3. ANONYMOUS AND CCA SECURE PRE CONSTRUCTION

3.1 Cryptographic Assumptions

Let G, G_T be two cyclic groups of order q, a ℓ_1–bit prime, and g be a generator of G. Let e be a bilinear map: $e: G\times G \to G_T$ satisfying: (i) $\forall x, y \xleftarrow{R} \mathbb{Z}_q$, $e(g^x, g^y) = e(g,g)^{xy}$, (ii) $e(g,g) \neq 1$, and (iii) e can be computed efficiently.

Let H_0, H_1, H_2, H_3 be secure hash functions modeled as random oracles, s.t. $H_0 : G \to G, H_1 : \{0,1\}^{\ell_2} \times G_T \to \mathbb{Z}_q, H_2 : G\times G_T \times G \times \{0,1\}^{\ell_2} \to G, H_3 : \{0,1\}^{6\ell_1+\ell_2} \times G_T \to \mathbb{Z}_q$ and $H_4 : \mathbb{Z}_q \to \mathbb{Z}_q$, where ℓ_2 is another security parameter. Let F_1, F_2 be two secure pseudorandom generators, where $F_1 : G_T \to \{0,1\}^{\ell_2}$ and $F_2 : G_T \to \{0,1\}^{6\ell_1+\ell_2}$.

Decisional Bilinear Diffie-Hellman (DBDH) Given (g, g^x, g^y, g^z, Q) where $x, y, z \xleftarrow{R} \mathbb{Z}_q$ and $Q \xleftarrow{R} G_T$, for any probabilistic polynomial algorithm $\mathcal{A}$, the advantage of $\mathcal{A}$ determining $Q \stackrel{?}{=} e(g,g)^{xyz}$ is negligible to security parameter ℓ_1 at most, where the advantage is defined as

$$|\Pr[\mathcal{A}(g, g^x, g^y, g^z, e(g,g)^{xyz}) = 1] - \Pr[\mathcal{A}(g, g^x, g^y, g^z, Q) = 1]|.$$

Squared Decisional Bilinear Diffie-Hellman (SDBDH) [25] Given (g, g^x, g^y, Q) where $x, y \xleftarrow{R} \mathbb{Z}_q$ and $Q \xleftarrow{R} G_T$, for any probabilistic polynomial algorithm $\mathcal{A}$, the advantage of $\mathcal{A}$ determining $Q \stackrel{?}{=} e(g,g)^{x^2y}$ is negligible to security parameter ℓ_1 at most, where the advantage is defined as

$$|\Pr[\mathcal{A}(g, g^x, g^y, e(g,g)^{x^2y}) = 1] - \Pr[\mathcal{A}(g, g^x, g^y, Q) = 1]|.$$

3.2 Our Construction

The anonymous and CCA secure PRE scheme can be constructed as follows:

setup(1^ℓ): Given the security parameter ℓ, it obtains two secondary security parameters ℓ_1, ℓ_2, and instantiates H_0, H_1, H_2, H_3, H_4, F_1, F_2 and the bilinear map (q, g, G, G_T, e) as in section 3.1, where q is a ℓ_1-bit prime and the message $\mathsf{m} \in \{0,1\}^{\ell_2}$. In addition, let $g_1 \xleftarrow{R} G$ and set

$$\mathsf{Param} = \{q, g, g_1, G, G_T, e\}.$$

KeyGen(i): For use i, this algorithm selects $a_i \xleftarrow{R} \mathbb{Z}_q$ and sets

$$\mathsf{sk}_i = a_i, \mathsf{pk}_i = g^{a_i}.$$

ReKeyGen($\mathsf{sk}_i, \mathsf{pk}_j$): This algorithm generates the re-encryption key by selecting $s, t, w \xleftarrow{R} \mathbb{Z}_q$ and setting $\mathsf{rk}_{i\to j} = (\mathsf{rk}_1, \mathsf{rk}_2, \mathsf{rk}_3, \mathsf{rk}_4, \mathsf{rk}_5, \mathsf{rk}_6)$ as

$$(H_0(\mathsf{pk}_i)^{-\mathsf{sk}_i} \cdot \mathsf{pk}_j^{H_4(s\cdot \mathsf{sk}_i)},\ g^{H_4(s\cdot \mathsf{sk}_i)} g_1^t,\ g^t,\ g^w,\ e(\mathsf{pk}_j, \mathsf{pk}_j)^{tw},\ e(\mathsf{pk}_j, g)^{tw})$$

Note that rk_5 cannot be altered due to unknown t and w. Thus, the re-encryption key rk cannot be manipulated (Manipulating $\mathsf{rk}_5, \mathsf{rk}_6$ will be detected in Dec when decrypting first level ciphertexts.)

Enc($\mathsf{pk}_i, \mathsf{m}$): Given $\mathsf{m} \in \{0,1\}^{\ell_2}$ and pk_i, this algorithm generates a second level ciphertext by selecting $R \xleftarrow{R} G_T$, computing $r = H_1(\mathsf{m}, R)$, and setting $\mathsf{C} = (\mathsf{C}_1, \mathsf{C}_2, \mathsf{C}_3, \mathsf{C}_4, \mathsf{C}_5)$ as

$$(g^r, \quad R \cdot e(\mathsf{pk}_i, H_0(\mathsf{pk}_i))^r, \quad \mathsf{m} \bigoplus F_1(R), \quad g_1^r, \quad H_2(\mathsf{C}_1, \mathsf{C}_2, \mathsf{C}_3, \mathsf{C}_4)^r)$$

Here we apply the Fujisaki-Okamoto (FO) transformation [13] to generate C.

ReEnc($\mathsf{rk}_{i \to j}, \mathsf{C}$): This algorithm first checks

$$e(g, \mathsf{C}_5) \stackrel{?}{=} e(\mathsf{C}_1, H_2(\mathsf{C}_1, \mathsf{C}_2, \mathsf{C}_3, \mathsf{C}_4)).$$

If the equation does not hold, it aborts; otherwise it re-encrypts $\mathsf{C} = (\mathsf{C}_1, \mathsf{C}_2, \mathsf{C}_3, \mathsf{C}_4, \mathsf{C}_5)$ to a first level ciphertext under pk_j as follows:

- Let $T_1 = \mathsf{C}_1 = g^r$, $T_2 = \mathsf{C}_2 \cdot e(\mathsf{C}_1, \mathsf{rk}_1) = R \cdot e(g^r, \mathsf{pk}_j^{H_4(s \cdot \mathsf{sk}_i)})$, $T_3 = \mathsf{C}_3 = \mathsf{m} \bigoplus F_1(R)$ and $T_4 = \mathsf{C}_4 = g_1^r$, and set $\Gamma = T_1 || T_2 || T_3 || T_4 || \mathsf{rk}_2 || \mathsf{rk}_3 || \mathsf{rk}_4$.
- Select $R' \xleftarrow{R} G_T$ and let $r' = H_3(\Gamma, R')$, and set a first level ciphertext $\mathsf{C}' = (\mathsf{C}'_1, \mathsf{C}'_2, \mathsf{C}'_3)$ as

$$(\mathsf{rk}_6^{r'}, R' \mathsf{rk}_5^{r'}, \Gamma \bigoplus F_2(R'))$$

The intermediate ciphertext (T_1, T_2, T_3) cannot be manipulated because r, m, R are correlated with each other and the relation among them will be verified in decryption. It is worth noting that we apply FO transformation again to generate C' in order to achieve the CCA security for the first level ciphertext.

Dec: It decrypts the ciphertext correspondingly:

- Given a second level ciphertext $\mathsf{C} = (\mathsf{C}_1, \mathsf{C}_2, \mathsf{C}_3, \mathsf{C}_4, \mathsf{C}_5)$, it decrypts with $\mathsf{sk}_i = a_i$:
  1. If $e(g, \mathsf{C}_5) \neq e(\mathsf{C}_1, H_2(\mathsf{C}_1, \mathsf{C}_2, \mathsf{C}_3, \mathsf{C}_4))$, then output $\perp$;
  2. Otherwise let $R = \mathsf{C}_2 / e(g^r, H_0(\mathsf{pk}_i))^{\mathsf{sk}_i}$, and have $\mathsf{m} = \mathsf{C}_3 \bigoplus F_1(R)$;
- Given a first level ciphertext $\mathsf{C}' = (\mathsf{C}'_1, \mathsf{C}'_2, \mathsf{C}'_3)$, it decrypts with $\mathsf{sk}_j = a_j$:
  1. Compute $R' = \mathsf{C}'_2 / \mathsf{C}_1'^{\mathsf{sk}_j}$, let $\Gamma = \mathsf{C}'_3 \bigoplus F_2(R')$, and parse $\Gamma = T_1 || T_2 || T_3 || T_4 || \mathsf{rk}_2 || \mathsf{rk}_3 || \mathsf{rk}_4$.
  2. If $e(\mathsf{rk}_3, \mathsf{rk}_4)^{\mathsf{sk}_j H_3(\Gamma, R')} \neq \mathsf{C}'_1$, then return $\perp$. This is to verify rk_5 and rk_6 without being manipulated.
  3. Let $R = T_2 (\frac{e(\mathsf{rk}_3, T_4)}{e(\mathsf{rk}_2, T_1)})^{\mathsf{sk}_j}$ so that $\mathsf{m} = T_3 \bigoplus F_1(R)$.
  4. Let $r = H_1(\mathsf{m}, R)$ and verify $T_1 \stackrel{?}{=} g^r$. If so, return m; $\perp$ otherwise.

Correctness of the PRE scheme can be verified. In the construction, we can see that we use FO transformation twice to assure CCA security for the first and second level ciphertexts. In addition, The PRE scheme is collusion-safe [6] even that user j and the cloud collude together. Intuitively, user j cannot derive $\mathsf{pk}_j^{H_4(s \cdot \mathsf{sk}_i)}$ from the re-encryption key $\mathsf{rk}_{i \to j}$, so that he is unable to infer $H_0(\mathsf{pk}_i)^{-\mathsf{sk}_i}$ and decrypt user i's second level ciphertexts.

3.3 Security Analysis

We show the theorem regarding CCA security for second level ciphertexts as follows. Similarly, we can prove our scheme achieves CCA security for first level ciphertexts and omit it here.

THEOREM 1. *Assume that the DBDH assumption holds, the* PRE *scheme is* CCA *secure in the random oracle model for second level ciphertexts.*

PROOF. The challenger $\mathcal{C}$ maintains random oracles as follows:

- Oracle $\mathcal{O}_{H_0}$: If $H_0(\mathsf{pk})$ has been queried before, it retrieves β from $\mathcal{O}_{H_0}$ according to pk; otherwise it selects $\beta \xleftarrow{R} \mathbb{Z}_q$, lets $H_0(\mathsf{pk}) = (g^y)^\beta$, and adds (pk, β) into $\mathcal{O}_{H_0}$. It returns $(g^y)^\beta$.
- Oracles $\mathcal{O}_{H_1}$, $\mathcal{O}_{H_2}$, $\mathcal{O}_{H_3}$,$\mathcal{O}_{H_4}$, $\mathcal{O}_{F_1}$ and $\mathcal{O}_{F_2}$ are modeled as random oracles and we skip their details.

Suppose the challenger $\mathcal{C}$ is given a DBDH instance of (g, g^x, g^y, g^z, Q), where $x, y, z \xleftarrow{R} \mathbb{Z}_p$, and $Q \xleftarrow{R} G_T$, and x, y, z are unknown. $\mathcal{C}$ simulates the CCA-security game with $\mathcal{A}$ by letting $g_1 = g^c$, where $c \xleftarrow{R} \mathbb{Z}_q$ is known to $\mathcal{C}$, and proceeds the game as follows.

Phase 1: $\mathcal{A}$ can challenge the oracles in polynomially may times and $\mathcal{C}$ responds as follows:

$\mathcal{O}_{\mathsf{KeyGen}}(i)$: $\mathcal{C}$ responds as follows:

- $i \in \mathbb{U}_h$: If user i has been queried before, it retrieves pk_i from $\mathcal{O}_h$; otherwise $\mathcal{C}$ selects $a_i \xleftarrow{R} \mathbb{Z}_q$, lets $\mathsf{pk}_i = (g^x)^{a_i}$, and adds (i, pk_i, a_i) into $\mathcal{O}_h$. It returns pk_i to $\mathcal{A}$, where it implicitly defines $\mathsf{sk}_i = x \cdot a_i$.
- $i \in \mathbb{U}_e$: If user i has been queried before, it returns $(\mathsf{pk}_i, \mathsf{sk}_i)$ from $\mathcal{O}_e$; otherwise $\mathcal{C}$ selects $b_i \xleftarrow{R} \mathbb{Z}_q$, lets $\mathsf{pk}_i = g^{b_i}, \mathsf{sk}_i = b_i$, adds $(i, \mathsf{pk}_i, \mathsf{sk}_i)$ into $\mathcal{O}_e$, and returns $(\mathsf{pk}_i, \mathsf{sk}_i)$ to $\mathcal{A}$.

$\mathcal{O}_{\mathsf{ReKeyGen}}(\mathsf{pk}_i, \mathsf{pk}_j)$: $\mathcal{C}$ generates $\mathsf{rk}_{i \to j} = (\mathsf{rk}_1, \mathsf{rk}_2, \mathsf{rk}_3, \mathsf{rk}_4, \mathsf{rk}_5, \mathsf{rk}_6)$ for a pair of users i and j by selecting $s, t, w \xleftarrow{R} \mathbb{Z}_q$, and :

- If $i \in \mathbb{U}_e$, let $\mathsf{rk}_1 = H_0(\mathsf{pk}_i)^{-\mathsf{sk}_i} \mathsf{pk}_j^{H_4(s \cdot \mathsf{sk}_i)}$, $\mathsf{rk}_2 = g^{H_4(s \cdot \mathsf{sk}_i)} g_1^t$, $\mathsf{rk}_3 = g^t, \mathsf{rk}_4 = g^w, \mathsf{rk}_5 = e(\mathsf{pk}_j, \mathsf{pk}_j)^{tw}$ and $\mathsf{rk}_6 = e(\mathsf{pk}_j, g)^{tw}$. $\mathcal{C}$ returns $\mathsf{rk}_{i \to j}$ to $\mathcal{A}$.
- If $i \in \mathbb{U}_h$ and $j \in \mathbb{U}_h$, let $\mathsf{rk}_1 = \mathsf{pk}_i^\gamma$, $\mathsf{rk}_2 = (g^y)^{a_i \beta_i / a_j} g^{a_i \gamma / a_j} g_1^t$, $\mathsf{rk}_3 = g^t$, $\mathsf{rk}_4 = g^w$, $\mathsf{rk}_5 = e(\mathsf{pk}_j, \mathsf{pk}_j)^{tw}$ and $\mathsf{rk}_6 = e(\mathsf{pk}_j, g)^{tw}$, where $\gamma \xleftarrow{R} \mathbb{Z}_p$, then $\mathcal{C}$ returns $\mathsf{rk}_{i \to j}$ to $\mathcal{A}$. Note that $\mathsf{rk}_{i \to j}$ is a valid re-encryption key. Let us implicitly define $H_4(s \cdot \mathsf{sk}_i) = (a_i \beta_i y + \gamma a_i)/a_j$ (note s, sk_i are unknown to $\mathcal{A}$) so that

$$\begin{aligned} \mathsf{rk}_1 &= \mathsf{pk}_i^\gamma = g^{-y\beta_i x a_i + y \beta_i x a_i + \gamma a_i x} \\ &= (g^y)^{-\beta_i a_i x} g^{a_j x \frac{1}{a_j}(y \beta_i a_i + \gamma a_i)} \\ &= H_0(\mathsf{pk}_i)^{-a_i x} \mathsf{pk}_j^{H_4(s \cdot \mathsf{sk}_i)} \end{aligned}$$

- Otherwise returns $\perp$.

$\mathcal{O}_{\mathsf{ReEnc}}(\mathsf{pk}_i, \mathsf{pk}_j, \mathsf{C})$: Given a second level ciphertext $\mathsf{C} = (\mathsf{C}_1, \mathsf{C}_2, \mathsf{C}_3, \mathsf{C}_4, \mathsf{C}_5)$, $\mathcal{C}$ does:

- If $e(g, \mathsf{C}_5) \neq e(\mathsf{C}_1, H_3(\mathsf{C}_1, \mathsf{C}_2, \mathsf{C}_3, \mathsf{C}_4))$ or $i \in \mathbb{U}_h$ and $j \in \mathbb{U}_e$, output $\perp$.
- Query $\mathcal{O}_{\mathsf{ReKeyGen}}(\mathsf{pk}_i, \mathsf{pk}_j)$ to obtain $\mathsf{rk}_{i \to j} = (\mathsf{rk}_1, \mathsf{rk}_2, \mathsf{rk}_3, \mathsf{rk}_4, \mathsf{rk}_5, \mathsf{rk}_6)$.
- Execute ReEnc by taking as input C and $\mathsf{rk}_{i \to j}$, and output $\mathsf{C}' = (\mathsf{C}'_1, \mathsf{C}'_2, \mathsf{C}'_3)$.

$\mathcal{O}_{\mathsf{Dec}}(\mathsf{pk}_i, C)$: To decrypt C for user i, $\mathcal{C}$ does:

- If $i \in \mathbb{U}_e$, run algorithm Dec by taking as input the secret key b_i and the ciphertext C, and return the output.
- If C is a second level ciphertext, i.e., $\mathsf{C} = (\mathsf{C}_1, \mathsf{C}_2, \mathsf{C}_3, \mathsf{C}_4, \mathsf{C}_5)$, verify $e(g, \mathsf{C}_5) \stackrel{?}{=} e(\mathsf{C}_1, H_3(\mathsf{C}_1, \mathsf{C}_2, \mathsf{C}_3, \mathsf{C}_4))$. If not hold, then output $\perp$; otherwise search $\mathcal{O}_{H_1}$ for the tuple (m, R, r) where $r = H_1(\mathsf{m}, R)$ and the oracle $\mathcal{O}_{F_1}$, such that $\mathsf{C}_1 = g^r$ and $\mathsf{C}_3 = \mathsf{m} \bigoplus F_1(R)$. If such tuple exists, then return m; otherwise return $\perp$.
- If C is a first level ciphertext, i.e., $\mathsf{C}' = (\mathsf{C}'_1, \mathsf{C}'_2, \mathsf{C}'_3)$, search $\mathcal{O}_{H_3}$ for the tuple (Γ, R', r'), where $r' = H_3(\Gamma, R')$ and $\mathcal{O}_{F_2}$, such that $\mathsf{C}'_3 = \Gamma \bigoplus F_2(R')$. Then, parse Γ as $T_1, T_2, T_3, T_4, \mathsf{rk}_2, \mathsf{rk}_3, \mathsf{rk}_4$. Search $\mathcal{O}_{H_1}$ for the tuple (m, R, r), where $r = H_1(\mathsf{m}, R)$ and the oracle $\mathcal{O}_{F_1}$, such that $T_1 = g^r$ and $T_3 = \mathsf{m} \bigoplus F_1(R)$. If such tuple exists, return m, else return $\perp$.

Challenge: Once $\mathcal{A}$ decides that Phase 1 is finished, it outputs a public key pk^* and two messages $\mathsf{m}_0, \mathsf{m}_1$ of the same length, and sends them to $\mathcal{C}$. $\mathcal{C}$ returns $(\mathsf{C}^*_1, \mathsf{C}^*_2, \mathsf{C}^*_3, \mathsf{C}^*_4, \mathsf{C}^*_5)$ as follows: select $R^* \stackrel{R}{\leftarrow} G_T$ and let $\mathsf{C}^*_1 = g^z$, $\mathsf{C}^*_2 = R^* Q^{a^* \beta^*}$, $\mathsf{C}^*_3 = \mathsf{m}_\lambda \bigoplus F_1(R^*)$, $\mathsf{C}^*_4 = g_1^z = (g^z)^c$ and $\mathsf{C}^*_5 = (g^z)^{\theta^*}$, where $\theta^* \stackrel{R}{\leftarrow} \mathbb{Z}_q$.

If $Q = e(g,g)^{xyz}$, $(\mathsf{C}^*_1, \mathsf{C}^*_2, \mathsf{C}^*_3, \mathsf{C}^*_4, \mathsf{C}^*_5)$ is a valid ciphertext for m_λ under pk^*. To see it, we implicitly let $H_3(\mathsf{C}^*_1, \mathsf{C}^*_2, \mathsf{C}^*_3, \mathsf{C}^*_4) = g^{\theta^*}$, and have

$$\begin{aligned}
\mathsf{C}^*_1 &= g^z, \\
\mathsf{C}^*_2 &= R^* Q^{a^* \cdot \beta^*} = R^* e((g^x)^{a^*}, (g^y)^{\beta^*})^z = R^* e(\mathsf{pk}^*, H_0(\mathsf{pk}^*))^z, \\
\mathsf{C}^*_3 &= \mathsf{m}_\lambda \bigoplus F_1(R^*), \\
\mathsf{C}^*_4 &= (g^z)^c = g_1^z, \\
\mathsf{C}^*_5 &= (g^z)^{\theta^*} = (g^{\theta^*})^z = H_3(\mathsf{C}^*_1, \mathsf{C}^*_2, \mathsf{C}^*_3, \mathsf{C}^*_4)^z,
\end{aligned}$$

where $H_0(\mathsf{pk}^*) = (g^y)^{\beta^*}$, $\mathsf{pk}^* = (g^x)^{a^*}$.

Phase 2: $\mathcal{C}$ and $\mathcal{A}$ proceed the same as in Phase 1 while complying with constraints defined in the CCA-security game.

Guess: Finally, $\mathcal{A}$ returns a guess $\lambda' \in \{0, 1\}$. If $\lambda' = \lambda$, $\mathcal{C}$ outputs $Q = e(g,g)^{xyz}$; otherwise, $\mathcal{C}$ returns $Q \neq e(g,g)^{xyz}$.

This completes the simulation. In Phase 2, if $Q = e(g,g)^{xyz}$, then the ciphertext $(\mathsf{C}^*_1, \mathsf{C}^*_2, \mathsf{C}^*_3, \mathsf{C}^*_4, \mathsf{C}^*_5)$ is a valid ciphertext of m_λ, so the probability of $\mathcal{A}$ outputting $\lambda' = \lambda$ is $\frac{1}{2} + \mu$; if Q is an element randomly that is selected from G_T and independent from z, then the probability of $\mathcal{A}$ outputting $\lambda' = \lambda$ is $\frac{1}{2}$, because the ciphertext has no information about m_λ. Therefore, the probability of $\mathcal{C}$ correctly guessing $Q \stackrel{?}{=} e(g,g)^{xyz}$ with the instance of (g, g^x, g^y, g^z, Q) is $\frac{1}{2}(\frac{1}{2} + \mu + \frac{1}{2}) = \frac{1}{2} + \frac{\mu}{2}$.

□

Theorem 2 states that our scheme achieves our anonymity notion for re-encryption keys. Correspondingly, we can show that our scheme also achieves the anonymity for second level ciphertexts and first level ciphertexts, which are skipped here.

THEOREM 2. *Assume that SDBDH assumption holds, our scheme achieves the anonymity for re-encryption keys in Definition 3 in the random oracle model.*

The challenger $\mathcal{C}$ maintains random oracles as follows:

- Oracle $\mathcal{O}_{H_0}$: if $H_0(\mathsf{pk})$ has been queried, it retrieves $H_0(\mathsf{pk})$ from $\mathcal{O}_{H_0}$; otherwise select $\beta \stackrel{R}{\leftarrow} \mathbb{Z}_q$, let $H_0(\mathsf{pk}) = g^\beta$, and add (pk, β) into $\mathcal{O}_{H_0}$. It returns g^β.
- Oracles $\mathcal{O}_{H_1}$, $\mathcal{O}_{H_2}$, $\mathcal{O}_{H_3}$, $\mathcal{O}_{H_4}$, $\mathcal{O}_{F_1}$ and $\mathcal{O}_{F_2}$ are modeled as random oracles and we skip their details here.

The proof strategy is that $\mathcal{C}$ randomly selects an uncorrupted user J from the set of uncorrupted users and lets J be the targeted user in the Challenge phase. That is, if $j^* = J$ in the Challenge phase, the challenger will proceed the anonymous game; otherwise abort.

Proof of Theorem 2 Suppose $\mathcal{A}$ breaks the anonymous game with the probability $\frac{1}{2} + \mu$, then we can construct the challenger $\mathcal{C}$ solving $Q \stackrel{?}{=} e(g,g)^{x^2 y}$ for the instance (g, e, g^x, g^y, Q) with probability $\frac{1}{2} + \frac{\mu}{2n}$ at least, where n is the number of users in the PRE scheme, i.e., $|\mathbb{U}_h| + |\mathbb{U}_e| = n$.

Recall that $\mathcal{C}$ maintains a key list storing re-encryption keys for (i,j): $(i \to j, \{(\mathsf{rk}_{i \to j}, query)\})$. Assume $\mathcal{C}$ selects user J before proceeding the game. Given an instance (g, e, g^x, g^y, Q), $\mathcal{C}$ selects $c \stackrel{R}{\leftarrow} \mathbb{Z}_q$, lets $g_1 = g^c$, and proceeds the anonymous game to determine $Q \stackrel{?}{=} e(g,g)^{x^2 y}$ as follows.

Phase 1: $\mathcal{A}$ queries oracles below in polynomially many time:

$\mathcal{O}_{\mathsf{KeyGen}}(i)$: $\mathcal{C}$ responds as follows:

- $i \in \mathbb{U}_h$: If user i has been queried before, $\mathcal{C}$ retrieves pk_i from $\mathcal{O}_h$; otherwise (i) $i = J$, $\mathcal{C}$ selects $a_i \stackrel{R}{\leftarrow} \mathbb{Z}_q$, lets $\mathsf{pk}_i = (g^x)^{a_i}$, and adds (i, a_i, pk_i) into $\mathcal{O}_h$, (ii) $i \neq J$, $\mathcal{C}$ selects $a_i \stackrel{R}{\leftarrow} \mathbb{Z}_q$, lets $\mathsf{pk}_i = g^{a_i}$, and adds (i, a_i, pk_i) into $\mathcal{O}_h$. $\mathcal{C}$ returns pk_i to $\mathcal{A}$. Note that we explicitly define $\mathsf{sk}_i = x \cdot a_i$ when $i = J$.
- $i \in \mathbb{U}_e$: If the query has been queried before, then $\mathcal{C}$ returns $(\mathsf{pk}_i, \mathsf{sk}_i)$ from $\mathcal{O}_e$; else $\mathcal{C}$ selects $a_i \stackrel{R}{\leftarrow} \mathbb{Z}_q$, lets $\mathsf{pk}_i = g^{a_i}, \mathsf{sk}_i = a_i$, and adds $(i, \mathsf{pk}_i, \mathsf{sk}_i)$ into $\mathcal{O}_e$. It returns $(\mathsf{pk}_i, \mathsf{sk}_i)$ to $\mathcal{A}$.

$\mathcal{O}_{\mathsf{ReKeyGen}}(\mathsf{pk}_i, \mathsf{pk}_j)$: Given $\mathsf{pk}_i, \mathsf{pk}_j$, $\mathcal{C}$ obtains $(i \to j, \{(\mathsf{rk}_{i \to j}, query)\})$ and

- If $\{(\mathsf{rk}_{i \to j}, query)\}$ is `null` or all $\mathsf{rk}_{i \to j}$ have been queried before (i.e., all indicators $query = 1$), then
    1. If $i = J$, it generates $\mathsf{rk}_{J \to j}$ by selecting $s, w, v \stackrel{R}{\leftarrow} \mathbb{Z}_q$ and letting: $\mathsf{rk}_1 = (g^x)^{-a_i \beta_i} \mathsf{pk}_j^\gamma$, $\mathsf{rk}_2 = g^\gamma g_1^t$, $\mathsf{rk}_3 = g^t$, $\mathsf{rk}_4 = g^w$, $\mathsf{rk}_5 = e(\mathsf{pk}_j, \mathsf{pk}_j)^{tw}$, $\mathsf{rk}_6 = e(\mathsf{pk}_j, g)^{tw}$, where $\gamma \stackrel{R}{\leftarrow} \mathbb{Z}_q$. We implicitly define $H_4(s \cdot \mathsf{sk}_i) = \gamma$, and we can see $\mathsf{rk}_{i \to j}$ is a valid re-encryption key.

2. Otherwise let $\mathsf{rk}_{i \to j} = (\mathsf{rk}_1, \mathsf{rk}_2, \mathsf{rk}_3, \mathsf{rk}_4, \mathsf{rk}_5, \mathsf{rk}_6)$ as

$$(H_0(\mathsf{pk}_i)^{-\mathsf{sk}_i} \cdot \mathsf{pk}_j^{H_4(s \cdot \mathsf{sk}_i)},\ g^{H_4(s \cdot \mathsf{sk}_i)} g_1^t,\ g^t,\ g^w,\ e(\mathsf{pk}_j, \mathsf{pk}_j)^{tw},\ e(\mathsf{pk}_j, g)^{tw})$$

It adds $(\mathsf{rk}_{i \to j}, query = 1)$ to $\{(\mathsf{rk}_{i \to j}, query)\}$ and returns $\mathsf{rk}_{i \to j}$;

- Else, it chooses $\mathsf{rk}_{i \to j}$ randomly from $\{(\mathsf{rk}_{i \to j}, query)\}$ where $query = 0$, sets $query = 1$ correspondingly, and returns $\mathsf{rk}_{i \to j}$.

$\mathcal{O}_{\mathsf{ReEnc}}(\mathsf{pk}_i, \mathsf{pk}_j, \mathsf{C})$: Given a second level ciphertext $\mathsf{C} = (\mathsf{C}_1, \mathsf{C}_2, \mathsf{C}_3, \mathsf{C}_4, \mathsf{C}_5)$, $\mathcal{C}$ proceeds as follows:

- If $e(g, \mathsf{C}_5) \neq e(\mathsf{C}_1, H_3(\mathsf{C}_1, \mathsf{C}_2, \mathsf{C}_3, \mathsf{C}_4))$, $\mathcal{C}$ outputs $\perp$.
- If the set $\{i \to j, (\mathsf{rk}_{i \to j}, query)\}$ is `null`, $\mathcal{C}$ generates a re-encryption key $\mathsf{rk}_{i \to}$ as in $\mathcal{O}_{\mathsf{ReKeyGen}}$, and adds $(\mathsf{rk}_{i \to}, query = 0)$ to the key list; otherwise, $\mathcal{C}$ selects $\mathsf{rk}_{i \to j}$ randomly from the set $\{i \to j, (\mathsf{rk}_{i \to j}, query)\}$.
- $\mathcal{C}$ applies the algorithm ReEnc by taking input C and $\mathsf{rk}_{i \to j}$, and outputs $\mathsf{C}' = (\mathsf{C}'_1, \mathsf{C}'_2, \mathsf{C}'_3)$.

$\mathcal{O}_{\mathsf{Dec}}(\mathsf{pk}_i, \mathsf{C})$: Given pk_i and C, $\mathcal{C}$ does:

- If $i \neq J$, $\mathcal{C}$ applies the algorithm Dec by taking input the private key a_i and the ciphertext C, and returns the output.
- If $i = J$ and C is a second level ciphertext, i.e., $\mathsf{C} = (\mathsf{C}_1, \mathsf{C}_2, \mathsf{C}_3, \mathsf{C}_4, \mathsf{C}_5)$, $\mathcal{C}$ verifies $e(g, \mathsf{C}_5) \stackrel{?}{=} e(\mathsf{C}_1, H_3(\mathsf{C}_1, \mathsf{C}_2, \mathsf{C}_3, \mathsf{C}_4))$. If it does not hold, $\mathcal{C}$ outputs $\perp$; else $\mathcal{C}$ searches $\mathcal{O}_{H_1}$ for the tuple (m, R, r), where $r = H_1(\mathsf{m}, R)$ and $\mathcal{O}_{F_1}$, such that $\mathsf{C}_1 = g^r$ and $\mathsf{C}_3 = \mathsf{m} \bigoplus F_1(R)$. If such tuple exists, $\mathcal{C}$ returns m; else returns $\perp$.
- If $i = J$ and C is a first level ciphertext, i.e., $\mathsf{C}' = (\mathsf{C}'_1, \mathsf{C}'_2, \mathsf{C}'_3)$, $\mathcal{C}$ searches $\mathcal{O}_{H_3}$ for the tuple (Γ, R', r'), where $r' = H_3(\Gamma, R')$, and $\mathcal{O}_{F_2}$, such that $\mathsf{C}'_3 = \Gamma \bigoplus F_2(R')$. Then, $\mathcal{C}$ parses Γ as $T_1, T_2, T_3, T_4, \mathsf{rk}_2, \mathsf{rk}_3, \mathsf{rk}_4$, and searches $\mathcal{O}_{H_1}$ for the tuple (m, R, r), where $r = H_1(\mathsf{m}, R)$, and $\mathcal{O}_{F_1}$, such that $T_1 = g^r$ and $T_3 = \mathsf{m} \bigoplus F_1(R)$. If such tuple exists, $\mathcal{C}$ returns m; else returns $\perp$.

Challenge: Once $\mathcal{A}$ decides that Phase 1 is finished, it outputs (i^*, j^*), where $i^*, j^* \in \mathbb{U}_h$. If $j^* \neq J$, $\mathcal{C}$ aborts; otherwise $\mathcal{C}$ has $\mathsf{rk}^* = (\mathsf{rk}_1^*, \mathsf{rk}_2^*, \mathsf{rk}_3^*, \mathsf{rk}_4^*, \mathsf{rk}_5^*, \mathsf{rk}_6^*)$:

$$(H_0(\mathsf{pk}_i)^{-\mathsf{sk}_i} \cdot \mathsf{pk}_J^{H_4(s \cdot \mathsf{sk}_i)},\ g^{H_4(s \cdot \mathsf{sk}_i)} g^{yc},\ g^y,\ g^w,\ Q^{a_J^2 w},\ e(\mathsf{pk}_J, g^y)^w)$$

$\mathcal{C}$ adds $(\mathsf{rk}^*, query = 1)$ to the set of $\{(\mathsf{rk}^*, query)\}$. $\mathcal{C}$ selects $\lambda \stackrel{R}{\leftarrow} \{0, 1\}$, and delivers rk^* to $\mathcal{A}$ if $\lambda = 0$, or a random key from re-encryption key space if $\lambda = 1$.

Note that if $Q = e(g, g)^{x^2 y}$, rk^* is a valid re-encryption key for (i^*, j^*) since $\mathsf{rk}_5^* = e(g, g)^{x^2 y w a_J^2} = e(g^{a_J x}, g^{a_J x})^{yw} = e(\mathsf{pk}_J, \mathsf{pk}_J)^{yw}$.

Phase 2: $\mathcal{C}$ proceeds the game as that in the Phase 1 by following the constraints specified in the anonymous game.

Guess: Finally, $\mathcal{A}$ returns a guess $\lambda' \in \{0, 1\}$. If $\lambda' = \lambda$, $\mathcal{C}$ outputs $Q = e(g, g)^{x^2 y}$; $\mathcal{C}$ returns $Q \neq e(g, g)^{x^2 y}$.

This completes the simulation. Note $\mathsf{rk}_1^*, \mathsf{rk}_2^*, \mathsf{rk}_3^*$ are distributed uniformly and independently because of independent and random pk_j, $H_4(s\mathsf{sk}_i)$ and c. If $Q = e(g, g)^{x^2 y}$ (meaning $\mathsf{rk}_{i^* \to j^*}$ is a valid re-encryption key of (i^*, j^*)), $\mathcal{A}$ will output $\lambda' = \lambda$ with the probability of $\frac{1}{2} + \mu$; if Q is a random element in G_T independent from $e(g, g)^{x^2 y}$, $\mathcal{A}$ will output $\lambda' = \lambda$ with the probability of $\frac{1}{2}$ since the challenged re-encryption key reveals no information about (i^*, j^*). Hence, the probability of $\mathcal{C}$'s correctly guessing $Q \stackrel{?}{=} e(g, g)^{x^2 y}$ with the instance of (g, e, g^x, g^y, Q) is $\frac{1}{2}(\frac{1}{2} + \frac{\mu}{|\mathbb{U}_h|} + \frac{1}{2}) \geq \frac{1}{2} + \frac{\mu}{2n}$, because the probability of $\mathcal{C}$ proceeding the game is $\frac{1}{|\mathbb{U}_h|}$. Therefore, if $\mathcal{A}$ can break the anonymous game with a probability of $\frac{1}{2} + \mu$, we can solve the SDBDH problem at least with a probability of $\frac{1}{2} + \frac{\mu}{2n}$.

4. PERFORMANCE EVALUATION

We implement the proposed PRE scheme co-operating with Amazon Web Services (AWS) [1], an Infrastructure-as-a-Service (IaaS) cloud platform. In particularly, we deploy the proxy re-encryption as a service in Amazon EC2, provide simple API for application integration, and adopt Amazon S3 as storage server for ciphertexts. As a reference application, we develop a secure email forwarding application based on it and demonstrate its efficiency and feasibility.

4.1 Implementation

We implement the PRE in C language based on the Pairing-based Cryptography (PBC) library [4]. We instantiate the random oracles with OpenSSL/SHA256 and the converting function `element_from_hash` of PBC, and let each data block with length of 64 Bytes, e.g. $\ell_2 = 512$. The bilinear map is instantiated with two different parameters:

- `a.param`: The group order is 160 bits long, and the order of the base field is 512 bits long. It offers a level of security that is equivalent to 1024-bit DLOG. The operations is more efficient compared with other kinds of parameters [4].
- `e.param`: The group order is 160 bits long, and the order of the base field is 1024 bits long. It also offers a level of security equivalent to 1024-bit DLOG, but the specified pairing is not as efficient as that of `a.param`.

4.2 Asymptotic Complexity Comparison

Table 1 describes the asymptotic complexity for the proposed PRE scheme, and summarizes the security properties with the three anonymous schemes in the state of the art. We can see that the scheme [5] achieves CPA security and the scheme [19] achieves CCA security, both in the random oracle model. However, both schemes cannot achieve the anonymity as we defined. While the scheme [20] is proved to achieve the anonymity property as their defined, we find that their scheme does satisfy the anonymity notion we defined in the present paper. Unfortunately, [15] proved that the scheme [20] cannot attain CCA security as they claimed due to the attack [15]. In contrast, the proposed scheme in this paper not only achieves CCA security in the random oracle model, but also attains the desired anonymity property.

4.3 Efficiency of PRE Operations

To evaluate the efficiency of algorithms in the proposed PRE scheme, we run experiments on a machine with Linux

	Scheme [5]	Scheme [19]	Scheme [20]	Scheme in this Paper
Property				
Security Model	RO	RO		RO
Semantic Security	CPA	CCA	[CCA]*	CCA
Satisfying our anonymity	No	No	Yes	Yes
Bilinear Map?	Yes	No	Yes	Yes
Assumption	DBDH, Decision Linear	DDH, CCA-secury SKE	5-EDBDH, DDH CCA-secure SKE Strongly unforgeable SIG	DBDH
Complexity				
ReKeyGen	1P +4E	2E+ 1Enc	11E	2P +8E
Enc	3E	4E+ 1Enc	1P+ 5E+ 1ENC+ 1SIGN	1P +4E
ReEnc	2P+2E	2E	5P + 6E + 1VER	3P +2E
Dec (2nd level ciphertext)	1P + 1E	3E + 1DEC	5P+ 2E+ 1DEC +1VER	3P +1E
Dec (1st level ciphertext)	1E	2E+ 1DEC	7E+ 1 DEC	3P +4E

Table 1: Comparison between prior schemes and ours, where SKE denotes a one time symmetric encryption scheme, SIG denotes a one time signature scheme, P denotes a pairing operation, E denotes an exponentiation operation, ENC denotes an encryption operation of SKE, DEC denotes an decryption operation of SKE, SIGN denotes a signing operation of SIG, and VER denotes a verification operation of SIG. * The scheme [20] is not CCA secure shown in [15] (CT-RSA'13).

OS, Intel Duo CPU E7500 2.93GHz and 2GB RAM. We average the execution time by running each experiment 20 times and show them in Table 4.3. We can see that ReKeyGen is most costly compared with other algorithms. Fortunately, this operation is executed infrequently. We observe that the performance of the PRE scheme is quite acceptable in practice with the bilinear map specified by `a.param`, since the operations only require around 10-14 milliseconds except the re-encryption key generation.

Operation	a.param (ms)	e.param (ms)
ReKeyGen	20.17	56.89
Enc	10.69	30.22
ReEnc	11.86	35.69
Dec(2nd level ciphertext)	10.79	32.47
Dec(1st level ciphertext)	12.37	39.49

Table 2: Efficiency of operations of the proposed PRE scheme.

4.4 Implementation of Proxy Service

To investigate the utilization of our PRE, we implement the proxy service on top of two AWS services: EC2 and S3, where EC2 provides a virtualized environment to launch virtual machine instances with optional computing resources (CPU frequency/core/RAM) and S3 is a cloud-based storage system to store data in buckets and provides management interface, i.e., writing, reading and deletion.

We implement the proxy service as a PHP web server running on an EC2 virtual machine where the bilinear map is specified by `a.param`. The proxy service provides a simple HTTP API ReEnc(rk, `s3-url2`, `s3-url1`), where rk is a re-encryption key, `s3-url2` is the URL of a second level ciphertext object in S3, and `s3-url1` is the URL of a first level ciphertext object (after re-encrypting `s3-url2`) in S3. When the re-encryption has been done, a successful HTTP response is sent out to notify that the operation is executed successfully and the first level ciphertext has been stored to the location specified by `s3-url1`. Note that the proxy service itself does not manage any content. If necessary, the proxy service should be granted permissions to read/write data objects in S3. In addition, we can easily extend our proxy service to support other cloud storage services such as SQL (e.g., RDS) and NoSQL data (e.g., SimpleDB).

4.5 Secure Email Forwarding with Anonymous Proxy Service

As a case study, we have developed a secure email forwarding application with our proxy service in AWS.

System overview: As shown in Figure 1, our application consists of three parts: (i) a web-based email client (email sender/receiver here) provides regular browser interface for users to login and send/read emails. To keep the email confidential, it employs our PRE scheme to perform encryption and decryption, together with necessary functions, i.e., downloading ciphertext from S3. (ii)A email server, which is to manage incoming emails and handle them, and (iii) the proxy service deployed in EC2.

A secure email forwarding typically takes the following steps. First, Alice sends to Bob the email in encryption form (encrypting email body, and optional attachment) via the email client (step 1). Upon receiving it, the email server will upload the encrypted email body to `s3-url2` (step 2), and invoke the proxy service via the API ReEnc(`rk, s3-url2, s3-url1`) with a re-encryption key so that the re-encrypted email can be decrypted by Carol (step 3). The proxy service will parse `rk`, fetch second level ciphertexts specified by `s3-url2` from S3, perform the re-encryption, write re-encrypted ciphertexts to the location specified by `s3-url1`, and return `HTTP OK` to the email server (step 4). Finally the email server will send to Carol the final email stored in the location specified by `s3-url1` (step 5), so that Carol can decrypt and read it with its email client (step 6).

We use open source Hastymail [3] as the email client, which is written in PHP. We extend Hastymail with three important plugins: encryption, decryption, and key management. The encryption plugin encrypts the email that will be sent out and the decryption plugin decrypts the encrypted emails (before or after re-encrypted) that are downloaded from S3. On the other hand, we use Apache JAMES [2] as the email server, which is responsible to upload the incom-

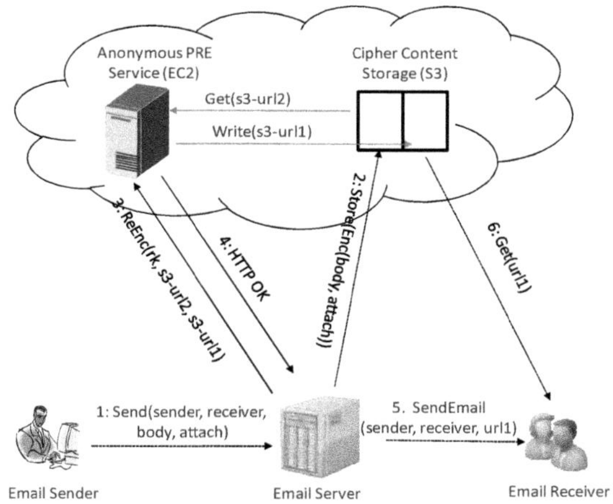

Figure 1: System overview of cloud-based email forwarding service with anonymous PRE.

ing email objects to S3, invoke the proxy service, and send (or broadcast) forwarding emails to appropriate receivers.

Experiment evaluation: We evaluate the system performance with two different EC2 instances:

- Small Instance: One core CPU of 1 ECU and 1.7GB memory;
- Medium Instance: Two core CPU of 5 ECUs and 1.7GB memory,

where an ECU provides the equivalent CPU capacity of 1.0-1.2 GHz 2007 Opteron or 2007 Xeon processor. In particular, we are interested in the execution time on the re-encryption operation by the proxy service.

We model the scenario that the proxy service receives 1,000 re-encryption requests simultaneously from the email server. The sizes of plaintexts for emails are 8KB, 32KB, and 128KB respectively, which are close to the size of emails in reality. we measure the execution time by the proxy service, including downloading second level ciphertexts from S3, performing re-encryption operations, and uploading first level ciphertexts to S3. Note here we do not encrypt plaintext with hybrid encryption methodology [14]: Encrypt the symmetric key with the PRE, and then encrypt plaintext with symmetric encryption. Instead we divide plaintexts into multiple blocks and encrypt each block individually.

As shown in Figure 2, we can see that the performance of the proxy service is acceptable. Taking the Medium Instance as an example, an email of 8KB can be re-encrypted around 2.3 second, and an email of 128KB around 40 seconds. Second, the computation capability has a positive influence on the re-encryption operations: the operation in the Medium Instance costs less time than that in the Small Instance.

Security properties: We use our anonymous PRE scheme to reduce the trust of cloud for email forwarding, which is ideal for large volume email sending, e.g., group email distribution. As an incoming email is encrypted with a user's (or an organization's) public key, the cloud based proxy service cannot access the encrypted content without its private key, which is stored in an isolated domain (Hastymail in our case). Furthermore, since users' private keys are maintained locally and re-encryption keys are generated out of cloud,

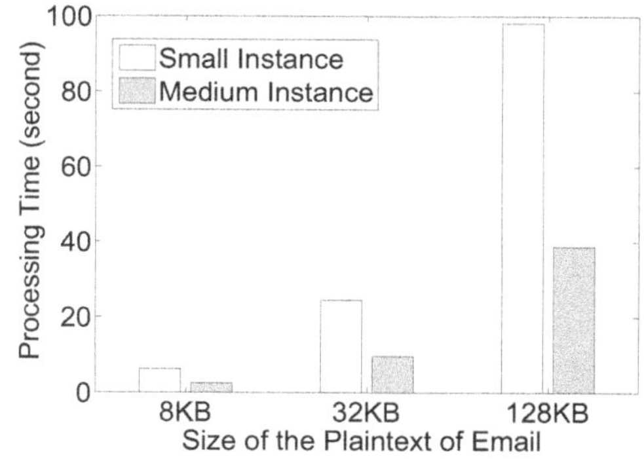

Figure 2: Average processing time for re-encryption in the cloud (one request).

the cloud cannot infer any identities information due to the anonymous property in our PRE scheme. Therefore, the identities of the re-encryption participants are kept private.

5. RELATED WORK

The cryptographic primitive of Proxy Re-Encryption (PRE) was formalized in [8] and has become an important building block for constructing cryptographic solutions to many application problems [6, 10, 11, 23, 24]. Various features of PRE have been investigated: e.g. [5] initiated the anonymity property, [9, 17] constructed CCA security PRE, [12] proposed efficient PRE construction and [21] enriched the PRE with conditional re-encryption feature.

The anonymity (key privacy) of PRE was first initiated in [5], where they assumed that only one re-encryption key existing for each pair of users. In addition, their proposed PRE scheme achieved security against chosen-plaintext attacks based on the DBDH assumption, and left constructing anonymous CCA-secure PRE as an open problem. Another anonymity notion came from the work [19], where allowed multiple re-encryption keys for each pair of users while lacking access to the re-encryption oracleïijŇ which weakened the adversary's capability as explained in Section 1. Their proposed scheme [19] achieved their defined anonymity and enjoyed the security against chosen-ciphertext attack in the random oracle. Another work [20] claimed attaining the security against chosen-ciphertext attack and the anonymity property simultaneously, but later was proved not CCA secure.

In order to achieve chosen-ciphertext security, the work [9] first formalized the notion of security against chosen-ciphertext attacks for PRE and presented an efficient construction satisfying that. The subsequent work on achieving CCA security can be found in [12, 17, 22, 16, 18]. To achieve both anonymity and CCA security in PRE, the construction is quite difficult, since the CPA-to-CCA translations, such as the Fujisaki-Okamoto transformation cannot be applied directly [5, 20].

6. CONCLUSION

We consider the identity privacy problem for proxy re-encryption, which is useful when cloud users outsource re-encryption operations to public clouds. We propose a new anonymity notion by comprehensively considering the limitations of existing anonymity notions. We then present an efficient construction, which achieves the anonymity and security against chosen-ciphertext attack in random oracle simultaneously. We implement and deploy our proposed scheme in Amazon Web Services, based on which we develop the prototype of secure email forwarding with anonymous re-encryption. Our evaluation shows that the performance is acceptable for many web-based applications. Our future work includes designing anonymous and CCA secure PRE in the standard model.

7. REFERENCES

[1] Amazon web service. `http://aws.amazon.com/`.

[2] Apache james. `http://projects.apache.org/projects/james.html`.

[3] Hastymail. `http://www.hastymail.org/`.

[4] Pairing-based cryptography library. `http://crypto.stanford.edu/pbc/`.

[5] G. Ateniese, K. Benson, and S. Hohenberger. Key-private proxy re-encryption. In *Proceedings of the The Cryptographers' Track at the RSA Conference 2009 on Topics in Cryptology*, CT-RSA '09, pages 279–294, Berlin, Heidelberg, 2009. Springer-Verlag.

[6] G. Ateniese, K. Fu, M. Green, and S. Hohenberger. Improved proxy re-encryption schemes with applications to secure distributed storage. volume 9, pages 1–30, New York, NY, USA, February 2006. ACM.

[7] M. Bellare, A. Boldyreva, A. Desai, and D. Pointcheval. Key-privacy in public-key encryption. In *Proceedings of the 7th International Conference on the Theory and Application of Cryptology and Information Security: Advances in Cryptology*, ASIACRYPT '01, pages 566–582, London, UK, UK, 2001. Springer-Verlag.

[8] M. Blaze, G. Bleumer, and M. Strauss. Divertible protocols and atomic proxy cryptography. In *In EUROCRYPT*, pages 127–144. Springer-Verlag, 1998.

[9] R. Canetti and S. Hohenberger. Chosen-ciphertext secure proxy re-encryption. In *Proceedings of the 14th ACM conference on Computer and communications security*, CCS '07, pages 185–194, New York, NY, USA, 2007. ACM.

[10] Y.-R. Chen, C.-K. Chu, W.-G. Tzeng, and J. Zhou. Cloudhka: A cryptographic approach for hierarchical access control in cloud computing. In *Proceedings of the 11th International Conference on Applied Cryptography and Network Security*, ACNS'13, pages 37–52, Berlin, Heidelberg, 2013. Springer-Verlag.

[11] Y.-R. Chen, J. D. Tygar, and W.-G. Tzeng. Secure group key management using uni-directional proxy re-encryption schemes. In *INFOCOM*, pages 1952–1960, 2011.

[12] R. H. Deng, J. Weng, S. Liu, and K. Chen. Chosen-ciphertext secure proxy re-encryption without pairings. In *Proceedings of the 7th International Conference on Cryptology and Network Security*, CANS '08, pages 1–17, Berlin, Heidelberg, 2008. Springer-Verlag.

[13] E. Fujisaki and T. Okamoto. Secure integration of asymmetric and symmetric encryption schemes. In *Proceedings of the 19th Annual International Cryptology Conference on Advances in Cryptology*, CRYPTO '99, pages 537–554, London, UK, 1999. Springer-Verlag.

[14] D. Hofheinz and E. Kiltz. Secure hybrid encryption from weakened key encapsulation. In *CRYPTO*, pages 553–571, 2007.

[15] T. Isshiki, M. H. Nguyen, and K. Tanaka. Proxy re-encryption in a stronger security model extended from ct-rsa2012. In *CT-RSA*, pages 277–292, 2013.

[16] X. Jia, J. Shao, J. Jing, and P. Liu. Cca-secure type-based proxy re-encryption with invisible proxy. In *CIT*, pages 1299–1305, 2010.

[17] B. Libert and D. Vergnaud. Unidirectional chosen-ciphertext secure proxy re-encryption. In *Proceedings of the Practice and theory in public key cryptography, 11th international conference on Public key cryptography*, PKC'08, pages 360–379, Berlin, Heidelberg, 2008. Springer-Verlag.

[18] T. Matsuda, R. Nishimaki, and K. Tanaka. Cca proxy re-encryption without bilinear maps in the standard model. In *Proceedings of the 13th international conference on Practice and Theory in Public Key Cryptography*, PKC'10, pages 261–278, Berlin, Heidelberg, 2010. Springer-Verlag.

[19] J. Shao, P. Liu, G. Wei, and Y. Ling. Anonymous proxy re-encryption. volume 5, pages 439–449. John Wiley & Sons, Ltd, 2012.

[20] J. Shao, P. Liu, and Y. Zhou. Achieving key privacy without losing cca security in proxy re-encryption. In *Journal of Systems and Software*, 2011.

[21] J. Weng, R. H. Deng, X. Ding, C.-K. Chu, and J. Lai. Conditional proxy re-encryption secure against chosen-ciphertext attack. In *ASIACCS*, pages 322–332, 2009.

[22] J. Weng, Y. Yang, Q. Tang, R. H. Deng, and F. Bao. Efficient conditional proxy re-encryption with chosen-ciphertext security. In *Proceedings of the 12th International Conference on Information Security*, ISC '09, pages 151–166, Berlin, Heidelberg, 2009. Springer-Verlag.

[23] H. Xiong, X. Zhang, W. Zhu, and D. Yao. Cloudseal: End-to-end content protection in cloud-based storage and delivery services. In *SecureComm*, pages 491–500, 2011.

[24] K. Yang, X. Jia, and K. Ren. Attribute-based fine-grained access control with efficient revocation in cloud storage systems. In *ASIACCS*, pages 523–528, 2013.

[25] F. Zhang, R. Safavi-Naini, and W. Susilo. An efficient signature scheme from bilinear pairings and its applications. In *Public Key Cryptography*, pages 277–290, 2004.

Efficient, Context-Aware Privacy Leakage Confinement for Android Applications without Firmware Modding

Mu Zhang
Department of EECS
Syracuse University
Syracuse, USA
muzhang@syr.edu

Heng Yin
Department of EECS
Syracuse University
Syracuse, USA
heyin@syr.edu

ABSTRACT

As Android has become the most prevalent operating system in mobile devices, privacy concerns in the Android platform are increasing. A mechanism for efficient runtime enforcement of information-flow security policies in Android apps is desirable to confine privacy leakage. The prior works towards this problem require firmware modification (i.e., modding) and incur considerable runtime overhead. Besides, no effective mechanism is in place to distinguish malicious privacy leakage from those of legitimate uses. In this paper, we take a bytecode rewriting approach. Given an unknown Android app, we selectively insert instrumentation code into the app to keep track of private information and detect leakage at runtime. To distinguish legitimate and malicious leaks, we model the user's decisions with a context-aware policy enforcement mechanism. We have implemented a prototype called `Capper` and evaluated its efficacy on confining privacy-breaching apps. Our evaluation on 4723 real-world Android applications demonstrates that `Capper` can effectively track and mitigate privacy leaks. Moreover, after going through a series of optimizations, the instrumentation code only represents a small portion (4.48% on average) of the entire program. The runtime overhead introduced by `Capper` is also minimal, merely 1.5% for intensive data propagation.

Categories and Subject Descriptors

D.2.4 [**Software Engineering**]: Software/Program Verification—*Validation*; D.4.6 [**Operating Systems**]: Security and Protection—*Information flow controls*

General Terms

Security

Keywords

Android; Privacy leakage; Context-aware policy; Bytecode rewriting

ASIA CCS'14, June 4–6, 2014, Kyoto, Japan.

http://dx.doi.org/10.1145/2590296.2590312.

1. INTRODUCTION

Android continues to dominate in the battle to be the top smartphone system in the world, and ranked as the top smartphone platform with 52 percent market share (71.1 million subscribers) in Q1 2013. The success of Android is also reflected from the popularity of its application markets. Tens of thousands of Android apps become available in Google Play while popular apps (e.g., Adobe Flash Player 11) have been downloaded and installed over 100 million times.

Meanwhile, privacy concerns in the Android platform are increasing. Previous studies [12, 13, 19, 31, 36, 38] have exposed that both benign and malicious apps are stealthily leaking users' private information to remote servers. Efforts have also been made to detect and analyze privacy leakage either statically or dynamically [12, 13, 17, 21, 24, 25, 34]. Nevertheless, a good solution to defeat privacy leakage at runtime is still lacking. We argue that a practical solution needs to achieve the following goals:

- **Information-flow based security.** Privacy leakage is fundamentally an information flow security problem. A desirable solution to defeat privacy leakage would detect sensitive information flow and block it right at the sinks. However, most of prior efforts to this problem are "end-point" solutions. Some earlier solutions extended Android's install-time constraints and enriched Android permissions [14, 29]. Some aimed at enforcing permissions in a finer-grained manner and in a more flexible way [6, 8, 27, 39]. Some attempted to improve isolation on various levels and each isolated component could be assigned with a different set of permissions [5, 22, 30]. In addition, efforts were made to introduce supplementary user consent acquisition mechanism, so that access to sensitive resource also requires user approval [23, 32]. All these "end-point" solutions only mediate the access to private information, without directly tackling the privacy leakage problem.
- **Low runtime overhead.** An information-flow based solution must have very low runtime overhead to be adopted on end users' devices. To directly address privacy leakage problem, Hornyack et al. proposed AppFence to enforce information flow policies at runtime [19]. With support of TaintDroid [12], AppFence keeps track of the propagation of private information. Once privacy leakage is detected, AppFence either blocks the leakage at the sink or shuffle the information from the source. Though effective in terms of blocking privacy leakage, its efficiency is not favorable. Due to the taint tracking on every single Dalvik bytecode instruction, AppFence incurs significant performance overhead.
- **No firmware modding.** For a practical solution to be widely adopted, it is also crucial to avoid firmware modding. Unfor-

tunately, the existing information-flow based solutions such as AppFence require modifications on the stock software stack, making it difficult to be deployed on millions of mobile devices.

- **Context-aware policy enforcement.** Many apps need to access user's privacy for legitimate functionalities and these information flows should not be stopped. Therefore, to defeat privacy leakage without compromising legitimate functionality, a good solution needs to be aware of the context where a sensitive information flow is observed and make appropriate security decisions. To the best of our knowledge, we are not aware that such a policy mechanism exists.

In this paper, we aim to achieve all these design goals by taking a bytecode rewriting approach. Given an unknown Android app, we selectively rewrite the program by inserting bytecode instructions for tracking sensitive information flows *only* in certain fractions of the program (which are called taint slices) that are potentially involved in information leakage. When an information leakage is actually observed at a sink node (e.g., an HTTP Post operation), this behavior along with the program context is sent to the policy management service installed on the device and the user will be notified to make an appropriate decision. For example, the rewritten app may detect the location information being sent out to a Google server while the user is navigating with Google Map, and notify the user. Since the user is actively interacting with the device and understands the context very well, he or she can make a proper decision. In this case, the user will allow this behavior. To ensure good user experiences, the number of such prompts must be minimized. To do so, our policy service needs to accurately model the context for the user's decisions. As a result, when an information leakage happens in the same context, the same decision can be made without raising a prompt. After exploring the design space of the context modeling and making a balance between sensitivity, performance overhead, and robustness, we choose to model the context using *parameterized source and sink pairs*.

Consequently, our approach fulfills all the requirements: 1) actual privacy leaks are captured accurately at runtime, with the support of inserted taint tracking code; 2) the performance overhead of our approach is minimal, due to the static dataflow analysis in advance and numerous optimizations that are applied to the instrumentation code; 3) the deployment of our approach is simple, as we only rewrite the original app to enforce certain information flow policies and no firmware modification is needed; 4) policy enforcement is context-aware, because the user's decisions are associated with abstract program contexts.

We implement a prototype, `Capper`[1], in 16 thousand lines of Java code, based on the Java bytecode optimization framework Soot [3]. We leverage Soot's capability to perform static dataflow analysis and bytecode instrumentation. We evaluate our tool on 4723 real-world privacy-breaching Android apps. Our experiments show that rewritten programs run correctly after instrumentation, while privacy leakage is effectively eliminated.

Contributions.

In summary, this paper makes the following contributions:

- We propose a bytecode rewriting approach to the problem of privacy leaks in Android applications. It requires no firmware changes and incurs minimal performance impact.

[1] `Capper` is short for Context-Aware Privacy Policy Enforcement with Re-writing.

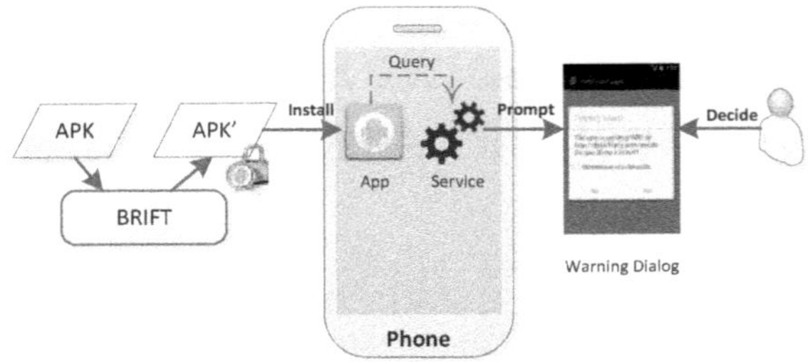

Figure 1: Architecture of `Capper`

- We design a novel mechanism to model program contexts with user knowledge. This helps differentiate between benign operations on sensitive data and actual privacy leakage.

- We evaluate `Capper` on 4723 real Android apps. The experiments show that our approach is both effective and efficient. We demonstrate that rewritten programs run correctly after instrumentation, while privacy leakage is effectively eliminated. We show that only a small portion (2.48% on average) of the program needs to be instrumented and after a series of optimizations the final program size increases only 4.48% on average. We also show that our runtime overhead is minimal, merely 1.5% for intensive data propagation.

2. APPROACH OVERVIEW

In this section, we present an overview of our technique. Further, we define the problem scope and provide a running example.

2.1 Key Techniques

Figure 1 depicts an overview of our techniques. When a user is about to install an app onto his Android device, this app will go through our bytecode rewriting engine (BRIFT) and be rewritten into a new app, in which sensitive information flows are monitored by the inserted bytecode instructions. Therefore, when this new app is actually running on the device and is observed to send out sensitive information, this behavior (along with the program context) will be reported to the policy management service for decision.

If this behavior under this program context is observed for the first time, the policy management service will prompt the user to make a proper decision: either allow or deny such a behavior. The user's decision will be recorded along with the program context, so the policy management service will make the recorded decision for the same behaviors under the same context.

Therefore, our solution to defeat privacy leakage consists of the following two enabling techniques.

(1) Bytecode Rewriting for Information Flow Control.

Given a bytecode program, the goal of our bytecode rewriting is to insert a minimum amount of bytecode instructions into the bytecode program to trace the propagation of certain sensitive information flows (or taint). To achieve this goal, we first conduct static dataflow analysis to compute a number of program slices that are involved in the taint propagation. Then we insert bytecode instructions along the program slices to keep track of taint propagation at runtime. Further, we perform a series of optimizations to reduce the amount of inserted instructions. More details are presented in Section 3.

(2) Context-aware Policy Enforcement.

The user allows or denies a certain information flow in a specific context. The key for a context-aware policy enforcement is to properly model the context. The context modeling must be sensitive enough to distinguish different program contexts, but not too sensitive. Otherwise, a slight difference in the program execution may be treated as a new context and may cause unnecessarily annoying prompts to the user. Further, the context modeling should also be robust enough to counter mimicry attacks. An attacker may be able to "mimic" a legitimate program context to bypass the context-aware policy enforcement. We present more details about the context modeling and policy enforcement in Section 4.

2.2 Problem Scope

Our proposed solution is designed to enforce user preferred privacy policy on innocent Android apps. Our solution can be used to block privacy leakage in most of current Android malware apps, but a dedicated malware author can still find ways to circumvent our confinement. For instance, malware can exfiltrate private information through side channels (such as implicit flows and timing channels). Most of previous solutions (including dynamic monitoring and static analysis approaches) share the same limitation. Moreover, the proposed technique (again shared by most of previous solutions) cannot handle native components and Java reflective calls in a general way. In rare occasions, our system will raise a warning to the user that the rewritten app may still be unsafe if we observe a JNI call or a reflective call appears on the information propagation path. According to our experimental evaluation in Section 5, only a small fraction (5%) of apps belong to this category. In this case, a security-conscious user may decide not to use this unsafe app or resort to other solutions.

2.3 Running Example

To elaborate the whole process, we use a synthetic running example to explain our approach. Figure 2 presents our synthetic running example in Java source code. More concretely, the example class extends an Android `Activity` and overrides several callbacks including `onStart()`, `onResume()` and `onDestroy()`. When the `Activity` starts, `onStart()` method will get the device identifier by calling `getIMEI()`, which returns the real device ID if it succeeds or empty string otherwise. On receiving the return value from `getIMEI()`, the program stores it to a static field `deviceId`. Further, both `onResume()` and `onDestroy()` read the device ID from this static field but use it for different purposes. While `onResume()` shows the device ID on screen via a `Toast` notification, `onDestroy()` encrypts it and sends it to a remote server through a raw socket. In Section 3 and 4 , we show how to perform bytecode rewriting and mitigate privacy leakage with this example.

3. BYTECODE REWRITING

We leverage our `BRIFT`[2] engine to insert the information flow control logic into a given Android app. BRIFT takes the following steps to rewrite a bytecode program: 1) it first translates the Dalvik executable (i.e., DEX file) to an intermediate representation (IR) to facilitate analysis and instrumentation; 2) it performs application-wide static dataflow analysis on IR to identify program slices for information leakage; 3) to keep track of data propagation and prevent the actual information leakage, it instruments the IR by inserting new IR statements along the program slices; 4) to further improve performance, it applies a series of optimization methods to remove redundant and unnecessary IR statements; and 5) in the end, it generates a new Dalvik executable from the IR and uses it

[2]It is short for Bytecode Rewriting for Information Flow Tracking

```
public class Leakage extends Activity{
  private byte key = DEFAULT_KEY;
  private String addr = DEFAULT_ADDR;
  private static String deviceId;

  public String getIMEI(){
    TelephonyManager manager = (TelephonyManager)
     getSystemService("phone");
    String imei = manager.getDeviceId();
    if(imei==null){
      imei = "";
    }else{
      imei = manager.getDeviceId();
    }
    return imei;
  }

  public byte crypt(byte plain){
    return (byte)(plain ^ key);
  }

  public void post(String addr, byte[] bytes){
    OutputStream output = conn.getOutputStream();
    output.write(bytes, 0, bytes.length);
    ...
  }

  public void toastIMEI(String imei){
    Context app = getApplicationContext();
    String text = "Your IMEI is " + imei;
    int duration = Toast.LENGTH_SHORT;
    Toast toast = Toast.makeText(app, text, duration);
    toast.show();
  }

  public void onStart(){
    Leakage.deviceId = getIMEI();
  }

  public void onResume(){
    toastIMEI(Leakage.deviceId);
  }

  public void onDestroy(){
    String imei = Leakage.deviceId;
    byte[] bytes = imei.getBytes();
    for(int i=0; i<bytes.length; i++){
      bytes[i] = crypt(bytes[i]);
    }
    post(addr, bytes);
  }
}
```

Figure 2: Java Code for the Running Sample

to repackage the new .apk file. We give a brief explanation for each step as below. For more details, please refer to our prior work [35].

3.1 Converting DEX into IR

An Android app generally consists of two parts, resources and a Dalvik executable file. Our bytecode rewriting is performed on the Dalvik executable file, so the resources remain the same, and will be repackaged into the new app in the last step. To convert DEX into IR, we first convert the DEX into a Java bytecode program using dex2jar [1][3] and then translate the Java bytecode into an intermediate representation with Soot [3]. More specifically, Soot produces Jimple IR to facilitate subsequent dataflow analysis and instrumentation.

3.2 Application-wide Dataflow Analysis

On Jimple IR, we perform flow-sensitive context-sensitive interprocedural analysis to track the propagation of certain *tainted* sensitive information and detect if the taint propagates into the sinks (e.g., Internet and file system). The result of this forward dataflow

[3]It is also possible to use alternative tools, such as Dare [28], ded [13], etc., for this conversion.

analysis is a taint propagation graph. If one or more sinks appear in this graph, it indicates a potential information leakage. Then for each sink in the graph, we perform backward dependency analysis to compute a "slice". Taint propagation outside this slice is irrelevant to the leakage and thus can be ignored. We call this slice *taint slice*, because it represents a program slice that contributes to a leakage from an information source to a sink. We present the analysis result for the running example in Appendix A.

3.3 Static Instrumentation

Static dataflow analysis is usually conservative and may lead to false positives. Therefore, we insert instrumentation code in these taint propagation slices. The inserted code serves as runtime checks to actually keep track of the taint propagation while the Android application is running. The sinks are also instrumented to examine the taint and confine the information leakage.

We create shadows, for each data entity defined or used within the slices, to track its runtime taint status. The data entities outside the slices do not need to be shadowed, because they are irrelevant to the taint propagation. We create shadows for different types of data entities individually. Static or instance fields are shadowed by adding boolean fields into the same class definition. A local variable is shadowed with a boolean local variable within the same method scope, so that compiler optimizations can be applied smoothly on related instrument code.

Shadowing method parameters and return value requires special considerations. Firstly, the method prototype needs modification. Extra "shadow parameters" are added to parameter list to pass the shadows of actual parameters and return value from caller to callee. Secondly, parameters are passed-by-value in Java, and therefore primitive-typed local shadow variables (boolean) need to be wrapped as objects before passing to a callee. Otherwise, the change of shadows in the callee cannot be reflected in the caller. To this end, we define a new class `BoolWrapper`. This class only contains one boolean instance field, which holds the taint status, and a default constructor, as shown below. Notice that the Java `Boolean` class cannot serve the same purpose because it is treated the same as primitive boolean type once passed as parameter.

```
public class BoolWrapper extends java.lang.Object{
  public boolean b;
  public void <init>(){
    BoolWrapper r0;
    r0 := @this: BoolWrapper;
    specialinvoke r0.<java.lang.Object: void <init>()>();
    return; }
}
```

With the created shadows, we instrument sources, data propagation code and sinks. At the source of information flow, we introduce taint by setting the corresponding shadow variable to "true". For data propagation code, we instrument an individual instruction depending on its type. 1) If the instruction is an assignment statement or unary operation, we insert a definition statement on correlative shadow variables. 2) If it is a binary operation, a binary OR statement is inserted to operate on shadow variables. If one of the operators is a constant, we replace its shadow with a constant "false". 3) Or, if it is a function call, we need to add code to bind shadows of actual parameters and return value to shadow parameters. 4) Further, if the instruction is a API call, we model and instrument the API with its taint propagation logic.

We generally put APIs into the following categories and handle each category with a different model. "get" APIs have straightforward taint propagation logic, always propagating taint from parameters to their return values. Therefore, we generate a default rule, which propagates taint from any of the input parameters to the return value. Similarly, simple "set" APIs are modeled as they propagate taint from one parameter to another parameter or "this" reference. APIs like `Vector.add(Object)` inserts new elements into an aggregate construct and thus can be modeled as a binary operation, such that the object is tainted if it is already tainted or the newly added element is tainted. APIs like `android.content.ContentValues.put(String key, Byte value)` that operate on (key, value) pairs can have more precise handling. In this case, an element is stored and accessed according to a "key". To track taint more precisely, we keep a taint status for each key, so the taint for each (key, value) pair is updated individually.

Then, at the sink, we insert code before the sink API to check the taint status of the sensitive parameter. If it turns out the critical parameter is tainted, the inserted code will query a separate policy service app for decision and a warning dialog is then displayed to the user.

We also devise taint cleaning mechanism. That is, if a variable is redefined to be an untainted variable or a constant outside taint propagation slices, we thus insert a statement after that definition to set its shadow variable to 0 (false).

3.4 Optimization

We further optimize the added instrumentation code. This is to remove the redundant bytecode instructions that are inserted from the previous step. As Soot's built-in optimizations do not apply well on this instrumentation code, we devise three custom optimization techniques to safely manipulate the instrumentation code and remove redundant ones. Thereafter, the optimized code is now amenable to the built-in optimizations. Consequently, after going through both custom and built-in optimizations, the added instrumentation code can be reduced to a minimum, ensuring the best performance of the rewritten bytecode program.

To be more specific, we have devised four steps of optimizations, described as follows.

- **O1**: In instrumentation, we add a shadow parameter for every single actual parameter and return value. However, some of them are redundant because they don't contribute to taint propagations. Therefore, we can remove the inserted code which uses solely these unnecessary shadow parameters.
- **O2**: Next, we remove redundant shadow parameters from parameter list and adjust method prototype. Consequently, instrumentation code, that is used to initialize or update the taint status of these shadow parameters, can also be eliminated.
- **O3**: Further, if inserted taint tracking code is independent from the control-flow logic of a method, we can lift the tainting code from the method to its callers. Thus, the taint propagation logic is inlined.
- **O4**: After custom optimizations, instrumentation code is amenable to Soot's built-in optimization, such as constant propagation, dead code elimination, etc.

3.5 Code Generation

At last, we convert the modified Jimple IR into a new package (.apk file). More concretely, we translate the Jimple IR to Java package using Soot, and then re-target Java bytecode to Dalvik bytecode with Android SDK. In the end, we repackage the new DEX file with old resources and create the new .apk file.

3.6 Rewritten Running Example

Figure 3 presents the rewritten program after the instrumentation and optimizations. For the sake of readability, we present the rewritten code in Java as a "diff" to the original program, even though the rewritten program is actually generated on the Jimple IR level. The statements with numeric line numbers are from the original program, whereas those with special line number "**I**" are inserted statements. The underlines mark either newly introduced code or modified parts from old statements. We hereby use this code to exemplify our design and implementation choices.

We can see that a boolean variable `deviceId_s0_t` is created to shadow the static field `deviceId`. `"s0"` denotes the source label which distinguishes different taint sources, while `"_t"` is the suffix for shadow in our implementation. Then in `onStart()`, the shadow variable `deviceId_s0_t` is set to be the `"status"` field in an object `ret_s0_wrapper`.

`ret_s0_wrapper` is an object of `"BoolWrapper"` structure which is introduced for the purpose of wrapping and passing primitive-typed shadow variables. In `Start()`, such an object is created and passed to `getIMEI(BoolWrapper)`, and further will be updated in the latter with the shadow of return value.

The shadow return value of `getIMEI(BoolWrapper)` is obtained from the local shadow variable `imei_s0_t`, which is initialized to be "true" if privacy access branch is taken (Ln.12), or cleaned to be "false" if `imei` is set as a constant (Ln.10). Without a cleaning mechanism, the value of corresponding shadow variable will remain "true" even if the taint status has already changed.

In the method `onDestroy()`, `deviceId` is used and sensitive data can thus be propagated to `"bytes"` array. In the meantime, `bytes_s0_t`, the shadow of `"bytes"` array is also assigned with `deviceId_s0_t`. We here choose to keep one single shadow for an entire array for efficiency. Further, the array is passed to the `crypt()` method in a loop and we update its taint status in every iteration. It is notable that taint propagation was devised in the callee (i.e., `crypt()`) at the beginning. However, due to optimizations, the taint logic in `crypt()` has been lifted up to the body of `onDestroy()` and further optimized there.

In the end, the shadow of the byte array is wrapped and passed to `post()`, where a sink API `OutputStream.write()` is encountered. We check the taint status of its first parameter (i.e., data packet) and query the policy service for decision if it is tainted.

```
1  public class Leakage extends Activity{
     ...
4    private static String deviceId;
I    public static boolean deviceId_s0_t;
     ...
6    public String getIMEI(BoolWrapper ret_s0_wrapper){
       ...
8      String imei = manager.getDeviceId();
9      if(imei==null){
10       imei = "";
I        imei_s0_t = false;
11     }else{
12       imei = manager.getDeviceId();
I        imei_s0_t = true;
13     }
I      ret_s0_wrapper.status = imei_s0_t;
14     return imei;
15   }
     ...
21   public void post(String addr, byte[] bytes,
         BoolWrapper bytes_s0_wrapper){
I      boolean bytes_s0_t = bytes_s0_wrapper.status;
22     OutputStream output = conn.getOutputStream();
I      boolean isAllow = false;
I      if(bytes_s0_t == true)
I        isAllow = queryPolicyService(0, 0, addr);
I      if(isAllow){
23       output.write(bytes, 0, bytes.length);}
I      else{ ... }
24     ...
25   }
     ...
35   public void onStart(){
I      BoolWrapper ret_s0_wrapper = new BoolWrapper();
I      ret_s0_wrapper.status = false;
36     Leakage.deviceId = getIMEI(ret_s0_wrapper);
I      Leakage.deviceId_s0_t = ret_s0_wrapper.status;
37   }
     ...
43   public void onDestroy(){
44     String imei = Leakage.deviceId;
45     byte[] bytes = imei.getBytes();
I      boolean bytes_s0_t = Leakage.devicdId_s0_t;
46     for(int i=0; i<bytes.length; i++){
47       bytes[i] = crypt(bytes[i]);
I        bytes_s0_t = bytes_s0_t || false;
48     }
I      BoolWrapper bytes_s0_wrapper = new BoolWrapper();
I      bytes_s0_wrapper.status = bytes_s0_t;
49     post(addr, bytes, bytes_s0_wrapper);
50   }
51 }
```

Figure 3: Java Code for the Rewritten Program

4. CONTEXT-AWARE POLICY

Once our inserted monitoring code detects an actual privacy leakage, policy service will enforce privacy policy based on user preferences. To be specific, the service app inquires user's decision upon detection and offers the user options to either "one-time" or "always" allow or deny the specific privacy breaching flow. The user can then make her decision according to her user experience and the policy manager will remember users preference for future decision making situations if the "always" option is chosen.

There exist two advantages to enforce a privacy policy with user preference history. Firstly, it associates user decisions with certain program contexts and can thus selectively restrict privacy-related information flow under different circumstances. Privacy-related outbound traffic occurs in both benign and malicious semantics. However, from dataflow analysis perspective, it is fairly hard to distinguish between, for example, a coordinates-based query towards a benign map service and a location leakage via some covert malicious process within, say, a wallpaper app. On the contrary, it is fairly straight-forward for a user to tell the difference because she knows the application semantics. With human knowledge, it is possible to avert overly strict restriction and preserve usability to the largest extent.

Secondly, it avoids repetitive warning dialogs and improves user experience. Once an "always" decision is made, this decision will be remembered and used for the same scenario next time. Thus, the user doesn't need to face the annoying dialog message over and over again for the exactly identical situation.

However, it is non-trivial to appropriately model the program context specific to a user decision and the challenge lies in the way semantics is extracted from a dataflow point of view. We hereby discuss some possible options and our solution.

4.1 Taint Propagation Trace

To achieve high accuracy, we first consider using the exact execution trace as pattern to represent a specific information flow. An execution trace can be obtained at either instruction or method level. It consists of all the instructions or methods propagating sensitive data from a source to a sink, and therefore can uniquely describe a dataflow path. When a user decision is made for a certain information flow, its execution trace is computed and saved as a pattern along with user preference. Next time when a new leakage instance is detected, the trace computation will be done on the new flow and compared with saved ones. If there exists a match, action taken on the saved one will be applied correspondingly.

Nevertheless, there exist two major drawbacks with this approach. Firstly, dynamic tracing is considerably heavy-weight. Comparison of two traces is also fairly expensive. This may affect the responsiveness of interactive mobile apps. Secondly, each dataflow instance is modeled overly precisely. Since any execution divergence will lead to a different trace pattern, even if two leakage flows occur within the same semantics, it is still difficult to match their traces. This results in repeated warning messages for semantically equivalent privacy-related dataflows.

4.2 Source and Sink Call-sites

Trace-based approach is too expensive because the control granularity is extremely fine. We therefore attempt to relax the strictness and achieve balance in the accuracy-efficiency trade-off. We propose a call-site approach which combines source-sink call-sites to model privacy flow. That is to say, information flows of same source and sink call-sites are put into one category. Once an action is taken on one leakage flow, the same action will be taken on future sensitive information flow in the same category. To this end, we introduce labels for source and sink call-sites. Information flows starting from or arriving at these call-sites are associated with corresponding labels, so that they can be differentiated based on these labels.

With a significant improvement of efficiency, this approach is not as sensitive to program contexts as the traced-based one - different execution paths can start from the same origin and end at the same sink. However, we rarely observed this inaccuracy in practice because the app execution with same source and sink call-sites usually represents constant semantics.

4.3 Parameterized Source and Sink Pairs

In addition to source/sink call-sites, parameters fed into these call-sites APIs are also crucial to the semantic contexts. For example, the user may allow an app to send data to certain trustworthy URLs but may not be willing to allow access to the others. Therefore, it is important to compare critical parameters to determine if a new observed flow matches the ones in history.

Notice that checking parameters can minimize the impact of mimicry attack. Prior research shows that vulnerable Android apps are subject to various attacks [9, 16, 18, 24, 37]. For instance, an exposed vulnerable app component can be exploited to leak private information to an attacker-specified URL. Without considering the URL parameter, it is difficult, if not possible, to distinguish internal use of critical call-sites from hijacking the same call-sites to target a malicious URL. Once a flow through some call-sites is allowed and user preference is saved, mimicking attack using same call-sites will also get approved. On the contrary, a parameter-aware approach can differentiate outgoing dataflows according to the destination URL, and thus, exploitation of a previously allowed call-sites will still raise a warning.

API Description	Source or Sink	Critical Parameter
Send data to Internet	Sink	destination URL
Send SMS message	Sink	target phone number
Query contacts database	Source	source URI

Table 1: APIs and Critical Parameters

Besides the URL of a Internet API, we also consider some other critical combinations of an API and its parameter. Table 1 summarizes our list. The target of a sink API is sensitive to security. Similar to Internet APIs, target phone numbers are crucial to `sendTextMessage()` APIs and thus need watching. On the other hand, some source call-sites also need to be distinguished according to the parameters. For instance, the API that queries contacts list may obtain different data depending on the input URI (e.g., `ContactsContract.CommonDataKinds.Phone` for phone number, `ContactsContract.CommonDataKinds.Email` for email).

4.4 Implementation

We implement the policy service as a separate app. This isolation guarantees the security of the service app and its saved policies. In other words, even if the client is exploited, the service is not affected or compromised, and can still correctly enforce privacy policies.

The service app communicates with a rewritten client app solely through Android IPC. Once a client app wants to query the service, it encapsulates the labels of source and sink call-sites as well as the specific critical parameter into an `Intent` as extra data payload. The client app is then blocked and waiting for a response. Since this transaction is usually fast, the blocking won't affect the responsiveness of the app mostly. On the service side, it decodes the data and searches for a match in its database. If there exists a match, it returns immediately with the saved action to the client. Otherwise, the service app will display a dialog message within a created `Activity`. The user decision is saved if the user prefers, or not saved otherwise. Either way, user's option is sent back to the client. On receiving the response from service, the rewritten app will either continue its execution or skip the sink call-site with respect to the reply.

It is noteworthy that we have to defend against spoofing attack and prevent forged messages from being sent to a client app. To address that, we instrument the client app to listen for the service reply with a dynamically registered `BroadcastReceiver`. When a broadcast message is received, the receiver is immediately unregistered. Thus, attack window is reduced due to this on-demand receiver registration. Further, to restrict who can send the broadcast, we protect the receiver with a custom `permission`. Broadcaster without this `permission` is therefore unable to send messages to the client app. To defeat replay attack, we also embed a session token in the initial query message, and the client app can therefore authenticate the sender of a response message.

Similarly, we need to protect a policy service from spoofing, too. The service app has to check the caller identity from a bound communication via `getCallingUid()`, so that a malicious application cannot pretend to be another app and trick the service to configure the policies for the latter.

4.5 Policy Enforcement in Running Example

We distinguish an information flow based on call-sites and their critical input. Therefore, here in this example, `queryPolicyService()` takes three parameters. The first "0" and second "0" represent the labels of source and sink call-sites, respectively. The third one is an object taking the critical input and is specific to a call-site API.

With the reply from policy service (i.e., `isAllow`), the enforcement logic devised in the app will be exercised. If the user decision is to block the dataflow, we need to properly skip the `output.write()` and disable the leakage.

5. EXPERIMENTAL EVALUATION

To evaluate the efficacy, correctness and efficiency of `Capper`, we conducted experiments on real-world Android applications. In the policy setting, we consider IMEI, owner's phone number, location, contacts to be the sensitive information sources, and network output APIs (e.g., `OutputStream.write()`, `HttpClient.execute()`, `WebView.loadUrl()`, `URLConnection.openConnection()` and `SmsManager.sendTextMessage()`) as the sinks. The action on the sink can be "block" or "allow". User can also check an "always" option to have the same rule applied to future cases of the same semantic context. Note that this policy is mainly for demonstrating the usability of `Capper`. More work is needed to define a more complete policy for privacy leakage confinement.

We first present our experiment setup and in Section 5.1. We then discuss summarized analysis results in Section 5.2, and describe a detailed analysis in Section 5.3. Finally we measure the runtime performance in Section 5.4.

5.1 Experiment Setup

We collect 11,939 real-world Android applications from Google Play, and perform a preparatory package-level investigation into these apps.

Use of Native Components.

Out of the 11,939 apps, 2631 of them enclose at least one native library in the package. This shows that a small portion of Android apps (22%) need auxiliary native code to function. In addition, we discover that a large amount of these native libraries are commonly used across these apps. These native libraries are often used for video/audio processing, encoding/decoding, etc. For example, libandroidgl20.so, an OpenGL graphical library for Android system, is used by 265 apps.

Framework Compatibility.

Fragmentation is a well-known issue for Android platform. Apps are developed with different versions of framework SDK, as well as supporting libraries including Google Maps, Google Analytics, Admob, and therefore require different sets of Google APIs for analysis and instrumentation. In our experiment, we prepare a set of specific libraries which consist of Android SDK of API level 16 (Android 4.1, Jelly Bean), Google Maps of API level 16, Google Analytics SDK v2 and Google Admob SDK, version 6.2.1. We then inspect the Manifest files and exclude those apps that don't fit into our setting. In the end, we obtain 4915 applications and use them as our experiment sample set. Of course, to use `Capper` in the field, multiple sets of APIs are needed to accommodate diverse SDK requirements in the apps.

We then perform bytecode rewriting on these apps to enable runtime privacy protection. We conduct the experiment on our test machine, which is equipped with Intel(R) Xeon(R) CPU E5-2690 (20M Cache, 2.90GHz) and 200GB of physical memory. The operating system is CentOS 6.3 (64bit).

To verify the effectiveness and evaluate runtime performance of the rewritten apps, we further run them on a real device. Experiments are carried out on Google Nexus S, with Android OS version 4.0.4.

5.2 Summarized Analysis Results

Figure 4 illustrates the partition of 4915 realworld apps. Amongst these apps, `Capper` did not finish analyzing 314 of them within 30 minutes. These apps are fairly large (many over 10 MB). Application-wide dataflow analysis is known to be expensive for these large programs. We further extended the analysis timeout to 3 hours, and 122 more apps were successfully analyzed and rewritten. Given sufficient analysis time, we believe that the success rate can further increase from currently 96% to nearly 100%.

Out of the 4723 apps that were completely processed by `Capper`, 1414 apps may leak private information, according to our static analysis, and `Capper` successfully performed bytecode rewriting on them. We observed that most of them leak IMEI and location information. These types of information are frequently sent out by apps due to analytic or advertisement reasons. Apps may also sometimes leak owner's phone number or phone numbers from contacts. For the rest of them (67%), static analysis couldn't find a viable path from the sensitive information sources to the network output sinks. It means that these apps do not leak private information, so no rewriting is needed for these apps.

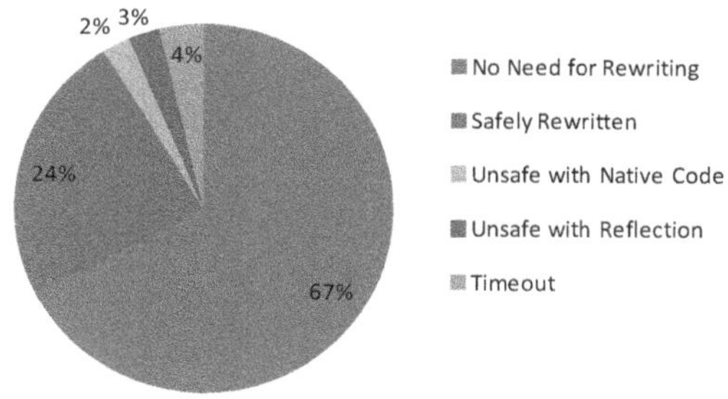

Figure 4: Bytecode Rewriting Results on 4915 Realworld Android Apps

For these 1414 apps that were rewritten, we further investigate their use of native code and reflection. Our study shows that unknown native code is invoked within the taint slices for 118 (2%) apps. As a bytecode-level solution, our system cannot keep track of information flow processing in the native code. So the information flow may be broken on these unknown native calls. The rest 3% contain reflective calls within the slices. If the class name and method name cannot be resolved statically, we do not know how information is propagated through this function. Therefore, totally 5% apps may be unsafe and may not be fully enforced with the specified policies. The best suggestion for the end user is not to use these unsafe rewritten apps due to the potential incompleteness in policy enforcement. More discussion on this issue is presented in Section 6.

We compute the taint propagation slice for each single leakage instance, and conduct a quantitative study on them. Figure 5a gives the number of generated taint propagation slices for every app. While most of the apps retrieve privacy-related information moderately, some apps leak user's privacy through up to 31 taint slices. Such apps usually enclose various Ads libraries, each of which acquires private data separately.

Figure 5b shows the proportional size of the slices, compared to the total size of the application. We can see that most of the program slices represent a small portion of the entire application, with the average proportion being 2.48%. However, we do observe that for a few applications, the slices take up to 54% of the total size. Some samples (e.g., com.tarsin.android.dilbert) are fairly small. Although the total slice size is only up to several thousands Jimple statements, the relative percentage becomes high. Apps like de.joergjahnke.mario.android.free and de.schildbach.oeffi operate on privacy information in an excessive way, and due to the conservative nature of static analysis, many static and instance fields are involved in the slices.

We measure the program size on different stages. We observe that the increase of the program size is roughly proportional to the slice size, which is expected. After instrumentation, the increased size is, on average, 10.45% compared to the original program. Figure 6 further visualizes the impact of the four optimizations to demonstrate their performance. The six curves on the figure represent the relative size of the program, compared to the original application, on different processing stages, respectively. The baseline stands for the size of the original program, while the top curve is that of instrumentation stage. We can see that 1) for most of these apps, the increase of program size due to instrumentation is

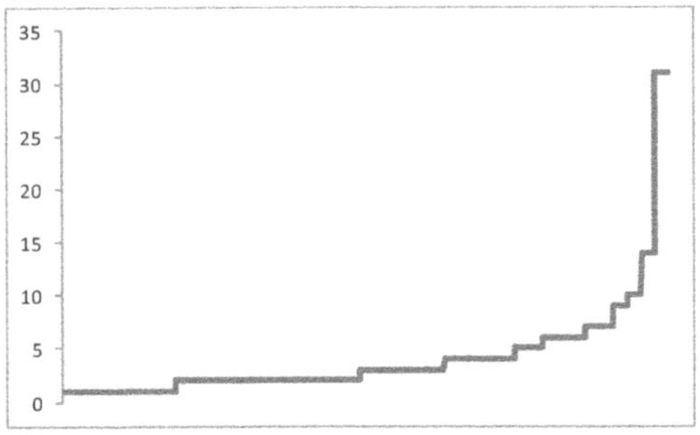

(a) **Number of Taint Slices.** X-axis is app ID; Y-axis is the number of taint slices.

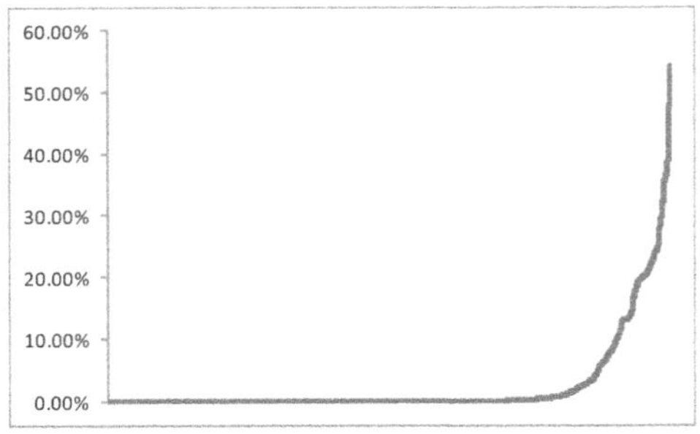

(b) **Proportional Size of Slices.** X-axis is app ID; Y-axis is the proportional size of slices.

Figure 5: Results for Taint Propagation Slices

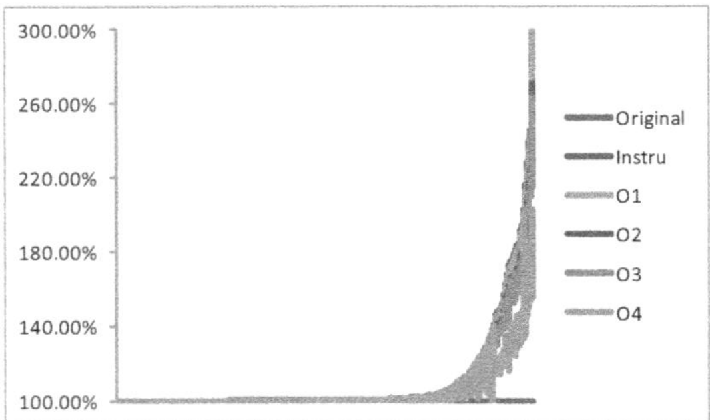

Figure 6: **Optimization Impact on LOC.** X-axis is app ID, while Y-axis is the proportional app size. The result is sorted based on Y-axis. Six curves quantify these sizes at different stages.

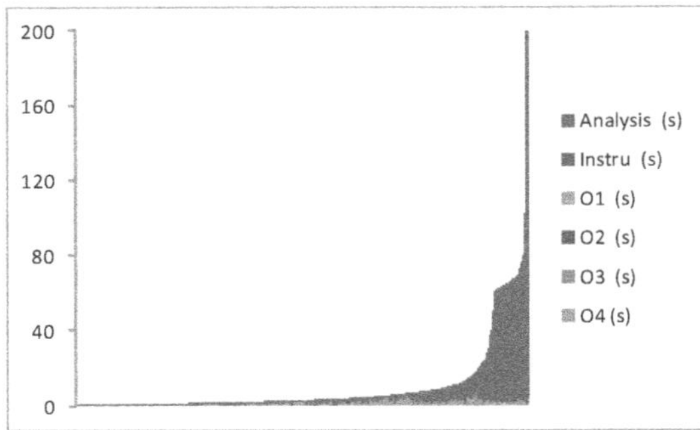

Figure 7: **Inspection & Rewriting Runtime.** X-axis is app ID, and Y-axis is the cumulative time for analysis, instrumentation and optimizations. The result is sorted based on Y-axis.

fairly small; and 2) these optimizations are effective, because they significantly reduce the program sizes. In the end, the average size of inserted code drops to 4.48%.

5.3 Detailed Analysis

Here we present the detailed analysis results of ten applications, and demonstrate the effectiveness of context-aware privacy policy enforcement. To this end, we rewrite these apps with `Capper`, and run them in a physical device along with our policy service app. We further manually trigger the privacy leakage components in the app, so that inserted code would block the program and query policy service for decision. The service will then search its own database to see if there exists a rule for the specific dataflow context of the requesting app. If a corresponding rule exists, service replies to requester immediately. Otherwise, a dialog is displayed to the user asking for decision. The user can also check the "always" option so that current decision will be saved for further reference (Figure 8). Notice that, in order to test the context-awareness of our approach, we always check this option during the experiment. Therefore, from the logcat information on the service side, we may observe and compare the number of queries an app makes with the amount of warning dialogs prompted to the user. We also compute the number of information flow contexts with trace-based model for comparison.

Table 2 lists the summarized results including number of queries, prompts and trace-based contexts. For these apps, the prompt number is often equal to or sometimes slightly smaller than the amount of trace-based dataflow contexts, while the number of queries is usually much larger than that of prompts. This means leakage contexts are modeled correctly: disparate contexts are usually treated differently in our callsite-based approach; and equivalent contexts are enforced with the same rule. The fundamental reason is that Android apps are often componentized while a separate component exercises a dedicated function.

Firstly, different types of private information are accessed through separate execution paths. Some apps (ID 2, 3) retrieve both device identifier and location information, and send them at separate sinks. Similarly, mabilo.ringtones.app leaks both geolocation data and user's phone number.

Secondly, the same type of privacy-related data can be retrieved from isolated packages but serves as different purposes. These apps (ID 4, 7, 10) consist of a main program and advertisement components, both of which produce outgoing traffic taking IMEI or location data. Take net.flixster.android as an example. In this movie app, location data is both sent to flixster server for querying theaters and to Ads server for analytical purpose.

Further, the same private data can be accessed in one package but contributes to different use cases. For instance, com.rs.autorun obtains device identifier via `getDeviceId()` API call in the first place. Then the app sends IMEI at multiple sinks to load advertisement `View`, retrieve configuration or upload analytical information including demographics, ratings, etc. Each semantic context is captured from the perspective of taint propagation trace. However, due to the use of same sink call-site, all the analytical traffics are considered to be with the same semantic context in the call-site model. Though call-site-based model is not as sensitive to context as the trace-based approach, it is still able to differentiate the contexts of Ads `View`, configuration file loading and analytical dataflow, according to disparate sink call-sites.

We also observe inconsistency between traced-based contexts and real program semantics. That lies in apps (ID 1, 6, 7, 8, 9,

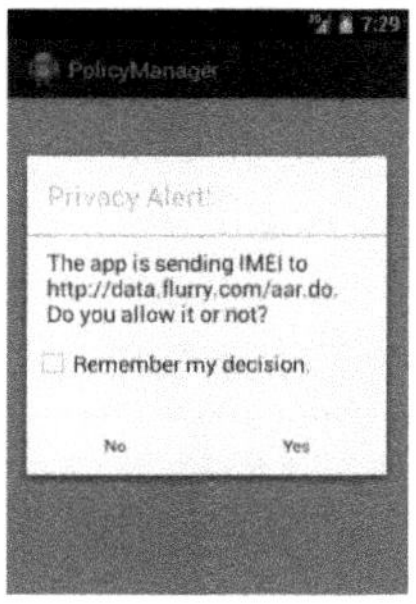

Figure 8: Warning Dialog

ID	App-Version	Queries	Prompts	Trace-based Contexts
1	artfulbits.aiMinesweeper-3.2.3	5	2	2
2	com.avantar.wny-4.1.5.1	3	2	2
3	com.avantar.yp-4.1.5	4	2	2
4	com.bfs.papertoss-1.09	3	2	2
5	com.rs.autorun-1.3.1	10	4	6
6	com.skyfire.browser-2.0.1	4	2	2
7	com.startapp.wallpaper.browser-1.4.15	5	3	3
8	mabilo.ringtones.app-3.6	5	3	3
9	mabilo.wallpapers-1.8.4	4	2	2
10	net.flixster.android-2.9.5	6	3	3

Table 2: Effectiveness of Context-aware Policy Enforcement

10) which acquire location information, where the number of trace-based contexts exceeds that of actual contexts. Geographic location is obtained either approximately from `getLastKnownLocation()`, or from a real-time update by registering a listener through `requestLocationUpdates()` and receiving updates via callback `onLocationChanged(Location)`. Some apps adopt both ways so as to achieve higher accuracy. For instance, artfulbits.aiMinesweeper reads location data by calling `getLastKnownLocation()` at the very beginning of the program, stores it into an instance field, and then periodically updates it with the aforementioned callback. Consequently, two separate paths achieve one sole purpose and thus should be considered as of equivalent context. However, from either trace or call-site point of view, there exist two separate contexts. Despite the disparity, we believe that this would at most introduce one extra prompt. Further, it is also reasonable to split this context into two, because one conducts a one-time access while the other obtains data repeatedly.

5.4 Performance Evaluation

We evaluate both offline rewriting time cost and runtime performance.

Rewriting Performance.

Figure 7 illustrates the time consumption of analysis and rewriting for 4723 Android apps in our experiment. To be specific, it depicts the execution time of analysis, instrumentation, and four optimization phases. We do not show the bytecode conversion time here, because code conversion by dex2jar is usually within several seconds and thus not significant as compared to the other steps. We find that more than 83.6% of the apps are processed within 10 seconds and the majority (92.8%) can be rewritten within 1 minute. However, still a few of them cost excessive time to finish. Global data-flow analysis dominates the overall processing time, especially for those privacy-breaching apps. In comparison, the time consumption of instrumentation and optimizations is fairly small.

Runtime Performance.

We compare the runtime overhead of bytecode rewriting with that of dynamic taint analysis in TaintDroid (on Android gingerbread version 2.3.4). In principle, if an app leaks private information only occasionally, the rewritten version would have much better performance than the original version on TaintDroid. This is because in the rewritten app nearly no instrumentation code is added on non-leaking execution paths whereas TaintDroid has to monitor taint propagation all the time.

Rather, we would like to compare the performance when the taint is actively propagated during the execution. This would be the worst-case scenario for `Capper`. Specifically, we build two customized applications for the measurement. Both leak IEMI string via `getDeviceId()` API, decode the string to a byte array, encrypt the array by doing XOR on every byte with a constant key, reassemble a string from the encrypted byte array, and in the end, send the string out to a specific URL through a raw socket interface. The only difference is that one merely sends the IMEI string, while the other also appends extra information of totally 10KB to the IMEI string before encryption. In other words, the former conducts a short-period data transfer while the latter manipulates the outgoing message within a much longer period. We expect that the execution of the first one to be mainly under `mterp` interpretation mode and the execution of the second to be boosted by JIT.

	Orig.	Orig. on TaintDroid	Rewritten
Short	30ms	130ms	34ms
Long	10583ms	15571ms	10742ms

Table 3: Runtime Performance Evaluation

We measured the execution time from `getDeviceId()` to the network interface. We observed that the rewritten application runs significantly faster than the original on TaintDroid, and only yields fairly small overhead compared to the original one running on Android, for both short-period and long-period data propagation. Table 3 illustrates the result of runtime measurement. While our approach causes 13% and 1.5% overhead for short and long data propagation respectively, TaintDroid incurs 330% and 47% overhead. The results also show that the presence of JIT significantly reduces runtime overhead, in both approaches. However, though newer version of TaintDroid (2.3.4 and later) benefits from JIT support, the overhead caused by dynamic instrumentation is still apparently high.

To further confirm the runtime overhead of the rewritten programs, we conduct an experiment on Google Nexus S, with Android OS version 4.0.4. It is worth mentioning that such verification on real device requires considerable repetitive manual efforts and thus is fairly time consuming. We therefore randomly pick 10 apps from the privacy-breaching ones, rewrite them, run both the original app and secured one on physical device, and compare the runtime performance before and after rewriting. We rely on the timestamps of Android framework debugging information (logcat logs) to compute the app load time as benchmark. The app load time is measured from when Android `ActivityManager` starts an `Activity` component to the time the `Activity` thread is displayed. This includes application resolution by `ActivityManager`, IPC and graphical display. Our observation complies with prior experiment result: rewritten apps usually have insignificant slowdown, with an average of 2.1%, while the maximum runtime overhead is less than 9.4%.

6. DISCUSSION

In this section, we discuss the limitations of our system and possible solutions. We also shed light on future directions.

Soundness of Our Bytecode Rewriting.

Our static analysis, code instrumentation, and optimizations follow the standard program analysis and compiler techniques, which have been proven to be correct in the single threading context. In the multi-threading context, our shadow variables for local variables and function parameters are still safe because they are local to each individual thread, while the soundness of shadow fields depends on whether race condition vulnerability is present in original bytecode programs. In other words, if the accesses to static or instance fields are properly guarded to avoid race condition in the original app, the corresponding operations on shadow fields are also guarded because they are placed in the same code block. However, if the original app does have race condition on certain static or instance fields, the information flow tracking on these fields may be out of sync.

We modeled Android APIs for both analysis and instrumentation. We manually generate dedicated taint propagation rules for frequently used APIs and those of significant importance (e.g., security sensitive APIs). Besides, we have general default rules for the rest. It is well-recognized that it is a non-trivial task to build a fairly complete API model, and it is also true that higher coverage of API model may improve the soundness of our rewriting. However, previous study [7] shows that a model of approximately 1000 APIs can already cover 90% of calls in over 90,000 Android applications. In addition, it is also possible to automatically create a better API model by analyzing and understanding Android framework, and we leave it as our future work.

Tracking Implicit Flow.

It is well known that sensitive information can propagate in other channels than direct data flow, such as control flow and timing channels. It is extremely challenging to detect and keep track of all these channels. In this work, we do not consider keeping track of implicit flow. This means that a dedicated malicious Android developer is able to evade `Capper`. This limitation is also shared by other solutions based on taint analysis, such as TaintDroid [12] and AppFence [19]. Serious research in this problem is needed and is complementary to our work.

Java Reflection.

A study [15] shows that many Android applications make use of Java reflection to call undocumented methods. While in 88.3% cases, the class names and method names of these reflective calls can be statically resolved, the rest can still cause problems. In our experiment, we seldom encounter this situation, because even though some apps indeed use reflective calls, they are rarely located within the taint propagation slices. That is, these reflective calls in general are not involved in privacy leakage. We could use a conservative function summary, such that all output parameters and the return value are tainted if any of input parameter is tainted, but it might be too conservative. A more elegant solution might be to capture the class name and the method name at runtime and redirect to the corresponding function summary, which enforces more precise propagation logic. We leave this as our future work.

Native Components.

Android applications sometimes need auxiliary native components to function, while, unfortunately, static bytecode-level analysis is not capable of keeping track of information flow within JNI calls. However, many apps in fact use common native components, which originate from reliable resources and are of widely recognized dataflow behavior. Thus, it is possible to model these known components with offline knowledge. In other words, we could build a database for well-known native libraries and create proper function summaries for JNI calls, and therefore exercise static data propagation through native calls with the help of such summaries.

7. RELATED WORK

In this section, we discuss previous work that is related to code rewriting and optimization and privacy leakage detection and mitigation on mobile platforms.

Bytecode Rewriting.

Many efforts are made to rewrite apps for security purposes. The Privacy Blocker application [2] performs static analysis of application binaries to identify and selectively replace requests for sensitive data with hard-coded shadow data. I-ARM-Droid [10] rewrites Dalvik bytecode, where it interposes on all the invocations of these API methods to implement the desired security policies. Aurasium [32] repackages Android apps to sandbox important native APIs and watch the applications' behaviors for security and privacy violations. Livshits and Jung [23] implemented a graph-theoretic algorithm to place mediation prompts into bytecode program and thus protect resource access. In comparison, we proposed a new bytecode rewriting technique to track information flow and enforce information-flow based policies.

Instrumentation Code Optimization.

We reduce code instrumentation overhead by performing various static analysis and optimizations. Several other works share the same insight. To find error patterns in Java source code, Martin et al. optimized dynamic instrumentation by performing static pointer alias analysis [26]. To detect numerous software attacks, Xu et al. inserted runtime checks to enforce various security policies in C source code, and remove redundant checks via compiler optimizations [33]. While we share the same insight, our work deals with Dalvik bytecode programs and specific instrumentation methods are completely different.

Privacy Leakage Detection.

Egele et al. [11] studied the privacy threats in iOS applications. They proposed PiOS, a static analysis tool to detect privacy leaks in Mach-O binaries. TaintDroid is a dynamic analysis tool for detecting and analyzing privacy leaks in Android applications [12]. It modifies Dalvik virtual machine and dynamically instruments Dalvik bytecode instructions to perform dynamic taint analysis. Enck et al. [13] proposed a static analysis approach to study privacy leakage as well. They convert a Dalvik executable to Java source code and leverage a commercial Java source code analysis tool Fortify360 [20] to detect surreptitious data flows. CHEX [24] is designed to vet Android apps for component hijacking vulnerabilities and is essentially capable of detecting privacy leakage. It converted Dalvik bytecode to WALA [4] SSA IR, and conducted static dataflow analysis with WALA framework. AndroidLeaks [17] is a static analysis framework, which also leverages WALA, and identifies potential leaks of personal information in Android applications on a large scale. Mann et al. [25] analyzed the Android API for possible sources and sinks of private data and thus identified exemplary privacy policies.

Privacy Leak Mitigation.

Based on TaintDroid, Hornyack et al. [19] proposed AppFence to further mitigate privacy leaks. When TaintDroid discovers the data dependency between source and sink, AppFence enforces privacy policies, either at source or sink, to protect sensitive information. At source, it may provide the app with fake information instead of the real one; at sink, it can block sending APIs. AppFence requires modifications in the Dalvik virtual machine to track information flow and incurs considerable performance overhead (14% on average according to TaintDroid [12]). In contrast, `Capper` takes a bytecode rewriting approach. There is no hurdle for deployment, and due to static dataflow analysis and a series of optimizations, the new application rewritten by `Capper` can achieve higher efficiency.

8. CONCLUSION

We developed a bytecode rewriting approach to defeat privacy leakage in Android applications. Given an unknown Android app, we firstly selectively rewrite the program by inserting bytecode instructions along taint propagation slices for potential information leakage. Then to differentiate true leakage with benign sensitive dataflow, we leverage user's semantic knowledge and devise a context-aware policy enforcement mechanism. Our evaluation on 4723 real-world Android applications demonstrates that `Capper` can effectively track and mitigate privacy leaks. Moreover, after going through a series of optimizations, the instrumentation code only represents a small portion (4.48% on average) of the entire program. In addition, the runtime overhead introduced by `Capper` is also minimal, merely 1.5% for intensive data propagation.

9. ACKNOWLEDGMENT

We would like to thank anonymous reviewers for their comments. This research was supported in part by NSF Grant #1018217, NSF Grant #1054605 and McAfee Inc. Any opinions, findings, and conclusions made in this material are those of the authors and do not necessarily reflect the views of the funding agencies.

10. REFERENCES

[1] dex2jar. http://code.google.com/p/dex2jar/.

[2] Privacy blocker. http://privacytools.xeudoxus.com/.

[3] Soot: a java optimization framework. http://www.sable.mcgill.ca/soot/.

[4] T.j. watson libraries for analysis. http://wala.sourceforge.net.

[5] J. Andrus, C. Dall, A. V. Hof, O. Laadan, and J. Nieh. Cells: A Virtual Mobile Smartphone Architecture. In *Proceedings of the 23rd ACM Symposium on Operating Systems Principles (SOSP'11)*, October 2011.

[6] A. R. Beresford, A. Rice, N. Skehin, and R. Sohan. MockDroid: Trading Privacy for Application Functionality on Smartphones. In *Proceedings of the 12th Workshop on Mobile Computing Systems and Applications (HotMobile'11)*, March 2011.

[7] K. Z. Chen, N. Johnson, V. D'Silva, S. Dai, K. MacNamara, T. Magrino, E. X. Wu, M. Rinard, and D. Song. Contextual Policy Enforcement in Android Applications with Permission Event Graphs. In *Proceedings of the 20th Annual Network and Distributed System Security Symposium (NDSS'13)*, February 2013.

[8] M. Conti, V. T. N. Nguyen, and B. Crispo. CRePE: Context-Related Policy Enforcement for Android. In *Proceedings of the 13th International Conference on Information Security (ISC'10)*, October 2010.

[9] L. Davi, A. Dmitrienko, A.-R. Sadeghi, and M. Winandy. Privilege Escalation Attacks on Android. In *Proceedings of the 13th International Conference on Information Security (ISC'10)*, October 2011.

[10] B. Davis, B. Sanders, A. Khodaverdian, and H. Chen. I-ARM-Droid: A Rewriting Framework for In-App Reference Monitors for Android Applications. In *Proceedings of the Mobile Security Technologies Workshop (MoST'12)*, May 2012.

[11] M. Egele, C. Kruegel, E. Kirda, and G. Vigna. PiOS: Detecting Privacy Leaks in iOS Applications. In *Proceedings of 18th Annual Network and Distributed System Security Symposium (NDSS'11)*, February 2011.

[12] W. Enck, P. Gilbert, B.-G. Chun, L. P. Cox, J. Jung, P. McDaniel, and A. N. Sheth. TaintDroid: An Information-Flow Tracking System for Realtime Privacy Monitoring on Smartphones. In *Proceedings of the 9th USENIX Symposium on Operating Systems Design and Implementation (OSDI'10)*, October 2010.

[13] W. Enck, D. Octeau, P. McDaniel, and S. Chaudhuri. A Study of Android Application Security. In *Proceedings of the 20th Usenix Security Symposium*, August 2011.

[14] W. Enck, M. Ongtang, and P. McDaniel. On Lightweight Mobile Phone Application Certification. In *Proceedings of the 16th ACM Conference on Computer and Communications Security (CCS'09)*, November 2009.

[15] A. P. Felt, E. Chin, S. Hanna, D. Song, and D. Wagner. Android Permissions Demystified. In *Proceedings of the 18th ACM Conference on Computer and Communications Security (CCS'11)*, October 2011.

[16] A. P. Felt, H. J. Wang, A. Moshchuk, S. Hanna, and E. Chin. Permission Re-delegation: Attacks and Defenses. In *Proceedings of the 20th USENIX Security Symposium*, August 2011.

[17] C. Gibler, J. Crussell, J. Erickson, and H. Chen. AndroidLeaks: Automatically Detecting Potential Privacy Leaks in Android Applications on a Large Scale. In *Proceedings of the 5th International Conference on Trust and Trustworthy Computing (TRUST'12)*, June 2012.

[18] M. Grace, Y. Zhou, Z. Wang, and X. Jiang. Systematic Detection of Capability Leaks in Stock Android Smartphones. In *Proceedings of the 19th Annual Network and Distributed System Security Symposium (NDSS'12)*, February 2012.

[19] P. Hornyack, S. Han, J. Jung, S. Schechter, and D. Wetherall. These Aren't The Droids You're Looking For: Retrofitting Android to Protect Data from Imperious Applications. In *Proceedings of the 18th ACM Conference on Computer and Communications Security (CCS'11)*, October 2011.

[20] C. Inc. Hp fortify source code analyzer. http://www.cigital.com/training/elearning/fortify-source-code-analyzer.

[21] J. Kim, Y. Yoon, K. Yi, and J. Shin. SCANDAL: Static Analyzer for Detecting Privacy Leaks in Android Applications. In *Proceedings of the Mobile Security Technologies Workshop (MoST'12)*, May 2012.

[22] M. Lange, S. Liebergeld, A. Lackorzynski, A. Warg, and M. Peter. L4Android: A Generic Operating System Framework for Secure Smartphones. In *Proceedings of the 1st ACM Workshop on Security and Privacy in Smartphones and Mobile Devices (SPSM'11)*, October 2011.

[23] B. Livshits and J. Jung. Automatic Mediation of Privacy-Sensitive Resource Access in Smartphone Applications. In *Proceedings of the 22th Usenix Security Symposium*, August 2013.

[24] L. Lu, Z. Li, Z. Wu, W. Lee, and G. Jiang. CHEX: statically vetting Android apps for component hijacking vulnerabilities. In *Proceedings of the 2012 ACM Conference*

on Computer and Communications Security (CCS'12), October 2012.

[25] C. Mann and A. Starostin. A Framework for Static Detection of Privacy Leaks in Android Applications. In *Proceedings of the 27th Annual ACM Symposium on Applied Computing (SAC'12)*, March 2012.

[26] M. Martin, B. Livshits, and M. S. Lam. Finding Application Errors and Security Flaws Using PQL: A Program Query Language. In *Proceedings of the 20th Annual ACM SIGPLAN Conference on Object-oriented Programming, Systems, Languages, and Applications (OOPSLA'05)*, October 2005.

[27] M. Nauman, S. Khan, and X. Zhang. Apex: Extending Android Permission Model and Enforcement with User-defined Runtime Constraints. In *Proceedings of the 5th ACM Symposium on Information, Computer and Communications Security (ASIACCS'10)*, April 2010.

[28] D. Octeau, S. Jha, and P. McDaniel. Retargeting Android Applications to Java Bytecode. In *Proceedings of the ACM SIGSOFT 20th International Symposium on the Foundations of Software Engineering (FSE'12)*, November 2012.

[29] M. Ongtang, S. McLaughlin, W. Enck, and P. McDaniel. Semantically Rich Application-Centric Security in Android. In *Proceedings of the 2009 Annual Computer Security Applications Conference (ACSAC'09)*, December 2009.

[30] S. Shekhar, M. Dietz, and D. S. Wallach. AdSplit: Separating Smartphone Advertising from Applications. In *Proceedings of the 20th Usenix Security Symposium*, August 2012.

[31] C. Wu, Y. Zhou, K. Patel, Z. Liang, and X. Jiang. AirBag: Boosting Smartphone Resistance to Malware Infection. In *Proceedings of the 21th Annual Network and Distributed System Security Symposium (NDSS'14)*, February 2014.

[32] R. Xu, H. Saïdi, and R. Anderson. Aurasium: Practical Policy Enforcement for Android Applications. In *Proceedings of the 21st USENIX Conference on Security Symposium*, August 2012.

[33] W. Xu, S. Bhatkar, and R. Sekar. Taint-enhanced Policy Enforcement: A Practical Approach to Defeat a Wide Range of Attacks. In *Proceedings of the 15th Conference on USENIX Security Symposium*, July 2006.

[34] Z. Yang, M. Yang, Y. Zhang, G. Gu, P. Ning, and X. S. Wang. AppIntent: Analyzing Sensitive Data Transmission in Android for Privacy Leakage Detection. In *Proceedings of the 20th ACM Conference on Computer and Communications Security (CCS'13)*, November 2013.

[35] M. Zhang and H. Yin. AppSealer: Automatic Generation of Vulnerability-Specific Patches for Preventing Component Hijacking Attacks in Android Applications. In *Proceedings of the 21th Annual Network and Distributed System Security Symposium (NDSS'14)*, February 2014.

[36] Y. Zhou and X. Jiang. Dissecting Android Malware: Characterization and Evolution. In *Proceedings of the 33rd IEEE Symposium on Security and Privacy (Oakland'12)*, May 2012.

[37] Y. Zhou and X. Jiang. Detecting Passive Content Leaks and Pollution in Android Applications. In *Proceedings of the 20th Network and Distributed System Security Symposium (NDSS'13)*, February 2013.

[38] Y. Zhou, Z. Wang, W. Zhou, and X. Jiang. Hey, You, Get Off of My Market: Detecting Malicious Apps in Official and Alternative Android Markets. In *Proceedings of 19th Annual Network and Distributed System Security Symposium (NDSS'12)*, February 2012.

[39] Y. Zhou, X. Zhang, X. Jiang, and V. W. Freeh. Taming Information-Stealing Smartphone Applications (on Android). In *Proceedings of the 4th International Conference on Trust and Trustworthy Computing (TRUST'11)*, June 2011.

APPENDIX

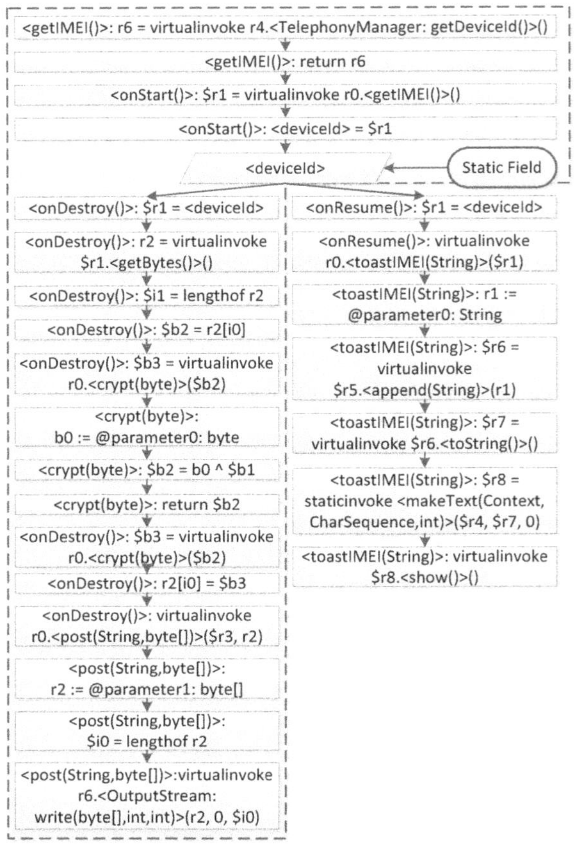

Figure 9: Taint Propagation Tree for the Running Example.

A. TAINT PROPAGATION TREE FOR RUNNING EXAMPLE

Figure 9 illustrates the result for applying the dataflow analysis on the running example. While the entire graph shows the taint propagation tree, the subgraph surrounded by dotted lines is the taint slice for the critical information flow (i.e. IMEI leakage). Each node represents a Jimple statement and its function call context. This tree starts at the invocation of `getDeviceId()` in `getIMEI()`. The source data is thus obtained and further propagated back to `onStart()` via return value. Then, in `onStart()`, IMEI is stored into a static field. Taking the static field as the source of the next iteration, the graph further expands into two branches. In the right branch, the static field is read from `onResume()` and then passed to `toastIMEI()` for display; In the left branch, the static field is accessed from `onDestroy()` which further propagates the data to `crypt()` and `post()` sequentially, and thus sends it out to the network. From this graph, we can see that the left branch is actually leading to privacy leakage and thus is our target to instrument. The right branch is irrelevant to leakage and thus removed from the taint slice.

Malware Detection with Quantitative Data Flow Graphs

Tobias Wüchner
Technische Universität München
Garching b. München, Germany
wuechner@cs.tum.edu

Martín Ochoa
Technische Universität München
Garching b. München, Germany
ochoa@cs.tum.edu

Alexander Pretschner
Technische Universität München, Germany
Garching b. München, Germany
pretschn@cs.tum.edu

ABSTRACT

We propose a novel behavioral malware detection approach based on a generic system-wide quantitative data flow model. We base our data flow analysis on the incremental construction of aggregated quantitative data flow graphs. These graphs represent communication between different system entities such as processes, sockets, files or system registries. We demonstrate the feasibility of our approach through a prototypical instantiation and implementation for the Windows operating system. Our experiments yield encouraging results: in our data set of samples from common malware families and popular non-malicious applications, our approach has a detection rate of 96 % and a false positive rate of less than 1.6 %. In comparison with closely related data flow based approaches, we achieve similar detection effectiveness with considerably better performance: an average full system analysis takes less than one second.

Categories and Subject Descriptors

K.6.5 [**Security and Protection**]: Invasive software

Keywords

Malware detection; behavioral malware analysis; intrusion detection; data flow tracking; quantitative data flows

1. INTRODUCTION

Our societies increasingly depend on the confidentiality of important business information like intellectual property as well as on the integrity of critical information systems and infrastructures. At the same time, rising complexity and rapidly increasing prevalence of malware threatens exactly these important security demands. Highly sophisticated and aggressive so-called advanced persistent threats like Stuxnet, Duqu, or Flamer very clearly suggest that we more than ever depend on sophisticated security measures to ensure a timely detection of such malicious activities.

ASIA CCS'14, June 4–6, 2014, Kyoto, Japan.

http://dx.doi.org/10.1145/2590296.2590319.

Malware detection is often done on the basis of signatures. By a-priori hashing parts or complete binaries, or extracting characteristic byte sequences of known malware samples, vendors of anti-malware technology create extensive collections of characteristic malware signatures that are used to later detect and re-identify new samples found in the wild by malware scanners. While this approach continues to be the main basis of most commercial anti-virus products, it also suffers from several limitations. There always is an inevitable time interval between the release of a new, unknown malware type and the specification and distribution of the corresponding detection signatures. Within this time interval, the malware cannot be detected through signatures. The rapidly increasing frequency of new malware types found in the wild, accompanied by comparably slow signature update and distribution intervals [29], indicate that this indeed is a conceptual and practical shortcoming of signature based approaches. Moreover, authors of current malware proactively try to counteract attempts to identify malware through signatures by packing or encrypting malware binaries or using other obfuscation techniques [20].

To address this challenge, recent malware detection research has focused on the detection of malware and malicious activities through behavioral analysis [5, 15, 7, 30]. This research ranges from approaches that utilize machine-learning, and in particular text-mining, to extract and later detect malware specific behavior patterns [17, 30], to approaches that extract unique dependency graphs between system calls that were executed by malware and match them against unknown malware samples [22].

These approaches significantly raise the bar for malware to prevent its detection. However, advanced static or behavioral obfuscation techniques [3, 27, 33] like reordering system call sequences, injecting bogus sequences of calls, or alternating between semantically equivalent ones, pose a new challenge to the effectiveness of such approaches.

The ideas presented in this paper tackle this problem by basing malware behavior detection on an abstraction of concrete system events to induced data flows between system entities. This abstraction renders reordering, injection, and replacement attacks ineffective, as they do not alter the resulting data flow graphs, making this approach more resilient against behavioral obfuscation attacks than comparable behavior-based detection approaches.

As a side effect, the used abstractions lead to smaller sets of behavioral profiles and heuristics that are necessary to detect a wide range of malware types. By aggregating semantically similar and related flows between system entities during the construction of our data flow graphs, we can furthermore keep the underlying data structures light-weight and efficient. Considering the findings of Frederikson et al. [11] that malware detection through behavioral matching in general cannot be done efficiently, simplifications as used in our approach are particularly helpful in keeping detection efficiency within reasonable boundaries.

Problem: In sum, the main problem tackled by this paper is to efficiently and effectively detect malware and malicious activities while being resilient against behavioral obfuscation techniques as used by current malware.

Solution: We tackle this problem with a generic behavioral malware detection approach that is based on the analysis of quantitative data flows at the OS level. By aggregating and abstracting concrete system events into resulting data flows between relevant system entities, we build graphs that represent the data flow behavior of all entities of a system. Based on these graphs we then specify and later on try to detect data flow patterns that are characteristic for specific types of malware. As a proof-of-concept we show an instantiation of our generic approach for Microsoft Windows operating systems.

Contributions: The original contributions of this paper are thus as follows: **a)** To the best of our knowledge, we are the first to make use of quantitative data flow analysis for detecting malware. **b)** We introduce a generic model to specify malware detection heuristics based on aggregated data flow graphs. **c)** We present a proof of concept instantiation of this model to detect malware in Microsoft Windows operating systems and **d)** We show that our approach is efficient (because of comparably light-weight data structure due to underlying abstractions and aggregations) and effective (a proof-of-concept evaluation indicates a high detection rate and precision).

Organization. In Section 2 we introduce the general ideas and present the data flow model and graph construction as well as the corresponding malware detection concept. In Section 3 we instantiate our approach for Microsoft Windows operating systems and present representative data-flow based malware detection heuristics. In Section 4 we analyze the runtime and detection performance of our prototype. In Section 5 we then give an overview of related work in the area of behavioral malware detection and put our work into context. Finally we conclude in Section 6.

2. PROPOSED APPROACH

In this section we present our aggregated quantitative data flow approach for malware detection and analysis. We proceed in two steps. We start by presenting a generic model that can be instantiated for various system types, and that provides a data structure suitable for data flows analysis. Then, we discuss how to use this data structure for the task of malware detection.

The basic idea is to base malware detection on the analysis of system-wide quantitative data flows. System-wide data flows in this context mean all flows of data between different system entities that happened within a specific time frame. *System entities* denote here all conceptual sources and sinks of data. In the case of operating systems, this includes resources like processes, sockets, or files. Data flows between system entities are caused by the execution of specific data flow related events. For operating systems, an example is

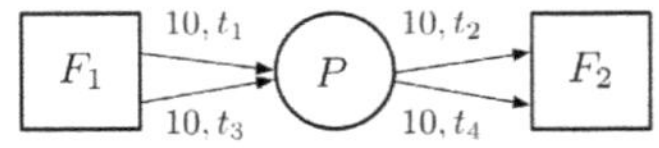

(a) Accurate log

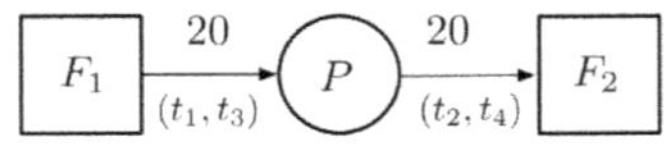

(b) Aggregated

Figure 1: Abstraction from single system events

file system events that, if called by a process, lead to a flow of data between the calling process and the involved file.

We describe such system-wide data flows with data flow graphs. Our data flow graphs contain nodes and edges: nodes represent system resources that were at least once involved in a data flow; and edges represent the actual data flows between these entities.

Example Suppose process P reads 10 Bytes from file F_1, then writes them to file F_2, and it repeats this process twice. An accurate log of this events would keep track of each single system event and their timestamp, as depicted in Figure 1a. As a built-in optimization, we aggregate these flows into single weighted events as depicted in Figure 1b together with a record of the first system event and the last one.

In Section 2.1 we formalize this notion and the graph updating algorithm. In Section 2.2 we discuss how to analyze such graphs with graph invariants.

2.1 Generic Data Flow Model

Our goal is to perform malware detection with quantitative data flow graphs (QDFGs), denoted by $\mathcal{G}$. They represent data flows (edges) in-between relevant resources of a system (nodes). QDFGs are incrementally built by runtime monitors that capture all relevant system-level events, $\mathcal{E}$, that move data from one resource to another, and therefore induce a change of the QDFG. QDFGs hence evolve over time: events cause either the creation or the update of nodes or edges in a data flow graph.

More precisely, QDFGs are elements of the set $\mathcal{G} = \overline{N} \times \overline{E} \times \overline{A} \times ((\overline{N} \cup \overline{E}) \times \overline{A} \to \mathit{Value}^{\overline{A}})$ for a set of nodes, $\overline{N}$, a set of edges, $\overline{E} \subseteq \overline{N} \times \overline{N}$, a set of attribute names, $\overline{A}$, and a set of labeling functions drawn from $((\overline{N} \cup \overline{E}) \times \overline{A}) \to \mathit{Value}^{\overline{A}}$ that map an attribute $a \in \overline{A}$ of a node or an edge to a value drawn from set $\mathit{Value}^{\overline{A}}$.

In a QDFG $G = (N, E, A, \lambda) \in \mathcal{G}$, nodes N represent data flow related system entities and edges E data flows between them. Attributes A are needed to keep our model flexible enough to be instantiated for various types of systems. They represent characteristics of data flows and system entities that are important for malware detection and analysis. Edges, for instance, have an attribute *size* that represents the amount of transferred data of the respective flow. The labeling function λ retrieves the value of an attribute assigned to a node or an edge, in this example the size of the flow that corresponds to an edge.

QDFGs are intuitively to be read as follows: If there has been a flow of data in-between the system entities corresponding to two nodes, there is an edge between these nodes. Data flows are caused by system events. Among other things, this is the case if a process reads from a file; writes to a registry; or writes to a socket. At the level of a QDFG, we are not interested precisely which event has caused the flow. Instead, we model events $(src, dst, size, t, \lambda) \in \mathcal{E}$ as tuples where $src \in \overline{N}$ is the originating system entity, $dst \in \overline{N}$ the destination system entity, $size \in \mathbb{N}$ is the amount of transferred data, $t \in Value^{time}$ is a time-stamp (defined below) and λ holds other attributes of the involved entities. Examples will be provided in Section 3.1.2. As mentioned above, a runtime monitor will then observe all events at, say, the OS level, and use the characterization of an event by set $\mathcal{E}$ as a data transfer to update a QDFG.

In order to define how exactly the execution of an event modifies a QDFG, we need some notation for updating attribute assignments. For any node/edge, attribute pair $(x, a) \in (N \cup E) \times \overline{A}$, we define $\lambda[(x, a) \leftarrow v] = \lambda'$ with λ' identical to λ for all values but for (x, a) where $\lambda'(x, a) = v$.

For brevity's sake, we agree on some syntactic sugar to represent multiple synchronous updates:

$$\lambda[(x_1, a_1) \leftarrow v_1; \ldots; (x_k, a_k) \leftarrow v_k] = (\ldots(\lambda[(x_1, a_1) \leftarrow v_1])\ldots)[(x_k, a_k) \leftarrow v_n].$$

The composition of two labeling functions is defined as:

$$\lambda_1 \circ \lambda_2 = \lambda_1[(x_1, a_1) \leftarrow v_1; \ldots; (x_k, a_k) \leftarrow v_n]$$

where $v_i = \lambda_2(x_i, a_i)$ and $(x_i, a_i) \in \mathsf{dom}(\lambda_2)$.

We consider the aggregation of flows and system entities to be one distinct feature of our approach. Such aggregations are needed to keep the resulting graphs within reasonable limits as illustrated in Fig. 1. This in particular means that entities with the same name (e.g. multiple running instances of the same program) are represented by the same node. Furthermore, flows between the same pair of system entities are represented by one edge where we simply sum the resulting transferred amount of data rather than creating two different edges.

In order to aggregate flows caused by similar events between the same entities edges get assigned a time interval attribute $time \in \overline{A}$ such that $Value^{time} \subseteq \mathbb{N} \times \mathbb{N}$. This interval represents the first and the last point in time where an event was executed that either led to the creation or update of one specific edge as illustrated in Fig. 1b.

Using the auxiliary functions $min, max : Value^{time} \rightarrow \mathbb{N}$ with $min((t_1, t_2)) = t_1$ and $max((t_1, t_2)) = t_2$ we can finally precisely define how an event updates a QDFG by function $update : \mathcal{G} \times \mathcal{E} \rightarrow \mathcal{G}$ defined in Figure 2.

$$update(G, (src, dst, s, t, \lambda')) = \begin{cases} \begin{pmatrix} N, \\ E, \\ A \cup \mathsf{dom}(\lambda'), \\ \lambda \begin{bmatrix} (e, size) \leftarrow \lambda(e, size) + s; \\ (e, time) \leftarrow (min(\lambda(e, time)), t) \end{bmatrix} \circ \lambda' \end{pmatrix} & \text{if } e \in E \\ \begin{pmatrix} N \cup \{src, dst\}, \\ E \cup \{e\}, \\ A \cup \mathsf{dom}(\lambda'), \\ \lambda \begin{bmatrix} (e, size) \leftarrow s; \\ (e, time) \leftarrow (t, t) \end{bmatrix} \circ \lambda' \end{pmatrix} & \text{otherwise} \end{cases}$$

where $e = (src, dst)$ and $G = (N, E, A, \lambda)$

Figure 2: Graph update function

In addition to the state update function we need a few auxiliary functions as basis for the definition of malware detection heuristics. Because their definition is standard, we omit a formalization. Function $pre : \overline{N} \times \mathcal{G} \rightarrow 2^{\overline{N}}$ computes all immediate predecessor nodes of a node of the graph. Conversely, $suc : \overline{N} \times \mathcal{G} \rightarrow 2^{\overline{N}}$ computes the immediate successors of a node. Functions $in, out : \overline{N} \times \mathcal{G} \rightarrow 2^{\overline{E}}$ compute the set of incoming and outgoing edges of a node. If P denotes the set of all finite sequences, function $paths_{from} : \overline{N} \times \mathcal{G} \rightarrow 2^{P}$ calculates all (temporally consistent) paths without loops that originate from a given node n. The intuition is that there is a data flow from n to each node in the path. Conversely, and finally, function $paths_{to} : \overline{N} \times \mathcal{G} \rightarrow 2^{P}$ computes all those paths without loops in the graph that have the argument node as last element. For the accuracy of our analysis it is important that paths satisfy a temporal consistency property (for a discussion on soundness of this approximation see Appendix A).

2.2 Malware Detection

We now have a basis for specifying malware-specific (quantitative) data flow heuristics. These heuristics will enable us to discriminate between benign and potentially malicious system entities. Typical examples for such heuristics include restrictions on orders or specific sequences of flows that are characteristic for certain malware types.

We express such malware data flow heuristics as first-order logic predicates on properties of the introduced QDFGs. The set $\Phi_{\mathrm{mw}} := \Phi_{\mathrm{rep}} \cup \Phi_{\mathrm{mpl}} \cup \Phi_{\mathrm{qnt}}$ contains all specified malware replication, manipulation, and quantitative heuristics that model specific classes of malware behavior. We will define these heuristics in Section 3.2 and formalize them in Appendix B. The motivation for our separation of heuristics is that we want to differentiate between heuristics that detect replication and those that detect the system manipulation behavior of a malware. This separation also allows us to increase the detection specificity by combining different types of heuristics. In addition we will also introduce quantitative heuristics to leverage quantitative data flow aspects in order to increase detection rates. Note that the sets of heuristics are not necessarily disjoint.

The detection of potentially malicious entities at runtime is then done by (1) continuously updating the QDFG and (2) by iterating over all system entities in the graph and matching the specified detection heuristics against them.

More specifically, for an entity to be considered malicious at least one replication and either a manipulation or quantitative heuristic must match.

To use our generic approach for platform–specific detection of malware one must provide platform–specific instantiations of both, data flow model and detection heuristics. This in particular means that (1) all interesting entity types of the target platform must be mapped to nodes in our model; and that (2) all system events must be mapped to corresponding changes of QDFGs as defined by the update function. Furthermore platform–specific instances of abstract heuristics must be specified, based on the previously defined system entities and events.

3. INSTANTIATION FOR WINDOWS

To demonstrate feasibility and effectiveness of our approach, we instantiated and implemented our generic model for the Microsoft Windows operating system family. We identified relevant system entities as potential sources or sinks of malware activities as well as system events that lead to data flows between them. Based on these entity and event definitions, we specify several Windows-specific data flow based malware detection heuristics.

To gather the necessary runtime information, we made use of a user-space monitor based on Windows API function call interposition. It intercepts all process interactions with respect to the identified set of relevant system events. More details on the design and technical implementation of the monitor can be found in [31].

3.1 Instantiated Model

3.1.1 System Entities

Based on a inductive study on process interactions and resulting data flows within Windows operating systems we identified a set of system resources that can be considered as sources or sinks of data flows, and thus as entities in our generic model. We use an attribute $type \in \overline{A}$ to describe an entity's type: **Processes** interact with the file system, registry, and sockets and cause data flows from or to these entities. Nodes that represent processes are assigned P as value of the *type* attribute. **Files** persistently store data and can be either read or written to by processes. Nodes that represent files are always implicitly assigned F as value of the *type* attribute. **Sockets** are connection points to remote systems. Processes can either read or write data from them, causing data flows from or to the respective remote systems. Socket nodes are always assigned S as value of the *type* attribute. **Registry Keys** persistently store settings and other Windows configuration data and can be either read or written to by processes. Nodes that represent registry keys are assigned R as value of the *type* attribute.

3.1.2 System Events

To model interactions that are relevant from a data flow perspective, we model several Windows API functions by abstract events. These will be used in the update function of Section 2.1, and thus by the runtime monitor, to build the QDFG. Due to the considerable complexity of the Windows API we concentrate on a subset of the Windows API that is commonly used by malware to interact with system resources. For brevity's sake we sometimes simplify some aspects of these functions like parameter types (e.g. use file names instead of file handlers) or enriched them with additional information that is usually not directly given by the function's parameters.

In the following we only describe one representative of each type of events which model all semantically (in terms of induced data flows) equivalent events; e.g. the WriteFile function that represents all Windows API functions that induce a data flow from a process to a file. In the prototypical implementation of our approach we considered and intercepted a wide range of semantically equivalent events for each class.

File System Operations

- **ReadFile(Ex)** Using this function a process reads a specified amount of bytes from a file to its memory.
  Relevant Parameters: Calling Process (P_C), Source File (F_S), ToReadBytes (S_R), File Size (S_F)
  Mapping: $(F_S, P_C, S_R, t, \emptyset[(F_S, size) \leftarrow S_F]) \in \mathcal{E}$
- **WriteFile(Ex)** Using this function a process can write a specific number of bytes to a file.
  Relevant Parameters: Calling Process (P_C), Destination File (F_D), ToWriteBytes (S_W), File Size (S_F)
  Mapping: $(P_C, F_S, S_W, t, \emptyset[(F_D, size) \leftarrow S_F]) \in \mathcal{E}$

Registry Operations

- **RegQueryValue(Ex)** Using this function a process reads the value of a specific registry key.
  Relevant Parameters: Calling Process (P_C), Source Key (K_S), ToReadBytes (S_R)
  Mapping: $(K_S, P_C, S_R, t, \emptyset) \in \mathcal{E}$
- **RegSetValue(Ex)** Using this function a process can write data to a specific registry key.
  Relevant Parameters: Calling Process (P_C), Destination Key (K_D), ToWriteBytes (S_W)
  Mapping: $(P_C, K_S, S_W, t, \emptyset) \in \mathcal{E}$

Socket Operations

- **Recv** Using this function a process can read a specific number of bytes from a network socket.
  Relevant Parameters: Calling Process (P_C), Source Address (IP Port) (A_S), ToReadBytes (S_R)
  Mapping: $(A_S, P_C, S_R, t, \emptyset) \in \mathcal{E}$
- **Send** Using this function a process can send a specific number of bytes to a network socket.
  Relevant Parameters: Calling Process (P_C), Destination Address (IP Port) (A_D), ToWriteBytes (S_W)
  Mapping: $(P_C, A_D, S_W, t, \emptyset) \in \mathcal{E}$

Process Operations

- **CreateProcess(Ex)** Through this function a process can trigger the creation of another process, using a specific executable file as binary image.
  Relevant Parameters: Caller Process (P_C), Callee Process (P_D), Binary Name (F_B), Binary Size (S_B)
  Mapping: $(P_C, P_D, S_B, t, \emptyset[(P_D, size) \leftarrow S_B]) \in \mathcal{E}$
- **ReadProcessMemory** Using this function a process can read a specific number of bytes from the memory of another process.
  Relevant Parameters: Calling Process (P_C), Source Process (P_S), ToReadBytes (S_R)
  Mapping: $(P_D, P_C, S_R, t, \emptyset) \in \mathcal{E}$
- **WriteProcessMemory** By this function one process can write a specific number of bytes to the memory of another one.
  Relevant Parameters: Calling Process (P_C), Destination Process (P_D), ToWriteBytes (S_W)
  Mapping: $(P_C, P_D, S_W, t, \emptyset) \in \mathcal{E}$

3.2 Heuristics

Based on the generic data flow model, Windows system entities and the mapping of Windows API calls to events, we can now present specific malware detection heuristics that make use of (quantitative) data flows and data flow properties. We used these for our prototype to detect potentially malicious processes and for the experiments in Section 4. These heuristics were deductively defined on the basis of malware behavior databases [28] and academic malware analysis reports [2]. In the following, we will say that a "heuristic triggers" if according to this heuristic, malware is present.

The basic idea of constructing such heuristics is to identify characteristic data flows and flow properties that correspond to typical high-level behavior of malware such as "*a malicious process tries to replicate itself by infecting other benign binaries*", like e.g. seen for the Parite worm, or "*a malicious process tries to replicate itself via email*", as e.g.

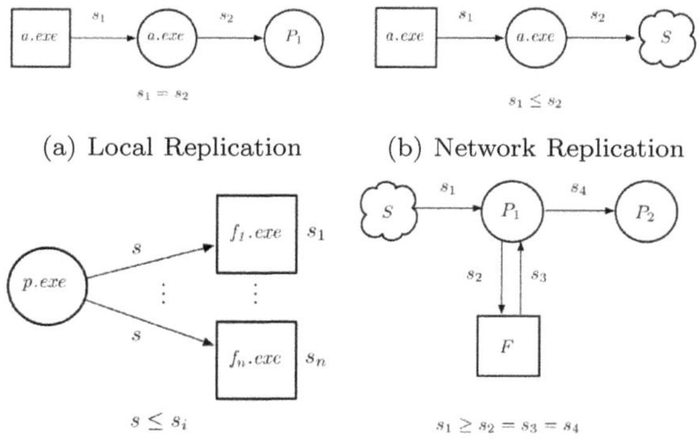

(a) Local Replication (b) Network Replication (c) Binary Infection (d) Reload Payload

Figure 3: Replication Heuristics

common for email worms like MyDoom. These characteristic data flows or properties than represent a set of potentially malicious activities that can later be re-identified in data flow graphs generated at runtime.

Not all of these heuristics in themselves are sufficiently specific and expressive to always discriminate between malware and goodware. An example for this is a heuristic that triggers if a process downloads payload from the internet and starts it as a new process. Although such behavior is typical for so-called dropper malware that install additional malware (so-called eggs) using this technique, it also matches the behavior of benign web installers. Yet, by combining several heuristics, we can achieve a sufficient specificity and precision do correctly discriminate between good- and malware in most cases.

As we focus on the detection of Windows malware in this paper, the following heuristics are specifically designed for Windows operating systems and make use of Windows-specific flow properties. Nevertheless many of these heuristics can be generalized to other operating systems as they e.g. resemble generic high-level worm replication behavior that is also typical for Linux-based malware.

Each of the following heuristic specification consists of a natural language description of the corresponding flow pattern, and a brief description of the rationales behind the heuristic. In addition we visually illustrated some basic flow patterns that correspond to these heuristics (see Figure 3), where boxes represent file nodes, circles represent process nodes, and clouds represent socket nodes. Due to space limitations we restricted the visual descriptions to the category of replication heuristics.

Formalizations of all heuristics are provided in Appendix B.

3.2.1 Replication Heuristics

The heuristics in this class capture activities targeting infection of a local or remote system with malware. That can e.g. be achieved by appending malicious binaries to a set of benign system programs, injecting malicious code into other processes, or sending binaries to remote network nodes.

Local Replication (ϕ_{rep_1}) Triggers if a process node has at least one flow from a file node that has the same name as the process, followed by at least one flow to another process. To increase the precision of the pattern the amount of flown data from file to process must be the same as the amount of data that flows between the two processes (as e.g. observed for Trojans like Agent). *Rationale:* This heuristic covers characteristic data flows caused by a malicious process trying to replicate itself by spawning clone processes from the own binary image.

Network Replication (ϕ_{rep_2}) Similar to the local replication pattern, this heuristic triggers if there exists at least one flow between a process and a file of similar name and a flow from this process to a network socket. To increase specificity the amount of data sent to the socket must be at least as big as the amount of data read from the file (as e.g. observed for Email Worms like MyDoom). *Rationale:* This heuristic covers data flows that are typical for a malware that tries to replicate itself by sending its binary image over the network to infect remote systems.

Binary Infection (ϕ_{rep_3}) This heuristic triggers if there exist multiple flows (at least two) from a process to executable binary files. To reduce false positives an additional quantitative constraint is as follows. The amount of transferred data to the benign executables must be at least as high as the amount of data from the binary image of the process to the process; and the size of the target binary files must be greater than 0. This to some extent ensures that at least the size of the malware image is appended to already existing binaries. *Rationale:* These data flows resemble malware activities that are targeted at replication through infection of other program's executables. This usually happens through malware appending its own code to benign binaries (as e.g. observed for Viruses like Parite).

Download and Start Payload (ϕ_{rep_4}) This heuristic trigers if there is a flow from a socket node to a process node, a flow from this process to a executable binary file node, a flow from this file node back to the process node, and then a flow from this process node to a new process node with a similar name as the file node. To increase detection specificity we increase the additional quantitative constraint that all flows of this pattern must have the same quantities, except for the first flow from the socket node that may also be bigger due to additional meta- and network control data. This to some extent ensures that at least the downloaded size of payload is propagated to a binary file and then to a new malicious process. *Rationale:* This data flow pattern subsumes malware behavior that targets reloading and executing additional malicious payload from the internet (observed for Droppers as e.g. used by the Conficker virus).

3.2.2 Manipulation Heuristics

This class of heuristics contains certain flow patterns that correlate with specific high-level semantics for activities that fall under the broad category of manipulation of system integrity or data confidentiality. Such heuristics for example include activities that target leaking sensitive data to untrusted locations like the internet, modifications of the registry to e.g. add autostart entries, or opening backdoors for further malicious activities.

Leak Cached Internet Data (ϕ_{mpl_1}) Whenever we detect a flow of data from a dedicated internet cache file (in our prototype identified by the absolute file path containing either "*Cookies*" or "*Temporary Internet Files*" as substring) to a process that afterwards sends data to a socket, this heuristic triggers. The specificity of this heuristic is increased by demanding that the flow from the leaking process to the remote socket node must be as least as big as the flow from the cache file to the process. *Rationale:* This heuristic captures the data flow behavior of a malicious process trying to steal potentially sensitive data like cookies from dedicated internet cache folders by sending them to a remote network location (as e.g. observed for various samples of the generic Infostealer malware family).

Spawn Shell (ϕ_{mpl_2}) This heuristic triggers if a command line shell process node (in Windows identified by the name of the process node containing the sub-string "*cmd.exe*") has an incoming or outgoing data flow connection to at least one socket. For simplicity's sake we currently only consider processes with an indirect connection with a maximum distance of at maximum two hops to a socket. *Rationale:* This heuristic describes data flows caused by malware trying to glue a command shell to a listening socket to open a backdoor (as e.g. observed for Backdoors like Autorun).

Deploy System Driver (ϕ_{mpl_3}) This heuristic triggers if we detect a flow between a process and a system driver binary, identified by its name containing the system driver extension "*.sys*", followed by a flow from this system driver file to one of Window's driver loading utilities (in our current implementation we consider "*wdreg.exe*" and "*sc.exe*"). To increase the specificity of this heuristic we also demand that the flow from the potentially malicious processes to the system driver file and from the file to the driver loading utility node must be of the same size. *Rationale:* Today, many sophisticated malware types make use of root kit technology to take over full control of a compromised system and hide their behavior from anti malware software. This heuristic thus describes the data flows that correlate with malware attempts to deploy and load malicious system drivers to the Windows kernel to inject its root kit functionality (as e.g. seen for the ZeroAccess root kit).

3.2.3 *Quantitative Heuristics*

The heuristics of this class capture typical quantitative data flow properties of malware to discriminate malicious processes from benign ones. Examples for such properties are characteristics of distributions or quantitative relationships between edge or node types. The thresholds for these heuristics were inductively derived through analyzing a set of eleven malware samples, distinct from the ones used for the evaluation.

Single-hop Data Amount Entropy (ϕ_{qnt_1}) This heuristic calculates the normalized entropy of the data amount distributions of all outgoing edges of a potentially malicious process and triggers if the corresponding distribution is too uniform. More precisely, for this heuristic to trigger, the normalized entropy (actual entropy divided by hypothetical entropy under uniform distribution) of the measured distribution must be higher than 0.8, indicating an almost uniform outgoing data flow distribution. *Rationale:* A lot of malware types replicate themselves by infecting other binaries or injecting code into other system processes. This often results in almost uniform data amount distributions of the outgoing edges of the corresponding graph nodes.

Registry Call Ratio (ϕ_{qnt_2}) This quantitative heuristic calculates the relative ratio of flows from the Windows registry with respect to the overall communication of a process. A high percentage of registry-related edges within all in-edges of a node is considered indicator for malicious activities. A threshold for this that turned out to work well in practice was a registry edge ratio of 0.8. *Rationale:* Malware often performs a lot of registry queries to probe the state of the infected system before starting its actual malicious activities. This results in a comparably high ratio of registry-related flows in the first moments after process startup.

Malware Family	All	Act.	Det. (N/Q)	Det.Rt.(all) (N/Q)	Det.Rt.(act.) (N/Q)
Agent	2	2	2/2	100% / 100%	100% / 100%
Agobot	6	4	4/4	67% / 67%	100% / 100%
Autorun	7	4	4/4	57% / 57%	100% / 100%
Bagle	5	1	0/1	0% / 20%	0% / 100%
Bancos	5	2	2/2	40% / 40%	100% / 100%
Infostealer	2	2	2/2	100% / 100%	100% / 100%
MyDoom	4	2	0/1	0% / 25%	0% / 50%
Parite	7	3	2/3	29% / 43%	67% / 100%
SpyEye	6	3	3/3	50% / 50%	100% / 100%
Total	44	23	19/22	43.18% / 50%	82.61% / 95.65%

Table 1: Detection Rate

4. EVALUATION

In general, it is difficult to objectively assess the effectiveness and precision of any behavior-based malware detection technique. This is because experiment outcomes heavily depend on chosen goodware and malware evaluation sets, malware activity during behavior recording, and counter-analysis measures employed by the malware.

To shed light on the general feasibility of our concepts and to evaluate our prototype we thus conducted a proof-of-concept study based on a representative set of goodware and malware. Within this study we investigated the effectiveness and efficiency of our detection approach. In terms of effectiveness we mainly focused on detection and false positive rates, where detection rate is defined as the fraction of correctly detected malware samples in all analyzed malware samples, and false positive rate by the ratio of goodware samples, wrongly classified as malware, within the entire set of analyzed goodware samples. In terms of efficiency we analyzed average detection time and space consumption.

We conducted two types of tests. In both we installed malware or goodware samples within our monitored environment and recorded their behavior in terms of calls to the Windows API to dedicated log files. These log files then built the basis for our actual graph generation and heuristic matching approach that in the end lead to the classification of processes into malicious and benign processes.

Malware Tests: For this type of tests we manually installed various samples from a representative set of malware families and recorded their behavior. In addition, we launched a small set of benign applications to increase the interaction diversity, introduce some non-determinism of the overall system behavior, and thus limit the detection bias for the further processing steps. The main goal of these test was to get a sufficiently large data base of malicious processes to reason about detection precision, in particular to derive an average false negative rate. To analyze a representative set of malware types, we picked samples from a public malware database[1] according to the prominent malware types as mentioned on the website of an anti-malware vendor[2].

[1] `http://openmalware.org/`
[2] `http://www.symantec.com/security_response/`

Goodware Tests: The intention of this type of tests was to get a data basis for reasoning about false positives. For this purpose we installed and executed a set of knowingly benign programs into our monitored environment. To increase the diversity of the behavior logs we furthermore performed simple tasks like opening or saving files using these programs. To get a representative set of analyzed goodwares, we installed the 20 most popular programs from `http://download.com`. In addition, we used multiple standard Windows programs that were already pre-installed on the evaluation machine.

All tests were conducted on a Windows 7 Service Pack 1 installation, running within a Oracle VirtualBox instance that was assigned two 2.7 Ghz cores and 4GByte of RAM. The host system itself was running a Windows 8 installation powered by a Intel i7 Quadcore 2.7 Ghz CPU and 8 GByte of RAM. The data collection part was done within the Windows 7 VirtualBox instance, whereas the actual behavioral analysis was conducted offline on the host system.

Note that our detection approach does not require an initial learning phase as it entirely depends on deductively defined set of static data flow heuristics. As basis for the subsequent analysis we performed 44 malware and 21 goodware tests, resulting in 65 activity logs, each containing a trace of process behavior monitored over a period of 5 minutes.

4.1 Effectiveness

For each of the collected malware and goodware logs we generated a quantitative data flow graph, as described in Section 2.1. The corresponding malware test graphs thus represented the behavior of 44 unique samples of the 10 malware families: Agent, Agobot, Autorun, Bagle, Bancos, Infostealer, MyDoom, Parite, and SpyEye.

One of the reasons for the comparably limited evaluation set of 10 different malware families is in the fact that we conducted our tests in a realistic state-of-the-art execution environment and thus picked Windows 7 SP1 as evaluation platform. This choice made it particularly hard to install many malware types like Nimda, Ramnit, or NetSky, because of their incompatibility with the used OS.

Moreover, some of the analyzed malware types had built-in anti-analysis measures that for example detected the presence of certain virtual machine files and settings and due to that stopped all further activities [24]. One example for this were the various samples of the Sality worm that we failed to analyze due to their awareness of being executed in a VirtualBox environment.

Furthermore, many of the analyzed malware samples did not show any significant activities during the 5 minute monitoring period. This inactivity was due to event-based activity mechanisms that were not triggered during our analysis; the corresponding malware was aware of being analyzed and thus did not start its usual infection routines; or it had deferred activity that we simply did not catch within our short monitoring period. This led us to further subdivide the set of malware samples into active and inactive ones. As our approach entirely relies on analysis of runtime behavior, we do not consider non-detected inactive malware samples to be real false negatives.

For the goodware tests we constructed graphs that represented the behavior of 2199 samples of 131 different known benign programs, ranging from standard pre-installed Windows programs like notepad or paint, over various installation routines for software like Oracle's Java, or Adobe's Flash Player, to a variety of third party software, including Microsoft Office products, anti-virus scanners, webcam software, or archiving or music production tools.

Goodware Family	Smp.	FP (N/Q)	FP Rate (N/Q)
Installer	261	14/18	5.36% / 6.90%
Std. Programs	1194	2/6	0.17% / 0.50%
3rd Party	744	6/11	0.81% / 1.48%
Total	2199	22/35	1.00% / 1.59%

Table 2: False Positive Rate

On these graphs we then conducted the analysis steps, as described in Section 2.2, using the heuristics described in Section 3.2, to classify each graph node into the categories *malicious* and *benign*. To further analyze the effect of quantitative properties on detection effectiveness we conducted the test both with and without using quantitative heuristics. As depicted in Table 1, we were able to detect all analyzed malware families. In sum, with respect to the active malware samples that we analyzed, we achieved a detection rate of about 83% without, and about 96% with using quantitative heuristics. This clearly underlines our hypothesis on the usefulness of quantitative aspects for detection effectiveness.

Our detection technique is sensitive to web installation routines as e.g. used by the Java or Flash update processes and thus quite often misclassified them as malware. The comparably high false positive rate of up to 7% on installer routines can be explained by the fact that, from the perspective of the employed heuristics, a web installation process in fact does similar things as a malware reloading additional payload from the internet. To cope with this problem we would thus need to accompany the corresponding detection heuristics with additional, more-specific detection patterns. Considering all analyzed samples of non-malicious processes, we achieved an aggregated false positive rate of about 1.0% for the non-quantitative case, and 1.6% if quantitative heuristics were used (see Table 2). This loss in detection precision when using quantitative heuristics can be explained by the limited specificity of quantitative heuristics in comparison to non-quantitative ones.

4.2 Efficiency

A crucial requirement for all malware detection and analysis approaches is their efficiency. In particular, if such an approach should be used for runtime malware detection, time efficiency is highly relevant since slow detection gives malware the change to interact with the system for some time without being stopped and thus increases the chances for a sophisticated malware to purge its traces of spread in a way that is hard to be later coped with. On the other hand, if a detection approach is to be used for forensics, space efficiency is of crucial importance to minimize to-be stored forensic data. For that reason we considered both, time and space aspects for our efficiency evaluation.

To get a realistic baseline for these efficiency evaluations we built the graphs on the logs that were also used for the goodware and malware effectiveness test. In addition we incorporated a log of a system were we tried to simulate a realistic usage behavior. This included web surfing, checking emails, writing and opening documents in Microsoft Word, listening to some music files in a media player, as well as

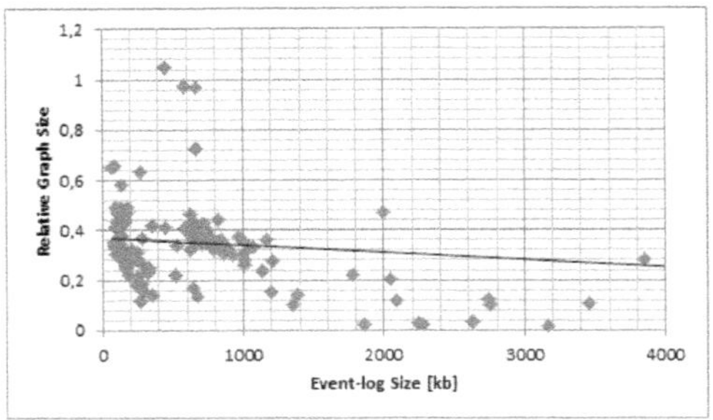

Figure 4: Scaling factor - graph to log size [kb]

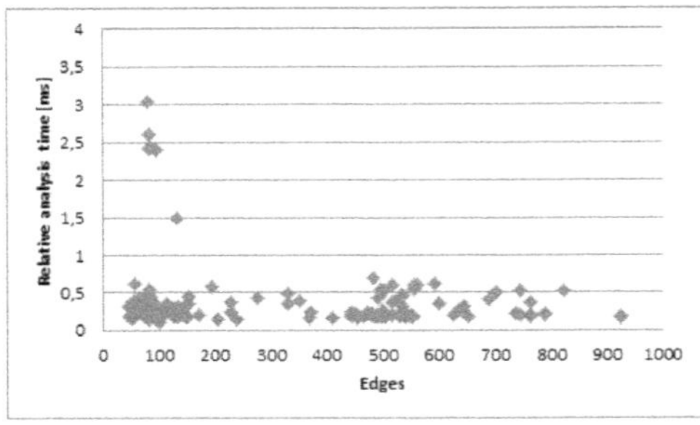

Figure 6: Relative analysis time per edge

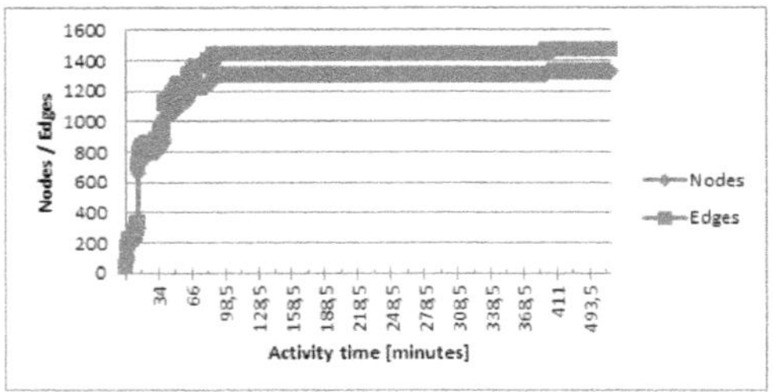

Figure 5: Graph growth - total complexity over time

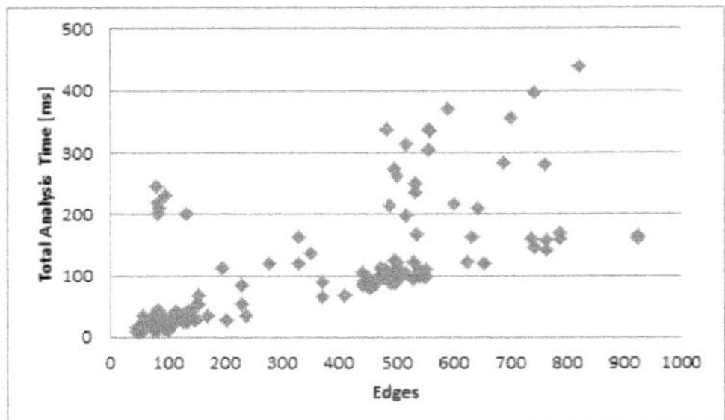

Figure 7: Absolute analysis time per edge

copying files between different folders of the file system. This log captured the behavior of this system during a period of about 9 hours.

4.2.1 Space Efficiency

In terms of space efficiency we first analyzed the relationship between raw log file sizes and the sizes of the corresponding generated graphs. Due to the way we built our graphs, in particular the aggregation as defined by the *update* function, we expected to see an increasing scaling factor between graph and log size for increasing log file sizes. The findings depicted in Figure 4 support this hypothesis, as we can see that while the size of a log file increases, the average relative graph size and thus the scaling factor decreases. With the exception of some outliers we can see an average scaling factor of about 40% for small logs of less than 1 MByte, going down to 10-20% for bigger log files.

These findings indicate that the amount of data that need to be stored in order to perform full-system malware detection and gives rise to optimism w.r.t. scalability.

In addition to this scaling factor analysis we also investigated the average graph growth and complexity over time. Due to our aggregation algorithms we assumed that after some time of system usage, the graph would not grow as fast as in the beginning of a system run. This is because after a while most of the connections between system entities should be present (e.g. because all necessary registry keys, files, and processes have been touched or run at least once) and future activities should only result in node or edge attribute updates.

Figure 5 supports this assumption, as we can see slow growth of graph complexity over time with a short complexity jump in the beginning. This slow growth during normal usage suggests that our approach also scales in terms of space complexity over time and thus, by construction, results in reasonably small graph sizes.

4.2.2 Time Efficiency

For reasoning about time efficiency we analyzed the relative time it took to match a graph node against the set of heuristics with respect to the graph size in terms of number of edges (see Figure 6). As we can see, the relative analysis time is independent of the graph size and, with the exception of some outliers, within the range of 1-2ms per node.

In absolute terms this means that the detection time is quasi-linear in the amount of edges of the graph (see Figure 7). For graphs of a maximum size of 1000 edges, which roughly corresponds to the behavior of a system with average activity over a period of about 60 minutes (see Figure 5), the complete graph analysis can be conducted in under 500ms.

With an average detection time of less than one second for a complete graph analysis, we consider our approach sufficiently fast to be usable for runtime detection. Our QDFT graphs typically only grow slowly under normal usage because of the applied aggregation steps of our model, with occasional peaks whenever new programs are started. This means that, although linear w.r.t. graph complexity, the necessary analysis time also only grows very slowly with respect to system runtime.

Note that all the heuristics presented in this paper are of a local nature (checking only a small neighborhood of a given node). Since atomic system events also impact a small portion of the graph, one does not need to re-check it entirely in each step, but it suffices to analyze the impact of the system event in a local neighborhood. Therefore we limited the efficiency analysis to graphs constructed after a few minutes of activity since the analysis times are representative for updates to bigger graphs in that time lapse. In general such a local reasoning is however not possible since interesting heuristics could include system-wide properties which force the re-verification of the complete graph.

Monitor Overhead: For space reasons, we do not include a dedicated discussion on the performance of the event monitor. In general, the computational overhead induced by the monitor under normal operation conditions is in the order of magnitude of about 20% and thus cannot be considered a show-stopper [31].

In sum, our measurements indicate sufficient efficiency of our approach and give rise to optimism w.r.t scalability.

5. RELATED WORK

As mentioned in the introduction, although still popular, signature-based malware detection is ineffective against unknown or obfuscated malware and thus can, when used in isolation, be considered insufficient to cope with modern malware. Behavior-based approaches in contrast are typically able to detect unknown malware because they focus on detecting malware by analyzing its behavior and not its persistent representation.

In the past decades, a plethora of work has been published in the broad area of behavior-based malware and intrusion detection and analysis [7]. This work can be be categorized according to several dimensions: targeted level of abstraction (e.g. host- vs. network-based), underlying detection model (misuse- vs. anomaly-based), or type of used analysis (static vs. dynamic analysis).

Because of the considered level of behavioral abstraction and system-external deployment, network based detection approaches exhibit several advantages over host-based approaches, including a lower likelihood to get disabled or circumvented by malware. These advantages, however, also come with a core limitation: By design, they work at a system rather than a process level, and therefore they cannot analyze the behavior of individual processes and thus in general provide less fine-grained behavior information than host based approaches. This in particular means that they usually cannot provide information about compromised or leaked system resources. Futhermore, network-based approaches are significantly challenged if malware uses advanced obfuscation or encryption techniques to blur or hide its network behavior [26].

Since our work focuses on host-based malware detection, we limit ourselves to review host-based behavioral malware detection approaches in the following. A seminal idea or Forrest et al. [9] in host-based malware detection through process behavior analysis is to profile benign and malicious processes through characteristic sequences of their interactions with the system, e.g., through issued system calls. The idea was later caught up by more elaborate text-mining and specifically n-gram based approaches that used machine learning to improve accuracy and precision [19, 13, 17, 25, 30, 6].

Our work differs from these approaches in two ways: First, these latter typically do not assign any explicit semantics to the used n-grams. By construction they can thus detect the presence of malware but cannot yield a deeper analysis of high-level malware behavior. Our solution, in contrast, gives a clear high-level semantics of observed malware behavior patterns. Besides detecting and pin-pointing to infections, our approach thus also establishes a basis fore more comprehensive behavioral analysis, e.g., to reason about malware intentions and attack goals. Second, approaches of the cited kind are typically sensitive to advanced behavioral obfuscation techniques like reordering system calls, randomly inserting bogus calls, or substituting calls with semantically equivalent calls. Due to the used abstraction from concrete system calls to induced data flows, which are oblivious to these obfuscation methods, our approach by construction is more robust against many obfuscation mechanisms as used by modern malware [3, 27, 33].

An orthogonal line of research on behavioral malware detection bases on the analysis of dependencies and interrelationships between activities like system call invocations of processes. After the extraction of characteristic call dependencies of different knowingly malicious processes they can be used to re-identify certain dependency patterns in unknown behavior graph samples in order to discriminate between malicious and non-malicious processes. This behavior-focused line of research can be roughly subdivided into the categories: approaches that are based on the derivation and later re-identification of potentially malicious call-dependency (sub-)graphs [16, 21, 22, 12, 18], approaches that infer high-level semantics for call-dependency graphs or sequences [5, 4, 23], and approaches that tackle the data flow aspects of potentially malicious behavior [32, 10, 14, 15].

One of the first call-graph based approaches was proposed by Kolbitsch et al. [16] who introduced the idea of deriving call-graphs from known malware samples that represent dependencies between different runtime executions of system calls, their arguments, and return values and using them as behavioral profiles for later re-identification in unknown executables. This idea was later refined by clustering and deriving near-optimal graphs to increase precision [12], or anticipate malware metamorphism [18]. Recent work in this field aimed at reducing the amount of to-be maintained behavior-graphs by mining specific invariants and paths from graphs of samples from same malware families [21, 22]. These approaches have several advantages over n-gram based ideas. Deriving and maintaining call-graph databases typically requires less sampling and storage effort than n-gram based approaches and is often more resilient to reordering or bogus call insertion obfuscation techniques.

Although we also base on the construction and analysis of behavioral graphs, we base our graph generations on quantitative data flows between system entities rather than on dependencies between single system calls. This provides better resilience against reordering and semantic obfuscation as the data flow based graph construction is less affected by shuffling and replacement of semantically equivalent calls. Also related approaches often make use of NP-complete algorithms like sub-graph isomorphism analysis which has a negative impact on the time-efficiency of these approaches. Our approach in contrast is of linear time complexity in terms of graph size. Besides quantitative aspects we furthermore differ from clustering approaches as presented by Park et. al. [21, 22] in that we construct per-system rather than per-process data flow graphs which widens the detection scope to inter-process behavior.

A seminal work of the third large pillar of behavioral malware detection was presented by Christodorescu et al. [5, 4, 12]. The basic idea of these type of approaches is to give high-level semantics to observed malware behavior. Rather than matching behavior on a purely syntactic and structural level, these approaches try to extract and re-identify characteristic behavior at a semantic level. Follow-up work further enriched this idea with formal semantics for identified malware behavior [23]. The semantic perspective of these approaches typically leads to better resilience against more simple obfuscation like call re-ordering. This is because, although resulting in mutations of call-graphs and thus challenging normal call-graph based approaches, such obfuscation attempts do not change the semantic dimension of the malware behavior and therefore cannot easily trick semantics-based approaches.

The main commonality with this line of research is that we also base our analysis on graphs and give high-level semantics for specific of malware behavior patterns. However, in contrast to the aforementioned approaches we base the construction of our behavior graphs on the analysis of *data* rather than *control* flows. As mentioned before, this abstraction increases the resilience against advanced obfuscation like permutations between semantically equivalent functionality, which is usually not given by such approaches [5]. The data flow perspective, as abstraction from control flows, furthermore reduces the set of sub-graphs or properties we need to maintain in order to detect malicious activities, which has a positive impact on detection efficiency. Intuitively, this is because one data flow property often subsumes multiple control flow properties.

The last category of related work tackles the data flow perspective of malicious behavior. One of the most prominent examples for this family of approaches is the Panorama system of Yin et al. [32] that leverages dynamic data flow analysis for the detection of malicious activities. The basic idea of Panorama is to profile data flow behavior of malicious processes through fine-grained system-wide taint analysis and match it against manually specified data flow properties. Similarly, our approach uses system-wide data flow graphs to represent process and system behavior and match them against FOL data flow invariants. However, we make use of quantitative flow aspects to increase invariant specificity and thus detection precision. Moreover, we incorporate dedicated graph aggregation, simplification, and abstraction steps which helps to keep data structures lean and maintainable, resulting in little performance impact, whereas Panorama induces performance overhead of up to 2000% which renders it unsuitable for runtime detection purposes. We mainly differ from data dependency graph based work like the one presented by Elish et al. [8] in that we leverage quantitative flow aspects for our analysis and have a system- rather than a program-centric scope by founding our analysis on data dependencies between system entities instead of individual program points.

In sum, the main difference between our work and related contributions is that to the best of our knowledge we are the first to leverage quantitative data flow aspects for the behavior-based detection of malware. Our approach also offers more resilience to behavioral obfuscations like call reordering or semantic replacements. In addition, graph simplification allows us to optimize storage and computational efforts, resulting in a superior space and detection time efficiency.

6. DISCUSSION AND CONCLUSION

We have proposed a novel approach to leverage quantitative data flow analysis and graph analysis for the detection of malicious activities. Through the specification of heuristics in form of malware-specific quantitative data flow patterns, we can then identify data flow activities that relate to the presence of malware. To demonstrate the practicability of our generic model, we presented an exemplary instantiation for Microsoft Windows operating systems based on a prototype that builds on top of a user-mode monitor, capturing process activities in form of data flows induced by process calls to the Windows API.

On the basis of a proof-of-concept evaluation we showed, that our approach is able to effectively discriminate between malware and goodware with competitively high detection (up to 96%) and low false positive rates (less than 2%) compared to related approaches from literature [5, 16, 32]. These results are based on preliminary measurements and thus do not necessarily generalize due to the relatively small sample size and inherent bias in the selection of analyzed malware and goodware. For future work we thus plan to extend our evaluation to a larger set of malware and goodware samples, as well as to longer system runs to more deeply investigate graph complexity over time.

The evaluation results also indicate good space and time efficiency: the complexity of the data flow graphs turned out to only grow slowly over time for normal system usages and we observed a linear relationship between the graph complexity and the time it takes to perform a full system malware detection. The full detection time for average system activity remains under one second with an average detection overhead of less than one millisecond per graph edge. In comparison to the data-flow based malware detection approaches closest to ours [32] we achieved a better performance with comparable detection and false positive rates. These preliminary results indicate that our approach is suited for multiple malware-related application areas including runtime malware detection and analysis, as well as offline forensics, and has better time and space efficiency than most related approaches.

Limitations: Although using quantitative data flows as abstraction of malware activities raises the bar for malware to hide its presence through obfuscation, the quantity-based detection mechanisms are challenged if the malware obfuscates flow quantities by e.g. blurring malicious flows by scattering them over time or adding bogus data flows. We acknowledge the threat arising from the so-called base-rate fallacy [1] on the effectiveness of intrusion and malware detection approaches, including ours. According to this paradox, even a low false-positive rate of less than 2% can render an approach ineffective if malicious activities are considerably less frequent than benign ones. To cope with these problems and to further reduce false positives we plan to come up with more elaborate and thus more resilient combinations of (potentially adaptive) quantitative heuristics.

In addition, our current implementation is solely based on static data flow heuristics which only allows us to detect malware that has the specified behavioral characteristics. Although we used a wide range of behavioral descriptions of different malware families to derive our heuristics, new malware could thus simply achieve its goals in a way that we did not anticipate. To thwart this issue we intend to investigate the effectiveness of state-of-the-art machine-learning based anomaly detection on the basis of quantitative data flows.

Also the security of our prototype itself is out of the scope of this paper. Sophisticated malware could for example try to disable the event monitor to evade detection. We plan to counteract this threat by moving our monitor down the stack to the kernel layer which would give us a certain degree of tamper-resilience against user-mode malware. In sum, we have shown that quantitative data flow analysis can be used for effective, efficient, and resilient malware detection.

Acknowledgments This work was done as part of the DFG's Priority Program SPP 1496 "Reliably Secure Software Systems," ref. numbers PR-1266/1-2.

7. REFERENCES

[1] S. Axelsson. The base-rate fallacy and the difficulty of intrusion detection. *ACM Transactions on Information and System Security (TISSEC)*, 3(3):186–205, 2000.

[2] U. Bayer. *Large-Scale Dynamic Malware Analysis.* PhD thesis, Technische Universität Wien, 2009.

[3] J.-M. Borello and L. Me. Code obfuscation techniques for metamorphic viruses. *Journal in Computer Virology*, pages 211–220, 2008.

[4] M. Christodorescu, S. Jha, and C. Kruegel. Mining specifications of malicious behavior. In *Proceedings of the 1st India Software Engineering Conference*, pages 5–14, 2008.

[5] M. Christodorescu, S. Jha, S. Seshia, D. Song, and R. Bryant. Semantics-Aware Malware Detection. *2005 IEEE Symposium on Security and Privacy (S&P'05)*, pages 32–46, 2005.

[6] G. Creech and J. Hu. A semantic approach to host-based intrusion detection systems using contiguous and discontiguous system call patterns. *Computers, IEEE Transactions on*, pages 1–1, 2013.

[7] M. Egele, T. Scholte, E. Kirda, and C. Kruegel. A survey on automated dynamic malware-analysis techniques and tools. *ACM Computing Surveys (CSUR)*, page 6, 2012.

[8] K. O. Elish, D. Yao, and B. G. Ryder. User-centric dependence analysis for identifying malicious mobile apps. In *Workshop on Mobile Security Technologies*, 2012.

[9] S. Forrest, S. Hofmeyr, a. Somayaji, and T. Longstaff. A sense of self for Unix processes. *Proceedings of Symposium on Security and Privacy*, pages 120–128, 1996.

[10] M. Fredrikson, M. Christodorescu, J. Giffin, and S. Jhas. A declarative framework for intrusion analysis. In *Cyber Situational Awareness*, pages 179–200. 2010.

[11] M. Fredrikson, M. Christodorescu, and S. Jha. Dynamic behavior matching: A complexity analysis and new approximation algorithms. *Automated Deduction-CADE-23*, pages 252–267, 2011.

[12] M. Fredrikson, S. Jha, M. Christodorescu, R. Sailer, and X. Yan. Synthesizing Near-Optimal Malware Specifications from Suspicious Behaviors. *2010 IEEE Symposium on Security and Privacy*, pages 45–60, 2010.

[13] A. K. Ghosh, A. Schwartzbard, and M. Schatz. Learning program behavior profiles for intrusion detection. In *Proceedings of the 1st Conference on Workshop on Intrusion Detection and Network Monitoring - Volume 1*, pages 6–6, 1999.

[14] S. T. King and P. M. Chen. Backtracking intrusions. In *ACM SIGOPS Operating Systems Review*, pages 223–236, 2003.

[15] E. Kirda, C. Kruegel, G. Banks, G. Vigna, and R. A. Kemmerer. Behavior-based spyware detection. In *Proceedings of the 15th Conference on USENIX Security Symposium*, 2006.

[16] C. Kolbitsch and P. Comparetti. Effective and Efficient Malware Detection at the End Host. *USENIX*, 2009.

[17] A. Lanzi, D. Balzarotti, C. Kruegel, M. Christodorescu, and E. Kirda. Accessminer: Using system-centric models for malware protection. In *Proceedings of the 17th ACM Conference on Computer and Communications Security*, pages 399–412, 2010.

[18] J. Lee, K. Jeong, and H. Lee. Detecting metamorphic malwares using code graphs. *Proceedings of the 2010 ACM Symposium on Applied Computing*, 2010.

[19] W. Lee, S. J. Stolfo, and P. K. Chan. Learning patterns from unix process execution traces for intrusion detection. In *AAAI Workshop on AI Approaches to Fraud Detection and Risk Management*, pages 50–56, 1997.

[20] P. O'Kane, S. Sezer, and K. McLaughlin. Obfuscation: The hidden malware. *Security Privacy, IEEE*, 2011.

[21] Y. Park and D. Reeves. Deriving common malware behavior through graph clustering. *Proceedings of the 6th ACM Symposium on Information, Computer and Communications Security*, 2011.

[22] Y. Park, D. S. Reeves, and M. Stamp. Deriving common malware behavior through graph clustering. *Computers & Security*, 2013.

[23] M. Preda, M. Christodorescu, S. Jha, and S. Debray. A semantics-based approach to malware detection. *ACM SIGPLAN Notices*, pages 1–12, 2007.

[24] T. Raffetseder, C. Krügel, and E. Kirda. Detecting system emulators. In *Information Security*, pages 1–18. 2007.

[25] K. Rieck, P. Trinius, C. Willems, and T. Holz. Automatic analysis of malware behavior using machine learning. *Journal of Computer Security*, pages 639–668, 2011.

[26] C. Rossow, C. Dietrich, and H. Bos. Large-scale analysis of malware downloaders. In *Detection of Intrusions and Malware, and Vulnerability Assessment*, pages 42–61. 2013.

[27] M. I. Sharif, A. Lanzi, J. T. Giffin, and W. Lee. Impeding malware analysis using conditional code obfuscation. In *NDSS*, 2008.

[28] Symantec. Malware database, Nov. 2013.

[29] P. Szor. *The Art of Computer Virus Research and Defense*. 2005.

[30] C. Wressnegger, G. Schwenk, D. Arp, and K. Rieck. A close look on n-grams in intrusion detection: anomaly detection vs. classification. In *Proceedings of the 2013 ACM workshop on Artificial intelligence and security*, pages 67–76, 2013.

[31] T. Wüchner and A. Pretschner. Data loss prevention based on data-driven usage control. In *Software Reliability Engineering (ISSRE), 2012 IEEE 23rd International Symposium on*, pages 151–160, Nov 2012.

[32] H. Yin, D. Song, M. Egele, C. Kruegel, and E. Kirda. Panorama: Capturing system-wide information flow for malware detection and analysis. In *Proceedings of*

the 14th ACM Conference on Computer and Communications Security, pages 116–127, 2007.
[33] I. You and K. Yim. Malware obfuscation techniques: A brief survey. In *Broadband, Wireless Computing, Communication and Applications (BWCCA), 2010 International Conference on*, pages 297–300, 2010.

APPENDIX

In the following, we will use projections $!_i$ with $(x_1, \ldots, x_k)!_i = x_i$ for $1 \leq i \leq k$. We use the same notation to address a specific element y in the i-th position of a sequence Y.

A. TEMPORAL CONSISTENCY

For the accuracy of our analysis it is important that we consider paths between nodes that have a certain temporal consistency. Consider the following example. Process P_1 reads from file F at time t_1. Then process P_2 writes to file F at time $t_2 > t_1$. Then, although it is possible to find a path from P_2 to P_1 in the data-flow graph, there has not been an actual flow from P_2 to P_1, because of the order in which the events happened. We characterize this temporal consistency with the following theorem.

THEOREM 1. *Let $p = (e_1, \ldots, e_k) \in P$. A flow from $e_1!_1$ to $e_k!_2$ is possible if and only if:*

$$max_{i=1\ldots j-1}(min(\lambda(e_i, time))) < max(\lambda(e_j, time))$$

for $0 \leq j \leq k$.

PROOF. Clearly, there is a flow from node n to node n' if an only if there is connected path from n to n' of length k and an increasing sequence of k timestamps such that data is transferred through the connecting nodes. By induction on k, it is easy to see that if the proposition holds, it is possible to construct such a sequence. On the other hand if the proposition does not hold, this is impossible, because for some j, there is a predecessor minimum which is greater than the current maximum time-stamp, so that the sequence can not be increasing. □

Note that this characterization is still an approximation: consider a similar example as before, now process P_2 writes from file F at time t_1. Then process P_1 reads from file F at time $t_2 > t_1$. In this case although possible, there is no guarantee of an actual flow in an information theoretical sense from P_2 to P_1, since we do not know whether P_1 reads the portion of F written by P_2

B. FORMALIZATION OF HEURISTICS

In the following, we provide formalizations of the heuristics described in Section 3.2. These formalizations come as predicates $\phi \subseteq \overline{N} \times \mathcal{G}$ that are to be read as follows. If $\phi(n, G)$ is true for some node n in a given QDFG G, then the heuristics corresponding to ϕ suggests that malware is present. This means that the evaluation must be performed for each node.

To simplify the description, we define a sub-string function to extend heuristics definitions with string comparisons: $ss : \mathcal{S} \times \mathcal{S} \rightarrow \{0, 1\}$ which evaluates to true, iff the first provided string is a sub-string of the second string parameter.

B.1 Replication Heuristics

Local replication is formalized as

$$\phi_{\mathrm{rep}_1}(n, G) := \exists p = (e_1, e_2, \ldots) \in paths_{from}(n) \bullet (n, Type) = F \wedge (e_1!_2, type) = P \wedge ss(e_1!_2, n) \wedge (e_2!_2, Type) = P \wedge (e_1, size) = (e_2, size).$$

Network replication is formalized as

$$\phi_{\mathrm{rep}_2}(n, G) := \exists p = (e_1, e_2, \ldots) \in paths_{from}(n) \bullet (n, Type) = F \wedge (e_1!_2, type) = P \wedge ss(e_1!_2, n) \wedge (e_2!_2, Type) = S \wedge (e_1, size) \leq (e_2, size).$$

Binary infection is formalized as

$$\phi_{\mathrm{rep}_3}(n, G) := |\{(e_1, \ldots) \in paths_{from}(n) | (n, Type) = P \wedge (e_1!_2, Type) = F \wedge ss(\text{``}.exe\text{''}, e_1!_2) \wedge (e_1!_2, size) > 0\}| \geq 2$$

Download and Start Payload is formalized as

$$\phi_{\mathrm{rep}_2}(n, G) := \exists p = (e_1, e_2, e_3, e_4, \ldots) \in paths_{from}(n) \bullet (n, Type) = S \wedge (e_1!_2, type) = P \wedge (e_2!_2, type) = F \wedge ss(\text{``}.exe\text{''}, e_2!_2) \wedge e_3!_2 = e_2!_1 \wedge (e_4!_2, type) = P \wedge (e_1, size) \geq (e_2, size) = (e_3, size) = (e_4, size).$$

B.2 Manipulation Heuristics

Leaked Cached Internet Data is formalized as

$$\phi_{\mathrm{mpl}_1}(n, G) := \exists p = (e_1, e_2, \ldots) \in paths_{from}(n) \bullet (n, type) = F \wedge (e_1!_2, type) = P \wedge (ss(\text{``}Cookie\text{''}, n) \vee ss(\text{``}Temporary\ Internet\ Files\text{''}, n)) \wedge (e_2!_2, type) = S \wedge (e_1, size) \leq (e_2, size).$$

Spawn Shell is formalized as

$$\phi_{\mathrm{mpl}_2}(n, G) := \exists n' \in (pre(n) \cup suc(n)) \bullet (n, type) = S \wedge (n', type) = P \wedge ss(\text{``}cmd.exe\text{''}, n').$$

Deploy System Driver is formalized as

$$\phi_{\mathrm{rep}_3}(n, G) := \exists p = (e_1, e_2, \ldots) \in paths_{from}(n) \bullet (n, Type) = P \wedge (e_1!_2, type) = F \wedge ss(\text{``}.sys\text{''}, e_1!_2) \wedge (e_2!_2, Type) = P \wedge (e_1, size) = (e_2, size) \wedge (ss(\text{``}wdreg.exe\text{''}, e_2!_2) \vee ss(\text{``}sc.exe\text{''}, e_2!_2)).$$

B.3 Quantitative Heuristics

Single-hop Data Amount Entropy is formalized as

$$\phi_{\mathrm{qnt}_1}(n, G) := (n, type) = P \wedge NE\left(\bigcup_{e \in (in(n) \cup out(n))} \frac{(e, size)}{\sum_{e' \in (in(n) \cup out(n))} (e', size)}\right) \geq 0.8$$

with the normalized entropy NE defined as:

$$NE(S) := \frac{-\sum_{s_i \in S} s_i * \log(s_i)}{\log(|S|)}.$$

Registry Call Ratio is formalized as

$$\phi_{\mathrm{qnt}_2}(n, G) := (n, type) = P \wedge \frac{|\{e | e \in in(n) \wedge (e!_1, type) = R\}|}{|in(n)|} \geq 0.8.$$

Abstract Model Counting: A Novel Approach for Quantification of Information Leaks

Quoc-Sang Phan
Queen Mary University of London
q.phan@qmul.ac.uk

Pasquale Malacaria
Queen Mary University of London
p.malacaria@qmul.ac.uk

ABSTRACT

We present a novel method for *Quantitative Information Flow* analysis. We show how the problem of computing information leakage can be viewed as an extension of the *Satisfiability Modulo Theories* (SMT) problem. This view enables us to develop a framework for QIF analysis based on the framework DPLL($\mathcal{T}$) used in SMT solvers. We then show that the methodology of *Symbolic Execution* (SE) also fits our framework. Based on these ideas, we build two QIF analysis tools: the first one employs CBMC, a bounded model checker for ANSI C, and the second one is built on top of Symbolic PathFinder, a Symbolic Executor for Java. We use these tools to quantify leaks in industrial code such as C programs from the Linux kernel, a Java tax program from the European project HATS, and anonymity protocols.

Categories and Subject Descriptors

H.1.1 [**Systems and Information Theory**]: Information theory; D.4.6 [**Security and Protection**]: Information flow controls; D.2.4 [**Software/Program Verification**]: Formal methods, Model checking

Keywords

Quantitative Information Flow; Model Checking; Symbolic Execution; Satisfiability Modulo Theories

1. INTRODUCTION AND BACKGROUND

Quantitative information flow analysis (QIF [14, 23]) is a rigorous approach to *"measure"* information leakage. The motivation for this approach is that absolute security is often not achievable and programs with *"small"* leaks are usually accepted as secure. QIF has attracted considerable attention in recent years and has been applied to the formal analysis of, for example, confidentiality of software [21, 5, 18, 27, 26], loss of anonymity in communication protocols [10], and leakage of information via side-channel [22, 17].

ASIA CCS'14, June 4–6, 2014, Kyoto, Japan.

http://dx.doi.org/10.1145/2590296.2590328.

To introduce QIF, consider the data sanitization program P from [27, 26], shown in Figure 1. Clearly only integer

```
base = 8;
if (H < 16) then O = base + H;
else O = base;
```

Figure 1: Data sanitization

values from 8 to 23 are possible outputs of this program. An attacker has hence available 16 possible output observations: observing outputs 9 .. 23 will know the secret H is 1 .. 15 and observing 8 will know the secret is 0 or greater than 15. Assuming the attacker has no prior knowledge of the secret H apart that is a 32 bits variable his *a-priori* probability of guessing the value of H in one try is $\frac{1}{2^{32}}$, and the expected probability of guessing the secret in one try after observing the outputs is:

$$\frac{15}{2^{32}} + \frac{2^{32}-15}{2^{32}}\frac{1}{2^{32}-15} = \frac{15}{2^{32}} + \frac{1}{2^{32}} = \frac{16}{2^{32}}$$

We can measure the leakage of the program as the difference (of the $-\log$ base 2) between the probability of guessing the secret before and after observing the outputs of the program; in this case:

$$-\log(\frac{1}{2^{32}}) - (-\log\frac{16}{2^{32}}) = \log(16) = 4$$

The fact that $\log(16) = \log$ (number of output observations) is not a coincidence. In fact a fundamental QIF result (the channel capacity theorem [24, 33]) shows that leakage for a program is always less or equal to the log of the number of observables of the program. More importantly the theorem holds if we consider not only the above notion of leakage based on the probability of guessing the secret [33] but also if we consider the notion of leakage based on information theory measuring the number of bits leaked [14].

For these reasons counting the number of observables is the basis of state-of-the-art QIF analysis, e.g. [18, 26, 22, 21], and also the basis for this work. The channel capacity theorem also justifies the following:

Definition 1. Given a program P, QIF is the problem of counting N, the number of possible outputs of P.

However the problem of an automated QIF analysis is still very challenging. A simpler problem, called bounding QIF, is considered in [34, 18]: deciding if a program P leaks less than a constant q. In previous work, Yasuoka and Terauchi have proved that bounding QIF is not a *k-safety* problem for any k [34]. Cerny et al. then proved that in the case of Shannon entropy, bounding QIF is PSPACE-complete [12]. So QIF and bounding QIF remain a huge challenge.

1.1 Overview and Contributions

In order to better frame the contributions of this paper let us consider again the program P in Figure 1. In the computer memory, O is stored as a bit vector $b_1b_2..b_{32}$ such that the first 27 bits, $\{b_1,..,b_{27}\}$, are 0 (otherwise O will exceed 23) and the last 5 bits range from 01000 to 10111.

Suppose we have a logical formula φ_P that describes the behaviour of P which contains a set of variables $p_1, p_2, ..p_{32}$ representing the bits of the output O. A model of φ_P then provides a truth assignment for the p_i which corresponds to a concrete value of the output O. In this way, the problem of counting all possible outputs, is reduced to the model counting problem on the logical formula φ_P. We name this problem *abstract model counting*, from the traditional *model counting* (#SAT) problem.

In summary, we introduce a theory-based technique which provides a dramatic improvement on state-of-the-art QIF analysis implementations. On the theoretical side, this work establishes a connection between fundamental verification algorithms and QIF. This connection is exploited to mitigate the state explosion problem by developing a novel approach for QIF based on SMT. More specific contributions are:

1. Introduction of a new research problem, #SMT, and its applications to QIF and Symbolic Execution [20].

2. A framework, called #DPLL($\mathcal{T}$), to build a solver for #SMT-based QIF.

3. The methodology of Symbolic Execution re-casted as #DPLL($\mathcal{T}$).

4. Two prototyping tools for QIF analysis: **sqifc** built on top of CBMC [15] and **jpf-qif** built on top of Symbolic PathFinder [32].

5. Analysis of complex code, including new vulnerabilities from the National Vulnerability Database of the US government [2] and anonymity protocols.

The rest of the paper is organized as follows: we describe the #SMT problem and our approach to QIF in Section 2. To illustrate the approach, we provide case studies of real-world applications in Section 3. Related work is mentioned in Section 4. Section 5 concludes our work.

2. ABSTRACT MODEL COUNTING

Before introducing our approach, Symbolic QIF (or SQIF), we recall the SMT problem, and define the new problem #SMT.

Satisfiability Modulo Theories (SMT) is the problem of checking the satisfiability of logical formulas over one or more first-order theories $\mathcal{T}$. *Boolean abstraction* of an SMT formula φ, denoted by $\mathcal{BA}(\varphi)$, is a bijective function that maps Boolean atoms into themselves and theory atoms (or $\mathcal{T}$-atoms) into fresh Boolean atoms. For example, below is a SMT formula φ w.r.t. the theory of *Linear Arithmetic* and its Boolean abstraction:

$$\begin{array}{ll} \varphi := \{\neg(x+y>1) \vee A_1\} & \mathcal{BA}(\varphi) := \{\neg B_1 \vee A_1\} \\ \quad \wedge \{(x+y>1) \vee \neg A_2\} & \quad \wedge \{B_1 \vee \neg A_2\} \\ \quad \wedge \{\neg A_3 \vee (y-z<7)\} & \quad \wedge \{\neg A_3 \vee B_2\} \end{array}$$

We extend the traditional SMT problem to define a new research problem, namely #SMT:

Definition 2. Given a formula φ w.r.t. combinations of background theories $\mathcal{T}$ and its Boolean abstraction $\mathcal{BA}(\varphi)$, **propositional abstract model counting** or #SMT is the problem of computing the number of models of $\mathcal{BA}(\varphi)$ which are consistent with φ. Such models of $\mathcal{BA}(\varphi)$ are also called *abstract models* of φ.

Note that most SMT theories permit an infinite number of models, but #SMT is always a finite number. Note also that the result of #SMT depends on the syntax of the formula, i.e. in our context the program syntax. For instance, the two formulas φ_1, φ_2 as follows are equivalent but will have different results in #SMT: $\varphi_1 = (x > 0) \vee (x < 0)$ and $\varphi_2 = \neg(x = 0)$.

State-of-the-art SMT solvers are in general the integration of two components: (i) an *enumerator* integrating a SAT solver enumerates truth assignments satisfying the Boolean abstraction of the input formula; (ii) $\mathcal{T}$-solvers validate the consistency w.r.t. theories $\mathcal{T}$ of the (partial) assignment produced by the SAT solver. Naturally, an SMT solver can be extended into a #SMT solver by replacing the SAT solver with a #SAT solver that can explicitly enumerate all models.

2.1 Symbolic QIF as a #SMT problem

The key idea behind SQIF is that instead of checking every concrete value one by one, we process multiple values at a time. To this aim, we need a representation denoting a set of values. We consider a set of atomic propositions $\Phi := \{p_1, p_2, .., p_M\}$, in which each p_i corresponds to the bit b_i of the output O. For example the proposition $p_1 \wedge \neg p_2$ represents a family of sets representing up to 2^{M-2} concrete values: all the bit configurations over M bits where the first bit is 1 and the second bit is 0.

```
for all output bits b_i, 1 ≤ i ≤ M do
    if (b_i == 1) then
        p_i = True
    else
        p_i = False
    end if
end for
```

Figure 2: Symbolic representation

Obviously, without any constraints Φ can represent up to 2^M possible values. With the constraints on the output O imposed by the program P, the number of models of Φ is down from 2^M to a number N that we need to count. To generate the formula of these constraints: the program P, to which the code in Figure 2 has been appended at the end, is first transformed into a logical formula φ_P w.r.t. theories $\mathcal{T}$, e.g. by translating statements into Static Single Assignment (SSA) form. Once P is encoded as a logical formula φ_P, then we can apply model checking on P to verify the satisfiability of φ_P. In other words, a model checker like CBMC is used as a $\mathcal{T}$-solver.

$$\text{Program} \longleftrightarrow \text{Logical formula}$$
$$\text{Model checker} \longleftrightarrow \mathcal{T}\text{-solver}$$

If one accepts the view that each p_i is a Boolean abstraction of the $\mathcal{T}$-atom expressing the constraints on bit b_i, then the QIF problem of counting N can be viewed as a #SMT problem. In other words, with this view the QIF analysis (Definition 1) is a #SMT problem.

The transformation from programs to logical formulas is also exactly what bounded model checkers like CBMC do: once a program is converted into a logical formula then its satisfiability is checked with a SAT solver or an SMT solver. We however can also use non SAT-based model checkers, e.g. Java PathFinder (JPF) [1], as a $\mathcal{T}$-solver. Our approach does not depend on a programming language or the type of model checker.

At this point we have defined the notation of a symbolic representation Φ of the state space of the output O. In the next section, we will describe a DPLL-based framework to systematically explore Φ.

2.2 A #DPLL($\mathcal{T}$) for QIF

The first practical approach for #SAT is an extension of DPLL [11] that enumerates all models. Modern #SAT solvers, e.g. RelSat [9] and c2d [16], are more efficient thanks to smarter approaches that exploit the structure of the clauses and avoid explicitly enumerating models. In the context of #SMT, however, explicit enumeration of abstract models is necessary since we need to check the consistency of each abstract model w.r.t. the background theory $\mathcal{T}$. The Symbolic QIF framework we propose here is a #DPLL($\mathcal{T}$) tailored for QIF, by combining a simple DPLL-based #SAT solver and a $\mathcal{T}$-solver. Hence, this variant of #DPLL($\mathcal{T}$) is a #SMT solver in the context of QIF.

A high level framework to explore the state-space and quantify the leaks of confidential data is described by the procedures `SymbolicQIF` and `SymCount` in Figure 3 and 4.

function SYMBOLICQIF(Φ, φ_P)
  $\Psi = \epsilon$, $pc = \epsilon$, $N = 0$, $i = 1$
  EarlyPrunning(Φ)
  SymCount($\Phi, \Psi, \varphi_P, N, pc, i$)
return Ψ, $\log_2(N)$
end function

Figure 3: Symbolic QIF analysis

Φ, Ψ, φ_P and N are passed by reference, while pc and i are passed by value. Φ is the symbolic representation of the output described in the previous section, φ_P is the formula representing the program P and Ψ is the set of models of φ_P. N is the cardinality of Ψ, and the procedure `SymbolicQIF` returns $\log_2(N)$ as the channel capacity. M is the size of the output data type, e.g. $M = 32$ if O is a 32-bit integer, and i is the depth of the recursive call. The parameter pc is a partial assignment of Φ, it is incrementally updated when the search progresses. In `SymCount`, $\mathcal{T}$-solver(φ_P, pc) means the $\mathcal{T}$-solver is called to check if there is a model of φ_P where pc is (assigned to) *True*.

We illustrate the algorithm `SymCount` by running it on a simple example (we ignore temporarily lines 2 and 3 that will be clarified in section 2.4). Consider again the case study

1: **function** SYMCOUNT($\Phi, \Psi, \varphi_P, N, pc, i$)
2: **if** ($N \geq 2^k$) **then return** *Insecure*
3: **end if**
4: Extract p_i from Φ
5: $pc_1 \leftarrow pc \wedge p_i$
6: **if** ($\mathcal{T}$-solver(φ_P, pc_1)) **then**
7: **if** ($i == M$) **then**
8: $\Psi \leftarrow \Psi \cup \{pc_1\}$
9: $N \leftarrow N + 1$
10: **else**
11: SymCount($\Phi, \Psi, \varphi_P, N, pc_1, i + 1$)
12: **end if**
13: **end if**
14: $pc_2 \leftarrow pc \wedge \neg p_i$
15: **if** ($\mathcal{T}$-solver(φ_P, pc_2)) **then**
16: **if** ($i == M$) **then**
17: $\Psi \leftarrow \Psi \cup \{pc_2\}$
18: $N \leftarrow N + 1$
19: **else**
20: SymCount($\Phi, \Psi, \varphi_P, N, pc_2, i + 1$)
21: **end if**
22: **end if**
23: **end function**

Figure 4: Symbolic counting for QIF

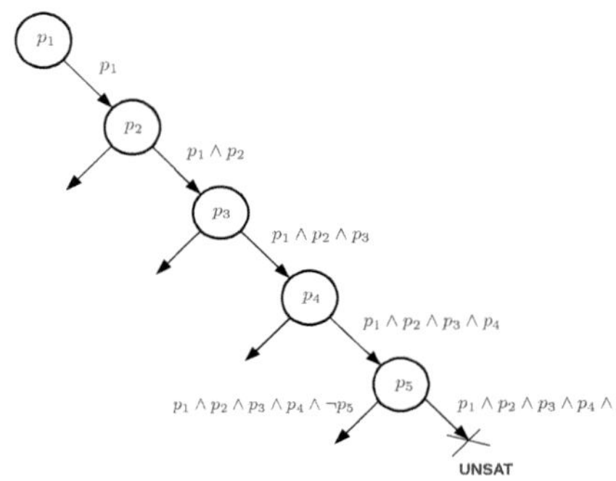

Figure 5: Partial exploration path of SQIF for the data sanitisation program from Figure 1.

of the data sanitization program in Figure 1. Only integer values from 8 to 23 are possible outputs of this program, which means the number of possible outputs is $N = 16$. At the beginning, all variables are initialised as in Figure 3, the method `EarlyPrunning` employs a heuristic that will be discussed later in this section. The method `SymCount` is then called to count the number of possible models of φ_P. When a variable $p_i \in \Phi$ is selected, we systematically explore in the same way for both p_i and $\neg p_i$. Hence, the block of code from line 5 to line 13, and the one from line 14 to line 22 in Figure 4 are symmetric: we only explain the first one.

A partial run of `SymCount` on the illustrative example is depicted in Figure 5. At the first call of `SymCount`: $i = 1$, the variable p_1 is in consideration and it is added to pc in line 5. Since pc is initialised to be empty, $pc_1 = p_1$. The $\mathcal{T}$-solver is called to check if there is a model of φ_P where p_1 is (assigned to) *True*. This can be done by using assertion to check the validity of $\neg p_1$ in a program as follows:

assert $!p_1$;

A model checking tool like JPF or CBMC can be used as a $\mathcal{T}$-solver to verify this assertion and it will return $True$ if the assertion fails, and $False$ otherwise. In this example, the $\mathcal{T}$-solver would return $True$ since p_1 stands for "first bit is 1" and all odd values from 9 to 23 are possible outputs satisfying the condition p_1. Hence, SQIF proceeds by calling `SymCount` with $i = 2$. Similarly, the procedure progresses until calling `SymCount` with $i = 5$, which means it needs to verify:

$$\textbf{assert}\ !(p_1\ \&\&\ p_2\ \&\&\ p_3\ \&\&\ p_4\ \&\&\ p_5);$$

This time the $\mathcal{T}$-solver would return $False$, since $p_1 \wedge p_2 .. \wedge p_5$ represents a set of outputs of which each element is at least $2^0 + 2^1 + .. + 2^4 = 31$, while the possible range of O is only from 8 to 23. For a program with an output of 32-bits, by using `EarlyPrunning`, SQIF trims a set of 2^{27} concrete values represented by the family of sets:

$$\{\Phi := \{p_1, p_2, .., p_{32}\} : p_1 \wedge p_2 \wedge p_3 \wedge p_4 \wedge p_5\}$$

This is how the state-space explosion problem is mitigated.

At the depth $i = 5$ as above, if SQIF takes the path of $\neg p_5$ from line 14, then the $\mathcal{T}$-solver returns $True$ ($O = 15$ is one of the models). Hence, the procedure continues with $i = 6$, and from this point until $i = 32$, only the path of $\neg p_i$ is SAT. At $i = 32$, SQIF finds a full path 00..01111 which represents an output $O = 15$. This path is added to Ψ, and SQIF increases N. Finally, at the end of the method `SymbolicQIF`, we have $\Psi = \{8, 9, .., 23\}$ and $N = 16$, thus we can conclude that the data sanitization program in Figure 1 leaks at most 4 bits.

The method `EarlyPrunning` implements the idea that if p_1 is unsatisfiable, then $p_1 \wedge C$ is also unsatisfiable for any C. Therefore, at the beginning of the `SymbolicQIF`, all p_i are checked for satisfiability, and the results are stored for later use. We note that `EarlyPrunning` speeds up `SymbolicQIF` dramatically when the number of possible models (outputs of the program) is small.

We have developed a prototyping tool for QIF analysis of C programs, **sqifc** built on top of CBMC.

2.3 Symbolic Execution as #DPLL($\mathcal{T}$)

Symbolic Execution (SE) [20] is a powerful technique, widely used in many domains of application such as test data generation, partial verification, symbolic debugging, and program reduction. Here we argue that:

Suppose a program is encoded into a logical formula then a Symbolic Executor can be viewed as a #SMT solver for this formula.

Intuitively, if we see a program as a logical formula, then a concrete execution of the program corresponds to a model of that formula. A symbolic path, which represents a set of concrete executions, can be viewed as corresponding to the Boolean abstraction of the set of models. Thus, a Symbolic Executor, returning all symbolic paths of a program, can be viewed as a #SMT solver.

Program	$\longleftrightarrow$	Logical formula
Concrete execution	$\longleftrightarrow$	Model of the formula
Symbolic path	$\longleftrightarrow$	Boolean abstraction of models

Example 1. To illustrate the idea, consider a simple C program as follows:

```
if (x > 1) { y = x < 5 ? x + 10 : x;} else y = 0;
```

We denote the propositional variables: C_1 as $(x > 1)$, C_2 as $(x < 5)$, A_1 as $(y_1 = x + 10)$, A_2 as $(y_2 = x)$, and A_3 as $(y_3 = 0)$. In this way, the program can be viewed as a Static Single Assignment-like (SSA) logical formula:

$$(C_1 \rightarrow ((C_2 \rightarrow A_1) \wedge (\neg C_2 \rightarrow A_2))) \wedge (\neg C_1 \rightarrow A_3)$$

This is a formula modulo the theory of *linear arithmetic*. In the Boolean abstraction of the formula, A_1, A_2 and A_3 are pure literals and can be removed. The formula has hence three models that can be written as:

$$\{C_1 \wedge C_2, C_1 \wedge \neg C_2, \neg C_1\}$$

This is also the set of possible symbolic paths generated by running SE on the program.

```
function SymEx(P, σ, pc, l)
    Execute assignment statements, update σ
    if (l = EOF) then
        Ψ ← Ψ ∪ {pc}
        Σ ← Σ ∪ {σ}
        return
    end if
    Extract {c, l⊤, l⊥} from if-statement
    if (T-solver(pc ⊢ c)) then
        SymEx(P, σ, pc, l⊤)
    else if (T-solver(pc ⊢ ¬c)) then
        SymEx(P, σ, pc, l⊥)
    else
        pc1 ← pc ∧ c
        if (T-solver(pc1)) then
            SymEx(P, σ, pc1, l⊤)
        end if
        pc2 ← pc ∧ ¬c
        if (T-solver(pc2)) then
            SymEx(P, σ, pc2, l⊥)
        end if
    end if
end function
```

Figure 6: Symbolic Execution

The above example suggests we can see SE as #SMT solver, we will now derive SE in the #DPLL($\mathcal{T}$) framework. Let us consider a program in SSA form and consisting of only assignment statements and conditionals. Tools such as CBMC and Soot [4] transform ANSI C and Java programs into SSA to verify properties.

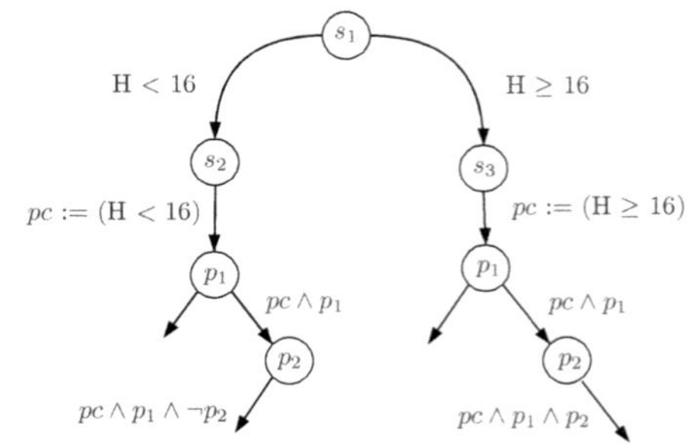

Figure 7: Partial exploration path of SQIF-SE for the data sanitisation program from Figure 1.

The algorithm of SE is depicted in Figure 6. Here σ is a symbolic environment, i.e. a map from program variables to formulas over symbolic inputs. The parameter pc holds the current path condition. At the end of the procedure, Ψ will be the set of all path conditions and Σ will be the set of all final symbolic environments, one for each path condition. Statements in the program P are identified by their program location l. For a conditional statement `if (c)` I `else` I', symbols $l_\top$ and $l_\perp$ denote the locations of the first statements in I and I' respectively. Notice that in `SymEx` lines 9 to 12 can be viewed as $\mathcal{T}$-propagation, and lines 14 to 21 can be viewed as splitting in DPLL($\mathcal{T}$) [28].

In `SymEx` $\mathcal{T}$-solver($pc \vdash c$) calls the solver to check whether c is a consequence of pc and $\mathcal{T}$-solver(pc) calls the solver to check whether pc is satisfiable.

We believe that the insight of SE as #DPLL($\mathcal{T}$) paves the way for the development of efficient Symbolic Executors, by exploiting techniques that have been successful in SMT such as non-chronological backtracking and clause learning [31].

2.3.1 SQIF by Symbolic Execution:

With the view of SE as #DPLL($\mathcal{T}$), we are able to make a Symbolic Executor work as `SymbolicQIF` with little effort. The key idea here is to enumerate all concrete values from symbolic executions.

For a program P that takes symbolic inputs $i_1, i_2, ..i_\alpha$, and produces an output O, the result of running SE on P is as follows:

$$O = \left\{ \begin{array}{ll} f_1(i_1, i_2.., i_\alpha) & \text{if } pc_1 \\ f_2(i_1, i_2.., i_\alpha) & \text{if } pc_2 \\ \cdots & \cdots \\ f_\beta(i_1, i_2.., i_\alpha) & \text{if } pc_\beta \end{array} \right\}$$

where $f_1, f_2, ..f_\beta$ are formulas over symbolic inputs $i_1, i_2, ..i_\alpha$. $pc_1, pc_2, ..pc_\beta$ are the path conditions. Notice f_i expresses a symbolic final value for O, i.e. in terms of `SymEx` instead of $f_i(i_1, i_2.., i_\alpha)$ we could write $\sigma_i(O)$ for $\sigma_i \in \Sigma$. The following proposition was proved by King [20]:

PROPOSITION 1.

$$\forall i, j \in [1, \beta] \wedge i \neq j, \ pc_i \wedge pc_j = \perp$$

which means that path conditions are mutually exclusive.

Definition 3. For a path condition pc_i obtained from SE, the concretization set of pc_i, denoted $\mathcal{CS}(pc_i)$, is the set of all concrete values of output O that can be reached by executing the program following pc_i.

Consider again the *Example 1* in which there are three path conditions: $pc_1 = C_1 \wedge C_2$, $pc_2 = C_1 \wedge \neg C_2$, $pc_3 = \neg C_1$. The corresponding concretization sets of these path conditions are: $\mathcal{CS}(pc_1) = [12..14]$, $\mathcal{CS}(pc_2) = [5..2^M]$, $\mathcal{CS}(pc_3) = [0]$, where M is the number of bits of the variable x. The set of all possible values of output O is formed by the union of concretization sets of all paths, and thus:

$$N = \left| \bigcup_{i=1}^{\beta} \mathcal{CS}(pc_i) \right|$$

The set $\mathcal{CS}(pc_i)$ can be computed by inserting the code in Figure 2 at the end of the program and run SE: we add M conditions, each one tests whether bit b_i of the output O is 0 or 1. These M conditions test all the bits of the output O. Exploring all possible combinations of these conditions leads to enumerating all possible values of O. We denote by SQIF-SE the implementation of SQIF using SE. A partial exploration path of SQIF-SE is described as in Figure 7. SE as implemented by Symbolic PathFinder (SPF) returns a concrete values for each possible path. The number of distinct concrete values is the N that we need to count.

SQIF-SE is implemented into a prototyping tool **jpf-qif** built on top of SPF. The tool works on Java programs.

2.4 Soundness and Completeness

By soundness of the SQIF approach we mean that given Ψ, $\log_2(N)$ returned by `SymbolicQIF`(Φ, φ_P), each element of Ψ is a model of φ_P i.e. corresponds to a possible value of the output of the program P. By completeness of SQIF, we mean that Ψ is the set of all models of φ_P i.e. all values of the output of P.

THEOREM 1. *Given a sound (resp. complete) $\mathcal{T}$-solver the SQIF approach is sound (resp. complete) i.e.* `SymCount` *solves the QIF problem (Definition 1).*

PROOF SKETCH 1. *The SQIF algorithm as described in Figure 4 is based on DPLL which itself is a depth-first search procedure. As the search space is a binary tree with bounded depth M, the number of bits of the output, the depth-first search procedure is complete. The soundness of SQIF is guaranteed by the soundness of the $\mathcal{T}$-solver, i.e. model checker.*

In reality $\mathcal{T}$-solvers are only complete in particular domains. Moreover, even with sound and complete $\mathcal{T}$-solvers, a large leak requires an exponential number of calls to the $\mathcal{T}$-solver and so in practice SQIF is complete only for programs with *small* leaks. SQIF-SE relies on a Symbolic Executor, and hence it is complete in programs with a bounded model of runtime behaviour, which means programs have no recursion or unbounded loops. These are well-known issues in SE and handling them is orthogonal to our work. Since our tools are based on bounded model checker and bounded SE, we choose to analyse only bounded programs. Notice however that Theorem 1 holds for general $\mathcal{T}$-solvers.

Because of these practical issues about completeness, it has been proposed to shift the focus from the question *"How much does it leak?"* to the simpler quantitative question *"Does it leak more than k?"* [18, 34]. This approach not only makes the problem easier to analysis, but it is also more intuitive in term of security, because the user policy, i.e. *threshold* k, is encoded in the analysis. The ultimate goal of security analysis is to determine whether a program is *secure* or *insecure*. As discussed in the previous section, the goal of QIF is to relax security policy from *non-interference* to an acceptable threshold k *bits of interference*, so that we can tolerate "*small*" leak, and accept more programs as secure. The SQIF approach can also be used in the same way: with a user policy k, if SQIF finds out more than $\mathcal{K} = 2^k$ possible outputs, we can stop the procedure and conclude that the program is *insecure*. This is the meaning of lines 2 and 3 of function `SymCount` in Figure 4.

A straightforward consequence of the Theorem 1 is that, assuming a sound $\mathcal{T}$-solver, given a user policy k, `SymCount` never returns *secure* for a program leaking more than k bits. This can be formally expressed as:

COROLLARY 1. *SQIF is sound w.r.t a user policy k.*

3. CASE STUDIES

Only few papers present QIF static code analysis of real-world applications: examples are [18], [22] and the more recent [21]. Of these three approaches, [22] uses a different attacker model, namely cache side-channels and so is not directly comparable with our approach. The other two, [18] and [21], use the same attacker model as we do but are at the moment both restricted to C programs, and hence only comparable to **sqifc**. We will concentrate on [18], to which we refer as **selfcomp**, because it is based on the well-known concept of self-composition [7]. **sqifc** is compared to [21] in section 3.7. For the analysis of anonymity protocols, we compare **sqifc** against **QUAIL** [3, 10], a state-of-the-art quantitative analyser for probabilistic programs. The case studies broadly fall in three categories:

- the first category, consisting of case studies from the National Vulnerability Database of the US government [2], is aimed to demonstrate how our analysis is able to deal with complex C-code,
- the case studies CRC and Tax show the applicability to quantify leakage in applications which leak by design,
- the case studies Grade and Dining cryptos protocols show how our technique, even if it is unable to analyse probabilistic programs, is able to computing channel capacity for anonymity protocols.

The experiments are conducted on a desktop machine with Intel Core i5 3.3GHz and 8GB of memory.

3.1 CVE-2011-2208

This case study is an example of a program that leaks information when the attacker can control the public input. It is taken from the National Vulnerability Database (NVD) of the US government [2], and it is released on 13/06/2012. The system call `osf_getdomainname`, depicted in Figure 8, in

```
1   int osf_getdomainname(char __user *name, int namelen)
2   {
3     unsigned len;
4     int i, error;
5
6     error = verify_area(VERIFY_WRITE, name, namelen);
7     if (error)
8       goto out;
9
10    len = namelen;
11    if (namelen > 32)
12      len = 32;
13
14    down_read(&uts_sem);
15    for (i = 0; i < len; ++i) {
16      __put_user(system_utsname.domainname[i],
17          name + i);
18      if (system_utsname.domainname[i] == '\0')
19        break;
20    }
21    up_read(&uts_sem);
22   out:
23     return error;
24  }
```

Figure 8: arch/alpha/kernel/osf_sys.c

the Linux kernel before 2.6.39.4 leaks sensitive information from kernel memory. This is caused by an integer signedness error: the signed parameter `namelen` is assigned to the unsigned variable `len` in line 10, so a negative value can be transformed into a big positive one. Therefore, although the condition in line 11 restricts `namelen` to 32, the number of characters returned to the user via the structure `name` may be much greater including bytes from kernel memory.

In order to quantify the information leakage caused by this vulnerability, we chose the thresholds of security policy $\mathcal{K} = 64$ and $\mathcal{K} = 256$, which means the program is secure if it leaks less than 6 and 8 bits respectively. After the times in Figure 11 , **sqifc** and **selfcomp** conclude that the program is insecure. We then apply the patch provided for this vulnerability, and run **sqifc** again. This time, **sqifc** found only one possible value for `name`, which means a leak of zero bit. Hence, we prove that the patch fixed the leak.

3.2 CVE-2011-1078

This case study is also taken from NVD, and it is released on 21/06/2012. The function `sco_sock_getsockopt_old` in the Linux kernel before 2.6.39, depicted in Figure 9, leaks sensitive information from kernel memory. As in line 24,

```
1   static int sco_sock_getsockopt_old(
2       struct socket *sock, int optname,
3       char __user *optval, int __user *optlen)
4   {
5     struct sock *sk = sock->sk;
6     struct sco_conninfo cinfo;
7     int len, err = 0;
8     ...
9
10    lock_sock(sk);
11
12    switch (optname) {
13      case SCO_OPTIONS:
14        ...
15
16      case SCO_CONNINFO:
17        ...
18
19        cinfo.hci_handle = sco_pi(sk)->conn->hcon->handle;
20        memcpy(cinfo.dev_class,
21          sco_pi(sk)->conn->hcon->dev_class, 3);
22
23        len = min_t(unsigned int, len, sizeof(cinfo));
24        if (copy_to_user(optval, (char *)&cinfo, len))
25          err = -EFAULT;
26          break;
27          ...
28        }
29
30        release_sock(sk);
31        return err;
32  }
```

Figure 9: net/bluetooth/sco.c

`cinfo` is copied to the user. Although its total size is 5 bytes, and all bytes are correctly assigned, when compiled it includes an additional padding byte for alignment purposes. This padding byte is not zeroed out, and hence it contains kernel memory, and is leaked to the user. Results of the analysis for $\mathcal{K} = 8$ and $\mathcal{K} = 64$, are shown in Figure 11.

3.3 Cyclic Redundancy Check

The program in Figure 10 performs Cyclic Redundancy Check[1] (CRC) and shifts right the result `sft` bits. We also have a Java version of the program to test with **jpf-qif**. We quantify the amount of information of the confidential input `ch` revealed by observing the output of function `GetCRC8`. We analyse this program with **sqifc**, **jpf-qif** and **selfcomp** for `sft` values of 3 and 5 giving a maximum leakage for this program of 5 (**selfcomp** times out on this case) and 3 bits respectively which is consistent with the design of the program. Results of the analysis for are shown in Figure 11. In the case value of `sft` is 5, i.e. $\mathcal{K} = 8$, **selfcomp** is faster as the state-space is still small enough, and **selfcomp** requires only one call to CBMC. When `sft` = 3, i.e. $\mathcal{K} = 32$, the state-space explosion makes **selfcomp** fail to solve. SQIF

[1]http://en.wikipedia.org/wiki/Cyclic_redundancy_check

```
unsigned char GetCRC8(
        unsigned char check , unsigned char ch)
{
  int i, sft ;
  for ( i = 0 ; i < 8 ; i++ ) {
    if ( check & 0x80 ) {
      check<<=1;
      if ( ch & 0x80 ) { check = check | 0x01;}
      else { check =check & 0xfe; }
      check = check ^ 0x85;
    } else {
      check <<=1;
      if ( ch & 0x80 ) { check = check | 0x01; }
      else { check = check & 0xfe; }
    }
    ch<<=1;
  }
  check >>= sft;
  return check;
}
```

Figure 10: Cyclic Redundancy Check

requires several calls to the solver, but it is less vulnerable to state-space explosion.

3.4 Tax Record

Balliu et al. [6] provided a very interesting case study of information flow security in Java programs derived from the EU-funded FP7-project HATS. The program contains 8 classes/interfaces and 267 LoC. In our analysis we assume the year 2011-2012 basic tax rate in UK, which is applied for a person whose income does not exceed 35 thousand pounds per annum, is $F = 20\%$[2]. Thus, the tax is less than 7 thousands pound per annual. We assume that donations to charities is below the amount of tax to be paid. Obviously, one cannot pay more than what one earns. Following [6] we are interested in leaks of a taxpayer's income and donations to a Tax checker.

3.4.1 QIF vs. Declassification

Balliu et al. considered two cases of declassification: the first one, called taxChecker1, is associated with the policy "$income \times F\% + donation > payment$", and the second one, called taxChecker2, is associated with the policy "$income \times F\% + donation - payment$". They claimed that: *"The value declassified in the taxChecker1 case, resp. taxChecker2 case, is a lower bound, resp. upper bound, of the value revealed to the tax checker in the fixed tax rate variant."*

We notice in this sentence the use of terms like *"value revealed"* and *"bound"*: the authors were trying to describe *quantitative* concepts. From the result of **jpf-qif**, we can give hence quantitative answers to these questions. In the case of *taxChecker1*, the observable is whether the payment is greater or smaller than the sum of the tax and donations, which means there are 2 possible outputs. This corresponds to the leak of 1 bit. In other words, the user policy or threshold $k = 1$. Regarding the taxChecker2 case, under the assumptions listed above, the leakage is upper bounded by 4.86 bits obtained in 24.988 seconds.

3.5 The Grade Protocol

This case study was used to illustrate protocol analysis in [19, 10]. This anonymity protocol is designed to enable a group of students to compute the sum of their grades (e.g., to compute the average) without revealing individual grades.

[2]Since SPF can only handle conditions with integer values, we simplify the code by replacing $(income \times 20)/100$ with tax as an integer. The simplification we made does not change the secrecy, i.e. entropy, of $income$, so it will not affect the result of our analysis.

We denote $S_1, ..., S_k$ be the k students arranged in a ring, each one is given a secret grade g_i between 0 and $m - 1$. To compute the sum of g_i without disclosing them, the students produce k random numbers between 0 and $n = (m - 1)k + 1$ such that the number r_i is known only to the students S_i and $S_{(i+1)\%k}$. Each student s_i then outputs a number $d_i = g_i + r_i - r_{(i+1)\%k}$ and the sum of all grades is equivalent to the sum of the outputs modulo n.

```
int func(){
  size_t S = 5, G = 5, i = 0, j = 0;
  size_t n = ((G-1)*S)+1, sum = 0;
  size_t numbers[S], announcements[S], h[S];

  for (i = 0; i < S; i++) h[i] = nondet_int() % G;

  for (i = 0; i < S; i++)
        numbers[i] = nondet_int() % n;

  while (i<S) {
    j=0;
    while (j<G) {
      if (h[i]==j)
        announcements[i] =
          (j+numbers[i]-numbers[(i+1)%S])%n;
      j=j+1;
    }
    i=i+1;
  }

  for (i = 0; i < S; i++)
    sum += announcements[i];

  return sum % n;
}
```

Figure 12: The Grade protocol

This protocol is implemented as a probabilistic program in both [19] and [10]. Here we implement it in standard ANSI C with the built-in non-deterministic functions of CBMC. The source code, shown on Figure 12, is based on the one provided in [10]. The array `h[S]` stores the grades of all students, i.e. the secret. The attacker can observe `sum % n`.

To compare **QUAIL** with our tool, **sqifc**, we repeat the experiment of the authors for the grade protocol with the tool and examples provided in [3]. However, **QUAIL** timed out after 1 hours for most of the cases, as showed in Figure 15 (we had the same results of leakage with the authors in the cases the tool did not time out). Therefore, we take the result in Figure 13 directly from the paper [10]. Comparing Figure 13 and Figure 14, it is easy to realise that the bounds on the leaks, measured by **sqifc**, do not exceed the real leaks, measured by **QUAIL**, by more than 1 bit, while **sqifc** required no more than 1 minutes in all cases as showed in Figure 16.

3.6 The Dining cryptos protocol

This case study is a variation of the dining cryptographers protocol of Chaum [13], one of the most popular problem in anonymity protocol. There is a group of cryptographers gathering around a table for dinner. After the meal, they are informed that the bill has been paid by someone, who could be one of them or the National Security Agency (NSA). Even though the cryptographers respect each other's right to make an anonymous payment, they want to find out whether the NSA paid. To determine this, they use a protocol as follows: each pair of adjacent cryptographers toss a coin hidden from everybody else, so that each cryptographer only knows the values of the coin shared with the one on his left and with the one on his right; then each cryptographer declares aloud the exclusive OR of the two coins he sees, i.e. 0 if they have the same value and 1 otherwise. However if the payer is one

Case Study	LoC	Language	**sqifc** time	**jpf-qif** time	**selfcomp** time
Data Sanitization	< 10	C/Java	11.898	20.695	timed out
CVE-2011-2208 (64)	> 200	C	22.759	-	119.117
CVE-2011-2208 (256)		C	88.196	-	timed out
CVE-2011-1078 (8)	> 200	C	10.380	-	13.853
CVE-2011-1078 (64)		C	37.899	-	timed out
CRC (8)	< 30	C/Java	1.209	8.386	0.498
CRC (32)		C/Java	8.657	9.357	timed out
Tax Record	267	Java	-	24.988	-

Figure 11: Times in seconds, timeout is 30 minutes. "-" means inapplicable.

(a)

		Students			
		2	3	4	5
Grades	2	1.500	1.811	2.030	2.198
	3	2.197	2.525	2.745	2.910
	4	2.655	2.984	3.201	3.365
	5	2.999	3.325	3.541	timed out

Figure 13: Leakage measured by QUAIL

(b)

		Students			
		2	3	4	5
Grades	2	1.585	2.000	2.322	2.585
	3	2.322	2.807	3.170	3.459
	4	2.807	3.322	3.700	4.000
	5	3.170	3.700	4.087	4.392

Figure 14: Leakage measured by sqifc

```
1  size_t func(){
2
3    size_t N = 5, output = 0, i = 0;
4    size_t coin[N], obscoin[2], decl[N];
5    size_t h;
6
7    h = nondet_uchar() % (N+1);
8
9    for (i = 0; i < N; i++){
10     coin[i] = nondet_uchar() % 2;
11   }
12
13   for (i = 0; i < N; i++){
14     decl[i] = coin[i] ^ coin[(i+1)%N];
15     if (h==i+1){
16       decl[i] = !decl[i];
17     }
18     i = i+1;
19   }
20
21   for (i = 0; i < N; i++){
22     output = output + decl[c];
23   }
24
25   return output;
26 }
```

Figure 18: The Dining cryptos protocol

of the cryptographers, he declares the opposite. In the end, if the sum of all declared values is even, then it is concluded that the NSA paid the bill. On the other hand, the sum is odd means one of the cryptographers did it.

We are interested in knowing how much information about the payer can be leaked by the sum of all declared values (in the dining cryptographers the observation are the declared values instead). The input code for the protocol is depicted in Figure 18. `h` is the identity of the payer, i.e. the secret, `output` is the observable. The coin toss is modelled by a built-in non-deterministic function in line 10. This model is less precise than implementation in probabilistic programs where it is possible to select random values from a specific distribution. By modelling with non-deterministic function and computing channel capacity, we can only compute the maximum leakage in all possible distributions. The channel capacity computed by **sqifc** is showed in Figure 17.

3.7 Optimizing SymCount

One source of inefficiency in the implementation of **sqifc** is that: in each call to CBMC, the transformation from the source code to the logical formula φ_P is recomputed. This can be very costly when the program is large or many calls to CBMC are needed. A simple optimisation to tackle this problem is to use CBMC to compute φ_P once and for all, and then use a SAT or SMT solver to check φ_P together with the appropriate assertion at line 6 or 15 of `SymCount`. We denote the resulting implementation **sqifc+**: it analyses CRC(8) in 0.289 and CRC(32) in 0.475 seconds respectively: an average improvement well over 1000% over **sqifc**.

We believe the performance of **sqifc+** is comparable to the technique in [21] for programs with small leaks but it is outperformed when analysing programs with large leaks (a precise comparison is not possible as all but one programs in [21] have large leaks), however we don't see this as a big issue: the main point of QIF is to determine whether a program leaks a small amount and hence can be considered a secure program, and while the meaning of "small leak" is context dependent it is difficult to see contexts where leaks much larger than 10 bits can be considered small.

4. RELATED WORK

Meng and Smith introduce an *approximate* technique to calculate an upper bound on channel capacity in [26]. The authors' implementation of the method is largely manual, and we proposed an automation for it in [30]. While the work of Meng and Smith is very inspiring, the technique can be very imprecise, for example when the leaks are sparse in the state space. Moreover, the user policy is not encoded in the analysis which makes it infeasible when the leaks are not small. Take an example of a program that leaks all 32 bits of integral confidential data, it needs to make 64 calls to STP solver to determine that all bits are *Non-fixed*. Then, in order to determine two bit patterns of $(31*32)/2 = 496$ pairs of *Non-fixed* bits, it needs to make another $496 * 4 = 1984$ calls to STP solver, so it is 2048 calls in total.

The first automated method for QIF was proposed by Backes et al. [5]. The method can be divided into two stages: first, it employs model checking to compute an equivalence relation $\mathcal{R}$ on the set of confidential inputs w.r.t. observable outputs; secondly, if this relation $\mathcal{R}$ can be represented by a system of *linear integer inequalities* $A\bar{x} \geqslant \bar{b}$, which means it is a bounded integer *polytopes*, then a variant of Barvinok's algorithm [8] can be used to count the number of integer

(c)

		Students			
		2	3	4	5
Grades	2	1.306	241.483	-	-
	3	28.613	-	-	-
	4	508.313	-	-	-
	5	-	-	-	-

Figure 15: Elapsed time in seconds of QUAIL

(d)

		Students			
		2	3	4	5
Grades	2	5.657	7.029	10.767	9.469
	3	9.145	11.597	17.987	20.930
	4	10.095	16.872	21.869	18.579
	5	14.639	20.666	33.298	40.399

Figure 16: Elapsed time in seconds of sqifc

cryptos	3	4	5	6	50	100	200	300
Channel capacity	2	2.32	2.59	2.81	5.672	6.658	7.651	8.234
Time in seconds	2.145	3.496	3.632	18.634	46.970	158.517	587.670	3326.915

Figure 17: The dining cryptos protocol analysed by sqifc

solutions of $\mathcal{R}$. While this work is important as the first effort on automation of QIF analysis, it is not clear however how this approach can be applied to real-world programs because of, for example, bit-wise operators in the CRC case study or non-linear relations and so on.

Closer to our work is the paper of **selfcomp** [18] discussed in the previous section. However, as already outlined their approach to address the question *"Does it leak more than k?"* is quite different from ours. Köpf et al. [22] also apply QIF to real-world applications, i.e. leakage of cache side-channels; their technique is based on abstract interpretation and hence not based on bounded models. Because of this however they over-approximate channel capacity.

A preliminary version of the algorithm `SymCount` has been presented in a workshop [30]. In our previous work, we also used Symbolic Execution for *qualitative* information flow analysis [29]. A recent paper [21] explores QIF in a pure logical framework. The approach is powerful and elegant, however it is more limited when compared to our approach as it relies on the solver to generate models whereas our approach can use any solver instead. For example we can analyse Java by using JPF as a solver for bytecode even if JPF doesn't generate a model in the sense of [21].

McCamant and Ernst released FlowCheck [25], a tool for security testing based on dynamic taint analysis. What FlowCheck measures is the number of tainted bits, not an information-theoretic bound, so it is significantly different from our approach. Another tool is described in [27], it is able to analyse large programs using the notion of channel capacity in the context of dynamic taint analysis, while our approach is based on verification techniques. In this sense, our work comes with stronger theoretical guarantees.

5. CONCLUSION AND FUTURE WORK

We introduce *Abstract Model Counting*, a novel approach based on SMT for the quantification of information leaks for real-world applications. Although our implementation is far from being optimised, it drastically outperforms the existing technique based on self-composition. Our approach is applicable to programs with difficult data structures such as pointers, and to Java bytecode.

An original contribution of this work on the theoretical side is: the establishment of connections between measuring confidentiality leaks and fundamental verification algorithms like Symbolic Execution, SMT solvers and DPLL. As a first consequence of these connections we have developed new QIF techniques implemented on two prototype tools for C and Java respectively. We have demonstrated the potential of these tools on C and Java code and argued that while measuring large leaks remains an infeasible task, the most interesting case, i.e. verifying whether a program only leaks a small amount of the secret may be dramatically improved by the techniques here introduced.

An immediate direction for investigation is: instead of dealing with programs as hidden formulas as in this paper, we may view it as an SMT formula w.r.t. the theory of Quantified Bit-Vector, and work directly with the formula. Other interesting directions include to explore the possibility of analysing anonymity protocols under specific probability distributions.

6. ACKNOWLEDGEMENTS

We thank Dino Distefano, Nikos Tzevelekos, Vladimir Klebanov and the anonymous reviewers for their valuable constructive comments. Pasquale Malacaria's research was supported by grant EP/K032011/1.

7. REFERENCES

[1] Java PathFinder. `http://babelfish.arc.nasa.gov/trac/jpf/`.

[2] National Vulnerability Database. `http://nvd.nist.gov/`.

[3] QUAIL. `https://project.inria.fr/quail/`.

[4] Soot: a Java Optimization Framework. `http://www.sable.mcgill.ca/soot/`.

[5] Backes, M., Kopf, B., and Rybalchenko, A. Automatic discovery and quantification of information leaks. In *Proceedings of the 2009 30th IEEE Symposium on Security and Privacy* (Washington, DC, USA, 2009), SP '09, IEEE Computer Society, pp. 141–153.

[6] Balliu, M., Dam, M., and Guernic, G. L. Encover: Symbolic exploration for information flow security. In *Proceedings of the 2012 IEEE 25th Computer Security Foundations Symposium* (Washington, DC, USA, 2012), CSF '12, IEEE Computer Society, pp. 30–44.

[7] Barthe, G., D'Argenio, P. R., and Rezk, T. Secure information flow by self-composition. In *Proceedings of the 17th IEEE workshop on Computer Security Foundations* (Washington, DC, USA, 2004), CSFW '04, IEEE Computer Society, pp. 100–.

[8] Barvinok, A. I. A polynomial time algorithm for counting integral points in polyhedra when the

dimension is fixed. *Math. Oper. Res. 19*, 4 (Nov. 1994), 769–779.

[9] Bayardo, R. J. RelSat: A Propositional Satisfiability Solver and Model Counter. `http://code.google.com/p/relsat/`.

[10] Biondi, F., Legay, A., Traonouez, L.-M., and Wasowski, A. Quail: A quantitative security analyzer for imperative code. In *Proceedings of the 25th international conference on Computer Aided Verification* (Berlin, Heidelberg, 2013), CAV'13, Springer-Verlag.

[11] Birnbaum, E., and Lozinskii, E. L. The good old davis-putnam procedure helps counting models. *J. Artif. Int. Res. 10*, 1 (June 1999), 457–477.

[12] Cerny, P., Chatterjee, K., and Henzinger, T. A. The complexity of quantitative information flow problems. In *Proceedings of the 2011 IEEE 24th Computer Security Foundations Symposium* (Washington, DC, USA, 2011), CSF '11, IEEE Computer Society, pp. 205–217.

[13] Chaum, D. The dining cryptographers problem: unconditional sender and recipient untraceability. *J. Cryptol. 1*, 1 (Mar. 1988), 65–75.

[14] Clark, D., Hunt, S., and Malacaria, P. A static analysis for quantifying information flow in a simple imperative language. *J. Comput. Secur. 15*, 3 (Aug. 2007), 321–371.

[15] Clarke, E., Kroening, D., and Lerda, F. A tool for checking ANSI-C programs. In *Tools and Algorithms for the Construction and Analysis of Systems (TACAS 2004)* (2004), vol. 2988 of *Lecture Notes in Computer Science*, Springer, pp. 168–176.

[16] Darwiche, A. The c2d Compiler. `http://reasoning.cs.ucla.edu/c2d/`.

[17] Doychev, G., Feld, D., Köpf, B., Mauborgne, L., and Reineke, J. Cacheaudit: A tool for the static analysis of cache side channels. In *Proceedings of the 22Nd USENIX Conference on Security* (Berkeley, CA, USA, 2013), SEC'13, USENIX Association, pp. 431–446.

[18] Heusser, J., and Malacaria, P. Quantifying information leaks in software. In *Proceedings of the 26th Annual Computer Security Applications Conference* (New York, NY, USA, 2010), ACSAC '10, ACM, pp. 261–269.

[19] Kiefer, S., Murawski, A. S., Ouaknine, J., Wachter, B., and Worrell, J. Apex: an analyzer for open probabilistic programs. In *Proceedings of the 24th international conference on Computer Aided Verification* (Berlin, Heidelberg, 2012), CAV'12, Springer-Verlag, pp. 693–698.

[20] King, J. C. Symbolic execution and program testing. *Commun. ACM 19*, 7 (July 1976), 385–394.

[21] Klebanov, V., Manthey, N., and Muise, C. Sat-based analysis and quantification of information flow in programs. In *Quantitative Evaluation of Systems*, vol. 8054 of *Lecture Notes in Computer Science*. Springer Berlin Heidelberg, 2013, pp. 177–192.

[22] Köpf, B., Mauborgne, L., and Ochoa, M. Automatic quantification of cache side-channels. In *Proceedings of the 24th international conference on Computer Aided Verification* (Berlin, Heidelberg, 2012), CAV'12, Springer-Verlag, pp. 564–580.

[23] Malacaria, P. Assessing security threats of looping constructs. In *Proceedings of the 34th annual ACM SIGPLAN-SIGACT symposium on Principles of programming languages* (New York, NY, USA, 2007), POPL '07, ACM, pp. 225–235.

[24] Malacaria, P., and Chen, H. Lagrange multipliers and maximum information leakage in different observational models. In *Proceedings of the third ACM SIGPLAN workshop on Programming languages and analysis for security* (New York, NY, USA, 2008), PLAS '08, ACM, pp. 135–146.

[25] McCamant, S., and Ernst, M. D. Quantitative information flow as network flow capacity. In *Proceedings of the 2008 ACM SIGPLAN conference on Programming language design and implementation* (New York, NY, USA, 2008), PLDI '08, ACM, pp. 193–205.

[26] Meng, Z., and Smith, G. Calculating bounds on information leakage using two-bit patterns. In *Proceedings of the ACM SIGPLAN 6th Workshop on Programming Languages and Analysis for Security* (New York, NY, USA, 2011), PLAS '11, ACM, pp. 1:1–1:12.

[27] Newsome, J., McCamant, S., and Song, D. Measuring channel capacity to distinguish undue influence. In *Proceedings of the ACM SIGPLAN Fourth Workshop on Programming Languages and Analysis for Security* (New York, NY, USA, 2009), PLAS '09, ACM, pp. 73–85.

[28] Nieuwenhuis, R., Oliveras, A., and Tinelli, C. Solving sat and sat modulo theories: From an abstract davis–putnam–logemann–loveland procedure to dpll(t). *J. ACM 53*, 6 (Nov. 2006), 937–977.

[29] Phan, Q.-S. Self-composition by symbolic execution. In *2013 Imperial College Computing Student Workshop* (Dagstuhl, Germany, 2013), vol. 35 of *OpenAccess Series in Informatics (OASIcs)*, Schloss Dagstuhl–Leibniz-Zentrum fuer Informatik, pp. 95–102.

[30] Phan, Q.-S., Malacaria, P., Tkachuk, O., and Păsăreanu, C. S. Symbolic quantitative information flow. *SIGSOFT Softw. Eng. Notes 37*, 6 (Nov. 2012), 1–5.

[31] Prosser, P. Hybrid algorithms for the constraint satisfaction problem. *Computational Intelligence 9* (1993), 268–299.

[32] Păsăreanu, C. S., Visser, W., Bushnell, D., Geldenhuys, J., Mehlitz, P., and Rungta, N. Symbolic pathfinder: integrating symbolic execution with model checking for java bytecode analysis. *Automated Software Engineering* (2013), 1–35.

[33] Smith, G. On the foundations of quantitative information flow. In *Proceedings of the 12th International Conference on Foundations of Software Science and Computational Structures* (Berlin, Heidelberg, 2009), FOSSACS '09, Springer-Verlag, pp. 288–302.

[34] Yasuoka, H., and Terauchi, T. On bounding problems of quantitative information flow. *Journal of Computer Security 19*, 6 (2011), 1029–1082.

ConXsense – Automated Context Classification for Context-Aware Access Control

Markus Miettinen
Technische Universität Darmstadt
markus.miettinen@trust.cased.de

Stephan Heuser
Technische Universität Darmstadt
stephan.heuser@trust.cased.de

Wiebke Kronz
Technische Universität Darmstadt
wiebke.kronz@cased.de

Ahmad-Reza Sadeghi
Technische Universität Darmstadt
ahmad.sadeghi@trust.cased.de

N. Asokan
Aalto University and University of Helsinki
asokan@acm.org

ABSTRACT

We present *ConXsense*, the first framework for context-aware access control on mobile devices based on context classification. Previous context-aware access control systems often require users to laboriously specify detailed policies or they rely on pre-defined policies not adequately reflecting the true preferences of users. We present the design and implementation of a context-aware framework that uses a probabilistic approach to overcome these deficiencies. The framework utilizes context sensing and machine learning to automatically classify contexts according to their security and privacy-related properties. We apply the framework to two important smartphone-related use cases: protection against device misuse using a dynamic device lock and protection against sensory malware. We ground our analysis on a sociological survey examining the perceptions and concerns of users related to contextual smartphone security and analyze the effectiveness of our approach with real-world context data. We also demonstrate the integration of our framework with the *FlaskDroid* [7] architecture for fine-grained access control enforcement on the Android platform.

Categories and Subject Descriptors

D.4.6 [**Operating Systems**]: Security and Protection—*Access controls, Invasive software*

Keywords

Mobile security; Context sensing; Privacy policies; Context-awareness

1. INTRODUCTION

Mobile devices today are equipped with a wide variety of sensors for sensing the context of the device. Applications that make use of this information are becoming increasingly popular. Examples include location-based applications like *Foursquare* and *Tencent WeChat*, augmented reality applications like *Layar*, *Wikitude*, *Google Goggles* and *HERE City Lens* among many more. Even mainstream applications like social network apps support context-based enhancements.

The improved sensing capabilities of modern smart devices also provide an attractive attack surface against the contextual privacy of users, as the recent development of sensory malware shows: malicious code, typically a Trojan Horse appearing to be a legitimate app, uses the sensors of the device to extract sensitive information from the surroundings of the user. Context-aware access control can be used to encounter this threat by limiting the access of untrusted 3rd-party applications to context information.

Various context-aware access control mechanisms and systems have been proposed. Some of these works are based on modifications of the RBAC model [12, 13] in which context-awareness is realized through roles that are triggered based on context parameters. Other approaches use explicit policies conditioned on contextual parameters [33, 2, 11, 5] or rules for expressing higher-level contextual preferences [21].

All of these works are based on *user-defined* or *pre-defined* policies. User-defined policies are very laborious to set up and maintain. This can be encountered with pre-defined policies provided by system administrators or app vendors, but these are inaccurate and inflexible: they cannot adequately capture and adapt to the highly personal and dynamic nature of individual users' contexts and privacy preferences. In our work, we overcome these deficiencies by using automatic context classification as a basis for access control decisions instead of static access control policies.

Furthermore, improved sensing capabilities also provide better possibilities to encounter threats arising from the context, like the threat of physical device misuse. Current static device locking methods severely deteriorate device usability with unnecessary password prompts in low-risk contexts, causing many users to leave their device unprotected [38]. Some earlier works attempted to improve device locking by using context information to probabilistically determine a level of confidence in the user's authenticity [31, 19]. We take a different approach: we do not try to authenticate users, but adjust device locking criteria according to the perceived security risk level of a context.

ASIA CCS'14, June 4–6, 2014, Kyoto, Japan.

http://dx.doi.org/10.1145/2590296.2590337.

To ground our work we use an interdisciplinary approach in which a sociological study is used to identify the concerns and perceptions of smartphone users in different contexts.

Contributions. Our contributions are as follows:

- We introduce *ConXsense*, the first context-aware access control framework for smartphones that uses **context profiling** and **automatic, adaptive and personalized context classification** for making context-aware access control decisions.
- We apply our framework to two important smartphone use cases: **protecting against device misuse**, and **defending against sensory malware**. ConXsense, however, is also applicable to a wide range of other security and privacy-related use cases.
- We apply **context profiling** and **machine learning** techniques on real-world data collected in a user study and evaluate the efficiency of automatic context classification in addressing the aforementioned threats.
- We integrate ConXsense with the *FlaskDroid* [7] architecture for fine-grained access control enforcement on the Android platform in order to realize the first adaptive, personalized and context-aware access control system of its kind for mobile devices.

The rest of this paper is structured as follows. A description of the problem and the ConXsense framework is given in Sections 2 and 3. In Section 4 we introduce the results of a sociological study on users' concerns and perceptions related to smartphones and present use cases addressing these concerns in Section 5. The design and implementation of our context model are described in Sections 6 and 7. The results of a user study evaluating the performance of context classification are presented in Section 8, and Section 9 shows its integration with the *FlaskDroid* architecture. After summarizing related work in Section 10, we conclude with outlines of future work in Section 11.

2. PROBLEM DESCRIPTION

While the idea of context-aware access control is not new [12, 21, 13, 11], currently proposed solutions mostly rely on policies specifying access control rules conditioned on values of contextual parameters.

User-specified policies have the potential to correctly reflect the user's true security and privacy preferences, but the amount of work required to set up and maintain a comprehensive set of context-dependent policies is high. Average users of mobile devices are hardly willing to spend significant amounts of time maintaining their policy set. In addition, it is questionable, whether regular users are capable to fully understand the implications of the policy settings they define. A study concerning location sharing policies [33] showed that the initial accuracy of location disclosure rules specified by users was only 59% and improved to 65% after users modified the rules based on a review of concrete enforcement decisions resulting from these rules. A recent study on the users' willingness to share their data with prominent single-sign on services [3] showed that the *majority* of users did not correctly understand the sharing implications of a sign-on dialog directly presented to them. These results suggest that the users' practical ability to control their security and privacy settings is limited.

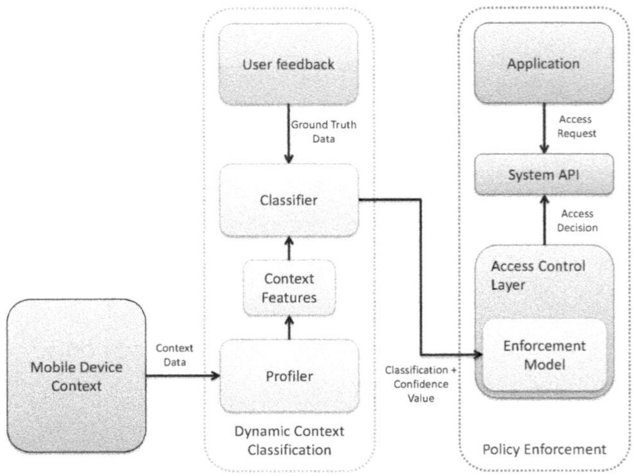

Figure 1: Context-based access control enforcement in ConXsense

An approach to tackle this problem of complexity and required user effort is to simplify things for users by pre-defined policies provided by administrators or app vendors. While this effectively reduces the user's burden, it fails to address the individual needs and privacy preferences of users. Pre-defined policies are by necessity only generalizations and not capable of accurately capturing concrete contexts and situations in individual users' lives. Also the fact that the privacy preferences of users may vary significantly from person to person can be very difficult to address using pre-defined policies.

It seems also unlikely that the privacy and security implications of pre-defined policies would be fully understood by regular users. This may lead to undesired situations: users under- or overestimating the level of privacy and security protection that the pre-defined policy provides to them.

User- or pre-defined policies alone are not sufficient to capture the highly dynamic and highly personal nature of a user's context (i.e., the ambient environment the device finds itself in) due to the problems outlined above. We aim at encountering these deficiencies by designing a context-aware access control framework that captures and adapts to the user's perception of the context and performs automatic context classification for making fine-grained context-aware access control decisions without the need for users to explicitly define contextual constraints. In the following section we describe the ConXsense framework in more detail.

3. FRAMEWORK DESCRIPTION

The ConXsense framework provides context-aware access control decisions by performing automatic classification of the context with regard to its security-relevant properties. The classification is based on machine learning models and user feedback providing ground truth information for training these models. Figure 1 shows a high-level overview of the framework.

The framework architecture is driven by context data observed with the sensors of the mobile device. The data are fed to a Profiler to calculate features describing the context. The Profiler implements a context model and aggregates profiles for relevant objects (e.g., significant places of the user or devices the user encounters) in the model. The Profiler evaluates incoming observations based on the profiles and the context model, and periodically calculates feature vectors characterizing the current context of the user.

Apart from sensed context data, the framework obtains input through user feedback. This feedback can be derived from explicit user interaction (e.g., feedback given through the device's UI) or by monitoring the user's actions.

The Classifier uses the context feature vectors and user feedback events to train and update the context classification models. Once the models have been trained, they are used to classify new observations with regard to the context's security and privacy-relevant properties. The classification estimate of the Classifier and its associated confidence value are forwarded to the Access Control Layer, which takes them into account when making access control decisions. The framework can be used to address any use case for which contextual factors play a role, and it can accommodate any sensors, resources, functionalities, communication links or other data objects for which the Access Control Layer provides enforcement support.

In the following, we instantiate the ConXsense framework for protecting the privacy of the user. We consider two central use cases we identified and demonstrate the applicability and effectiveness of our approach by evaluating it with real-world contextual data obtained from a user study.

4. USER SURVEY

To investigate smartphone users' perceptions and concerns with regard to their smartphones in different contexts, we conducted a user survey following a *Mixed Methods* [40] approach commonly applied in sociological studies. We designed a statistical-quantitative survey [41] using quantitative questions to identify facts by statistical analysis [1] combined with open-ended, qualitative questions for investigating the underlying reasons for the users' perceptions.

The survey was answered by 122 participants aged 18-56 including people from different household types and representing different organizational positions. The participants were recruited using word-of-mouth, electronic communications like e-mail and social networks, targeting particularly smartphone users, to obtain a cross-sectional sample of different age groups and backgrounds. Thus, the set of respondents in our sample is representative of the target group of our framework, namely active smartphone users.

The survey contained questions on which contexts and contextual factors users deem relevant for their perceptions of contextual privacy and security. The answers to the open-ended questions confirmed our initial assumptions that two major context-related concerns dominate the users' minds. Firstly, people are concerned about *device misuse*, i.e., that their device is stolen and/or misused without their knowledge. The second concern relates to *privacy exposure*: users fear that private or confidential context information related to their life is revealed to unauthorized parties.

In some earlier studies on contextual behavior patterns of mobile device users, two central contexts have been used: "home" and "work" [43]. Also lifetime studies in social sciences suggest that these contexts are the most important contexts in average users' lives [37]. Therefore, we included dedicated questions about these context types as prototypes of very familiar contexts. Tables 1 and 2 show the results.

Table 1: Perceptions of Home vs. Work

Context	Privacy exposure		Risk of misuse	
	high	low	low	high
Home	46%	17%	94%	4%
Work	42%	21%	55%	40%

Table 2: Influence of people on the perceived privacy exposure and risk of misuse in the context

Question	Yes	No
Low risk of misuse depends on people	66%	14%
High risk of misuse depends on people	68%	11%
High privacy exposure depends on people	39%	43%
Low privacy exposure depends on people	36%	42%

4.1 Survey Results

Risk of device misuse. As can be seen in Table 1, the majority of people (94% and 55%, respectively) perceive "home" and "work" as having a low risk of misuse. This is explained by answers to open-ended questions, like "(...) places like home or office tend to remain secure regardless of time of day", supporting the intuition that familiar places are commonly perceived as having a low risk of misuse. While it is not surprising that "home" is perceived as safe, perceptions of "work" are more diverse [10], as reflected in our survey results. A significant fraction of people perceive "work" as a context with high risk of misuse. The reasons for this are indicated in several answers to the open-ended questions, e.g., "At work there are people around that I don't know and I don't trust them." This suggests that the familiarity of the context alone is not a sufficient indicator for estimating the risk level, also the people in context play an important role.

From Table 2 we can see that the people present in the context clearly affect the perceived risk of device misuse in that context. A clear majority of respondents stated that a low or high risk of device misuse is dependent on the persons present. From the responses to open-ended questions, we identified that the feeling of low risk is particularly caused by people that are *familiar* to the user (e.g., "I trust my friends and colleagues"). Similarly, the presence of *unfamiliar* persons in the context was indicated as a reason for perceiving the context as having a high risk of device misuse (e.g., "Where there are people around me that I don't know, I don't feel secure", or "Unknown people represent threat").

This underlines the fact that location information alone is not a sufficient basis for access control decisions. Also other context information affecting the perceptions of security need to be taken into account.

Privacy exposure. The data in Table 1 suggest that a significant fraction of respondents feel that a familiar context also has high privacy exposure, i.e., contains private or confidential context information related to the user.

Table 2 shows, however, that the perception of privacy exposure does not appear to be affected by the presence of people. More respondents believe that the people present in the context do not contribute to the level of privacy exposure of the context.

Conclusions and Discussion. Based on the analysis of the survey results above, we see that two main factors affect users' perceptions on privacy exposure and risk of misuse in contexts: the familiarity of the context itself and the familiarity of persons present in the context. Therefore, we need to design our context model in a way that we can (1) identify relevant contexts and model their familiarity, and, (2) track encounters with other persons and measure their familiarity by observing their mobile devices. In Section 6 we construct such a context model.

The analysis presented above supports our *common* understanding and shows which factors typically influence the perception of contexts. However, exceptions exist, like, e.g., those 4% who consider home a high-risk environment. Reasons for this can be various. Answers to open-ended questions suggest that even in familiar contexts the perception of risk of misuse changes when untrusted people appear, or, it is caused by what we call the "Toddler Scenario", i.e., the influence of familiar people (e.g., a young child, or spouse) considered as "clueless" or "honest but curious", causing a person to consider the risk of device misuse significant also in familiar surroundings. To investigate these special cases, more detailed questions on familiar contexts would need to be included. However, sociological literature suggests that questions about such contexts are perceived as intrusive and will therefore not be answered [4, 10]. This concern was also reflected in some of the feedback we received about the online questionnaire. Hence, and because exceptional cases seem to be a marginal phenomenon, we focus on the common cases and address more exceptional cases in subsequent studies.

5. USE CASES

Based on the user survey, we focus on the most prominent concerns expressed by the users: fear of device misuse and disclosure of private or confidential context information. To mitigate these concerns, we identified following use cases.

5.1 Misuse Protection: Usable Device Lock

Several surveys [9, 38] point out that many mobile users do not use device locks (also known as idle screen locks) to protect their phones even though that would effectively protect against device misuse. One reason for this is that screen locks and other similar access control techniques on mobile devices today are both too inflexible and hard to use. A solution could be to make the locking mechanism more usable, so that users would be more willing to use device locking. The approach taken by Gupta et al. [17] was to use context data to adapt the locking time out of the device lock in different contexts. We adopt this approach and want to use the estimated *risk of device misuse* in a context as a means to decide, whether and how fast to lock the device in case it is not used.

Adversary model. For this use case, the adversary is a person in the context with physical access to the device. The person may be malicious (a thief) or honest-but-curious (a colleague or sibling) or "clueless" (a small child).

Goal. We want to protect the applications and data on the device from potential threats in the context by limiting the potential damage arising from someone physically accessing the device without the user's approval. Therefore, we want to minimize the chances that an unauthorized person in the context has access to the user's data. We do this by configuring the device lock dynamically based on the risk of device misuse in the context, while trying to strike a balance between maximizing protection on one hand and minimizing user annoyance of having to unlock the device in low-risk contexts on the other hand.

5.2 Resisting Sensory Malware

Sensory malware is an emerging class of malicious applications (typically Trojans) that use the context sensors of a mobile device to collect potentially sensitive information from the user's context. Prominent examples of sensory malware are *Stealthy Video Capturer* [44] (video via camera), *(sp)iPhone* [25] (keystrokes via accelerometer) *Soundcomber* [36] (spoken secrets via microphone), or the recent *PlaceRaider* [42] Trojan (3D models via camera). Users may also have granted sensor access privileges to benign apps which use them too intrusively: for instance an augmented reality app may take pictures of surroundings even when the user is not actively using augmented reality, as a means of enriching the app vendor's data collection.

Adversary Model. For this use case, the adversary is an app already installed on the device. We assume that the application has been granted the necessary privileges during installation and has therefore access to the contextual sensors on the mobile device, but cannot circumvent the access control system[1]. The application may be a Trojan Horse (e.g., sensory malware) or a benign but somewhat intrusive application.

Goal. We aim at protecting sensitive information in the context of the device from the adversary. We do this by preventing or limiting the ability of the adversary to gather information from contexts with high *privacy exposure*, i.e., contexts that contain information that the user would want to protect from the adversary. Such information can be either *private*, i.e., information about the user herself, or, *confidential*, i.e., other sensitive information not directly related to the user. The user's home (private) and workplace (confidential) are examples of typical contexts with high privacy exposure.

6. CONTEXT MODEL

In this section, we present a context model used to extract context features reflecting the familiarity of contexts and the persons in the context. The context features are input for the Classifier and used for classifying contexts as having high or low privacy exposure and/or risk of misuse. The context model is based on two main concepts: *Contexts of Interest (CoI)* for modelling the familiarity of contexts and *Bluetooth devices* for modelling familiar and unfamiliar people in context.

6.1 Detection of Contexts of Interest (CoIs)

For our purpose, *Contexts-of-Interest* (CoIs) correspond to locations that a user often visits and/or spends a significant amount of time in, e.g., home, workplace, grocery store, etc. We consider two kinds of CoIs: *GPS-based CoIs* which are geographical areas on the surface of the earth, and *WiFi-based* CoIs that are characteristic sets of WiFi access points usually observed in a specific place and thus identifying the RF environment there. GPS CoIs capture significant places of the user in outdoor areas, and WiFi CoIs cover also indoor locations in urban areas, where GPS can't be used but coverage of WiFi access points typically is available. By combining both types of CoIs, we can identify and detect most significant places that users typically visit.

[1]Malware that uses operating system (root) exploits to circumvent the enforcement of the context-aware access control system is outside the scope of this paper.

6.1.1 GPS-based CoIs

To identify GPS-based CoIs, we adopt the notions of *stay points* and *stay regions* as introduced by Zheng et al. [46] and developed further by Montoliu et al. [26]. The identification of GPS-based CoIs is based on position observations obtained via GPS.

The sequence of GPS observations is divided into *GPS stay points*, which represent visits of the user to different places, during which the user stays within a radius of $r_{sp} = 100$ m from the first GPS observation. In order for a visit to be considered a stay point, the visit is also required to last longer than $t\_min_{sp} = 10$ min and not to contain observation gaps longer than $t\_gap_{sp} = 5$ min.

We calculate for each stay point an average position $pos_{\bar{sp}}$ as the average of all position observations belonging to the stay point, i.e., $pos_{\bar{sp}} = (lat_{\bar{sp}}, lon_{\bar{sp}})$, s.t. $lat_{\bar{sp}} = \frac{\sum_{k=1}^{n} lat_k}{n}$, and $lon_{\bar{sp}} = \frac{\sum_{k=1}^{n} lon_k}{n}$. The average position of a stay point represents the predominant location where the user has been located during her visit to the stay point.

The average positions $pos_{\bar{sp}}$ of individual stay points are aggregated to form rectangular geographical areas of at most $gps_{max} = 100$ m width and length. An area is a *GPS-based Context-of-Interest*, if (i) the user has visited the area more than $f\_min_{coi} = 5$ times and (ii) has spent longer than $t\_min_{coi} = 30$ min in total in the area.

Example. As an illustrative running example, let us consider a user who regularly commutes between her workplace and home. Other places she regularly visits are a grocery store and a public sports facility. She usually carries her smartphone with her, which continuously senses her GPS location and other context data.

When the user goes to the grocery store and stays there for 15 minutes, i.e., longer than $t\_min_{sp} = 10$ min and moves only within a radius of $r_{sp} = 100$ m, a stay point sp of duration $\mathsf{dur}(sp) = 15$ min will be generated. The average of all position observations pos_i during the stay point visit will be the stay point average position $pos_{\bar{sp}}$, most likely located in or near the grocery store. Waypoints along her daily commuting routes, however, would not generate any stay points, since on her way she does not spend sufficiently long time in the same limited area.

If our user visits the grocery store 10 times and stays each time for 15 minutes, ten stay points will be generated. These average positions will be aggregated into a GPS-based CoI C, because their total stay duration of 2 hours and 30 minutes is longer than the required $t\_min_{coi} = 30$ min and there are more than the required $f\_min_{coi} = 5$ stay points falling inside the CoI. The area of the CoI will be the smallest rectangle containing all the stay point average positions $pos_{\bar{sp}}$.

6.1.2 WiFi-based CoIs

For identifying WiFi-based CoIs, WiFi access point observations rf_i are used. Each observation consists of the MAC address of a detected WiFi access point and the timestamp of the observation. The sequence of individual WiFi observations is divided into *WiFi snapshots*, which are subsequences corresponding to observations obtained during a single WiFi scan of duration $t\_max_{wifi} = 10$ sec.

Following the notion of stay points for GPS observations, we extend this concept to WiFi and divide the sequence of WiFi snapshots into so-called *WiFi stay points*. The similarity between snapshots is determined by calculating the *Jaccard distance*[2] between the first snapshot and subsequent snapshots one-by-one. As long as the Jaccard distance between the snapshots is less than or equal to 0.5, which means that the intersection of the snapshots is at least as large as half of their union, the subsequent snapshots are assigned to the stay point. The staypoint is considered complete, if the Jaccard distance to new WiFi snapshots grows beyond 0.5 or there is a gap between consecutive WiFi snapshots that is longer than t_gap_{sp}.

These criteria for WiFi stay points were selected, because it is not uncommon that WiFi access points are missed in scans [14]. This is apparently not dependent on the signal strength of the missed access point, so one needs to take into account that even very strong access point beacons will be missed from time to time.

A WiFi stay point has a characteristic set of access points $\mathsf{char}(wifi\_sp)$ that includes those access points that occur at least in half of all WiFi snapshots of the stay point. A set of access points is a *WiFi-based CoI*, if there are at least f_min_{coi} WiFi stay points having this set of access points as their characteristic set of access points, and the stay points have a duration of at least t_min_{coi} in total.

Example. When our example user arrives at her workplace, a WiFi snapshot $wifi$ is recorded. This snapshot and following snapshots having a Jaccard distance of less than or equal to 0.5 to the first one form a WiFi stay point $wifi\_sp$, given that the time difference of the first and last snapshot is greater than t_min_{sp} and there are no gaps in the WiFi snapshot observations longer than t_gap_{sp}. The characteristic set $\mathsf{char}(wifi\_sp)$ of access points of this stay point consists of access points mostly observed at the workplace. During subsequent visits to the workplace, more WiFi stay points with the same characteristic set will be generated. If at least f_min_{coi} such stay points have been observed and the total visit duration $\mathsf{dur}(wifi\_sp)$ of these stay points reaches t_min_{coi}, the characteristic set constitutes a WiFi-based CoI C for the user's workplace.

6.2 Context Detection

Once the GPS- and WiFi-based CoIs have been identified, new incoming GPS, WiFi and Bluetooth observations can be used to identify the location context and social context of the user at any point in time.

6.2.1 Location context

The location context of the user is defined in terms of the CoIs that the user visits at a specific point in time.

DEFINITION 1 (VISITS). *A user's* visit V_C *to a GPS-based CoI* $C = (lat_{min}, lon_{min}, lat_{max}, lon_{max})$ *is a sequence of position observations* $pos_i = (lat_i, lon_i)$ *falling within the CoI and having timestamps at most* ϵ_V *apart from each other:* $V_C = (pos_1, pos_2, \ldots, pos_n)$*, where* $\forall pos_i \in V_C : lat_{min} < lat_i \wedge lon_{min} < lon_i \wedge lat_i < lat_{max} \wedge lon_i < lon_{max}$*, and* $\forall i, 1 < i \leq n : t(pos_i) - t(pos_{i-1}) < \epsilon_V$*. Similarly, a visit* V_C *to a WiFi-based CoI* C *is a sequence of WiFi snapshots* $wifi$ *falling within the CoI and having timestamps at most* ϵ_V *apart from each other. That is,* $V_C = (wifi_1, wifi_2, \ldots, wifi_n)$*, where* $J_\delta(C, wifi_i) \leq 0.5$ *and*

[2]The Jaccard distance measures the dissimilarity between two sets A and B as $J_\delta(A, B) = \frac{|A \cup B| - |A \cap B|}{|A \cup B|}$

$\forall i, 1 < i \leq n : t(wifi_i) - t(wifi_{i-1}) < \epsilon_V$. *We denote the set of all visits* V_C *of the user to CoI* C *with* $\mathcal{V}_C$.

DEFINITION 2 (LOCATION CONTEXT). *A* location context L_t *at timestamp* t *is the set of CoIs* C *that the user is visiting during that point of time.*

Note, that CoIs can be overlapping, which means that a user can be visiting several CoIs simultaneously. If the user is not visiting any of the CoIs at a specific point in time, the corresponding location context will be empty.

6.2.2 Social context

In order to capture *people* in the user's surroundings, we observe their mobile devices that can be sensed through proximity sensing technologies like Bluetooth (BT). Bluetooth has a range of approximately 30 meters given a direct line of sight, so its physical properties quite well reflect our notion of a context comprising the space immediately observable by the user (e.g., a room). Bluetooth has been commonly used in ubiquitous computing literature to model the presence of persons in a perimeter (cf., e.g., [27]). To capture only devices that are typically carried by persons, we filter the BT observations by their device class so that we consider only mobile devices like cell phones, headsets, PDAs and other portable devices.

Some users may not keep Bluetooth enabled and discoverable on their devices or always carry their devices with them. Therefore, we will not always be able to reliably detect the presence of all persons in the context using Bluetooth alone. However, this is not necessary, since our probabilistic framework utilizes Bluetooth as one factor for identifying the type of context the user is in and not as a 'tripwire' for detecting potentially malicious users. Especially in public contexts where many persons are present and the likelihood that at least some Bluetooth devices can be detected is high, Bluetooth works well as a context classification factor. In addition, familiar, known devices (e.g. devices of family and friends) can be polled even if they are in hidden mode, if the BDADDR of the target device is known. For example, two devices that are paired can detect each other this way even if they remain invisible to other devices.

The social context is defined in terms of the devices that are detected in the user's context at a specific point in time.

DEFINITION 3 (ENCOUNTERS). *An* encounter E_d *of a user with a device* d *is a sequence of Bluetooth observations* bt_i *of device* d *with timestamps that are at most* ϵ_E *apart from each other:* $E = (bt_1, bt_2, \ldots, bt_n)$, *where* $\forall i, 1 < i \leq n : bt_i = d \wedge t(bt_i) - t(bt_{i-1}) < \epsilon_E$. *We denote the set of all encounters of the user with a device* d *with* $\mathcal{E}_d$.

When our example user arrives at her workplace, her device obtains a Bluetooth observation $bt_1 = d$ of her colleague's device d. This observation and any subsequent device observations $bt_i = d$ of the colleague's device form an encounter E_d with the colleague's device, as long as the time distance between consecutive device observations is less than $\epsilon_E = 5$ minutes. The purpose of allowing gaps of this size is to be able to handle missed device observations not uncommon with Bluetooth sensing.

DEFINITION 4 (DEVICE CONTEXT). *The* device context D_t *at timestamp* t *is the set of devices* d *that are encountered during that point of time.*

DEFINITION 5 (FAMILIAR DEVICES). *The set of* familiar devices $\mathcal{D}_{fam}$ *is the set of all such devices that the user has encountered at least* f_min_{famdev} *times and for which the total duration of the encounters is at least* t_min_{famdev}.

Familiar devices d for our example user would be the mobile devices of familiar people like her spouse or her colleagues at work which she has encountered more often than $f\_min_{famdev} = 5$ times and the total duration of these encounters is longer than $t\_min_{famdev} = 30$ minutes.

6.3 Context Profiles

Based on the above context model, context profiles are aggregated for the user: a *CoI profile* $CoIs$ and a *device profile* $Devs$. The CoI profile $CoIs = \{\mathcal{C}, P\}$ consists of the set of all identified CoIs $\mathcal{C}$, and a mapping $P : \mathcal{C} \rightarrow \mathbb{N} \times \mathbb{R}, C \mapsto (visits_C, dur_C)$ providing the total amount $visits_C$ and total duration dur_C of visits to each CoI $C \in \mathcal{C}$.

Similarly, the device profile $Devs = \{\mathcal{D}, \mathcal{D}_{fam}, O\}$ consists of the set of all encountered devices $\mathcal{D}$, the set of familiar devices $\mathcal{D}_{fam}$ and a mapping $O : \mathcal{D} \rightarrow \mathbb{N} \times \mathbb{R}, d \mapsto (enc_d, dur_d)$ providing the total amount enc_d and total duration dur_d of encounters with each device $d \in \mathcal{D}$.

6.4 Context Features

Based on the context model, we define following features:

Context familiarity features.

Let $\mathcal{C}^{\text{GPS}}$ denote the subset of all GPS-based CoIs and $\mathcal{C}^{\text{WiFi}}$ the subset of all Wifi-based CoIs in $\mathcal{C}$. Then we have:

$f^{\text{GPS}}_{\text{max}_{\text{dur}}}$: maximum total visit time of any GPS-based CoI in current location context

$$f^{\text{GPS}}_{\text{max}_{\text{dur}}}(t) = \begin{cases} \max_{C \in \{\mathcal{C}^{\text{GPS}} \cap L_t\}} dur_C, & L_t \cap \mathcal{C}^{\text{GPS}} \neq \emptyset \\ 0, & \text{otherwise} \end{cases}$$

$f^{\text{GPS}}_{\text{max}_{\text{dur}}}$: number of visits to the GPS-based CoI with the maximum total visit time

$$f^{\text{GPS}}_{\text{max}_{\text{dur}}}(t) = \begin{cases} visits_{C_i}, & i = \arg\max_{C \in \{\mathcal{C}^{\text{GPS}} \cap L_t\}} dur_C \wedge \\ & L_t \cap \mathcal{C}^{\text{GPS}} \neq \emptyset \\ 0, & \text{otherwise} \end{cases}$$

$f^{\text{WiFi}}_{\text{max}_{\text{dur}}}$: maximum visit time of any WiFi-based CoI in the location context

$$f^{\text{WiFi}}_{\text{max}_{\text{dur}}}(t) = \begin{cases} \max_{C \in \{\mathcal{C}^{\text{WiFi}} \cap L_t\}} dur_C, & L_t \cap \mathcal{C}^{\text{WiFi}} \neq \emptyset \\ 0, & \text{otherwise} \end{cases}$$

$f^{\text{WiFi}}_{\text{max}_{\text{freq}}}$: number of visits to the WiFi-based CoI with the maximum total visit time

$$f^{\text{WiFi}}_{\text{max}_{\text{freq}}}(t) = \begin{cases} visits_{C_i}, & i = \arg\max_{C \in \{\mathcal{C}^{\text{WiFi}} \cap L_t\}} dur_C \wedge \\ & L_t \cap \mathcal{C}^{\text{WiFi}} \neq \emptyset \\ 0, & \text{otherwise} \end{cases}$$

Device familiarity features.

$f^{\text{BT}}_{\text{num}}$: Number of Bluetooth devices and familiar Bluetooth devices in device context D_t

$$f^{\text{BT}}_{\text{num}}(t) = |D_t|, \; f^{\text{BT}}_{\text{fam}}(t) = |D_t \cap \mathcal{D}_{fam}|$$

$f^{\text{BT}}_{\text{fam}_{\text{avg-time}}}$: Average encounter time of familiar devices in D_t

$$f^{\text{BT}}_{\text{fam}_{\text{avg-time}}}(t) = \begin{cases} \frac{\sum_{d \in \{D_t \cap \mathcal{D}_{fam}\}} dur_d}{|D_t \cap \mathcal{D}_{fam}|}, & D_t \cap \mathcal{D}_{fam} \neq \emptyset \\ 0, & \text{otherwise} \end{cases}$$

$f^{\mathrm{BT}}_{\mathrm{fam}_{\mathrm{avg\text{-}freq}}}$: Average number of encounters of familiar devices in D_t

$$f^{\mathrm{BT}}_{\mathrm{fam}_{\mathrm{avg\text{-}freq}}}(t) = \begin{cases} \frac{\sum_{d \in \{D_t \cap \mathcal{D}_{fam}\}} enc_d}{|D_t \cap \mathcal{D}_{fam}|}, & D_t \cap \mathcal{D}_{fam}| \neq \emptyset \\ 0, & \text{otherwise} \end{cases}$$

The Profiler calculates context feature values based on a history of observation data and labels them based on user feedback. The feature values are used by the Classifier to train machine learning-based classifiers for classifying new observations. In the following sections, we show how we applied this context model on real-world context data to evaluate the effectiveness of the model and the Classifier.

7. IMPLEMENTATION

To evaluate the ConXsense framework, we created a prototype implementation consisting of a Data Collector app, a Profiler and Classifier. The output of the Classifier was integrated with the Access Control Layer (cf. section 9) to provide enforcement.

7.1 Data Collector

For collecting context data, we implemented a Data Collector app for Android. It uses a background Service to collect context data in intervals of 60 seconds. This is a required tradeoff between the battery lifetime and the quantity of collected data for reaching a battery lifetime of at least a working day (12h) on, e.g., the Samsung Galaxy Nexus and Nexus S devices. The collected data comprise location information, nearby Bluetooth devices and WiFi access points, acceleration sensor information as well as information about user presence and her interaction with apps (Activities).[3]

The Data Collector app also collects *ground truth data*. The user regularly reports the perceived risk of device misuse in the current context by specifying the context to be "safe" (low risk of misuse) or "unsafe" (high risk of misuse). In addition, users are asked to classify the current context as "home" or "work", if the context has high privacy exposure due to context information being either *private* or *confidential*, respectively, or, "public" if the context has low privacy exposure. By using concise words that are easy to follow and relate to helped us in keeping the user interaction as simple as possible. To avoid misunderstandings, an introductory explanation was given to study participants beforehand.

The users provided the above feedback for the current context either by using context feedback buttons on the device's UI or by using dedicated NFC tags provided to the participants for triggering context reporting (cf. Figure 2). The feedback UI was either spontaneously invoked by the user, or, if no ground truth had been provided during the last two hours, the app reminded the user to do so via sound, vibration and flashing LED notifications. Context and ground truth data were stored in a SQLite database and periodically uploaded to a server via HTTPS.

7.2 Profiler and Classifier

We implemented the functionality of the Profiler as off-line data processing scripts utilizing `bash` shell scripting, `awk` and `Python`. The scripts were used to identify individual GPS

[3]Data Collector is a generic solution collecting more data than required by the current Profiler.

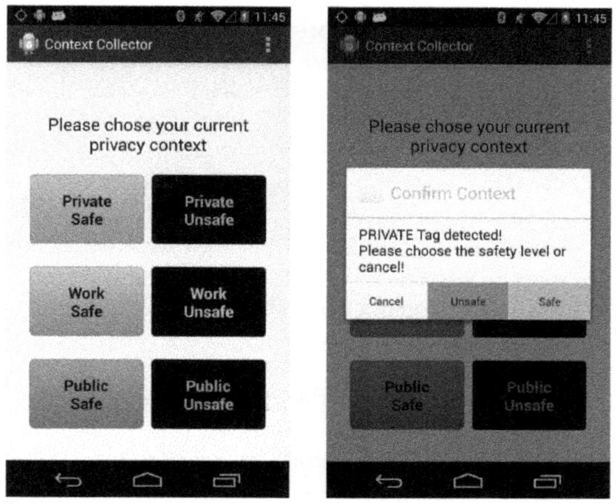

(a) Feedback using Context Feedback Buttons (b) Feedback using Context NFC Tags.

Figure 2: Android Data Collector App

and WiFi CoIs for each user, and to calculate the familiarity of Bluetooth devices that the users had encountered during the data collection period. Scripts were also used for extracting the context feature vectors.

The functionality of the Classifier was realized and evaluated using the Weka data mining suite [18] and its provided algorithm implementations for k-NN, Random Forest and Naïve Bayes classifiers.

8. EVALUATION

To evaluate the context classification, the Data Collector app was installed on the Android smartphones of 15 test users having technical and non-technical backgrounds. A test user group of this size is large enough for verifying the validity of the concept and is in line with previous works evaluating context-aware access control by Riva et al. [31] ($n = 9$) and Sadeh et al. [33] ($n = 12$ and $n = 19$). Users provided context and feedback data over a period of 68 days, 56 days per user on the average. The total dataset contained data from 844 distinct user days. On the average, users provided ground truth feedback on 46 days of the data collection period, resulting in a ground truth dataset containing 3757 labeled data points.

From the collected data, the Profiler calculated personal context profiles and context features. The features were used by the Classifier to train classification models for predicting the privacy exposure and misuse risk levels of contexts. The context labels obtained through user feedback were used to attach class labels to the context feature vectors.

Each test user provided at least 50 or more feedback labels. This would roughly correspond to the user providing 2-3 feedbacks per day over a period of three weeks, which seems like a manageable burden on the user. After this initial training period of the Classifier, the need for explicit user feedback would significantly diminish. The user would need to provide only occasional corrective feedback in cases of incorrect predictions of the Classifier.

In constructing the Classifier, we experimented with three different machine learning algorithms: 1) A k-nearest neighbors (kNN) classifier, which bases its prediction on comparing a testing datapoint to the n closest observations to it in the training dataset. The prediction is the most frequent class label in this set of observations. 2) A Naïve Bayes (NB) classifier is a simple probabilistic classifier which has been successfully used, e.g., in spam e-mail detection [34]. 3) Random Forest (RF) is an ensemble method that is commonly used for classification tasks. It randomly picks subsets of input attributes and trains decision trees for them. It uses the most frequently predicted label provided by this set of tree classifiers as the final prediction. For each participant, we trained the Classifier using the labeled context feature vectors and evaluated the performance of the classifiers using 10-fold cross-validation.

We assume that by default restrictive protection measures are in place (access to sensors disabled, device lock active). The Classifier's task is therefore to predict situations, in which the protections could be relaxed, i.e., if the context has low privacy exposure or a low risk of device misuse.

Even though most accurate results would be obtained by direct measurement of on-line enforcement on users' mobile devices, we had to rely on an offline evaluation of the Classifiers performance, since we wanted to be able to experiment with several different machine learning algorithms. Implementing or porting several different algorithms on the mobile device and conducting a separate user study for each of them was not feasible given the resource limitations. Therefore we intend to evaluate the performance of on-line enforcement in a subsequent user study involving devices with enhanced device locking functionality.

Protecting against device misuse. Figure 3 shows the average receiver operating characteristic (ROC) curves of the classifiers for users who provided at least five feedback datapoints for each context class.

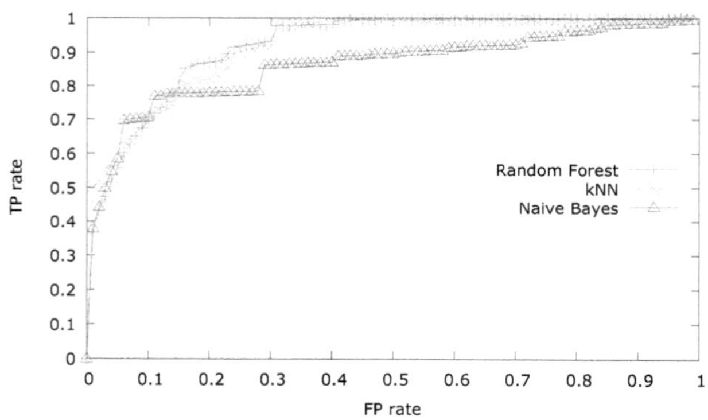

Figure 3: Average receiver operating characteristic (ROC) curves for classifying contexts with low risk of device misuse.

All classifiers perform reasonably well on the testing data, providing usable results for practical use. The classifiers reach a true positive rate of approximately 70% with a fairly moderate false positive rate of 10%. This would mean that by applying a relaxed device locking scheme in low-risk contexts, we can potentially reduce the amount of unnecessary authentication prompts shown to the user by 70%. Only one time in ten would a relaxed locking mechanism be enforced while the user is in a context with higher risk of misuse. This means that a thief or other unauthorized user would likely have a less than 10% chance of finding the device in an unlocked state, when obtaining physical access to it. These results clearly outperform the progressive authentication scheme presented by Riva et al. [31], who report a reduction of 42% in unnecessary authentication prompts presented to the user.

Protecting against sensory malware. Figure 4 shows the average performance of the classifiers in identifying contexts with low privacy exposure.

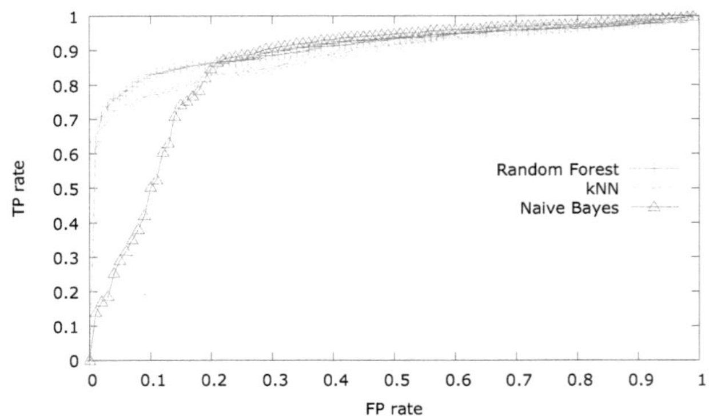

Figure 4: Average ROC curves for classifying contexts with low privacy exposure.

For this use case, the Random Forest and kNN classifiers provide best performance. They reach a true positive rate of 70% at a very low false positive rate of 2-3.5%. This would mean that if a sensory malware protection scheme with a 'default deny' policy is enforced, only in less than 3.5% of the cases would access control be relaxed in contexts with high privacy exposure. In practice, this would severely limit a sensory malware application's ability to extract useful sensitive information about the user.

Through the use of a default deny policy, our framework errs by default on the safe side, i.e., sensory malware is by default denied access to sensor information. The true positive rate of 70% means that our scheme is able to relax the access restrictions to sensors in public or low-privacy exposure contexts in 70% of the cases. The remaining 30% can be handled through manual overriding of the default policy by the user. Fortunately, the use of context information by many apps is often user-driven, i.e., sensor data are utilized, when the user is actively using the app (e.g., using a navigation app to locate a nearby restaurant). Adding an override confirmation dialog to the user interaction in such situations should therefore be easy, since the device already is in the focus of the user's attention. This approach also has the benefit that the overriding action can be used as additional ground truth data for updating the classification model and thus improving subsequent classification accuracy.

9. ENFORCEMENT

To verify the applicability of our framework to practical access control enforcement, we integrated it with an Access Control Layer for which we adopted and adapted the *FlaskDroid* [7] architecture, a fine-grained mandatory access control framework for Android 4.0.4 (cf. Figure 5). We now show how the combination of ConXsense and *FlaskDroid* can address the previously defined use-cases, namely *Resisting Sensory Malware* and *Usable Device Lock* (cf. Section 5). For our implementation we use a Samsung Galaxy Nexus smartphone.

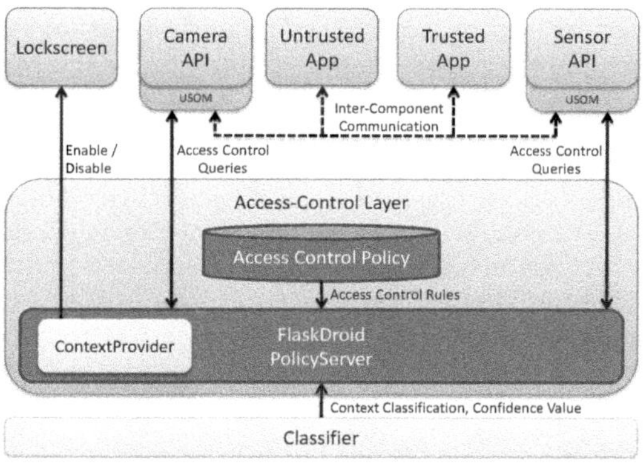

Figure 5: Enforcement of Context-based policies

9.1 Implementation

FlaskDroid extends *Security Enhanced Android (SEAndroid)* [39] with fine-grained type enforcement on Android's middleware layer. In *FlaskDroid*, Android components that provide access to sensitive resources, such as the SensorService which provides access to sensor information, act as User-Space Object Managers (USOMs) which control access to resources they manage. More specifically, USOMs control *operations* from *subjects* (i.e., apps) to *objects* (e.g., data) using *types* assigned to *subjects* and *objects*.

At boot time, *FlaskDroid's* PolicyServer (cf. Figure 5) parses an Access Control Policy and proceeds to assign app types (e.g., *trusted* or *untrusted*) to all installed apps based on application metadata (e.g., package name or developer signature). Apps installed by the user are assigned types during their installation. Whenever apps request access to a USOM, for example the SensorService to query the device's sensors or the CameraService to take pictures, the USOM queries the PolicyServer, which is part of Android's SystemServer, for access control decisions. *FlaskDroid* supports conditional access control rules by means of ContextProviders that evaluate the current context and enable or disable rules at runtime.

To meet our goals we extended *FlaskDroid* with additional USOMs and implemented a ConXsense ContextProvider. It uses the context classification information and confidence values provided by the Classifier to activate or deactivate conditional rules at runtime (cf. Figure 5) and to influence the Lockscreen behaviour. The ContextProvider can be tuned with individual user-, use-case and sensor-specific thresholds for the expected confidence values. These thresholds could be set, e.g., by specifying a desired maximal false positive rate and adjusting the confidence threshold accordingly based on the observed historical performance of the context classifier. Access to more sensitive context sensors like GPS could require a higher prediction confidence than less sensitive sensors like the magnetometer.

Mitigation of Sensory Malware. To mitigate, respectively reduce the effects of sensory malware (e.g., *Placeraider* [42] or SoundComber [36]), access control on the sensors of a device is required. For example, *Placeraider* uses the device's camera and the acceleration sensor to covertly construct 3D images of the surroundings of the user. We transformed Android's CameraService into an USOM which filters queries to the *takePicture* and *startPreviewMode* methods. Furthermore, we used *FlaskDroid* to filter acceleration sensor events delivered to SensorEventListeners registered by apps. It should be noted that *FlaskDroid's* original implementation of the SensorManager USOM is insufficient to block sophisticated attacks, since the SensorManager is loaded into the memory space of (potentially malicious) apps. Thus, we replaced *FlaskDroid's* SensorManager USOM with a corresponding USOM in Android's SensorService, which is not under the control of apps.

Similarily, the combination of ConXsense and *FlaskDroid* can address also other variants of sensory malware, such as *Soundcomber* [36], by identifying the relevant Android APIs, instrumenting them as USOMs and extending the *FlaskDroid* policy with corresponding conditional rules.

Usable Device Lock. To allow for changes in the Android Lockscreen policy based on the current risk for device misuse, we use the ConXsense ContextProvider to configure Android's Lockscreen dynamically at runtime. We modified Android's Settings component to be notified by our ContextProvider about changes in the current risk for device misuse by means of a Broadcast Intent. We further modified Android's LockPatternKeyguardView which is used to display the Lockscreen to query the Settings component for context information. While the device is used in a context with *low* risk for device misuse, the LockPatternKeyguardView class automatically dismisses the Lockscreen. Whenever the device is rebooted or the risk for device misuse changes to *high*, a low-watermark mechanism ensures that the Lockscreen is always displayed regardless of the current risk for device misuse. This mechanism is required to prevent an attacker from bypassing the Lockscreen by changing the context, emulating a context the user considers to have low risk for device misuse or rebooting the device. In addition, to mitigate the effect of sensory malware which uses the acceleration sensor as a side channel to derive user credentials (e.g., Lockscreen PIN or password) [45, 30, 8], we use the SensorService USOM, our ContextProvider and corresponding conditional access control rules to block access to the acceleration sensor by 3rd-party apps while the Lockscreen is displayed.

9.2 Evaluation

Mitigation of Sensory Malware. To mitigate the effects of the *PlaceRaider* [42] sensory malware we designed a *FlaskDroid* policy to assign the type *trusted* to all preinstalled system apps (e.g., the camera app), and the type *untrusted* to all 3rd-party apps. In a real-world scenario this trust level could be derived from the app's reputation in an app market. We use conditional access control rules for the CameraService and SensorService USOMs to prevent all *untrusted* apps from accessing the acceleration sensor and the camera when the risk for privacy exposure is *high*.

We tested our implementation using a slightly modified version of the *PlaceRaider* malware generously provided to us by its authors[4]. By installing the malware on our device and logging the context information and access control decisions we verified that *FlaskDroid* successfully filtered all data delivered from Android's SensorService and CameraService components to the *untrusted PlaceRaider* app when the risk for privacy exposure was *high*, thus rendering the attack futile. We further verified that *trusted* apps could still use the sensors and the camera. No false positives or false negatives emerged during the evaluation of the Access Con-

[4]The sample we received is incompatible with Android 4.0.4.

trol Layer, which is not surprising since it merely enforces context-dependent access control rules.

To evaluate the performance impact of the Access Control Layer we implemented an app which automatically triggers 10,000 access control queries by reading sensor data and taking pictures. On average, the Access Control Layer caused an overhead μ of 4.9 ms (standard deviation σ 17.6 ms) for the SensorService and CameraService USOMs on a Samsung Galaxy Nexus smartphone. The high standard deviation σ is caused by the garbage collector used in Android's Dalvik Virtual Machine: While studying Android's system logs we noticed that during the irregularly slow access control queries, which are responsible for the high standard deviation, the garbage collector started and caused a stall. Overall, 95% of all access control decisions are handled in less than 4.2 ms, which we consider reasonable.

Usable Device Lock. To test our implementation of the context-aware device lockscreen we modified the Android operating system to periodically wake the device from sleep and switch on the screen. We furthermore installed a synthetic malware, which registers SensorEventListeners in Android's SensorService to be notified of acceleration sensor readings. By logging and analyzing the Lockscreen behavior, context information and sensor readings we verified that the Lockscreen was only automatically dismissed in valid situations and that our synthetic malware did not receive any sensor readings while the Lockscreen was active.

10. RELATED WORK

In the digital society, context data have been extensively used to analyze numerous aspects of human everyday life. Examples range from the prediction of health status by interpreting context data [24] to analyzing ethnographics [20] or person matching based on similar interests [15]. Our framework brings this idea of contextual analysis to the area of security and privacy protection for the most important tool of modern life - the smartphone.

A number of works have approached the problem of context-aware access control. Contrary to our work, all of them rely on user-defined or pre-defined policies in the form of role definitions, conditions on context parameters, or context-dependent rules. For example, Covington et al. [12] use a *Generalised Role Based Access Control* (GRBAC) model utilizing Environment Roles that are activated and deactivated based on context observations, and Damiani et al. [13] utilize roles in their spatially-aware RBAC model using location as a component for access control decisions.

Others have used user- or pre-defined policies conditioned on context parameters. Examples include Sadeh et al. [33] who investigate a policy definition and management system for the *PeopleFinder* application and Kelley et al. [23], who introduced a user-controllable policy learning system that builds on incremental policy improvements proposed to the users based on recorded history events. For mobile devices, Bai et al. propose a solution for fine-grained usage control on Android [2]. Their work extends the UCON access control model [35] by using context information (e.g., location and time) as an additional input for policy decisions.

Hull et al. [21] present the *Houdini* framework for mitigating the complexity that value-based customization of policies implies by using user-provided higher-level preferences to generate rules for privacy enforcement. They mention the possibility for automatically-learned preferences, but do not provide support for such automation at the time of writing.

Many recent papers have addressed context-aware access control enforcement on mobile devices. For example, Conti et al. [11] describe the *CRePe* framework for Android for enforcement of context-dependent access control policies allowing or denying access to specific resources depending on the currently detected active context. In the *MOSES* framework [32] Rusello et al. propose a combination of dynamic taint tracking using the *TaintDroid* architecture [16] and policy enforcement on Android's middleware layer to enable context based access control on resources and apps with the goal of providing isolated environments called security profiles. Similarly, the *TrustDroid* [6] architecture provides lightweight security domain isolation on Android with basic support for context-based network access control policies. Saint [29] features a context-aware fine-grained access control framework for Android, which focuses on enabling app developers to define context-dependent runtime constraints on inter-app communication. Nauman et al. present *Apex* [28], which extends the Android operating system with conditional permissions. It provides to some extent support for context-based access control by allowing the user to define context-dependent resource restrictions (e.g., based on the time of day). All of these works heavily rely on user- or pre-defined rules, whereas our work relies on dynamic context classification utilizing machine learning as a source for access control enforcement. Also, in contrast to *MOSES*, *TrustDroid* and *Apex*, our access control architecture is based on the more generic and flexible *FlaskDroid* platform [7], which is also able to cover (most of) the use cases described in *Saint*.

A recent patent application by Bell et al. [5] discloses a system using context-triggered policies controlling the access of applications to sensors and other resources on a smartphone. Also their approach relies on either pre-defined policies or policies uploaded to the devices by external entities.

Addressing the problem of more usable user authentication on mobile devices, Riva et al. [31] use various contextual clues to (partially) authenticate the user by estimating the likelihood that the user is in proximity and use this information to configure the device lock. Similarly, Hayashi et al. [19] introduce *Context-Aware Scalable Authentication*, an approach which uses the location of the device in a probabilistic framework to determine the active authentication factors to be used for user authentication (e.g., PIN or password) on smartphones. Although we cover a similar use case as these papers, our approach is very different. We do not authenticate the user, but rather adjust device locking behavior based on automatic classification of the context according to its perceived risk level.

Kang et al. [22] introduced the idea of time-based clustering of position observations, which Zheng et al. [46] used to introduce the concepts of stay points and stay regions, further developed by Montoliu et al. [26]. We adopt a slightly modified form of the notion of stay regions to define our GPS-based CoIs. In addition, we also extend the notion of a stay points to non-locational data in the form of WiFi stay points. Dousse et al. [14] have successfully demonstrated the use of WiFi fingerprints for identifying and detecting places based on WiFi. We adopt a simplified version of their place identification scheme considering only intersections of WiFi snapshots for our WiFi-based CoI detection.

Gupta et al. [17] were the first to use context profiling and the notion of CoI and device familiarity for estimating the 'safety' level of a context. Their system relied on a simple heuristic model based on time-discounted familiarity measures and suffered from having to specify a fixed threshold for distinguishing between context classes, which fails to take into account context- and user specific differences. Since we apply a sophisticated context model and more powerful machine learning models for context classification, our approach is capable to take better into account also context- and user-specific differences in perceptions of risk level and privacy exposure.

11. CONCLUSIONS AND FUTURE WORK

In this paper, we described ConXsense, a context-aware access control framework for mobile devices utilizing automated classification of contexts based on sensed context data. We applied it to two concrete smartphone-related use cases: defending against sensory malware and device misuse. We showed that context classification can be used for context-aware access control enforcement, effectively addressing true security concerns that smartphone users have. In this, however, we do not see the task merely as a prediction problem, but rather we consider true contextuality as a continuous process of learning from and adapting to the individual needs and preferences of smartphone users.

Having validated the effectiveness of ConXsense, the next step is to evaluate its usability. We plan to implement on-device versions of the Profiler and Classifier and create a mobile app for user studies focusing on the usability aspects related to our framework. We intend also to develop further richer context models incorporating more context sensors, and addressing other context-aware access control use cases.

12. REFERENCES

[1] B. Alan and E. Bell. *Business Research Methods.* Oxford University Press, Incorporated, 2007.

[2] G. Bai, L. Gu, T. Feng, Y. Guo, and X. Chen. Context-aware usage control for android. In *Security and Privacy in Communication Networks*, pages 326–343. Springer, 2010.

[3] L. Bauer, C. Bravo-Lillo, E. Fragkaki, and W. Melicher. A comparison of users' perceptions of and willingness to use google, facebook, and google+ single sign-on functionality. In *Workshop on digital identity management (DIM) in conjunction with the 20th AMC Conference on Computer and Communications Security (ACM CCS 2013)*, Berlin, Germany, Nov. 2013.

[4] U. Beck. *Risk Society: Towards a New Modernity.* Association with Theory, Culture & Society. SAGE Publications, 1992.

[5] M. Bell and V. Lovich. Apparatus and methods for enforcement of policies upon a wireless device. US. Patent 8254902, Aug. 2012.

[6] S. Bugiel, L. Davi, A. Dmitrienko, S. Heuser, A.-R. Sadeghi, and B. Shastry. Practical and lightweight domain isolation on android. In *1st ACM workshop on Security and privacy in smartphones and mobile devices*, SPSM '11, pages 51–62, New York, NY, USA, 2011. ACM.

[7] S. Bugiel, S. Heuser, and A.-R. Sadeghi. Flexible and fine-grained mandatory access control on Android for diverse security and privacy policies. In *22nd USENIX Security Symposium (USENIX Security '13).* USENIX, 2013.

[8] L. Cai and H. Chen. Touchlogger: Inferring keystrokes on touch screen from smartphone motion. In *6th USENIX Conference on Hot Topics in Security*, HotSec'11, pages 9–9, Berkeley, CA, USA, 2011. USENIX Association.

[9] C. Camp. The BYOD security challenge: How scary is the iPad, tablet, smartphone surge? WeLiveSecurity Blog post, February 2012.

[10] S. Cohen and L. Taylor. *Escape Attempts: The Theory and Practice of Resistance in Everyday Life.* Taylor & Francis, 1992.

[11] M. Conti, B. Crispo, E. Fernandes, and Y. Zhauniarovich. CRêPE: A system for enforcing fine-grained context-related policies on android. *Information Forensics and Security, IEEE Transactions on*, 7(5):1426–1438, 2012.

[12] M. Covington, P. Fogla, Z. Zhan, and M. Ahamad. A context-aware security architecture for emerging applications. In *18th Annual Computer Security Applications Conference*, pages 249 – 258, 2002.

[13] M. L. Damiani, E. Bertino, B. Catania, and P. Perlasca. GEO-RBAC: A spatially aware RBAC. *ACM Trans. Inf. Syst. Secur.*, 10(1), Feb. 2007.

[14] O. Dousse, J. Eberle, and M. Mertens. Place Learning via Direct WiFi Fingerprint Clustering. In *IEEE 13th International Conference on Mobile Data Management (MDM)*, pages 282–287, 2012.

[15] N. Eagle and A. Pentland. Social serendipity: mobilizing social software. *Pervasive Computing, IEEE*, 4(2):28–34, 2005.

[16] W. Enck, P. Gilbert, B.-G. Chun, L. P. Cox, J. Jung, P. McDaniel, and A. N. Sheth. TaintDroid: an information-flow tracking system for realtime privacy monitoring on smartphones. In *9th USENIX conference on Operating systems design and implementation*, OSDI'10, pages 1–6, Berkeley, CA, USA, 2010. USENIX Association.

[17] A. Gupta, M. Miettinen, N. Asokan, and M. Nagy. Intuitive security policy configuration in mobile devices using context profiling. In *International Conference on Privacy, Security, Risk and Trust (PASSAT), and 2012 International Confernece on Social Computing (SocialCom)*, pages 471–480. IEEE, Sept. 2012.

[18] M. Hall, E. Frank, G. Holmes, B. Pfahringer, P. Reutemann, and I. H. Witten. The weka data mining software: an update. *SIGKDD Explor. Newsl.*, 11(1):10–18, Nov. 2009.

[19] E. Hayashi, S. Das, S. Amini, J. Hong, and I. Oakley. CASA: context-aware scalable authentication. In *Ninth Symposium on Usable Privacy and Security*, SOUPS '13, pages 3:1–3:10, New York, NY, USA, 2013. ACM.

[20] J. Höflich and M. Hartmann. *Mobile Communication in Everyday Life: Ethnographic Views, Observations and Reflections.* Frank & Timme, 2006.

[21] R. Hull, B. Kumar, D. Lieuwen, P. Patel-Schneider, A. Sahuguet, S. Varadarajan, and A. Vyas. Enabling

context-aware and privacy-conscious user data sharing. In *2004 IEEE International Conference on Mobile Data Management*, pages 187 – 198, 2004.

[22] J. H. Kang, W. Welbourne, B. Stewart, and G. Borriello. Extracting places from traces of locations. *SIGMOBILE Mob. Comput. Commun. Rev.*, 9(3):58–68, July 2005.

[23] P. G. Kelley, P. H. Drielsma, N. M. Sadeh, and L. F. Cranor. User-controllable learning of security and privacy policies. In *1st ACM Workshop on Workshop on AISec*, AISec '08, pages 11–18, New York, NY, USA, 2008. ACM.

[24] A. Madan, M. Cebrian, D. Lazer, and A. Pentland. Social sensing for epidemiological behavior change. In *12th ACM International Conference on Ubiquitous Computing*, Ubicomp '10, pages 291–300, New York, NY, USA, 2010. ACM.

[25] P. Marquardt, A. Verma, H. Carter, and P. Traynor. (sp)iphone: Decoding vibrations from nearby keyboards using mobile phone accelerometers. In *18th ACM Conference on Computer and Communications Security*, CCS '11, pages 551–562, New York, NY, USA, 2011. ACM.

[26] R. Montoliu, J. Blom, and D. Gatica-Perez. Discovering places of interest in everyday life from smartphone data. *Multimedia Tools Appl.*, 62(1):179–207, 2013.

[27] F. Naini, O. Dousse, P. Thiran, and M. Vetterli. Population size estimation using a few individuals as agents. In *2011 IEEE International Symposium on Information Theory Proceedings (ISIT)*, pages 2499 – 2503, July 2011.

[28] M. Nauman, S. Khan, and X. Zhang. Apex: extending android permission model and enforcement with user-defined runtime constraints. In *ACM Symposium on Information, Computer and Communications Security*, ASIACCS '10, pages 328–332, New York, NY, USA, 2010. ACM.

[29] M. Ongtang, S. Mclaughlin, W. Enck, and P. Mcdaniel. Semantically rich application-centric security in android. In *2009 Annual Computer Security Applications Conference*, ACSAC '09, 2009.

[30] E. Owusu, J. Han, S. Das, A. Perrig, and J. Zhang. Accessory: Password inference using accelerometers on smartphones. In *Twelfth Workshop on Mobile Computing Systems & Applications*, HotMobile '12, pages 9:1–9:6, New York, NY, USA, 2012. ACM.

[31] O. Riva, C. Qin, K. Strauss, and D. Lymberopoulos. Progressive authentication: deciding when to authenticate on mobile phones. In *21st USENIX Security Symposium*, 2012.

[32] G. Russello, M. Conti, B. Crispo, and E. Fernandes. Moses: supporting operation modes on smartphones. In *17th ACM symposium on Access Control Models and Technologies*, SACMAT '12, pages 3–12, New York, NY, USA, 2012. ACM.

[33] N. Sadeh, J. Hong, L. Cranor, I. Fette, P. Kelley, M. Prabaker, and J. Rao. Understanding and capturing people's privacy policies in a mobile social networking application. *Personal and Ubiquitous Computing*, 13:401–412, 2009.

[34] M. Sahami, S. Dumais, D. Heckerman, and E. Horvitz. A bayesian approach to filtering junk e-mail. In *Learning for Text Categorization: Papers from the 1998 workshop*, volume 62, pages 98–105, 1998.

[35] R. Sandhu and J. Park. Usage control: A vision for next generation access control. In V. Gorodetsky, L. Popyack, and V. Skormin, editors, *Computer Network Security*, volume 2776 of *Lecture Notes in Computer Science*, pages 17–31. Springer Berlin Heidelberg, 2003.

[36] R. Schlegel, K. Zhang, X. Zhou, M. Intwala, A. Kapadia, and X. Wang. Soundcomber: A stealthy and context-aware sound trojan for smartphones. In *Network & Distributed System Security Symposium (NDSS'11)*, pages 17–33, 2011.

[37] R. Sennett. *The Uses of Disorder: Personal Identity and City Life*. Sociology: History. W. W. Norton, Incorporated, 1992.

[38] R. Siciliano. More than 30% of people don't password protect their mobile devices. McAfee Blog Central, February 2013.

[39] S. Smalley and R. Craig. Security Enhanced (SE) Android: Bringing Flexible MAC to Android. In *Network & Distributed System Security Symposium (NDSS'13)*. The Internet Society, 2013.

[40] A. Tashakkori and C. Teddlie. *Handbook of Mixed Methods in Social & Behavioral Research*. SAGE Publications, 2003.

[41] C. Teddlie and A. Tashakkori. *The Quantitative Tradition: Basic Terminology and two Prototypes*, chapter 1, pages 5–6. SAGE Publications, 2009.

[42] R. Templeman, Z. Rahman, D. Crandall, and A. Kapadia. PlaceRaider: Virtual theft in physical spaces with smartphones. In *Network & Distributed System Security Symposium (NDSS'13)*, Feb. 2013.

[43] H. Verkasalo. Contextual patterns in mobile service usage. *Personal and Ubiquitous Computing*, 13(5):331–342, Mar. 2008.

[44] N. Xu, F. Zhang, Y. Luo, W. Jia, D. Xuan, and J. Teng. Stealthy video capturer: A new video-based spyware in 3G smartphones. In *Second ACM Conference on Wireless Network Security*, WiSec '09, pages 69–78, New York, NY, USA, 2009. ACM.

[45] Z. Xu, K. Bai, and S. Zhu. Taplogger: Inferring user inputs on smartphone touchscreens using on-board motion sensors. In *5th ACM Conference on Security and Privacy in Wireless and Mobile Networks*, WISEC '12, pages 113–124, New York, NY, USA, 2012. ACM.

[46] V. W. Zheng, Y. Zheng, X. Xie, and Q. Yang. Collaborative location and activity recommendations with GPS history data. In M. Rappa, P. Jones, J. Freire, and S. Chakrabarti, editors, *19th International Conference on World Wide Web*, pages 1029–1038, New York, NY, USA, 2010. ACM.

On the Feasibility of Software Attacks on Commodity Virtual Machine Monitors via Direct Device Assignment

Gábor Pék
CrySyS Lab, BME
Budapest, Hungary
pek@crysys.hu

Andrea Lanzi
Univ. degli Studi di Milano
Milan, Italy
andrea.lanzi@unimi.it

Abhinav Srivastava
AT&T Labs Research
New Jersey, USA
abhinav@research.att.com

Davide Balzarotti
Eurecom
Sophia Anitpolis, France
balzarot@eurecom.fr

Aurélien Francillon
Eurecom
Sophia Antipolis, France
francill@eurecom.fr

Christoph Neumann
Technicolor, Rennes, France
christoph.neumann
@technicolor.com

ABSTRACT

The security of virtual machine monitors (VMMs) is a challenging and active field of research. In particular, due to the increasing significance of hardware virtualization in cloud solutions, it is important to clearly understand existing and arising VMM-related threats. Unfortunately, there is still a lot of confusion around this topic as many attacks presented in the past have never been implemented in practice or tested in a realistic scenario.

In this paper, we shed light on VM related threats and defences by implementing, testing, and categorizing a wide range of known and unknown attacks based on directly assigned devices. We executed these attacks on an exhaustive set of VMM configurations to determine their potential impact. Our experiments suggest that most of the previously known attacks are ineffective in current VMM setups.

We also developed an automatic tool, called PTFuzz, to discover hardware-level problems that affects current VMMs. By using PTFuzz, we found several cases of unexpected hardware behaviour, and a major vulnerability on Intel platforms that potentially impacts a large set of machines used in the wild. These vulnerabilities affect unprivileged virtual machines that use a directly assigned device (e.g., network card) and have all the existing hardware protection mechanisms enabled. Such vulnerabilities either allow an attacker to generate a host-side interrupt or hardware faults, violating expected isolation properties. These can cause host software (e.g., VMM) halt as well as they might open the door for practical VMM exploitations.

We believe that our study can help cloud providers and researchers to better understand the limitations of their current architectures to provide secure hardware virtualization and prepare for future attacks.

ASIA CCS'14, June 4–6, 2014, Kyoto, Japan.

http://dx.doi.org/10.1145/2590296.2590299.

Categories and Subject Descriptors

D.4 [**Operating Systems**]: Security and Protection; D.2.5 [**Software Engineering**]: Testing and Debugging—*error handling and recovery*

Keywords

I/O virtualization; Virtual Machine Monitor; Passthrough; Interrupt attack; DMA attack; MMIO; PIO

1. INTRODUCTION

Due to the increasing demand towards server consolidation, virtualization has become a key element of IT infrastructures. For example, the ability to create and manage virtual servers is one of the pillars of Infrastructure-as-a-Service (IaaS) cloud services, such as Amazon EC2 [1] and Google Compute Engine [2]. For this reason, both software and hardware vendors are constantly developing and releasing new technologies to satisfy the ever-growing customer expectations in terms of security, privacy, performance, and usability.

In the last ten years, a large number of papers [3, 4, 5, 6, 7, 8] have been presented to either secure, or enhance the performance and capabilities of VMMs. Several works [9, 10, 11, 12, 13, 14] also mention and implement possible attacks. Unfortunately, most of them are described only from a theoretical point of view, and only a few have been actually implemented and thoroughly tested in realistic settings. Moreover, even when a proof-of-concept implementation exists, it is often difficult to understand what the prerequisites are for the attack to work, what the real impact is, and to which extent the results can be generalized to other environments and/or VMMs. Most of these questions are difficult to answer, and it is not uncommon also for experts to disagree on these points. Finally, to make things even more complex, current VMMs are rapidly evolving. Each new release contains new technologies that can potentially introduce new vulnerabilites as well as new countermeasures that can make existing attacks obsolete.

For example, several techniques have recently been introduced to increase the efficiency and security of I/O operation for guest virtual machines (VMs). *Direct device assignment* (also known as device passthrough) is such a mechanism, where the VMM assigns a device exclusively to one VM instead of sharing it with other virtual machines. This is achieved by directly mapping the device into a VM address space, redirecting the corresponding interrupts to the correct VM. Clearly, assigning the hardware to be directly controlled by a VM improves the performance. At the same time, this approach also introduces a wide range of security problems that eventually led hardware manufacturers to introduce hardware assisted protection extensions for the CPU and chipset.

In this paper, we demonstrate a wide range of known *and* unknown attacks that can be launched via device passthrough. First, we chose to re-implement attacks that have been proposed by security researchers in order to systematically study their impact and their limitations against recent versions of Xen and KVM virtual machine monitors. We believe that repeating experiments is fundamental in computer science, as well as in many other scientific fields (e.g., physics) to validate the results of different researchers. For this reason, we carefully replicated our tests under seven different VMM configurations.

Second, we complemented the existing attacks by exploring new directions and unknown corner cases. In particular, we propose two *novel* attacks, one based on the modification of the Peripheral Component Interconnect express (PCIe) configuration space and the other based on the creation of host-side Non-Maskable Interrupts (NMIs). More precisely, our interrupt attack is the consequence of a misunderstanding between the hardware and software. In addition, it is the only interrupt attack to date that works on configurations in which all available hardware protections are turned on. By discussing our results with vendors, we realized that our attack is pervasive and especially affects Intel based server platforms.

To perform our experiments, we implemented several tools designed to reveal configuration weaknesses, VMM vulnerabilities, or deeper hardware problems. Some attacks were manually tested, for example by remapping specific I/O memory ranges and trying to read or write them. In other cases, however, it was impossible to manually cover the space of all possible values, so we implemented a fuzzer, called PTFuzz, to thoroughly explore different problems.

In summary, this paper makes the following contributions:

- We re-implement a wide range of previously proposed attacks to evaluate the threat that they carry on contemporary VMMs.
- We introduce two *novel* attacks for *passthrough devices*: A new variation of an attack against the PCIe configuration space *and* an interrupt attack that violates the security settings in all tested configurations. While the former was discovered manually, the latter was revealed by a fuzzer, called PTFuzz, that we built to automatically reveal low-level problems during DMA operations. In addition, PTfuzz revealed another unexpected hardware behaviour during testing interrupt attacks.
- We test all the attacks on various configurations of two commodity VMMs (Xen and KVM), and discuss how different features contribute to the security of these VMMs. On the one hand, our experiments show that it can be quite difficult to properly configure a VMM to operate securely. In addition, we show that in some circumstances the overall security can only be guaranteed by disabling device passthrough for untrusted guests. On the other hand, once the system is properly configured, most of the attacks (except our new interrupt attacks) are either ineffective or restricted to the attacker's virtual machine.

2. BACKGROUND

A virtualized environment consists of three main software components: the host operating system (or privileged VM), a number of guest operating systems running inside isolated virtual machines (VMs), and a Virtual Machine Monitor (VMM) responsible for controlling the access to hardware resources[1]. In reality, the distinction between these three components is not always clear. For example, in Type I VMMs (such as Xen), there is no host OS but only the VMM and a privileged VM (e.g., Xen's Dom0) that manages other unprivileged guest virtual machines. Type II VMMs (such as KVM), however, include a host OS which also contains the hypervisor in charge of uniformly managing all the system resources.

Prior to the introduction of specific hardware support, the execution of unmodified guest OSs (i.e., full virtualization) was implemented by performing instruction emulation, for example, by using *binary translation*. Performance was further improved by the introduction of *paravirtualization*, however, this requires a modified version of the guest OS.

As these pure software solutions have various weaknesses in terms of scalability, performance and security, a new approach called *hardware assisted virtualization* was introduced by AMD/V [15] and Intel-VT [16] technologies.

In the rest of this section, we will introduce the main technologies (both hardware and software) that are required to understand the security of VMMs and the experiments we present in this paper.

2.1 Direct Device Assignment

One of the main tasks of the VMM is to control how guest virtual machines can access physical I/O devices. Three main approaches exist to perform this task: emulation, paravirtualization and direct device assignment (also known as *direct access* or *passthrough*). The first two techniques share virtualized I/O devices among multiple virtual machines. On the contrary, the passthrough approach assigns one physical device exclusively to one VM that has full control and direct access to most parts of the assigned hardware. This has the advantage of significantly reducing the main bottleneck of virtual environments: the overhead of I/O operations [17, 18, 19, 20, 21]. Unfortunately, direct device assignment also raises several security concerns. In fact, bus mastering capable directly assigned devices can initiate DMA transfers, and have access to arbitrary memory locations [10]. A malicious virtual machine may misuse them to access the memory of other VMs. Moreover, buggy device drivers can also be the root cause of system instability [22, 23, 24, 25]. These problems can be mitigated by using an IOMMU, as explained later in this section.

2.2 PCI/PCIe Address Space Access

On the x86 architecture, a PCI device can be accessed in two different ways: using a Port Mapped I/O (PIO) or using a Memory Mapped I/O (MMIO) mechanism. Each PCI device configuration is stored in the device configuration memory. This memory is accessible either by using special PIO registers or through an MMIO space. The configuration space is typically accessed by the BIOS or the operating system kernel to initialize or configure the Base Address Registers (BAR). Base Address Registers are defined by the PCI standard and used to specify the address at which the device memory is mapped in the PIO or MMIO address spaces.

Access to configuration space registers is usually emulated for fully virtualized guests, and in some cases also for privileged VMs. In this case, whenever a guest accesses a configuration space, the request is intercepted by the VMM, which incurs a significant performance overhead. Therefore, in order to improve the performance, some VMMs (e.g., KVM) allow to directly pass PIO or

[1]We deliberately use the term *VMM* instead of *hypervisor*, as the latter traditionally is not capable of providing a full-fledged guest environment and does not support multiple VMs.

MMIO accesses [21], except for the accesses targeting the device configuration memory.

2.3 Hardware IOMMU

To improve the isolation, performance, and security of I/O devices, hardware supported I/O Memory Management Units (IOMMUs) were introduced [26]. In particular, Intel VT-d [27] provides hardware support for DMA and interrupt virtualization. DMA virtualization (a.k.a. DMA remapping) enables system software to create multiple isolated DMA protection domains by allocating a subset of the host physical memory to a specific domain.

The DMA isolation is performed by restricting memory access from I/O devices to a specific physical memory domain set. More precisely, the DMA isolation mechanism is able to exclusively assign a set of physical pages to a particular I/O device. For this purpose, the VT-d architecture defines a multi-level page table structure for the DMA address translation.

2.4 Interrupt Remapping

In a multiprocessor environment, hardware interrupts are handled either by the per-processor Local Advanced Programmable Interrupt Controller (LAPICs) or by the external I/O APIC, which is part of the system chipset. LAPICs are responsible for receiving and sending local interrupts from various sources, including special pins in the processor, the APIC timer, or the performance-monitoring counters. LAPICs can also receive interrupts via the Inter-Processor Interrupt (IPI) mechanism to get notifications from other processors. Finally, interrupts can also originate from external interrupt sources (e.g., I/O devices) that are connected to the I/O APIC. In this case, the I/O APIC translates these requests to corresponding interrupt messages using its *redirection table*, and delivers them to the target LAPIC. The LAPIC then decides whether to forward the interrupt to the processor or not.

There are two main types of interrupts that can be generated by I/O devices: legacy interrupts and Message Signaled Interrupts (MSI). Legacy interrupts use dedicated wires, while MSI interrupts use an in-band mechanism. MSIs are created by a DMA write to the memory mapped LAPIC region as step (1) and step (2) of the *numerical* path in Figure 3 show it. Such interrupts encode their own attributes (interrupt vector, destination processor, delivery mode, etc.) into the address and data of the DMA request. Basically, it means that a guest VM with a directly assigned device can also use this mechanism to signal an MSI to a physical processor via a simple DMA write operation. However, this can be fatal for a system as an arbitrary interrupt vector could be called from unprivileged guests [9].

To protect against such interrupt-based attacks, Intel introduced the interrupt remapping architecture as a part of the VT-d technology (see block *IR* in Figure 3). This mechanism is responsible for isolating and routing device interrupts to corresponding virtual machines. More precisely, when VT-d is turned on, all the interrupt requests (both MSI and legacy interrupts) are extended with a *source-id* attribute to identify the device that issues the interrupt request. Moreover, the *new, remappable* MSI format uses only simple attributes such as the *index* value that points out an entry in the so-called *interrupt remapping table* to find a requested interrupt vector. In this way, the device cannot call an arbitrary interrupt vector directly, but only after the validation of the hardware. After successful validation, interrupts are remapped by the hardware module to the corresponding physical interrupt vectors with the proper attributes (e.g., delivery mode). However, if Extended Interrupt Mode (x2APIC mode) [27] is disabled, *old, compatibility*-format MSI interrupts can still be generated if VMM software enables them during runtime.

2.5 A Closer Look at Commodity VMMs

Since direct device assignment has a large impact on the overall system security and performance, we discuss that in more detail in the case of the two VMMs we use in our tests: Xen and KVM.

Xen

Xen supports two types of passthrough modes: the software-only Xen PCI passthrough for paravirtual guests, and the hardware IOMMU based passthrough available for both paravirtualized and fully virtualized (HVM) guests. The software-only paravirtual Xen PCI passthrough requires VMM intervention to handle DMA requests [28]. From a security point of view, software-only paravirtual Xen PCI passthrough gives full control over the device, which allows a compromised paravirtualized guest to write arbitrary machine memory locations using a DMA attack. In contrast to that, the hardware IOMMU based passthrough allows for remapping all the DMA requests by the corresponding DMA remapping hardware units. As Xen enables device passthrough for HVM guests only when hardware based IOMMU is turned on, it is a more secure solution. In this paper, we test only the hardware *IOMMU based* passthrough model as this is the preferred configuration in current public clouds. In addition, the software-only paravirtual passthrough is well-known to be insecure as it does not use a hardware IOMMU, we therefore do not evaluate it in this paper.

KVM

KVM guests normally use either emulated devices or virtio devices to perform I/O operations. Virtio is an efficient I/O virtualization abstraction layer that allows the development of paravirtualized drivers for guests. Similarly to Xen, direct device assignment is only allowed when the hardware based protection (either Intel VT-d or AMD-V) is turned on. In this setting, PCI/PCIe devices can be assigned directly to a guest VM, thus allowing these devices to be used almost at native speed with minimal I/O overhead.

3. SETUP AND TEST CONFIGURATION

In this paper, we describe the implementation, validation, and execution of three classes of software-based virtualization attacks based on direct device assignments. The attacks we present are based on abusing the PCI/PCIe configuration space to generate device memory collisions, on performing unauthorized memory access through DMA and MMIO regions, and on generating interrupts to the VMM from a guest VM.

3.1 Threat Model

In our experiments, we run each attack against different hardware and VMM configurations, according to two possible attack scenarios. In the first scenario, we assume that the attacker has full access to a guest machine configured with a pass-through device. This is a common setup for IaaS cloud providers that offer, for example, direct access to video cards (e.g., Amazon EC2 Cluster GPU).

In the second scenario, we assume that the attacker is able to control or compromise the privileged VM (e.g., by exploiting vulnerabilities such as CVE-2008-3687, or CVE-2007-4993). Even though this case is certainly more difficult to achieve, it still represents an important threat model that needs to be carefully evaluated. In fact, the privileged VM is often a large piece of software, therefore, it is more prone to contain vulnerabilities that can be exploited by an attacker. However, unrestricted access to the privileged VM does not give full privileges over the physical machine [10]. For example, VMMs (e.g., Xen) execute the privileged VM (Dom0) with the role of a host OS, and strictly divide the physical address space and privileges between Dom0 and the VMM. In other words, the VMM is specifically designed to be protected against a malicious privileged VM.

We also launched our attacks on KVM's host OS to identify the differences with Xen's Dom0. However, we performed this test only for completeness, as host OS privileges on KVM are equivalent of having entire control over the VMM as well.

3.2 VMM and Hardware Setup

For our experiments, we installed the last versions of Xen and KVM available at the time we ran our tests (i.e., Xen 4.2 and KVM 3.5). Table 1 shows the default boot settings for both VMMs and the configurations we used in our tests.

Xen 4.2 came with a set of new virtual machine management tools named XL that support passthrough devices by default. KVM enables both DMA and Interrupt remapping by default, as well as the x2APIC mode if it is supported by the hardware. x2APIC combined with interrupt remapping is known to be a *secure* configuration against interrupt attacks [9]. Device passthrough is instead not enabled by default, but it can be manually turned on by the administrator.

Properly configuring a VMM can be a daunting and confusing task, even for experienced system administrators. For example, hardware IOMMU requires the support from the CPU, the BIOS, and the motherboard chipset. Unfortunately, these dependencies are not always correctly documented for VMMs. For example, our original test machine was equipped with an i5-2400 CPU (with IOMMU support), but contained a BIOS and chipset (H67) without IOMMU support. Both KVM and Xen refused to put our network card in passthrough mode in this setup. However, after updating the BIOS to a new version with IOMMU support, KVM let us put the device in passthrough mode. This means that in practice KVM trusted the Advanced Configuration and Power Management Interface (ACPI) data structures reported by the updated BIOS, but did not pay attention to the real chipset capabilities. This may carry serious threat for integrated devices which have no PCIe Function Level Reset (FLR) capabilities [29]. More precisely, an integrated device assigned to a guest VM can be configured to send DMA requests continuously to memory addresses belonging to the host OS/privileged VM. While the device is assigned to the guest VM, all these requests are blocked by the IOMMU hardware. When the device is reassigned to the host OS/privileged VM, the VMM first resets the device via an FLR or bridge-level reset, and then reconfigures the IOMMU hardware to allow device access to the host OS/privileged VM memory. However, if the VMM cannot reset the device (e.g., FLR capability is missing), the device keeps sending DMA requests which now overwrite host OS/privileged VM memory addresses.

In conclusion, KVM lets the administrator believe the device is in a secure passthrough mode, while the support is actually incomplete. To prevent this issue, system administrators are advised to carefully check whether the CPU, the BIOS *and* the motherboard chipset support hardware IOMMU. This is a clear example of configurations problems related to properly setting up passthrough devices. For this reason, we executed our attacks on *another* machine with Intel i5-2500 CPU, Q67 chipset and Intel VT-d support enabled in the BIOS. The machine was equipped with an Intel 82579LM PCIe network card that was used as passthrough device for the experiments. The guest OSs were running Linux kernel 2.6.32-5-amd64 and 3.5.0.

3.3 Results Overview

In the rest of the paper, we use an abbreviated notation to refer to the scenario and the target of each attack. We use the following notation:

- Guest-to-VMM (**g⇒vmm**) attacks.
  This is the most critical scenario, in which an attacker controlling a guest VM can launch an attack against the system VMM.
- Guest-to-Host (**g⇒h**) attacks.
  An attacker, with full control on a guest virtual machine, can compromise the host OS/privileged VM. Even though it is not as powerful as the previous one, the consequences of this attack are often as serious.
- Host-to-VMM (**h⇒vmm**) attacks.
  As we explained above, the VMM is often separated and protected from the privileged guest VM (e.g., Xen Dom0). In this attack, an attacker who was able to gain control in the privileged guest OS can escalate her privileges in the machine by launching an attack against the VMM. As we highlighted before, we tested our attacks on KVM host OS only to show the differences with the Xen Dom0 case.
- Guest-to-Guest (**g⇒g**) attacks.
  These attacks aim at compromising a target guest VM starting from a separate guest VM controlled by the attacker.
- Guest-to-Self (**g**$\circlearrowright$) and Host-to-Self (**h**$\circlearrowright$) attacks.
  These are less severe scenarios in which the attack is confined inside the attacker's virtual machine. For this reason, we also refer to these attacks as *intra-guest* and *intra-host* attacks. In most of the cases, since the attacker has already root privileges on the same virtual machine, the consequences of these attacks are negligible. However, we still report these cases for completeness. Also, they may still be relevant if the attacker does not fully control the machine, but can exploit a vulnerability that allow her to run the attack, or the system has to provide some security properties in an untrusted environment (e.g., as presented by Zhou et al. [30]).

The previous classification is based only on the originator and target of each attack. We intentionally use this approach, instead of a more traditional one based on the possible consequences of each attack (e.g., Denial of Service (DoS), code execution, information leakage, etc), because it better summarizes the results of our tests in terms of violating the *isolation* property. In fact, our main goal is to clarify which attack works under which conditions. The fact that it can be later used to DoS the VMM, or steal some information from other virtual machines, highly depends on other environmental conditions that are not under our control (e.g., the presence of other vulnerabilities in the system, and the capabilities and motivation of the attacker). However, we will briefly describe and comment on the possible consequences of each successful attack, case by case, in the next three sections.

All the attacks, presented in this paper are summarized in Table 2. The second column (*Ref*) reports the original source in which the attack was first proposed. The table also shows the *Previous Status* of the attack, (i.e., whether we found any evidence that the attack had been successfully implemented before our study). A value of *NC* (not confirmed) means that the attack was only theoretically described, *C* (confirmed) means that it was already tested in practice by other authors, and *NEW* means that the attack is proposed for the first time in this paper.

Feature	Default Values Xen	Default Values KVM	Our Xen Setup Dom0	Our Xen Setup HVM-1	Our Xen Setup HVM-2	Our Xen Setup HVM-3	Our Xen Setup HVM-4	Our KVM Setup Host OS	Our KVM Setup HVM-1
VT-d DMA Remapping	✓	✓	✓	✓	✓	✓	✓	✓	✓
VT-d Dom0 DMA passthrough	✗	✓	✓	✓	✓	✓	✓	✓	NA
VT-d interrupt remapping	✓	✓	✓	✗	✗	✓	✓	✓	✓
Direct Configuration Space Access	✗	NA	✗	✓*	✗	✗	✗	✓	✗
x2APIC mode on the Host	✓	✓	✓	✗	✗	✗	✓	✓	✓

Table 1: Test Configurations. The table shows both the default and test configurations in our Xen 4.2 and KVM 3.5 setup on an Intel Core (Quad) i5-2500 CPU 3,30 GHz CPU and Q67 motherboard chipset. While the *Default Values* column is placed only for comparison purposes, the *Our Xen Setup* and *Our KVM Setup* columns summarize those configurations we tested our attacks on. For example, the HVM-4 configuration on Xen means that all the hardware protection features were enabled in this configuration, but we did not give direct configuration space access to the passthrough device being attached to the Xen guest VM. The sign *NA*, refers to a cell that cannot be evaluated in the given configuration.
*Direct PIO access to device configuration memory was granted explicitly.

Attack	**Ref.**	**Previous Status**	Xen Host	Xen HVM-1	Xen HVM-2	Xen HVM-3	Xen HVM-4	KVM Host	KVM HVM-1
PCI/PCIe Configuration Attacks									
PCI/PCIe config. space access (PIO)	[31]	C*	h↻	g↻	g↻	g↻	g↻	h↻	g↻
PCIe config. space access (MMIO)	-	**NEW**	h↻	NA	g↻	g↻	g↻	h↻	g↻
I/O port overlapping (PIO)	[30]	NC	h↻	g↻	g↻	g↻	g↻	-	g↻***
I/O memory overlapping (MMIO)	[30]	NC	h↻	NA	g↻	g↻	g↻	h↻	g↻
Unauthorized Memory Access									
Unauthorized MMIO memory region access	[30]	NC	h↻	g↻	g↻	g↻	g↻	h↻	g↻
DMA	[10]	C**	h↻	g↻	g↻	g↻	g↻	h↻	g↻
Interrupt Attacks									
NMI	-	**NEW**	h↻	*g⇒vmm*	*g⇒vmm*	*g⇒vmm*	*g⇒vmm*	*g⇒vmm*	*g⇒vmm*

Table 2: Overview of the results of the attacks implemented in our study.
* The attack was previously confirmed as h↻, g⇒h, and g⇒vmm against an old version of Xen.
** The attack was previously confirmed as h⇒vmm, against an old version of Xen without DMA remapping hardware.
*** KVM detects the port overlapping and kills the guest. The state of CPU registers is also dumped in the Host OS.

Each cell in the table lists the results of a given attack against a particular configuration of Xen and KVM, according to the abbreviations introduced above. Whenever the attack was not applicable, it is marked as *NA*. Finally, we mark in red color the most critical results, i.e., any successful guest-to-host or guest-to-VMM attacks. We do not highlight here the unexpected hardware behavior we discovered while carrying out interrupt attacks. The unexpected behaviors are described in Section 6.

The next three sections present an in-depth analysis of the three classes of attacks and the result of our experiments.

4. DEVICE MEMORY COLLISION ATTACKS

In this section, we systematically examine how a VM can access the configuration space of directly assigned devices, and what security risks are associated to these actions. In particular, by reconfiguring a device, an attacker can create a *conflict* with another device. Therefore, without enforcing the proper PCI/PCIe configuration space access restrictions, an attacker could ex-filtrate data from one virtual machine to another that is under her control. Moreover, unmediated PCI/PCIe configuration space accesses can result in either privilege escalation [31] or DoS attack against the host/privileged VM. All the attacks we present are implemented by modifying the *e1000e* device driver of an Intel 82579LM *PCIe* network card.

PIO Attack against the PCI/PCIe Configuration Space

Duflot et al. [31] described the dangers of enabling a VM to directly access the configuration registers of a PCI device via the PIO space. The authors showed that delegating PIO access to userspace or a guest virtual machine can lead to several attacks, such as privilege escalation between isolated virtual machines.

According to the literature, KVM emulates PIO accesses (using QEMU code [32]), thus, accessing directly the configuration space I/O ports is not possible in normal circumstances. Xen originally allowed direct access to the PIO configuration space from Dom0, but this was eventually emulated as well [33]. However, direct access can still be allowed to fully virtualized guests (HVM) via a guest configuration option. There is no clear conclusion still (e.g.,[34]) whether certain guest VM configurations are insecure if direct PCI/PCIe configuration space accesses are enabled for passthrough devices.

For this reason, we decided to test this condition to show what the real risks are in a practical scenario. In our experiments, we modified the e1000e network driver to overwrite the PIO Base Address Register (BAR) in the configuration address space of arbitrary devices (identified by their *source-id*) by writing to the `0xcf8` I/O port. The goal of our test was to address PCI devices that were invisible from our VM. We tested our attack in various setups as shown in Table 2, but all cases turned out to be ineffective on current Xen and KVM versions. The reason is that PIO configuration space accesses are always emulated, no matter what configurations we used. In other words, we could access only the devices of our VM, therefore restricting the attack to an *intra-guest* or *intra-host* scenario.

MMIO Attack against the PCIe Configuration Space

PCI Express (PCIe) devices have an extended configuration space that can be accessed via traditional memory operations (i.e., MMIO). To test this situation, we implemented a *new* device configuration space attack that can be launched via the MMIO with the goal of manipulating the memory mapped registers of the target device.

Similarly to the PIO access attack, we addressed the PCIe configuration space of the targeted devices by using their source-id [35], and then tried to modify some of their configuration registers (e.g., BAR). Again, we were not able to address devices that were not in the scope of our VM, thus the attack is limited to an *intra-guest* or *intra-host* scenario.

PIO Overlapping Attack

Zhou et al. [30] proposed several device-related attacks that could affect already compromised operating systems. For example, PIO overlapping is similar to the PIO configuration space attack, but in this case the attacker can only reconfigure the configuration space of a specific device she controls. In particular, by changing the PIO BAR register of a directly assigned PCI/PCIe device, an attacker can overwrite the BAR value with the one of another device attached to another VM. In this way, the device memory of the two devices will overlap, leading to data ex-filtration from one device to the other.

To test this attack, we modified our e1000e PCIe network card driver by changing the PIO BAR value of the card with the value of the keyboard. We observed unresponsive keyboard and mouse under Xen both in case of Dom0 (with dom0-passthrough mode enabled) and HVM guests. On a KVM host, however, the port overlapping was successful but without any apparent effect. Interestingly, when the attack was launched from the KVM guest (HVM-1), the host kernel detected our overlap attempt, and killed the guest VM instantly. Additionally, the host OS provided a clear debug message about a hardware error that occurred during the registration of the I/O port read operation for the keyboard.

MMIO Overlapping Attack

In an MMIO overlapping attack (Figure 1), an attacker controlling one guest VM with an assigned passthrough device can access the device memory space of another device attached to another VM.

The attack was implemented by changing the MMIO BAR values of our PCIe passthrough network card to overlap with the BAR value of a graphics card. In all configurations, we observed that the Ethernet card became unresponsive inside the attacker VM. In contrast with the previous attack, we did not find any mechanisms implemented in Xen and KVM to notify users about these overlapping I/O memories.

To summarize the results, all the configurations that we tested are protected against PIO/MMIO configuration space manipulations in both Xen and KVM.

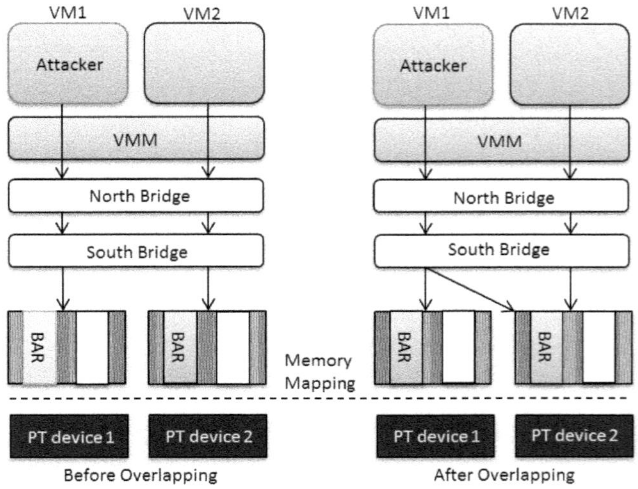

Figure 1: MMIO overlapping attack. An attacker on VM1 sets the MMIO Base Address Register (BAR) value of a passthrough device (PT device1) to that of another device (PT device 2), assigned to VM2. As a result of this manipulation, the attacker can get access to the device memory of PT device 2.

5. UNAUTHORIZED MEMORY ACCESS

In this section, we describe two types of attacks to access protected memory regions via unauthorized memory device requests. These attacks can be used to steal and ex-filtrate information in a cloud environment, or to control devices assigned to other VMs.

Unauthorized MMIO Region Access

A device can be accessed through physical memory in two ways: using MMIO and using Direct Memory Access (DMA). As the authors mention in [30], an attacker can manipulate the device behavior by writing into these memory regions. The attack can be accomplished in two steps: 1) the attacker remaps an MMIO region, belonging to a victim device, into a new virtual address by using `ioremap_nocache` Linux kernel function, 2) she injects malicious code/data into the remapped memory region by using the `iowrite32()` Linux kernel function. By doing so, the memory of the victim device is manipulated and can be controlled by the attacker.

In order to test the protection mechanisms offered by Xen and KVM, we implemented a proof-of-concept attack in which we overwrote the entire MMIO address space of a *second* network adapter by modifying the e1000e driver of the *attacker* network card. As the second adapter, which had Internet connection, was assigned to the same VM as the attacker network card, we could access its MMIO space. In our tests on Xen and KVM guests, the second adapter's Internet connection was lost and the guests became isolated from the network.

The same experiment was also performed on our KVM host, and it completely crashed the operating system. Therefore, we can conclude that none of the tested VMMs implemented a detection technique for checking these types of unauthorized memory region modifications. However, these attacks only work in *intra-guest* and *intra-host* scenarios.

DMA Attack

User-space processes are prevented from accessing protected memory regions by a memory controller known as Memory Manage-

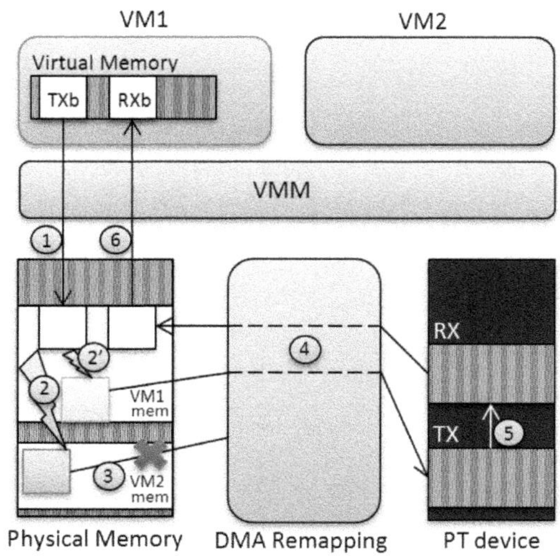

Figure 2: Intra-guest DMA attack. An attacker, controlling VM1, can read/write arbitrary intra-guest memory locations by a loopback mode passthrough device (PT device).

ment Unit (MMU). However, drivers that communicate to PCI/PCIe devices can directly access any physical memory address space by using Direct Memory Access (DMA) operations. Since the physical address space includes the whole system memory, a malicious driver could potentially read and write the entire memory of the system. To prevent this from happening, hardware vendors designed an hardware protection mechanism (called IOMMU). As we already explained in Section 2, IOMMU is a memory management unit that maps I/O bus addresses to physical memory addresses for all DMA memory transactions on the bus. The role of the IOMMU is similar to that of a traditional MMU: 1) it translates the memory I/O address range of one device to the corresponding real physical address, and 2) it prevents any unauthorized access from one device address space to another. Even though the IOMMU establishes memory barriers among different device address spaces, which parts of the memory should be assigned to which devices remains an open research problem [36]. Since it is not clear how different VMMs deploy such a protection mechanism, we implemented and tested different DMA attacks under three main threat models: intra-guest, guest-to-guest and guest-to-host.

To launch the attack, we put our passthrough network card into loopback mode similarly to Wojtczuk [10] to directly connect the card's internal transmission buffer (TX) to the receiving buffer (RX) (i.e., to receive all the packets that were sent by the card). We then associated a transmission (TXb) and a receiver buffer (RXb) to the DMA channel by using the `dma_map_single()` function. This allows us to link the guest virtual address of the transmission buffer (TXb) to the physical address that we want to access (Figure 2).

After the setup phase was completed, we performed two different experiments. First, we tried to perform a DMA operation using a physical memory location belonging to a different virtual machine. In this case (points 2 and 3 in Figure 2), the DMA Remapping Engine (DMAR) successfully blocked the attack as one VM is not allowed to access the memory of other VMs for I/O operations. We then repeated the operation using a physical address belonging to another driver that runs inside the attacker VM (step 2' in Figure 2). This time, the DMA operation succeeded as the DMA remapping was not setup to create intra-guest protection domains. As a result (points 4 to 6 in Figure 2), the stolen data was transferred into the card's internal TX buffer, and then into the RX buffer thanks to the loopback mode. Finally, another DMA transaction moves the content of RX buffer to the receiver buffer in the VM (RXb), making the data accessible to the driver (and therefore to the attacker). A similar approach can also be used to perform an arbitrary memory write operation.

We implemented our DMA attacks by extending the e1000e network driver. It is important to note that *DMA remapping was always turned on* during our attack, otherwise we could not have put the network card into passthrough mode.

We were able to successfully run *intra-guest* and *intra-host* DMA attacks on both VMMs to retrieve the code of the kernel pages of the guest OS. Considering the *guest-to-guest* case, we verify that both VMMs implement DMA remapping correctly and does not allow inter-guest DMA operations. We obtained the same results for guest-to-host attacks, as the protection isolated the host address space, and the guest was redirected to its own address space.

6. INTERRUPT ATTACKS

In this section, we present a number of interrupt-related attacks. In particular, we introduce a novel attack that evades *all* currently available hardware and software protection mechanisms. After reporting this attack to vendors, we concluded that the problem stems from a misunderstanding between the hardware and software, and cannot be resolved by existing technologies without limiting platform capabilities. We also describe other unexpected hardware conditions that we discovered by fuzzing DMA operations.

Interrupt attacks could be used to DoS a VMM or a privileged VM, or, in more severe cases, even to execute arbitrary code inside them.

6.1 Abusing Message Signalled Interrupts

Recent PCIe devices generate interrupts by using the Message Signalled Interrupt (MSI) technology. Wojtczuk et al. [9] demonstrated that MSIs can also be generated by enforcing a device's scatter-gather mechanism during a DMA transaction by writing to a specific MMIO space that belongs to the LAPIC (0xfeexxxxx). In this case, the passthrough device writes specific information (e.g., interrupt vector, and delivery mode) to that predefined interrupt address range, which results in an interrupt generation with the preset interrupt vector. From an attacker's point of view, MSIs are advantageous as they can be generated without the need to compromise the firmware of a device: only the device driver has to be under her control. Practical interrupt attacks via passthrough devices have already been discussed in previous works [9], where the authors showed how an attacker could execute arbitrary code with VMM privileges by invoking Xen hypercalls from a guest OS.

However, interrupt remapping introduced remappable-format MSIs, which prevent an attacker from generating MSI interrupts with arbitrary interrupt vectors (i.e., compatibility-format MSI) as the *numerical* path on Figure 3 shows it. The only way to entirely forbid the generation of compatibility-format MSIs is to switch on the x2APIC mode (Section 2.4). In our experiments, we observed that x2APIC mode is turned on by default in KVM, but needs to be manually selected in older versions of Xen. This is considered to be the most secure configuration. To the best of our knowledge, we present here the first attack that succeeds when both interrupt remapping and x2APIC mode are enabled.

Fuzzing the Interrupt Generation

To test for the presence of low-level problems in the interrupt generation and handling phase, we designed and implemented a tool called PTFuzz, by extending Intel's e1000e network driver. PT-

Fuzz is optimized to launch any type of MSI by fuzzing both the MSI *address* and its *data* components as well as the size of DMA requests. It works by writing data (i.e., MSI data component) to the LAPIC MMIO range using DMA. As PTFuzz is capable of fuzzing each field of an MSI separately, it can be fine-tuned to create both *compatibility* and *remappable* MSIs formats. The operation of PT-Fuzz can be summarized in a few steps (see Figure 2 for context information):

1. Prepare a transmission buffer (TXb) in the guest OS, and populate it with the MSI *data* component.
2. Prepare a receiver buffer (RXb) in the guest OS.
3. Change the physical address of the RXb buffer according to the MSI *address* component to point to the memory mapped interrupt space (i.e., MMIO LAPIC).
4. Move the MSI data component via a DMA transaction into the card's internal TX buffer.
5. Send the data in loopback mode into the card's RX buffer.
6. Move the MSI data from the card's internal RX buffer into the corresponding MMIO LAPIC address range specified by the MSI address (0xfeexxxxx) with a given DMA request size.
7. If the MSI data component is fuzzed, then select a new MSI data value and repeat from Step 1.
8. If the MSI address component is fuzzed, then select a new MSI address value and repeat from Step 3.

Fuzzing the entire MSI data and address spaces would require an extensive amount of work to manually verify and validate each result. For this reason, we decided to focus our effort on those MSI fields that were either more interesting from an attacker's point of view, or had clear constraints set by the vendors.

In particular, here we present the results we obtained by fuzzing the *vector* field of a compatibility format MSI *data* component and the *don't care* field of a remappable format MSI *address* component. Whenever we observed an unexpected hardware behavior as a result of our test cases, we instrumented the code of the VMM to collect all the information required to understand the problem in detail. The following two sections discuss our results.

6.2 Interrupt Vector Fuzzing

In our first experiment, we fuzzed the *vector* field of the compatibility format MSI *data* as well as the size of the MSI request. During the tests, we noticed that the VMM/privileged VM received a *legacy* Non-Maskable Interrupt (NMI) for some values of the *vector*. This happens even when all the existing hardware protections mechanisms were turned on. In addition, we got the same results when the size of the MSI request had not conformed with the required MSI transmission size (i.e., it was not 32-bit long).

Non-Maskable Interrupts are normally generated as a result of hardware errors that must be immediately handled by the CPU, in order to prevent system damage. From an architectural perspective, NMIs are exceptions and not interrupts. This is a subtle, but very important difference. Interrupts are asynchronous events that are handled when the CPU decides to do so. On the contrary, exceptions are synchronous events that are served instantly. In our case, the most important difference is that devices do not extend NMIs with the source-id information. As a consequence, NMIs are *not* subject to interrupt remapping. This is a very significant point.

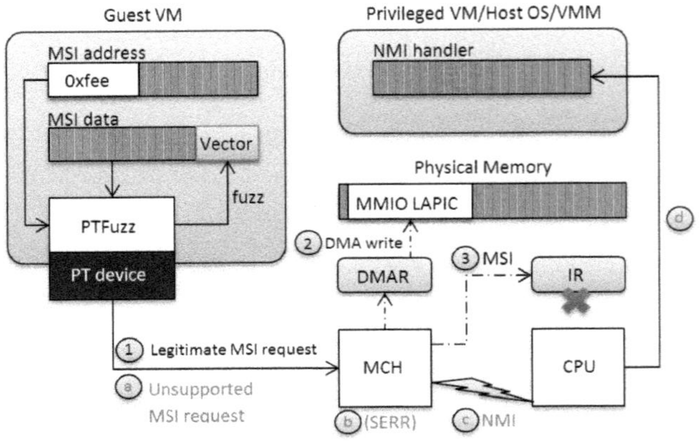

Figure 3: Interrupt generation by PTFuzz. This figure describes two interrupt generation cases indicated by the *numerical* and *alphabetical* paths. On the *numerical* path, PTfuzz requests a legitimate MSI (1) by a DMA write operation to the MMIO LAPIC (2) which is first verified by the DMA remapping engine (DMAR). As a result, a compatibility-format MSI is generated (3) that is blocked by the interrupt remapping engine (IR). The *alphabetical* path, however, shows *our* unsupported MSI request (a), which the platform detects and blocks. However, when System Error Reporting is enabled, the platform sets the SERR status bit on the Memory Controller Hub (MCH) PCI Device (b). As a result, a host-side Non-maskable Interrupt (NMI) is *directly* delivered to the physical CPU (c) executing the privileged VM/host OS/VMM. SERR induced NMIs, however, may cause host software halt or trigger the host-side NMI handler (d) which opens the door for Guest-to-VMM escapes.

Another key observation is that we did not generate an MSI that was delivered as an NMI. Our tests indirectly generated a *host-side legacy* NMI to one of the physical CPUs (i.e., Bootstrap Processor - BSP). More precisely, as a result of performing an unsupported MSI request by a DMA transaction to the memory mapped interrupt space, the platform blocks the MSI request and raises a PCI System Error (SERR#) which is delivered as NMI to report hardware errors. In our case, the SERR status bit is set by the platform on the Memory Controller Hub - MCH (BDF 00:00.0) PCI device. Thus, the unchecked host-side NMI is forwarded to the physical CPU executing the privileged VM/host OS/VMM. Depending on privileged VM/host OS/VMM kernel configuration, such an NMI may be handled by the privileged VM/host OS/VMM or can result in a host software halt (*panic*). Figure 3 gives a high-level overview about the attack. When we took a closer look at this issue, we noticed that the NMI was spawned when a compatibility format MSI is requested with vector numbers below 16 or with an invalid request size (i.e., not 32-bit long). The reason for the former lies in the fact that MSI cannot deliver interrupts with vector less than 16 [16].

All these operations are executed at the chipset level, and it took a considerable amount of time and effort to understand all the details. After discussing the problem with the Xen security group and Intel Product Security Incident Response Team (Intel PSIRT), we concluded that we identified a platform problem that affects all the machines which enable System Error Reporting. As System Error Reporting is an essential feature on server machines to report legitimate hardware errors for providing Reliability, Availability, Serviceability (RAS), this attack seriously threatens the main security feature of hardware virtualization: the isolation of virtual machines.

The *main* difference with previous interrupt attacks is that our NMI injection attack works on configurations where interrupt remapping is enabled. In fact, the DMA Remapping Engine cannot protect against our DMA write as the attacker intends to manipulate only legitimate, intra-guest physical addresses. Second, the interrupt remapping is circumvented as NMIs are considered to be exceptions by the architecture, so no source information is added during their delivery. Without source-id the interrupt remapping Engine is not able to validate the interrupt. In addition, the NMI was indirectly spawned by the Memory Controller Hub (and *not* by our passthrough device) which is handled by the host. Finally, x2APIC mode, which forbids to reenable compatibility format MSIs during runtime, is also circumvented.

NMI Injection Evaluation

We successfully verified our NMI injection attack on both Xen 4.2 and KVM 3.5.0 in the configurations shown in Table 1, however, every VMM, which runs on a platform with System Error Reporting enabled, can be affected. In order to be sure that the attack overcomes all the available protection mechanisms, we enabled DMA and interrupt remapping as well as x2APIC mode on the privileged VM/host (this configuration was known to be safe against all known interrupt attacks).

Our physical NMI can have three different scenarios with respect to its impact depending on the configuration of the privileged guest/host/VMM kernel. First, we *simulate* a legitimate hardware error induced purely by software from the guest VM which is reported to the privileged VM/Host OS/VMM. As a result, the system administrator believes that the MCH has some serious hardware problems and the motherboard must be replaced as soon as possible. This fact on its own leads to an indirect Denial of Service attack against the host. Second, depending on the privileged guest/host OS/VMM kernel configuration, the system can halt as it cannot recover from NMIs that were signalled as a result of a PCI System Error (`SERR#`). Note that we could reproduce this case as well, which means a direct Denial of Service attack against the host. Finally, if the host kernel does not halt, the attacker has still chance to execute arbitrary code on the host by means of this host-side NMI.

To achieve this, we have to take into consideration similar interrupt attacks that were used in the past to execute arbitrary code [9] by exploiting a race condition. A similar race condition could be used in our case as well:

1. Prepare a shellcode that is made of four parts: a) The code to execute in the VMM, b) reference to a swapped page, c) padding, d) pointer to the code to execute

2. The attacker needs to count the number of pages between the location of the page fault handler entry in the Interrupt Descriptor Table (IDT) and that of the VMM stack to set the length of padding (c) in the shellcode. This padding is used to span that distance and overwrite the page fault entry in the IDT with a pointer (d), that points to the code (a) to be executed in the VMM.

3. Place the shellcode in the MMIO address space of the guest VM that the attacker controls. As the copy operation from the MMIO space is slow enough (MB/s) it can be interrupted with high probability.

4. As hypercalls contain code snippets that copy memory from guest VM space into that of the VMM, call legitimate hypercalls in a loop to catch the very moment when the corresponding function (i.e., *copy_from_user()*) copies the guest buffer with the shellcode.

5. Create a host-side NMI from the guest via a malformed MSI request to interrupt the hypercalls.

6. Modify a register value (e.g., rax) inside the interrupted copy operation in the hypercall by the NMI handler (race condition) to control the length of copy operation. For example, the NMI handler can return with a large value (e.g., error code) in the rax register which register indirectly influences the length of copy operation (e.g., $mov\ rcx, rax$).

7. While copying the shellcode into the VMM space the hypercall handler will end up in a page fault, as we placed a reference to a swapped page (b) into our shellcode. However, the page fault handler entry had already been overwritten, so the injected code (a) is launched.

This exploit sequence is difficult to apply in our case because hardware interrupt handlers (e.g., NMI) do not modify saved register states (see point 6 in the list above). Thus, they cannot influence the behavior of the interrupted handler (e.g., hypercall). However, the NMI injection attack is pervasive and works on all Intel platforms which enable System Error Reporting, which is a typical configuration for server platforms (e.g., IaaS clouds).

Mitigation

As we discussed above, there is no publicly known hardware protection mechanism available against our NMI injection attack. We responsibly reported the problems and received a Xen Security Advisory (XSA-59) and a CVE number (CVE-2013-3495) from Xen and MITRE, respectively. In addition, after a long discussion period with Xen and Intel, we concluded that there is *no ideal* solution available against our attack. Considering mitigations, SERR reporting can either be disabled on the Memory Controller Hub, or system software can block SERR error signaling due to Unsupported Request error resulting from malformed MSI requests. The former advice is quite intrusive as it suppresses all the system errors coming from the MCH, which affects legitimate hardware errors as well. At the same time, this is supported by all the chipsets. The second option is a more fine-grained solution, however, according to recent debates [37] between Xen and Intel, it seems that the problem cannot be put to rest as software patches are required every time a new chipset/processor is released. In addition, these patches disable SERR which may affect legitimate requests. In summary, both of the above mitigations can be a daunting and very expensive operation especially for cloud operators who expose VM instances for public use with passthrough devices (e.g., Amazon EC2).

6.3 Don't Care Field Fuzzing

In our second test, we used PTFuzz to modify the *don't care* field of remappable format MSI address. *don't care* fields should never influence the behavior of the hardware if manipulated. Interestingly, this is not the case for remappable format MSIs. In our experiments, we combined a remappable format MSI *data* with a corresponding MSI *address* component in a way to create an Interrupt Remapping Table *index* larger than the number of entries in that table. When the fuzzer modified the *don't care* field against a fully protected KVM guest, we observed that three different types of interrupt faults were generated on the host OS/VMM (Figure 4).

```
INTR-REMAP: Request device [00:19.0] fault index 77ff
INTR-REMAP:[fault reason 32] Detected reserved fields in
the decoded interrupt-remapped request
INTR-REMAP: Request device [00:19.0] fault index 8fff
INTR-REMAP:[fault reason 32] Detected reserved fields in
the decoded interrupt-remapped request
```

DC=0

```
INTR-REMAP: Request device [00:19.0] fault index ffff
INTR-REMAP:[fault reason 32] Detected reserved fields in
the decoded interrupt-remapped request
```

DC=1, DC=2

```
INTR-REMAP: Request device [00:19.0] fault index ffff
INTR-REMAP:[fault reason 34] Present field in the IRTE
entry is clear
```

DC=3

Figure 4: Raising different types of interrupt faults on the KVM host by fuzzing the *don't care* (DC) field of a remappable format MSI address. Note that both the fault reason and the fault index values (Interrupt Remapping Table Entries - IRTE) are changing on different DC values.

Interrupt Remapping Fault Evaluation

This case is very similar to the NMI injection attack in the sense that the attacker can spawn a partially controllable host-side hardware fault by fabricating unexpected conditions. We do highlight here that this case also opens a door towards practical guest-to-VMM escapes. Theoretical exploitation scheme can either be a similar race condition presented in Section 6.2 or a buffer overflow by influencing the fault reason or the fault index values in the hardware fault handler. Until now, we could not identify a problem in VMM software that allows for practical exploitation. At the same time, hardware problems are orthogonal to VMM implementation bugs, thus, it is enough to find a single problem in any VMM implementation, and the attacker can succeed.

All the above problems demonstrate the hardware does not always follow the specifications from vendors or the synergy is missing between hardware and software for flawless collaboration.

7. RELATED WORK

To the best of our knowledge, we are the first who systematically discuss and implement a wide range of attacks that exploit the device passthrough technology. However, a considerable amount of related work exists in the three attack areas that we cover in this paper. More information about possible attacks in hardware virtualization can be read in [38].

Attacks via the PCI/PCIe configuration space.

Zhou et al. [30] presented several attacks (e.g., MMIO overlapping) via the PCI/PCIe configuration space. However, the attacks were presented in a different context, and the authors' focus was more on the development of a small hypervisor to prevent these device passthrough attacks from causing damage in a compromised OS. On the contrary, we aim at revealing design, configuration, and implementation weaknesses in commodity VMMs that can be abused to escalate privileges, read restricted memory regions and perform DoS attacks.

A privilege escalation attack via PIO based PCI/PCIe configuration space accesses was discussed for USB UHCI [39] controllers by Duflot et al. [40, 31]. The authors were able to manipulate the secure level of OpenBSD and escalate root access in privileged domains (e.g., Xen Dom0) from arbitrary guests by evading Intel VT-x protection. Since Xen does not allow direct configuration space access any more [33], our PIO attacks were confined inside the attacker guest. We faced the same issues with KVM as well.

DMA attacks. The introduction of DMA opened the door to a new set of attacks. By misusing DMA transactions either a native or a virtualized system can be compromised by reading/writing arbitrary physical memory locations. A long list of DMA attacks exists in the literature, based on USB *On-The-Go* controllers [41], PCI cards [42, 43], or FireWire controllers [44, 45, 46, 47, 48]. Even though, most of these attacks were presented for native environments, proof-of-concept codes for virtual environments exist as well [10]. The main difference with our paper is that *none* of the previous works examined the impact and limitations introduced by existing DMA protection mechanisms (e.g., DMA remapping).

Interestingly, a DMA attack can also be launched by a code residing on the northbridge [49, 14]. From one aspect, this higher privileged code is advantageous for an attacker. However, malicious DMA transactions are still ineffective on systems with DMA remapping enabled (e.g., Intel VT-d is turned on).

Interrupt Attacks. Wojtczuk et al. [9] demonstrated that the x86-64 architecture is vulnerable against Message Signalled Interrupt (MSI) based attacks. Later, Müller et al. [50] pointed out a similar interrupt attack on PowerPC. However, both of the attacks worked only without an active interrupt remapping engine. The authors showed that an attacker can force the generation of unmediated MSIs in these cases, allowing her to send specific interrupts to the physical CPU. This attack even allowed Wojtczuk et al. [9] to execute arbitrary code with VMM privileges in a given Xen installation. In contrast to that, our host-side NMI interrupt cannot be blocked with currently available protection mechanisms (e.g., interrupt remapping engine) without limiting platform functionalities. Also, we can launch our attack from fully-virtualized (HVM) guests that are known to be more isolated than their paravirtualized counterparts (e.g., because of the hardware-supported protection ring for the VMM code).

Protection Evasion. While we focus on *circumventing* all the hardware protection mechanisms currently available, other approaches try to disable them. For example, an attacker can modify hardware-level data structures (e.g., Interrupt Descriptor Table) or configuration tables (e.g., DMA remapping table) [51] to turn off IOMMU. Another approach aims at making the illusion of a non-parsable DMA remapping table. To achieve this, an attacker has to set a zero length for such a table during boot time. Another class of attacks aim at modifying the metadata exposed by I/O controllers to mislead the IOMMU. One such an attack is described by Lone-Sang et al. [13]. Here, the attackers could map two I/O devices into the same physical memory range by impersonating a PCI Express device with a legacy PCI device. This attack, however, requires physical access to the victim machine.

We partially discuss a similar approach in Section 3, where we presented a problem to circumvent the interrupt remapping engine on KVM by updating a BIOS on a motherboard that originally does not support this technology. In this way, an attacker could use a passthrough device without the appropriate protections enabled.

Recently, an interrupt remapping source validation flaw was reported by the Xen security team (CVE-2013-1952). More precisely, MSI interrupts from bridge devices do not provide source information, so the interrupt remapping table cannot check the originator bridge. In this way, a VM that owns a bridge can inject arbitrary interrupts to the system via MSI interrupts.

8. CONCLUSIONS

In this paper, we presented and tested a wide range of pass-through attacks on commodity VMMs. Some of them were already publicly known while others were presented for the first time in this paper. To discover new vulnerabilities, we designed and implemented an automatic fuzzer called PTFuzz. This tool successfully detected various unexpected hardware behaviors while running on commodity VMMs.

Our experiments showed that software patches (e.g., when the device configuration space is emulated) and robust hardware protections can indeed prevent all previously discovered attacks. Nonetheless, we demonstrated that the proper configuration of these protection mechanisms can be a daunting task. Unfortunately, VMMs remain vulnerable to sophisticated attacks. In this paper, we discovered and implemented an interrupt attack that leverages unexpected hardware behaviour to circumvent all the existing protection mechanisms in commodity VMMs. To the best of our knowledge, this is the first attack that exhibits such a behaviour and to date it seems that there is no easy way to prevent it on Intel platforms.

The fact that we discovered a major vulnerability as well as an unexpected hardware behaviour in Intel platforms does not necessarily mean that VMMs are threatened in the wild, but certainly raises an alarm to cloud operators. We believe that our study can help them to better understand the limitations of their current architectures to provide secure hardware virtualization and to prepare for future attacks.

Acknowledgment

The research leading to these results was partially funded by the European Union Seventh Framework Programme (contract N 257007) and by the French National Research Agency through the MIDAS project. We would also like to thank anonymous reviewers for their valuable comments, Mariano Graziano for running certain experiments with DMA attacks as well as Pipacs from PaX team, Olivér Pintér and Hunger for their technical advices.

Special thank goes to Rafal Wojtczuk <rafal@bromium.com>, Jan Beulich from Xen Security and Intel PSIRT for technical discussions and feedback on the interrupt attack. Additional thanks to Csaba Krasznay from HP Hungary for providing extra machines to thoroughly test the interupt attack.

9. REFERENCES

[1] Amazon EC2. `http:/aws.amazon.com/`.

[2] Google Compute Engine. `https://cloud.google.com/products/compute-engine/`.

[3] Arvind Seshadri, Mark Luk, Ning Qu, and Adrian Perrig. Secvisor: a tiny hypervisor to provide lifetime kernel code integrity for commodity oses. In *Proceedings of twenty-first ACM SIGOPS symposium on Operating systems principles*, SOSP '07, pages 335–350, New York, NY, USA, 2007. ACM.

[4] Zhi Wang and Xuxian Jiang. Hypersafe: A lightweight approach to provide lifetime hypervisor control-flow integrity. In *Proceedings of the 2010 IEEE Symposium on Security and Privacy*, SP '10, pages 380–395, Washington, DC, USA, 2010. IEEE Computer Society.

[5] Jonathan M. McCune, Yanlin Li, Ning Qu, Zongwei Zhou, Anupam Datta, Virgil D. Gligor, and Adrian Perrig. TrustVisor: Efficient TCB Reduction and Attestation. In *IEEE Symposium on Security and Privacy*, pages 143–158, 2010.

[6] Abel Gordon, Nadav Amit, Nadav Har'El, Muli Ben-Yehuda, Alex Landau, Assaf Schuster, and Dan Tsafrir. ELI: bare-metal performance for I/O virtualization. *SIGARCH Comput. Archit. News*, 40(1):411–422, March 2012.

[7] Ahmed M. Azab, Peng Ning, Zhi Wang, Xuxian Jiang, Xiaolan Zhang, and Nathan C. Skalsky. Hypersentry: enabling stealthy in-context measurement of hypervisor integrity. In *Proceedings of the 17th ACM conference on Computer and communications security*, CCS '10, pages 38–49, New York, NY, USA, 2010. ACM.

[8] Eric Keller, Jakub Szefer, Jennifer Rexford, and Ruby B. Lee. Nohype: virtualized cloud infrastructure without the virtualization. In *Proceedings of the 37th annual international symposium on Computer architecture*, ISCA '10, pages 350–361, New York, NY, USA, 2010. ACM.

[9] Rafal Wojtczuk and Joanna Rutkowska. Following the White Rabbit: Software attacks against Intel®VT-d technology, April 2011.

[10] Rafal Wojtczuk. Subverting the Xen Hypervisor - Xen 0wning Trilogy part I. *Black Hat USA*, aug 2008.

[11] Rafal Wojtczuk. Preventing and Detecting Xen Hypervisor Subversions - Xen 0wning Trilogy part II. *Black Hat USA*, aug 2008.

[12] Joanna Rutkowska and Alexander Tereshkin. Bluepilling the Xen Hypervisor - Xen 0wning Trilogy part III. *Black Hat USA*, aug 2008.

[13] Fernand Lone Sang, Eric Lacombe, Vincent Nicomette, and Yves Deswarte. Exploiting an I/OMMU vulnerability. *MALWARE*, 2010.

[14] Patrick Stewin and Iurii Bystrov. Understanding DMA Malware. In *Proceedings of the 9th Conference on Detection of Intrusions and Malware & Vulnerability Assessment*, 2012.

[15] AMD. AMD 64 Architecture Programmer's Manual: Volume 2: System Programming. *AMD Pub. no. 24593 rev. 3.20*, 2011.

[16] Intel. Intel® 64 and IA-32 Architectures Software Developer's Manual - Combined Volumes: 1, 2A, 2B, 2C, 3A, 3B and 3C, Aug 2012.

[17] Jiuxing Liu. Evaluating standard-based self-virtualizing devices: A performance study on 10 GbE NICs with SR-IOV support. In *IEEE Int'l Parallel & Distributed Processing Symp. (IPDPS)*, pages 1–12, April 2010.

[18] Jiuxing Liu, Wei Huang, Bulent Abali, and Dhabaleswar K. Panda. High performance VMM-bypass I/O in virtual machines. In *Proceedings of the annual conference on USENIX '06 Annual Technical Conference*, ATEC '06, pages 3–3, Berkeley, CA, USA, 2006. USENIX Association.

[19] Himanshu Raj and Karsten Schwan. High performance and scalable I/O virtualization via self-virtualized devices. In *Proceedings of the 16th international symposium on High performance distributed computing*, HPDC '07, pages 179–188, New York, NY, USA, 2007. ACM.

[20] P. Willmann, J. Shafer, D. Carr, A. Menon, S. Rixner, A.L. Cox, and W. Zwaenepoel. Concurrent direct network access for virtual machine monitors. In *High Performance Computer Architecture, 2007. HPCA 2007. IEEE 13th International Symposium on*, pages 306 –317, feb. 2007.

[21] Ben-Ami Yassour, Muli Ben-Yehuda, and Orit Wasserman. Direct device assignment for untrusted fully-virtualized virtual machines. Technical report, 2008.

[22] Thomas Ball, Ella Bounimova, Byron Cook, Vladimir Levin, Jakob Lichtenberg, Con McGarvey, Bohus Ondrusek, Sriram K. Rajamani, and Abdullah Ustuner. Thorough static analysis of device drivers. *SIGOPS Oper. Syst. Rev.*, 40(4):73–85, April 2006.

[23] Jorrit N. Herder, Herbert Bos, Ben Gras, Philip Homburg, and Andrew S. Tanenbaum. Failure resilience for device drivers. In *Proceedings of the 37th Annual IEEE/IFIP International Conference on Dependable Systems and Networks*, DSN '07, pages 41–50, Washington, DC, USA, 2007. IEEE Computer Society.

[24] Joshua LeVasseur, Volkmar Uhlig, Jan Stoess, and Stefan Götz. Unmodified device driver reuse and improved system dependability via virtual machines. In *Proceedings of the 6th conference on Symposium on Opearting Systems Design & Implementation - Volume 6*, OSDI'04, pages 2–2, Berkeley, CA, USA, 2004. USENIX Association.

[25] Dan Williams, Patrick Reynolds, Kevin Walsh, Emin Gün Sirer, and Fred B. Schneider. Device driver safety through a reference validation mechanism. In *Proceedings of the 8th USENIX conference on Operating systems design and implementation*, OSDI'08, pages 241–254, Berkeley, CA, USA, 2008. USENIX Association.

[26] Intel. Intel® Virtualization Technology for Directed I/O. *Intel® Technology Journal*, 10, August 2006.

[27] Intel. Intel® Virtualization Technology for Directed I/O, Feb 2011.

[28] Paul Barham, Boris Dragovic, Keir Fraser, Steven Hand, Tim Harris, Alex Ho, Rolf Neugebauer, Ian Pratt, and Andrew Warfield. Xen and the art of virtualization. In *Proceedings of the nineteenth ACM symposium on Operating systems principles*, SOSP '03, pages 164–177, New York, NY, USA, 2003. ACM.

[29] Intel. Intel 6 Series Chipset and Intel C200 Series Chipset. May 2011.

[30] Zongwei Zhou, Virgil D. Gligor, James Newsome, and Jonathan M. McCune. Building verifiable trusted path on commodity x86 computers. In *Proceedings of the 2012 IEEE Symposium on Security and Privacy*, SP '12, pages 616–630, Washington, DC, USA, 2012. IEEE Computer Society.

[31] Loïc Duflot and Laurent Absil. Programmed I/O accesses: a threat to Virtual Machine Monitors? *PacSec*, 2007.

[32] Intel. Intel Graphics Virtualization on KVM. *KVM Forum*, Aug 2011.

[33] Emulation of PCI configuration space access. `http://xenbits.xen.org/hg/xen-4.2-testing.hg/rev/1ac2a314aa3c`.

[34] Joanna Rutkowska. pciback: question about the permissive flag. XEN-devel mailing list, Available at `http://old-list-archives.xenproject.org/archives/html/xen-devel/2010-07/msg00257.html`, July 2010.

[35] Sam Fleming. Accessing PCI Express* Configuration Registers Using Intel Chipsets. December 2008.

[36] Nadav Amit, Muli Ben-Yehuda, Dan Tsafrir, and Assaf Schuster. vIOMMU: efficient IOMMU emulation. In *Proceedings of the 2011 USENIX conference on USENIX annual technical conference*, USENIXATC'11, pages 6–6, Berkeley, CA, USA, 2011. USENIX Association.

[37] XSA-59 blog. `http://www.gossamer-threads.com/lists/xen/devel/318464?page=last`.

[38] Gábor Pék, Levente Buttyán, and Boldizsár Bencsáth. A survey of security issues in hardware virtualization. *ACM Comput. Surv.*, 45(3):40:1–40:34, July 2013.

[39] Intel. Universal Host Controller Interface (UHCI), Mar 1996.

[40] Loïc Duflot. Contribution à la sécurité des systèmes d'exploitation et des microprocesseurs. In *PhD thesis, Universite de Paris*, Oct 2007.

[41] David Maynor. 0wn3d by everything else - USB/PCMCIA Issues. *CanSecWest/core05*, May 2005.

[42] Brian D. Carrier and Joe Grand. A hardware-based memory acquisition procedure for digital investigations. *Digital Investigation*, 2004.

[43] Christophe Devine and Guillaume Vissian. Compromission physique par le bus PCI. In *Proceedings of the 7th Symposium sur la Sécurité des Technologies de l'Information et des Communications*, SSITC 2009, pages 169–193, June 2009.

[44] Damien Aumaitre. Voyage au coeur de la mémoire. In *Proceedings of the 6th Symposium sur la Sécurité des Technologies de l'Information et des Communications*, SSITC 2008, pages 378–437, June 2008.

[45] Adam Boileau. Hit by a Bus: Physical Access Attacks with Firewire. *Ruxcon*, 2006.

[46] Maximillian Dornseif. 0wned by an iPod. *PacSec*, 2004.

[47] Michael Becher, Maximillian Dornseif, and Christian N. Klein. FireWire - all your memory are belong to us. *CanSecWest/core05*, May 2005.

[48] Antonio Martinm. FireWire memory dump of a windows XP computer: a forensic approach. Technical report, 2007.

[49] Alexander Tereshkin and Rafal Wojtczuk. Introducing Ring -3 Rootkits. *Black Hat USA*, 2009.

[50] Kevin Müller, Daniel Münch, Ole Isfort, Michael Paulitsch, and Georg Sigl. Decreasing system availability on an avionic multicore processor using directly assigned pci express devices. In *EUROSEC 2013*, Apr 2013. Prag.

[51] Rafal Wojtczuk, Joanna Rutkowska, and Alexander Tereshkin. Another Way to Circumvent Intel Trusted Execution Technology, December 2009.

After We Knew It:

Empirical Study and Modeling of Cost-effectiveness of Exploiting Prevalent Known Vulnerabilities Across IaaS Cloud

Su Zhang
Kansas State University
zhangs84@ksu.edu

Xinwen Zhang
Samsung Research America
xinwen1.z@samsung.com

Xinming Ou
Kansas State University
xou@ksu.edu

ABSTRACT

Infrastructure as a Service (IaaS) cloud has been attracting more and more customers as it provides the highest level of flexibility by offering configurable virtual machines (VMs) and computing infrastructures. Public VM images are usually available for customers to customize and launch. However, the 1 to N mapping between VM images and running instances in IaaS makes vulnerabilities propagate rapidly across the entire public cloud. Besides, IaaS cloud naturally comes with a larger and more stable attack surface and more concentrated target resources than traditional surroundings. In this paper, we first identify the threat of exploiting prevalent vulnerabilities [1] over public IaaS cloud with an empirical study in Amazon EC2. We find that attackers can compromise a considerable number of VMs with trivial cost. We then do a qualitative cost-effectiveness analysis of this threat. Our main result is a two-fold observation: in IaaS cloud, exploiting prevalent vulnerabilities is much more cost-effective than traditional in-house computing environment, therefore attackers have stronger incentive; Fortunately, on the other hand, cloud defenders (cloud providers and customers) also have much lower cost-loss ratio than in traditional environment, therefore they can be more effective for defending attacks. We then build a game-theoretic model and conduct a risk-gain analysis to compare exploiting and patching strategies under cloud and traditional computing environments. Our modeling indicates that under cloud environment, both attack and defense become less cost-effective as time goes by, and the earlier actioner can be more rewarding. We propose countermeasures against such threat in order to bridge the gap between current security situation and defending mechanisms. To our best knowledge, we are the first to analyze and model the threat with prevalent known-vulnerabilities in public cloud.

[1] in our experiments, we treat vulnerabilities with 30% or higher prevalence as prevalent vulnerabilities

ASIA CCS'14, June 4–6, 2014, Kyoto, Japan.

http://dx.doi.org/10.1145/2590296.2590300.

Categories and Subject Descriptors

D.2.4 [**Software Engineering**]: Software/Program Verification—*Statistical methods*; K.6.1 [**Management of Computing and Information Systems**]: Project and People Management—*Strategic information systems planning*; K.6.5 [**Management of Computing and Information Systems**]: Security and Protection ;

General Terms

Security, Measurement, Management

Keywords

Cloud Computing, Vulnerability Management, Game Theory, Virtual Machine Images, Patching Management

1. INTRODUCTION

Public cloud delivers computing resources with service-oriented, multi-tenant, and pay-as-you-go manner. According to the forms of offered resources, cloud computing can be Software as a Service (SaaS) such as Google Apps which provide individual applications to cloud customers (or users), Platform as a Service (PaaS) such as Microsoft Azure which offers a platform with a set of pre-configured software and programming environment, and Infrastructure as a Service (IaaS) such as Amazon Web Services (AWS) which allows users to run a number of virtual machines (VMs). In general, users in IaaS have the highest level of flexibility, e.g., to deploy their own infrastructures, systems, and applications according to their business requirements, by completely controlling and customizing their VMs. At the same time, IaaS users have more responsibility to secure their infrastructures and systems [1, 2].

Problem: In this paper, we do a comprehensive analysis on threats from VM images used in public cloud, based on an empirical study of known vulnerabilities in Amazon Machine Images (AMIs), which are VM images running on AWS Elastic Compute Cloud (EC2). Typically in an IaaS cloud, users can choose either private images (uploaded or customized by themselves) or public images (uploaded by others) to run their VMs. The public images could be uploaded by various types of publishers, including IT companies, open-source communities, and individuals. AWS is currently leading the market among IaaS providers. There are more than 6,000 public images published on EC2.

Security issues of public images in AWS have been reported in previous research work [1, 3]. Bugiel et al. [3] scanned a number of public images and found out that image publishers may leave unwanted information (e.g. passwords, keys, and other credentials) in their images and form backdoors in the cloud. They proposed several operational solutions to these issues. Balduzzi et al. [1] did a similar but more comprehensive experiments on EC2 by scanning a larger number of images and identified more security issues including software vulnerabilities. However, these work do not provide any further analysis and modeling of attack and defense in cloud environment, which have very different cost-effectiveness properties compared with traditional computing environment according to our study in this paper. Although risk assessment approaches [4, 5, 6, 7, 8, 9, 10, 11] have been largely applied over traditional network surroundings, both Grobauer et al. [12] and Shrobe [13] have pointed out that prevalent vulnerabilities should be considered as a cloud-specific threat, under the homogeneous system environments in public cloud. However, they do not systematically analyze the impact of exploiting prevalent vulnerabilities in the cloud.

Even though security bulletins have been setup by Amazon to notify users about vulnerability information, previous experience has told us that significant effort is needed to bridge the gap between the provided service and current security situation. Specifically, we find that Amazon security bulletin usually releases critical vulnerability information more than two weeks later than original release date, e.g., by software vendors or community (cf. Section 2 for our study result). The exploit window could be even longer since there is no guarantee that every cloud user will and will be able to apply the update with the release, even though he is notified. Also, a cloud provider may not be able to identify all known vulnerabilities on its platform. For known vulnerabilities, this attack window is way longer than it should be [14]. Besides, the prevalence of individual vulnerabilities has not been considered when publishing security bulletins. For example, Amazon only use CVSS score [15] to indicate the severity of vulnerabilities, which is indicative for individual vulnerabilities on traditional in-house servers. However, threat from the prevalence of individual vulnerabilities should be re-evaluated under cloud environment. A prevalent image with known vulnerabilities can be instantiated by a large number of users in cloud, therefore it may generate large number of security holes for attackers. Attackers can do penetration test over public images, from where they can identify prevalent known vulnerabilities of running VMs and launch the same attack repeatedly to different instances. If the prevalent vulnerabilities indeed spread over the cloud, the attacker obtains an ideal cost-effective vehicle by exploiting the vulnerabilities to a large number of VMs. Therefore, with the new computing model of public cloud, it is easier for attackers to launch attacks through prevalent vulnerabilities.

On the other side, cloud also provides an ideal venue to deploy defense mechanisms in large-scale. For example, with the homogeneous cloud environment, automatic patching becomes more efficient than in traditional in-house environment. A number of patching frameworks have been proposed towards known security holes in cloud [16, 17]. However, there is no empirical study and analysis on the cost and gain effectiveness of defending in cloud.

Contributions: Consider these two aspects, we believe that public IaaS cloud introduces a completely new venue to consider attack and defense strategies, to maximum each side's benefit with minimum costs. For the first in this line of research, we empirically analyze the cost and effectiveness for exploiting known vulnerabilities under two different environments (traditional in-house and public IaaS cloud). We take AWS in our study since we can find more publicly available information than other IaaS providers. We first identify with real data analysis that prevalent known vulnerabilities are very common in AWS AMIs, and demonstrate with real penetrations test that attack with these vulnerabilities is very trivial by malicious cloud users. We then statically analyze that both attack and patch are more cost-effective in cloud than under traditional environment. By statically we mean our analysis is over one time spot. To further investigate the relationship and strategy of attackers and defenders in cloud environment, we map these scenarios into a two-player game theoretic model. Our model indicates that the current security of public cloud needs significant improvement. We then construct risk-gain analysis to simulate the evolution of the cost-effectiveness from defenders and attackers under different circumstances. Our results show that cloud defender should be more responsive and proactive when hardening cloud platform as the attack surface increases dramatically compared to traditional computing environment. Moreover, our model illustrates that both attack and defense are more time-sensitive in cloud as they become less cost-effective as time goes by. We then propose countermeasures according to the evaluation results. Figure 1 summarizes our contributions in this paper.

Roadmap: Section 2 states our approach and finds of identifying security vulnerabilities and threats from prevalent vulnerabilities in AWS. We conduct cost-effectiveness analysis for both attackers and defenders in Section 3. We construct a game theoretical model and a risk-gain analysis in Section 4. In Section 5 we provide countermeasures based on the results of our model. We discuss several limitations of our modeling in Section 6. We present related work in Section 7 and conclude this paper in Section 8.

2. EMPIRICAL STUDY: METHODOLOGY AND FINDS

2.1 Background

Amazon EC2 We do our experiments on public images over Amazon EC2. As a leading IaaS cloud provider, Amazon EC2 provides a platform by allowing different principals sharing their images publicly. Open source organizations like BitNami [2] and Ubuntu, IT companies such as Oracle and Amazon itself, and arbitrary number of individual contributors have published over 6,000 public images. Like potential attackers, we do penetration test over these images by launching corresponding VMs in order to analyze the weakness of running instances in the cloud.

Nessus Vulnerability Scanner Nessus [3] is a commercial vulnerability scanner developed from an open source product. It checks against configuration settings of a host and outputs a detailed report including security vulnerabilities, warnings, and system information, which can be from 50 to hundreds of pages. Therefore it is usually difficult for cloud administrators and users to read reports one by one in order to understand all security details in the cloud.

National Vulnerability Database (NVD) NVD [4] is an open database maintained by National Institute of Standards and Technology (NIST), which is regarded as one of the most comprehensive open vulnerability databases. Each entry in NVD is indexed by a Common Vulnerability Exposure(CVE), which is associated severity base score with a set of characteristics for that vulnerability. The base score is called "Common Vulnerability Scoring System (CVSS) base score" ranging from 0 to 10. The score indicates the overall severity of the vulnerability (the higher the worse).

2.2 Methodology

Penetration test over public images is a straightforward approach to identify prevalent vulnerabilities. Figure 2 illustrates our overall methodology. When scanning available public images on Amazon

[2] `http://bitnami.org/`

[3] `http://www.tenable.com/products/nessus`

[4] `http://nvd.nist.gov/`

Empirical study: vulnerability scanning and penetration test with public AMIs in EC2.

$\xrightarrow{Identify}$

Prevalent known vulnerabilities are common in AMIs. Real exploits are viable : e.g., more than half (11 out of 20) of tested hosts can be "killed" by one prevalent vulnerability (CVE-2011-3192).

$\xleftarrow{Incent}$

Statically analyzing the *cost-effectiveness* over the threat. The results indicate both attack and patch are more *cost-effective* in IaaS cloud than under traditional environment.

$\xrightarrow{Induce}$

Tactical game modeling and risk-gain analysis between attackers and defenders.

$\xleftarrow{Reveal}$

Both attack and defense become *less cost-effective* as time goes by. Each side has strong incentive to act as early as possible

$\xrightarrow{Infer}$

Countermeasures against such threats with reduced expected cost: increase defender's *responsiveness* and *activeness* while protecting cloud platform.

Figure 1: Contribution map of this paper.

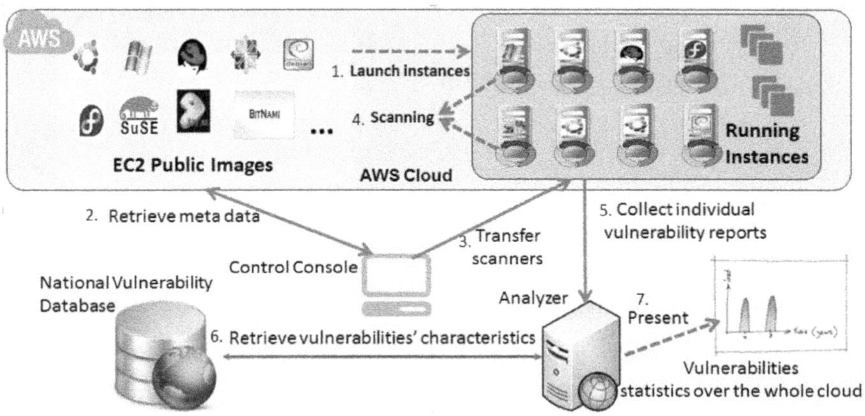

Figure 2: Methodology of our empirical study.

EC2, we first select a number of representative images to investigate, then launch one instance for each selected image. We then adopt a dedicated scanning server to transfer Nessus vulnerability scanner to each instance, and start scanning by running our script on each target instance [5]. After the scanning is complete, our script transfers all scanning reports to the scanning server. We retrieve the characteristics of each vulnerability by looking it up at the NVD. Based on the distribution of vulnerabilities and their characteristics, we obtain a single vulnerability report of all launched instances.

We launch and scan 80 public images in EC2. The selection of these images is based on the distribution of the operating system (OS) types and versions of public AMIs, with the assumption of the similar distribution of launched VM instances in the cloud.

2.3 What We Find

A considerable amount of prevalent vulnerabilities exist in AMIs. Similarly to what other researchers have found [3, 1], our scanning reveals a large number of vulnerabilities existing in public AMIs. Besides, we have identified several prevalent ones among all of these detected vulnerabilities. Table 1 lists the top prevalent vulnerabilities from our scanning. The prevalence indicates the probability of the vulnerability's existence among all images we have scanned. We find out that most (8 out 9) of them are critical vulnerabilities (with a CVSS score 7-10) by NVD standard, most (8 out of 9) of them can be accessed remotely, most (8 out 9) of them can be easily accessed, and most of them (7 out of 9) can be utilized by attackers to crush corresponding applications completely.

Attackers can identify prevalent vulnerabilities without scanning individual VM instances. Amazon EC2 allows users to select public images based on platforms (OS types, versions, and pre-installed applications). Figure 3 shows the public images distribution based on OS types [6]. As we can see, more than half of the images are Ubuntu based. A closer look into the Ubuntu images indicates that more than half of them are either 10.04 or 12.04. Therefore under this circumstance, an attacker can keep monitoring newly released vulnerabilities affecting these prevalent OSes and application frameworks. The attacker can also leverage known vulnerabilities that have not been patched by the publishers of the

[5]Thanks for Amazon's approval for our scanning and penetration tests

[6]The data was collected in September 2012, which may change with new releases of AMIs.

Table 1: Windows between Original Release and Amazon Announcement of Prevalent Known Vulnerabilities

CVE	CVSS Base Score	Prevalence	Original Release	Amazon Announce	Attack Window in (days)
CVE-2012-4244	7.8	0.59	09/14/2012	09/28/2012	14
CVE-2012-3955	7.1	0.58	09/14/2012	N/A	> 26
CVE-2012-3817	7.8	0.52	07/25/2012	08/07/2012	13
CVE-2012-2807	10	0.49	09/07/2012	N/A	> 33
CVE-2012-2337	7.2	0.46	05/18/2012	07/30/2012	73
CVE-2011-3102	10	0.45	05/16/2012	N/A	> 117
CVE-2012-1033	5.0	0.45	02/08/2012	06/22/2012	135
CVE-2012-1667	8.5	0.45	06/05/2012	06/22/2012	17
CVE-2012-2110	7.5	0.34	04/19/2012	05/03/2012	15

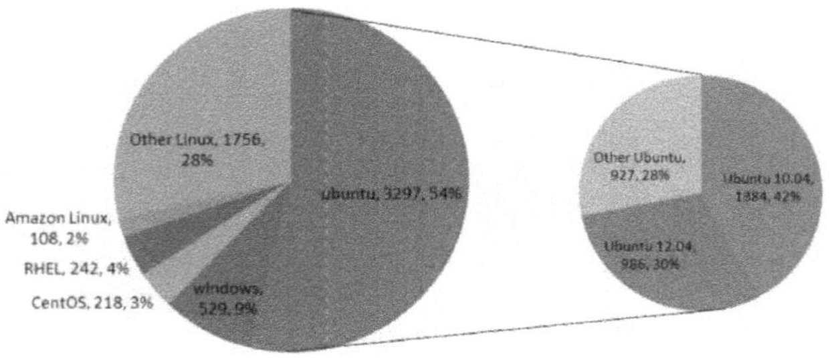

Figure 3: Public images distribution by OS in Amazon EC2.

100% of requests can be serviced before DoS attack.

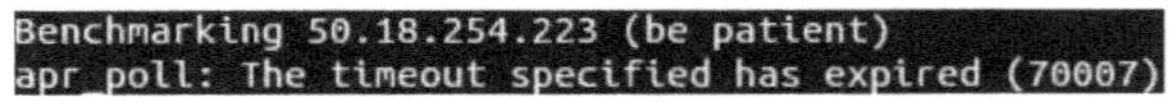

The server stops responding after DoS attack.

Figure 4: Benchmarking results of a server before and after launching apache killer.

AMIs or the administrators of running instances, due to the patch window gap that we have observed in EC2 (explain shortly).

As a result, statistical analysis of OS and application distributions can help attackers in identifying the weaknesses and prevalent vulnerabilities in the cloud. This provides a scope of target victims and reduces the cost for large scale scanning and penetration. Attackers can roughly understand the overall potential weakness by simply noticing the latest vulnerabilities associated with the most prevalent OSes and applications installed in public images.

The patch window is long enough for attackers to exploit. We study several critical vulnerabilities and find that the gap between their original releases and Amazon's notifications is usually longer than two weeks (cf. Table 1). Attackers could easily launch 1-day exploit repeatedly in the entire cloud. The length of exploit window depends on the activities of cloud stakeholders (cloud provider and customers) such as the date of notification and their hardening and patching mechanisms. Moreover, not all known vulnerabilities can be easily detected by the cloud provider. As we have noticed, a large amount of exploitable vulnerabilities have not been notified by Amazon after a long time of their original releases. Therefore, attackers have enough time to prepare and launch attacks. Even worse, existing study has shown that more than 40% of small companies (under $50M revenue) do not have patch management [18] deployed in cloud, which consists of a considerable amount of current IaaS customers [19].

Running VMs in IaaS cloud offers more stable attack surfaces. VMs in IaaS cloud are more stable than traditional endpoints from an attacker' perspective. First of all, the IP range of each cloud provider is stable and can be predicted easily. Attackers could identify the location of their target VMs by playing several tricks [20]. Besides, a vast number of EC2 users are service providers with high availability requirement [19]. Therefore their applications and port configurations are relatively easy to detect. Attackers could reuse configuration information obtained previously to launch large scale attacks afterwards (for new vulnerabilities on the same or similar applications and systems). However, this does not work well under traditional in-house environments since the IP addresses of end hosts are changing more frequently, and most in-house servers are behind firewalls, and it is much more costly for an attacker to launch large scale attacks in order to locate a large number of victims under such heterogeneous environment.

2.4 Case Study: Penetration Testing on VMs in EC2

To confirm the viability of exploiting with prevalent vulnerabilities in EC2, we conduct a penetration test towards running VMs launched from vulnerable AMIs upon Amazon's approval. We first identify a prevalent vulnerability CVE-2011-3192, which is referred as "Apache Killer". We note that this vulnerability was not detected by Nessus in our scanning but it exists in 11 out of 20 AMIs [7] that we investigated with Ubuntu 10.04, most of which have been published for more than one year. Surprisingly, no security advisory on Amazon has been published for this vulnerability. We simply launch another instance in EC2 as an attacker with Metasploit [21] installed. By following the online instruction, we simply setup Metasploit with the number of packets sent to the target VM for DoS attack. We successfully crashed the Apache server running on all of the target VMs by sending 400 packets. The attack can be defended by running one line command (`sudo apt-get update`) to patch the vulnerability.

In order to verify the DoS attack, we use ApacheBench to test the response of the target server. As shown in Figure 4, before the exploit, all requests are served by the server; while after the attack, the ApacheBench could not receive any response, indicating the server is completely crashed.

We observe that the attack is very easy to launch with little interaction from the attacker. Therefore, crushing a large number of

[7] For safety reason we omit the AMI IDs here.

web service hosts is trivial from the attacker's perspective if any one of these vulnerable AMIs is widely used.

3. STATIC COST-EFFECTIVENESS ANALYSES

Our empirical study has demonstrated that homogeneous settings in popular public cloud not only enhance the efficiency of computing power, but also bring new economic considerations for both attackers and defenders. Towards a first study on this, we do a comprehensive cost-effectiveness analysis by comparing exploiting prevalent vulnerabilities in public IaaS cloud and traditional in-house computing environments. While we refer a single *attacker* in both cases, a *defender* refers to service owners in traditional case and all cloud stakeholders (both cloud platform provider and cloud customers) in IaaS.

Assumptions: Our analysis is based on the assumption that VM images are publicly available and used by cloud customers, but we do not require either each image or certain percentage of images are instantiated in the cloud. We further assume that prevalent types of images (OS types, versions, and application frameworks) are also prevalent in the VMs of the cloud.

Results: Our analysis reveals that *both attack and defense are more cost-effective in cloud than in traditional in-house environment.* Attack surface under cloud environment has been enlarged with an increased density of potential victims. Moreover, attack cost has been decreased in cloud because the homogeneous nature of public cloud platforms reduces the effort required for target locating and vulnerability reconnaissance. On the other hand, cloud stakeholders (providers and customers) can manage patch with batch processing, which can patch larger attack surface per unit time than that in traditional environment.

3.1 Cost-effectiveness Analysis for Attacker

3.1.1 Cost of Attacker

A cyber attack usually involves the following costs [22, 13]: (1) locating target victims, (2) identifying vulnerabilities of victims, (3) choosing vulnerabilities , (4) obtaining exploits, and (5) dealing with defense mechanisms. For target victims in the cloud and traditional in-house environment, the costs (3) and (4) are the same. Therefore our analysis focuses on (1), (2), and (5), and our results indicate that IaaS cloud provides dramatically lower costs for attackers in these aspects.

Identifying victims. Under traditional environment, attackers could obtain target IP addresses in a straightforward way (e.g. by looking up DNS server). However, the external firewall deployed by most in-house servers may make the IP addresses untraceable. For certain types of threats like botnet or non-targeted DoS attacks by cyber terrorists, continuous (in terms of IP address) nodes with weak defending mechanisms but stable and high bandwidth are on the top of their target list. Consider that most bots in popular botnets such as "Conficker" have small bandwidth only [23], we believe high quality bots in cloud are very appealing and can significantly increase the competitive strength of a bot master in botnet market, thus give strong incentive for attackers.

Consider a botnet master that needs to harvest N bots with a certain vulnerability v. Assuming for each reachable host, the probability of having v is ρ_v. Ideally, the search space of the vulnerable hosts under traditional environment is the whole IP address space (3,706,452,992), e.g., by generating random target IP addresses to exploit. Consider the factors that not every IP is assigned a host,

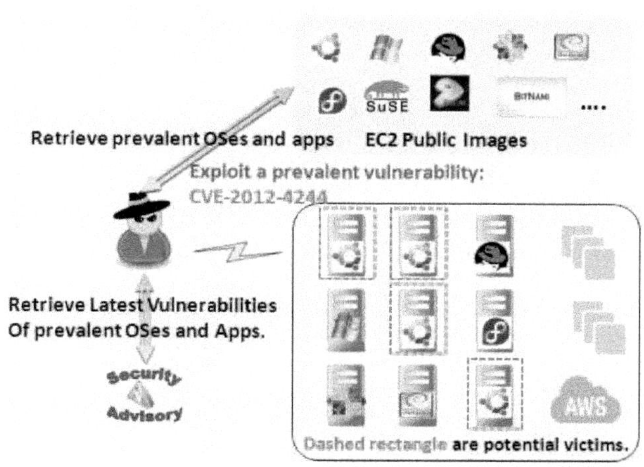

Figure 5: Attacks under IaaS cloud

and not each host is accessible, let δ_i be the probability that a single IP address is reachable in the Internet. Therefore the attacker needs to have at least $N/\rho_v\delta_i$ tries. However, under public IaaS cloud environment, the exploring range is significantly shrunk as the cloud provider offers the location and IP range publicly. For EC2, the total IP addresses is around 1,500,000 [24]. Besides, most of these IPs are located in a centralized manner as the IP addresses of VMs on the same data center are usually assigned continuously [20]. With the high density of VMs running in a single data center, launching exploit to the cloud usually has much higher hit ratio δ_c. Therefore the attacker needs $N/\rho_v\delta_c$, where $\delta_c \gg \delta_i$, which indicates that the attacker needs dramatically less cost in cloud.

Identifying vulnerabilities. Under traditional environment, if the attacker wants to utilize known vulnerabilities to exploit a host, he may have to scan over the target machine, which can be easily blocked by firewalls. Researchers have proposed several passive scanning approaches in order to bypass IDS or firewall [25, 22], which may lower the scanning cost but still take a considerable amount of time and rely on some other assumptions (e.g., host administrators never modify packet headers).

On the other side, this vulnerability scanning cost can be reduced dramatically in public cloud environment (cf. Figure 5). As shown in our study in Amazon EC2, attackers could obtain the information of VM images (OS and applications installed) by browsing public image description pages. A brute force scanning on all images can help the attacker to decide the distributions of systems and applications in VMs, although in a rough manner. This information can reduce the cost to identify existing vulnerabilities of VMs running in the cloud. Furthermore, the attacker can keep tracking newly-released vulnerabilities associated with these prevalent OSes or applications in public images. Once a new vulnerability is released, it may exist on a large number of VMs in the cloud. Consider the usual patching window gap that we have observed in the last section, the attacker has plenty of time to develop and launch exploits, e.g., to harvest bots with vulnerable VMs. Therefore, identifying known vulnerabilities over the cloud is dramatically faster than that under traditional environment.

Dealing with hardening mechanisms of hosts. Customers on IaaS cloud usually have limited hardening support from the cloud provider, e.g,. Amazon EC2 only provides each instance an external firewall called security group, but no patching management. At the same time, a large number of cloud customers are small-sized service providers [18], and usually do not have strong motivation of hardening their systems as large companies. This results in a weak link for the cloud provider. Once an attacker has managed to exploit a prevalent vulnerability among the VMs of these small companies, a large scale of attack can result in loss for both the cloud customers and the cloud provider.

However, under traditional environment, an enterprise level service provider usually has dedicated team to maintain their platforms, which are usually hardened with several layers of firewalls in order to protect their data and infrastructure. The in-depth defense mechanisms increase the difficulty level for an attacker to compromise the server. It is extremely hard for an attacker to compromise a large number of hosts at the same time.

Therefore, we conjecture that compromising or bypassing hardening systems costs less under public cloud than that in traditional environment. Consider the cloud provider as a special service provider. Since it provides high flexibility of customizing infrastructure to its customers, its own defense mechanism is less tightly controlled compared to traditional in-house service providers, which makes it much easier to penetrate.

3.1.2 Gains of Attacker

An attacker could access confidential information for social or commercial benefits. Besides, the attacker could gain from the loss of his competitors by disrupting or disabling their services. These gains are the same under both cloud and traditional environment. One cloud specific gain is that upon compromising, high-quality bots on the cloud are denser than that in traditional computing environment with higher bandwidth and availability, which makes cyber terrorists easier to identify their targets.

3.1.3 Summary of Cost-effectiveness for Attacker

Considering similar gains of compromising a fixed set of hosts, the cost of the attacker is lowered by launching large scale attacks in an IaaS cloud, with lower costs in identifying enough number of vulnerable hosts, identifying exploiting vulnerabilities, and dealing with hardening mechanisms. Furthermore, exploiting prevalent vulnerabilities in the cloud usually brings the attacker more competing benefits with higher quality of bots than exploiting targets individually under traditional environment. Therefore, *the cost-effectiveness ratio for an attacker is lower in public cloud than that in traditional computing environment; that is, it is more economically efficient for an attacker to launch attacks in cloud.*

3.2 Cost-effectiveness Analysis for Defender

We refer the single term defender as all stakeholders that benefit from defending attacks, including the cloud provider and all of its customers. While facing attacks, the visible cost paid by the defender is the hardening cost, and the gain is the loss of being exploited by attackers, or the commercial benefits from the services that otherwise are disrupted or disabled by attacks.

3.2.1 Costs for Defender

Hardening cost against known vulnerabilities is mainly from patching [26]. The cost per unit by patching in-house hosts is more pricey than batch patching over the cloud, since the batch processing lowers the hardening cost in cloud than in house servers [16].

3.2.2 Loss (or Gains) of Defender

Avoiding potential exploit effectiveness is the gain from the cloud provider's perspective. Exploiting effectiveness has a considerable overlap with an attacker's potential gains. Specifically, classical losses including that of service availability, data integrity, and confidentiality are the same for the defender in both cloud and traditional environment. Most of these losses are transferred to the attacker's benefit. However, there are cloud specific losses caused by large scale attacks, including neighborhood loss, user reputation loss for services, cloud provider reputation loss, and cloud utility misuse.

Neighborhood loss. As aforementioned, an attacker can lookup the IP range of a cloud provider's data center easily. The attacker could rent a VM and launch a large scale exploits to the VMs in the same data center. The attacker does not need to know the exact IP address of his target. Instead, all VMs on the same data center with the same vulnerability can be exploited. This expanded attack surface causes exponentially higher loss than that in traditional computing environment.

Reputation loss for cloud customers. Cloud customers usually are web service providers, and can lose their reputation from their own users upon being compromised. Even though this type of loss is invisible and indirect, it may completely affect the end users' confidence in continuing their services. Threats from prevalent vulnerabilities enlarge such fears as a large number of services on the same cloud platform may exist.

Reputation loss of cloud provider. Even worse than user's reputation loss for cloud customers, the cloud provider's reputation can dramatically drop given a considerable amount of their VMs are compromised. Typically, the healthy including safety level of a cloud provider impacts the number of its users. A customer based survey [27] indicates that a cloud provider's reputation is the most important factor when a customer chooses which provider to go with.

Cloud utility misuse. Once an attacker has managed to deploy bots on one type of VMs in public cloud, he potentially could create a botnet with a large number of machines, which can be powerful enough for crushing other services over the Internet. This further enlarges the cloud provider's reputation loss. As for monetary loss, existing study has pointed out that a DDoS attack could cause up to $19M/hour loss for availability-sensitive services like E-banking. For each DDoS attack, the cost can be up to $100M [28].

3.2.3 Summary of Cost-effectiveness for Defender

The cloud provider can patch prevalent vulnerabilities with a cheaper unit cost than patching in-house servers individually. At the same time, the effectiveness of exploiting prevalent vulnerabilities in IaaS cloud is exponentially higher than the same attacks under traditional environment, consider much denser potential victims with the same vulnerabilities in cloud. Furthermore, the defender has extra cloud-specific losses such as cloud provider's reputation loss and cloud utility misuses. Therefore, our conclusion is that *the cloud defender has much lower cost-effectiveness ratio than in traditional computing environment, which indicates that with the same cost spent by the defender, he achieves more economic benefit in cloud.*

4. TACTICAL GAME MODELING BETWEEN ATTACKER AND DEFENDER

Above cost-effectiveness analysis statically considers the costs and gains for both attackers and defenders. However, in real world several factors impact the relative costs and benefits of each side, and thus both rational attackers and defenders adjust their behaviors by considering these dynamic factors to achieve maximum benefits. Among these, the time-since-release has been considered as one of the main affecting factors that impacts the effectiveness of exploiting known vulnerabilities. This comes from an assumption that more VMs are patched for a given vulnerability as time goes by. Therefore, the sooner the attacker acts, the larger number of victim hosts can be hit with the same cost. On the other side, the sooner the defender acts, he can patch more VMs thus prevent more loss with lower cost. Moreover, patching a more prevalent vulnerability (by means of the vulnerability distribution in images and VMs) results in more cost-effectiveness ratio for both the attacker and defender, since it costs more for the attacker to identify vulnerable victims, and brings less gain for the defender to patch the vulnerability.

Therefore, we believe the dynamic cost-effectiveness ratios result in a game-based tactics between the attacker and defender. In this section, we construct a game theoretic model in order to illustrate the actions that rational attackers and defenders should take. We further map different cost-effectiveness scenarios into cost density functions to show their evolutions. Our model indicates that both the attacker and defender have stronger incentive to act earlier, and their actions become less cost-effective as time goes by. After certain moment, the defender only needs to maintain the security level (the prevalence of the vulnerability) as the patching cost may exceed the cost from residual risk. The attacker may also lose the motivation of launching further attacks after certain point as the attack gain may not be able to compensate the attack cost due to the drop of the vulnerability prevalence. Therefore the threat from prevalent vulnerabilities can be greatly mitigated as long as the defender patches security holes in a timely and proactive manner. However, cloud customers should be advised to protect their systems against targeted attacks as this is not a cloud specific threat.

4.1 Game Theory Background

An N-player game can be represented as a function G ($S_1, S_2, \dots, S_N, u_1, u_2, \dots, u_N$), where S_i $(0 < i < N)$ is a strategy set $(s_{i1}, \dots, s_{im})$ for player i, and s_j $(s_j \in S_i)$ is a complete strategy available for player i. Player i has a probability distribution $P_i = (p_{i1}, \dots, p_{im})$, where p_{ik} is the probability of s_{ik} being adopted by player i. The payoff for player i is $u_i(S_1, \dots, S_n)$ $(1 < j < n)$, where S_j is the strategy adopted by user j. For an N-player game theory, the expected payoff for player i is:

$$v_i(p_1, \dots, p_n) = \sum_{m_1=1}^{M_1} \cdots \sum_{m_n=1}^{M_n} \left[\prod_{k=1}^{n} P_{km_k} \right] u_i(S_{1m_1}, \dots, S_{nm_n}), \quad (1)$$

where M_j is the pure strategy numbers available to player j. For a 2-player game, the expected payoff of player 1 is:

$$v_1(p_1, p_2) = \sum_{m_1=1}^{M_1} \sum_{m_2=1}^{M_2} P_{1m_1} P_{2m_2} u_1(S_{1m_1}, S_{2m_2}), \quad (2)$$

where p_1 and p_2 are two sets of probability distributions adopted by the two players, respectively. Each distribution consists of a number of probabilities (sum up to 1), each of which indicates the chance of a strategy adopted by the player. S_{1m1} and S_{2m2} represent the strategies adopted by p_1 and p_2, respectively.

4.2 Game Theory Modeling

We consider player 1 as the attacker and player 2 as the defender. Player 1 has two strategies: attack (S_{11}) or stay idle (S_{12}). Player 2 also has two strategies: patching (S_{21}) or stay unpatched (S_{22}). P_{ij} indicates the probability of S_{ij} being adopted. We say that K_1 is a proactive action adopted by each player, meaning attack and patch for the attacker and the defender, respectively. K_2 means a passive action: stay idle for the attacker and leave the platform unpatched for the defender. Given each of the two players has two possible strategies, there are four conditions as follows.

- Both players choose K_1. The cloud defender needs to pay cost ($-CP$) in order to patch his platform in a timely manner. On the other side, the attacker has to pay the cost ($-AC$) of exploiting but without gaining from the hardened platform.
- When both players choose K_2, obviously both get 0.
- When the attacker chooses K_1 and the defender chooses K_2, the attacker gains ($+AG$) from exploiting by paying attack cost ($-AC$). The defender suffers the cost of being exploited ($-CD$).
- When the attacker chooses K_2 and the defender chooses K_1, the attacker gets 0 and the defender pays patch cost ($-CP$) to keep the platform up-to-date.

We use P_S and P_A to denote the probability of being proactive for the defender and the attacker, respectively. Given the four possible conditions, their expected payoffs (V_A and V_S) in the game are:

$$\begin{aligned} V_A &= -AC \times P_A P_S + 0 \times (1 - P_A) \times (1 - P_S) \\ &\quad +AG \times P_A \times (1 - P_S) + 0 \times (1 - P_A) \times P_S \\ &\quad = AG \times P_A \times (1 - P_S) - AC \times P_A P_S \quad (3) \end{aligned}$$

$$\begin{aligned} V_S &= -CP \times P_A P_S + 0 \times (1 - P_A) \times (1 - P_S) \\ &\quad -CD \times P_A \times (1 - P_S) - CP \times (1 - P_A) \times P_S \\ &= -CD \times P_A \times (1 - P_S) - CP \times P_S \quad (4) \end{aligned}$$

The equations indicate that the expected payoffs of both players depend on both of their determinations of being proactive. Without exploiting intention, the attacker does not gain anything. When being more aggressive, he has an increased potential gain (when facing an unconscious defender) with the cost of launching attacks. A passive defender may end up losing nothing given the attacker is passive as well. However, this assumption is unrealistic as cyber attacks are ubiquitous. The defender (especially under cloud environment) should have a reasonable expectation on the density of attacks per unit time in order to balance the tradeoff between hardening cost and risk properly. Visualizing the game between the attacker and the defender can assist cloud stakeholders to better understand current security situation and make hardening plans accordingly.

4.3 Tactical Modeling between Attacker and Defender

We consider the events of instantiating images by different customers in an IaaS cloud are independent, and the instantiation rate is a relatively stable value given the large number of customers. Therefore the instantiation of images with each prevalent vulnerability can be modeled with an exponential distribution, and the probability density function (PDF) can be expressed in Equation 5, where t is time and λ is the arrival rate of instantiation events in the cloud. A larger λ means a denser event and higher risk density of the vulnerability. Therefore, the prevalence of the vulnerability determines the value of λ, and the PDF can be regarded as a risk density function. The risk density keeps decreasing as time goes by. This is because less and less vulnerable targets available (either

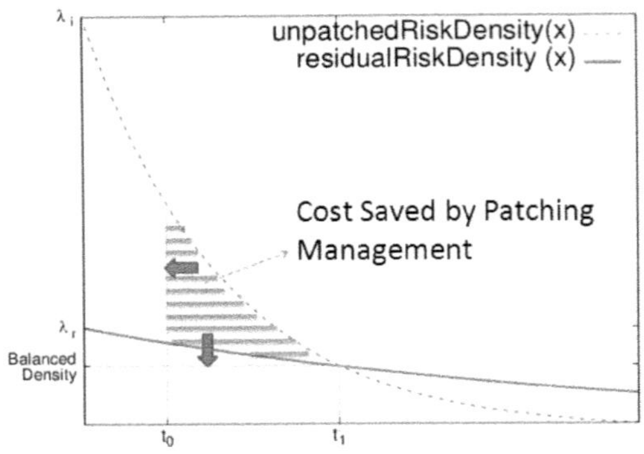

Figure 6: Cost density distribution for cloud defender.

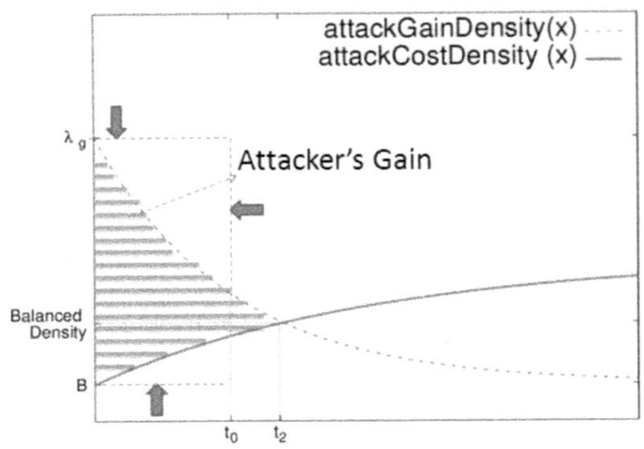

Figure 7: Cost and gain density distribution for cloud attacker.

patched by the VM users or already exploited by the attacker) to the attacker.

$$f(t,\lambda) = \begin{cases} \lambda e^{-\lambda t} & t \geq 0 \\ 0 & t < 0 \end{cases} \tag{5}$$

4.3.1 *Tactical Modeling for Defender*

Figure 6 illustrates the cost-effectiveness from the defender's perspective with two different strategies. A defender with little or no security awareness has a higher rate parameter (risk density) than a defender with appropriate patching management. The value of t_0 indicates the exploit window of a prevalent vulnerability. Therefore starting from t_0, the defender can choose to deploy patch to the vulnerability. Then the risk density is dropped to the patched risk density curve. A rational defender has a lower risk density because the sum of residual risk and patch cost is regarded lower than the unpatched risk cost density. At the moment t_1, the two curves have a point of intersection. Starting from t_1, the defender only needs to maintain the security level. This is because the patch cost density has exceeded the residual risk density [8]. The value of t_1 is decided by the two rate parameters with Equation 6.

$$\begin{aligned} \lambda_1 e^{-\lambda_1 t_1} &= \lambda_2 e^{-\lambda_2 t_1} \\ t_1 &= \frac{\ln^{\lambda_i} - \ln^{\lambda_r}}{\lambda_i - \lambda_r} \end{aligned} \tag{6}$$

Therefore, the risk that could possibly be reduced by a rational defender can be expressed with Equation 7 and is marked in Figure 6, where λ_i and λ_r are risk density rates of before and after the patch has been deployed. As indicated in Figure 6, minimizing the value of t_0 and rate parameter (λ_2) of residual risk density can maximally reduce the risk.

$$\begin{aligned} R(\lambda_i, \lambda_r) &= \int_{t_0}^{t_1} \lambda_i e^{-\lambda_i t} dt - \int_{t_0}^{t_1} \lambda_r e^{-\lambda_r t} dt \\ &= (1 - e^{-\lambda_i t})\Big|_{t_0}^{t_1} - (1 - e^{-\lambda_r t})\Big|_{t_0}^{t_1} \end{aligned} \tag{7}$$

4.3.2 *Tactical Modeling for Attacker*

The density of the attacker's potential gain through exploiting is similar as but slightly lower than the unpatched cloud loss due to being exploited, since some loss like neighborhood loss cannot be gained by the attacker. Therefore, the attacker's potential gain conforms to a PDF as well. The attack cost has both maximum and minimum values given a fixed number of to-be exploited targets. The maximum value is paid while brute-forcing over the whole cloud platform (if there are not enough hosts that can be compromised in the whole platform) and the minimum cost is paid while exploiting each target with minimum cost (each attack succeeds at its first attempt). The cost is negatively correlated to the exploiting effectiveness because exploiting vulnerabilities with higher density costs less than utilizing sparsely distributed security holes. Therefore, the attack cost can be mapped to a variant of a cumulative probability function (CPF) shown in Equation 8. The only difference between the attack cost model and CPF is the constant B, which represents the basic cost of each attack, e.g., target reconnaissance and vulnerability detection. λ_e refers to the cost density of failed attack attempts.

$$F(t, \lambda_e) = \begin{cases} 1 - e^{-\lambda_e t} + B & t \geq 0 \\ 0 & t < 0 \end{cases} \tag{8}$$

Figure 7 indicates the attacker's cost-effectiveness as time goes by. Consider a defender with strong security awareness which deploys patch at t_0, the attacker's gain is then decreased dramatically. If the defender is unconscious, attacks could last until t_2 as the gain through attacks after t_2 cannot compensate the attacker's cost of launching these exploits. Equations 9 indicates the attacker's gain by exploiting unpatched ($t_p = t_2$) and well hardened ($t_p = t_0$) platform, respectively. λ_g means the density of attacker's gain and λ_c means the attack cost density. In general the attacker loses the motivation of attacks after t_0 or t_2 whichever comes first. t_2 can be calculated through solving Equation 10. Given t_0 and t_2, the attacker's gain reduced by a rational defender can be obtained through Equations 9 and is the marked area in Figure 7.

$$\begin{aligned} G(\lambda_g, \lambda_c) &= \int_0^{t_p} \lambda_g e^{-\lambda_g t} dt - \int_0^{t_p} (1 - e^{-\lambda_c t}) dt - t_p \times B \\ &= (1 - e^{-\lambda_g t})\Big|_0^{t_p} - (t + \frac{1}{\lambda_c})\Big|_0^{t_p} \\ t_p &= \begin{cases} t_2 & t_0 \geq t_2 \\ t_0 & t_0 < t_2 \end{cases} \end{aligned} \tag{9}$$

$$\lambda e^{-\lambda_g t_2} = (1 - e^{-\lambda_c t_2}) \tag{10}$$

4.3.3 *Two-player Game*

The game between the attacker and defender can be seen in Figure 8. At the starting point, both attack and defense are impacting. However, both of them become less cost-effective as time goes

[8]residual risk density refers to the risk density left after the patch has been deployed

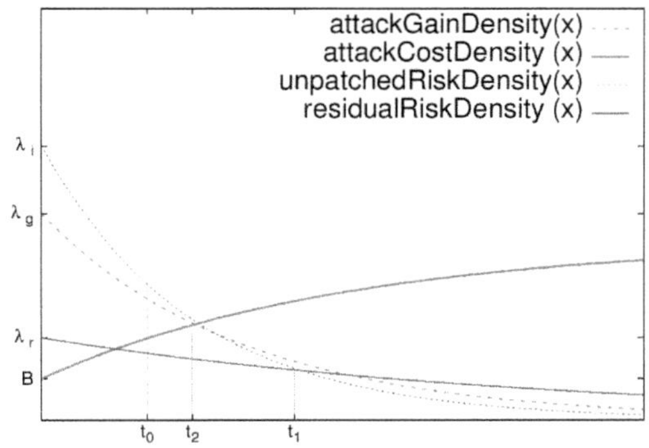

Figure 8: Game between attacker and defender in cloud.

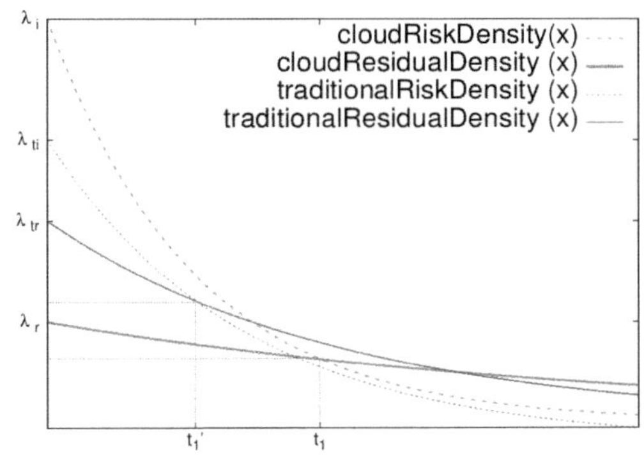

Figure 9: Cost-effectiveness comparison between traditional and cloud environments.

by. There are three noteworthy moments. t_1 is the moment when the attacker's cost and gain get balanced, after that a rational attacker stops launching attacks. t_2 is the moment when the cloud defender's cost is minimized and further patching costs higher than the residual risk. t_1 is not necessarily less than t_2. When $t_1 < t_2$, a rational attacker stops attacking but the cloud defender continues patching as the expected potential loss is greater than patching cost, and the cloud defender stops hardening its platform until t_2. When $t_1 \geq t_2$, the defender's cost and gain get balanced first, and he stops patching but maintains the security level. However, a rational attacker continues launching attacks under this circumstance as he can still obtain more than attack cost. When $t_1 \geq t_2$, we say there is a range for both the attacker and the defender can be satisfied. If $t_1 < t_2$, the attacker stops launching attacks as the expected gain cannot compensate attack cost. The defender only needs to maintain the security level under this circumstance. After t_0 the defender has patch available to the vulnerability. If the defender deploys patch, both t_1 and t_2 could arrive earlier up to t_0 because both rate parameters of the exploiting effective density and attacker gain density drop. Therefore, not only could an smaller t_0 reduce the attacker's gain and exploiting effectiveness, it could also end the game between attacker and defender earlier.

4.3.4 *Cost-effectiveness Comparison between Cloud and Traditional Computing Environment*

In order to compare attacks under cloud and traditional computing environment, and investigate how much risk can be reduced by rational defenders, we model the cost-effectiveness from both the attacker's and the defender's perspective. We use the risk density functions (Equations 7 and 9) to answer the following questions:

- How much risk can be reduced by a rational defender in the cloud?
- How much risk can be reduced by a rational defender in traditional in-house environment?
- How much more gain can the attacker obtain when facing an unconscious cloud defender than a rational defender?
- How much more gain can the attacker obtain when facing an unconscious defender than a rational defender in traditional environment?

In Section 3 we have analyzed that prevalent vulnerabilities lead to lower patching expense but higher potential loss in cloud than under traditional environment. Therefore under the cloud environment, the risk density is higher but the patch cost density is lower than those under traditional environment. Figure 9 illustrates the comparison. For cloud environment, the rate parameters before and after patch deployed are denoted by λ_i and λ_r. While λ_{ti} and λ_{tr} represent rate parameters under traditional environment (before and after patch deployed, respectively). As we can see, the defender in the cloud can achieve a better stable security level than in traditional because of the lower cost in patching. The time t_1' does not need to be greater than t_1 [9]. If the cloud defender can handle hardening work appropriately, it can achieve a lower security level with shorter period of time. Figure 9 also tells us that it is urgent for the cloud defender to harden the cloud platform as the gap between the potential loss and hardening cost is dramatically enlarged compared to that under traditional environment. Without patch deployed, the potential loss in the cloud is exponentially higher , i.e., $R(\lambda_i, \lambda_r) \gg R(\lambda_{ti}, \lambda_{tr})$.

4.4 Summary

Through dynamic cost-effectiveness analysis with gaming modeling, we have observed that both attack and defense are more cost-effective in the cloud, and they become less cost-effective as time goes by. Three factors determines the game between the two parties: the defender's willingness (P_S), responsiveness (t_0), and activeness (λ_r). In a nutshell, the cloud defender should be willing to harden its cloud platform in a timely and proactive manner.

5. COUNTERMEASURES

Our gaming modeling indicates that in order to reduce the risk with prevalent known vulnerabilities in cloud, which is the cost marked in Figure 6, two parameters (t_0 and the rate parameter of residual risk density) need to be minimized.Which means that the defender should be more responsive and proactive to known vulnerabilities. Minimizing t_0 means eliminating 1-day exploits, i.e., keeping all instances up-to-date and maintaining running instances without severe known security holes. As this is difficult to achieve, keeping all public images up-to-date may be more feasible. We propose the following three countermeasures for cloud providers and customers.

Patching public VM images. Public VM images like AMIs should be up-to-date when being launched by users. The cloud provider should setup policy in order to make sure unpatched images should not be launched. Two options are available in order to achieve this

[9] t_1 and t_1' represent the moment when the attacker's cost and gain get balanced under traditional and cloud environment respectively

requirement: the provider can either force a user to update the image before it is launched, or the provider or image publishers can update public images offline periodically [16]. This could reduce the boot time at user end during launching.

Maintaining running instances. Every time when launching an image, the image should be required to check against a configuration file in order to make sure all default apps are up to date. The configuration file can be provided by the image publisher. Cloud users can customize the configuration file on their own. Cloud users should also be responsible for the applications installed by themselves.

Give patching priority to prevalent vulnerabilities. As Figure 6 indicates, higher prevalence is more time sensitive. Therefore, considering the prevalence (along with impact factors) of vulnerabilities is needed when making patching plans. The moment (t_d) of deploying a patch to a specific vulnerability can be inferred from a preset threshold of tolerable risk. Given similar impact, a higher prevalent vulnerability usually has a smaller t_d.

Shuffling cloud infrastructure smartly. Introduce a new defensive mechanism, which could make the configuration of the cloud platform as an animation rather than a static picture. Similar to patching vulnerabilities periodically, configurations (e.g.IP address, topology or applications) can be changed time to time. This type of moving target defense paradigms [29, 30, 31] could significantly mitigate security holes on the cloud.

6. LIMITATIONS AND DISCUSSIONS

Our model has a number of limitations. First of all, we only consider prevalent vulnerabilities in large-scale cloud. We do not provide an aggregated metric indicating the security level of the whole cloud platform and individual VM systems. Cloud stakeholders can use our model to further calculate a metric for finer-grained modeling. The calculation can be based on environmental factor or impact factor of identified vulnerabilities.

Secondly, we do not have accurate statistics regarding cloud customers' system information of running VMs, e.g., exactly how many VMs are launched for a particular image, and how many users usually patch their VMs in timely manner. In our model we take a simple estimation by assuming that the prevalence of instances is similar to that of public images.

7. RELATED WORK

Security issues regarding the public images in Amazon EC2 have been studied. Sensitive information leak has been detected by Bugiel et al. [3]. They also suggested several solutions for various cloud specific threats. More comprehensive experiments over EC2 have been conducted by Balduzzi et al. [1]. They scanned a larger number of public AMIs and found more security issues like software vulnerabilities and malwares. However, neither of them evaluate potential threat from prevalent known software vulnerabilities, which we believe is the most straightforward and efficient way for attackers to intrude an IaaS cloud.

Game theory has been used for modeling attacks and defenses. Activities (exploiting and hardening) between attackers and defenders perfectly conform to a 2-player game. Yan et al. [32] model a game between DDoS attackers and defenders. Khirwadkar [33] constructs a game theoretic model between attackers and defenders by using Fictitious-Play approach in order to make sure the two parties are not under complete information environment. Game theory based analysis regarding network security is surveyed in [34].

Another line of work is to visualize economic incentive from defender's perspective [35, 14, 36, 37, 26, 28], which helps the defender appropriately allocate resources to security-related tasks. Studer et al. [35] evaluate DDoS attacks from both technical and economic points of view, and provide evaluation on monetary loss due to these attacks in addition to the economic appraisal by [28]. Frei et al. [37] visualize time lengths between vulnerability disclosure date, patch date, and exploit date, and believe these time periods represent the current status of security industry. However, they do not consider the date of patch deployment, which is captured in our model to evaluate the dynamic threat of individual platforms or systems. Richardson et al. [26] conduct a survey indicating that 62.3% respondents apply patch after a security incident happens. A report by Mellberg [18] indicates that only 59% of small companies ($\leq$ \$50M revenue) have patch management which conforms to the number investigated by Richardson et al. [26]. This motivates our modeling study in this paper since a large number of IaaS users are individuals and small companies [19].

8. CONCLUSION

We identify the threat of exploiting prevalent vulnerabilities in IaaS cloud with an empirical study and real penetration test in Amazon EC2. We pinpoint that such threat exponentially increases the risk level of cloud due to two factors: the prevalent vulnerabilities can spread quickly on public cloud as one image could potentially be instantiated by a large number of users, and the nature of the cloud enables more cost-effective attacks than traditional in-house computing environment. We analyze the cost and effectiveness of exploiting and defending prevalent vulnerabilities under traditional and cloud environments. Our results indicate that both cloud attackers and defenders have lower cost-effectiveness ratio, which enables a game-like tactical scenario between them. To further illustrate the influence of dynamic cost-effectiveness nature, we build a 2-player game theoretic model and a risk-gain analysis to capture the risks associated with two types (rational or unconscious) of attackers and defenders. Our result reveals that both attack and defense become less cost-effective in cloud as time goes by, which suggests the defender should be more responsive and proactive under cloud environment. We stir up them with a number of possible countermeasures against such threat.

9. ACKNOWLEDGEMENTS

Su Zhang and Xinming Ou were partially supported by the Air Force Office of Scientific Research award FA9550-12-1-0106 and U.S. National Science Foundation awards 0954138 and 1018703. Any opinions, findings and conclusions or recommendations expressed herein are those of the authors and do not necessarily reflect the views of the above agencies.

10. REFERENCES

[1] M. Balduzzi, J. Zaddach, D. Balzarotti, E. Kirda, and S. Loureiro, "A security analysis of amazon's elastic compute cloud service," in *Proc of the 27th Annual ACM SAC*, 2012.

[2] *AWS Customer Agreement.* http://aws.amazon.com/agreement/: Amazon Web Services LLC., 2012.

[3] S. Bugiel, S. Nürnberger, T. Pöppelmann, A. Sadeghi, and T. Schneider, "Amazonia: when elasticity snaps back," in *Proc of the 18th ACM CCS*, pp. 389–400, 2011.

[4] S. Zhang, D. Caragea, and X. Ou, "An empirical study on using the national vulnerability database to predict software vulnerabilities," in *Database and Expert Systems Applications*, pp. 217–231, Springer, 2011.

[5] H. Huang, S. Zhang, X. Ou, A. Prakash, and K. Sakallah, "Distilling critical attack graph surface iteratively through minimum-cost sat solving," in *Proceedings of the 27th Annual Computer Security Applications Conference*, pp. 31–40, ACM, 2011.

[6] J. Homer, S. Zhang, X. Ou, D. Schmidt, Y. Du, S. R. Rajagopalan, and A. Singhal, "Aggregating vulnerability metrics in enterprise networks using attack graphs," *Journal of Computer Security*, vol. 21, no. 4, pp. 561–597, 2013.

[7] S. Zhang, X. Ou, A. Singhal, and J. Homer, "An empirical study of a vulnerability metric aggregation method," in *The 2011 International Conference on Security and Management (SAM'11), special track on Mission Assurance and Critical Infrastructure Protection (STMACIP'11)*, 2011.

[8] S. Zhang, X. Ou, and J. Homer, "Effective network vulnerability assessment through model abstraction," in *Detection of Intrusions and Malware, and Vulnerability Assessment*, pp. 17–34, Springer, 2011.

[9] H. Holm, M. Ekstedt, and D. Andersson, "Empirical analysis of system-level vulnerability metrics through actual attacks," *IEEE Transactions on Dependable and Secure Computing*, vol. 9, no. 6, pp. 825–837, 2012.

[10] W. P. WD, F.-X. A. THA, K. M. THA, and D. Date, "Posecco-prototype for vulnerability autonomous assessment and remediation," 2013.

[11] H. Holm, *A Framework and Calculation Engine for Modeling and Predicting the Cyber Security of Enterprise Architectures*. Kth royal institute of technology, dissertation trita-ee, issn 1653-5146; 2014:001, KTH Royal Institute of Technology, 2014. ISBN 978-91-7595-005-1.

[12] B. Grobauer, T. Walloschek, and E. Stocker, "Understanding cloud computing vulnerabilities," *Security & Privacy, IEEE*, vol. 9, no. 2, pp. 50–57, 2011.

[13] H. Shrobe, "What if we got a do-over?," in *Proc of the 2012 ACM Workshop on CCSW*, ACM.

[14] L. Bilge and T. Dumitras, "Before we knew it: an empirical study of zero-day attacks in the real world," in *ACM CCS*, 2012.

[15] P. Mell, K. Scarfone, and S. Romanosky, "A complete guide to the common vulnerability scoring system version 2.0," in *Published by FIRST-Forum of Incident Response and Security Teams*, pp. 1–23, 2007.

[16] W. Zhou, P. Ning, X. Zhang, G. Ammons, R. Wang, and V. Bala, "Always up-to-date: scalable offline patching of vm images in a compute cloud," in *Proc of the 26th ACSAC*, 2010.

[17] L. Litty and D. Lie, "Patch auditing in infrastructure as a service clouds," in *ACM SIGPLAN Notices*, vol. 46, pp. 145–156, ACM, 2011.

[18] J. Mellberg, *Take patch management to the next level.* https://www.brighttalk.com/webcast/8113/54861: Secunia, 2012.

[19] *Customer Success. Powered by the AWS Cloud.* http://aws.amazon.com/solutions/case-studies/: Amazon Web Services LLC., 2008.

[20] D. Talbot, "Vulnerability seen in amazon's cloud-computing," tech. rep., MIT Tech Review, 2009.

[21] D. Maynor, *Metasploit Toolkit for Penetration Testing, Exploit Development, and Vulnerability Research*. Syngress, 2007.

[22] A. Ghosh, S. Noel, and S. Jajodia, "Mapping attack paths in black-box networks through passive vulnerability inference," tech. rep., DTIC Document, 2011.

[23] S. Shin and G. Gu, "Conficker and beyond: a large-scale empirical study," in *Proceedings of the 26th ACSAC*, 2010.

[24] *Amazon Web Services Discussion Forums.* https://forums.aws.amazon.com/forum.jspa?forumID=30: Amazon Web Services LLC.

[25] R. Lippmann, D. Fried, K. Piwowarski, and W. Streilein, "Passive operating system identification from tcp/ip packet headers," in *Workshop on Data Mining for Computer Security*, p. 40, Citeseer, 2003.

[26] R. Richardson, "15th annual 2010/2011 computer crime and security survey," tech. rep., Computer Security Institute, 2011.

[27] P. Koehler, A. Anandasivam, M. Dan, and C. Weinhardt, "Cloud services from a consumer perspective," *AMCIS 2010 Proc.*

[28] F. Consulting, *DDoS: A Threat You Can't Afford To Ignore.* Jan. 2009.

[29] R. Zhuang, S. Zhang, S. A. DeLoach, X. Ou, and A. Singhal, "Simulation-based approaches to studying effectiveness of moving-target network defense," in *National Symposium on Moving Target Research*, 2012.

[30] R. Zhuang, S. Zhang, A. Bardas, S. A. DeLoach, X. Ou, and A. Singhal, "Investigating the application of moving target defenses to network security," in *Resilient Control Systems (ISRCS), 2013 6th International Symposium on*, pp. 162–169, IEEE, 2013.

[31] I. Unruh, A. G. Bardas, R. Zhuang, X. Ou, and S. A. DeLoach, "Compiling abstract specifications into concrete systems–bringing order to the cloud," tech. rep., Kansas State University, 2013.

[32] G. Yan, R. Lee, A. Kent, and D. H. Wolpert, "Towards a bayesian network game framework for evaluating ddos attacks and defense," in *ACM CCS*, 2012.

[33] T. Khirwadkar, *Defense against network attacks using game theory*. PhD thesis, University of Illinois, 2011.

[34] S. Roy, C. Ellis, S. Shiva, D. Dasgupta, V. Shandilya, and Q. Wu, "A survey of game theory as applied to network security," in *System Sciences (HICSS), 2010 43rd Hawaii International Conference on*, IEEE.

[35] R. Studer, "Economic and technical analysis of botnets and denial-of-service attacks," *Communication systems IV*, p. 19, 2011.

[36] T. Forbath, P. Kalaher, and T. O'Grady, "The total cost of security patch management," tech. rep., Wipro Product Strategy & Architecture, 2005.

[37] S. Frei, M. May, U. Fiedler, and B. Plattner, "Large-scale vulnerability analysis," in *Proc of the 2006 SIGCOMM workshop on Large-scale attack defense*, ACM.

PROSPECT

Peripheral Proxying Supported Embedded Code Testing

Markus Kammerstetter
Vienna University of Technology
mk@iseclab.org

Christian Platzer
Vienna University of Technology
cplatzer@iseclab.org

Wolfgang Kastner
Vienna University of Technology
k@auto.tuwien.ac.at

ABSTRACT

Embedded systems are an integral part of almost every electronic product today. From consumer electronics to industrial components in SCADA systems, their possible fields of application are manifold. While especially in industrial and critical infrastructures the security requirements are high, recent publications have shown that embedded systems do not cope well with this demand. One of the reasons is that embedded systems are being less scrutinized as embedded security analysis is considered to be more time consuming and challenging in comparison to PC systems. One of the key challenges on proprietary, resource constrained embedded devices is dynamic code analysis. The devices typically do not have the capabilities for a full-scale dynamic security evaluation. Likewise, the analyst cannot execute the software implementation inside a virtual machine due to the missing peripheral hardware that is required by the software to run. In this paper, we present PROSPECT, a system that can overcome these shortcomings and enables dynamic code analysis of embedded binary code inside arbitrary analysis environments. By transparently forwarding peripheral hardware accesses from the original host system into a virtual machine, PROSPECT allows security analysts to run the embedded software implementation without the need to know which and how embedded peripheral hardware components are accessed. We evaluated PROSPECT with respect to the performance impact and conducted a case study by doing a full-scale security audit of a widely used commercial fire alarm system in the building automation domain. Our results show that PROSPECT is both practical and usable for real-world application.

Categories and Subject Descriptors

D.2.5 [**Testing and Debugging**]: Debugging aids; D.4.7 [**Organization and Design**]: Real-time systems and embedded systems; C.2.0 [**General**]: Security and protection

ASIA CCS'14, June 4–6, 2014, Kyoto, Japan.
Copyright 2014 ACM 978-1-4503-2800-5/14/06 ...$15.00.
http://dx.doi.org/10.1145/2590296.2590301.

Keywords

embedded system, security, device tunneling, dynamic analysis, fuzz testing

1. INTRODUCTION

Embedded systems are omnipresent in today's world. From small digital clocks over home appliances such as washing machines and multimedia devices to medical appliances or smart phones, embedded technology provides tremendous advantages compared to general purpose systems. One key aspect is the possibility to create tailored hardware devices to fulfill a very specific task. With exactly the right amount of memory, processing power and interfaces, embedded devices are cheaper, smaller and faster than their general-purpose computing counterparts. However, a good amount of embedded devices are aimed at functionality rather than security. In fact, recent publications have shown that the security of embedded devices is especially bad [23, 8, 10, 14]. One reason is, that security audits on embedded devices are considered to be far more challenging and time consuming than on general purpose PC systems. Considering the common case in which the security analyst has no access to the source code of the system under test, there is a broad gap between state-of-the-art security analysis techniques for PCs and for embedded systems. Liu et al. [11] and Austin et al. [1] give an overview of the wide area of vulnerability discovery techniques that are available for PC systems. The techniques range from sophisticated static analysis techniques over dynamic analysis and fuzz testing to advanced dynamic taint analysis and symbolic or concolic execution [16, 4]. However, for embedded systems, the situation is different. Mainly due to custom proprietary hardware, undocumented peripherals and strict system limitations, the prevalent vulnerability discovery techniques are still based on static analysis [9, 3, 22].

At the same time, using the wide range of dynamic analysis or taint analysis and symbolic execution tools is in general not possible due to the limitations of the embedded system under test. One solution would be to take the investigated application from its original context and run it in a virtual machine that provides the necessary resources and facilities for a full dynamic evaluation. To emulate the embedded device, however, the connected peripheral hardware needs to be available from within the virtual machine as well. The usual way is to emulate the peripheral hardware. Yet, for proprietary hardware this is not possible due to the following reasons. First, the analyst would need comprehensive information on how all peripheral hardware devices work in order to emulate the hardware behavior in software. Since peripheral hardware is likely to be proprietary, this information is not available and, subsequently, the analyst can not emulate the hardware. Second, even if the information is available to the analyst, adding full support for new peripheral hardware components to a virtual machine implementation is not an easy task. It is likely that the implementation would take the analyst a tremendous amount of time that renders the whole dynamic security analysis infeasible.

To amend this problem, we take a different approach and introduce PROSPECT, a proxy capable of tunneling arbitrary peripheral hardware accesses from within a virtual machine to the embedded system under test. The result is a virtualized execution environment for embedded software implementations with a completely transparent connection to the actual peripheral hardware components of the system under test. PROSPECT thus enables the analyst to leverage any powerful dynamic analysis techniques of her choice to discover vulnerabilities on embedded devices with minimal effort. We developed and continuously improved PROSPECT over a duration of more than 10 months during which our system evolved. In addition, we conducted a case study to prove the effectiveness of PROSPECT and used the system to undertake a full scale security analysis of a widely used proprietary fire alarm system in the building automation domain. Summing up, the contributions presented in this paper are as follows:

- We introduce PROSPECT, a transparent proxy for tunneling peripheral hardware accesses from within a virtual analysis environment to the embedded system under test. Our system can overcome prevalent analysis limitations by enabling dynamic instrumentation inside arbitrary analysis environments.
- We provide a MIPS based proof-of-concept implementation that has continuously evolved over a duration of more than 10 months.
- We evaluate and discuss our approach with a detailed analysis of the system's performance and usability.
- We utilized PROSPECT to conduct a case study by running a full-scale security audit of a widely used commercial fire alarm system in the building automation domain showing that PROSPECT is both practical and usable for real-world application.

2. CHALLENGES IN EMBEDDED SECURITY ANALYSIS

Assuming that the reader is familiar with the general field of information security, in this chapter, we briefly outline binary code analysis and highlight fuzz testing as exemplary, widely established techniques to discover software vulnerabilities. We point out, that dynamic analysis is one of the key requirements for efficient fuzz testing as well as for manual in-depth analysis approaches usually done as soon as fuzz testing discovers a potential security vulnerability. After presenting dynamic analysis techniques for PC systems, we continue by providing a general overview of how typical medium to large scale embedded systems are made up and why the presented dynamic analysis approaches are frequently not applicable to embedded systems. Besides, the chapter shows why the approach PROSPECT takes is promising as it can overcome the described challenges and enable dynamic analysis in general, regardless of the analysis limitations on the system under test.

2.1 Binary Code Analysis

Vendors are typically profit-driven and try to push their newest software products to market as soon as possible. Depending on their efforts to avoid software vulnerabilities, a released software implementation may contain numerous security flaws such as stack smashing or use-after-free vulnerabilities [17]. At that point, an arms race between attackers and the vendor begins. Attackers try to exploit the vulnerabilities for their own ill-gotten gain such as industrial espionage, spreading malware or setting up botnets [20, 7] while vendors try to patch newly discovered bugs.

For proprietary software implementations, the source code is usually not available. Thus, in order to discover vulnerabilities in these implementations, security analysts need to rely on techniques that can be applied to binary code. In a recent survey [11], Liu et al. describe a number of common techniques to discover software vulnerabilities. While analysts can resort to static analysis that does not require the execution of the program under test, static analysis suffers from a number of drawbacks hindering penetration tests. For instance, object orientated code makes frequent use of function pointers that are hard to resolve, if the program is not being executed. With dynamic analysis, the program is being executed and the analyst can trace and instrument the current execution path of the program under test. However, unless advanced techniques such as multipath exploration [13] are employed, the analyst needs to generate different program inputs to analyze different execution paths.

2.2 Fuzz Testing: A Common Technique to discover Software Vulnerabilities

Generating different program inputs to reach different execution paths is also one of the key ideas of *fuzz testing*, a widely established technique to discover software vulnerabilities [11, 5, 2]. With fuzz testing, input data to the program are generated automatically either at random or by mutating previously obtained program input. At the same time, the analyst can employ dynamic analysis to monitor the program execution and detect program anomalies such as crashes, illicit memory accesses or endless loops causing high CPU utilization. If an anomaly is detected, the generated input data are likely to have caused the abnormal behavior. This is a starting point for a more thorough manual program analysis, usually also within a dynamic analysis environment.

Practical results [11, 17, 5, 2] have shown that fuzzing is both a viable and established technique to discover software vulnerabilities. However, since fuzzers can be highly application specific, it might be necessary to implement new fuzzing tools for each penetration test. Also, we would like to stress that although fuzz testing is widely used, it is not the only technique to discovery software vulnerabilities efficiently. One key observation at this point is that dynamic instrumentation is required for both efficient fuzz testing and the manual analysis that is usually done after the fuzzer discovers a potential security vulnerability.

2.3 Dynamic Code Analysis on PC Systems

In general, a PC system can be divided into hardware, an operating system (including kernel and drivers) and software applications. The analyst has the freedom to dynamically instrument any of these layers. The easiest way to instrument a program is to debug it with a state-of-the-art-debugger such as *gdb* or *Ida Pro*. The drawback here is that the program can easily detect that it is being instrumented and behave differently. For instance, the program might just exit instead of performing its usual functionality. On the next level, the analyst can instrument the operating system to analyze the program's behavior. For instance, CWSandbox [24] uses this approach by hooking the operating system libraries. This allows the analyst to trace the behavior of the application, but at the same time hinders typical techniques for debugging (e.g. single stepping through code). On the lowest level, the analyst can instrument the hardware using Virtual Machine Introspection (VMI) [6], which makes it hard for the investigated software to detect that it is being analyzed. Although the target of the analysis is the application itself, the downside of this approach is the need to analyze the surrounding operating system as well. Therefore, the necessary effort is higher than applying a regular debugging technique.

2.4 A typical Embedded System

Embedded systems can be divided into small, medium and large scale embedded systems [19, 14]. Depending on their size, their system configuration can differ tremendously.
Small scale embedded systems such as electronic toys, digital clocks or pocket calculators are built around strongly resource constrained microcontrollers. Typically, there is no operating system and the firmware of these systems comprises a single program that is contained in an on-chip Flash memory. In contrast, medium and large scale embedded systems such as smart phones, wireless routers or field level components of SCADA systems are based on more powerful controllers. Typically, they run a customized operating system (e.g. Linux) and the product-specific implementation of an embedded product often comprises custom kernel code, drivers and several applications. At the heart of these systems commonly lies a powerful System-On-Chip (SoC) controller that includes a CPU, ROM, SRAM and a number of internal peripherals and I/O controllers.

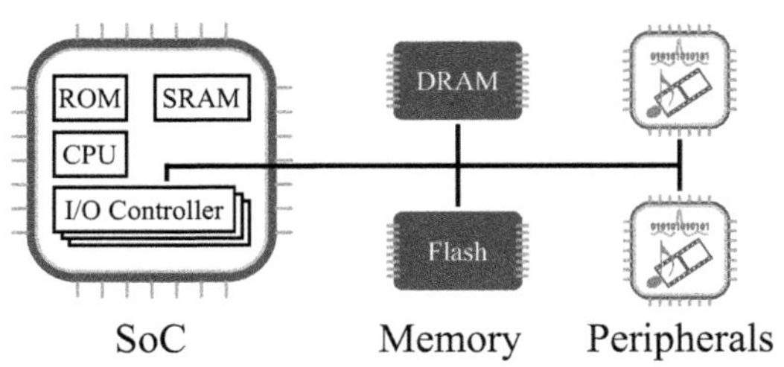

Figure 1: A Typical Medium to Large Scale Embedded System

A typical separation of components is shown in Figure 1. Upon power-up, the CPU in the SoC controller will execute the first-stage bootloader code contained in internal ROM and perform low-level initializations. After that, the SoC can access external memories (such as Flash and SDRAM) to boot into a second-stage bootloader and, consequently, into the operating system (OS) kernel. At that point, the OS can load a number of additional drivers to support external peripherals and then start the product specific processes. While the general operation of embedded systems is similar to PC systems, it is the external peripherals that make embedded systems so special. External peripherals are typically customly designed by the system manufacturers ranging from product specific sensors and actuators to custom communication interfaces. Taking modern smart phones as an example, such external peripherals could be charging controls, wireless radios, GPS receivers, magnetic or accelerations sensors, driving circuits for the vibrating alert, speech compression DSPs and many more. These external peripherals are what actually transforms an off-the-shelf SoC system into a valuable everyday product.

2.5 Challenges of Dynamic Code Analysis on Embedded Systems

In contrast to PC systems, employing dynamic analysis techniques on embedded systems can be more challenging. Typically, embedded devices are resource constrained, access to the file system is limited and the kernel's functionality and tools available on the device are just a minimal set of functions necessary for the product to operate properly [14]. The main reason for these constraints is that including additional functionality on the embedded systems would result in increased embedded resource requirements and ultimately in higher manufacturing costs. From this perspective, the presented analysis approaches for PC systems are hard to apply to their embedded counterparts:

1. Using a debugger to instrument the program is only feasible if the OS kernel includes debugging support (e.g. through `ptrace()` in the case of Linux). Running a state-of-the-art debugger on the system might not be possible due to resource constraints (e.g. in terms of memory consumption) or due to missing support (e.g on legacy systems or on systems where `ptrace()` support was not compiled into the kernel to save memory space).

2. Instrumenting the operating system would require kernel modifications or loading custom kernel modules. Embedded systems often run customized minimal kernel configurations to keep resource consumption and boot-up delays low. As a result, instrumenting the operating system might not be feasible.

3. Instrumenting the hardware would require not only virtualization of the system architecture, but also of all the necessary peripheral devices. However, as peripheral devices and their drivers are often proprietary, the information required to emulate them might not be publicly available. Besides, writing emulation code for all peripheral hardware devices would cause a tremendous overhead, considering that the analyst's goal is dynamic code analysis of only a small set of programs.

These challenges show that while on PC systems there is a wide range of established and well working vulnerability discovery techniques, the situation is different on embedded systems. In theory, all of those techniques could be applied to embedded systems as well. However, practically, embedded systems frequently lack support for these techniques and thus make it much harder to discover software vulnerabilities. We believe that this is also the reason, why static analysis techniques are still so prevalent for those systems.

3. PERIPHERAL DEVICE FORWARDING

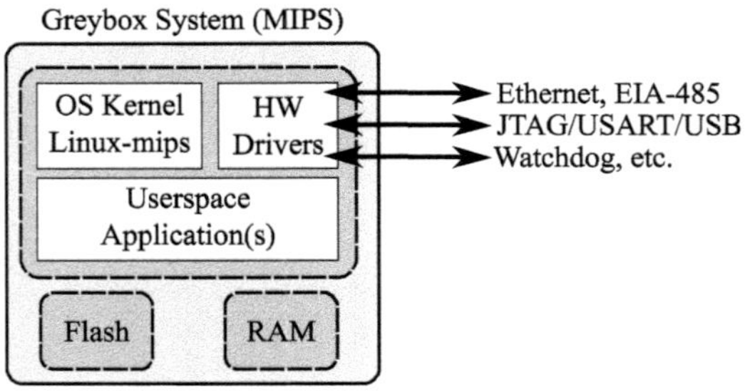

Figure 2: A typical Greybox System Example

Figure 2 shows a typical greybox embedded system example from a security analyst's point of view. The analyst's goal is to test one or more userspace applications on the embedded system for security vulnerabilities. This could, for instance, be a network daemon that is exposed to external attackers over a network connection. Yet, due to the challenges portrayed in Section 2, the analyst is unable to perform dynamic code analysis on the target system.

That is, the system lacks system resources, analysis tools are not available or can not be run and the userspace application, the analyst is interested in, can not be executed in a virtual environment as the peripheral hardware is missing there. However, one key observation is that userspace applications commonly communicate through character devices with potentially proprietary drivers and, consequently, with the peripheral hardware. Also, the communication interfaces to exchange data with the driver, and therefore with the kernel, are limited and can be considered standardized.

This is where PROSPECT comes into play. The basic idea of the system is to create virtual character devices inside another physical or virtual analysis environment. PROSPECT must intercept system calls used for communication with the character device from within the operating system kernel, forward them to the appropriate device on the embedded system and execute them there. Any responses need to be fed back to the analysis environment so that the intercepted system calls can return the data from the embedded remote system. Block devices, on the other hand, are generally used to access storage media which are emulated by the analysis virtual machine (i.e. qemu) anyways. To the analyst, PROSPECT constitutes a transparent forwarding solution for character device communication and thus allows her to conduct dynamic analysis techniques that were previously infeasible. Even software running on legacy systems lacking support for state-of-the-art analysis tools can be analyzed this way. As a result, PROSPECT allows to overcome typical challenges an embedded security analyst typically needs to face today.

3.1 Character Device Access

In order to forward peripheral hardware accesses, we need to know which system calls are generally used to interact with character devices. Targeting Linux systems, we gathered information on the supported `file_operations` of all included character device drivers in three different Linux kernel versions (Linux-2.4.20, Linux-2.6.38.1 and Linux-3.4.4) by analyzing the source code of all available drivers (514 files in total). We chose these specific kernel versions to get an idea which system calls are used to access character devices on legacy systems (i.e. Linux-2.4 and Linux-2.6) as well as on current kernel versions (i.e. Linux-3.4). Table 1 shows how many of the character device driver source code files actually define `file_operations`. It can be seen that the number of files decreases with newer kernels. We believe that this is due to increased abstraction in the Linux kernel requiring driver authors to write less supporting code.

Linux-2.4.20			Linux-2.6.38.1			Linux-3.4.4		
files	fops	fops %	files	fops	fops %	files	fops	fops %
264	77	29.17	143	62	43.36	107	54	50.47

Table 1: Analyzed Device Drivers on different Linux Kernel Versions

Table 2 shows which `file_operations` (i.e. which system calls) are used to interact with character device drivers in the different Linux kernel versions in relation to the number character device source code files. For instance, on Linux-2.4.20, there are 77 files that define `file_operations` and, out of these, 83.12% define a custom handler for the `open` system call. Some of the system calls in older kernel versions have been superseded by newer ones. For instance, the `ioctl` call in Linux-2.4.20 has been replaced by `unlocked_ioctl` and `compat_ioctl` for performance reasons in newer kernel versions.

Syscall	2.4.20	2.6.38.1	3.4.4
aio_fsync	-	0.00	0.00
aio_read	-	1.61	1.85
aio_write	-	1.61	1.85
check_flags	-	0.00	0.00
compat_ioctl	-	6.45	7.41
fallocate	-	0.00	0.00
fasync	28.57	11.29	12.96
flock	-	0.00	0.00
flush	14.29	-	-
fsync	0.00	3.23	3.70
get_unmapped_area	2.60	1.61	1.85
ioctl	84.42	-	-
llseek	6.49	32.26	29.63
lock	0.00	0.00	0.00
mmap	18.18	12.90	14.81
open	83.12	74.19	77.78
poll	32.47	20.97	25.93
read	68.83	82.26	85.19
readdir	0.00	0.00	0.00
readv	0.00	-	-
release	77.92	62.90	66.67
sendpage	0.00	0.00	0.00
setlease	-	0.00	0.00
splice_read	-	0.00	0.00
splice_write	-	0.00	0.00
unlocked_ioctl	-	51.61	50.00
write	62.34	50.00	55.56
writev	0.00	-	-

Table 2: Usage of Linux `file_operations` in Character Device Drivers (Percentage) for different Linux versions

In theory, PROSPECT could forward any of the system calls visible in Table 2. However, for performance reasons, it is beneficial to handle some of those calls locally. In fact, PROSPECT could execute system calls such as **flush**, **sync**, **fasync** or **aio_fsync** locally, if device access on the remote device is kept synchronized. Due to the delay imposed by the connection to the remote system, however, this would have a negligible effect. On the other side, system calls such as **splice_read**, that have been introduced for performance reasons, can use their regular counterparts (i.e. **read**) without breaking their basic functionality. With PROSPECT, we thus focus on *basic* character device operations that are broadly used by the majority of the character device drivers we analyzed. Specifically, PROSPECT can handle the **file_operations** listed in Table 3. The first column shows the name of the system call. For each system call, we specify if the system call is supported by PROSPECT, which system call is used to implement it and whether the call is handled locally or forwarded to the remote system.

Syscall	supported	implemented through	local/ remote
aio_fsync	yes	fsync	local
aio_read	yes	read	remote
aio_write	yes	write	remote
check_flags	no	-	-
compat_ioctl	yes	ioctl	remote
fallocate	no	-	-
fasync	yes	fsync	local
flock	no	-	-
flush	yes	fsync	local
fsync	yes	fsync	local
get_unmapped_area	no	-	-
ioctl	yes	ioctl	-
llseek	yes	llseek	remote
lock	no	-	-
mmap	no	-	-
open	yes	open	remote
poll	yes	poll	remote
read	yes	read	remote
readdir	no	-	-
readv	no	-	-
release	yes	release	remote
sendpage	no	-	-
setlease	no	-	-
splice_read	yes	read	remote
splice_write	yes	write	remote
unlocked_ioctl	yes	ioctl	remote
write	yes	write	remote
writev	no	-	-

Table 3: Basic file_operations supported by PROSPECT

With the exception of **mmap**, all operations that are frequently used for character device communication are supported. This is due to the fact that FUSE (Filesystem in Userspace) does not support direct **mmap** calls for character devices at the moment (see Section 7).

However, special consideration was necessary for the **ioctl** system call, as its exact behavior can frequently not be inferred prior to the actual execution.

3.2 IOCTL Mechanism and its Shortcomings

The IOCTL (I/O control) mechanism allows more flexibility in the communication with underlying device files. In general, there are two types of IOCTLs: Well-formed and unrestrictive IOCTLs. The difference is that well-formed IOCTLs have information about the type of the call encoded in the request number, whereas unrestricted IOCTLs do not provide this kind of information.

```
#define _IOC(dir,type,nr,size)    \
((dir << _IOC_DIRSHIFT)|(type << _IOC_TYPESHIFT)|\
 (nr  << _IOC_NRSHIFT) |(size << _IOC_SIZESHIFT))
```

Listing 1: Encoding for well-formed IOCTLs

Listing 1 shows how information such as the direction (e.g. read, write or none/execute), the request number or the amount of data (size) are encoded in the **ioctl** request parameter. By decoding this parameter prior to the actual **ioctl** call, it is possible to determine the direction of the data transfer and whether the provided parameter is a constant or a pointer to memory. In this case, PROSPECT could forward the request to the target system.

However, for unrestricted IOCTLs and prior to the actual **ioctl** execution, PROSPECT would have no way to determine the direction of the data, how much data should be transferred and whether a provided parameter is supposed to be a pointer or not. Since unrestricted IOCTLs are commonly used for device driver communication, we had to address this issue in the design of PROSPECT. We solved the challenge by introducing a concept we denote *Dynamic Memory Tunneling* which is described in Section 4.3.

4. IMPLEMENTATION

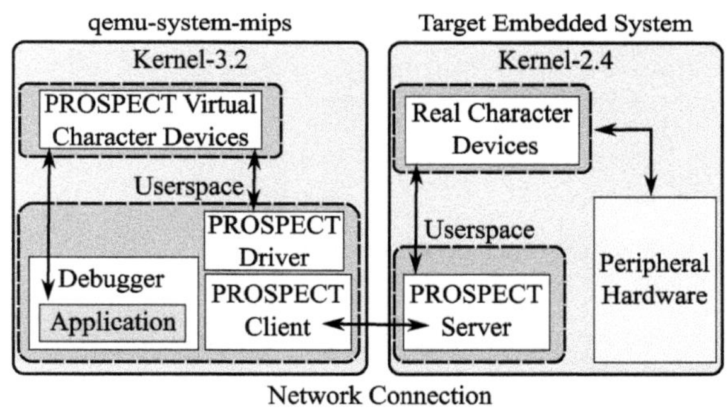

Figure 3: Peripheral Character Device Forwarding

As sketched in Sections 2.2 and 2.5, we assume that the analyst would like to dynamically instrument a binary on an embedded system that heavily accesses peripheral devices. While infeasible without PROSPECT, the application can now be executed inside an arbitrary analysis environment. Figure 3 provides a schematic overview of PROSPECT. On the left side, the application that should be analyzed is being executed within an arbitrary state-of-the-art debugger. However, instead of directly accessing the peripheral hardware through a character device, the application actually interacts with the *virtual* character devices that were generated through PROSPECT. At this point, PROSPECT intercepts the system calls defined in **file_operations** and forwards them to the userspace PROSPECT client. The client decides whether the system call should be executed locally or on the remote system. If remote execution is required, it communicates with the lightweight PROSPECT

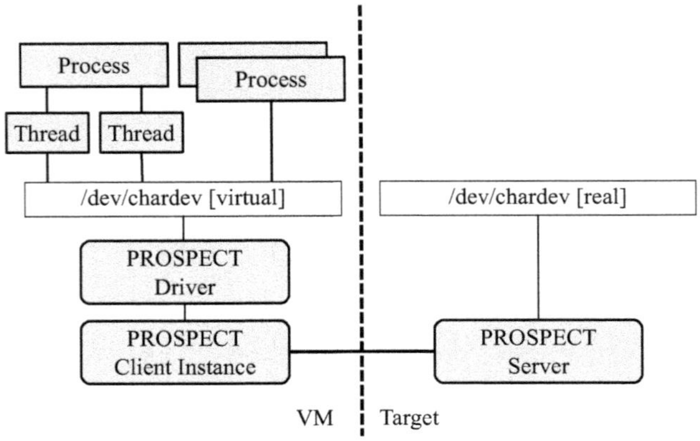

Figure 4: Concurrent Device Access

server on the target system. The server has very low system requirements and can thus be executed on a wide range of embedded systems. Once the system call has been executed on the target system, any results are fed back into the software application under analysis.

In order to generate virtual character devices and intercept system calls, parts of PROSPECT need to run in kernel context. While we could have realized all parts of PROSPECT in kernel space, we decided that the major part of our implementation should be in user space. In comparison to a full kernel space implementation, a user space centric implementation has the advantage of increased system stability, security and, most of all, more flexibility. We implemented PROSPECT from scratch and our overall implementation consists of roughly 7,500 lines of C code. In summary, PROSPECT comprises:

- A lightweight kernel driver utilizing the FUSE [15] kernel framework.
- A userspace driver combined with the PROSPECT client
- A lightweight server component running on the target system.

The PROSPECT lightweight server needs to be executed on the target system. Assuming that the security analyst typically has full physical access to the embedded device under test, we believe that this is a viable option. For instance, the analyst could use the bootloader console to get root level access to the operating system and then simply copy the PROSPECT statically linked binary to the device by using an attached storage medium or a networked remote machine as source.

Since our lightweight kernel driver utilizes the FUSE kernel framework, PROSPECT has the advantage that it is applicable to a wide range of operating systems, including Linux, FreeBSD, NetBSD, OpenSolaris, Android and OS X.

4.1 Concurrent Device Accesses

On typical embedded systems, a character device might be accessed by multiple threads or processes concurrently. Likewise, a single process or thread might interact with multiple devices at the same time. PROSPECT can handle these scenarios by using a client/server architecture (Figure 3) with multiple synchronization mechanisms. On the target system, there is a single PROSPECT server that can handle multiple incoming connections. Each client represents a character device that is forwarded to the target system, whereas each client can handle concurrent devices accesses by multiple threads and/or processes (Figure 4). PROSPECT relies on POSIX thread synchronization mechanisms (i.e. mutexes) to sustain the order of all accesses throughout the system.

4.2 File Descriptor Tracking

PROSPECT needs to keep track of file descriptors. Essentially, there are three cases we need to consider: (1) single processes, (2) child processes (i.e. created with `fork()`) and (3) threads. As file descriptors work on a per-process basis, they are only unique within the context of a process. Whenever a new process is spawned, new file descriptors returned by `open()` typically start at 3 (as 0,1 and 2 are already used for *stdin*, *stdout* and *stderr*, respectively). Considering two different processes, both processes may receive the same file descriptor (i.e. 3), but it may correspond to completely different files with different properties (e.g. file offsets or permissions). If a process uses `fork()` to spawn a child process, it will inherit all open file descriptors from its parent, but any new file descriptors it receives at a later point will be unique to the child process. In contrast, threads behave much like a single process, as all file descriptors they receive are shared between them. As a result, both the PROSPECT client as well as the server would need to be aware of the type of process or thread in order to emulate normal operating system behavior.

PROSPECT tackles this challenge by taking a different approach. Instead of emulating the behavior of a real system, it uses *globally unique* file descriptors on the server side and supplies them in a synchronized way to all clients. More specifically, we implemented the PROSPECT server as a single process but with multiple threads to handle different connections. For that reason, all file descriptors it receives from the target's OS kernel are unique within the server and, ultimately, within all PROSPECT clients and all processes and/or threads accessing virtual character devices as well.

4.3 Dynamic Memory Tunneling

In Section 3.2, we explained how the IOCTL mechanism is used for more flexible device driver communication. However, unlike well-formed IOCTLs, their unrestricted counterparts do not provide any data exchange information (i.e. information on direction and the amount of data that should be exchanged with the driver). As unrestricted IOCTLs are frequently used, we considered different approaches to address this challenge in PROSPECT.

Both, the userspace application(s) accessing a character device as well as the character device driver are aware of the parameters for unrestricted IOCTLs. A userspace application may not use all unrestricted IOCTLs the driver supports. However, the driver implementation always includes all supported unrestricted IOCTLs as well as the information on how data can be exchanged with them. Even better, device driver code is typically structured in a known way so that it can be loaded by the operating system. For that reason, we could extract the kernel image and device drivers from the target system and employ static (or even dynamic) code analysis techniques on the binaries to extract a data exchange rule-set for all available unrestricted IOCTLs. The drawback of this approach is that PROSPECT would need to be aware of operating system specifics (such as architecture, kernel version, kernel configuration, etc.). Thus, it would be hard to use PROSPECT on a wide range of different systems without major modifications. On the other side, extracting a rule-set from the userspace application, the analyst wants to work with, might be a challenge on its own (i.e. due to code size, program obfuscation or required manual code analysis).

Another approach we considered is that instead of extracting a rule set, PROSPECT could dynamically observe any unrestricted IOCTLs during program execution and learn from them. However, this is not always feasible, as the analysis would need to take place on the target system that does not necessarily support dynamic analysis in the first place. In fact, one of the goals of PROSPECT is to enable dynamic analysis on embedded systems, that might not support it for the reasons mentioned in Section 2.5.

Since any analysis required to gain information on unrestricted IOCTL parameters should not depend on the capabilities of the target system, we implemented *dynamic memory tunneling*. The key idea of dynamic memory tunneling is to always transfer a memory buffer to the target system if the IOCTL parameter is a possible pointer to a memory location. Accordingly, for each unrestricted IOCTL call, we need to answer the following questions:

- Is the parameter a valid pointer?
- How much data should be transferred to/from the target?

To determine whether the IOCTL parameter is a valid pointer, we use a heuristic. For each unrestricted IOCTL call, our system retrieves the PID (process ID) of the program that currently accesses the character device. For that PID it retrieves all mapped memory regions from the OS kernel (i.e. through `/proc/PID/maps`) and filters out any regions that are not suitable for a buffer (i.e. memory regions that are not read- and writable at the same time). If the parameter value is in one of the remaining memory regions, PROSPECT assumes that the parameter is a pointer and a data transfer with the target is initiated.

The question remains *how much* memory should be transferred to and from the target system. During our experiments we observed that the amount of data exchanged with unrestricted IOCTLs was below the page size (typically 4096 bytes on Linux) in all cases. To allow exceptions with larger buffer sizes, we experimentally limited the maximum size to 3*PAGESIZE = 12KiB. However, PROSPECT can be easily reconfigured with increased limits. Besides the configured limit, the amount of memory that is actually transferred, can be limited through the mapped memory region boundaries as well.

During execution, for any unrestricted IOCTL call with a valid pointer as parameter, PROSPECT takes the following steps:

1. Given the pointer address ADDR and the PID of the calling process, use the kernel driver to read up to 3*PAGESIZE bytes from the mapped memory region of the corresponding userspace process.
2. Transfer the buffer to the PROSPECT server on the target system and execute the unrestricted IOCTL call on a local copy of the transferred buffer.
3. Once `ioctl()` returns, compare the transferred buffer with the potentially modified local copy of the buffer to determine how many bytes were changed in the local copy.
4. In addition to the `ioctl()` *return* and *errno* values, send back the content of the local copy buffer to the corresponding client. The size of the transfer is limited through the last byte in the buffer that has actually changed (see Step 3).
5. Given the pointer address ADDR and the PID of the calling process, use the kernel driver to overwrite the corresponding memory region of the userspace process (i.e. starting at ADDR) with the content of the response buffer.
6. Return the `ioctl()` *return* and *errno* values to the calling process.

Through dynamic memory tunneling, PROSPECT can forward unrestricted IOCTLs with arbitrary read, write and execute operations.

5. EVALUATION

To provide a well-founded discussion of our system, we evaluated PROSPECT in two ways. First, we collected system call timing information to determine the performance impact PROSPECT causes in comparison with the native system. Second, we conducted a case study over more than 6 months by running a full-scale security audit of a widely used commercial fire alarm system in the building automation domain.

5.1 Evaluation of Performance Impact

On a 324 MHz embedded Linux MIPS system with 16MiB RAM, we used the *strace* tool to collect timing information for the system calls that are used for basic character device access (see Table 3 in Section 3.1 for details). Table 4 shows the userspace system calls we monitored.

Operation	Function
`close()`	Close device
`ioctl()`	I/O Control mechanism
`lseek()`	Seek to a given position
`_newselect()`	System call used for `poll()`
`open()`	Open device
`read()`	Read data from device
`write()`	Write data to device

Table 4: System Calls used for Character Device Access

To collect timing information, we ran a userspace application that makes heavy use of all of the system calls in Table 4. In order to determine how much longer the forwarded system calls take, we ran the application with PROSPECT in our analysis environment (qemu-system-mips) as well as natively on the embedded MIPS system. For both executions we used *strace* to create system call logs with timing

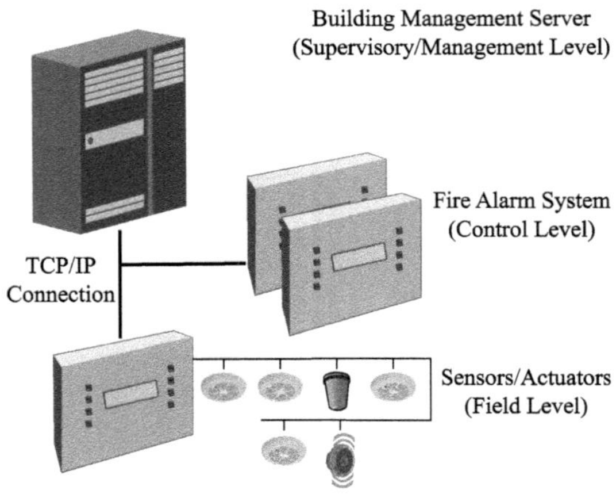

Figure 5: Proprietary Fire Alarm System

information. For our measurements we collected timing information for 196,075 system calls on the analysis environment and for 166,972 system calls on the embedded MIPS system. To compare the execution time of the system calls, we created custom analysis scripts to keep track of the file descriptors. This way, we were able to consider only timing information for calls made on character devices that are forwarded when PROSPECT is used. The results are visible in Table 5 in Section 6.1.

5.2 Case Study: Security Audit of a Proprietary Fire Alarm System

Under a legally binding non-disclosure agreement, we were able to employ PROSPECT to conduct a full-scale security audit of a widely used fire alarm system over a time frame of more than 6 months. A schematic overview of the overall fire alarm system is visible in Figure 5. On the lower side of the picture there is the fire alarm system that has a field level bus with a number of sensors (such as smoke detectors) and actuators (such as alarm lights or sirens) attached to it. Typically, there is one fire alarm system in a building and the sensors/actuators are situated in the rooms or on the outside of each building. Each fire alarm system is connected over a network connection (i.e. via TCP/IP) to one central building management server that is responsible for all fire alarm systems in multiple buildings. Thus, the server can manage the fire alarm systems and necessary steps can be taken in case there is a fire alarm. From the security perspective, the TCP/IP connection between the fire alarm systems and the building management server is interesting. After all, if an attacker could get access to the fire alarm systems over the building network or even the Internet, it might be possible to trigger false alarms or to disable fire alarms which would lead to a dangerous situation for the persons in the building.

On a technical level, the fire alarm system we analyzed is a customized embedded Linux system with custom drivers, custom peripheral hardware components and several proprietary userspace programs that make up the overall fire alarm system implementation. The userspace programs make heavy use of multi-threading (pthreads) and the `fork` mechanism. In the running state, there is a total of 29 multi-threaded fire-alarm system specific processes, spawning multiple threads depending on the handled networking communication. In total, there are 5 different hardware peripherals that are accessed concurrently by the different processes and threads. As soon as the whole system is up and running, any network communication is processed. The system resources are very limited and the fire alarm implementation consumes nearly all available resources.

Due to the resource constraints, it is not possible to run a debugger on the system. Thus, dynamic analysis on the device is not possible either and the code that handles the network communication cannot be analyzed in another environment, as the device specific peripheral hardware would be missing there. As a result, the software application(s) would not start up in the first place. In this case, the analyst would be limited to static analysis and/or very basic security testing techniques.

To conduct a security audit of the fire alarm system implementation that handles the network communication, we employed PROSPECT to run the fire alarm system software implementation inside a virtual analysis environment. In this case, we utilized *qemu*, an open source virtualization environment that also supports the MIPS architecture. The center of Figure 6 shows the multi threaded userspace application with all connected installations for a complete analysis. It concurrently interacts with 5 different peripheral devices which are handled by multiple PROSPECT client instances, each handling exactly one character device. For automated fuzz testing of the network protocol implementation, we set up three different machines. On the left, there is the Fire Alarm Control VM that runs the manufacturer's software to communicate with the fire alarm system over a network connection. We used this machine to generate network traffic and capture it (*Packet Capture*) to obtain packets that can be used as input data for our fuzzer. Accordingly, the fuzzer can generate randomized traffic that looks very similar to the original communication protocol by taking packets from the captured network traffic, randomizing a single byte at a random position within the packet each test run and replaying the communication towards the userspace application under test. This allows us to use a single fuzzer implementation for a broad range of proprietary network protocols without the need to know protocol specifics or the requirement to develop a new fuzzer for each protocol. The downside of this approach is the limitation of the test cases to the captured network communication: If feasible protocol states are not captured during the capture phase, our fuzzer will not be able to test them. At the same time, we used a debug server to run the userspace applications we want to analyze. Through the Debugger VM (with a state-of-the-art debugger), the fuzzer can thus monitor the state of the software application and whether the test packets it sent, caused an exception such as a memory access violation. In this case, the fuzzer stores the network packets that led to the exception for later (manual) analysis.

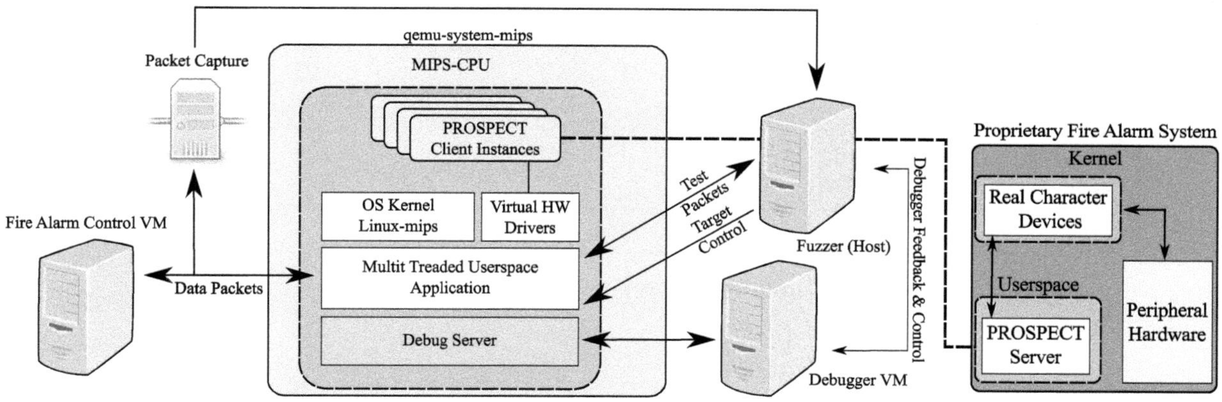

Figure 6: Security Analysis Environment

6. RESULTS AND DISCUSSION

6.1 Performance Impact

Table 5 shows the average performance impact of our system (Section 5.1). The values are arithmetic means over all recorded system calls. More specifically, the average number of `read()` accesses is the average of all read accesses from 166,972 native and 196,075 forwarded system calls, respectively. It clearly shows that for system calls that can be forwarded without further consideration (i.e. `lseek()`, `read()`, `write()` and `_newselect()`), the slowdown is practically insignificant as the main use of PROSPECT is program debugging (i.e. single stepping) and dynamic code analysis. Our results show that with PROSPECT the `_newselect()` call was slightly faster than on the native system. This is due to the nature of the system call. It blocks as long as either the given timeout is reached or one of the monitored file descriptors is ready. As this is closely related to the behavior of peripheral hardware (e.g. sleep modes), small variances in the recorded values are unavoidable.

In contrast, the `ioctl()` and `open()` calls cause a significant slowdown. The `ioctl()` slowdown is caused by the dynamic memory tunneling mechanism described in Section 4.3 whereas the `open()` slowdown is due to the connection establishment between the PROSPECT client and server. On the virtual analysis environment, we were unable to capture `close()` calls on virtual character devices which is why we can not provide a performance comparison. However, as `close()` also works on an existing PROSPECT connection and no special considerations are necessary for the call, we believe that the performance impact is comparable to the `lseek()`, `read()`, `write()` and `_newselect()` calls. Furthermore, Table 5 also lists the frequency of each specific system call. It shows that the most frequently used calls are also the fastest. For instance, `write()`, `read()`, `seek()` and `_newselect()` account for 95,71% of all forwarded system calls. The distribution between system calls for native and forwarded execution slightly varied between analysis runs due to the internal state of the peripheral hardware.

6.2 Proprietary Fire Alarm System Security Audit

During our fire alarm security analysis (Section 5.2), we conducted extensive fuzz testing with the setup shown in Figure 6. During analysis, PROSPECT successfully forwarded more than 500,000 system calls per analysis run to the target system without issues. Likewise, we were able to manually debug and single-step through the fire alarm application code. Our fuzz tests revealed a previously unknown zero-day vulnerability that was reported to the manufacturer. Our case study shows that even under demanding real-life requirements (29 multi-threaded processes that concurrently access 5 different hardware peripherals), our system performed well and enabled us to conduct both dynamic analysis and extensive fuzz testing to discover vulnerabilities.

7. LIMITATIONS AND FUTURE WORK

Due to the nature of PROSPECT, it has a number of limitations that need to be considered. At the moment, our system uses TCP/IP over a network connection between the virtual analysis system and the embedded target system. However, if the userspace application under analysis changes the network configuration, this would also bring down the PROSPECT connection. Similarly, if the target system has no network interface, PROSPECT can not be used. We plan to add support for different communication interfaces (such as serial links) to PROSPECT so that it is usable in these cases as well. Another limitation is that PROSPECT requires *pthreads* on the target system and only runs on Linux right now. Another limitation is the missing `mmap` support for character devices due to the missing support in FUSE. Since `mmap` calls can be forwarded just the same (i.e. by using a similar approach as described in Section 4.3), we plan to implement full `mmap` support in future versions.

As PROSPECT requires only very little supported functionality on the target system and FUSE has been ported to a number of operating systems (Section 3), our system could be easily ported to different architectures and operating systems as well. At least for some implementations, the considerable slowdown caused by PROSPECT might lead to issues. However, this situation also occurs when single-stepping through programs and solutions, such as altering the information returned by timing related system calls, exist. Also, our system does not provide any security features at the moment.

Another consideration was briefly discussed in Section 3. When accessing devices on UNIX systems, their access rights are determined by the device's permissions. The client implementation needs to create virtual character devices and

Syscall	Native [%]	Native [ms]	Fwd. [%]	Fwd. [ms]	Diff. [ms]	Slowdown [x]
`write()`	21.27	6.07	22.79	25.39	19.32	3.18
`lseek()`	28.14	0.12	18.88	2.31	2.2	18.65
`ioctl()`	1.6	0.89	4.27	117.15	116.26	130.37
`_newselect()`	14.8	43.27	17.14	40.85	-2.41	-0.06
`read()`	34.16	1.03	36.9	3.29	2.26	2.19
`close()`	0.01	0.1	0.0	N/A	N/A	N/A
`poll()`	0.0	N/A	0.0	N/A	N/A	N/A
`open()`	0.02	0.9	0.02	684.62	683.72	757.37

Table 5: PROSPECT Slowdown

therefore requires root privileges. In contrast, the PROSPECT server can be run as any user on the target system. It is however recommended to run it as root, simply to ensure that all devices are accessible. Through PROSPECT, the investigated process inherits the device access permissions from the server. As a result, it could be possible for an investigated process to access devices even though that would not be possible under normal circumstances. This property is not necessarily a limitation per se, as it constitutes an additional possibility to influence system behavior during analysis.

With regard to the high slowdown for unrestricted `ioctl()` calls, our implementation still provides room for improvement. For instance in future implementations, instead of querying the */proc* file system, we could implement a more efficient mechanism to minimize execution time.

8. RELATED WORK

When dealing with security analysis on embedded systems, most research approaches use static analysis to achieve their goal. For instance, Khare et al. presented some of the key problems that need to be faced when using static analysis techniques on a large embedded code base [9]. In their work they focus on the static analysis of source code to improve the overall security of embedded systems.

In contrast, Ramakrishnan and Gopal do not require access to source code as their static program analysis techniques run on embedded binaries [22]. However, they do not focus on embedded security or vulnerability discovery.

In [18], Zili Shao et al. introduce a mixed hardware/-software system to check for and protect embedded systems from buffer overflow attacks. Their system works during program execution, but is more focused on vulnerability protection than on vulnerability discovery.

In [21], Sumpf and Brakensiek introduced device driver isolation within virtualized embedded platforms. The approach presented here can be considered the most closely related system compared to PROSPECT. The authors created device drivers with a generalized interface to provide homogeneous access for virtual machines. In contrast to PROSPECT, however, the implementation of the driver must be known. Furthermore their system is limited to L4 microkernels and not suitable for unknown peripheral devices.

9. CONCLUSION

PROSPECT turned out to be a valuable tool that enabled us to conduct a full-scale dynamic security analysis of a widely used fire alarm system. Without PROSPECT, dynamic analysis would have been infeasible due to the limitations of the fire alarm embedded system. We believe that PROSPECT's approach has a high practical impact. It allows to overcome the limitations of static analysis that are common for embedded vulnerability discovery. The general concept is applicable to a wide range of embedded systems, including smart phones or field level SCADA components.

10. ACKNOWLEDGEMENTS

The research leading to these results has received funding from the Austrian Research Promotion Agency (FFG) under grants 836276 (SG2), 834005 (Fire-IP) and the European Union Seventh Framework Programme under grant agreement n. 257007 (SysSec). We would like to thank the anonymous reviewers for their helpful feedback and improvement suggestions. We would like to thank Trustworks [12] for providing valuable insights and tools that made this research possible.

11. REFERENCES

[1] A. Austin and L. Williams. One technique is not enough: A comparison of vulnerability discovery techniques. In *Empirical Software Engineering and Measurement (ESEM), 2011 International Symposium on*, pages 97–106, 2011.

[2] S. Bekrar, C. Bekrar, R. Groz, and L. Mounier. Finding software vulnerabilities by smart fuzzing. In *Software Testing, Verification and Validation (ICST), 2011 IEEE Fourth International Conference on*, pages 427–430, 2011.

[3] D. Brylow, N. Damgaard, and J. Palsberg. Static checking of interrupt-driven software. In *Proceedings of the 23rd International Conference on Software Engineering*, ICSE '01, pages 47–56, Washington, DC, USA, 2001. IEEE Computer Society.

[4] S. K. Cha, T. Avgerinos, A. Rebert, and D. Brumley. Unleashing mayhem on binary code. In *Security and Privacy (SP), 2012 IEEE Symposium on*, pages 380–394, 2012.

[5] W. Drewry and T. Ormandy. Flayer: Exposing application internals, 2007.

[6] T. Garfinkel and M. Rosenblum. A virtual machine introspection based architecture for intrusion detection. In *In Proc. Network and Distributed Systems Security Symposium*, pages 191–206, 2003.

[7] S. Karnouskos. Stuxnet worm impact on industrial cyber-physical system security. In *IECON 2011 - 37th Annual Conference on IEEE Industrial Electronics Society*, pages 4490–4494, 2011.

[8] M. Kermani, M. Zhang, A. Raghunathan, and N. Jha. Emerging frontiers in embedded security. In *VLSI Design and 2013 12th International Conference on Embedded Systems (VLSID), 2013 26th International Conference on*, pages 203–208, 2013.

[9] S. Khare, S. Saraswat, and S. Kumar. Static program analysis of large embedded code base: an experience. In *Proceedings of the 4th India Software Engineering Conference*, ISEC '11, pages 99–102, New York, NY, USA, 2011. ACM.

[10] P. Koopman. Embedded system security. *Computer*, 37(7):95–97, July 2004.

[11] B. Liu, L. Shi, Z. Cai, and M. Li. Software vulnerability discovery techniques: A survey. In *Multimedia Information Networking and Security (MINES), 2012 Fourth International Conference on*, pages 152–156, 2012.

[12] Trustworks KG. *http://www.trustworks.at (retrieved 2013-04-17)*, 2013.

[13] A. Moser, C. Kruegel, and E. Kirda. Exploring multiple execution paths for malware analysis. In *Proceedings of the 2007 IEEE Symposium on Security and Privacy*, SP '07, pages 231–245, Washington, DC, USA, 2007. IEEE Computer Society.

[14] S. Parameswaran and T. Wolf. Embedded systems security-an overview. *Design Automation for Embedded Systems*, 12(3):173–183, 2008.

[15] F. Project. Filesystem in userspace. *http://fuse.sourceforge.net/ (retrieved 2013-04-17)*, 2013.

[16] E. Schwartz, T. Avgerinos, and D. Brumley. All you ever wanted to know about dynamic taint analysis and forward symbolic execution (but might have been afraid to ask). In *Security and Privacy (SP), 2010 IEEE Symposium on*, pages 317–331, 2010.

[17] K. Serebryany, D. Bruening, A. Potapenko, and D. Vyukov. Addresssanitizer: a fast address sanity checker. In *Proceedings of the 2012 USENIX conference on Annual Technical Conference*, USENIX ATC'12, pages 28–28, Berkeley, CA, USA, 2012. USENIX Association.

[18] Z. Shao, C. Xue, Q. Zhuge, M. Qiu, B. Xiao, and E. H.-M. Sha. Security protection and checking for embedded system integration against buffer overflow attacks via hardware/software. *IEEE Transactions on Computers*, 55(4):443–453, 2006.

[19] K. V. Shibu. *Introduction To Embedded Systems*. McGraw-Hill Education, 2009.

[20] B. Stone-Gross, M. Cova, L. Cavallaro, B. Gilbert, M. Szydlowski, R. Kemmerer, C. Kruegel, and G. Vigna. Your botnet is my botnet: analysis of a botnet takeover. In *Proceedings of the 16th ACM conference on Computer and communications security*, CCS '09, pages 635–647, New York, NY, USA, 2009. ACM.

[21] S. Sumpf and J. Brakensiek. Device driver isolation within virtualized embedded platforms. In *Consumer Communications and Networking Conference, 2009. CCNC 2009. 6th IEEE*, pages 1–5, 2009.

[22] R. Venkitaraman and G. Gupta. Static program analysis of embedded executable assembly code. In *Proceedings of the 2004 international conference on Compilers, architecture, and synthesis for embedded systems*, CASES '04, pages 157–166, New York, NY, USA, 2004. ACM.

[23] J. Viega and H. Thompson. The state of embedded-device security (spoiler alert: It's bad). *Security Privacy, IEEE*, 10(5):68–70, 2012.

[24] C. Willems, T. Holz, and F. Freiling. Toward automated dynamic malware analysis using cwsandbox. *Security Privacy, IEEE*, 5(2):32–39, 2007.

Scanning of Real-world Web Applications for Parameter Tampering Vulnerabilities

Adonis P.H. Fung[†], Tielei Wang[‡], K.W. Cheung[†], and T.Y. Wong[†]

[†] The Chinese University of Hong Kong, Shatin, NT, Hong Kong

[‡] Georgia Institute of Technology, Atlanta, GA, USA

phfung@ie.cuhk.edu.hk,tielei@gatech.edu,{kwcheung@ie,tywong@cse}.cuhk.edu.hk

ABSTRACT

Web applications require exchanging parameters between a client and a server to function properly. In real-world systems such as online banking transfer, traversing multiple pages with parameters contributed by both the user and server is a must, and hence the applications have to enforce workflow and parameter dependency controls across multiple requests. An application that applies insufficient server-side input validations is however vulnerable to parameter tampering attacks, which manipulate the exchanged parameters. Existing fuzzing-based scanning approaches however neglected these important controls, and this caused their fuzzing requests to be dropped before they can reach any vulnerable code.

In this paper, we propose a novel approach to identify the workflow and parameter dependent constraints, which are then maintained and leveraged for automatic detection of server acceptances during fuzzing. We realized the approach by building a generic blackbox parameter tampering scanner. It successfully uncovered a number of severe vulnerabilities, including one from the largest multi-national banking website, which other scanners miss.

Categories and Subject Descriptors

H.3.5 [**Online Information Services**]: Web-based services; K.4.4 [**Electronic Commerce**]: Security

Keywords

parameter tampering; parameter dependency; in-context fuzzing; state-aware fuzzing

1. INTRODUCTION

Web applications typically require traversing multiple pages with parameters exchanged between a client and a server to complete even a single action. Figure 1 depicts a simplified workflow of an online banking transfer application used by the HSBC bank, in which a user can transfer a certain amount of money (i.e., `AMT`) from his account `FROM` only to an authorized account `TO`. While user-supplied transaction details (i.e.,`FROM`, `TO`, `AMT`) are taken from input elements of a form, those server-generated ones such as session ID (`SESSID`) and the one-time use tokens working against Cross-Site Request Forgeries ($\text{CSRF}_{1\&2}$) are respectively set in Cookies and hidden fields. In Step_A, client-side validations are applied to restrict and instantly prompt the user for input corrections before the form can be submitted. Upon a valid submission, the ServHandler_A verifies the CSRF_1 token, validates the user inputs, and responds with a review page for Step_B. The user confirms the transaction by submitting Req_B, and finally the ServHandler_B executes the actual banking transfer and returns an acknowledgment page for user's reference at Step_C. It is worth noting that ServHandler_B enforces, among others, that the received token CSRF_2 and `TO` account respectively match with their previously stored values (i.e., $\texttt{sess.CSRF}_2$ and `sess.TO`).

ASIA CCS'14, June 4–6, 2014, Kyoto, Japan.

ACM 978-1-4503-2800-5/14/06 ...$15.00.

http://dx.doi.org/10.1145/2590296.2590324 .

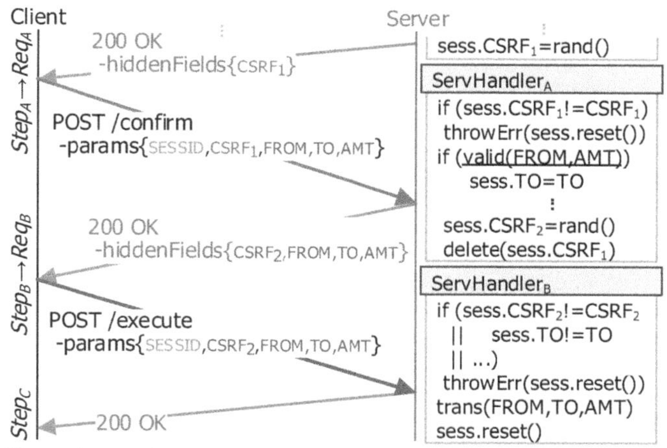

Figure 1: A vulnerable banking transfer application enforces workflow and parameter dependency controls across multiple requests

Such kind of web applications are however vulnerable to parameter tampering that is known to attack insecure direct object references, which is ranked No. 4 in the OWASP Top 10 Web Application Security Risks [26]. The vulnerability often arises from a misconception that the object references directly exposed as parameters to the client-side (and their validations) are assumed immutable, and thus improper or insufficient validations were applied at the server [10]. As shown in the motivating example, the server does not validate whether the `TO` account is authorized (i.e., `TO` is missing at `valid(FROM,AMT)` in ServHandler_A). Hence, an attacker who has compromised a victim's session can tamper the `TO` parameter and bypass any associated client-side validations in order to commit unauthorized banking transfers.

The parameter tampering vulnerability revealed above is however hardly discoverable despite many research efforts that were dedicated to web vulnerability scanning [5,7–9,11,13,29,32]. There are two fundamental reasons. First, blackbox fuzzing-based scanners such as [1,7,20,25] cannot preserve the intended workflow. It is because they literally work in a "crawl-once-fuzz-many" manner, that captures a set of requests only once during crawling, and these requests will become the only bases to generate subsequent fuzzing requests. However, the one-time use tokens such as $\text{CSRF}_{1\&2}$ expire as soon as they are accepted by the server during crawling. Regardless of how parameters are mutated, subsequent fuzzing attempts that reuse such expired tokens will all be rejected.

Second, existing blackbox scanners neglect cross-request parameter dependencies. To uncover the vulnerbility in the banking example, the `TO` account from Req_A and the one later sent in Req_B must be equal. It is because ServHandler_A stores the user-supplied parameter `TO` from Req_A into `sess.TO`. When receiving Req_B, ServHandler_B enforces that `TO` in Req_B must match with the stored `sess.TO`. If they are different, Req_B will be rejected before any parameters can reach the vulnerable code. None of the blackbox fuzzing tools can identify this constraint and maintain the required parameter dependencies across the requests. While a state-aware fuzzer is recently proposed to observe the workflow control [11], its fuzzing requests are still insensitive towards cross-request dependencies. For other approaches that consider parameter relationships [33,34], they are largely manual and protocol-specific.

This paper presents Cross-Request Scanner (CRS), a novel approach that respects and leverages the intended workflow and parameter dependency controls while scanning for parameter tampering vulnerabilities. CRS consists of two phases: capturing and fuzzing. In the capturing phase, CRS records a set of valid user actions, identifies the one-time tokens, tracks the cross-request parameter dependencies, and learns key features (e.g., locations of submit buttons and reflected parameters) that indicate a server acceptance from rendered server responses.

In the fuzzing phase, CRS sequentially replays the user actions to fetch new responses while keeping those confirmed one-time and dependent parameters intact so as to preserve the intended workflow and parameter dependency. Other parameters are mutated and placed back to the application itself for validations. Only those client-side rejected parameters are then forcefully submitted by bypassing client-side validations. Finally, it reports a vulnerability if the server accepts the mutated parameters and gives responses that are in line with those key features learned in the initial valid submissions (e.g., submit buttons reappeared, parameters reflected).

While CRS takes a set of manually provided user actions, we argue that it is unavoidable in discovering parameter tampering vulnerabilities (i.e., unlike discovering XSS by simply asserting a popup dialog after an injection of what comprises `alert(1)`). Referring to the banking example, a parameter tampering vulnerability can be resulted by mutating only a digit in the `TO` account. Therefore, it is clear that the semantic meaning and underlying consequence of a mutation can be domain-specific, and thus known only to humans. Existing work also corroborate the needs of manual effort [12,34]. CRS requires the least amount of manual assistance among blackbox parameter tampering scanners [1,7,20,25].

The contributions of this paper are as follows:

- A field study on online banking applications to understand their workflow and implementations, and how they can be intercepted for vulnerability scanning.
- A novel approach that respects the intended workflow and cross-request parameter dependency while fuzzing, as well as to correlate the dependency in both requests and responses for automatic detection of server acceptances.
- An "in-context fuzzing" technique to build a blackbox vulnerability scanner that drives fuzzing in the application context allowing dynamic features to be preserved, and thus improving coverage and accuracy.
- The discovery of real-world vulnerabilities that are uncovered only by our scanner, which existing approaches miss.

The rest of this paper is organized as follows: Section 2 describes the online banking transfer applications of different banks. Section 3 discusses the CRS approach. Section 4 provides some technical background on the web applications, followed by the implementation of the CRS scanner. Section 5 evaluates the scanner, and details the vulnerabilities uncovered. Section 6 presents related work. Finally, we conclude.

2. MOTIVATING EXAMPLES

This paper focuses on real-world applications, and that makes the testing intrinsically blackbox and more challenging owing to the lack of server-side source code. This section summarizes four representative banking transfer applications, which are among the most security-critical operations being carried out over the Internet. They include Citibank, HSBC, Bank of China (BOC), and Bank of East Asia (BEA), with their headquarters respectively located at the US, UK, China, and Hong Kong. The unauthorized transfers that are made possible in HSBC and BEA are discussed in Section 5.3.

2.1 Workflow Design

As outlined in Figure 1, all banks adopt a three-step workflow design to receive instructions of banking transfers.

Step_A. A user specifies a source (i.e., `FROM`) and a destination (i.e., `TO`) account besides setting an amount (i.e., `AMT`) to transfer. The government mandates that the user can transfer his money only to third-party accounts that are authorized through an out-of-band channel. HSBC accepts unauthorized accounts to be specified in this step, and provides on-the-fly authorization in the next step, as shown in Figure 3. Citibank and BOC users can pre-authorize an account beforehand in a separate online form with an One-Time Password (OTP) that is received through SMS. BEA offers only offline authorization (i.e., must register an account by person in a physical branch). Finally, the user submits Req_A by clicking "Go".

Step_B. The user reviews the transaction details returned by the server. If an HSBC user has specified an unauthorized account in Step_A, he needs to enter an OTP token from his own hardware device for on-the-fly authorization, as detailed in Section 5.3.1. The user finally submits again by clicking "confirm" to send Req_B.

Step_C. The transfer instruction is acknowledged with a transaction number. The transaction details are shown for user's reference.

2.2 Workflow Implementation

Notably, HSBC, BOC and BEA implement each step of the workflow in a separate page, while Citibank integrates all steps in a single AJAX page with the use of `XMLHttpRequest` API. Their workflow implementations are outlined as follows:

Step_A. Client-side code is implemented to restrict the user-supplied input parameters (i.e., `FROM`, `TO`, `AMT`) before they can be submitted (as Req_A) together with a CSRF_1 token that is server-generated and placed in a hidden field. All banks apply some client-side pre-processing (e.g., manipulating values of hidden fields) before validating and submitting the form. The submission approaches vary from one bank to another, as detailed in Section 4.1.2.

ServHandler_A. The server verifies whether the CSRF_1 token matches with what was previously stored. Upon validating other parameters that represent the transaction details, the server stores them temporarily. Finally, it returns a review page in which a newly generated CSRF_2 token is embedded in a hidden field. Notice that

Table 1: The website features that are essential for effective fuzzing by blackbox web vulnerability scanners

	Websites Studied							Param. Tampering Scanners			Web Vulnerability Scanners	
	HSBC	BEA	BOC	HSB	Citibank	Webjet	Jetstar	CRS	NoTamper [7]	Proxy-based [1, 20, 25]	Traditional [2, 31]	State-aware [11]
Multi-request Applications	√	√	√	√	√	√		√			√	√
AJAX Applications					√	√	√	√		√		
Workflow Enforcement	√	√	√	√	√	√		√				√
One-time Use Tokens	√	√	√	√	√			√				
Parameter Dependency	√		√	√		√		√				
Client-side Pre-processing	√	√	√	√	√			√				

besides defending against CSRF, both $\text{CSRF}_{1\&2}$ tokens can also serve the purposes of enforcing the intended workflow and preventing duplicate transactions owing to their nature of one-time uses.

Step$_B$. It echoes all transaction-related parameters visually for user's review, and that a confirming click will naturally include the hidden CSRF_2 token in the submission Req_B. In HSBC, an OTP parameter may be solicited for account authorization. For HSBC and BOC, this step also serves to resubmit those transaction parameters gathered from Step_A by embedding them in hidden fields.

ServHandler$_B$. The server again verifies the CSRF_2 token beforehand. In HSBC, the OTP parameter, if provided, will then be verified. HSBC and BOC further ensure if some transaction-related parameters match with those stored at ServHandler_A. The server finally executes the transfer with the transaction parameters.

Step$_C$. The transaction details and a reference number are shown.

2.3 Intrinsic Limitations of Existing Scanners

We verify that the banks enforce the workflow design and parameter dependency across requests by empirically and systematically running a series of experiments in their banking transfer applications. We first interact with an application through its user interface (UI), and capture a pair of submission requests from a valid transaction, which is referred to as $\{\text{Req}_{A.o}, \text{Req}_{B.o}\}$. Next, we prepare a mutated pair of requests $\{\text{Req}_{A.m}, \text{Req}_{B.m}\}$, in which all `AMT` parameters are incremented by "1".

Neglecting Intended Workflow and One-time Tokens. With this mutated set of requests, we however found that they were all rejected by the server through the following experiments. First of all, the requests were replayed according to a sequence of a few $\text{Req}_{A.m}$s and then some $\text{Req}_{B.m}$s, of which the sequence obviously violates the intended workflow. The requests were all rejected. We then proceed to sequentially replay $\{\text{Req}_{A.m}, \text{Req}_{B.m}, \text{Req}_{A.m}, \text{Req}_{B.m}\}$, but they were still rejected despite observing the workflow.

The server actually responds differently to requests that are initiated by re-interacting with the application as usual. Therefore, when we interact with the UI and specify the same user-supplied values (including the incremented `AMT`) as in those mutated requests, the new requests are accepted as expected. We investigated all the requests generated through multiple times of UI interactions. We then found some distinct server-generated tokens were introduced to every request. Since replaying $\text{Req}_{A.o}$ that was once accepted by the server would result in a failure, we conclude that these tokens are of one-time uses.

Breaking Cross-request Parameter Dependency. As discussed in Section 5.3.1, it is found that HSBC and BOC submit some transaction-related and other parameters twice in both Req_A and Req_B. To understand the relationship between the parameters, we thus run the remaining three possible pairs of request combinations $\{\text{Req}_{A.o}, \text{Req}_{B.m}\}$, $\{\text{Req}_{A.m}, \text{Req}_{B.o}\}$, and $\{\text{Req}_{A.m}, \text{Req}_{B.m}\}$, in which the one-time tokens are observed. Here, all transaction-related parameters are "slightly" mutated one by one.

- When running $\{\text{Req}_{A.o}, \text{Req}_{B.m}\}$, it is found that some parameters mutated only at $\text{Req}_{B.m}$ are actually disregarded, while their corresponding values given at $\text{Req}_{A.o}$ are instead honored by the server. This result shows that these parameters must be mutated at Req_A during fuzzing. Mutating them at $\text{Req}_{B.m}$ can be ineffective.
- For $\{\text{Req}_{A.m}, \text{Req}_{B.o}\}$, server rejections are resulted since some parameter values are inconsistent between the request pair. Clearly, the server enforces certain parameters to be equal across the requests.
- Likewise, for $\{\text{Req}_{A.m}, \text{Req}_{B.m}\}$, server rejections depend on whether some parameters are mutated in such a way that the required dependency are broken across both requests.

In a nutshell, existing scanners [1, 2, 7, 11, 20, 25, 31] all suffer from these limitations despite the prevalence of multi-request applications. The limitations are generic and intrinsic to all web vulnerability scanners. Hence, most attack vectors in their fuzzing attempts are incapable of reaching the vulnerable code.

These findings are confirmed by running the publicly available scanners [1,2,20,25,31], and analyzing their fuzzing patterns against a banking transfer website mimicked by us. We also carefully read through the descriptions of those tools that are unavailable to us [7, 11]. We attribute the main reason for such limitations to their fundamental scanner design. All blackbox scanners are common in crawling a website only once, and will rely on this static set of captured requests for mutation and fuzzing. Therefore, it is unsurprising that they do not even work well with applications that have applied token-based CSRF defenses. However, it is non-trivial as to how such a scanner design can be patched to identify, renew, and relate a token from a former response to a corresponding fuzzing request as well as handling the synchronization issues.

3. THE CRS APPROACH

We aim at addressing not only the problems concerned but also other dynamic characteristics that have made scanning of real-world web applications difficult. It is hard to resolve all these issues in the existing scanner design largely owing to their *crawl-once-and-replay-many* and stateless fuzzing approaches.

Hence, this paper proposes a parameter tampering scanner called Cross-Request Scanner (CRS), which structurally changes the traditional fuzzing approach. Table 1 provides a quick comparison of various scanners, which shows their support to those website features that are essential for effective fuzzing. Here we outline our approach and its design considerations, which has enabled the discovery of some previously unknown vulnerabilities.

3.1 Overview of CRS

Figure 2 depicts the high-level architecture of CRS, which is a blackbox parameter tampering scanner designed to find parameters that are client-side rejected yet server-side accepted [10]. It comprises the capturing and fuzzing phases:

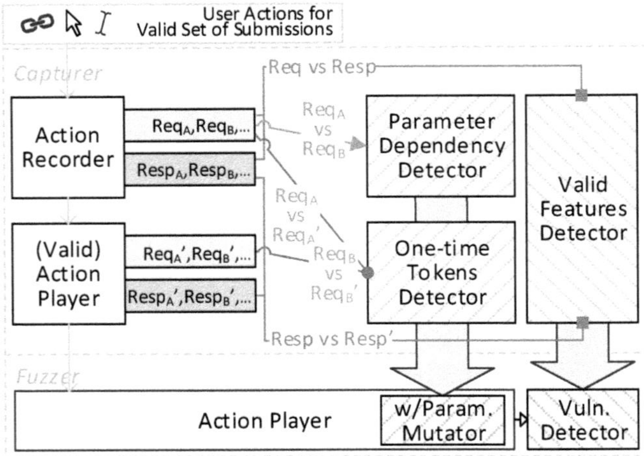

Figure 2: The architecture of Cross-Request Scanner (CRS)

Capturing Phase. While running CRS as a browser add-on, an analyst provides an initial valid set of submissions by interacting with a testing application as usual in the browser. CRS captures the user actions for later replays. Meanwhile, it tracks the parameter dependency across the submission requests, and thus a parameter with its value being the same as in the last request is marked dependent. From the server responses, it identifies some candidates of key features such as locations of submit buttons and reflected parameters, that can represent an acceptance by the server. It then replays the original user actions to get a second valid set of submissions, and classifies those parameter values that differ from the initial submissions as token candidates. In these two valid submissions, those key feature candidates that cannot be reproduced will be dropped. Finally, it confirms that each token candidate is of one-time use if a rejection is resulted upon repeating the same request.

Fuzzing Phase. To observe the intended workflow and one-time use tokens, CRS sequentially replays the user actions and keeps the tokens intact during fuzzing. Each parameter is mutated and placed back to the application to undergo its client-side validations. The dependent parameters are exempted from fuzzing after the candidates are mutated, submitted, and actually confirmed to result in server rejections. Next, those parameters that are rejected by the client-side are forcefully submitted with the validations bypassed. With such a rejected parameter, CRS reports a vulnerability if the server reacts in such a way that the expected workflow and key features can be reproduced as in the valid submissions.

3.2 Design Considerations

Here we explain the underlying considerations of the approach.

Preserving Intended Workflow. Sequentially fuzzing a whole set of requests, one after another, is a necessity to preserve the intended workflow. CRS achieves this by replaying user actions.

Respecting One-time Use Tokens. One-time use tokens are by definition those server-generated parameters that differ across two requests even though an identical set of user actions are provided. Before any user inputs are entered, these tokens are readily present either in hidden fields or the query string of submission URLs. This important clue can help eliminate many false classifications. However, proxy-based scanners [1, 20, 25] which capture a request at proxy level (i.e., outside the browser context) obviously possess no such knowledge. To extract these tokens, complex state maintenance and even synchronization issues are anticipated if we are to modify existing scanners to fetch a previous response for token extraction before making every fuzzing request. In contrast, CRS proposes to identify and fuzz directly in the browser so that these tokens are inherently recognizable and well-preserved. After confirming that they are of one-time uses, CRS excludes them from being mutated during fuzzing.

Respecting Parameter Dependency. Given the two valid sets of requests, CRS marks a parameter as dependent candidate if its value is equal to any parameters in the last request. This simple classification might be an overkill, so CRS still fuzzes each dependent candidate once for confirmation. Hence, only those that result in server rejections will be confirmed as dependent. To preserve the confirmed dependency, the fuzzer mutates such a parameter only in the first request it appeared but not in any successive ones. For instance, if a parameter value in Req_B is confirmed to be dependent to one in Req_A, then it is mutated only at Req_A but kept intact at Req_B. In fact, this algorithm is also good for locating session-based tokens of which the values are present in multiple requests and will expire only after the session is terminated.

Preserving Client-side Preprocessing. Web applications implement their client-side logic using JavaScript. Without any page loading, modern applications may dynamically add or drop input fields in response to a user action. In the banking examples studied, HSBC, BOC, HSB and BEA even manipulate some hidden fields before performing form validations and submissions. AJAX-driven websites such as Citibank use the asynchronous `XMLHttpRequest` API. Existing scanners are however ignorant to all of them. It may look intuitive to preserve these features simply by running the applications in a full-blown browser during testing. But this actually poses a challenge in preserving these client-side executions while mutating parameters, to be detailed in Section 4.3.2.

Detecting Client-side Rejection. Some existing approaches infer the validation rules by coding analysis [7, 8]. Given a blackbox environment, it is however difficult to preserve complex and dynamic validations that may even depend on AJAX feedbacks. Instead, to be generic, CRS places a mutated parameter back into the application itself to determine whether a submission is forbidden, and if so, the parameter must be rejected by client-side validations and will be used for fuzzing. Concerning the mutation algorithm, it heuristically derives new values (e.g., $+1$, $\times -1$) from either a user-given or default value besides adopting some static values from [20]. Although it may not be as exhaustive as what can be generated through code analysis, it suffices in the current study.

Detecting Server-side Acceptance. Most existing blackbox scanners use edit distances for response classifications [1, 7, 25]. However, this approach often fails in classifying JSON-formatted [19] feedbacks that are commonly used in AJAX applications. For responses such as `{success:1}` and `{success:0}`, the zero edit distance between them makes server acceptances hardly discernible from rejections. In particular, NoTamper [7] also requires an analyst to provide a baseline pair of valid and invalid submissions, such that a fuzzed response can be clustered to the one with closer edit distance. In contrast, CRS requires only one valid set of submissions, and is able to figure out the invalid responses which must fail to reproduce the expected submit buttons, workflow, and reflected parameters. The concept of button detection is similar to a proposal that clusters server responses into different states according to their outgoing hyperlinks [11]. But here, CRS can support those responses that may contain no hyperlinks and those with indistinguishable edit distances. It is because the classification is applied to those DOM elements that receive visual changes [23] upon AJAX feedbacks, rather than tapping directly to the response data.

4. IMPLEMENTATION

To realize our approach as a usable tool, this section first presents a background study on how parameters are gathered, validated, and submitted in web applications in general. Next, we detail the implementation of the core components, including the Capturer and Fuzzer, of the scanner.

4.1 Technical Background of Web Applications

4.1.1 Sources of Parameters and Validations

An HTML form typically encloses a variety of input controls to take users' input, and each of which is associated with a name and optionally a default value (e.g., with the `value` attribute). Such a name/value pair then contributes a request parameter during form submission. On the other hand, server-generated values are typically embedded in hidden fields, or hardcoded at the query string of submission URLs.

The choice of an input control can obviously impose a restriction on the input format that a user is supposed to follow. For instances, two radio boxes denoting genders with values defaulted to `M` and `F` can prevent users from entering unexpected values, whereas the use of a hidden field is a means of validation that it must be equal to the given (or default) value.

In addition, applications can be programmed to apply explicit client-side validations with JavaScript and HTML 5 API [18]. For instances, application typically enforces string-valued input to be composed of only alphanumeric characters, and that numeric input to be within a proper range (e.g., $age >= 18$). If a form fails the validations, the submission must be forbidden.

These explicit validations and those imposed by input controls are all referred to as client-side validations. Notice that they are implemented only for improved usability. Input validations must also be implemented at the server for security purposes.

4.1.2 Form Submissions

Client-side validations must be applied before an actual submission by registering an event handler to either the `submit` event of the form or the `click` event of a clickable element. In this paper, the former approach is referred to as the *event-based form submission*, and the latter one as *programmatic form submission*, whereas those submitted using the `XmlHttpRequest` API are referred to as the *AJAX form submission*. Their behaviors, as detailed below, essentially govern how they can be intercepted for fuzzing:

Event-based Form Submission. When a user clicks a submit button (e.g., `<input type=image|submit>`), or hits "Enter" in a text field, the `submit` handler of the form is invoked. If its return value is set to `true`, the form proceeds to submit and will trigger a page load; otherwise, the submission can be forbidden. JavaScript validations are applied inside this handler, and thus the form is submitted only if it is properly validated (i.e., `return validated(form)`).

Programmatic Form Submission. When employing an (click) event that is non-specific to form submission, the event handler must explicitly invoke the `submit()` method for a form submission. Clearly, this approach will trigger a page load but not the `submit` event. The invocation is typically restricted by the form validity (i.e., `validated(form) && form.submit()`).

AJAX Form Submission. Modern applications submit a form at the background without reloading the page. To achieve this with the `submit` event handler, `false` is always returned to cancel the default submission and thus the page load. There is no page load problem when using other event handlers such as `onclick`. When the form passes the validations, the event handler will invoke a custom function (e.g., `sendAJAX()`), that is made to encode the name/value input pairs as request parameters, and finally submit a request using the well-known `XMLHttpRequest` API.

4.2 The Capturer of CRS

When the add-on is being launched alongside the browser, the Capturer actually begins by recognizing the form submission approach that is being used. Even before any user actions, it has already interposed on the `submit()` method of every form, and registered an handler to the `beforeunload` event. If the `submit()` method is called, the form submission approach is a programmatic one. If the `beforeunload` handler is first fired (i.e., not initiated by the `submit()` method), then it is clearly an event-based form submission. Otherwise, the form submission is using AJAX.

Here we present the implementation of the smaller modules including the Action Recorder, Action Player, Parameter Dependency Detector, One-time Token Detector, and Valid Features Detector.

4.2.1 Action Recorder

The Action Recorder is responsible for capturing the URLs, HTTP requests and responses of an initial valid set of submissions. The request URL and parameters are obtained from the attributes and input elements of the corresponding form, while the responses are also readily accessible by similar DOM API calls.

On the other hand, it listens to all keystrokes and clicking events, and takes the unique id attributes or otherwise XPath positions [22] as references to those target elements that receive the events. This is implemented by registering event handlers at the `document` level, so that they are recorded before propagating down to the target elements or possibly canceled by the intermediate ones.

4.2.2 Action Player

With the captured user actions, the Action Player of the Capturer can replay them to obtain the second set of valid submissions. This is achieved by synthesizing and replaying the events with the `initEvent()` and `initMouseEvent()` APIs. In general, the implementations of the event recorder and player is similar to Selenium, which is an open-source recording and replaying tool [30].

4.2.3 One-time Tokens Detector

This detector concerns only server-generated parameters that are originated from hidden fields and query string of submission URLs. Working as a browser add-on, CRS can easily sort out these parameters by DOM inspection. The name/value pairs in the query string are then properly decoded using the `decodeURIComponent()` API. Among these server-generated parameters, it identifies those parameters that have the same name yet distinct values across each corresponding pair of requests between the initial and second valid sets of submissions.

Each of these identified candidates is confirmed of one-time use if making an identical request will indeed lead to a server rejection. Given a non-AJAX form, it is relatively easy to tamper the corresponding hidden field or submission URL and reuse the token in order to spoof an identical request. A server rejection, which is literally a lack of any of the key features, can then be asserted. However, for forms submitted over AJAX, more complex techniques to be detailed in Section 4.3.2 and 4.2.5 are similarly used here to spoof an identical request as well as to find if any key features are missing. The names of these confirmed parameters are recorded, and they will be preserved when fuzzing other parameters.

4.2.4 Parameter Dependency Detector

This detector is actually responsible only for identifying candidates of dependent parameters, which are subject to further confirmation by the Fuzzer. First, CRS applies regular expressions to determine the value types. For instance, `/^[\d,]+(?:\.\d+)?$/` is used to test for numbers. With any commas stripped, the numeric values are casted into float using the `parseFloat()` API, while all other values are trimmed. When comparing the parameters across the requests of the initial valid set of submissions, it neglects the names but considers only those transformed values. A candidate parameter is finally considered dependent to another parameter of the last request only if two values are identical. The references (i.e., id attribute or XPath location) to these candidates are recorded.

4.2.5 *Valid Features Detector*

This module is to determine the key features that indicate reproducible acceptances by the server. The references to the candidate elements of key features are recorded throughout the initial valid set of submissions. In the second valid set of submissions, the extracted features are relocated in the rendered server responses. Hence, the final key features to be used are all verified to be reproducible in both valid set of submissions.

First of all, the buttons that are clicked and captured in the Action Recorder automatically qualify as the key features since they are always needed to follow the intended workflow.

Next, CRS extracts a number of other key features by locating user-supplied parameters that are visually reflected in the rendered responses. This is achieved by searching for the presence of a parameter value in the `textContent` and `value` attributes of every leaf node through DOM tree traversal. This technique is commonly used in search engine keyword highlighting [36]. Nevertheless, CRS handles number matching differently in order to tolerate formatting issues that are introduced by the server. For instance, `12345` is first converted to a regular expression object, i.e., `\/1[^\d]?2[^\d]?3[^\d]?4[^\d]?5\/`, and can thus find its presence in a node content such as `$12,345.00`. If a value has resulted in multiple occurrences that exceed a configurable limit[1], the candidate parameter is disqualified. Obviously, each parameter is mutated based on its specific features.

In case no parameter reflections can be identified, CRS will heuristically search for some keywords that indicate sever acceptance with the same DOM traversal approach. The case insensitive keyword choices include "success, done, complete(d), execute(d), ok(ay), or update(d)" but must also exclude "not, n't, fail(ed), err(or) or sorry". Since the extension to multi-lingual support is trivial, so a string is now tested only as follows:

```
/\b(?:success(?:ful)?|done|completed?|executed?|
    ok(?:ay)?|updated?)\b/i.test(string)
&& !/\b(?:not|sorry|fail(?:ed)?|err(?:or)?)\b
    |(?:[a-z]n\'t\b)/i.test(string)
```

The approximate string matching algorithms [24] may better perform in some applications, but they are not used here for less complexity. In case of no identifiable features, the analyst will be prompted to provide a regular expression statement for asserting the server acceptance. We so far did not encounter such a manual need in our experiments.

The CRS approach focuses on the rendered responses to locate key features even for AJAX applications. It generally ignores the raw response data as replied from the server, but simply allows the testing application itself to react accordingly and make DOM changes. In this regard, CRS is so designed to leverage the application itself to generate the required `XMLHttpRequests`. So, the relevant `onstatechange` handlers that respond to the AJAX feedbacks can be triggered.

[1]For instance, a single-character value such as 1 or 0 will likely occur everywhere. While a maximum of 3 times is generally reasonable for applications that reflect parameters, here we do not quest for a magic number but leave it configurable.

```
1 while (action = userActionList.next()) {
2   if (action.isSubmissionClick()
3       && param = paramList.nextCandidate()
4       && !param.isOneTimeToken()
5       && !param.isDependencyDetected()) {
6     getClientRejected(param)
7     form.forceSubmission()
8     detectServerAcceptance()
9   } else {
10    action.replay()
11    paramList.addNewlyAppearedFields()
12  }
13 }
14 function getClientRejected(param) {
15   if (mutated = param.nextMutated()) {
16     form.interceptSubmission(function() {
17       form.cancelSubmission()
18       getClientRejected(param)
19     })
20     form.fillIn(mutated)
21     action.replay()
22     paramList.addNewlyAppearedFields()
23   }
24 }
```

Listing 1: The core algorithm of the Fuzzer

On the other hand, CRS limits the scope of feature searching to accurately the part that changes after the AJAX form submission. To implement this, CRS registers a callback function to the `MutationObserver` API [23] right before the submit button is clicked. After the application has made some DOM changes, the callback function will be invoked with those DOM objects that receive the changes, where the feature extraction algorithm will be applied to those visible objects. Only if no visual changes are ever made, CRS will use the HTTP status code and response data to determine server acceptances. However, we did not encounter such a case in the websites we tested.

4.3 The Fuzzer of CRS

The Fuzzer begins by confirming the list of dependent parameters. It replays the captured user actions up to the page where a candidate dependent parameter is found. The value of which is then mutated to ensure that it differs from that of the last request to make a dependency breaking attempt. Finally, the dependency is confirmed if a server rejection is encountered. To assert this, a fuzzing technique that is also applied to other non-candidate parameters is used and described as follows.

Listing 1 outlines the core algorithm of the Fuzzer. It sequentially replays the captured user actions (Line 1 & 10) and stops before a submission click (Line 2). Parameters that are confirmed of one-time use (Line 4) or dependent to a previous request (Line 5) are exempted from fuzzing. Other parameters are mutated one by one with respect to its default or user-given value (Line 15). The mutated parameter is then placed back to the form, and the corresponding events (e.g., `onclick`, `onchange`) are also triggered (Line 20). Any newly appeared fields will also be captured here for later mutation (Line 11 & 22). Upon replaying the submission click event (Line 21), the web application itself validates the form concerned. If a submission is attempted, that means the mutated parameter is accepted by the client-side validations (Line 16). The Fuzzer will however cancel the submission (Line 17), and repeatedly mutate the parameter until it is rejected by the client-side (Line 18). With that client-side rejected parameter, the Fuzzer bypasses the validations to force a form submission (Line 7). Finally, it asserts a server acceptance by locating all the valid key features (Line 8), and is able to report those parameters that are rejected by the client-side validation but accepted by the server as vulnerable to parameter tampering attacks.

Those smaller modules including the Parameter Mutator and Vulnerability Detector are detailed as follows. The discussion on Action Player is omitted as it is the same as that in the Capturer.

4.3.1 *Parameter Mutator*

This module is responsible for generating mutated values. The default values, or otherwise analyst-provided ones form the bases for mutations. First, CRS mutates the numeric portion of this existing value in order to derive some integral, decimal, negated, incremented, decremented, and multiplied versions (e.g., `parseInt()`, $+n/1000$, $-n$, $+n$, $\times - 1$, $\times n$, where n comes from some hard-coded and randomized integers).

CRS then determines the input types by inferring from the whole value (e.g., `/[\d,\.]+/` for numbers), type attributes (e.g., `date` from HTML 5), class attributes (e.g., alphanumeric, datepicker; as often employed by JavaScript validation libraries [28]), name attributes, and field labels (e.g., tel, date). For boolean values that are likely represented in `1`, `0`, `Y`, `N`, `T`, `F`, `true`, or `false`, new values are derived by negating the boolean. For certain input types such as date, time and percentage, CRS adds some relevant hardcoded values (e.g., `2013-9-22`, `23:59`, `111%`). Optionally, the Mutator is configurable to also output test cases for violating the input types and other field restrictions such as `required` and `maxlength` (e.g., concatenating an existing value with itself by multiple times).

Here some of the hardcoding values are borrowed from a tool called TamperData [20]. It is certain that this heuristic input generation module is imperfect, and can be further enhanced by performing extra coding analysis [3,7,8]. However, the current setting is found sufficient in our experiments.

4.3.2 *Vulnerability Detector*

This subsection mainly enumerates how to intercept and cancel submission attempts (client-side accepted parameters) as well as force a submission (client-side rejected parameters) for each form submission approach. Interestingly, this involves flipping the original decision on whether to proceed a submission. With a fuzzing attempt that is client-side rejected, CRS can then discern server acceptances by detecting those valid features found by the Capturer.

Intervening in Event-based Form Submission. To intercept the submission, CRS interposes on the `onsubmit` handler of the form to wrap the original one. Our handler disables HTML 5 automatic validations by setting `form.noValidate` to `false`. It then discerns the parameter validity by examining the return values of the original `onsubmit` handler and `form.checkValidity()` method that respectively reflect the results of JavaScript and HTML 5 validations. If an accepted parameter is encountered (i.e., both returned `true`), CRS will return `false` in our `onsubmit` handler to cancel the submission. For rejected parameters, CRS forces the submission by returning `true` in our handler.

Intervening in Programmatic Form Submission. To intercept the programmatic submission, CPS overrides the `submit()` method of the form. To discern parameter validity, we cannot rely on the return value which is always `void`. Instead, we know that our method will be called only with client-side accepted parameters. We will then simply ignore the submissions for these parameters. For other (i.e., rejected) parameters, CPS deliberately calls the original `submit()` method to force submissions.

Intervening in AJAX Form Submission. Intervening in AJAX submissions is the most challenging implementation for the following reasons. First, we do not assume web applications to use any particular JavaScript libraries such as jQuery [28]. Second, in contrast to the previous approaches of which the event and method are directly associated with a form object, `XMLHttpRequest` multiplexes all kinds of HTTP requests that are non-specific to form submissions (i.e., without a function like `form.ajaxSubmit()` that can be intercepted similarly). Third, owing to the asynchronous nature, multiple AJAX requests can simultaneously exist, such as refreshing a placeholder for advertisements and dynamic validations that involve server feedbacks (e.g. nickname uniqueness). Hence, it is non-trivial to distinguish which request is responsible for the form submission concerned.

We solve this problem by first intercepting the methods `open()` and `send()` at the prototype level of `XMLHttpRequest`, which are invoked before making a request. It is necessary to intercept both `open()` and `send()` methods, through which input parameters are provided respectively for GET and POST requests.

To distinguish the particular request that corresponds to the form submission, CPS appends a nonce to the value of an existing (hidden) input control[2], of which its validity is unaffected. Hence, the AJAX request that consists of this nonce can be isolated in our intercepted methods. Here, an invocation of our intercepted `send()` method implies that the parameter is client-side accepted. CPS discards the submission by ignoring it.

For client-side rejected parameters, the application will not even instantiate the `XMLHttpRequest`. Given a simple application, it may be feasible to reproduce the instantiation by program slicing. But we instead develop a more succinct approach. CPS achieves a forced submission by reusing the set of valid parameters to trigger a submission request. But then the parameters are substituted with the client-side rejected ones at the intercepted methods. The nonce is also removed during so before sending the requests.

5. EVALUATIONS

This section focuses on evaluating the proposed scanning approach in terms of its practicality and effectiveness. Practicality considers how well CRS can automate and intercept real-world applications, while effectiveness measures the vulnerability scanning capabilities. All experiments are conducted with an entry-level PC using Firefox. The lightweight implementation actually incurs only negligible performance overhead, and that the scanning time is dominated by the server responsiveness and a configurable delay deliberately introduced to avoid "DoS-ing" the servers. We thus omit here a benchmark on performance overhead. If needed, the fuzzing time can be further reduced by using a headless browser [27].

This section also briefly discusses some insights behind the severe vulnerabilities uncovered with the scanner, and shares how they are responsibly reported and subsequently resolved [34].

5.1 Ethical Concerns

For the practicality evaluation which generates no tampered requests, there are no ethical issues. For the effectiveness evaluation, we turned tampering on in real-world web applications. In the worst case scenarios, the tampered banking transfer requests could possibly result in money transferred either from our account to an unknown account or from an unknown account to ours. We thus tested only the interbank transfer applications which all require at least two days to take effect, and hence we have sufficient time to manually cancel (or make instant transfer before) any unwanted transactions. To further limit the risk, all requests are capped to use only a small amount of money during the automated fuzzing. To confirm a vulnerability to be a working exploit, we only manually

[2]Alternatively, we can inject a hidden field with a nonce value, so that it will be submitted along with other field values.

made online transfers from and to accounts that are owned by us at different banks. All findings were promptly disclosed to the affected parties. We were grateful for being formally recognized by the government and banks' officials as "good citizens".

5.2 Empirical Results

We tested a total of seven applications, including five online banking transfer applications including HSBC, BEA, Citibank, BOC, and Hang Seng Bank (HSB), followed by two traveling websites including Jetstar airline and an online travel agent Webjet. These banks are chosen since their branches are in close geographical proximity to our institution, so that we can minimize the overhead of visiting them for opening bank accounts. The traveling websites are chosen because of a plan to visit Australia, where the headquarters of Jetstar and Webjet are located.

Practicality Evaluation. We found that CRS can practically drive all the testing applications to run successfully. In this regard, CRS outperforms the existing scanners, which fail to support many critical features that are required for effective scanning, as tabulated in Table 1. Some scanners cannot even run the applications due to their lack of JavaScript and AJAX support.

We are unaware of any unsupported form designs except those with non-standard input controls and those built with plug-ins such as Adobe Flash. This limitation is however non-specific to CRS but also other parameter tampering scanners [1, 7, 8, 20].

Effectiveness Evaluation. We evaluated that CRS is effective in uncovering some previously unknown vulnerabilities even in banking websites. Table 2 summarizes the confusion matrix of the vulnerability scanning results, which is further discussed below.

- *True Positives*. The vulnerabilities uncovered in two banking websites are separately detailed in Section 5.3. CRS discovered another vulnerability in an AJAX page of the official Jetstar website. There is a restriction on tracking on-time performance only from the last 10 days, but it is found bypassable. We confirmed manually that it allowed us to check the performance of a randomly selected flight, which departed even three years ago. Given that the information was once (when within last 10 days) publicly accessible, we did not approach the organization for a patch. This finding serves to demonstrate the support of AJAX applications by CRS.
- *True Negatives*. In our experiments, CRS found no vulnerabilities in BOC, Citibank and HSB. We manually analyzed their client-side source code and classified them as true negatives largely because the servers have mapped each account number to a unique index (rather than using the actual account number). Thus, a tampered index could not go beyond a pre-defined mapping of authorized accounts that is maintained at the server. It is indeed a proper parameter tampering defense, as recommended by OWASP [26].
- *False Positives*. We are unaware of any false positives so far.
- *False Negatives*. Finding false negatives requires a set of known and unpatched vulnerabilities, which is intrinsically difficult in our blackbox evaluation. We managed to manually discover only one vulnerability in a travel booking website Webjet. It was missed because the lack of domain knowledge on airport code. More specifically, only some Australia airports such as HBA would cause the vulnerability. This limitation is non-specific to CRS but also any other scanners. We believe that this vulnerability is discoverable only by chance even with a human (when planned to visit Australia). We contacted Webjet, which appreciated our finding and fixed the vulnerability.

Table 2: The confusion matrix of the CRS scanning results

	Positives	**Negatives**
True	HSBC, BEA, Jetstar	Citibank, BOC, HSB
False	/	Webjet

5.3 Case Studies and Vulnerability Disclosure

Here we discuss the parameter tampering vulnerabilities uncovered in HSBC and BEA by CRS, as well as our encounters of responsible vulnerability disclosures. We once expected banks to be well scrutinized by existing scanners and security audit. For instance, the Acunetix web vulnerability scanner being used by HSBC is also adopted by NASA and even the Pentagon [2]. Being one of the largest multinational banks, HSBC also won the "Best Information Security Initiatives" award in the world's best consumer and corporate Internet banks [15]. However, their existing mitigation approaches have apparently failed. Their application designs may provide some insights on why the vulnerabilities would evade the detection of their existing approaches.

5.3.1 *Bypassed OTP Requirement in HSBC*

Figure 3 shows two screenshots of the interbank transfer application of HSBC, which correspond to Step_A and Step_B in Figure 1.

Legitimate Use Cases. When transitioning from Step_A to Step_B, the server first verifies the one-time token and cross-request parameter dependency. The logic flow then depends on a radio button that indicates whether the account `TO` is authorized (registered).

If the *upper* radio button is chosen, the server will make use of the corresponding "Account Holder's Name and Account Number" and "Bank Code and Name" fields for further format verification. Therefore, the account number format should match with a regular expression `/^[a-zA-Z]{1,20}~~\d{1,12}$/`. It is however unlikely that checksum verification can be applied to the `TO` account number since its definition is totally up to another bank. Given an authorized account, the user still has to click "confirm" in the review page.

If the *lower* radio button is chosen, the server will take an authorized account from the corresponding "Bank Code and Name", "Account No.", and "Account Holder's Name" fields. The review page will then ask the user for an OTP generated from a dedicated hardware device. This second factor authentication is to assure that the transfer is authorized by the legitimate user. In either case, the bank sends out an SMS to the user. The `TO` account number is however partially masked, and that neither the holder name nor registered status are provided.

Vulnerability Details. CRS is first provided with an initial valid set of user actions that go through the complete workflow to transfer $1 from our account to an authorized account. CRS then automates the rest of the discovery, and reported several parameter tampering possibilities for the `TO` parameter. Among the scanning results, the simplest possibility was to increment the numeric portion of the original value by one (i.e., `FUND RECEIPIENT~~290 123456883`).

We manually confirmed this vulnerability by transferring money out from our HSBC account, and were able to receive it in an unauthorized account of our own in another bank. It is likely that the mutated (i.e., unauthorized) account number was handled by the logic branch responsible for authorized accounts. Hence, the most-trusted OTP was completely bypassed! It is reasonable that even a transaction-signing device [17] could not help in this regard.

As a consequence, an attacker transferring his money to an "unauthorized" account can dispute the transaction on the basis that it does not correspond to a use of OTP. Alternatively, he can steal

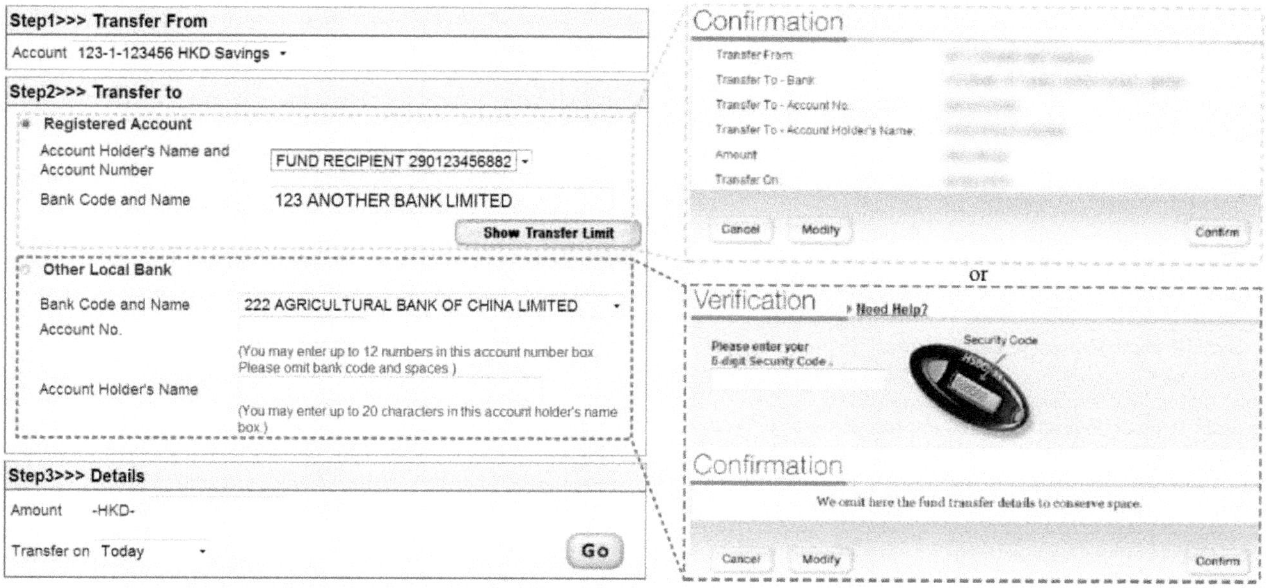

The first page that takes transaction details ($Step_A$) | The review page to confirm the transaction ($Step_B$)

Figure 3: The online banking transfer application of HSBC responds with a different review page based on the choice of radio buttons

money from those victims whose sessions can be hijacked or whose credentials can be purchased from underground communities.

Existing scanners miss this vulnerability due to the enforcements of one-time use tokens, cross-request parameter dependency, and client-side pre-processing.

Disclosure. It was threatening that two out of four banks (by the time we ran the first set of experiments) were confirmed as being vulnerable, in spite of the limited applications we scanned. This made us believe that the prevalence of parameter tampering vulnerabilities were heavily under-estimated in online banks. Having failed to contact the right representative of HSBC, we anonymized its name and reported our findings to the government authority responsible for maintaining monetary and banking stability. The authority took our findings seriously and met with us in person to avoid any discloses through a wire. Promptly after the meeting, the authority alerted all licensed banks to request them for a check and possible fix, which may explain that no further vulnerabilities were later found in other banks. It later forwarded to us a technical clarification request from HSBC, which rolled out a patch in two days. The authority and HSBC expressed their gratitude in writing.

5.3.2 *Unauthorized Transfer in Bank of East Asia*

Here we outline only the findings that are specific to BEA.

Legitimate Use Case. The interbank transfer application of BEA allows transfers only to registered accounts, which can be authorized only by visiting a physical branch. In other words, one can never make an online transfer to any unregistered accounts as a protection. No SMS and email notifications were implemented.

Vulnerability Details. Similar to HSBC, CRS was able to report a vulnerability that result in unauthorized transfers owing to the lack of proper server-side validations. We manually confirmed the vulnerability by transferring $10,000 from our account to an unregistered account of our own.

We noticed an interesting implementation that a hidden field called `MACcode` is set at the client-side before any form validations and submission. Its value is prepared by concatenating the transaction parameters (i.e., `FROM`, `TO`, `AMT`) and encoding the result by the Base64 scheme. The server was found rejecting those requests if the `MACcode` received does not align with the transaction parameters. Since CRS places a mutated parameter back to the application, the parameter can undergo the same `MACcode` algorithm at the client-side. So, it is clear that such an algorithm cannot protect message authenticity, as opposed to its confusing name.

Existing scanners miss this vulnerability owing to the enforcements of client-side pre-processing and intended workflow.

Disclosure. More than a week after our experiments, we disclosed the vulnerability directly to BEA. Apparently, no monitoring alarms were triggered regardless of the large transaction amount. They acknowledged our finding, and promptly fixed it within a day. Their system was later enhanced by dispatching email notifications.

6. RELATED WORK

6.1 Parameter Tampering Scanners

Blackbox. Blackbox scanners are not tied to any specific frameworks and languages used on the server-side. This makes them often more generic than whitebox approaches. In general, they all work by first crawling an application to capture any requests encountered, then fuzzing it by replaying the requests with some mutated parameters. Proxy-based parameter tampering scanners include the HTTP fuzzer in Acunetix [1], WebScarab [25], and TamperData [20]. They accept per-request fuzzing, and thus cannot automatically observe the intended workflow. They also require considerable amount of manual configurations such as specifying (a) a self-signed SSL certificate for interceptions of encrypted traffic [14], and; (b) even explicit value range of each parameter.

NoTamper [7] outperforms proxy-based parameter tampering by reducing the manual efforts needed. Similar to CRS, it automates parameter generation based on the client-side validations. With static symbolic execution and constraint solving (that currently support the event-based form submissions only), it is able to generate an exhaustive set of parameters that are rejected by the client-side. This approach can complement the Parameter Mutator of CRS. It however requires an analyst to provide two (i.e., valid and invalid) initial sets of requests though, so as to discern whether the server accepts the mutated requests.

To preserve the intended workflow during fuzzing, research work is found only for scanning other web vulnerabilities such as XSS. A state-aware fuzzer [11] is able to detect whether a fuzzing attempt has triggered a state change. If changed, it backtracks to the previous state by page traversal. It thus allows every state to be completely fuzzed by all candidate parameters before moving on to the next state. However, this stateful scanner can handle static web pages only, i.e., AJAX applications are not supported.

Nonetheless, all these scanners are limited owing to their fundamental scanner design. It is very hard to enhance them in handling the one-time use tokens, cross-request parameter dependencies, and client-side pre-processing. Their fuzzing requests are thus likely barred from reaching vulnerable code.

On the other hand, there are studies that evaluate the effectiveness of existing web vulnerability scanners. According to [6], the commercial scanners being evaluated are found not to be as comprehensive as they are claimed to be. This evaluation however covers only vulnerabilities like XSS, and it does not cover parameter tampering. According to [12], the study found that none of its evaluated scanners could find a parameter tampering vulnerability. It also suggests that high-level domain knowledge on the application is needed, but can hardly be known without a human.

PAPAS [5] focuses only on a specific variant of parameter tampering, namely the parameter pollution vulnerabilities. Its success relies on the use of a server-side parameter precedence algorithm that allows malicious parameter to take over the precedence of an existing parameter. Its scanning approach is thus very similar to finding reflected vectors such as XSS, and that is different from finding more general parameter tampering vulnerabilities.

Whitebox. When server-side source code is available, whitebox scanners can be used to compare the inconsistencies between client-side and server-side validations.

WAPTEC [8] extends the NoTamper [7] approach by applying similar coding analysis to the server-side validations. The additional knowledge eliminates the manual effort required, and improves the selection of candidate parameter. But it still suffers from the limitations of NoTamper such as the negligence of the cross-request parameter dependency.

ViewPoints [3] discovers validation inconsistencies between the client-side and server-side by differential string analysis. It supports only a specific framework of the Java web applications. Besides reporting those parameters that are client-rejected yet server-accepted, its goal is to also report parameters that are client-accepted yet server-rejected. Eliminating this latter class of inconsistencies from the application can improve in usability but not its security.

In general, what can be validated from the server and client sides is intrinsically inconsistent since the server is always more knowledgeable (e.g., access to DB) than the client, and thus these approaches must report many false positives. It is also difficult to first annotate all the expected inconsistencies particularly in real-world complex applications before running these tools.

6.2 Parameter Tampering Mitigations

InteGuard [35] is a whitebox protection approach that operates a server-side proxy to verify the parameters exchanged between the server and a client as well as those further exchanged with a third-party server. It relies on a human to provide some valid transactions for analyzing the parameter dependencies in its learning phase. Then its online defense is to drop subsequent requests that violate the expected dependencies. Its mitigation is limited only to those parameters triggered by human. CRS can automatically explore the client-side events to uncover new parameters, which can be hardly exhausted by a human in the training phase.

Some development frameworks such as .NET [4] and Java [16] can replicate the server-side validations to become client-side code. However, they are often limited to simple validations that are purposely programmed for replications. Swift [9] proposes that developers should annotate those parameters and codes that are sensitive to run only on server-side or safe for both sides to facilitate replication. But again, it is demanding to annotate even a simple program.

Server-side validations and sanitizations are still fundamental defenses against parameter tampering. For client-side validations aiming at delivering better user experience, HTML 5 Validations [18] and JavaScript libraries such as jQuery [28] can be deployed.

6.3 Others

Compared to [33, 34] which also explored parameter relationships, CRS systematically analyzes all the parameter dependencies between different tuples of requests and responses, as shown in Figure 2. As a result, CRS can automatically detect server acceptances by analyzing `Req vs Resp` and `Resp vs Resp'`, which makes a significant improvement over the manual and protocol-specific approaches as with [33,34]. The proposed model checking also requires human effort in accurately transforming a subset of logic replica from the original application [34].

Some existing work also involve in replaying user actions, but none of which have identified the advantage of fuzzing inside the application context, that is, by intercepting the submission requests for fuzzing. Mugshot [21] deterministically captures and replays user actions and other JavaScript functions for failure and usability analysis. Kudzu [29] enhances its code coverage by exploring client-side events for the discovery of more client-side injection vulnerabilities. Ripley [32] maintains a server-side replica of the client-side logic in a shadow browser hosted in a trusted proxy, and attempts to automatically replicate and replay the client-side events in the replica for integrity check. Although it ensures the computation integrity of the client-side code, it does not eliminate the need for server-side validations. Acunetix Web Vulnerability Scanner [2] is able to generate some user action events while scanning for XSS vulnerabilities.

7. CONCLUSION

We studied a number of real-world web applications to understand their implementations, and how they can be intercepted for vulnerability scanning. Existing parameter tampering scanners do not consider the enforcements of, among others, the intended workflow, one-time use tokens, and parameter dependency across requests, which are all common in multi-request applications. Their effectiveness of vulnerability scanning is thus severely limited. We proposed the novel CRS approach to respect all these enforcements. We realized the approach by building a generic blackbox parameter tampering scanner. In our evaluation, it is practical to drive real applications to run for fuzzing. The importance of this work is demonstrated by the vulnerabilities uncovered in real-world applications including banks, which existing scanners miss. The scanning approach can also be extended to the discovery of other web application vulnerabilities including XSS and CSRF.

Acknowledgements

This work is partially supported by the Sir Edward Youde Memorial Fellowship. We appreciate and thank HSBC and Hong Kong Monetary Authority for their prompt follow-up. Special thanks are due to Chris Smith, Clara Ho, Thomas Yung, Esmond Lee, Shu-pui Li, and James Tam for their support. We thank for the valuable comments from Shuo Chen, Kehuan Zhang and anonymous reviewers.

8. REFERENCES

[1] Acunetix. Http fuzzer. http://www.acunetix.com/blog/docs/http-fuzzer-tool/.

[2] Acunetix. Web vulnerability scanner. http://www.acunetix.com/vulnerability-scanner/.

[3] M. Alkhalaf, S. R. Choudhary, M. Fazzini, T. Bultan, A. Orso, and C. Kruegel. Viewpoints: differential string analysis for discovering client- and server-side input validation inconsistencies. In *Proceedings of the 2012 International Symposium on Software Testing and Analysis*, ISSTA 2012, pages 56–66, New York, NY, USA, 2012. ACM.

[4] ASP. Net validation controls. http://msdn.microsoft.com/en-us/library/debza5t0.aspx.

[5] M. Balduzzi, C. T. Gimenez, D. Balzarotti, and E. Kirda. Automated discovery of parameter pollution vulnerabilities in web applications. In *Proceedings of the 18th Annual Network and Distributed System Security Symposium*, NDSS'11, San Diego, CA, USA, 2011. The Internet Society.

[6] J. Bau, E. Bursztein, D. Gupta, and J. Mitchell. State of the art: Automated black-box web application vulnerability testing. In *Proceedings of the 2010 IEEE Symposium on Security and Privacy*, SP '10, pages 332–345, Washington, DC, USA, 2010. IEEE Computer Society.

[7] P. Bisht, T. Hinrichs, N. Skrupsky, R. Bobrowicz, and V. N. Venkatakrishnan. Notamper: automatic blackbox detection of parameter tampering opportunities in web applications. In *Proceedings of the 17th ACM conference on Computer and communications security*, CCS '10, pages 607–618, New York, NY, USA, 2010. ACM.

[8] P. Bisht, T. Hinrichs, N. Skrupsky, and V. N. Venkatakrishnan. Waptec: whitebox analysis of web applications for parameter tampering exploit construction. In *Proceedings of the 18th ACM conference on Computer and communications security*, CCS '11, pages 575–586, New York, NY, USA, 2011. ACM.

[9] S. Chong, J. Liu, A. C. Myers, X. Qi, K. Vikram, L. Zheng, and X. Zheng. Secure web applications via automatic partitioning. In *Proceedings of 21st ACM SIGOPS symposium on Operating systems principles*, SOSP '07, pages 31–44, New York, NY, USA, 2007. ACM.

[10] CWE. Cwe-472: External control of assumed-immutable web parameter. http://cwe.mitre.org/data/definitions/472.html.

[11] A. Doupé, L. Cavedon, C. Kruegel, and G. Vigna. Enemy of the state: a state-aware black-box web vulnerability scanner. In *Proceedings of the 21st USENIX conference on Security symposium*, Security'12, pages 26–26, Berkeley, CA, USA, 2012. USENIX Association.

[12] A. Doupé, M. Cova, and G. Vigna. Why johnny can't pentest: an analysis of black-box web vulnerability scanners. In *Proceedings of the 7th international conference on Detection of intrusions and malware, and vulnerability assessment*, DIMVA'10, pages 111–131, Berlin, Heidelberg, 2010. Springer-Verlag.

[13] V. Felmetsger, L. Cavedon, C. Kruegel, and G. Vigna. Toward automated detection of logic vulnerabilities in web applications. In *Proceedings of the 19th USENIX conference on Security*, USENIX Security'10, pages 10–10, Berkeley, CA, USA, 2010. USENIX Association.

[14] A. P. H. Fung and K. W. Cheung. Sslock: Sustaining the trust on entities brought by ssl. In *Proceedings of the 5th ACM Symposium on Information, Computer and Communications Security*, ASIACCS '10, pages 204–213, New York, NY, USA, 2010. ACM.

[15] Global Finance. World's best internet banks 2011. http://www.gfmag.com/tools/best-banks/11485-worlds-best-internet-banks-2011.html.

[16] Google Web Toolkit. Validation framework. concept of operations. http://code.google.com/p/gwt-validation/wiki/ConceptOfOperations.

[17] HSBC. Faq - security device. https://www.hsbc.com.hk/1/2/hk/misc/otphelp.

[18] HTML 5. Association of controls and forms. http://dev.w3.org/html5/spec/association-of-controls-and-forms.html.

[19] JSON. Javascript objection notation. http://json.org/.

[20] A. Judson. Tamper data :: Add-ons for firefox. https://addons.mozilla.org/en-US/firefox/addon/tamper-data/.

[21] J. Mickens, J. Elson, and J. Howell. Mugshot: deterministic capture and replay for javascript applications. In *Proceedings of the 7th USENIX conference on Networked systems design and implementation*, NSDI'10, pages 11–11, Berkeley, CA, USA, 2010. USENIX Association.

[22] Mozilla. Introduction to using xpath in javascript. https://developer.mozilla.org/en/Introduction_to_using_XPath_in_Javascript.

[23] Mozilla. Mutationobserver. https://developer.mozilla.org/en-US/docs/DOM/MutationObserver.

[24] G. Navarro. A guided tour to approximate string matching. *ACM Computing Surveys*, 33(1):31–88, Mar. 2001.

[25] OWASP. Fuzzing with webscarab. https://www.owasp.org/index.php/Fuzzing_with_WebScarab.

[26] OWASP. Top 10 2013 A4-Insecure Direct Object References. https://www.owasp.org/index.php/Top_10_2013-A4-Insecure_Direct_Object_References.

[27] PhantomJS. Headless webkit with javascript api. http://phantomjs.org/.

[28] J. Resig. jquery. http://jquery.com/.

[29] P. Saxena, D. Akhawe, S. Hanna, F. Mao, S. McCamant, and D. Song. A symbolic execution framework for javascript. In *Proceedings of the 2010 IEEE Symposium on Security and Privacy*, SP '10, pages 513–528, Washington, DC, USA, 2010. IEEE Computer Society.

[30] Selenium. Web browser automation. http://seleniumhq.org/.

[31] Skipfish. Web application security scanner. https://code.google.com/p/skipfish/.

[32] K. Vikram, A. Prateek, and B. Livshits. Ripley: automatically securing web 2.0 applications through replicated execution. In *Proceedings of the 16th ACM conference on Computer and communications security*, CCS '09, pages 173–186, New York, NY, USA, 2009. ACM.

[33] R. Wang, S. Chen, and X. Wang. Signing me onto your accounts through facebook and google: A traffic-guided

security study of commercially deployed single-sign-on web services. In *Proceedings of the 2012 IEEE Symposium on Security and Privacy*, SP '12, pages 365–379, Washington, DC, USA, 2012. IEEE Computer Society.

[34] R. Wang, S. Chen, X. Wang, and S. Qadeer. How to shop for free online – security analysis of cashier-as-a-service based web stores. In *Proceedings of the 2011 IEEE Symposium on Security and Privacy*, SP '11, pages 465–480, Washington, DC, USA, 2011. IEEE Computer Society.

[35] L. Xing, Y. Chen, X. Wang, and S. Chen. Integuard: Toward automatic protection of third-party web service integrations. In *Proceedings of the 20th Annual Network and Distributed System Security Symposium*, NDSS'13, San Diego, CA, USA, 2013. The Internet Society.

[36] S. Yang. Search engine keyword highlighting with javascript. `http://scott.yang.id.au/code/se-hilite/`.

The Harvester, the Botmaster, and the Spammer: On the Relations Between the Different Actors in the Spam Landscape

Gianluca Stringhini, Oliver Hohlfeld[†], Christopher Kruegel, and Giovanni Vigna
Department of Computer Science, UC Santa Barbara
[†]RWTH Aachen University
{gianluca, chris, vigna}@cs.ucsb.edu, oliver@comsys.rwth-aachen.de

ABSTRACT

A spammer needs three elements to run a spam operation: a list of victim email addresses, content to be sent, and a botnet to send it. Each of these three elements are critical for the success of the spam operation: a good email list should be composed of valid email addresses, a good email content should be both convincing to the reader and evades anti-spam filters, and a good botnet should efficiently sent spam. Given how critical these three elements are, figures specialized on each of these elements have emerged in the spam ecosystem. Email harvesters crawl the web and compile email lists, botmasters infect victim computers and maintain efficient botnets for spam dissemination, and spammers rent botnets and buy email lists to run spam campaigns.

Previous research suggested that email harvesters and botmasters sell their services to spammers in a prosperous underground economy. No rigorous research has been performed, however, on understanding the relations between these three actors. This paper aims to shed some light on the relations between harvesters, botmasters, and spammers. By disseminating email addresses on the Internet, fingerprinting the botnets that contact these addresses, and looking at the content of these emails, we can infer the relations between the actors involved in the spam ecosystem. Our observations can be used by researchers to develop more effective anti-spam systems.

Categories and Subject Descriptors

K.4.1 [**Computers and Society**]: Abuse and crime involving computers

Keywords

Botnets; Spam; Cybercrime; Underground Economy

ASIA CCS'14, June 4–6, 2014, Kyoto, Japan.

http://dx.doi.org/10.1145/2590296.2590302.

1. INTRODUCTION

Email spam is a wealthy business for cyber criminals. Recent research showed that a successful spam campaign can generate revenues between $400,000 and $1,000,000 [11, 12]. Given this profitability, a whole economy has emerged around email spam. Similar to legitimate economic ecosystems, many different parties are involved in a spam campaign. On the one side, the spammer needs to have a good list of target email addresses for the campaign to be effective, as well as a botnet able to efficiently send emails to them [21]. On the other side, spammers need an effective infrastructure to sell the illicit goods that they advertise. This infrastructure includes the websites that sell the goods, the shipping facilities, and the payment processors [15]. Thus, there can be three main parties involved in the spam ecosystem: the email harvester, the botmaster, and the spammer.

Studying the relationship among these different parties involved in the spam ecosystem deepens the understanding of the spam underground economy and can pave the way for new spam mitigation techniques. In this way, it first helps to estimate the magnitude of the spam problem and can reveal new trends. Second, it allows to identify bottlenecks and critical points in the spamming pipeline; these critical points can be used to develop mitigation techniques to fight such threats. For these reasons, previous work analyzed *individual* aspects of the parties involved in the process. In particular, researchers studied the harvesting process of email addresses on the web [9, 20], the structure and operation of spamming botnets [5, 18, 21], or the email templates used by spammers [13, 14]. Other work focused on studying the financial conversion of spam [11, 12] or the workflow that goes from when an illicit good is purchased to when it gets delivered [15]. These recent advances in the understanding of individual parties now open the question on their *relationship*.

To the best of our knowledge, no research has focused on the operational relations and the interactions among the different parties in the spam ecosystem. Some work addressed *economic* interactions of some of the different players on the underground market [21]. This work suggested that spammers buy email lists from email harvesters, rent botnets from botmasters, and then use them to send spam. However, the question on their *operational* relation and the interactions among *multiple* parties has not been answered yet. Thus, a complete understanding of relations and interactions of players in the spam ecosystem is still missing. Open research questions include the following aspects. Do some spammers harvest email addresses by themselves? Do some spammers rent multiple botnets to send the same type of spam? And if they do, do they use the same email list across different botnets?

This paper presents the first analysis of the relations among email harvesters, botmasters, and spammers. In an attempt to contribute to answering these questions, we run a multi-step experiment. In the first step, we set up a large number of email addresses, each pointing to a mailserver under our control and advertise them on web pages. Then, we record the accesses to those web pages, to fingerprint the email harvesters. We then log the connections that we receive on our mailserver. Since the email addresses that we disseminated on the web are not used for legitimate purposes, we assume that any connection that we receive is generated by a botnet (or by a mailserver operated by spammers). We then apply a technique known as *SMTP dialects* [22] to assess which botnet or mailserver generated each connection. As a last step, we analyze the content of the spam emails that we receive, and group them into *spam campaigns*. Our assumption is that a single spammer will be responsible for each spam campaign. Such assumption has been confirmed by previous work [21]. After having logged this information, we compare the different datasets, checking whether the same spammer has rented multiple botnets, and whether multiple spammers share the same email list or botnet.

The results of this study give us new insights into how spammers operate. In particular, our findings suggest that spammers typically rent a single botnet and that a fraction of them set up their own mail transfer agents (MTAs) to spread spam. Another interesting discovery is that spammers tend to stick with a single list of email addresses for long periods of time, even years.

In summary, this paper makes the following contributions:

- We perform a large-scale experiment that tracks how email addresses are harvested, which botnets are contacting the harvested addresses, and what type of spam they are sending.
- We provide detailed statistics about the email harvesters, the spamming botnets, and the spam campaigns that we observed. We make novel observations on the way email harvesters operate and on the geographic distribution of the bots in large botnets.
- We analyze the relations between email harvesters, botmasters, and spammers. We show that, with rare exceptions, spammers purchase their email lists from professional email harvesters and rent a single botnet to send spam.
- We discuss how our observations can aid researchers in spam mitigation. We argue that the consistent habits of spammers in terms of the email lists and botnets they use can be leveraged for detection.

2. METHODOLOGY & DATA COLLECTION

The analysis infrastructure that we used in our measurement is composed of three parts:

1. **Email Harvester Logging.** In this part, we first advertise a large number of unique email addresses on the web. Each email address is only displayed once and points to a mailserver under our control. To be able to correlate received spam with harvesting information, we log web page retrieval logs for each issued email address. This approach thus allows us to identify which harvester fetched a certain email address.
2. **SMTP Dialect Fingerprinting.** Previous research showed that each botnet, email client, and mail transfer agent (MTA) uses a different implementation of the SMTP protocol [22]. This allows us to fingerprint the email engine of a host that is talking to a mailserver. We leverage this technique to fingerprint the different botnets and MTAs that send emails to the harvested email addresses.
3. **Spam Campaign Analysis.** To avoid easy detection, spammers slightly alter the content of their spam emails over time. However, previous research showed that it is possible to group spam campaigns by looking at the domains of the URLs that are advertised in the email body [27]. We leverage a similar technique, and identify spam campaigns that are carried out by the same spammer.

Site	Description	# of Addresses	# of Emails
A	Private blog	1	72
B	Gaming web site	274	1,511
C	Mail archive	187	387
D	Private web page	4	74
E	Spamtrap page	71	153

Table 1: Number of advertised email addresses (ids) and number of received spam emails per web site. As it can be seen, the gaming web site is the one whose addresses received the most spam.

In the remainder of this section, we describe the three parts of our data analysis infrastructure in detail.

2.1 Email Harvester Logging

We identify email harvesters by using a methodology that relies on issuing unique spamtrap email addresses via the web [9]. As the addresses are uniquely generated for each page request, their usage can be directly mapped to a specific page request once the first spam email is received. To allow for this mapping, we log basic information such as the requesting IP addresses, timestamps, and HTTP header information for all page requests. This per-request information allows us to analyze further properties such as the user agent strings submitted by the harvester bots.

The generated addresses are embedded into nine low-profile web pages of various type. Table 1 provides a description of the websites and statistics about the advertised email addresses. This methodology is implemented in web sites by including a server-side dynamic script that generates unique email addresses for each page request and logs information about the visitors. Each web site advertises six different spamtrap addresses, each being displayed with one of the following presentation and obfuscation techniques: *i)* a *mailto:* link, *ii)* non-linked, plain-text address, *iii)* address obfuscated in the form of *user [at] domain [dot] tld*, *iv)* address obfuscated using JavaScript code, *v)* address included in a hidden data field of a web form, and *vi)* plain-text address inside an HTML comment. All of the above described addresses consist of random strings of 10 characters each (*RND*

IDs, e.g., "jdi4gj8bzx"). We use random strings as they are difficult to guess and, therefore, we can be confident that a spammer who targets those addresses obtained them from the harvesters, and did not randomly guess them. In addition to random strings, we issue realistic looking addresses containing random combinations of first and last names generated from phone book records (e.g., "john.doe"). Compared to random strings, the assumption is that realistic looking addresses are harder to identify as fake addresses, but are also easier to guess.

Email addresses are advertised by appending different domains and Top Level Domains (TLDs). Our email domains are handled by several mail exchange servers located in different networks. These servers provide us with the unfiltered email feed via IMAP. We consider any email sent to those addresses as spam. As our SMTP dialect classification (see next section) relies on detailed SMTP transaction logs, we needed to capture detailed traffic traces at each mail exchange server. Unfortunately, this was only possible at one server due to administrative restrictions in other networks.

The data collection started on December 14, 2012, and ended on May 15, 2013. In this period, the system received 2,197 spam emails sent to 613 unique spamtrap addresses. The summary of the number of emails received per web site is reported in Table 1.

During the measurement period, the mail exchange server also received 1,299 emails sent to 75 email addresses that were not advertised by the system. Out of this set, 115 emails were addressed to `admins@foo.tld`, `info@foo.tld`, `contact@foo.tld`, `contactus@foo.tld`, and `sales@foo.tld`, where `foo.tld` denotes the domain advertised on the web and assigned to the mail exchange server. The remaining 1,184 emails were addressed to external email domains, including `163.com`, `gmail.com`, and `yahoo.com.tw`. As none of our mailservers is configured as an open relay, these mails were declined.

Despite the size small size of the dataset, it enabled us to observe interesting interactions between the different actors in the spam landscape. Our results therefore provide a first step in getting an understanding on how different parties involved in the spam process cooperate, which ultimately aims at gaining a better understanding of the online underground economy.

2.2 SMTP Dialect Fingerprinting

In our previous work, we showed that it is possible to reliably fingerprint an SMTP client by analyzing the SMTP messages that it exchanges with the mailserver. More precisely, each SMTP implementation, both in legitimate programs and in malware, shows differences in the way it implements the SMTP protocol [22]. We call these variations of the SMTP protocol *SMTP dialects* [22]. To identify different botnets, we extract the SMTP dialect spoken by each client trying to send an email to the mailserver.

The SMTP protocol is defined as an alternating dialogue between a client and a server. The messages sent by the client are called *SMTP commands*, while the messages sent by the server are called *SMTP replies* [1]. The client first specifies the sender of the email (in the form of an email address), one or more recipients, and then asks for permission to send the actual email content (with a `DATA` command). If the server grants this permission, the client starts transmitting the content of the email, otherwise the connection is aborted (typically because of an error). To study the SMTP dialect spoken by a client, we are only interested in the sequence of commands and replies until the `DATA` command is issued, or an error is reported.

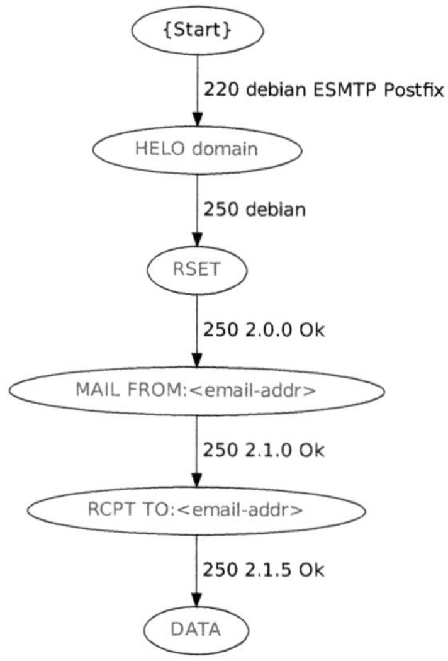

Figure 1: An example of an SMTP dialect. The transitions are labeled with server replies, while the states are labeled with client commands. Reaching the `DATA` command represents and email correctly being sent.

In our previous work, we defined an SMTP dialect **D** as a state machine

$$\mathbf{D} =< \Sigma, S, s_0, T, F_g, F_b >,$$

where Σ is the input alphabet (composed of server replies), S is a set of states, each labeled with a client command, s_0 is an initial state, and T is a set of transitions. $F_g \subset S$ is a set of good states, representing an email being processed correctly, while $F_b \subset S$ is a set of bad states, representing an error in the email sending process. Since SMTP commands include variable fields (such as email addresses), we abstract specific fields of the commands into regular expressions. In particular, we substitute fully-qualified domains, IP addresses, host names, and email addresses with generic identifiers. This operation is described in detail in our previous paper [22].

To build an SMTP dialect, we capture the SMTP conversations between a client and the mailserver and iteratively build the state machine, as described in [22]. Figure 1 shows an example of an SMTP dialect. The transitions represent server replies, while the states represent client commands. In this particular case, the client first announces itself and its domain (`HELO` command), then sends a `RSET` command, specifies the sender and the recipient email addresses (with the `MAIL` and `RCPT` commands, respectively), and starts sending the content of the email.

2.2.1 *Learning the Dialects Spoken by Botnets*

As we said, we are interested in understanding what botnet or MTA generated the emails that have been sent to the mailserver. To this end, we need previous knowledge about which SMTP dialects are spoken by different botnets and MTAs. To accomplish this task, we analyzed the SMTP conversations generated by the malware samples submitted to *Anubis*, a popular sandbox malware analysis system [2]. For each malware sample, we first learned the SMTP dialect spoken by it. Then, we grouped together all the samples that speak the same dialect.

We analyzed the malware samples submitted to Anubis for the period between January 1, 2013 and May 15, 2013. In total, 18,849 submitted samples connected to a mailserver and started an SMTP conversation. These samples include spamming botnets, self-propagating worms that send a copy of themselves over email, and generic malware that sends an email to their botmaster as a heartbeat signal. The sandbox environment did not allow any SMTP connection to the outside, but redirected them to a local mailserver. This way, we were able to log the SMTP conversations generated by the malware samples. In total, the malware samples that we analyzed speak 72 different SMTP dialects. As we will show in Section 3.2, these dialects cover the vast majority of the hosts that contacted the email addresses that we disseminated on the web.

To assign a name to each dialect, we proceeded as follows. First, we grouped all the malware samples that speak the same dialect together. Then, we collected the name given to those malware samples by popular antivirus programs, by using `Virustotal` [25]. Finally, we assigned as a name for the malware family the most common label assigned to the samples that speak that dialect by the antivirus programs in `Virustotal`. This approach has been already used in previous work, and it proved to be reliable [22].

Not all spam is sent by botnets though [24]. Some spammers set up their own mailservers and use them to send spam, instead of setting up botnets. To identify this type of spam, we need to learn the dialects spoken by popular Mail Transfer Agents (MTAs). To this end, we set up a number of virtual machines, and installed a different MTA on each of them. More precisely, we used Virtualbox as our virtualization environment — we set up Ubuntu Linux 11.10 virtual machines, and set up one of the Exim, Postfix, Qmail, and Sendmail MTAs on each of them; we also set up a Windows Server 2008 virtual machine, and ran Microsoft Exchange 2010 on it. On each virtual machine, we set up a script that sent emails automatically to a mailserver under our control. We then leveraged the SMTP conversations generated by the virtual machines to learn the dialects spoken by each MTA. As we already noted, each MTA speaks a different dialect from the others [22].

2.3 Spam Campaign Analysis

We call a spam operation a *spam campaign*. Broadly speaking, a spam campaign is composed by a set of emails that advertise the same product. Typical goods advertised in spam emails are pharmaceutical products, counterfeit goods, dating sites, and others [21]. In this paper, we consider a spam campaign as being indicative of a single spammer. This assumption is motivated by the fact that previous work showed that each spammer sets up his/her email templates when sending spam [21]. In principle however, the same spammer might run multiple spam campaigns at the same time. We perform a more comprehensive analysis of these assumptions in Section 3.4.

Even if they advertise the same type of goods, the spam emails belonging to the same campaign are not identical. Spammers add some variations in the content, in the subject lines, and in the advertised URLs to avoid easy detection by template-based anti-spam techniques [19, 27]. For this reason, we have to adopt more advanced similarity techniques to group spam emails into spam campaigns. We extract four features that characterize an email; in the following, we describe them in detail. We consider two emails as belonging to the same campaign if they match any of these four criteria.

Subject Line. Subject lines are important in spam emails, because they are the first piece of information seen by a victim, and might lure them into opening the full email. Spammers need to make their subject lines captivating, but also vary them enough to avoid easy detection. We consider two emails as belonging to the same spam campaign if their subject lines are either identical or share four or more words.

URL domain. Miscreants change the domains that they use to host their malicious web pages quite often. Since purchasing domains has a non-negligible cost, however, they use each of them for multiple emails. For this reason, we consider two emails as belonging to the same spam campaign if they advertise a URL that shares the same domain. A similar technique has been leveraged by previous research [27].

Mailer. Spammers often use fake mail user agent strings in the email headers (mailer). This mailer is often the same for the emails belonging to the same campaign [21]. Therefore, we group together emails that share the same mailer.

Sender email address. From our observations, we noticed that most spammers set the `From` address in their emails. We also observed that this from address is often shared by multiple emails in the same campaign. For this reason, we group together emails that share the same sender address.

2.4 Assumptions & Limitations

The methodology that we follow in this paper is based on a set of assumptions. In the following, we discuss these assumptions in detail.

Different actors in the spam chain engage in a market economy. We assume the presence of three different roles, i.e., the harvester, the botmaster, and the spammer. As suggested by previous work [21], these roles are likely to be represented by different entities that engage in a market economy. For example, email addresses are collected by the harvester and then sold to spammers who rent botnets for the spam dissemination. In other cases, the spammer and the harvester might represent the same entity.

Different usage pattern in the harvesting and spamming process are indicative for the different actors. While we cannot observe the different actors directly, we assume that they can be fingerprinted by different observable usage pattern. For instance, short turnaround times in which spam arrives almost immediately after harvesting [9, 20] can be *indicative* for cases in which the harvesting is performed by the spammer. In turn, long turnaround times of up to multiple years, however, can be *indicative* of cases in which email addresses were sold on the market. Conversely, spammer and harvester are likely to be two independent entities. We note that this first step provides *indications* rather than strict evidence.

Email addresses are being harvested from the web. In this paper, we only focus on e-mail addresses that were harvested from public web pages by using crawlers. We remark that there are other ways to harvest email addresses, such as malicious software locally running on compromised machines [14]. These further harvesting techniques are, however, out-of-scope of this paper.

SMTP dialects are indicative for different botnets. To identify different botnets, we rely on SMTP dialect fingerprinting. We assume that this technique can reliably distinguish between malware families that send spam or between misused MTAs. This assumption is supported by our previous work, in which we show that all the SMTP implementations that we encountered in the wild are different [22].

A single campaign is indicative for a single spammer. Spam campaigns advertise goods, point to scam web pages, or disseminate malware. We assume that such campaigns are run by an entity that we refer to as a spammer. The spammer himself remains invisible to us and only the launched campaigns can be observed. Previous work showed that spammers use individual templates for composing spam mails [21] and thus supports our hypothesis. In case of a joint campaign run by multiple spammers, individual entities cannot be differentiated by our approach and are merged into distinct observable campaigns. Thus, we cannot derive exact figures on the number of spammers observed.

The assumed behavior of the harvester, the botmaster, and the spammer are based on indirect measurements of both the harvesting and the spamming process. The nature of the applied indirect measurements yields correlations among the behavior of different actors in the spam chain. However, our approach does not allow us to derive *exact* figures and causal relationships for the involved actors. Despite these limitations, this work provides a novel first step in understanding these relationships.

3. ANALYSIS OF THE COLLECTED DATA

In the following, we first analyze the harvesters that fetched our email addresses. Then, we analyze the botnets (or MTAs) that sent the emails and we study the spam campaigns that targeted our email addresses. Finally, we discuss the relations among the three actors involved in the spam delivery process (harvesters, botnets, and spammers).

3.1 Analysis of the Harvesters

In total, the spamtrap email addresses in our dataset were harvested by 75 unique IP addresses. Note that the number of IP addresses does not map to the number of harvesters. In distributed infrastructures, for instance, multiple IP addresses can belong to the same harvesting entity. A distributed infrastructure helps in two ways: it is more efficient, and it is stealthier. From what we observed in our experiments, however, the main activity concentrates on a small set of IPs. In particular, four IP addresses harvested 70% of the email addresses, which ended up receiving 74% of the total spam.

To classify the harvesters that crawled the web sites, we manually analyzed the dataset. We consider two IP addresses as belonging to the same harvester if *i)* they are located in the same autonomous system or if *ii)* they announce the same user agent string or share patterns in the HTTP headers. While several distinct harvester bots can run in the same AS, we consider the submitted user agent string pattern to be one characteristic of the harvesting software being used.

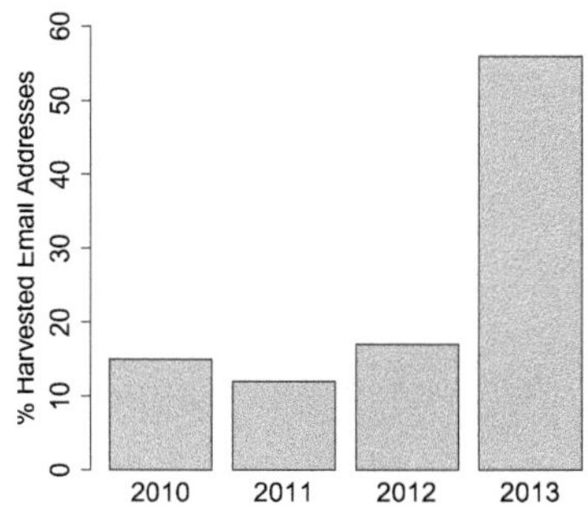

Figure 2: Harvesting year. As it can be seen, most addresses have been harvested during 2013.

In total, we observed nine distinct harvesters, which are summarized in Table 4. Five harvesters used a single IP address, while the others were distributed. The largest distributed harvester (C) was observed on 56 distinct IP addresses located in a residential DSL access network in Germany. One unique characteristic of this harvester are random-looking user agent strings. The total number of machines used by the harvester is likely to be different from the number of IP addresses, as residential users in this network get new dynamic IP addresses assigned every 24 hours. While the 56 IP addresses could in theory belong to the same physical machine, we observed several parallel crawling activities from multiple IP addresses. This indeed suggests a distributed harvesting infrastructure.

Interestingly, the size of the harvester, estimated by the number of IP addresses, does not correlate with harvesting activity and spam volume received by the harvested email address: The largest number of email addresses was collected by a harvester (D) that was using only three IP addresses.

We assume user agent strings to be a main characteristic of a harvesting software. Table 4 also shows example user agents for the email harvesters that we observed. Some of the user agent strings mimic legitimate browsers, while others identify software libraries or consist of random strings. In some cases, such as harvester I, the user agent does not change at subsequent requests. For some harvesters, the user agent is constantly changed, arguably to avoid easy detection. At the extreme is harvester C, which sets a different random string as user agent after each request.

We observe two interesting patterns in the harvesters that contacted us. Firstly, the Java user agent used by harvester D correlated with high harvesting activity and caused large spam volumes. Earlier observations of this user agent in the context of harvesting [9, 20] suggest that this harvesting software has existed for at least eight years and thus to be a stable pattern in the harvesting landscape.

As we observed earlier [9], in some cases addresses that we returned only to harvesters presenting the user agent of the Google bot received spam. This denotes the case of harvester F that not only presents a legitimate user agent, but

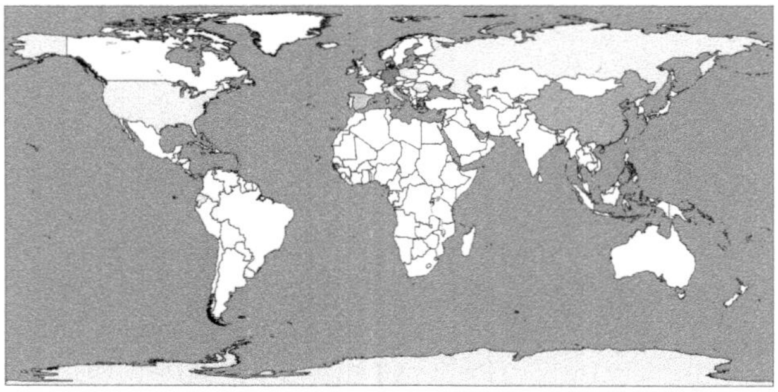

Figure 3: Country distribution of the email harvesters. 73% of the harvester IP addresses were located in Germany, while 9% of them came from China.

also originates from the Google AS. It suggests that harvesters use search engines as a proxy to either *i)* hide their own identity or *ii)* optimize the harvesting process itself. We identified harvesting software that offers the functionality of querying search engines. For example, the advertisement for ECrawl v2.63 [17] states: "Access to the Google cache (VERY fast harvesting)," while the description of the Fast Email Harvester 1.2 reports that the "collector supports all major search engines, such as Google, Yahoo, MSN" [6].

It is interesting to look at where the harvesters are located. By using the Maxmind geolocation database [16], we map harvester IP addresses to geolocation. We additionally map harvester IP addresses to AS numbers. We observe harvesters from ten countries (eleven Autonomous Systems), respectively. Figure 3 shows the country distribution of the IP addresses that harvested the email addresses that we disseminated. A darker color in the map represents a larger fraction of IP addresses from that country. As it can be seen, Germany is the country hosting the largest number of harvesters (73% of the total), followed by China (9%), and Spain (5%). The prevalence of German IP addresses can be explained with the fact that the IP addresses of harvester C, which is composed of 56 IP addresses, are all located in Germany. On the other hand, the IP addresses of harvester D, which was the one that was able to gather the highest number of IP addresses, are located in the Netherlands.

We next focus on harvesting activity periods. The harvesting time of email addresses that received spam during the measurement dates back to 2010. We show the number of addresses harvested per year in Figure 2. We split the harvesting activity in activity periods. We define activity periods as periods of time in which the harvester connected to our pages at least once in each of two consecutive hours. The number of activity periods with their respective start and end time is shown in Table 2. The harvesting behavior that we observed during an activity period was typically intense, with a larger number of crawled web sites in a small time period of several seconds to minutes.

We investigated what happens to e-mail addresses after they have been harvested by focusing on the usage of harvested addresses. Concretely, we denote the time between the address being harvested and the first spam email received at that address as the *turnaround time* and show their median value in Table 3. Harvester D and G show

Harvester	Activity Periods	Start	Stop
A	2	2010-07-02	2010-07-02
B	1	2010-10-30	2010-10-30
C	41	2010-02-10	2010-10-20
D	3	2011-01-08	2013-04-06
E	1	2011-01-15	2011-01-15
F	1	2013-03-29	2013-03-29
G	1	2012-08-30	2012-08-30
H	4	2012-10-19	2012-12-05
I	4	2011-08-27	2012-02-16

Table 2: Activity periods per harvester. As it can be seen, some harvesters were active in bursts for short periods of time, while others were constantly observed for very long periods.

Harvester	Median Turnaround Time
A	26 days
B	15 days
C	343 days
D	5 days
E	548 days
F	35 days
G	5 days
H	42 days

Table 3: Email turnaround times. This table shows after how many days from the harvesting the first spam email was received.

the fastest turnaround of 5 days, while medium turnaround times of less than two months are observed for harvester A, B, F and H. Harvester C and E show the longest turnaround time of more than one year. Long turnaround times suggest emails being sold on the market and used by entities other than the harvester. As previous research showed [21], the purchase of email lists on underground sites is heavily influenced by the reputation of the creator of the list. A reason for longer turnaround times might be that the reputation of the harvester is not yet established, and therefore spammers are less likely to purchase his lists.

3.2 Analysis of the SMTP Dialects

We learned the SMTP dialects for all the clients that sent emails to the mailserver, as described in Section 2.2. We discarded any SMTP conversation that generated an error, or for which the client abruptly closed the connection. Therefore, each SMTP conversation analyzed in this section corresponds to an email being delivered to the mailserver. We logged 2,024 correctly sent emails in total.

Our system identified seven different dialects among the clients that sent emails to the mailserver. A summary of these results is shown in Table 5. As it can be seen, the mailserver was targeted by three of the largest active spamming botnets (*Cutwail*, *Lethic*, and *Kelihos*). It was also targeted by *MyDoom*, which is a generic name used by antivirus companies to refer to email-spreading worms. Our mailserver was also contacted by two types of MTAs, set up by miscreants to send spam (*Postfix* and *Sendmail*). Note that, in principle, multiple spammers might use the same botnet, or set up the same MTA to send spam. We discuss this possibility in Section 3.4.

The *modus operandi* of the spammers using each botnet, worm, and MTA setup is rather different. For instance, the spammers using Lethic did not send emails only to harvested email address, but also to generic ones (e.g., `info`, `admin`). All other setups leveraged the email addresses harvested by

Harvester	# of IPs	# of Email Addresses	Sample User Agent
A	1	2	Mozilla/4.0 (compatible; MSIE 6.0; Windows NT 5.1; SV1; Alcohol Search;)
B	1	1	Mozilla/4.0 (compatible; Synapse)
C	56	60	r5wRofjnmtbqqrea5igfhmjisyqjikweoepo
D	3	415	Java/1.6.0_04
E	1	2	Mozilla/4.0 (compatible; MSIE 7.0; Windows NT 5.1; Trident/4.0;)
F	1	2	Mozilla/5.0 (compatible; Googlebot/2.1; +http://www.google.com/bot.html)
G	1	20	libwww-perl/6.04
H	2	13	Mozilla/5.0 (Windows; U; Windows NT 6.1; rv:11.0)
I	9	20	Mozilla/4.0(compatible; MSIE 5.0; Windows 98; DigExt)

Table 4: Summary of the observed email harvesters. For each email harvester, we include the number of IP addresses used, as well as the number of email addresses collected by the harvested, and a "sample" user agent. For those harvesters that vary their user agent, we included a random one among the ones used.

Botnet or MTA	Harvesters	Campaigns Sent	# of Email Addresses	# of Emails	# of IPs
Cutwail	A,B	A,B	3	244	243
Kelihos	C	C	5	8	5
Lethic	D,None	D	29	533	101
Mydoom	C,D,E,F,G	*	431	1,191	52
Postfix	C,D,H	E,F,G	41	43	5
Sendmail	B,C	H	5	5	4

Table 5: Summary of the SMTP dialects, the email lists, and the spam campaigns observed. The horizontal line separates dialects that belong to botnets or generic malware from those that belong to regular Mail Transfer Agents (MTAs). "None" means that the botnet sent emails to email addresses that were not harvested, but that are popular default addresses (e.g., `admin`). We omitted the list of campaigns spammed by Mydoom, for simplicity.

one or more harvesters. The way in which these addresses are used varies according to the type of setup too. In general, botnets tend to send several emails to each harvested address, while MTAs limit themselves to one email per address, on average.

Table 5 also shows the number of IP addresses that we observed belonging to each botnet and MTA. As it can be seen, botmasters use different strategies while managing their bots: Each email sent by Cutwail came from a different IP address (i.e., bot), while Lethic bots are reusing their email addresses. The time at which the different botnets or MTAs contacted the mailserver also varies. In particular, the Cutwail botnet constantly sent spam emails to our harvested addresses during the observation period, sending a small number of emails per day, while Lethic started contacting the mail server in April 2013, sending a higher number of emails. Mydoom, on the other hand, focused its activity during March 2013. A summary of the activity of the various botnets and MTAs that contacted us is pictured in Figure 4. The size of the circles is proportional to the number of emails sent by each botnet or MTA during that day.

As a last element, the different botnets show a very different country distribution of their bots: Figure 5 shows the country distribution for the Cutwail botnet. As it can be seen, most Cutwail bots are located in Korea (18% of the total), India (13%), and Serbia (9%). Lethic, on the other hand, has 92% of its bots located in South Korea (see Figure 6). This country distribution is not necessarily representative of all Cutwail and Lethic instances: as previous research showed, spammers rent single instances of command and control servers and buy their malware installations separately [3,21]; spammers can go as far as selecting the countries in which they want their bots to be located. Therefore, our observation suggests that the botnet users that sent spam to us purchased their bots in a small number of countries. Other instances (and customers) of the same botnet might show very different country distributions. The fact that each spammer uses bots located in different countries is consistent with previous work, which showed that the physical location of a bot does not influence the overall spamming performance of the botnet [10].

On the other hand, the Mydoom worm has most of its victims in Poland (19% of the total IP addresses) and in the United States (17%) (see Figure 7). We omit Kelihos because this botnet sent a very small amount of spam, and the map would not be meaningful.

We also wanted to understand in which countries spammers set up their mailservers to send spam. Figure 8 shows the country distribution of the Postfix and Sendmail installations that contacted the mailserver. Two servers were located in Russia, while the United States and Canada hosted one server each. The United Kingdom and Spain also hosted one server.

3.3 Analysis of the Spam Campaigns

We applied the clustering technique described in Section 2.3 to the emails that we received. In total, we obtained 63 spam campaigns. Table 6 reports a summary of some of these campaigns. We omitted the 55 spam campaigns carried out by Mydoom. We suspect that Mydoom might be a generic label that antivirus companies give to unknown malware samples, and therefore analyzing the different spammers grouped under this label is not very meaningful. For this reason, we did not analyze this botnet any further.

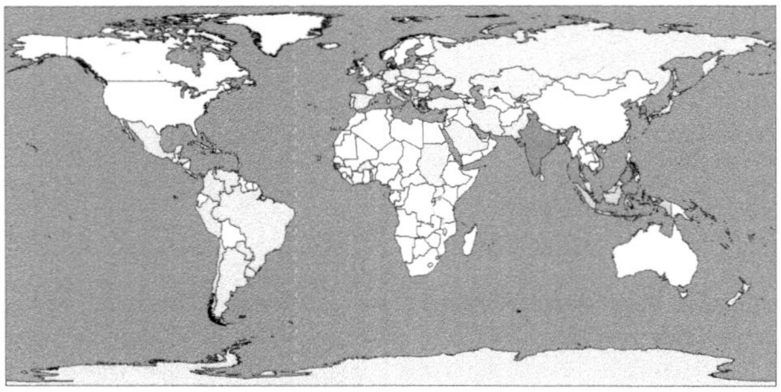

Figure 5: Country distribution of the Cutwail botnet. Most bots are in South Korea (18%), followed by India (13%).

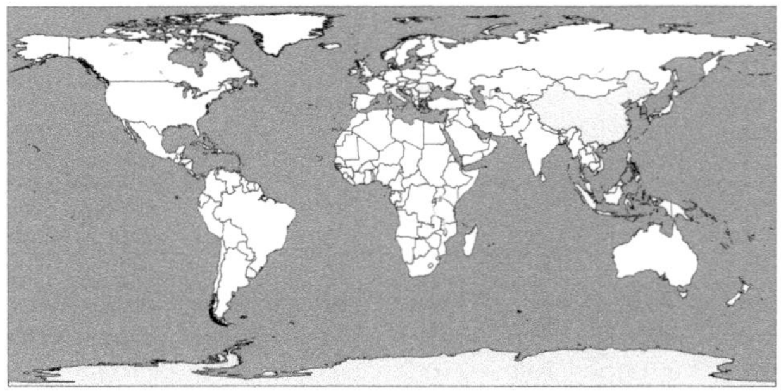

Figure 6: Country distribution of the Lethic botnet. The vast majority of the bots are located in South Korea (92%).

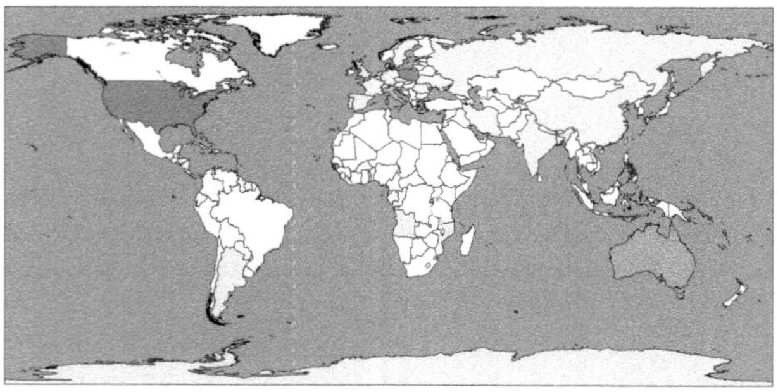

Figure 7: Country distribution of the Mydoom worm. The countries with most bots are Poland (19%) and the United States (17%).

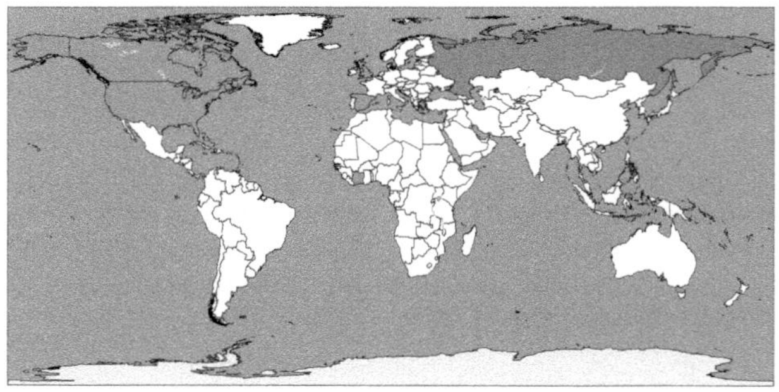

Figure 8: Country distribution of the MTAs used to send spam (Postfix and Sendmail). Interestingly, there are a number of rogue mailservers located in Western Europe and North America.

Campaign	# of Emails	Topic
A	64	Counterfeit goods
B	180	Online dating
C	8	Financial scam
D	533	Search Engine Optimization
E	7	Email marketing
F	6	Phishing scam
G	30	Phishing scam
H	5	Phishing scam

Table 6: Summary of the observed spam campaigns. The topic of the campaign was selected by manual analysis of the spam emails. We omitted the campaigns carried out by Mydoom for simplicity.

As it can be seen in Table 6, the spam campaigns that we logged cover a large variety of goods and services. Surprisingly, we did not observe any email advertising pharmaceutical products, which has been the focus of the majority of the underground economy research in the past [11]. While this might arguably be an artifact in our dataset, it might also suggest that spammers are moving on to exploring other ways of generating revenue, such as blackhat Search Engine Optimization (SEO). We leave a detailed investigation of changes in spamming trends for future work.

3.4 Relations Between the Actors

In this section, we discuss the relations between the different parties involved in the spam delivery process: email harvesters, spammers, and botmasters.

First, we try to understand how many spammers contacted the spamtrap system. The basic relations are reported in Table 5. As we mentioned, we consider a specific spam campaign as being indicative of a single spammer. However, a spammer might perform multiple spam campaigns, either at the same time, or at two different points in time. We consider two campaigns as being carried out by the same spammer if both the botnets or MTAs and the email lists used to carry out the two campaigns are the same.

Interestingly, all the botnets that we observed were used by a single spammer each. Lethic and Kelihos carried out a single spam campaign, while Cutwail carried out two different campaigns, at two distinct points in time. However, both campaigns used the email lists A and B. Therefore, we associate them to the same spammer. On the other hand, we identified three different installations of Postfix, each carrying out a different campaign, and each one using a different email list. We consider these three servers as being managed by three different spammers.

We next investigated whether email harvesters collect email addresses to sell them, or whether spammers are doing the harvesting themselves. The intuition here is that if the email

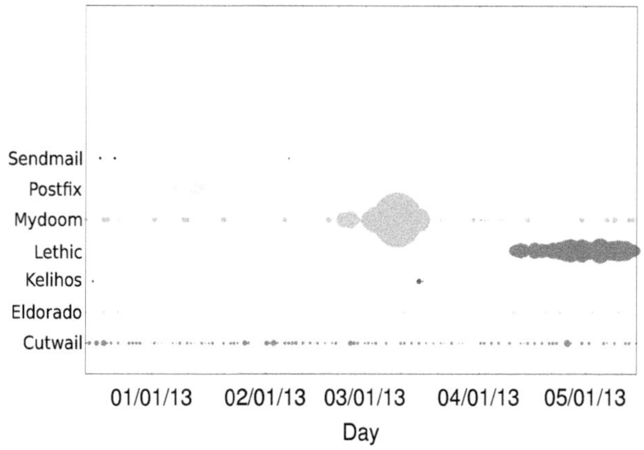

Figure 4: Email activity of the different botnets / MTAs per day. Each line represents a different dialect, and the diameter of the circles is a function of the number of emails sent by clients speaking that dialect during a given day.

addresses collected by a harvester are used by multiple spammers, they have likely been purchased on the black market. On the other hand, if a spammer is using a set of email addresses exclusively, he might have harvested them himself. Our findings lead us to speculate that harvesters C and D are likely to be ran by professional harvesters, who are selling their email lists on the black market. This is supported by the fact that multiple spammers used them for their spamming operations: the email list harvested by harvester C was used by spammers that rented Kelihos, Mydoom, Postfix, and Sendmail. Similarly, the email list sold by harvester D was used by Lethic, Mydoom, and Postfix users. The fact that multiple spammers purchased these email lists suggests that these harvesters are successfully collecting email addresses and advertising their email list. This is further supported by the fact that harvester C is the one with the largest infrastructure among the logged one (56 IP addresses), and that harvester D was the most successful one, with 415 harvested email addresses. It is also interesting that the first spam email that was received by one of the email addresses harvested by D arrived after five days from the harvesting (see Table 3). This shows that the operators of D are very efficient in harvesting email addresses and selling them on the black market. The operators of harvester B probably also sold their email list, since it has been used by both Cutwail and Postfix.

The emails harvested by two harvesters were used only by a single spammer (E, H). This might suggest that in these cases the spammers and the harvesters are the same entity, and are using the email addresses that they harvested exclusively for launching their spam campaigns. This intuition is supported by the fact that one of the Postfix installations was located in the same country as harvester H, which collected the email addresses used by that server (Spain). Interestingly, the email addresses collected by harvester I were not used by any spam setup.

4. DISCUSSION

Previous research showed that reputation is key for the success of a cybercriminal [21]. For example, an email harvester is more likely to sell his email lists if he is a respected member of the underground community, and a botmaster is more likely to rent his botnet to spammers if he has proven that his botnet works well in delivering spam. In the experiments performed for this paper, we found evidence of this behavior. Spammers seem to stick with the same email harvesters, as well as with the same botnets, for long periods of time. This suggests that spammers establish some sort of customer loyalty with harvesters and botmasters, and that this relationship hardly breaks (in the absence of major events, such as botnet takedowns).

The fact that spammers are using the same botnet and email list for long periods of time can be leveraged by security researchers for detection. For example, a system that was recently proposed observes bots as they contact different email servers, in practice fingerprinting the email list that the bots are using [23]. By observing a small number of bots that are known to belong to a botnet, this system is able to find more bots that use the same email list. Since spammers use the same email list for long periods of time, this approach could prove to be a very effective method to track spambots in the wild. Similarly, spammers that keep using the same botnet can be effectively detected by techniques that fingerprint the email engine used by such botnets [22]. Moreover, since spammers seem to rely on a single botnet at a time, taking down the botnet that they are using can have significant effects on their business. This observation makes techniques that identify command and control servers particularly important [4, 7, 26].

The fact that spammers concentrate their bots in a small number of countries could further help in the detection. Previous research showed that the geographical distance between spamming bots and their victims is higher on average than the distance between legitimate email senders and recipients [8]. Similarly, having spambots that are concentrated in few far countries can be used as a strong indicator for a mailserver performing spam detection.

As we said previously, we did not observe any pharmaceutical spam sent to the email addresses that were harvested. This is somewhat surprising, since much of previous research focused on studying spam schemes that advertise pharmaceuticals [11, 12]. Besides being caused by measurement artifacts, another reason for this discrepancy might be that pharmaceutical spam has been steadily declining over the last two years, as recent reports noted [24]. Alternatively, it could be that large pharmaceutical affiliate programs harvest their own email addresses, and that they directly provide them to their affiliates, who do not have to look for email lists on the black market.

Note that our findings are based on *correlations* among the observed behavior of different actors in the spam chain—the harvester, the botmaster, and the spammer. Despite the correlative nature of our analysis and the limited dataset size, the collected data enables us to observe interesting interactions between the different actors in the spam landscape. Thus, we see our work as a promising first step toward understanding how different parties involved in the spam process cooperate, which ultimately improves our understanding of the online underground economy. We expect additional data to deepen this understanding and plan to expand this preliminary study in future work. The next steps include going beyond our correlation analysis to establishing causal relationships among the different spam actors.

5. RELATED WORK

A wealth of research has been conducted on email spam. By studying the underground economy surrounding spam, as well as the challenges that spammers and botmasters face, researchers can develop new mitigation techniques that attackers cannot easily evade. Previous research falls in two main fields: *Studying the conversion of spam* and *Studying the spam delivery infrastructure.*

Studying the conversion of spam. Studying to what extent the goods advertised in spam emails are purchased helps in dimensioning the spam ecosystem, and in understanding how much money spammers can make. Kanich et al. infiltrated the Storm botnet, and modified the spam emails sent by the botnet to point to their fake pharmaceutical site [11]. This way, they were able to track the number of users that would have purchased the counterfeit goods. In a follow-up work, Kanich et al. studied a large rogue pharmaceutical website [12]. By leveraging a vulnerability in the website that allowed to enumerate any order that was made, they estimated the size of the whole spam operation. Levchenko et al. studied the workflow of spam-advertised goods, from when a good is purchased, to when it is delivered to the customer [15]. They were able to identify the financial institutions involved in transactions related to the spam business. Although studying the economic conversion of spam is very important, it goes beyond the scope of this paper. Instead, we look at how the different entities operating in the spam delivery business operate and are related.

Studying the spam delivery infrastructure. When studying the spam delivery infrastructure, it is important to understand how the different parties involved in it operate. Previous work studied how miscreants collect email addresses on the web [9,20]. This research showed how automated harvesters operated, and suggested some simple obfuscation techniques that can prevent them to read email address, while still making them intelligible to humans.

A wealth of research has been conducted in studying the command and control (C&C) infrastructure of spamming botnets, and how botmasters manage their bots. Stone-Gross et al. analyzed a number of C&C servers from the Cutwail botnet, studying how spammers used them, and the challenges that they had to face [21]. Cho et al. infiltrated the MegaD botnet, providing interesting insights on how a large-scale botnet operates. A number of infiltration operations have been performed against peer-to-peer botnets, showing how these botnets work, and the type of spam that they send [13,18].

Another interesting aspect is understanding how miscreants purchase infected machines. Caballero et al. [3] showed that there are complex schemes, made of malware-delivery networks that can download the payload that is required by customers on a large number of infected machines.

Although previous research suggested that there is a rich underground economy trading all the components required to set up a successful spam campaign (email lists, botnets, and malware installations) [21], no work actually studied these dynamics. Our paper provides a first look at this phenomenon, focusing on the relations between email harvesters, botnets, and spammers.

6. CONCLUSIONS

In this paper, we analyzed how the different actors involved in the spam delivery process cooperate, and what type of resources are shared among them. Our preliminary study suggests that spammers typically rely on a number of professional email harvesters to populate their email lists. Also, our findings suggest that spammers typically rent a single botnet, instead of using multiple ones at the same time. This work is a first step in understanding how spammers operate, and how the underground economy landscape look like. We hope that the insights provided in this paper will help researchers in finding the weak points in the spam delivery chain, and in developing better mitigation techniques.

7. ACKNOWLEDGMENTS

This work was supported by the Office of Naval Research (ONR) under Grant N000140911042, the Army Research Office (ARO) under grant W911NF0910553, and Secure Business Austria.

8. REFERENCES

[1] RFC 821: Simple Mail Transfer Protocol. `http://tools.ietf.org/html/rfc821`.

[2] U. Bayer, A. Moser, C. Kruegel, and E. Kirda. Dynamic analysis of malicious code. *Journal in Computer Virology*, 2(1):67–77, 2006.

[3] J. Caballero, C. Grier, C. Kreibich, and V. Paxson. Measuring Pay-per-Install: The Commoditization of Malware Distribution. In *USENIX Security Symposium*, 2011.

[4] J. Caballero, P. Poosankam, C. Kreibich, and D. Song. Dispatcher: Enabling Active Botnet Infiltration Using Automatic Protocol Reverse-Engineering. In *ACM Conference on Computer and Communications Security (CCS)*, 2009.

[5] C. Cho, J. Caballero, C. Grier, V. Paxson, and D. Song. Insights from the Inside: A View of Botnet Management from Infiltration. In *USENIX Workshop on Large-Scale Exploits and Emergent Threats (LEET)*, 2010.

[6] eMarkSofts. Fast email harvester 1.2. `http://fast-email-harvester.smartcode.com/info.html`, 2009.

[7] G. Gu, R. Perdisci, J. Zhang, and W. Lee. BotMiner: Clustering Analysis of Network Traffic for Protocol- and Structure-independent Botnet Detection. In *USENIX Security Symposium*, 2008.

[8] S. Hao, N. A. Syed, N. Feamster, A. G. Gray, and S. Krasser. Detecting Spammers with SNARE: Spatio-temporal Network-level Automatic Reputation Engine. In *USENIX Security Symposium*, 2009.

[9] O. Hohlfeld, T. Graf, and F. Ciucu. Longtime Behavior of Harvesting Spam Bots. In *ACM SIGCOMM Conference on Internet Measurement*, 2012.

[10] J. Iedemska, G. Stringhini, R. Kemmerer, C. Kruegel, and G. Vigna. The Tricks of the Trade: What Makes Spam Campaigns Successful? In *International Workshop on Cyber Crime*, 2014.

[11] C. Kanich, C. Kreibich, K. Levchenko, B. Enright, G. Voelker, V. Paxson, and S. Savage. Spamalytics:

An Empirical Analysis of Spam Marketing Conversion. In *ACM Conference on Computer and Communications Security (CCS)*, 2008.

[12] C. Kanich, N. Weaver, D. McCoy, T. Halvorson, C. Kreibich, K. Levchenko, V. Paxson, G. Voelker, and S. Savage. Show Me the Money: Characterizing Spam-advertised Revenue. *USENIX Security Symposium*, 2011.

[13] C. Kreibich, C. Kanich, K. Levchenko, B. Enright, G. M. Voelker, V. Paxson, and S. Savage. On the Spam Campaign Trail. In *USENIX Workshop on Large-Scale Exploits and Emergent Threats (LEET)*, 2008.

[14] C. Kreibich, C. Kanich, K. Levchenko, B. Enright, G. M. Voelker, V. Paxson, and S. Savage. Spamcraft: An Inside Look at Spam Campaign Orchestration. In *USENIX Workshop on Large-Scale Exploits and Emergent Threats (LEET)*, 2009.

[15] K. Levchenko, A. Pitsillidis, N. Chachra, B. Enright, M. Félegyházi, C. Grier, T. Halvorson, C. Kanich, C. Kreibich, H. Liu, et al. Click trajectories: End-to-end analysis of the spam value chain. In *IEEE Symposium on Security and Privacy*, 2011.

[16] MaxMind. GeoIP. `http://www.maxmind.com/app/ip-location`.

[17] Northworks Solutions Ltd. Ecrawl v2.63. `http://www.northworks.biz/software.html`, 2012.

[18] C. Nunnery, G. Sinclair, and B. B. Kang. Tumbling Down the Rabbit Hole: Exploring the Idiosyncrasies of Botmaster Systems in a Multi-Tier Botnet Infrastructure. In *USENIX Workshop on Large-Scale Exploits and Emergent Threats (LEET)*, 2010.

[19] A. Pitsillidis, K. Levchenko, C. Kreibich, C. Kanich, G. M. Voelker, V. Paxson, N. Weaver, and S. Savage. botnet Judo: Fighting Spam with Itself. In *Symposium on Network and Distributed System Security (NDSS)*, 2010.

[20] M. Prince, B. Dahl, L. Holloway, A. Keller, and E. Langheinrich. Understanding how spammers steal your e-mail address: An analysis of the first six months of data from project honey pot. In *Collaboration, Electronic messaging, Anti-Abuse and Spam Conference (CEAS)*, 2005.

[21] B. Stone-Gross, T. Holz, G. Stringhini, and G. Vigna. The Underground Economy of Spam: A Botmaster's Perspective of Coordinating Large-Scale Spam Campaigns. In *USENIX Workshop on Large-Scale Exploits and Emergent Threats (LEET)*, 2011.

[22] G. Stringhini, M. Egele, A. Zarras, T. Holz, C. Kruegel, and G. Vigna. B@BEL: Leveraging Email Delivery for Spam Mitigation. In *USENIX Security Symposium*, 2012.

[23] G. Stringhini, T. Holz, B. Stone-Gross, C. Kruegel, and G. Vigna. BotMagnifier: Locating Spammers on the Internet. In *USENIX Security Symposium*, 2011.

[24] Symantec Corp. State of spam & phishing report. `http://www.symantec.com/content/en/us/enterprise/other_resources/b-intelligence_report_02-2013.en-us.pdf?om_ext_cid=biz_socmed_AR_pv_180313_scom_socialmedia_SIRFeb13`, 2013.

[25] VirusTotal. Free Online Virus, Malware and URL Scanner. `https://www.virustotal.com/`.

[26] P. Wurzinger, L. Bilge, T. Holz, J. Goebel, C. Kruegel, and E. Kirda. Automatically Generating Models for Botnet Detection. In *European Symposium on Research in Computer Security (ESORICS)*, 2009.

[27] Y. Xie, F. Yu, K. Achan, R. Panigrahy, G. Hulten, and I. Osipkov. Spamming Botnets: Signatures and Characteristics. *SIGCOMM Comput. Commun. Rev.*, 38, August 2008.

pTwitterRec: A Privacy-Preserving Personalized Tweet Recommendation Framework

Bisheng Liu and Urs Hengartner
Cheriton School of Computer Science
University of Waterloo, Waterloo, ON, Canada
{bisheng.liu, urs.hengartner}@uwaterloo.ca

ABSTRACT

Twitter is one of the most popular Online Social Networks (OSNs) nowadays. Twitter users retrieve information from other users by subscribing to their tweets. Twitter users, especially those who have many followees, may receive hundreds or even thousands of tweets daily. Currently, all tweets are shown to users in chronological order. Consequently, a Twitter user may accidentally overlook useful and interesting tweets because the user is overwhelmed by the huge volume of uninteresting tweets. Researchers in the recommendation system community have proposed using recommendation techniques such as collaborative filtering to predict users' preference of tweets and highlight those tweets in which users are most likely to be interested. At the same time, while OSNs such as Twitter have enabled people to conveniently share information and interact with each other online, OSN users are getting increasingly concerned about their online privacy. Researchers in the security community have proposed using techniques such as encrypted tweets to protect users' privacy. In this paper, we propose a privacy-preserving personalized tweet recommendation framework, *pTwitterRec*, in a Twitter-like social network where users' tweets are hidden from the OSN provider. *pTwitterRec* provides users with personalized tweet recommendations while keeping users' tweets and interests hidden from the OSN provider as well as other unauthorized entities. *pTwitterRec* splits the tweet recommendation task between the provider and a semi-trusted third party, so that neither can derive users' sensitive information alone while working together to provide users with personalized tweet recommendations. We implement a prototype and demonstrate through evaluation that *pTwitterRec* incurs tolerable overhead on today's smartphones.

Categories and Subject Descriptors

H.3.3 [**Information Search and Retrieval**]: Information filtering; J.4 [**Computer Applications**]: Social and behavioral sciences; K.4.1 [**Computers and Society**]: Public Policy Issues – Privacy

ASIA CCS'14, June 4–6, 2014, Kyoto, Japan.

http://dx.doi.org/10.1145/2590296.2590304

Keywords

Privacy Protection; Tweet Recommendations; Personalization

1. INTRODUCTION

Twitter is a popular online social networking website and microblogging service that allows users to conveniently share short messages of up to 140 characters, known as "tweets", with their online followers. With more than 550 million active registered Twitter users nowadays, approximately 58 million tweets are generated per day [38]. Twitter users on average follow 80 people [29], which leads to hundreds or even thousands of new tweets received by each user every day. Currently, all tweets are shown to users in chronological order, which may lead to users missing some informative and interesting tweets simply because users are overwhelmed by other tweets that do not interest them at all. Researchers [10, 14, 21] have proposed using various recommendation techniques that utilize all kinds of information available on Twitter (such as users' tweet history and social relations) to rank tweets and display those tweets that might interest the user most on top.

In the meantime, users of Online Social Networks (OSNs) such as Twitter are increasingly concerned about privacy issues [30]. In general, OSN providers are considered to be trustworthy, as they have a valuable reputation to maintain and any suspicion of malicious behaviors could potentially lead to a significant loss of users. As a result, users trust OSN providers by default to properly safeguard and manage the contents published by users. Unfortunately, users' privacy is at risk by placing trust completely on OSN providers. For example, OSNs' Terms of Service typically include clauses that explicitly/implicitly allow the provider to mine user content for the purpose of delivering targeted advertising or reselling to third party services [12]. Also, in regions where OSNs are closely monitored by unscrupulous and suppressive governments [32], it is crucial to guarantee that only users' explicitly authorized followers/friends can access their data. Researchers in the security community have proposed several approaches [3, 12, 16, 23] to achieve this goal by delegating control over content to end users.

The contributions of this paper are as follows: Our work is the first, to our best knowledge, to propose a privacy-preserving personalized tweet recommendation framework, *pTwitterRec*. We enhance an existing personalized tweet recommendation algorithm with a few cryptographic protocols and split the recommendation task between the provider of the Twitter-like service and a semi-trusted third party, so that users obtain personalized tweet recommendations without leaking any sensitive information to unauthorized entities. We demonstrate the practicality through implementation and evaluation of the overhead incurred by *pTwitterRec*. *pTwitterRec* only introduces minimum overhead on the user side while achieving the privacy goal, compared with the original tweet recommendation algorithm, which was designed with no privacy in mind. In this paper, we positively answer the following question: in a Twitter-like OSN, can we provide users with *the benefits of personalized tweet recommendations* while *keeping the contents of users' tweets and users' interests hidden from the provider as well as other unauthorized parties*?

The remainder of this paper is organized as follows: In Section 2, we overview the related work. In Section 3, we introduce the background of our work. In Section 4, we describe our system and threat models. In Section 5, we present in detail our proposed privacy-preserving personalized tweet recommendation framework *pTwitterRec*. In Section 6, we discuss the security and privacy aspects and a possible extension of *pTwitterRec*. We describe the server-side implementation in Section 7. We analyze and evaluate the overhead incurred by *pTwitterRec* in Section 8. Finally we conclude our work in Section 9.

2. RELATED WORK

2.1 Tweet Recommendations

Researchers have proposed recommendation systems for Twitter. Chen et al. [9] focus on recommending URLs on Twitter that a Twitter user might find interesting. Hannon et al. [17] develop a followee recommender system for Twitter that utilizes Twitter's real-time information as a source of recommendation knowledge. Diaz-Aviles et al. [13] propose using collaborative filtering to recommend hash tags on Twitter in real-time.

Some researchers focus on recommending tweets that are interesting to users. Duan et al. [14] propose using *learning to rank* algorithms to rank tweets based on the user query. Their approach considers quality of tweets and authority of the publishers but does not consider user personalization. Ramage et al. [31] propose using latent variable topic models like *Labeled LDA* to map the content of the Twitter feed into dimensions and then filter Twitter feeds for users. Their approach uses content-based filtering and does not consider users' social relations. Naveed et al. [21] propose using a learning approach based on pure content features to predict the probability of a message being retweeted. Their work does not consider user personalization, either. Chen et al. [10] propose using collaborative ranking to recommend tweets that are personally interesting to a user. Their approach considers not only explicit features such as quality of the tweet and authority of the publisher, but also tweet topic level latent factors and social relation latent factors. Experiments on real-world data show that their approach outperforms other tweet recommendation algorithms in terms of *mean average precision* (MAP).

Our work is based on the tweet recommendation algorithm proposed by Chen et al. [10]. In addition, we provide users with personalized tweet recommendations while preserving user privacy.

2.2 Privacy-preserving Recommendations

Privacy for traditional recommender systems such as collaborative filtering has been extensively studied. Canny [7, 8] propose using homomorphic encryption and a peer-to-peer protocol to provide privacy for model-based collaborative recommender systems. Polat and Du [25–28] propose that customers adopt randomized perturbation techniques to disturb their private data before sending the data to the service provider for recommender systems. Aïmeur et al. [1] propose using a semi-trusted third party to distill encoded sensitive customer information, which can be used to produce recommendations but cannot be decrypted by any of the concerned parties alone.

In personalized tweet recommendations, tweets are regarded as items and many unique Twitter features such as content information and social relation information need to be utilized to improve recommendation accuracy. None of the abovementioned approaches can be trivially adapted to offer personalized tweet recommendations while preserving user privacy.

2.3 Privacy-preserving OSNs

There has been significant work in OSN privacy. Our work is most related to approaches that aim to protect social network users' privacy from a curious OSN provider. Systems such as *FlyByNight* [22], *NOYB* [16] and *Facecloak* [23] store users' data with the untrusted provider but protect its content with encryption. Conti et al. [11] propose establishing a virtual private network between friends on OSNs to share sensitive information. Singh et al. [34] propose *Twitsper*, a wrapper around Twitter that enables private group communication among Twitter users while preserving Twitter's business interests. Feldman et al. [15] propose *Frientegrity*, a framework where an OSN provider observes only encrypted data and cannot deviate from correct execution without being detected. De Cristofaro et al. [12] propose *Hummingbird*, a variant of Twitter that protects users' tweets as well as users' interests from a semi-trusted OSN provider.

Our work, however, focuses primarily on protecting users' privacy from a curious OSN provider while offering users personalized tweet recommendations. Our privacy-preserving tweet recommendation framework *pTwitterRec* can be built upon any of the abovementioned approaches as long as the OSN provider is able to distribute tweets to the corresponding followers without learning the tweets.

3. BACKGROUND

3.1 Twitter

Twitter is one of the most popular OSNs that enable users to send and read *tweets*, which are text messages limited to 140 characters. A user receives tweets from other users by subscribing to their tweets. Twitter terminology relevant to this paper includes:

- *Publisher*: A user who posts a tweet.
- *Follower*: A user who follows others' tweets.
- *Followee*: A user whose tweets are being followed by others.
- *Tweets*: short messages posted by a user/publisher.
- *Retweets*: someone else's tweets that a user chooses to share with all of the user's followers.
- *Service Provider* (*SP*): the centralized entity of Twitter that maintains all user profiles and tweets, and distributes users' tweets to followers.

Tweets are public by default; that is, any registered user can read other users' public tweets. However, upon registration, a user has the option of keeping the tweets only visible to the user's approved Twitter followers, known as *protected tweets*. Nonetheless, all tweets published by users are not hidden from the SP.

3.2 Personalized Tweet Recommendations

Recommending useful tweets to a user is a challenging problem. The key of the problem is how to use any information available on Twitter to decide whether or not a user is interested in a tweet. Such information available on Twitter includes the quality of the tweet, the authority of the publisher, the user's previous tweets, etc. With such information as input, the SP adopts various machining learning techniques such as *Collaborative filtering* [4, 6], *LDA* [5] or *RankSVM* [19] to learn a model to predict users' interests in tweets. Among existing recommendation algorithms for social updates [5, 10, 14, 18, 19, 21, 35], we adopt the collaborative personalized tweet recommendation algorithm proposed by Chen et al. [10] as the building block of our privacy-preserving tweet recommendation framework *pTwitterRec*. We choose their algorithm over others because: ***a)*** their tweet recommendation model not only incorporates explicit tweet features such as the quality of the tweet and the authority of the publisher, but also uses topic level latent factors of tweets to capture users' interests and uses latent factors to model users' social relations; ***b)*** their model outperforms other up-to-date recommendation models with reasonable computation cost. For example, the empirical results show that their method achieves 46.84% and 17.41% improvements compared with the RankSVM method and joint matrix factorization method [35] in terms of Mean Average Precision (MAP).

We briefly describe their tweet recommendation algorithm. For a given user u and two received tweets k and h, assuming that the ranks of tweets k and h are r_k^u and r_h^u respectively (user u is more interested in tweet k than tweet h if r_k^u is larger/higher than r_h^u), the authors model the probability of the orders of tweets k and h for user u as follows:

$$P(r_k^u > r_h^u \mid u) = \frac{1}{1+e^{-(y_{u,k}-y_{u,h})}} \tag{1}$$

where $y_{u,k}$ represents the predicted rating of user u for tweet k.

Then, the authors define the rank preference set D as follows:

$$D = \{<u,k,h> \mid k \in Re(u), h \notin Re(u)\} \tag{2}$$

where $Re(u)$ represents the set of tweets user u has retweeted. D is built based on the assumption that *users are more interested in those tweets that they have retweeted than those they have not retweeted.* For a tuple $<u, k, h>$ in D, an ideal rating prediction model $y_{u,k}$ maximizes the probability of the ranking order that user u ranks tweet k higher than tweet h. To solve this problem for all tuples in D, it is equivalent to solve the following objective by learning the optimal parameters for the rating prediction model $y_{u,k}$:

$$\min \sum_{<u,k,h\in D>} \ln(1+e^{-(y_{u,k}-y_{u,h})}) + \text{regularization} \tag{3}$$

Finally, the authors define the prediction model $y_{u,k}$ as follows:

$$y_{u,k} = \sum_{j\in F} b_j r_j^{u,k} + p_u^T\left(\frac{1}{Z^k}\sum_{w\in T_k} q_w + \alpha d_{p(k)}\right) \tag{4}$$

In the first part of equation 4, the authors use $\sum_{j\in F} b_j r_j^{u,k}$ to capture the impact of explicit features (such as the quality of the tweet and the authority of the publisher) on user u's rating of tweet k, where $r_j^{u,k}$ is the j-th explicit feature computed from tweet k regarding user u, F is the set of explicit features and b_j is the system-wide weight corresponding to the j-th explicit feature, which is to be learned in the prediction model. The second part of equation 4 considers a latent factor model (described in Appendix A.1). In brief, the authors use $p_u^T \sum_{w\in T_k} q_w$ to capture the impact of words contained in tweet k on user u's rating of the tweet, where p_u is the low dimensional representation of user u in the latent feature space R^d, T_k is the word set contained in tweet k and q_w represents the low dimensional representation of word w in the latent feature space R^d; the authors use $p_u^T d_{p(k)}$ to capture the impact of the social relation between user u and the publisher of tweet k on user u's rating of the tweet, where $d_{p(k)}$ is the low dimensional representation of the publisher of tweet k in the latent feature space R^d. In equation 4, Z^k is the normalization term defined as the cardinality of the word set T_k, and α is a predefined system-wide parameter that indicates the importance of social relations relative to words contained in the tweet.

Using D as the training datasets, by solving objective 3, the SP learns the parameters of the tweet rating prediction model: the system-wide weight vector b, the latent factor for user u denoted as p_u, the latent factor for each word w denoted as q_w and the latent factor for the publisher of tweet k denoted as $d_{p(k)}$. Note that among all parameters to be learned in the prediction model, only the value of p_u depends on user u and all other parameters are global values. To solve objective 3, the authors perform stochastic gradient descent (as described in Section 3.3). After the prediction model $y_{u,k}$ is learned, the SP estimates a user's rating for a tweet using equation 4.

3.3 Stochastic Gradient Descent

Chen et al. [10] adopt stochastic gradient descent to solve objective 3. For each tuple $<u, k, h>$ in D, the SP computes the descent of each parameter as follows and updates the parameters by moving in the direction of negative gradient:

$$\frac{\partial \ell}{\partial p_u} = \hat{e}\left(\frac{1}{Z^k}\sum_{w\in T_k} q_w - \frac{1}{Z^h}\sum_{w\in T_h} q_w + \alpha(d_{p(k)} - d_{p(h)})\right) - \lambda_1 p_u \tag{5}$$

$$\frac{\partial \ell}{\partial q_w^k} = \frac{1}{Z^k}\hat{e}p_u - \lambda_2 q_w^k, \quad \frac{\partial \ell}{\partial q_w^h} = -\frac{1}{Z^h}\hat{e}p_u - \lambda_2 q_w^h \tag{6}$$

$$\frac{\partial \ell}{\partial d_{p(k)}} = \alpha\hat{e}p_u - \lambda_3 d_{p(k)}, \quad \frac{\partial \ell}{\partial d_{p(h)}} = \alpha\hat{e}p_u - \lambda_3 d_{p(h)} \tag{7}$$

$$\frac{\partial \ell}{\partial b_j} = \hat{e}(r_j^{u,k} - r_j^{u,h}) - \lambda_4 b_j \tag{8}$$

$$\text{where } \hat{e} = 1 - \frac{1}{1+e^{-(y_{u,k}-y_{u,h})}} \tag{9}$$

Here, q_w^k represents the latent factor of word contained in tweet k. The algorithm loops over all tuples in D and updates the parameters accordingly.

4. SYSTEM AND THREAT MODEL

4.1 System Model

In *pTwitterRec*, we assume a privacy-preserving Twitter-like social network where tweets posted by users are hidden from the SP. We assume that users install a client application to participate in the social network. In the remainder of the paper, we refer to the client software installed on user u's device as user u for simplicity. In *pTwitterRec*, upon registration, each user's account is protected by default; that is, a user's tweets are only visible to the user's explicitly authorized followers. In addition, the user's tweets are hidden from the SP as well. We assume that a user encrypts the tweets using a secret key (not known by the SP) shared only among the user's authorized followers before posting them to *pTwitterRec*. The SP is responsible for storing encrypted tweets published by users and delivering those tweets to their corresponding followers. How to construct *pTwitterRec* such that it meets the abovementioned assumptions is out of the scope of our work; as described in the related work, systems such as FlyByNight [22] and Hummingbird [12] can be adapted to implement *pTwitterRec*.

For tweet recommendations, to prevent the SP from learning a user's interests, in *pTwitterRec*, we introduce a semi-trusted third party server, denoted as the *word server* (WS). Users, the SP and the WS cooperate and learn the personalized tweet recommendation model. More specifically, users are mainly responsible for collecting and preparing training samples that are used to learn the recommendation model, the SP is responsible for computing the weight parameters for explicit features, the latent factors of users as recipients of tweets and the latent factors of users as publishers of tweets while the WS is responsible for computing the latent factors of words in the tweet vocabulary. By separating the latent factors of words from the latent factors of users, neither the SP nor the WS can learn the contents of users' tweets and users' interests without colluding with each other (more details in Section 5).

4.2 Threat Model

In *pTwitterRec*, we assume both the SP and the WS to be honest but curious; that is, they follow our protocol, but are curious about *passively* learning the contents of users' tweets and users' interests. More specifically, we assume that neither the SP nor the WS creates spurious users or falsifies user requests in order to learn secrets from each other. We consider this assumption to be reasonable in OSNs, because it is not in OSN providers' best interests to lose users as a result of any suspicion of malicious behaviors [12]. Furthermore, we assume that the SP and the WS do not collude.

As mentioned in the system model, we assume that a user's tweets are encrypted with a secret key shared only among the user's approved followers. No entities can decrypt the tweets without the appropriate decryption key. Both the SP and the WS are interested in learning the contents of a user's tweets. In addition, both the SP and the WS are interested in inferring users' interests by learning users' preference of specific words. For example, a user who exhibits a strong preference for words "Ford" and "Toyota" is most likely to be interested in cars.

Furthermore, we assume that the social relations between users are not hidden from the SP in *pTwitterRec*. *pTwitterRec* works for Twitter-like systems where user's social relations and the contents of users' tweets are both hidden from the provider. However, *pTwitterRec* may lose some recommendation accuracy if neither the SP nor users are able to compute some of the explicit features that depend on user's social relations (more details in Section 5.3).

5. pTwitterRec

In this section, we present the main components of *pTwitterRec*.

5.1 Design Overview

The *main challenges* are: ***a)*** when using stochastic gradient descent to learn the recommendation model, for any given tuple <u, k, h> in D, update the parameters of the model using equations 5-9 without revealing the words contained in tweets k and h to any unauthorized entities; ***b)*** when the model is learned, only user u is allowed to compute $p_u^T q_w$ where p_u is the latent factor of user u as the recipient of tweets and q_w is the latent factor of word w, because the result of $p_u^T q_w$ represents user u's preference of word w and thereby potentially reveals user u's interest.

We make the following *observations* in relation to equations 5-9: ***a)*** computing $\hat{e}$ in equation 9 does not require knowing the specific words contained in tweets k and h. Instead, we only need to know the result of $\frac{1}{Z^k}\sum_{w\in T_k} q_w - \frac{1}{Z^h}\sum_{w\in T_h} q_w$; ***b)*** Similarly, updating p_u using equation 5 and updating $d_{p(k)}$ using equation 7 only require knowing the result of $\frac{1}{Z^k}\sum_{w\in T_k} q_w - \frac{1}{Z^h}\sum_{w\in T_h} q_w$; ***c)*** updating b_j using equation 8 only requires knowing the result of $(r_j^{u,k} - r_j^{u,h})$ which is the difference between the explicit features computed from tweets k and h regarding user u, and the result of $\frac{1}{Z^k}\sum_{w\in T_k} q_w - \frac{1}{Z^h}\sum_{w\in T_h} q_w$; ***d)*** finally, updating q_w using equation 6 does not require to know the identity of user u. Instead, we only need to learn the result of $\hat{e}p_u$.

Intuition. Based on the above observations, we split the task of learning the parameters of the recommendation model among user u, the SP and the WS. User u is responsible for selecting tweets k and h which constitute the tuple <u, k, h>. User u and the SP cooperate to compute explicit features from tweets k and h and compute $(r_j^{u,k} - r_j^{u,h})$ without revealing the content of the tweets to the SP. The SP is responsible for updating b_j, P_u and $d_{p(k)}$ while the WS is responsible for updating q_w. The SP updates b_j, P_u and $d_{p(k)}$ upon receiving the result of $\frac{1}{Z^k}\sum_{w\in T_k} q_w - \frac{1}{Z^h}\sum_{w\in T_h} q_w$ from the WS without learning the words contained in tweets k and h. The WS updates q_w upon receiving the result of $\hat{e}p_u$ from the SP without learning the identity of user u. As a result, neither the SP nor the WS can calculate $p_u^T q_w$ without a coalition between them.

The main components of *pTwitterRec* include: ***a)*** word indexing, ***b)*** explicit feature computation and training sample submission, ***c)*** model learning, and ***d)*** tweet publishing, receiving and ranking. We will describe each component in details in following subsections.

Table 1. Explicit features (tweet k published by user p received by user u)

Feature	Category	Description	Computed By
Co-follow Score	Relation	The similarity of followee sets of between user u and user p	SP
Mention Score	Relation	The number of times user u has mentioned user p in his previous tweets	SP
Friend	Relation	1 when user u and user p follow each other and 0 otherwise	SP
Relevance to Tweet History	Content-relevance	The relevance between tweet k and the posting history of user u	User u
Relevance to Retweet History	Content-relevance	The relevance between tweet k and the retweeted history of user u	User u
Relevance to Hash Tags	Content-relevance	The count of words in tweet k that ever appeared as hash tags through user u's posting history	User u
Length of Tweet	Twitter Specific	The number of words contained in tweet k	User u
Hash Tag Count	Twitter Specific	The number of hash tags contained in tweet k	User u
URL Count	Twitter Specific	The number of URLs contained in tweet k	User u
Retweet Count	Twitter Specific	The number of times tweet k has been retweeted	SP
Mention Count	Publishers' Authority	The times user p is mentioned in all tweets	SP
Followee Count	Publishers' Authority	The number of users who user p follows	SP
Follower Count	Publishers' Authority	The number of users who follow user p	SP
Tweet Count	Publishers' Authority	The number of tweets ever posted by user p	SP

5.2 Word Indexing

In *pTwitterRec*, user u is responsible for selecting tweets k and h (where tweet k is some tweet that user u has previously retweeted and tweet h is some tweet that user u has not retweeted) and preparing the tuple $<u, k, h>$ in D before submitting it to the SP. User u intends to keep the content of the tweets, i.e., the words contained in tweets k and h, hidden from the SP. In addition, even though the WS only manages the latent factor of words and will not learn the identity of user u at the model learning stage (more details in Section 5.3), user u wants to keep the content of the tweets hidden from the WS as well, because the tweets may contain some words that potentially reveal the identity of user u. On the other hand, in order to update the latent factor of each word contained in tweets k and h, the WS must be able to uniquely index each word. Therefore, each word contained in D must be uniquely indexed in a manner that the WS does not learn the mapping between the word and the corresponding index.

Since all users communicate with the SP, we require the SP to be the central server responsible for indexing words using some secret that is unknown to the WS. Note that when users request the indexes of words from the SP, users want to keep the words and the corresponding indexes hidden from the SP. We propose that the SP adopts a *deterministic commutative encryption* scheme such as *Pohlig-Hellman encryption* [24], denoted as E_{comm}, to generate the unique index for each word. Loosely speaking, an encryption scheme is *commutative* if a message encrypted by key k_1 first and then by key k_2 can be decrypted by the decryption key corresponding to k_1 to reveal the message singly encrypted by k_2. Assuming that user u is requesting the index of word w from the SP, the protocol works as follows: during system setup, both the SP and user u generate a separate secret encryption key for the commutative encryption scheme, denoted as k_{sp} and k_u respectively. Then user u encrypts word w using E_{comm} with the secret key k_u and sends the encrypted result to the SP. Let the encrypted result be $E_{comm}(w, k_u)$. Because the SP does not know the corresponding decryption key for k_u, the SP cannot learn word w. Upon receiving $E_{comm}(w, k_u)$, the SP further encrypts it using E_{comm} with the SP's secret key k_{sp} and sends $E_{comm}(E_{comm}(w, k_u), k_{sp})$ back to user u. Finally, user u decrypts $E_{comm}(E_{comm}(w, k_u)$ with the corresponding decryption key for k_u. Because of the commutative property of the encryption scheme E_{comm}, user u obtains $E_{comm}(w, k_{sp})$ and computes $index_w = H(E_{comm}(w, k_{sp}))$ where H is the SHA-224 hash function and $index_w$ is the index of word w. Because of the deterministic property of the encryption scheme E_{comm}, the index of word w is unique in the whole system. In order to reduce the online computational and communication overhead on the user side, an alternative approach is to require that the SP pre-computes the indexes of popular words and users pre-download the indexes beforehand without revealing their interests to the SP. For some obscure words that are not pre-computed by the SP, users adopt the commutative encryption scheme as mentioned above to request the indexes from the SP.

5.3 Explicit Feature Computation and Training Sample Submission

For each tweet in D, information such as the quality of the tweet (e.g., the number of URLs contained in the tweet) and the authority of the publisher (e.g., the number of followers) can be indicated as features, which explicitly reflect the possibility of a user retweeting the tweet, known as explicit features. Chen et al. [10] propose four categories of explicit features: relation features, content-relevance features, twitter-specific features and publishers' authority features.

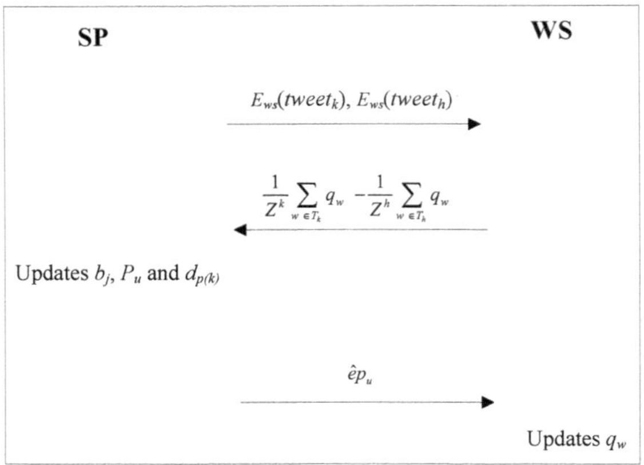

Figure 1. Privacy-preserving model learning.

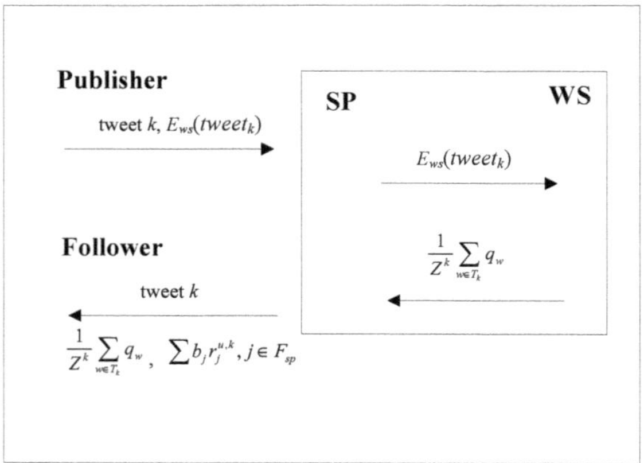

Figure 2. Tweet publishing, receiving and ranking.

In *pTwitterRec*, we split the task of computing explicit features between users and the SP (as listed in Table 1). Users are responsible for computing those features that depend on the content of the tweet, for example, *relevance to tweet history* feature, which estimates the relevance between the tweet and the user's previous tweet history. The SP is responsible for computing those features that depend on non-sensitive global information that is available to the SP, for example, *co-follow score* feature, which estimates the similarity of the followee sets of the recipient and the publisher of the tweet.

For a given tuple $<u, k, h>$ in D, user u computes the explicit features that she is responsible for computing. Let the j-th explicit feature computed from tweets k and h be $r_j^{u,k}$ and $r_j^{u,h}$ respectively. User u calculates $r_j^{u,k}$ - $r_j^{u,h}$ and attaches the result to the tuple before sending it to the SP.

Finally, user u cannot simply replace each word contained in tweets k and h with the corresponding index when submitting the tuple $<u, k, h>$ to the SP, because the SP can conveniently learn each word by decrypting the index with its decryption key. We propose that during system setup, the WS generates a pair of public and private keys (Puk_{ws}, Prk_{ws}) for a probabilistic public-key encryption scheme denoted E_{ws}. For tweet k in the tuple, user u randomly mixes the order of the indexes of all words contained in tweet k, concatenates all indexes altogether, and encrypts the indexes using E_{ws} with the WS's public key Puk_{ws}. Consequently, the SP learns neither the indexes of words contained in the tweet nor the frequency of each word contained in D while the WS only learns the index of each word at the model learning stage. The WS does learn the frequency of each word and might be able to correlate the most popular words with their indexes at certain probabilities. However, we argue the impact of such attacks is negligible for reasons explained in Section 6.

As a result, for a given tuple $<u, k, h>$ in D, the final data submitted to the SP by user u is as follows:

$$< u, \{r_j^{u,k} - r_j^{u,h} \mid j \in F_u\}, p(k), p(h), E_{ws}(tweet_k), E_{ws}(tweet_h) > \quad (10)$$

Where $E_{ws}(tweet_k)$ denotes the encrypted set of indexes of words contained in tweet k as previously described, F_u denotes the set of explicit features computed by user u, and $p(k)$ denotes the identities of the publisher of tweets k. Upon receiving the data submitted by user u, the SP computes explicit features (as listed in Table 1) that the SP is responsible for computing from tweets k and h. Combined with the data received from user u, we denote the final training dataset for the given tuple $<u, k, h>$ in D as $d<u, k, h>$.

5.4 Model Learning

For tweet k received by user u, in addition to explicit features computed as described in Section 5.3, Chen et al. [10] use a latent factor model (details in Appendix A.1) to capture user u's interests in tweet k and propose three categories of latent features: the latent factors of user u as a recipient of tweet k in the latent feature space R^d denoted as p_u, the latent factor of the publisher of tweet k in R^d denoted as $d_{p(k)}$, and the latent factor of each word w contained in tweet k in R^d denoted as q_w. User u's interest in tweet k is captured by measuring the affinity between user u and the words contained in tweet k and the affinity between user u and the publisher of tweet k in the latent feature space R^d. At the model learning stage, the SP and the WS cooperate to learn the values of these latent factors, in addition to the weight vector for explicit features by performing stochastic gradient descent as described in Section 3.3.

In *pTwitterRec*, during system setup, the SP initializes the weight b_j for all explicit features, the latent factor p_u of each user as the recipient of tweets and the latent factor $d_{p(k)}$ of each user as the publisher of tweets with random values. For each training dataset $d<u, k, h>$ corresponding to $<u, k, h>$ in D, the SP and the WS engage in the following protocols (as depicted in Figure 1):

a) The SP forwards the encrypted set of word indexes (denoted as $E_{ws}(tweet_k)$ and $E_{ws}(tweet_h)$) contained in $d<u, k, h>$ to the WS. The WS obtains the corresponding word indexes by decrypting with its private key Prk_{ws}. If the WS has never come across the index of word w before, the WS initializes the latent factor for word w with random values, denoted as q_w. Then, the WS calculates $\frac{1}{Z^k}\sum_{w\in T_k} q_w - \frac{1}{Z^h}\sum_{w\in T_h} q_w$ and sends the result back to the SP. Note that the WS does not know the actual words but only learns the index of each word contained in tweets k and h.

b) Upon receiving $\frac{1}{Z^k}\sum_{w\in T_k} q_w - \frac{1}{Z^h}\sum_{w\in T_h} q_w$ from the WS, the SP calculates $\hat{e}$ using equation 9 and updates parameters b_j, p_u and $d_{p(k)}$ using equations 5, 7 and 8.

c) The SP computes $\hat{e}p_u$ and sends the result to the WS. The WS updates q_w for each word w contained in tweets k and h

using equation 6. Note that the WS does not learn the identity of user u.

The SP and the WS loop over all training datasets in D and update the parameters of the tweet recommendation model in the same manner as mentioned above. At the end of the model learning stage, the SP learns b_j for each explicit feature, p_u for users as recipients of tweets and $d_{p(k)}$ for users as publishers of tweets while the WS learns q_w for words in the tweet vocabulary.

5.5 Tweet Publishing, Receiving and Ranking

Once the tweet recommendation model is learned, it can be used to predict users' interests in tweets and rank the tweets accordingly (as depicted in Figure 2).

In *pTwitterRec*, users are primarily responsible for ranking tweets with the help of the SP and the WS. When the recommendation model is learned, user u requests from the SP her personal latent factor p_u, the latent factors of all her followees as publishers, denoted as d_f where user f is a followee of user u, and the system-wide weight b_j for explicit features. Note that user u only needs to retrieve these parameters once.

When publishing a tweet, the user looks up the indexes of words contained in the tweet to be published, mixes the order of these indexes randomly and concatenates them together, encrypts the indexes using E_{ws} with the WS's public key Puk_{ws} and attaches the encrypted indexes to the tweet before sending it to the SP. Similarly to model learning, the SP forwards the encrypted indexes to the WS, which calculates $\frac{1}{Z^k}\sum_{w\in T_k} q_w$ for words contained in the tweet and sends the result back to the SP. The SP computes the sum of explicit features (denoted as $\sum b_j r_j^{u,k}, j \in F_{sp}$ where F_{sp} denotes the set of explicit features that the SP is responsible for computing), attaches the sum along with $\frac{1}{Z^k}\sum_{w\in T_k} q_w$ which was previously received from the WS to the tweet before distributing it to corresponding followers.

Upon receiving the tweet and the attached values, user u decrypts the tweet, calculates the explicit features that the user is responsible for computing, and computes the predicted rating for the tweet using equation 4. Tweet ranking works as follows: When the actual user, not the *pTwitterRec* client software, wants to read her tweets, this process is done for all tweets that have arrived since her last update and then the tweets are shown to her in ranked order.

6. DISCUSSION

In this section, we discuss the security and privacy aspects of *pTwitterRec* and a possible extension.

6.1 Security Analysis

We discuss possible attacks against *pTwitterRec*.

Frequency analysis attacks. At the model learning stage, the WS decrypts the encrypted indexes of the words contained in the tweets submitted by users as described in Section 5.4. Therefore, the WS learns the frequency of each word that has appeared in all tweets contained in the training datasets D while not knowing the actual words. Should the WS have the background knowledge of the popularity of each word in the tweet vocabulary, the WS might be able to correlate the most popular words with their indexes at certain probabilities. However, we argue that those words that are most vulnerable against such frequency analysis attacks are exactly those words that are most common among all users and therefore reveal little personal information regarding an individual user. In regards of the SP, even though the SP knows the identities of the users included in D, the SP cannot learn the frequencies of words because the indexes were encrypted using probabilistic encryption scheme E_{ws} with the WS's public key Puk_{ws}.

Collusion attacks. In our threat model, we assume that the SP and the WS do not collude. In addition, since the SP and the WS are honest-but-curious adversaries, they would not create phantom users to interact with other parties. The SP might try to collude with some legitimate users. A collusion between the SP and a user does not reveal the indexes of words contained in other users' tweets as they are encrypted using probabilistic encryption scheme E_{ws} (we require that E_{ws} is also secure against chosen-plaintext attacks.) with the WS's public key Puk_{ws}. However, the SP can learn the latent factors of some words through the colluding user and thereby infer other users' interests. Similarly, a collusion between the WS and a user discloses the mapping of words and corresponding indexes. However, we claim that users who collude with either the SP or the WS lose some of their own privacy. A collusion among a group of users does not pose threats to other users, because in *pTwitterRec* users are only allowed to obtain their own personal latent factors from the SP, as described in Section 5.5.

Poisoning attacks. Some malicious users may inject false training datasets such as falsified explicit features to render the tweet recommendation model less effective. Prior work such as Orca [2] has been proposed to detect such poisoning attacks. Poisoning attacks are not introduced as a result of adopting *pTwitterRec*. We leave the full investigation of the impact of such attacks on the recommendation accuracy and the applicability of existing defense mechanisms to future work.

6.2 Privacy Analysis

In this subsection, we examine the user information disclosed to the SP and the WS at each stage of *pTwitterRec* and analyze the privacy threats.

Word indexing. When user u requests the index of word w from the SP, the SP learns neither word w nor the corresponding index, because word w is encrypted using commutative encryption with a secret key known only to user u. Upon receiving the index of word w from the SP, user u caches the index corresponding to word w locally so user u does not need to request the index of the same word again in the future. Therefore, the SP learns no information other than that user u has made such a request. If the SP pre-computes the indexes for all popular words in the tweet vocabulary as described in Section 5.2, user u reveals no personal information by downloading such indexes from the SP in advance.

Explicit feature computation and training sample submission. For a given tuple $<u, k, h>$ in D, when user u finishes calculating the explicit features for tweets h and k and submitting the corresponding training dataset to the SP as described in Section 5.3, the SP learns: ***a)*** the identities of the publishers of tweets k and h, which is not private information in our threat model; ***b)*** the encrypted indexes for words contained in tweets k and h, which are encrypted using E_{ws} with the WS's public key Puk_{ws}. The SP learns neither the words contained in the tweets nor their indexes. In addition, the SP does not even learn how frequent the same word has appeared among all tweets in D because E_{ws} is a probabilistic encryption scheme; ***c)*** the difference between the explicit features (computed by user u) computed from tweets k and h, denoted as $\{r_j^{u,k} - r_j^{u,h} \mid j \in F_u\}$. Among all explicit features computed by user u, features *Relevance to Tweet History*, *Relevance to Retweet History* and *Relevance to Hash Tags* do not leak any personal information about user u because all tweets received and published by user u are hidden from the SP. Features *Length of Tweet*, *Hash Tag Count* and *URL Count* do reveal the number of words, the number of hash tags and the number of URLs contained in a tweet. However, we do not consider such information to be sensitive for user u. In addition, user u only submits the difference between those features computed from tweets k and h; ***d)*** the SP computes some explicit features of tweets k and h as listed in Table 1. However, those features only depend on non-sensitive information, which is already available to the SP, such as user u's social relations, and therefore do not leak any private information about user u.

Model learning. At the model learning stage, the SP and the WS cooperate to update the parameters of the tweet recommendation model. For a given tuple <u, k, h> in D, ***a)*** at the first step of the protocol, the SP only forwards the encrypted indexes for words contained in tweets k and h to the WS. The WS does not learn the original words contained in tweets k and h but only learns their indexes. In addition, the WS learns neither the identity of user u nor the identity of the publishers of tweets k and h. Furthermore, we require that users randomly mix the order of indexes of words contained in the tweet before encrypting and submitting them, so the WS cannot identify words by analyzing the pattern of the order of words appearing in tweets. The WS does learn the frequency of each word that has appeared in all tweets contained in D while not knowing the actual words. However, as analyzed in Section 6.1, such frequency analysis attacks reveal little personal information regarding each individual user. At the end of the first step, the SP learns the result of $\frac{1}{Z^k}\sum_{w \in T_k} q_w - \frac{1}{Z^h}\sum_{w \in T_h} q_w$ from the WS, which does not reveal the individual latent factor of each word because all word indexes were encrypted using probabilistic encryption scheme E_{ws} with the WS's public key Puk_{ws}; ***b)*** at the third step of the protocol, the WS learns the result of $\hat{ep}_u$ from the SP, which does not reveal the identity of user u; ***c)*** at the end of the model learning stage, the SP learns the latent factor p_u of user u as recipients of tweets and the latent factor $d_{p(k)}$ of user $p(k)$ as the publisher of tweet k (note that p_u is a vector in the latent feature space R^d and p_u alone does not disclose any personal information of user u). The SP is able to learn the closeness of the social relation between users u and $p(k)$ by computing $p_u^T d_{p(k)}$. However, in *pTwitterRec*, we assume that the social relations between users are not hidden from the SP, as described in the threat model; ***d)*** the SP cannot replace the WS by updating the latent factors of words as well, because the indexes for words are encrypted by user u using the probabilistic encryption scheme with the WS's public key; ***e)*** the WS cannot replace the SP, because the WS cannot compute the model all by itself without knowing the explicit features, the identity of the recipient of the tweet, and the identity of the publisher of the tweet, which are only known to the SP.

Tweet publishing, receiving and ranking. For tweet k received by user u, the SP and the WS both only learn the value of $\frac{1}{Z^k}\sum_{w \in T_k} q_w$ for all words contained in tweet k but do not know the words contained in tweet k. In addition, neither the SP nor the WS can infer user u's interest by computing $p_u^T q_w$ for any word w (which represents user u's preference over word w) without colluding with each other. Furthermore, for user u, we require that user u is only allowed to retrieve her own personal latent factor p_u from the SP and therefore user u cannot learn other users' interests.

6.3 Extension

In *pTwitterRec*, the SP is not only responsible for managing the social relations between users and distributing users' tweets to their followers as an OSN provider, but also responsible for recommending personalized interesting tweets to users (in cooperation with the WS and users) as a recommendation service provider. However, *pTwitterRec* can be conveniently adapted to support a third-party privacy-preserving tweet recommendation service that is independent of the OSN provider. The benefit of implementing *pTwitterRec* as a third-party service is that there would be no requirements of any changes to the existing OSN provider while still providing users with personalized tweet recommendations (and hiding the contents of users' tweets and user's interests from the tweet recommendation service provider).

With the new *pTwitterRec* client application, users receive/publish tweets from/to the OSN provider, and interact with the third-party tweet recommendation service provider (consisting of a separate SP and WS) to learn the recommendation model without leaking any sensitive information to the recommendation service provider. Upon the completion of the model learning stage, users are able to rank tweets received from the OSN provider. *pTwitterRec* may lose some recommendation accuracy because the recommendation service provider is unable to compute some explicit features such as features that depend on users' social relations. However, users may be able to compute such features if they know their followees' social relations.

7. IMPLEMENTATION

To demonstrate the practicality of our framework, we implemented a prototype that simulates the model learning stage of *pTwitterRec*, which is the core component of our framework. The prototype consists of: a server acting as the SP that takes the training datasets D as input and updates the weight b_j for each explicit feature, the latent factor p_u of user u as the recipient of the tweets, and the latent factors $d_{p(k)}$ and $d_{p(h)}$ of users $p(k)$ and $p(h)$ as publishers of tweets k and h for every tuple <u, k, h> in D; another server acting as the WS that communicates with the SP as described in Section 5.4 and updates the latent factor q_w of each word w contained in D.

Our prototype uses the *SVDFeature* toolkit [37] to implement gradient stochastic descent, which is used for updating abovementioned parameters at the model learning stage. We choose *SVDFeature* since it is open source and well-documented. *SVDFeature* is a toolkit designed to efficiently solve large-scale collaborative filtering problems with auxiliary information by performing gradient stochastic descent. Unlike traditional approaches that require writing a specific solver for each recommendation model, *SVDFeature* provides a general solution for collaborative filtering problems and allows developing new recommendation models by defining new features.

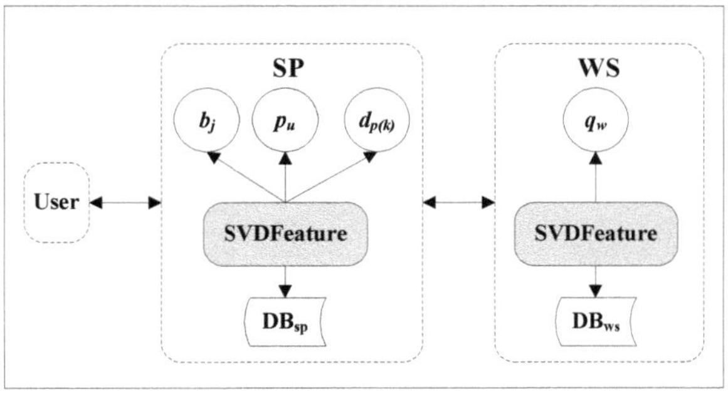

Figure 3. Server-side architecture.

In our prototype, we define the explicit features described in Section 5.3 as global features in *SVDFeature*, the latent factors of users (as recipients of tweets) as user features in *SVDFeature*, and the latent factors of words contained in the tweet vocabulary in addition to the latent factors of users (as publishers of tweets) as item features in *SVDFeature*. Figure 3 depicts the architecture of our prototype. The SP and the WS each maintains a separate database. At the end of the model learning stage, the SP stores in its database the final values of the system-wide weight b_j for each explicit feature, the latent factor p_u of each user as the recipient of tweets, and the latent factors $d_{p(k)}$ of each user as the publisher of tweets; the WS stores in its database the latent factor q_w of each word in the tweet vocabulary. We leave the implementation of the complete framework to future work.

8. EVALUATION

In this section, we analyze and evaluate the overhead particularly on the user side due to the introduction of our privacy protection framework *pTwitterRec*, compared with the original tweet recommendation algorithm [10] with no user privacy protection. Our framework only adds privacy protection to the tweet recommendation algorithm without modifying the original recommendation model [10]. Thus, there is no loss of recommendation accuracy (please refer to [10] for the thorough evaluation of recommendation accuracy).

We assume that users run the *pTwitterRec* client application on a smartphone with limited computation power and memory. In our evaluation, we use a Google Nexus Four phone featuring a 1.512 GHz quad-core Krait CPU and 2 GB of RAM. On the other hand, we assume that both the SP and the WS have reasonably unlimited computation power and storage space. We use an 8 core server featuring Intel Xeon 2.40 GHz CPU with 8 GB RAM as the SP/WS. We assume that there is a fast and persistent network connection between the SP and the WS and the communication overhead between them is negligible. We analyze the overhead at each stage of our framework in following subsections.

8.1 Word Indexing

As described in Section 5.2, assuming that user u does not know the index of word w, user u first encrypts word w using commutative encryption E_{comm} with her secret key k_u and then sends the encrypted word to the SP. The SP further encrypts the received encrypted word using E_{comm} with its secret key k_{sp} and returns the result to user u. Finally, user u obtains the index of word w by decrypting the result received from the SP with her decryption key and then computing the hash value of the result using SHA-224. Therefore, to obtain the index of a new word, it requires user u to perform one encryption and one decryption using commutative

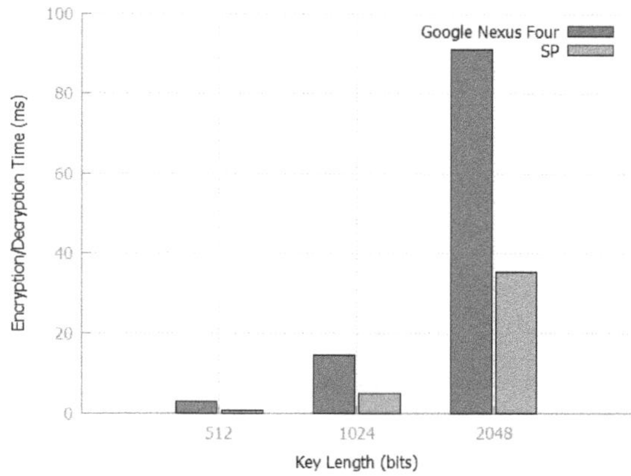

Figure 4. Pohlig-Hellman encryption/decryption.

encryption E_{comm} and perform one hash function while it requires the SP to perform one encryption using E_{comm}. The computational cost for carrying out one hash function is negligible and therefore we only evaluate the computational cost for commutative encryption/decryption. We adopt *Pohlig-Hellman encryption* (described in Appendix A.2) as E_{comm} for our evaluation because of its deterministic commutative property (note that any encryption scheme that is both *deterministic* and *commutative* can be used as E_{comm} in our protocol, as described in Section 5.2). We measure the execution time of a single *Pohlig-Hellman* encryption/decryption on the smartphone and on the server. We vary the key length, carry out 10,000 runs for each key length and average the results. Figure 4 shows the results. With a 2048-bit key, it takes approximately 91.1 ms for the smartphone and 35.2 ms for the SP to carry out one *Pohlig-Hellman* encryption/decryption. The communication overhead for user u is to send and receive one encrypted word. Therefore, with a 2048-bit key size, the communication overhead for user u is approximately 512 bytes to obtain the index of one word. It is reported that there are approximately 15 words [36] in each tweet on average. Assuming that each user submits n (n = 392 in [10]) tweets to the SP as training datasets, the total communication overhead for a user to obtain all indexes from the SP is less than 7.5n KB and the total computational overhead is less than 2.7n seconds. Note that user u caches the index of word w locally and thereby only needs to request the index of word w from the SP once even if word w appears in multiple tweets. In addition, to further reduce the overhead on the user side, as described in Section 5.2, we propose that the SP precomputes the indexes for popular words and users pre-download the indexes for these popular words beforehand without revealing their interests to the SP.

8.2 Explicit Feature Computation and Training Sample Submission

In *pTwitterRec*, users are responsible for computing six of the explicit features for each tweet contained in the training samples. Compared with the cryptographic overhead evaluated in Section 8.1, the computational overhead incurred by explicit feature computation is negligible for users. For each tweet contained in the training samples, *Relevance to Tweet History* feature and *Relevance to Retweet History* feature each takes four bytes, and the remaining four integer-value features each takes two bytes.

Furthermore, users encrypt the indexes of words contained in the tweet using probabilistic encryption E_{ws} with the WS's public key Puk_{ws}. The size of each word index is 28 bytes (recall that users

Table 2. User side overhead (each user submits n tweets for training)

	Computational Overhead	Communication Overhead
Word Indexing	<$2.7n$ seconds	<$7.5n$ KB
Explicit Feature Computation and Training Sample Submission	$0.1n$ seconds	$0.7n$ KB
Model Learning	none	none
Tweet Publishing and Receiving (one tweet)	Publisher: 91.1 ms Receiver: none	Publisher: 0.7 KB Receiver: 8 bytes
Tweet Ranking	negligible	none

adopt SHA-224 to compute the indexes for words) and therefore the plaintext of all indexes for a tweet is 420 bytes on average. We propose that users encrypt all indexes using *Advanced Encryption Standard* (AES) in CBC mode with a random secret key k_r and then encrypt the secret key using RSA with the WS's public key Puk_{ws} (note that any *probabilistic* public-key encryption scheme can be used as E_{ws} in our protocol, as described in Section 5.3). The size of the ciphertext is approximately equal to the size of (all word indexes + one AES block + initialization vector + the ciphertext of the secret AES key k_r encrypted using RSA), which is about 0.7 KB in total with a 2048-bit RSA key. The computational overhead for encrypting word indexes is dominated by encrypting k_r using RSA. With the same key size, the computational cost for RSA encryption/decryption is the same as Pohlig-Hellman encryption/decryption (see Figure 4) because the compute-intensive part for both encryption schemes is one modular exponentiation. Therefore, the computational overhead at this stage for the user to submit n tweets is approximately $0.1n$ seconds and the communication overhead is approximately $0.7n$ KB for a user.

8.3 Model Learning

Once the SP has received all training samples from users, the SP only interacts with the WS at the model learning stage. Therefore, there is no overhead on the user side. Compared with the original recommendation algorithm [10], we split the model learning task between the SP and the WS. As we assume that the communication overhead between the SP and the WS is negligible, the only overhead incurred by *pTwitterRec* is the cost for the WS to decrypt and obtain the indexes for words contained in tweets, so that the WS can update the corresponding latent factors of these words.

8.4 Tweet Publishing, Receiving and Ranking

When publishing a tweet, the publisher carries out one probabilistic encryption E_{ws} to encrypt the indexes of all words contained in the tweet in the same manner as described in Section 8.2 and attaches the result to the tweet before publishing it. Therefore, to publish a tweet, the computational overhead for the publisher is approximately 91.1 ms and the communication overhead is approximately 0.7 KB on average. The overhead incurred on the server side is that the WS needs to perform one decryption to obtain the word indexes for each tweet. As described in Section 5.5, the SP attaches the results of $\sum b_j r_j^{u,k}$ and $\frac{1}{Z^k}\sum_{w \in T_k} q_w$ to the tweet before forwarding it to the followers. Therefore, the communication overhead for the followers to receive a tweet is approximately the size of two floating point number, which is eight bytes. We do not consider here the overhead incurred by decrypting tweets using the publisher's secret key that is shared only among the publisher's followers, which is out of the scope of our work.

For tweet ranking, upon receiving a tweet from the SP, the user only needs to compute the explicit features and then predicts the rating for the tweet using equation 4. Therefore, the overhead incurred by tweet ranking on the user side is negligible and there is no communication overhead.

8.5 Overall Overhead

Users may run the client application on a smartphone with limited computation power and memory. Therefore, we illustrate the feasibility of *pTwitterRec* by analyzing the overall overhead incurred on the user side. We summarize the results in Table 2.

For model learning, assuming that each user submits n tweets to the SP for training, the computational overhead for a user is approximately $2.7n$ seconds and the communication overhead is approximately $7.5n$ KB in total assuming that the user requests the index of every single word contained in the tweets. Note that a user only needs to submit training samples once and the tweet recommendation model can be learned offline between the SP and the WS. Therefore, there are no strict real-time requirements for a user to submit training samples and it can take place when the user's phone is not busy and when it has a Wi-Fi connection to the Internet.

To publish a tweet, the computational overhead for the publisher is 91.1 ms and the communication overhead is 0.7 KB. The publisher can choose to not participate in tweet recommendations by just publishing tweets without attaching the encrypted word indexes. However, the publisher's followers may overlook her tweets as the followers cannot predict the ratings for her tweets and rank her tweets. For every received tweet, there is no computational cost for the receiver and the communication overhead for the receiver is eight bytes per tweet.

For tweet ranking, the computational overhead for the user is negligible and there is no communication overhead.

Summary. The user side overhead incurred by *pTwitterRec* for tweet recommendation model learning is reasonable and the model learning between the SP and the WS can take place offline. The overhead for publishing and receiving tweets incurred by *pTwitterRec* is small and the overhead for ranking tweets is negligible.

9. CONCLUSIONS

In this paper, we present *pTwitterRec*, the first privacy-preserving personalized tweet recommendation framework that provides users with the benefits of tweet recommendations while keeping the content of tweets and users' interests hidden from other unauthorized entities including the provider. We introduce a semi-trusted third server (WS) to compute the tweet recommendation model, in cooperation with users and the SP. The implementation and evaluation show that *pTwitterRec* is practical and only introduces reasonable overhead. Our future work includes implementing the complete framework of *pTwitterRec* and evaluating the performance in the real world.

10. ACKNOWLEDGMENTS

We thank the anonymous reviewers for their helpful comments. This work is supported by a Google Focused Research Award, the Ontario Research Fund, and the Natural Sciences and Engineering Research Council of Canada.

11. REFERENCES

[1] Aïmeur, E., Brassard, G., Fernandez, J.M. and Mani Onana, F.S. Alambic: a privacy-preserving recommender system for electronic commerce. *International Journal of Information Security*. 7, 5 (2008), 307–334.

[2] Bay, S.D. and Schwabacher, M. Mining distance-based outliers in near linear time with randomization and a simple pruning rule. *Proceedings of the 9th ACM SIGKDD International Conference on Knowledge Discovery and Data Mining* (2003), 29–38.

[3] Beato, F., Kohlweiss, M. and Wouters, K. Scramble! your social network data. *Proceedings of the 11th International Conference on Privacy Enhancing Technologies* (2011), 211–225.

[4] Billsus, D. and Pazzani, M.J. Learning collaborative information filters. *Proceedings of the 15th International Conference on Machine Learning* (1998), 46–54.

[5] Blei, D.M., Ng, A.Y. and Jordan, M.I. Latent dirichlet allocation. *Journal of Machine Learning research*. 3, (2003), 993–1022.

[6] Breese, J.S., Heckerman, D. and Kadie, C. Empirical analysis of predictive algorithms for collaborative filtering. *Proceedings of the 14th conference on Uncertainty in Artificial Intelligence* (San Francisco, CA, USA, 1998), 43–52.

[7] Canny, J. Collaborative filtering with privacy. *Proceedings of 2002 IEEE Symposium on Security and Privacy* (2002), 45–57.

[8] Canny, J. Collaborative filtering with privacy via factor analysis. *Proceedings of the 25th Annual International ACM SIGIR Conference on Research and Development in Information Retrieval* (New York, NY, USA, 2002), 238–245.

[9] Chen, J., Nairn, R., Nelson, L., Bernstein, M. and Chi, E. 2010. Short and tweet: experiments on recommending content from information streams. *Proceedings of the SIGCHI Conference on Human Factors in Computing Systems* (2010), 1185–1194.

[10] Chen, K., Chen, T., Zheng, G., Jin, O., Yao, E. and Yu, Y. Collaborative personalized tweet recommendation. *Proceedings of the 35th International ACM SIGIR Conference on Research and Development in Information Retrieval* (2012), 661–670.

[11] Conti, M., Hasani, A. and Crispo, B. Virtual private social networks. *Proceedings of the 1st ACM Conference on Data and Application Security and Privacy* (2011), 39–50.

[12] De Cristofaro, E., Soriente, C., Tsudik, G. and Williams, A. Hummingbird: privacy at the time of Twitter. *Proceedings of 2012 IEEE Symposium on Security and Privacy (SP)* (May 2012), 285 –299.

[13] Diaz-Aviles, E., Drumond, L., Schmidt-Thieme, L. and Nejdl, W. Real-time top-n recommendation in social streams. *Proceedings of the 6th ACM Conference on Recommender Systems* (2012), 59–66.

[14] Duan, Y., Jiang, L., Qin, T., Zhou, M. and Shum, H.-Y. An empirical study on learning to rank of tweets. *Proceedings of the 23rd International Conference on Computational Linguistics* (2010), 295–303.

[15] Feldman, A.J., Blankstein, A., Freedman, M.J. and Felten, E.W. Social networking with Frientegrity: privacy and integrity with an untrusted provider. *Proceedings of the 21st USENIX Conference on Security Symposium* (Berkeley, CA, USA, 2012), 31–31.

[16] Guha, S., Tang, K. and Francis, P. NOYB: Privacy in online social networks. *Proceedings of the 1st Workshop on Online Social Networks* (2008), 49–54.

[17] Hannon, J., Bennett, M. and Smyth, B. Recommending twitter users to follow using content and collaborative filtering approaches. *Proceedings of the 4th ACM Conference on Recommender Systems* (2010), 199–206.

[18] Hong, L., Bekkerman, R., Adler, J. and Davison, B.D. Learning to rank social update streams. *Proceedings of the 35th International ACM SIGIR Conference on Research and Development in Information Retrieval* (2012), 651–660.

[19] Joachims, T. Optimizing search engines using clickthrough data. *Proceedings of the 8th ACM SIGKDD International Conference on Knowledge Discovery and Data Mining* (2002), 133–142.

[20] Koren, Y., Bell, R. and Volinsky, C. Matrix factorization techniques for recommender systems. *Computer*. 42, 8 (2009), 30–37.

[21] Kunegis, N.N.T.G.J. and Alhadi, A.C. Bad news travel fast: a content-based analysis of interestingness on twitter. *Proceedings of ACM Web Science Conference* (2011).

[22] Lucas, M.M. and Borisov, N. Flybynight: mitigating the privacy risks of social networking. *Proceedings of the 7th ACM Workshop on Privacy in the Electronic Society* (2008), 1–8.

[23] Luo, W., Xie, Q. and Hengartner, U. Facecloak: an architecture for user privacy on social networking sites. *Proceedings of International Conference on Computational Science and Engineering* (2009), 26–33.

[24] Pohlig, S. and Hellman, M. An improved algorithm for computing logarithms over GF (p) and its cryptographic significance. *Information Theory, IEEE Transactions on*. 24, 1 (1978), 106–110.

[25] Polat, H. and Du, W. Achieving private recommendations using randomized response techniques. *Advances in Knowledge Discovery and Data Mining*. (2006), 637–646.

[26] Polat, H. and Du, W. Privacy-preserving collaborative filtering. *International Journal of Electronic Commerce*. 9, 4 (2003), 9–35.

[27] Polat, H. and Du, W. Privacy-preserving collaborative filtering using randomized perturbation techniques. *Proceedings of the 3rd IEEE International Conference on Data Mining* (Washington, DC, USA, 2003), 625–628.

[28] Polat, H. and Du, W. SVD-based collaborative filtering with privacy. *Proceedings of the 2005 ACM symposium on Applied Computing* (New York, NY, USA, 2005), 791–795.

[29] Qu, Z. and Liu, Y. Interactive group suggesting for Twitter. *Proceedings of the 49th Annual Meeting of the Association*

for Computational Linguistics: Human Language Technologies (Short Papers) (2011), 519–523.

[30] Rainie, L., Kiesler, S., Kang, R. and Madden, M. 20130905. Anonymity, privacy, and security online. *Pew Internet & American Life Project.* *http://www.pewinternet.org/PPF/r/213/report_display.asp,*

[31] Ramage, D., Dumais, S.T. and Liebling, D.J. Characterizing microblogs with topic models. *Proceedings of the 4th International AAAI Conference on Weblogs and Social Media* (2010).

[32] Reeves, S. Internet is double-edged sword in Arab revolts. *http://middle-east-online.com/english/?id=46109*

[33] Rennie, J.D. and Srebro, N. Fast maximum margin matrix factorization for collaborative prediction. *Proceedings of the 22nd International Conference on Machine Learning* (2005), 713–719.

[34] Singh, I., Butkiewicz, M., Madhyastha, H.V., Krishnamurthy, S.V. and Addepalli, S. Twitsper: tweeting privately. *IEEE Security Privacy*. 11, 3 (2013), 46–50.

[35] Yang, S.-H., Long, B., Smola, A., Sadagopan, N., Zheng, Z. and Zha, H. Like like alike: joint friendship and interest propagation in social networks. *Proceedings of the 20th International Conference on World Wide Web* (2011), 537–546.

[36] RT this: OUP Dictionary team monitors Twitterer's tweets. *http://blog.oup.com/2009/06/oxford-twitter/*

[37] SVDFeature toolkit. *http://svdfeature.apexlab.org/wiki/Main_Page*

[38] Twitter statistics. *http://www.statisticbrain.com/twitter-statistics/*

A: Appendix

A.1 Latent Factor Model

Collaborative recommendation techniques based on latent factor models have been proved to be effective in improving recommendation accuracy [20, 33]. In a basic latent factor model, users and items are mapped to a joint low-dimensional latent factor space R^d. Let p_u be the low dimensional representation of user u in the latent feature space R^d and q_i be the low dimensional representation of item i in R^d. The predicted rating of user u for item i is computed as the affinity between user u and item i in the latent feature space, i.e., the inner product of p_u and q_i in R^d.

For tweet recommendations, directly applying the basic latent factor model faces the problem of data sparsity due to the lack of retweet data. Chen et al. [9] propose decomposing the latent factor of a tweet (i.e., an item in the basic latent model) into a combination of the latent factors of words contained in the tweet. Therefore, for a given tweet k, $p_u^T \sum_{w \in T_k} q_w$ captures the impact of the words contained in tweet k on user u's rating of the tweet, where T_k is the word set contained in tweet k and q_w represents the low dimensional representation of word w in the latent feature space R^d. Furthermore, Chen et al. propose representing the publisher of tweet k as a latent factor (denoted as $d_{p(k)}$) in R^d as well and measuring the possibility of user u retweeting tweet k by considering the affinity of user i and the publisher of tweet k in the latent feature space. Therefore, $p_u^T d_{p(k)}$ captures the impact of the social relation between user u and the publisher of tweet k on user u's rating of the tweet. The values of p_u, q_w and $d_{p(k)}$ are learned through the training as described in Section 5.4.

A.2 Pohlig-Hellman Encryption

The Pohlig-Hellman encryption scheme [24] is similar to RSA. Different keys are used for encryption and decryption. However, it is not a public-key scheme, because the keys are easily derivable from each other; both the encryption and decryption keys must be kept secret.

Given a large prime p with no small factors of p - 1, each party chooses a random (e, d) pair such that $e \times d = 1 \pmod{p-1}$ where the encryption key is e and the decryption key is d. For a given message M, the encryption of M is $M^e \pmod{p}$ and for a given ciphertext C, the decryption of C is $C^d \pmod{p}$. It is straightforward to prove that the Pohlig-Hellman encryption scheme is both deterministic and commutative.

Pohlig-Hellman leaks the information whether the plaintext message M is quadratic residue (mod p) or not. In our framework, the SP computes the index of each word by encrypting the word using Pohlig-Hellman. Because the *SP* is honest but curious in the threat model, the *SP* would not manipulate the distribution of word indexes at the risk of being caught. Although we use Pohlig-Hellman encryption for examples in this paper, any encryption scheme that is both *deterministic* and *commutative* can be used in our protocol.

Shades of Gray: A Closer Look at Emails in the Gray Area

Jelena Isacenkova
Eurecom
Sophia Antipolis
06410 France
jelena.isacenkova@gmail.com

Davide Balzarotti
Eurecom
Sophia Antipolis
06410 France
balzarotti@eurecom.fr

ABSTRACT

Every day, millions of users spend a considerable amount of time browsing through the messages in their spam folders. With newsletters and automated notifications responsible for 42% of the messages in the user's inboxes, inevitably some important emails get misclassified as spam. Unfortunately, users are often unable to take security related decisions, and tools provide no assistance to easily distinguish harmless commercial messages from the ones that are most certainly malevolent.

Most of the previous studies focused on the detection of spam. Instead, in this paper we look into the often overlooked area of gray emails, i.e., those messages that cannot be clearly categorized one way or the other by automated spam filters. In particular, we analyze real-world emails by grouping them into clusters of bulk email campaigns. Our approach is able to automatically classify and reduce by half the gray emails area with only 0.2% false positives.

Moreover, we identify a number of campaign features that can be used to predict the campaign category and we discuss their effectiveness and their limitations. Our experiments show that a large fraction of emails in the gray area are composed of legitimate bulk emails: newsletters, notifications, and marketing offers. The latter appears to be a large e-marketing business industry that has grown into a complex infrastructure for sending legitimate bulk emails. To the best of our knowledge, this is the first real-world empirical study of such emails.

Keywords

Gray emails, classification, botnet generated campaigns, commercial campaigns, Nigerian scam, newsletters, phishing, challenge response system

1. INTRODUCTION

Nowadays, many antispam filters provide a good level of protection against large-scale unsolicited email campaigns. However, as spammers have improved their techniques to increase the chances of reaching their targets, also antispam solutions have become more aggressive in flagging suspicious emails.

On one side, this arms race has lead to a steady increase in the detection rate. On the other, it also contributed to the increase of the false positives, with serious consequences for the users whenever an important message is erroneously flagged as spam. Moreover, at the border between legitimate user emails and spam lies a gray area of messages that are hard to automatically classify. This area often contains newsletters and commercial offers which were originally solicited, but that are not anymore interesting for the users [9]. More in general, it includes messages that are not flagged by traditional antispam filters, but that are not necessarily wanted by the users. In 2012, Hotmail estimated that gray emails were the source of 75% of all spam complaints. Another Email Intelligence Report published by ReturnPath [28] pointed out that 16% of emails containing advertisements or marketing information are normally flagged as spam and, therefore, never reach user mailboxes. At first glance, many people would consider this "side-effect" as an advantage. However, it has been estimated that only one-third of users consider such messages as spam, while two-thirds prefer to receive unsolicited commercial emails from already known senders [7]. A more recent report shows that despite the mailboxes being overloaded, consumers still read 18% of subscribed marketing emails, and continue to sign up for email offers and mailing lists [28], with the result that newsletters and automated notifications sum up up to 42% of inbox messages. For these reasons, it is a well known fact that most of the users regularly check their spam folder to verify that no important messages have been misclassified by the antispam filter.

Unfortunately, this process is very time-consuming. Antispam solutions are not very helpful in this direction, and do not usually provide any additional information to help users in quickly identifying marketing emails, newsletters, or "borderline" cases that may be interesting for the users.

Even worse, when users skim through their spam messages looking for something that looks legitimate, they need to take a decision on which email can be trusted, which one is just annoying, and which can pose a real security threat. Unfortunately, several studies showed that most users are very bad in taking these kind of security-related decisions [19], and this is one of the reasons why we need automated spam filters in the first place. For example, a recent survey conducted in 2010 [17] by the Messaging Anti-Abuse Working Group reported that 57% of the people who have accessed spam messages admitted to have done so intentionally, be-

ASIA CCS'14, June 4–6, 2014, Kyoto, Japan.
Copyright 2014 ACM 978-1-4503-2800-5/14/06 ...$15.00.
http://dx.doi.org/10.1145/2590296.2590344 .

cause they were unsure whether the suspicious message was spam or not.

While most of the existing research deals with the problem of efficiently and accurately distinguishing spam from ham, in this paper we focus on the thin line that separates the two categories. In particular, we limit our study to the often overlooked area of gray emails [31], i.e., those ambiguous messages that cannot be clearly categorized one way or the other by automated spam filters. We start from the assumption that spam filters are good in detecting most of the spam, and if the filter has "good reasons" to believe that a message is unsolicited or that it contains malicious content (e.g., by employing an antivirus, a black list, or by matching a signature of a known scam message), there would be no reason for most users to double-check that decision.

We start our study by analyzing a real deployment of a challenge-response antispam solution to measure the extent of this gray area. We use system's quarantined emails that already exclude the majority of the ham and spam messages as an approximation of the gray emails category. According to our data, after the obvious spam and ham emails have been eliminated, users still manually check on average five to six messages per day. On average, 1.5% of these messages have an attachment with 9% of them being malicious. However, some of these messages also contain interesting content, as proved by the fact that users read and whitelist an average of 1.5 messages per day. We also confirm the belief that ordinary users are not very good in telling spam and ham apart.

Under these premises, we analyze the messages in the gray area in order to improve our understanding about them and the reasons that make them difficult to categorize. In particular, we adopt a three-phase approach based on message clustering, classification, and graph-based refinement. Extracted email features are applied in a context of email campaigns instead of individual emails. Our technique is able to automatically classify half of the gray emails, corresponding to 15% of all email traffic, with only 0.2% of false positives. Moreover, our results show a number of interesting characteristics of commercial marketing campaigns, which constitute to a large fraction of the gray area. To the best of our knowledge, this is the first empirical study of legitimate bulk emails.

2. BACKGROUND

Email-based marketing is a common practice for advertisement and sales, and it is used both to maintain communication with current customers, as well as to acquire new ones. Unfortunately, when users' inboxes started to get overloaded with various types of bulk messages, mailbox maintenance became highly time-consuming. As a result, email filters were introduced to protect users from unsolicited messages, starting a multi-million anti-spam protection industry and a battle that is far from being over. In fact, even though direct mail marketing has a higher response rate (3.4%) than email marketing (0.12%) [8], the low cost of emails still makes electronic messages a very attractive solution.

Marketers often use professional marketing tools in order to maximize their campaign delivery rates. These tools help to clean non-existing emails from customer lists, to deal with recipient complaints, to avoid hitting spam traps, and even provide detailed campaign delivery statistics. Today running an email marketing campaign is a complex operation, and more and more solicited bulk emails fall into the recipient spam folders. In fact, these folders often contain messages that cannot be clearly categorized by automated spam filters. This gray area is responsible for 75% of the spam complaints [9] and it contains both legitimate and harmless bulk emails, and malicious messages that can result in a computer infection or in stolen personal data. However, users also appear to be ineffective in distinguishing one class from the other [17, 19] and often (70%) take their decision based only on the sender field and subject line.

For clarity, in this study we separate bulk emails into two categories: legitimate and spam. The first includes solicited (subscribed newsletters and notifications) or *potentially* solicited (advertisements) messages sent according to legal regulations (e.g. the CAN-SPAM Act [1] and the E-Privacy Directive [3]). The second category contains instead unsolicited, malicious, or illegal promotion emails.

The distribution of legitimate marketing campaigns became a large business where specialized companies provide as a service professional email marketing tools, and also sell categorized email lists for marketers looking for new clients. The collection of such lists is legal: when users subscribe to some services and fill out a form, they might – by choice or by default – agree to share their information with the third-parties. Hence, at some point users do agree to receive the advertisements.

Related work

Many filtering solutions, often used in combination with each other, exist to detect and mitigate spam.

In our approach we focus on the analysis of the senders behavior. Pathak et al. [20] suggested to analyze the sending behavior of spammers, while Ramachandran et al. [27, 26] used behavioral blacklists to classify sender IP addresses based on their behavior. Ramachandran observed that spammers exhibit recognizable sending patterns, based on which behavior fingerprints can be build. Qian et al. [25] proposed to rely on the reputation of IP clusters, e.g. BGP clusters, and combine it with DNS information, improving the precision of public IP-based blacklists by 50%. Hao et al. [10] built an automated reputation engine, called SNARE, aiming at distinguishing legitimate senders from spammers based on a number of non-content email features. West et al. [30] built a reputation model to predict the behavior of spammers. The model relies on spatial and temporal features that can be especially useful in partial-knowledge situations. The model managed to classify up to 50% of the spam emails that were not identified by the blacklists. The advantage of such network-level detection techniques is that they tend to react faster to spam campaigns than typical blacklisting services.

The study closest to our research was performed by Qian et al. [24], where the authors proposed a content-based unsupervised email campaign clustering algorithm, and also recognized the problem of classifying legitimate campaigns in a real-world dataset. In particular, they tried to filter out legitimate bulk emails by using certain keywords and a threshold of IPs per campaign. While the latter can be efficient when dealing with campaigns sent by botnets, it is ineffective against other malevolent campaigns sent from webmail accounts. We demonstrate in our study that such campaigns tend to mimic the traits of legitimate campaigns and are difficult to identify based only on sender characteristics.

To our knowledge, there are no known studies performed on legitimate bulk emails, and only few have studied the gray emails phenomenon [32, 31, 6]. Yih et al. [31] argued that filtering gray emails with even an optimal spam filter is a very difficult task. Therefore, the authors proposed to treat gray emails separately and rely on user feedback to label messages. Their experiments, performed on a dataset that is similar to the one we used in our study, showed that classifying emails on per-campaign basis yielded a higher precision and data coverage compared to a per-email treatment. However, the email or campaign class may depend on the user [6, 7]. Therefore, Chang et al. [6] studied how to combine user feedback with user preferences to improve the classification results. Youn et al. [32] proposed an ontology-based technique to provide personalized gray email filtering based on user behavior. Although we agree that the personalization of gray email is crucial, our results also suggest that user feedback might be unreliable for class prediction.

As spam is primarily sent in bulk emails, many studies try to identify it through the analysis of bulk email campaigns ([16, 21, 29, 13]). Kanich et al. [13] studied spam campaigns by infiltrating a botnet and evaluated their conversion rate from a marketing perspective. Clustering spam emails by URLs and their redirections was first proposed by Li et al. [16]. Pathak et al. [21] tried to cluster spam campaigns using URLs, but it proved to be a challenging task due to URL obfuscation. Thomas et al. [29] confirmed the problem and proposed a new technique to filter URLs in real-time. Finally, Qian et al. [24] identified email campaigns based on their content similarity and Pitsillidis et al. [23] proposed to automatically extract spam campaign templates from regular expressions extracted from the messages.

As we mentioned at the beginning, most of the previous work on the field is focused on identifying spam and its campaigns. In this paper, we exclude most of the spam and legitimate messages and focus instead on the borderline area between them.

3. METHODOLOGY

This section presents the dataset we used in our experiments and the techniques we adopted to process and analyze the email messages. Since it would be impossible to classify each email in isolation, we adopted a multi-layered approach to group them into similar campaigns (a solution proven to be effective by several previous studies [31, 24, 21]). In particular, we start by clustering them based on the email headers. We then extract a set of features based on a number of campaign attributes and we use them to train a classifier in order to predict the campaign class. Finally, we employ a graph-based refinement technique to further increase the coverage and precision of our classification.

3.1 Data Collection

The amount and diversity of the available data is crucial in order to successfully identify email campaigns. Messages should be collected from multiple feeds, cover numerous recipients, several organizations, and for a long period of time [21, 22]. Our email dataset fulfills these requirements as it was collected from a commercial Challenge-Response (CR) spam system deployed in tens of different organizations. A CR filter is a software that automatically replies with a challenge (in our case a CAPTCHA) to any previously-unknown sender of incoming emails. If the sender solves the challenge, the message is delivered to the recipient and the sender is added to a whitelist; if not, it remains in a quarantined folder, where its recipient can manually view and whitelist/blacklist it. Since in our study we want to focus on the borderline area that contains the emails that cannot be easily classified as legitimate or spam, we installed a sensor in the CR system to intercept any quarantined message. These emails have successfully passed through a number of traditional antispam filters including virus scanners, reverse DNS, and DNS blacklisting verification. Moreover, users never had any previous conversation with the sender. Therefore, we can consider this dataset as pre-filtered from obvious legitimate and spam emails.

Sometimes this set is referred to as a gray zone [6] that stores emails of uncertain class. Email categories often found in this group include traditional spam and scam messages, automated notifications, newsletters, and commercial offers. Due this variety, users need to manually check these messages from time to time looking for any interesting or missing email.

We also instrumented the CR-system to collect additional information (see Table 1): opened emails by the users, and whitelisted messages (thus showing that the user manually classified them as legitimate). This provides insights on the users ability to distinguish harmless from harmful messages. Finally, our sensor collected the delivery status information, e.g. sent, bounced, and delivered, for each challenge email sent back by the CR system.

In our experiments we relied on statistical email data that we collected from companies of different sizes. The monitoring period covered 6 months, from August 2011 to January 2012. During this period around 11 million messages were delivered to the monitored mail servers (Table 1). 29.4% of them belonged to the class of gray messages. To protect the privacy of both the users and the companies involved in the study, the data we used in our experiments did not include the email bodies, and the headers were sanitized and analyzed in an aggregated form.

3.2 Email Clustering

The task of grouping emails into campaigns has already been covered by several previous studies ([15, 23, 16, 24, 21]). Previous results were very successful in identifying email campaigns, but, unfortunately, often relied on the content of the email body. Our dataset is limited to the email headers, thus forcing us to use a different approach based only on the email subjects. The main limitation of this technique is that the email subjects have to be long enough to minimize the chances of matching different messages by coincidence.

The obvious solution for grouping similar subjects would be to apply some text mining algorithm, but our input text is short and it is important to preserve the word order. Hence, we decided to use a simple approach based on "almost exact" text matching, extended to include subjects with a variable part. The latter could be a varying phrase in the subject, including random words, identifiers, or user names. We use word n-grams of a decreasing length (between 70 and 8), with a sliding window that permits to skip over varying parts of the subjects. Our implementation is based on an existing n-grams extraction library (Ngram Statistics Package [4]), a standard list of stop-words, and a number of custom scripts to match the extracted n-grams and assign them to clusters.

Table 1: General statistics

Mail servers	13	White emails	2,806,415	Challenges solved	166,279
Active users	10,025	Black emails	5,066,141	Users whitelisted emails	42,384
Total messages	11,203,905	Gray emails	3,331,349	Users viewed emails	104,273

Table 2: Cluster features

Group A	
Sender IPs	Distribution of network prefixes (/24)
Sender names	Distribution of email sender names
Sender add.domain	Distribution of email domain names
Sender add.prefix	Distribution of email prefixes
Group B	
Rejections	Percentage of rejected emails at MTA
White emails	Percentage of whitelisted emails
Challenges bounced	Percentage of bounced challenges
CAPTCHAs solved	Percentage of solved challenges
Unsubscribe header	Percentage of Unsubscribe headers
Group C	
Number of recipients per email	Normalized number of unique recipients per email
Recipient's header	Location of recipient's email: To/Cc/Bcc/Mixed
Countries	Distribution of countries based on originating IPs

The process starts by searching for the longest n-gram (70) and then decreasing the length until enough similar matches (with a threshold of 30 emails per cluster) are found to create a cluster. This algorithm is efficient on long subjects but problematic on short ones, thus limiting our analysis to subjects containing at least 10 characters and 3 words. In this phase we successfully clustered 50% of all emails in 12,250 clusters. Cluster sizes varied between 30 and 8,468 messages.

3.3 Feature-based Classification

To be able to differentiate and classify the identified clusters, we extract a set of eleven features grouped in three categories (see Table 2).

Group A: Features in this group reflect the similarity of a certain feature inside a cluster. The values are expressed as a range between 0 and 1, where 0 indicates a high distribution (low data similarity) and 1 indicates a low distribution (high data similarity) in the cluster. The feature similarity is defined as:

$$a(C) = 1 - u/t$$

where u is the number of unique or similar feature values, and t is the number of total emails. This group contains four features measuring the similarity of sender IP prefixes and email addresses, and the similarity of the sender names. In particular, we split the email domain address into two parts: the *email prefix* and the *email suffix*. The suffixes are grouped by removing numerical differences (e.g., between `abc10.com` and `abc22.com`). When similar suffixes are found, they are merged until there are no similar values left. *Email prefixes* are instead compared using a variation of the Levenshtein distance algorithm in which a threshold is computed based on the length of the email prefix itself. In this way, the similarity score is normalized to account for the fact that, for example, a two-chars difference for short strings is somehow equivalent to a six-chars difference for longer ones.

Group B: Features of this group reflect the percentage of messages in a cluster that have a certain feature value. There are five features in this group: *CAPTCHA solved*, *rejections*, *white emails*, *challenges bounced*, and *unsubscribe header*. The first measures the percentage of challenges that were solved by the senders. The *challenges bounced* are instead emails not delivered because the recipient did not exist, or did not accept emails from the sender. Whenever an email was sent to multiple recipients, we were also able to compute the percentage of *white emails* (i.e., the percentage of recipients that had already whitelisted the sender) and the percentage of incoming email *rejections* (i.e., the percentage of recipients that were rejected by the Mail Transfer Agent - normally because the corresponding addresses did not exist on the server). Finally, the *unsubscribe header* feature evaluates the percentage of emails that contained the unsubscribe header. The latter is generally used by commercial messages and notifications providing the users an option to unsubscribe from the list.

Group C: Features in this groups are computed in different ways. *Recipients per email* estimates the average number of recipients per email. The *Recipient's header* feature indicates the location of email recipient address in the email headers: *To*, *Cc*, *Bcc*, or *Mixed* when multiple locations are used in the same campaign. Finally, the *countries* feature reflects the number of countries (based on the sender IP geolocation) in the cluster.

Manual Labeling

Before performing our classification, we need to build a training set. Obviously, the result of our manual labeling process depends on the actual definition of spam that we adopt in our experiments. By definition, spam is an unsolicited email that is usually sent in bulk. However, there is no reliable way to verify if a certain email is solicited, i.e., if the recipient has subscribed to it or not. Moreover, the notion of spam is somehow subjective and it may not be the same for all the users. Some commercial campaigns are probably unsolicited, and therefore *could be* considered as spam. However, when such emails are sent by professional marketing companies according to the country regulations, it becomes unclear how they should be treated by antispam filters. This is also the main reason why they are considered as gray emails in the first place.

In this paper we take a conservative approach, and flag as spam only campaigns with potentially illegal content that may involve malicious, fraudulent or illegal online activities. This includes different "business models": illegal product sellers, malware spreading emails, personal data and credential thieves, or advanced fee fraud specialists. Finally, we consider any email belonging to a commercial marketing campaign as legitimate (in the sense that general antispam filters should not block them, unless they are specifically instructed to do so by the user).

Although email labeling might be difficult even with the full email content, it can be facilitated by enriching emails with aggregated campaign features. All the campaign features are stored and viewed in an aggregated form, thus never providing access to any distinct email information. A particular case is represented by the *email subject*, a textual information that would be difficult to aggregate without textual data. As we group emails based on subject similarity, we also keep an aggregated copy of the campaign subject.

During the sampling, we relied on the domain knowledge of the analyst and on the additional information (e.g., average number of recipient per email, and number of originating countries), that would not be available to a user reading only one message at a time. Often a subject is enough to make a labeling decision, but in cases when it is not, aggregated header information is used by the analyst. For example, if the message subject resembles a private communication but the email has been sent in 50 identical copies to different recipient, this is more likely to be a scam than a real personal message. In the same way, a message promoting a new product or services online, sent in thousands of copies from over 30 different countries and with multiple recipient per email is probably an illegitimate campaign.

To build the training set, we randomly selected 2,000 campaigns and performed a manual labeling of them. We labeled 1,581 (79%) as legitimate and 419 (21%) as spam campaigns. This preliminary classification confirms that the majority of spam was already filtered out from the gray dataset.

Classification

Using the eleven features presented above, we trained a binary classifier. To select a classifier we referred to the results presented by Kiran et al. [14], in which the authors demonstrated that, on spam datasets, ensemble classifiers perform better than single classifiers. Based on this conclusion, for our classification task we decided to use a supervised Random Forest ensemble classifier.

We first performed a cross validation test in which we randomly split the sampled data into two groups including respectively 70% and 30% of the data. We then trained the Random Forest classifier (configured with 500 trees and three random variables per split) on the first group, and we tested the extracted model on the second one. For each cluster, the algorithm returned a score ranging between -1 (for spam) and 1 (for legitimate). A score close to zero indicates that the classifier was uncertain about the sample.

Since our set includes classes of very different sizes, we use the Matthews Correlation Coefficient (MMC) to measure the classification quality. Our model achieved MCC of 0.75, where the value is between [-1,..1], and 1 represents a perfect prediction. The model produced 0.9% false positives (i.e., legitimate campaigns being misclassified as spam) and 10% false negatives (i.e., spam being misclassified as legitimate). These rates suggest that the set of attributes we identified are effective in separating the two types of campaigns. We also noticed that while our classifier identified legitimate campaigns well, it had a higher probability of misclassifying spam campaigns. A further interpretation of this phenomenon is described in section 5.

Finally, we applied the model extracted from our training set to predict the classification of the remaining unlabeled campaigns. Results are presented in Table 3.

Table 3: Campaign classification results

Campaign type	Manual sampling	%	Unlabeled	%
Legitimate	1,581	79%	8,398	81.9%
Spam	419	21%	1,852	18.1%
Total	2,000		10,250	

Table 4: Attribute values per campaign category

Attribute	Legitimate	Spam Min / Mean / Max	Gray
Countries	1 - 1.2 - 6	7 - 29 - 123	1 - 5 - 80
IPs	0.13 - 0.9 - 1	0 - 0.06 - 0.82	0 - 0.7 - 1
Sender email domain	0.2 - 0.98 - 1	0 - 0.3 - 1	0 - 0.85 - 1
Sender email prefix	0.03 - 0.98 - 1	0 - 0.09 - 1	0 - 0.81 - 1
Senders	0 - 0.98 - 1	0 - 0.3 - 1	0 - 0.8 - 1
Unsubscribe header	0 - 0.5 - 1	0 - 0 - 0.3	0 - 0.3 - 1
Bounced	0 - 0 - 1	0 - 0.1 - 1	0 - 0.1 - 0.9
CAPTCHAs	0 - 0 - 1	0 - 0 - 1	0 - 0.1 - 1
White emails	0	0	0.001
Rejections	0 - 0 - 0.4	0 - 0.23 - 1	0 - 0.1 - 0.7
Rec.per email	1 - 1 - 1.1	1 - 3 - 16	1 - 1.1 - 8
Recipient header	*To*, *Bcc*, *Mixed* shares 0.76 - 0.04 - 0.2	0.3 - 0.1 - 0.6	0.4 - 0.33 - 0.3

3.4 Graph-based Refinement

Although we achieved a relatively high accuracy using our classifier, we still found that for some campaigns our algorithm gave uncertain results. Luckily, the vast majority of the campaigns are located at the extremes of the classifier scores, either close to 1 (legitimate), or to -1 (spam). Campaigns become much more scarce in the range between [-0.8..0.8]. This gray area inside the gray area represents cases for which our technique was unable to automatically assign a definitive category.

Using these two thresholds, we can refine our classification and split the data into three classes: legitimate (77% of the total campaigns), spam (16%), and gray (6.4%). The minimum, average, and maximum values for each attribute in the three classes are summarized in Table 4. Since most of the false positives and false negatives are located in the gray area, we focused on improving the classification of those messages by using a graph-based technique.

In particular, we built a graph in which nodes represent campaigns and edges model the fact that two campaigns share a combination of sender IP address and email domain name. These links created networks of campaigns sent from the same mailing infrastructure. To avoid false connections that might appear between campaigns when they use webmail providers (spoofed or not), we removed those links from the graph.

The resulting graph contained 9,891 connected campaigns and 608 isolated subgraphs. By visually looking at the subgraphs, we noticed that the majority consisted of a predominant class (either spam or legitimate nodes) sometimes intermixed with gray nodes (see an example in Figure 1). This seems to suggest that gray campaigns also belong to the same class as the other nodes in the same group, since they are sent using the same infrastructure.

Additionally, our graph contains a Giant Component – a graph linking together 52% of all the campaigns – for which it is impossible to decide which class it belongs to. There-

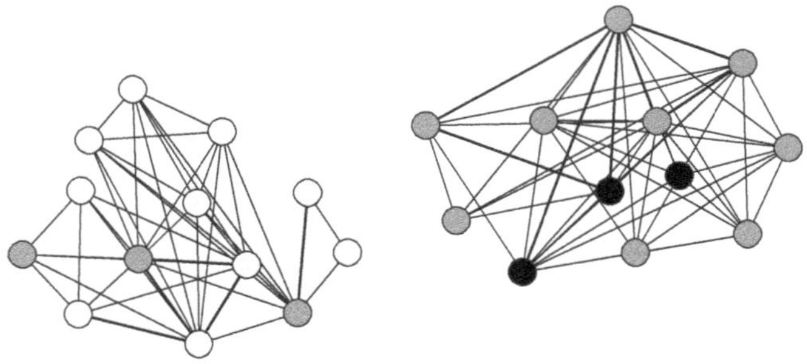

Figure 1: Subgraphs with mixed campaign classes: white for legitimate, gray for gray, black for spam

Table 5: Refining the campaign classification using graph analysis. Classification errors evaluated on 2,000 sampled campaigns

	RandomForest	Graph analysis
False Positives	0.9%	0.2%
False Negatives	8.6%	7.6%
Gray area	6.4%	2.9%

fore, we apply a community finding algorithm [5] that groups all the nodes into interconnected communities, also called groups, decomposing the Giant Component into smaller parts. We end up with 660 groups, for most of which we can accurately associate a single class. When gray campaigns are in the same group with any other class, we assign gray campaigns to the class of its group.

While this technique works well for most of the groups, some noise is still introduced in the results by the presence of loosely connected nodes. These are nodes that get erroneously connected to a group due to emails reusing the subjects of legitimate campaigns. To remove these connections, for each node we compute a graph metric called *clustering coefficient*. The coefficient for loosely connected nodes is equal to 0, whereas it approaches 1 for tightly connected nodes. As a result, we re-classify all the gray nodes with a clustering coefficient greater than zero and that belong to a group of either legitimate or spam campaigns. To decide on the class of the group, we compute the mean of classifier score of all nodes in the group: groups above 0.2 are considered legitimate, and groups below this threshold are considered spam.

Using this approach we were able to re-classify over half of the gray campaigns (427). This reduced the false positives from 0.9% to 0.2% (see Table 5 for more information). The entire dataset is now split into legitimate (80%), spam (17%) and gray (2.9%) messages (an increase of 3% for legitimate campaigns and 1% for spam). Again, our method performs better with legitimate messages. This is due to legitimate campaigns forming stronger networks (reusing the same mailing infrastructure over time) than malicious campaign.

4. ATTRIBUTE ANALYSIS

In this section we analyze the characteristics of spam and legitimate campaigns, and compare our findings to the ones presented in previous spam studies [21, 24].

The Random Forest classifier provides some information about the relevance of each feature. Interestingly, the least important attributes are the ones in Group B, and in particular the percentage of already whitelisted emails in the cluster. The most important ones are the distributions of countries and IP addresses, followed by the average number of recipients, and the sender email address similarity. The latter proved to be useful because spammers often change sender emails, while legitimate campaigns use a single or several repetitive patterns.

In particular, we found the number of originating countries to be the most indicative parameter, whereas previous research often relied on the IP address distribution (e.g. [24]).

4.1 The Role of IPs and Geolocation

IP address variation is often regarded as a strong indicator of botnet activity and often used as a reliable metric to detect spam. However, it is unclear what should be adopted as a threshold for this metric, how many different IPs should alert us of a distributed malicious activity, or how accurately we can classify email campaigns simply by looking at their IP address distribution.

In a previous study of spam campaigns, Qian et al. [24] used a threshold of 10 IPs per campaign to separate spam campaigns from legitimate ones. To evaluate this threshold, we applied it on our gray dataset as shown in Figure 2 (a). The graph plots the distribution of unique IP prefixes for both spam and legitimate campaigns. Around 90% of the legitimate campaigns are indeed below the 10 IP threshold, while 90% of the spam is above - resulting in a global error rate of 9.2% (to be precise, our measure is based on /24 subnetworks and not on single IP addresses, and therefore the real error rate is much higher than 9.2%). In comparison, this error is 5 times higher than the one of our classifier.

By looking at Figure 2 (a), we notice that above 50 IP prefixes there are few legitimate campaigns left and 99.8% of legitimate campaigns are below this threshold. However, half of the spam campaigns are located above the threshold and another half in between the two thresholds (10-50). This suggests that there is not a single value that separates the two classes with an acceptable error rate.

When we look at IP country distribution, the results improve considerably as some legitimate campaigns have many IP prefixes, but originate from few countries. This could be explained by one commercial campaign being distributed by several marketing companies in different locations. In contrast, the vast majority of spam campaigns originate from multiple IP prefixes *and* multiple countries. In fact, by using a six-countries threshold (the one chosen by our classifier) we misclassify only 0.4% of legitimate and 12% of spam campaigns - resulting in a total error rate of 2.8%. Figure 2 (b) shows the classification error.

Finally, we investigate closer this group of spam campaigns with few origins. Interestingly, the classifier for most of them gave a weak score, between 0 and -0.5. The graph refinement was ineffective for them, because these campaigns did not appear at all in our graph. At a closer manual inspection, these cases mainly corresponded to phishing and Nigerian scams. Several of these campaigns are sent in low volume and for short periods of time using webmail accounts, thus hiding under benign IP addresses.

4.2 Recipient-Oriented Attributes

The email recipient can be specified in three different headers: *To*, *Cc*, and *Bcc*. Interestingly, we found no campaigns using the *Cc* header, and some campaigns that seem to randomly change the location of the recipient over time

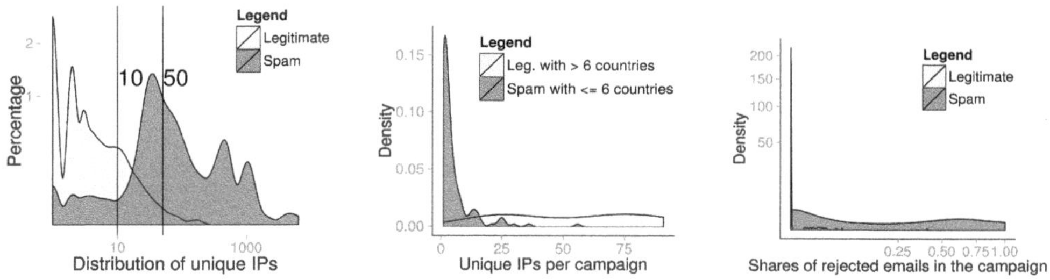

(a) Logarithmic plot of unique IP prefix distribution

(b) Campaigns with a threshold of 6 countries

(c) Emails rejections per campaign

Figure 2: Attribute distributions in campaigns

Table 6: *To/Bcc/Mixed* recipient header distribution

	To	*Bcc*	*Mixed*
Legitimate	75%	5%	20%
Spam	30%	12%	58%
Gray	20%	53%	27%

Table 7: *Unsubscribe* header presence in campaigns

Campaigns	Header present	Missing header
Spam	225 (10%)	2,013 (90%)
Legitimate	5,064 (51%)	4,948 (49%)
Emails		
Spam	2,710 (0.6%)	482,133 (99%)
Legitimate	506,352 (43%)	668,153 (57%)

(we categorize them as *Mixed*). We also looked at the number of recipients per incoming email and at the number of non-existing email accounts (rejected at MTA-in because of non-existent user) in multiple recipient emails. We look at these three features together as they are often more informative when combined than when taken individually.

Around 75% of the legitimate campaigns use the *To* header (Table 6), whereas spammers often mix different headers in the same campaign. The *Bcc* header is adopted by both campaign types, although less frequently. However, it is very common among gray campaigns: in fact, half of them use exclusively this header to specify the recipient. Again, this is very common between the previously mentioned scam campaigns.

Since the campaigns located in the gray zone often use the *Bcc* field, they have shorter recipient lists including on average only 1.2 recipients per email. In contrast, 94% of legitimate campaigns have a single recipient, while spammers tend to include an average of at least three recipients per email.

However, these features alone cannot be used to reliably separate spam from legitimate messages. For example, 36% of spam campaigns used only one recipient per email, and in 30% of the cases specified in the *To* header. Interestingly, by combining these two criteria with the fact that these campaigns also have high IP prefix distribution, we can deduct that they originate from infected machines or botnets.

When some of the messages in a campaign are rejected, it is an indicator that the sender's recipient list was unverified or not up-to-date. Although sometimes users make typos while providing their email addresses, a higher rejection ratio, as shown in Figure 2 (c), along with multiple recipients is a good indicator of spammer activity. In fact, only 1% of spam campaigns sent with two recipients per email have a rejection ratio lower than 0.1. Thus, the combination of these two characteristics performs well for campaign classification.

4.3 Newsletter Subscription Header

One of our features counts the presence of the *List-Unsubscribe* header in the emails. This header is intended specifically to indicate bulk email senders in order to treat such emails separately, and normally points to a URL or email address that can be used to unsubscribe from a mailing list[1]. This header is recommended to be used by regular bulk senders. Another recommendation for bulk email is to use the *Precedence: bulk* header. However, since in our dataset this header was used only in a few messages, we focus on the more common *List-Unsubscribe* header.

Figure 3 shows the percentage of each campaign type that uses the unsubscribe header. Only 10% of the spam campaigns adopt the header, counting only for a total of 0.6% of the spam messages. While legitimate campaigns tend to use the header in most of their emails, around half of the campaigns do not use it at all. This is due to several different email marketing companies advertising the same campaign, where some include the header, and some do not. In total, around half of the legitimate campaigns include the header (Table 7), and 27% of all legitimate campaigns have the header present in all messages.

In conclusion, we find it uncommon for spammers to use the *Unsubscribe* header, but at the same time legitimate campaigns use it in only half of their emails. While this attribute seems to be a good feature to identify marketing campaigns, spoofing the *Unsubscribe* header is extremely easy and could be done with minimal additional costs for spammers.

5. EMAIL CAMPAIGNS

In this section we present four categories of email campaigns that we identify in the gray area. We already separated spam from legitimate campaigns. We further divide

[1]In general an unsubscribe option is also included in the body of the message, but we could not check for this case since we had no access to email bodies.

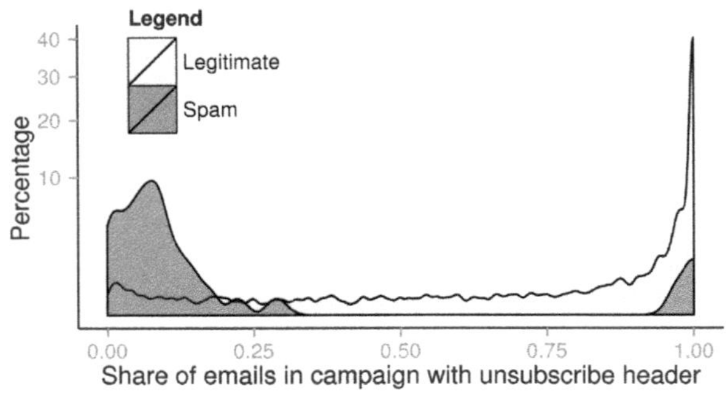

Figure 3: Newsletter subscription header distribution. Only the cases where the header is present are plotted

the spam in two categories: the one generated by distributed and dynamic infrastructures (likely sent by botnet or infected machines) from the smaller campaigns sent by few IPs.

We also split the legitimate campaigns into two groups. The first sent by private marketing companies as a service to distributes legitimate bulk advertisements, i.e., commercial campaigns. The second including newsletters that are sent to the users subscribed to a web services or mailing lists, and the automatically generated notifications (e.g. for online registrations). Again, the first ones are delivered by large infrastructures, while the second ones are often sent from a limited and constant set of IP addresses.

To identify these four categories in our dataset, we adopt a number of simple heuristics. As *commercial campaigns* we mark legitimate campaigns that belong to the biggest interconnected component of the graph described in Section 3.4. These are campaigns that are spread over many different networks and domain names as such campaigns are sometimes sent by several different e-marketing services providers, thus forming a large graph of interconnected campaigns. We consider the remaining scattered legitimate campaigns as *newsletters and notifications* as they rely on more static and isolated email delivery infrastructures. Botnet-generated campaigns are instead approximated by the spam clusters that are sent from more than six different countries and by more than 20 unique /24 IP prefixes. Finally, we manually sample over 350 of the remaining spam campaigns to identify *scam* and *phishing campaigns*.

All the categories are visualized in Figure 4, and the mean values of their features are summarized in Table 8.

5.1 Commercial Campaigns

This is the largest category in our dataset covering 42% of the identified campaigns, with an average of 148 emails each. By looking manually at these clusters, we confirm that these messages are mainly generated by professional email marketers sending. We were able to identify some of the main players (both national and international), and often confirmed that they actually run a legal business. On their websites, they repeatedly underline the fact that "they are not spammers", and that they just provide to other companies a way to send marketing emails within the boundaries of the current legislation. In fact, they also offer an online procedure for users to opt-out and be removed from future communications. These companies also use wide IP address ranges to run the campaigns, probably to avoid being blacklisted. Moreover, we find quite interesting that some of these

Table 8: Feature mean values per campaign category. **Note:** User actions were evaluated only on campaigns with actions

Attribute		Commercial	Newsletter	Botnet	Scam
Countries		1.4	1.14	28.2	2.74
Recipients per email		1.00	1.00	2.80	1.16
Recipient header (%)	*To*:	0.75	0.77	0.31	0
	Bcc:	0.07	0	0.12	0.83
	Mixed:	0.18	0.22	0.57	0.17
Sender email prefix		0.97	0.98	0.12	0.94
Sender email domain		0.96	0.99	0.31	0.97
IP distribution		0.84	0.94	0.08	0.86
Unique IPs		6	2	172	5
Rejections		0	0	0.24	0.02
Senders		0.97	0.98	0.34	0.95
Bounced		0.01	0.02	0.09	0.14
Unsubscribe header		0.59	0.39	0.01	0
CAPTCHAs		0.006	0.007	0	0.007
White emails		0.007	0.004	0.004	0.02
Period (days)		28	19	59	41
Viewed emails		3.6	6	7.3	2.9
Whitelisted emails		2.9	4	1.26	2.25
CAPTCHAs solved		19	26	1.7	7.6
Campaigns		5,113	3,597	2,107	150

companies also provide a pre-compiled list of emails (already categorized by user interests) that can be used to acquire new clients.

Therefore, email recipients can be taken both from *cold lists* (i.e., people who are not yet customers), or from current customer lists. As a result, different marketers send many different email campaigns, thus forming a large interconnected network of campaigns, as captured by our graph. As the senders also rely on cold lists, it is crucial to ensure that recipients can unsubscribe from the unsolicited advertisements. Indeed, commercial campaigns have the highest rate of *unsubscribe* headers.

On average, this class of campaigns lasts for 26 days, but some also continue for several months. Different email marketing companies are often involved in sending a single campaign, where each company is only active during a certain time frame. Also, each marketing service provider has its own dedicated range of IP addresses, which explains sometimes high IP address variance and high geographical distribution of campaigns in this group. As a comparison, newsletters (Figure 4, upper-left part) use on average three times less of unique IP addresses than a professional marketer.

To conclude, commercial campaigns can be highly distributed, but, at the same time, they often adopt consistent email patterns with similar sender names and email addresses.

5.2 Newsletter Campaigns

The newsletter senders rely mostly on static and small mailing infrastructure. The sender is often the actual company distributing the emails, with typically a small and fixed IP address range. This category contains half of the emails of the previous one (probably because most of the legitimate mailing lists do not get into the quarantined area as they are already whitelisted by their customers) and covers around

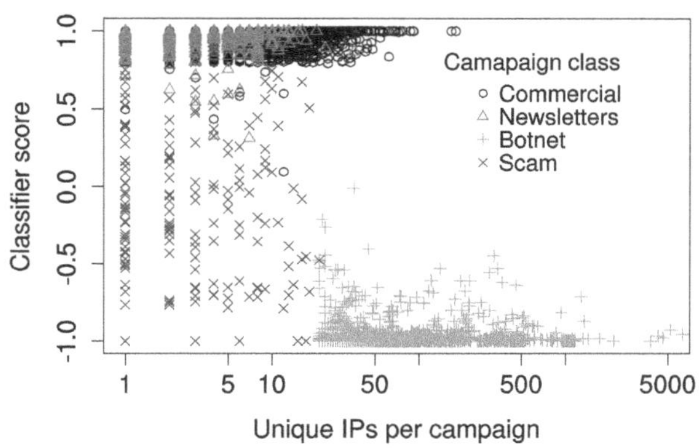

Figure 4: Email campaign classes distribution

30% of the total campaigns with an average size of 90 emails each.

A manual inspection seems to confirm that these campaigns consist mainly of notifications and newsletters sent by online services to which users have subscribed in the past. The senders are geographically localized (we encountered only one exception of a distributed newsletter campaign) and have extremely consistent sending patterns. Since we cluster campaigns based on their subjects, newsletters tend to last for very short periods of time. In addition, they normally use valid email recipient lists, and exhibit the lowest IP address, country, and sender email address variations. Only the use of the *Unsubscribe* header seems inconsistent, as only 39% of emails use it. However, this can be explained by the fact that notification emails normally do not use this header - only newsletters are subject to optional subscription. The consistent patterns in the email headers of this category indicate that the senders are making an effort to build a reputation and successfully deliver their correspondence. Not surprisingly, this is also the category that is whitelisted most often by the users.

5.3 Botnet-Generated Campaigns

Unsurprisingly, Table 8 shows that botnet-generated campaigns have highly dynamic attribute values, making them the easiest category to identify automatically. This category contains clusters that accounts for only 17% of all campaigns (also because most of the spam emails were already excluded from the gray emails by other antispam filters). Botnet campaigns have the highest geographical distribution as they are sent by infected computers from all over the world: 172 unique /24 networks per campaign, spread on average over 28 countries. Another prevalent characteristic is the use of multiple recipient emails sent using unverified email lists. Consequently, this leads to the highest email rejection rates (24%), and highest bounced CAPTCHA requests. The *Unsubscribe* header is rarely used, and sender email addresses have low similarities.

On average, botnet campaigns are the ones lasting the longest, with one drug-related campaign sent slowly over the entire six-months period of our experiments. Pathak et al. [21] also studied the length of *spam* campaigns, reporting a maximum length of 99 days over a dataset spanning 150 days. Our campaigns are substantially longer than that, maybe due to different datasets (we collected directly from user mail servers, not from open-relays), different email grouping methods (similar subject vs. URLs), or to changes in the behavior of spammers over time.

Despite the easily recognizable characteristics of these campaigns, users show a surprisingly high interest in these emails. This category has the highest number of email views per campaign, suggesting that users are often curious about products promoted and sold on the black market [18].

5.4 Scam and Phishing Campaigns

These campaigns contain phishing and Nigerian scam emails. Fraudsters trick their victims using threatening messages or by trying to seduce them with huge monetary gains. The characteristics of this category largely resemble those of commercial campaigns, thus making it difficult to automatically separate these campaigns without analyzing the email body. In fact, most of these campaigns belong to the gray area of our classifier. This is the reason why we needed to verify this set manually. These kind of threats are more likely to be identified by content-based detection techniques, e.g., by looking at email addresses and phone numbers [12], or URL [21, 29] included in the body.

We found only 12,601 of such emails, with an average campaign size of 84 emails. Phishing campaigns often spoofed the email addresses using well known company names (e.g. banks, eBay, Paypal), whereas Nigerian scammers relied mostly on webmail accounts [12]. In this case, many senders solved the CAPTCHA challenge – confirming that there is usually a real person behind these kinds of scams. The IP addresses from where the CAPTCHAs were solved are mostly located in West-African countries, like Nigeria or Ivory Coast. None of the messages in this category include an *Unsubscribe* header.

Unfortunately, users seemed to often fall victims to this type of attack, as they opened and even whitelisted messages in these campaigns.

6. USER BEHAVIOR

Our dataset also provides information about which actions were performed by the users on the quarantined emails. In particular, we collected information regarding the messages that were read, added to a user whitelist or blacklist, and the CAPTCHA that was later solved by the sender. These data can give us some useful insights on the ability of average users to identify suspicious emails.

Table 9 presents three user action statistics. As expected, user activity involves mainly legitimate and gray campaigns. In fact, the main reason for users to go through the emails in this folder is to spot missed notifications or undelivered benign messages. However, a large fraction of users also opened spam messages, maybe attracted by some deceiving subjects. As shown in Table 8 and Figure 5 (a), the highest campaign viewing rates are produced by botnet-generated campaigns, overpassing even newsletters. Over 3,888 spam emails were viewed by users during our six-month experiments, resulting in the fact that *one out of five users* has viewed at least one spam message, and, on average, *opened 5 of them*[2].

After a manual inspection of botnet-generated campaigns where the emails were read and whitelisted, we confirmed that those campaigns were promoting illegal products, e.g.

[2]Unfortunately, from our dataset we are unable to tell how many users downloaded attachments or followed links included in the message body.

Table 9: User actions performed on campaigns

	Viewed	Whitelisted	CAPTCHA solved
Legitimate	42%	12%	3.5%
Spam	25%	6%	0.2%
Gray	40%	17%	10%

drugs and pirated software. This may suggest two things: either users have problems in distinguishing legitimate emails from harmful, or some users are genuinely interested in the products promoted by spammers. It is difficult to draw conclusions as both hypotheses might be true for different users, but, clearly, most of them are unaware of the security threats involved in opening malicious emails.

Meanwhile, we should compare the reported statistics of viewed emails with the number of emails that actually got whitelisted – an action that could be interpreted as the equivalent of clicking the "Not Spam" button provided by several webmail services. The number of whitelisted emails per botnet-generated campaign (1.26 emails, Table 8) is the lowest among all the categories, suggesting that most users successfully differentiate them. However, we notice that scam/phishing campaigns have almost the same number of emails being whitelisted per campaign as commercial campaigns (2.25 vs 2.9). This suggests that users might have difficulties in differentiating these categories. It is important to remember that this category was manually sampled by domain experts, which is not the case for the typical users as most of them are untrained and are more likely to fall for these kind of fraud.

To further measure how significant this phenomenon is, we compute that there is a 0.36% probability that a certain user whitelists a legitimate email and 0.0005% that she whitelists a spam message. These numbers may seem low, but they rapidly increase when multiplied by the number of users and the number of messages received. In total, an average of 3.9 emails get whitelisted per legitimate campaign compared to 1.1 emails per spam campaign.

The last question we want to answer is whether the fact that the senders solve some CAPTCHAs in a campaign could be a good indicator of its legitimacy. Unfortunately, it is not and for two reasons. First, most of the legitimate campaign senders are automated tools, since a large potion of gray emails consists of newsletters, online notifications, and marketing emails. Secondly, although the general tendency is that users solve more CAPTCHAs within legitimate classes (Figure 5 (b)), as shown in Table 8, also scam and phishing campaigns have high CAPTCHA solved rates (7.6) compare with other categories. Finally, the rare cases of botnet-generated campaigns solving few CAPTCHAs correspond to challenges delivered to spoofed addresses by spammers as previously described by Isacenkova et al. [11].

To conclude, user-generated actions on gray emails are erroneous and thus are inaccurate to use for prediction. They often open even potentially dangerous emails, ignoring security risks. These results are in line to what has been tested in a user study conducted by Onarlioglu et al. [19].

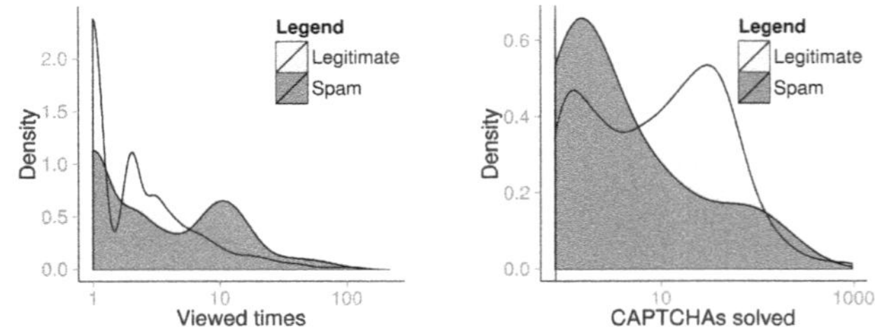

(a) Viewed emails (b) CAPTCHAs solved

Figure 5: Number of user actions taken per campaign

7. UNCLUSTERED EMAILS

Our campaign classification covers half of the emails in the quarantined area, with 0.2% false positive rate. One may wonder what is inside the remaining 50% that is left outside our clustering approach. Qian et al. [24] concluded that the majority of legitimate emails should not be classifiable into clusters because of the content uniqueness generated by humans. Additionally, since most of the spam and legitimate emails were already filtered out from our dataset, the exact proportion may be different.

We could try to approximate the content of the unclustered part by assuming that the legitimate campaign senders always rely on a stable hosting infrastructure (as described in Section 3.4). In this case, for every legitimate campaign we can try to find messages sent by the same subnetwork and domain name in the unclassified email set. Using this technique, we found that 26% of the emails were sent from senders that were also responsible for legitimate campaigns. Almost 40% were sent from webmail providers. The spam set had a very low number of matches in the unclustered set, which is expected since most of these emails are sent from compromised machines that change over time.

Even though this heuristic can only provide a rough approximation of what is inside the remaining 50% of the messages, it can still be used (as part of a more complex system) to automatically separate marketing campaigns from more dangerous forms of spam.

8. DISCUSSION AND CONCLUSIONS

In this paper we presented a system to identify and classify campaigns of gray emails. As an approximation of this set, we chose to use the quarantined folder of a challenge-response antispam filter, since it is already clean from obvious spam and ham messages.

Our analysis unveiled the most and the least predictive email campaign class attributes. We also demonstrated that previous techniques used for email campaign classification [24] did not provide acceptable results in our settings, confirming that the gray area contains the hardest messages to classify. Additionally, we confirmed and extended some of the findings of previous studies regarding botnet campaigns [21].

Our system could be used in different ways. First of all, it can help understanding how large commercial campaigns work, how they originate, and how they differ from other unsolicited emails. It could also serve as an input to automatically place marketing campaigns and newsletters in a separate folder, so that users can clearly differentiate these messages from other forms of spam. In fact, the users in our study often opened botnet-generated emails and were especially prone to errors when dealing with scam and phishing messages; we believe that a separate folder dedicated to legitimate bulk emails would create an extra layer between the users and the malicious messages, thus allowing users to focus on the bulk folder when looking for missing and misclassified emails. Interestingly, after we completed our study, a similar solution was deployed by GMail [2], to place user newsletters, notifications, and other commercial email into distinctive categories.

We also found out that our classification method based on sender behavior works well for any campaign except scam. We believe that the latter would benefit largely from content-based email analysis, e.g. URL or emails/phones clustering. Finally, we demonstrated that by using a graph-based refinement method, legitimate email campaigns can often be identified based only on sender information, and can be categorized as newsletters or commercial advertisement. This is a particularly promising result in the direction of empirical study of legitimate bulk emails.

9. ACKNOWLEDGEMENTS

The research leading to these results has received funding from the European Union Seventh Framework Programme (FP7/2007-2013) under grant agreement nr. 257007. We also thank MailInBlack for providing the data that was used in our study.

10. REFERENCES

[1] CAN-SPAM Act: Controlling the Assault of Non-Solicited Pornography And Marketing Act of 2003.

[2] Inbox tabs and category labels. `http://gmailblog.blogspot.fr/2013/05/a-new-inbox-that-puts-you-back-in.html`.

[3] Directive 2002/58 on Privacy and Electronic Communications, concerning the processing of personal data and the protection of privacy in the electronic communications sector (Directive on privacy and electronic communications). , 2002.

[4] S. Banerjee and T. Pedersen. The design, implementation and use of the ngram statistics package. *ITPCL*, 2003.

[5] V. D. Blondel, J.-L. Guillaume, R. Lambiotte, and E. Lefebvre. Fast unfolding of communities in large networks. *Journal of Statistical Mechanics: Theory and Experiment*, 2008(10):P10008, 2008.

[6] M.-W. Chang, W.-T. Yih, and R. Mccann. Personalized spam filtering for gray mail. *CEAS*, 2008.

[7] D. Fallows. Spam: How it is hurting email and degrading life on the internet, 2003.

[8] Direct Marketing Association. Response Rate Report, 2012.

[9] D. M. A. DMA. Email deliverability review whitepaper, 2012.

[10] S. Hao, N. Syed, N. Feamster, A. Gray, and S. Krasser. Detecting spammers with SNARE: Spatio-temporal network-level automatic reputation engine. In *Proc. of the 18th conference on USENIX security symposium*, pages 101–118. USENIX Association, 2009.

[11] J. Isacenkova and D. Balzarotti. Measurement and evaluation of a real world deployment of a challenge-response spam filter. *ACM SIGCOMM, IMC*, 2011.

[12] J. Isacenkova, O. Thonnard, A. Costin, D. Balzarotti, and A. Francillion. Inside the scam jungle: A closer look at 419 scam email operations. *IWCC*, 2013.

[13] C. Kanich, C. Kreibich, K. Levchenko, B. Enright, G. M. Voelker, V. Paxson, and S. Savage. Spamalytics: An empirical analysis of spam marketing conversion. *CCS*, 2008.

[14] P. Kiran and I. Atmosukarto. Spam or not spam–that is the question. *Tech. rep., University of Washington*, 2009.

[15] A. Kolcz and A. Chowdhury. Hardening fingerprinting by context. *CEAS*, 2007.

[16] F. Li and M. han Hsieh. An empirical study of clustering behavior of spammers and groupbased anti-spam strategies. *CEAS*, 2006.

[17] MAAWG. Email Security Awareness and Usage Report, 2012.

[18] D. McCoy, A. Pitsillidis, G. Jordan, N. Weaver, C. Kreibich, B. Krebs, G. M. Voelker, S. Savage, and K. Levchenko. Pharmaleaks: Understanding the business of online pharmaceutical affiliate programs. *USENIX*, 2012.

[19] K. Onarlioglu, U. O. Yilmaz, D. Balzarotti, and E. Kirda. Insights into user behavior in dealing with internet attacks. *NDSS*, 2012.

[20] A. Pathak, Y. Hu, and Z. Mao. Peeking into spammer behavior from a unique vantage point. In *Proc. of the 1st Usenix Workshop on Large-Scale Exploits and Emergent Threats*, pages 1–9. USENIX Association, 2008.

[21] A. Pathak, F. Qian, Y. C. Hu, Z. M. Mao, and S. Ranjan. Botnet spam campaigns can be long lasting: Evidence, implications, and analysis. *SIGMETRICS*, 2009.

[22] A. Pitsillidis, C. Kanich, G. M. Voelker, K. Levchenko, and S. Savage. Taster's choice: a comparative analysis of spam feeds. *IMC*, 2012.

[23] A. Pitsillidis, K. Levchenko, C. Kreibich, C. Kanich, G. M. Voelker, V. Paxson, N. Weaver, and S. Savage. Botnet judo: Fighting spam with itself. *NDSS*, 2010.

[24] F. Qian, A. Pathak, Y. C. Hu, Z. M. Mao, and Y. Xie. A case for unsupervised-learning-based spam filtering. *SIGMETRICS*, 2010.

[25] Z. Qian, Z. M. Mao, Y. Xie, and F. Yu. On network-level clusters for spam detection. In *NDSS*, 2010.

[26] A. Ramachandran and N. Feamster. Understanding the network-level behavior of spammers. In *ACM SIGCOMM Computer Communication Review*, volume 36, pages 291–302. ACM, 2006.

[27] A. Ramachandran, N. Feamster, and S. Vempala. Filtering spam with behavioral blacklisting. In *Proc. of the 14th ACM conference on computer and communications security*, pages 342–351. ACM, 2007.

[28] Return Path. Email Intelligence Report, Q3 2012.

[29] K. Thomas, C. Grier, J. Ma, V. Paxson, and D. Song. Design and evaluation of a real-time url spam filtering service. *IEEE Symposium on Security and Privacy*, 2011.

[30] A. G. West, A. J. Aviv, J. Chang, and I. Lee. Mitigating spam using spatio-temporal reputation. Technical report, DTIC Document, 2010.

[31] W.-t. Yih, R. McCann, and A. Kolcz. Improving spam filtering by detecting gray mail. *CEAS*, 2007.

[32] S. Youn and D. McLeod. Spam decisions on gray e-mail using personalized ontologies. *SAC*, 2009.

Practical User Authentication Leveraging Channel State Information (CSI)

Hongbo Liu
Department of CIT
Indiana University Purdue University Indianapolis (IUPUI)
Indianapolis, IN, USA
hl45@iupui.edu

Yang Wang
Department of ECE
Stevens Institute of Technology
Hoboken, NJ, USA
ywang84@stevens.edu

Jian Liu
Department of ECE
Stevens Institute of Technology
Hoboken, NJ, USA
jliu28@stevens.edu

Jie Yang
Department of CSE
Oakland University
Rochester, MI, USA
yang@oakland.edu

Yingying Chen
Department of ECE
Stevens Institute of Technology
Hoboken, NJ, USA
yingying.chen@stevens.edu

ABSTRACT

User authentication is the critical first step to detect identity-based attacks and prevent subsequent malicious attacks. However, the increasingly dynamic mobile environments make it harder to always apply the cryptographic-based methods for user authentication due to their infrastructural and key management overhead. Exploiting non-cryptographic based techniques grounded on physical layer properties to perform user authentication appears promising. In this work, we explore to use channel state information (CSI), which is available from off-the-shelf WiFi devices, to conduct fine-grained user authentication. We propose an user-authentication framework that has the capability to build the user profile resilient to the presence of the spoofer. Our machine learning based user-authentication techniques can distinguish two users even when they possess similar signal fingerprints and detect the existence of the spoofer. Our experiments in both office building and apartment environments show that our framework can filter out the signal outliers and achieve higher authentication accuracy compared with existing approaches using received signal strength (RSS).

Categories and Subject Descriptors

C.2 [**COMPUTER-COMMUNICATION NETWORKS**]: General—*Security and protection*

General Terms

Design, Experimentation, Measurement, Performance

ASIA CCS'14, June 4–6, 2014, Kyoto, Japan.

http://dx.doi.org/10.1145/2590296.2590321.

Keywords

Channel state information, user authentication, wireless networks

1. INTRODUCTION

The rapid advancement of wireless technologies are making the wireless networks ubiquitous and people can access network services at anytime and anywhere. However, securing wireless networks is challenging due to the shared nature of wireless medium as adversaries can eavesdrop or intercept any wireless transmission [16]. For example, an adversary can passively monitor wireless networks to obtain valid device identities and further launch identity-based attacks, which serves as a basis for launching a variety of malicious attacks across multiple network layers [6]. Indeed, such identity-based attacks are easy to launch in WiFi networks, where the Access Points (AP) can be spoofed, resulting in Denial of Service (i.e., rogue AP attack) [30]. Although existing cryptographic based authentication techniques (such as WiFi Protected Access and 802.11i) can protect data frames, an attacker can still spoof the 802.11 management frames [22]. In addition, the increasingly dynamic mobile environments make it harder to utilize cryptographic-based authentication, due to its infrastructural and key management overhead [2, 5, 7].

Recently authentication based on non-cryptographic methods are proposed to compliment and enhance the existing cryptography based schemes [6, 9, 3]. For example, the channel based authentication schemes use the Received Signal Strength (RSS) of wireless packets or the Channel Impulse Response (CIR) of a single frequency to generate fingerprints of the wireless channel to perform user authentication [6, 21]. The rational behind these schemes is that both RSS and CIR present unique spatial properties due to path loss and multi-path effects. An adversary, resided at a different location from the legitimate user, will incur different RSS or CIR profiles. However, the RSS and CIR extracted from a single frequency only provide coarse-grained information of the wireless channel and thus the effectiveness of user authentication is largely limited. For example, the RSS-based authentication can hardly distinguish two users with similar signal signatures even though they may be located far away from each other [6].

In this paper, we exploit the fine-grained physical layer information made available from orthogonal frequency-division multiplexing (OFDM) to perform user authentication. The channel response from multiple subcarriers of OFDM provides detailed Channel Sate Information (CSI) [10], which could become an ideal candidate for achieving accurate user authentication. Specifically, we show that CSI can be utilized to accurately authenticate users with similar signal fingerprints and discriminate the legitimate user from a spoofing attacker. The detailed channel information has the power to enable user authentication at per packet level, making it a promising utility to achieve user authentication at a much higher granularity (in both spatial and temporal domains) than existing channel-based (i.e., RSS and CIR) approaches. In this work, we conduct user authentication by associating each individual user with his own wireless device, which is not accessible by other users. Each wireless device represents a distinct user in the network. Thus user authentication could be performed by examining the channel state information of the associated wireless device.

CSITE [14] applies a sliding-window based technique to CSI measurements to build the user profile for authentication purpose. They assume the CSI collection is benign (without the presence of an identity-based attacker) when building the user profile. However, in practice the identity based attacker could be present at any time. Thus, the CSI measurements could be a mixture of readings from both the legitimate user and the spoofer, leading to a misclassification of the user profile and falsely authenticate the spoofer. To tackle such challenges raised from real-world scenarios, we study how to construct the user profile even when a spoofer is present and perform robust user authentication under various adversarial scenarios, e.g., when the legitimate user is not present but the spoofer is active. In particular, we propose a framework consisting of two main components: *Attack-resilient Profile Builder* and *Profile Matching Authenticator*. The *Attack-resilient Profile Builder* has the capability to accurately construct the user profile of the legitimate user even when the spoofing attacker is present. We further develop a *Profile Matching Authenticator* grounded on machine-learning based techniques to perform robust per-packet user authentication in real-time based on CSI measurements. In addition, we are among the first to study the effect of different modulation and coding scheme rates to CSI to achieve accurate user authentication.

We summarize the main contributions of our work as follows:

- We show that it is feasible to perform user authentication by utilizing CSI from OFDM even when the users possess similar signal fingerprints, making the fine-grained user authentication achievable in practice.
- We develop an user authentication framework that has the capability to build the user profile under the presence of the spoofing attack and achieves higher authentication accuracy compared with existing channel based (e.g., RSS-based) methods.
- We validate the framework by conducting real experiments in both office and apartment environments using off-the-shelf WiFi devices. Experimental results confirm that our framework is highly robust and effective in user authentication under various attacking scenarios without requiring any additional overhead on wireless devices.

The rest of the paper is organized as follows. In Section 2, we put our work in the context of the related studies. The attack model and our framework overview are described in Section 3, and the feasibility of using CSI to perform user authentication is presented in Section 4. In Section 5, we detail the proposed Attack-resilient Profile Builder based on clustering analysis. The Profile Matching Authenticator grounded on machine learning techniques is described in Section 6. We discuss the experimental setup and methodology, and further present the performance evaluation results of our proposed CSI-based authentication framework in both office and apartment environments in Section 7. Finally, we conclude our work in Section 8.

2. RELATED WORK

The traditional approach to provide user authentication is to use cryptographic-based authentication. For example, Wu et al. [28] have introduced a secure and efficient key management (SEKM) framework. SEKM builds a Public Key Infrastructure (PKI) by applying a secret sharing scheme and an underlying multicast server group. Wool [27] implements a key management mechanism with periodic key refresh and host revocation to prevent the compromise of authentication keys. The application of cryptographic authentication requires reliable key distribution, management, and maintenance mechanisms, which reduce its usability in a dynamic mobile wireless environment (i.e., lacks of a fixed key management infrastructure) or resource-constrained wireless networks (i.e., limited resources on wireless devices).

Recently non-cryptographic based authentication has drawn considerable attention [31]. In general, non-cryptographic solutions can be categorized into four groups: software based, hardware based, biometric and physical-trait based, and channel-signature based. Software based authentication basically relies on the unique characteristics of the software programs or protocols running on the devices [25, 9], whereas hardware based authentication leverages the unique hardware traits such as channel-invariant radiometric [3, 23] and clock skews [18, 13] to identify users. Biometric and physical-trait based authentication relies on the behavioral modalities including on-screen touch and finger movement patterns [8, 20]. And channel-signature based authentication schemes are proposed to use either Received Signal Strength (RSS) [29, 6, 30, 32, 15] or Channel Impulse Response (CIR) [26, 21] to identify users. The major advantage of using channel signatures is that it exploits the naturally available random and location-distinct characteristics of the wireless channel, which is very hard to falsify, for user authentication.

For the channel based user authentication using RSS, a series of approaches [29, 6, 30] have been proposed to detect identity-based attacks, determine the number of attackers when multiple adversaries masquerading as the same node identity, and localize the adversaries. Reciprocal Channel Variation-based Identification (RCVI) [32] exploits the reciprocity of RSS variance to decide if all packets come from a single or more than one sender. Ensemble [15] leverages a user's growing collection of trusted devices that analyze variations in RSS to determine whether the pairing devices are in physical proximity to each other. It is important to note that although RSS is available on the current wireless devices, RSS is known to be sensitive to the multipath effects and affected by the transmission power level. As a result, a legitimate user may be mistakenly regarded as the malicious user due to the inherent RSS variance. Different from RSS which is readily available in the existing wireless infrastructure, CIR is usually extracted from the specialized devices such as Field-Programmable Gate Array (FPGA) [26] and Universal Software Radio Peripheral (USRP) [21], which limit its practical usage in real-world scenarios.

Different from the previous work, we propose to use Channel State Information (CSI), a readily available fine-grained channel information from the current commercial hardware (i.e., 802.11 a/g/n devices), which represents both amplitude and phrase for each subcarrier on the 802.11 a/g/n OFDM system. Exploiting CSI has the potential to achieve much higher granularity (in both spatial and temporal) for user authentication than applying existing channel based (i.e., RSS and CIR) authentication methods. The most related work to us is CSITE [14], which utilizes CSI magnitude measurements averaged over time to generate profiles for legitimate users. They assume the CSI collected over time is benign and there is no identity-based spoofing attack present when building the profile. However, in practice the spoofing attack could present at any time. Thus, the profiles built under such attacks cannot represent legitimate users and may lead to authenticate malicious users falsely. In our work, we develop an Attack-resilient Profile Builder, which has the ability to detect the presence of spoofing attacks when building profiles for legitimate users. Furthermore, we study the effect of different modulation and coding scheme rates to CSI to achieve a higher accuracy of user authentication under both single antenna and multiple antenna cases.

3. ATTACK MODEL AND SYSTEM OVERVIEW

In this section we first introduce the attack model we consider in this work. We then present the flow of our proposed CSI-based user-authentication framework.

3.1 Attack Model

User authentication is a technique of confirming the identity of a user. Based on the user authentication result, a system can determine whether a user is allowed to access certain restricted services, such as restricted access of certain web sites and enterprise data retrieval [24]. User authentication is particularly challenging in wireless networks as it is very hard, if not impossible, to physically confirm the truth of a user's identity due to the open nature of the wireless medium. In our user-authentication framework, we focus on the identity-based attack, in which an adversary can collect a legitimate user's identity and then masquerades as the legitimate user to pass the user authentication process [6]. The identity-based attack is very harmful as once passing the user authentication, the adversary can gain certain access privileges and further launch a variety of malicious attacks. For example, an adversary could easily obtain the Media Access Control (MAC) address of a legitimate WiFi device by passively monitoring the wireless traffic and then impersonate as the legitimate device by changing its MAC address. Another example is that by masquerading as an authorized wireless access point (AP) or an authorized client, an attacker could launch a variety of attacks including session hijacking, denial-of-service (DoS) attacks, or falsely advertise services to wireless clients [30].

In this work, we consider the identity-based attack can be present at any time. That is, different from the previous work, which only considers the presence of such an attack during the authentication phase, we take the view point that the identity-based attacks could be present at any time in real-world scenarios even when building profiles for legitimate users. Once such an attack is present in the network, the adversary spoofs the legitimate user's device identity (e.g., WiFi device's MAC address) to send out packets. Once the attacker obtains the legitimate user's device identity, it can access the network with or without the presence of the legitimate user. Furthermore, the spoofer can be either static or mobile, whereas the legitimate device is mostly placed at a fixed position but could be moved from one location to another (e.g., the user walks from one office room to a meeting room). The movement of the device can be detected using the existing techniques [19, 17, 4] (e.g., examining the variance of the wireless signal). In addition, we assume the attacker does not have the capability to capture and replay the CSI, thus the attacker cannot alter or jam the signals.

3.2 System Overview

Our basic idea is to profile the user by exploiting the readily available fine-grained CSI extracted from orthogonal frequency-division multiplexing (OFDM) based wireless networks, such as 802.11 a/g/n networks. CSI reveals the wireless channel response depicting the amplitudes and phases of every OFDM subcarrier. In general, CSI measurements from each user present a unique pattern corresponding to the wireless communication channel. Such CSI patterns can be extracted and utilized to uniquely identify each user. If the observed wireless packet (from a wireless device identity) contains a different CSI pattern from the legitimate profile, the network will raise an alert indicating possible identity-based attack and fails the user authentication on the specific device identity.

Our proposed user authentication framework, as depicted in Figure 1, consists of two main components: Attack-resilient Profile Builder and Profile Matching Authenticator. The network implementing this framework will keep monitoring the wireless traffic and examining CSI measurements from each packet based on the device's identity.

Attack-Resilient Profile Builder: The novelty of our profile builder is that it has the capability to build the actual user profile under the presence of the spoofer when building the user profile. When building the user profile for a specific user identity (ID), the presence of the spoofer will cause the CSI measurements collected from this ID containing the mixture signal information from both the legitimate user and spoofer. As a result, the profile built under such a scenario is thus undermined by the spoofer, leading to mistakenly authenticate the spoofer or deny the legitimate user's access. Our profile builder employing clustering analysis can separate the CSI measurements (from the legitimate user) from the ones (from the spoofer) and determine the presence of the spoofer. It can thus ensure the legitimacy of the user profile construction.

Furthermore, when the legitimate user moves from current location to another, e.g., from office to a meeting room, our framework can adaptively rebuild the user's profile. This rebuilding procedure can be user triggered or triggered after detecting the user movement based on existing techniques [19, 17, 4].

Profile Matching Authenticator: This component examines the real-time CSI measurements per packet from a device ID and performs user authentication by perform-

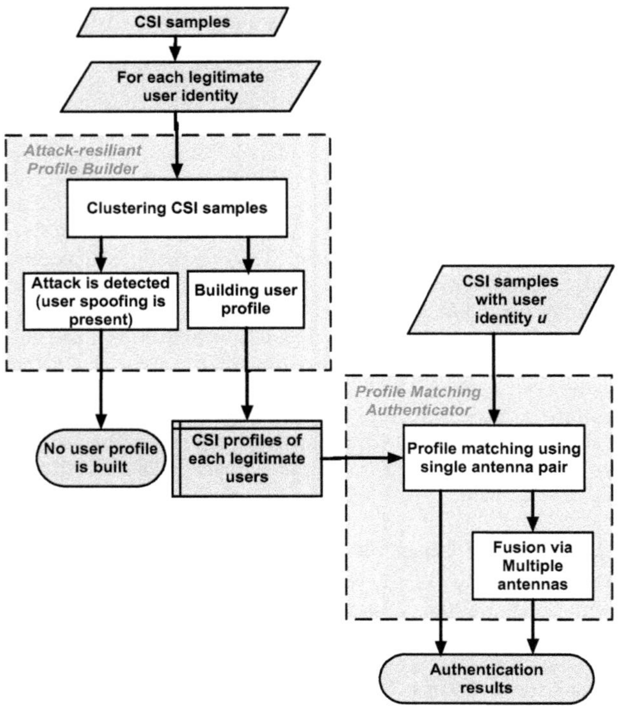

Figure 1: Overview of the CSI-based user authentication framework.

ing user profile matching. It is grounded on the machine-learning based techniques and raises an alert if the profile matching fails. Our authenticator aims to achieve fine-grained user authentication as it can work at per packet level - authenticating each packet of the device ID. It is capable to authenticate different users even when they possess similar signal fingerprints due to the complex environment setup in real-life. The authenticator works well under both single antenna as well as multiple-antennas cases (using data fusion).

4. FEASIBILITY STUDY OF CSI-BASED USER AUTHENTICATION

In this section, we first provide the background of CSI measured from OFDM subcarriers. We then discuss the feasibility of using CSI for user authentication. We next present our data pre-processing techniques applied to CSI measurements for more reliable user authentication.

4.1 Preliminary

Our authentication framework exploits the CSI measured from OFDM subcarriers, a reliable and fine-grained description of channel characteristics, for user authentication. OFDM technique has been extensively used in wireless communication systems to improve the communication performance by utilizing the frequency diversity of wireless channels. For example, OFDM is used in popular wireless networks including IEEE 802.11$a/g/n$, WiMAX, $4G$ and Digital Subscriber Line (DSL). OFDM is a method of encoding data streams on multiple carrier frequencies. In particular, Data in OFDM is split into multiple streams, which are coded and modulated respectively into different subcarriers. The

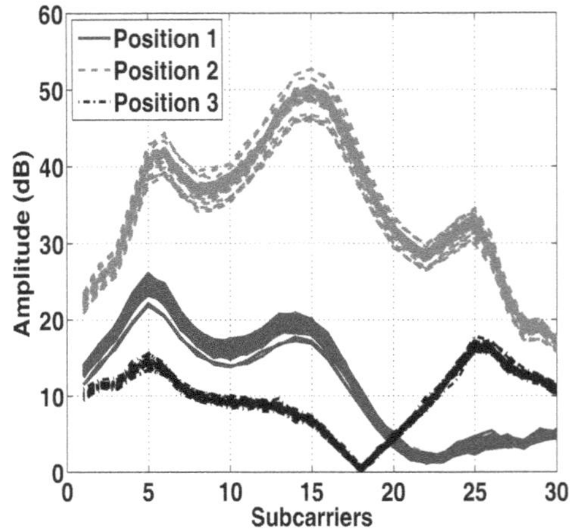

Figure 2: Example for channel state information of OFDM that is collected at three different positions.

frequency of each subcarrier is designed to be orthogonal to each other, so that the interference during transmission is minimized. For example, for the OFDM employed by the 802.11$a/g/n$ physical layer, a relatively wideband channel (or carrier) with 20 or 40 MHz is partitioned into 54 or 108 subcarriers for data transmission, so that each subcarrier can be used as a narrowband channel. This inspires us to exploit the channel state information (CSI) extracted from OFDM subcarriers for user authentication, which can provide a finer granularity of the channel information and has the potential to achieve higher accuracy for user authentication in practice. Figure 2 depicts the amplitude of channel state information across 30 subcarrier groups at three different positions. For each position, the CSI of 50 packets are measured from an Intel WiFi 5300 card in a laptop [11].

4.2 Feasibility study

To be able to use CSI for user authentication, the measured CSI from different devices should satisfy the *uniqueness* requirement. That is, the CSI measured at different devices resided at different locations should be distinct, while the CSI collected from different packets emitted by the same device should be similar, if not identical. We observe in Figure 2 that the amplitude of CSI at different subcarriers is different due to frequency diversity. Furthermore, the CSI shape from these three devices at different locations are distinct. This is because the CSI is the reflection of the complicated wireless channel and is affected by the wireless environment due to reflection, refraction, shadowing, etc. The CSI decorrelates with location rapidly. If two users are located at different locations, the profile of CSI should differ significantly. Additionally, we observe that the CSI of multiple packets from the same device at a fixed location exhibit the same trend, which indicates that an unique profile could be built for each user and serves as the basis for user authentication.

Note that compared to the RSS, which only provides overall received power for each packet, CSI provides fine-grained channel information, i.e., channel responses on multiple subcarriers. Therefore, instead of deploying multiple landmarks or monitors to collect multi-dimensional RSS reading for user authentication purpose, a single monitor can provide multi-dimensional channel state information sufficient for user authentication. Furthermore, since the widely adopted IEEE 802.11n standard[1] already defines a mechanism to exchange detailed CSI between a pair of wireless devices, employing CSI as an unique means for user authentication will not involve extra communication cost for the prevalent WiFi networks.

Data Preprocessing: In our study, we observe that the mean amplitude value of CSI measurement may shift over time. We call such a mean value shift as *temporal bias*, and it will result in inaccurate CSI profile construction for user authentication. Therefore, our framework develops a data preprocessing strategy to cope with CSI samples to mitigate the effects caused by such temporal bias.

In particular, we observe a shift on the amplitude of a specific subcarrier due to the interference presented at either transmitter or receiver. Figure 3 (a) plots the curve of the CSI sample in a packet and many curves are collected over time. It shows that the amplitude of each subcarrier in CSI samples varies over time. Our data preprocessing strategy adjusts the mean value of the CSI sample (from a specific packet) to zero. This helps to reduce the overall variance across the subcarriers on CSI measurements before performing user authentication. To illustrate, we denote the raw CSI sample per packet from a particular user u as a k-dimensional vector C_u, and the preprocessed CSI sample can be obtained as:

$$C_u = C_u - 1_{1\times K}\frac{1}{K}\sum_{k=1}^{K} C_u(k), \qquad (1)$$

where K is the number of subcarriers within a single CSI sample, and $1_{1\times K}$ is a K-length all-one vector. After applying the data preprocessing strategy, the updated CSI samples will have smaller variance and reduced amplitude bias on each subcarrier as shown in Figure 3(b). In addition, the wireless devices in the 802.11n network are usually equipped with multiple-antennas. Thus, the CSI samples collected from each channel between the transmitting antenna i and receiving antenna j of two communicating devices will go through the pre-process as shown in equation 1, where C_u will be replaced by $C_u^{i,j}$.

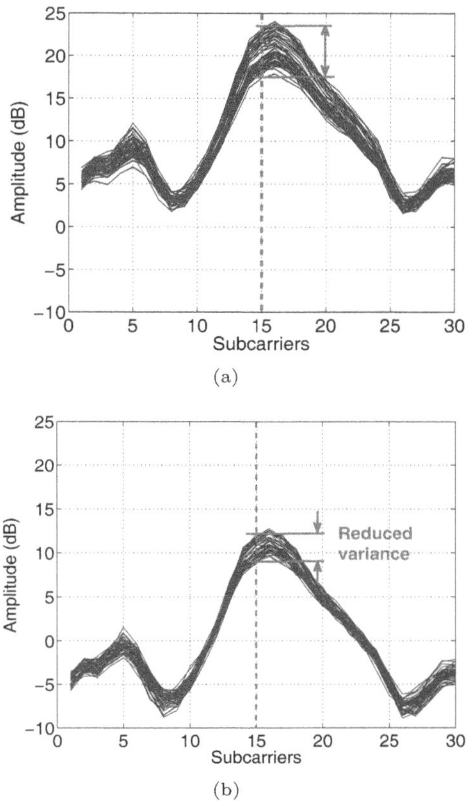

Figure 3: CSI samples before and after data processing.

5. ATTACK-RESILIENT USER PROFILE BUILDER

In this section, we describe the attack-resilient profile builder which employs clustering analysis on CSI measurements to determine whether the network environment is benign or the spoofer is present when constructing the user profile.

5.1 Basic Idea

Since the spoofing attack could be present at any time, we need to determine whether a spoofer is present when constructing a user profile. Our attack-resilient profile builder aims to ensure the legitimacy of the user profiles even under a malicious wireless environment. The relational behind our attack-resilient profile builder is that the CSI measurements of each device presents unique spatial characteristics: the CSI has strong spatial correlation with the device's location. Although the wireless channel may fluctuate over time, the CSI of wireless packets from one device at a fixed location should be clustered together in the multi-dimensional signal space constructed by CSI measurements. For example, the 30 subcarriers obtained in our experiments can form a 30-dimensional CSI space, and the amplitudes of the CSI from the 50 packets in Position 1 are clustered together (i.e., has a constant shape) in CSI space as shown in Figure 2. Furthermore, the CSI measurements of the wireless packets collected from another device resided at a different location (Position 2) should form a different cluster in the CSI space. Thus, when the environment is benign, the CSI measurements from a particular device identity should be clustered together and form one cluster in the CSI space, while under the spoofing attack, the spoofer utilizes the same device identity as the legitimate user to transmit packets, and the CSI readings of the device identity are the mixture readings from both legitimate user and the spoofer, resulting in more than one CSI cluster.

To determine whether the network environment is benign, Our framework applies clustering analysis to partition the CSI from one device identity into two clusters. Under normal conditions without spoofing, the distance between the partitioned two CSI clusters should be small since there is basically only one cluster from a single device at a physical location. However, under a spoofing attack, there is more than one devices at different physical locations claiming the same device identity. As a result, more than one CSI clusters will be formed in the CSI space. Therefore, the distance between two partitioned clusters will be large as the cluster centers are derived from the different CSI clusters associated with different locations in physical space. Therefore, by examining the distance between the two partitioned CSI clusters, any presence of the spoofing attack can be determined

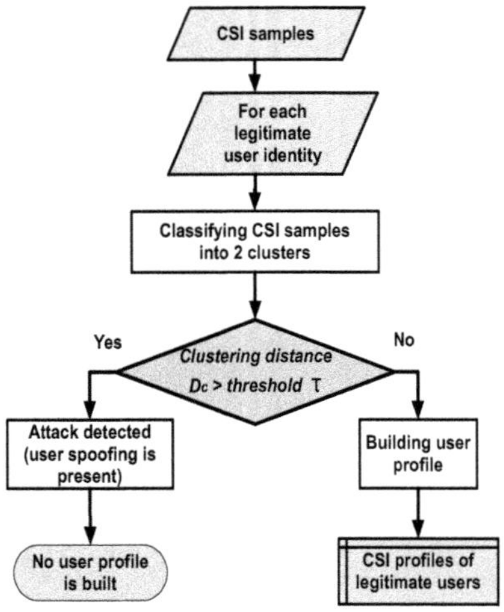

Figure 4: Work Flow for the Attack-Resilient Profile Builder.

when building user profiles. The flow of the Attack-resilient Profile Builder is shown in Figure 4. Only when there is no spoofing attack present, the profile of the legitimate user will be built.

5.2 Algorithm Description

5.2.1 *Modulation and Coding Scheme Study*

WiFi devices usually use a fixed range of modulation and coding scheme (MCS) for data transmission. We find in our experiments that the modulation and coding scheme occasionally changes to a different one and then switches back due to the variation of the wireless channel. And the occasionally changed modulation and coding scheme creates outliers in the CSI measurements. Thus, our framework first performs outlier filtering based on the modulation and coding scheme used for packet transmission before conducting clustering analysis. In particular, MCS is a specification of the high-throughput (HT) physical layer (PHY) parameter in 802.11n standard [1]. It contains the information of the modulation order (e.g., BPSK, QPSK, 16-QAM, 64-QAM), the forward error correction (FEC) coding rate, etc. Each 802.11n packet header (at 2.4GHz band) contains a 16-bit MCS, which can be extracted together with the CSI sample of each packet.

Figure 5(a) shows the raw CSI measurements for a wireless device with two clusters formed in our experiments. Under such cases, the MCS rate is changing according to the channel condition, and we can observe CSI samples resulting from different MCS rates. For these cases we find the MCS values are greater than 263, different from most of the other testing cases in both the lab and apartment environments. We thus filter out CSI for the packets with MCS value greater than 263, which corresponds to single spatial stream with transmission rate 60Mbps [1]. After filtering out the outliers, the CSI coming from the rest of the packets exhibit the similar shape (i.e., form one cluster in the CSI space) as shown in Figure 5(b).

5.2.2 *Clustering Analysis*

We utilize the K-means algorithm to partition the filtered CSI measurements from the device identity u into two clusters. The K-means algorithm is one of the most popular iterative descent clustering methods [12]. The squared Euclidean distance is chosen as the dissimilarity measure. If there are S CSI samples from the device u, the K-means clustering algorithm partitions S CSI samples into K disjoint subsets L_k containing S_k sample points so as to minimize the sum-of-squares criterion:

$$J_{min} = \sum_{k=1}^{K} \sum_{C_{u,s} \in L_k} ||C_{u,s} - \mu_{\mathbf{k}}||^2, \quad (2)$$

where $C_{u,s}$ is a CSI vector representing the CSI value for the sth packet and $\mu_{\mathbf{k}}$ is the geometric centroid of the sample points for L_k in CSI space. In our cluster analysis, we choose $K = 2$. We further choose the distance between two centroids as the test statistic $\mathbf{T}$ for identity-based attack detection,

$$D_c = ||\mu_{\mathbf{k}} - \mu_{\mathbf{k'}}|| \quad (3)$$

with $k, k' \in \{1, 2\}$.

Under normal conditions in a benign network environment, the distance between the centroids from the K-means cluster analysis in CSI space should be close to each other, because there is only one cluster from a single device u at a physical location. However, when a spoofer is present, there is more than one devices residing at different physical locations, claiming the same device identity. The distance between two partitioned CSI clusters thus will be large. Through the analysis above, we show that the clustering

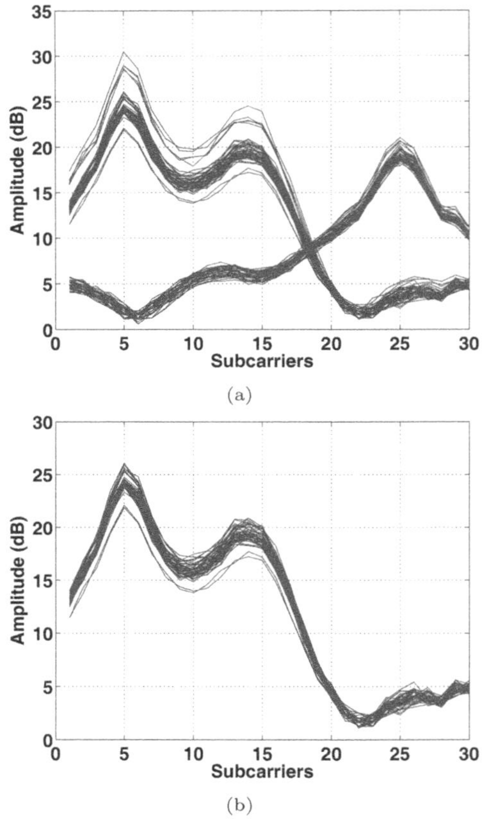

Figure 5: CSI samples before and after filtering based on MCS rate.

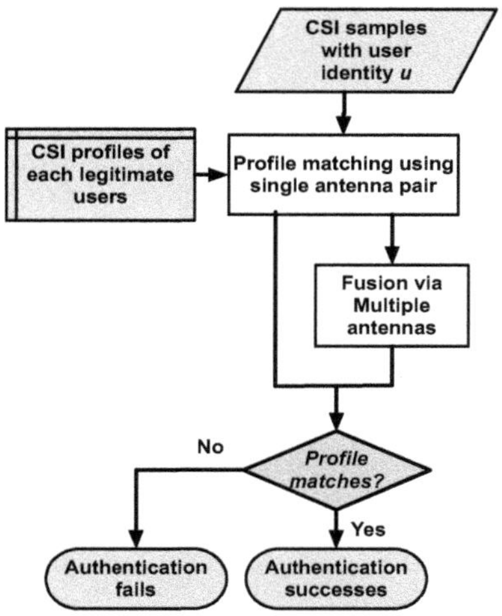

Figure 6: Work Flow for the Profile Matching Authenticator.

method has the capability of detecting the presence of the spoofer by applying the threshold τ to the D_c as following:

$$\begin{cases} D_c > \tau & \text{attacker is present;} \\ D_c \le \tau & \text{normal condition.} \end{cases} \quad (4)$$

5.2.3 *User Profile Building*

If the CSI samples are collected in a benign environment, the framework deposits the pre-processed CSI samples, C_u, as the profile for user u for future profile matching based authentication. We note that the user profile only requires a small number of packets, i.e. less than 100 packets.

If the user moves from one location to another (e.g., walks from his office to a meeting room), the user authentication framework will adaptively rebuild the user's profile. Following are possible two ways to update the user's profile: 1) the user can actively trigger the profile updating after he moves to a new place; 2) the profile updating can be triggered by detecting the user movement using existing techniques operating on wireless signals [19, 17, 4].

6. USER AUTHENTICATION LEVERAGING PROFILE MATCHING

In this section, we present our profile matching authenticator which uses machine-learning based methods for packet-level user authentication.

6.1 Basic Idea

The basic idea of our profile matching authenticator is using machine learning to determine whether the CSI measurement for the incoming packet with the user identity u matches the profile constructed at the profile builder. If the incoming CSI sample matches the user profile, the corresponding packet can be authenticated successfully as from the user u. Otherwise, the user authentication fails. Figure 6 illustrates the work flow of our profile matching authenticator. In particular, the profile matching scheme works at the packet level, which minimizes the latency of the authentication process. In addition, the packet-level authentication can also be used to monitor and count the number of packets injected by the attacker.

6.2 Approach Description

We next present the profile matching method using the CSI samples from a single antenna. We then present the profile matching using CSI samples from multiple antennas to improve the performance of user authentication.

6.2.1 *Profile Matching using a Single Antenna Pair*

We perform the profile matching via the support vector machine (SVM) technique, which is a computationally efficient way of learning good separating hyperplanes in a high dimensional feature space. The CSI samples are used as features in the SVM to perform profile matching for each user. We first study the case using a single antenna pair for profile matching.

In this study, we consider the profile matching as a two-class pattern classification problem. The CSI sample C_u with user identity u denotes the data to be classified, where $u = 1, \cdots, U$ (with U as total number of legitimate users), and let scalar y denote its class ($y \in \{-1, 1\}$). We use $\{(C_{u,s}, y_{u,s}), s = 1, ..., S\}$ to denote a set of CSI samples associated with the user identity u. The challenge is how to construct a decision function $f(C_u)$ that correctly classifies the input CSI data, which could be different from all the constructed profiles.

If the constructed CSI user profiles are linearly separable, we can represent them with a linear function in the following form:

$$f(C_u) = w^T C_u + b \quad (5)$$

such that $f(C_{u,s}) \geq 0$ for $y_{u,s} = 1$ and $f(C_{u,s}) \leq 0$ for $y_{u,s} = -1$, where w and b represent the hyperplane $f(C_u) = 0$ separating two classes.

We seek to find such a hyperplane that maximizes the separating margins between the two classes. In particular, this hyperplane can be found by minimizing the following cost function:

$$\min J(w, \xi) = \frac{1}{2}\|w\|^2 + \Gamma \sum_{s=1}^{S} \xi_{u,s} \quad (6)$$

subject to the following constraints:

$$y_{u,s}(w^T \Phi(C_{u,s}) + b) \geq 1 - \xi_{u,s}, \xi_{u,s} \geq 0, s = 1, \cdots, S, \quad (7)$$

where $\Phi(\cdot)$ is a non linear operator mapping the CSI profile C_u to a higher dimensional space, Γ indicates the significance of the constraint violations with respect to the distance between the points and the hyperplane and ξ is a slack variable vector.

The mapping between the input CSI samples $C_{u,s'}$ and user profile $C_{u,s}$ is constructed in the form of the kernel function $Kernel(\cdot, \cdot)$, such as $Kernel(C_{u,s}, C_{u,s'}) = \Phi^T(C_{u,s})\Phi(C_{u,s'})$. Particularly, we choose a polynomial kernel as the mapping function and the problem in Equation 6 can be expressed as:

$$\max_{\alpha_s}\{\sum_{s=1}^{S} \alpha_s - \frac{1}{2}\sum_{s=1}^{S}\sum_{s'=1}^{l} \alpha_u (y_{u,s} y_{u,s'} Kernel(C_{u,s}, C_{u,s'}))\alpha_{s'}\} \quad (8)$$

subject to the constraints:

$$\alpha_s \geq 0, \sum_{s=1}^{S} \alpha_s y_{u,s} = 0, \quad (9)$$

where α_s is the Lagrange multipliers associated with equation 7. Thus, the profile matching classifier for input CSI sample $C_{u,s'}$ is derived as:

$$f(C_{u,s'}) = sign(\sum_{s=1}^{S}(\alpha_s y_{u,s} Kernel(C_{u,s'}, C_{u,s}) + b)). \quad (10)$$

And the authentication result is determined as:

$$f(C_{u,s'}) = \begin{cases} 1 & success \\ -1 & failure. \end{cases} \quad (11)$$

6.2.2 *Fusion via Multiple Antennas Pairs*

When multiple antennas are available, we can further improve the performance of the user authentication accuracy. For example, we can employ a simple majority voting process to combine the independent profile matching results from different antenna pairs. Assume that the input CSI samples with user identity u between the transmitting antenna i and receiving antenna j are represented as $C^{i,j}_{u,s'}$, all the independent results from different antenna pairs consist of the voting set $\Omega = \{f(C^{i,j}_{u,s'}), 1 \leq i \leq I, 1 \leq j \leq J\}$, where I and J are the numbers of transmitting and receiving antennas respectively. Finally, the authentication result is given by:

$$f'(C_{u,s'}) = sign(\sum_{i=1}^{I}\sum_{j=1}^{J} f(C^{i,j}_{u,s'})). \quad (12)$$

If $f'(C_{u,s'}) = 1$, the authentication successes; otherwise it fails.

7. PERFORMANCE EVALUATION

In this section, we present the performance evaluation of the proposed CSI-based user authentication framework in two types of real environments, laboratory and apartment. We show that the CSI-based authentication framework is resilient to attacks, and outperforms existing RSS-based authentication methods.

7.1 Experimental Setup

We conduct experiments in a 802.11n WiFi network with two laptops (i.e., Lenovo T500 and T61) serving as monitors that collect the wireless packets. These two laptops run Ubuntu 10.04 LTS with the 2.6.36 kernel and are equipped with Intel WiFi Link 5300 wireless card. Both Intel wireless cards' drivers we installed are able to collect CSI information from frames transmitted in HT rate [1]. A commercial wireless access point, Linksys $E2500$, is sending out packets that can be captured by these two monitors. We use the *ping* command on two laptops to simulate the authentication packets continuously transmitted over the network. The packet rate is set to 10 packets/second. For each packet, we extract CSI for 30 subcarrier groups, which are evenly distributed in the 56 subcarriers of a 20 MHz channel [11]. We also record the RSS value of each packet for comparison.

We conduct experiments in two indoor environments, i.e., a laboratory and an apartment. The laboratory represents the typical office environment, which has office cubicle and many furniture that create complex multipath effects in a large room. The apartment, on the other hand, represents the typical home environment with small rooms and simple furniture. The size of these two environments are $11m \times 12m$ and $11m \times 6m$, respectively. The experimental setups in these two environments are shown in Figure 7. The numbered circles in the figures are the positions used to collect

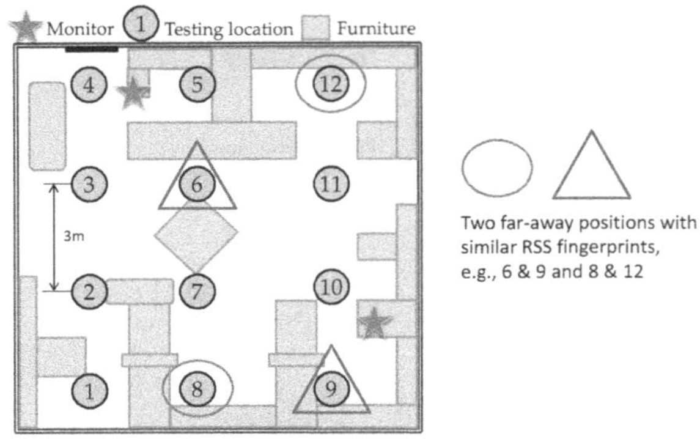

(a) Laboratory

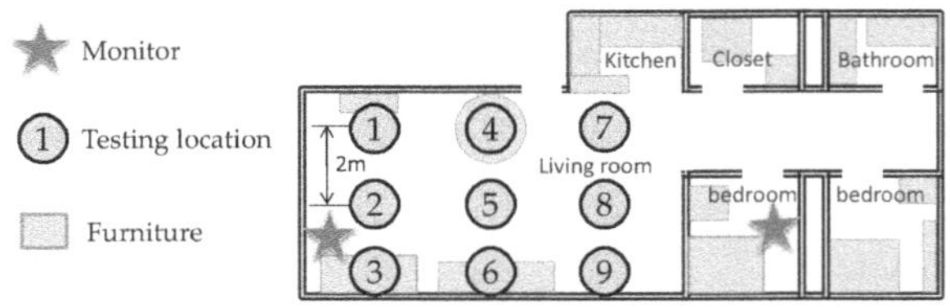

(b) Apartment

Figure 7: Experimental setups in (a) Laboratory and (b) Apartment.

CSI data for evaluating our user authentication framework, and the two red stars represent two network monitors.

7.2 Experimental Methodology

In the experiments, we collect 400 packets at each location, and both CSI and RSS values of each packet are recorded. When using RSS measurements for user authentication, we employ the RSS values collected from two network monitors as the two-dimensional feature vector for clustering and profile matching, while our proposed CSI-based authentication framework only uses the CSI measurements from one network monitor to perform user authentication.

To evaluate the performance of our proposed framework, we examine two main attacking scenarios: **1)** In the first attacking scenario, both the legitimate user and the attacker are present at the same time in the network. **2)** In the second attacking scenario, after the attacker obtains the legitimate user's identity, only the attacker is active in the network. In order to obtain the statistical results, we choose all possible point pairs in both experimental environments and treat one point as the position of the legitimate user and the other point as the position of the attacker. We run the proposed framework through all possible combinations of point pairs. There are a total of 66 pairs for laboratory environment and 36 pairs for apartment environment. The experimental results are presented in the following sections for the attack resilient profile builder and profile matching authenticator.

7.3 Metrics

In order to evaluate the performance of our proposed user authentication framework, we define the following two metrics, attack detection ratio and authentication accuracy.

Attack detection ratio (during profile building): We define the attack detection ratio $\bar{R}$ as the number of correctly detecting the presence of spoofing attacks over the total number of experiments with spoofing attacks. The spoofing attacks presented when building the user profile belong to the attacking scenario 1. Given a total number of P attacking cases the attack detection ratio can be written as:

$$\bar{R} = \frac{1}{P}\sum_{p=1}^{P} H_p \qquad (13)$$
$$s.t.\ \ H_p = \begin{cases} 0 & D_c \leq \tau \\ 1 & D_c > \tau, \end{cases}$$

where D_c is the distance between two centroids of clusters formed in the profile builder, and τ is the threshold used for spoofing attack detection.

Authentication accuracy (during user authentication): We define the authentication accuracy A_p as the number of correctly classified packets over the total number of packets collected in the pth attacking run. The attacks could belong to either the attacking scenario 1 or 2. We use $N_{u,p}$ to denote the number of packets that are sent by a legitimate user u and are correctly determined as from the user u by our system. Similarly, we use $N'_{u,p}$ to denote the number of packets sent by the adversary using the identity of the legitimate user u and are correctly determined as not from the user u. We then define the authentication accuracy for the pth experimental run as:

$$A_p = \frac{N_{u,p} + N'_{u,p}}{N_{a,p}}, \qquad (14)$$

where $N_{a,p}$ is the total number of packets received with user identity u, and $N_{u,p} + N'_{u,p} \leq N_{a,p}$.

We further define the *average authentication accuracy* and *worst authentication accuracy* as shown below to evaluate the general and worst-case performance.

- **Average authentication accuracy:** Given P testing cases, the average authentication accuracy is given as:

$$A_{avg} = \frac{1}{P}\sum_{p=1}^{P} A_p. \qquad (15)$$

- **Worst authentication accuracy:** The worst authentication accuracy chooses A_p from the attacking case with the smallest number of $N_{u,p}$ and $N'_{u,p}$:

$$A_{worst} = \min_{p} A_p. \qquad (16)$$

7.4 Evaluation Results

7.4.1 Attack Detection Study During Profile Building

We first compare the effectiveness of our Attack-resilient Profile Builder when determining the presence of a spoofer (during profile building) using CSI to that using RSS. We examine the attack detection ratio by varying the threshold τ. As shown in Figure 8, the results show that the averaged detection ratio for the proposed CSI based approach achieves 0.92 with the optimal distance threshold $17dB$ in Figure 8 (a), while the maximum detection ratio for the RSS-based method is only 0.4 with distance threshold $2dB$ as shown in Figure 8 (b). This observation indicates that our profile builder can effectively determine whether the network environment is benign or a spoofer is present when building the user profiles.

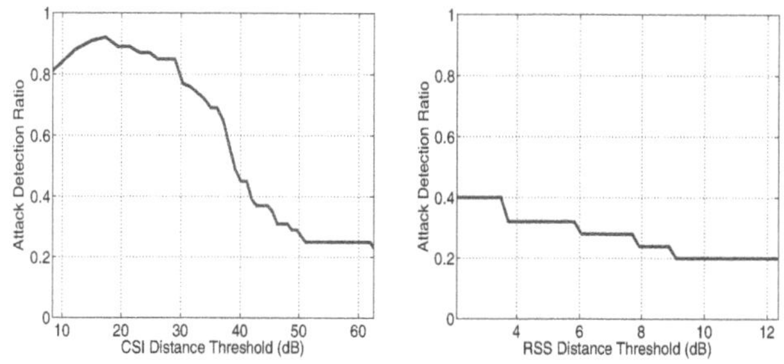

(a) CSI-based (b) RSS-based

Figure 8: Attack-resilient Profile Builder: Attack detect ratio versus cluster distance threshold when a spoofer is present.

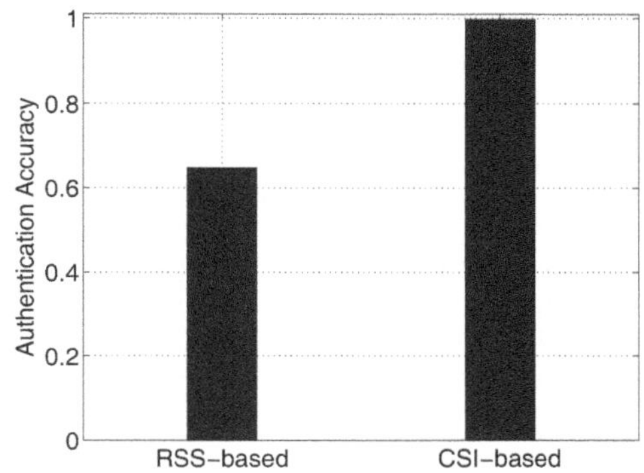

Figure 9: Performance of the Profile Matching Authenticator: Authentication accuracy when two users possess similar RSS fingerprints.

7.4.2 Authentication Accuracy Study

Discriminating two far-away users with similar RSS fingerprints: Due to the irregularity of wireless signal propagation, two geographical distant users may share similar RSS signatures. For example, in Figure 7 (a), two positions 6 and 9 are about $6 - 7m$ away from each other, but their RSS fingerprints obtained from our same network monitor look similar; positions 8 and 12 present the same signal phenomenon. This makes RSS-based user authentication schemes suffer poor performance when two legitimate users (but physically separated) present the similar signal fingerprints. In particular, we observe that the authentication accuracy for RSS-based method degrades to only around 0.64 as shown in Figure 9. However, our proposed CSI-based method could still achieve the authentication accuracy close to 1. The results confirm that CSI measurements provide fine-grained information on differentiating users, even when their RSS measurements are similar.

Comparison with RSS-based method: We next study the overall performance of our CSI based user authentication method. Figure 10 shows the comparison of the authentication accuracy when using CSI-based and RSS-based methods in two different environments (i.e., a laboratory and an apartment). We note that the RSS-based method relies on RSS values collected from two network monitors to perform user authentication, while our proposed CSI-based authentication framework only uses the CSI measurement

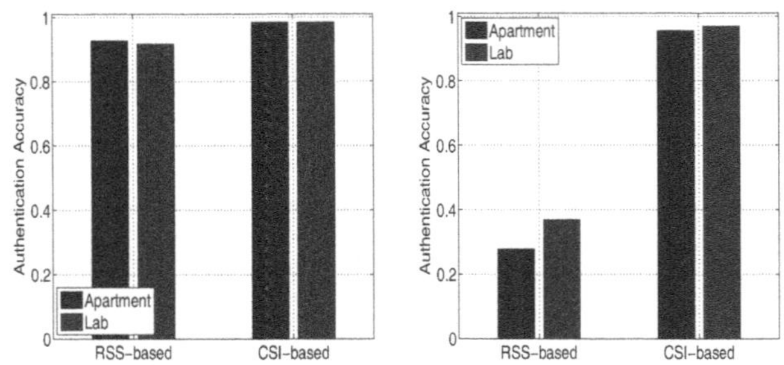

(a) A_{avg} (b) A_{worst}

Figure 10: User authentication accuracy comparison between CSI-based and RSS-based methods.

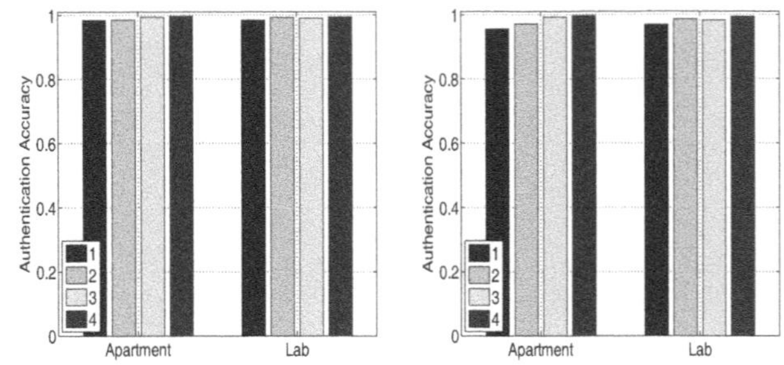

(a) A_{avg} (b) A_{worst}

Figure 11: CSI-based user authentication accuracy when involving single and multiple antennas.

from one antenna at one network monitor. We observe that our proposed CSI-based method outperforms the RSS-based method in both experimental environments. Specifically, Figure 10 (a) shows that the average authentication accuracy for CSI-based method is very high (above 0.984), and the RSS-based method has a lower authentication accuracy (i.e., 0.92). Furthermore, we show that the worst authentication accuracy for RSS-based method reduces to around 0.27 and 0.36 in the apartment and laboratory environments respectively, whereas our CSI-based method maintains the high authentication accuracy over 0.95 as presented in Figure 10 (b). These observations strongly indicate the robustness of our CSI-based user authentication framework even when only a single antenna is used on WiFi devices.

Impact from single/multiple antennas: We further examine the performance when employing measurements from multiple antennas. We expect that using measurements from multiple antennas can provide better reliability for user authentication. Figure 11 shows that both the average and worst authentication accuracy exhibit an increasing trend when more antennas are used. In particular, the authentication accuracy of using single antenna in the apartment and laboratory environments is over 0.95. When the number of antenna pairs (i.e., a set of transmitting and receiving antennas) increases from 1 to 4, the average authentication accuracy in laboratory and apartment further improves, and the worst authentication accuracy improves even more. We also observe that when using 3 antenna pairs in the laboratory environment the authentication accuracy has a slightly drop when comparing to that of using 2 antenna pairs. This is because although current commodity wireless devices are usually equipped with multiple antennas, the main antennas usually have better quality of signal reception. Therefore, including the CSI samples from the main antennas (i.e., using 1 or 2 antenna pairs in our experiments) results in better stability of user authentication.

Impact from user profile size: Finally, we study how the number of packets (i.e., user profile size) employed to build the user profile affects the performance of our framework. We vary the size of user profile from 1 sample to 200 samples, and the corresponding average authentication accuracy is shown in Figure 12. When the size of user profile increases, the authentication accuracy increases and then maintains at a high level (i.e., over 0.95). We note that even if the profile of each user contains only 1 CSI sample, the authentication accuracy is still over 0.91. These results demonstrate that our profile builder is highly effective in our CSI-based user authentication framework.

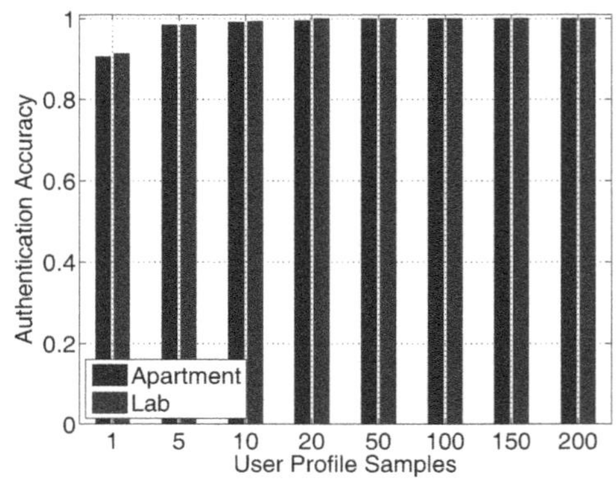

Figure 12: Impact of user profile size on CSI-based user authentication accuracy.

8. CONCLUSION

In this paper, we study utilizing channel state information (CSI) to perform practical user authentication in wireless networks. The fine-grained channel information revealed in CSI has the potential to perform accurate user authentication. We propose a CSI-based user authentication framework including Attack-resilient User Profile Builder and Profile Matching Authenticator. The Attack-resilient Profile Builder employs clustering analysis to intelligently determine whether the network environment is benign without the presence of the identity-based attack when constructing the profile for the legitimate user. The Profile Matching Authenticator performs packet level user authentication grounded on Support Vector Machine (SVM). It has the capability to distinguish two users even when they possess the similar signal fingerprints. Our extensive experiments conducted in both lab and apartment environments confirm the feasibility of exploiting CSI to perform accurate user authentication. The evaluation results show that the CSI-based approach is highly effective as compared with methods directly applying received signal strength.

9. ACKNOWLEDGMENTS

This work was supported in part by the National Science Foundation under grant numbers CNS-1318751, CNS-1318748 and Army Research Office W911NF-13-1-0288.

10. REFERENCES

[1] IEEE Std. 802.11n-2009: Enhancements for higher throughput, 2009. Available at http://www.ieee802.org.

[2] B. Azimi-Sadjadi, A. Kiayias, A. Mercado, and B. Yener. Robust key generation from signal envelopes in wireless networks. In *Proceedings of the 14th ACM conference on Computer and communications security*, pages 401–410, 2007.

[3] V. Brik, S. Banerjee, M. Gruteser, and S. Oh. Wireless device identification with radiometric signatures. In *Proceedings of the 14th ACM international conference on Mobile computing and networking*, pages 116–127, 2008.

[4] G. Chandrasekaran, M. A. Ergin, M. Gruteser, R. P. Martin, J. Yang, and Y. Chen. Decode: Exploiting shadow fading to detect comoving wireless devices. *IEEE Transactions on Mobile Computing*, 8(12):1663–1675, 2009.

[5] O. Cheikhrouhou, A. Koubaa, M. Boujelben, and M. Abid. A lightweight user authentication scheme for wireless sensor networks. In *IEEE/ACS International Conference on Computer Systems and Applications (AICCSA)*, pages 1–7, 2010.

[6] Y. Chen, J. Yang, W. Trappe, and R. P. Martin. Detecting and localizing identity-based attacks in wireless and sensor networks. *IEEE Transactions on Vehicular Technology*, 59(5):2418–2434, 2010.

[7] O. Delgado-Mohatar, A. FÃžster-Sabater, and J. M. Sierra. A light-weight authentication scheme for wireless sensor networks. *Ad Hoc Networks*, 9(5):727–735, 2011.

[8] S. Govindarajan, P. Gasti, and K. S. Balagani. Secure privacy-preserving protocols for outsourcing continuous authentication of smartphone users with touch data. *IEEE Transactions on Information Forensics and Security*, 8(1):136–148, 2013.

[9] F. Guo and T.-c. Chiueh. Sequence number-based mac address spoof detection. In *Recent Advances in Intrusion Detection*, pages 309–329, 2006.

[10] D. Halperin, W. Hu, A. Sheth, and D. Wetherall. Predictable 802.11 packet delivery from wireless channel measurements. In *ACM SIGCOMM Computer Communication Review*, volume 40, pages 159–170, 2010.

[11] D. Halperin, W. Hu, A. Sheth, and D. Wetherall. Predictable 802.11 packet delivery from wireless channel measurements. In *ACM SIGCOMM Computer Communication Review*, volume 40, pages 159–170, 2010.

[12] T. Hastie, R. Tibshirani, and J. Friedman. *The Elements of Statistical Learning, Data Mining Inference, and Prediction*. Springer, 2001.

[13] S. Jana and S. K. Kasera. On fast and accurate detection of unauthorized wireless access points using clock skews. *IEEE Transactions on Mobile Computing*, 9(3):449–462, 2010.

[14] Z. Jiang, J. Zhao, X.-Y. Li, J. Han, and W. Xi. Rejecting the attack: Source authentication for wi-fi management frames using csi information. In *Proceedings of the IEEE International Conference on Computer Communications (INFOCOM)*, May 2013.

[15] A. Kalamandeen, A. Scannell, E. de Lara, A. Sheth, and A. LaMarca. Ensemble: cooperative proximity-based authentication. In *Proceedings of the 8th international conference on Mobile systems, applications, and services*, pages 331–344, 2010.

[16] T. Karygiannis and L. Owens. Wireless network security. *NIST special publication*, 800:48, 2002.

[17] K. Kleisouris, B. Firner, R. Howard, Y. Zhang, and R. P. Martin. Detecting intra-room mobility with signal strength descriptors. In *The ACM International Symposium on Mobile Ad Hoc Networking and Computing (MobiHoc)*, pages 71–80, 2010.

[18] T. Kohno, A. Broido, and K. C. Claffy. Remote physical device fingerprinting. *IEEE Transactions on Dependable and Secure Computing*, 2(2):93–108, 2005.

[19] J. Krumm and E. Horvitz. Locadio: Inferring motion and location from wi-fi signal strengths. In *MobiQuitous*, pages 4–13, 2004.

[20] L. Li, X. Zhao, and G. Xue. Unobservable re-authentication for smartphones. In *Proceedings of the Network and Distributed System Security Symposium (NDSS)*, February 2013.

[21] S. Mathur, R. Miller, A. Varshavsky, W. Trappe, and N. Mandayam. Proximate: proximity-based secure pairing using ambient wireless signals. In *Proceedings of the 9th international conference on Mobile systems, applications, and services*, pages 211–224, 2011.

[22] S. Mathur, W. Trappe, N. Mandayam, C. Ye, and A. Reznik. Radio-telepathy: extracting a secret key from an unauthenticated wireless channel. In *Proceedings of the 14th ACM international conference on Mobile computing and networking*, pages 128–139, 2008.

[23] N. T. Nguyen, G. Zheng, Z. Han, and R. Zheng. Device fingerprinting to enhance wireless security using nonparametric bayesian method. In *Proceedings of the IEEE International Conference on Computer Communications (INFOCOM)*, pages 1404–1412, 2011.

[24] L. O'Gorman. Comparing passwords, tokens, and biometrics for user authentication. *Proceedings of the IEEE*, 91(12):2021–2040, 2003.

[25] J. Pang, B. Greenstein, R. Gummadi, S. Seshan, and D. Wetherall. 802.11 user fingerprinting. In *Proceedings of the 13th annual ACM international conference on Mobile computing and networking*, pages 99–110, 2007.

[26] D. Shan, K. Zeng, W. Xiang, P. Richardson, and Y. Dong. Phy-cram: Physical layer challenge-response authentication mechanism for wireless networks. *IEEE Journal on Selected Areas in Communications*, 31(9):1817–1827, 2013.

[27] A. Wool. Lightweight key management for ieee 802.11 wireless lans with key refresh and host revocation. *ACM/Springer Wireless Networks*, 11(6):677–686, 2005.

[28] B. Wu, J. Wu, E. Fernandez, and S. Magliveras. Secure and efficient key management in mobile ad hoc networks. In *Proceedings of the 19th IEEE International Parallel and Distributed Processing Symposium (IPDPS)*, 2005.

[29] J. Yang, Y. Chen, and W. Trappe. Detecting spoofing attacks in mobile wireless environments. In *6th Annual IEEE Communications Society Conference on Sensor, Mesh and Ad Hoc Communications and Networks*, pages 1–9, 2009.

[30] J. Yang, Y. Chen, W. Trappe, and J. Cheng. Detection and localization of multiple spoofing attackers in wireless networks. *IEEE Transactions on Parallel and Distributed Systems*, 24(1):44–58, 2013.

[31] K. Zeng, K. Govindan, and P. Mohapatra. Non-cryptographic authentication and identification in wireless networks. *Wireless Communications*, 17(5):56–62, 2010.

[32] K. Zeng, K. Govindan, D. Wu, and P. Mohapatra. Identity-based attack detection in mobile wireless networks. In *Proceedings of the IEEE International Conference on Computer Communications*

Outsourceable Two-Party Privacy-Preserving Biometric Authentication

Hu Chun
Dept. of Computer Science
Missouri S&T
Rolla, Missouri 65409
chwrc@mst.edu

Yousef Elmehdwi
Dept. of Computer Science
Missouri S&T
Rolla, Missouri 65409
ymez76@mst.edu

Feng Li
Dept. of Computer Science
Missouri S&T
Rolla, Missouri 65409
lftrd@mst.edu

Prabir Bhattacharya
School of Computing Sciences and Informatics
University of Cincinnati
Cincinnati, Ohio 45221
bhattapr@ucmail.uc.edu

Wei Jiang
Dept. of Computer Science
Missouri S&T
Rolla, Missouri 65409
wjiang@mst.edu

ABSTRACT

Biometric authentication, a key component for many secure protocols and applications, is a process of authenticating a user by matching her biometric data against a biometric database stored at a server managed by an entity. If there is a match, the user can log into her account or obtain the services provided by the entity. Privacy-preserving biometric authentication (PPBA) considers a situation where the biometric data are kept private during the authentication process. That is the user's biometric data record is never disclosed to the entity, and the data stored in the entity's biometric database are never disclosed to the user. Due to the reduction in operational costs and high computing power, it is beneficial for an entity to outsource not only its data but also computations such as biometric authentication process to a cloud. However, due to well-documented security risks faced by a cloud, sensitive data like biometrics should be encrypted first and then outsourced to the cloud. When the biometric data are encrypted and cannot be decrypted by the cloud, the existing PPBA protocols are not applicable. Therefore, in this paper, we propose a two-party PPBA protocol when the biometric data in consideration are fully encrypted and outsourced to a cloud. In the proposed protocol, the security of the biometric data is completely protected since the encrypted biometric data are never decrypted during the authentication process. In addition, we formally analyze the security of the proposed protocol and provide extensive empirical results to show its runtime complexity.

ASIA CCS'14, June 4–6, 2014, Kyoto, Japan.

http://dx.doi.org/10.1145/2590296.2590343.

Categories and Subject Descriptors

K.6 [**Management of Computing and Information Systems**]; K.6.5 [**Security and Protection**]: Authentication

General Terms

Security

Keywords

Security; Cloud Computing; Biometric Authentication

1. INTRODUCTION

In recent years, biometric authentication has increasingly gained importance for various application domains. Those systems which include fingerprint-, face- and iris- authentication systems are widely used in enterprise, civilian and law enforcement. Such systems typically consist of an entity whose databases hold biometric records and users/clients who send the entity their biometric recordings for authentication [15]. During the process of biometric authentication, the systems need to identify whether candidate biometric readings from users match the records in the entity's biometric database. There are potential privacy concerns regarding biometric authentication: biometric matching process would cause a leakage of user's biometric data especially running on untrusted servers. Biometric data are usually very sensitive because they could uniquely identify a person. Thus, the leakage of biometric data to malicious parties can lead to a violation of personal privacy. To avoid this privacy concern, privacy-preserving biometric authentication (PPBA) protocols have been developed, e.g., [5, 6, 13, 15, 43]. Under the existing PPBA protocols, a user's biometric data record is never disclosed to the entity, and the entity's biometric database is never exposed to the user.

Due to cost efficiency and operational flexibility of the cloud computing paradigm [1,8,30], an entity has the opportunity to outsource its data and their relevant computations to a cloud which can provide on-demand services. To outsource biometric authentication tasks, the entity's biometric database needs to be encrypted before outsourced to a cloud.

This is because it is difficult for the cloud to actually guarantee the confidentiality of sensitive data. The challenge arises due to several well-documented security risks faced by existing cloud service providers [14,22,40,41,48,52]. One such risk for instance, is that when a breach occurs in the cloud, any sensitive data stored in the clear (i.e., not encrypted) can be easily exposed to the attacker.

As mentioned previously, the goal of PPBA protocols is to perform biometric authentication without disclosing the involved biometric data to the participating parties, except for their own data. The input data to the existing PPBA protocols are not encrypted, and it is not straightforward to modify these protocols to solve the outsourced biometric authentication problem because the cloud cannot access the original/non-encrypted biometric database. Different from existing PPBA, an entity's biometric database is encrypted under an outsourceable privacy-preserving biometric authentication (O-PPBA) protocol.

1.1 Problem Definition

Let $D = \{v_1, \ldots, v_n\}$ denote an entity's biometric database with n biometric data records. Each v_i, $1 \leq i \leq n$ is a m-dimension vector representation of a biometric data record. Let $[D] = \{[v_1], \ldots, [v_n]\}$ denote the encryption of D where each $[v_i]$ is encrypted component-wise. Suppose Bob is a user who wants to be authenticated using his biometric image data denoted by u. Here u is represented using the same method as the records in D. An O-PPBA protocol can be defined as follows with $[D]$ and [u] as the inputs:

$$\text{O-PPBA}([D], [u], t) \rightarrow b \tag{1}$$

When $b = 1$, there is a biometric data record v_i in D such that the distance between u and v_i is at most t distance apart; otherwise, $b = 0$. t is defined by the underlying biometric authentication system, and it varies from system to system. t also depends on the biometric data used for authentication. How to determine the best value for t is out of the scope of this paper, so we just assume t is publicly know parameter. During an execution of O-PPBA, $[D]$ and $[u]$ are never decrypted to maximize the confidentiality protection of D and u.

We inherit the common structure of the existing PPBA systems which mainly consist of two phases: distance computation, and matching and retrieval [15]. In the distance computation phase, either Euclidean or Hamming distance between the feature vectors of biometric records v_i's in D and the user's biometric data record u are calculated pairwise. After that in matching and retrieval phase, those distances are compared with a pre-defined threshold t to decide whether u matches some v_i with t-distance apart. Some biometric authentication protocols such as face recognition [13] need a feature extraction phase to get the biometric feature vectors; however, in this paper, we assume that feature extraction phase as a pre-computation stage to produce the feature vectors in D and u.

1.2 Our Contributions

In this paper, we propose fully secure O-PPBA protocol. Our protocol meets the following privacy requirements:

- Contents of D or any intermediate results should not be revealed to the cloud.
- Bob's biometric image data u should not be revealed to the cloud.
- The output b should not be revealed to the cloud.
- Data access patterns, such as the biometric data records corresponding to the matching or comparison results with u, should not be revealed to Bob and the cloud.
- After sending his encrypted biometric data to the cloud, Bob never participates in any intermediate computation. Therefore, our protocols incur low computation overhead on Bob.

We emphasize that the intermediate results seen by the cloud in our protocol are either newly generated randomized encryptions or random numbers.

1.3 Overview of the Proposed Protocol

Let P_1 denote a cloud service provider who stores $[D]$ and performs biometric authentication based on $[D]$, $[u]$ and t. When outsourced biometric data $[D]$ are encrypted with a fully homomorphic encryption scheme [17], P_1 can perform any possible computations over the encrypted data. However, fully homomorphic encryptions have yet to be practical due to their extremely high computation costs.

In our proposed O-PPBA protocol, in addition to P_1, we will utilize another independent cloud service provider P_2 and use an additive homomorphic encryption scheme (AH-Enc) to encrypt each v_i and u component-wise to produce $[v_i]$ and $[u]$. There are several AH-Enc schemes, and without loss of generality, we adopt the Paillier cryptosystem [38] for its simple implementation and being semantically secure. $[D]$ is outsourced and stored at P_1, and only P_2 has the corresponding decryption key. Therefore, $[D]$ and $[u]$ cannot be decrypted by P_1 without accessing the decryption key.

To solve the proposed O-PPBA problem, one might suggest using garbled circuits [24] for every secure computation between P_1 and P_2. This is logical for simple tasks (e.g., secure comparison), where such an approach can be quite efficient. However, biometric authentication is complex process consisting of several sub-components. In Section 4.1, we present these sub-components and investigate the most efficient and secure way to implement them. The proposed O-PPBA combines homomorphic encryption and garbled circuit to take advantages offered by each approach. This hybrid approach leads to a more efficient protocol as shown in Section 5.

The rest of this paper is organized as follows: Section 2 overviews the work related image retrieval and existing PPBA protocols, Section 3 presents technical background and threat models, Section 4 presents our proposed O-PPBA protocol, Section 5 provides empirical results showing the run time complexity of the proposed protocol, and we summarize our contributions and future research in Section 6.

2. RELATED WORK

Since our work is directly related to the concept of secure multiparty computation (SMC), in this section, we first provide a high level discussion of SMC. In addition, we provide an overview of content based image retrieval techniques and the existing privacy-preserving biometric identification protocols. The formulation of privacy-preserving biometric identification (PPBI) is slightly different from privacy-preserving biometric authentication (PPBA) which is considered in this paper.

A PPBI protocol generally returns the profile of an person whose biometric data record stored at the server matches the user's input biometric data record. On the other hand, a PPBA protocol only returns a single bit to indicate if there is a match or not. The existing PPBI protocols can be easily modified to satisfy the PPBA problem statement definition. From a technical perspective, the difference between PPBI and PPBA is negligible. Since there is a lack of exiting work directly related to PPBA, here we will mainly present the work related to PPBI and discuss the reasons why the existing PPBI protocols cannot be directly applied to solve the outsourceable PPBA problem.

2.1 Secure Multiparty Computation

Secure multiparty computation (SMC) was first introduced by Yao's Millionaire problem [51] where Alice and Bob want to know who is richer without disclosing their actual wealth to each other. Suppose there are n parties $P_1, \ldots, P_n$ who hold private inputs $a_1, \ldots, a_n$ respectively. An SMC protocol allows $P_1, \ldots, P_n$ to collaboratively compute a function f on inputs $a_1, \ldots, a_n$ without disclosing a_i to P_j where $1 \leq i, j \leq n$ and $i \neq j$. To achieve that, the participating parties have to exchange messages and perform some local computations until all the parties get the desired output. In general, we need to make sure that the messages exchanged should not disclose any information regarding each party's private input.

2.2 Content based Image Retrieval

Biometric authentication or identification is a special case of content based image retrieval (CBIR). In a CBIR system, a desirable image is retrieved from a large image database based on the similarity of some common attributes which are called features. There are two kinds of features: the global and local. Global features usually include color, texture and shape which are well known and studied in image retrieval. Local features are usually used in a localized circumstance which needs to recognize objects more precisely.

The basic way to separate images is to use color. Thus, color is a very important visual feature for image retrieval. In existing literatures many color space models are available. The RGB model is the most commonly used color space model that represents colors by red (R), green (G) and blue (B). In most RGB systems, the values of red, green and blue are depending upon the nature of the primaries in a certain imaging device [46]. Thus, other models such as HSI, HSV, LAB, LUV and YCrCb have been proposed to overcome of RGB shortcomings. When those color spaces models, the color histogram scheme is the most effective way to represent a image since color histograms are invariant to orientation and scale [9,31]. However, color histogram can hardly characterize the spatial structures of images; as a result, other descriptors have been proposed such as compact color moments, the color coherence vector and color correlograms [23].

Texture is another important characteristics of an image. Various algorithms have been designed for texture analysis such as gray level co-occurrence matrices [39], the Tamura texture feature [21], and Gabor filtering [7]. Co-occurrence matrix is a popular representation of texture feature of an image which is constructed based upon the orientation and distance between image pixels [39]. Tamura texture feature is another popular representation which is based upon the human mental study in visual perception of texture [21]. Gabor filters are very effective that applying signal processing and wavelet transform methods in texture analysis [7]. The wavelet transform is used for image classification based on multi-resolution decomposition of images.

In addition, shape features are also playing a critical role in CBIR because human beings can recognize objects solely based on shapes. Main method for shape features is the use of moment invariants [47]. Usually shape feature extraction requires the use of image segmentation, where an image needs to be divided into different regions.

Beside of those global feature-based algorithms (color, texture, shape), local feature-based algorithms are more precise but time-consuming. Several types of local descriptors have been proposed in the literature [3,28,32,42,49]. One very effective technique is termed as scale-invariant feature transfer (SIFT) [32] which extracts features that do not change when exposed to a set of image transformations. Speed-Up Robust Features (SURF) [3] is another local feature based technique which is faster than other descriptors including SIFT. In addition, SIFT has its advantages in rotation and illumination changes against SURF [33].

2.3 Privacy-Preserving Biometric Authentication / Identification

To the best our knowledge, Erkin et al. [13] proposed the first privacy-preserving biometric face recognition protocol based on the standard Eigenfaces recognition algorithm. The protocol is a secure two-party computation protocol where one party (client) wants to learn whether its candidate biometric reading matches for one or more records in the other party's (server's) database without disclosing any information except the final result. The protocol computes Euclidean distances between face image feature vectors from client and server's face image database, and it returns the profile information associated with the facial image data record that has the smallest distance to the client's input biometric data. At the end, the client only knows the profile information without knowing other biometric data and their associated profiles stored at the server, and the server knows nothing, even regarding the profile information returned to the client. The data exchanged during an execution of the protocol are encrypted by an additive homomorphic encryption scheme, but the data stored at the sever are not encrypted. Therefore, the server knows the contents of its biometric database.

Sadeghi et al. [43] developed a hybrid privacy-preserving face recognition protocol which improved the efficiency of Erkin's work. This protocol follows the problem setting of Erkin's work and also uses additive homomorphic encryption (the Paillier cryptosystem) to securely compute Euclidean distances. On the other hand, Garbled circuits [24,50] are used for finding the minimum distance. The authors also proposed a method of packing multiple values together into a single ciphertext before blinding. This can save communication cost significantly.

Huang et al. developed an efficient privacy-preserving biometric identification protocol for fingerprint recognition [15]. The basic algorithm for fingerprint identification is based on $FingerCode$ [27]. In the main system, the server and a client jointly perform the protocol to retrieve the identity record from the server's database whose fingerprint best matches the client's input fingerprint reading. The protocol provides the same security guarantee as the previously mentioned protocols. In addition, similar to Sadeghi's work, this protocol also combines additive homomorphic encryption with garbled circuits. However, the protocol improves efficiency for both distance-computing phase and matching phase compared to Sadeghi's work. The protocol separates retrieval step from matching phase, and it uses the by-product of evaluating the garbled circuit in the matching phase to perform the oblivious retrieval efficiently. In the retrieval phase, the protocol utilizes a backtracking tree to obliviously and efficiently recover the profile corresponding to the closest matching vector.

Different from calculating Euclidean distance, Blanton and Gasti [6] developed a privacy-preserving identification protocol for iris codes based on Hamming distance. In their protocol, the client who possesses an iris reading would also like to learn whether his or her reading matches one or more records in an iris database managed by the server. The contents of the server's database are never disclosed to the client, but the client learns the comparison results between his or her input iris record and every record in the server's database. The implementation of the protocol also uses both additive homomorphic encryption and garbled circuits, and it reduces the complexity of the circuits used for comparison based on an optimization that permits XOR gates to be evaluated for free. The proposed techniques can be applied in protocols where $FingerCode$ and Euclidean distances are adopted to improve the performance compared to the existing Euclidean distance based solutions.

SCiFI [37] is a realization of a privacy-preserving face identification system which uses a component-based face identification technique which building a binary index into a vocabulary representation. The adopted image representation technique is robust against different viewing conditions, such as illumination, occlusions, and changes in appearance (like wearing glasses). The protocol utilizes Hamming distance to measure image similarity, and its implementation were based on additive homomorphic encryption and oblivious transfer [34].

Although the aforementioned privacy-preserving biometric identification / authentication protocols protect the confidentiality of both server and client's biometric data, our problem setting is quite different from these protocols. In our problem domain, the biometric database is encrypted and outsourced to a server (or a cloud), and the server does not have the key to decrypt the data. Thus, the server does not know anything regarding the original biometric database. Since the previously proposed solutions require the server to perform computations on the original biometric data, these solutions cannot be applied to solve this outsourced biometric authentication problem.

Recently, Blanton and Aliasgari [5] developed a secure approach to outsourcing computations of matching iris biometric data records. The setting of their work is very similar to ours. Two protocols were proposed for either single server-setting or multiple-server setting. In their single-server setting, the protocol uses predicate encryption scheme [29, 45] that allows the server to perform non-interactive computations. The predicate encryption scheme is not as secure as additive homomorphic encryption. As a result, our proposed protocol offers much better confidentiality protection of the biometric data. Under the multiple-server setting, the protocol adopts a secret sharing scheme (e.g., Shamir [44]) to "encrypt" the outsourced biometric database. However, the protocol requires at least three independent servers to perform the intermediate computations. Our proposed protocol requires only two servers, so it is more practical.

In addition, the protocol mainly focuses on calculating Hamming distance, whereas our proposed protocol can compute Euclidean and Hamming distances. Since both distances are commonly used to image retrieve according to different kinds of biometric data, our protocol offers more generality. Another different is that at the end of protocol execution, the server can know which encrypted biometric data record matches the client's input. This access pattern leakage can violate the security guarantee of the underlying encryption scheme [26]. Because our protocol does not disclose this information to any participating party, our protocol offers the same security protection as the encryption scheme used to encrypt the outsourced biometric data.

3. SECURITY DEFINITIONS AND ADVERSARY MODELS

In this section, we first discuss the encryption scheme used to build the proposed protocols. Since the notion of security varies from different application domains, we also present the security threat or adversary models that best match the proposal application domain.

3.1 Additive Homomorphic Encryption

The proposal protocol adopts an additive homomorphic probabilistic public key encryption (AH-Enc) scheme as the building block. Let E_{pk} and D_{pr} be the encryption and decryption functions in an AH-Enc scheme with public key pk and private key pr. Without pr, no one can discover x from $E_{pk}(x)$ in polynomial time. Since the encryption and decryption keys are unique in our problem domain, we will adopt the succinct notation $[x]$ to represent an encryption or ciphertext of x. an AH-Enc has the following properties:

- The encryption function is additive homomorphic: $[x_1 + x_2] = [x_1] \times [x_2] \mod N^2$;
- Given a constant c and $[x]$, $[c \cdot x] = [x]^c \mod N^2$;
- The encryption function has semantic security as defined in [20], i.e., a set of ciphertexts do not provide additional information about the plaintext to an adversary with polynomial-bounded computing power. In other words, two encryptions of x differs with very high probability. This is the probabilistic property of the AH-Enc system.

Any AH-Enc system is applicable, but in this paper, we adopt the Paillier encryption scheme [38] for its implementation simplicity. Informally speaking, the public key in the system is (g, N), where N is resulted from multiplication of two large prime numbers and $g \in \mathbb{Z}^*_{N^2}$ is randomly chosen. When computations are performed on ciphertexts, we need to perform a modulo N^2 operation at the end (e.g., $[x_1 + x_2] = [x_1] \times [x_2] \mod N^2$). Because N is unique in the proposed protocols, we will drop or eliminate this modulo N^2 operation whenever the context is clear.

3.2 Threat / Adversary Models

In general, there is a conceptual difference between *privacy* and *security*. However, in this paper, we will not differentiate the two terms. Regarding a distributed protocol, security is generally related to the amount of information leaked during the protocol execution. To maximize security

Table 1: Common Notations

SMC	Secure Multiparty Computation
PPBA	Privacy-Preserving Biometric Authentication
O-PPBA	Outsourceable PPBA
AH-Enc	Additive homomorphic encryption
v_i or u	m-dimension feature vector representation of a biometric data image
$[v_i]$ or $[u]$	A component-wise encryption of v_i, using an AH-Enc scheme
D	A biometric database with n records: $v_1, \ldots, v_n$
$[D]$	An encryption of D: $[v_1], \ldots, [v_n]$
P_1 or P_2	A cloud service provider

protection, we use the security definitions in the literature of secure multiparty computation (SMC).

SMC-based secure protocols generally assume there basic adversarial models: semi-honest (or honest but curious), malicious and covert [2, 18]. Semi-honest adversaries follow the protocol faithfully, but can try to infer the secret information of the other parties from the data they see during the protocol execution. Malicious adversaries may do anything to infer secret information. On the other hand, under the covert adversary model, malicious behaviors can be detected without disclosing private information. Almost all practical SMC-based protocols are secure under the semi-honest model, and using zero-knowledge proofs [19], these protocols can be transformed into protocols secure under the malicious model. Also, it is hard to imagine that two well-established cloud service providers can collude to damage their reputations and customer base. Therefore, we will adopt the semi-honest model. In addition, since the covert model provides a nice balance between the semi-honest model and the malicious model, we will also proposed strategies to make the proposed protocol secure under the covert model. Briefly, the following definition captures the security definition under the semi-honest model.

DEFINITION 1. *Let a_i be the input of party P_i, $\prod_i(\pi)$ be P_i's execution image of the protocol π and b_i be the result computed from π for P_i. π is secure if $\prod_i(\pi)$ can be simulated from $\langle a_i, b_i \rangle$ and distribution of the simulated image is computationally indistinguishable from $\prod_i(\pi)$.*

A formal way to prove the security of a protocol under the semi-honest model is to use the simulation approach [18]. In our security proofs, we will adopt this method.

4. THE PROPOSED TWO-PARTY O-PPBA PROTOCOL

We will follow the same notations as given in Sections 1.1 and 1.3. For clearness, commonly used notations for this paper are given in Table 1. According to the number of participants, an SMC protocol can be classified into either two-party or multi-party protocol. In our problem domain, it is more cost effective to use two cloud service providers, so we will focus on developing a two-party O-PPBA protocol. For a functionality as complex as biometric authentication, the best way to implement an efficient two-party secure protocol is to combine homomorphic encryption approach and garbled circuit. This hybrid approach was adopted in [36] to produce a secure protocol that is more efficient than either homomorphic encryption approach or garbled circuit approach alone. The key challenges to utilize the hybrid approach are:

- Break a complex functionality into a set of simpler sub-components (or sub-functionalities).
- Determine which approach to use to implement each sub-component securely.

Next we will dissect O-PPBA into sub-components and identify the most efficient approach, between homomorphic encryption or garbled circuit, to implement each component.

4.1 Sub-Components of O-PPBA

To implement an O-PPBA protocol, first each biometric image needs to be represented as a feature vector. This pre-processing step can be implemented using the existing image representation techniques as summarized in Section 2.2. For the rest of this paper, we assume that the feature vector of each biometric image is given as part of the input to an O-PPBA protocol.

According to Equation 1 and based on the description given in Section 1.1, an O-PPBA protocol (with input $[D] = \{[v_1], \ldots, [v_n]\}$, $[u]$ and t) consists three main sub-components or protocols that need to be performed sequentially. According to the Composition Theorem [18], when a protocol is implemented based on a set of secure primitives, and for the protocol to be secure, the intermediate results produced from these primitives must be in the form of random shares. By random shares, we mean that the actual value is divided into two additive random shares, each of which is independently and uniformly distributed in a group (e.g., $\mathbb{Z}_N = \{0, 1, \ldots, N-1\}$). The actual value can be reconstructed by adding the two shares modulo N. Next we describe each sub-component and its outcomes.

(1) *Distance computation*: This component computes the distance between u and each v_i, for $1 \leq i \leq n$. Note that the distance is between the actual feature vectors, but the input should be the encrypted feature vectors $[u]$ and $[v_i]$. During the computation, $[u]$ and $[v_i]$ are never decrypted to preserve the confidentiality of u and v_i. Let d_i denote the distance between u and v_i. The output of this component returns two random shares d_i' and d_i'' for each d_i such that $d_i' + d_i'' \mod N = d_i$.

(2) *Comparing with the threshold*: Once the distances are computed, these distances need to be compared with the threshold t, to find out if u is one of $v_1, \ldots, v_n$. Distance less than t indicating u matches some biometric record in D. Again, all these computations are based on encrypted data or random shares. More specifically, the (d_i', d_i'') pairs and the threshold t are the input for this sub-component. Let b_i denote the comparison result between d_i and t. $b_i = 1$ if $d_i \leq t$; otherwise $b_i = 0$. The output of this component returns two random shares b_i' and b_i'' for each b_i such that $b_i' + b_i'' \mod N = b_i$.

(3) *Combining the comparison results*: As long as there is a b_i equal to 1, we can conclude that u matches some v_i in D. Then authentication succeeds. The (b_i', b_i'') are the input for this sub-component. Let b_f denote the final authentication result. If $b_f = 1$, then authentication

succeeds. On the other hand, $b_f = 0$, authentication fails. The output of this component returns two random shares b'_f and b''_f such that $b'_f + b''_f \mod N = b_f$.

Note that, it is possible for the last component to return b_f directly, but b'_f and b''_f are more useful in case b_f serves as an intermediate result for a more complex protocol. Base their need, the participating parties can decide the appropriate output. Without loss of generality, this paper adopts b'_f and b''_f as the final outcome of the proposed O-PPBA protocol.

4.2 Efficient and Secure Implementation of Each Sub-Component

According the descriptions of the sub-components given in the previous section, this section investigates how to implement them efficiently and securely. Depending on the specific functionality or computation, we will identify the most efficient and secure method (either homomorphic encryption based approach or garbled circuit) to implement each sub-component.

4.2.1 Secure Distance Computation

As mentioned previously, since biometric data have multiple types and each type can be represented in various ways, here we will implement secure sub-protocols to compute two most common distance metrics adopted in the existing PPBI work (summarized in Section 2.3): Euclidean distance and Hamming distance. Both metrics have their advantages and disadvantages, and an entity can decide which metric to use for its O-PPBA protocol.

Euclidean Distance.

Suppose v_i and u are m-dimensional vectors, and the content of the individual dimension is represented by $v_i\langle j\rangle$ ($u\langle j\rangle$), where $1 \leq j \leq m$. The Euclidean distance between v_i and u can be computed as follows:

$$\text{Euclidean\_Dist}(v_i, u) = \sqrt{\sum_{j=1}^{m}(v_i\langle j\rangle - u\langle j\rangle)^2}$$

When comparing two distances, the square root does not make any difference. Thus, in our implementation, we will drop the square root to compute the square of the Euclidean distance between v_i and u:

$$\text{Euclidean\_Dist}^2(v_i, u) = \sum_{j=1}^{m}(v_i\langle j\rangle - u\langle j\rangle)^2 \qquad (2)$$

According to the above equation, the main challenge is to compute $v_i\langle j\rangle^2$, $u\langle j\rangle^2$, and $v_i\langle j\rangle \cdot u\langle j\rangle$ from $[v_i\langle j\rangle]$ and $[u\langle j\rangle]$ (where $[v_i\langle j\rangle]$ and $[u\langle j\rangle]$ are encryptions of $v_i\langle j\rangle$ and $u\langle j\rangle$). The key steps to securely compute Euclidean_Dist$^2(v_i, u)$ are given by Algorithm 1 where computations are only based on either encrypted or randomized data. At step 1(a) of the algorithm, x_j is a randomized difference between $v_i\langle j\rangle$ and $u\langle j\rangle$, and r_j is randomly chosen to hide the actual difference. According to the additive homomorphic property of the encryption scheme, $[x_j]$ can be computed as follows:

$$[v_i\langle j\rangle - u\langle j\rangle + r_j] \leftarrow [v_i\langle j\rangle] \times [u\langle j\rangle]^{N-1} \times [r_j]$$

Since P_2 has the decryption key, it can decrypt $[x_j]$ to get x_j. Then P_2 computes the square of x_j and sends the encrypted results (e.g., $[x_1], \ldots, [x_m]$) to P_1. Because P_1 knows r_j and

Algorithm 1 Secure_Distance$^e([v_i], [u]) \rightarrow (d'_i, d''_i)$

Require: P_1 has $[v_i]$ and $[u]$; P_2 has the decryption key

1: P_1:
   - (a) $[x_j] \leftarrow [v_i\langle j\rangle - u\langle j\rangle + r_j]$, where $r_j \in_R \mathbb{Z}_N$ and $1 \leq j \leq m$
   - (b) Send $[x_1], \ldots, [x_m]$ to P_2

2: P_2:
   - (a) Perform decryption to get $x_1, \ldots, x_m$
   - (b) Compute $[(x_1)^2], \ldots, [(x_m)^2]$, and send them to P_1

3: P_1:
   - (a) Obtain $[(v_i\langle j\rangle - u\langle j\rangle)^2]$ by eliminating r_j^2 and $2r_j(v_i\langle j\rangle - u\langle j\rangle)$ from $[(x_j)^2]$, for $1 \leq j \leq m$
   - (b) $[d_i] \leftarrow [sum_{j=1}^{m}(v_i\langle j\rangle - u\langle j\rangle)^2]$
   - (c) Compute $[d_i + r]$, where $r \in_R \mathbb{Z}_N$
   - (d) Set $d'_i = N - r$ and send $[d_i + r]$ to P_2

4: P_2:
   - (a) Perform decryption on $[d_i + r]$ to get $d_i + r$
   - (b) Set $d''_i = d_i + r$

$[v_i\langle j\rangle - u\langle j\rangle]$, it can easily compute $[r_j^2]$ and $[2r_j(v_i\langle j\rangle - u\langle j\rangle)]$. Since $[(x_j)^2] = [(v_i\langle j\rangle - u\langle j\rangle)^2 + 2r_j(v_i\langle j\rangle - u\langle j\rangle) + r_j^2]$, P_1 can obtain $[(v_i\langle j\rangle - u\langle j\rangle)^2]$ by:

$$[(v_i\langle j\rangle - u\langle j\rangle)^2] \leftarrow [(x_j)^2] \times ([v_i\langle j\rangle - u\langle j\rangle]^{2r_j} \times [r_j^2])^{N-1}$$

From here, $[d_i]$ can be directly derived:

$$[d_i] \leftarrow [(v_i\langle 1\rangle - u\langle 1\rangle)^2] \times \cdots \times [(v_i\langle m\rangle - u\langle m\rangle)^2]$$

The rest of the steps are straightforward.

Hamming Distance.

When v_i and u are binary vectors, Hamming distance can be used to determine how close v_i and u are. Hamming distance can be computed as follows:

$$\text{Hamming\_Dist}(v_i, u) = m - \sum_{j=1}^{m} v_i\langle j\rangle \cdot u\langle j\rangle \qquad (3)$$

According to the above equation, the main challenge is to compute $v_i\langle j\rangle \cdot u\langle j\rangle$ from $[v_i\langle j\rangle]$ and $[u\langle j\rangle]$. The key steps to securely compute Hamming_Dist(v_i, u) are given by Algorithm 2 where computations are only based on either encrypted or randomized data. At step 1(a) of the algorithm, x_{j_1} and x_{j_2} are randomizations of $v_i\langle j\rangle$ and $u\langle j\rangle$ respectively, and r_{j_1} and r_{j_2} are randomly chosen to hide the actual values of $v_i\langle j\rangle$ and $u\langle j\rangle$. According to the additive homomorphic property of the encryption scheme, $[x_{j_1}]$ and $[x_{j_2}]$ can be computed as follows:

$$[v_i\langle j\rangle + r_{j_1}] \leftarrow [v_i\langle j\rangle] \times [r_{j_1}]$$

$$[u\langle j\rangle + r_{j_2}] \leftarrow [u\langle j\rangle] \times [r_{j_2}]$$

Algorithm 2 Secure_Distance$^h([v_i],[u]) \rightarrow (d_i', d_i'')$

Require: P_1 has $[v_i]$ and $[u]$; P_2 has the decryption key

1: P_1:

(a) $[x_{j_1}] \leftarrow [v_i\langle j\rangle + r_{j_1}]$ and $[x_{j_2}] \leftarrow [u\langle j\rangle + r_{j_2}]$, where $r_{j_1}, r_{j_2} \in_R \mathbb{Z}_N$ and $1 \le j \le m$

(b) Send $([x_{1_1}],[x_{1_2}]),\dots,([x_{m_1}],[x_{m_2}])$ to P_2

2: P_2:

(a) Perform decryption operation to get $(x_{1_1}, x_{1_2}),\dots,$ (x_{m_1}, x_{m_2})

(b) Compute $[x_{1_1} \cdot x_{1_2}],\dots,[x_{m_1} \cdot x_{m_2}]$, and send them to P_1

3: P_1:

(a) Obtain $[v_i\langle j\rangle \cdot u\langle j\rangle]$ by eliminating $r_{j_1} \cdot r_{j_2}$, $r_{j_2} \cdot v_i\langle j\rangle$ and $r_{j_1} \cdot u\langle j\rangle$ from $[x_{j_1} \cdot x_{j_2}]$, for $1 \le j \le m$

(b) $[d_i] \leftarrow [m - \sum_{j=1}^{m} v_i\langle j\rangle \cdot u\langle j\rangle]$

(c) Compute $[d_i + r]$, where $r \in_R \mathbb{Z}_N$

(d) Set $d_i' = N - r$ and send $[d_i + r]$ to P_2

4: P_2:

(a) Perform decryption on $[d_i + r]$ to get $d_i + r$

(b) Set $d_i'' = d_i + r$

Since P_2 has the decryption key, it can decrypt $([x_{j_1}],[x_{j_2}])$ to get (x_{j_1}, x_{j_2}) at step 2(a). Then P_2 computes the multiplication of $x_{j_1} \cdot x_{j_2}$ and sends the encrypted results to P_1. Because P_1 knows r_{j_1}, r_{j_2}, $[v_i\langle j\rangle]$ and $[u\langle j\rangle]$, it can easily compute $[r_{j_1} \cdot r_{j_2}]$, $r_{j_2} \cdot v_i\langle j\rangle$ and $r_{j_1} \cdot u\langle j\rangle$. Since $[x_{j_1} \cdot x_{j_2}] = [v_i\langle j\rangle \cdot u\langle j\rangle + r_{j_1} \cdot r_{j_2} + r_{j_2} \cdot v_i\langle j\rangle + r_{j_1} \cdot u\langle j\rangle]$, at step 3(a), P_1 can obtain $[v_i\langle j\rangle \cdot u\langle j\rangle]$ by:

$$[v_i\langle j\rangle \cdot u\langle j\rangle] \leftarrow [x_{j_1} \cdot x_{j_2}] \times ([r_{j_1} \cdot r_{j_2}] \times [r_{j_2} \cdot v_i\langle j\rangle] \times [r_{j_1} \cdot u\langle j\rangle])^{N-1}$$

From here, $[d_i]$ can be directly derived at step 3(b):

$$[d_i] \leftarrow [m] \times ([v_i\langle 1\rangle \cdot u\langle 1\rangle] \times \cdots \times [v_i\langle m\rangle \cdot u\langle m\rangle])^{N-1}$$

The rest of the steps are fairly obvious. All above computations are based on the additive homomorphic property of the encryption schemes. The two sub-protocols are more efficient than garbled circuit based solutions, and detailed analysis is provided in Section 5. The security analysis of both protocols is presented in Section 4.3.2.

4.2.2 *Securely Comparing with the Threshold*

To implement the second sub-component securely, we need a secure comparison protocol that takes random shares (i.e., d_i' and d_i'') and a threshold t as input and returns two random shares b_i' and b_i'', such that $b_i' + b_i'' \mod N = 1$ if $d_i \le t$; otherwise $b_i' + b_i'' \mod N = 0$. The inputs of most existing secure comparison protocols [4,10,11,16,35] are non-encrypted or non-random shares, so they are not directly applicable in our problem domain. On the other hand, garbled circuit has been known for its efficiency to securely evaluate simple functionalities, such as comparison. In addition, garbled circuit only requires one round of communication and can

Algorithm 3 O-PPBA$([D],[u],t) \rightarrow b$

Require: P_1 has $[D]$ and $[u]$, P_2 has the decryption key, and t is a public parameter

1: P_1 and P_2 jointly execute Secure_Distance$([v_i],[u])$, for $i = 1$ to n

2: P_1 and P_2 jointly execute Secure_Comparison(d_i', d_i'', t), for $i = 1$ to n

3: P_1: $\alpha \leftarrow \sum_{i=1}^{n} b_i' \mod N$

4: P_2: $\beta \leftarrow \sum_{i=1}^{n} b_i'' \mod N$

5: P_1 and P_2 jointly execute Secure_Comparison$(\alpha, \beta, 0)$

6: $b \leftarrow b_f' + b_f'' \mod N$

be easily modified to fit our problem domain. As a result, we adopt the fast garbled circuit method [24] to implement this sub-component.

Technical details on how to produce and evaluate a garbled circuit are well documented in [24]. In this paper, we will skip these technical details. Instead, we assume that Secure_Comparison$(d_i', d_i'', t) \rightarrow (b_i', b_i'')$ is the protocol to implement the sub-component and it is constructed using a garbled circuit, where d_i' and d_i'' are private input values from P_1 and P_2 respectively, and t is publicly known parameter. The protocol returns b_i' to P_1 and b_i'' to P_2.

4.2.3 *Securely Combining the Comparison Results*

As discussed in Section 4.1, the third sub-component / functionality is to identify the existence of a comparison result that is equal to 1. To maximize security guarantee, the individual comparison results cannot be disclosed; otherwise, the first two sub-components would be sufficient. Now the challenge is to find out whether there is a comparison result of 1 without disclosing which encrypted biometric record $[v_i]$ matches $[u]$. Since a server only knows if two encrypted biometric data records match, we may think that disclosing the matching result is harmless. However, according to [26], the matching result must not be leaked to preserve the security guarantee of the underlying encryption scheme.

To prevent the matching or comparison results from disclosing to P_1 and P_2, the design of our protocol is based on the following observations:

OBSERVATION 1. *Let $b_1,\dots,b_n$ be the n actual comparison results from comparing $d_1,\dots,d_n$ with the threshold t, where $d_1,\dots,d_n$ are the distances between u and each of $v_1,\dots,v_n$. Then $b_f = 1$ if and only if $0 < \sum_{i=1}^{n} d_i$.*

OBSERVATION 2. *Let $\alpha = \sum_{i=1}^{n} b_i'$ and $\beta = \sum_{i=1}^{n} b_i''$. Then we have $\alpha + \beta \mod N = \sum_{i=1}^{n} b_i$.*

From the above observations, it is not hard to see that this sub-component can be implemented using the same secure comparison protocol as discussed in Section 4.2.2. More specifically, Secure_Comparison$(\alpha, \beta, 0) \rightarrow (b_f', b_f'')$ is the protocol to implement the sub-component and it is constructed using a garbled circuit, where α and β are private input values from P_1 and P_2 respectively, and 0 is a public parameter. The protocol returns b_f' to P_1 and b_f'' to P_2 such that $b_f' + b_f'' \mod N = b_f$.

4.3 The O-PPBA Protocol

Once we have proper secure implementations of the three sub-components, we can build an O-PPBA protocol directly based on these components. The key steps of the O-PPBA protocol are given in Algorithm 3. Here we assume that a user's encrypted biometric data record $[u]$ has been received by P_1, and it is encrypted using the same public key as the one to encrypt D to produce $[D]$, where $[D]$ is encrypted by the entity who owns the biometric database D.

Step 1 of Algorithm 3 securely computes the distance between u and each of $v_1, \ldots, v_n$. P_1 and P_2 receive $d'_1, \ldots, d'_n$ and $d''_1, \ldots, d''_n$ as their private output respectively. Note that in the protocol, we do not specify which distance metric (either Euclidean or Hamming). Depending on the type of biometric data and the feature vector, the entity who outsourced its biometric authentication to P_1 and P_2 can decide the appropriate metric to use. Secure_Distance^e and Secure_Distance^h in Algorithm 3 are interchangeable without affecting the security and the correctness of O-PPBA.

The output from step 1 serves as the input for step 2. At the end of step 2, P_1 receives $b'_1, \ldots, b'_n$ and P_2 receives $b''_1, \ldots, b''_n$. P_1 and P_2 independently compute α and β which are input for step 5 of the algorithm. Step 5 returns b'_f to P_1 and b''_f to P_2. To obtain the actual authentication result, P_2 can send d''_f to P_1, and b_f can be reconstructed by adding the two random shares modulo N. Steps 2, 3 and 5 of Algorithm 3 correspond to the three sub-component and their implementations investigated in Sections 4.1 and 4.2.

4.3.1 Complexity Analysis

Here we analyze both computation and communication complexities of the proposed O-PPBA protocol. First, we analyze the computation complexity for each sub-protocol. For the Secure_Distance^e protocol, the number of multiplications and encryptions is bounded by $O(m)$, where m is the vector size. To derive this upper bound, we need to examine each step of the protocol. At step 1, the protocol performs $2m$ encryptions and $2m$ multiplications. Here we treat $[u\langle j\rangle]^{N-1}$ as one encryption although it is slightly less expensive than an encryption operation. Step 2(a) performs m decryptions. A decryption has a similar cost as an encryption, so we count m encryptions for step 2(a). Step 2(b) performs m encryptions and m multiplications. Step 3(a) performs $3m$ encryptions and $2m$ multiplications since we count the two exponentiations as two encryptions. Step 3(b) requires $m-1$ multiplications. The computations for the rest of the steps are constant. Therefore, the total number of multiplications and encryptions for this sub-protocol is bounded by $O(m)$. In addition, because an encryption operation is generally several order of magnitude more expensive than a multiplication, we can claim the computation complexity of Secure_Distance^e is bounded by $O(m)$ encryptions. Similarly, we can derive the same asymptotic bound for Secure_Distance^h.

The inputs to the Secure_Comparison protocol are two random shares with size bounded by N, so the initial phase of the garbled circuit needs $O(\log N)$ gates to add the shares. The resulting distance value is much smaller than N is our problem domain. Therefore, the total number of gates in the garbled circuit is bound by $O(\log N)$. Since the fast garbled circuit evaluation method proposed in [24] is every efficient and use symmetric key encryption to garble the circuit. We can expect that the total computation cost of the Secure_Comparison protocol is about performing several homomorphic encryption operations, so $O(m)$ encryptions provide an appropriate upper bound for Secure_Comparison. The O-PPBA protocol executes the Secure_Distance protocol n times and the Secure_Comparison protocol $n+1$ times. As a consequence, the total computation complexity of O-PPBA is bound by $O(mn)$ encryptions.

To analyze the communication complexity, we calculate an asymptotic bound on the number of bits exchanged between P_1 and P_2. Let k denote the number of bits to represent N. Then the communication complexity of Secure_Distance is bound by $O(mk)$. Also, for a sufficiently large m, the communication complexity of Secure_Comparison is bound by $O(mk)$. As a result, the total communication complexity of O-PPBA is bounded by $O(mnk)$ in bits.

4.3.2 Security Analysis and Extensions to Other Adversary Models

The O-PPBA protocol is secure under the semi-honest adversary model of SMC. Since the protocol is a sequential composition of sub-protocols, to prove the security of O-PPBA, we first need to prove the security of each sub-protocol. The security of Secure_Distance^e depends on the size of the encryption key. In general, N needs to be at least 1024 bit long, and then we can say that the Paillier encryption scheme possesses semantic security. Thus, in our proof, we assume N is 1024-bit or larger. Under the semi-honest model, the security guarantee is very easy to proof because the computations are performed on either encrypted data or randomized data. To be more clear, here we analyze step-by-step how the original biometric data records are protected or never disclosed.

At step 1(a) of Algorithm 1, the computations are directly performed on each pair of $[v_i\langle j\rangle]$ and $[u\langle j\rangle]$ and they are never decrypted, no information is leaked regarding v_i and u as long as the encryption scheme is semantically secure. The only place where the original data could be disclosed is at step 2(a) since decryption operations are performed on the intermediate computation results. However, because $x_j = v_i\langle j\rangle - u\langle j\rangle + r_j \mod N$, and r_j is randomly chosen and only known to P_1, x_j is a uniformly distributed in $\mathbb{Z}_N$ from the view point of P_2. Therefore, x_j does not leak any information regarding v_i and u to P_2. The rest of the computations is based on either encrypted or randomized data. As a consequence, if P_1 and P_2 do not collude, no information related to v_i and u is ever disclosed to the two parties. Note that collusion is prohibited under the semi-honest model.

The Secure_Distance^h protocol has the same structure as the Secure_Distance^e protocol, and it is secure under the semi-honest model as well. Secure_Comparison is implemented using a garbled circuit which is also secure under the semi-honest model [24]. Since all these sub-protocols of O-PPBA produce random shares as intermediate results, according to the sequential Composition Theorem [18], the O-PPBA protocol is also secure under the semi-honest model.

Justification of the Use of the Semi-Honest Model.

This adversary model assumes that the participating parties follow the prescribed steps of the protocol. The model may not be appropriate for many situations when we do not have any background knowledge about the parties, e.g., P_1 and P_2 in our case. On the other hand, the semi-honest model suits our problem domain very well because we assume P_1 and P_2 are two cloud service providers. Today, cloud service providers are legitimate and well-known companies like Google, Amazon and Microsoft. It is hard to believe any two of these companies collude to discover the original biometric data. Their reputations are invaluable assets and need to be protect at all costs. Therefore, we can safely assume P_1 and P_2 are semi-honest.

Since a user only sends his or her encrypted biometric data $[u]$ and never participate in any intermediate computations, how the user behaves is irrelevant to the security of the protocol. Just like any authentication protocol, a user can try to probe the system using different passwords, which is out of scope of this paper. However, there does exist technique to either prevent or mitigate this probing attacking. These techniques are independent from but their functionalities complement the proposal O-PPBA protocol. Also, the initial set-up of the biometric authentication system is performed by the entity who owns the biometric database D. All these issues are irrelevant to the security of the O-PPBA protocol. Thus, we will not discuss them any further.

Extension to Other Adversary Models.

In case P_1 and P_2 are not as trustworthy as the existing cloud service providers, we need to extend the O-PPBA protocol to satisfy other adversary models, such as malicious and covert [2] models. Protocols that satisfy the malicious model are generally very expensive and do not have much practical value. This is also evidenced by the fact that almost all practical SMC-protocols are secure under the semi-honest model. In addition, input modification is an open problem in SMC [18]. Before executing an SMC protocol, a participating party can provide wrong input. Since each party's input is private, there is no way to verify the input provided by the party is its actual input. This phenomenon is called input modification, and no solution exists under the general setting of SMC. Because each sub-protocol is non-interactive, any malicious behavior can only lead to a wrong computation result. Under this situation, the malicious behavior can be reduced to input modification. Thus, from a theoretical perspective, to extend the O-PPBA protocol to satisfy the malicious model does not have much value.

On the other hand, the covert model provides both practical value and added security guarantee. In this model, although the honest behavior of a participating party cannot be enforced, a malicious behavior is detectable. Thus, a protocol secure under the covert model is much more efficient than in the malicious model. Here we highlight the key steps involved to make the proposed O-PPBA protocol satisfy the covert model. We will adopt the dual execution strategy proposed in [25]. First, the entity outsources two encrypted copies $[D]_1$ and $[D]_2$ of D. $[D]_1$ is stored at P_1 and encrypted using the public key generated by P_2 (who has the corresponding decryption key). Similarly, $[D]_2$ is stored at P_2 and encrypted using the public key generated by P_1 (who has the corresponding decryption key). Now the proposed O-PPBA protocol can be executed twice with $([D]_1, u)$ and $([D]_2, u)$ as the respective input. Also, the roles of P_1 and P_2 are switched after the first execution. When the final outputs are inconsistent between the two executions, we know one of the parties behaved maliciously. The complexity of this modified protocol is twice as much as the original O-PPBA protocol. Again, since we assume P_1 and P_2 are cloud service providers, the proposed O-PPBA protocol, secure under the semi-honest model, is sufficient and practical.

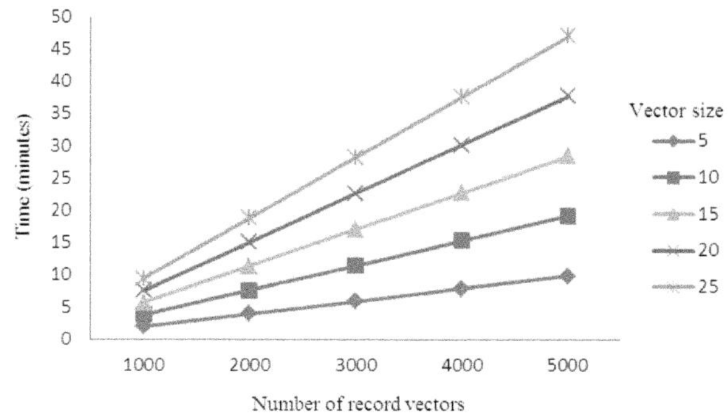

(a) Secure squared-Euclidean distance

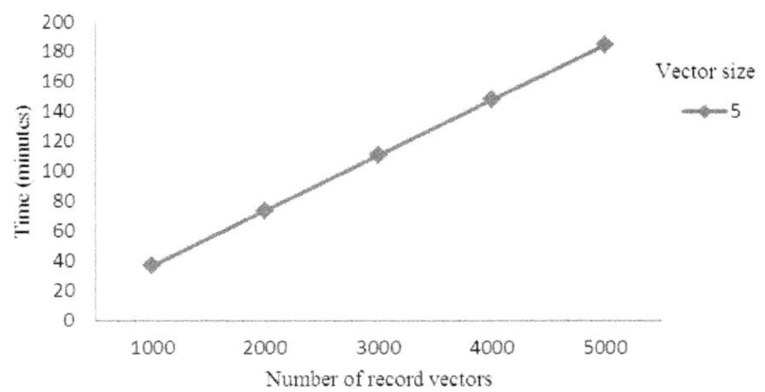

(b) Secure circuit comparison for $m = 5$

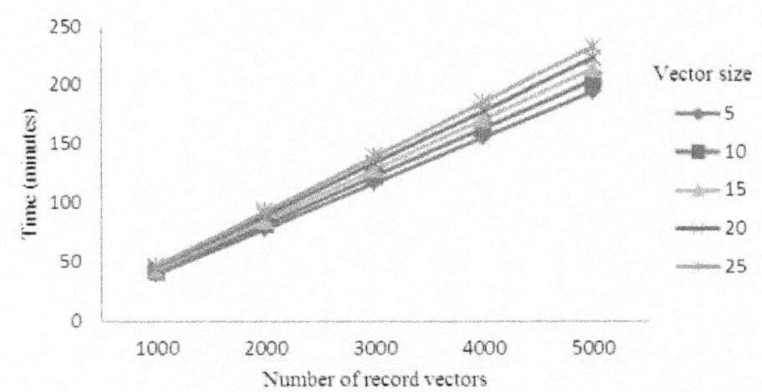

(c) O-PPBA execution time

Figure 1: Time complexities of secure squared-Euclidean distance, secure circuit comparison and O-PPBA for varying values of n, and m

5. PERFORMANCE EVALUATION

In this section, we discuss the performance of the O-PPBA protocol in details under different parameter settings. We look at the performance in term of the execution time. Recall that the proposed protocol is a sequential composition of three sub-protocols. We implemented each sub-protocol and measured their performance on a range of inputs.

We randomly generated synthetic datasets depending on the parameter values in consideration. The advantage of using these synthetic datasets is that we can perform a more elaborated analysis on the computation costs of the proposed protocols under different parameter settings. We randomly generated biometrics feature vectors depending on the parameter values in consideration, such as n- number of record vectors and m-vector size. We encrypted these feature vectors component-wise, using the Paillier cryptosystem [38] with a 1024-bit modulus in our experiments, and the encrypted feature vectors were stored on our machine. Based on this dataset, we performed the O-PPBA protocol. All experiments were done using a Linux machine with an Intel® Xeon® Six-Core^{TM} CPU 3.07 GHz processor and 12GB RAM running Ubuntu 12.04 LTS.

5.1 Performance of O-PPBA

To begin with, we analyze the computation costs of the Secure_Distance^e sub-protocol (Step 1 of Algorithm 3) by varying m and n. We then analyze the computation costs of the secure comparison sub-protocols (Steps 3 and 5 of Algorithm 3) by varying n because m is irrelevant in our secure comparison task.

Secure_Distance^e is implemented using Paillier encryption in C language on top of the GNU multiple precision arithmetic library (https://gmplib.org/). As shown in Figure 1(a), the computation cost grows linearly with n and m. For example, when $m = 5$, the computation time of Secure_Distance^e increases from 1.987 to 9.921 minutes when n is varied from 1000 to 5000.

We build the Secure_Comparison sub-protocol on top of FastGC [24], a Java-based framework that allows users to define boolean circuits. After the circuits are constructed, the framework encrypts the circuits, performs oblivious transfer, and evaluates the garbled/encrypted circuits. The FastGC provides is an 80-bit security level which matches the security level of the homomorphic encryption scheme that we used in our implementation. Since the size of inputs for this stage are fixed by 1024 bits modulus which are random shares of a 1024 bit number, m does not affect the performance for this stage. We evaluated the computation costs of this secure comparison by fixing $m = 5$ and varying values of n. Following from Figure 1(b), the running time of secure circuit comparison varies from 37.45 to 185.013 minutes when n is changed from 1000 to 5000 respectively. Thus, we observed that the running time of secure circuit comparison grows almost linearly with n.

Based on above results, as shown in Figure 1(c), the computation costs of O-PPBA protocol scales approximately linearly with n and m. For example, when $m = 5$, the computation time of O-PPBA increases from 39.032 to 194.934 minutes when n is varied from 1000 to 5000. Based on that, the computation time for O-PPBA is dominated by the time required to compare the encrypted distance vectors. However, when m is sufficiently large (e.g., over 100), the run time complexity of Secure_Distance^e will be greater than Secure_Compare. This is consistent with the upper bound derived in Section 4.3.1.

For $n = 5000$, $m = 25$ and the encryption key size is 1024, the communication cost is roughly 16MB. The time that takes to transmit 16MB of data is significantly less than the computation time. Therefore, this communication complexity could be ignored in the proposed protocol.

5.2 Justification of Using AH-Enc to Implement Secure_Distance

As we claimed that pure garbled circuit based implementation of O-PPBA is not efficient, here we empirically justify

Share size	Distance size	SM-GC	SM-HE
1024	10	1.752s	0.02984s
1024	20	1.792s	0.02985s

Table 2: Garbled circuit vs. homomorphic based secure multiplication

the proposed hybrid implementation is more efficient. Since secure multiplication (SM) is the main building block and performance bottle neck for securely computing the distance in both Euclidean and Hamming metrics, we analyze and compare the computation costs of two different implementations of SM: homomorphic encryption approach (SM-HE) and garbled circuit approach (SM-GC). We compared the running times of the two implementations for varying number of bits required to perform multiplication. Based on the results shown in Table 2, we observed that the running time of each implementation is independent from the input size, and the computation cost of SM-GC is significantly higher than that of SM-HE. For example, the computation time of multiplying two 10-bit numbers using SM-GC is 1.752 seconds whereas in SM-HE is 0.02984 second. Therefore, we adopted homomorphic encryption approach to implement Secure_Distance.

5.3 Performance Improvement

If biometric authentication needs to be done in real time, clearly the proposed O-PPBA protocol is not practical even though it is the best two-party protocol we know of. One main advantage of the proposed protocol is that the computations of the sub-components can be parallelized. For example, at steps 1 and 2 of Algorithm 3, each secure distance computation or secure comparison are independent and can be performed at the same time. Since we assume P_1 and P_2 are cloud service providers, the O-PPBA protocol can take advantage of highly parallel computing capability. If P_1 and P_2 have n nodes available to execute O-PPBA, step 1 can be performed within a second, and step 2 can be performed a little bit over 2 seconds. Thus, the total running time would be around 5 seconds. In general, SMC-based privacy-preserving protocols are very expensive. For real-time applications like biometric authentication, using cloud is the only way to make them practical.

6. FUTURE WORK

In this paper, we proposed an outsourceable and privacy-preserving biometric authentication (O-PPBA) protocol. A main difference from the existing privacy-preserving biometric identification protocols is that the input biometric data of O-PPBA are encrypted. In addition, our protocol does not leak data access patterns, so the proposed O-PPBA protocol is more secure than the existing solutions. Furthermore, we adopted a hybrid approach to implement O-PPBA, in order to take advantages of both homomorphic encryption and garbled circuit based approaches.

Although our construction of O-PPBA is the most efficient secure two-party implementation known today, the empirical results clearly show it is still not practical. As a future work, we will implement it using a cloud to drastically improve its run time complexity. Also, we will utilize more than two parties and the secret sharing based secure multiparty computation framework [12] to produce more efficient O-PPBA protocols.

7. ACKNOWLEDGMENTS

We would like to thank the anonymous reviewers for their constructive feedback. This material is based upon work supported by the Office of Naval Research under award No. N000141110256 and NSF under award No. CNS-1011984.

8. REFERENCES

[1] M. Armbrust, A. Fox, R. Griffith, A. D. Joseph, R. Katz, A. Konwinski, G. Lee, D. Patterson, A. Rabkin, I. Stoica, and M. Zaharia. A view of cloud computing. *Communications of the ACM*, 53:50–58, April 2010.

[2] Y. Aumann and Y. Lindell. Security against covert adversaries: Efficient protocols for realistic adversaries. *Journal of Cryptology*, April 7 2009.

[3] H. Bay, T. Tuytelaars, and L. Gool. Surf: Speeded up robust features. In A. Leonardis, H. Bischof, and A. Pinz, editors, *Computer Vision âĂŞ ECCV 2006*, volume 3951 of *Lecture Notes in Computer Science*, pages 404–417. Springer Berlin Heidelberg, 2006.

[4] I. F. Blake and V. Kolesnikov. One-round secure comparison of integers. *Journal of Mathematical Cryptology*, 3(1):37–68, May 2009.

[5] M. Blanton and M. Aliasgari. Secure outsourced computation of iris matching. *Journal of Computer Security*, 20(2):259–305, 2012.

[6] M. Blanton and P. Gasti. Secure and efficient protocols for iris and fingerprint identification. In *Computer Security–ESORICS 2011*, pages 190–209. Springer, 2011.

[7] W. M. B.S. Manjunathi. Texture features for browsing and retrieval of image data. Aug. 1996.

[8] R. Chow, P. Golle, M. Jakobsson, E. Shi, J. Staddon, R. Masuoka, and J. Molina. Controlling data in the cloud: outsourcing computation without outsourcing control. In *Proceedings of the 2009 ACM workshop on Cloud computing security*, CCSW '09, pages 85–90. ACM, 2009.

[9] C. W. C.M. Pun. Fast and robust, color feature extraction for content-based image retrieval. 2005.

[10] I. Damgård, M. Geisler, and M. Krøigaard. Efficient and secure comparison for on-line auctions. In *Proceedings of the 12th Australasian conference on Information security and privacy*, pages 416–430. Springer-Verlag, 2007.

[11] I. Damgard, M. Geisler, and M. Kroigard. Homomorphic encryption and secure comparison. *International Journal of Applied Cryptology*, 1(1):22–31, 2008.

[12] I. Damgård, M. Keller, E. Larraia, V. Pastro, P. Scholl, and N. Smart. Practical covertly secure mpc for dishonest majority âĂŞ or: Breaking the spdz limits. In J. Crampton, S. Jajodia, and K. Mayes, editors, *Computer Security âĂŞ ESORICS 2013*, volume 8134 of *Lecture Notes in Computer Science*, pages 1–18. Springer Berlin Heidelberg, 2013.

[13] Z. Erkin, M. Franz, J. Guajardo, S. Katzenbeisser, I. Lagendijk, and T. Toft. Privacy-preserving face recognition. In *Privacy Enhancing Technologies*, pages 235–253. Springer, 2009.

[14] T. Ermakova, B. Fabian, and R. Zarnekow. Security and privacy system requirements for adopting cloud computing in healthcare data sharing scenarios. 2013.

[15] D. Evans, Y. Huang, J. Katz, and L. Malka. Efficient privacy-preserving biometric identification. In *Proceedings of the 17th conference Network and Distributed System Security Symposium, NDSS*, 2011.

[16] J. Garay, B. Schoenmakers, and J. Villegas. Practical and secure solutions for integer comparison. In *Proceedings of the 10th international conference on Practice and theory in public-key cryptography*, pages 330–342. Springer-Verlag, 2007.

[17] C. Gentry. Fully homomorphic encryption using ideal lattices. In *Annual ACM Symposium on Theory of Computing*, pages 169–178, Bethesda, MD, USA, 2009.

[18] O. Goldreich. *The Foundations of Cryptography*, volume 2, chapter Encryption Schemes. Cambridge University Press, 2004.

[19] O. Goldreich, S. Micali, and A. Wigderson. Proofs that yield nothing but their validity or all languages in NP have zero-knowledge proof systems. *Journal of the ACM*, 38:690–728, 1991.

[20] S. Goldwasser, S. Micali, and C. Rackoff. The knowledge complexity of interactive proof systems. In *Proceedings of the 17th Annual ACM Symposium on Theory of Computing*, pages 291–304, Providence, Rhode Island, U.S.A., May 6-8 1985.

[21] T. Y. H. Tamura, S. Mori. Texture features corresponding to visual perception. June 1978.

[22] K. Hashizume, D. G. Rosado, E. Fernández-Medina, and E. B. Fernandez. An analysis of security issues for cloud computing. *Journal of Internet Services and Applications*, 4(1):1–13, 2013.

[23] J. Huang, S. R. Kumar, M. Mitra, W.-J. Zhu, and R. Zabih. Image indexing using color correlograms. In *Computer Vision and Pattern Recognition, 1997. Proceedings., 1997 IEEE Computer Society Conference on*, pages 762–768. IEEE, 1997.

[24] Y. Huang, D. Evans, J. Katz, and L. Malka. Faster secure two-party computation using garbled circuits. In *Proceedings of the* 20th *USENIX Security Symposium*, page 35, August 2011.

[25] Y. Huang, J. Katz, and D. Evans. Quid-pro-quo-tocols: Strengthening semi-honest protocols with dual execution. In *IEEE Symposium on Security and Privacy*, pages 272–284, May 2012.

[26] M. S. Islam, M. Kuzu, and M. Kantarcioglu. Access pattern disclosure on searchable encryption: Ramification, attack and mitigation. In *Proceedings of the* 19th *Annual Network & Distributed System Security Symposium (NDSS)*, February 2012.

[27] A. K. Jain, S. Prabhakar, L. Hong, and S. Pankanti. Filterbank-based fingerprint matching. *Image Processing, IEEE Transactions on*, 9(5):846–859, 2000.

[28] C. K. Milkolajczyk. A performance evaluation of local descriptors. Oct. 2005.

[29] J. Katz, A. Sahai, and B. Waters. Predicate encryption supporting disjunctions, polynomial equations, and inner products. In *Advances in*

Cryptology–EUROCRYPT 2008, pages 146–162. Springer, 2008.

[30] K. Kumar and Y.-H. Lu. Cloud computing for mobile users: Can offloading computation save energy? *Computer*, 43(4):51 –56, april 2010.

[31] G.-H. Liu and J.-Y. Yang. Content-based image retrieval using color difference histogram. *Pattern Recognition*, 46(1):188 – 198, 2013.

[32] D. Lowe. Distinctive image features from scale-invariant keypoints. *International Journal of Computer Vision*, 60(2):91–110, 2004.

[33] O. G. Luo Juan. A comparison of sift, pca-sift and surf. 2009.

[34] M. Naor and B. Pinkas. Oblivious transfer and polynomial evaluation. In *Proceedings of the Thirty-first Annual ACM Symposium on Theory of Computing*, pages 245–254, Atlanta, Georgia, United States, 1999. ACM Press.

[35] A. E. Nergiz, M. E. Nergiz, T. Pedersen, and C. Clifton. Practical and secure integer comparison and interval check. In *Proceedings of the IEEE Second International Conference on Social Computing*, pages 791–799, 2010.

[36] V. Nikolaenko, U. Weinsberg, S. Ioannidis, M. Joye, D. Boneh, and N. Taft. Privacy-preserving ridge regression on hundreds of millions of records. In *IEEE Symposium on Security and Privacy*, May 2013.

[37] M. Osadchy, B. Pinkas, A. Jarrous, and B. Moskovich. Scifi-a system for secure face identification. In *IEEE Symposium on Security and Privacy*, pages 239–254. IEEE, 2010.

[38] P. Paillier. Public key cryptosystems based on composite degree residuosity classes. In *Advances in Cryptology - Eurocrypt '99 Proceedings, LNCS 1592*, pages 223–238, Prague, Czech Republic, May 2-6 1999. Springer-Verlag.

[39] I. D. R.M. Haralick, K. Shangmugam. Textural feature for image classification. Nov. 1973.

[40] J. J. Rodrigues, I. de la Torre, G. FernÃąndez, and M. LÃşpez-Coronado. Analysis of the security and privacy requirements of cloud-based electronic health records systems. *Journal of medical Internet research*, 15(5), 2013.

[41] M. D. Ryan. Cloud computing security: The scientific challenge, and a survey of solutions. *Journal of Systems and Software*, 2013.

[42] J. P. S. Belongie, J. Malik. Shape matching and object recognition using shape contexts. Apr. 2002.

[43] A.-R. Sadeghi, T. Schneider, and I. Wehrenberg. Efficient privacy-preserving face recognition. In *Information, Security and Cryptology–ICISC 2009*, pages 229–244. Springer, 2010.

[44] A. Shamir. How to share a secret. *Communications of the ACM*, 22(11):612 – 613, November 1979.

[45] E. Shen, E. Shi, and B. Waters. Predicate privacy in encryption systems. In *Theory of Cryptography*, pages 457–473. Springer, 2009.

[46] S. W. S.M. Lee, J.H. Xin. Evaluation of image similarity by histogram intersection. Aug. 2005.

[47] M. B. W. Burger. Principles of digital image processing: core algorithms. 2009.

[48] B. Wang, S. S. Chow, M. Li, and H. Li. Storing shared data on the cloud via security-mediator. In *International Conference on Distributed Computing Systems-ICDCS 2013*, 2013.

[49] R. S. Y. Ke. Pca-sift: a more distinctive representation for local image descriptors. 2004.

[50] A. C. Yao. How to generate and exchange secrets. In *Proceedings of the 27th IEEE Symposium on Foundations of Computer Science*, pages 162–167. IEEE, 1986.

[51] A. C.-C. Yao. How to generate and exchange secrets. In *Foundations of Computer Science, 1986., 27th Annual Symposium on*, pages 162–167. IEEE, 1986.

[52] H.-J. Yu, H.-S. Lai, K.-H. Chen, H.-C. Chou, J.-M. Wu, S. Dorjgochoo, A. Mendjargal, E. Altangerel, Y.-W. Tien, C.-W. Hsueh, et al. A sharable cloud-based pancreaticoduodenectomy collaborative database for physicians: Emphasis on security and clinical rule supporting. *Computer methods and programs in biomedicine*, 2013.

Understanding OSN-Based Facial Disclosure Against Face Authentication Systems

Yan Li, Ke Xu, Qiang Yan, Yingjiu Li, Robert H. Deng
School of Information Systems, Singapore Management University
{yan.li.2009, kexu.2013, qiang.yan.2008, yjli, robertdeng}@smu.edu.sg

ABSTRACT

Face authentication is one of promising biometrics-based user authentication mechanisms that have been widely available in this era of mobile computing. With built-in camera capability on smart phones, tablets, and laptops, face authentication provides an attractive alternative of legacy passwords for its memory-less authentication process. Although it has inherent vulnerability against spoofing attacks, it is generally considered sufficiently secure as an authentication factor for common access protection. However, this belief becomes questionable since image sharing has been popular in online social networks (OSNs). A huge number of personal images are shared every day and accessible to potential adversaries. This OSN-based facial disclosure (OSNFD) creates a significant threat against face authentication.

In this paper, we make the first attempt to quantitatively measure the threat of OSNFD. We examine real-world face-authentication systems designed for both smartphones, tablets, and laptops. Interestingly, our results find that the percentage of vulnerable images that can used for spoofing attacks is moderate, but the percentage of vulnerable users that are subject to spoofing attacks is high. The difference between systems designed for smartphones/tablets and laptops is also significant. In our user study, the average percentage of vulnerable users is 64% for laptop-based systems, and 93% for smartphone/tablet-based systems. This evidence suggests that face authentication may not be suitable to use as an authentication factor, as its confidentiality has been significantly compromised due to OSNFD. In order to understand more detailed characteristics of OSNFD, we further develop a risk estimation tool based on logistic regression to extract key attributes affecting the success rate of spoofing attacks. The OSN users can use this tool to calculate risk scores for their shared images so as to increase their awareness of OSNFD.

Categories and Subject Descriptors

K.6.5 [**Management of Computing and Information Systems**]: Security and Protection—*Authentication*; I.4.9 [**Image Processing and Computer Vision**]: Applications

ASIA CCS'14, June 4–6, 2014, Kyoto, Japan.

http://dx.doi.org/10.1145/2590296.2590315.

Keywords

Face authentication; online social networks; OSN-based facial disclosure

1. INTRODUCTION

Online social networks (OSNs) have been an essential part of modern social life. As the platforms for experience sharing and social interaction, numerous personal data including personal images are being published in OSNs such as Facebook, Google+, and Instagram at every moment. According to a recent report by Facebook, 350 million personal images are published by users on Facebook every day [40]. It is very likely that these images contain facial images where the users' faces can be clearly seen. The large base number indicates that these shared personal images could become an abundant resource for potential attackers to exploit, which introduces the threat of OSN-based facial disclosure (OSNFD).

OSNFD may have a significant impact on the current face authentication systems, which is one of promising biometrics-based user authentication mechanisms. Face authentication have been widely available on all kinds of consumer-level computing devices such as smartphones, tablets, and laptops with built-in camera capability. Popular face authentication systems include Face Unlock [10], Facelock Pro [8], and Visidon [38] on smartphones/tablets, Veriface [24], Luxand Blink [25], and FastAccess [39] on laptops. These systems provide attractive alternatives of legacy passwords, as face authentication requires zero memory efforts from users and usually has higher entropy than legacy password as users tend to choose easy-to-guess passwords [28]. Previously, the major obstacle for an adversary to compromise face authentication is that physical proximity is required to capture a victim's facial images. However, this is no longer necessary since the appearance of OSNFD. OSNFD provides abundant exploitable resources affecting the applicability of face authentication as it compromises its confidentiality, which is one of fundamental requirements for authentication [14, 18]. The facial images used for face authentication are no longer secrets and can be disclosed in large scale due to OSNFD.

In this paper, we make the first attempt to provide a quantitative measurement on the threat of OSNFD against face authentication. We investigate real-world face-authentication systems designed for both smartphones, tablets, and laptops. These systems recognize users by analyzing facial images captured by built-in cameras. Our study collects users' facial images published in OSNs and uses them to simulate the spoofing attacks against these systems. Since all target systems including Google's Face Unlock [10, 8, 38, 24, 25, 39] are closed-source and do not provide any programmable testing interfaces, enormous efforts are made for image collection and testing. We also build a dataset containing important image attributes that are common in real-life photos but rarely used in prior controlled study on face authentication [6, 13].

Our study reveals interesting results indicating that face authentication may not be suitable to use as an authentication factor. Although the percentage of vulnerable images that can be used for spoofing attacks is moderate, the percentage of vulnerable users that are subject to spoofing attacks is high. On average, the percentage of vulnerable users is 64% for laptop-based systems, and 93% for smartphone/tablet-based systems. Our results also show the difference between systems designed for smartphones/tablets and laptops, as smartphones/tablets have to be accessible in more varied environments. Further investigation shows the quality of images is a more important factor affecting the success rate of spoofing attacks compared to quantity. A user who uploads a few clear facial images is more vulnerable than another user who uploads much more facial images of lower quality due to makeup, illumination, or other negative effects. All these findings show that OSNFD has significantly compromised the confidentiality of face authentication.

In order to understand more detailed characteristics of OSNFD, we further develop a risk estimation tool based on our dataset. Logistic regression is used to extract key attributes affecting the success rate of spoofing attacks. It achieves a precision of 81%, a recall of 83%, and an F1 score of 82% on average. It can help users evaluate the risk of uploading an image by calculating a risk score based on the extracted attributes, which makes them aware of the threat of OSNFD.

The contributions of this paper are summarized as follows:

- We investigate the threat of OSN-based face disclosure (OSNFD) against face authentication. Our results suggest that face authentication may not be suitable to use as an authentication factor, as its confidentiality has been significantly compromised by OSNFD.
- We make the first attempt to quantitatively measure the threat of OSNFD by testing real-world face authentication systems designed for smartphones, tablets, and laptops. We also build a dataset containing important image attributes that significantly affect the success rate of spoofing attacks. These attributes are common in real-life photos but rarely used in prior controlled study on face authentication [6, 13].
- We use logistic regression to extract key attributes that affect the success rate of spoofing attacks. These attributes are further used to develop a risk estimation tool to help users measure the risk score of uploading images to OSNs.

2. PRELIMINARIES

2.1 Face Authentication

Face authentication is a biometrics-based user authentication mechanism, which verifies a user's identity by using information extracted from the user's facial features. As illustrated in Figure 1, a typical face authentication system uses a camera to capture the user's facial image/video as input, and then verifies it with enrolled biometric information for the claimed identity. The objective of a face authentication system is to recognize a user as long as the input is collected from the legitimate user, while rejecting the inputs from all other users.

Two key modules are involved in this verification process. The first module is the face detection module, which identifies the face region and removes irrelevant information of an image. The processed image is then passed to the next module named face match-

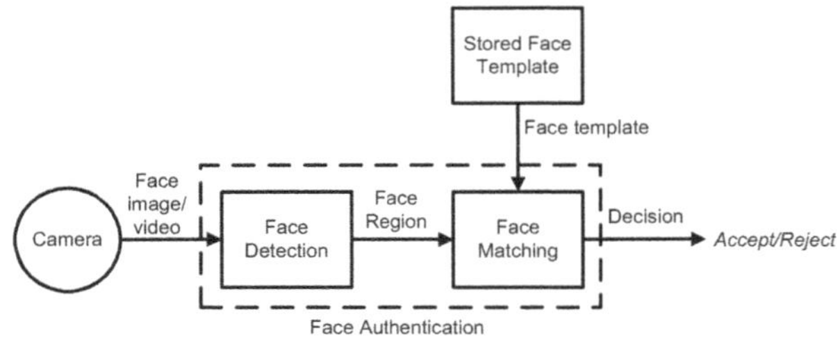

Figure 1: Work flow of a typical face authentication system

ing. This module computes a similarity score for the input image based on an enrolled face template containing key features which can be used to distinguish a user from other users and imposters. Different algorithms may be used for these two modules, but all face authentication systems generally have these two modules and follow this work flow. In the end, a face authentication system outputs the final decision (i.e. accepting or rejecting a claim) according to whether or not the similarity score is higher than a matching threshold. This threshold is carefully chosen so as to achieve a proper balance between false rejection rate and false acceptance rate.

2.2 OSN-based Facial Disclosure and Threat Model

The OSN-based facial disclosure (OSNFD) addresses the issue when users' face biometrics are involuntarily disclosed by sharing personal images in OSNs. These disclosed face biometrics would raise security risks against face authentication systems.

It is a well-known limitation of face authentication that it is subject to spoofing attacks based on captured face biometrics, where an adversary attempts to circumvent user authentication by replaying a victim's facial images/videos collected at an early time. As shown in Figure 1, a face authentication system is not expected to tell whether an input image is from a live user or from a captured image/video, as they are all valid inputs from a legitimate user collected at different times. Nevertheless, the impact of these attacks was believed to be limited due to the requirement that an adversary had to be physically close to a victim in order to collect the required information. Therefore, it is generally considered sufficiently secure as an authentication factor for common access protection [5], as we observe that many face authentication systems [10, 8, 38, 24, 25, 39] such as Google's Face Unlock and Lenovo's Veriface, are widely available on all kinds of consumer-level computing devices. Considering its zero-memory requirement, it does provide an attractive alternative for legacy passwords.

However, this belief may be questionable since OSNFD becomes a common phenomenon. OSNFD supplies an adversary with abundant facial images to exploit and makes large-scale identity theft possible for those who use face authentication. Our work investigates the OSNFD threat and quantitatively measures its impacts. We consider OSNFD-based attacks where an adversary attempts to forge a valid input from image resources disclosed from OSNFD so as to pass face authentication. Our study focuses on image-based attacks unless explicitly mentioned.

The OSNFD threat may be mitigated with liveness detection technologies, which rely on extra information sources or heuristic algorithms to distinguish a live user from a captured image/video. All the existing sophisticated liveness detection technologies associate with considerable costs, which will be explained later in Section 5.2. This may explain that only weak liveness detection technologies are currently deployed on the face authentication systems designed for consumer-level computing devices [29, 19]. For example, eye blinking detection is a common heuristic used by many face authentication systems [10, 38, 29] including Google's Face Unlock; however, it can be easily bypassed using two facial images as demonstrated in [31]. Similar tricks can also apply to other weak liveness detection mechanisms such as head rotation detection [29, 31]. Even worse is that the existing liveness detection mechanisms are disabled by default in most popular face authentication systems [10, 8, 38, 24, 25, 39], as they may have negative impacts on accessibility.

3. DATA COLLECTION AND EMPIRICAL ANALYSIS

In order to quantitatively measure the impacts of OSNFD, we conduct a user study to collect real personal images that have been shared in OSNs. The collected images are used to test against real-world face-authentication systems chosen from the most popular face authentication products in terms of user base [37, 11]. This section describes the detailed process of data collection and the results of our empirical analysis. We use the following classifications in our discussion.

First, we classify the security settings of a face authentication system into *low* and *high*. Most of face authentication products [10, 8, 38, 24, 25, 39] provide very limited choices on security settings that generally affect the recognition threshold used in the face matching module. For example, Google's Face Unlock [10] does not provide any option for users to adjust its security strength. Most of our tested products [8, 38, 24, 25, 39] only have two options for users, labeled as "high accessibility" (i.e. low security) and "high security". Only Lenovo's Veriface [24] provides a scrollbar for users to adjust its security strength from the lowest to the highest. Therefore, we use "low" to indicate that a target system enforces the weakest security protection, and use "high" to indicate the strongest security protection achievable to the system.

Second, we classify face authentication systems into *mobile* and *traditional*. A system is labeled as mobile if it is used for smartphones or tablets, while a traditional system is used for laptops or desktops. A mobile system is usually more tolerant to varied environments, as it should be accessible no matter where a user uses the device. Laptops is considered as traditional as it is not expected to be used from anywhere at any time like what users expect smartphones and tablets.

Third, we classify users into different groups according to the pattern of their sharing behaviors. As observed in our study, it is quite common that a user tends to upload edited images where facial landmarks are significant changed to create better visual appeal. Therefore, it is also an important factor that needs to be considered.

These classifications represent three major factors that affect the effectiveness of OSNFD-based attacks, which are security settings, target platforms, and user behaviors, respectively. We use them as controlled parameters to evaluate the severity of OSNFD, and more sophisticated statistical analysis will be given in the next section to identify the key attributes that can be used to mitigate the OSNFD threat.

3.1 Data Collection

There are 74 participants involved in our study including 36 males and 38 females with age range between 19 and 35. Most of these participants are students in our university. Each participant is paid with 10 dollars as compensation. The study is conducted in a quiet room. The study consists of three parts. In the first part, we ask each participant to select and download 20 *facial* images published within the last 12 months in popular OSNs such as Facebook, Google+, Instagram, etc. A facial image is defined as an image where a participant's face can be seen. But the participant's face may be affected by many negative effects such as blur, occlusion (e.g. covered by a sunglasses), head rotation (e.g. non-frontal head pose). All these effects will be examined in our study.

In the second part, we capture the participant's facial images with 35 controlled head poses and 5 facial expressions using a Canon EOS 60D (18.0-megapixel DSLR CMOS camera). The resulting images are 5184×3456 in size with inner pupil distance of the subjects typically exceeding 400 pixels. 35 controlled head poses are specified by both horizontal and vertical rotation. Rotation angles are represented as (rot_H, rot_V) where rot_H corresponds to the angle of horizontal rotation while rot_V corresponds to the angle of vertical rotation. The value range of rot_H contains $0°$, $10°$ to left/right, $20°$ to left/right, $30°$ to left/right while the value range of rot_V contains $0°$, $10°$ to up/down, $20°$ to up/down. We choose these boundary values according to the common restriction of existing face authentication systems [1], where a participant should not pass user authentication if rot_H exceeds $30°$ or rot_V exceeds $20°$ degrees. On the other hand, 5 facial expressions include neutral expression, smile without showing teeth, smile showing teeth, closed eyes, and open mouth. Continuous lighting system is used to eliminate the shadow on the participants' faces.

We use a helmet equipped wit a gyroscope to control head rotation of the participants. The use of gyroscope has advantages over the other approaches, which includes attaining theoretical accuracy of less than 1 degree, ignoring the head position, measuring only orientation, not affected by metallic interference [27]. For each head pose, we firstly ask the participants to face to the DSLR camera and help them adjust their heads to frontal position in the way similar to [13]. Then the participants rotate their heads to the required angles with help of the gyroscope. The gyroscope generates real-time rotation angles and broadcasts them via WiFi. This rotation information will be received and displayed on an iPad screen, and shown to the participants. Thirdly, we ask the participants to hold their head poses and one of our researchers then removes the helmet gently and quickly in order to avoid movement of the heads during helmet removal. After that, the images of each head pose are captured immediately.

In the final part, the participant will be asked to fill in a questionnaire for collecting the participant's attitudes towards usage of face authentication systems and sharing behaviors in OSNs.

3.2 Empirical Results

Based on the collected images, we inspect the realistic threat of OSNFD against the latest version of popular real-world face authentication systems. We use the common experiment procedure similar to prior work [22, 6], which is described as follows: The frontal image is first used to enroll each participant into a face authentication system. Then we use a participant's own OSN images to test whether it can be used to log in a target face authentication system for his/her own account. The participant's OSN images are displayed on an LCD screen with resolution 1600×900 pixels, and the result whether a target system can be spoofed by an OSN image will be recorded for each system and each image.

Our analysis uses two basic metrics, namely *vulnerable images* and *vulnerable users*. A vulnerable image, denoted by $VulImage$, is defined as a facial image which is wrongly accepted as a genuine user by a face authentication system during user authentication and therefore enables an adversary to circumvent the face authentication system. A vulnerable user, denoted by $VulUser$, is a user enrolled in a face authentication system who has at least one vulnerable image published in OSNs.

Table 1 shows that the face authentication systems are vulnerable to the OSNFD in general. On average, 39% of the OSN images and 77% of the participants are vulnerable. Among popular face authentication systems, Visidon is more vulnerable in low security level, for which 68% of the images and 97% of the participants are vulnerable. Especially for Google's Face Unlock that comes as a built-in feature of all Android-based systems whose version is higher than 4.0 [10], 45% of the OSN images and 86% of the participants are vulnerable.

Table 1: Overall percentage of $VulImage$ and $VulUser$

	$VulImage\%$	$VulUser\%$
Face Unlock	45%	86%
Facelock Pro	46%	96%
Visidon	68%	97%
Veriface	27%	73%
Luxand Blink	20%	41%
FastAccess	33%	80%
Average	39%	77%

Although the percentage of vulnerable images is moderate, the quantity of the vulnerable images is large due to the huge amount of images in OSNs. These large amount of vulnerable images create resources online for potential attacks. Even worse, users share their personal images with their friends in OSNs, most of them tend to publish the images where the users' faces can be clearly viewed for easier recognition. Consequently, the percentage of vulnerable users would be high as observed in our study. The following subsections will further analyze the detailed characteristics of these vulnerable images and users from three major perspectives, security settings, target platforms, and user behaviors.

3.2.1 *Impacts of Security Settings*

Security settings specify the security strength of a face authentication system against potential attacks. As previously explained, most of face authentication products [10, 8, 34, 23, 24, 35] provide very limited choices on security level. So we focus our analysis on lowest and highest security level that can be provided by each system, which are denoted as low security and high security, respectively. Since there is only one security level in Face Unlock and the observed security strength of Face Unlock is comparable to the other systems in low security level, we classify its security level as low. As expected, Figure 2 shows that the face authentication systems in low security level are facing more severe OSNFD threat than those in high security level. On average, 40% of the images and 79% of the participants are vulnerable for the face authentication systems in low security level while 8% of the images and 30% of the participants are vulnerable for the face authentication systems in high security level.

The change of security settings generally affects the recognition threshold in the face matching module. As the security level is raised, the recognition threshold becomes higher which imposes more restrictions for matching between login facial image and prestored facial image. Therefore the face authentication imposes more rigid restrictions on the login facial image. The major restrictions observed in our study are head pose and lighting condition.

For head pose, we use *acceptable head pose range* to measure the tolerance of a face authentication system on head pose variations. It describes the head rotation range of head poses with which at least 50% of the participants successfully log in the face authen-

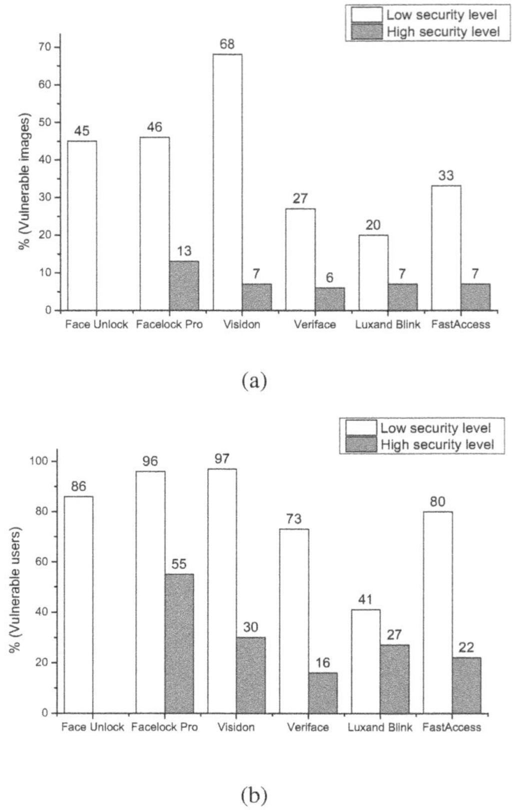

Figure 2: Percentage of $VulImage$ and $VulUser$ in different security levels

tication systems. In these tests, we use participant's frontal image for enrollment and use the images collected with controlled head poses as test inputs (i.e. login images). Figure 3 shows the average results computed from all tested systems, where each closed curve corresponds to the acceptable head pose range. The results for each individual system that indicate the difference between high security and low security are similar to Figure 3, which are not shown.

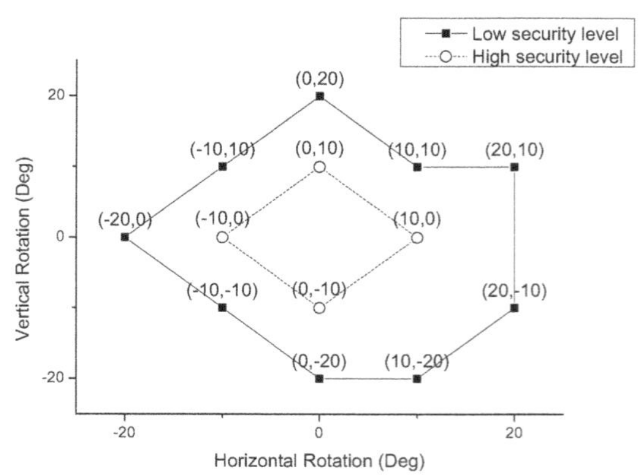

Figure 3: Tolerance of the rotation range of head pose

For lighting condition, we further classify it into different types of illumination and low lighting [9, 43, 20]. The face authentication systems in low security level are observed to have higher tolerance for variation of lighting conditions than the systems in high security level. In our study, illumination is observed in 27% (394 out of 1440) of the OSN images while low lighting is observed in 18% (266 out of 1440) of the OSN images. On average, 81% of the OSN images with illumination and 79% of the OSN images with low lighting cannot be used to log in the face authentication systems in low security level while 96% of the OSN images with illumination and 94% of the OSN images with low lighting cannot be used to log in the systems in high security level.

On the other hand, a face authentication system in low security level has higher tolerance for varied login environments, which is necessary for the system to be usable in the complex environments. As a tradeoff for higher security strength, the false rejection rates in high security level may be significantly increased. As shown in the follow-up experiment described in Section 5.1, the false rejection rate could be as high as 85%. This will cause a significant concern on the accessibility. From our questionnaire on user perception, 70% of the participants think it is important to successfully log in their smartphones, tablets, or laptops at the time they want to use. If the face authentication system is not always functional, 67% of the participants give up using the system which causes the serious accessibility problem to their devices. This may also explain why the popular face authentication systems always use low security level by default.

3.2.2 *Impacts of Target Platforms*

The target platform of a face authentication system imposes the platform-specific requirements on both security and usability. In our tested systems, Face Unlock, Facelock Pro, and Visidon are targeting for mobile platform, while Veriface, Luxand Blink, and FastAccess are targeting for traditional platform.

Figure 4 shows that the OSNFD threat for mobile platform is generally more severe than the OSNFD threat for traditional platform. On average, in low security level, 53% of the images and 93% of the participants are vulnerable for the face authentication systems on mobile platform while 27% of the images and 64% of the participants are vulnerable for the systems on traditional platform. In high security level, 10% of the images and 43% of the participants are vulnerable for the face authentication systems on mobile platform while 7% of the images and 22% of the participants are vulnerable for the face authentication systems on traditional platform.

These results clearly show the difference caused by platform-specific requirements. Compared to a traditional system, a mobile system is usually designed to be more robust and more tolerant to varied environments such as outdoor environment in order to meet accessibility expectation by users. Meanwhile it leads to the more severe OSNFD threat for mobile platform based systems. This difference is confirmed by the results of our questionnaire, which shows that 91% of the participants believe that it is important to log in smartphones or tablets in both indoor and outdoor environment while only 36% of the participants think it is important to log in laptops in both indoor and outdoor environment.

This difference is also revealed in our tests on head pose and lighting condition. Figure 5 shows the face authentication systems targeting for mobile platform have higher tolerance for variations of the head poses than the systems targeting for traditional platform.

Our tests on lighting conditions further show the face authentication systems targeting for mobile platform are more tolerant to variations of the lighting conditions. In our study, 81% of the OSN images with illumination and 77% of the OSN images with low lighting cannot be used to log in the face authentication systems

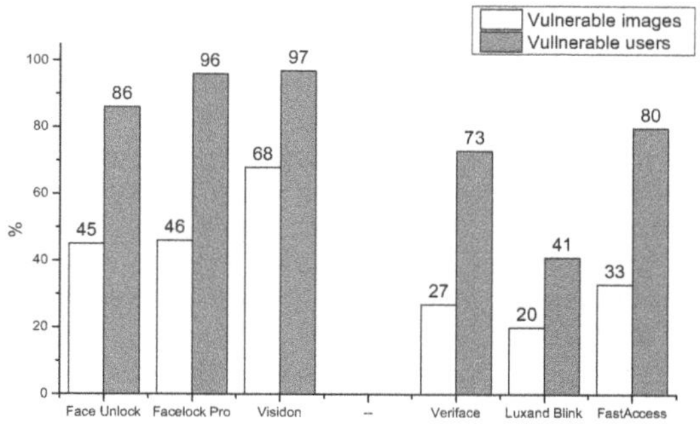

(a) Low security level

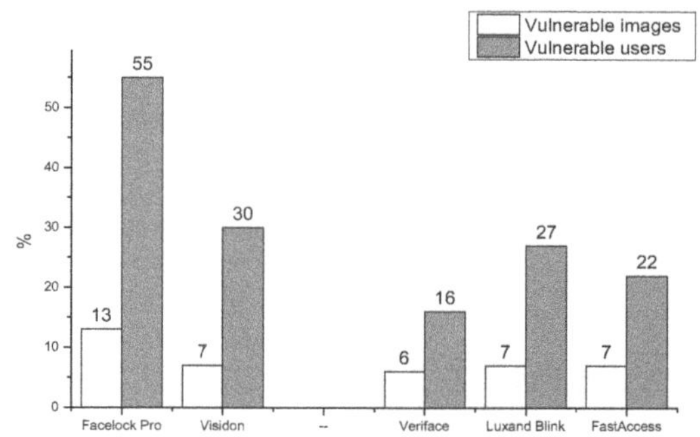

(b) High security level

Figure 4: Difference in $VulImage$ and $VulUser$ between systems targeting for mobile platform and traditional platform.

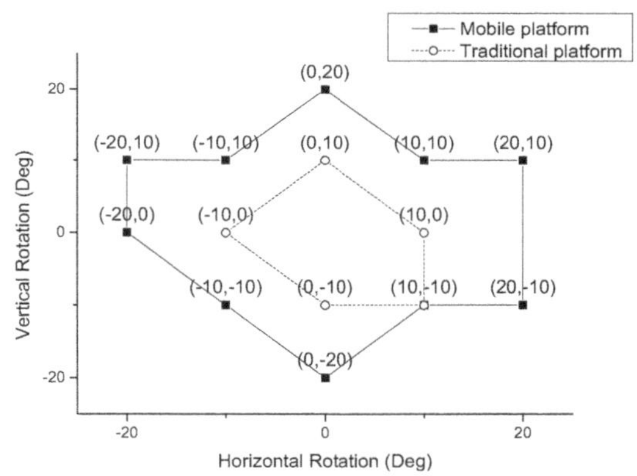

Figure 5: Difference in the tolerance of the rotation range of head pose.

targeting for mobile platform, while these rates increase to 96% for the images with illumination and 96% for the images with low lighting on traditional platform.

3.2.3 *Impacts of User Behaviors*

The difference in user behavior is another major factor influencing the quality of shared images that decides whether these images can be eventually used for successful OSNFD-based attacks. Our study reveals that the participants who publish more facial images in OSNs are not necessarily more vulnerable than those who publish less facial images in OSNs. In fact, the OSNFD threat is more severe among the participants who publish facial images with higher quality in OSNs.

To illustrate the impact of user behaviors, we use the different sharing behaviors and the different OSNFD threat between females and males as example. In our study, female participants are reported to publish facial images in OSNs more frequently than male participants in general. On average, each of the female participants publishes 65 facial images per year while each of the male participants publishes 34 facial images per year. However, the OSNFD threat for the females is less severe than that for the males, as shown in Figure 6.

This can be explained by the lower quality of the OSN images published by the females. We find that the female participants are more likely to publish blurred images, edited images, or images with their makeup. The blur, edit, and makeup can degrade the quality of an image and therefore lead to the difficulty in face recognition [16, 7]. In our study, 12% of the OSN images suffer from these negative effects. Among these low quality images, 61% are published by the females while only 39% of the images are published by the males. All of these blurred, makeup, or edited images fail to pass at least one face authentication system.

4. STATISTICAL ANALYSIS AND RISK ESTIMATION

Although the OSNFD threat is significant as shown in the previous section, we observe the effectiveness of OSNFD-based attacks may be significantly reduced by manipulating certain attributes of facial images. In this section, we extract these key attributes via statistical analysis and use them to develop an estimation tool for end users to calculate the risk of their shared images.

4.1 Key Attributes Affecting OSNFD-based Attacks

From the theoretical perspective, there are still many challenges for face recognition algorithms. These challenges also become key attributes that limit the effectiveness of OSNFD-based attacks. The common attributes addressed in the prior study [1] include head pose, lighting condition, facial expression, facial occlusion, and image resolution. Beside these traditional attributes, we also observe blur, facial makeup, and editing (using Photoshop-like software) as the extra key attributes which often appear in the real world images shared in OSNs, though they are usually not considered in the controlled settings of traditional study on face authentication. We describe the details of these key attributes as follows.

Head pose is a prominent challenge to face recognition. The performance of face recognition algorithms in face authentication can be significantly affected if the head pose in a login image and the head pose in the pre-stored facial image are different [43]. The affecting variations of a head pose mainly include two out-of-plane rotations, namely horizontal rotation and vertical rotation [27].

Lighting condition is another prominent challenge in the realm of face recognition. The variation of lighting conditions mainly includes illumination and low lighting [9, 43, 20]. The illumination is mainly caused when direct light shoots on the 3D structure of a face and strong shadows can be casted which diminish facial features [9, 43]. The illumination can be classified into side illumination and top/bottom illumination [9]. Low lighting is another negative lighting condition, which usually happens when a facial image is taken in dim environment or with extreme bright background. The low lighting may diminish facial features since the luminance in face region is too low for face recognition algorithms to recognize [20].

Facial expression such as smile, surprise, etc, can change face geometry and therefore affect the performance of face recognition algorithms [1]. The common facial expressions include neutral expression, smile without showing teeth, smile showing teeth, closed eyes, open mouth, and other expressions.

Facial occlusion often happens in real world due to additional accessories on face, such as sunglasses, scarf, hands on face, etc. The occlusion can result in the failure of face appearance representation or imprecise facial feature searching and localization, and therefore have negative influence on the performance of face recognition algorithms. The common facial occlusions include forehead occlusion, eyebrow occlusion, eye occlusion, cheek occlusion, and mouth occlusion [1].

The **resolution** of an image can affect accuracy of facial landmark localization and therefore influence the performance of face recognition algorithms. As the resolution of face images decreases, the performance of the face recognition algorithms drops [43].

The **blur** in a facial image causes difficulty in accurate localization of edges of facial region and facial landmarks (i.e. eyes, nose, mouth, etc) by face recognition algorithms and therefore harms the performance of the algorithms.

Facial **makeup** can substantially change the appearance of a face and facial landmarks, such as the alternations of perceived facial shape, nose shape, location of eyebrows, etc. These alternations by the facial makeup, especially by non-permanent facial makeup, challenge face recognition significantly [7].

The **editing** of an image introduces noise pixels and change the appearance of the face in the image [2, 7]. Face recognition algorithms can be affected by these noises and appearance changes due to the edited image.

All these attributes significantly degrade the image quality and therefore lead to the failure of OSNFD-based attacks. They are used as input parameters to build our risk estimation tool in the next section.

4.2 Risk Estimation Model

We use binomial logistic regression [15] to model the impact of the key attributes introduced in the previous subsection. The notions of these attributes are defined in Table 2. Then the key attributes of each image can be represented by an input parameter vector, denoted as $V = (rot_H, rot_V, ill_{sd}, ill_{tb}, dm, bg, FEx_n, FEx_s, FEx_{st}, FEx_{ce}, FEx_m, FEx_{other}, Occ_{fh}, Occ_{eb}, Occ_{eye}, Occ_{chk}, Occ_{mh}, res, blur, mk, ed)$.

For the output, we assign an OSN image to either a positive class or a negative class. The positive class means the image can be used to pass the login of a specific face authentication system, otherwise the image will be in the negative class.

Binomial logistic regression is a classic probabilistic classification model [15], which accepts multiple predictor variables as inputs, and predicts the outcome for a dependent variable which has only two possible types, such as "positive" vs "negative". Thus it is a proper tool to calculate the probability of an image assigned to the positive class based on the key attributes extracted from an OSN image. Given a parameter vector V_i of a facial image i and a face authentication system in a security level, the regression function is

$$\ln\left(p_i/(1-p_i)\right) = \beta_0 + \beta_1 v_1 + \cdots + \beta_m v_m \qquad (1)$$

where p_i is the probability that an image i is assigned to the positive class, v is a parameter in V_i, and β is a regression coefficient. The risk score of the facial image i is the value of p_i. The facial image

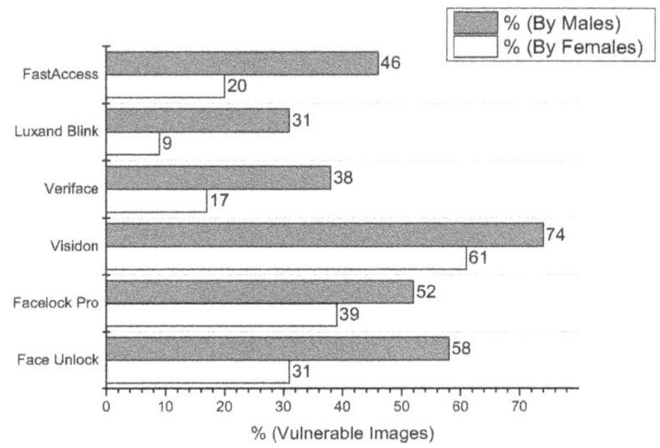

(a) $VulImage\%$ in low security level

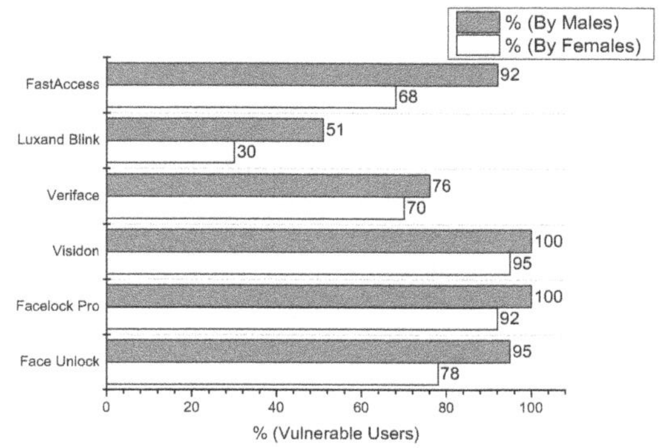

(b) $VulUser\%$ in low security level

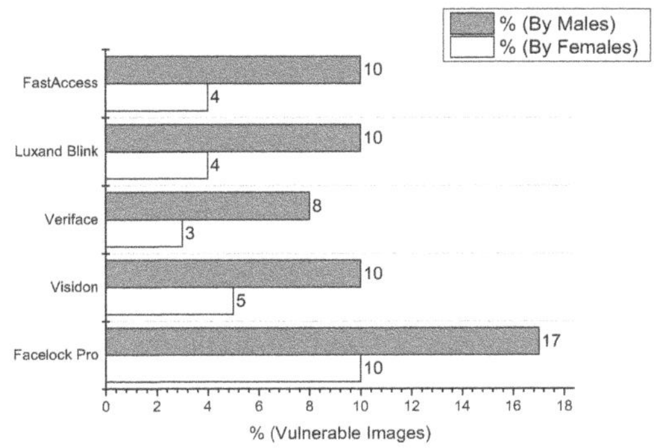

(c) $VulImage\%$ in high security level

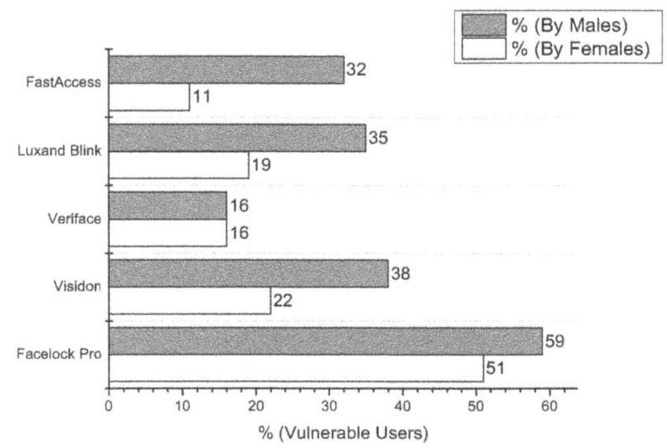

(d) $VulUser\%$ in high security level

Figure 6: Difference in $VulImage$ and $VulUser$ between females and males

Table 2: Parameters related to the key attributes

Attribute	Parameter	Notation
Head pose	Horizontal rotation	rot_H
	Vertical rotation	rot_V
Lighting condition	Side illumination	ill_{sd}
	Top/bottom illumination	ill_{tb}
	Dimness	dm
	Bright background	bg
Facial expression	Neutral	FEx_n
	Smile without showing teeth	FEx_s
	Smile showing teeth	FEx_{st}
	Closed eyes	FEx_{ce}
	Open mouth	FEx_m
	Other expressions	FEx_{other}
Facial occlusion	Occluded forehead	Occ_{fh}
	Occluded eyebrow	Occ_{eb}
	Occluded eye	Occ_{eye}
	Occluded cheek	Occ_{chk}
	Occluded mouth	Occ_{mh}
Resolution	Resolution	res
Blur	Blur	$blur$
Facial makeup	Makeup	mk
Edit	Edit	ed

i is assigned to the positive class if $p_i \geq 0.5$. Otherwise, i is assigned to the negative class. The correctness of these assignments is verified with the ground truth data collected from the previous empirical analysis.

For each combination of face authentication system and its security level, we examine the model fitting of binomial logistic regression and the significance of the parameters by using the real world OSN images and run binomial logistic regression on SAS software [33]. The likelihood ratio test and wald statistic [15] for all the face authentication systems are smaller than 0.0001.

Our statistical analysis shows the most influential attributes are resolution res, occluded eye Occ_{eye}, makeup mk, and illumination ill_{sd}. Resolution res has positive impact on the risk of OSNFD. It is because higher resolution contributes to more accurate facial landmark localization and results in better performance of face recognition and increases the risk of OSNFD. The occluded eye Occ_{eye}, makeup mk, and illumination ill_{sd} have negative impact and lower the risk of OSNFD. In particular, the occluded eye leads to decrease in the performance of face recognition algorithms, as accurate localization of eyes is important for the alignment process in all major face recognition algorithms [1]. Makeup can significantly change the appearance of the face and the facial landmarks and therefore lowers the performance of face recognition. The illumination is a prominent attribute which causes difficulty in face recognition since it diminishes facial features.

The parameters related to other attributes, including head pose and facial expression, are generally not statistically significant. Among the collected OSN images, the variations of head pose and facial expression are limited since users are usually cooperative when these images are captured and tend to publish the images from which they are easily recognized. As observed in our study, the head poses in most OSN images are within the acceptable head pose ranges of the face authentication systems, which causes the insignificance due to lack of samples with extreme head pose. On the other hand, facial expressions observed in most OSN images are only mild-mannered expressions including neutral expression, smile without showing teeth, smile showing teeth, closed eyes, open mouth. These common expressions do not have significant impact as they have been well handled in current face recognition algorithms [1]. Other extreme facial expressions, such as making faces, do significantly affect the face recognition, but they are observed in only 5% of the OSN images.

4.3 Model Evaluation

To evaluate the performance of the proposed risk estimation tool, we use cross-validation method. In each round, for each of the face authentication systems in a specific security level, we randomly choose 80% of the OSN images to train the model and use the risk estimation tool to automatically classify the rest of the images. The above process is repeated by 10 rounds. The performance is measured by standard classification evaluation metrics, including precision, recall, and F1 score [32].

Precision is defined as the percentage of the true positive images among the images assigned to the positive class by the risk estimation tool, which can be calculated by $tp/(tp + fp)$ where tp is the number of true positive images and fp is the number of false positive images. Recall is defined as the percentage of the true positive images detected by the risk estimation tool among the positive images in ground truth, which can be calculated by $tp/(tp + fn)$ where tp is the number of true positive images and fn is the number of false negative images. F1 score considers both the precision and the recall, which can be calculated by $\text{F1} = 2 \times \text{precision} \times \text{recall}/(\text{precision} + \text{recall})$.

Table 3 shows the performance evaluation metrics of the risk estimation tool. On average, the risk estimation tool achieves a precision of 81%, a recall of 83%, and an F1 score of 82%. The performance evaluation indicates that the risk estimation tool detects most of the vulnerable images which can lead to successful OSNFD-based attacks if these images are published in OSNs.

Table 3: Effectiveness of our risk estimation tool

System	Security level	Precision	Recall	F1 score
Face Unlock	N/A	73%	77%	75%
Facelock Pro	Low	70%	69%	69%
	High	81%	75%	78%
Visidon	Low	79%	90%	84%
	High	86%	92%	89%
Veriface	Low	79%	68%	73%
	High	90%	98%	94%
Luxand Blink	Low	84%	87%	85%
	High	87%	90%	88%
FastAccess	Low	77%	67%	72%
	High	89%	95%	92%
Average	N/A	81%	83%	82%

5. DISCUSSION

5.1 Tradeoff between Security and Accessibility

Clear tradeoffs between security and accessibility can be observed in our tested systems, which are decided by security settings and target platforms as analyzed in Section 3.2. The increasing security strength inevitably decreases the accessibility. We conduct a follow-up experiment to collect quantitative evidence for the impact of these tradeoffs.

20 participants from the main user study are invited for this follow-up study. The participants need to enroll their faces in the 6 face authentication systems in low/high security level in a meeting room with normal lighting, respectively. To mimic the different login environment, the experiments are conducted between 2pm-4pm in a sunny day at four fixed indoor/outdoor locations, including 1) a meeting room with normal lighting condition, 2) a meeting room with dim lighting condition, 3) outdoor ground in the sunshine, and 4) shelter of building. This setting simulates a situation when a user registers in one place, but tries to access the system in many other places. The participants are asked to login by using each face authentication systems. In this experiment, there are no OSN images, but only live legitimate users who attempt to access a face authentication system. Each participant has at most three attempts for each login before we record it as a false rejection.

Table 4 shows the false rejection rates of the face authentication systems in low security level are lower than those of the face authentication systems in high security level in overall. Moreover, the face authentication systems on mobile platform have lower false rejection rates than those on traditional platform. The highest observed false rejection rate is 85% for Veriface in high security level. This accessibility degradation could be a disaster for end users. In our questionnaire, 91% of the participants believe that it is important to log in smartphones and tablets in both indoor and outdoor environments, while 36% of the participants think that it is important to log in laptops in both indoor and outdoor environments. If a face authentication system is set to high security level in order to mitigate the OSNFD threat, the system will be less tolerant for complex environments and violate the users' need of accessibility.

Table 4: Significant increase in false rejection rates when using high security level settings. The increments of false rejection rates are more significant for traditional platform-based systems (the last three systems).

System	Security level	Room+ normal lighting	Room+ dim lighting	Outdoor ground	Shelter
Face Unlock	N/A	0%	5%	10%	0%
Facelock Pro	Low	0%	10%	10%	0%
	High	0%	45%	60%	25%
Visidon	Low	0%	5%	5%	0%
	High	5%	55%	65%	50%
Veriface	Low	0%	25%	35%	20%
	High	10%	60%	85%	60%
Luxand Blink	Low	0%	30%	50%	45%
	High	5%	55%	70%	55%
FastAccess	Low	0%	15%	30%	15%
	High	5%	55%	65%	55%

5.2 Costs of Liveness Detection

Liveness detection could be a mitigation for OSNFD-based attacks, which is designed to distinguish between a live face and a facial image in front of the camera. The most common liveness detection mechanisms deployed on popular face authentication systems are eye-blinking and head rotation detection, as they have the advantages of no additional hardware support, requiring moderate image quality, and involving relatively low usability cost. This is important to all consumer-level products that are price-sensitive and accessibility-first. However, these two mechanisms can be easily bypassed with one or two pre-catched images as shown in [31]. The practicality of these attacks is also verified by our experiments.

Besides these two simple mechanisms, several sophisticated liveness detection techniques have been proposed for face authentication. However, all of them are associated with considerable costs as shown in Table 5 [29]. Their costs include requiring additional hardware, high quality images, ideal environment that are usually not universally available, and high user collaborations that may cause inconvenience. This indicates they may not be suitable for consumer-level face authentication systems. It still remains a challenge to deploy reliable and practical liveness detection in face authentication systems that can be used by the public.

Table 5: Costs associated with existing liveness detection mechanisms for face authentication. * sign indicates a requirement involves a significant cost for end users or device manufacturers.

Liveness detection	Image quality	Additional hardware	Usability cost
Eye blinking	Low	No	Low
Mouth movement	Middle	No	Middle
Degradation	High*	No	Low
Head movement	High*	No	Middle
Facial expressions	High*	No	Middle
Facial thermogram	N/A	Yes*	Low
Multi-modal	N/A	Yes*	Middle/High*
Facial vein map	N/A	Yes*	Middle
Interactive response	N/A	Yes*	High*

5.3 Implications of Our Findings

Face authentication does provide an attractive alternative of user authentication for its non-intrusive and zero-memory procedure. However, the appearance of OSNFD brings a significant threat to question the practicality of face authentication as a usable authentication factor. Nowadays, a huge amount of personal facial images/videos have been published in OSNs that can be accessible to potential adversaries without the previously required physical proximity. Therefore, face biometrics can now be disclosed in large scale and acquired by adversaries remotely. Face biometrics are no longer secrets only owned by the users and can be disclosed to anyone who has access to victim's personal images shared in OSNs.

Raising the security level of face authentication systems could mitigate the OSNFD threat by scarifying the accessibility, which leads to the inconvenience for legitimate users. Liveness detection is another major countermeasure to mitigate the spoofing attack against the face authentication systems. Unfortunately, existing liveness detection techniques available on consumer-level computing devices can be easily circumvented by one or two images. More reliable liveness detection like multi-modal mechanisms usually relies on using additional authentication factor (e.g. another biometrics such as voice and fingerprint). This introduces another liveness detection problem for the additional authentication factor, which may not be reliable. For example, voice and fingerprint can also be spoofed. Even worse, more serious privacy concerns will rise if a system requires to collect many biometrics information from a user [42], which may eventually cause the rejection of the liveness detection mechanism.

As the emergence of OSNFD, the face biometrics is losing confidentiality which is one of the fundamental requirements for a usable authentication factor. Moreover, the existing liveness detection techniques are either too weak to defend against the OSNFD or too difficult to be deployed on the consumer-level devices. All these findings suggest that face authentication may not be a proper authentication factor unless we can resolve the discovered problems.

5.4 Limitations

Ecological validity is a challenge to any user study. Like most prior research [12, 35, 3], our study only recruits students in university. These participants are more active in using consumer-level computing devices and sharing images in OSNs. Thus the evaluation of the OSNFD may vary with other populations.

In the user study design, it is still a challenge to collect facial images with precisely controlled head poses [27]. Like the prior head pose data sets [13, 23, 34], the accuracy of the head poses in our data set may be affected by the poor ability of the participant to accurately direct his/her head, the unconscious movement of human beings and limit of resources. In another experiment of examining the false rejection rates of the face authentication systems, we choose 4 locations to mimic different login environments in daily life. Since it is impossible for all the participants to do the tests at the same time and at the same physical positions, the background of image inputs captured by the camera may change.

Another challenge in our study is to accurately estimate parameters [21] such as head pose, illumination, and makeup in our collected OSN dataset. Since the accuracy of automatic labeling tools is limited [1, 30], we manually label the OSN images with the help of automatic tools and follow the similar validating methodology used in prior study [21, 17, 41]. For each OSN image, we estimate the head pose with typical head pose estimation algorithms including POSIT and LGBP [27]. And we manually validate the estimation of the head pose by comparison between the OSN image and the participant's images with controlled head poses. We manually label the parameters related to lighting conditions according to the shadow and histogram of face region similar to the approaches in [21, 17]. The parameters related to facial expressions are label by comparing the OSN image with the images captured in our user study, which is similar to [21, 17]. We use popular face detection software Picasa to mark the face region with a rectangle in the image and calculate the resolution of the face region. The parameters related to the attributes of blur, makeup, and edit are labeled in the way similar to [21, 17, 41].

It is also possible to further improve our risk estimation tool. To our best knowledge, our work is the first attempt to semi-automatically detect the vulnerable images that can be used to attack face authentication. Our current risk estimation tool can serve as a baseline for future improvement by refining the key parameters and the statistical model. It is also valuable to incorporate automatic high accuracy labeling for those hard-to-label attributes like illumination and facial makeup, once the ongoing research [27, 9, 7] resolves these challenges.

6. RELATED WORK

In this section, we summarize the closely related work in terms of face recognition, spoofing attack, and liveness detection.

In face recognition, holistic approaches and local landmark based approaches are the two major types of popular face recognition algorithms [1, 43]. The holistic approaches, such as PCA-based algorithms and LDA-based algorithms, use the whole face region as input. Local landmark based approaches extract local facial landmarks such as eyes, nose, mouth, etc and feed locations and local statistics of these local facial landmarks into a structure classifier.

Face authentication is an important application of face recognition, which validates a claimed identity based on comparison between a facial image and an enrolled facial image and determines either accepting or rejecting the claimed identity [26]. Trewin et al. [36] show that the face authentication is faster and causes lower interruption of user memory recall task than voice, gesture, and typical password entry. Another advantage of face authentication is that it provides stronger defense against repudiation than token based authentication and password based authentication [28]. Besides face authentication, face identification is another application of face recognition, which compare a facial image with multiple registered users and identifies the user in the facial images. The face identification can cause privacy leakage in OSNs due to the identifiable personal images published in OSNs [3, 12]. Compared to their work, our study focuses on investigating the impact of the shared personal images that can be used to attack face authentication systems.

It is a well-known fact that face authentication is subject to spoofing attacks. An attacker can pass the authentication by displaying images or videos of a legitimate user in hard copy or on the screen [5]. But it is generally believed sufficiently secure as an authentication factor for common access protection, as an adversary usually has to be physically proximate to a victim in order to collected required face biometrics. Our findings indicate that this belief is not valid as the emergence of OSNFD. Face biometrics can now be disclosed in large scale and acquired by a remote adversary.

Liveness detection is the major countermeasure designed to mitigate the risk of spoofing attacks. Interaction based approach, multimodal based approach, and motion based approach are three popular types of liveness detection [29, 19, 4]. Interaction based approaches require real-time responses from claimants, including eye blink, head rotation, facial expression, etc. However, these approaches can be bypassed with one or two images [31]. Multimodal based approaches take face biometric and other biometrics into consideration together such as voice, facial thermogram, etc [29]. The multi-modal based approaches require additional hardware and specific environment. Motion based approaches are based on the detection of involuntary motions of a 3D face, such as involuntary rotation of head [19]. The approaches require high quality images captured with ideal lighting condition. Compared to these approaches, our estimation tool addresses this problem from a different perspective. Since OSNFD significantly compromise the confidentiality of face authentication, our tool is designed to increase the users' awareness before they publish their personal images so as to reduce the number of exploitable images available to an adversary.

7. CONCLUSION

In this paper, we investigated the threat of OSN-based facial disclosure (OSNFD) against some real-world face authentication systems. Our results show that the face authentication systems are vulnerable to OSNFD-based attacks. We analyzed the characteristics of these attacks from three major perspectives including security settings, target platforms and user behavior. The key attributes of the OSNFD were further extracted to develop a risk estimation tool that can help users understand the risks associated with their personal images shared in OSNs. Our work made the first step in systematically understanding the OSNFD. Quantitative evidence indicates that face authentication may not be a proper authentication factor as the confidentiality of face biometrics has been significantly compromised by OSNFD.

8. ACKNOWLEDGMENTS

The authors would like to thank Swee Won Lo (School of Information Systems, Singapore Management University) for her help and discussion on the user study and data collection. The authors would also like to thank Jianhui Huang (School of Information Systems, Singapore Management University) for his help and discussion on the the risk estimation model.

9. REFERENCES

[1] A. F. Abate, M. Nappi, D. Riccio, and G. Sabatino. 2d and 3d face recognition: A survey. *Pattern Recognition Letters*, 28(14):1885–1906, 2007.

[2] M. Abdel-Mottaleb and M. H. Mahoor. Assessment of blurring and facial expression effects on facial image recognition. In *Advances in Biometrics*, pages 12–18, 2005.

[3] A. Acquisti, R. Gross, and F. Stutzman. Faces of facebook: Privacy in the age of augmented reality. *BlackHat USA*, 2011.

[4] A. Anjos and S. Marcel. Counter-measures to photo attacks in face recognition: a public database and a baseline. In *Biometrics (IJCB), 2011 International Joint Conference on*, pages 1–7, 2011.

[5] B. Biggio, Z. Akhtar, G. Fumera, G. Marcialis, and F. Roli. Security evaluation of biometric authentication systems under real spoofing attacks. *Biometrics, IET*, 1:11–24, 2012.

[6] I. Chingovska, A. Anjos, and S. Marcel. On the effectiveness of local binary patterns in face anti-spoofing. In *Biometrics Special Interest Group (BIOSIG), 2012 BIOSIG - Proceedings of the International Conference of the*, pages 1–7, 2012.

[7] A. Dantcheva, C. Chen, and A. Ross. Can facial cosmetics affect the matching accuracy of face recognition systems? In *Biometrics: Theory, Applications and Systems (BTAS), 2012 IEEE Fifth International Conference on*, pages 391–398, 2012.

[8] Facelock.mobi. http://www.facelock.mobi/facelock-for-apps.

[9] A. S. Georghiades, P. N. Belhumeur, and D. J. Kriegman. From few to many: Illumination cone models for face recognition under variable lighting and pose. *Pattern Analysis and Machine Intelligence, IEEE Transactions on*, 23(6):643–660, 2001.

[10] Google. http://www.android.com/about/ice-cream-sandwich/.

[11] Google. https://play.google.com/store/apps?hl=en.

[12] R. Gross and A. Acquisti. Information revelation and privacy in online social networks. In *Proceedings of the 2005 ACM workshop on Privacy in the electronic society*, pages 71–80, 2007.

[13] R. Gross, I. Matthews, J. Cohn, T. Kanade, and S. Baker. Multi-pie. *Image and Vision Computing*, 28(5):807–813, 2010.

[14] A. J. Harris and D. C. Yen. Biometric authentication: assuring access to information. *Information Management & Computer Security*, 10(1):12–19, 2002.

[15] D. W. Hosmer Jr, S. Lemeshow, and R. X. Sturdivant. *Applied logistic regression*. Wiley. com, 2013.

[16] F. Hua, P. Johnson, N. Sazonova, P. Lopez-Meyer, and S. Schuckers. Impact of out-of-focus blur on face recognition performance based on modular transfer function. In *Biometrics (ICB), 2012 5th IAPR International Conference on*, pages 85–90, 2012.

[17] G. B. Huang, M. Mattar, T. Berg, E. Learned-Miller, et al. Labeled faces in the wild: A database forstudying face recognition in unconstrained environments. In *Workshop on Faces in'Real-Life'Images: Detection, Alignment, and Recognition*, 2008.

[18] A. K. Jain, A. Ross, and S. Pankanti. Biometrics: A tool for information security. *Trans. Info. For. Sec.*, 1(2):125–143, 2006.

[19] K. Kollreider, H. Fronthaler, and J. Bigun. Non-intrusive liveness detection by face images. *Image and Vision Computing*, 27(3):233–244, 2009.

[20] S. G. Kong, J. Heo, B. R. Abidi, J. Paik, and M. A. Abidi. Recent advances in visual and infrared face recognitionąła review. *Computer Vision and Image Understanding*, 97(1):103–135, 2005.

[21] N. Kumar, A. C. Berg, P. N. Belhumeur, and S. K. Nayar. Attribute and simile classifiers for face verification. In *Computer Vision, 2009 IEEE 12th International Conference on*, pages 365–372, 2009.

[22] I. Lab. https://www.idiap.ch/dataset/replayattack.

[23] K.-C. Lee, J. Ho, and D. J. Kriegman. Acquiring linear subspaces for face recognition under variable lighting. *Pattern Analysis and Machine Intelligence, IEEE Transactions on*, 27(5):684–698, 2005.

[24] Lenovo. http://en.wikipedia.org/wiki/VeriFace.

[25] Luxand. http://www.luxand.com/.

[26] H. Moon and P. J. Phillips. The feret verification testing protocol for face recognition algorithms. In *Automatic Face and Gesture Recognition, 1998. Proceedings. Third IEEE International Conference on*, pages 48–53, 1998.

[27] E. Murphy-Chutorian and M. M. Trivedi. Head pose estimation in computer vision: A survey. *Pattern Analysis and Machine Intelligence, IEEE Transactions on*, 31(4):607–626, 2009.

[28] L. O'Gorman. Comparing passwords, tokens, and biometrics for user authentication. *Proceedings of the IEEE*, 91(12):2021–2040, 2003.

[29] G. Pan, L. Sun, Z. Wu, and S. Lao. Eyeblink-based anti-spoofing in face recognition from a generic webcamera. In *Computer Vision, 2007. ICCV 2007. IEEE 11th International Conference on*, pages 1–8, 2007.

[30] P. J. Phillips, P. J. Flynn, T. Scruggs, K. W. Bowyer, J. Chang, K. Hoffman, J. Marques, J. Min, and W. Worek. Overview of the face recognition grand challenge. In *Computer vision and pattern recognition, 2005. CVPR 2005. IEEE computer society conference on*, volume 1, pages 947–954, 2005.

[31] J. Rice. http://www.androidpolice.com/2012/08/03/android-jelly-beans-face-unlock-liveness-check-circumvented-with-simple-photo-editing/.

[32] C. J. V. Rijsbergen. *Information Retrieval.* Butterworth-Heinemann, 1979.

[33] SAS. http://www.sas.com/.

[34] T. Sim, S. Baker, and M. Bsat. The cmu pose, illumination, and expression database. *Pattern Analysis and Machine Intelligence, IEEE Transactions on*, 25(12):1615–1618, 2003.

[35] F. Stutzman, R. Gross, and A. Acquisti. Silent listeners: The evolution of privacy and disclosure on facebook. *Journal of Privacy and Confidentiality*, 4(2):2, 2013.

[36] S. Trewin, C. Swart, L. Koved, J. Martino, K. Singh, and S. Ben-David. Biometric authentication on a mobile device: a study of user effort, error and task disruption. In *Proceedings of the 28th Annual Computer Security Applications Conference*, pages 159–168, 2012.

[37] VagueWare.com. http://www.vagueware.com/top-globally-popular-face-recognition-software/.

[38] Visidon. http://www.visidon.fi/en/Home.

[39] S. Vision. http://www.sensiblevision.com/en-us/home.aspx.

[40] K. Wagner. http://mashable.com/2013/09/16/facebook-photo-uploads/.

[41] Z. Wang, A. C. Bovik, H. R. Sheikh, and E. P. Simoncelli. Image quality assessment: From error visibility to structural similarity. *Image Processing, IEEE Transactions on*, 13(4):600–612, 2004.

[42] J. D. Woodward. Biometrics: Privacy's foe or privacy's friend? *Proceedings of the IEEE*, 85(9):1480–1492, 1997.

[43] W. Zhao, R. Chellappa, P. J. Phillips, and A. Rosenfeld. Face recognition: A literature survey. *ACM Computing Surveys (CSUR)*, 35(4):399–458, 2003.

Tracing and Revoking Leaked Credentials: Accountability in Leaking Sensitive Outsourced Data

Hua Deng
School of Computer
Wuhan University
Wuhan, P. R. China
denghua@whu.edu.cn

Qianhong Wu
School of Electronic and Information Engineering
Beihang University, P.R. China
qianhong.wu@buaa.edu.cn

Bo Qin
School of Information
Renmin University of China
Beijing, P. R. China
bo.qin@ruc.edu.cn

Sherman S. M. Chow
Department of Information Engineering
Chinese University of Hong Kong, Hong Kong
sherman@ie.cuhk.edu.hk

Josep Domingo-Ferrer
Department of Computer Engineering and Mathematics
Universitat Rovira i Virgili
Catalonia
josep.domingo@urv.cat

Wenchang Shi
School of Information
Renmin University of China
Beijing, P. R. China
wenchang@ruc.edu.cn

ABSTRACT

Most existing proposals for access control over outsourced data mainly aim at guaranteeing that the data are only accessible to authorized requestors who have the access credentials. This paper proposes TRLAC, an *a posteriori* approach for tracing and revoking leaked credentials, to complement existing *a priori* solutions. The tracing procedure of TRLAC can trace, in a black-box manner, at least one traitor who illegally distributed a credential, without any help from the cloud service provider. Once the dishonest users have been found, a revocation mechanism can be called to deprive them of access rights. We formally prove the security of TRLAC, and empirically shows that the introduction of the tracing feature incurs little costs to outsourcing.

Categories and Subject Descriptors

E.3 [**Data**]: Data Encryption

Keywords

Cloud computing; Data security; Access control; Accountability; Leakage; Tracing; Broadcast encryption

1. INTRODUCTION

In recent years, cloud computing has emerged as one of the most promising computing paradigms. For example, it has been used in healthcare applications such as mobile health monitoring [30], patient-controlled encryption [12], etc. In the context of storage, a user can outsource a huge amount of data to a cloud storage server maintained by a cloud service provider (CSP). Both the user and any authorized peers can access (and process) the outsourced data from anywhere anytime. In this way, users can obtain storage and computing resources on demand without local hardware and software maintenance burden.

Security and privacy are widely recognized to be one of the main barriers for the public to accept cloud computing (e.g., [31, 33]). Numerous existing approaches (to be reviewed in Section 2) have been proposed, but most of them are *a priori* or only provide *outsider security* in the sense that only those insiders who hold some appropriate access credentials (or secret keys) can retrieve the data in plaintext, while those outsiders who have no credentials cannot. This is insufficient since the insiders may be hacked or may simply intentionally leak their credentials for other benefits. Unfortunately, while it is crucial to obtain electronic evidence in a court of law after leakage incident [18], it can be challenging to enforce digital forensics analysis in cloud computing due to the separation of the data ownership and its physical access control, and few efforts have been made to facilitate digital forensics analysis of credential leakage. Countermeasures should be adopted to trace and then revoke the compromised credentials to minimize the exposure risks to future data. This observation motivates us to investigate an *a posteriori* approach to enhance the access control over outsourced data.

Our contribution includes the following aspects. We propose TRLAC, a system for tracing and revoking leaked access credentials for accessing data outsourced to clouds, by extending an existing identity-based broadcast encryption [14] and leveraging optimal fingerprint codes [23] to encode each authorized user's credential (which is the decryption key for the encryption system). In our TRLAC system, users are organized in different groups and given credentials associated with their groups' identities and fingerprint codes. Before outsourcing data, the data owners can encrypt them by specifying a set of groups in which the members should be granted access. When credential leakage has occurred, even if multiple credentials are embedded in a pirate decoder box, a tracing procedure can be run in a black-box manner (without knowing how the decoder box was produced) to trace at least one compromised key among those used to create the

ASIA CCS'14, June 4–6, 2014, Kyoto, Japan.
Copyright 2014 ACM 978-1-4503-2800-5/14/06 ...$15.00.
http://dx.doi.org/10.1145/2590296.2590342 .

decoder box. The tracing procedure does not require the help of the CSP, who may not even know that a tracing procedure has been invoked. When compromised credentials are found out by the tracing procedure, the owners can revoke the privileges associated to those credentials for accessing the outsourced data.

We conduct a thorough analysis of the proposed TRLAC scheme. Its security is formally reduced to the security of the collusion resistance of the underlying fingerprint codes and the semantic security (against chosen-plaintext attacks) of the identity-based broadcast encryption scheme. We also perform a comprehensive performance evaluation. Both the theoretical analysis and the experimental results confirm that our scheme can trace illegal credentials almost without any extra cost to file creation and access procedures in cloud storage. The cost of the user admission procedure is affected more by the introduction of tracing, yet it is pretty acceptable to a typical administrator machine which act as a key distribution center. The revocation mechanism only requires few computations and we will show empirically that it is very cost-effective. These advantageous features make our scheme a promising solution to secure sensitive data that are being outsourced to untrusted clouds.

The rest of this paper is organized as follows. Section 2 reviews the related work in the literature. Section 3 presents our system framework and a threat model. We present our TRLAC construction in Section 4. In Section 5, the security of TRLAC is formally analyzed. We evaluate the performance of our TRLAC system both theoretically and experimentally in Section 6. Section 7 concludes the paper.

2. RELATED WORK

It is essential for the owners to validate that their data are kept intact to guarantee availability. Sebé and Domingo-Ferrer *et al.* [26] identified the requirements to remotely check integrity of the data stored by a third party. Ateniese *et al.* [2] proposed a model of provable data possession (PDP) and realized the first PDP scheme. Various privacy concerns of PDP have also been addressed. To not only outsource the data storage but also its integrity auditing, we have a privacy-preserving scheme [33] which enables a third party auditor (TPA) to simultaneously perform multiple auditing tasks, without allowing the TPA to infer the data being audited. For enterprise uses, preserving anonymity of the uploader from the view of the cloud also matters, and that can be achieved with the help of a security-mediator in [31], without letting the mediator link the upload to the identity of the user, or learn the data being uploaded.

One way to allow only authorized users to access the service is authentication. Chow *et al.* [10] proposed SPICE, a simple privacy-preserving identity-management for cloud environment, which provided various features such as delegatable verification from one CSP to another CSP, yet not covered by previous privacy-preserving authentication schemes. Qin *et al.* [25] proposed an identity-based signcryption scheme for proving a user's access right. A scheme with public verifiability (e.g., [11]) can further allow verification of signcryption without requiring the verifier to know the encrypted content. These solutions, even though employed cryptographic techniques, require trusting the server to act according to the authentication results.

The standard way to achieve data privacy is to encrypt the data before they are outsourced. The users allowed to access the digital content are given credentials in the form of secret decryption keys. Some early works (e.g., [27]) adopt traditional public key encryption, such as RSA, which can be cumbersome regarding key management and public-key validation before encryption. To circumvent these problems, Boneh and Franklin proposed the first practical identity-based encryption (IBE) [4], in which the users' public keys are their identities (e.g., email addresses, telephone numbers). In the one-to-many encryption scenario, Delerablée [14] presented an identity-based broadcast encryption (IBBE) to enable a sender to encrypt his data once by specifying a set of identities so that the receivers with the specified identities can decrypt the same ciphertext. Recent works (e.g., [19, 15]) have employed attribute-based encryption (ABE) such as multi-authority ABE (e.g., [8]) to provide flexible and fine-grained access to encrypted data, although this is achieved by sacrificing the efficiency of encryption and decryption to some extent.

Cloud users should be able to retrieve selected items without downloading and decrypting all outsourced files and then searching locally. Encryption schemes which satisfy this requirement are called searchable encryption. Examples include deterministic encryption (e.g., [3, 36]) and public-key searchable encryption with post-search privacy [34] and for multi-dimensional search [32].

All the aforementioned works only provide *a priori* approaches to secure outsourced data. For tracing traitors who leaked decryption keys, Boneh *et al.* [6, 7] constructed two collusion-resistant public-key broadcast encryption schemes, with ciphertext size being sub-linear in the sub-linear in the total number of users in the whole system. Note that in the first scheme [6], encryption can only be done to all the system users. That is different from the second scheme [7], in which the encryptor can *revoke* some set of users from accessing the plaintext. In ABE, multiple users could decrypt the same ciphertext, as long as their credentials satisfy the condition pre-defined by the encryptor. Liu *et al.* [22] proposed a white-box-traceable ABE, which is weak since the white-box traceability model assumes dishonest users to be traced have directly disclosed their credentials. Subsequently, they constructed black-box traceable ABE ([20, 21]) based on the Boneh *et al.*'s constructions ([6, 7]). These schemes [6, 7, 22, 20, 21] suffer from the lower efficiency when compared with prime-order group construction in general. In view of the lower efficiency of composite-order groups, Garg *et al.*'s construction [16] is built in prime-order bilinear groups. On the other hand, Boneh and Naor [5] proposed a way to achieve traitor tracing functionality for public-key encryption by exploiting fingerprint codes. Their technique supports constant size ciphertext. Note that saving ciphertext size is a major efficiency concern in broadcast encryption. By applying their technique, Guo *et al.* [17] presented an identity-based encryption scheme which supports traitor tracing, yet their scheme is not a broadcast one since only a single recipient can be specified during encryption.

The issue of leakage of sensitive data in cloud computing has already attracted some attention. Chow *et al.* [9] proposed a dynamic secure provenance scheme which can record the data ownership as an evidence if there is a dispute later. Similar to our scheme, the encryption part of their solution also extends the IBBE scheme proposed by Delerablée[14]. Tan *et al.* [28] presented an auditing methodology that enables tracking data transferred out of clouds, and provides

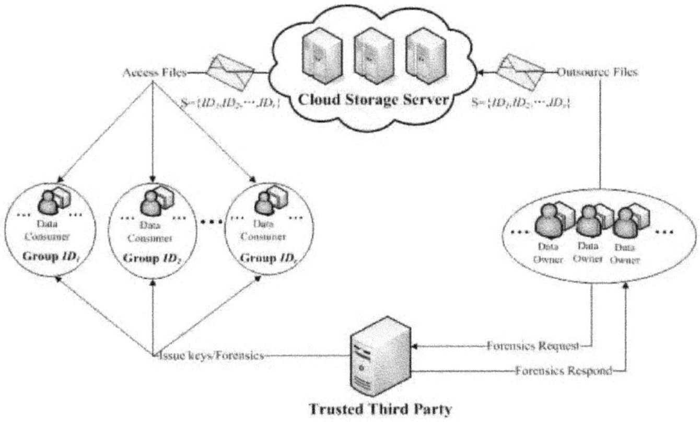

Figure 1: System Model

a countermeasure in case of data leakage. Pappas *et al.* [24] proposed a CloudFence framework to provide data owners with tracking capabilities to independently audit the treatment of their data. Zhang *et al.* [35] presented rule-based data provenance tracing algorithms to detect operations performed on files, especially those which can harm data confidentiality.

3. DEFINITIONS AND MODELS

3.1 System Model

As depicted in Fig. 1, our TRLAC framework consists of four parties as follows:

- Cloud Storage Provider (CSP): a party which provides storage service for cloud users, i.e., data owners and data consumers in clouds.
- Data Owners: the users who encrypt and outsource their data to CSP for sharing with data consumers.
- Data Consumers: the users who download the shared data from CSP and then decrypt them.
- Trusted Third Party / Administrator (admin): an authority who setups the system by publishing the system parameters, and is trusted to distribute private keys for data consumers only after they passed the identity verification. Also, upon a data owner's request, the admin will execute the forensics analysis and return the result to the data owner.

i All cloud users are organized in distinct groups associated with different identities. One user in multiple groups will be assigned to multiple keys corresponding to different groups (identities). The data owners interact with CSP to store their data. They can specify an access policy, i.e., a set $S = \{ID_1, ID_2, \cdots, ID_r\}$, so that the data consumers in these groups can access their data. The CSP is thought to have sufficient storage space and computation resources. The admin (e.g., the IT center of a company that employs the cloud storage systems) is assumed to be unbiased in the sense that it will correctly respond to the users' forensics analysis requests.

3.2 Security Model and Assumption

The CSP is assumed not to be fully trustable. It may be curious about the users' uploaded files or collude with some cloud users for accessing the files without authorization. Unauthorized users and intruders may also try to access the users' files. Therefore, a user needs to encrypt his files before outsourcing them to the CSP so that only authorized ones can decrypt with assigned credentials. The problem is that some users' credentials may be leaked, e.g., if their devices storing their credentials were hacked. Some authorized users may also intentionally leak their credentials. For instance, an employee who is unsatisfied with his company could leak his credentials for revenge.

We make the minimum assumption that the data owners can be informed on successful illegal access to their data. Similar to [21] for simplifying data leakage in the cloud, we assume that there exists a *pirate decryptor* ($\mathcal{PD}$), that is, a procedure created by the leaked credentials (equivalently treated as the decryption keys), that allows unauthorized parties to access the user's files. The output of $\mathcal{PD}$ is visible to the admin. We require that a tracing procedure can find out at least one of the leaked credentials used to produce $\mathcal{PD}$. The tracing procedure should fulfill its task without any knowledge about how $\mathcal{PD}$ is created, since the attacker may try to create an obfuscated algorithm for decryption to avoid being traced. The tracing procedure could be executed in a passive way in the sense that the admin only needs to observe and analyze the outputs of $\mathcal{PD}$, by supplying inputs which are indistinguishable to $\mathcal{PD}$.

4. OUR TRLAC SCHEME

We first review some basic techniques used in constructing the TRLAC scheme. We then give our construction.

4.1 Preliminaries

Bilinear Map. Let $\mathbb{G}$ and $\mathbb{G}_T$ be two multiplicative cyclic groups of prime order p and let g be a generator of $\mathbb{G}$. A bilinear map $e : \mathbb{G} \times \mathbb{G} \to \mathbb{G}_T$ has the following properties:

1. Bilinearity: for all $u, h \in \mathbb{G}$ and $a, b \in \mathbb{Z}_p$, it holds that $e(u^a, h^b) = e(u, h)^{ab}$;
2. Non-degeneracy: $e(g, g) \neq 1$.

We say that $\mathbb{G}$ is a bilinear group if the group operations in $\mathbb{G}$ and the target group $\mathbb{G}_T$, and the bilinear map e, are all efficiently computable.

Fingerprint codes. We are mainly interested in binary fingerprint codes and follow their definition in [5].

- A set $\Gamma = \{\omega^{(1)}, \cdots, \omega^{(n)}\} \subseteq \{0,1\}^l$ will be called an (l, n)-code. The codeword $\omega^{(i)}$ will be assigned to the i-th user, for $1 \leq i \leq n$, where $\omega^{(i)} = \omega_1^{(i)} \cdots \omega_l^{(i)}$ and n is the number of users.
- Let set $\mathbb{W} = \{\omega^{(1)}, \cdots, \omega^{(t)}\} \subseteq \{0,1\}^l$, where $t \leq n$. A codeword $\omega^* \in \{0,1\}^l$ is called *feasible* for $\mathbb{W}$ if for all $i = 1, \cdots, l$ there is a $j \in \{1, \cdots, t\}$ such that $\omega_i^* = \omega_i^{(j)}$.
- For a set $\mathbb{W} \subseteq \{0,1\}^l$ we say that the feasible set of $\mathbb{W}$, denoted by $F(\mathbb{W})$, is the set of all codewords that are feasible for $\mathbb{W}$.

A fingerprint code scheme consists of a generation algorithm $\mathbf{Gen}_{FC}$ and a tracing algorithm $\mathbf{Tra}_{FC}$. The algorithm $\mathbf{Gen}_{FC}$ can efficiently generate a fingerprint code Γ of n l-bit codewords, with each codeword being assigned to one user. Given a feasible codeword $\omega^* \in F(\mathbb{W})$, the algorithm $\mathbf{Tra}_{FC}$ can efficiently find out at least one codeword $\omega \in \mathbb{W}$, where $\mathbb{W} \subseteq \Gamma$ and $|\mathbb{W}| \leq t$. Our scheme exploits the Nuida *et al.*'s fingerprint codes [23] which is an improvement of the well-known Tardos's scheme [29]. Nuida *et al.*'s fingerprint codes achieve a shorter length, about 1/20 of Tardos's fingerprint codes, for the same security level. To provide traceability against at most t colluders among n users, Nuida*et al.*'s fingerprint codes require the codeword length to be

$$l \geq -\frac{1}{\log T(t)}\left(\log\frac{n}{\epsilon} + \log\frac{c}{c-1} + \log\log\frac{c}{\epsilon}\right), \quad (1)$$

where $T(t) < 1$ is parameterized by t, $c > 1$ is a constant and ϵ denotes the probability that an innocent user is accused.

4.2 Our Proposal

4.2.1 Basic idea

We construct the TRLAC scheme by using the fingerprint codes [23] and following the Boneh and Naor's paradigm. This paradigm requires generating a pair of public and secret keys for each bit position of the fingerprint codes when the system is set up, which causes the system public keys to grow linearly with the length of codes. We overcome this problem by embedding the information about fingerprint codes not in the system setup phase but only in the identity-based private key generation procedure of the IBBE scheme [14]. More specifically, in generating a private key for a user, we append the bit value of each position of the user's codeword to the end of the identity of the group which this user belongs to. Then we independently hash the concatenated strings (of each bit of the codeword and the identity) and finally produce a private key on the hash results. The user is unable to modify the fingerprint code embedded in the private key (due to the one-wayness of the hash and security of the identity-based key).

By using the underlying broadcast encryption scheme, data owners can specify sets of group identities that they want to share data with before outsourcing them to clouds. Data consumers in any group with identity included in the specified set can access the outsourced data using their credentials (identity-based private key) issued by the admin.

In case that credentials are leaked for creating a decoder box $\mathcal{PD}$ which allows unauthorized access, the tracing procedure of TRLAC can find out the users compromising their credentials in two steps. First, the tracing procedure enabled by Boneh and Naor's technique can trace the feasible codeword associated with the illegal credential used by $\mathcal{PD}$. Second, given this feasible codeword, the tracing algorithm of the underlying fingerprint codes can output a set of codewords associated with the users who leaked their credentials.

Finally, once the dishonest users are traced, the admin can revoke access rights from the groups involving the dishonest users by updating the ciphertexts.

4.2.2 Construction

We are now ready to describe our TRLAC scheme as consisting of the following procedures.

System Setup: The admin calls the **Setup** algorithm to create master public key parameters MPK and a master secret key MSK. MPK is public to other parties and MSK must be kept secret.

$(MPK, MSK) \leftarrow$ **Setup**(): This algorithm selects a bilinear group $\mathbb{G}$ of prime order p with generator g. Next, it randomly chooses $h \in \mathbb{G}, \gamma \in \mathbb{Z}_p^*$ and computes

$$u = g^{\gamma}, h^{\gamma}, h^{\gamma^2}, \cdots, h^{\gamma^m},$$

where m is the maximal size of a set of groups with each member as decryptor. The algorithm also chooses a hash function[1] $H : \{0,1\}^* \to \mathbb{Z}_p^*$. It sets the master public key and secret key, respectively, as

$$MPK = \left(u, h, h^{\gamma}, \cdots, h^{\gamma^m}, e(g,h), H\right), \qquad MSK = (g, \gamma).$$

User Admission: When a new user, denoted by (ID, i), $1 \leq i \leq n$, in group ID wants to join the system, the admin will first check whether this user is valid or not. If that is a new ID, this algorithm calls the code generation algorithm $\mathbf{Gen}_{FC}$ to generate a set of codewords

$$\Gamma = \{\omega^{(1)}, \cdots, \omega^{(n)}\}$$

where n is the maximum number of cloud users in each group. The admin picks a codeword, denoted by $\omega^{(i)} \in \Gamma$, that has not been used before, and then calls the **KeyGen** algorithm to generate a private key for this user.

$SK_{ID,i} \leftarrow$ **KeyGen**$(MSK, (ID, i))$: This algorithm uses MSK, the group identity ID and the index i to produce a private key for user (ID, i). For each j from 1 to l, it computes

$$ID_j = ID|j|\omega_j^{(i)}$$

and outputs the private key as

$$SK_{ID,i} = \{K_j\}_{j=1}^{l} = \{g^{\frac{1}{\gamma + H(ID_j)}}\}_{j=1}^{l},$$

We note that the unique codeword $\omega^{(i)}$ is embedded in the private key; thus, this key is solely associated with the user. Hence, to trace a leaked key, we just need to trace the associated fingerprint code $\omega^{(i)}$.

File Creation: A data owner creates a file to be stored in CSP by the following steps. First, the owner encrypts the file with a random symmetric session key of some symmetric cryptosystem such as AES. Second, the owner encrypts the symmetric session key DEK with the identities of the groups the owner wants to share his file with. The procedure runs as follows.

$CT \leftarrow$ **Encrypt**(MPK, S, M): This algorithm takes as inputs MPK, a set of group identities $S = \{ID_z\}_{z=1}^{r}$ and message $M \in \mathbb{G}_T$, where $r \leq m$ and M is a representation of the symmetric key DEK to be encrypted. For forensics analysis, it randomly picks $j \in \{1, 2, \cdots, l\}$ and calls the following algorithm twice by respectively taking in as inputs

$$\{ID_{z,j} = ID_z|j|0\}_{z=1}^{r} \text{ and } \{ID_{z,j} = ID_z|j|1\}_{z=1}^{r}.$$

$CT' \leftarrow$ **Encrypt**$'(MPK, \{ID_{z,j}\}_{z=1}^{r}, M)$: This algorithm runs as follows.

[1]The hash function will be modeled as a random oracle in the security proof. On the other hand, one can apply modification as described by the original paper for a proof without random oracle [14].

- Choose a random $s \in \mathbb{Z}_p^*$ and compute:

$$C_0 = Me(g,h)^s, C_1 = u^{-s}, C_2 = h^{s\prod_{z=1}^{r}(\gamma+H(ID_{z,j}))}.$$

- Output $CT' = (C_0, C_1, C_2)$.

We use CT_0' and CT_1' to denote the output of the above algorithm on input $ID_z|j|0$ and $ID_z|j|1$, respectively. The **Encrypt**() algorithm finally outputs

$$CT = (j, CT_0', CT_1').$$

This CT, together with the ciphertext of data encrypted under the symmetric key, forms the data to be outsourced.

File Access: When a user requests a file from CSP, the server returns the corresponding encrypted file. The user first recovers the symmetric key by decrypting CT and then uses this symmetric key to decrypt the body of the file. The **Decrypt** algorithm outputs the symmetric key as follows.

$M/\perp \leftarrow$ **Decrypt**$(MPK, CT, S, SK_{ID_k,i})$: It takes as inputs MPK, ciphertext

$$CT = (j, CT_0', CT_1')$$

of an encrypted file, private key $SK_{ID_k,i}$ of user (ID_k, i) and the set

$$S = \{ID_z\}_{z=1}^{r}$$

of group identities. If S does not include ID_k, this algorithm returns an invalid symbol $\perp$. Otherwise, it decrypts the ciphertext as follows.

The algorithm chooses K_j from $SK_{ID_k,i}$. If $\omega_j^{(i)} = 0$, which means $ID_{k,j} = ID_k|j|0$, it also chooses CT_0' (otherwise, chooses CT_1') and computes:

$$M' = \left(e\left(C_1, h^{\Delta_{k,j}}\right) \cdot e\left(K_j, C_2\right)\right)^{\frac{1}{\prod_{z=1,z\neq k}^{r} H(ID_{z,j})}}$$

with

$$\Delta_{k,j} = \frac{1}{\gamma}\left(\prod_{z=1,z\neq k}^{r}(\gamma + H(ID_{z,j})) - \prod_{z=1,z\neq k}^{r} H(ID_{z,j})\right).$$

Then it recovers M by $M = C_0/M'$.

Correctness. If CT is well formed for S, $M' = e(g,h)^s$ since

$$\begin{aligned} M' &= \left(e\left(g^{-\gamma s}, h^{\Delta_{k,j}}\right) \cdot \right. \\ &\qquad \left. e\left(g^{\frac{1}{\gamma+H(ID_{k,j})}}, h^{s\prod_{z=1}^{r}(\gamma+H(ID_{z,j}))}\right)\right)^{\frac{1}{\prod_{z=1,z\neq k}^{r} H(ID_{z,j})}} \\ &= \left(e\left(g,h\right)^{-s\prod_{z=1,z\neq k}^{r}(\gamma+H(ID_{z,j}))+s\prod_{z=1,z\neq k}^{r} H(ID_{z,j})} \cdot \right. \\ &\qquad \left. e\left(g,h\right)^{s\prod_{z=1,z\neq k}^{r}(\gamma+H(ID_{z,j}))}\right)^{\frac{1}{\prod_{z=1,z\neq k}^{r} H(ID_{z,j})}} \end{aligned}$$

Thus, $M = C_0/M'$.

For a user (ID_k, i), if his codeword has a 0 in the j-th position, then he only has the private key for $ID_k|j|0$. Thus, he can only decrypt the ciphertext component CT_0'. Otherwise, he can only decrypt CT_1'. Note that a user can only have a key for either $ID_k|j|0$ or $ID_k|j|1$ in the position j.

Forensics Analysis: When the owner found a $\mathcal{PD}$ from having access to his files stored in the cloud without his authorization, he can call the admin to run this procedure and find out the users who have taken part in creating this $\mathcal{PD}$.

Usually, the $\mathcal{PD}$ is *imperfect* in the sense that it decrypts the ciphertexts only with a probability less than one. This issue has been extensively discussed and a robust fingerprint code can be employed in this case [5]. Hence, in the rest of this paper, we assume that the $\mathcal{PD}$ is perfect, i.e.,

$$\Pr[\mathcal{PD}(\mathbf{Encrypt}(MPK, S, M)) = M] = 1.$$

When the admin receives a request to perform forensics analysis on a $\mathcal{PD}$ with respect to a set S of group identities, it first calls the **Trace** algorithm.

$\mathbb{T} \leftarrow$ **Trace**$(MPK, \mathcal{PD}, S)$: This algorithm takes as inputs MPK and a $\mathcal{PD}$ which is supposed to be a box which can decrypt the ciphertexts generated for $S = \{ID_z\}_{z=1}^{r}$. Note that due to the security of the underlying identity-based system, decryption keys for identities outside S should not be able to decrypt the ciphertexts generated for S.

It works in two steps. First, to trace the feasible codeword associated with the illegal credential used by $\mathcal{PD}$, This algorithm chooses each j from 1 to l and does the following.

1. Randomly choose two distinct symmetric keys M_j, M_j'.

2. Compute the ciphertexts

$$CT_0' \leftarrow \mathbf{Encrypt}'(MPK, \{ID_z|j|0\}_{z=1}^{r}, M_j),$$

$$CT_1' \leftarrow \mathbf{Encrypt}'(MPK, \{ID_z|j|1\}_{z=1}^{r}, M_j').$$

3. Take ciphertext $CT^* = (j, CT_0', CT_1')$ as the input of $\mathcal{PD}$. Define the output of $\mathcal{PD}$ as M_j^* and set

$$\omega_j^* = \begin{cases} 0 & \text{if } M_j^* = M_j, \\ 1 & \text{otherwise.} \end{cases}$$

Finally, the algorithm uses all ω_j^* for $j = 1, 2, \cdots, l$ to form

$$\omega^* = \omega_1^*\omega_2^*\cdots\omega_l^*,$$

which is the feasible codeword associated with the illegal credential.

Second, the algorithm takes this codeword ω^* as input of the tracing algorithm $\mathbf{Tra}_{FC}$ of the underlying fingerprint code scheme. For a suspected group, this tracing algorithm then outputs a set

$$\mathbb{T} \subseteq \{1, \cdots, n\}.$$

Since our system is traceable against t-collusion attack (more details in the next section), the set $\mathbb{T}$ is a subset of the users whose credentials were leaked. The admin returns this set to the data owner so that the owner can take further countermeasures (e.g., lawsuit).

User Revocation: After the forensics analysis traced to $ID_{k,j}$, the data owner can revoke the access rights of this group to access his files. To revoke group ID_k from set S, the owner asks the admin to update the C_2 component of CT_0' and CT_1' by computing

$$C_2 \leftarrow (C_2)^{\frac{1}{\gamma+H(ID_{k,j})}}$$

with $ID_{k,j} = ID_k|j|0$ for CT_0' and $ID_{k,j} = ID_k|j|1$ for CT_1' respectively.

4.2.3 Discussions on Our Revocation Mechanism

Here, we just describe a simple update mechanism for the ciphertext assuming the old one is securely erased and no adversary has previously obtained an old copy. For higher security, we recommend to use the provably-secure update mechanism proposed by Chow *et al.* [9].

The construction of the C_2 component, the crucial component enabling ciphertext-update, bears similarities as a pairing-based accumulator (e.g., [1]) which is also useful for revocation, our approach is conceptually different. On the other hand, one may view the update of C_2 component as something like proxy re-encryption (PRE) (e.g., [13]). However, in a typical identity-based PRE scheme, it will be the data owner who owns the identity-based private key to be responsible for generating a transformation key, such that only the ciphertexts encrypted with respect to this particular identity can be transformed to one for another identity. In our case, all computational tasks are performed by the admin, which can transform every ciphertext, even though it is the data owner who initiated the revocation procedure.

5. FORMAL SECURITY ANALYSIS

In this section, we evaluate the security of our TRLAC scheme. Intuitively, we require TRLAC to have semantical security and traceability. The former states that someone having no appropriate credential cannot get any useful information about the file created by the data owner, and the latter states that, if someone accesses the uploaded file with an illegal credential, then the admin can find out at least one original credential used to produce the illegal one. The two security properties are formally defined by two games: one is the semantic security game (*Game 1*) and the other is the traceability game (*Game 2*).

Game 1: In this game, to capture the access attempts from unauthorized users colluding with CSP, we define an attacker which is able to query the users' private keys.

The semantic security states that any polynomial-time attacker cannot distinguish the ciphertexts of two equal-length messages encrypted to the challenge set, provided that the attacker cannot query for private keys which can be used to decrypt the challenge ciphertext.

More formally, the attacker can choose to be challenged on a set of group identities, $S^* = \{ID_z^*\}_{z=1}^r$, and ask for any private key of $(ID_k, i \in [1, n])$ on the condition that $ID_k \notin S^*$. This game played between an adversary $\mathcal{A}$ and a challenger is defined as follows.

Init: The adversary $\mathcal{A}$ outputs a set $S^* = \{ID_z^*\}_{z=1}^r$ of group identities that it wants to attack.

Setup: The challenger runs the setup algorithm to obtain a master public key MPK and give it to adversary $\mathcal{A}$.

Phase 1: The adversary $\mathcal{A}$ specifies a user's identity (ID_k, i). In response, the challenger creates a key for this identity by calling the **KeyGen** algorithm, and sends this key to $\mathcal{A}$.

Challenge: The adversary $\mathcal{A}$ outputs two equal-length messages M_0 and M_1 with an extra restriction that any queried group identity is not involved in S^*. The challenger flips a coin $\beta \in \{0, 1\}$, encrypts M_β under identity S^*, and returns the ciphertext CT^* to $\mathcal{A}$.

Phase 2: This is the same as Phase 1 with the constraint that any group identity queried in this phase must not be included in S^*.

Guess: The attacker outputs a guess $\beta' \in \{0, 1\}$.

The advantage of an attacker $\mathcal{A}$ in this game is defined as

$$Adv_{\mathcal{A}}^S = |P[\beta = \beta'] - 1/2|.$$

DEFINITION 1. *A TRLAC system is semantically secure against chosen-plaintext attacks if any polynomial-time adversary $\mathcal{A}$ has only a negligible advantage in the above game.*

Game 2: In this game, we define an adversary which can collude with authorized users by querying their private keys (these users are then regarded as traitors who leaked their keys). Then the adversary can use these keys to create a $\mathcal{PD}$ through which one can illegally access data without directly identifying the traitors. The adversary terminates the key queries by outputting the pirate decryptor as a challenge. Formally, this game is defined as follows.

Setup: The challenger runs the setup algorithm to obtain the master public key MPK and give it to adversary $\mathcal{A}$.

Query: For a query on (ID, i) from $\mathcal{A}$, the challenger responds by calling the **KeyGen** algorithm and returning the key $SK_{ID,i}$ to $\mathcal{A}$.

Challenge: The adversary $\mathcal{A}$ outputs a pirate decryptor $\mathcal{PD}$ for a set S^* of group identities.

Trace: The challenger runs the **Trace**$(MPK, \mathcal{PD}, S^*)$ algorithm and outputs a set $\mathbb{T} \subseteq \{1, \cdots, n\}$ for the suspected group. Let $\mathbb{S}$ be the set of users with private keys queried by $\mathcal{A}$. The adversary wins this game if the following conditions hold:

1. The set $\mathbb{T}$ is empty or is not a subset of $\mathbb{S}$.
2. There are at most t private key queries with group identities included in S^*.
3. The pirate decryptor $\mathcal{PD}$ is perfect, i.e.,

$$\Pr[\mathcal{PD}(\mathbf{Encrypt}(MPK, S^*, M)) = M] = 1.$$

The first condition is straightforward and the third one is an assumption which can be dealt with by other means as previously described. The second condition is required by the underlying fingerprint codes [23]. Since this scheme is secure against at most t colluders, it is also required that there are at most t queried private keys that can be used to directly decrypt the encryption with respect to set S^*.

The advantage of an attacker $\mathcal{A}$ in this game is defined as

$$Adv_{\mathcal{A}}^T = \Pr[\mathcal{A} \text{ wins}].$$

DEFINITION 2. *A TRLAC system is t-collusion resistant if for all polynomial-time adversary $\mathcal{A}$ we have that $Adv_{\mathcal{A}}^S$ and $Adv_{\mathcal{A}}^T$ are negligible in* Game 1 *and* Game 2, *respectively.*

The t-collusion resistant security implies that: 1) there is semantic security and 2) at least one member of any collusion of at most t members can be found out.

The following formal claim guarantees that our TRLAC is semantically secure and traceable.

THEOREM 1. *Our TRLAC scheme is t-collusion resistant if the fingerprint codes scheme [23] is t-collusion resistant and the underlying IBBE scheme [14] is semantically secure against chosen-plaintext attacks. Formally, let l be the length of the fingerprint code and $|\mathcal{M}|$ the size of the message space. Then, for all $t > 0, n \geq t$, any polynomial-time attacker breaks our TRLAC system with advantage at most*

$$Adv_{\mathbb{A}}^{T} \leq l \cdot Adv_{\mathbb{A}}^{S} + \epsilon + \frac{l}{|\mathcal{M}|}.$$

If the TRLAC scheme is semantically secure, then the advantage $Adv_{\mathbb{A}}^{S}$ of any adversary breaking its semantic security is negligible. The code length l is much less than the message space size $|\mathcal{M}|$, so $l/|\mathcal{M}|$ is a negligible quotient. Since the underlying fingerprint codes scheme has been shown ϵ-secure, the advantage $Adv_{\mathbb{A}}^{T}$ of any adversary breaking the scheme's traceability is negligible, which means that the TRLAC scheme is t-collusion resistant. The proof of this theorem is given in the full version.

6. PERFORMANCE EVALUATION

In this section, we evaluate the TRLAC scheme both theoretically and experimentally.

6.1 Theoretical Analysis

We first analyze the computational complexity of the proposed scheme in each of its procedures. In this analysis, we treat the underlying fingerprint scheme as a black-box and let $O(\mathbf{Gen}_{FC})$ and $O(\mathbf{Tra}_{FC})$ be the computation complexity of $\mathbf{Gen}_{FC}$ and $\mathbf{Tra}_{FC}$, respectively. We focus on the most time-consuming operations, i.e., exponentiation and pairing, conducted in groups $\mathbb{G}$ and $\mathbb{G}_T$. Their computation times are respectively denoted by τ_{exp} and τ_{pair}. (We do not differentiate exponentiations in $\mathbb{G}$ from those in $\mathbb{G}_T$.) Also, we do not differentiate a multi-base exponentiation from a single-base one, as the latter is only slightly more efficient. The time to sample a random element in $\mathbb{G}$ is approximately equal to (indeed, slightly less than) the time to compute an exponentiation. We do not take into account the time costs of the symmetric encryption and decryption in our evaluation, since both are negligible when compared to the asymmetric encryption and decryption.

Table 1 summarizes the computation cost of each procedure in TRLAC. In this table, m denotes the maximal size of the set of groups in which each member can access a stored file, and $|S| \leq m$ denotes the size of set S specified in encryption. Table 1 clearly reveals the performance cost incurred by the *a posteriori* forensics analysis approach in securing outsourced cloud data. In addition to the unavoidable process of forensics analysis, only the system setup and user admission procedures are affected. We stress that both procedures are only executed once in an offline stage independent of files outsourcing. Adding credential leakage traceability hardly affects neither file creation nor access: the users can create files and access them normally without any significant overhead. These features render our TRLAC scheme a promising solution to *a posteriori* protection of data outsourced to an untrusted third party.

Table 2 compares our TRLAC scheme with other schemes achieving traceability of leaked credentials in terms of performance, tracing manner (black-box or white-box), bilinear group type (prime-order or composite-order) and revocation support. In this table, the schemes in [6], [7] and [16] are devised for the broadcast encryption and N denotes the number of total users in the systems. The works from [22] to [21] following [7] aim to provide traceability for attribute-based encryption, thus their performance depends on the number of attributes, in which $|\mathcal{U}|$ denotes the size of the attribute universe, $|\gamma|$ the size of the set γ of attributes associated with a user, $|\mathbb{A}|$ the size of an access structure associated with a ciphertext, and $|\gamma^*|$ denotes the size of a set γ^* satisfying the access structure. The work [17] supports identity-based traitor tracing system, in which a data owner can choose only one identity (i.e. group) to access his data at a time, in contrast to a set of groups in our TRLAC scheme.

Table 1: Computation

Operation	Computational Complexity
System Setup	$1\tau_{pair} + (m+2)\tau_{exp} + O(\mathbf{Gen}_{FC})$
User Admission	$l \cdot \tau_{exp}$
File Creation	$2 \cdot (\|S\| + 4)\tau_{exp}$
File Access	$2 \cdot \tau_{pair} + \|S\| \cdot \tau_{exp}$
Forensics Analysis	$2l \cdot (\|S\| + 4)\tau_{exp} + O(\mathbf{Tra}_{FC})$
User Revocation	$2 \cdot \tau_{exp}$

It can be seen that all the schemes, except ours, [16], and [17], are constructed in composite-order groups. Note that the performance of operations in composite-order groups is much (about one order) lower than those in prime-order bilinear groups for the same security level. For instance, the scheme [16] is shown to encrypt 6 times faster and decrypt 10 times faster than [6] for the same level of security. Compared to our TRLAC scheme, however, the decryption time of [16] is linear in the size of the vector space which is used to simulate the orthogonality of composite-order groups. Moreover, this scheme [16] (as well as [6, 7, 20, 21]) requires the ciphertext size to be linear in the square root of the number of total users N, which means that the encrypted files to be outsourced to the cloud will be quite large.

Table 2 reveals the superior practicality of our scheme. Let m be the maximal size of the set of groups. It can be seen that the ciphertext size and pairing computations in decryption are both constant, which provides a cost-effective way for users to securely outsource and access their files. Although the scheme of [17] achieves the same encryption and decryption efficiency, it does not support revocation, which is seen as an important mechanism to protect data security after the tracing results come out. Compared to other schemes, the public key size of our TRLAC scheme is also short, since the parameter m is usually less than the size of total attributes in [22, 20, 21], the square root of the number of total users in [6, 7, 16], and the code length in [17]. Although the private key size is linear in the code length l (which can be relatively short by setting reasonably big ϵ and small t in a practical scenario), the key generation algorithm is only executed once by the admin in an offline stage independent of outsourcing any files. This confirms the practical attractiveness of our solution.

6.2 Experimental Analysis

We conducted a series of experiments on a PC with 4-core Intel Core i3-2130 CPU running at 3.4GHz, 2.0G RAM, us-

Table 2: Comparison with Related Work

	|Public key|	|Private key|	|Ciphertext|	$e(\cdot,\cdot)$ in Decryption	Black-box	Prime-order	Revocation
[6]	$3+4\sqrt{N}$	1	$6\sqrt{N}$	3	√	×	×
[7]	$5+9\sqrt{N}$	$1+\sqrt{N}$	$7\sqrt{N}$	4	√	×	√
[16]	$2+3\sqrt{N}$	$1+\sqrt{N}$	$7\sqrt{N}$	$2+2\lvert\vec{v}\rvert$	√	√	√
[22]	$\lvert\mathcal{U}\rvert+4$	$\lvert\gamma\rvert+4$	$2\lvert\mathbb{A}\rvert+3$	$2\lvert\gamma^*\rvert+1$	×	×	×
[20]	$\lvert\mathcal{U}\rvert+7+8\sqrt{N}$	$\lvert\gamma\rvert+3$	$2\lvert\mathbb{A}\rvert+8\sqrt{N}$	$2\lvert\gamma^*\rvert+5$	√	×	×
[21]	$\lvert\mathcal{U}\rvert+3+4\sqrt{N}$	$\lvert\gamma\rvert+4$	$2\lvert\mathbb{A}\rvert+9\sqrt{N}$	$2\lvert\gamma^*\rvert+6$	√	×	×
[17]	$6+2l$	2	6	2	√	√	×
Ours	$3+m$	l	6	2	√	√	√

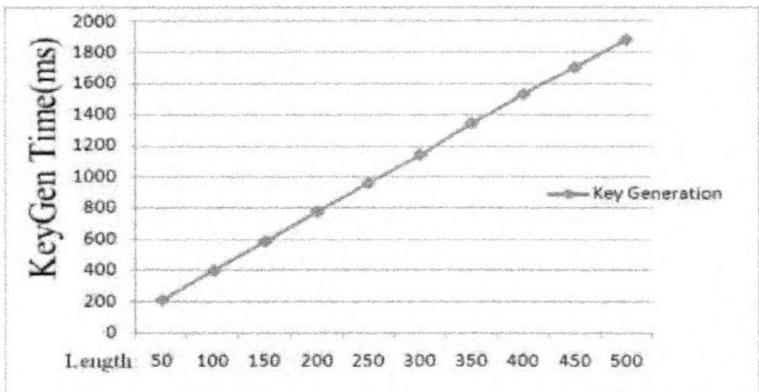

Figure 2: Time Consumed in User Admission

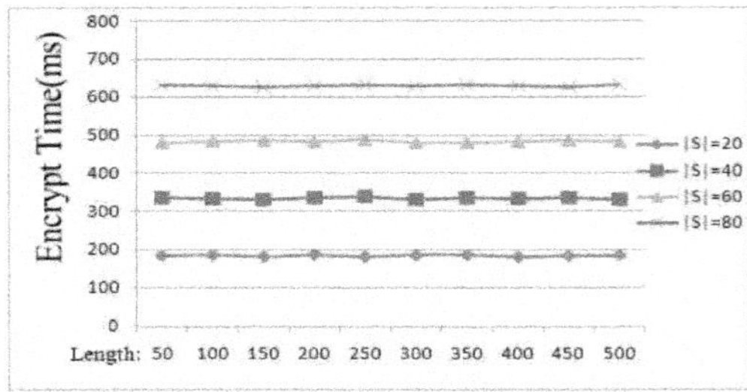

Figure 3: Time Consumed in File Creation

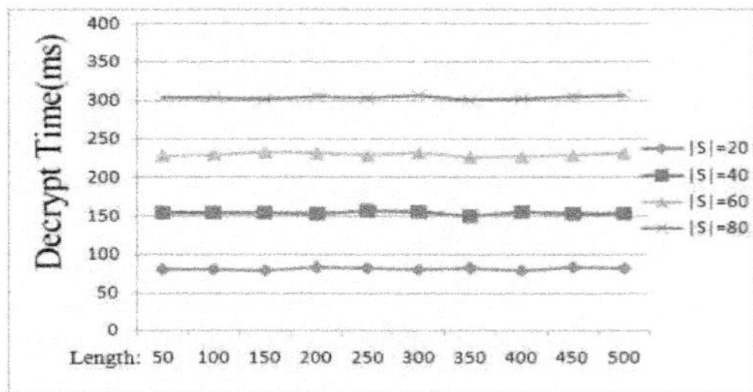

Figure 4: Time Consumed in File Access

ing the C programming language in Windows 7. The involved cryptographic operations (e.g., pairing, exponentiation) were implemented by using the Pairing-Based Cryptography library version 0.5.12 (available at `http://crypto.stanford.edu/pbc`). In the experiments, we evaluated the performance of each procedure of the TRLAC scheme.

We employed Nuida *et al.*'s fingerprint codes which have shorter length than Tardos codes. Recall that to achieve t-collusion resistant traceability with a total number n of users with error probability ϵ, the length of their fingerprint codes is given by Expression (1). Since the traceability is uniquely determined by the fingerprint code length l, we conduct experiments with different code length. Consider a practical scenario where the created file is allowed to be accessed by different departments of different companies and each department has usually a staff size n at most 100. It seems reasonable to assume that at most $t \leq 5$ staff member's credentials are compromised in normal circumstances. Suppose that tracing to an incorrect staff member has probability $\epsilon \approx 10^{-5}$. For such a practical scenario, according to Expression (1), we have that the fingerprint code has length $l \leq 50$. Thus, in the experiments, we set $l = 50, 100, \cdots, 500$. Besides, the system performance is also related to the maximal size m of set, which is determined at the setup phase, and the size $|S|$ of set S decided in encryption. For the above scenario, it seems reasonable to set the number of different companies to 100, i.e., $m = 100$. We thus conduct our experiments with $|S|$ equal to 20, 40, 60 and 80 as well.

The system setup procedure run by the admin outputs a master public key of size linear in m. For $m = 100$, the time consumed by this procedure turns out to be about 440.5ms, which is negligible for an admin whose equipment is often more powerful than a typical desktop PC.

Fig. 2 shows the time to register a user to the system. It can be seen that the time consumed by the user admission procedure grows linearly with the length of fingerprint codes. The lowest point means that, to trace $t \leq 5$ employees who leaked their credentials in a company's department of 100 staff, the required code length is about 50 bits, which results in a time about 200ms to produce a private key. If the number of dishonest employees leaking credentials increases to $t \leq 30$, the code length needs to grow to 500 bits and the time to produce a private key is near 1.9s (represented by the highest point). These results show that TRLAC can tolerate a large number of traitors who leaked their credentials while keeping a manageable cost for the admin.

Fig. 3 shows the time to create a file to be stored in the cloud. The four lines represent four different sizes of the set of encryption groups, respectively: 20, 40, 60, and 80. It can be seen that none of these lines varies as the code length grows. The time consumed by file creation is only linear in the size of encryption groups. Even for the largest value 80 (the file is intended to be shared with 80 groups), the time consumed by this procedure is about 630ms, which is a low cost for users to encrypt their data to be outsourced.

Fig. 4 shows the time to access a file. It can be seen that the time consumed by the file access procedure does not depend on the code length either. It only grows linearly with the size of encryption groups. The four lines represent the time costs associated with different sizes of the set of encryption groups, respectively. For the largest size of 80 groups, the time to access a file is only about 300ms. Therefore, with millisecond-level file creation and file access times, our TRLAC scheme provides an efficient protection for users to secure their outsourced data.

The group revocation procedure in our scheme is also very efficient in the sense that it only requires two exponentiations for a file. We tested that the time taken by the admin to revoke access rights of a group is around 16.4ms in our desktop PC. This procedure is only executed by the admin and does not take the user any time.

From the experimental analyses above, our TRLAC scheme provides an efficient way for users to protect the security of their outsourced data. Users can encrypt their data at a low cost before outsourcing them to clouds and the time for any authorized user to access the stored files is even less. The introduction of traceability incurs almost no extra cost for the file creation and access. Even for user admission, the procedure that is most affected by the introduction of traceability, the cost is acceptable. A user can also revoke access privileges of a group to access his files without having to do himself any computation.

7. CONCLUSION

This paper has presented countermeasures to fight against illegal leakage of credentials. We presented TRLAC, a system for tracing and revoking leaked credentials. Formal proofs show that the proposed scheme is t-collusion resistant. Finally, we conducted a comprehensive performance evaluation. Our analyses show that the proposed scheme has reasonable performance after incorporated the mechanism to trace and revoke compromised credentials.

8. ACKNOWLEDGEMENTS

This paper was supported by the National Key Basic Research Program (973 program) under project 2012CB315905, the Natural Science Foundation of China through projects 61370190, 61173154, 61003214, 61070192, 61021004, 61272501 and 61202465, the Beijing Natural Science Foundation under projects 4132056 and 4122041, the Research Funds of Renmin University of China through project 14XNLF02, the Fundamental Research Funds for the Central Universities through project 2012211020212 of Wuhan University, the Open Research Fund of The Academy of Satellite Application and the Open Research Fund of Beijing Key Laboratory of Trusted Computing, and by the European Commission under FP7 projects DwB (INFRA-2010-262608) and Inter-Trust (FP7-ICT-317731), the Spanish Government through projects TIN2011-27076-C03-01, IPT-2012-0603-430000, and TIN2012-32757.

Sherman Chow is supported by the Early Career Scheme and the Early Career Award of the Research Grants Council, Hong Kong SAR (CUHK 439713), and Direct Grant (4055018) of the Chinese University of Hong Kong.

Josep Domingo-Ferrer is partly supported as an ICREA-Acadèmia researcher by the Government of Catalonia. He holds the UNESCO Chair in Data Privacy, but the views expressed in this paper are his own and do not commit UNESCO.

9. REFERENCES

[1] T. Acar, S. S. M. Chow, and L. Nguyen. Accumulators and U-Prove Revocation. In *Financial Cryptography and Data Security*, pages 189–196. Springer, 2013.

[2] G. Ateniese, R. C. Burns, R. Curtmola, J. Herring, L. Kissner, Z. N. J. Peterson, and D. X. Song. Provable Data Possession at Untrusted Stores. In *ACM conference on Computer and Communications Security (CCS)*, pages 598–609. ACM, 2007.

[3] M. Bellare, A. Boldyreva, and A. O'Neill. Deterministic and Efficiently Searchable Encryption. In *Advances in Cryptology - CRYPTO*, pages 535–552. Springer, 2007.

[4] D. Boneh and M. K. Franklin. Identity-Based Encryption from the Weil Pairing. *SIAM J. Comput.*, 32(3):586–615, 2003.

[5] D. Boneh and M. Naor. Traitor Tracing with Constant size Ciphertext. In *ACM conference on Computer and Communications Security (CCS)*, pages 501–510. ACM, 2008.

[6] D. Boneh, A. Sahai, and B. Waters. Fully Collusion Resistant Traitor Tracing with Short Ciphertexts and Private Keys. In *Advances in Cryptology - EUROCRYPT*, pages 573–592. Springer, 2006.

[7] D. Boneh and B. Waters. A Fully Collusion Resistant Broadcast, Trace, and Revoke System. In *ACM conference on Computer and Communications Security (CCS)*, pages 211–220. ACM, 2006.

[8] M. Chase and S. S. M. Chow. Improving Privacy and Security in Multi-Authority Attribute-Based Encryption. In *ACM conference on Computer and Communications Security (CCS)*, pages 121–130. ACM, 2009.

[9] S. S. M. Chow, C.-K. Chu, X. Huang, J. Zhou, and R. H. Deng. Dynamic Secure Cloud storage with Provenance. In *Cryptography and Security: From Theory to Applications - Essays Dedicated to Jean-Jacques Quisquater on the Occasion of His 65th Birthday*, pages 442–464. Springer, 2012.

[10] S. S. M. Chow, Y.-J. He, L. C. K. Hui, and S. M. Yiu. SPICE – Simple Privacy-preserving Identity-management for Cloud Environment. In *Applied Cryptography and Network Security*, pages 526–543. Springer, 2012.

[11] S. S. M. Chow, S.-M. Yiu, L. C. K. Hui, and K. P. Chow. Efficient Forward and Provably Secure ID-Based Signcryption Scheme with Public Verifiability and Public Ciphertext Authenticity. In *International Conference on Information Security and Cryptology (ICISC)*, pages 352–369. Springer, 2004.

[12] C.-K. Chu, S. S. M. Chow, W.-G. Tzeng, J. Zhou, and R. H. Deng. Key-Aggregate Cryptosystem for Scalable Data Sharing in Cloud Storage. *IEEE Transactions on Parallel Distributed System*, 25(2):468–477, 2014.

[13] C.-K. Chu, J. Weng, S. S. M. Chow, J. Zhou, and R. H. Deng. Conditional Proxy Broadcast Re-Encryption. In *Australasian Conference on Information Security and Privacy (ACISP)*, pages 327–342. Springer, 2009.

[14] C. Delerablée. Identity-Based Broadcast Encryption with Constant Size Ciphertexts and Private Keys. In

Advances in Cryptology - ASIACRYPT, pages 200–215. Springer, 2007.
[15] H. Deng, Q. Wu, B. Qin, J. Domingo-Ferrer, L. Zhang, J. Liu, and W. Shi. Ciphertext-Policy Hierarchical Attribute-Based Encryption with Short Ciphertexts. *Information Sciences*, Elsevier, 2014. http://dx.doi.org/10.1016/j.ins.2014.01.035.
[16] S. Garg, A. Kumarasubramanian, A. Sahai, and B. Waters. Building Efficient Fully Collusion-Resilient Traitor Tracing and Revocation Schemes. In *ACM conference on Computer and Communications Security (CCS)*, pages 121–130. ACM, 2010.
[17] F. Guo, Y. Mu, and W. Susilo. Identity-Based Traitor Tracing with Short Private Key and Short Ciphertext. In *European Symposium on Research in Computer Security (ESORICS)*, pages 609–626. Springer, 2012.
[18] K. Kent, S. Chevalier, T. Grance, and H. Dang. Guide to Integrating Forensic Techniques into Incident Response. NIST Special Publication 800-86 Notes.
[19] M. Li, S. Yu, K. Ren, and W. Lou. Securing Personal Health Records in Cloud Computing: patient-centric and fine-grained data access control in multi-owner settings. In *Security and Privacy in Communication Networks*, pages 89–106. Springer, 2010.
[20] Z. Liu, Z. Cao, and D. S. Wong. Expressive Black-box Traceable Ciphertext-Policy Attribute-Based Encryption. Cryptology ePrint Archive, Report 2012/669, 2012.
[21] Z. Liu, Z. Cao, and D. S. Wong. Blackbox Traceable CP-ABE: how to catch people leaking their keys by selling decryption devices on eBay. In *ACM conference on Computer and Communications Security (CCS)*, pages 475–486. ACM, 2013.
[22] Z. Liu, Z. Cao, and D. S. Wong. White-box Traceable Ciphertext-Policy Attribute-Based Encryption supporting Any Monotone Access Structures. *IEEE Transactions on Information Forensics and Security*, 8(1):76–88, 2013.
[23] K. Nuida, S. Fujitsu, M. Hagiwara, T. Kitagawa, H. Watanabe, K. Ogawa, and H. Imai. An Improvement of Discrete Tardos Fingerprinting Codes. *Designs, Codes and Cryptography*, 52(3):339–362, 2009.
[24] V. Pappas, V. P. Kemerlis, A. Zavou, M. Polychronakis, and A. D. Keromytis. CloudFence: Data Flow Tracking as a Cloud Service. In *Research in Attacks, Intrusions, and Defenses*, pages 411–431. Springer, 2013.
[25] B. Qin, H. Wang, Q. Wu, J. Liu, and J. Domingo-Ferrer. Simultaneous Authentication and Secrecy in Identity-Based Data Upload to Cloud. *Cluster Computing*, 16(4):845–859, 2013.
[26] F. Sebé, J. Domingo-Ferrer, A. Martinez-Balleste, Y. Deswarte, and J.-J. Quisquater. Efficient Remote Data Possession Checking in Critical Information Infrastructures. *IEEE Transactions on Knowledge and Data Engineering*, 20(8):1034–1038, 2008.
[27] U. Somani, K. Lakhani, and M. Mundra. Implementing Digital Signature with RSA Encryption Algorithm to Enhance the Data Security of Cloud in Cloud Computing. In *Parallel Distributed and Grid Computing (PDGC)*, pages 211–216. IEEE, 2010.
[28] Y. S. Tan, R. K. Ko, P. Jagadpramana, C. H. Suen, M. Kirchberg, T. H. Lim, B. S. Lee, A. Singla, K. Mermoud, D. Keller, et al. Tracking of Data Leaving the Cloud. In *Trust, Security and Privacy in Computing and Communications (TrustCom)*, pages 137–144. IEEE, 2012.
[29] G. Tardos. Optimal Probabilistic Fingerprint Codes. *Journal of the ACM (JACM)*, 55(2):10, 2008.
[30] Y. Tong, J. Sun, S. S. M. Chow, and P. Li. Cloud-Assisted Mobile-Access of Health Data with Privacy and Auditability. *IEEE Journal of Biomedical and Health Informatics*, 18(2):419–429, 2014.
[31] B. Wang, S. S. M. Chow, M. Li, and H. Li. Storing Shared Data on the Cloud via Security-Mediator. In *International Conference on Distributed Computing Systems (ICDCS)*, pages 124–133. IEEE, 2013.
[32] B. Wang, Y. Hou, M. Li, H. Wang, and H. Li. Maple: Scalable Multi-Dimensional Range Search over Encrypted Cloud data with Tree-Based Index. In *ACM Symposium on Information, Computer and Communications Security (ASIACCS)*, 2014. To Appear.
[33] C. Wang, S. S. M. Chow, Q. Wang, K. Ren, and W. Lou. Privacy-Preserving Public Auditing for Secure Cloud Storage. *IEEE Transactions on Computers*, 62(2):362–375, 2013.
[34] P. Xu, H. Jin, Q. Wu, and W. Wang. Public-Key Encryption with Fuzzy Keyword Search: a provably secure scheme under keyword guessing attack. *IEEE Transactions on Computers*, 62(11):2266–2277, 2013.
[35] O. Q. Zhang, R. K. Ko, M. Kirchberg, C. H. Suen, P. Jagadpramana, and B. S. Lee. How to Track Your Data: rule-based data provenance tracing algorithms. In *Trust, Security and Privacy in Computing and Communications (TrustCom)*, pages 1429–1437. IEEE, 2012.
[36] Z. Zhang, Y. Chen, S. S. M. Chow, G. Hanaoka, Z. Cao, and Y. Zhao. All-but-One Dual Projective Hashing and Its Applications. In *Applied Cryptography and Network Security (ACNS)*. Springer, 2014. To Appear.

Sufficient Conditions for Vertical Composition of Security Protocols

Sebastian Mödersheim
DTU Compute
Lyngby, Denmark
samo@imm.dtu.dk

Luca Viganò
Department of Informatics
King's College London, UK
luca.vigano@kcl.ac.uk

ABSTRACT

Vertical composition of security protocols means that an application protocol (e.g., a banking service) runs over a channel established by another protocol (e.g., a secure channel provided by TLS). This naturally gives rise to a compositionality question: given a secure protocol P_1 that provides a certain kind of channel as a goal and another secure protocol P_2 that assumes this kind of channel, can we then derive that their vertical composition $P_2[P_1]$ is secure? It is well known that protocol composition can lead to attacks even when the individual protocols are all secure in isolation. In this paper, we formalize seven easy-to-check static conditions that support a large class of channels and applications and that we prove to be sufficient for vertical security protocol composition.

Categories and Subject Descriptors

C.2.0 [**Computer-Communication Networks**]: Security and protection; C.2.2 [**Computer-Communication Networks**]: Network Protocols—*Protocol verification*

Keywords

Security protocols; protocol composition; verification; static analysis; model checking

1. INTRODUCTION

It is preferable to verify small or medium-size security protocols (such as TLS) in isolation because: (1) The composition of several protocols immediately leads to very complex systems that are infeasible for formal verification, be it manual or automated; (2) one should not have to repeat a security proof of all existing protocols whenever a new protocol is added to a system (i.e., the verification should be independent of what other protocols may later be used on the same network); and (3) one should strive for general and reusable results, e.g., that TLS provides a secure channel no matter what application it is used for. Similarly, the verification of an application protocol that relies on a secure channel should be completely independent of how (i.e., by which other protocol) that channel is actually realized.

In general, however, the composition of secure protocols may lead to attacks even when the individual protocols are all secure in isolation. Compositional reasoning thus aims at identifying conditions for security protocols that are sufficient to prove a statement of the form: whenever secure protocols (that satisfy the conditions) are composed, then also their composition is secure.

There are several results for the *parallel* composition of security protocols (e.g., [11, 12]), i.e., when two or more protocols are used (independently) on the same network. The general idea is here that the message formats of the involved protocols need to be sufficiently different, so that message parts of one protocol cannot be accidentally mistaken for message parts of another protocol, to avoid any risk that confusions could be exploited by an intruder. Note that, in general, such conditions are sufficient for compositionality[1] but not necessary: some protocols with confusable protocol formats may still be sound to compose when confusions cannot be exploited by an intruder.

Another line of work concerns *sequential* protocol composition (e.g., [10, 12, 14, 18, 20]), where the result of one protocol, e.g., a shared session key, becomes input to a second, subsequent secure channel protocol. One may interpret TLS as an example of sequential composition where the TLS handshake protocol establishes a pair of symmetric keys and the TLS transport protocol uses them to encrypt messages of an application protocol. A disadvantage of this view is that we must consider the agglomeration of TLS transport with the application protocol, while we would rather like to have a clear-cut dividing line between channel protocol and application protocol, as is common in the layered Internet.

For such a view of layered protocols we will use the term *vertical* protocol composition, in contrast to sequential and parallel composition that we refer to as *horizontal* compositions. Maurer et al. [24] (but see also the more recent [22, 23]) have initiated an idea to capture very different means of communication, based on cryptography, protocols, and non-technical means (e.g., trust relationships or humans who know each other) with a notion of *channels* that may build on each other. For instance, a banking service may run over a secure channel that is provided by another protocol such as TLS. Another example is Diffie-Hellman that allows

[1]In this paper, we use the terms *compositionality* and *composability* interchangeably.

ASIA CCS'14, June 4–6, 2014, Kyoto, Japan.

http://dx.doi.org/10.1145/2590296.2590330.

two agents A and B to establish secure channels with each other, provided that they already have authentic channels; how exactly these channels are realized does not matter for Diffie-Hellman.

In [27], we used the concepts that Maurer et al. had presented informally in [24] and gave a formal definition in a transition-system model for security protocols. In particular, channels can be both *assumptions* of a protocol (e.g., the authentic channels in Diffie-Hellman) and *goals* of a protocol (e.g., that Diffie-Hellman establishes secure channels).[2] This naturally gives rise to a compositionality question: given a secure protocol P_1 that provides a certain kind of channel as a goal (e.g., TLS) and another secure protocol P_2 that assumes this kind of channel (e.g., a banking service), is it then possible to derive that their vertical composition $P_2[P_1]$ (e.g., a banking service over TLS) is secure?

We can distinguish two aspects for the potential failure of such a composition:

1. In [27], we considered what we call the *logical aspect:* a mismatch between the behavior of a channel as an assumption and as a goal.

2. But there is also a *static aspect:* an interference between the message formats (when message parts of P_1 could be confused with message parts of P_2).

In [27], we proved only the logical aspect of the compositionality question for our notion of channels, while for the static aspect we simply *assumed* that the composed protocols do not interfere with each other. In fact, this assumption is a *semantical* condition that involves the set of all concrete runs of the composed protocols—as opposed to a simple syntactic check on the protocols. We suggested there that this could maybe be solved similar to existing disjointness notions in parallel protocol composition, but left this complex problem open.

Contributions.

This open problem of how to deal with the static aspect of vertical protocol composition turns out to be intricate for two main reasons. First, in contrast to all horizontal composition types, the vertical composition has to deal with messages that are composed from the channel protocol P_1 and the application protocol P_2, because the payload messages of P_2 are *embedded* into message-templates of P_1 that are used for transferring messages with the desired properties. Second, we have that the channel protocol is *parameterized* over a payload message.[3] We want to be able to use standard existing verification methods to verify P_1, especially independent of payload messages of a particular P_2. This is in fact why we call this problem the static aspect: we want to see this independent of the dynamic behavior of P_2 using a form of abstract interpretation for the payload.

We define a precise interface for the abstract payload in a "pure" P_1 that is suitable for all standard protocol verification methods. This further gives rise to the notion of *static vertical composition* $P_1^{P_2}$, where "statically" all possible payloads of a protocol P_2 are inserted into P_1 and this serves as an interface to the results of [27]. Building on this notion, the main contributions of this paper are:

(1) We give a set of seven syntactic conditions on P_1 and P_2 that are easy to check statically. In a nutshell, they require the disjointness of the message formats of P_1 and P_2, and that the payloads of P_2 are embedded into P_1 under a unique context to define a sharp borderline. Our seven conditions are satisfied by a large class of protocols in practice. In fact, we believe (and discuss in detail at the end of Section 4) that our conditions are in line with the general principles of prudent engineering for security protocols [1].

(2) We give a compositionality result that shows that the seven conditions are sufficient for static vertical composition, i.e., if P_1 and P_2 are secure in isolation (which can be established using any classical method) and they satisfy the seven conditions, then also $P_1^{P_2} \parallel P_2$ is secure, where $\parallel$ denotes parallel composition. That, in turn, is sufficient for the result in [27] to infer that $P_2[P_1]$ is secure. The proof of our compositionality result can be found in [28].

Finally we also discuss how to extend the result to channel protocols that support more than one channel type and to an arbitrary number of message transmissions, and illustrate this for a TLS-based example. These results are left informal though, since the general vertical protocol composition framework of [27] needs to be extended to this end.

Related Work.

Like the previous results in horizontal protocol composition (see [2, 13, 16, 17] in addition to the works already cited above), our result requires disjoint message formats of the different protocols involved to avoid confusions. Vertical protocol composition, however, makes a difference in that the several layers of a protocol stack can be verified independently, even though messages of the composed protocols are themselves composed from the different layers. For instance, in contrast to [10], we can consider an application protocol completely independent from a transport layer (such as TLS).

The work most similar to ours is [15], which also considers vertical protocol composition. The difference is that [15] supports only one particular kind of channel protocol, namely one that establishes a pair of symmetric keys (one for each communication direction) and then encrypts all messages of the application protocol with the key for the respective direction. In contrast, our results in the present paper are compatible with many channel types (for which the logical connection between channels as assumptions and as goals has to be proved like in [27]) and the transmission over the channel is not limited to symmetric encryption but may be any realization of the desired channel type. Despite being less general in this respect, [15] allows for arbitrary stacks where the same protocol may occur several times, which is here excluded due to disjointness.

Vertical protocol composition is conceptually close to the view of many cryptographers such as [22, 23, 24] and the Universal Composability (UC) framework [8]. The original UC has however very restrictive assumptions that forbid its application to many practical compositions, e.g., that different protocols use the same key-material. Recent extensions and modifications of UC have improved the situation drastically [21]. A detailed comparison is difficult here be-

[2] In fact, later papers [22, 23] have more formal notions of channels as well, but very remote from transition systems.

[3] As we describe in more detail below, the fact that the payload is used as a placeholder for data from an arbitrary protocol makes this a complex problem that cannot be solved simply by requiring the two protocols to be disjoint (which is the typical solution for other kinds of compositionality).

cause the UC-works, and similarly the other cryptographic approaches, are rooted in the cryptographic world based on the indistinguishability of an ideal and a real system, while our approach is based on trace-based protocol semantics and properties (and treats cryptography as black boxes). Works are emerging that bridge the gap between the cryptographic and the symbolic world, but this is beyond the scope of our paper. Rather, we are interested in obtaining results that can be immediately applied with the established protocol verification approaches and we formalize sufficient conditions that are both easy to check and satisfied by many protocols in practice.

Organization.
Section 2 contains some formal preliminaries. To ease the reading, we first (Section 3) discuss our compositionality theorem that shows that the seven conditions that we formalize in this paper are sufficient for static vertical composition and then (Section 4) describe the conditions and illustrate the role that they play in the theorem. In Section 5, we discuss an extension of our compositionality result, and we draw conclusions in Section 6.

2. PRELIMINARIES: PROTOCOL MESSAGES AND TRANSITION SYSTEM

2.1 Messages

Following the line of black-box cryptography models, we employ a term algebra to model the messages that participants exchange. Let Σ be a countable signature and $\mathcal{V}$ be a countable set of variable symbols disjoint from Σ. The signature is partitioned into the set Σ^0 of constants and the set Σ_p of "public" operations. As a convention, we denote variables with upper-case letters and constants with lower-case letters. We use standard notions about terms such as *ground* (without variables), *atomic*, etc. We write $\mathcal{T}_\Sigma$ to denote the set of ground terms and $\mathcal{T}_\Sigma(\mathcal{V})$ to denote all terms.

The constants represent agents, keys, nonces, and the like. The function symbols of Σ_p represent operations on messages that every agent can perform. In this paper, we use the following function symbols: $\{m\}_k$ represents the asymmetric encryption of message m with a public or private key k; $\{|m|\}_k$ represents the symmetric encryption of m with symmetric key k (we assume that this primitive includes also integrity protection such as a MAC); and $[m_1, \ldots, m_n]_n$, for every $n \geq 2$, represents the concatenation of n messages $m_1, \ldots, m_n$ (we use this family of operators to abstract from the details of structuring messages in the implementation).

We also use a set of meta-symbols Σ_m that we refer to as *mappings*. We use them to specify mappings that do not necessarily correspond to operations that agents can perform on messages, e.g., $\mathsf{pubk}(s)$ and $\mathsf{privk}(s)$ represent the public and private keys resulting from a seed s. Moreover, $\mathsf{pk}(A)$ may represent the seed for the public key of agent A to model a fixed public-key infrastructure. Most importantly, we use the mapping $\mathsf{payload}(A, B)$ to denote an *abstract* payload message that A wants to send to B (we will make precise the details of payload messages below). Formally, these mappings are injective functions on Σ^0 (rather than function symbols of the term algebra). As a consequence, the expression $\mathsf{payload}(A, B)$ represents a constant of Σ^0, and is thus regarded as atomic.

2.2 Transition system (ASLan)

For concreteness, as a formal protocol specification language, we use here the *AVANTSSAR Specification Language ASLan* [5, 3] but all our results carry over to other protocol formalisms such as strands, the applied π calculus, and so on. ASLan is (i) expressive enough that many high-level languages (e.g., BPMN or Alice-and-Bob-style languages such as the one we will consider in the following for channels and composition) can be translated to it, and (ii) amenable to formal analysis (e.g., with the AVANTSSAR Platform [3]).

ASLan provides the user with an expressive language for specifying security protocols and their properties, based on set rewriting. At its core, ASLan describes a *state-transition system*, where states are sets of *facts* (i.e., predicates that express something that holds true in a give state) separated by dots ("."). These facts model the state of honest agents, the knowledge of the intruder, communication channels, and goal-relevant information. Transitions are specified as *rewriting rules* over sets of facts. We give here one example of an ASLan transition rule, pointing to the references for more details. Consider the following message exchange (that is part of the protocol P_1 that we will consider in Figure 1 below)

$$A \to B: \{\{[\mathsf{p}, A, B, \mathsf{payload}(A, B)]_4\}_{\mathsf{privk}(\mathsf{pk}(A))}\}_{\mathsf{pubk}(\mathsf{pk}(B))}$$

in which A first signs[4] with its private key a payload, along with information on sender and receiver that is needed to achieve a secure channel. The tag p signals that this concatenation contains the payload transmission. A then encrypts the message with B's public key.

This message exchange is formalized by two ASLan rules, one for the sender and one for the receiver. One way to model the sender's transition is as follows:

$$\begin{aligned}&\mathsf{state}_{\mathcal{A},P_1}(A, \mathit{step1}, \mathit{SID}, B) \Rightarrow\\&\mathsf{state}_{\mathcal{A},P_1}(A, \mathit{step2}, \mathit{SID}, B).\\&\mathsf{iknows}(\{\{[\mathsf{p}, A, B, \mathsf{payload}(A, B)]_4\}_{\mathsf{privk}(\mathsf{pk}(A))}\}_{\mathsf{pubk}(\mathsf{pk}(B))})\end{aligned}$$

where $\mathsf{state}_{\mathcal{A},P_1}(\ldots)$ formalizes the local state of an honest agent in role $\mathcal{A}$ of protocol P_1. Here we have chosen to model this state as consisting of the agent's name A, its step number in the protocol execution, a session identifier SID, and the name of the intended communication partner B. A, B and SID are here variables that allow for matching against arbitrary concrete facts. In contrast, *step1* is a constant, i.e., this rule can only be applied to an agent that is currently in this stage of the protocol execution. On the right-hand side of the rule, there is the updated state of the honest agent and a message that the agent sends out. Since we assume that the intruder can read all messages that are sent on insecure channels, we immediately add this message to the intruder knowledge, as formalized by the fact $\mathsf{iknows}(\cdot)$. The local state of an honest agent does not necessarily carry all the knowledge of the agent (like $\mathsf{payload}(A, B)$) but it is sufficient that it contains all those variables on which the terms depend that the agent is supposed to send and receive.

It is standard to define what the intruder can deduce (e.g., encryption and decryption with known keys) by rules on $\mathsf{iknows}(\cdot)$ facts to obtain a Dolev-Yao-style model. We usually also allow that the intruder may completely control

[4]For simplicity, we model signing by asymmetric encryption with a private key. If one wishes to distinguish signing and encryption, one may of course use instead a dedicated operator like $\mathsf{sign}(\mathsf{privk}(\mathsf{pk}(A)), M)$ and all results hold similarly.

several "compromised" agents (including knowing their long-term secrets). We use the predicate $\mathsf{dishonest}(\cdot)$ that holds true for every agent under the intruder's control (from the initial state on), and the predicate $\mathsf{honest}(\cdot)$ that holds for all other agents.

We describe the goals of a protocol by *attack states*, i.e., states that violate the goals, which are in turn described by *attack rules*: a state at which the attack rule can fire is thus an attack state. For instance, we can formulate a *secrecy goal* as follows. We add the fact $\mathsf{secret}(M, \{A, B\})$ to the right-hand side of an honest agent rule, whenever a message M is supposed to be a secret between A and B, and then give the following attack rule, which expresses that, whenever the fact $\mathsf{secret}(M, \{A, B\})$ holds for two honest agents A and B, and the intruder has learned the message, then we can derive the fact attack:

$$\mathsf{secret}(M, \{A, B\}).\mathsf{iknows}(M).\mathsf{honest}(A).\mathsf{honest}(B) \Rightarrow \mathsf{attack} \quad (1)$$

Definition 1. (Secure protocol) We say that a protocol is *secure* when no attack state is reachable.

Note that our focus, like in most security papers, is on safety properties and they can always be expressed as reachability problems. There are a few papers that also consider liveness (e.g., [4]), but this generally also requires fairness assumptions on the channels as otherwise an intruder could simply block communication indefinitely. We leave for future work the investigation if such resilient channels can be combined with our approach.

3. CHANNELS AND COMPOSITION

The most common type of security protocol composition is running two protocols in parallel over the same network, which is easy to define for many protocol formalisms. For instance, in a strand notation, we simply consider the union of the strands of the two protocols. Similarly, in ASLan we will simply consider the union of the rules of the two protocols (as well as the unions of initial states and goal rules).

There is, however, a subtlety about this in ASLan due to its expressiveness. Recall that in the previous example of a transition rule in ASLan we have noted explicitly the protocol in the name of the state fact. If we did instead use the same fact $\mathsf{state}_{\mathcal{A}}$ in several protocols and build the union, then we might obtain executions that do not make much sense. So, in general, we assume that the state facts of different protocols are disjoint to avoid this kind of collisions. For other facts it can, however, make sense to use the same predicate in several protocols. Obviously, $\mathsf{iknows}(\cdot)$ and attack shall be shared by protocols, but one may also formalize a database of an agent A as the set of messages msg for which a fact $\mathsf{db}(A, msg)$ holds. This database can then be "shared" across different protocols that A participates in. As this makes composition much more difficult, we will exclude this by assuming the following notion of protocol independence:

Definition 2. (Execution independence of two protocols) We say that two protocols P_1 and P_2 are *execution independent* if they are formulated over disjoint sets of facts, except for $\mathsf{iknows}(\cdot)$ and attack.

Execution independence is neither necessary nor sufficient for parallel compositionality (or other composition types), but it only simplifies the problem: we reduce ourselves to protocols that can interfere with each other only in terms of exchanged messages.

Three further remarks are in order. First, note that execution independence does not exclude protocols where agents for instance maintain protocol-specific databases over several protocol sessions, it only excludes that a database can be shared over several protocols. Second, note that for security goals we also have protocol-specific facts, e.g., $\mathsf{secret}_{\mathsf{P}_1}$, but that is not a restriction and even helps to identify in which protocol the goals were violated. Finally, note that the definition of execution independence is trivial for strands and the applied π calculus: they cannot express dependent protocols in this sense.

Definition 3. (Parallel Composition $P_1 \parallel P_2$ and Composability) For two execution independent protocols P_1 and P_2 specified in ASLan, we define their *parallel composition* as the union of the initial states, transition rules, and goal rules, respectively. We denote the resulting ASLan specification with $P_1 \parallel P_2$.

We say that P_1 and P_2 are *composable in parallel* if the following holds: if P_1 and P_2 are secure in isolation, then also $P_1 \parallel P_2$ is secure.

A similar definition can be given for the composition of Alice-and-Bob-style protocols modulo their translation to ASLan.

The main idea to ensure parallel compositionality is that messages of the composed protocols should have sufficiently different formats so that no message part of one protocol can be mistaken for one of another. For simple Alice-and-Bob-style protocols, this is already sufficient, but in general more complex situations may occur. For instance, if a web-service maintains a database of transactions that it was involved in, and several of the composed protocols involve reading or writing in this database, then this can result in a "side-channel" that may break compositionality.

3.1 Channels as Assumptions, Channels as Goals

Channels may be used both as protocol assumptions (i.e., when a protocol relies on channels with particular properties for the transmission of some of its messages) and as protocol goals (i.e., a protocol's objective is the establishment of a particular kind of channel). Considering channels as assumptions allows us to enhance the standard insecure communication medium with security guarantees for message transmission. We can express this, e.g., in an Alice-and-Bob-style notation, where a secure end-point of a channel is marked by a bullet, as follows:

- $A \rightarrow B : M$ represents an *insecure channel* from A to B, meaning that the channel is under the complete control of the intruder.
- $A \bullet\!\!\rightarrow B : M$ represents an *authentic channel* from A to B, meaning that B can rely on the fact that A has sent the message M and A meant to send it to B.
- $A \rightarrow\!\!\bullet B : M$ represents a *confidential* (or *secret*) *channel* from A to B, meaning that A can rely on the fact that only B can receive the message M.
- $A \bullet\!\!\rightarrow\!\!\bullet B : M$ represents a *secure channel*, i.e., a channel that is both authentic and confidential.

P_1 :

$$\begin{array}{lccl} A & \rightarrow & B & : \{\{[\mathsf{p}, A, B, \mathsf{payload}(A,B)]_4\}_{\mathsf{privk}(\mathsf{pk}(A))}\}_{\mathsf{pubk}(\mathsf{pk}(B))} \\ \hline A & \bullet\!\!\rightarrow\!\!\bullet & B & : \mathsf{payload}(A,B) \end{array}$$

P_2 :

$$\begin{array}{lccl} D & \rightarrow & C & : [N, C, D]_3 \\ C & \bullet\!\!\rightarrow\!\!\bullet & D & : [h(N), M]_2 \\ \hline C & \bullet\!\!\rightarrow\!\!\bullet & D & : M \end{array}$$

$P_1^{P_2}$:

$$\begin{array}{lccl} A & \rightarrow & B & : \{\{[\mathsf{p}, A, B, m_{A,B}]_4\}_{\mathsf{privk}(\mathsf{pk}(A))}\}_{\mathsf{pubk}(\mathsf{pk}(B))} \\ \hline A & \bullet\!\!\rightarrow\!\!\bullet & B & : m_{A,B} \end{array}$$

$P_2[P_1]$:

$$\begin{array}{lccl} D & \rightarrow & C & : [N, C, D]_3 \\ C & \rightarrow & D & : \{\{[\mathsf{p}, C, D, [h(N), M]_2]_4\}_{\mathsf{privk}(\mathsf{pk}(C))}\}_{\mathsf{pubk}(\mathsf{pk}(D))} \\ \hline C & \bullet\!\!\rightarrow\!\!\bullet & D & : M \end{array}$$

Figure 1: Abstract channel protocol P_1 (top left) and application protocol P_2 (top right), their static vertical composition $P_1^{P_2}$ (bottom left) and their vertical composition $P_2[P_1]$ (bottom right).

These are some examples of channel types, but note that, in fact, the details of the supported channel types do not matter for the results of this paper.

In [27], we also give a definition of channels as goals, e.g., to express that it is the goal of a protocol to authentically transmit a certain message. This gives rise to a vertical composition question: given a *channel protocol* that provides a certain kind of channel as a goal and an *application protocol* that assumes this kind of channel, is it safe to compose the two? While [27] tackles the "logical aspect" of this question, we look in this paper at the "static aspect", i.e., the potential problems that arise from inserting the messages of one protocol into another protocol. In particular, for compositional reasoning we want to be able to verify channel protocol and application protocol separately. This means, especially, that we want to verify the channel protocol for an *abstract payload* that is independent of the application that uses the channel (and this requires more than mere protocol disjointness).

The easiest and most intuitive way to define vertical composition is at the level of Alice-and-Bob notation, and we use here the formal language AnB [26, 27], which can be automatically translated to ASLan so that we can connect to and exploit our ASLan formalization of protocols. It is possible to give corresponding definitions on the ASLan level as well, but due to the handling of local state facts it would be technically quite involved and distracting from our main point.

An *AnB specification* of a protocol is, in a nutshell, a description of a protocol as an exchange of messages; the goal is specified as a result below a horizontal line using the channel notation about some message terms of the protocol.

Definition 4. (Abstract Channel Protocol) Let $\kappa(A, B)$ range over a set of defined channel types (e.g., $A \bullet\!\!\rightarrow B : M$) and $\mathsf{payload}(A, B)$ be a mapping from pairs of agents to (abstract) payloads. An *abstract channel protocol* for $\kappa(A, B)$ is an AnB specification that has $\kappa(A, B) : \mathsf{payload}(A, B)$ as a goal. Moreover, we require that every agent A initially knows $\mathsf{payload}(A, B)$ for every communication partner B (recall the notion of knowledge given in Section 2).

An example of an abstract channel protocol is P_1 in Figure 1. The message exchange was already explained in Section 2, and we declare the goal to be the transmission of the abstract payload over a secure channel.

Definition 5. (Application Protocol) An *application protocol* for channel $\kappa(A, B)$ is an AnB specification that contains as part of its message exchange one step $\kappa(A, B) : t$ with some message term t.

An example of an application protocol is P_2 in Figure 1, in which D first sends to C a nonce N, together with both agent names, as a challenge on an insecure channel, and then C sends back to D the hashed nonce $h(N)$ paired with a message M on a secure channel; the goal of this protocol is the secure transmission of the message M between the two agents.

3.2 Vertical Protocol Composition

Definition 6. (Vertical Composition $P_2[P_1]$) Let P_1 be an abstract channel protocol for $\kappa(A, B)$ and P_2 an application protocol for $\kappa(C, D)$.[5] The *vertical composition* $P_2[P_1]$ is defined by replacing in P_2 the step $\kappa(C, D) : t$ with the entire protocol P_1 under the replacement $[A \mapsto C, B \mapsto D, \mathsf{payload}(A, B) \mapsto t]$.

An example is given in Figure 1, where $\mathsf{payload}(A, B) \mapsto [h(N), M]_2$.

As already mentioned, we separate the vertical composition question into a logical aspect (that is already handled in [27]) and a static aspect. For this, we need two further definitions related to this composition. We now define the notion of static vertical composition; it is based on a static characterization of all the messages that can occur in any run of the protocol P_2 as a payload:

Definition 7. Let P_2 be an application protocol and let $\kappa(C, D) : t$ be the step that uses an abstract channel $\kappa(C, D)$ to transmit message t. Consider the set of all ground terms t_0 that are instance of t in any run of P_2 for a fixed pair (C, D) of agents. We define $\mathcal{M}_{C,D}$ to be an *arbitrary* superset of this set of payload messages.

For the example protocol P_2 from Figure 1, the payload messages sent by an honest agent C has always the form $[h(N), M]_2$, where N is any message that C has received in the first step (supposedly from D) and M is a fresh nonce. We can bound the values that are possible for M since they are freshly created by C; let us say we have a distinguished subset $M_{C,D}$ of all constants (for each pair C and D of agents), from which these are taken. Then the set of all

[5] To avoid confusion, we assume here disjoint role names; but when there is no risk of confusion, later on in the paper, we will use the same role names in the two protocols.

payload messages that can ever occur here are a subset of $\mathcal{M}_{C,D} = \{[h(N), M]_2 \mid N \in \mathcal{T}_\Sigma \wedge M \in M_{C,D}\}$. Note that it is difficult to bound the set of values that variable N can take: it is (potentially) under the control of the intruder and basically depends on what he knows at the time, so we take the largest possible choice, namely, the set $\mathcal{T}_\Sigma$ of all ground terms. (In fact, for dishonest C we usually have to set $\mathcal{M}_{C,D} = \mathcal{T}_\Sigma$ as the intruder can send any term from his knowledge; the case of dishonest C is however uncritical for the rest.)

This example shows why we do not require $\mathcal{M}_{C,D}$ to be *exactly* the set of all payload messages that can occur, but allow *any* superset. This over-approximation is typical of static analysis. As a rule of thumb, very large, coarse over-approximations make computations easier, but also increase the risk of false positives, i.e., protocols that do not satisfy our sufficient conditions even though they are composable. In our case, a coarse over-approximation can lead to false positives, since we will later assume that the intruder gets all payloads $\mathcal{M}_{C,D}$ whenever the receiver D is dishonest or secrecy of the payload is not a goal (and C is honest). Suppose we had in the example protocol instead of the hash $h(N)$ directly the nonce N; this would mean that the intruder knows $[N, \cdot]_2$ for every $N \in \mathcal{T}_\Sigma$, i.e., then with $\mathcal{M}_{C,i}$ he initially knows *every* term, trivially giving us false positives. In such a case, we would need to resort to a full-fledged static-analysis approach—in this example, intuitively, using the fact that the intruder learns only nonces N that he himself sent earlier. As the entire approach is already quite complex, we chose not to consider this complication in this paper.

Definition 8. (Static Vertical Composition $P_1^{P_2}$) Let P_1 be a channel protocol for $\kappa(A, B)$ and P_2 an application protocol for the channel $\kappa(C, D)$, and let $\mathcal{M}_{C,D}$ be the set of ground messages that C can transmit over the channel $\kappa(C, D)$ in any run of the protocol P_2. The *static vertical composition* $P_1^{P_2}$ is the protocol that results from P_1 by replacing $\mathsf{payload}(A, B)$ when it is first sent by A with a non-deterministically chosen element of $\mathcal{M}_{C,D}$, and all the following occurrences of $\mathsf{payload}(A, B)$ must be the same element of $\mathcal{M}_{C,D}$.

An example is given in Figure 1, where we write $m_{A,B}$ to denote an arbitrary message, non-deterministically chosen, from the set $\mathcal{M}_{A,B}$.

The protocol $P_1^{P_2}$ represents a certain "concretization" of P_1 with "random" payload messages from P_2.[6] This notion is valuable because it indeed allows us to divide the composition problem into two aspects, a logical and a static one:

Definition 9. (Static Vertical Composability) Given an abstract channel protocol P_1 and an application protocol P_2 as in the definitions above, we say that P_1 and P_2 are *statically vertically composable* if the following implication holds: if P_1 and P_2 are secure in isolation, then also $P_1^{P_2} \parallel P_2$ is secure.

These notions are used in [27] to show the following compositionality result:

THEOREM 1 ([27]). *If channel protocol P_1 and application protocol P_2 are secure protocols in isolation and they are both statically vertically composable and composable in parallel, then $P_2[P_1]$ is secure.*

In this paper, we call this result the logical aspect of the problem, because it proves that the definitions of channels as assumption and as goals have "compatible" behavior, and what remains to show is static vertical composability. It turns out that the static aspect is in fact quite intricate and solving this open problem is the main contribution of this paper: the rest of this paper will concentrate on giving conditions that can be easily checked syntactically and proving that they are sufficient for a pair of protocols to be statically vertically composable, i.e., satisfying Definition 9.

As a result, we can check in isolation, with any protocol verification method, a channel protocol P_1 with abstract payload as well as an application protocol P_2 that uses the respective channel type. If this channel type is part of the ones defined in [27] and the sufficient conditions of this paper are satisfied for P_1 and P_2, then we can combine Theorem 1 with our Theorem 2 (given below) to infer that $P_2[P_1]$ is secure.

3.3 The Static Aspect of Vertical Protocol Composition

We are now ready for our main result, namely that the seven conditions that we will define in Section 4 are sufficient for static vertical composability, i.e., if P_1 and P_2 are secure, then so is $P_1^{P_2} \parallel P_2$. Or, in other words, that we can reduce an attack against $P_1^{P_2} \parallel P_2$ to an attack against one of the component protocols.

THEOREM 2. *Consider two protocols P_1 and P_2 that satisfy all the seven conditions defined in Section 4. If there is an attack against $P_1^{P_2} \parallel P_2$, then there is an attack against P_1 or against P_2.*

Since we lack space to give the proof of this theorem (the proof is given in [28] and spans several pages), let us at least give a proof sketch, and then illustrate the proof by means of a detailed example, which also provides further motivation for the conditions themselves, which we will formalize in the next section.

PROOF SKETCH. In the proof, we employ the constraint reduction technique that we refer to as the *lazy intruder* (see, e.g., [6, 9, 25, 29]). While this technique is originally a verification technique (for a bounded number of sessions), we use it here for a proof argument for our compositionality result (for an unbounded number of sessions). The key idea of the lazy intruder is to model "symbolic executions" where variables in the messages that honest agents receive from the insecure network (i.e., from the intruder) are left uninstantiated. We use intruder *constraints* of the form

$$IK \vdash t$$

where t is a (symbolic) term that an agent is able to receive and the set IK of messages is the current intruder knowledge. We use the fact that we can check satisfiability of such constraints using the lazy intruder calculus, and that we can reduce insecurity to satisfiability of lazy intruder constraints.

We thus assume we are given lazy intruder constraints for an attack against the composition $P_1^{P_2}$ for any channel protocol P_1 and application protocol P_2 that satisfy our seven conditions. We then show that over all reductions with the

[6] [27] instead uses the notion P_1^*, which, however, may be confusing here as it does not denote the protocol from which the payloads come.

lazy intruder calculus, the seven conditions and some further invariants are preserved, in particular, that the attack never requires a confusion between P_1 and P_2 messages. This is because the lazy intruder technique never instantiates variables whose concrete value is irrelevant for the attack (this is why we call it *lazy* in the first place); these still admit "ill-typed" instantiations (confusing P_1 and P_2), but they always also admit well-typed instantiations. As a consequence, we can show that there exists an attack against P_1 in isolation or against P_2 in isolation. □

3.4 Illustration

We illustrate the proof at hand of a concrete example. Let us turn again to the example protocols P_1, P_2, $P_1^{P_2}$ and $P_2[P_1]$ from Figure 1, and let us now consider a slight variant of the protocol P_1 in which we deliberately insert an authentication vulnerability. This allows us to illustrate the different steps in the construction of the proof—that an attack against $P_2[P_1]$ can be reduced to an attack against either P_1 or P_2. Moreover, it also helps to illustrate and motivate the conditions that we introduce below.

Note that the message in P_1 mentions both the sender and the intended receiver as part of the signature. Let us now consider a variant without these two names:

P_1 :

$$\begin{array}{llll} A & \rightarrow & B & : \{\{[\mathsf{p}, \mathsf{payload}(A,B)]_2\}_{\mathsf{privk}(\mathsf{pk}(A))}\}_{\mathsf{pubk}(\mathsf{pk}(B))} \\ \hline A & \bullet\!\!\rightarrow\!\!\bullet & B & : \mathsf{payload}(A,B) \end{array}$$

that also gives accordingly the following variants of the compositions $P_1^{P_2}$ and $P_2[P_1]$:

$P_1^{P_2}$:

$$\begin{array}{llll} A & \rightarrow & B & : \{\{[\mathsf{p}, m_{A,B}]_2\}_{\mathsf{privk}(\mathsf{pk}(A))}\}_{\mathsf{pubk}(\mathsf{pk}(B))} \\ \hline A & \bullet\!\!\rightarrow\!\!\bullet & B & : m_{A,B} \end{array}$$

$P_2[P_1]$:

$$\begin{array}{llll} D & \rightarrow & C & : [N, C, D]_3 \\ C & \rightarrow & D & : \{\{[\mathsf{p}, [h(N), M]_2]_2\}_{\mathsf{privk}(\mathsf{pk}(C))}\}_{\mathsf{pubk}(\mathsf{pk}(D))} \\ \hline C & \bullet\!\!\rightarrow\!\!\bullet & D & : M \end{array}$$

As we already remarked above, it turns out that, for our proof, a symbolic representation of traces is very useful to make the arguments about intruder actions concise. This representation is often used in model checking, sometimes briefly referred to as the lazy intruder technique, but our results are of course independent of any such technology. A *symbolic trace* of a protocol consists of a sequence of send and receive actions of the honest agents, in which we have variables for each subterm of a received message where the agent is willing to accept an arbitrary value; this variable can then occur in subsequent sending actions. Although we do not note it explicitly here, every sent message is directly added to the intruder knowledge, and every received message must be constructed by the intruder. For instance, the following is one symbolic trace for the protocol $P_2[P_1]$:

d sends $m_1 = [n, c, d]_3$
c receives $m_1' = [N, c, D]_3$
c sends $m_2' = \{\{[\mathsf{p}, [h(N), m]_2]_2\}_{\mathsf{privk}(\mathsf{pk}(c))}\}_{\mathsf{pubk}(\mathsf{pk}(D))}$
d receives $m_2 = \{\{[\mathsf{p}, [h(n), M]_2]_2\}_{\mathsf{privk}(\mathsf{pk}(c))}\}_{\mathsf{pubk}(\mathsf{pk}(d))}$

where the constants n and m are the concrete nonces that d and c created for N and M, respectively. When c receives m_1', every value for nonce N and for the claimed sender D is possible, and the answer m_2' that c sends depends on these two variables. In contrast, when d receives m_2, it must be encrypted for d and contain the nonce n sent earlier. A requirement for such a trace to exist is that the intruder can indeed construct all the messages that are received, using what he learned. For this symbolic trace, we thus have the constraints

$$IK_0 \cup \{m_1\} \vdash m_1' \quad \wedge \quad IK_0 \cup \{m_1, m_2'\} \vdash m_2 ,$$

Here, IK_0 is the set of initially known messages: it includes all public constants, i.e., all agent names, public keys, the private keys of the dishonest agents (like $\mathsf{privk}(\mathsf{pk}(i))$), as well as the payloads for dishonest receivers, i.e., $\mathcal{M}_{C,D} = \{[h(N), M]_2 \mid N \in \mathcal{T}_\Sigma, M \in M_{C,D}\}$ for honest C and dishonest D and where $M_{C,D}$ is the subset of nonces that C freshly creates for D. Thus, from IK_0 the intruder can derive $h(t)$ for every term t, and he can derive all nonces that honest agents will create for him, but this does not include n and m since these are created for honest agents. (However n is derivable from the first message m_1.) Note that the symbolic representation with the constraints corresponds exactly to the set of *ground* traces that are possible.

The core of the lazy intruder is a constraint reduction technique to find (a finite representation of) all solutions of the constraints. In this case, we have, for instance, the solution $D = d$, $N = n$, $M = m$ that corresponds to one normal execution of the protocol between two honest agents c and d with the intruder as a "network node" simply forwarding all messages. We can, however, also express that the symbolic trace violates authentication, namely if c and d at the end do not agree on the concrete values of the (relevant) protocol variables, namely whenever $M \neq m$ or $D \neq d$ (the nonce N itself is not part of any authentication goals). There is indeed such a solution: $D = i$, $M = m$, and $N = n$. This means that the intruder started a session with c, playing under his real name in role D and using the nonce n from the other session with the honest d. The intruder can then decrypt the message m_2' (since it is encrypted with his public key) and re-encrypt it with the public key of d, completing the attack.

The logical part of the composition problem (i.e., what is proved in [27]) shows that such an attack on $P_2[P_1]$ can be transformed into one on $P_1^{P_2} \parallel P_2$. For our example, the transformed symbolic attack would look like this (annotating for each step which of the protocols it belongs to):

P_2 : d sends $m_1 = [n, c, d]_3$
P_2 : c receives $m_1' = [N, c, D]_3$
P_2 : c sends on a secure channel $c \bullet\!\!\rightarrow\!\!\bullet D$: $[h(N), m]_2$
$P_1^{P_2}$: c sends $m_2' = \{\{[\mathsf{p}, [h(N), m]_2]_2\}_{\mathsf{privk}(\mathsf{pk}(c))}\}_{\mathsf{pubk}(\mathsf{pk}(D))}$
$P_1^{P_2}$: d receives $m_2 = \{\{[\mathsf{p}, X]_2\}_{\mathsf{privk}(\mathsf{pk}(c))}\}_{\mathsf{pubk}(\mathsf{pk}(d))}$
P_2 : D receives on a secure channel $c \bullet\!\!\rightarrow\!\!\bullet D$: $[h(N), m]_2$

Here, the abstract channel of P_2 runs in parallel with a corresponding step from $P_1^{P_2}$ with exactly the same payload message (which is possible since in $P_1^{P_2}$ the agent c non-deterministically picks a message from the set of all payload messages $\mathcal{M}_{c,D}$). Also note that d receiving m_2 in $P_1^{P_2}$ does not require a particular form of payload anymore (in contrast to the message m_2 in the $P_2[P_1]$ trace).

The intruder deduction constraints for the received messages are again the same (modulo the said change of m_2). The requirement for the attack is also similar: $D \neq d$ or

$X \neq [h(N), m]_2$, and we have again the attack for the solution $D = i$ (and $X = [h(N), m]_2$ with N arbitrary).

Now the goal of this paper to show that such a $P_1^{P_2} \parallel P_2$ attack can indeed be reduced to an attack against P_1 in isolation or against P_2 in isolation.

To that end, we look at how the lazy intruder technique would check the satisfiability of the constraints

$$IK_0 \cup \{m_1\} \vdash m_1' \ \wedge \ IK_0 \cup \{m_1, m_2'\} \vdash m_2 \ \wedge \\ (D \neq i \vee M \neq m).$$

The point for using the lazy intruder here is that the technique is complete, i.e., if the constraints have a solution, then the reduction rules find a solution, and that the *laziness* precludes making any instantiations of variables that are not required for solving the constraints.

One reduction rule is *unification*: for constraint $IK \vdash t_1$, if there is a term $t_2 \in IK$ that is unifiable with t_1 under the most general unifier σ, then we can solve this constraint and apply σ to all remaining constraints. However at this point we are lazy: we do not apply the unification rule if t_1 or t_2 is a variable; we do not make a choice when any value t_1 is fine, and do not analyze any value t_2 that the intruder himself created earlier. One of the conditions below (namely, (Καπανεύς)) in fact says that the structure of all messages and non-atomic submessages in the protocols P_1 and P_2 must be sufficiently disjoint; roughly speaking, P_1 stuff cannot be unified with P_2 stuff. The exclusion of atomic submessages (i.e., variables and constants) is necessary because a random nonce does not indicate whether it "belongs" to P_1 or P_2. Thus, in any unification step of the lazy intruder, t_1 and t_2 can only be unifiable if they belong to the same protocol. In the example, neither m_1 nor m_1' can be unified with m_2 or m_2'.

Other intruder operations are *analysis* of messages in the knowledge (e.g., in the example the intruder can decrypt m_2'), as well as *generating* terms on the sender side (in the example, the intruder can generate m_2 by encrypting with $\mathsf{pubk}(\mathsf{pk}(d))$ the message obtained from decrypting m_2'). More generally, this allows us to show that each constraint for generating a $P_1^{P_2}$ message can be solved without using any P_2 messages in the knowledge and vice versa. Thus, we can reduce it to a problem of "pure" constraints that contain only messages from one protocol each. That, however, by the notion of protocol independence (cf. Definition 8, required below in (Τυδεύς)) means that we can simply split the constraints into a $P_1^{P_2}$ part and a P_2 part, and they represent an execution in isolation of $P_1^{P_2}$ and of P_2, respectively. Moreover, one of the two executions is then an attack against the respective protocol. In our case, the two $P_1^{P_2}$ steps of the trace together with the constraint $IK_0 \cup \{m_2'\} \vdash m_2$ alone entail an attack against $P_1^{P_2}$: the attack is the solution $D = i$ and $X = [h(n), m]_2$.

What remains to show is that this implies also an attack on P_1. This follows merely by replacing the payload $[h(n), m]_2$ in m_2' with the abstract payload $\mathsf{payload}(c, D)$. In fact, as part of the conditions below we will label every payload sent by an honest agent with this abstract payload (reflecting the intentions of the agent). Similarly, the receiver-side payload X is labeled with d's expectations of a payload from C for d. The solution $C = c$ and $D = i$ is the authentication attack. This concludes the illustration of the proof.

We thus solved the static vertical composition question as it was left open in [27]. We emphasize once again that the results are independent both of the verification technique used for verifying the atomic components and of the formalism employed to model protocols such as rewriting, strands, or process calculi.

4. THE CONDITIONS

We now finally present our seven conditions on a pair of protocols that are sufficient for the vertical composition result (cf. Theorem 2); actually, in some cases, the conditions are sets of related sub-conditions. For each condition, we also highlight the specific role it plays in the proof. We label the conditions with the names of the Ἑπτὰ ἐπὶ Θήβας [19].

4.1 Structural Properties (Τυδεύς)

The first condition is that P_1 is a channel protocol providing a $\kappa(A, B)$ channel and P_2 is an application protocol relying on a $\kappa(A, B)$ channel according to Definitions 4 and 5, so that the compositions $P_2[P_1]$ and $P_1^{P_2}$ (Definitions 6 and 8) are actually defined. Let also $\mathcal{M}_{A,B}$ be defined with respect to P_2 according to Definition 8. We further assume that P_1 and P_2 are execution independent (Definition 2).

The execution independence is used in the "splitting step" of the proof, where we have an execution of $P_1^{P_2}$ and P_2 in parallel and where we already know that the intruder does not need to use messages from either protocol to attack the other. Execution independence then allows us to conclude that the sub-traces of the respective protocols are valid traces.

4.2 Constants (Ἱππομέδων)

We require that the set $\mathcal{A}$ of constants of the protocols is partitioned into 4 pairwise disjoint subsets $\mathcal{A} = \mathcal{P} \uplus \mathcal{S} \uplus \mathcal{F} \uplus \mathcal{L}$ where:

- $\mathcal{S}$ is the set of *secret constants*, e.g., long-term private keys of honest agents, or long-term shared keys shared by only honest agents; we assume that these are never transported (they can of course be used for encryption/signing).
- $\mathcal{P} \subseteq M_0$ is the set of *public constants*, e.g., agent names, long-term public keys, long-term private keys of dishonest agents, long-term shared keys that are shared with a dishonest agent; these are part of the initial knowledge M_0 of the intruder.
- $\mathcal{F}$ is the set of the *fresh constants*, i.e., whenever an agent randomly generates new keys or nonces, they will be picked uniquely from this set. As is standard, the intruder by default does not know the fresh constants created by honest agents, but may learn them from messages that the agents send. $\mathcal{F}$ is further partitioned into the two disjoint subsets $\mathcal{F}_1$ and $\mathcal{F}_2$ of fresh constants of P_1 and P_2, respectively.
- $\mathcal{L}$ is the set of *abstract payloads* (i.e., those denoted by $\mathsf{payload}(A, B)$). These may only occur in P_1, and are replaced by concrete payloads in $P_1^{P_2}$ and $P_2[P_1]$. We discuss the initial knowledge of the abstract payloads below.

The partitioning of the constants plays a role in proving that for each message that the intruder has to produce for protocol P_2, he needs only (composed) P_2 messages, public constants, and fresh constants from $\mathcal{F}_2$. (And a similar property holds for $P_1^{P_2}$.) If, however, the considered attack were to use a secret constant from $\mathcal{S}$, then there would be a simpler attack already (and we would not need to worry about the construction of further messages with the exposed secret). The abstract payloads $\mathcal{L}$ only come back into the picture in the final step of the proof, when we reduce the $P_1^{P_2}$ attack to a P_1 attack.

4.3 Disjointness (Καπανεύς)

We require that the message formats are sufficiently different to distinguish P_1 *terms* and P_2 *terms*—except for constants (like agent names, nonces, and keys) since constants (a) may be shared between protocols (e.g., agent names and keys) and (b) by construction usually cannot be attributed to a unique protocol, (e.g., nonces).

- The *message patterns MP* are the terms that represent messages sent and received by honest agents in the ASLan protocol description, where we ensure by renaming of variables that distinct elements of MP have disjoint variables. Let *SMP* be the *non-atomic subterms* of the message patterns (with the same variable renaming). For instance, for the protocols of Figure 1, *MP* and *SMP* are as shown in Figure 2, where we write A, B, C, D as placeholders for arbitrary agents for the sake of readability. We require message patterns not to be atomic:[7] $MP(P_i) \cap (\mathcal{V} \cup \Sigma^0) = \emptyset$ for $i \in \{1, 2\}$; moreover, non-atomic subterms must be disjoint: $SMP(P_1) \sqcap SMP(P_2) = \emptyset$, where $M \sqcap N = \{\sigma \mid \exists m \in M, n \in N.\ m\sigma = n\sigma\}$. We exclude atomic message patterns since otherwise we'd have messages for which we cannot ensure that they are attributed to a unique protocol.
- By the previous item, the following labeling is possible on all message patterns in the protocol description. Every non-atomic subterm m is labeled either P_1 or P_2, in symbols $m : P_i$. There is only one unique such labeling because the spaces of non-atomic subterms of the P_i must be disjoint.
- Next, we can also label the atomic subterms except public and secret constants in a unique way: we label them by the label of the next surrounding operator. We will make one exception from this rule below for the payload (the payload is of type P_2 but it is embedded into a P_1 context), but, in order not to break the flow of the argument, we postpone this a bit.
- We additionally require that the sets of variables used in the descriptions of P_1 and P_2 are disjoint, and that fresh constants are chosen from the disjoint sets $\mathcal{F}_i$. Therefore, no variable or constant can have an ambiguous labeling.

Forbidding atomic messages in *MP* may seem like a restriction, e.g., we cannot send simply a single nonce N as message. However, observe that we only require to put that nonce into a bit of context e.g., $[tag, N]_2$, where *tag* could be a constant identifying the protocol, as it is in practice often done with port numbers.

This condition is used in the proof when we consider how the lazy intruder constraints of a given attack can be solved. The message to construct is an instance of a subterm of *MP*. It is either non-atomic or atomic. If it is non-atomic (i.e., is an instance of a term in *SMP*), then it belongs to a unique protocol P_1 or P_2 and unification is only possible with other *SMP* messages of that protocol that are in the knowledge of the intruder. If it is atomic, then it is either a constant (and handled by arguments provided by the previous condition) or a variable. Note that the variable is thus labeled by the last surrounding context. This is in fact the key where the lazy intruder comes into play: we leave constraints where the term to generate is just a variable, i.e., any term the intruder knows will do. However, during other reduction steps, the variable may get instantiated. In this case, again by this condition, the instantiated term will have the same label as the variable (i.e., whether it belongs to P_1 or P_2). Thus, at the end of the day, we obtain that all P_2 terms can be constructed using only P_2 knowledge and public constants (and similar for $P_1^{P_2}$ terms).

4.4 Disjointness of Concrete Payloads (Πολυνείκης)

We require that $\mathcal{M}_{A,B}$ comprise only of ground P_2 terms. Moreover, the concrete sets of payload terms $\mathcal{M}_{A,B}$ must be pairwise disjoint for honest senders, i.e., $\mathcal{M}_{A,B} \cap \mathcal{M}_{A',B'} = \emptyset$ whenever A and A' are honest and ($A \neq A'$ or $B \neq B'$).[8] This does not imply that honest agents or the intruder can recognize from a payload who is (the claimed) A and B.

This condition allows us to unambiguously label every concrete payload with its original sender (even when the message has been forwarded and manipulated by the intruder) and the intended recipient. This labeling makes several constructions in the proof easier as we explain below.

To see that this condition is actually feasible, consider for instance the concrete example of $\mathcal{M}_{A,B}$ in Section 3.2.

4.5 Payload Type and Context (Ἐτέοκλος)

We now make some provisions about the handling of payload messages in the protocols. We begin with an overview and then give the precise conditions. First, we label those subterms in the message patterns that represent payloads sent or received by honest agents. This is, of course, no restriction but requires that during the translation from AnB to ASLan we need to keep track of which subterms of messages represent payloads, and we thus simply speak of messages of type Payload (this is made precise below). Second, we require that these payload subterms when sent or received by honest agents are always embedded into a unique *payload context* $C_P[\cdot]$ that unambiguously signalizes the subterm is meant as a payload and so that no other message parts are accidentally interpreted as payloads (this is also made precise below). We require that this context is an n-tuple of the form $[m_1, \ldots, m_n]_n$ where one of the m_i is the payload and the other m_i are all constants, e.g., tags or agent names. For instance, our example abstract channel protocol P_1 in Figure 1 uses the context $C_P(A, B)[\cdot] = [\mathsf{p}, A, B, \cdot]_4$. Note that we here actually allow that contexts may be parameterized over additional information such as the involved agents, but for simplicity of notation we only write $C_P[\cdot]$ whenever no confusion arises. Note also that the context alone does not protect the payload against manipulation or even reading by other parts, as this depends on the goal of the channel protocol. Moreover, we will assume that an intruder can always create such contexts.

The precise requirements about the labeling and the occurrence of contexts are as follows:

1. ($C_P[\cdot]$ identifies payload.) In P_1 and $P_1^{P_2}$ terms: For every term $C_P[m]$ it holds that m is typed Payload, and all Payload-typed messages m occur as $C_P[m]$. More-

[7] Recall that mappings like $\mathsf{pk}(a)$ map from atoms to atoms and thus $\mathsf{pk}(a)$ also counts as atomic in the sense of this definition.

[8] This could be achieved by inserting a constant into the payload chosen from a set $\mathcal{X}_{A,B}$ of a family of disjoint sets $\mathcal{X}_{A,B}$.

$$
\begin{aligned}
MP(P_1) &= \{ \{\{[\mathsf{p}, A, B, \mathsf{payload}(A,B)]_4\}_{\mathsf{privk}(\mathsf{pk}(A))}\}_{\mathsf{pubk}(\mathsf{pk}(B))}, \{\{[\mathsf{p}, A_1, B_1, X_1]_4\}_{\mathsf{privk}(\mathsf{pk}(A_1))}\}_{\mathsf{pubk}(\mathsf{pk}(B_1))} \} \\
SMP(P_1) &= MP(P_1) \cup \{ \{[\mathsf{p}, A_2, B_2, \mathsf{payload}(A_2,B_2)]_4\}_{\mathsf{privk}(\mathsf{pk}(A_2))}, \{[\mathsf{p}, A_3, B_3, X_3]_4\}_{\mathsf{privk}(\mathsf{pk}(A_3))}, \\
&\quad \mathsf{pubk}(\mathsf{pk}(B_4)), [\mathsf{p}, A_5, B_5, \mathsf{payload}(A_5,B_5)]_4, [\mathsf{p}, A_6, B_6, X_6]_4, \mathsf{privk}(\mathsf{pk}(A_7)), \mathsf{p}, \mathsf{payload}(A_8,B_8) \} \\
MP(P_2) &= \{ [N_1, C_1, D_1]_3, [h(N_2), M_2]_2 \} \\
SMP(P_2) &= MP(P_2) \cup \{ h(N_2) \}
\end{aligned}
$$

Figure 2: MP and SMP for the example protocols of Figure 1.

over, in $P_1^{P_2}$ such a message m is a concrete payload from P_2 and is thus labeled as belonging to P_2, while in P_1, we have abstract payloads that are labeled P_1.

2. ($C_P[\cdot]$ has blank-or-concrete payloads): each payload that occurs under $C_P[\cdot]$ (i.e., in all P_1 messages) is either ground or a variable. The ground case represents an honest agent sending a concrete payload from $\mathcal{M}_{A,B}$, and we thus additionally label it $\mathsf{spayload}(A,B)$. The variable case means that an agent receives a payload, and we thus label it $\mathsf{rpayload}(A,B)$ (where B is the name of the receiver and A is the supposed sender). The fact that we here allow only a variable means that the channel protocol P_1 is "blind" for the structure of the payload messages from P_2, and thus any value is accepted. We also require that if a variable occurs as payload under $C_P[\cdot]$, then all other occurrences of that variable are also under $C_P[\cdot]$.

3. (Payloads in P_2.) In P_2 terms, the message m that is transmitted as payload over the $\kappa(A,B)$-channel is of type Payload and every ground instantiation $m^{\mathcal{I}}$ must be a member of $\mathcal{M}_{A,B}$. Similarly to the labeling for $P_1^{P_2}$ in the previous item, m is either ground and labeled $\mathsf{spayload}(A,B)$, or it is a symbolic term (not necessarily a variable) and labeled $\mathsf{rpayload}(A,B)$.

4. ($C_P[\cdot]$ cannot be confused in P_1.) $\{t\} \sqcap \{C_P[s] \mid s \in \mathcal{T}_\Sigma(\mathcal{V})\} = \emptyset$ for any $t \in SMP(P_1)$ where $t \neq C_P[t']$ for any term t'.[9] By (Καπανεύς), it also follows that $C_P[\cdot]$ is disjoint from P_2-typed message parts as it belongs to P_1.

This assumption ensures that every subterm m of a $P_1^{P_2}$ term that is of type Payload is either a variable or ground. If it is a variable it is labeled $\mathsf{rpayload}(A,B)$, whereas if it is ground, then $m \in \mathcal{M}_{A,B}$ for some uniquely determined A and B and this is indicated by the appropriate label $\mathsf{spayload}(A,B)$. This property is preserved over all constraint reductions in the proof. In particular, we cannot unify payload with non-payload subterms. Note that when we unify a concrete payload with a variable (as respective subterms of a message), the variable will be replaced with the concrete ground payload and will be again labeled with an $\mathsf{spayload}(A,B)$ term. This is even true if the variable was labeled with $\mathsf{rpayload}(A',B')$; this may then be the source of the attack, but observe that when the goal did not include authentication, it may be not be an attack in itself. Finally, the labels give us the argument for the final step of the proof, when we have isolated a $P_1^{P_2}$ attack and want to transform it to a P_1 attack: then we can replace every concrete payload m labeled $\mathsf{spayload}(A,B)$ simply with the abstract $\mathsf{payload}(A,B)$ and obtain a valid P_1 attack.

[9]This is not a consequence of the fact that $t \neq C_P[t']$ for any t' as t may contain variables.

4.6 Abstract Payloads (Παρθενοπαῖος)

In the channel protocol P_1 with abstract $\mathsf{payload}(A,B)$, we require that the intruder knows initially

$$\{\mathsf{payload}(A,B) \mid \mathsf{dishonest}(A) \vee \mathsf{dishonest}(B)\}$$

if the channel-type $\kappa(A,B)$ includes secrecy (i.e., if it is $A \rightarrow\!\bullet\, B$ or $A \bullet\!\!\rightarrow\!\bullet\, B$, which we can denote by $secrecy \in \kappa(A,B)$); otherwise, the intruder initially knows all payloads $\{\mathsf{payload}(A,B)\}$. With this, we assume that the intruder may "in the worst case" know all payloads that are not explicitly secret (even though he may not find out the actual payload in a concrete run of $P_2[P_1]$ or $P_1^{P_2}$). This is essential for the soundness of the payload abstraction in the sense that when a concrete payload is known (and this fact is not yet a violation of a secrecy goal), then the intruder knows also the corresponding abstract payload.

This condition is thus used in the last step of the proof when we transform a $P_1^{P_2}$ attack into a P_1 attack and thus replace concrete payloads with abstract payloads: if the attack includes that the intruder can produce a concrete payload m labeled $\mathsf{spayload}(A,B)$, then either we already had earlier a secrecy violation (thus there exists a shorter attack) or it is one of the public payloads, and the intruder thus knows $\mathsf{payload}(A,B)$.

4.7 Properties of Concrete Payloads (Ἀμφιάραος)

For the concrete payloads, we similarly require that all payloads that are not explicitly secret are included in the initial intruder knowledge of $P_1^{P_2}$ and P_2, i.e., initially the intruder knowledge M_0 contains at least:

$$\bigcup_{\mathsf{honest}(A) \wedge (\mathsf{dishonest}(B) \vee secrecy \notin \kappa(A,B))} \mathcal{M}_{A,B}.$$

Moreover, all the other—secret—payloads (when A and B are honest and $\kappa(A,B)$ entails secrecy) must be considered as secrets in P_1 and P_2 (and thus they are also secrets in $P_1^{P_2}$). This can be expressed in ASLan for instance by adding the fact $\mathsf{secret}(M, \{A,B\})$ in every transition where an honest agent sends a payload M labeled $\mathsf{spayload}(A,B)$ or receives a payload M labeled $\mathsf{rpayload}(A,B)$ and using the general attack rule (1).[10]

This condition is, of course, similar to the previous one on abstract payloads. We use it in the proof in two ways: as already explained before, whenever in the attack the intruder uses a payload that is supposed to be secret, we already have a simpler attack to reduce to. Conversely, whenever

[10]Pedantically, to fulfill the condition of protocol independence, we should use two distinct facts secret_{P_1} and secret_{P_2} for secrecy in the respective subprotocols.

the intruder uses a payload that is not supposed to be secret, then this is already part of the initial knowledge. This is the closing stone in the proof, because the payloads are the only non-atomic submessages shared between the two protocols $P_1^{P_2}$ and P_2, and having these always in the initial knowledge (when not secret) allows us thus to solve $P_1^{P_2}$ constraints using only $P_1^{P_2}$ messages and P_2 constraints only using P_2 messages.

Discussion.

We like to point out that most of the conditions imposed here actually are, in a sense, in line with the prudent engineering principles of security protocols of Abadi and Needham [1].

- Execution independence in (Τυδεύς): we have a general notion of security protocols that may have databases; for simplicity, we do not deal with the interactions that can arise from different protocols sharing a database. In fact, one may argue that it is prudent engineering that channel and application protocols should indeed not have a shared database, but rather separate data-spaces except long-term keys.
- (Ἱππομέδων): it should be consistent over all protocols which items are secrets and which are not. (The other aspects of this condition are modeling aspects.)
- (Καπανεύς) corresponds to the central prudent engineering principle that every message should clearly indicate what it means, hence, it should not be a mere collection of data but rather have enough identifiers so that the meaning of each piece of data is unique.
- (Πολυνείκης) similarly requires that the payloads are unique for honest sender/receiver pairs (even though the names do not need to be recognizable). This condition is indeed a restriction that does not necessarily follow from prudent engineering and that many protocols in practice may not adhere to; we will thus try to lift in future work.
- (Ἐτέοκλος) is again in line with the paradigm that every message should say what it means, and in this case the integration of two protocols that results from inserting a message in a transport protocol should have a clear distinction between "letter and envelope", so to speak.
- (Παρθενοπαῖος) is actually not directly a requirement on the design of the channel protocol, but that it should satisfy its goals even under the assumption that all payloads are known whenever they are not explicitly secret from the intruder (even though the intruder in practice may sometimes not know all non-secret payloads). In fact, we believe that this is again in the spirit of prudent engineering.
- (Ἀμφιάραος) is the analogon of the previous property for the channel protocol.

5. EXTENSION TO MORE MESSAGES

As we remarked above, our seven conditions appear complex because they are formulated at a deep technical level, but they actually reflect realistic static properties that are satisfied by many protocols and that are easy syntactical checks. Now, we want, however, to discuss what are the limitations of the composability result so far and how we can extend it to the case of more messages for what concerns both the static aspect and the logical aspect of vertical protocol composition.

The composability result of [27] refers to only one single payload message of the application protocol being transmitted over the channel provided by the channel protocol. There are two reasons why this is a limitation. First, if the channel protocol is complex (and consisting of many steps), it is not desirable to execute this entire protocol for every message transmission of an application protocol. Second, disjointness conditions would not even allow repeated applications of the composability result, i.e., $P_2[P_1[P_1]]$ when we have two messages in P_2 that should be transmitted over a channel provided by P_1.

Our conjecture is that there is no insurmountable obstacle to allowing the definition of a channel protocol for more than one message transmission. One obvious way to go is to generalize the channel protocol to the transmission of several payload messages $\mathsf{payload}_1(A_1, B_1), \ldots, \mathsf{payload}_k(A_k, B_k)$ for a fixed number k of transmissions (the endpoints of the channels may differ); these transmissions would be over k different channel types $\kappa_i(A_i, B_i)$; they would be reflected by k disjoint contexts $C_P^i[\cdot]$, and the application protocol can then transmit k messages with associated concrete payload message sets $\mathcal{M}_{A,B}^i$ (for $1 \leq i \leq k$). These payload message sets would have to be disjoint unless $\kappa_i(A_i, B_i) = \kappa_j(A_j, B_j)$. The respective extensions of the definitions and proofs are notationally involved, but conceptually simple, so we avoided them here.

More generally, we also like to allow the transmission of an unbounded number of messages over a channel. The most prominent examples for this are, of course, secure channel protocols like TLS that establish a pair of symmetric keys (one for client-to-server transmissions, and one for server-to-client; see also [14]). We discuss an example based on TLS in more detail in [28]; this includes a suitable notation for the transmission protocol(s), i.e., how payload messages are handled. Note that we are here focussing only on the channel's transmission properties for the single messages such as authentication and secrecy, not for their relationship such as their ordering, completeness or replay protection.

Again, there is no fundamental problem in extending our static vertical composition result for arbitrary message transmissions as long as, again, the message spaces $\mathcal{M}_{A_i,B_i}^i$ for the different used channel types are disjoint. In particular, observe that we require honest receivers in the channel protocol to accept any payload that is embedded into the proper context; thus, the abstraction of the payload in the pure P_i works, independent of whether there is just one concrete payload message per session or many of them.

We also conjecture that the principles of vertical protocol composition of [27] can also be extended to arbitrary payload transmissions. However, we leave it for future work.

6. CONCLUSIONS

We have formalized seven static conditions that are sufficient for vertical protocol composition for a large class of channels and applications. Our results tell us that we can check in isolation — with any protocol verification method[11] — a channel protocol P_1 with abstract payload, as well as an application protocol P_2 that uses the respective channel type. If this channel type is part of the ones defined in [27] and the sufficient conditions of this paper are satisfied for P_1 and P_2, then we can combine Theorems 1 and 2 to infer that $P_2[P_1]$ is secure.

As we have already partly mentioned above, there are a number of interesting directions for future work, in particular, allowing for negative checks also on the channel protocol when considering finer abstractions and formalizing the extension of our sufficient conditions to the case of more messages for what concerns both the static aspect and the logical aspect of vertical protocol composition.

7. ACKNOWLEDGMENTS

The work presented in this paper was partially supported by the EU FP7 Projects no. 318424, "FutureID: Shaping the Future of Electronic Identity" (futureid.eu) and no. 257876, "SPaCIoS: Secure Provision and Consumption in the Internet of Services" (spacios.eu), and by the PRIN 2010-2011 Project "Security Horizons". Much of this work was carried out while Luca Viganò was at the Dipartimento di Informatica, Università di Verona, Italy.

8. REFERENCES

[1] M. Abadi and R. M. Needham. Prudent engineering practice for cryptographic protocols. *IEEE Trans. Software Eng.*, 22(1):6–15, 1996.

[2] S. Andova, C. Cremers, K. Gjøsteen, S. Mauw, S. Mjølsnes, and S. Radomirović. A framework for compositional verification of security protocols. *Information and Computation*, 206:425–459, 2008.

[3] A. Armando, W. Arsac, T. Avanesov, M. Barletta, A. Calvi, A. Cappai, R. Carbone, Y. Chevalier, L. Compagna, J. Cuéllar, G. Erzse, S. Frau, M. Minea, S. Mödersheim, D. von Oheimb, G. Pellegrino, S. E. Ponta, M. Rocchetto, M. Rusinowitch, M. Torabi Dashti, M. Turuani, and L. Viganò. The AVANTSSAR Platform for the Automated Validation of Trust and Security of Service-Oriented Architectures. In *TACAS*, LNCS 7214, pp. 267–282. Springer, 2012.

[4] A. Armando, R. Carbone, and L. Compagna. LTL Model Checking for Security Protocols. In *CSF 20*, pp. 385–396. IEEE CS, 2007.

[5] The AVANTSSAR Project: Deliverable 2.3: ASLan (final version), 2010. Available at `www.avantssar.eu`.

[6] D. Basin, S. Mödersheim, and L. Viganò. OFMC: A symbolic model checker for security protocols. *International Journal of Information Security*, 4(3):181–208, 2005.

[7] B. Blanchet. From secrecy to authenticity in security protocols. In *SAS'02*, LNCS 2477, pp. 342–359. Springer, 2002.

[8] R. Canetti. Universally composable security: A new paradigm for cryptographic protocols. In *FOCS'01*, pp. 136–145. IEEE CS, 2001.

[11] Such as ProVerif [7] or the AVANTSSAR Platform [3], where for bounded-session tools compositionality only holds for those bounded sessions.

[9] Y. Chevalier, R. Küsters, M. Rusinowitch, and M. Turuani. Deciding the security of protocols with Diffie-Hellman exponentiation and products in exponents. In *FST TCS*, LNCS 2914. Springer, 2003.

[10] S. Ciobâca and V. Cortier. Protocol composition for arbitrary primitives. In *CSF 23*. IEEE CS, 2010.

[11] V. Cortier and S. Delaune. Safely composing security protocols. *Form Method Syst Des*, 34(1):1–36, 2009.

[12] A. Datta, A. Derek, J. C. Mitchell, and D. Pavlovic. Secure protocol composition. In *FMSE'03*, pp. 11–23. ACM, 2003.

[13] S. Delaune, S. Kremer, and M. D. Ryan. Composition of password-based protocols. In *CSF 21*, pp. 239–251. IEEE CS, 2008.

[14] T. Gibson-Robinson and G. Lowe. Analysing applications layered on unilaterally authenticating protocols. In *FAST*, LNCS 7140, pp. 164–181. Springer, 2011.

[15] T. Groß and S. Mödersheim. Vertical protocol composition. In *CSF 24*, pp. 235–250. IEEE CS, 2011.

[16] J. D. Guttman. Authentication tests and disjoint encryption: a design method for security protocols. *Journal of Computer Security*, 3–4(12):409–433, 2004.

[17] J. D. Guttman. Cryptographic protocol composition via the authentication tests. In *FOSSACS*, LNCS 5504, pp. 303–317. Springer, 2009.

[18] J. D. Guttman and F. J. Thayer. Protocol independence through disjoint encryption. In *CSFW 2000*, pp. 24–34, 2000.

[19] G. O. Hutchinson. *Aeschylus. Seven against Thebes.* Clarendon Press, Oxford, 1985.

[20] A. Kamil and G. Lowe. Understanding abstractions of secure channels. In *FAST*, LNCS 6561, pp. 50–64, Springer, 2011.

[21] R. Küsters and M. Tuengerthal. Composition Theorems Without Pre-Established Session Identifiers. In *CCS 18*, pp. 41–50. ACM, 2011.

[22] U. M. Maurer. Constructive cryptography – A new paradigm for security definitions and proofs. In *TOSCA 2011*, LNCS 6993, pp. 33–56. Springer, 2011.

[23] U. M. Maurer and R. Renner. Abstract Cryptography. In *ICS*, pp. 1–21. Tsinghua U.P., 2011.

[24] U. M. Maurer and P. E. Schmid. A calculus for security bootstrapping in distributed systems. *J. Comp. Sec.*, 4(1):55–80, 1996.

[25] J. K. Millen and V. Shmatikov. Constraint solving for bounded-process cryptographic protocol analysis. In *CCS*, pp. 166–175. ACM, 2001.

[26] S. Mödersheim. Algebraic Properties in Alice and Bob Notation. In *Ares'09*, 2009.

[27] S. Mödersheim and L. Viganò. Secure pseudonymous channels. In *ESORICS 14*, LNCS 5789, pp. 337–354. Springer, 2009.

[28] S. Mödersheim and L. Viganò. Sufficient Conditions for Vertical Protocol Composition (Extended Version). TR-2014-07, DTU Compute, Denmark, 2014. Available at `imm.dtu.dk/~samo`.

[29] M. Rusinowitch and M. Turuani. Protocol insecurity with a finite number of sessions, composed keys is NP-complete. *Theor. Comput. Sci.*, 299:451–475, 2003.

Evading Android Runtime Analysis via Sandbox Detection

Timothy Vidas
Carnegie Mellon University
tvidas@cmu.edu

Nicolas Christin
Carnegie Mellon University
nicolasc@andrew.cmu.edu

ABSTRACT

The large amounts of malware, and its diversity, have made it necessary for the security community to use automated dynamic analysis systems. These systems often rely on virtualization or emulation, and have recently started to be available to process mobile malware. Conversely, malware authors seek to detect such systems and evade analysis. In this paper, we present techniques for detecting Android runtime analysis systems. Our techniques are classified into four broad classes showing the ability to detect systems based on differences in behavior, performance, hardware and software components, and those resulting from analysis system design choices. We also evaluate our techniques against current publicly accessible systems, all of which are easily identified and can therefore be hindered by a motivated adversary. Our results show some fundamental limitations in the viability of dynamic mobile malware analysis platforms purely based on virtualization.

Categories and Subject Descriptors

D.4.6 [**Operating Systems**]: Security and Protection

Keywords

Evasion; malware; android; security; sandbox

1. INTRODUCTION

In the past couple of years, mobile devices have become sophisticated computing environments with increased computing power and network connectivity. This has made them considerably closer to traditional computing platforms such as PCs, than to the telephones they were initially designed to replace. As a result of this trend, security threats that traditionally only applied to PCs can now also be encountered on mobile devices. In particular, as miscreants discover that mobile devices can be targeted and exploited for financial gain, new forms of malware are created to do so. Some mobile malware is designed to work in tandem with PC-oriented malware while other focuses on mobile devices exclusively [18,36,40].

When a new piece of malware is discovered, it must be analyzed in order to understand its capabilities and the threat it represents. One popular method of analysis, *dynamic analysis*, consists of executing the malware in a controlled environment to observe effects to the host system and the network.

On traditional PCs, the controlled environment used for dynamic analysis is often created through host virtualization. PC malware authors have consequently taken to design malware that can detect virtual environments [19,24,30,34], and exhibit alternative, benign behavior, rather than the malicious behavior which would occur on actual hardware. This kind of evasion allows malware to thwart dynamic analysis systems, and has fueled an arms race between those improving the realism of virtualized environments and those wishing to detect them.

However, virtualization technology has considerably matured in the past few years, and a number of users have migrated physical machines to virtual instances. Today, production services may be run in corporate virtualization "farms" or even in space rented in a "cloud." As a result, virtualized environments are not merely used for sandboxing malware anymore, but have become commonplace for a number of applications. In turn, the ability for malware to detect a virtual environment is losing its usefulness, as virtualization is no longer a near-certain indication that dynamic malware analysis is taking place.

On the other hand, there are, so far, only limited use cases for virtual environments on mobile devices. Likewise, emulated environments are typically only used by developers or dynamic analysis systems. For this reason, mobile malware authors may still employ virtualization or emulation detection to alter behavior and ultimately evade analysis or identification.

In this paper we contribute several techniques that can be used to detect a runtime analysis in Android. Some of these techniques are specific to the Android framework or a virtualized environment (e.g., emulator), and could be quite easily thwarted, while others, based for instance on resource availability, are more general, and much harder to defend against. All of the techniques we present require minimal or no privileges, and could be invoked from typical applications found in online marketplaces.

The primary contribution of this paper is thus to demonstrate that dynamic analysis platforms for mobile malware that purely rely on emulation or virtualization face fundamental limitations that may make evasion possible.

The rest of this paper is organized as follows. We start by presenting related work in Section 2. We then propose different emulation detection techniques in Section 3. In Section 4 we address an obvious countermeasure to some detection techniques by demonstrating alternate implementations of the methods described in Section 3. We evaluate how current systems fare against the proposed techniques in Section 5 before discussion results in Section 6, and concluding in Section 7.

ASIA CCS'14, June 4–6, 2014, Kyoto, Japan.
Copyright 2014 ACM 978-1-4503-2800-5/14/06 ...$15.00.
http://dx.doi.org/10.1145/2590296.2590325.

2. RELATED WORK

Automated runtime analysis systems are a popular method of processing large volumes of malware, or as an alternative to having skilled personnel perform lengthy manual analysis. For desktop operating systems there are numerous free [12] and commercial [39] systems that perform such analysis. More recently, a few systems [1,2,3,4,10,13,25] have been proposed for dynamic analysis of mobile malware. Because of their novelty, these systems remain less mature than their desktop counterparts.

PC malware writers responded to the advent of automated systems by finding creative solutions to detect whether code was running in virtualized environments. Virtualization detection routines have been implemented in numerous ways from detecting a vendor-specific API, such as VMWare's communication channel [24], to observing environmental effects of a single CPU instruction [34].

Upon detection, malware may exhibit alternate behavior, hiding its true purpose. This runtime change in control flow results in a different execution path through the malicious software. In 2008, Chen et al. observed that PC malware exhibited reduced behavior in nearly 40% of unique samples when run in debugged environment, and 4% of samples when run in a virtualized environment. However, the samples that exhibit alternate behavior due do environment accounted for 90% of attacks during particular time periods [15]. Moser et al. propose a system for analyzing multiple execution paths by presenting different input and environments to subsequent executions of the same malware [26]. While this system investigates different execution paths, virtualization is not one of the changes used to effect a different execution.

The detection of analysis environments is not limited to detecting the virtualization component itself. Holz et al. describe numerous techniques for detecting honeypots [22]. Some techniques are indeed rooted in virtualization detection, but others focus on other environmental components such as the presence of a debugger.

The concept of evasion has also been subject to a considerable amount of research in the context of network intrusion detection systems (NIDS). Handley et al. observe that a skilled attacker can "evade [network] detection by exploiting ambiguities in the traffic stream" [21]. These ambiguities are classified into three categories: incomplete system implementation, incomplete knowledge of the traffic recipient's system, or incomplete network topology knowledge. Numerous others describe evasion attacks due inconsistencies between the NIDS and the victim computer [14,16,20,27,32].

The most closely related work to ours offers emulator detection techniques for the PC [33]. Raffetseder et al. detail some "general" detection methods and well as a few that specifically detect the Intel x86 version of the QEMU emulator. At a high level, we explore similar general detection techniques targeting the Android emulator. There is scant similar academic research in evading mobile malware analysis; however there have a been a few industry presentations [28, 31] that look at evasion particular to Google Bouncer. Both of these presentations address some API related detections (which we generalize in Section 3.1) as well as detections that specifically target Bouncer, such as source IP addresses associated with Google. Our work here is more general, in that it tries to pinpoint more fundamental limitations in dynamic analysis on mobile devices. A more general industry presentation by Strazzere explores several Android API-based detections as well as a specific QEMU detection and is complimentary to our research [35].

3. EMULATOR DETECTION

Fundamentally, the concept of emulator detection is rooted in the fact that complete system emulation is an arduous task. By discovering or observing differences between virtual and physical execution an attacker can create software virtualization checks that can be used to alter overall program behavior. Such differences may be an artifact of hardware state not correctly implemented in the virtual CPU, hardware or software components that have yet to be virtualized, or observable execution duration.

In this section we detail several virtualization detection techniques and discuss the results of experimental evaluation of these techniques. The techniques require few or no permissions and work on commodity devices in the standard consumer software configuration. As with any consumer Android device, applications are governed by Linux access control and are thus limited to user-mode processor execution (e.g. devices are not "rooted" or "jailbroken").

We evaluate the detection techniques using emulator instances on similar Windows, Mac, and Linux hosts (each with an i7 processor, 8 GB RAM) as well as six physical devices from major U.S. cellular carriers. We divide detection techniques into the following categories: differences in behavior, performance, hardware and software components, and those resulting from system design choices. For ease in comparison, the first three roughly coincide with existing work in PC emulator detection [33].

3.1 Differences in behavior

Since virtualization is often defined in terms of execution being indistinguishable from that of a real machine, in some sense, any virtualization detection technique can be perceived as a difference in behavior. However, here we focus on behavioral differences specific to software state and independent of system performance.

Detecting emulation through the Android API.

The Android API provides an abstract interface for application programmers. Since many Android devices are smartphones, the API provides a rich interface for telephony operations as well as methods for interacting with other hardware and local storage.

Table 1 enumerates several API methods that return particular values when used with an emulated device. Each of the API-value pairs in Table 1 can be used to explicitly detect an emulated device or used in conjunction with other values in order to determine a likelihood. For example, if the `TelephonyManager.getDeviceId()` API returns all 0's, the instance in question is certainly an emulator because no physical device would yield this value.

Similarly, emulator instances adopt a telephone number based on the Android Debug Bridge (ADB) port in use by the emulator. When an emulator instance starts, the emulator reserves a pair of TCP ports starting with 5554/5555 (a second instance would acquire 5556/5558) for debugging purposes. The adopted telephone number is based on the reserved ports such that the initial emulator instance adopts precisely 1-555-521-5554. Therefore, if the `TelephonyManager.getLine1Number()` API indicates that the device phone number is in the form 155552155xx, then the device is certainly an emulator. Such a number would never naturally be used on a device because the 555 area code is reserved for directory assistance [9]. The presence of the 555 area code may also be used in other emulator detections such as the pre-configured number for voicemail.

Other values in Table 1 are certainly used by the emulator but may also be used by some real devices. Consider the Mobile Country Code (MCC) and Mobile Network Code (MNC) values obtained via the `TelephonyManager.getNetworkOperator()` method. The emulator always returns values associated with T-Mobile USA. Since there are certainly real devices that use the same codes, checks based on the MCC and MNC need to be

API method	Value	meaning
Build.ABI	armeabi	is likely emulator
Build.ABI2	unknown	is likely emulator
Build.BOARD	unknown	is emulator
Build.BRAND	generic	is emulator
Build.DEVICE	generic	is emulator
Build.FINGERPRINT	generic††	is emulator
Build.HARDWARE	goldfish	is emulator
Build.HOST	android-test††	is likely emulator
Build.ID	FRF91	is emulator
Build.MANUFACTURER	unknown	is emulator
Build.MODEL	sdk	is emulator
Build.PRODUCT	sdk	is emulator
Build.RADIO	unknown	is emulator
Build.SERIAL	null	is emulator
Build.TAGS	test-keys	is emulator
Build.USER	android-build	is emulator
TelephonyManager.getDeviceId()	All 0's	is emulator
TelephonyManager.getLine1 Number()	155552155xx†	is emulator
TelephonyManager.getNetworkCountryIso()	us	possibly emulator
TelephonyManager.getNetworkType()	3	possibly emulator (EDGE)
TelephonyManager.getNetworkOperator().substring(0,3)	310	is emulator or a USA device (MCC)‡
TelephonyManager.getNetworkOperator().substring(3)	260	is emulator or a T-Mobile USA device (MNC)
TelephonyManager.getPhoneType()	1	possibly emulator (GSM)
TelephonyManager.getSimCountryIso()	us	possibly emulator
TelephonyManager.getSimSerial Number()	89014103211118510720	is emulator OR a 2.2-based device
TelephonyManager.getSubscriberId()	310260000000000‡‡	is emulator
TelephonyManager.getVoiceMailNumber()	15552175049	is emulator

Table 1: Listing of API methods that can be used for emulator detection. Some values clearly indicate that an emulator is in use, others can be used to contribute to likelihood or in combination with other values for emulator detection. † xx indicates a small range of ports for a particular emulator instance as obtained by the Android Debug Bridge (ADB). Emulator instances begin at 54 and will always be an even number between 54 and 84 (inclusive). ‡ 310 is the MCC code for U.S. but may also be used in Guam. †† The value is a prefix.‡‡ An emulator will be in the form MCC + MNC + 0's, checking for the 0's is likely sufficient.

augmented with other data. If another check establishes that the device is a Verizon device, but the MNC shows T-Mobile, this may indicate a modified emulator that is returning spoofed values.

Table 1 also contains several values from the `android.os.Build` class which contains information about the current software build. Retail devices will have system properties that detail the actual production build. An emulator will have build properties based on the SDK build process used to create the emulator binary, such as the `Build.FINGERPRINT`. The fingerprints listed in Table 2 clearly show a pattern followed by the SDK build process. Even though the SDK documentation warns "Do not attempt to parse this value," testing for the presence of "generic," "sdk," or "test-keys" yields perfect results for emulator detection when compared to our sample of physical devices.

Experiments with physical devices led to some counter-intuitive findings for some values. For example, the `Build.ABI` value on the emulator is "armeabi" which is a plausible value for all devices with an ARM processor (nearly all devices). However, the API returned an empty string when used on a Motorola Droid. Similarly, a `Build.HOST` value starting with "android-test" was also found on the Droid. As shown in Table 3, the `Build.HOST` value is not as useful for emulator detection as other `Build` values.

Detecting emulated networking.

The emulated networking environment is often quite different than that found on physical devices. Each emulator instance is isolated from the host PC's network(s) via software. The network address space is always 10.0.2/24. Furthermore, the last octet of the virtual router, host loopback, up to four DNS resolvers, and the

Device	Build.HOST
Emulator	apa27.mtv.corp.google.com
Emulator	android-test-15.mtv.corp.google.com
Emulator	android-test-13.mtv.corp.google.com
Emulator	android-test-25.mtv.corp.google.com
Emulator	android-test-26.mtv.corp.google.com
Emulator	vpbs30.mtv.corp.google.com
Emulator	vpak21.mtv.corp.google.com
Motorola Droid	android-test-10.mtv.corp.google.com
HTC EVO 4G	AA137
Samsung Charge	SEI-26
Samsung Galaxy Tab7	SEP-40
Samsung Galaxy Nexus	vpak26.mtv.corp.google.com

Table 3: Build values collected from various instances.

emulator's address are always known (1, 2, 3–6, and 15, respectively). Unlike ADB, which reserves adjacent, incrementing TCP ports, the network schema is the same for every emulator instance, even if several instances are simultaneously running on one host.

While it is possible that a network to which a real device is connected may exhibit exactly the same network layout, it is unlikely. Devices configured with cellular data plans will often user carrier DNS resolvers and have a carrier DHCP lease for the device IP. WIFI networks to which a device connects are also unlikely to be configured in exactly this way, and are unlikely to exhibit the quiet nature of a /24 network solely allocated to one emulated device.

Accessing network information is relatively straightforward using standard Java techniques. A trivial detection for the emulated

Device	Fingerprint
Emulator	generic/sdk/generic/:1.5/CUPCAKE/150240:eng/test-keys
Emulator	generic/sdk/generic/:1.6/Donut/20842:eng/test-keys
Emulator	generic/sdk/generic/:2.1-update1/ECLAIR/35983:eng/test-keys
Emulator	generic/sdk/generic/:2.2/FRF91/43546:eng/test-keys
Emulator	generic/sdk/generic:2.3.3/GRI34/101070:eng/test-keys
Emulator	generic/sdk/generic:4.1.2/MASTER/495790:eng/test-keys
Emulator	generic/sdk/generic:4.2/JB_MR1/526865:eng/test-keys
Motorola Droid	verizon/voles/sholes/sholes:2.0.1/ESD56/20996:user/release-keys
Motorola Droid	verizon/voles/sholes/sholes:2.2.1/FRG83D/75603:user/release-keys
HTC EVO 4G	sprint/htc_supersonic/supersonic:2.3.3/GRI40/133994.1:user/release-keys
Samsung Charge	verizon/SCH-I510/SCH-I510:2.3.6/GINGERBREAD/EP4:user/release-keys
Samsung Galaxy Nexus	google/mysid/toro:4.1.1/JRO03O/424425:user/release-keys

Table 2: Listing of `Build.FINGERPRINT`'s collected from various instances. Emulator instances clearly include common substrings not found in physical devices.

network would be to check for the four known IP addresses. The false positives on this approach would be low and suffice in most situations. In order to obtain networking information and to interact with the network, the Android application would need to request the ACCESS_NETWORK_STATE and INTERNET permissions.

Detecting the underlying emulator.
The underlying emulator, QEMU, is employed to drive the hardware emulation of the Android emulator. As such, any QEMU detection techniques such as using CPU bugs [33] or virtual address allocation [17] can also be employed against the Android emulator. These techniques, however, require to run so-called native code, that is, software that executes on the processor instead of Android's Dalvik VM. Such software must be compiled with the Native Development Kit (NDK), and is only found in 4.52% of applications [41]. Hence, malware that attempts to detect the underlying emulator using native code may actually be easy to flag as suspicious.

Some CPU based detection mechanisms rely upon privileged instructions which cannot be used as part of a typical application. Android uses Linux for privilege separation and each application is installed under a different user ID. As is common in modern operating systems the application code (both Dalvik and native code) executes in user-mode. In order to use privileged instructions the application must gain elevated privileges by "rooting" the device. While this is certainly possible [37], many of the other techniques discussed in this paper appear much simpler to deploy.

3.2 Differences in performance

The emulator, unassisted by hardware, is at a natural disadvantage when it comes to processing speed. Translating the instructions for execution indeed inherently causes a performance penalty. However, the emulator is typically run on a PC with considerably more processing resources than a mobile device. Thus, it is plausible that, even with the instruction translation penalty, an emulator could approximate the performance of a physical device. We tested this hypothesis by 1) measuring CPU performance and 2) measuring graphical performance.

3.2.1 CPU performance

Some hardware features often used for performance measurements are unavailable to the application executing in user-mode. For example, the performance counters on ARM processors are enabled via the CP15 register and may only be enabled from the privileged kernel—which will not be accessible unless the phone is rooted. This limitation also poses a significant barrier to using many processor benchmarking software suites, which require higher privilege than an Android application possesses.

Device	Average Round Duration (Seconds)	Standard Deviation
PC (Linux)	0.153	0.012
Galaxy Nexus (4.2.2)	16.798	0.419
Samsung Charge (2.3.6)	22.647	0.398
Motorola Droid (2.2)	24.420	0.413
Emulator 2.2	62.184	7.549
Emulator 4.2.2	68.872	0.804

Table 4: Pi calculation round duration on tested devices using AGM technique (16 rounds). The tested devices are noticably slower at performing the calculations than related devices running similar software.

We instead turn to a crude method of benchmarking: evaluating the duration of lengthy computations. We created a Java Native Interface (JNI) application for Android using the NDK. Our application calculates the first 1,048,576 digits of Pi using the method described by Ooura [29]. Pi is calculated over 16 rounds of increasing precision using Arithmetic-Geometric Mean (AGM) making extensive use of Fast Fourier Transforms, square roots, multiplication, etc.

The AGM calculation shows significantly different results when comparing emulated instances with similar physical devices. Table 4 shows the average and standard deviation for several tested devices. For instance, executing the native application on a 4.2.2 emulator results in an median round duration of 68.8 seconds with a total execution time of 1101.9 seconds. A 4.2.2 Galaxy Nexus demonstrates a 16.8 second median round duration, and takes 268.8 seconds to complete. Comparatively, the PC hosting the emulator executes the same code 2.5 seconds with a median of 0.15 second/round (Linux PC). Round durations show statistically significant differences between emulated and non-emulated environments (Wilcoxon test, $W = 256$, $p < .001$), which in turn demonstrates the viability of the this emulation detection technique.

3.2.2 Graphical performance

We also investigated differences in the video frame rate across various hardware and emulator instances. To that effect, we created an Android application that uses Android's `SurfaceHolder` callback method as part of the `SurfaceView` class. A thread continuously monitors the `SurfaceHolder` canvas and calculates a

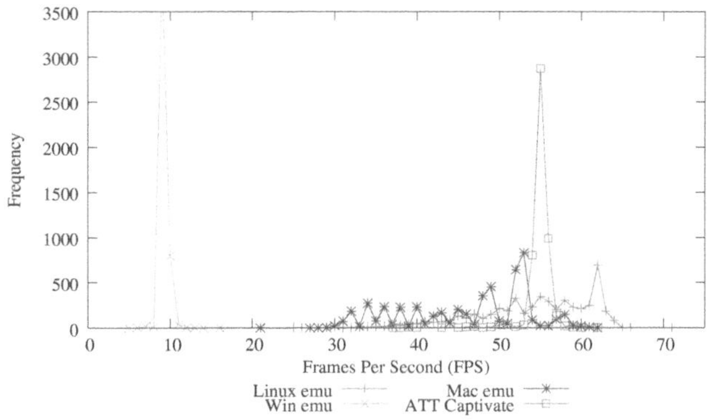

Figure 1: Android 2.2 FPS measurements: Windows exhibits a very low frame rate. The hardware device, ATT captivate, clearly has a very tight bound on framerate at 58-59 FPS. All emulators are statistically different from the real device (Wilcoxon, $p < .001$).

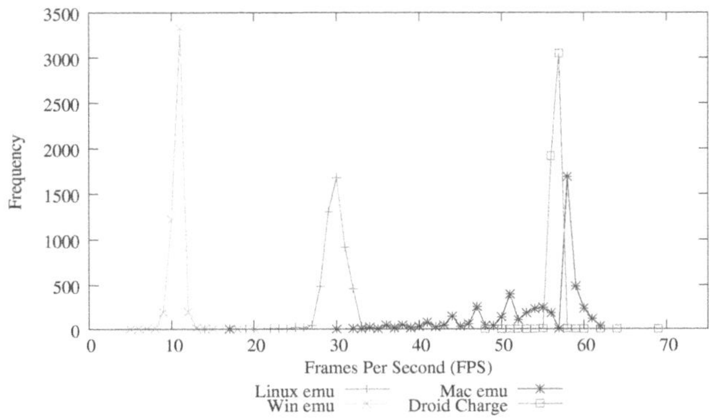

Figure 2: Android 2.3.x FPS Measurements: The Droid Charge registers the majority frame readings between 57 and 58, while the emulators show lower, more distributed readings. The emulators are 2.3.3; the Droid Charge is 2.3.6. All emulators are statistically different from the real device (Wilcoxon, $p < .001$)

Frame Per Second (FPS) value. We sampled 5,000 values for each device.

We ran each emulator instance serially on a 4-core i7 host with 8 GB of RAM and at no time did the the system monitor indicate that any PC resources were a limiting factor. Each emulator and physical device was cold booted and left idle for five minutes prior to testing, and the instances were not otherwise used.

Figures 1–3 show that physical devices typically exhibit both a higher and much more consistent FPS rate. For example, the Galaxy Nexus (4.2.2) shows 58 or 59 FPS for quite near the duration of the experiment. However, a similar emulator shows both much lower FPS near 11 and exhibits more of a bell curve with observable measurements between 9 and 14. Also, some frame rates simply would not occur on a commodity device, such as the 150+ FPS reported occasionally by a 3.2 emulator.

From the experimental data, heuristics can be devised to detect emulators in a host-OS agnostic way across all versions of Android. One such heuristic is shown in Figure 4. The intuition behind the heuristic is that the emulators generally exhibit slower and less tightly bounded FPS rates, often representing a bell curve. Each of the physical devices, on the other hand, exhibit relatively high

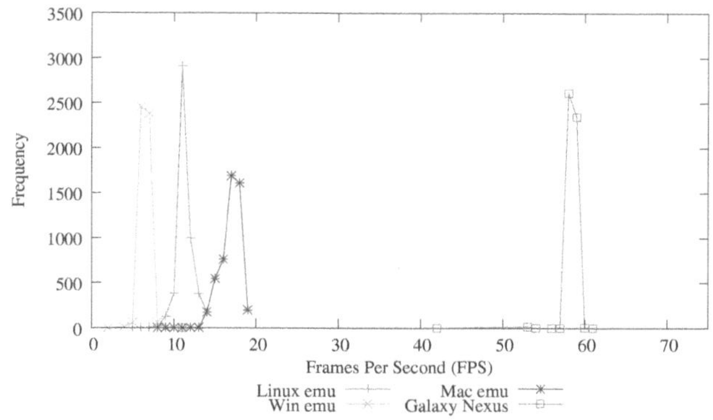

Figure 3: Android 4.2.2 FPS Measurements: Emulators clearly show a low rate, and more of a bell curve than the Galaxy Nexus which shows almost entirely 59-60 FPS. All emulators are statistically different from the real device (Wilcoxon, $p < .001$).

```
for a value: v
 IF
  > 80% of samples fall within v-1..v+1
 AND
  v is > 30 FPS
 THEN
  the sampled device is a physical device
 ELSE
  the sampled device is an emulator
```

Figure 4: Sample heuristic using Frames Per Second (FPS) to determine if an Android application is executing on a physical device, indicated be high and closely-coupled FPS values.

and tightly coupled rates. By identifying FPS distributions that are less coupled or slower, emulator instances can be identified.

Versions of the Android SDK after Revision 17 allow for limited emulator GPU acceleration, though only on Mac and Windows systems. This feature is only meant to work for emulator instances of Android 4.0.3 or later [11], but we tested several configurations anyway. Figures 5 and 6 show FPS results from Mac and Windows emulators and GPU-assisted emulators.

On the Mac, the 4.2.2 emulator instance, the only supported platform, appears to behave considerably more like a physical device than the 4.2.2 emulator without assistance from the host GPU. However, the GPU-assisted 4.2.2 emulator still registers visible FPS rates in the 30-60 and 60-65 ranges, not the tightly coupled plot of almost exclusively 59-60 FPS as observed in Figure 3. The difference between the GPU-assisted 4.2.2 emulator on the Mac and a real Galaxy Nexus, like all of the timing results, is statistically significant (Wilcoxon test, $W = 8.1 \times 10^6$, $p < .001$). On the other hand, GPU assistance on Windows emulators does not considerably improve upon collected values.

3.3 Differences in components

Modern devices are composed of complex combinations of hardware subsystems that are all meant to work in concert. These subsystems all have their own physical implementations and often vary from what is provide with the Android emulator. Likewise, devices are shipped with proprietary software that drives special hardware, interacts with web services, or implements specific functions such as digital rights management. These hardware and software components can both be used to differentiate physical devices from virtual instances.

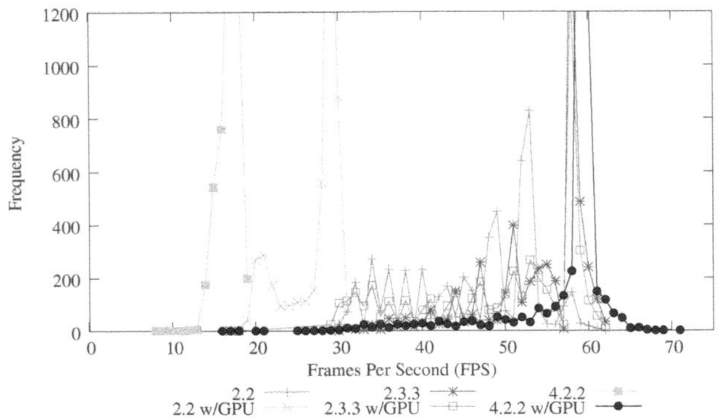

Figure 5: GPU-Accelerated Emulator (Mac): The only supported version, 4.2.2, shows significant improvement when using the host GPU (AMD Radeon 6750M - 1GB RAM). The GPU-assisted 4.2.2 emulator more closely resembles a physical device, but still exhibits a visible tail through the 30-60 FPS range.

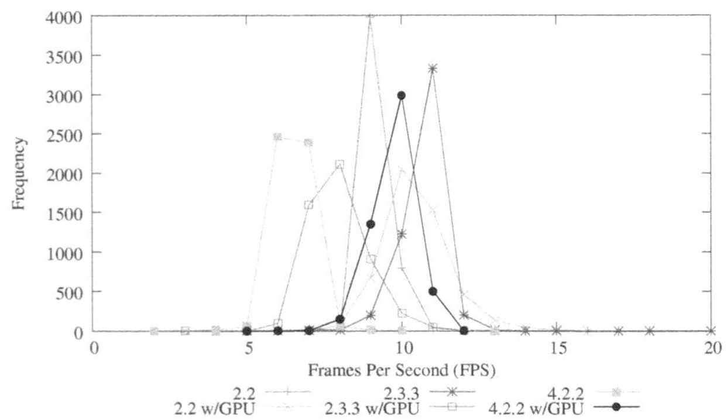

Figure 6: GPU-Accelerated Emulator (Windows): Using the GPU (NVidia 545 GT - 1GB RAM) in Windows did not have a significant effect Note: the scale of this graph is much different than other FPS graphs in this section.

3.3.1 Hardware components

With errors in hardware design, such as CPU bugs, indistinguishable emulation of a processor is an arduous task. Emulation of a complete hardware system is even more difficult. Since emulated environments must appear similar to a physical device, other components such as I/O ports, memory management chips and networking devices must all somehow be made available to emulated software. Similar to virtual IDE/SCSI devices exhibiting certain characteristics that facilitate PC emulator detection [33], differences can be observed in the Android emulator. We focus on two classes of differences, those observable due to emulated hardware (or lack of) and those observable due to omitted software.

Hardware components.

Much like specific hardware values present in PC components, values for various hardware components are observable in Android. For example, the CPU serial number is world-readable as part of `/proc/cpuinfo`. Emulator CPUs always show a value of sixteen 0's, while real ARM CPUs return a unique 16-character hexadecimal string. Similarly, current CPU frequencies can be retrieved from `/sys/devices/system/cpu-/cpu0/cpufreq/cpuinfo_min_f req` and `max_freq` on a Galaxy Nexus, but these files are not present in a 4.2.2 emulator.

Sensor	**Android Version**	**Moto. Droid**	**Samsung Charge**	**HTC EVO 4G**	**Galaxy Nexus**
Accelerometer	1.5	1	1	1	1
Ambient Temperature	4.0	-	-	-	0
Gravity	2.3	-	1	1	2
Gyroscope	1.5	0	1	0	2
Light	1.5	1	1	1	1
Linear Acceleration	2.3	-	1	1	2
Magnetic Field	1.5	1	1	1	1
Orientation	1.5	1	1	1	2
Pressure	1.5	0	0	0	1
Proximity	1.5	1	1	1	1
Relative Humidity	4.0	-	-	-	0
Rotation Vector	2.3	-	1	1	2
Temperature	1.5	1	0	0	0
Total		6	9	8	15

Table 5: `Sensor` types, the earliest version of Android to support each type, and observed sensor counts on four devices.

In addition to board-level design decisions such as the use of different memory types [38], devices employ a myriad of motion, environmental and positional hardware sensors often not found on PCs. Even budget devices often have GPS receivers, Bluetooth, accelerometers, temperature sensors, ambient light sensors, gravity sensors, etc. More recent or expensive devices often have additional capabilities perceived as market-differentiators such as Near Field Communication (NFC) chips, air pressure sensors, or humidity sensors.

The sensor types supported as of API 14 (Android 4.x) are shown in Table 5. Some types of sensors are not natively supported on older devices. Observing the type and quantity of sensors on a particular device can easily be performed via an the `SensorManager` API. The size of the list returned from `getSensorList()` for each type of sensor shown in Table 5 reveals the quantity of each type. Even early devices such as the Motorola Droid have many types of sensors.

Simply observing the number of devices may be sufficient for emulator detection, but this metric is relatively easy to spoof by modifying the SDK. A modified emulator may simply return lists of an appropriate size for each sensor type. More advanced emulator detection could be performed by interacting with each sensor. This type of emulator detection would require significant modification to the emulator, such as emulating the entire functionality of a sensor along with synthetic data.

Recent versions of the SDK facilitate adding some virtual hardware to an emulator instance. Figure 7 enumerates the configuration settings for several supported device types, one of each may be added to an emulator instance. However, this support is limited to later versions of Android, and the degree to which the virtual device emulates a physical device varies.

As an example, we implemented an application to continuously monitor the accelerometer, a very common sensor that requires no permission to be accessed. Since we are interested gathering data as close as possible to the real-time readings we poll using the fastest setting (`SENSOR_DELAY_FASTEST`). Since the accelerometer measures acceleration (m/s^2) along all three axes, we subtract the acceleration force of gravity (9.81) from the vertical

```
hw.sensors.temperature=yes
hw.camera.back=emulated
hw.gpu.enabled=yes
hw.gsmModem=yes
hw.sensors.magnetic_field=yes
hw.accelerometer=yes
hw.audioOutput=yes
hw.battery=yes
hw.sensors.proximity=yes
hw.lcd.backlight=yes
hw.sensors.orientation=yes
hw.camera.front=emulated
hw.gps=yes
```

Figure 7: Android Virtual Device (AVD) configuration settings to add emulated hardware. These settings can be added to the device ini file in order to indicate the virtual presence of hardware sensors such as the accelerometer, or temperature sensor.

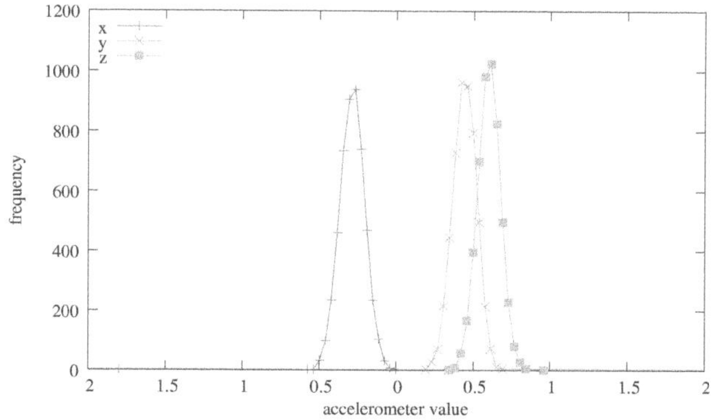

Figure 9: Accelerometer values: Measurements from 5000 data points gathered as quickly as possible from a Samsung Galaxy Nexus (4.2.2) (vertical value adjusted for gravity).

axis to normalize the recorded values. In this way, an accelerometer of a stationary device should register 0 for all three axes.

Figure 9 shows measurements for a physical device are closely coupled, but are neither always constant for any axis nor 0. A virtual device with an emulated accelerometer yields exactly the same value on every axis for every sampled data point. Regardless of Android version in the emulator or the host OS on which the emulator is used, the values are always 0.0, 9.77622, 0.813417 (x, y, and z). A device that is actually being used will show a drastically wider distribution along all axes.

Similar detections can be created for other sensors, either to detect an emulator exactly, via known emulator values, or by determining a heuristic for detect a physical device based on hardware ranges. Furthermore, similar detections can be created for other hardware subsystems such as Bluetooth which is often found on physical devices but is not present at all in the emulator. Simply testing to see if a valid handle is returned from `BluetoothAdapter.getDefaultAdapter()` will indicate that the device has a Bluetooth capability and is thus a physical device.

Software components relating to hardware.

Detection techniques very similar to the sensor detections discussed above can be created for the camera(s) and for readings akin to sensors such as the battery level. The battery could be monitored over time to ensure the battery level changes or depletes. The exception, of course, is if the device is plugged in and is thus constantly at 100%. The level and charging status can be observed using the `BatteryManager` API as shown in Figure 8. The battery level on the emulator is exclusively set at 50% or the two components are two known constants (level is 0 and scale is 100).

Another detection relates to special software added by manufactures in order to support certain hardware. Manufacturers often add special hardware to device as a market-differentiator to consumers or in order to take advantage of hardware not natively supported by Android. Such support is added via kernel modules, and like many Linux-based systems, Android detections could consist of looking at what might be loaded from `/sys/module` or the `/lib/modules` directory and what is currently inserted via the `lsmod` command or `/proc/modules` interface. As with other detection techniques, kernel module detection can take a high-level approach by counting (a 4.2.2 emulator shows 26, a physical Galaxy Nexus shows 72), or a more granular approach.

One specific example of such software is kernel modules added by Samsung in order to take advantage of Samsung memory and the proprietary RFS (Robust FAT File System) [38] instead of the common Linux Memory Technology Device (MTD) system. Simply listing `/proc/modules` on the Samsung Charge reveals that modules for RFS are loaded on the device. To improve detection, the compiled modules (`/lib/modules/rfs_fat.ko` and `rfs_glue.ko`) can be inspected for `modinfo`-like information or for specifically known byte sequences.

3.3.2 Software components

In addition to the software that specifically supports hardware, consumer Android devices are shipped with a variety of additional software. This software ranges from pre-installed applications to services designed specifically to interface with "cloud" resources or enable Digital Rights Management (DRM). Clear omissions from the emulator are the applications and supporting software for Google's Internet services. The marketplace application, Google Play, the Google Maps API, Google Talk, the Google services used to handle authentication and session information, and other similar software are found on nearly every consumer Android device, but are not included in the emulator. Observing `GoogleLoginService.apk`, `GoogleServicesFramework.apk`, `Phonesky.apk` or `Vending.apk` in `/system/app` likely indicates a real device. Carrier-added applications such as Verizon's backup software (`VZWBackupAssistant.apk`) can be observed the same way and similarly indicate real device.

Instead of or in addition to inspecting files, an API can be used to query the installed applications in an instance. The `PackageManager`'s `getInstalledPackages(0)` interface can be used to obtain a list of all installed applications. The list can then be queried for the Java-style package names such as `com.google.android.gsf` or `com.android.vending`. The associated application for each list item can also be located indirectly through `applicationInfo.sourceDir` which will provide the full path to the APK.

Android's `ContentResolver` can also be used to query the system for the presence of a software service. For instance, the Google Services Framework identifier can be queried with `ContentResolver.query(content: //com.google.android.gsf.services, null,null,"android_id",null)`. The emulator does not support this service and will always return `null` for this query.

In addition to observing the presence (or absence) of software services, variations in software component behavior can be observed. For instance, when establishing an interactive shell to an instance via ADB, the behavior is different between an emulator

```
int level = batteryStatus.getIntExtra(BatteryManager.EXTRA_LEVEL, -1);
int scale = batteryStatus.getIntExtra(BatteryManager.EXTRA_SCALE, -1);
float batteryPct = level / (float)scale;

boolean isCharging = status == BatteryManager.BATTERY_STATUS_CHARGING ||
                     status == BatteryManager.BATTERY_STATUS_FULL;
```

Figure 8: Battery level emulator detection example. The battery level is obtained via two Android Intents [8]. If batteryPct is exactly 50% or the level is exactly 0 and the scale is exactly 100, the device in question is likely an emulator. The level could be monitored over time to ensure it varies, and the charging status could be used to determine if the battery should be constant (at 100%).

and a physical device. In particular, in an emulator shell the effective Linux user id is root (0). This difference is caused by a check in ADB called `should_drop_privileges` which inspects two "read-only" system properties: `ro.kernel.qemu` and `ro.secure`. The inspection verifies that the instance is running the emulated kernel and that the "secure" setting is zero meaning that the root shell should be permitted.[1]

There are no APIs for inspecting properties such as `ro.secure`, but the properties are loaded from the `default.prop` file at system boot. Standard Java file methods can be used to read this file and therefor examine settings such as `ro.secure`. Even though this file is not likely to be modified, obtaining the properties in this way may not reflect the runtime state of the instance. We will explore other ways of obtaining actual runtime values in Section 4.

3.4 Differences due to system design

Modern runtime analysis systems must cope with certain constraints that do not affect consumer devices. In particular runtime systems must generally process a considerable volume of malware as the number of daily unique samples is quite large and reportedly growing. This phenomenon has been observed for years in the realm of PC malware and early signs indicate a similar growth pattern for mobile malware. Unfortunately, this requirement for additional scale is often at odds with resource availability. It is simply not economically viable to purchase thousands of physical devices or to run thousands of emulators simultaneously, forever. For these reasons, critical design decisions must be made when designing a runtime analysis system and the effects of these decisions can be used as a form of runtime-analysis detection. We outline two classes of design decisions that may influence an attackers ability to detect or circumvent analysis: those shared with PC runtime analysis systems and those specific to Android.

PC system design decisions, such execution time allotted to each sample or how much storage to allocate to each instance, have been explored in the PC realm. Many of these same decisions must be made for a mobile malware runtime analysis system. System circumvention, such as delaying execution past the maximum allotted execution time, is also shared with PC techniques.

Android-specific design decisions revolve around the inherent differences between a device that is actively used by an individual and a newly created instance (virtual or physical). If an attacker can determine that a device is not actually in use, the attacker may conclude that there is no valuable information to steal or that the device is part of an analysis system.

Metrics for determining if the device is (or has been) in use include quantities such as the number of contacts and installed applications, and usage indicators such as the presence and length of text messaging and call logs. These and many more indicators are available programatically as part of the Android API, but many require the application to request particular permissions. Runtime analysis system detection using these metrics is not as clear-cut as the other techniques we presented. These values depend upon knowing the average or minimum quantities present on the typical consumer device, and would be rife with false positives if the quantities were not evenly distributed among all users. Some work shows that these values are indeed not evenly distributed as a small user study showed eight of 20 participants downloaded ten or fewer applications while two of 20 downloaded more than 100 [23].

[1]The method also employs a second check for `ro.debuggable` and `service.adb.root`; if these are both 1, privileges will not be dropped even if `ro.secure` is set to 1.

4. MINIMIZING THE PERMISSIONS NEEDED

Some of the detections mentioned in this paper require certain application-level permissions. For example, to detect if Bluetooth is present on a device the application must request the `android.permission.BLUETOOTH` or `BLUETOOTH_ADMIN` permission. Other resources, such as the accelerometer require no permission to access.

All the techniques described in previous sections require only a very limited set of application permissions and the make use of existing APIs that are unlikely to change substantially in the foreseeable future. However, using the advertised APIs also has a offensive drawback: Designers of automated analysis systems could attempt to address the specific APIs we have utilized instead of completely addressing the downfalls of the emulation environment. For example, mitigating the device ID check by simply hooking the call to `TelephonyManager.getDeviceId()` and causing the return value to not be all 0's. To demonstrate how such an approach is short-sighted defensively, we present two techniques for retrieving runtime system properties even though there is no programmatic API in the SDK. We can then use these properties to create alternate implementations of nearly every detection we have detailed.

We offer two additional techniques for obtaining system properties: reflection and runtime `exec` (subprocess). Example code can be found in Figure 11 in the Appendix. In the reflection example, the `android.os.SystemProperties` class is obtained via the `ClassLoader`. The `get` method can then be obtained from the class and used to retrieve specific properties. This example retrieves settings we've already discussed, such as the `ro.secure`, the battery level and the `Build` tags. The `exec` example is more general and simply prints a list of all runtime properties be executing the "getprop" binary and parsing the output.

5. EVALUATION

Our techniques were developed in a relatively isolated test environment. We thus need to measure the effectiveness of our techniques against real analysis systems. We identified publicly available Android sandbox systems via literature review, industry referral, and via Internet searches. Candidate systems had to have a public, automated interface to be considered. Ideally, a candi-

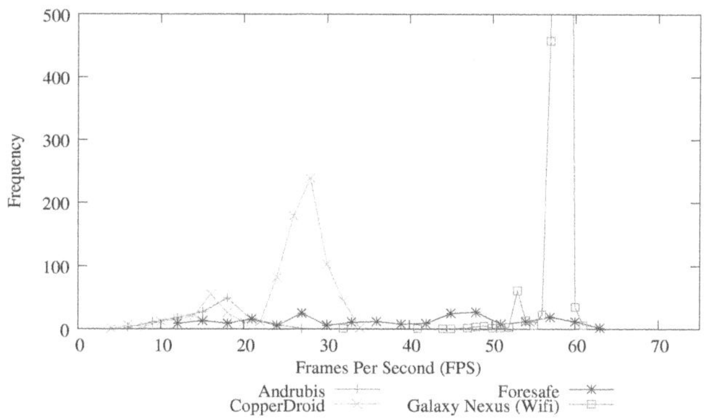

Figure 10: FPS measurements for sandboxes: For comparison, a physical Galaxy Nexus was re-measured using the same application. The physical device shows strong coupling at 59 FPS and all of the sandboxes demonstrate loose coupling and wide distribution, indicating that they all make use of virtualization.

date system also provides a publicly accessible output – typically as some form of report.

Our candidate sandboxes were Andrubis [2], SandDroid [10], Foresafe [6], Copperdroid [3], AMAT [1], mobile-sandbox [7] and Bouncer [25]. Each sandbox presents a slightly different interface, but are all meant to be accessible as web services. Likewise, each sandbox is the result of different levels of developmental effort and therefore embodies various levels of product maturity.

Mobile-sandbox constantly displayed a message indicating that 0 static and 308,260 dynamic jobs were yet to be processed. We were only ever able to observe static analysis output of mobile-sandbox. Similarly, SandDroid seemed to not route or otherwise filtered outbound network traffic, and the SandDroid reports only displayed results of static analysis so it was not possible to test our evasion techniques on SandDroid.

AMAT's online instance does not appear to be in working order, immediately stating that any uploaded application was "not malware." AMAT did not provide any further reasoning as to why this message was displayed, but uploading APK files did result in the overall analysis number incrementing with each submission. When using Foresafe, an action would occasionally fail, and a server-side error would be displayed to the user. Even so, refreshing the page and repeating the action always seemed to solicit the desired effect.

Google's Bouncer does not immediately meet our minimal requirement of having a public interface, but we attempted to include it given its importance on deployed applications. Not much about the inner workings of Bouncer has been made available. Without the ability to directly submit applications for analysis, and without the ability to directly view reports, interaction with Bouncer is widely unpredictable. Indeed, even after submitting several, increasingly offensive, applications into the Google Play marketplace, we never observed any connections coming from Bouncer. It is possible that Bouncer has altered the decision process for selecting which applications to run (e.g. only those with more than 10K downloads, or those with negative reviews) or has been changed to disallow connections to the Internet following other work on profiling the inner workings of Bouncer [28,31].

5.1 Behavior evaluation

As shown in Table 6, the SDK and `TelephonyManager` detection methods prove successful against all measured sandboxes. Many of the simple detection heuristics outlined in Table 1 are similarly successful. However, some of the `Build` parameters, such as `HOST`, `ID`, and `manufacturer` require a more complex heuristic in order to be useful. Detecting the emulated networking environment was also very successful as the sandboxes all employed the default network configuration.

Detection method	Andrubis	CopperDroid	ForeSafe
getDeviceId()	Y†	Y	Y
getSimSerial Number()	Y	Y	Y
getLine1 Number()	Y	Y‡	Y
MCC	Y	Y	Y
MNC	Y	Y	Y
FINGERPRINT	Y	Y	Y
BOARD	Y	Y	Y
BRAND	Y	Y	Y
DEVICE	Y	Y	Y
HOST	N	N	N
ID	N	N	N
manufacturer	N	N	N
MODEL	N	N	Y
PRODUCT	N	N	Y
serial	Y	N	N
TAGS	Y	Y	Y
radio	N	N	N
USER	N	N	N
NetCountry	y	N	N
NetType	y	N	N
PhoneType	y	N	N
SimCountry	y	N	N
VMNum	Y	Y	Y
SubscriberID	Y†	Y	Y
Networking	Y	Y	Y
bluetooth	Y	Y	Y
ro.secure	Y	Y	Y
sensors	Y	Y	Y
contacts	Y	Y	Y
call log	Y	Y	Y
performance	Y	Y	Y

Table 6: Evaluation of detections. An uppercase Y indicates that the system was detected as an emulator, a lowercase y indicates that the system may be an emulator, and an uppercase N indicates that the detection mechanism did not succeed. † This detection was actually designed to detect a particular tool in the same manner as described in Section 3.1, and we discuss the detection in the Section 6.‡ the number is not exactly an emulator number, but the area code is 555 which is not valid.

5.2 Performance evaluation

The graphical performance measurements further indicate that all of the measured sandboxes are built using virtualization. Figure 10 shows measurements from the sandboxes as well as a hardware device. As with the emulators sampled in section 3.2, each of the sandboxes exhibit a lower, loosely coupled values. Unlike in our own test environment, we have no control over the duration of execution in the measured sandboxes. Due to premature termination, we only received a subset of the 5,000 measurements the application should have generated (604, 814, and 229 for Andrubis, CopperDroid, and Foresafe, respectively).

Sensor	Andrubis	CopperDroid	ForeSafe
Accelerometer	0	1	0
Ambient Temperature	0	0	0
Gravity	0	0	0
Gyroscope	0	0	0
Light	0	0	0
Linear Acceleration	0	0	0
Magnetic Field	0	0	0
Orientation	0	0	0
Pressure	0	0	0
Proximity	0	0	0
Relative Humidity	0	0	0
Rotation Vector	0	0	0
Temperature	0	0	0
Total	0	1	0

Table 7: `Sensor` counts, as evaluated from different Android sandbox systems. Very different from table 5, the sandboxes exhibit very few sensors.

5.3 Hardware and software component evaluation

None of the measured sandbox systems made effort to emulate hardware sensors. As shown in Table 7, only CopperDroid handles accelerometer events, and no sandbox handles any other sensor type. Likewise, the sandboxes report exact, unchanging values for the battery level (0) and scale (100) as used in the emulator.

5.4 System design evaluation

We elected to only measure coarse data in regard to potentially sensitive items such as address book contacts and call logs. With the wide distribution of our test applications to public sandboxes and Google Play, we wanted to reduce the risk of incidentally receiving any private information. For this reason, we only collected the total counts of contacts, call logs, and applications installed. Even so, these total counts are likely enough to discern if a device is realistically in use as the sandboxes report very low values. Better heuristics could certainly be developed over time. Andrubis reports 63 applications installed and Foresafe reports 46 apps, but neither sandbox has any of the Google services apps such as Google Talk, YouTube, or Google Service Framework installed. Andrubis shows 5 contacts and 3 call logs, indicating that some thought has been given to making Andrubis look like a device in use. The standard emulator has no contacts and no call logs, which is also what Foresafe shows.

In addition to the duration shown in the various sandbox reports, we attempted to measure the execution time. We did this by creating an application that embedded the system timestamp (`System.currentTimeMillis()`) in repeated UDP packets sent out from the sandbox. By comparing the largest and smallest value received, we can approximate the duration of execution. For instance, Foresafe may report a "Processing Time" of 106 seconds, yet for the same submission we observe timestamp values indicating an execution time of 68 seconds. Similarly, When Andrubis reports an analysis duration of 306 seconds we observe 248 seconds and when CopperDroid reports 731 seconds, we observe 399 seconds. The additional time listed by each sandbox may include some operations other than exclusively executing the application.

6. DISCUSSION

Some of the emulation detections presented in this work are relatively simple to mitigate. For instance, unexpected values could be returned for many of the API methods listed in Table 1. Some security tools, such as DroidBox [4], have started to take this step. However, DroidBox does not raise the bar very high as the new values are set to a known constant. For example, the `TelephonyManager` device identifier is always 357242043237517, and the subscriber identifier is always 310005123456789 [5]. When other security tools make use of software packages such as DroidBox, they become subject to evasion due to DroidBox detections. Such is the case for Andrubis. A sandbox system designer must be thoughtful about *how* these detections are mitigated. As demonstrated in section 4, reflection and runtime exec can be used to observe many system values in different ways, a good mitigation will handle all such cases.

Perhaps the easiest mitigations to counter are those that rely on the high-level state of the device, such as the number of contacts and the call log. Populating a sandbox with a copious address book makes such a detection considerably more difficult for an attacker.

Yet other detection mechanisms we have presented are far more difficult to counter. Techniques rooted in detecting virtualization itself, such as those we presented via timing, present a difficult hurdle for mobile sandbox system designers as they essentially require to redesign the emulator to obtain timing measurements that closely resemble those obtained on actual hardware. While it may be possible to reduce the wide discrepancy we have observed through our measurements, one can easily imagine the next step of this arms race would be to build up a hardware profile based on various measurements (CPU, graphics, ...) over several benchmarks rather than the simple Pi calculation we relied upon. We conjecture it could be possible to pinpoint the exact hardware used with such a technique—and of course, to detect any emulation.

7. CONCLUSION

As with many malware-related technologies, the detection of dynamic analysis systems is one side of an arms race. The primary reason emulator detection is more applicable here than for PCs is that practical use cases have developed for virtualizing general purpose computers – a phenomenon that has yet to occur for mobile devices. Virtualization is not broadly available on consumer mobile platforms. For this reason, we believe that mobile-oriented detection techniques will have more longevity than corresponding techniques on the PC.

We have presented a number of emulator and dynamic analysis detection methods for Android devices. Our detections are rooted in observed differences in hardware, software and device usage. From an implementation perspective, the detection techniques require little or no access beyond what a typical application would normally be granted. Such detections can significantly raise the bar for designers of dynamic analysis systems as they must universally mitigate all detections. Of those, hardware differences appear to be the most vexing to address: a very simple evaluation of the frame-per-second rate immediately led us to identify malware sandboxes, without requiring advanced permissions. Likewise, accelerometer values would yield definitive clues that the malware is running in a sandboxed environment. Whether concealing such hardware properties can be done in practice remains an open problem, on which we hope the present paper will foster research, lest malware sandboxes be easily detected and evaded.

Acknowledgments

This research was partially funded by the National Science Foundation under ITR award CCF-0424422 (TRUST).

8. REFERENCES

[1] AMAT: Android Malware Analysis Toolkit. http://sourceforge.net/projects/amatlinux/.
[2] Andrubis. http://anubis.iseclab.org/.
[3] CopperDroid. http://copperdroid.isg.rhul.ac.uk/copperdroid/.
[4] DroidBox. https://code.google.com/p/droidbox/.
[5] Droidbox device identifier patch. https://code.google.com/p/droidbox/source/browse/trunk/droidbox23/framework_base.patch?r=82.
[6] Foresafe. http://www.foresafe.com/scan.
[7] mobile-sandbox. http://mobilesandbox.org/.
[8] Monitoring the Battery Level and Charging State | Android Developers. http://developer.android.com/training/monitoring-device-state/battery-monitoring.html.
[9] North American Numbering Plan Adminstration search. www.nanpa.com/enas/area_code_query.do.
[10] SandDroid. http://sanddroid.xjtu.edu.cn/.
[11] Using the Android Emulator | Android Developers. http://developer.android.com/tools/devices/emulator.html.
[12] U. Bayer, P. Comparetti, C. Hlauschek, C. Kruegel, and E. Kirda. Scalable, behavior-based malware clustering. In *NDSS*, 2009.
[13] T. Blasing, L. Batyuk, A. Schmidt, S. Camtepe, and S. Albayrak. An android application sandbox system for suspicious software detection. In *MALWARE'10*, 2010.
[14] D. J. Chaboya, R. A. Raines, R. O. Baldwin, and B. E. Mullins. Network intrusion detection: automated and manual methods prone to attack and evasion. *Security & Privacy, IEEE*, 4(6):36–43, 2006.
[15] X. Chen, J. Andersen, Z. M. Mao, M. Bailey, and J. Nazario. Towards an understanding of anti-virtualization and anti-debugging behavior in modern malware. In *Dependable Systems and Networks With FTCS and DCC, 2008. IEEE International Conference on*, pages 177–186, 2008.
[16] H. Dreger, A. Feldmann, V. Paxson, and R. Sommer. Operational experiences with high-volume network intrusion detection. In *Proc. CCS*, pages 2–11. ACM, 2004.
[17] M. F. and P. Schulz. Detecting android sandboxes, Aug 2012. https://www.dexlabs.org/blog/btdetect.
[18] A. Felt, M. Finifter, E. Chin, S. Hanna, and D. Wagner. A survey of mobile malware in the wild. In *Proc. SPSM*, pages 3–14. ACM, 2011.
[19] P. Ferrie. Attacks on more virtual machine emulators. *Symantec Technology Exchange*, 2007.
[20] P. Fogla and W. Lee. Evading network anomaly detection systems: formal reasoning and practical techniques. In *Proc. CCS*, pages 59–68. ACM, 2006.
[21] M. Handley, V. Paxson, and C. Kreibich. Network intrusion detection: Evasion, traffic normalization, and end-to-end protocol semantics. In *Proc. USENIX Security*, 2001.
[22] T. Holz and F. Raynal. Detecting honeypots and other suspicious environments. In *Information Assurance Workshop, 2005. IAW'05. Proceedings from the Sixth Annual IEEE SMC*, pages 29–36. IEEE, 2005.
[23] P. G. Kelley, S. Consolvo, L. F. Cranor, J. Jung, N. Sadeh, and D. Wetherall. A conundrum of permissions: Installing applications on an android smartphone. In *USEC'12*, pages 68–79. Springer, 2012.
[24] B. Lau and V. Svajcer. Measuring virtual machine detection in malware using dsd tracer. *Journal in Computer Virology*, 6(3):181–195, 2010.
[25] H. Lockheimer. Android and Security, Feb 2012. http://googlemobile.blogspot.com/2012/02/android-and-security.html.
[26] A. Moser, C. Kruegel, and E. Kirda. Exploring multiple execution paths for malware analysis. In *Security and Privacy, 2007. SP'07. IEEE Symposium on*, 2007.
[27] D. Mutz, G. Vigna, and R. Kemmerer. An experience developing an ids stimulator for the black-box testing of network intrusion detection systems. In *Computer Security Applications Conference, 2003. Proceedings. 19th Annual*, pages 374–383. IEEE, 2003.
[28] J. Oberheide and C. Miller. Dissecting the android bouncer. *SummerCon2012, New York*, 2012.
[29] T. Ooura. Improvement of the pi calculation algorithm and implementation of fast multiple precision computation. *Transactions-Japan Society for Industrial and Applied Mathematics*, 9(4):165–172, 1999.
[30] R. Paleari, L. Martignoni, G. F. Roglia, and D. Bruschi. A fistful of red-pills: How to automatically generate procedures to detect cpu emulators. In *Proc. WOOT*, volume 41, page 86. USENIX, 2009.
[31] N. J. Percoco and S. Schulte. Adventures in bouncerland. *Black Hat USA*, 2012.
[32] T. H. Ptacek and T. N. Newsham. Insertion, evasion, and denial of service: Eluding network intrusion detection. Technical report, DTIC Document, 1998.
[33] T. Raffetseder, C. Krügel, and E. Kirda. Detecting system emulators. In *Information Security*. Springer, 2007.
[34] J. Rutkowska. Red pill... or how to detect vmm using (almost) one cpu instruction. *Invisible Things*, 2004.
[35] T. Strazzere. Dex education 201 anti-emulation, Sept 2013. http://hitcon.org/2013/download/Tim\%20Strazzere\%20-\%20DexEducation.pdf.
[36] T. Vidas and N. Christin. Sweetening android lemon markets: measuring and combating malware in application marketplaces. In *Proc. 3rd CODASPY*, pages 197–208. ACM, 2013.
[37] T. Vidas, D. Votipka, and N. Christin. All your droid are belong to us: A survey of current android attacks. In *Proc. WOOT*. USENIX, 2011.
[38] T. Vidas, C. Zhang, and N. Christin. Toward a general collection methodology for android devices. *DFRWS'11*, 2011.
[39] C. Willems, T. Holz, and F. Freiling. Toward automated dynamic malware analysis using cwsandbox. *Security & Privacy, IEEE*, 5(2):32–39, 2007.
[40] Y. Zhou and X. Jiang. Dissecting android malware: Characterization and evolution. In *Proc. IEEE Symp. on Security and Privacy*, 2012.
[41] Y. Zhou, Z. Wang, W. Zhou, and X. Jiang. Hey, you, get off of my market: Detecting malicious apps in official and alternative android markets. In *Proc. NDSS*, 2012.

9. APPENDIX

```java
private void logRuntimeSystemPropsReflect(){
  logAprop("ro.secure");
  logAprop("ro.product.name");
  logAprop("ro.debuggable");
  logAprop("status.battery.level_raw");
  logAprop("ro.build.host");
  logAprop("ro.build.tags");
  logAprop("net.gprs.local-ip");
  logAprop("net.eth0.gw");
  logAprop("net.dns1");
  logAprop("gsm.operator.numeric");
  logAprop("ro.kernel.qemu");
  logAprop("ro.kernel.qemu.gles");
  logAprop("ro.kernel.android.qemud");
}
private void logAprop(String s){
  Log.e("reflect."+s,getPropViaReflect(s));
}

//the actual reflection to obtain a handle to the hidden android.os.SystemProperties
private String getPropViaReflect(String s){
  String ret="";
  try{
    ClassLoader cl = theActivity.getBaseContext().getClassLoader();
    Class<?> SystemProperties = cl.loadClass("android.os.SystemProperties");

    @SuppressWarnings("rawtypes")
    Class[] paramTypes = { String.class };
    Method get = SystemProperties.getMethod("get", paramTypes);

    Object[] params = { s };
    ret = (String) get.invoke(SystemProperties, params);
  } catch(Exception e){
    e.printStackTrace();
  }
  return ret;
}

private void logRuntimeSystemPropsExec(){
  try
  {
    String line;
    java.lang.Process p = Runtime.getRuntime().exec("getprop");
    BufferedReader input = new BufferedReader(new InputStreamReader(p.getInputStream()));
    while ((line = input.readLine()) != null)
    {
      //quick line parsing
      int split = line.indexOf("]: [");
      String k = line.substring(1,split);
      String v = line.substring(split+4,line.length()-1);
      Log.e("runprop."+k,v);
    }
    input.close();
  }
  catch (Exception err)
  {
    err.printStackTrace();
  }
}
```

Figure 11: This listing uses reflection (top) and a runtime exec (bottom) to obtain runtime `SystemProperties` information. In either case the information is logged to the system log, for detection purposes this value would be evaluated in accordance with the detection techniques presented in earlier sections. This code listing obtains information in completely different ways than those detailed in the earlier sections of the paper without using the official API and without requiring additional permissions. This code obtains values for the battery level, the Build configuration, network IP settings, and cellular provider MCC and MNC.

VirtualSwindle: An Automated Attack Against In-App Billing on Android

Collin Mulliner
Northeastern University
Boston, MA
crm@ccs.neu.edu

William Robertson
Northeastern University
Boston, MA
wkr@ccs.neu.edu

Engin Kirda
Northeastern University
Boston, MA
ek@ccs.neu.edu

ABSTRACT

Since its introduction, Android's in-app billing service has quickly gained popularity. The in-app billing service allows users to pay for options, services, subscriptions, and virtual goods from within mobile apps themselves. In-app billing is attractive for developers because it is easy to integrate, and has the advantage that the developer does not need to be concerned with managing financial transactions. In this paper, we present the first fully-automated attack against the in-app billing service on Android. Using our prototype, we conducted a robustness study against our attack, analyzing 85 of the most popular Android apps that make use of in-app billing. We found that 60% of these apps were easily and automatically crackable. We were able to bypass highly popular and prominent games such as Angry Birds and Temple Run, each of which have millions of users. Based on our study, we developed a defensive technique that specifically counters automated attacks against in-app billing. Our technique is lightweight and can be easily added to existing applications.

Categories and Subject Descriptors

K.6.5 [**Software**]: Security and Protection

General Terms: security

Keywords: Mobile Application; App Protection; Payment; Smartphone Security

1. INTRODUCTION

Since 2008, centralized mobile application markets for smartphones such as Apple's App Store and Google's Play Store have radically changed the way applications are installed on mobile devices. Users can now easily search for, read reviews on, and install mobile apps from central repositories that come pre-configured on the device. Furthermore, such centralized market places also provide the advantage that updating installed applications is simpler and more efficient.

One recent development in the competition for providing new app market-based services and, hence, creating new revenue streams for app market providers is *in-app purchasing*. This feature first appeared in Apple's iOS 4 in 2010, and allows users to pay for options, services, subscriptions, and virtual goods from within apps themselves. In March 2011, Google followed suit, and provided a service they term in-app billing [12].

The idea behind selling commercial services in the apps themselves is to allow users to first try out, use, and test an application before they are offered the option of buying additional services. For example, the first three levels of a game might be offered for free, but the user might be asked to pay for the ability to activate and access subsequent levels in the game. Similarly, some games allow users to play for free, but offer to improve the gaming experience by selling game-related tools to the player. For instance, in an aerial dogfighting game, a fighter plane that is higher performance might only be available to the player through an in-app purchase. Of course, in-app purchasing is not only useful for game developers. For example, ComiXology's Comics is a free app, but the comics themselves cost money and must be acquired through in-app purchases.

In Android's in-app billing, any developer can integrate the service in their application without needing a special contract with Google. The only requirements are the possession of *a*) a Google play developer account, and *b*) a Google Wallet merchant account. Hence, it is very easy for any developer to integrate in-app billing functionality in her application, and she is not unnecessarily burdened with having to go through a tedious registration process. For Google, making in-app billing accessible and easy to use is important because it receives a 30% sales commission on each in-app purchase. The advantage for the developer, on the other hand, is that she does not need to be concerned with credit card transactions and billing cycles. Furthermore, the in-app billing service offered by Google provides libraries that are straightforward to use, and that can be integrated into existing apps with ease.

One important question with respect to in-app billing is how secure these operations are. In a detailed document, Google discusses the security and design of in-app billing, and provides best-practice recommendations and guidelines to app developers who are planning to use the in-app billing service [13] on Android. One of the recommendations is that, if practical, the developer should perform signature verification to authorize Google-supported purchases on a remote server, and not on the device itself. The explanation provided is that implementing purchase verification on a remote server makes it difficult for attackers to break the verification process by analyzing the application code. Another recommendation is that the developer should obfuscate in-app billing code using a tool such as ProGuard so that it is difficult for an attacker to reverse engineer security protocols and other application components. Furthermore, developers are encouraged to perform method inlining, construct strings on the fly instead of defining them as constants, and use Java reflection to call methods as further obfuscation techniques.

ASIA CCS'14, June 4–6, 2014, Kyoto, Japan.

http://dx.doi.org/10.1145/2590296.2590335.

The key insight behind these obfuscation recommendations is that using these techniques will help minimize attacks that give users access to protected virtual goods while bypassing the in-app billing implementation.

Note that the discussion in the in-app billing security and design recommendations provided to app developers assumes that the majority of anticipated attacks will directly target application code through reverse engineering and manual analysis. This is a time-consuming and tedious task if the code is obfuscated. In fact, this assumption also seems to be popular among some developers. For instance, the discussion attached to Google's official recommendations document contains claims that it is not important to worry about the small number of people who have the time and knowledge to hack one instance of the app [13].

In this paper, we present the first fully-automated attack against the in-app billing service on Android. Instead of taking the manual approach of trying to reverse engineer, decompile, and patch individual apps that use in-app billing services, our generic attack uses a dynamic Dalvik instrumentation approach we have developed to inject arbitrary code into a running process. Hence, we are able to modify the behavior of any Dalvik-based Android app at runtime. Our attack code is launched as a simple app named VirtualSwindle. Our attack app runs in the background and, when invoked, automatically attacks every app using in-app billing that relies upon on-device signature verification, allowing the attacker to access digital content and services without paying for them. Hence, the bar for gaining illicit access to paid services in Android apps is significantly lowered.

Using our prototype, we conducted a robustness study against our attack, and analyzed 85 popular apps that made use of in-app billing. Our findings show that 60% of the apps we analyzed employed on-device signature verification, and were therefore easily crackable. Only 36% of the applications that we tested took in-app billing security seriously by performing the signature checks on a remote server as recommended in the in-app billing developer guidelines. Note that our paper *does not show a weakness* in Google's in-app billing architecture. Rather, it shows that many app developers *do not seem to be aware* of how easily the in-app billing functionality in their applications could potentially be bypassed if they do not rigorously follow Google's guidelines.

From an economic perspective, the amount an attacker could steal in pirated in-app items can easily add up to several hundred dollars, equivalent to the cost of a new Android phone. We found that items offered through in-app billing cost between $1 and $99 (see Figure 8), while a new Android phone (e.g., Nexus 5) costs around $399. Hence, given an average observed item cost of $20 which we draw from our empirical evaluation, an attacker need only steal 20 items to offset the cost of a new phone. In practice, attackers could quite easily steal significantly larger sums.

This paper makes the following contributions.

- We present and describe a novel dynamic Dalvik instrumentation approach. Our approach is able to instrument Dalvik applications by intercepting and mapping Dalvik methods to equivalent, attacker-provided native methods. Furthermore, our tool is able to load and inject arbitrary Dalvik code into a running process. Hence, we are able to change the behavior of any Dalvik-based Android process at runtime without tampering with application code signatures.

- We present a novel attack against Google Play's in-app billing service on the Android platform. Our attack is generic and, once launched, automatically attacks every application that uses in-app billing on the targeted device that relies upon on-device signature verification. As our attack is dynamic, any static protection mechanism that uses code obfuscation (e.g., reflection or variable renaming) is ineffective and easily evaded.

- We counter the popular developer folk wisdom that following the simple obfuscation guidelines in the in-app billing documentation will significantly deter attackers from compromising their apps. We performed empirical experiments, testing our attack on 85 popular apps that make use of in-app billing, and found that 60% of the apps we analyzed were automatically and easily crackable using our attack prototype. Among the crackable apps were well-known, extremely popular apps such as Angry Birds and Temple Run. We present detailed reports on the in-app billing defenses implemented by these 85 popular Android apps.

- We developed a lightweight countermeasure that prevents fully automated attacks like ours. Our countermeasure is based on replicating and obfuscating code specific to the billing process. The aim of the technique is to force attackers to perform manual analysis of applications in order to crack them. Our method can be integrated into existing applications with low effort.

- We have posted an anonymous video of our attack demo on YouTube at `http://www.youtube.com/watch?v=Jx5GGINNGoc`. We hope that the video will be educational for developers, and will motivate them to better secure their applications.

The rest of this paper is organized as follows. The next section gives background information on in-app billing. Section 3 discusses the threat model we assume in this work. Section 4 describes our automated attack against in-app billing. Section 5 presents our evaluation and experiments. Section 6 presents and discusses our lightweight countermeasure. Section 7 discusses related work, and Section 8 concludes the paper.

2. BACKGROUND: IN-APP BILLING

In this section, we first provide background information on in-app billing for the Android platform before presenting details of our attack.

2.1 The In-App Billing Architecture

The architecture of the Android in-app billing service consists of four components; three are mandatory and one is optional. The first component is the Android Play Store application, which is used to download applications from the Play Store. The Play Store app exposes the `MarketBillingService` interface that is used by applications to interact with the billing system. The second component is the back-end Play Store server that is hosted by Google. The aim of the Play Store server is to perform the actual financial transaction requested by remote apps. The third component in the architecture is the application on the device that uses the in-app billing service. The application communicates with Google's Play Store by using the `MarketBillingService` API. The fourth optional component is a server-side service that can be deployed by the application developer. The application developer can use this optional service to provide services for users of his apps such as content distribution or data storage. In the context of in-app billing, the developer can also use it to authorize in-app billing transactions. Figure 1 depicts the architecture of the in-app billing service.

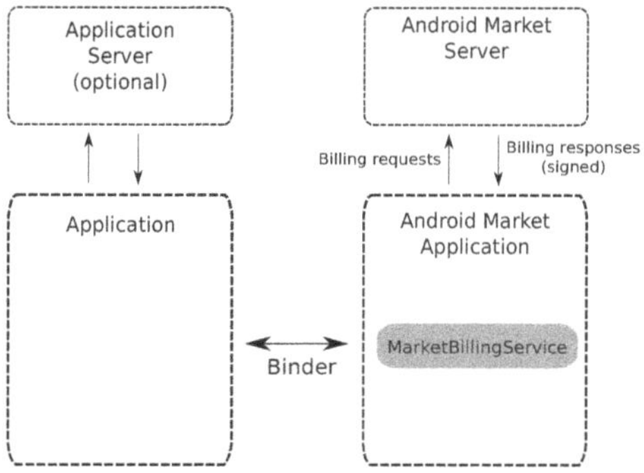

Figure 1: The Android in-app billing architecture [12].

2.2 In-App Billing: Developer's Perspective

Developers that wish to include in-app billing services in their apps need to perform three basic steps.

1. **Add in-app billing code to their application**. This is the code that talks to the Play Store app on the Android device that provides the in-app billing service.
2. **Register items in the Android Play Store**. These items are the digital services that users can purchase inside the application. For example, an artifact could be the ammunition that is needed for a powerful weapon that the user has picked up in a game. Note that every item that can be purchased has to be registered on the Play Store back-end server so that it can be sold as a digital service through in-app billing.
3. **Generate a public key pair**. For in-app billing to be activated, a private key needs to be uploaded by the developer to the Play Store server. It is then used to sign each in-app purchase. The public key is embedded into the application by the developer, and is used to verify the signature of the purchase data that is provided by the Google in-app billing service.

Once these steps are completed by the developer, in-app billing can be used in the app. Note that applications do not need to go through any testing process, and they do not need any special permissions from Google to be able to use in-app billing. Clearly, Google, as the in-app billing provider, is interested in making this process as easy and as low-overhead as possible for developers.

2.3 Purchasing an Item with In-app Billing

An application that has in-app billing functionality uses two interfaces to the Android Play Store app. The main interface is the `sendBillingRequest` method call. This method takes a `Bundle` (i.e., an object that holds key-value mappings) as an argument, and returns another Bundle as the result. The second interface is a broadcast receiver. The broadcast receiver is used to receive `Intents`, which are abstract descriptions of an operation to be performed, from the Android Play Store app. Note that the in-app billing process is highly asynchronous and, therefore, all state changes are signaled via `Intents`.

To purchase an item, three steps have to be taken. First, the application issues the `REQUEST_PURCHASE` command using the `sendBillingRequest` method. The Play Store replies with a Bundle that contains a `REQUEST_ID` and a `PendingIntent`, which is a special `Intent` that is used to display the payment screen. Figure 2 shows a screenshot of the payment screen from the popular game Temple Run.

Figure 2: Payment screen from the game Temple Run.

Once the user completes the payment process, the Play Store application sends an `IN_APP_NOTIFY Intent` to the application, and indicates that the payment has been successfully received. The application responds with the `GET_PURCHASE_INFORMATION` command. The Play Store application then follows with a `PURCHASE-_STATE_CHANGED Intent`. This `Intent` contains detailed information about the completed in-app purchase. That is, it contains purchase information that has been generated by the Play Store server, and that has been signed with the developer's private key.

After the application receives the signed purchase information, it checks the signature of the data sent by the Play Store app, and confirms the sale with a `CONFIRM_NOTIFICATIONS` command. At this point, the purchase is now complete. Figure 3 shows the command and Intent exchange between an application that uses in-app billing and the Android Play Store app.

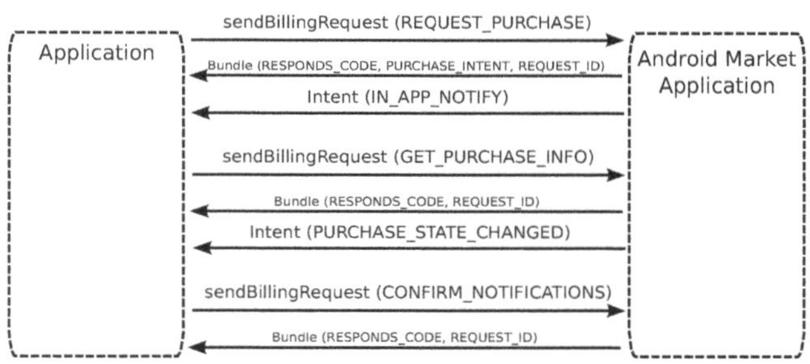

Figure 3: Method calls and `Intents` for a payment [12].

3. THREAT MODEL

In this section, we describe the threat model that we assume for our attack against in-app billing. We first discuss the motivation of the attacker, and then describe the prerequisites for the attack.

3.1 The Attacker

The attacker is the owner of an Android device, and is interested in using in-app services without paying for them. Hence, by launching an attack, the attacker aims to automatically subvert the in-app billing process. The defenders are *a*) the in-app billing service on the device that is responsible for in-app purchases and that receives a commission on each sale, and *b*) the application developer who is interested in making her application as difficult to crack as possible (e.g., but following security recommendations in the in-app billing documentation [13]).

3.2 The Prerequisites

For our attack to succeed, there are two prerequisites that need to be fulfilled. The first prerequisite is that the attacker has full control over her own device, and that she can gain root access. We believe that this assumption is realistic, as rooting an Android device is straightforward, and a wealth of documentation on the topic is available. Furthermore, popular tools such as SuperOneClick [6] allow technically unsophisticated users to automatically root Android devices. Note that unlike Apple's iOS, Google and most Android device manufacturers tolerate users acquiring root access to their devices. For example, HTC has an official site to unlock the bootloader of their devices [14]. An unlocked boot loader allows one to easily root a phone by installing a modified firmware such as CyanogenMod [7].

Rooting a device normally consists of installing an `su` (superuser) binary with setuid root permissions in `/system/xbin`. This process is as simple as downloading a ZIP archive to the `/sdcard` path of an Android device, and installing its contents using the Android recovery boot loader that is present on all devices.

Also, note that rooting an Android device does not mean that the device's security guarantees are necessarily void. For example, SuperSU [4] has a GUI application that allows the user to selectively give super-user privileges to individual applications. Thus, the user keeps control over which applications have root privileges on her device.

The second prerequisite for a successful automated attack is that the application developer performs signature verification on the device using the functionality provided by Google's in-app billing service. As our experiments in Section 5 demonstrate, this assumption is realistic based on empirical measurements. That is, the majority of the apps we analyzed – including highly popular games such as Angry Birds – performed on-device signature verification, relied on existing libraries for this task, and were therefore vulnerable.

4. ATTACKING IN-APP BILLING

Our attack against in-app billing is straightforward, and works by emulating and subverting the `MarketBillingService` inside the Android Play Store application on the device itself. The `MarketBillingService` has one function, `sendBillingRequest`, that is exposed to applications as an Inter-Process Communication (IPC) endpoint. As discussed in Section 2, `sendBillingRequest` takes a `Bundle` as an argument, and returns another `Bundle` as a result.

In the attack, we dynamically subvert and modify the Play Store application on the device. In other words, at runtime, we replace the `sendBillingRequest` method with our own code. Our version of `sendBillingRequest` then generates the answer `Bundles` and `Intent` that make the calling app believe that the purchase was successful.

For our attack to be successful, we only have to overcome a single security check located inside the in-app billing-enabled victim app. In particular, this check is the signature verification of the purchase data returned to the application by the Android Play Store. To overcome the signature check, we replace the standard Dalvik library method `java.security.Signature.verify` with our own method that always returns true, indicating success. Thus, we can disable signature verification with ease if the programmer has chosen to do on-device verification, and relies on the provided functionality. Note that we replace the verification function globally on the device. Hence, we do not need to attack vulnerable applications individually. In order to not break signature verification for the rest of the device we only return true if the input is our fake signature.

To be able to launch a dynamic attack against the in-app billing service, we had to develop novel tools for the dynamic instrumentation of Dalvik binaries. In this section, we describe the implementation of our attack and the tools we developed in detail.

4.1 Dynamic Dalvik Instrumentation

As a part of our attack, we created a dynamic Dalvik instrumentation approach, and implemented a library called *libddi*. Our library consists of several components, and allows us to intercept and map any Dalvik method to an alternative native function implementation provided by the attacker. Furthermore, we are also able to inject additional, arbitrary Dalvik code into a running process, and perform full dynamic instrumentation of any process that is running on the Android platform.

The Dalvik Virtual Machine on Android devices supports the invocation of native code that is loaded from shared libraries using the Java Native Interfaces (JNI) mechanism. The basic idea behind our instrumentation approach is to abuse the JNI layer of Dalvik, and to modify any interpreted Dalvik method and to replace it with a corresponding native variant that is provided by the attacker.

In the following, we describe the main features of our instrumentation tool in more detail, and discuss some of the technical challenges we faced.

4.1.1 Library Injection

Our instrumentation tool is bootstrapped through a well-known library injection technique (i.e., [5]) that we had to adjust for the ARM platform. This technique is based on executing a few instructions on the stack that invoke *dlopen(2)*, and that load the shared library into the process. The code is executed once the dynamic linker loads the shared library, and executes the library's *init* function.

4.1.2 Redirecting Dalvik Methods to Native Code

Just like the Java VM, the Dalvik VM supports calling native code loaded from shared libraries using the JNI mechanism. The key insight behind our instrumentation approach is that Dalvik calls can be replaced with native calls. In fact, this is functionality that has to exist in the VM as a feature to be able to implement and provide JNI functionality.

A method in the Dalvik VM is represented by a *method struct*. The method struct contains several fields that are related to the actual code being executed. The `insns` field points to the Dalvik bytecode if this is a Dalvik function, and the `nativeFunc` field points to a JNI helper function if the method is native; in this case, `insns` will point to the actual native code. Furthermore, the `registersSize` and `jniArgInfo` fields contain information related to method parameters, and the `accessFlags` field holds information concerning method visibility (i.e., public vs. private) and whether the method is implemented using native or managed code.

To modify an existing method in Dalvik and map it to a different native call, all of these fields must be adjusted accordingly. For example, the `jniArgInfo` field has to be set so that the JNI helper will scan the method signature to determine how the arguments are passed, and the `registersSize` field has to be adjusted with the number and type of arguments. Furthermore, the `accessFlags` have to be modified to indicate that the method is native. Finally, the actual function pointer has to be set to the field `insns`, and the field `nativeFunc` has to be pointed at the JNI helper function. The last step is performed using the `dvmUseJNIBridge` function in the Android `libdvm` library.

Figure 4 depicts an example of how the existing `verify` method of the `java.security.Signature` class can be redirected to an arbitrary native implementation. In the first step, a handle to the class `java.security.Signature` has to be obtained using the Android `dvmFindLoadedClass` function. In the second step, a method handle has to be acquired for the method in question. This is done by invoking the libdvm function `dvmFindVirtualMethod-`

```
cls = dvmFindLoadedClass("Ljava/security/Signature;");
Method *m = dvmFindVirtualMethodHierByDescriptor(
  cls, "verify", "([B)Z");
m->registersSize = 2;
m->jniArgInfo = 0x40000000;
m->accessFlags = m->accessFlags | 0x0100;
dvmUseJNIBridge(m, verify);
```

Figure 4: An example of redirecting a Dalvik method to native code. Here, the method `boolean java.security.Signature.verify(byte[])` is hijacked.

```
int verify(JNIEnv* env, jobject obj, jobject bytearray)
{
  return 1;
}
```

Figure 5: Native code to replace `java.security.Signature.verify(byte[])` with a function that always returns true.

`HierByDescriptor` and passing the method's name and signature. As described above, the method meta data is adjusted and redirected to the arbitrary, native implementation of `verify`.

Figure 5 shows the replacement function for the method `java.security.Signature.verify`, which follows the JNI call standard. The first argument is the JNI environment. This is followed by the instance object and the actual method parameters – in this case, a byte array.

4.2 Loading Arbitrary Dalvik Classes into an Existing Process

The ability to redirect any existing Dalvik method and map it to an arbitrary native call is useful and powerful in terms of dynamic instrumentation. However, our instrumentation approach also allows us to load additional, arbitrary Dalvik classes into an existing process. In other words, we are able to write instrumentation and attack code in Java. Clearly, being able to write attack code in Java has the advantage that it is easier to build new functionality as it makes it straightforward to interact with existing Dalvik libraries. In comparison, developing code in C/C++ has a much higher overhead.

To load classes into a running process, the Dalvik executable (known as a DEX file) has to be loaded from disk. This is done using the `openDexFile` function, provided by Android's libdvm, through our libddi instrumentation library. Second, we have to define the class and tell the class loader which class to load from the DEX file. This is done by calling the libdvm function `defineClass`. After the class has been loaded, it can be used just like any other class in the VM. One can create new instances, dispatch methods to those instances, and also call static methods.

Figure 6 depicts our instrumentation library libddi in operation. After the library is injected into a running process, it intercepts and patches methods that the attacker wishes to instrument, and then loads attacker-provided Dalvik classes into the target process.

4.3 Calling Patched Methods

Once a Dalvik method has been intercepted and redirected to a native method provided by the attacker, there exists no direct path to call the original method. That is, every time the method is looked up through standard Android functions such as `dvmFindVirtualMethodHierByDescriptor`, the method structure that is returned

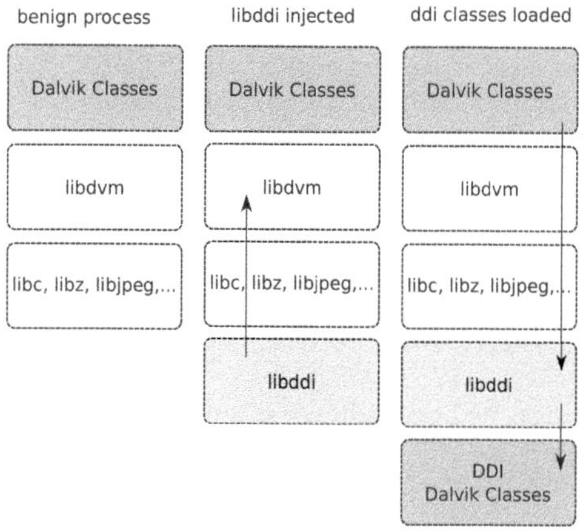

Figure 6: The DDI instrumentation library in operation. The benign process consists of native libraries, the Dalvik VM, and the Dalvik classes. In the first step, our libddi library is injected into the process. Then, libddi uses the Dalvik VM to change the Dalvik methods to point to native code. Once the native code is executed, arbitrary Dalvik classes can be loaded and executed.

points to our alternative native method implementation. The only way to call the original, replaced Dalvik code is to patch the internal method structure to make it point back to the original implementation.

4.4 Obtaining a Context

Unfortunately, interacting with the Android system from the instrumented code is not always straightforward. In many instances, an `android.content.Context` class is needed. A `Context` object allows the sending of `Intents` using the `sendBroadcast` method. Normally, a developer does not need to be concerned with obtaining a handle on the `Context` object because every Android application is a subclass of `android.content.Context`. However, if additional attacker-provided classes are loaded into a running process, the loaded classes do not have a reference to the existing `Context` instance, and hence cannot interact with the Android framework.

We had to design two techniques for obtaining a reference to the current application's `Context` object. These techniques work well in practice, and allow us to launch successful attacks against the in-app billing infrastructure on the device. In the following, we describe the two techniques we use.

4.4.1 Using the ActivityThread

If the injected code is running inside an application that is currently in the foreground, we use a static method belonging to the `ActivityThread` class to obtain a `Context` reference by calling the method `currentApplication`. The `ActivityThread` class manages the main thread of an Android application process. This technique is generic, and works in most situations. Furthermore, it can be implemented purely in Java.

4.4.2 Scraping the Instance Object

Unfortunately, in some cases the application does not run in the foreground. Hence, the `ActivityThread` approach does not work.

If the instrumented method is not a static method, the method call always has the instance object as the first argument passed to the method. We now have multiple options for acquiring a `Context` reference depending on what kind of class we are dealing with.

a) If the method is part of a class or a subclass of `Context`, then the instance object provides a valid `Context`. Well-known subclasses of `Context` are the three cornerstones of the Android application framework, namely `Service`, `Activity`, and `Application`.

b) If the class is an inner-class of any one of those classes, we simply need to access the enclosing class. The Java compiler generates a synthetic member field for such purposes named `this$0` that allows us to obtain a `Context` reference.

c) If the class has any member variable that stores a reference to a `Context`, this variable can be accessed to obtain a handle to that `Context`. In fact, this is frequently used by application developers as they also need an easy method to acquire a `Context` object to be able to interact with the Android framework.

All of the three above methods can be implemented using reflection using Java or C/C++. However, if the `Context` is acquired via C/C++, it has to be transferred to the Java world through the JNI interface.

4.5 Attacking In-App Billing

The implementation of the automated attack against in-app billing is based on the dynamic Dalvik instrumentation approach we discussed in Section 4.1. That is, we use libddi to subvert in-app billing.

In the first step, the `com.android.vending` process is hijacked by injecting libddi into the process, where `com.android.vending` is the Android process that is responsible for authorizing in-app purchases. To interact with the application process and the Dalvik VM, we need our injected code to execute in an application thread. Therefore, we hijack a common, frequently called function. We determined that `epoll_wait`, a low-level function that waits for events on a set of file descriptors, is a suitable choice since it is called frequently by the Android framework, and thus by every application. Once our version of `epoll_wait` is called, the in-app billing method `sendBillingRequest` is redirected to our own native implementation.

In the second step, whenever `sendBillingRequest` is invoked, our attack code is executed. The attack code then loads Dalvik classes that we have written into the vending process. The ability to use Dalvik classes in the attack is important because we need to be able to communicate with in-app billing victims using the standard Android communication mechanisms (e.g., `Intents`).

Our Dalvik attack engine is responsible for emulating the Android billing process, and has four basic components. A handler component first parses the request received via `sendBillingRequest` from the in-app billing victim application. Here, we extract application-specific values such as the purchased item names. A second component then generates the appropriate answers based on the extracted request data. A third component is responsible for sending back answers to the victim app as `Bundles` and `Intents`. Finally, a fourth component provides a state tracking mechanism that is used by our native attack code to query the state of the Dalvik component of the attack.

Patching `java.security.Signature.verify` is done by loading a small native library into the *zygote process*. Note that on Android systems, this process is automatically mapped into all other Dalvik processes. Hence, using this approach, our attack code only needs to be injected once into the zygote for it to be automatically propagated to every process running on the system.

4.6 Launching the Attack

The attack against in-app billing is executed as soon as the victim application sends a `REQUEST_PURCHASE` request through the `sendBillingRequest` call to the Play Store application. Our native, subverted implementation of `sendBillingRequest` operates as a central dispatcher. It receives requests from the victim applications as `Bundles`, and forwards these `Bundles` to our request handler in the attack engine. The attack consists of four main steps.

4.6.1 *Interception of* `REQUEST_PURCHASE`

Once the purchase request is intercepted, the corresponding `Bundle` is parsed and relevant data such as the package name and the item ID are extracted. `REQUEST_PURCHASE` is a special request in the context of our attack in the sense that it indicates a valid and legitimate purchase request from the victim app. Hence, the result that is returned to the victim has to make sense. Therefore, we pass this request and its parameters to the original, legitimate implementation of `sendBillingRequest`. We then take the answer generated by the Play Store app and pass it back to the victim app. The Play Store then builds a `PendingIntent` as shown in the example in Figure 2.

4.6.2 *Sending* `IN_APP_NOTIFY`

This `Intent` is be sent to indicate that the purchase was carried out by the user. The `Intent` needs to be delayed until `sendBillingRequest` has returned and the victim application has a defined state. Therefore, we create a thread and delay it for five seconds before sending the `Intent` to the victim application. We chose five seconds as the delay time as it worked well in our experiments.

4.6.3 *Handling* `GET_PURCHASE_INFORMATION`

The handling of this request is an important part of the attack. Here, we generate the JSON object that contains all the purchase information such as the product ID, the state of the purchase, and the order ID.

Under normal conditions, this JSON object would be generated and signed by the remote Play Store server. However, since we are not really performing a purchase and are only making the victim app believe that the purchase has been successful, we need to generate this JSON object ourselves. For the attack to succeed, we do not care about having a valid signature and, hence, fill the signature field with a fake signature that we Base64 encode. This is done to ensure that the field passes the Base64 decoding check in the victim app.

The two fields `inapp_signed_data` and `inapp_signature` are sent via a `PURCHASE_STATE_CHANGED Intent` back to the victim application. Figure 7 shows a real-world example of data that is sent in the `inapp_signed_data` field for the popular game Temple Run.

4.6.4 *Confirming the purchase*

If satisfied with the signature verification step, the victim app can now send a `CONFIRM_NOTIFICATIONS Intent` through the `sendBillingRequest` method. We can then detect that our attack has succeeded. Note that as we intercept and subvert the on-device signature verification libraries, any app that relies on this functionality will be automatically cracked.

4.7 Dealing with the Play Store User Interface

Our attack against in-app billing works completely automatically, without any user interaction, immediately after the `REQUEST_PURCHASE Intent` is received by our subverted version of `sendBillingRequest`. Under normal conditions, whenever an in-app purchase succeeds, the payment dialog shown by the Play Store app

```
{ "nonce": -9149971711919728712,
  "orders":
  [{
    "notificationId": "1",
    "packageName": "com.imangi.templerun",
    "orderId": 6120396686557988119,
    "purchaseState": 0,
    "purchaseTime": 0,
    "productId": "com.imangi.templerun.iap.coinpack.d"
  }]
}
```

Figure 7: Automatically-generated purchase data for the game Temple Run.

is closed as soon as the payment process is completed. However, since our attack does not actually complete the payment process in the Play Store application, pressing the back button in the Play Store app to go to a different view would normally cancel the purchase. Hence, a `CANCEL` message would be sent to the victim app. In our experiments, we observed that some apps will cancel an in-app purchase if they receive a `CANCEL` message from the Play Store after a transaction. To mitigate this problem, we also patched the `sendResponseCode` method in the Play Store application to suppress the `CANCEL` message from being sent when the payment dialog is closed via the back button.

4.8 Cheating with In-Game Currency

We adapted our attack for all games that have in-game currency. In such apps, a currency is defined in the game that allow users to save and purchase in-game items. For example, a magic sword might cost the player 100 gold coins, and these gold coins might be purchased using traditional currency through in-app billing. With this simple extension, we can create automated loops to continuously buy currency for cheating purposes, or for jumping ahead in the game's high-score rankings.

This extension requires sending the `IN_APP_NOTIFY Intent` and restarting the in-app purchase process as soon as the last step of payment is completed. Hence, an in-app item can be bought hundreds of times without having to manually interact with the user interface for each purchase.

4.9 Making the Attack Easy to Use

To make the attack prototype easy to launch and use, we created an Android app called VirtualSwindle that an attacker can launch with the simple touch of a finger. The app runs in the background, and automatically cracks every in-app billing app that relies upon on-device signature verification as discussed in the previous sections. The reader is referred to an anonymous YouTube video located at `http://www.youtube.com/watch?v=Jx5GGINNGoc` for a demonstration of the attack in action.

5. EVALUATION

The aim of our evaluation is to determine how effective our automated attack would be against popular apps that use in-app billing, and to gain insights into how security-aware app developers are today. We tested VirtualSwindle on 85 apps from the Google Play Store. Furthermore, we manually analyzed and reverse engineered these apps to determine what kinds of security precautions, if any, they were taking.

In the following, we describe how we selected the in-app billing apps we tested for robustness, how we executed the tests, and how we performed our security analyses.

5.1 Ethical Considerations

Checking popular applications to see if their in-app functionality can be bypassed could be considered an ethically sensitive issue. Clearly, one question that arises is if it is ethically acceptable and justifiable to test an attack tool on real applications. We believe that realistic experiments are the only way to reliably estimate success rates of attacks in the real world. Unfortunately, criminals do not have any second thoughts about discovering vulnerabilities in the wild, or launching attacks. We note that VirtualSwindle only performed a client-side attack on each application, and the attack had no server-side effect on the tested applications (i.e., an in-app transaction was never really completed). Furthermore, if the attack succeeded, we stopped interacting with the app, and made sure that no server-side logs were affected (e.g., online high scores). Also, the vulnerable apps we tested only had in-app currency that was generated on the device, and the virtual currency was deleted once the app was uninstalled.

5.2 Selection Process for In-App Billing Apps

Determining if an application is using in-app billing is not a straightforward process. Although in-app billing does require a special permission (i.e., `com.android.vending.BILLING`), it is not possible to search the Play Store for all apps that support this feature. Furthermore, just because the permission is present and the application asks for it does not necessarily mean that the application uses in-app billing.

One possible, straightforward idea to discover which apps use in-app billing would be to crawl the Play Store and to look at the descriptions of the apps in the Play Store. However, app developers are not obliged to disclose that they have in-app billing enabled in their applications. Furthermore, currently, Google does not make an effort to mark applications in the Play Store as being in-app billing enabled.

To select applications for testing, we developed some simple heuristics to narrow down the selection choice to apps that had a high probability of having in-app billing functionality. To determine if an app has in-app billing services, we first check if the billing permission is present. Furthermore, if we determine that an application has any of the following three characteristics, we decide that it will likely support in-app billing.

a) The game has an in-app currency, and the player has to acquire it. It is likely that she has to buy it through in-app billing.

b) The game has multiple levels. In many games, in-app billing can be used to buy additional levels.

c) The game is ad-supported. In many cases, in-app billing can be used to remove ads, or to upgrade to the full version.

Using these simple heuristics, we selected 100 candidate apps based on popularity, and downloaded them from the Play Store's `Top Free` and `Top Grossing` categories.

Once an application is installed and executed, we can observe calls to the vending API by intercepting `sendBillingRequest` invocations to determine if the app is indeed using in-app billing. However, once again, this is not always as straightforward as one might expect. About half of the applications we tested use the `CHECK_BILLING_SUPPORTED` request during startup to determine if the device is capable of supporting in-app billing. Unfortunately, the other half check for in-app billing only just before the purchase task is about to be executed.

Hence, we had to manually interact with most of the apps to determine if they were in-app billing capable. This entailed playing

Figure 8: Purchasing coins in the game Big Win Slots.

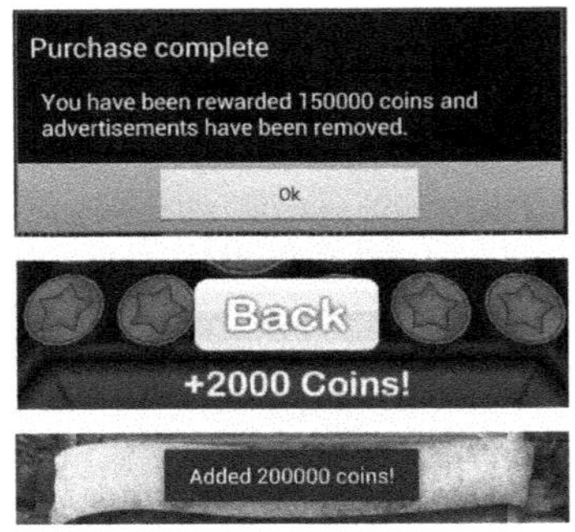

Figure 9: Purchase confirmations from three different apps: Hill Climb Racing, Coin Dozer, and Temple Run.

many games and attempting to, for example, buy digital content. In 85 apps, we were able to trigger the in-app billing functionality, and used our attack prototype on these apps. Note that our list of apps includes highly popular games such as Angry Birds, Temple Run, and Flow Free that have millions of users. For instance, Angry Birds is reported to have 500 million users.

In our test set, we observed item prices between $0.99 USD and $99 USD. It is not uncommon for games to sell currency packs for differing amounts. Figure 8 shows a screenshot from the game Big Win Slots where the user is prompted to buy in-game coins in exchange for real currency. In contrast, the removal of ads and game levels usually cost around $2.00 USD.

5.3 Attack Experiments

Once we had selected 85 popular apps that were confirmed to use in-app billing, the next step of the evaluation was to determine how effective our attack was against these applications. If our attack was successful (i.e., the fake in-app purchase worked), we quit the application, and restarted it to see if it remembered the items that we had purchased. If, on the other hand, the application was not vulnerable to our attack, we inspected the Android Debug Bridge (ADB) log to identify countermeasures the application might have implemented. Furthermore, we reverse engineered the application to gain a deeper understanding of its countermeasures.

In our experiments, we used multiple indicators to determine if an application was vulnerable. First, an obvious indicator of a successful attack is positive visual feedback from the app after a purchase that indicates that the items have successfully been purchased. Figure 9 depicts the purchase confirmation messages from three applications drawn from our test set. Second, we observed the log output from our code that runs inside the vending process. The log shows us the exact state of the purchase action. Third, the log output of our patched signature verification function served as a useful indicator for on-device verification.

If an app was not vulnerable, the first obvious indication that the attack had failed was that there was no visual confirmation of success. Furthermore, the log message for the `CONFIRM_NOTIFICATIONS` command would be missing, and there might be general log messages indicating the use of remote signature verification. Note that if the signature verification is performed remotely, the log file for the subverted `java.security.Signature.verify` method will be empty.

We manually ran VirtualSwindle for each test app. To trigger the in-app purchase request, in some cases we had to go through a lengthy interaction with the app in question.[1]

[1]We note that many virtual zombies were killed in the course of this research.

5.4 Analysis of Security Countermeasures

Of the 85 apps we analyzed in our experiments, 51 (60%) were automatically cracked by VirtualSwindle. 33 apps were not cracked automatically, and we determined that one application still contained the Play Store test item that is provided for testing purposes (`android.test.purchased`).

One of the goals of our evaluation was to investigate to what extent popular apps follow Google's in-app billing security recommendations [13]. For our test set, we first downloaded all 85 applications to our test device. Note that this was not straightforward for all apps: three apps used App Encryption, a content security feature that was introduced with Android 4.1. To bypass App Encryption, we had to execute the applications and manually copy the decrypted files from the `/mnt/aesc` directory to the `/sdcard` directory before we could download them to our test device.

Second, we disassembled each of the 85 applications using Apktool [1]. Apktool unpacks the APK files and disassembles the DEX classes, among other functions. We were then able to manually analyze the disassembled applications and investigate the security countermeasures employed by the applications. The reverse engineering and analysis effort was largely manual, but we did use some simple guidelines.

5.4.1 *Locating the billing code*

In many cases, obfuscated apps will still contain the well-known names of the calls to the Android framework and imported interfaces (e.g., `sendBillingRequest`).

5.4.2 *Checking if Java reflection is used*

If `sendBillingRequest` cannot be located, it is likely that the application is using Java reflection [16] to dynamically resolve classes and methods to further obfuscate the application. The use of reflection can often be quickly ascertained by checking the code for the string "reflect".

5.4.3 *Checking for the use of dynamic strings*

Google advises developers to manually assemble strings that are related to in-app billing such as `inapp_signed_data` and `inapp_signature` [13]. If these strings are not found, it is likely that the application is constructing them on the fly, or is obfuscating them in some other way.

5.4.4 *Checking network traffic*

For all applications in our test set that we were not able to crack automatically, we also analyzed the network traffic they produced during the purchase process. To accomplish this, we installed and executed tcpdump directly on the Android device.

5.5 Findings and Key Insights

Table 1 in the Appendix summarizes our key findings for each of the 85 apps that we analyzed. It lists whether or not the application is vulnerable to our automated attack, and the type of countermeasures we identified in each application.

Seven of the vulnerable applications in our test set included countermeasures such as code obfuscation and reflection. We discovered these countermeasures only after manually analyzing the apps, since our attack was dynamic, and thus not affected by such techniques.

One finding that was surprising was that Big Win Slots, a popular app with over one million installs, does not perform any signature verification at all. Based on our testing, we knew that the application was vulnerable. However, we discovered that the on-device signature was never triggered during these tests. Further investigation revealed that the developer, in fact, was not checking for valid purchase signatures.

In our test set, we found evidence that some developers indeed take in-app billing security seriously. For example, Grab Money Slots uses on-device signature verification, but implements it in native code. Naturally, such code is more difficult to attack automatically. As another example, Outdoor Atlas, an app that provides access to maps that can be purchased via in-app billing, performs signature verification on a remote server, and does not deliver maps to the device there until the purchase had succeeded. Clearly, the developers of this app were following the remote signature and content distribution recommendations in the Google in-app billing guidelines [12].

We found one app, KungFu, that still contained the in-app billing test item (`android.test.purchased`). We conclude that the developer probably evaluated in-app billing, added in-app billing functionality, but had not yet enabled it.

All other non-vulnerable applications implemented server-side signature verification. In some rare cases, only server-side signature checks are performed. In most cases, though, the server-side signature check is an addition to the on-device signature checks. Hence, some developers seem to be doing a good job in securing their in-app functionality.

We also observed that in a large number of applications, the disassembled billing code was identical to the code used in other applications. We discovered that this was because many applications were using the in-app billing example code provided by Google. Note that as a security precaution, Google explicitly warns developers against reusing the provided example code as-is. Specifically, 38 of the vulnerable apps we analyzed reused Google's example in-app billing code verbatim, while 15 of the vulnerable apps not vulnerable to our attack also showed evidence of code reuse.

6. COUNTERMEASURES

After determining that most countermeasures we found during our evaluation did not stop our attack, we investigated possible countermeasures. We recognize that there is no silver bullet defense against offline attacks based on manual reverse engineering. The only way to counter static code patching attacks is to design applications in a way that they require heavy interaction with a server component, thus making client-side patching approaches useless. But many applications do not require a server component for their actual functionality and, therefore, developers do not wish to invest time and money to include a server component in their application. Therefore, we investigated ways to improve the client-side security of the billing process against automated attacks. We focused on methods that are lightweight, easy to adopt, and do not incur the additional costs of a server component.

Our work shows that the use of reflection and obfuscation do not protect against instrumentation-based automated attacks. The weak point of the applications cracked by our automated attack is the easily identifiable and patched purchase data signature verification routine. We concluded that a viable working countermeasure is to not rely on signature verification code provided by the Android libraries.

6.1 Hardening the Signature Check Code

A basic assumption of instrumentation-based automated attacks is that all important symbol, class, method, and attribute names are known to the attacker. This is especially true if the names are part of a standard API. Our proposed defense against VirtualSwindle-like attacks is to introduce artificial diversity by replacing fixed names with dynamic names. This forces the attacker to invest time to disassemble and analyze every individual application, and drives up the per-target costs for the attacker.

Our approach for replacing fixed function names with dynamic functions names requires multiple steps. First, the developer must inline the functionality required for signature verification to the application. Second, the application must be modified to use the inline signature verification code instead of that provided by the Java framework via `java.security.Signature`. Third, the names of classes and methods comprising the signature verification code must be randomized on a per-application basis.

6.2 Hardening Implementation

We implemented and evaluated our approach by creating an example application named `com.example.paymenttest`. For the signature verification, we leveraged SpongyCastle[2], an Android version of the well known open source Java cryptographic library BouncyCastle. We implemented our approach in three steps: *a*) we renamed the package `org.spongycastle` to `com.example.payment test`, *b*) copied the library source files into the application's source directory, and *c*) randomized the imports in the application's source to reflect the renaming of the SpongyCastle package.

To implement the renaming of classes and methods, we used the well-known obfuscation tool ProGuard. ProGuard is already deeply integrated into the Android build process and can easily be enabled in the application's build configuration. However, switching on ProGuard is not sufficient for our purposes since, by default, ProGuard renames symbols in a deterministic fashion. For example, `org.example.cryptotest.crypto.digests.SHA1Digest` might always be mapped to `org.example.cryptotest.b.a.b`. To address this, we implemented randomized renaming through ProGuard's ability to accept a user-provided dictionary to map input symbols to obfuscated symbols. Therefore, instead of renaming `crypto.digests.SHA1Digest` to `b.a.b`, we can rename it to a random obfuscated symbol that changes with each application build.

The result of our compile-time obfuscation technique is that the signature verification code now is part of the actual application, shares the same namespace, and all known symbols are removed from the library. We verified our method through unpacking and inspecting a number of APKs created using these steps. We found no common names besides the applications MainActivity class, which serves as an application entry point specified in the application manifest that must remain unmodified.

6.3 Discussion

We believe our approach for hardening the signature verification code against automated attacks provides a beneficial trade-off between developer effort and improved security. Not every appli-

[2]https://github.com/rtyley/spongycastle

cation developer has the resources to deploy a back-end server for his application. Furthermore, our approach can be easily added to existing applications with minimal effort.

7. RELATED WORK

It is well-known that strong security properties are difficult to guarantee on remote devices controlled by untrusted and potentially malicious users. Much work in the trusted systems domain has examined this problem [19, 17, 23]. Unfortunately, at the same time, security systems have been built in the past that have relied solely on client-side enforcement. For example, smart-card systems that are widely used by European governments often rely on functionality provided by the operating system, and can often easily be bypassed [20]. Our work shows that many app developers seem not to be aware of dynamic attacks against their applications that can easily subvert in-app purchasing. We show that the current difficulty bar for the attacker is very low, automated attacks are possible, and that the popular protection techniques such as reflection and obfuscation can often easily be evaded.

To the best of our knowledge, we are the first to examine the security of Android's in-app billing in detail and to present a real-world, practical attack that compromises its security. There has been some recent work that has looked at the security of Apple's in-app purchasing service, however. For instance, the In-AppStore project [26] created an attack against the Apple iOS in-app payment system. This attack is different than ours, as it is based on redirecting the device's network traffic to the In-AppStore servers. For the redirection, an attackers has to change the DNS settings on the iOS device and install a custom SSL certificate. Note that the security measures of Apple's in-app payment architecture are not comparable to Android's in-app billing before iOS version 6 – for instance, Apple did not digitally sign any of the purchases prior to that iOS release.

Other work has demonstrated attacks against in-app billing [18], but this approach is based creating an alternate Android store that contains modified APKs. The techniques described in this work require disassembling, modifying, and re-packaging all applications. In the process, they render about 20% of the applications non-functional. Additionally, they break the APK signature which renders the application update mechanism provided by the Google Play Store non-functional. The user must also download applications from their store and not Google Play. As a result, their attack is far from being executed in reality and does not pose a real threat to Google and developers.

In contrast, our attack is fully dynamic and only takes place on the device. We do not need to modify application APKs. Users can install applications from the Google Play Store. Our attack can be switched on and off on the device since it does not carry out any permanent changes. Finally, we do not need to touch the target application APK as it exists on device storage at all.

Our work is also related to research that has been performed on game security. For example, previous work has investigated the potential for cheating in games by passively monitoring application memory in order to extract data that is helpful for the cheater [3]. Other work has looked at ways to improve the resilience of games against cheating by building in server-side checks [15, 2]. These works, however, are not concerned with in-app billing. In a recent DEFCON talk, Stracener and Barnum presented ways to cheat in YoVille, a popular game on Facebook [21]. As part of this work, they were able to create and steal in-game items. Unlike VirtualSwindle, however, the presented attacks were manual and game-specific.

Our dynamic Dalvik instrumentation approach shares similarities with other work that was carried out in parallel, specifically the Xposed [22] framework and Cydia Substrate for Android [11]. These two projects were created for device modding and require replacing system components such as zygote. Our approach targets stock Android devices and does not rely on replacing core components of the Android system. We released the source code for our DDI implementation at `http://github.com/crmulliner/ddi/`.

There has also been some work that has investigated approaches for the static instrumentation of Dalvik code. I-ARM [8] builds a reference monitor that is statically patched into an application binary. The authors disassemble the application's DEX classes, and statically modify their existing behavior by adding their own classes and replacing method calls to point to their newly added code. After the modification, they have to recompile the application.

Similarly, Aurasium [24] builds a reference monitor into application binaries. The Dalvik code is not patched, but new classes and native code are added to ensure that the instrumentation code is run first. Once the instrumentation code runs, functionality that the authors are interested in (e.g., native socket accesses) can be intercepted. Clearly, such approaches are not effective if the code is obfuscated and protected against static analysis and disassembly. Also, note that the package signature of the instrumented applications are broken when they are patched statically. In comparison, our approach does not need access to source code. Our modifications are in-memory only, and thus we do not break code signing. Furthermore, our modifications can be inserted or removed at runtime.

DroidScope [25] presents a dynamic malware analysis system for Android. The system is based on an Android emulator that the authors instrument in order to be able to track the execution of binary samples. The instrumentation is lightweight and allows the authors to produce Dalvik execution traces. In comparison, our Dalvik dynamic instrumentation library provides the capability to perform in-depth instrumentation of Dalvik classes as well as the native code of running Android applications as well as the Android system itself. In contrast, DroidScope only instruments the VM, while our main focus is the instrumentation of the applications (although we can also instrument the VM).

Recently, there have also been work that has investigated the privacy behavior of Apple as well as Android apps. For example, Enck et al. [10] present TaintDroid, an efficient, system-wide dynamic taint tracking and analysis system capable of simultaneously tracking multiple sources of sensitive data. Using TaintDroid, the authors monitor the behavior of 30 popular third-party Android applications, and discovered 68 instances of potential misuse of users' private information across 20 applications. Similarly, Egele et al. [9] present PiOS, a tool for statically analyzing iOS apps for privacy threats. PiOS uses static analysis to detect data flows in Mach-0 binaries compiled from Objective-C code. Our work is orthogonal to these projects, and focuses on subverting existing functionality on an Android system to break the security of in-app billing.

8. CONCLUSION

Android's in-app billing service allows developers to provide mobile apps for free, but charge users for digital services from within the apps themselves. In this paper, we present VirtualSwindle, the first fully-automated attack against Google Play's in-app billing service. To the best of our knowledge, the work we present in this paper is the first to provide an in-depth analysis of how app developers are using Android's in-app billing service, and to measure the robustness of these apps against automated attack.

We present an attack that is able to automatically compromise the security of many popular Android apps. One of the goals of this work is to *raise awareness* among developers, and to counter the popular folk wisdom that following the obfuscation guidelines in Google's in-app billing documentation will significantly deter attackers from compromising their apps. We show that this is indeed not the case, and that dynamic attacks can be performed against many popular apps with ease.

We performed empirical experiments and tested our attack prototype on 85 popular apps that make use of in-app billing. We present detailed reports on the in-app security defenses implemented by these apps. 60% of the apps we analyzed were automatically and easily crackable using our attack prototype.

Based on our findings we created a lightweight countermeasure that protects against automated attacks. Our countermeasure is easy to adopt and improves the security of existing applications against automated attacks such as VirtualSwindle.

Acknowledgements

This work was supported by the Office of Naval Research (ONR) under grant N000141310102. Engin Kirda thanks Sy and Laurie Sternberg for their generous support.

9. REFERENCES

[1] Apktool Developers. android-apktool - A tool for reverse engineering Android apk files. `http://code.google.com/p/android-apktool/`, November 2012.

[2] Bethea, D., Cochran, R. A., and Reiter, M. K. Server-side verification of client behavior in online games. In *17th ISOC Network and Distributed System Security Symposium (NDSS)* (2010).

[3] Bursztein, E., Hamburg, M., Lagarenne, J., and Boneh, D. OpenConflict: Preventing Real Time Map Hacks in Online Games. In *IEEE Symposium on Security and Privacy* (May 2011).

[4] Chainfire. SuperSU. `https://play.google.com/store/apps/details?id=eu.chainfire.supersu&hl=en`, November 2012.

[5] Clowes, S. injectso - Modifying and Spying on running processes under Linux and Solaris. `http://www.blackhat.com/presentations/bh-europe-01/shaun-clowes/bh-europe-01-clowes.ppt`, 2001.

[6] CLShortFuse. SuperOneClick. `http://forum.xda-developers.com/showthread.php?t=803682`, November 2012.

[7] CyanogenMod Developers. CyanogenMod. `http://www.cyanogenmod.org/`, November 2012.

[8] Davis, B., Sanders, B., Khodaverdian, A., and Chen, H. I-ARM-Droid: A Rewriting Framework for In-App Reference Monitors for Android Applications. In *Workshop on Mobile Security Technologies (MoST)* (May 2012).

[9] Egele, M., Kruegel, C., Kirda, E., and Vigna, G. PiOS: Detecting Privacy Leaks in iOS Applications. In *Network and Distirbuted Systems Security Symposium (NDSS)* (2 2011).

[10] Enck, W., Gilbert, P., Chun, B., Cox, L. P., Jung, J., McDaniel, P., and Sheth, A. N. TaintDroid: An Information-Flow Tracking System for Realtime Privacy Monitoring on Smartphones. In *Symposium on Operating Systems Design and Implementation (OSDI)* (2010).

[11] Freeman, J. Cydia Substrate for Android. `http://www.cydiasubstrate.com/`.

[12] Google. In-app Billing. `http://developer.android.com/guide/google/play/billing/`, November 2012.

[13] Google. In-app Billing Security and Design. `http://developer.android.com/guide/google/play/billing/billing_best_practices.html`, November 2012.

[14] HTC. Unlock Bootloader. `http://htcdev.com/bootloader/`, November 2012.

[15] Mitterhofer, S., Platzer, C., Kirda, E., and Kruegel, C. Server-side Bot Detection in Massively Multiplayer Online Games. *IEEE Security and Privacy Magazine* (5 2009).

[16] Oracle. The Reflection API. `http://docs.oracle.com/javase/tutorial/reflect/index.html`, November 2012.

[17] Petroni Jr, N., Fraser, T., Walters, A., and Arbaugh, W. An architecture for specification-based detection of semantic integrity violations in kernel dynamic data. In *USENIX Security Symposium* (2006).

[18] Reynaud, D., Song, D., Tom Magrino, E. W., and Shin, R. POSTER: FreeMarket: Shopping for free in Android applications. In *ISOC Network and Distributed System Security Symposium (NDSS)* (February 2012).

[19] Seshadri, A., Luk, M., Shi, E., Perrig, A., van Doorn, L., and Khosla, P. Verifying code integrity and enforcing untampered code execution on legacy systems. In *ACM Symposium on Operating System Principles (SOSP)* (2005).

[20] Spalka, A., Cremers, A., and Langweg, H. Trojan Horse Attacks on Software for Electronic Signatures. In *Informatica* (2002).

[21] T. Stracener and E. A. Smith and S. Barnum. So Many Ways to Slap a Yo-Ho: Hacking Facebook and YoVille. `http://www.defcon.org/images/defcon-18/dc-18-presentations/Stracener-Smith-Barnum/DEFCON-18-Stracener-Smith-Barnum-So-Many-Ways.pdf`, August 2010.

[22] Vollmer, R. Xposed. `http://repo.xposed.info/`.

[23] Watson, R. N. M. TrustedBSD: Adding Trusted Operating System Features to FreeBSD. In *USENIX Annual Technical Conference, FREENIX Track* (2001), pp. 15–28.

[24] Xu, R., Saidi, H., and Anderson, R. Aurasium: Practical Policy Enforcement for Android Applications. In *USENIX Security Symposium* (August 2012).

[25] Yan, L. K., and Yin, H. DroidScope: Seamlessly Reconstructing the OS and Dalvik Semantic Views for Dynamic Android Malware Analysis. In *USENIX Security Symposium* (August 2012).

[26] ZonD80. Getting started to receive your in-app for free on iOS. `http://system.in-appstore.com/`, Ocrober 2012.

Appendix

Table 1 below summarizes our key findings for each of the 85 apps that we analyzed.

#	Name	Notes
1	**Angry Birds**	
	Angry Gran Run	
	Bad Piggies	
	Big Win Slots	does not verify the signature
	Clouds & Sheep	
	Coin Dozer	
	Contract Kill 2	
	Dead Trigger	
	Death Dome	
10	**Defender II**	
	Design My House	
	DH Reloaded	
	Drag Racing Bike Edition	reflection + obfuscation
	Family Feud & Friends	
	Flow Free	
	GYRO	
	Happy Street	reflection + obfuscation
	Hill Climb Racing	
	Infinite Monsters	
20	**Jaws**	reflection + obfuscation
	Jellyflop	
	Jetpack Joyride	
	Millionaire Slots	
	Monster Pet Shop	
	My Country Online	
	Ninja Fishing	
	NinJump Deluxe	
	Plague Inc	
	Prize Claw	
30	**Robinson**	
	Rule the Kingdom	
	Slot Machnie Delux	
	Slots Journey	
	Smurfs' Village	
	Stardom	
	Style Me Girl	
	Subway Surf	
	Super Dynamite Fishing	
	Tank Hero	
40	**TapFish**	
	Temple Run	
	The Tribez	
	Tiny Monsters	reflection + obfuscation
	Tiny Tribe	
	Tiny Village	reflection + obfuscation
	Top Stylist	
	Tractor Pull	
	TripleTown	
	Zombie Frontier	reflection + obfuscation
50	**Zombie**	reflection + obfuscation
	Zombirds	

(a) Listing of 51 popular Android apps that were successfully automatically cracked by VirtualSwindle. An empty notes entry indicates that no security countermeasures were present.

#	Name	Notes
1	Arcane Empires	server-side verification
	BigWin Football	server-side verification
	Bingo Bash	server-side verification
	Bingo Blitz	server-side verification
	Bubble Mania	server-side verification
	Camelot	server-side verification
	Crime City	obfuscation + reflection + server-side verification
	Crime Inc.	server-side verification
	DerbyDays	obfuscation + server-side verification
	Dragon Story	server-side verification
10	Fatal Frontier	server-side verification
	Grab Money Slots	signature check in native code
	Hello Kitty Cafe	server-side verification
	Indestructable	server-side verification
	KungFu	only contains the developer test item `android.test.purchased`
	Legned	server-side verification
	Life is Crime	server-side verification
	Little Dragons	server-side verification
	Live Holdem Pro	obfuscation + reflection + server-side verification
	Modern War	server-side verification
20	Outdoor Atlas	server-side verification (content needs to be downloaded)
	PIMD	server-side verification
	Pumkins Vs Monsters	obfuscation + reflection + server-side verification
	Pumpkin Festival	server-side verification
	Restaurent Story	server-side verification
	Slot City	obfuscation + reflection + server-side verification
	Slotmania	server-side verification
	Slots	server-side verification
	SongPop Free	server-side verification
	Strikefleet Omega	server-side verification (blocks billing after failed attempt)
30	Stupid Zombies	server-side verification
	Texas Poker	obfuscation + reflection + server-side verification
	TinyFarm	server-side verification
	Zynga Poker	obfuscation + reflection + server-side verification

(b) Listing of 34 popular Android apps that employ countermeasures against in-app billing attacks.

Table 1: Security analysis of 85 Android apps that use in-app billing.

DroidRay: A Security Evaluation System for Customized Android Firmwares

Min Zheng, Mingshen Sun, and John C.S. Lui
Department of Computer Science and Engineering
The Chinese University of Hong Kong

ABSTRACT

Android mobile devices are enjoying a lion's market share in smartphones and mobile devices. This also attracts malware writers to target the Android platform. Recently, we have discovered a new Android malware distribution channel: *releasing malicious firmwares with pre-installed malware to the wild.* This poses significant risk since users of mobile devices cannot change the content of the malicious firmwares. Furthermore, pre-installed applications have "*more permissions*" (i.e., silent installation) than other legitimate mobile apps, so they can download more malware or access users' confidential information.

To understand and address this new form of malware distribution channel, we design and implement "*DroidRay*": a security evaluation system for customized Android firmwares. DroidRay uses both static and dynamic analyses to evaluate the firmware security on both the application and system levels. To understand the impact of this new malware distribution channel, we analyze 250 Android firmwares and 24,009 pre-installed applications. We reveal how the malicious firmware and pre-installed malware are injected, and discovered 1,947 (8.1%) pre-installed applications have signature vulnerability and 19 (7.6%) firmwares contain pre-installed malware. In addition, 142 (56.8%) firmwares have the default signature vulnerability, five (2.0%) firmwares contain malicious *hosts* file, at most 40 (16.0%) firmwares have the native level privilege escalation vulnerability and at least 249 (99.6%) firmwares have the Java level privilege escalation vulnerability. Lastly, we investigate a real-world case of a pre-installed zero-day malware known as `CEPlugnew`, which involves 348,018 infected Android smartphones, and we show its degree and geographical penetration. This shows the significance of this new malware distribution channel, and DroidRay is an effective tool to combat this new form of malware spreading.

ASIA CCS'14, June 4–6, 2014, Kyoto, Japan.

http://dx.doi.org/10.1145/2590296.2590313.

1. INTRODUCTION

In the past few years, we have experienced an exponential growth of mobile devices. Among the popular platforms, Android is enjoying a lion's share of mobile market. According to the recent report by the International Data Corporation (IDC) [13], Android market share in smartphone dominates nearly 80% worldwide during the second quarter of 2013. In addition, sales of smartphones grows another 32.7% in 2013, and the shipments could exceed 958.8 million units. According to VR-ZONE [30], US, UK and Japan only contributed 20.5% of the total shipments of smartphones in Q2, 2013, while the major bulk of smartphones (or 79.5%) were manufactured in countries such as China, India and others. According to the China Daily [5], shipments of smartphones on the Chinese mainland hit 18 million in April, 2012, accounting for more than half of the mobile phone market, with more than 77% of the shipment was contributed by local brands targeting mid-end and low-end customers. These statistics show that there exist a large percentage of "*low-end smartphones*" produced by low cost manufacturers in developing countries and these devices domain the Android smartphone market. Therefore, the exponential growth of Android and the abundance of low-end smartphones attract hackers to develop new ways to distribute malware.

The conventional approach to spread Android malware is by uploading the malware to Android app markets. However, with the passage of time, people pay more attention on malware detection. As of today, nearly all of the app markets scan their apps before publishing them to the public.

Recently, we have discovered that malware writers are using new channels to distribute malware: "*Malware writers pay money to manufacturers of low-cost mobile devices to pre-install malware in their devices, or they release malicious firmwares with pre-installed malware to the wild*". Note that for some manufacturers, their business line is to produce low-cost smartphones or mobile devices. To improve their sales, they usually prefer to "*pre-install*" as many applications as possible. So with the financial offer given by malware writers and their own business needs, these manufacturers have the economic incentive to include these applications (even if some of them are malware) [17] [31]. Figure 1 depicts the approach to distribute the pre-installed apps in firmwares. The manufacturer receives money (and malware) from hackers. Then the manufacturer produces and sales these smartphones to customers with these pre-installed malware in the devices. Finally, malware writers gain control of the victims' devices. As an evidence of this form of malware distribution channel, we found that jSMSHider and Oldboot are malware family which targets custom firmwares and these familes were reported by Lookout [15] and Qihoo360 [41].

Another closely related distribution channel which we discovered was that malware writers *release firmwares of mobile devices on the Internet* in order to attract potential manufacturers or customers to download. In fact, some low-cost manufacturers often download firmwares from the wild and use them in their production. Of course, these firmwares may contain many vulnerabilities and pre-installed malware. We carried out our investigation and found that there are many customized firmwares download sites available on the Internet (e.g., [22, 32, 16, 7]).

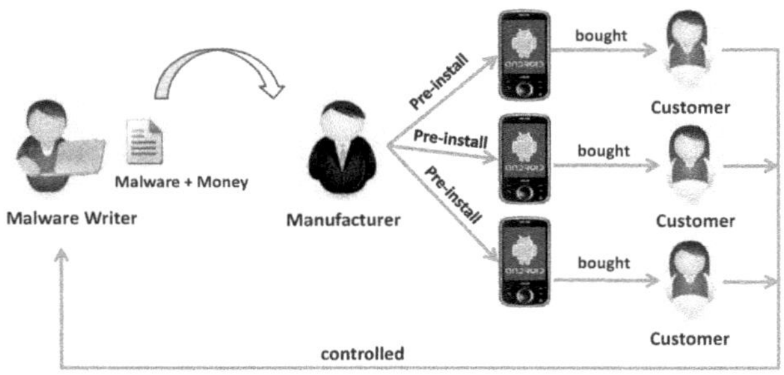

Figure 1: Malicious Android firmware distribution

The firmware contains the operating system (e.g., Android kernel) as well as some "*pre-installed*" mobile applications. Usually, users of mobile devices cannot change the content in the firmwares unless they have the root privilege or they have jailbroken the device. In addition, pre-installed applications usually have *more* permissions than other mobile applications which are downloaded from various sites (e.g., Google Play or other third party markets). Due to the enhanced permissions, pre-installed applications can use system-level APIs to perform privileged operations such as silent installation, which implies they can download more malware from the wild. In [12], authors investigate whether the pre-installed applications have *capability leak*, which means that an application can gain access to permissions without explicitly requesting them. They reported that most of these Android devices have more than 100 pre-installed applications and they pose a high risk of capability leak. However, their research only focused on the capability leak detection of pre-installed applications. It is very dangerous that if hackers release some infected firmwares in the wild, or include malware in the firmwares, it is difficult for users to determine the security level of these pre-installed applications. Further complicating the situation is that these pre-installed applications cannot be uninstalled unless users have the root privilege. In addition, not only can the hackers add malware in the firmware, but also modify the Android system. For example, the hackers can change the *iptables* to redirect users' internet visit or leave some back doors in the firmware system for the further actions.

To address the security problems of malicious firmware and pre-installed applications, we propose "*DroidRay*", a security evaluation system for customized Android firmwares. The system uses both static and dynamic analyses to evaluate the firmware security on both the application and system levels. The main contributions of this paper are:

- We design a security evaluation system for customized Android firmwares on both the application level and system level. We study how the malicious firmwares and malware are injected into the market. In particular, we use DroidRay to perform application signature vulnerability detection and malware detection on the application level (see Sec. 4). Then it performs system signature vulnerability detection, network security analysis, and privilege escalation vulnerability detection for the customized Android firmware on the system level (see Sec. 5).

- We use "*DroidRay*" to systematically analyze 250 customized Android firmwares and 24,009 pre-installed applications. On application level, we successfully discovered 1,947 (8.1%) applications have signature vulnerability and 19 (7.6%) firmwares contain pre-installed malware. On system level, we discovered 142 (56.8%) firmwares have the default signature vulnerability, five (2.0%) firmwares contain malicious *hosts* file, at most 40 (16.0%) firmwares have the native level privilege escalation vulnerability and at least 249 (99.6%) firmwares have the Java level privilege escalation vulnerability (see Sec. 4, 5).

- To show the influence of pre-installed Android malware, we investigate a real world case of a pre-installed zero-day Android malware known as `CEPlugnew`, which involves 348,018 infected Android smartphones. We investigate the degree of its penetration as well as its infected geographical regions (see Sec. 6).

The paper is organized as follows: In Section 2, we briefly overview the background on Android firmware. Then we discuss the system design and analysis methodology of DroidRay in Section 3. In Section 4, we present our systematic study of 24,009 pre-installed applications to show their security problems. In Section 5, we present our systematic study of 250 customized Android firmwares. In Section 6, we present our detailed analysis of a real world malware to illustrate the Android malware ecosystem. Related work is given in Section 7 and Section 8 concludes.

2. BRIEF OVERVIEW OF ANDROID FIRMWARE

In this paper, Android firmware refers to a "*packed binary system image*" which can be written to a non-volatile storage, say a device's flash memory. "*Flashing*" is a process of writing data to the internal memory on smartphones. Normally, one needs to flash a firmware to a smartphone in order to upgrade (or even downgrade) the system software.

There are two types of firmwares: (1) firmware with "*recovery partition*" and, (2) firmware "*without recovery partition*". The recovery partition can be considered as an alternative boot partition which lets the device boot into a recovery console for performing advanced recovery and maintenance operations. For example, it can perform an update using the "`update.zip`" file on the microSD card. There are two types of recovery partitions, one is the "*official recovery partition*", the other is the "*customized recovery partition*". The official recovery partition will check the public key information of the firmware. Only the official firmwares can be flashed into an Android device. The custom recovery partition does not check whether the public key is official or not, so users can flash third-party firmwares into Android devices. Usually, if an Android smartphone has a recovery partition, users could just download those firmwares without recovery partition, and then perform the flashing.

All firmwares have three core components: (1) the "system" folder, (2) the "META-INF" folder and (3) the "boot.img" file and several optional components (e.g., the "data" folder). The "system" folder contains most of the system files, and the "/system/app" directory on the Android device is where the pre-installed applications with system level privilege are stored. In addition, the "/system" folder is read-only by default, which means user cannot uninstall the pre-installed applications unless the user has the root privilege. The "META-INF" folder contains the installation script and signature information of the firmware. Because firmware's developers can create their own installation scripts, they can put their applications into the "/system/app" folder or other folders. Malware writers who create malicious firmwares often craft a script which can copy pre-installed applications into "/system/app" folder or "/data/app" folder. Therefore, the pre-installed apps can be in any sub-directory because malware writers can inject various installation scripts. In order to bypass the malware detection, the malware writer may place the malware into another folder, or even encrypt these applications if necessary. This is the reason why some pre-installed applications are not stored in the "/system/app" folder of the firmware. This also points to the weakness of current Android anti-virus software since they only inspect applications in the /system/app folder. Last but not least, the "boot.img" is the Linux kernel which is used in the Android device. This img file also contains many initialization scripts for system booting, so the hackers can perform modification in order to hide their malicious intent.

3. SYSTEM DESIGN AND ANALYSIS METHODOLOGY

DoridRay is a security evaluation system for customized Android firmwares. The system uses Android firmwares as the input, then the system analyzes both Android firmwares as well as pre-installed applications. After the analysis, DroidRay outputs the analysis report of these firmwares and pre-installed applications. In the analysis process, DoridRay uses both static analysis and dynamic analyses to evaluate the firmware security on application level and system level. The architecture of DroidRay is depicted in Figure 2.

Let us discuss the methodology we use to carry out the security analysis of various Android firmwares. The methodology can be summarized as the following steps:

- We download and collect firmwares from different Android firmware forums and websites.
- After we obtain these firmwares, we use DroidRay to analyze the configuration files (e.g., "/system/build.prop" file) to obtain the firmware information. The information includes firmware name, product model and Android version, etc.
- DroidRay uses both static and dynamic methodologies to extract and analyze the pre-installed applications in the Android firmware. Specifically, we carry out two forms of security analysis: (a) application signature vulnerability detection and, (b) malware detection. The details are presented in Section 4.
- DroidRay uses both static and dynamic methodologies to analyze the system security of the Android firmware. Specifically, we carry out three forms of security analysis: (a) system signature vulnerability detection, (b) network security analysis, and (c) privilege escalation vulnerability detection. The details are presented in Section 5.
- DroidRay organizes all the analysis results of systems and pre-installed applications into the database and then outputs various reports which are classified by the signature, MD5 and package name. This helps security analysts use DroidRay to quickly identify and associate malware and vulnerabilities.

To show the effectiveness of our system, we used DroidRay to perform a large scale security analysis on 250 Android firmwares and 24,009 applications. To the best of our knowledge, this is the largest scale of Android firmware security analysis reported so far. We downloaded these Android firmwares from [22, 16, 36, 19, 29, 7, 4]. The statistics are summarized in Table 1. Because of the page limit, we put the full firmware information at https://www.dropbox.com/s/8rrmyqwzlqg3wjw/RomInfo.xls.

Firmware Information	Number
Total firmwares	250
Total number of apps in all firmwares	24,009
Average number of apps per firmware	96.04
Average size of a firmware	274.7MB
Android Version ($\geq$4.0)	210
Phone Models (e.g., Samsung Galaxy S4)	101

Table 1: Summary Statistics of 250 Firmwares

4. SECURITY EVALUATION OF PRE-INSTALLED APPLICATIONS

In this section, we briefly introduce how to pre-install and extract applications in the Android firmware, then we show our analysis methodologies and experiment results for Android pre-installed applications.

4.1 Introduction to Pre-installation

There are two methods to pre-install the applications in the Android firmware: One is putting the apk files to the "/system/app" folder or "/data/app" folder of the firmware. Then the system will pre-install these applications when it launches. The advantage of using this method is that the applications in the "/system/app" folder (not the "/data/app folder) can gain the system privilege. The drawback of this approach is that the applications cannot execute normally if it contains any native libraries i.e., libraries which are written in C/C++, such as foo.so. Because the Android system does not extract the native libraries for applications in the "/system/app" folder, the applications cannot find the related native libraries when it executes.

The other way is using the "pm install" command to create a pre-install script and add the trigger script to the "init.rd" file in the "boot.img" file. After that, the system will trigger the pre-install shell script the first time it

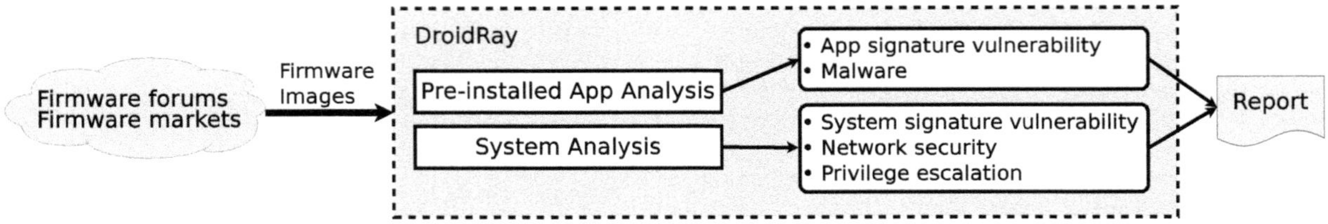

Figure 2: Architecture of DroidRay

launches. The advantage of using this method is it uses the normal installation process, so the application which contains native libraries can execute normally. The drawback is the pre-installed applications cannot obtain the system privilege.

In order to analyze the pre-installed applications, we need to extract all the `apk` files from the Android firmware. In DroidRay, our system uses both static and dynamic approaches to extract `apk` files. Since an `apk` file is in fact a zip file which includes `AndroidManifest.xml` and `classes.dex` file. The static approach of extracting `apk` files is to uncompress the Android firmware and extract all the files which has the zip magic number and contains `AndroidManifest.xml` file. The dynamic approach of extracting `apk` files is to flash Android firmware into the device and then use "`pm list packages`" and "`pm path`" command to obtain all the paths of these `apk` files in the device, and then use "`adb pull`" to extract all the `apk` files.

4.2 Application Signature Vulnerability Detection

In Android, application signature is very important for security and privacy. The Android system requires all installed applications be digitally signed with a certificate and the private key should be held by the application's developer. The Android system uses the certificate as a mean of identifying the author of an application and establishing trust relationships between applications. Note that if two applications have the same package name and same signature, they can replace each other due to the application update mechanism. In addition, if two applications are signed by the same certification and claim the same "`SharedUserId`" attribute in their `AndroidManifest.xml` files, they will share the same union permission set. Furthermore, with the same uid, they will have the permission to access each other's data. Therefore, if two applications have the same certificate but one of them is a malware, this implies the malware has penetrated into the system.

AOSP (Android Open source Project) comes with four signature key pairs in the "`build/target/product/security/`" folder. The platform key is used to sign core parts of the system. The shared key is used to sign home and contacts part of AOSP. The media key is used to sign media and download framework parts of AOSP. The test key is used to sign everything else. These signature key pairs are for the developers to build *test* Android firmwares. The signature information can be found in Table 2. The first column shows the MD5 value of the signature after signed. The second column shows the description of the signature. Because all of these four key pairs are created by the Android team, they have the same description. The last column shows the signature of file names. It is important for us to point out that developers should *not* use these default AOSP key pairs to build their released Android applications because everyone can obtain these key pairs from the AOSP. Therefore, it is in danger that an application with "`SharedUserId`" attribute is signed by the AOSP keys.

In order to detect application signature vulnerability, DroidRay first extracts the "`SharedUserId`" attribute from the `AndroidManifest.xml` file and the signature information from the `RSA` file of the application. Then DroidRay puts all of the information into the database and compares with the default signatures of AOSP. Note that we did not count the applications which share the same uid (as known as "`android.uid.system`") with the system platform. The reason is that these applications belong to the platform applications with the system level privilege, so we classify them as a part of system signature vulnerability. We will discuss this form of security analysis in Section 5.

Among 24,009 apps in 250 Android firmwares we analyzed, we discover that 5,712 apps have the "`SharedUserId`" attribute in their `AndroidManifest.xml` files. Moreover, 1,947 (34%) applications are signed by the default AOSP key pairs. Table 3 shows how many shared uid applications are signed by which key pairs (because of the page limit, the full list can be found at `https://www.dropbox.com/s/f7c5de4s55o2rk9/AppSign.zip`). This is quite alarming since malware writers can easily sign their malware with the default AOSP key pairs, and the malware can gain extra permissions and modify other applications' data if they have the same shared uid. For example, we discover that all the firmwares released by Cyanogenmod [22] have several vulnerable applications. In particular, `com.android.providers.media`, `com.android.providers.drm` and `com.android.providers.downloads` are signed by the default AOSP media key and they all have a same shared uid, "`android.media`". Also, `com.android.contacts`, `com.android.providers.contacts`, `com.android.providers.applications` and `com.android.providers.userdictionary` are signed by the default AOSP shared key and they all have a same shared uid, "`android.uid.shared`". Therefore, if the malware is signed by the default AOSP key (media or shared key) and claims the same shared uid ("`android.media`" or "`android.uid.shared`"), it can access all the data and get permissions (e.g., `READ_CONTACTS`, `WRITE_CONTACTS`, `WRITE_SETTINGS` and `ACCESS_DRM`) from vulnerable applications.

4.3 Malware Detection

DroidRay first uses anti-virus software (e.g. VirusTotal [11]) to scan all apks and filter out the "known" and common malware. For the remaining applications, DroidRay only retains the applications which have dangerous permissions (e.g., sending SMS message) or silent installation behavior. For the applications with dangerous permissions, DroidRay uses permission-to-api map table [1] to find the code section which uses the related API of dangerous per-

MD5 of Signature	Signature Description	Signature Type
8ddb342f2da5408402d7568af21e29f9	EMAIL=android@android.com,CN=Android,OU=Android, O=Android,L=Mountain View,ST=California,C=US	platform
e89b158e4bcf988ebd09eb83f5378e87	EMAIL=android@android.com,CN=Android,OU=Android, O=Android,L=Mountain View,ST=California,C=US	testkey
1900bbfba756edd3419022576f3814ff	EMAIL=android@android.com,CN=Android,OU=Android, O=Android,L=Mountain View,ST=California,C=US	media
5dc8201f7db1ba4b9c8fc44146c5bcc2	EMAIL=android@android.com,CN=Android,OU=Android, O=Android,L=Mountain View,ST=California,C=US	shared

Table 2: Default Signature Information

MD5 of Signature	Signature Description	# of App
cde9f6208d672b54b1dacc0b7029f5eb	CN=Android,OU=Android,O=Google Inc.,L=Mountain View,ST=California,C=US	767
8ddb342f2da5408402d7568af21e29f9	emailAddress=android@android.com,CN=Android,OU=Android,O=Android,L=Mountain View,ST=California,C=US	673
5dc8201f7db1ba4b9c8fc44146c5bcc2	emailAddress=android@android.com,CN=Android,OU=Android,O=Android,L=Mountain View,ST=California,C=US	518
1900bbfba756edd3419022576f3814ff	emailAddress=android@android.com,CN=Android,OU=Android,O=Android,L=Mountain View,ST=California,C=US	503
4a441695cb20427d284e7ded135925ad	emailAddress=android@htc.com,CN=Android,OU=Android,O=Android,L=Taoyuan,ST=Taoyuan,C=TW	268
f11fdf766b78025bf4035cb1b7ad483c	emailAddress=android.os@samsung.com,CN=Samsung Cert,OU=DMC,O=Samsung Corporation,ST=South Korea,C=KR	263
2eed75e85b154fb0c1013ecd16115c84	CN=Tencent,OU=Tencent,O=Tencent,L=Beijing,ST=Beijing,C=CN	255
e89b158e4bcf988ebd09eb83f5378e87	emailAddress=android@android.com,CN=Android,OU=Android,O=Android,L=Mountain View,ST=California,C=US	253
d087e72912fba064cafa78dc34aea839	emailAddress=android.os@samsung.com,CN=Samsung Cert,OU=DMC,O=Samsung Corporation,ST=South Korea,C=KR	241
ea75f0b73ee288cd683b7a11716b9f77	emailAddress=android@htc.com,CN=Android,OU=Android,O=Android,L=Taoyuan,ST=Taoyuan,C=TW	159
f31d93c0e9064bafa39cbe653360e6ba	emailAddress=android.os@samsung.com,CN=Samsung Cert,OU=DMC,O=Samsung Corporation,ST=South Korea,C=KR	128
701478a1e3b4b7e3978ea69469410f13	emailAddress=miui@xiaomi.com,CN=MIUI,OU=MIUI,O=Xiaomi,L=Beijing,ST=Beijing,C=CN	115

Table 3: App Signature Information

missions and then check whether it has malicious behavior or not. On the other hand, in order to find those applications with silent installation behavior, DroidRay disassembles each application and uses two silent installation code patterns to search the assemble code. One code pattern we used is using the hidden installation API, `android.content.pm.PackageManager.installPackage()`, to install the `apk` file. The other code pattern we used is `Runtime.exec()` which is to execute "`pm install`" command to install the `apk` file. After determining the code section, we continue to check whether it contains malicious behavior or not.

Among the 250 Android firmwares we analyzed, we discovered that 19 firmwares contain malware. This means about 7.6% Android firmwares contain pre-installed malware. Again, this is quite alarming since many low-cost manufactures use public firmwares for their products. We provide more detailed information of these 19 firmwares in Table 4.

- We discover that 19 firmwares contain the same Android malware which is known as "Agent". This is a premium SMS trojan. In addition, it has a special permission, `android.permission.INSTALL_PACKAGES`, as compared with other Android malware. Usually, a normal Android application cannot be installed in the smartphone if it has the `android.permission.INSTALL_PACKAGES` permission, because this is a privilege permission only reserved for system applications. However, pre-installed applications are different. Because they are stored in the "`/system/app/`" folder, these apps belong to the system applications. Therefore they possess the `android.permission.INSTALL_PACKAGES` permission. Once the malware has this permission, it can install other Android applications into the smartphone without notifying the user that a new application is being installed.
- We discover "JSmsHider", which is a premium SMS trojan that uses the HTTP protocol to receive and execute the command from some botnet masters.
- We discover "Stesec", which is a SMS trojan which makes phone calls to long-distance numbers or sends SMS premium rate phone numbers without the phone owner's knowledge.
- We discover "Hippo", which is another premium SMS trojan that can cause additional phone charges by sending SMS messages to some hard-coded premium-rated numbers in the mobile application.
- One malware family we want to emphasize is the "CE-Plugnew". In our security analysis, we discover that it uses various encryption techniques to bypass the anti-virus detection and hide in the firmwares. To gain a deeper understanding on this malware family and its business chain, we carried out a detailed study of this new malware family. Results and discussion will be presented in Section 6.

5. SECURITY EVALUATION OF THE SYSTEM

In this section, we discuss how we perform system security detection. The process can be divided into three aspects: (1) *system signature vulnerability detection*, (2) *network security vulnerability detection*, and (3) *privilege escalation vulnerability detection*.

MD5 of Firmware Image	Size (MB)	OS Version	Phone Model	# of Apps	Malware Path	Malware Name
3643C59163D102616BF547A465837C44	934	4.1.2	GT-I9300	244	/optional/other/digua/preload/digua.apk	Agent
5B7E06BCE9920E82CB0A8CBC0302BC7E	215	4.0.3	ZTE U970	83	/system/framework/framework.jar	Agent
5BFE256A10BDB9A44BA7F7AF78DDD3AC	225	4.0.4	GT-I9300	83	/system/app/BaiduReader.apk/assets/huafubao.apk	Agent
6B20E70C4AD84B1EE5F840E920E718EB	183	4.0.4	HUAWEI C8812	82	/system/app/168_(2216G7).apk	Agent
76099C37D57AC1A5659B7B312155733C	185	4.2.2	Galaxy Nexus	78	/system/preload/digua.apk	Agent
8BA7722157471E31946D500BDAAA7998	1026	4.2.1	GT-I9300	249	/optional/other/digua/preload/digua.apk	Agent
959A7ADC6F1A8AC4D8D266C4AB3EDD9E	262	4.1.2	X907	85	/system/app/YXPhoneBook.apk	JSmsHider
979DAF30377A1D85CD19F1CE71A7A5DC	87	2.3.7	LT15i	18	/system/app/Youni_1.1.16_1103.apk	Hippo
99DD205A5E6D2045CE3D57D157278FBF	207	4.0.4	Incredible S	74	/system/etc/product/applications/duoku.apk	Agent
A364CF949574DAEF8C30072F45504432	83	2.3.7	Blade	55	/system/app/BaiduReader.apk	Agent
BC3B5944A758A8B7734C152E096C80A6	226	4.0.4	GT-I9300	86	/system/app/iReader.apk	Agent
BE541971F46F5BCE0EDC0A397B608FF9	387	4.1.2	LT26i	164	/system/app/BaiduReader.apk	Agent
BEC16CFCB0C5FBE9E6F8D402D88BDB8B	937	2.2.2	ZTE-U V880	74	system/app/SecuritySms.apk	Stesec
D3ECD1333E7F46CE3E028CEA1CB3F224	628	4.1.2	GT-I9300	170	/system/etc/product/applications/duoku.apk	Agent
E9F033CD8C694A5BD56C7AE94A425C97	406	4.2.1	ZTE N986	156	/system/app/BaiduReader.apk	Agent
F4DF6D64A4F856CA1B53B400A33C55F4	113	2.3.7	GT-I9000	67	/system/app/youni_2.2.2.3.apk	Hippo
F62C11C7827BBA0374DB69B276910266	161	4.1.2	GT-I9300	64	/system/app/Plugnew.apk	CEPlugnew
F893F4BE1A0A280BD62887A2BF2C36C6	193	4.2.2	SGH-I897	83	/system/preload/digua.apk	Agent
FD2EA6A845A86AAB0122BB2ADF90F2C1	81	2.3.7	Wildfire S	55	/system/app/iReader.apk	Agent

Table 4: Malicious firmwares with pre-installed apps

5.1 System Signature Vulnerability Detection

As mentioned in Section 4, developers should not use the AOSP default key pairs to build their released Android applications because anyone can get these key pairs from the AOSP. For Android firmwares, it also have two signature mechanisms for integrity verification and system level permission control. However, our experiment result shows that there exist many Android firmwares which were signed by the default AOSP key pairs and this will create two types of default signature security problem:

(1) Android firmware default signature problem: The Android firmware signature mechanism is similar to other Android applications. The signing program first calculates the SHA1 value of each file in the firmware, then it uses a private key to encrypt these SHA1 values. The signing program will put the encrypted SHA1 values and the public key in the "`META-INF`" folder of the firmware. Before the firmware can be flashed to an Android device, the recovery partition will use the encrypted SHA1 values and its public key to check the integrity of each file as well as to verify the signature of the firmware. Note that the recovery partition of some manufacturers' products (e.g., Samsung) will check whether the public key is indeed its own key or not. If it is not, one cannot flash the firmware to the flash memory. However, many users may choose to turn off the signature verification process so to install the third-party firmwares.

By analyzing all of our 250 downloaded firmwares, we discovered that 206 (82.4%) firmwares have the *same public key*, which is the test key of the default key pairs provided by AOSP. The result of our analysis is showed in Table 5. For example, the fifth row of the table shows the public key information of the AOSP and there are *206* firmwares using this key pairs. Note that if malware writers use the AOSP default key pairs to create firmwares, this will give people the false impression that the Android firmware was created by the official Android open source project.

(2) Android system default signature problem: The system signature information is stored at: "`/system/framework/framework-res.apk/META-INF/CERT.RSA`". By using the pkcs7 function of the "`openssl`" library, the system can parse the signature information from "`CERT.RSA`". Note that the Android system signature is different from the Android firmware signature. The Android firmware signature is used to check the integrity of the files in the firmware. But the system signature is used for permission control. If one application has the same public key as the system, it can use the system level permissions.

By analyzing all of our 250 downloaded firmwares, we discovered that 142 (56.8%) Android firmwares have the *default public keys*, which are part of the default key pairs provided by AOSP [10]. This is alarming because if a malware writer uses the AOSP key pairs to sign their malware, then the malware can get the system level privilege. With the system level privilege, the malware can silently install new applications and modify other applications. The result of our analysis is showed in Table 6 (because of the page limit, the full list can be found at `https://www.dropbox.com/s/8fbl0yujqoaja1h/SystemSign.xls`). For example, the first row of the table shows the public key information of the AOSP and there are 134 Android firmwares using this key pairs.

5.2 Network Security Vulnerability Detection

Android is a derivative based on a modified Linux 2.6 with a Java programming interface, so it has components (e.g., hosts and iptables) similar to those of Linux to control network filtering and forward. In this subsection, we present the security issues of these components.

(1) Hosts security: The `hosts` file is a plain text file used by an operating system to map host names to IP addresses. For example, if the user wants to visit "`www.google.com`" and if there is a map record in the "`/etc/hosts`" file, the system will not request IP lookup from a DNS server but instead, it directly uses the IP address which is recorded in the `hosts` file. Therefore, it would be very dangerous if the hackers modify this file and add malicious redirection information. For example, if a user wants to visit some legitimate websites listed in the "`/etc/hosts`" file, a compromised system will

MD5 of Signature	Signature Information	# of Firmware
1f1b2fd4e0bded6ca5088afa287b5332	EMAIL=mobile@zte.com.cn, CN=zte.com.cn, OU=Product R&D Center I, O=ZTE Corporation, L=Nanjing, C=CN	1
5fd1d7579992cff701ea20873e8ac99f	CN=Smaritsan	2
ab82cce8af68057b7ab8867b5dd75d65	EMAIL=Android@amoi.com.cn, CN=Amoi, OU=Amoi, O=Amoi, L=Xiamen, ST=Fujian, C=CN	1
943e1151975cfd342a95f2a7512bbff8	EMAIL=12001@oppo.com, CN=12001, OU=M6, O=OPPO, L=DongGuang, ST=GuangDong, C=CN	1
e89b158e4bcf988ebd09eb83f5378e87	EMAIL=android@android.com,CN=Android,OU=Android,O=Android,L=Mountain View,ST=California,C=US	206
fcf645259f609183606ab55da67fc9db	EMAIL=oppo@oppo.com, CN=SmartPhone, OU=PLF, O=OPPO, L=ChangAn, ST=DongGuan, C=CN	2
fe3c74f0431ea0dc303a10b6af6470fc	EMAIL=bms@baidu.com,CN=BMS,OU=BaiduYi,O=Baidu,L=Haidian,ST=Beijing,C=CN	9
No Signature	No Signature Information	28
Total		250

Table 5: Firmware signature count with highlighted row indicating misleading signature

MD5 of Signature	Signature Information	# of Firmware
8ddb342f2da5408402d7568af21e29f9	emailAddress=android@android.com,CN=Android,OU=Android,O=Android,L=Mountain View,ST=California,C=US	134
d087e72912fba064cafa78dc34aea839	emailAddress=android.os@samsung.com,CN=Samsung Cert,OU=DMC,O=Samsung Corporation,ST=South Korea,C=KR	24
2eed75e85b154fb0c1013ecd16115c84	CN=Tencent,OU=Tencent,O=Tencent,L=Beijing,ST=Beijing,C=CN	13
701478a1e3b4b7e3978ea69469410f13	emailAddress=miui@xiaomi.com,CN=MIUI,OU=MIUI,O=Xiaomi,L=Beijing,ST=Beijing, C=CN	12
4abc4868a502c9c77b50ca9deb53b672	emailAddress=yi@baidu.com,CN=rom-platform,OU=BaidYi,O=Baidu,L=Haidian,ST=Beijing, C=CN	8
bb7bce1b1090fc3a6b67ebc88701acdd	emailAddress=mobile@huawei.com,CN=AndroidTeam,OU=TerminalCompany,O=Huawei, L=Shengzhen, ST=Guangdong,C=CN	9
0f92c3b692319a1daabac6c94b07fbee	emailAddress=Admin@dianxinos.com,CN=TAPAS,OU=SDG,O=TAPAS,L=BeiJing,ST=BeiJing, C=CN	5
10637522aa8f840170c50fcbe61227ac	CN=Smartisan	4
9e5b0111e0408bb405c819ea0784b69d	CN=Sony_Ericsson_E_Platform_Signing_Live_864f,O=Sony Ericsson Mobile Communications AB, C=SE	7
a7babf3e3872080766e5331943aafa58	emailAddress=android@htc.com,CN=Android,OU=Android,O=Android,L=Taoyuan,ST=Taoyuan, C=TW	6
75711ca27d4693cc27432c47ac8582c0	emailAddress=android@android.com,CN=Android,OU=Android,O=Android,L=Mountain View,ST=California,C=US	5
d4c6ea170fd9ef95572ab50318b695de	emailAddress=oppo@oppo.com,CN=SmartPhone,OU=PLF,O=OPPO,L=ChangAn,ST=DongGuan,C=CN	4
2bf07615199371b0c35ef2e23936b345	CN=lidroid,OU=lidroid,O=lidroid,L=xi'an,ST=shaanxi,C=CN	3
e89b158e4bcf988ebd09eb83f5378e87	emailAddress=android@android.com,CN=Android,OU=Android,O=Android,L=Mountain View,ST=California,C=US	3
8701cf44ad2623c4a5c89944b24d6417	CN=lidroid.com,OU=lidroid.com,O=xian,L=shaanxi,ST=SX,C=86	2
...	...	...
Total		250

Table 6: System signature count with highlighted row indicating AOSP default signatures

not connect the user to the legitimate server but instead, requests will be re-routed to some malicious websites.

To investigate this form of network security vulnerability, we use DroidRay to extract the **hosts** file from Android firmware and check whether it has malicious modifications or not. Note that some developers may use **hosts** file to block advertisements. They redirect the advertisement servers' host names to "127.0.0.1" in order to prevent the server from sending advertisement to the smartphone. In this case, we will treat it as a warning but not a malicious behavior. By analyzing all of our 250 downloaded firmwares, we discovered that 54 firmwares modified their **hosts** files and five Android firmwares contained malicious **hosts** file (please refer to Table 7). For example, the first row of Table 7 shows that "*HUAWEI*" Android firmware with 4.1.2 version has malicious **hosts** file which redirects Google and Youtube websites to malicious websites.

(2) Iptables security vulnerability: **iptables** is used to set up, maintain, and inspect the tables of IPv4 or IPv6 packet filter rules. It is more versatile than the **hosts** file specification because it can define many forwarding/filtering rules for each packet. Therefore, it is very dangerous if hackers add malicious rules in the **iptables**. In order to detect this form of vulnerability, we use DroidRay to perform the analysis. For the static analysis, DroidRay first searches all the initial scripts in the firmware and checks whether it has "**iptables**" command or not. Then DroidRay searches **iptables** configuration file from the "/system/etc/" folder. For the dynamic analysis, DroidRay executes the "**iptables --list-rules**" command to obtain all rules from the devices. If the system finds that the **iptables** rules are not none, DroidRay will report a warning to the analysts. Note that DroidRay will not consider the forward rules that redirect the advertisement servers' package to "127.0.0.1". By analyzing all of our 250 downloaded firmwares, we discovered that *two* Android firmwares modified their **iptables** rules and *no* Android firmware contains malicious **iptables** rules.

5.3 Privilege Escalation Vulnerability Detection

Privilege escalation vulnerabilities can be exploited by a malicious application to gain high level privileges (e.g., root and system levels) and execute malicious actions that would normally be restricted by the Android system. A number of such vulnerabilities (e.g., GingerBreak [2] and MasterKey [26]) were discovered in the core Android platform, affecting nearly all Android devices. Although manufacturers have tried their best to fix these vulnerabilities, unfortunately, privilege escalation vulnerabilities still remain unpatched on large populations of Android firmwares.

MD5 of firmware Image	Size (MB)	OS Version	Phone Model	# of Apps	Malicious Behavior
5EC3A725107D787C51F73055E2B2836B	473	4.1.2	HUAWEI U9508	127	Redirect google and youtube
5F262C7046904152ABC0DC0635694EA2	286	4.0.3	X907	92	Redirect facebook
67C031B8BCC97B2EBE672B30243C3050	306	4.0.3	X907	92	Redirect yahoo
8A3598500340843FF1D0609F42E852E7	428	4.1.2	LT26i	161	Redirect google
E43B91728003193EA4E889C20310FD5D	207	4.0.4	HUAWEI C8812	75	Redirect adobe and wikipedia

Table 7: Modified Firmwares with Malicious Hosts File

We use DroidRay to explore the existence of privilege escalation vulnerabilities on Android firmware systems. For the static analysis, we classify escalation vulnerabilities into *native level vulnerabilities* (e.g.,GingerBreak and ZergRush [24]) and *Java level vulnerabilities* (e.g., MasterKey). For native level vulnerabilities, DroidRay first extracts the potential vulnerable `elf` files from the Android firmware and then disassembles the potential vulnerable functions into ARM assemble language. Then the system compares the control flow of the potential vulnerable functions with the vulnerable functions stored in our vulnerability database. Note that for patching vulnerable files, developers need to add new judgement code into the vulnerable functions. This is the reason why we choose the control flow as the signature. For example, Android 2.2 (as known as Froyo) has a *RageAgainsttheCage* vulnerability. This vulnerability exploits the lack of checking for the return value of `setuid()` function in the `/system/bin/adb` file. After the initial process has the root privilege, the `adb` daemon attempts to call `setuid()` to set its uid to the shell privilege in its code:

```
setgid(AIL_SHELL);
setuid(AIL_SHELL);
```

However, the exploit attempts to fork as many "*adb*" processes as possible in order to make the "*setuid*" fail. In addition, the current `adb` code does not check whether the `setuid()` call was successful or not and it will keep running as a root process even if the call fails. To patch this vulnerability, Android 2.3 adds the privilege check after the `setuid()` call:

```
if (setgid(AIL_SHELL) != 0) {
    exit(0);
}
if (setuid(AIL_SHELL) != 0) {
    exit(0);
}
```

For Java level vulnerabilities, DroidRay first extracts the potential vulnerable `odex` or `jar` files from the Android firmware and then disassembles the potential vulnerable functions into Dalvik assemble language. Then the system compares the control flow of the potential vulnerable functions with the vulnerable functions stored in our vulnerability database. For example, Android 4.2 has a master key vulnerability. This vulnerability exploits the lack of checking for the duplicate name of the entries in the zip file. So hackers can create two files with the same name in order to bypass the signature verification:

```
LinkedHashMap<String, ZipEntry> mEntries
    = new LinkedHashMap<String, ZipEntry>();
for (int i = 0; i < numEntries; ++i) {
    ZipEntry newEntry = new ZipEntry(hdrBuf, bin);
    mEntries.put(newEntry.getName(), newEntry);
}
```

To patch this vulnerability, Android 4.3 adds the duplicate name check after the `mEtries` putting the name into the HashMap:

```
for (int i = 0; i < numEntries; ++i) {
    ZipEntry newEntry = new ZipEntry(hdrBuf, bin);
    String entryName = newEntry.getName();
    if (mEntries.put(entryName, newEntry) != null) {
        throw new ZipException("Duplicate" +
        "entry␣name:␣" + entryName);
    }
}
```

For dynamic analysis, DroidRay uses the "`adb`" to execute all real exploits in our vulnerability database and then checks whether the exploits are successful or not. Last but not least, DroidRay reports the potential privilege escalation vulnerabilities to the user.

Currently, our vulnerability database includes four native level vulnerabilities and three Java level vulnerabilities (please refer to Table 8). In Table 8, the first column shows the name of the vulnerability. The second column shows the check points of the vulnerability and the last column shows the type (native or Java) of the vulnerability. For example, the first row shows the *RageAgainsttheCage* vulnerability we discussed before. By analyzing all of our 250 downloaded firmwares, we discovered that most of firmwares can defend against native level vulnerabilities. However, nearly 99% firmwares have Java level vulnerabilities. The experiment result is summarized in Table 9. The first column is the name of the vulnerability. The second column indicates how many firmwares have this type of vulnerability, and the last column depicts the percentage of vulnerable firmwares.

vulnerability name	# of firmware	Percentage
RageAgainsttheCage [3]	1	0.4%
GingerBreak [2]	2	0.8%
ZergRush [24]	40	16.0%
CVE-2009-1185 [6]	40	16.0%
Masterkey1[26]	249	99.6%
Masterkey2[25]	249	99.6%
Masterkey3[27]	250	100.0%

Table 9: Experiment result of privilege escalation vulnerabilities

6. PRE-INSTALLED MALWARE CASE STUDY

As mentioned in Section 4, we discovered a malware named "CEPlugnew" in numbers of firmwares. In March of 2013, we captured this pre-installed zero-day Android malware family

vulnerability name	Check Point	Type
RageAgainsttheCage [3]	adb_main() function of /system/bin/adb elf file	native
GingerBreak [2]	handlePartitionAdded() function of /system/bin/vold elf file	native
ZergRush [24]	dispatchCommand() function of libsysutils.so elf file	native
CVE-2009-1185 [6]	uevent_kernel_multicast_recv() function of /system/bin/sysinit elf file	native
Masterkey1[26]	readCentralDir() function of java.util.zip.ZipFile class of /system/framework/core.jar	Java
Masterkey2[25]	getInputStream() function of java.util.zip.ZipFile class of /system/framework/core.jar and ZipEntry() function of java.util.zip.ZipEntry class of /system/framework/core.jar	Java
Masterkey3[27]	getInputStream() function of java.util.zip.ZipFile class of /system/framework/core.jar	Java

Table 8: vulnerability Description

and its management system. The system is used to send premium rate SMS and distribute pay per install applications. In this section, we present our investigation of this zero-day Android malware, its operating process and its business chain.

6.1 Zero-day Malware: CEPlugnew

As we mentioned in Section 4, malware writers can pay money to some smartphone manufacturers in order to pre-install apps in smartphones. By using DroidRay, we studied several firmwares of low-cost smartphones and successfully discovered a pre-installed zero-day malware. We call this malware `CEPlugnew` because its package name is `com.example.plugnew`. Firstly, it has `INSTALL_PACKAGES` and `SEND_SMS` permission, so DroidRay extracts it from firmware for further analysis. Secondly, by using dynamic analysis, we find it is an advanced malware using the `DexClassLoader` to dynamically decrypt and load an encrypted JAR file. In addition, because it is a pre-installed app with system privilege, it can download and install any application when it receives commands from the malware server. By reverse engineering, we were able to determine the malware servers' addresses (e.g., 42.121.120.*). Furthermore, we discover that one of their servers has the MSSQL SQL injection vulnerability. We exploit this vulnerability and obtain a large database and its malware manage system. Let us present our findings.

6.2 Malware Management System

The malware management system we obtained is a web-based system to manage and view the status of premium rate SMS messages and silent installation of mobile applications. The system was written in JSP and was created in 2009. At first, this system was used to control the Symbian-based malware. According to the modification record, the system was modified and began controlling Android-based malware in 2011. Firstly, this system has a dynamic web page, the malware on the controlled smartphones will visit this dynamic web page on the specified time with some essential parameters (e.g., IP address, time, IMEI, IMSI, version, and phone model). Then the system will record the information in the MSSQL database. Secondly, if the malware writers want to distribute an application, they only need to create a new task and enter parameters for this task (e.g., the download link and distribution numbers). On the other hand, the malware on the controlled smartphone will request the server for the task, and execute it on the specified time. Thirdly, this system can be used to send a large number of SMS messages to a host of phone numbers. In addition, malware writers can use this system to check their monthly profits from different telecommunications operators.

6.3 Database Analysis

We obtain the database snapshot from the malware writers' server. The database includes more than 348,018 unique International Mobile Equipment Identification (IMEI) and 415,607 unique International Mobile Subscriber Identification (IMSI). The statistics of the database is summarized in Table 10. We find that all the smartphones in the database were infected within five months (from 2012.10 to 2013.03). In addition, by querying the database on the IP distribution map, we can approximate the locations of these IP addresses. Table 11 shows the number of infected IP addresses in countries. Note that due to the page limit, we only list those countries which have more than 50 infected smartphones. Finally, we use Google map API [14] to generate an infected smartphone distribution map and it is depicted in Figure 3. From the map, we can see that some major cities in China, like Guangzhou, Beijing and Chengdu, have the high number of victims. Other countries like US and other European countries are not immune either since they have infected devices. To the best of our knowledge, this is the first real world case about the pre-installed malware which has more than 348,018 infected devices.

Database Information	Description
Unique IMEI	348,018
Unique IMSI	415,607
# of Phone Model	3,178
Unique IP Address	568,072
First log time	2012-10
Last log time	2013-03

Table 10: Statistics of infected smartphones

7. RELATED WORK

In this section, we present some related works which are related to Android malware, Android application security and Android firmware security.

In [8], authors presented the `ded` decompiler and carried out a study of 1,100 Android applications. Their analysis framework allows researchers to observe not only the existence of dangerous functionality, but also how it occurs within an Android app. Felt et al. studied 18 Android malware in [9]. Jia et al. [18] conducted a study on the run-time enforcement of information-flow. In [33], authors discussed how to enhance users' comprehension of Android permissions. ADAM [35] and DroidChameleon [23] are two systems to generate Android malware variants. [40] was the first paper to provide a systematic study on the detection of malicious applications on Android Markets. The authors successfully discovered 211 malware and carefully analyzed the malicious behaviors of the malware. DroidMOSS [37] is an Android system to detect repackaged applications using

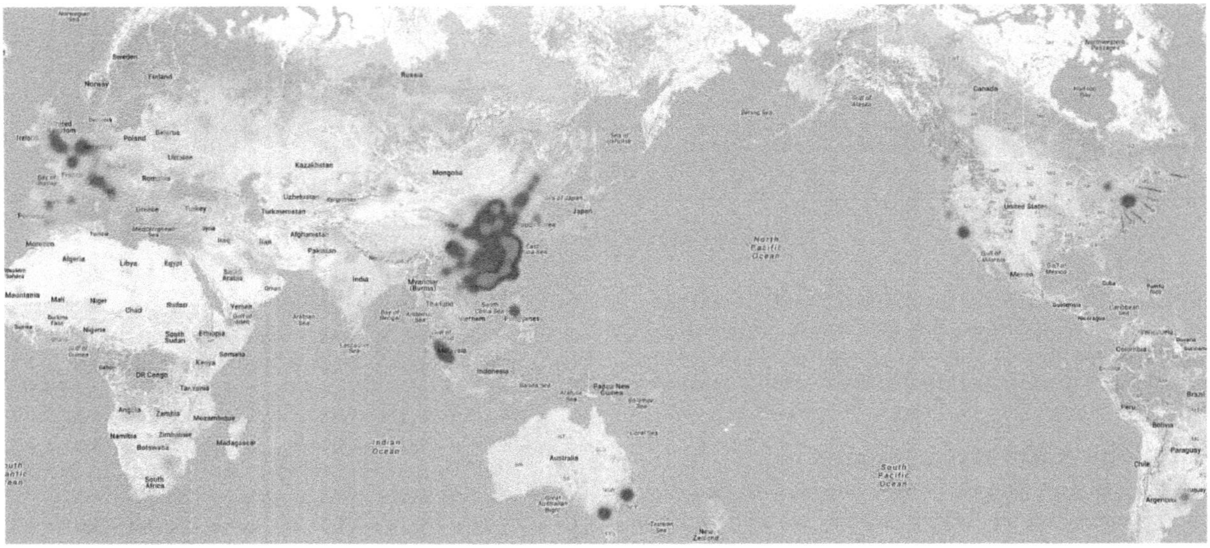

Figure 3: Distribution of infected Android devices around the world due to the pre-installed malware "CEPlugnew"

Country	# of Infected IP Addresses
CN-(CHINA)	561,657
TW-(TAIWAN)	1,299
HK-(HONG KONG)	891
KR-(REPUBLIC OF KOREA)	453
US-(UNITED STATES)	385
MY-(MALAYSIA)	305
VN-(VIET NAM)	202
RU-(RUSSIAN FEDERATION)	168
VE-(VENEZUELA)	165
MO-(MACAU)	159
SG-(SINGAPORE)	155
IT-(ITALY)	141
AU-(AUSTRALIA)	126
CA-(CANADA)	114
ES-(SPAIN)	105
GB-(UNITED KINGDOM)	105
TH-(THAILAND)	88
FR-(FRANCE)	81
DE-(GERMANY)	74
PH-(PHILIPPINES)	66
BG-(BULGARIA)	62
KZ-(KAZAKHSTAN)	62
ID-(INDONESIA)	61
NZ-(NEW ZEALAND)	58
AR-(ARGENTINA)	57
SA-(SAUDI ARABIA)	50

Table 11: Number of infected IP addresses in countries

fuzzy hashing. ContentScope [39] aimed to find the passive content leaks and pollution in Android applications. SmartDroid [34] can automatically reveal the UI-based trigger conditions. In [38], Zhou et al. studied characterization and evolution of Android malware with 1,260 samples. Kevin McNamee [21] showed us how to build a spyphone. However, all of the above mentioned works only focused on the detection and functionalities of Android malware and they did not focus on Android firmware security.

Woodpecker [12] analyzed each application in a smartphone firmware to explore the reachability of a dangerous permission from a public, unguarded interface. Lei et al. [20] studied ten representative stock Android images from five popular smartphone vendors and they found a lot of security problems on the permission usages of pre-installed applications. However, all of the above mentioned works only focused on the applications. XRay[28] is an app for scanning security vulnerabilities of Android system, so it cannot scan the firmwares. Our paper is the first detailed study on both pre-installed application security and system security for Android firmwares. In particular, we have done large scale experiments on 250 Android firmwares and performed a detailed case study on infected firmwares.

8. CONCLUSION

As malware writers are using firmwares to spread new malware, there is an urgent need to combat this new form of distribution channel. We present the design and implementation of "*DroidRay*": a security evaluation system for customized Android firmwares. The system uses both static and dynamic analyses to evaluate the firmware security on application level and system level. We carry out a comprehensive study on 24,009 pre-installed applications and 250 Android firmware systems, and discover compromised firmwares can contaminate the system and inject new malware into devices. We found 1,947 (8.1%) pre-installed applications have signature vulnerability and 19 (7.6%) firmwares contain pre-installed malware. In addition, we discovered 142 (56.8%) Android firmwares have the default signature vulnerability, five (2.0%) Android firmwares contain malicious *hosts* file, at most 40 (16.0%) Android firmwares have native level privilege escalation vulnerability and at least 249 (99.6%) Android firmwares have Java level privilege escalation vulnerability. In particular, we carry out detailed investigation on a real world pre-installed zero-day Android malware known as `CEPlugnew`, which involves 348,018 infected Android smartphones and reveal its geographical spread.

9. REFERENCES

[1] F. Adrienne, Porter, C. Erika, H. Steve, S. Dawn, and W. David. Android permissions demystified. In *Proceedings of ACM Conference on Computer and Communications Security (CCS)*, 2011.

[2] C-skill. Gingerbreak. `http://c-skills.blogspot.hk/2011/04/yummy-yummy-gingerbreak.html`, 2011.

[3] C-skill. Rageagainstthecage. `https://github.com/bibanon/android-development-codex/wiki/rageagainstthecage`, 2011.

[4] A. Central. Android central (rom market). `http://www.androidcentral.com/tags/firmware`, 2013.

[5] C. Daily. Low-end smartphone fight. `http://www.chinadaily.com.cn/bizchina/2012smartphone/2012-07/16/content_15703750.htm`, 2012.

[6] N. V. Database. Cve-2009-1185. `http://web.nvd.nist.gov/view/vuln/detail?vulnId=CVE-2009-1185`, 2009.

[7] DownloadAndroidROM. Downloadandroidrom (rom market). `http://downloadandroidrom.com/`, 2013.

[8] W. Enck, D. Octeau, P. McDaniel, and S. Chaudhuri. A study of android application security. In *Proceedings of the 20th USENIX conference on Security*, SEC'11, 2011.

[9] A. P. Felt, M. Finifter, E. Chin, S. Hanna, and D. Wagner. A Survey of Mobile Malware in the Wild. In *Proceedings of the 1st ACM workshop on Security and privacy in smartphones and mobile devices*, 2011.

[10] Google. Android open source project. `http://source.android.com`, 2008.

[11] Google. virustotal. `https://www.virustotal.com/`, 2013.

[12] M. Grace, Y. Zhou, Z. Wang, and X. Jiang. Systematic Detection of Capability Leaks in Stock Android Smartphones. In *Proceedings of the 19th Annual Network & Distributed System Security Symposium*, 2012.

[13] I. D. C. (IDC). Apple cedes market share in smartphone operating system market as android surges and windows phone gains, according to idc. `http://www.idc.com/getdoc.jsp?containerId=prUS24257413`, 2013.

[14] G. Inc. Google map apis. `http://developers.google.com/maps/`, 2012.

[15] L. Inc. Security alert: Malware found targeting custom roms (jsmshider). `https://blog.lookout.com/blog/2011/06/15/security-alert-malware-found-targeting-custom-roms-jsmshider/`, 2011.

[16] Ipmart. Ipmart (rom forum). `http://www.ipmart-forum.com/forum.php`, 2013.

[17] J. Janego. The security implications of custom android roms. `http://labs.neohapsis.com/2011/12/21/the-security-implications-of-custom-android-roms/`, 2012.

[18] L. Jia, J. Aljuraidan, E. Fragkaki, L. Bauer, M. Stroucken, K. Fukushima, S. Kiyomoto, and Y. Miyake. Run-time enforcement of information-flow properties on Android (extended abstract). In *Computer Security—ESORICS 2013: 18th European Symposium on Research in Computer Security*, Sept. 2013.

[19] Jidi. Rom jidi (rom market). `http://www.romjd.com/`, 2013.

[20] W. Lei, G. Michael, Z. Yajin, W. Chiachih, and J. Xuxian. The impact of vendor customizations on android security. In *Proceedings of ACM Conference on Computer and Communications Security (CCS)*, 2013.

[21] K. McNamee. How to build a spyphone. `Blackhat`, 2013.

[22] C. Mod. Cyanogen mod (rom forum). `http://www.cyanogenmod.org/`, 2013.

[23] V. Rastogi, Y. Chen, and X. Jiang. Droidchameleon: evaluating android anti-malware against transformation attacks. In *Proceedings of the ASIACCS '13*.

[24] Revolutionary. Zergrush. `http://forum.xda-developers.com/showthread.php?t=1296916`, 2011.

[25] saurik. Android bug superior to master key. `http://www.saurik.com/id/18`, 2009.

[26] saurik. Exploit and fix android master key. `http://www.saurik.com/id/17`, 2009.

[27] saurik. Yet another android master key bug. `http://www.saurik.com/id/19`, 2009.

[28] D. Security. Xray for android. `http://www.xray.io/#vulnerabilities`.

[29] Shendu. Rom shendu (rom market). `http://www.shendu.com/android/`, 2013.

[30] VR-ZONE. Research shows chinese manufacturers account for 20 percent of smartphones worldwide, india on the rise. `http://vr-zone.com/articles/research-shows-chinese-manufacturers-account-for-20-percent-of-smartphones-worldwide-india-on-the-rise/49868.html`, 2013.

[31] D. Walker. Pay-per-install pays big bucks in the mobile world. `http://www.scmagazine.com/pay-per-install-pays-big-bucks-in-the-mobile-world/article/258731/`, 2012.

[32] Xda. Xda-developers (rom forum). `http://www.xda-developers.com/`, 2013.

[33] L. Yang, N. Boushehrinejadmoradi, P. Roy, V. Ganapathy, and L. Iftode. Short paper: enhancing users' comprehension of android permissions. In *Proceedings of the second ACM workshop on Security and privacy in smartphones and mobile devices*, SPSM '12, 2012.

[34] C. Zheng, S. Zhu, S. Dai, G. Gu, X. Gong, X. Han, and W. Zou. Smartdroid: an automatic system for revealing ui-based trigger conditions in android applications. In *Proceedings of the second ACM workshop on Security and privacy in smartphones and mobile devices*, SPSM '12, 2012.

[35] M. Zheng, P. P. C. Lee, and J. C. S. Lui. Adam: an automatic and extensible platform to stress test android anti-virus systems. In *Proceedings of the 9th international conference on Detection of Intrusions and Malware, and Vulnerability Assessment*, DIMVA'12, 2013.

[36] Zhijia. Rom zhijia (rom market). `http://www.romzj.com/`, 2013.

[37] W. Zhou, Y. Zhou, X. Jiang, and P. Ning. DroidMOSS: Detecting Repackaged Smartphone Applications in Third-Party Android Marketplaces. In *Proceedings of the second ACM conference on Data and Application Security and Privacy*, 2012.

[38] Y. Zhou and X. Jiang. Dissecting Android Malware: Characterization and Evolution. In *Proceedings of the 33rd IEEE Symposium on Security and Privacy*, 2012.

[39] Y. Zhou and X. Jiang. Detecting passive content leaks and pollution in android applications. In *Proceedings of the 20th Annual Symposium on Network and Distributed System Security*, 2013.

[40] Y. Zhou, Z. Wang, W. Zhou, and X. Jiang. Hey, You, Get Off of My Market: Detecting Malicious Apps in Official and Alternative Android Markets. In *Proceedings of the 19th Annual Network & Distributed System Security Symposium*, 2012.

[41] H. Z. Zihang Xiao, Qing Dong and X. Jiang. Oldboot: the first bootkit on Android. `http://blogs.360.cn/360mobile/2014/01/17/oldboot-the-first-bootkit-on-android/`, 2014.

APKLancet: Tumor Payload Diagnosis and Purification for Android Applications

Wenbo Yang[*]
Shanghai Jiao Tong University
800 Dongchuan Road
Shanghai, China
talentyang@hotmail.com

Juanru Li*
Shanghai Jiao Tong University
800 Dongchuan Road
Shanghai, China
jarod@sjtu.edu.cn

Yuanyuan Zhang*
Shanghai Jiao Tong University
800 Dongchuan Road
Shanghai, China
yyjess@sjtu.edu.cn

Yong Li
Shanghai Jiao Tong University
800 Dongchuan Road
Shanghai, China
1120339057@sjtu.edu.cn

Junliang Shu
Shanghai Jiao Tong University
800 Dongchuan Road
Shanghai, China
s.junliang@gmail.com

Dawu Gu[†]
Shanghai Jiao Tong University
800 Dongchuan Road
Shanghai, China
dwgu@sjtu.edu.cn

ABSTRACT

A huge number of Android applications are bundled with relatively independent modules either during the development or by intentionally repackaging. Undesirable behaviors such as stealthily acquiring and distributing user's private information are frequently discovered in some bundled third-party modules, i.e., advertising libraries or malicious code (we call the module *tumor payload* in this work), which sabotage the integrity of the original app and lie as a threat to both the security of mobile system and the user's privacy.

In this paper, we discuss how to purify an Android APK by resecting the tumor payload. Our work is based on two observations: 1) the tumor payload has its own characteristics, so it could be spotted through program analysis, and 2) the tumor payload is a relatively independent module so it can be resected without affecting the original app's function. We propose APKLancet, an automatic Android application diagnosis and purification system, to detect and resect the tumor payload. Relying on features extracting from ad libraries, analytics plugins and an approximately 8,000 malware samples, APKLancet is capable of diagnosing an APK and discovering unwelcome code fragment. Then it makes use of the code fragment as index to employ fine-grained program analysis and detaches the entire tumor payload. More precisely, it conducts an automatic app patching process to preserve the original normal functions while resecting tumor payload. We test APKLancet by the Android apps bundled with representative tumor payloads from online sandbox system. The result shows that the purification process is feasible to resect tumor payload and repair the apps. Moreover, all of the above do not require any Android system modification, and the purified app does not introduce any performance latency.

*All three authors contributed equally to this work.
†Corresponding author.

ASIA CCS'14, June 4–6, 2014, Kyoto, Japan.
Copyright 2014 ACM 978-1-4503-2800-5/14/06$15.00.
http://dx.doi.org/10.1145/2590296.2590314.

Categories and Subject Descriptors

D.4.6 [**Security and Protection**]: (e.g., viruses, worms, Trojan horses);

General Terms

Security

Keywords

Program analysis; Third-party libraries; Malicious code; Android Security

1. INTRODUCTION

Smartphones such as Android phones are beneficial supplements to stationary computing: online payment, web surfing, email processing, etc. Being a functional cellular phone, smartphone maintains the contacts lists, geographic location, SMS and more, which are directly related to the user herself. As a result, with the booming of the market share of these mobile devices, Android attracts great attention of malicious activities that are rapidly increasing. Android applications are discovered gathering data such as GPS location, device identifiers, and even user's identity without proper notice or authorization from the end user. The unwanted behaviors, however, are usually introduced by the bundled third-party libraries or injected malicious code. These kinds of potentially undesirable third-party code, as we call *tumor payload* in this paper, introduce new security threat to benign apps and expose the users to privacy leakage or system compromising.

Typical tumor payload includes not only malicious code but also some advertising/analytics libraries. Most of the tumor payload choose to bundle with the popular apps which would bring in more profit for the publisher. The *Brightest*

Flashlight Free app for Android, which has been downloaded between 50 to 100 million times, has been secretly sending location and device data to advertisers[5]. For third-party ad libraries or analytics plugins that seem to be benign, they may also introduce potential security breaches. For instance, ad libraries have been observed the behavior of downloading code over HTTP and dynamically loading and executing at runtime without checking the integrity[3]. Attacker may hijack the network and replace the executable with malicious code.

Due to the fact that Android apps are vulnerable to repackaging attack, tumor payload bundling becomes even more popular. Attackers could simply modify the apps using sophisticated decompilation tools to inject extra code or change the user interface through tweaking resource files. According to Zhou and Jiang's study[24], about 86.0% of the malwares they analyzed are repackaged versions of legitimate apps with malicious payloads. BitDefender's survey on Google Play[1] shows that more than 4,000 apps out of about 420,000 apps are plagiarized or simply re-engineered from other app developers, adding new advertising SDK to original apps for profit. In third-party application market, the situation is even worse. The experiment in[23] displays the fact that 5% to 13% of apps hosted on these studied marketplaces are repackaged. Since bundling tumor payload with an app is becoming a common phenomenon in Android ecosystem, tackling the tumor payload is not only the issue of protecting the secure execution environment of Android app, or of constraining the undesirable behavior, but also of protecting the ecosystem of the Android OS.

From the end users point of view, not only do they want to detect but also to forbid the imposed function (mostly from the tumor payload) while remaining the expected app function. Several studies on detecting the tumor payload have been proposed at module level pairwise comparison and large-scale analysis[8, 9, 14, 22]. The issue here is how to repress the undesirable behaviors and restore a purified app to its normal status.

A coarse-grained approach is to forbid the unnecessary permissions that tumor payload has declared. Android OS grants and controls the permissions to an entire APK, so the injected tumor payload shares the same privilege that the original APK has declared. Avoiding declaring unnecessary permission could somehow protect the apps from permission abuse by malicious activities, but notice that many apps provide their own function based on privileged permissions, and the injected code itself could share those permissions to conduct malicious activities, so this method is not recommended.

There also exist several fine-grained access control approaches[15, 10, 20] by rewriting the APK and inserting instrumentation routines to monitor the API invocation and dynamically applying security countermeasures when detecting threats. We should notice that these countermeasures do not account for the fact that APK is composed of modules of equal status but treated as an entire package. So it still goes to the end user's judgment call on granting permission to the "benign" or "malicious" functions in the APK. This is a difficult task even for the savvy user with the help of advanced information flow analysis, not to mention the non-savvy users who have little knowledge on the mechanism behind the veil. An alternative approach suggests to isolate the unwanted code (typically, the advertising libraries) and execute it in another process with limited privilege[21, 18, 17]. The advantage is to ensure the function of legally inserted third-party advertising libraries to bring profit to developers. The problem is that it commonly requires Android system modification and thus is difficult to implement.

We found that in most cases tumor payload is simply inserted as an independent module (otherwise the decompilation and re-compilation process may fail and it will be hard to be deployed in large scale) in APK files. When executed, this module runs in a separated work flow and is loosely relevant to the original work flow. Moreover, the styles of integration of the tumor payload are limited and usually the integrating procedure is reversible. Thus, it is able to purify an app through properly analyzing the way of integration and precisely locating and resecting the tumor payload.

In this paper we propose *APKLancet*, a tumor payload diagnosis and purification system for Android app. APKLancet is an APK rewriting system focusing on resecting tumor payload (the resecting process is called *purification* in this work) and further repairing the purified app after the resecting. It diagnoses an APK to spot potential tumor code with tumor payload feature database. Then it partitions the entire tumor payload with program analysis. Rather than directly cutting the tumor code off and leaves the normal function unchanged, APKLancet will automatically detect the integration style of the tumor payload and correspondingly patches the APK file to prove that it can work properly after the purification. Finally, APKLancet conducts a verification process to assure that the purification does resect the unwanted behavior, and the operated app is able to work properly.

The contributions of this work include:

- We conduct a systematic study on the characteristics of different kinds of tumor payload as ad libraries, analytics plugins and malicious code. This serves as a first step towards resecting the tumor payload. Based on this study, we summarize typical integration styles of the tumor payload. We propose an effective purification and restoration process that adopts different strategies to trim the tumor payload and sew the APK back.

- We build a tumor payload feature database using the knowledge of ad libraries, analytics plugins and an approximately 8,000 malware samples to help finding suspicious code fragment in the app. The diagnosed suspicious code fragment is then used as index to partition the entire tumor payload from the app using code and data dependency analysis.

- The proposed APK purification approach directly operates on apps and does not need to modify the system. Compared with other access control schemes, our purification approach operated by APKLancet does not bring any extra runtime overhead to either the app or the system.

- We evaluated the effect of resecting a variety of representative tumor payloads such as malicious code *Geinimi* and ad library *Wooboo*. Our work shows that tumor payload is able to be split. Based on this fact, APKLancet provides a novel way of access control at the code level.

2. PRELIMINARIES

2.1 Tumor Payload

We define the term of tumor payload as the code that is loosely linked to the primary function of the host app and performs undesirable behaviors (e.g., collecting information without proper notice or authorization from the end user). Malicious code, ad libraries and analytics plugins that contain privacy-violated function (although they may bring profit to developer or help collecting information) can all be regarded as tumor payload.

2.1.1 *Malicious Code*

Among all kinds of potentially unwanted code, malicious code is perhaps the most dangerous one. Malicious code refers to the code that intentionally conducts undesirable behaviors without approval. On Android OS, malicious code has evolved from simple functions such as sending SMS without the authorization to sophisticated functions such as getting root privileges by exploits, receiving and executing commands from remote server. More works[12, 19] have described the details on such threats caused by malicious code. One example is the *Geinimi* malware, the first sophisticated malware for Android found in the wild in 2010. Many legitimate apps are infected by being repackaged and the malicious code that includes a backdoor-like functionality. Following Geinimi, the repackaging-based infections were soon arising by other variants such as the Trojan *ADRD*. Researchers found that 86.0% repackaged apps have included malicious payloads after analyzing more than 1200 Android malware samples in 49 different malware families[24].

2.1.2 *Ad Library*

Ad library is the most common third-party code among Android apps. According to [2], about 50% of the apps contain at least one ad library. Although users dislike ads popping in their apps, developers can gain profit from it (by user's clicking the ads) so it is not reasonable to classify the ad library as malicious code. However, if an app without advertising is modified by injecting ad library for profit, the intellectual property rights of the original author are violated, which harms the whole Android ecosystem. In this situation, the injected library is obviously considered to be unwanted code by both the end users and the developers.

2.1.3 *Analytics Plugin*

Being different from the ad library, analytics plugin is to help developer collect user engagement data from their applications and make decision according to huge amount of collected information. For instance, the Google Analytics SDK for Android can help Android developers to collect data such as the number of active users, location of the users who use the application, etc. Analytics plugin generally runs in background and does not intervene in any operation at the front-end. Same as ad lib, analytics plugin should not be defined as malicious code. The potential risk of analytic plugin is that it may collect data related to user's privacy.

2.2 Observations

Tumor payload has obvious characteristics. From the viewpoint of program analysis, the tumor payload is a module that is loosely linked to the primary function of the host app and can be effectively partitioned[22]. From the perspective of pattern matching, typical tumor payload often contains special meta-data information declared in the xml file of the APK. And from the viewpoint of behavior monitoring, tumor payload generally involves privileged permission requirement and sensitive API invoking.

Another observation is that although tumor payloads may be various, they are basically using the same repackaging techniques, and most repackaging processes are reversible. The typical repackaging process involves unpacking the original APK to extract bytecode part and resource part, decompiling bytecode, modifying existing code (injecting new code) and resource files, and repacking the modified contents into a new package. Most of the repackaging procedures do not make too much modification to the inside of the original code but only add extra functional modules due to the applicability and dissemination. The function of the original APK is often preserved, and the injected code is normally a third-party module that is well encapsulated. Therefore, it is feasible to split the tumor payload from the app and purify the host app because the injection is detachable.

3. APK PURIFICATION

APK purification is the process of resecting tumor code from an app. The goal is to resect the undesirable behaviors brought by the tumor code while preserving the original function. It relies on the observation that tumor code is not tightly interweaving with the major function of the APK. To this end, we propose **APKLancet**, a tumor code excision system to conduct the app purification process. APKLancet's work flow consists of four stages(Fig 1). At the first stage APKLancet mainly relies on existing tumor code features to diagnose the APK file and filter out possible code fragment related to tumor payload. At the second stage the filtered suspicious code fragment is used as index to partition the entire tumor payload from the benign code, the partitioning process is conducted using program analysis. The third stage is tumor code resection. The main purpose of this stage is to resect the tumor payload, and patch the benign code of the APK to prove the correctness of the normal control flow. Final stage, the purified APK is verified and the effect of tumor payload resection is measured.

3.1 The APKLancet System

APKLancet fulfils tumor payload excision task. The APKLancet system contains three main components: *APK analyzer*, *APK rewriter* and *APK verifier*.

3.1.1 *APK Analyzer*

The APK analyzer of APKLancet is used to analyze APK file comprehensively. The implementation is based on Androguard[11]. The APK analyzer parses manifest file and resource files to acquire declaration information of an app. Relying on a feature database built from existing knowledge of tumor payload, it then locates suspicious code fragment and partitions the entire tumor code payload according to the results from smali code analysis. Moreover, it analyzes the type of tumor payload and conducts a patching process to prove the purified APK work properly.

3.1.2 *APK Rewriter*

The APK rewriter is responsible for unpacking and decompiling APK file, and repacking the purified file into a new app. It is mainly based on APKtool[4]. The APK

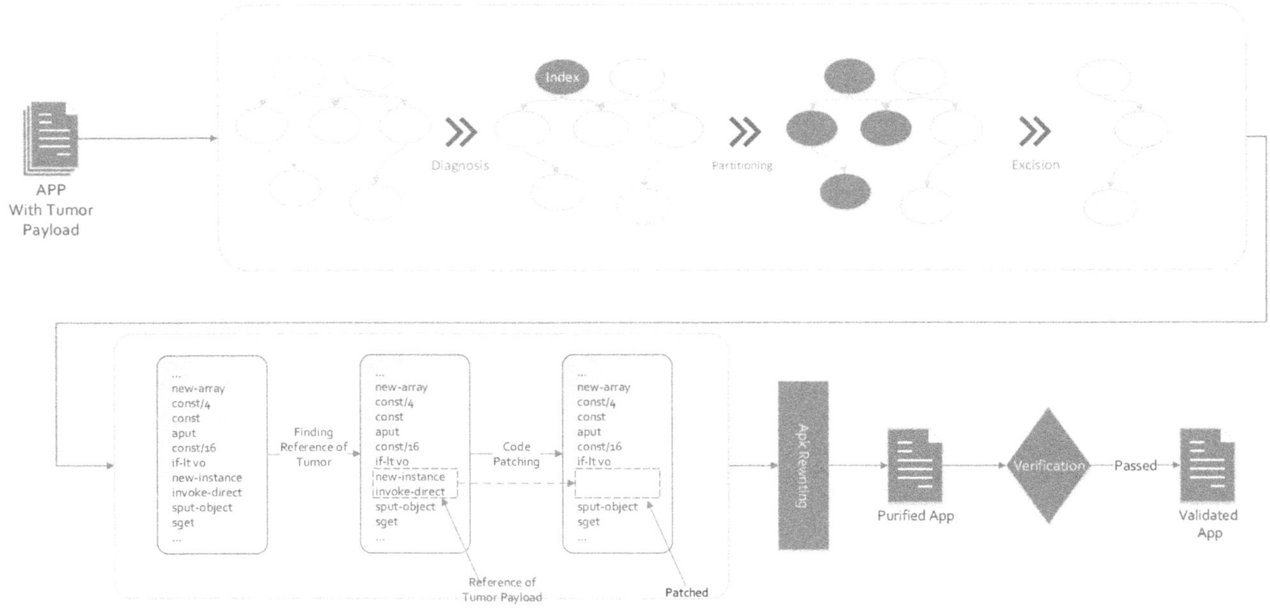

Figure 1: APK purification process

rewriter first unpacks the target APK file and decompiles the executable part into *smali* code, decoding manifest file and related resource files for the APK analyzer. Then, it receives the analyzing results from the APK analyzer, resects the tumor payload and repairs the "incision" in remained benign part. Finally, it reassembles the purified files into a new app.

3.1.3 APK Verifier

The APK verifier is mainly an automatic Android logging system to record and analyze app's execution status. It validates the purified app through dynamically recording its log output and corresponding events such as network access, and captures any possible exception that is introduced.

3.2 APK Diagnosis

To detect suspicious tumor payload, APKLancet conducts an approach that relies on existing knowledge database rather than analyzing the characteristics. The reason is that resecting tumor code from an app is aggressive and risky compared with solely detecting it. Any improper code resection will damage the benign function. What's worse, the effect of code resection may not be detected immediately but afterwards. Therefore, the strategy APKLancet adopts should be extremely conservative to prove that the diagnosis will not suffer from false positive.

To meet this requirement, APKLancet diagnoses an app using the existing knowledge of tumor payload. It first builds a tumor payload feature database summarized from known malicious code and popular third-party libraries. For malicious code, we have collected more than 8000 malware samples with 184 malware families from an automatic Android program analysis sandbox[6]. To build the database, we first randomly choose one app or two from each malware family and extract the feature. Then we use the knowledge to guide APKLancet to detect malicious payload in other malwares. For third-party libraries, we defined the tumor libraries after investigating popular ad libraries and analytics plugins since these libraries are more likely to be injected into benign apps for the profit. However, considering it may cause the result that legitimate apps bundled with tumor third-party libraries will also be the target of our system, we leave the issue discussed in Section 5.

The content of the database is the representative code fragment, as we called *index class*, of those tumor payloads. In the following, we discuss the details about extracting index class from malicious code and tumor libraries.

- *Malicious Code.* An index class of malware is responsible for certain events or functions connected to the malicious behaviors of the tumor payload. The advantage of building the feature database according to index classes instead of the whole payload is that it is common to malware that generating new variants. Even the tumor payload may be various, the index classes of one malware family are generally unchanged. Thus scanning these kinds of classes in tumor payload is essential for extracting feature.

  Since malicious code injecting aims to affect as much apps as possible, tumor payload of malware usually registers its own class as an entry point for convenience to assure it could be executed in most cases, which can avoid manual analysis to various app victims. Unlike application on traditional commodity computer platform, an Android application can have multiple entry points. APKLancet focuses on five types of classes (including inherited types) that can be registered as entry point. The first four are the basic components of Android: *Activity*, *Service*, *Broadcast Receiver* and *Content Provider*. The final class type, *android.app.Applic-*

ation, is the appointed class type of an app's main entry point and also considered in feature extracting. APKLancet only needs to scan these classes in a tumor payload and adds them into the tumor code feature database.

- *Third-party Library.* Unlike the malicious code, tumor third-party libraries such as popular ad libraries and analytic plugins are always well-documented, developer-friendly and less irregular. As a result, they usually offer a set of unified interfaces to developers for ease of use. It is not difficult for us to construct the tumor code feature database by selecting some of the most typical classes in the single library as the index classes(i.e., *AdView* in *AdMob*).

After constructing the feature database, APKLancet checks every class of an app that is one of the five entry point classes or representative classes of third-party libraries to find out the clue of tumor code. Different from signature-based detection of the malicious code that is frequently used in Antivirus, APKLancet compares the content of a class of the app with the feature database to identify the existence of any tumor code. In order to defeat the widely used code obfuscation technique, APKLancet leverages the fuzzy hashing content comparison technique proposed by DroidMOSS[23] to detect whether a class in an app is similar to one of the tumor classes in our database. If such a class is detected, APKLancet will label it as the index class to help conduct tumor payload partitioning in the next stage.

3.3 Tumor Payload Partitioning

After obtaining suspicious index classes, the next thing is to partition all of the tumor payload inside an app. In detail, the task is to identify the entire tumor payload including inserted executable code and its corresponding declaration in manifest file, extra injected resource files and additional libraries. To fulfil this task, APKLancet makes use of program analysis technique to traverse the entire payload from the detected index classes. According to the type of tumor code, APKLancet deals them with different strategies.

3.3.1 Third-party Library Partitioning

The method APKLancet partitions third-party library is mainly based on the knowledge of its insertion style. In most cases, third-party library is a relatively independent module which allows the partitioning with feasibility. The bundling of a third-party library generally involves adding three categories of information: a supporting Java jar file, special meta-data tag, possible elements declared in layout XML files and a small amount of modification to the original code mainly for inserting new advertising *View* class.

Because library provider more or less publishes document to illustrate how to integrate the lib into an app, APKLancet leverages this information for partitioning the inserted library with ease. The inserted libraries are usually Java jar files attached to the APK and can also be decompiled. If APKLancet identifies suspicious index class in these libraries, the whole Java jar file is labeled as the tumor payload (i.e., the whole package *com.google.ads.**). APKLancet further labels the inserted instructions in benign classes according to the reference relationship. In general, each class of benign code is searched to find any reference to any of the whole tumor libraries. For instance, an *AdView* class is created as follows:

```
adView = new AdView(this);
adView.setAdUnitId(MY_AD_UNIT_ID);
adView.setAdSize(AdSize.BANNER);
```

APKLancet could recognize the reference relationship of the class *AdView* with the payload library, and hence label these instructions(in smali code) as part of the tumor payload. Finally, the meta-data tag and the elements in resource files are also labeled as part of the tumor payload.

3.3.2 Malicious Code Partitioning

For malicious code in an infected app, the situation is much more sophisticated. Unlike the situation of third-party library, systematic knowledge is lacked in partitioning malicious code. There is no document information for malicious code and it usually uses transformation technique to avoid being detected. Furthermore, instead of being injected as an independent Java package (as the style of third-party libraries bundling), malicious payload is sometimes injected into an existing Java package of benign parts to make the identification more difficult, even the payload is still a relatively independent module from the viewpoint of functionality. Hence APKLancet makes use of program dependency analysis technique to help partition. APKLancet uses Algorithm 1 to search malicious code in an APK. The input of the algorithm include a set O of all classes in an APK and a set E containing the already identified malicious index classes. The output is a set M that contains the entire malicious class payload. The core part of the algorithm is the function $Find\_invoke\_dest()$. It is based on the program dependency graph of the app to extend the malicious class set. If the already identified malicious class invokes any method of a class that is not in system library, the invoked class should be added into the malicious class set.

Algorithm 1 Malicious Code Class Searching

Require:
The set of class in an APK, O;
The set of malicious class in O, E;
Ensure:
The set of malicious code class, M;

```
M = E
repeat
    D = ∅
    for all m in M do
        D ← Find_invoke_dest(m);
    end for
    for all d in D do
        if d in O AND d not in M then
            M ← d
        end if
    end for
until M is not modified
return M;
```

We choose a Java *class* as the basic unit in the algorithm for the reason that malicious payload is always composed of several complete classes. It is more likely for malware to construct a new class to perform malicious behavior instead of adding some malicious methods to specific benign classes because adding independent module is more suitable for large-scale deployment and needs less complicated manual analysis to various original apps to assure the modified apps still work.

3.4 Tumor Payload Resection

Although during tumor code partitioning stage an entire payload has been identified, tumor payload resection is nontrivial compared with the permission removal of app[16]. A payload contains both relatively independent third-party libraries and bundled code that is tightly interweaved with the host class. Therefore, simply resecting the entire payload will lead to an improper execution or even crash the app. Thus after partitioning tumor code payload, there still remains fixing work to be done. The key point is to repair the inserted code in benign code and information in the manifest file. APKLancet adopts a three-step repairing strategy, which is introduced in the following subsections.

3.4.1 Entry Point Reverting

An app declares many kinds of information in its manifest file. An inserted tumor code payload also declares its components in this file and adds or modifies entry points. In detail, we consider the following frequently used entry point modification approaches:

1. *Directly added entry point.* Tumor payload will directly register new *Service*, *Broadcast Receiver* and *Activity* in manifest file. Under certain condition, the tumor payload class is invoked.

2. *Main entry point tampering.* Some tumor code simply changes the original app's main entry point class (declared in the manifest file's *<application>* tag or changed the ACTION_MAIN Intent) to its own class. Through tampering the execution flow, it makes sure that the inserted module is invoked.

3. *Entry point inheritance modification.* One trick used by malicious code is to hide malicious entry point class through class inheritance. In this case, the original main entry point class is kept and malicious classes can hide themselves without being declared in manifest file. However, the inheritance relationship of main entry point class is modified. For instance, in Fig 2 the entry point class *com.normal.Activity* is originally inherited from *android.app.Activity*, after the infection its superclass is changed to *com.mal.Activity* which is a malicious class. When the entry point class is executed, the malicious function in its super class is firstly invoked.

In order to make a fixed app work properly, APKLancet needs to handle manifest file to resect the entry point items related to tumor payload. Moreover, if the main entry point class is modified to be a tumor code class, APKLancet tries to recover the main entry point through searching a *launcher* class. Once a launcher class is found, APKLancet will use it as the new main entry point class. If no launcher class can be found, APKLancet will further search for benign *Activity* referred by current entry point class code, and uses the first found *Activity* as new entry point class. If again there is no candidate, APKLancet uses the first *Activity* declared in manifest file as the new entry point class. For the case of *Entry point inheritance modification*, we need to find the

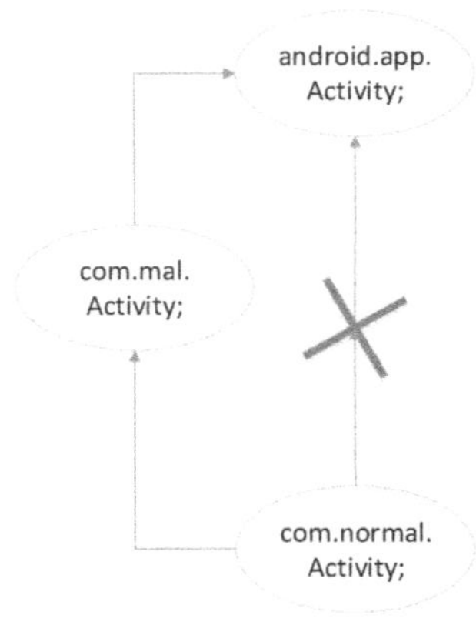

Figure 2: Entry Point Class Inheritance Modification

first super class of the original entry point class which is not in the tumor payload(i.e., *android.app.Activity* in Fig 2), and recover the inheritance relationship.

3.4.2 Benign Code Patching

APKLancet can identify every invoke instruction in decompiled smali code and check whether a benign code class invokes a method of tumor code class. Further, the invoking can be divided into two cases: 1) the invoked method is an inherited method that overwrites the base method, and it belongs to a class of entry point class type (inherits from *Activity*, *Service*, *Broadcast Receiver*, *Content Provider* or *Application* class), 2) the invoked method belongs to a common class of tumor code payload.

For the first case, the invoked methods in tumor code generally overwrite the methods of base class (such as *onCreate()*) and are special for Android application execution model. Resecting this kind of methods will crash the app. In this situation, APKLancet will replace the invoked methods in tumor code class with the methods of its direct base class (already fixed in inheritance recovery). For the second case, we consider the invoking instruction and its data-dependent instructions are inserted. Therefore, APKLancet analyzes the following instructions that depend on the return value of this invoking instruction, and patches the invoking instruction as well as following data-dependent instructions with *nop* instruction.

APKLancet will also scan the decompiled smali code to find any object reference relationship between benign code class and tumor code class. Again, if an object reference is found, APKLancet uses data dependency analysis to find other instructions and objects that are data-dependent to this object and then get it resected.

3.4.3 Payload Resection

After the fixing of benign code classes, APKLancet resects tumor code directly. In addition, APKLancet checks resource files related to tumor code. Native libraries(.so) and Java libraries(.jar) that are used by tumor code **only**, file under the *lib* and *assets* directory that are only referred by tumor code are all considered as part of the tumor payload, and should be resected.

Tumor payload	Classes resected	Items resected in manifest file	Resources resected	Reference patching	Entry point patching
ADRD	25	5	0	No	No
BaseBridge Variant.A	17	0	1	Yes	Yes
BaseBridge Variant.B	69	10	3	Yes	Yes
BaseBridge Variant.C	20	3	4	Yes	No
DroidDream	10	3	5	No	Yes
DroidKungFu	13	3	5	Yes	No
DroidKungFu2	13	3	5	Yes	No
Geinimi Variant.A	105	4	0	Yes	Yes
Geinimi Variant.B	85	3	0	No	Yes
PJAPPS	22	3	0	No	No

Table 1: Characteristic of Different Tumor Payload

3.5 Verification

APKLancet introduces a verification process to assure that the purified app is able to work properly and the purification process does remove the unwanted behavior. It evaluates the purification from the aspects of both feasibility and effectiveness.

3.5.1 Feasibility

APKLancet adopts a very conservative strategy, which does not allow new exception to crash the host app after the purification. The verification work for purified app contains two steps. First, the tested app is launched before purification and operated manually, and the Android's *logcat* output is collected. Second, after the purification the tested app is launched again with the same operation. APKLancet will check the *logcat* output and compare it with the previous record to determine whether the application is being executed normally or throws any exception or crashes due to the purification.

APKLancet does not adopt random test methodology such as testing using Android *Monkey*. Instead, to assure the purified APK is still able to work properly, APKLancet needs the involvement with manual test to deal with complex GUI interactions such as *password login*.

3.5.2 Effectiveness

APKLancet evaluates the effectiveness of the tumor code excision both statically and dynamically. The static evaluation approach adopted by APKLancet takes advantage of online malicious code analysis engine. The purified APK, if containing tumor code beforehand, is submitted to VirusTotal[7] to check whether the malicious feature still exists. This approach evaluates whether the purification does identify the malicious feature. The purified app is also executed on real device for APKLancet to collect *logcat* output and verify whether the features such as advertising is resected.

4. EVALUATION

4.1 General Testing

We tested APKLancet with repackaged apps from online sandbox system Sanddroid[6]. Table 1 shows the result that how APKLancet splits the typical tumor payloads. The result shows that for each payload at least 10 classes are resected during the purification process. To be more clear, we define different purification results of one malware family as different variants and label it in the form of *Variant.A*, etc. From the results, we can see that nearly all the malwares added or modified entry point of the original apps and it is quite common for malwares to conduct simple modification to benign part of the original app or add extra resource files such as native libraries or jar files to inject malicious behaviors.

In order to further effectively evaluate APKLancet, we randomly choose 16 apps from each malware family in our malware collection (we elaborately avoid those samples we used to build feature databases though the malware family they belong to should be included in our feature databases). The characteristic of the chosen apps is that not only do they contain either malicious code or third-party libraries (some of them contain both), but all of these apps are also able to execute well on latest version of the Android OS on mainstream devices. We evaluate the sophisticated result of malicious code purification. First, all of the tested apps worked properly and did not terminate by exception according to our manual test and Android's *logcat* output. Also, as Table 2 shows (malware family information given by AegisLab Antivirus), all of the samples experience a dramatic decrease in VirusTotal detection result after the purification, which means the tumor payload purification is effective and malicious behaviors are resected from these malwares to some extent. Although more than half of the samples are not detected by any anti-virus engines in VirusTotal, we also notice that a few anti-virus engines in VirusTotal still regard the purified apps as malicious. After manually checking those purified samples, we find that the same anti-virus engine classifies the sample as a different malware family in most cases. The root cause for the alert information is that some third-party libraries such as analytics plugins and ad libraries are still remained in the app, but are not defined as tumor payload either by APKLancet or other majority of Antivirus. Therefore, we treat this as false positive alert.

We also evaluate the effectiveness of resecting typical ad libraries. After purification of the tested app with *AdMob* library, advertisement in app's UI is gone.(See Fig 3). What's more, such outputs (i.e., URL of *AdMob* or Javascript code) that indicate the existence of *AdMob*, are not found in *logcat* output after purification. At the meantime, other log information created by benign code generally appears repeatedly before and after the purification. Another case is app with

Package Name	Malware Family	Before Purification	After Purification
com.appspot.swisscodemonkeys.steam	ADRD	26/47	3/47
com.bytedroid.liveprints	ADRD	35/47	0/44
com.caiping	BaseBridge	30/45	1/48
com.computertimeco.minishot.android	BaseBridge	32/48	0/47
com.game	BaseBridge	34/48	0/47
com.hyxen.taximeter.app	BaseBridge	34/48	0/45
com.power.SuperSolo	DroidDream	38/47	0/46
super.mobi.eraser	DroidDream	37/47	3/47
com.andtutu.stetris	DroidKungFu	33/47	0/46
com.eguan.update	DroidKungFu	34/47	0/47
com.bottleworks.dailymoney	DroidKungFu2	35/47	3/46
com.allen.txthej	DroidKungFu2	36/47	4/46
chaire1.mm	Geinimi	33/47	0/48
com.aac.cachemate	Geinimi	33/47	1/47
com.electricsheep.dj	Geinimi	33/48	1/47
cn.jingling.motu.photowonder	PJAPPS	32/47	0/46

Table 2: VirusTotal Detection Result

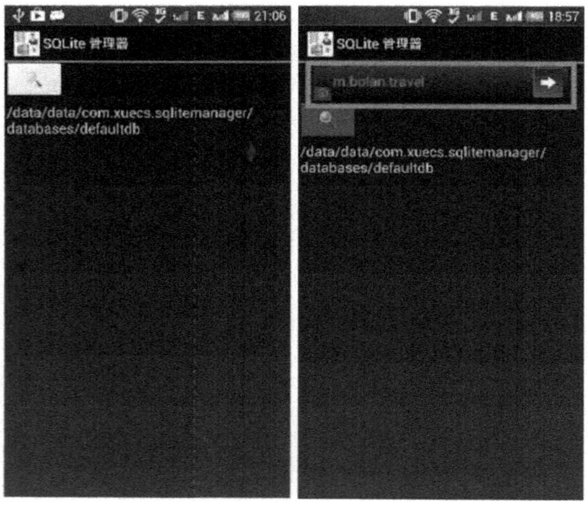

Figure 3: Advertisement Resection

Flurry library. If the *Flurry* library is loaded, *logcat* outputs the following information:

```
D/FlurryAgent: Starting new session
D/FlurryAgent: Sending report to: http://data.flurry.com/aar.do
D/FlurryAgent: Report successful
```

Such information would not be found in the purified app even for the same user operation is performed.

4.2 Case Study I: BaseBridge and Wooboo

The first case we studied is a repackaged app *com.caiping*. APKLancet extracts the fuzzy hashing feature of every entry point class of the apps. Compared with the feature database built before, in this app 10 classes (*com.android.view.custom.**) are detected to be tumor code index classes. Then APKLancet identifies the payload using Algorithm 1 taking these index classes as input, and finds out class *jackpal.androidterm.Exec* and all classes of *com.sec.android.providers.drm.** are also tumor code.

After locating tumor code payload, APKLancet discovers that the direct base class of main entry point *caiping* class, the *BaseAActivity* class, which is not declared in the manifest file, is suspicious and connected to the feature of *BaseBridge* malware family.

```
.class public Lcom/caiping/caiping;
.super Lcom/android/view/custom/BaseAActivity;
.source "caiping.java"
```

That means the malicious code modifies the class inheritance to make the *BaseAActivity* class execute before the original entry point class. If APKLancet simply resects the *BaseAActivity* class, the inheritance of *caiping* class is broken. APKLancet thus redirects the base class of *caiping* class to the base class of *BaseAActivity*, *android.app.Activity*.

After fixing the original inheritance of the main entry point class, APKLancet checks references in benign code and finds 4 method-invoking references (*onCreate*, *<init>*, *onCreateOptionsMenu* and *onOptionsItemSelected*) of the *BaseAActivity* class in benign code. All of these references locate in the main entry points class *com.caiping.caiping*. As we mentioned above, class *caiping* is a derived class of the malicious class *BaseAActivity*, and the base class of *BaseAActivity* is *android.app.Activity*. These 4 method-invoking references should point to the methods in class *android.app.Activity*, APKLancet hence patches the invoking instruction through replacing the invoked method's class from *BaseAActivity* to *android.app.Activity*. For the tumor object reference in this app, no data-dependent relationship is found and APKLancet just resects any direct reference of *Lcom/android/view/custom/BaseAActivity* in the benign code. APKLancet also cleans the declaration of the tumor code class in manifest file.

Finally, according to the string searched in smali code,

```
const-string v0, "androidterm"
invoke-static {v0},
    Ljava/lang/System;->
        loadLibrary(Ljava/lang/String;)V
```

The related *androidterm* library (libandroidterm.so) should be resected.

After the purification and repackaging, the new app is able to work. However, the test result of VirusTotal demonstrates that 15 out of 47 antivirus engines still report the app as malware and most of them classified it as *Wooboo* malware. We manually check the app and find that it contains an unauthorized advertising library *Wooboo*. So we add the *Wooboo* library's feature into APKLancet's database and re-execute the purification process. Relying on the knowledge of *Wooboo* directly, we regard the *WoobooAdView* as its index class and label the whole package where the index class locates as the payload. This time APKLancet partitions all classes of *com.wooboo.adlib_android.** as tumor payload.

In benign code APKLancet find four references of the tumor payload. All these references directly refer to the class *com.wooboo.adlib_android.WoobooAdView*, hence APKLancet recursively resects dependent instructions and definitions. After the purification, the purified app still works properly under manual testing. And all 47 engines of VirusTotal report no threat for this purified app.

4.3 Case Study II: Geinimi

The second case is an app *com.electricsheep.dj* containing malicious code of *Geinimi* malware family. According to APKLancet's feature database, the following classes are identified as the index classes,

```
com.geinimi.AdServiceReceiver;
com.geinimi.AdService;
com.geinimi.custom.Ad1020_102001;
```

Then, using the index classes as input, APKLancet executes Algorithm 1 and partitions classes *com.geinimi.** as the tumor code payload. After the partitioning of tumor code payload, APKLancet checks references in benign code and finds no reference to the tumor code payload. However, APKLancet finds that in manifest file the main entry point will be missing if the tumor code is resected. According to the fixing policy of APKLancet, the replaced main entry point should be first found in all launcher classes declared in its manifest file(See Fig 4). In this case, APKLancet finds *DroidJumpActivity* is the proper candidate and defines it as the new main entry point class. Further analysis shows that the inserted malicious entry point class will first perform its own function, and then starts the *DroidJumpActivity* class. The code fragments selected from several smali files to illustrate the behavior of launching the original entry point is showed as followed(code fragment of exception handler part is omitted):

```
AdService.smali:
...
  const-string v0,
    "com.electricsheep.dj.DroidJumpActivity"
  sput-object v0,
    Lcom/geinimi/AdService;->a:Ljava/lang/String;
...

AdActivity.smali:
...
  sget-object v1,
    Lcom/geinimi/AdService;->a:Ljava/lang/String;
  invoke-static {v1}, Ljava/lang/Class;->
    forName(Ljava/lang/String;)Ljava/lang/Class;
  move-result-object v0
  new-instance v1, Landroid/content/Intent;
  invoke-direct {v1, p0, v0},
    Landroid/content/Intent;->
      <init>(Landroid/content/Context;Ljava/lang/Class;)V
  invoke-virtual {p0, v1},
    Lcom/geinimi/AdActivity;->
      startActivity(Landroid/content/Intent;)V
...
```

It proves that APKLancet's fixing policy effectively recovers the original entry point.

4.4 Case Study III: AdMob and Flurry

In this subsection, two popular third-party libraries, *AdMob* and *Flurry*, are studied to illustrate the effectiveness of APKLancet's purification. Actually *AdMob* and *Flurry* are benign third-party ad libraries, but they may be injected into legitimate apps by attackers for profit. What's more, they are typical full functional third-party ad libraries and thus are good cases for demonstrating the excision process and evaluating the purification.

The case for illustrating *AdMob* purification is an app whose package name is *com.xuecs.sqlitemanager*. APKLancet lists the class *AdView* as index classes in the feature database and identifies the whole package of *com.google.ads.**, which contains the index class, as tumor payload. Then APKLancet resects all the method invoking and object references from the benign code to the tumor code, including 3 *invoke* instructions with the same pattern, 1 object reference and several further dependent instructions in benign code. For the case of *Flurry*, the sample is an app *com.electricsheep.dj*. Also, APKLancet constructs the feature database by listing *FlurryAgent* as index class and then resects the tumor payload *com.flurry.android.**. After that, APKLancet searches the benign code and finds several method invoking instructions related to tumor payload, including *onStartSession*, *onEvent*, *onEndSession*, etc.

One problem of the ad libraries purification is that Java class is often referred in resource files (i.e., layout XML or manifest). And this kind of information is not fixed and cannot be detected with the knowledge of feature database. For instacne, in *main.xml* file an *AdMob*'s *AdView* element is referred as:

```
<com.admob.android.ads.AdView android:id="@id/ad"
    android:layout_width="fill_parent"
    android:layout_height="48.0dip"
    admobsdk:backgroundColor="#ff00b8f5"
    admobsdk:textColor="#ffffffff"
    admobsdk:keywords="Android game droid jump" />
```

To solve this issue, the analysis of APKLancet for tumor payload not only deals with reference in code part but also in resource part. The patching of resource files is relatively easy because APKLancet could resect this kind of declaration directly.

5. LIMITATIONS

In this paper we do not focus on identifying the repackaged app which have been extensively studied[25]. One essential requirement for the repackaging detection is that the detection needs the knowledge of the original app. Actually, there is no one-size-fits-all approach to find the knowledge of the original app. It seems that the certificate of an APK could help identify its provenance. The problem is that Android allows either a certificate from the certificate authority or a self-signed certificate. Thus it is not able to trust an APK only through the certificate. Best practice suggests that Google Play is the trust source for validating APK. But even some APKs on Google Play are also repackaged version of other applications. And not all of the applications can be found on Google Play. Actually in China some famous applications(e.g., WeChat with more than 500 million users) cannot even be downloaded from Google Play. Thus, Our

```xml
<application android:label="@string/app_name" android:icon="@drawable/icon">
    <activity android:theme="@*android:style/Theme.NoTitleBar.Fullscreen" android:label="@string/app_name"
    android:name=".DroidJumpActivity" android:screenOrientation="portrait">
        <intent-filter>
            <category android:name="android.intent.category.LAUNCHER" />
        </intent-filter>
    </activity>
    <activity android:label="@string/app_name" android:name=".SettingsActivity" android:screenOrientation="
    portrait" />
    <meta-data android:name="ADMOB_PUBLISHER_ID" android:value="a14b5c886f95c4c" />
    <activity android:theme="@*android:style/Theme.NoTitleBar.Fullscreen" android:name="GameActivity"
    android:screenOrientation="portrait" />
    <receiver android:name="com.geinimi.AdServiceReceiver">
        <intent-filter>
            <action android:name="android.intent.action.BOOT_COMPLETED" />
            <category android:name="android.intent.category.LAUNCHER" />
        </intent-filter>
    </receiver>
    <service android:enabled="true" android:name="com.geinimi.AdService" android:permission="android.
    permission.INTERNET" />
    <activity android:label="@string/app_name" android:name="com.geinimi.custom.Ad1020_102001">
        <intent-filter>
            <action android:name="android.intent.action.MAIN" />
            <category android:name="android.intent.category.LAUNCHER" />
        </intent-filter>
    </activity>
</application>
```

Figure 4: Main Entry Point Fixing

APKLancet system focuses on the tumor payload ignoring whether it is a repackaged app or not. APKLancet adopts the policy of splitting any unrelated modules and resecting them to assure the security.

Since our work does not include repackaging detection, we do not distinguish whether the third-party libraries such as ad libraries are imported by the original developers or injected by malicious authors. We argue that the choice of purification of third-party libraries should depend on the end user. APKLancet hence just prompts the existence of any potentially unwanted ad library based on the permissions it requires, and the end user may decide whether to resect it or not.

Our work assumes that the tumor code is embedded as a module not closely interweaving with the host app. Although this assumption stands in most cases, some undesirable behaviors may still remains inside the application if the tumor code author binds the tumor code with the benign function cautiously. However this may not happen frequently for the cost is generally very high(a profitless work seldom lasts). What's more, we purify the apps according to the index classes in feature database, so benign apps that generally do not include the index classes will not be affect by APKLancet.

Finally, this work does not focus on the detection of malware. Our APKLancet relies on the tumor payload feature database built on existing knowledge of the undesirable code. As a result, APKLancet could only deal with the analyzed malicious tumor payload, and because APKLancet is mainly a static analysis based system, it is not able to control the dynamically loaded code. However, the goal of APKLancet is only to purify the application with undesirable code so that it is good enough to be used again. It adopts conservative strategy to only deal with apps that it can be purified. It is a simple but effective approach to prevent the known malicious tumor payload. APKLancet may not able to purify any tumor payload perfectly, but it helps deal with the known ones and can co-operate with other access control system to counter other unknown undesirable code.

6. RELATED WORK

6.1 Malware Analysis

Previous work on tumor payload analysis has mainly focused on malicious code analysis. Automated analysis tools are also developed to help detect malicious code and different evaluation schemes are adopted. **DroidRanger**[25] detects malicious applications by using both permission-based behavioral footprint and heuristics-based filtering scheme. **RiskRanker**[13] performs large-scale security risk analysis for zero-day malware detection. Researchers have also systematically characterize Android malwares from various aspects including installation methods, activation mechanisms as well as the nature of carried malicious payload[24].

Our study does not lead to malware detection. The purpose is to resect the tumor payload with the help of existing summarized knowledge. On one hand, malware detection and analysis contribute a lot to tumor payload identification. On the other hand, our APKLancet system pays attention to tumor payload, which contains not only malicious code but also potentially risky third-party libraries. It needs to address challenges brought by tumor payload purifying and host apps fixing.

Our work is the first to measure the effectiveness of tumor payload purification. Although our work relies on existing knowledge of tumor code, we believe that most tumor payload in repackaged applications are not novel, especially for its injection style.

6.2 Repackaging Detection

Tumor payload detection and analysis is closely connected to the problem of detecting repackaged legitimate app, which is often injected with malicious payload. Studies vary from pair-wise comparison to scalable detection. **DNADroid**[8] computes the similarity between two Android applications by comparing program dependency graph to detect application copying and cloning. And **DroidMOSS**[23] systematically detects repackaged apps on third-party Android marketplaces by applying fuzzy hashing technique to measure an app's similarity and then compares apps in pair. **AnDarwin**[9] uses a scalable approach rather than comparing apps pairwise to detect similar Android applications based on semantic information. **PiggyApp**[22] scalably detects *piggybacked* Android applications by organizing various feature vectors from apps into a metric space and applying line-arithmic search algorithm. The prior works mainly focus on the similarity of the repackaged app and the original one, while our work assumes that the target of our system contains not only the repackaged apps but also some apps with tumor payload injected by their authors. In this case, APKLancet can deal with the tumor payload without the support of the reference app.

6.3 Advertisement Splitting

Advertisement is controversial in Android app. An ad library embedded in an app may send information about the device and user to the ad server, thus raising concerns about user privacy. Studies suggest isolating the advertising or even separating it from the application process.

AdSplit[18] extends Android to separate advertising from applications and leverage QUIRE's mechanisms to let the remote server validate the authenticity of client-side behavior. **AFrame**[21] provides a developer a friendly method to isolate untrusted third-party code from the host applications including process, permission, display and input isolation. **AdDroid**[17] introduces a new advertising API and corresponding advertising permissions to separate privileged advertising functionality from host applications. All of these schemes require to extend the Android system trying to separate advertisement from host apps. In comparison, APKLancet does not need to modify the Android system and introduces no performance latency.

6.4 App Rewriting

Many fine-grained permission control systems use application rewriting technique to implement sensitive API invoking management. **Aurasium**[20] repackages applications to attach user-level sandboxing and policy enforcement code for the aim of monitoring applications' behavior about security and privacy violation. **In-App Reference Monitors**(I-ARM)[10] rewrites the Dalvik bytecode of applications to enforce the security policies the framework users specified towards a set of security-sensitive API methods. **Dr. Android**[15] introduces a novel framework to address the issue that many applications are allowed broader access than required by adding finer-grained permissions. APKLancet also rewrites the app. But instead of adding instrumentation code or extra libraries to monitor the behavior of the app, it directly resects the undesirable part to enforce access control policy, which is more concise.

7. CONCLUSION

Android apps are vulnerable to repackaging attack and the undesirable code (tumor code) bundling is becoming a popular way of spreading malicious behavior. Based on the fact that the tumor code in Android APK is usually characteristic and relatively independent in the app, it is possible to resect the tumor from the original APK. In this paper, we propose an effective tumor code diagnosis and purification system called APKLancet. It consists of three components, the APK analyzer, APK rewriter and APK verifier, and carries out the workflow by four stages: 1) diagnosing the tumor code relying on an existing knowledge database, 2) partitioning the tumor payload from the host app, 3) excision of the tumor code and restoring the benign function, and 4) verifying the app's benign function. APKLancet has been applied to apps with typical tumor payloads and our analysis indicates that it is feasible to defend the undesirable behaviors through app's purification.

8. ACKNOWLEDGEMENT

This work is supported by National Natural Science Foundation of China (No.61103040), National Science and Technology Major Projects (Grant No.2012ZX03002011), and Technology Innovation Project of Shanghai Science and Technology Commission (No.13511504000). We also appreciate Wenjun Hu, the author of SandDroid[6], for providing the valuable malware samples.

9. REFERENCES

[1] 1.2 percent of google play store is thief-ware, study shows. `http://tinyurl.com/kvf7xvc`. Online; accessed Nov-2013.

[2] Ad networks - android library statistics. `http://www.appbrain.com/stats/libraries/ad`.

[3] Ad vulna: A vulnaggressive (vulnerable & aggressive) adware threatening millions. `http://tinyurl.com/pv4wts3`. Online; accessed Nov-2013.

[4] android-apktool, a tool for reverse engineering android apk files. `http://code.google.com/p/android-apktool/`. Online; accessed Nov-2013.

[5] Android torch app with over 50m downloads silently sent user location and device data to advertisers. `http://tinyurl.com/mhfyv3r`. Online; accessed Nov-2013.

[6] Sanddroid - an automatic android program analysis sandbox. `http://sanddroid.xjtu.edu.cn/`. Online; accessed Nov-2013.

[7] Virustotal - free online virus, malware and url scanner. `https://www.virustotal.com/` note = Online; accessed Nov-2013,.

[8] J. Crussell, C. Gibler, and H. Chen. Attack of the clones: Detecting cloned applications on android markets. In *Computer Security–ESORICS 2012*, pages 37–54. Springer, 2012.

[9] J. Crussell, C. Gibler, and H. Chen. Andarwin: Scalable detection of semantically similar android applications. In *Computer Security–ESORICS 2013*, pages 182–199. Springer, 2013.

[10] B. Davis, B. Sanders, A. Khodaverdian, and H. Chen. I-arm-droid: A rewriting framework for in-app reference monitors for android applications. *Mobile Security Technologies*, 2012, 2012.

[11] A. Desnos. Androguard: Reverse engineering, malware and goodware analysis of android applications... and more (ninja!).

[12] A. P. Felt, M. Finifter, E. Chin, S. Hanna, and D. Wagner. A survey of mobile malware in the wild.

In *Proceedings of the 1st ACM workshop on Security and privacy in smartphones and mobile devices*, pages 3–14. ACM, 2011.

[13] M. Grace, Y. Zhou, Q. Zhang, S. Zou, and X. Jiang. Riskranker: scalable and accurate zero-day android malware detection. In *Proceedings of the 10th international conference on Mobile systems, applications, and services*, pages 281–294. ACM, 2012.

[14] S. Hanna, L. Huang, E. Wu, S. Li, C. Chen, and D. Song. Juxtapp: a scalable system for detecting code reuse among android applications. In *Detection of Intrusions and Malware, and Vulnerability Assessment*, pages 62–81. Springer, 2013.

[15] J. Jeon, K. K. Micinski, J. A. Vaughan, A. Fogel, N. Reddy, J. S. Foster, and T. Millstein. Dr. android and mr. hide: fine-grained permissions in android applications. In *Proceedings of the second ACM workshop on Security and privacy in smartphones and mobile devices*, pages 3–14. ACM, 2012.

[16] K. Kennedy, E. Gustafson, and H. Chen. Quantifying the effects of removing permissions from android applications.

[17] P. Pearce, A. P. Felt, G. Nunez, and D. Wagner. Addroid: Privilege separation for applications and advertisers in android. In *Proceedings of the 7th ACM Symposium on Information, Computer and Communications Security*, pages 71–72. ACM, 2012.

[18] S. Shekhar, M. Dietz, and D. S. Wallach. Adsplit: Separating smartphone advertising from applications. *CoRR, abs/1202.4030*, 2012.

[19] G. Suarez-Tangil, J. Tapiador, P. Peris-Lopez, and A. Ribagorda. Evolution, detection and analysis of malware for smart devices. 2013.

[20] R. Xu, H. Saïdi, and R. Anderson. Aurasium: Practical policy enforcement for android applications. In *Proceedings of the 21st USENIX Security Symposium*, 2012.

[21] X. Zhang, A. Ahlawat, and W. Du. Aframe: Isolating advertisements from mobile applications in android. 2013.

[22] W. Zhou, Y. Zhou, M. Grace, X. Jiang, and S. Zou. Fast, scalable detection of piggybacked mobile applications. In *Proceedings of the third ACM conference on Data and application security and privacy*, pages 185–196. ACM, 2013.

[23] W. Zhou, Y. Zhou, X. Jiang, and P. Ning. Detecting repackaged smartphone applications in third-party android marketplaces. In *Proceedings of the second ACM conference on Data and Application Security and Privacy*, pages 317–326. ACM, 2012.

[24] Y. Zhou and X. Jiang. Dissecting android malware: Characterization and evolution. In *Security and Privacy (SP), 2012 IEEE Symposium on*, pages 95–109. IEEE, 2012.

[25] Y. Zhou, Z. Wang, W. Zhou, and X. Jiang. Hey, you, get off of my market: Detecting malicious apps in official and alternative android markets. In *Proceedings of the 19th Annual Network and Distributed System Security Symposium*, 2012.

How Many Down? Toward Understanding Systematic Risk in Networks

Benjamin Johnson
University of California, Berkeley

Aron Laszka
Budapest University of Technology and Economics

Jens Grossklags
The Pennsylvania State University

ABSTRACT

The systematic risk of a networked system depends to a large extent on its topology. In this paper, we explore this dependency using a model of risk propagation from the literature on interdependent security games. Our main area of focus is on the number of nodes that go down after an attack takes place. We develop a simulation algorithm to study the effects of such attacks on arbitrary topologies, and apply this simulation to scale-free networks. We investigate by graphical illustration how the outcome distribution of such networks exhibits correlation effects that increase the likelihood of losing more nodes at once – an effect having direct applications to cyber-insurance.

Categories and Subject Descriptors

K.6.m [**Management of Computer and Information Systems**]: Miscellaneous—*Security, Insurance*; C.2.0 [**Computer Communication Networks**]: General—*Security and protection*

General Terms

Security, Economics, Measurement, Management, Theory

Keywords

Networks, Security, Topology, Cyber-insurance, Risk Mitigation, Economics of Security, Scale-Free Networks

1. INTRODUCTION

Researchers across the spectrum from industry, government, and academia have struggled for years to understand and remedy market failures in the cyber-insurance industry. These failures serve to motivate a tremendous need for a better understanding of systematic risk for real-world networks.

ASIA CCS'14, June 4–6, 2014, Kyoto, Japan.

http://dx.doi.org/10.1145/2590296.2590308.

One reason for these market failures is a lack of good data,[1] but this is certainly not the only problem. Risk correlation and interdependency combine together in networked systems to make understanding the problem hard. For example, risks to two different networked individuals can be highly correlated, due to vulnerabilities in a shared common platform, or due to a shared communication channel, or for a variety of other reasons. This problem is further exacerbated by misaligned incentives whereby network-benefiting security practices may not be cost-effective for some individuals.

This paper aims to address this problem by analyzing the systematic risk of a networked system that is subject to both direct risks based on individual investments, and indirect risks based on the network's topology. By *systematic risk*, we mean vulnerability to events which cause catastrophic losses, for example, a very large number of individuals in the network being compromised. Systematic risks are of special interest to cyber-insurers because, in contrast to non-systematic risks, they cannot be diversified by having a sufficiently large portfolio.

Our risk propagation model is borrowed from the literature on interdependent security games, where it has been used primarily to study the incentives of individuals within a networked system. Our focus here is rather on the state of the entire networked system. In particular, we are interested in understanding the distribution on the number of lost nodes within a network after an attack occurs.

To evaluate this focus, we implement a simulation algorithm that approximates the loss distribution for an arbitrary network topology. We then apply this simulation to randomly-generated scale-free networks. We find that the loss distribution derived from this topology differs significantly from the binomial distribution (i.e., the distribution that we would see if the risks to individuals were independent). Quantifying the risk in this scenario has applications for cyber-insurance.

The rest of the paper is organized as follows. In Section 2, we discuss related work. Section 3 describes our network risk model, which comes from the literature on interdependent security games. In Section 4, we apply a risk simulation based on our model to randomly-generated scale-free networks, and discuss the corresponding applications to cyber-insurance. Finally, Section 5 concludes the paper.

[1] Industry specialists gain valuable information from cybersecurity incident reporting. But these data may suffer from selection bias, and for a variety of reasons many incidents go unreported [13].

2. RELATED WORK

Our work is relevant to the fields of cyber-insurance, and security in networked systems. We also utilize insights from studies about the network structure of real-world networks. We review important works in these areas in the following subsections.

2.1 Cyber-insurance

A functioning market for cyber-insurance and a good understanding of the insurability of networked resources are both important, because they signal that stakeholders are able to manage modern threats that cause widespread damage across many systems [1, 6]. However, the market for cyber-insurance is developing at a frustratingly slow pace due to several complicating factors, which are discussed in the detailed review of the security economics and cyber-insurance literature by Böhme and Schwartz [8]. The outlined key challenges and the progress made by academics in addressing them serve as important motivators for our work.

A group of defenders might appear as a particularly appealing target to an attacker because of a high correlation in the risk profiles of the defended resources. For example, even though systems may be independently owned and administrated, they may exhibit similar software configurations leading to so-called monoculture risks [5]. Böhme and Kataria study the impact of correlation that is readily observable for an insurer, and found that the resulting insurance premiums to make the risks insurable would likely endanger a market for cyber-insurance [7]. Chen et al. study correlated risks by endogenizing node failure distribution and node correlation distribution [10]. In their work, they allow for different risk mitigation measures, but do not consider the impact on the insurability of risks, or different cases of interdependence.

Our research is complementary to the studies cited above: they investigate (the effect of) correlations arising from nodes having the same software configurations, while we study how correlations arise from nodes being connected to each other.

2.2 Security in Networked Systems

The problem of interdependence in networked systems has been considered in a variety of different ways in the academic literature [22]. Varian, for example, studies security compromises that result from the failure of independently-owned systems to contribute to an overall prevention objective (i.e., security is a public good) [29]. In this model, security compromises are often the result of misaligned incentives which manifest as coordination failures, such as free-riding on others' prevention investments. Grossklags et al. extend this work to allow for investments in system recovery (i.e., self-insurance) and find that it can serve as a viable investment strategy to sidestep such coordination failures [14]. However, the availability of system recovery will further undermine incentives for collective security investments. Johnson et al. add the availability of cyber-insurance to this modeling framework, and identify solution spaces in which these different investment approaches may be used as bundled security strategies [16].

A second group of economic models derives equilibrium strategies for containing the propagation of a virus or an attack in a network. For example, the models by Aspnes et al. as well as Moscibroda et al. would be applicable to the study of loss distributions; however, several simplifying assumptions in those models limit the generality of the results [2, 26]. Those limitations include the assumption that every infected node deterministically infects all unprotected neighbors.

A third class of propagation models that has been widely studied is the class of epidemic models, which describe how a virus spreads or extinguishes in a network. In the literature on epidemic models, the results of Kephart and White [20] are the closest to our analysis. Kephart and White study one of the simplest of the standard epidemic models, the susceptible-infected-susceptible (SIS) model, using various classes of networks.

Finally, a popular approach to model interdependent risk is taken by Kunreuther and Heal, and forms the basis for our formal analysis [15, 21]. The basic premise of this work is to separately consider the impact of direct attacks and propagated attacks. We explain the details of the model in Section 3. The model has been generalized to consider distributions of attack probabilities [17] and strategic attackers [9]. Similarly, Ogut et al. proposed a related model that allows for continuous (rather than binary) security investments [27]. Our model draws from these extensions by implicitly considering a continuum of risk parameters to study the distribution of outcomes.

2.3 Real-World Networks

The Internet and many other real-world networks have been shown to be scale-free [3]. For example, several studies have measured and made attempts to characterize properties of online social networks. Mislove et al. [25] studied a dataset with over 10 million nodes and over 300 million links to characterize properties of Flickr, YouTube, LiveJournal, and Orkut. They confirmed power law and scale free properties of these networks. More recent work has concentrated on Facebook, today's most popular online social networking platform (e.g., [12]). More generally, a scale-free network's degree distribution is a scale-free power law distribution, which is generally attributed to robust self-organizing phenomena. Recent interest in scale-free networks started with [4], in which the Barabási-Albert (BA) model is introduced for generating random scale-free networks. The BA model is based on two concepts: network growth and preferential node attachment. Li et al. introduce a new, mathematically more precise, and structural definition of "scale-free" graphs [24], which promises to offer a more rigorous and quantitative alternative. The networks discussed in our paper satisfy this definition as well.

3. MODEL OVERVIEW

Our modeling framework is grounded in a set of models introduced by Kunreuther and Heal [15, 21] in the context of interdependent security games. These models supply a mechanism for nodes in a network to be attacked, and to attack their immediate neighbors. The primary motivating purpose of these models and their myriad of extensions [9, 11, 17, 19] has been to understand what motivates networked individuals to invest in security.

Our focus in this paper differs from prior work in that we concentrate primarily on the inter-node risk transfer mechanism as opposed to individual operator decisions. Our research questions are to understand the factors contributing to the loss of a catastrophically large number of nodes, and to assess the probabilities with which these bad events may happen.

The Kunreuther–Heal risk propagation structure provides a convenient mechanism to address these questions. In this regime, each network node is exposed to risk from two different types of attacks – external and internal. A successful external attack results in a complete compromise of the node, allowing the node to attack its neighbors. A successful internal attack can results in the complete failure of a node but it does not allow the failed node to attack its neighbors.

3.1 Network Risk Model

More formally, consider a network of size N. Each node is connected to its neighbors and also to an outside system such as the internet. We thus divide threats against nodes into two types – those that originate from outside the network, and those that originate from within the network.

If a node is successfully attacked from outside the network, then the node becomes an attacker; while if a node is successfully attacked from within the network, it is simply damaged. We do not directly model the attacker in this framework. Rather, attacks occur probabilistically. An external attack against node i succeeds with probability p_i. If node i is compromised by an external attack, then q_{ij} is the conditional probability that an attack by node i against node j succeeds.

3.2 Loss Distribution

Once a set of attacks happen with their respective probabilities, we are interested in the aftermath from the perspective of the whole network. That is, we want to know how many total nodes went down from this attack.

To formalize this, let NL be the random variable that counts the total number of compromised nodes in an outcome of the model. Then we define the *loss distribution* as a set of $N+1$ numbers giving $\Pr[NL = k]$ for $k = 0, \ldots, N$.

3.3 Simulation

To compute a probability distribution on these outcomes, we use simulation. The simulation repeatedly chooses outcomes from a simulated attack following the external and internal attack success probabilities. The simulation proceeds as follows:

- For each node i, decide whether node i is directly compromised (or not) at random according to p_i.
- For each externally compromised node i, and for each of its non-compromised neighbors j, decide whether node i successfully attacks node j at random according to q_{ij}.
- Count the total number of nodes that have been compromised and call this the outcome. Add 1 to the number of occurrences of this outcome.
- After the empirical distribution becomes Cauchy within some epsilon, or after a fixed number of iterations, terminate the simulation and, for each outcome, output the number of occurrences over the number of iterations as the empirical probability of that outcome.

The running time of the simulation is polynomial in the size of the network, given a constant number of iterations. Furthermore, we know from the strong law of large numbers that this simulation converges to the actual function almost surely. To verify that the simulation is working, we randomly generated scale free networks using the Barabási-Albert (BA) model [4], and ran the simulation with varying number of iterations. In each case, the shape of the distribution settled down to a smooth form within a few tens of thousands of iterations.

Figure 1 shows a series of simulated distributions using a single network and with varying numbers of iterations. As can be seen from the figure, once the number of iterations is sufficiently high, the empirical distribution reaches a fixed state.

4. SCALE-FREE NETWORKS

The BA model generates scale-free graphs in stages, based on the principle of preferential attachment, meaning that the degrees of nodes with high degrees tend to get even higher as the graph grows. The parameters of the model are the initial clique size m_0, the number of edges added at each stage m, and the total size of the graph N. An instance of a graph with these parameters is constructed randomly as follows. We first initialize with a clique of $m_0 > m$ nodes. The remaining $N - m_0$ nodes are added one at a time, with each new node being randomly connected to m existing nodes with probabilities proportional to the degrees of the existing nodes.

4.1 Simulation Results

We study the risk of scale-free networks using various metrics. For each network, we compute the mean $E[NL]$, the variance $Var(NL)$, and the value of the quantile function Q_{NL} for probability 99.9%. In probability theory, the quantile function (also called the inverse cumulative distribution function) of a random variable gives, for a probability p, the lowest value such that the outcome of the random variable is less than or equal to the value with probability p. This value will play an important role in our cyber-insurance application example.

Besides comparing the loss distributions of various networks to each other, we also compare them to loss distributions without any interdependence effects. To derive loss distributions without interdependence effects, we assume that node compromises are completely independent events. In other words, we use binomial distributions with population size N for the comparisons. Finally, to make the comparisons fair, we set the mean of each binomial distribution equal to the mean of the actual distribution. Formally, we use the binomial distribution $B(\frac{E[NL]}{N}, N)$.

First, we study the effects of varying the compromise probabilities p and q. Figure 2 and Table 1 show the actual loss distributions and the corresponding binomial distributions for various internal and external compromise probability values. In each case, the network consists of $N = 500$ nodes, and it was generated using the B-A model with parameters $m_0 = 15$ and $m = 4$. We see that, for lower internal probabilities, the relationship between external compromise probability and the mean of total loss is roughly linear. For the other metrics, the relationships to the probabilities seem much less predictable.

By comparing the actual loss distributions to binomial distributions, we see a huge difference in variability. This means that, as expected, interdependence in networks causes

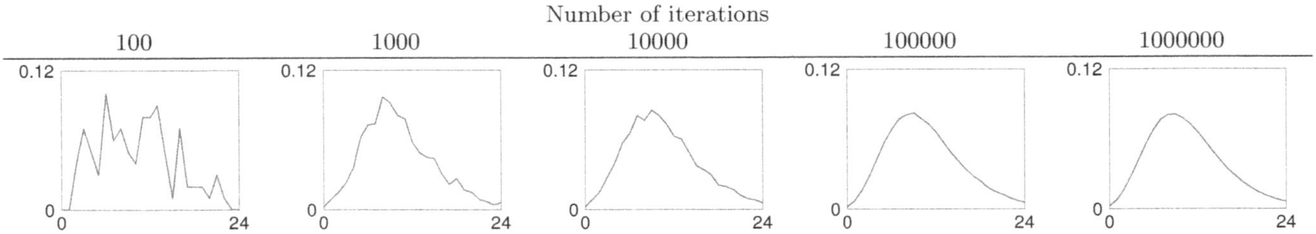

Figure 1: Loss distributions obtained from simulations with various numbers of iterations.

Table 1: Comparison of the actual loss distribution to the binomial distribution for various direct compromise and propagation probabilities, and constant network size $N = 500$.

p	q	$E[NL]$	Variance $Var(NL)$ actual	Variance $Var(NL)$ binomial	Quantile $Q_{NL}(0.999)$ actual	Quantile $Q_{NL}(0.999)$ binomial
0.005	0.025	3.01	4.25	2.99	12	10
	0.05	3.51	6.51	3.49	15	10
	0.1	4.52	12.45	4.48	22	12
	0.2	6.51	29.80	6.43	35	16
	0.4	10.42	84.54	10.21	59	22
0.01	0.025	6.01	8.43	5.94	17	15
	0.05	7.01	12.81	6.92	22	16
	0.1	9.00	24.28	8.84	30	19
	0.2	12.91	56.92	12.58	47	25
	0.4	20.46	156.24	19.62	77	35
0.02	0.025	11.99	16.49	11.70	27	24
	0.05	13.97	24.85	13.58	33	27
	0.1	17.85	46.10	17.21	44	32
	0.2	25.39	104.48	24.10	66	42
	0.4	39.58	270.16	36.45	105	59

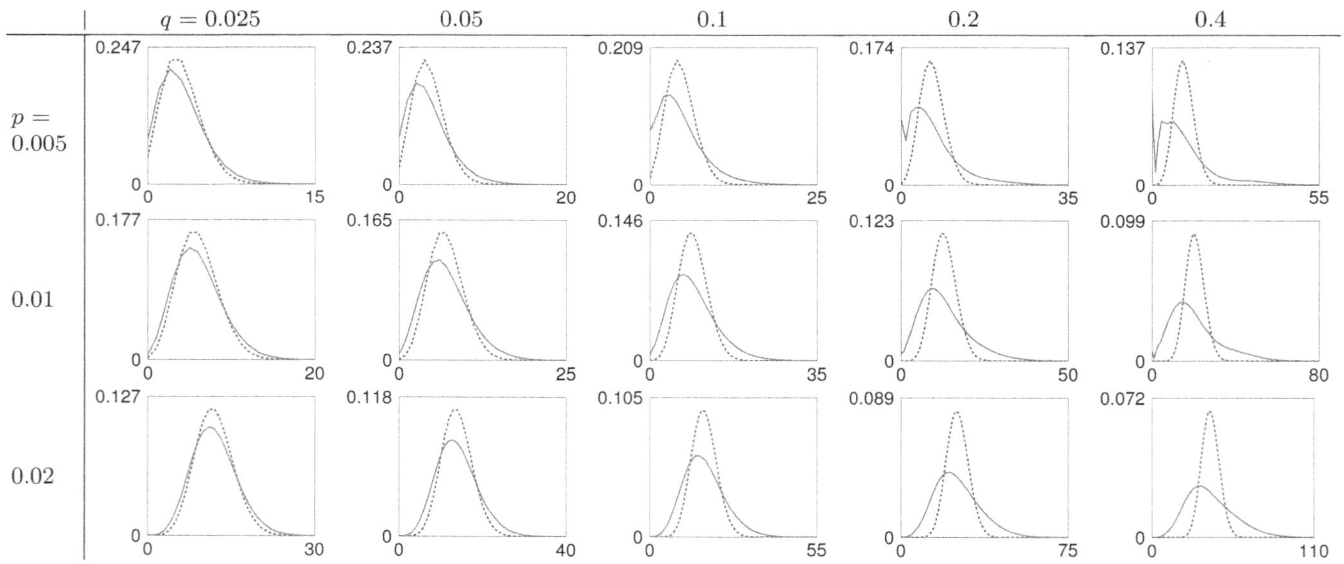

Figure 2: Comparison of the actual loss distribution (solid red) to the binomial distribution (dotted green) for various direct compromise and propagation probabilities, and constant network size $N = 500$. (Note that the slightly irregular subfigures for $p = 0.005$ and $q = 0.2$ or $q = 0.4$ are correctly drawn.)

high systematic risk. Furthermore, we see that increasing internal compromise probability has a much higher impact on systematic risk than increasing external compromise probability. Again, this is unsurprising, since internal compromises model the interdependence between the nodes, while external compromises model independent events.

Second, we study the effects of varying the size N of the network. Figure 3 and Table 2 show the actual loss dis-

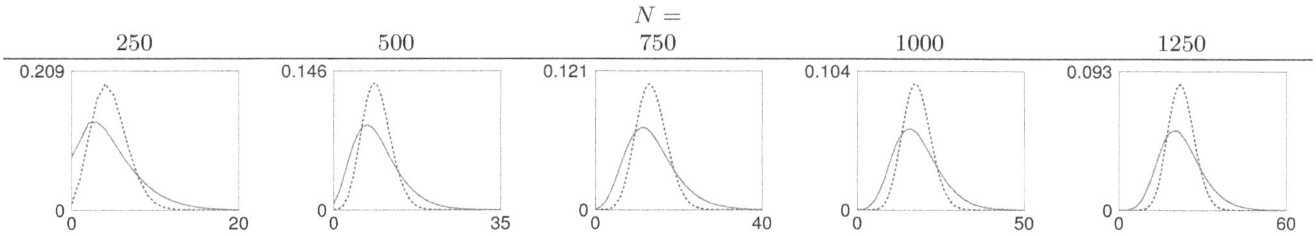

Figure 3: Comparison of the actual loss distribution (solid red) to the binomial distribution (dotted green) for various network sizes and constant $p = 0.01$, $q = 0.1$.

Table 2: Comparison of the actual loss distribution to the binomial distribution for various network sizes and constant $p = 0.01$, $q = 0.1$.

N	$E[NL]$	Var. $Var(NL)$		Quant. $Q_{NL}(0.999)$	
		actual	binomial	actual	binomial
250	4.55	12.13	4.46	21	12
500	9.01	23.98	8.84	30	19
750	13.45	37.16	13.21	39	26
1000	17.92	49.56	17.60	47	32
1250	22.37	61.75	21.97	55	38

tributions and the corresponding binomial distributions for various network sizes. In each case, the internal and external compromise probabilities are $p = 0.01$ and $q = 0.1$, and the network was generated using the B-A model with the same parameters as for the previous figure and table. The main observation here is that systematic risk does not disappear as the size of the network increases. This can be observed in both the figure and the table, which show that the difference between the actual loss distributions and the binomial distributions does not diminish. For example, the ratio between the variance of the actual distribution and the binomial distribution remains around 2.77 (more precisely, the ratios are 2.72, 2.71, 2.81, 2.82, and 2.81). In the following subsection, we will show that this has important implications for the viability of cyber-insurance.

4.2 Cyber-Insurance Example

The viability of cyber-insurance – just like any other insurance – depends on the diversifiability of risks. Diversifiability means that, in a large set of entities, the individual risks of the entities cancel out, and the aggregate risk of the whole set is relatively low. More specifically, for a sufficiently large set of entities, it is very unlikely that the total loss is much higher than its expected value, even when the individual entities themselves are very risky. In a competitive market, the diversifiability of risks leads to insurance premiums that are only marginally higher than the expected loss. Here, we show that underestimating the systematic risk of networked systems can have catastrophic consequences for an insurance provider, which highlights the importance of studying systematic risk.

Suppose that an insurer plans to provide coverage to a set of $N = 500$ networked entities, whose external and internal compromise probabilities are $p = 0.01$ and $q = 0.1$. We assume that the insurance provider is able to measure the average probability of a node being compromised, which is equal to $E[NL]/N = 1.8\%$ in this example. In practice, the insurer can obtain this value by randomly choosing nodes and measuring their probability of being compromised. On the other hand, the insurance provider is unable to learn the topology of the network, since this would require detailed data collection from a large number of nodes. Note that, for learning the network topology, random sampling is not a viable solution either [28].

To avoid bankruptcy, the insurance premiums are chosen so that the total losses exceed the sum of the premiums with only a very low probability, which is called the probability of ruin. Let us assume that the highest probability of ruin that an insurance provider can tolerate is 0.1%. Then, in the above example, the sum of the premiums has to be at least $Q_{NL}(0.999) = 30$ (see the actual quantile in Table 1). Now, consider an insurance provider who underestimates systematic risk, and assumes that individual risks are mostly independent. Based on this assumption, the insurer will calculate an incorrect sum premium $Q_{NL}(0.999) = 19$ (see the binomial quantile in Table 1). The consequences of this mistake can be catastrophic, as the probability of ruin for the incorrect sum premium is $\Pr[NL > 19] = 3.3\%$, more than 30 times the intended value.

5. CONCLUSIONS AND FUTURE WORK

Systematic risks in networked systems depend on both the network's topology and the security levels of individual nodes. In this work, we explored the loss outcomes of a model in which nodes face both external and internal risks. Applying the model to randomly generated scale-free networks, we found that the risk of catastrophe was substantially higher than if the node compromises were independent events, yielding an application to cyber-insurance.

Alongside this introductory work are many key questions, some of which we have already begun to study. The computational complexity of computing loss distributions for various classes of networks is addressed in [18]. Methods for better extrapolating the correct risk portfolio of a network from sample data on subnets are addressed in [23]. An important remaining research goal is to develop mechanisms for a cyber-insurer to estimate the direct risks of compromise and the probabilities of internode risk transfer for relevant real-world networks.

Acknowledgements: We thank the reviewers for their comments on an earlier draft of the paper. We gratefully acknowledge the support of the Penn State Institute for CyberScience and the National Science Foundation under ITR award CCF-0424422 (TRUST). In addition, this research was partially sponsored by the Army Research Laboratory and was partially accomplished under Cooperative

Agreement Number W911NF-13-2-0045 (ARL Cyber Security CRA). The views and conclusions contained in this document are those of the authors and should not be interpreted as representing the official policies, either expressed or implied, of the Army Research Laboratory or the U.S. Government. The U.S. Government is authorized to reproduce and distribute reprints for Government purposes notwithstanding any copyright notation here on.

6. REFERENCES

[1] R. Anderson. Liability and computer security: Nine principles. In *Proceedings of the Third European Symposium on Research in Computer Security (ESORICS)*, pages 231–245, Nov. 1994.

[2] J. Aspnes, K. Chang, and A. Yampolskiy. Inoculation strategies for victims of viruses and the sum-of-squares partition problem. *Journal of Computer and System Sciences*, 72(6):1077–1093, Sept. 2006.

[3] A.-L. Barabási. Scale-free networks: A decade and beyond. *Science*, 325(5939):412–413, July 2009.

[4] A.-L. Barabási and R. Albert. Emergence of scaling in random networks. *Science*, 286(5439):509–512, Oct. 1999.

[5] K. Birman and F. Schneider. The monoculture risk put into context. *IEEE Security and Privacy*, 7(1):14–17, Jan. 2009.

[6] R. Böhme. Towards insurable network architectures. *it - Information Technology*, 52(5):290–293, Sept. 2010.

[7] R. Böhme and G. Kataria. Models and measures for correlation in cyber-insurance. In *Workshop on the Economics of Information Security*, June 2006.

[8] R. Böhme and G. Schwartz. Modeling cyber-insurance: Towards a unifying framework. In *Workshop on the Economics of Information Security*, June 2010.

[9] H. Chan, M. Ceyko, and L. Ortiz. Interdependent defense games: Modeling interdependent security under deliberate attacks. In *Proceedings of the Twenty-Eighth Conference on Uncertainty in Artificial Intelligence (UAI)*, pages 152–162, Aug. 2012.

[10] P.-Y. Chen, G. Kataria, and R. Krishnan. Correlated failures, diversification, and information security risk management. *MIS Quarterly*, 35(2):397–422, June 2011.

[11] S. Dhall, S. Lakshmivarahan, and P. Verma. On the number and the distribution of the Nash equilibria in supermodular games and their impact on the tipping set. In *Proceedings of the International Conference on Game Theory for Networks (GameNets)*, pages 691–696, May 2009.

[12] M. Gjoka, M. Kurant, C. Butts, and A. Markopoulou. Practical recommendations on crawling online social networks. *IEEE Journal on Selected Areas in Communications*, 29(9):1872–1892, Oct. 2011.

[13] L. Gordon, M. Loeb, and W. Lucyshyn. Sharing information on computer systems security: An economic analysis. *Journal of Accounting and Public Policy*, 22(6):461–485, November–December 2003.

[14] J. Grossklags, N. Christin, and J. Chuang. Secure or insure?: A game-theoretic analysis of information security games. In *Proceedings of the 17th International World Wide Web Conference (WWW)*, pages 209–218, Apr. 2008.

[15] G. Heal and H. Kunreuther. Interdependent security: A general model. Working Paper No. 10706, NBER, August 2004.

[16] B. Johnson, R. Böhme, and J. Grossklags. Security games with market insurance. *Decision and Game Theory for Security*, pages 117–130, 2011.

[17] B. Johnson, J. Grossklags, N. Christin, and J. Chuang. Uncertainty in interdependent security games. *Decision and Game Theory for Security*, pages 234–244, 2010.

[18] B. Johnson, A. Laszka, and J. Grossklags. The complexity of estimating systematic risk in networks. Working paper, Feb. 2014.

[19] M. Kearns and L. Ortiz. Algorithms for interdependent security games. In S. Thrun, L. Saul, and B. Schölkopf, editors, *Advances in Neural Information Processing Systems 16*, pages 561–568. MIT Press, 2004.

[20] J. Kephart and S. White. Directed-graph epidemiological models of computer viruses. In *Proceedings of the IEEE Computer Society Symposium on Research in Security and Privacy*, pages 343–359, May 1991.

[21] H. Kunreuther and G. Heal. Interdependent security. *Journal of Risk and Uncertainty*, 26(2):231–249, 2003.

[22] A. Laszka, M. Felegyhazi, and L. Buttyán. A survey of interdependent security games. Technical Report CRYSYS-TR-2012-11-15, CrySyS Lab, Budapest University of Technology and Economics, Nov 2012.

[23] A. Laszka, B. Johnson, J. Grossklags, and M. Felegyhazi. Estimating systematic risk in real-world networks. In *Proceedings of the 18th International Conference on Financial Cryptography and Data Security (FC)*, 2014.

[24] L. Li, D. Alderson, J. Doyle, and W. Willinger. Towards a theory of scale-free graphs: Definition, properties, and implications. *Internet Mathematics*, 2(4):431–523, 2005.

[25] A. Mislove, M. Marcon, K. Gummadi, P. Druschel, and B. Bhattacharjee. Measurement and analysis of online social networks. In *Proceedings of the 7th ACM SIGCOMM Conference on Internet Measurement*, pages 29–42, 2007.

[26] T. Moscibroda, S. Schmid, and R. Wattenhofer. When selfish meets evil: Byzantine players in a virus inoculation game. In *Proceedings of the ACM Symposium on Principles of Distributed Computing*, pages 35–44, 2006.

[27] H. Ogut, N. Menon, and S. Raghunathan. Cyber insurance and IT security investment: Impact of interdependent risk. In *Workshop on the Economics of Information Security*, 2005.

[28] M. Stumpf, C. Wiuf, and R. May. Subnets of scale-free networks are not scale-free: Sampling properties of networks. *Proceedings of the National Academy of Sciences of the United States of America*, 102(12):4221–4224, 2005.

[29] H. Varian. System reliability and free riding. In J. Camp and S. Lewis, editors, *Economics of Information Security*, pages 1–15. Kluwer Academic Publishers, Dordrecht, The Netherlands, 2004.

Prover Anonymous and Deniable Distance-Bounding Authentication

Sébastien Gambs Cristina Onete
Université de Rennes 1 -Inria/IRISA
263 Avenue Général Leclerc
35000 Rennes, France
sebastien.gambs@irisa.fr
cristina.onete@gmail.com

Jean-Marc Robert
ETS Montréal
1100 rue Notre-Dame ouest
Montréal, Canada
Jean-Marc.Robert@etsmtl.ca

ABSTRACT

In distance-bounding authentication protocols, a verifier assesses that a prover is (1) legitimate and (2) in the verifier's proximity. Proximity checking is done by running time-critical exchanges between both parties. This enables the verifier to detect relay attacks (also called mafia fraud). While most distance-bounding protocols offer resistance to mafia, distance, and impersonation attacks, only few protect the privacy of the authenticating prover. One exception is the protocol due to Hermans, Peeters, and Onete, which offers prover untraceability with respect to a Man-in-the-Middle adversary. However in this protocol as well as in all other distance-bounding protocols, any legitimate verifier can identify, and thus track, the prover.

In order to counter the threats of possible corruption or data leakage from verifiers, we propose a distance-bounding protocol providing strong prover privacy with respect to the verifier and deniability with respect to a centralized back-end server managing prover creation and revocation. In particular, we first formalize the notion of *prover anonymity*, which guarantees that even verifiers cannot trace provers, and *deniability*, which allows provers to deny that they were authenticated by a verifier. Finally, we prove that our protocol achieves these strong guarantees.

Categories and Subject Descriptors

K.6.5 [**Management of Computing and Information Systems**]: Security and Protection—*Authentication*

Keywords

Privacy; Distance Bounding; Cryptography.

1. INTRODUCTION

Distance-bounding protocols [3] were originally designed to counter *relay attacks* [5] in authentication protocols. In these attacks, an adversary can illegitimately authenticate using two proxies that relay messages between a mobile device, known as a *prover*, and a terminal, known as a *verifier*. In distance bounding, the verifier uses an internal clock to repeatedly measure the roundtrip time of lightweight communication phases, thus checking that the prover is within his vicinity. These protocols essentially provide two functionalities: prover-to-verifier authentication and a prover-proximity check for the verifier.

As our capacity to manipulate large amount of data increases, the risks associated with the leak of personal information are also exploding. In this context, ensuring prover privacy with respect to Man-in-the-Middle (MIM) adversaries in authentication and distance-bounding protocols is no longer sufficient. In particular, in any authentication protocol insiders such as verifiers and the managing back-end server can potentially forward users' data to governmental agencies or to other third parties. Thus, our main motivation is to develop authentication schemes ensuring a strong degree of user privacy with respect to these insiders.

Distance bounding was originally introduced in a generic context [3]. However, due to the lightweight nature of the proximity check, it has been frequently used to address the threats posed by relay attacks in RFID authentication [1, 3, 6, 10, 13]. Strong privacy is unfortunately unattainable for symmetric-key protocols [14, 17], which is the usual setting for such schemes. Hence, our objective is to answer the following question:

- Can we design an efficient and secure distance-bounding authentication protocol, preserving prover privacy even against verifiers?

Our solution to this question follows the public-key approach of Brands and Chaum [3], Reid et al. [16], Bussard and Bagga [4], and Hermans-Peeters-Onete [12] (thereafter denoted as "HPO"). More precisely, the protocol we present is a modification of the HPO construction, which already provided good MIM-privacy guarantees [12]. However, our solution achieves even stronger privacy guarantees. Namely, our protocol provides privacy against honest-but-curious or malicious verifiers, and attains *prover deniability* with respect to the back-end server managing the provers' credentials. Our scheme is explicitly aimed at mobile devices more potent than regular RFID tags.

In summary, we (1) introduce the prover anonymity property as an indistinguishability game, with an adversary acting respectively as a MIM adversary, an honest-but-curious verifier, or a malicious verifier; (2) propose a secure, prover-anonymous and deniable distance-bounding protocol in a

ASIA CCS'14, June 4–6, 2014, Kyoto, Japan.
Copyright 2014 ACM 978-1-4503-2800-5/14/06 ...$15.00.
http://dx.doi.org/10.1145/2590296.2590331.

setting in which a *back-end server* handles prover creation and revocation, providing legitimate authentication credentials; (3) give concrete bounds for the security and privacy of this scheme. We prove correctness, soundness, impersonation security, mafia- and distance-fraud resistance for our protocol, as well as wide-strong prover anonymity and deniability with respect to the back-end server.

2. PRELIMINARIES

In this section, we describe the system model, the problem statement, and some relevant security and privacy notions.

2.1 System Model

We consider a distance-bounding authentication system with a single verifier V, a set of provers $\mathcal{P} = \{\mathsf{P}_1, \ldots, \mathsf{P}_k\}$, and a back-end managing server Srv.

The *server* Srv is offline most of the time and takes care of prover creation and revocation. At every update of $\mathcal{P}$, Srv updates the authentication information available on a public board $\mathcal{B}$. We associate Srv with a one-time private/public key pair (z, Z), used with an unforgeable signature scheme $\mathcal{S} = (\mathsf{SS.KGen}, \mathsf{Sign}, \mathsf{Vfy})$, and we assume that the server can self-certify these keys.

Each *prover* P_i has a key pair (x_i, X_i) for authentication. The public part X_i is stored on $\mathcal{B}$ and updated by Srv. In contrast, the private part x_i is known only by the prover and Srv. In our security models, an adversary may also register *insider* provers and obtain their private keys.

The *verifier* has a private/public key pair (y, Y) used for authentication and may also store auxiliary information in his internal state.

The *adversary* has access to the public information on the board $\mathcal{B}$, the private information of the insider provers, and, for our prover-anonymity and deniability models, to the full internal state of the verifier. We assume that the adversary can (1) change the information on $\mathcal{B}$, (2) corrupt provers to obtain their non-volatile state, or (3) act as a MIM between provers and verifiers. When the adversary acts a MIM, she can either strictly interact with one party or simply relay and modify messages exchanged between parties.

2.2 Problem Statement

We concretely aim to solve the following problems.

PROBLEM 1 (AUTHENTICATION PROBLEM). *Prevent an illegitimate party from authenticating to an honest verifier, while ensuring that legitimate parties always authenticate.*

PROBLEM 2 (DISTANCE-BOUNDING PROBLEM). *Prevent a prover (honest or malicious) from claiming to be in the verifier's proximity while he is, in fact, outside this proximity.*

PROBLEM 3 (PRIVACY PROBLEM). *Prevent MIM adversaries, honest-but-curious or malicious verifiers, and even the back-end server from learning the identity of a prover or linking two authentication sessions.*

These problems are addressed in the literature in slightly different settings. Specifically, the formal model of distance-bounding security presented by Dürholz et al. [6] defines mafia, distance, and (simulation-based) terrorist-fraud resistance, as well as lazy-phase impersonation security *for a single prover and a single verifier.* This model is used by many protocols [6, 7, 8, 12] as it is sufficiently formal to give precise security bounds. In contrast, the notion of prover privacy in authentication and distance bounding *must* assume the existence of *multiple provers.* The privacy framework for RFID authentication due to Hermans et al. [11], which is used in this work, considers many potentially corrupted provers. Ideally, one should also account for multiple provers in distance bounding. For instance, the recent work of Boureanu et al. [2] makes a step towards generalizing distance-bounding security to the multi-prover setting. However, this model is incompatible with the framework of Dürholz et al. [6], which is used to prove the security of the HPO protocol. As our construction relies on the approach of HPO, we use the model of [6].

Our objective is to develop a protocol attaining the impersonation, mafia-, and distance-fraud resistance of the single-prover model of Dürholz et al., and the strong correctness and soundness requirements of the multi-prover framework of Hermans et al. [11], but with stronger privacy properties. These properties are outlined in the following sections. However, due to space restrictions, we defer the complete model and relevant discussions to the full version of the paper [9].

2.3 Security and Privacy

Correctness and Soundness. Authentication protocols must respect two *security* properties: *correctness* (a legitimate prover should always authenticate) and *soundness* (an adversary should never authenticate except with negligible probability) [11, 17]. As these classical definitions do *not* capture the adversary's interaction with the public board $\mathcal{B}$, we update them to take this aspect into account in Section 3.

Since we allow prover corruption (yielding private keys) and insider-prover creation (yielding full internal states) in the soundness model, we must make two assumptions. First, the server Srv is assumed to revoke all corrupted provers upon corruption. Second, insider provers are not registered by Srv in the soundness game. We discuss these assumptions in more detail in the full version [9].

Privacy. We use the game-based definition of privacy due to Hermans et al. [11], which is an indistinguishability game. In this game, the adversary first picks two legitimate entities. An oracle chooses one of them and returns an anonymized handle associated with this prover to the adversary, thus enabling him to access the hidden prover. After interacting with him arbitrarily and repeating the process multiple times, the adversary must guess which entity was selected by the oracle. This approach guarantees session unlinkability, and thus prover untraceability, with respect to a MIM attacker. The adversary interacts with provers by means of oracles. We present the most relevant ones below and refer the reader to [11] for more details.

Prover Creation. This oracle generates a private/public key pair for a given prover identifier. As output, the adversary receives a handle P_i and the public key.

Insider Creation. The oracle creates a prover, and leaks the private/public keys and the handle to the adversary.

Draw and Release Provers. The adversary gives two prover handles to the $\mathsf{DrawProver}$ oracle and receives an anonymized handle to one of them through which the adversary can interact with the prover. When selected, the two provers become unreachable by the adversary. Releasing the handle allows the prover to interact with them again.

Interactions. Through oracles, the adversary can interact as a MIM between the verifier and the selected (anonymized) prover, launching sessions and relaying messages or changing/injecting arbitrary messages to any of the two parties.

Prover Corruption. The adversary can learn the non-volatile internal state of a chosen prover.

Result. The adversary learns the result (1 = acceptance, 0 = rejection) of an authentication session.

At the end, the adversary *wins* the game if she can identify which prover is consistently selected by DrawProver.

Following the classification of Vaudenay [17] and Hermans et al. [11], adversaries are known as *wide* or *narrow* depending on whether or not they query Result. In parallel, they are *weak* (if they cannot use Corrupt), *forward* (if only Corrupt can be used after a Corrupt query), *destructive* (if Corrupt destroys the prover's handle), or *strong* (if there is no restriction on the use of the oracles). The original model of [11] does not model insider provers. Thus, Peeters and Hermans [15] added *insider* privacy and obtained narrow-strong and wide-forward insider privacy by using public-key primitives. They formalized privacy as follows.

Definition 1 (MIM-Privacy). *A protocol is Γ-private if and only if for all polynomial time MIM adversaries $\mathcal{A}$ in class Γ, the adversary cannot win the privacy game with a non-negligible advantage over the guessing probability.*

Three aspects are not considered in the above model. First, the presence in our setting of the server Srv and its public board $\mathcal{B}$ introduces new adversary interactions.

More importantly, this definition does *not* guarantee prover privacy with respect to a legitimate verifier. In fact, most distance-bounding and authentication protocols (including [11, 12]) *always* allow the verifier to distinguish which prover has authenticated. We extend this notion to capture prover anonymity and unlinkability with respect to the verifier.

Finally, we require prover privacy with regard to Srv. In particular, we demand prover *deniability* with respect to a server, even if it has access to the verifier's full internal state.

Distance-Bounding Security. In the single-prover/single-verifier model of Dürholz et al. [6], the adversary can run adversary-prover or adversary-verifier sessions, or simply observe prover-verifier sessions. The verifier has a clock that can accurately measure the time elapsed between sending a challenge and receiving the response. If the round-trip time is measured, the round is *time-critical* (fast); otherwise it is called *lazy* (slow). We give informal definitions for the three properties defined in [6] below and refer to the full version for a discussion of these properties.

Definition 2 (Distance Fraud Resistance). *No legitimate prover located outside the prover's proximity should be able to authenticate.*

Definition 3 (Mafia Fraud Resistance). *No MIM adversary should authenticate to a verifier even in the presence of a prover, except by purely relaying messages.*

Definition 4 (Impersonation Resistance). *No MIM adversary should be able to authenticate to the verifier in the lazy phases except by purely relaying messages.*

This notion is independent of the notion of soundness as defined by Hermans et al. [12] (see [9]). While we advocate the use of schemes also achieving the strong notion of terrorist-fraud resistance, we leave this as future work and focus specifically on achieving strong priacy properties.

3. Prover Anonymity

In order to define prover anonymity, we extend the privacy model of Hermans et al. [11] in two directions: (1) by modeling the interactions of the adversary with the board $\mathcal{B}$ and (2) by generalizing the privacy notion to protect provers against malicious verifiers and the server Srv.

First, we introduce the ChangeBoard oracle allowing the adversary to alter the contents of $\mathcal{B}$ with her own input. We also propose (1) the notion of *prover anonymity*, requiring session unlinkability *even* if the verifier's full internal state is known, and (2) the notion of *deniability*, demanding that Srv cannot distinguish a real protocol transcript from a simulated one, even if the verifier reveals his full internal state.

For prover anonymity, we capture *honest-but-curious* and *malicious* verifier behavior as a *collusion* between an adversary and this verifier, thus extending the MIM-anonymity notion of [11]. As the honest-but-curious verifier always follows the rules of protocol, the corresponding colluding MIM adversary just acts as a simple proxy between the verifier and the prover. For a malicious verifier, the colluding MIM adversary is fully-functional and may interact solely with the verifier or the prover. We depict the definitions of prover anonymity and deniability in Figure 1.

We use a parameter flag to indicate verifier involvement and specify the oracle behavior. This flag can take one of three values: hon, hbc, mal, standing respectively for an honest, an honest-but-curious or a malicious verifier.

The Effect of flag. At the beginning of the privacy game, the adversary gives the value of flag. If flag $\in$ {hbc, mal}, the adversary receives the verifier's full internal state. In addition, whenever the verifier sends a message to the adversary (e.g., via SendVerifier or Launch queries), the adversary also receives an update of the internal state. This enables the adversary to check the legitimacy of the prover without issuing Result queries. Thus, for flag $\in$ {hbc, mal}, the verifier always behaves honestly, but passes on his full internal state to the MIM adversary. If flag = hbc, the adversary may only relay prover-verifier communication, modeled by the oracle Execute. In this case, the adversary cannot interact with Corrupt, CreateInsider, nor any other interaction oracle[1]. If flag = mal, the adversary cannot corrupt provers or create insiders, but may use any interaction oracle as in the original game. Finally, if flag = hon, the adversary runs the original MIM-privacy game, while also being able to modify the content of $\mathcal{B}$.

Extended Interaction Model. We introduce two additional oracles, namely ChangeBoard and Execute. The first oracle allows the adversary to change $\mathcal{B}$, while the second triggers an honest prover-verifier protocol execution in which the adversary acts as a proxy.

ChangeBoard($\mathcal{B}'$). This oracle changes the content of the public board $\mathcal{B}$ with the new content $\mathcal{B}'$.

Execute($\cdot$). When given as input a prover index I, this oracle executes the protocol between the prover I and the verifier.

[1]This restriction can be relaxed by allowing CreateProver and CreateInsider queries. This is equivalent to achieve deniability *and* honest-but-curious prover anonymity.

The prover index I is either an index $i \in \{1, \ldots, k\}$, for a number k of provers, or the anonymized handle as returned by DrawProver. The protocol is run by appropriate use of Launch, SendProver, and SendVerifier (we give more details about these oracles in [9]). At the end, the transcript of the protocol prot is returned (in case of an abort, a special symbol $\perp$ is appended at the end).

We also modify the following oracles, originally defined by Hermans et al. [11].

CreateProver. On prover creation, the private/public key pair is also stored by the server Srv, which updates the board $\mathcal{B}$ accordingly.

CreateInsider. When creating an insider, in the privacy game the key pair is registered with Srv and $\mathcal{B}$ as for legitimate provers. For the soundness model, the credentials are given to the adversary, but not to the server (as mentioned in Section 2.3).

SendProver. We extend this oracle for the soundness model such that it takes three inputs: a prover index, a message, and a protocol handle. The oracle sends that message to that prover within a specific protocol session, and receives the prover's response.

Corrupt. We extend this oracle for the soundness model such that the prover is immediately revoked after his corruption, and Srv updates its internal database and the board accordingly (as assumed in Section 2.3).

$\mathsf{SendVerifier}_{\mathsf{flag}}$. Depending on flag, this oracle either just sends a message to the verifier and receives his response, or it sends a message to the verifier and receives his full internal state and the response.

Note that the oracles SendProver, Corrupt, and CreateInsider run differently for the soundness and the privacy models. To distinguish these modes, we use the notation Oracle* if this oracle was run in the soundness model.

The games. In *extended correctness*, the adversary can query CreateProver, ChangeBoard, Result, and Execute. In this setting, she *wins* if for an honest execution Result returns 0.

For *extended soundness*, the adversary $\mathcal{A}$ can use CreateProver, CreateInsider*, ChangeBoard, Launch, SendProver*, SendVerifier, Result and Corrupt*. She *wins* if a session in which the prover was not queried returns Result = 1.

For the *prover anonymity* game, $\mathcal{A}$ selects flag $\in$ {hon, hbc, mal} and is given access to ChangeBoard, DrawProver, and Free. If flag = hon, $\mathcal{A}$ gets access also to CreateProver and Corrupt (depending on the adversary model). The adversary may also use Launch, SendProver, $\mathsf{SendVerifier}_{\mathsf{flag}}$, and possibly Result (if flag $\in$ {hon, mal}) or to Execute (if flag = hbc). If flag $\in$ {hbc, mal}, the use of Result is superfluous, as the verifier's state allows verification (making narrow and wide privacy equivalent). $\mathcal{A}$ *wins* if she can distinguish the hidden bit used by DrawProver. We preserve the same definition and adversary classes as Hermans et al. [11].

Finally, for *deniability* with respect to an honest-but-curious Srv[2], let $\mathsf{state}_\mathsf{V}$ denote the full internal state of the verifier V and let Sim be a simulator taking as input $\mathsf{state}_\mathsf{V}$ and returning a transcript τ_{Sim}. We require that the transcript of an honest session between V and a legitimate prover chosen by Srv is identical, from Srv's point of view, to a simulated

[2]This can be extended to a malicious server by adding further NIZK-PK in our protocol.

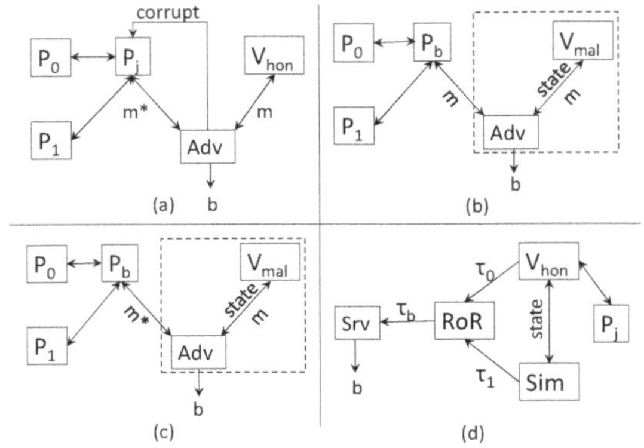

Figure 1: Prover anonymity (a) for flag = hon, (b) for flag = hbc, (c) for flag = mal, and (d) deniability.

transcript generated by V for the same state $\mathsf{state}_\mathsf{V}$. Formally, we introduce a real-or-random oracle DenyRoR outputting either the genuine protocol transcript of an honest prover-verifier session, or a simulated transcript run with the same state (depending on a hidden bit).

The adversary (i.e., Srv) is given access the verifier's state, and can create provers or query DenyRoR. She wins if she outputs the hidden bit of the latter oracle. The protocol is *perfectly deniable* if $\mathcal{A}$ wins with probability at most $\frac{1}{2}$.

4. OUR CONSTRUCTION

Our protocol extends the HPO protocol [12], which is narrow-strong and wide-forward-insider MIM-private, as well as correct, sound, and resistant to mafia- and distance-fraud.

In order to achieve wide-strong prover anonymity, we have modified the HPO protocol in two places (these changes are highlighted in bold font in Figure 2). First, during the nonce-exchange phase the prover uses a Non-Interactive Zero-Knowledge (NIZK) Proof of Knowledge system to derive an auxiliary session key. Second, during the authentication phase the prover uses this auxiliary key to authenticate anonymously. We thus obtain stronger prover anonymity guarantees while preserving the security properties of the HPO protocol. Our scheme also achieves deniability with respect to an honest-but-curious server Srv.

Setting. Let $\mathbb{G} = \langle P \rangle$ be a subgroup of prime order q of points on an elliptic curve $\mathcal{E}$ over a finite field $\mathbb{F}_q$. The point P is a generator of this group. We specify a homomorphic encryption scheme[3] $\mathcal{HE}$ = (HE.KGen, HEnc, HDec) with message-space $\mathbb{G}$, which is IND-RCCA and IK-CCA secure.

At each prover creation and revocation, Srv generates and self-certifies a private/public key pair (z, Z) to be used with an EUF-CMA signature scheme $\mathcal{S}$ = {SS.KGen, Sign, Vfy}. The certificates of old keys are placed on an authenticated revocation list.

Finally, the prover uses a NIZK-PK system $\mathcal{PK}$ = (par, Prove, Vf, Sim, Ext), in which the witness is a private/public encryption key pair and the randomness used to encrypt. The corresponding statement is that a specific ciphertext c

[3]We use EC Elgamal encryption: knowing $\mathsf{HEnc}(\mathsf{pk}, \mathrm{Q}_i)$, one can compute $\mathsf{HEnc}(\mathsf{pk}, r\mathrm{Q}_i) = r \circ \mathsf{HEnc}(\mathsf{pk}, \mathrm{Q}_i)$ (i.e., the multiplication of the ciphertext r times by itself).

is the encryption of the value Q_i with $i \in \{1, \ldots, k\}$ and publicly known values Q_i with probability exactly $\frac{1}{k}$. This scheme should have perfect completeness.

Prover setup. Prover creation associates each prover P_i, with a private key $x_i \in \mathbb{Z}_q$ and an auxiliary public key Q_i stored by P_i and Srv. The key Q_i is defined as $\prod_{j=1;j\neq i}^{k} x_j P$, for $i = 1, \ldots, k$, while the public key Q is defined as follows $Q \coloneqq \prod_{i=1}^{k} x_i P$. These values are updated dynamically at prover creation and revocation. The server generates a signature key pair, certifies it, signs the message $m \coloneqq Q_1, \ldots, Q_k, Q$, and publishes m and $\sigma \coloneqq \mathsf{Sign}(z, m)$ on $\mathcal{B}$.

Prover revocation. Whenever prover P_i is revoked, the server removes the key x_i from its database and updates the values Q_j, Q and σ in its database and on the board $\mathcal{B}$.

Protocol intuition. In our scheme the prover P_j, knowing his key x_j, demonstrates that he can compute $x_j Q_j = Q$. At each session, the (potentially malicious) verifier generates a random value r and expects to retrieve the value rQ from the string S sent by P_j. The prover is not given the value r explicitly. Instead, he computes $\mathsf{HEnc}(\mathsf{epk}, Q_i)$ under an ephemeral private/public key pair $(\mathsf{esk}, \mathsf{epk})$ known from himself only. Afterwards, the verifier uses the homomorphic property of the encryption scheme to return $\mathsf{HEnc}(\mathsf{epk}, rQ_i)$. Finally, the prover decrypts the value and computes $x_i(rQ_i) = rQ$.

Retrieving information from the board. We assume that the prover and the verifier *only* retrieve information from $\mathcal{B}$ if the authenticating signature σ and the corresponding certificate are valid. Our protocol is depicted in Figure 2.

Efficiency. In the HPO protocol, the prover had to compute two-point multiplications and two x-coordinate computations. In our protocol, we achieve prover anonymity and deniability at the expense of a total of four-point multiplications (including the computation of epk), one x-coordinate computation, one homomorphic encryption step, one decryption and one NIZK computation. We use the Elgamal encryption scheme, which is relatively fast. However, we use the NIZK-PK in black-box fashion, which might be relatively expensive. As our proof-of-concept protocol aims for NFC mobile-device implementation, the usual restrictions relevant in RFID scenarios no longer applies here.

On the verifier side, one x-coordinate computation is replaced by a point multiplication with respect to the HPO protocol. In addition, the verifier must compute the session key (one-point multiplication), verify the NIZK proof, and perform a homomorphic multiplication.

Security. The following theorem is stated informally here. Please refer to the full version of the paper for the complete formalization and the corresponding proofs.

THEOREM 1 (PROTOCOL SECURITY AND PRIVACY). *For the protocol in Figure 2, the following properties hold:*

- *If the signature scheme used for certification is unforgeable, the scheme achieves extended correctness.*
- *If the truncation of a DDH product is indistinguishable from random and the certification signature scheme is unforgeable, this scheme has a distance-fraud resistance of $\frac{3}{4}$ per round.*
- *If the truncation of a DDH product is indistinguishable from random, the certification scheme is unforgeable and the DLog problem is hard in $\mathbb{G}$, and if the protocol is sound, it has a mafia fraud resistance of $\frac{1}{2}$ per round.*
- *If the NIZK proof is sound, the DLog problem is hard, and the certification scheme is unforgeable, the protocol achieves extended soundness.*
- *If the NIZK proof is sound and ZK, the homomorphic encryption scheme is IND-RCCA and IK-CCA, this protocol is wide-strong-prover anonymous.*
- *The protocol is perfectly deniable with respect to an honest-but-curious server.*
- *If the truncation of a DDH is indistinguishable from random, the DLog problem is hard, and if the protocol is sound, the protocol is also impersonation secure.*

Limitations and Future Work. Our protocol can be seen as a proof-of-concept. While it gives strong anonymity and security guarantees, it currently lacks the property of terrorist-fraud resistance, an attack in which the prover helps the adversary authenticate such that the adversary cannot later authenticate on her own. It is especially hard to ensure this property at the same time as deniability and prover anonymity, since the typical terrorist-fraud countermeasure of linking time-critical responses by a key only guarantees the key's secrecy with respect to MIM adversaries. We also encourage research into attaining prover anonymity in a more efficient way, thus also finding solutions for resource-constrained hardware. Finally, another possible extension is to investigate generic compositions of classical distance-bounding protocols and private authentication, so as to determine how far prover anonymity is achievable in such scenarios.

Acknowledgements

This work has been supported by the ANR-11-INS-0013 LYRICS Project and by an NSERC discovery grant. We are grateful to Patrick Tague for his shepherding and to the anonymous reviewers for their useful comments.

5. REFERENCES

[1] G. Avoine and A. Tchamkerten. An efficient distance bounding RFID authentication protocol: Balancing false-acceptance rate and memory requirement. In *Proc. of ISC'09*, volume 5735 of *LNCS*, pages 250–261. Springer-Verlag, 2009.

[2] I. Boureanu, A. Mitrokotsa, and S. Vaudenay. Secure and lightweight distance-bounding. In *Proc. of LightSec'13*, volume 8162 of *LNCS*, pages 97–113. Springer-Verlag, 2013.

[3] S. Brands and D. Chaum. Distance-bounding protocols. In *Proc. of EUROCRYPT'93*, volume 765 of *LNCS*, pages 344–359. Springer-Verlag, 1993.

[4] L. Bussard and W. Bagga. Distance-bounding proof of knowledge to avoid real-time attacks. In *Proc. of Security and Privacy*, IFIP, pages 222–238. Springer-Verlag, 2005.

[5] Y. Desmedt, C. Goutier, and S. Bengio. Special uses and abuses of the Fiat-Shamir passport protocol. In

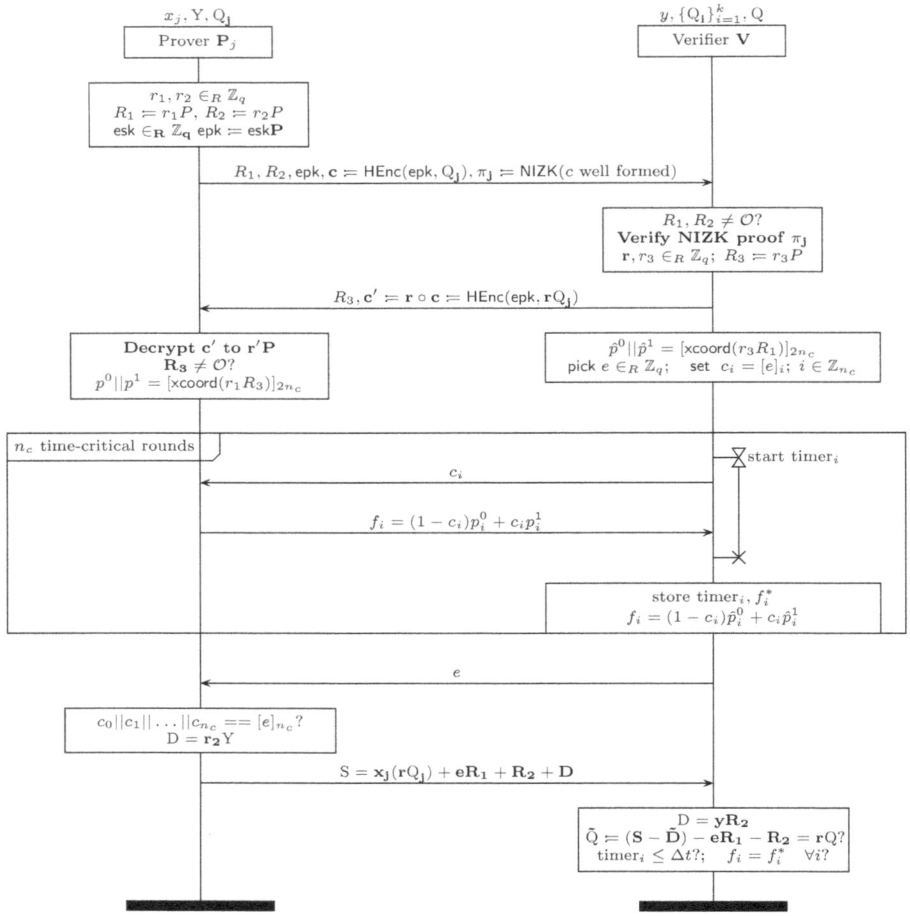

Figure 2: Our prover-anonymous and deniable distance-bounding construction.

Proc. of CRYPTO'87, volume 293 of *LNCS*, pages 21–39. Springer-Verlag, 1988.

[6] U. Dürholz, M. Fischlin, M. Kasper, and C. Onete. A formal approach to distance bounding RFID protocols. In *Proc. of ISC'11*, volume 7001 of *LNCS*, pages 47–62. Springer-Verlag, 2011.

[7] M. Fischlin and C. Onete. Subtle kinks in distance-bounding: an analysis of prominent protocols. In *Proc. WISec'13*, pages 195–206. ACM Press, 2013.

[8] M. Fischlin and C. Onete. Terrorism in distance bounding: Modeling terrorist fraud resistance. In *Proc. of ACNS'13*, volume 7954 of *LNCS*, pages 414–431. Springer-Verlag, 2013.

[9] S. Gambs, C. Onete, and J.-M. Robert. Prover anonymous and deniable distance-bounding authentication. Cryptology ePrint Archive, Report 2014/114, 2014. http://eprint.iacr.org/2014/114.pdf.

[10] G. P. Hancke and M. G. Kuhn. An RFID distance bounding protocol. In *Proc. of SecureComm'05*, pages 67–73. IEEE, 2005.

[11] J. Hermans, A. Pashalidis, F. Vercauteren, and B. Preneel. A new RFID privacy model. In *Proc. of ESORICS'11*, volume 6879 of *LNCS*, pages 568–587. Springer-Verlag, 2011.

[12] J. Hermans, R. Peeters, and C. Onete. Efficient, secure, private distance bounding without key updates. In *Proc. of WiSec'13*, pages 207–218. ACM Press, 2013.

[13] C. H. Kim and G. Avoine. RFID distance bounding protocol with mixed challenges to prevent relay attacks. In *Proc. of CANS'09*, volume 5888 of *LNCS*, pages 119–131. Springer-Verlag, 2009.

[14] R.-I. Paise and S. Vaudenay. Mutual authentication in RFID: Security and privacy. In *Proc. of ASIACCS'08*, pages 292–299. ACM, 2008.

[15] R. Peeters and J. Hermans. Wide strong private RFID identification based on zero-knowledge. Cryptology ePrint Archive, Report 2012/389, 2012.

[16] J. Reid, J. M. G. Nieto, T. Tang, and B. Senadji. Detecting relay attacks with timing-based protocols. In *Proc. of ASIACCS'07*, pages 204–213. ACM Press, 2007.

[17] S. Vaudenay. On privacy models for RFID. In *Proc. of ASIACRYPT'07*, volume 4883 of *LNCS*, pages 68–87. Springer-Verlag, 2007.

Why Eve and Mallory (Also) Love Webmasters

A Study on the Root Causes of SSL Misconfigurations

Sascha Fahl, Yasemin Acar, Henning Perl, Matthew Smith
FKIE, Fraunhofer
Bonn, Germany
{sascha.fahl,yasemin.acar,henning.perl,matthew.smith}@fkie.fraunhofer.de

ABSTRACT

Previous research showed that the SSL infrastructure is a fragile system: X.509 certificate validation fails for a non-trivial number of HTTPS-enabled websites resulting in SSL warning messages presented to users. Studies revealed that warning messages do not provide easy-to-understand information or are ignored by webbrowser users. SSL warning messages are a critical component in the HTTPS infrastructure and many attempts have been made to improve these warning messages. However, an important question has not received sufficient attention yet: Why do webmasters (deliberately) deploy non-validating, security-critical X.509 certificates on publicly available websites? In this paper, we conduct the first study with webmasters operating non-validating X.509 certificates to understand their motives behind deploying those certificates. We extracted the non-validating certificates from Google's webcrawler body of X.509 certificates, informed webmasters about the problem with the X.509 certificate configuration on their website and invited a random sample of the respective webmasters to participate in our study. 755 webmasters participated, allowing us insight into their motives. While one third of them admitted to having misconfigured their webserver accidentally, two thirds of them gave reasons for deliberately using a non-validating X.509 certificate.

Categories and Subject Descriptors

H.4 [**Information Systems Applications**]: Miscellaneous

General Terms

SSL, Webmasters, Usable Security, User Study

1. INTRODUCTION

For the authentication of a server during an SSL handshake, clients perform multiple validation steps to check whether the server's X.509 certificate is trustworthy or should better be rejected. Self-signed and expired certificates, certificates that were signed by an unknown CA, certificates that are not delivered with a complete issuer chain as well as certificates issued for the wrong hostname result in rejection. Whenever there is a problem with X.509 certificate validation, modern webbrowsers generate warning messages so users can decide how to proceed with the (possibly) critical X.509 certificate in question.

Further research revealed that misconfigurations of HTTPS-enabled webservers are a widespread issue. In 2009, the EFF conducted an internet-wide scan of all public IPv4 addresses on port 443 and collected the respective X.509 certificates[1]. Since then, multiple projects crawled the public part of the Internet for HTTPS certificates and analyzed different aspects of their deployment in the wild. Holz et al. [5], Akhawe et al. and the ICSI Certificate Notary [1] collected X.509 certificates either actively or passively and concluded certain properties of the current CA-based SSL infrastructure: While previous research provides valuable insights into the current SSL ecosystem, their focus is solely on technical aspects of SSL configurations or on the behavior of webbrowser users confronted with SSL warning messages but leaves out the following interesting questions: (1) Why are HTTPS-enabled websites operated with non-validating X.509 certificates at all? (2) How many misconfigured websites are frequently visited with webbrowsers and hence throw SSL warning messages? (3) For how many users do SSL warning messages occur unexpectedly? Based on the knowledge that a non-negligible percentage of SSL handshakes fail and that a large percentage of warning messages is dismissed by users[2], we conducted the first qualitative study with website administrators to investigate the root causes for X.509 misconfiguration that cause browser warning messages. We collected 755 study results to assess the motivation for the use of non-validating X.509 certificates on the web. We were interested in the reasons and motivation for webmasters to operate non-validating X.509 certificates, how these webmasters assess the operation of their non-validating certificates and the number of affected users and the protected data types. Additionally, we were interested in suggestions to improve the usability of certificate configuration.

Our findings suggest that a remarkable number of websites that operate non-validating X.509 certificates either do so intentionally or are not actively in use and hence do not trigger warning messages at all. However, we also find that many administrators misconfigure their HTTPS webservers due to the high complexity of SSL configuration options or

[1]https://www.eff.org/observatory

ASIA CCS'14, June 4–6, 2014, Kyoto, Japan.

http://dx.doi.org/10.1145/2590296.2590341.

due to a misunderstanding of the security features of SSL. Our contributions can be summarized as follows: (1) We conduct the first user-study with webmasters of HTTPS-enabled websites to identify the root causes for SSL warning messages in modern webbrowsers. (2) We find that a large amount of non-validating certificates is meant to be that way and clicking through them can be classified as deliberate. (3) We find that mainly websites with a manageable user count throw certificate validation errors. In many of these cases the users were previously informed, have probably been helped with the installation of the respective CA or trust the certificate and thus are not shown a warning message when browsing the site. (4) We report that a remarkable amount of websites employing non-validating certificates as can be found by crawlers are not meant to be actively used, are only ever accessed by crawlers and thus do not trigger real world warning messages for users. (5) We find that a substantial number of webmasters are overwhelmed by the complexity of SSL and the configuration parameters offered by HTTPS webservers. (6) We provide a list of suggestions to improve the usability of X.509 certificate configuration on webservers given by the webmasters.

2. BACKGROUND

The SSL protocol provides authentication based on the X.509 public key infrastructure[2], protects data confidentiality using symmetric encryption, and ensures data integrity with cryptographic message digests. SSL is commonly used to secure websites and mail servers, prevent network attackers from eavesdropping or replaying the client's messages, and is generally considered security best practice for websites using the HTTPS protocol[3].

2.1 Browser Certificate Validation

Basically X.509 certificate validation in browser software consists of the following steps: (1) check if the certificate was digitally signed by a trusted issuer, (2) check if the certificate is not already expired, (3) check if the certificate was issued for the requested hostname.

(1) This step verifies whether a server's certificate was issued by a trusted CA of which modern browsers usually include more than 100. Common reasons for failures in practice are X.509 certificates that were self-signed or signed by unknown CAs, e. g. CAs used in an enterprise context. (2) An X.509 certificate has a validity period of typically 12 or 24 months. In this step browsers check if the certificate was delivered within its validity period and otherwise reject it. (3) Finally, browsers check if the given certificate's common name or subject alternative names match the server's hostname. A widespread real world reason for hostname mismatches are certificates used for hostnames without the `www.` prefix although the certificate was only issued for the prefix or vice versa.

2.1.1 SSL Warning Messages

In case X.509 certificate validation fails, modern browsers show their users warning messages. These warning messages might imply that a Man-In-The-Middle attack occurred, i. e. that an attacker exchanged the server's original certificate with their own, to eavesdrop or alter data sent between the client and server. Another reason for failures are misconfigured servers, e. g. a webmaster did not update an already expired certificate or operates a certificate for an invalid hostname. In case browsers are certain that an attack is occuring, the presented warning message cannot be bypassed. If there is a chance that the warning message is a false positive (i. e. the website's administrator (deliberately) misconfigured the X.509 certificate), browsers will show a bypassable warning message, discouraging users from clicking through.

[2] https://www.ietf.org/rfc/rfc5280.txt
[3] https://tools.ietf.org/html/rfc2818

3. RELATED WORK

To the best of our knowledge, we present the first study with webmasters on the root causes of misconfigured X.509 certificates for HTTPS webservers. Although no other studies focused on the same topic, the motivation for our work is built on related work which we will discuss in this section. As mentioned above, several projects either actively or passively measured – or, respectively, are still measuring – the condition of the HTTPS ecosystem. Akhawe et al. [1] passively collected SSL handshakes of multiple US universities and 300,000 users over a period of nine months in 2012 and 2013, concentrating on the frequency of X.509 certificate validation errors in SSL handshakes. Overall, they found that 98.46% of the 3.9 billion SSL handshakes they monitored validated correctly, while 1.54% failed for different reasons: 70.51% used an unknown issuer, 2.99% a self-signed certificate, in 7.65% of all handshakes the certificate was expired and 18.82% of all handshakes generated hostname validation errors. Due to the unlikeliness of an actual Man-In-The-Middle attack, they assume all validation errors to be false positives. Durumeric et al. [3] presented ZMap – a fast internet-wide scanner – and conducted 110 scans of the world-wide HTTPS infrastructure over one year, collecting more than 42 million unique certificates of which 6.9 million were browser trusted. In 2009, Sunshine et al. [6] conducted lab studies with over 400 internet users to evaluate the effectiveness of browser SSL warning messages, as well as their human understandability, finding that participants made unsafe choices when confronted with warning messages. They suggest reducing the number of warning messages altogether, taking the decision whether to trust an unsafe connection or not out of the users' hands. In 2013, Akhawe and Porter Felt [2] used Firefox and Chrome's telemetry feature to measure click-through rates for SSL (and other) warning messages for different browsers in situ. Over a period of two months, they collected 16,704,666 SSL warning impressions for Chrome and 10,976 for Firefox. However, they were not able to see the respective handshakes or certificates that led to the warnings, thus they assume that almost all warning messages they saw were false positives.

4. WEBMASTER STUDY

While previous research either focused on a technological analysis of the deployed X.509 certificates in the wild or evaluated the users' behaviour when faced with an SSL warning message, our work incorporates the third important pillar in the SSL infrastructure: the webmasters of HTTPS-enabled websites. Knowing the technical reasons why SSL handshakes fail and produce warning messages and how users react to those warning messages are important aspects. However, to achieve a better understanding of the whole picture, we conduct the first study with webmasters to assess the root causes why webmasters operate non-validating X.509 certificates.

4.1 Methodology

To find websites that operate non-validating X.509 certificates, we gathered certificates deployed in the wild in a first step. We applied a technique different from previous work to collect X.509 certificates from websites: We used the body of certificates Google's webcrawler collected over a period of 12 months. The webcrawler collected X.509 certificates for 55,675,334 ($\sim$ 55.7 million) different hosts (identified as different domain names), resulting in a body of 4,487,463 X.509 certificates and their corresponding hostnames. This certificate body overcomes two essential problems common to other approaches reported in literature: (1) Actively crawling X.509 certificates for the complete IPv4 space such as Holz et al.[5] and the EFF SSL observatory resulted in a comprehensive map of IPv4 addresses and corresponding X.509 certificates - in this case one cannot deduce for which hostname the certificate was configured, hence post-validation does not allow for hostname verification. (2) Passively recording X.509 certificates similar to Akhawe et al. [1] only collects X.509 certificates for the websites their users visit - although they collected both X.509 certificates and SNI[4] values for the corresponding SSL handshakes, they might have missed an essential part of the HTTPS-enabled part of the Internet. The X.509 certificate body of Google's webcrawler provides both, an encompassing list of X.509 certificates and their corresponding hostnames of the publicly available part of the Internet and the possibility to perform all three steps of X.509 certificate validation in postprocessing steps: (1) CA signature validation, (2) expiration checks and (3) hostname verification. We used the webcrawler's certificate body and performed the following steps to select candidates for our study: Firstly, we re-validated all X.509 certificates, using the NSS library as proposed by Akhawe et al. [1] which gave us the following results:

Error Type	#Certificates	
Valid	3,876,497	(86.38%)
Self-Signed	89,981	(2.0%)
Expired	309,350	(6.89%)
Hostname Mismatch	146,941	(3.27%)
Unknown Issuer	64,694	(1.44%)

Altogether, our re-validation left us with 610,966 X.509 certificates that generate warning messages when users visit the corresponding websites. We picked a random sample of 50,000 of all failed X.509 certificates [5] and subsequently revisited all websites of our 50,000 certificate sample to learn the current SSL configuration status of the corresponding webserver. This left us with 46,934 X.509 certificates and their corresponding webservers.

We decided to get in contact with all of the affected webmasters. Therefore we started by extracting email addresses from the collected X.509 certificates. Whenever we found an email address pointing to a Certificate Authority's or a webhosting provider's info address, we ignored it. For all other email addresses, we ran DNS queries for MX entries for the email's domain. In case of a positive response, we stored the email address for contacting the webmaster later. In order to contact the webmasters for whom we did not find email addresses embedded in the certificate, we decided to send an email to `webmaster@domain.com`. Altogether, we sent 46,145 emails to email addresses either embedded in an X.509 certificate or to the domain's corresponding webmaster email address. We sent 40,480 emails to webmaster@domain.com and 5,664 to embedded addresses. 37,596 of those could not be delivered, leaving us with 8,549 successfully delivered emails. We received 755 complete responses to our survey, a response rate of 8.83%. We decided on a set of questions that would take only 5-7 minutes to answer, including two free text questions why the webmasters were using exactly this X.509 certificate on their website and the free text prompt to report problems with the configuration and wishes to make configurations for HTTPS more usable. We were mainly interested in the following aspects:

(1) **Reasons and Use Cases for employing HTTPS:** We were interested in how the website was primarily accessed, how many users were visiting it and in which context (e.g. commercial, private etc) the website was mostly used.

(2) **Technical Knowledge concerning SSL:** We asked several questions to asses how much the webmasters knew about SSL and if they had set it up themselves; we asked for estimations for the pricing of X.509 certificates and problems they had with SSL.

(3) **Risk Assessment Concerning Misconfigured SSL:** We asked how important SSL was for their website and how strong the risk for users was due to the non-validating certificate.

(4) **Complaints, Wishes and Suggestions for SSL:** In the end, we asked them to fill in a free text about if they had problems with configuring the certificate for their webserver, also asking them for complaints and ideas to "make things better".

4.2 Ethics

Our University has no formal IRB process, but the Privacy Officer also consults on ethical matters. The purpose of making contact with the affected webmasters was two-fold: (1) we intended to inform webmasters of the misconfiguration of their website and (2) kindly asked them to support our research. However, webmasters would benefit from our email without participating in the study.

We were aware that sending emails to all candidates at once could cause resentment in the recipients. To reduce negative side-effects, we specifically contacted the webmaster of the website by sending an email to the webmaster@domain address that is specifically intended for questions and comments concerning technical problems, as stated in RFC2142 [6]. However, we felt we were offering the administrators valuable information. Our results confirm our estimation of the situation: most webmasters reacted in a grateful or at least friendly way, some nicely explained why we saw the invalid certificate or thanked us for alarming them to the non-validating certificate and some of them said they wanted to fix the SSL configuration of their websites immediately.

[4]Server Name Indication (Cf. `http://www.ietf.org/rfc/rfc3546.txt`

[5]we conservatively estimated a success rate of reaching 10% of the administrators, and another 10% response rate to the study, which would have provided us with 500 answers

[6]https://www.ietf.org/rfc/rfc2142.txt

4.3 Study Results

Of the 755 webmasters, 154 (20.4%) operated websites with an expired certificate, for 250 (33.1%) websites hostname validation failed (13 were also expired), 160 (21,2%) websites used an X.509 certificate issued by a CA not included in the Mozilla truststore and 191 (25.3%) websites operated self-signed certificates.

4.3.1 Reasons and Use Cases for employing HTTPS

The primary access method was said to be via browsers in 681 cases, 15 by apps, 15 by embedded systems, and 44 stated they did not know. 319 webmasters estimated they had less than one hundred visitors per month, 165 estimated between one hundred and thousand, 95 between thousand an ten thousand, 66 between ten thousand and a hundred thousand, 19 between a hundred thousand and a million, 5 more than a million. Of the 134 webmasters who offered information about their websites' users, 84 (62.7%) said it was used only by themselves (primarily for administrative purposes), 11 (8,2%) said it was mostly used by friends and 39 (29,1%) said it was used by their company and colleagues. An important question of interest was why exactly the websites operated a non-validating X.509 certificate. Of the 495 webmasters who gave information as to why the certificate was configured in a way that would throw a warning message, 330 said they had configured it in such a way on purpose. W713, who operated a self-signed certificate, stated: *"The site is a development system not accessed by customers or the public and the warning message "issue" is known internally."*, while W49 stated: *"The X.509 certificate is used for access to sensitive parts of the site. It is only being used by skilled operators, i. e. people who are able to check the fingerprint of the certificate to determine its authenticity and then store it for subsequent uses."* W23 on the other hand mentioned: *"Using SSL with a commercial CA issued certificate that is not under total control by myself is inherently insecure, since every CA owner can hijack the security and all providers that acquired an intermediate CA certificate can do so. And in the last years we have seen how weak some CAs are protected against cybercriminals. So it's much more secure for users to accept a certificate that was signed by my own CA once and get cautious when it changes."* Another prominent statement came from W31: *"Our users are explicitly required to provision the CACert.org root CA before visiting the website. The website generates no warning then."* While 495 webmasters stated they use the questionable certificate deliberately, 165 webmasters said they had accidentally misconfigured their X.509 certificate. Again, the reasons for employing a non-validating certificate are manifold. W218 for example stated, *"I am the administrator of a website in the medical domain that must be HIPAA compliant and the HIPAA guidelines require HTTPS for websites. Since we did not want to spend money on a commercial X.509 certificate we decided to use a self-signed certificate."*, while W284 stated *"Actually you see the warning message because the certificate was issued for xxx.com and not www.xxx.com. If you click through the warning message you will be redirected to the correct website and will see no warning message at all."*. W98 stated *"I'm using one certificate for many sites (my server did not support SNI until a recent update), so I had to list every one of them in the alternative domain name. Since it is tiresome to add an additional entry for every one of them to account for the the correct subdomain, I did not bother [...] But your survey brought up to my attention this cases and I will fix the issue immediately"*
The *deliberate setup* group self-reported a mean SSL technical knowledge of 4.08, while the *misconfiguration* group reported a mean SSL technical knowledge of 3.80. The deliberate group rated their data sensitivity to be a mean of 2.48 out of 5, while the misconfiguration group rated it to be a 2.43. 101 of the participants stated that their websites were not actively in use or said that they were sure that there were no hyperlinks pointing to their website and hence no browser warning messages would ever be thrown.

4.3.2 Technical Knowledge Concerning SSL

We asked the webmasters who had set up the X.509 certificate for their HTTPS server. 613 stated they had set it up themselves, 63 certificates were set up by a coworker, 12 by a retired coworker, 68 by their service provider and 11 did not know who set up the certificate. We asked the participants to self-report their technical knowledge of SSL on a 5-point likert-scale between *very low* and *very high.* 12 self-reported their SSL knowledge as *very low*, while 236 said their technical knowledge of SSL was *very high.* In the mean they rated it as a 3.96. Many administrators were uninformed about the pricing of X.509 certificates and strongly overestimated the actual costs. At total of 87 (11.5%) webmasters did not know their configuration could lead to browser warning messages prior to our survey (those who did know reported a mean technical SSL knowledge to be 4.02, those who did not reported their mean technical SSL knowledge to be 3.50). One interesting finding was that six survey participants stated they do not need the features provided by CA-issued X.509 certificates. They argued that for their use cases they did not need the authenticity features CA-issued certificates provide but only rely on "strong encryption" to transport sensitive data. These statements demonstrate a lack of understanding of the SSL security features. Although they rely on strong encryption, they oversee the fact that without properly verifying the identity of the server, no secure communication channel can be established in a reliable way since a Man-In-The-Middle attacker could easily exchange the original with a malicious certificate.

4.3.3 Risk Assessment Concerning Misconfigured SSL

We asked the participants to rate the importance of HTTPS for the operation of their website on a 5-point likert-scale from *not important at all* to *very important.* 217 said that HTTPS is not important at all, while 190 stated that it is very important for their websites' users. In the mean they rated it as a 3.00. We also asked them to rate the sensitivity of the data their website serves via HTTPS on a 5-point likert-scale ranking from 1 as *not sensitive at all* to 5 as *very sensitive.* 252 rated the sensitivity of their data as not sensitive at all, while 81 rated it as very sensitive. In the mean they rated it as a 2.53. We also had them rate the risk the non-validating X.509 certificate they are using poses to their users. On a 5-point likert-scale they could choose from *very low* to *very high.* 524 rated the risk as very low, while 23 said the risk for their users was very high. In the mean they rated it as a 1.55 Of the 755 respondents, 612 stated their users never complained about the occurring warning message, 7 administrators reported they receive complaints at least once a week, 12 received complaints on a monthly ba-

sis, 26 on a yearly basis, 77 receive complaints less often and 21 could not remember how often they receive complaints. We had been looking for interesting correlations between certificate error types and certain self-reported values. However, except for the results described above, we did not find a statistically significant correlation that would have helped us predict what kind of error would occur because of which characteristic. This underlines the importance of increasing the usability of X.509 certificate configuration and deployment in general, as well as building in more failsafe mechanisms and generally taking the weight of correct and secure X.509 certificate configuration and deployment away from webmasters.
At the end of the study, we asked the webmasters to describe problems they encountered with setting up SSL for their website and suggestions they had to *make X.509 certificate configuration more usable*. We present their concerns and suggestions in what we call the *Admins' Wishlist*.

4.4 Admins' Wishlist

We asked our participants to describe improvements they would like to add to make X.509 certificate configuration for HTTPS webservers easier and what they think is missing in the current system. In the following section we analyze their statements and describe what most participants find lacking in the current system. Of the 755 responding administrators, 87 offered suggestions, some of them more than one. Their suggestions can be categorized into six different groups:

Lowering The Price: 13 of the participants mentioned that the current price range for X.509 certificates that do not throw warning messages in browsers is not adequate. They find that paying a high amount of money for such a low cost task such as digitally signing an X.509 certificate is not fair and they would like to see a change in the current pricing policy of commercial Certificate Authorities. They criticize that the current CA infrastructure *"is a money printing machine without providing strong security for both service providers and their users"* (W29). Nine of them asked for a CA that issues free certificates that are accepted by popular browsers. Four participants complained that they have to configure X.509 certificates for multiple subdomains and that current wildcard certificates are too expensive. They wished to get access to cheaper wildcard certificates to reduce the number of false positive warnings on their websites.

Allowing CACert: 45 websites operated an X.509 certificate issued by CACert[7]. 10 of these proposed to add the CACert root CA to all popular browsers to provide an alternative to the commercial CAs issuing trusted certificates. The motivation to use a CACert certificate was two-minded: 28 of the administrators preferred CACert certificates since they did not want to support the commercial CAs and are of the opinion that basic encryption mechanisms as provided by SSL should be accessible by everyone for free. The remaining (17) did not trust the centralized trust model of commercial CAs after the breaches of DigiNotar and Commodo. They argued that the CACert's web of trust model provides more security and better protection against Certificate Authority compromise attacks.

Better Support for Non-Validating Certificates: 15 participants complained that they were forced to use certificates issued by commercial CAs to avoid SSL warning messages. They can be categorized into three different groups: Seven participants would like to change the current trust model. While two did not describe their idea of a different trust model, three would prefer a trust-on-first-use-based model such as known from the Secure Shell[8] which would allow them to use a certificate of their choice. Two other responders would prefer the TACK trust model proposed by Moxie Marlinspike[9] since they explicitly did not trust commercial CAs. Five participants would like to have an easy way to use self-signed certificates without giving concrete ideas of how such a system could work and four participants wanted to have an easier-to-use mechanism to validate certificate fingerprints to be able to securely deploy self-signed certificates for their users. Three participants were using their own CA in an enterprise environment and criticized the complicated workflow of adding their custom CAs to their users' browsers.

Better Tool Support: Six survey participants suggested to improve the tool support to generate and configure X.509 certificates for webservers. They found the command line interface for the OpenSSL tool[10] too complicated and wished for better documentation. The SSL configuration options of popular webservers were also criticized. Particularly the configuration of virtual hosts was described as very complicated and error-prone and administrators generally requested a more easy-to-use mechanism to configure X.509 certificates for multiple hostnames on a single IP address.

Auto-Update Reminder: Eight survey participants who used an already expired certificate were not aware of that fact before we contacted them. They criticized the fact that they would not receive an automatic message when their certificate expired and would like to have a service that keeps an eye on the expiration date of their certificate: *"Ideally an automatic message would be sent out to not miss the date to re-new a server's certificate"* (W643).

5. DISCUSSION

Our study reveals new findings and helps to better understand previous work in the field. While Akhawe and Felt [2] desire a 0% click-through rate for SSL warning messages, in our study 330 of 755 website administrators stated that they deliberately operate non-validating X.509 certificates and that their users are informed of the warning message beforehand. In these cases, SSL warning messages are no unexpected security warnings, but can be seen as information dialogs that users expect and to which they react by clicking through the warning because their administrator told them to. Whenever websites with non-validating certificates are re-visited by users, and the users did not add the non-validating certificate or the browser-untrusted CA to their truststore, they will repeatedly click through the warning. Since Google Chrome does not open the change to its trust store in the warning menu, it is likely that users will click-through a warning message on every visit. This is one possible explanation for the huge difference in click-through rates as reported by Akahwe et al.[2]: They count every repeated click-through in Chrome, while they count click-throughs in Firefox only at the first visit to the respective website (which may or may not have occurred during the period of their data collection). Thus, our findings sup-

[7] `http://www.cacert.org`

[8] `http://tools.ietf.org/html/rfc4253`

[9] `http://tack.io/draft.html`

[10] `http://www.openssl.org/`

port the assumptions that Chrome's click-through rate is massively influenced by re-visits of websites that operate non-validating certificates.

We found that many webmasters reported that their site was either not in use any more, or that the SSL version of the specific domain we encountered had never been meant to be accessible for users at all and had respectively never been hyperlinked anywhere on the Internet. This attests to a very important finding: Studies using datasets of SSL certificates that were accumulated by certifictae crawlers are prone to massively overreport handshake failures and hence SSL warning messages in browsers not only by assuming a possibly not applicable set of trusted certificate issuers, but also by including unused websites.

We gained valuable insights from the free texts the webmasters wrote about problems with SSL and improvement suggestions. Many of them wished for more simplicity: 165 had accidentally misconfigured SSL. Some wished for either a simpler interface to set up a webserver, others wanted an automatic renewal for expiring certificates.

330 webmasters had configured their webservers in a non-validating way on purpose. 15 of them wished that there was a broadly-accepted alternative to commercial CAs; in general there were complaints about the pricing of CAs. This is a very interesting finding: 20 of the 85 webmasters who suggested improvements requested a free alternative to paid CA certificates. Obviously these webmasters were not aware of the fact that there are free alternatives[11] that provide free and trusted X.509 certificates, which demonstrates that there is not only the need for a better technical education but also for a broad and basic documentation, complete with examples and links for webmasters, who understandably do not call SSL their primary field of expertise.

6. LIMITATIONS

Population: We contacted webmasters from a random sample of 50,000 websites which operated non-validating X.509 certificates without considering the popularity of the given website. Our results imply that X.509 certificate warnings occur more frequently on websites with low traffic which is often regarded as unproblematic by their webmasters: they claim that their users are aware of the presence of an SSL warning message causative certificate.

Self-Selection Bias: All our participants were self-selected. They chose to fill out the survey, which could mean that more active webmasters answered.

Bounced emails: We tried to reach webmasters either by using the contact email address in the website's X.509 certificate or the webmaster@domain.com email address. 37,596 of all emails we sent were bounced. Hence, the majority of websites with non-validating X.509 certificates does neither follow best practices and nor provide an easy-to-find contact email address. It might be possible that those webmasters have different reasons for using a non-validating X.509 certificate on their websites.

Underreporting: Some of our conclusions are drawn from answers which were given as free text. Thus we do not have data on all of our participants for several issues: Some did not report on whether their website is in use/is meant to be used at all, while others did. Not all of the users report on who the SSL connection is intended for. Therefore it is possible that we underreport the websites which are out of use, as well as the websites which exist for webmasters' use only.

[11]e. g. `www.startssl.com`

7. CONCLUSIONS

We conducted the first study with webmasters who operate non-validating X.509 certificates on their HTTPS-enabled websites to understand their motives. Therefore, we used the body of 4,487,463 certificates Google's webcrawler had collected over 12 months. We identified 610,966 non-validating certificates, chose a random sample of 50,000 of these, established if they were still operating and non-validating certificates, extracted email addresses for their webmasters and emailed them. Of those emails, 8,549 were successfully delivered. Of these, 755 webmasters who operated websites with non-validating X.509 certificates responded to our study.

101 said that their website was not meant to be accessible, and that actual users would not have encountered the certificate as the webcrawler did. We found that of the 495 who reported on this issue, 330 said that their use of a non-validating certificate was deliberate, while only 165 explained it with an accidental misconfiguration. 44 of the webmasters (25% of those who had accidentally misconfigured their webserver) stated that they were confused about SSL configuration in general, strengthening the assumption already made by Fahl et al[4] that, while warning messages and user behavior are an important field of study, studies with IT professionals in general and webmasters and developers in particular are an important and often neglected issue. We confirm findings from Akahwe et al., who state that Google Chrome users tend to click through warning messages more easily: This goes well with our finding that many webmasters use non-validating certificates on purpose and inform their users about it. Clicking through these warnings will add the certificate to Firefox, while Google Chrome will show a new warning on each revisit.

8. REFERENCES

[1] D. Akhawe, B. Amann, M. Vallentin, and R. Sommer. Here's my cert, so trust me, maybe?: Understanding tls errors on the web. WWW '13, 2013.

[2] D. Akhawe and A. P. Felt. Alice in warningland: A large-scale field study of browser security warning effectiveness. In *USENIX Security Symposium*, 2013.

[3] Z. Durumeric, E. Wustrow, and J. A. Halderman. ZMap: Fast Internet-wide scanning and its security applications. In *22nd USENIX Security Symposium*, Aug. 2013.

[4] S. Fahl, M. Harbach, H. Perl, M. Koetter, and M. Smith. Rethinking ssl development in an appified world. CCS '13. ACM, 2013.

[5] R. Holz, L. Braun, N. Kammenhuber, and G. Carle. The ssl landscape: A thorough analysis of the x.509 pki using active and passive measurements. IMC '11, 2011.

[6] J. Sunshine, S. Egelman, H. Almuhimedi, N. Atri, and L. F. Cranor. Crying wolf: An empirical study of ssl warning effectiveness. SSYM'09. USENIX Association, 2009.

YourPassword: Applying Feedback Loops to Improve Security Behavior of Managing Multiple Passwords

Tiffany Hyun-Jin Kim* H. Colleen Stuart† Hsu-Chun Hsiao* Yue-Hsun Lin*
Leon Zhang* Laura Dabbish* Sara Kiesler*
* Carnegie Mellon University † Johns Hopkins University

ABSTRACT

Various mechanisms exist to secure users' passwords, yet users continue to struggle with the complexity of multiple password management. We explore the effectiveness of a feedback loop to improve users' password management. We introduce YourPassword, a web-based application that uses feedback to inform users about the security of their password behavior. YourPassword has two main components: a password behavior checker that converts password strengths into numerical scores and a dashboard interface that visualizes users' overall password behavior and provides visual feedback in real time. YourPassword not only provides a total score on all passwords, but also visualizes when passwords are too similar to each other. To test the efficacy of YourPassword, we conducted a between-subjects experiment and think-aloud test with 48 participants. Participants either had access to YourPassword, an existing commercial password checker, or no password tool (control condition). YourPassword helped participants improve their password behavior as compared with the commercial tool or no tool.

Categories and Subject Descriptors

K.6.5 [**MANAGEMENT OF COMPUTING AND INFORMATION SYSTEMS**]: Security and Protection—*Authentication*; H.5.2 [**INFORMATION INTERFACES AND PRESENTATION (e.g., HCI)**]: User Interfaces—*User-centered design*; H.1.2 [**MODELS AND PRINCIPLES**]: User/Machine Systems—*Human factors*

Keywords

Authentication; Feedback Loops; Password Management

1. INTRODUCTION

Password-based online authentication is a primary way users log in securely to various websites. According to a study conducted in 2007, a typical user types approximately eight passwords each day [9]. The same study suggests that users are reusing the same or very similar passwords on multiple websites, maintaining 25 passwords but actively using about 7 distinct passwords. Reuse of passwords increases the security risks of password breach, but people have trouble recalling many distinct passwords.

Password managers of various types attempt to help people manage multiple different passwords without having to remember them (e.g., LastPass,[1] SplashID[2]). Although these password managers are useful, they are vulnerable in different ways: reliant on the strength of a master password, open to physical attacks, or subject to usability and convenience issues because of lack of portability.

We take a different approach and explore the effectiveness of a feedback loop to improve users' multiple password management behavior. Previous research in behavioral science suggests that a feedback loop can provide people with timely information about their actions and opportunities to improve them [11]. We argue that by making people more aware of their own behavior and how it is linked to their security, we can lead them to make improvements.

In this paper, we present the YourPassword system, which explores how to apply feedback loops to remind users of their own password security behavior and encourage them to choose multiple dissimilar passwords. YourPassword algorithms measure the strength of the user's passwords and translate them into easily understandable scores. Our algorithm considers password similarities and reuse among different websites.

YourPassword is a web-based dashboard application implemented as a Chrome browser extension. It provides password information and advice to users based on the algorithms we developed. We conducted a user study to measure the usability and usefulness of YourPassword. Our results suggest that the feedback loops in YourPassword helped users become more aware of their password choices and create more secure passwords.

2. PROBLEM DEFINITION

Our goal is to encourage users to create unique, dissimilar, and strong passwords for different websites, and to periodically update their passwords. Doing so is a challenge because users favor convenient, simple, and memorable passwords. In addition, overly salient indicators may overwhelm people, making them feel inadequate and unmotivated. At the same time, overly subtle indicators will not catch people's

ASIA CCS'14, June 4–6, 2014, Kyoto, Japan.
Copyright 2014 ACM 978-1-4503-2800-5/14/06 ...$15.00.
http://dx.doi.org/10.1145/2590296.2590345.

[1] `https://lastpass.com/`
[2] `http://splashdata.com/splashid/`

attention. We provide a feedback loop that gives people information about the effectiveness of their own password choices in a way that will encourage them to exert more care over their password management behavior.

Assumptions. We assume that we can gather relevant password information for all the user's websites and analyze the user's passwords in real time. We also assume that the gathered passwords are securely stored on the user's local machine and that our application does not leak stored passwords. In Sections 4.2 and 6, we discuss an alternative approach to relax our assumptions.

Desired properties. The following usability and performance properties are desired for an effective password behavior indicator: easy to use and intuitive, motivating (to choose stronger and more unique passwords), timely (catching the password information in real time), and accurate.

Adversary model. Attackers may attempt to guess as many passwords as possible to gain access to users' sensitive information. Accessing one password may provide exponential benefits to the attacker if that password is reused on multiple websites.

3. PASSWORD BEHAVIOR CHECKER

We designed a password scoring mechanism that considers a multitude of parameters to evaluate a password's security level. Unlike existing mechanisms [4,5,7,13,14,23,24], our mechanism adjusts the score based on the similarity to all the passwords of a user and the corresponding website's sensitivity level: we apply stricter rules for those passwords for highly sensitive websites (e.g., bank, email) compared to the passwords for moderately sensitive websites (e.g., forum, classifieds).

Our password behavior checker is composed of 5 modules:

- **Individual password strength:** This module checks if the password has a certain number of characters (e.g., minimum 8 characters for sensitive websites), contains dictionary words or common passwords,[3] contains uppercase characters, contains special characters, and is composed of unique characters.
- **Password reuse:** This module checks if the same password is reused on multiple websites.
- **Website sensitivity:** This module checks if the same password is reused on multiple websites with different sensitivity levels.
- **Password encryption:** This module checks if the password is transmitted without encryption.
- **Password similarity:** This module calculates how similar a user's password is to his/her other passwords.

For each site u, we denote pw_u, the password for u, and ℓ_u, the sensitivity level of u. Our password behavior checker (PBC) computes a score S_u for this site given pw_u and ℓ_u as well as the passwords and sensitivity levels of other sites. Specifically, $S_u = PBC(pw_u, \ell_u, \{pw_i, \ell_i | \forall i \neq u\})$. S_u is the combination of the normalized scores from all 5 modules, and this score can be potentially updated whenever the user enters any password (since our algorithm considers similarities of all of his/her passwords). For most modules (except password similarity), website's sensitivity levels affect the

[3] For our prototype, we used the top 100 Adobe passwords that were recently exposed in November 2013.

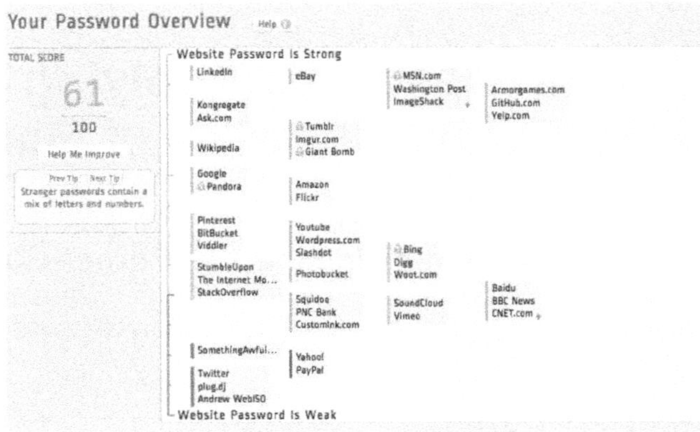

Figure 1: YourPassword dashboard.

generosity of the password scores as follows:

$$S_i \leq S_j \quad \forall \ell_i > \ell_j, pw_i = pw_j.$$

That is, if two sites have the same password but different sensitivity levels, the more sensitive site has a lower score.

Determining websites' sensitivity levels is a non-trivial task due to differences in individuals: a website that Alice considers to be sensitive may not be sensitive to Bob. On the other hand, any websites that are vulnerable to security and privacy breaches should be labeled as sensitive. Hence, YourPassword provides a default list of sensitive websites, such as financial corporations that are prone to phishing attacks.[4] Furthermore, YourPassword enables a user to update the list to include websites that (s)he considers to be sensitive.

The password behavior checker multiplies the fractional scores from the above five modules and outputs two scores: (1) a normalized score (0-100) for a recently entered password and (2) an average score for all of a user's passwords.

4. USER INTERFACE

The YourPassword interface visualizes a user's overall password behavior for all websites along with strength and uniqueness scores for each website's password.

4.1 YourPassword Description

YourPassword is a browser dashboard that displays:

- An overall score for a user's passwords based on their relative strength,
- Websites that share the same passwords,
- Visual groupings of websites with similar passwords,
- An individual score for each password based on its strength,
- A visual hierarchy, such that website groups with high scores are shown at top of the screen,
- A "Help me improve" button that displays multiple pieces of information to help users improve their password scores and security.

Figure 1 illustrates the YourPassword interface. The main display chart visualizes the user's overall password behavior. The scoring feedback is designed to range from 0 to 100 to make it easy for users to understand. To reinforce differences, we apply colors to differentiate score groupings (e.g., scores from 0 – 39, 40 – 69, 70 –100 are in red, orange, and green, respectively).

[4] http://docs.apwg.org/reports/APWG_GlobalPhishingSurvey_2H2011.pdf

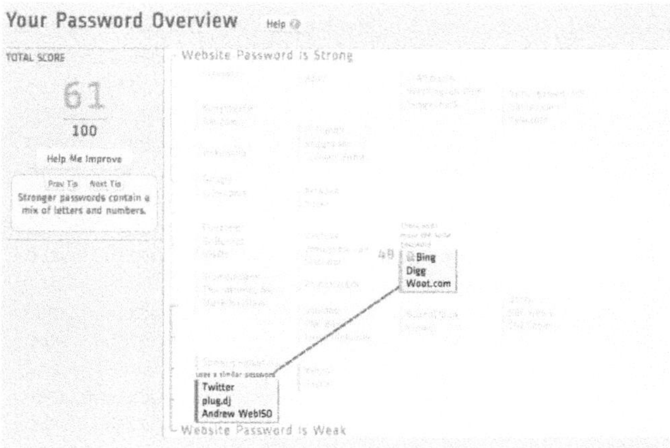

Figure 2: Individual node in the dashboard. When a user hovers over a node, the dashboard grays out the background and emphasizes the node, displaying the password's score along with links to other nodes with similar passwords.

Websites that share the same password are grouped together and displayed in the same node. In Figure 1, the user has a unique password for LinkedIn but shares the same password for Google and Pandora. (A node marked with the "+" sign indicates that a password is shared on more than 3 websites.) Sensitive websites are represented with a lock icon.

We apply the same coloring scheme to individual nodes to help users understand the relationship between the groups of websites and their password strengths. We also display an individual score for each password. When the user hovers over a node, it grays out the background and emphasizes the node, and the score for the password is displayed on the left side of the node. YOURPASSWORD also draws links to other nodes with similar passwords when a user hovers over a node (Figure 2). The "Help" button on top of the dashboard toggles the visibility of the tool tips (Figure 3).

The advice for improvement includes suggestions to update a specific website's password and reminders to update passwords regularly. The advice is dynamically updated as users enter their passwords, reducing potential habituation.

4.2 Implementation

We implemented YOURPASSWORD as a Google Chrome browser extension. The extension consists of three main modules – PASSWORD EXTRACTOR (PE), SCORE GENERATOR (SG), and PASSWORD DATABASE (PD).

Tracking is automatically accomplished by the PE module that monitors a user's login activities. After the installation, the PE module records the user's passwords at login pages by parsing the HTML source in the background and looking for the input field of a password type. When the user clicks the login button, the PE module captures the information $T = \{pwd, fn, d\}$, which includes the entered password (pwd), the password field name (fn), and the visited domain address (d), and then waits for a submission callback. Users may choose Chrome's incognito mode if they do not desire PE to track the credentials of particular websites.

The login information T is first saved at a temporary database, until a redirect page is loaded. If the redirect page has a password input field, we assume a login failure and delete the entry from the temporary database. Other-

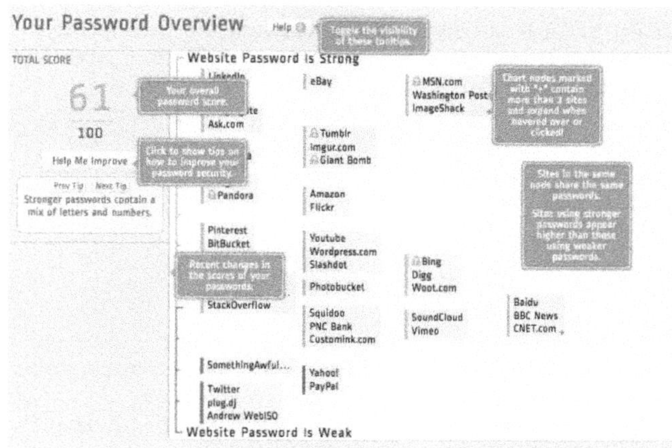

Figure 3: Help button. When a user clicks the "Help" button, tool tips for each section are displayed to help users understand the dashboard and interpret their current password behavior.

wise, we assume a successful login and load the temporary database into memory. When the login is successful, T is sent to the SG module using the Chrome extension API call `chrome.extension.sendRequest`. The SG module then calculates the score based on the currently entered password and all the previously stored passwords. To ensure privacy and secrecy of the passwords, the PD module encrypts and stores in the user's local machine the passwords in cleartext, total scores, individual module scores, T, and the website address.

Limitations. Some websites may prevent YOURPASSWORD from capturing passwords, for example by enabling javascripts. One possible solution is to ask users to manually enter passwords and their corresponding websites to YOURPASSWORD. Doing so would reduce the usability and convenience of appliance.

5. EVALUATION

We conducted a user study to evaluate whether YOURPASSWORD improves users' password behavior.

5.1 Method

The study was a between-subjects experiment in which participants played the role of a twin sibling, Robin, who suspects that eight personal accounts are potentially compromised by hackers. We gave the participant *Robin's* accounts and their corresponding passwords (Table 1). We asked the participant to improve the security of Robin's passwords. Two sets of passwords were similar to each other, and we reused the same password for two accounts. Six passwords, slightly modified, were among the most common in 2012.[5] Two were strings of random characters. We explained that hackers may steal private and sensitive information, including personal emails, private photos, private purchase history, personal medical history, as well as bank, credit card, and financial investment information. We emphasized that all Robin's accounts are equally important and sensitive, and have the same level of security risk.

The experiment had three conditions:

1. Control condition (CC): Participants were asked to up-

[5] `http://www.cnn.com/2012/10/25/tech/web/worst-passwords-2012/`

Table 1: A list of accounts and passwords for the experiment. We had two sets of passwords that were similar to each other, and the same password for two accounts.

Service	Password	Similar	Same
Amazon	!iloveyou	①	
American Express	Abcd123	②	
Bank of Oklahoma	passw0rd		✓
Etrade	eswr@U1ayP		
Facebook	passw0rd		✓
Gmail	@w43df2rxTL6^		
MyChart@Johns Hopkins	abcd123	②	
PayPal	iloveyou!	①	

date Robin's passwords. They were given no hints about the original or updated password strengths.

2. Microsoft password checker condition (MC): Microsoft's application allows users to check the strength of a password.[6] Participants in MC were asked to suggest new password(s), check each of them using Microsoft's password checker, and record the final passwords when they were happy with their strengths. They were allowed to try passwords multiple times until they were satisfied.
3. YOURPASSWORD condition (YC): Participants were asked to use YOURPASSWORD. After seeing the overall security of Robin's current passwords from the YOURPASSWORD application, they were asked to suggest new password(s), check each of them using YOURPASSWORD, and record the final passwords when they were satisfied. As in MC, they could repeat multiple times.

We hypothesized that participants in the YOURPASSWORD condition (YC) would suggest more password changes, stronger passwords, and more unique passwords.

5.2 Sample

We recruited 48 participants from Carnegie Mellon University's participant pool service. We also recruited local residents and students. We randomly assigned participants to each of the three conditions. Participants included 26 men and 22 women, ranging in age from 18 to 46 years old. Thirty-five were students, and of these students, 27 were majoring in engineering or computer science.

5.3 Procedure

A pretest asked participants if they had accounts with the websites listed in Table 1, if they thought it would be important to protect their personal data, how many unique passwords they currently had, and what strategy they used to remember their passwords. Participants were then randomly assigned to a condition and asked to follow the instructions described above. They were asked to think aloud and explain which password(s) they would update and their reason(s) for doing so. After the participants had reported their final password selections, they were asked to recall their final passwords for all eight accounts, including the passwords they did not suggest changing. We also asked participants whether they applied a policy to secure Robin's accounts, and what strategy they would use to remember the passwords they observed or created during the study.

5.4 General Observations

We observed that participants had fundamental security knowledge to create secure passwords *individually*. For example, all participants followed their own password policies to create a new password and proposed to update passwords that did not include a number, an uppercase character, or a symbol. However, without proper feedback, all participants in CC and MC conditions reused the same password on multiple websites, whereas all participants in YC proposed distinct passwords during our experiment.

Some participants in CC and MC conditions reused the same or similar passwords for services that are linked for usage. For example, two participants, one in CC and one in MC, reused the same or similar passwords for those services dealing with banking or credit card information (i.e., Amazon, American Express, Bank of Oklahoma, and PayPal). Also, one participant in MC mentioned that she would reuse the same password for Amazon, Facebook, and Gmail, since she logs into these services using the same email address.

Some participants did not trust the strength measurement using Microsoft's password checker, because they believed that their password policies would generate secure passwords. An interesting observation was that a number of participants used the initials of the services to create new passwords for memorability: not only these participants generated passwords that are meaningful to them but also linked with the services to tie individual passwords to the corresponding services.

Participants in YC immediately started to update the same or similar passwords after examining the feedback interface. On average, participants made 1.8 attempts ($\sigma = 0.71$, max $= 9$) to update the passwords for the accounts they wished to update. All participants tried hard to increase both individual password scores and overall score. However, they gave up after multiple attempts if the scores did not increase significantly.

5.5 Results

The results of an ANOVA test support the hypothesis that the feedback-based YOURPASSWORD interface (YC) improved participants' password behavior as compared with response to the commercial individual password checker (MC) or getting no feedback (CC). There were no effects of participants' education level, major field of study, occupation, age, or gender.

As shown in Table 2, participants' overall security level, use of unique passwords, and dissimilar passwords were significantly higher when they used the YOURPASSWORD application. The CC and MC conditions did not differ.

During the post-test, we measured how many final passwords participants could remember correctly. Memorability is an important issue because users may avoid passwords that are difficult to recall. We did not find statistically significant differences in the number of final passwords that participants remembered in different conditions. We also gave a 5-point Likert scale question to measure how useful participants found the application. Participants found both YOURPASSWORD and the commercial password checker somewhat useful but their usefulness scores were not significantly different. For the YC condition, we also asked how useful each feature in YOURPASSWORD was to the participants. On average, participants using YOURPASSWORD found the following features at least somewhat helpful: the total score ($\mu = 3.75, \sigma = .88$), individual score ($\mu = 4.58, \sigma = .56$), passwords similarity indicators ($\mu = 4.19, \sigma = .56$), grouping of the reused passwords ($\mu =$

[6] https://www.microsoft.com/security/pc-security/password-checker.aspx

Table 2: Summary of ANOVA test results for overall security, password uniqueness, similarity, memorability, usefulness, and likeliness to use to analyze the efficacy of **YourPassword** (YC) compared to individual password checker (MC) and no feedback (CC) ($N = 48$). The higher mean that is statistically significant from the others is highlighted in bold.

	Overall min: 0, max: 100		Uniqueness min: 0, max: 8		Similarity min: 0, max: 1		Memorability min: 0, max: 8		Usefulness min:1, max:5		Likeliness min:1, max:5	
	μ	$\sigma_{\bar{X}}$	μ	$\sigma_{\bar{X}}$	μ	$\sigma_{\bar{X}}$	μ	$\sigma_{\bar{X}}$	μ	σ	μ	σ
YC	**77.83**	**1.75**	**8.00**	**.00**	**.97**	**.01**	2.44	.70	4.28	.63	**4.31**	**.66**
MC	44.38	6.96	6.71	.49	.73	.06	4.06	.68	3.97	1.11	3.00	1.31
CC	44.46	8.54	5.60	.68	.71	.08	2.93	.71				
Results	$F(2,45) = 9.17$ $p < .0005$		$F(2,45) = 6.18$ $p = .004$		$F(2,45) = 5.74$ $p = .006$		$F(2,45) = 1.48$ $p = .239$		$F(1,31) = .96$ $p = .34$		$F(1,31) = 12.97$ $p = .001$	

μ: mean, $\sigma_{\bar{X}}$: standard error, σ: standard deviation

$4.59, \sigma = .91$), and placing passwords along the y-axis based on their scores ($\mu = 4.59, \sigma = .37$). Finally we asked participants in the MC and YC studies how likely it was that they would use the application to analyze their own password behavior. Participants were statistically significantly more likely to use YourPassword compared with the commercial password checker.

At the end of the study, we asked participants to share their strategies for remembering complex passwords. They mentioned writing passwords on paper, and sending themselves emails or text messages with passwords or password hints. Twenty participants said that they enable their browsers to remember their passwords. Just a few participants said that they would avoid storing their passwords for sensitive websites, such as banks or credit cards.

Our evaluation suggests that participants had sufficient security knowledge to create secure passwords individually. All participants followed their own password policies to create a new password. Several participants used the initials of the services to create new passwords for memorability. Participants also proposed updating passwords that did not include a number, an uppercase character, or a symbol. However, without feedback, all participants in the CC and MC conditions reused the same password on multiple websites, whereas all participants in YC proposed distinct passwords during our experiment. Because YourPassword suggests that users avoid reusing passwords, and our participants just did that, this feature may be especially valuable.

6. DISCUSSION

Regardless of its usability, any password manager must itself be safe. As is true of other password managers, YourPassword's current implementation stores encrypted passwords in a database so that YourPassword can accurately measure the similarity between a new password and old passwords. Unlike commercial password managers that ask users to generate a master encryption key, YourPassword's encryption key is a randomly generated string that is difficult for an attacker to break, and the user does not need to remember the key. Thus, the current implementation of YourPassword provides a better level of security compared with other password managers in the sense that the passwords are protected using a full-length random secret key that is hard to break even if the encrypted passwords are leaked. YourPassword can further increase the level of protection by storing the encryption key in sealed storage using the trusted computing technology. However, neither password managers nor YourPassword can defend against a strong adversary capable of stealing the encryption key.

We might further minimize the attack surface of YourPassword by storing the hashes of the passwords instead of storing the encrypted passwords. We can use two types of hash functions: a cryptographic hash function (e.g., SHA256) for exact matching, and a Locality Sensitive Hashing (LSH) function for fuzzy matching. Exact matching is needed to detect password reuse, whereas fuzzy matching is needed to evaluate the similarity between passwords. We can obtain an estimate of the distance between two passwords by using multiple LSH hashes with different threshold values. Since LSH is probabilistic, this modified version of YourPassword would eliminate the risk of master key leakage at the cost of the accuracy of a score. However, in contrast to cryptographic hash algorithms, LSH algorithms may suffer from preimage attacks – the attacker recovers the input from the hash value in short time (e.g., much fewer than 2^L attempts, where L is the hash length) – due to the additional distance information leaked to the attacker. We leave it as future work to formally investigate the trade-offs between security and score accuracy.

7. RELATED WORK

Feedback loops. Websites provide password strength meters to provide real-time feedback on the strength of a password as a user types. Such meters encourage users to create longer passwords [8,20]. YourPassword is different from this previous work in two aspects: YourPassword visualizes the relationship among all the user's passwords and provides feedback on the use of similar passwords.

Password vulnerabilities. Compromising less sensitive sites in order to attack sites with high security has been observed in websites using email addresses as user identifiers [3]. Several researchers have analyzed the actual deployment of such an attack [15,21], and many schemes have been developed to evaluate password strength based on attack resistance [4–7,14,23,24]. A recent study revealed that long passwords with no other restrictions provide resistance to guessing attacks, and that the dictionary check relies heavily on the choice of dictionary [13]. We designed our password strength checking algorithms to incorporate findings from these previous studies.

Human factors for password mechanism. Adams and Sasse emphasized the importance of considering human factors when designing security mechanisms, including passwords [1]. They noted the importance of making system security visible to users, such as providing feedback during password construction process. Users experience difficulties in creating and remembering attack-resistant passwords under strict policies [12, 16–19, 22]. Rather than aiming to replace passwords, our goal is to help users become aware of their password behavior based on feedback loops and encourage them to improve their password behavior.

Prior studies indicate that the majority of users reuse

their passwords across multiple websites [9, 10]. A large-scale password study also revealed that strong passwords are used at fewer sites on average compared to weak passwords [9]. Based on these findings, YourPassword aims to help users avoid sharing the same password on multiple websites by visualizing such information.

A recent proposal uses stories and pictures to help users create memorable passwords [2]. Such a scheme can be combined with YourPassword to help users create secure, unique, and memorable passwords.

8. CONCLUSION

People want to improve their password management behavior but they need help in doing so. Although various password managers have been developed to help users manage multiple, possibly unique passwords for various websites, they face security vulnerabilities and may not adequately change user behavior. Our solution is to apply feedback loops, the effectiveness of which has been demonstrated in the past, such as in speed-limit control systems [11]. By providing a non-invasive reminder about users' overall password behavior, they become more aware of their current actions and are encouraged to update weak and reused passwords to improve their security. The results of our experimental evaluation suggest further research to help users improve their own password behavior without relying on complex and possibly vulnerable external management tools.

9. ACKNOWLEDGMENTS

We gratefully thank Payas Gupta, Ruogu Kang, Peter Kinnard, Adrian Perrig, and Akshay Udiavar for their insightful feedback and help with the interface design and implementation. We also thank anonymous reviewers for their valuable comments. This research was supported by NSF under awards CNS-1040801 and CNS-1221006.

10. REFERENCES

[1] A. Adams and M. A. Sasse. Users are not the Enemy. *Communications of the ACM*, December 1999.

[2] J. Blocki, M. Blum, and A. Datta. Naturally Rehearsing Passwords. In *Proceedings of ASIACRYPT*, 2013.

[3] J. Bonneau and S. Preibusch. The Password Thicket: Technical and Market Failures in Human Authentication on the Web. In *Proceedings of WEIS*, 2010.

[4] W. E. Burr, D. F. Dodson, and W. T. Polk. Electronic Authentication Guideline. Technical report, NIST, 2006.

[5] C. Castelluccia, M. Durmuth, and D. Perito. Adaptive Password-Strength Meters from Markov Models. In *Proceedings of NDSS*, 2012.

[6] A. Das, J. Bonneau, M. Caesar, N. Borisov, and X. Wang. The Tangled Web of Password Reuse. In *Proceedings of NDSS*, 2014.

[7] M. Dell'Amico, P. Michiardi, and Y. Roudier. Password Strength: An Empirical Analysis. In *Proceedings of INFOCOM*, 2010.

[8] S. Egelman, A. Sotirakopoulos, I. Muslukhov, K. Beznosov, and C. Herley. Does My Password Go up to Eleven? The Impact of Password Meters on Password Selection. In *Proceedings of CHI*, 2013.

[9] D. Florencio and C. Herley. A Large-Scale Study of Web Password Habits. In *Proceedings of WWW*, 2007.

[10] S. Gaw and E. W. Felten. Password Management Strategies for Online Accounts. In *Proceedings of SOUPS*, 2006.

[11] T. Goetz. Harnessing the Power of Feedback Loops. Wired Magazine, June 2011.

[12] P. Inglesant and M. A. Sasse. The True Cost of Unusable Password Policies: Password Use in the Wild. In *Proceedings of CHI*, 2010.

[13] P. G. Kelley, S. Komanduri, M. L. Mazurek, R. Shay, T. Vidas, L. Bauer, N. Christin, L. F. Cranor, and J. Lopez. Guess again (and again and again): Measuring password strength by simulating password-cracking alrogithms. In *Proceedings of the IEEE Symposium on Security and Privacy*, 2012.

[14] A. Narayanan and V. Shmatikov. Fast Dictionary Attacks on Passwords Using Time-Space Tradeoff. In *Proceedings of CCS*, 2005.

[15] B. Prince. Twitter Details Phishing Attacks Behind Password Reset. eWeek, January 2010.

[16] R. W. Proctor, M.-C. Lien, K.-P. L. Vu, E. E. Schultz, and G. Salvendy. Improving Computer Security for Authentication of Users: Influence of Proactive Password Restrictions. *Behavior Research Methods, Instruments, & Computers*, 2002.

[17] R. Shay and E. Bertino. A Comprehensive Simulation Tool for the Analysis of Password Policies. *International journal of Information Security*, 2009.

[18] R. Shay, A. Bhargav-Spantzel, and E. Bertino. Password Policy Simulation and Analysis. In *Proceedings of ACM Workshop on Digital Identity Management*, 2007.

[19] J. M. Stanton, K. R. Stam, P. Mastrangelo, and J. Jolton. Analysis of End User Security Behaviors. *Computer & Security*, 2005.

[20] B. Ur, P. Kelley, S. Komanduri, J. Lee, M. Maass, M. L. Mazurek, T. Passaro, R. Shay, T. Vidas, L. Bauer, N. Christin, and L. F. Cranor. How Does Your Password Measure Up? The Effect of Strength Meters on Password Creation. In *Proceedings of USENIX*, 2012.

[21] A. Vance. If your Password is 123456, Just Make It HackMe. The New York Times, January 2010.

[22] K.-P. L. Vu, R. W. Proctor, A. Bhargav-Spantzel, B.-L. B. Tai, J. Cook, and E. E. Schultz. Improving Password Security and Memorability to Protect Personal and Organizational Information. *International Journal of Human-Computer Studies*, 2007.

[23] M. Weir, S. Aggarwal, B. de Medeiros, and B. Glodek. Password Cracking using Probablistic Context-Free Grammars. In *Proceedings of IEEE Symposium on Security and Privacy*, 2009.

[24] Y. Zhang, F. Monrose, and M. K. Reiter. The Security of Modern Password Expiration: An Algorithmic Framework and Empirical Analysis. In *Proceedings of CCS*, 2010.

Cyber Defenses for Physical Attacks and Insider Threats in Cloud Computing

Jakub Szefer
Yale University
jakub.szefer@yale.edu

Pramod Jamkhedkar
Princeton University
pjamkhed@princeton.edu

Diego Perez-Botero
Princeton University
diegop@cs.princeton.edu

Ruby B. Lee
Princeton University
rblee@princeton.edu

ABSTRACT

In cloud computing, most of the computations and data in the data center do not belong to the cloud provider. This leaves owners of applications and data concerned about cyber and physical attacks which may compromise the confidentiality, integrity or availability of their applications or data. While much work has looked at protection from software (cyber) threats, very few have looked at physical attacks and physical security in data centers. In this work, we present a novel set of cyber defense strategies for physical attacks in data centers. We capitalize on the fact that physical attackers are constrained by the physical layout and other features of a data center which provide a time delay before an attacker can reach a server to launch a physical attack, even by an insider. We describe how a number of cyber defense strategies can be activated when an attack is detected, some of which can even take effect before the actual attack occurs. The defense strategies provide improved security and are more cost-effective than always-on protections in the light of the fact that on average physical attacks will not happen often – but can be very damaging when they do occur.

Categories and Subject Descriptors

K.6 [**Managements of Computing and Information Systems**]: Security and Protection; H.1.2 [**Models and Principles**]: User/Machine Systems—*Human factors*

Keywords

Data Center Security; Physical Attacks; Insider Threats; Cloud Computing; Migration; Cloning; Virtual Machines

1. INTRODUCTION

Physical attacks on computers are less frequent and harder to launch, compared to software attacks. However, a physical attack may give an attacker absolute control over a secure sever, resulting in potentially greater damage. For this reason, most institutions that deal with highly sensitive data, including military and financial companies, go to great lengths to protect their servers and data centers from physical attacks. For example, to get into the building, one needs to scan one's hand, pass a guard, then go through a hallway where one is trapped if found suspicious. Also, some servers are locked in cages and separated from other systems [20]. Many physical attacks are, however, carried out by insiders who have authorized physical access to secure servers, making them difficult to prevent. Physical attacks on information technology (IT) infrastructures have been identified as one of the most overlooked aspects of IT security [12], and there has been no, or limited, cyber-physical defenses proposed. Furthermore, as cloud computing becomes prevalent, data centers will become prime targets for attackers.

Problem Overview: Defense mechanisms against physical attacks have typically followed two approaches: 1) physically controlled access and surveillance (entirely in physical space) and 2) design of secure servers with pervasive encryption and hashed storage (entirely in cyber space). On the one hand, physical access control mechanisms [11] may prevent unauthorized physical access to a certain degree, but are not effective against insider attacks. On the other hand, pervasive encryption, or continuous encryption of all memory (and swap disk space), is done by secure processor proposals, e.g. [22, 15, 6, 3], in which everything is automatically encrypted in DRAM. While the performance overhead may be acceptable, such architectures are not implemented in existing commodity processors – and hence are not available in current servers inside data centers.

Malicious Insiders: A particular concern is that a malicious cloud provider employee, who has "legitimate" physical access to the data center, can trivially launch physical attacks. This is precisely the scenario where our cyber-physical security countermeasures come into play. Today, any person, authorized or not, can launch physical attacks. In our proposed system, thanks to the use of the physical sensors, any sensitive data will be moved or scrubbed before an authorized employee or outsider has a chance to launch a physical attack. Note that we add the missing, physical, piece to the plethora of current, cyber-only, defenses. Also, our solution applies equally well to external attackers, insiders and maintenance personnel. Hence, our proposed solution is different from the existing ones, which are primarily aimed at keeping out the intruders, or are cyber-only mechanisms which focus on software attacks and not physical attacks.

ASIA CCS'14, June 4–6, 2014, Kyoto, Japan.
Copyright 2014 ACM 978-1-4503-2800-5/14/06 ...$15.00.
http://dx.doi.org/10.1145/2590296.2590310.

Our primary contributions are:

- A new cyber-physical defense strategy, where cyber defenses are used to protect against physical attacks (Section 2), including a new defense based on virtual machine (VM) cloning;
- Qualitative and quantitative analysis of four cyber defense strategies for physical attacks (Section 3); and
- A formalization of concepts and ideas needed to reason about physical attacks in data centers or other distributed networked systems (Section 4).

Key Advantages: Our cyber-physical defense framework is cost-effective. The cyber defenses against potential physical attacks are triggered only when the possibility of such an attack is detected by the surveillance and physical access control mechanisms. This precludes the need for pervasive encryption and hashing. It also offers a realistic solution against insider threats.

Paper Organization: Section 2 provides an overview of our cyber-physical defense architecture. Section 3 provides an analysis of the four defense strategies. Section 4 discusses physical attacks and equations needed to reason about them. Related work is described in Section 5 and we conclude in Section 6.

2. CYBER-PHYSICAL DEFENSES

Our work is based on a cloud computing paradigm where computation is performed inside VMs. Our goal is to protect code and data inside the VMs from physical attackers.

2.1 Threat Model and the Attacks

We aim to protect against physical attacks on compute, storage and networking equipment in a data center setting. This work is orthogonal to, and complements, work on defenses of these entities from cyber attacks. There is already a plethora of security research on software defenses, e.g. [4].

The main protected entities in our cyber-physical defense framework are the VMs running on the physical servers in a data center, which contain applications and data belonging to cloud customers. By extracting the contents of the VMs, an attacker can gain valuable information, including proprietary or sensitive data or programs belonging to cloud customers.

The human threat we are worried about is a physical attacker who has or gains physical access to a data center and the servers where the VMs are running. A physical attack can be carried out by different types of individuals including outsiders, maintenance individuals, insiders, etc. We assume that once an attacker has physical access to a machine, at that point in time the attack can be considered successful. Physical attacks include cold boot style attacks for extracting information from memory chips of the server [10], or stealing hard drives to extract data from the local disk. Attacks can also include turning off the power, or allowing the machine to overheat by turning off the cooling, to cause loss of availability to the VMs running on this server.

2.2 Attack Detection and Defense Timeline

Our defense framework against physical attacks is based on the time difference between potential attack detection and the actual attack, as shown in Figure 1, which we have first proposed in [24]. We now, however, consider three timestamps in our framework: time of detection (t_{detect}) denoting the time at which a physical attack is detected, and the time of attack (t_{attack}) denoting the time at which the attacker has physical contact with the equipment. We also consider $t_{pre-empt}$, which denotes a pre-attack time when some defenses can be pro-actively launched. The physical sensors mentioned previously are used to trigger a warning at t_{detect}. Scheduled events, such as maintenance, could be used to trigger pre-emptive actions at $t_{pre-empt}$.

Figure 1 shows different security mechanisms and their relationship with these three time stamps. Mechanisms shown in case A are preventive mechanisms that operate wholly in the physical space, and their effectiveness ends after an attack occurs. The goal of these measures is to delay t_{attack}, possibly forever (i.e., to shift t_{attack} as far right as possible). While these defenses may prevent outsider access, they are ineffective against insider attacks. Mechanisms shown in case B are detection mechanisms that operate in physical space, and their defensive purpose ends after an attack has been detected; although they can be utilized for evidence gathering as the attack proceeds, and for forensics afterwards. Pervasive encryption mechanisms shown in case C assume that an attacker can attack without any warning ($t_{detect} = t_{attack}$), and data is kept encrypted all the time. Such mechanisms, even though effective, either incur significant overhead, or require new hardware.

In our defense framework, we capitalize on the fact that effective detection mechanisms (case B) coupled with effective protection mechanisms (case A), both operating in the physical space, will induce a significant delay between t_{detect} and t_{attack}. The physical detection mechanisms (case B) would produce a warning at t_{detect} that can trigger appropriate cyber defense mechanisms, based on the expected time available for realtime response (T_r). We have identified four primary types of cyber defenses, which fall under cases D and E, that could be used against physical attacks to protect VMs. Our defenses consist of three reactive defenses (case D) and one proactive defense (case E).

1. *Migrate:* Applications and data are moved away from the physical servers being attacked so that when the attacker gains access to these servers, the data is no longer there.
2. *Encrypt:* Applications and data are encrypted within the servers, so that when the attacker gains access to the servers, the attacker cannot make use of the data since it is in encrypted form.
3. *Delete:* Applications and data are deleted from the servers so that when the attacker gains access to the servers, the data is no longer there.

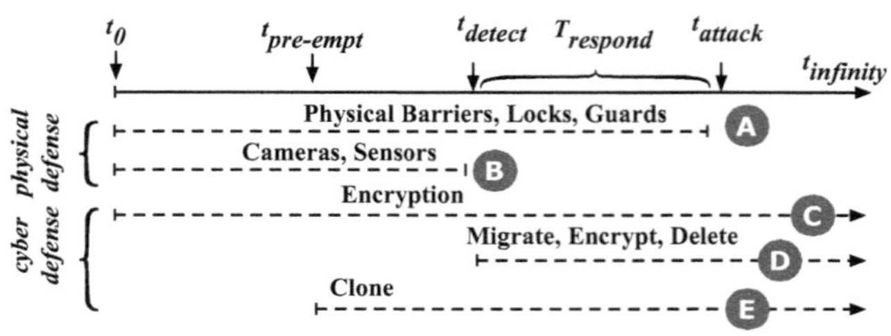

Figure 1: Defense strategy timeline. Our new proposed defense strategies are highlighted with Ⓓ and Ⓔ.

4. *Clone:* A VM with applications and data is cloned in anticipation of a potential attack; when an attack is detected we only need to erase the memory and any local storage on the victim server as a clone is already active and running in a different location.

Each defense strategy has its own limitations in terms of the time taken to carry out the response, practical feasibility, computation cost, and the security protections it offers; we present evaluation of these four in Section 3.

2.3 Cyber-Physical Defense Architecture

The Cyber-Physical Defense architecture consists of three main components: physical sensors, security management infrastructure, and compute equipment (e.g. servers).

2.3.1 Sensors and Physical Security Monitors

Data centers routinely include motion sensors, cameras, electronic locks on doors, etc., [19] and others can easily be added. These sensors provide an infrastructure that can signal an alert about an impending physical attack. Such a warning system provides various degrees of response times for defense mechanisms to be triggered.

We propose a physical security monitor which collects all the data from the attached sensors, formats it and converts it to the standard API (application programming interface) calls to the management infrastructure.

2.3.2 Security Management Infrastructure

The security manager integrates all the data from the various sensors. In order to calculate minimum response times based on attacker paths and hurdles, the data center floor plan, location of access doors, and location of servers can be automatically extracted from CAD (computer aided design) files describing the data center. The possible paths to a given server and the hurdles (e.g. locks on cages) can be pre-calculated, based on these inputs, to optimize reaction times to threats. The management software also calculates defense times for individual VMs based on bandwidth availability, server availability, safe destination servers, VM sizes, etc. The defense trigger mechanism also takes into consideration scheduled events (such as cleaning and maintenance) and mobility of data center personnel to trigger appropriate defenses. The defense strategies are translated into actual VM management commands so that the compute equipment can carry out the needed defensive countermeasures.

2.3.3 Compute Equipment

The cloud providers use management software such as OpenStack [17] to manage the actual compute servers. Figure 2 shows a possible realization of our cyber-physical defense system using the OpenStack cloud computing framework. The sensor and physical monitor infrastructure provides inputs via a modified Nova API. The inputs are then passed, via the Queue, to the management infrastructure which includes the Threat Evaluation and Defense Selection logic. This obtains floor plans and sensor locations from a CAD database. The defense triggers are passed via the message Queue to a modified Nova Compute server, which then carries out the defense strategies. Nova database is used by the OpenStack components to store (and retrieve) information about the different physical servers, status of the running VMs, etc.

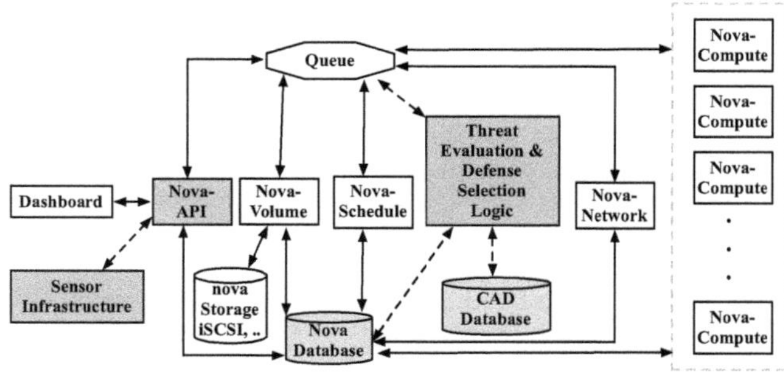

Figure 2: Our cyber-physical security architecture overlays onto the OpenStack cloud architecture. Modules shown in gray are OpenStack parts that would need to be added or modified.

3. FEASIBILITY OF CYBER DEFENSES

We now describe the defense strategies in more detail, and also evaluate the feasibility of our defenses with respect to the available attack response times. We follow the instance type definitions for Amazon's EC2 instances [1] (see Table 9 in the Appendix).

3.1 Migrate Strategy Analysis

When employing *migration* as a defense strategy, confidentiality, integrity and availability are all preserved after the attack; even if the attacker destroys or steals the equipment. Use of live VM migration allows for reduced downtime, and erasure of the source host's memory ensures that attacker does not gain information from the server he or she captures. Thus, our proposed defense is actually realized by complementing migration with the erasure or deletion of relevant RAM or local disk sectors[1], as described in Table 1.

Table 1: Migration based defense strategies.

Strategy	Details
Migrate + Erase RAM	The VM is migrated and the VM's main memory contents on the local machine need to be scrubbed.
Migrate + Erase RAM & Disk[1]	Same as "Migrate + Erase RAM", but if any of the VM's main memory has been swapped to local disk by the hypervisor, that disk space needs to be erased as well.
Migrate + Encrypt RAM	The VM is migrated, but the local main memory that was allocated to the VM is encrypted (local copy of encryption key is scrubbed).
Migrate + Encrypt RAM & Disk[1]	Same as "Migrate + Encrypt RAM", but any local disk contents (e.g. swapped memory of the VM) are encrypted (local copy of encryption key is scrubbed).

3.1.1 Migrate Strategy – Feasibility Analysis

The time taken to enact live migration as a defense depends on the type of applications which are running inside the VMs. We base our evaluation on the 7 types of workloads that most commonly arise in data centers [13], which are listed in Table 2.

To evaluate the migration strategy, our test bed is comprised of two hosts with identical hardware and software

[1]The local disk need not be erased or encrypted if always-on encrypted storage is used. The encryption key, however, still needs to be scrubbed from the system's main memory.

Table 2: Data Center Workloads

Workload	Benchmark
Mail Server	mstone [16] as remote SMTP client; smtp-sink [21] as SMTP server inside VM
App Server	Faban Benchmarking Framework [7] as remote client; Glassfish Server [9] with sample Java EE application inside VM
File Server	Dbench [5] inside VM
Web Server	Faban Benchmarking Framework [7] as remote client; Apache HTTP Server [2] inside VM
DB Server	Sysbench [23] inside VM
Stream Server	VideoLAN [26] inside VM; Wireshark [28] capturing stream packets remotely
Idle Server	No workload

configurations. Each host comes with dual quad-core Intel Nehalem CPUs (1.6GHz), on top of which a KVM hypervisor is running. The network connecting both hosts supports 1Gbps speeds. Meanwhile, the VMs being migrated come with 1 GB of dedicated RAM and 1 CPU core. For each workload, we ran 2-minute long benchmarks and performed migrations at five different migration points within that 2-minute interval; those results were then averaged. This solves the problem of variations due to the migration point [13].

The results are shown in Table 3. From the data, it can be seen that total migration time for a 1 GB VM (and thus the time needed to deploy the defense) is on the order of 10 seconds. The *liveness* of this strategy is clear: downtimes experienced by users are negligible (< 1 second) for all but one server workload. A key fact to bear in mind is how critical available bandwidth is to live migration. For instance, it took us 19.4 seconds to migrate an Idle Server when using a 100 Mbps link, but only 2.6 seconds with a 1 Gbps link. The overhead is the difference between execution time when migrating and when not migrating, divided by the time when not migrating.

Table 3: Migration Performance and Resource Usage with Data Center Workloads with 1Gbps link.

Server Type	Total Time (s)	Down -time (ms)	Data Sent (MB)	Over -head (%)	Avg. BW (Mbps)
Mail	8.9	300	800.39	15.71	702.86
App	7.5	4050	728.21	6.25	766.52
File	7.2	250	697.87	12.71	764.77
Web	7.2	250	645.33	10.08	707.08
DB	7.4	450	717.52	1.39	765.22
Stream	8.0	650	716.21	3.03	705.31
Idle	2.6	200	212.34	0.00	629.11

3.2 Cloning Strategy Analysis

When employing VM cloning as a pre-emptive defense strategy, confidentiality, integrity and availability are preserved. Cloning strategies are listed in Table 4. Cloning relies on proactively cloning the VM and running multiple clones of the VM; if any clone is in danger of attack, that clone is simply terminated while other clones keep running.

3.2.1 Cloning Strategy – Feasibility Analysis

The cost of cloning comes from the duplicate resources used as the VMs run, e.g. DRAM memory allocated to each clone. This can be dealt with by installing more resources.

Table 4: Cloning based defense strategies.

Strategy	Details
Clone and erase RAM	Scrub RAM containing VM's memory pages.
Clone and erase RAM & Disk	Scrub RAM and any disk containing VM's memory pages.

Also, to be able to use cloning as a defense strategy, there needs to be sufficient time to proactively clone the VMs. Cloning re-uses many of the facilities of migration and has almost identical total time. Details of the cloning strategy are omitted for space reasons, they are available in [18].

The time required to clone a 2GB VM ranges between 4 and 15 seconds if the full bandwidth of a 1Gbps link is available between the host machines. As with live migration, the bandwidth and current processor load will influence the cloning time. However, since cloning is proactive, the cloning time can be selected when there is available bandwidth and the servers are not under heavy load.

3.3 Encrypt Strategy Analysis

When employing encryption as a reactive defense strategy, confidentiality is preserved after the attack. Availability, however, is not preserved if the attacker destroys or steals the equipment and there is no redundant backup copies stored elsewhere. The defense is realized through encryption of relevant RAM or local disk sectors, as described in Table 5.

Table 5: Encryption based defense strategies.

Strategy	Details
Encrypt RAM	Encrypt all of VM's memory pages in RAM.
Encrypt RAM & Disk	Encrypt all of VM's memory pages in RAM and any memory that has been swapped to local disk.
Move to Encrypted Disk & Erase RAM	If swap space is already using encrypted storage, move all memory pages to swap space, and erase RAM contents.

3.3.1 Encrypt Strategy – Feasibility Analysis

Encryption will be affected by both by the algorithm used as well as the hardware available. We benchmark symmetric key encryption using the popular TrueCrypt [25] . Based on the speeds and the VM's RAM and local disk sizes (from Table 9) the times for encryption of RAM are obtained and shown in Table 6. On the test servers (see Section 3.1.1 on migration) the AES algorithm performed at 450 MB/s and Twofish at 409 MB/s. We also tested the encryption on a different system with Intel Core i7 processor with dedicated AES instructions. The AES algorithm benefited greatly from the new Intel AES-specific hardware instructions and achieved 2253 MB/s All measurements were done when the CPU was not utilized for any other purpose.

Table 6: Encryption of VMs' RAM (a) without and (b) with dedicated AES encryption instructions.

	Encrypt RAM	micro	m1.small	m1.medium	m1.large
(a)	AES	1.38 s	3.89 s	8.56 s	34.16 s
	Twofish	1.52 s	4.28 s	9.41 s	37.58 s
(b)	AES	0.27 s	0.77 s	1.71 s	6.82 s
	Twofish	1.52 s	4.28 s	9.41 s	37.58 s

3.4 Delete Strategy Analysis

When employing deletion as a defense strategy, confidentiality is preserved, but integrity and availability are not, as the applications or data are not available anymore after the deletion. The defense is realized through deletion of relevant RAM or local disk sectors, as described in Table 7.

Table 7: Delete based defense strategies.

Strategy	Details
Erase RAM	Scrub RAM containing VM's memory pages.
Erase RAM & Disk	Scrub RAM and any disk containing VM's memory pages.

3.4.1 *Delete Strategy – Feasibility Analysis*

RAM and disk erasure times depend on the write speeds of the memories and disks. Data can also be overwritten with a random pattern. Our results in Table 8 are for overwriting RAM and disks with zeros.

On the test servers (see Section 3.1.1) sequential writes to main memory can sustain 6481 GB/s. For disk, we use the 70 MB/s throughput (assuming the erase is just writing 0s at the full speed of the disks we have tested). Table 8 summarizes the times needed to perform the erase strategy for the different types of VMs.

Table 8: Erasing RAM and local disk of VMs.

Operation	micro	m1.small	m1.medium	m1.large
Erasing RAM	0.10 s	0.27 s	0.59 s	2.37 s
Erasing local disk	8.9 s	0.14 s	0.14 s	0.14 s

Note that *micro* instances have some local swap disk, while other instance types only have configuration files that count as data on local disk (they use remote persistent storage).

3.5 Comparing the Defense Strategies

We have presented details of the four defense strategies: migrate, clone, encrypt and delete. In our evaluation, the migration strategy takes longer (about 9s), compared to encrypting data or erasing the VM, but provides the most security, and availability is maintained. The encryption strategy is faster with less than 7 seconds even for the largest VMs, if AES-specific hardware instructions are available. The exception is when there is a lot of VM memory that has been swapped to disk and that disk has to be encrypted on the fly. Use of encrypted swap space, however, alleviates this problem. The fastest strategy, but also offering only confidentiality protection, is the delete strategy. All data is lost, but the attacker does not get to it. Alternatively, cloning is a very good strategy if there are enough resources to create clones, pre-emptively, of the VMs. The defense then is quite fast (as fast as the erasure strategy) because, if the attacker threatens one clone, the clone can simply be erased. Moreover, cloning can be configured to use less network resources and take more time.

4. REASONING ABOUT PHYSICAL ATTACK AND RESPONSE TIMES

The key to accurately determining the response time for a given VM is to calculate how "close" is the nearest potential threat from the server on which the VM is running. This calculation must be carried out taking into consideration the physical locations of different individuals in a data center, their type, and how easily each of those individuals can reach the server. We denote the current location of different individuals in a data center as the threat context. For a given threat context, the estimation of time to respond is not absolute, but relative to the type of security required by the VM. For instance, one VM may consider the presence of a maintenance person in the vicinity as a threat, whereas another VM may not consider it as a threat according to which security level was selected for the VM. Therefore, two VMs operating on the same server, under the same threat context, may perceive the same threat with different urgency and hence have different response times. The calculation of the estimated response time available for a given VM is carried out in the following steps:

1. Obtain the locations of all the potential attackers (i.e. the threat context) and the location of the host server.
2. For each attacker, calculate all paths from the attacker's position to the server.
3. Calculate the response time for each attacker based on the shortest path (in terms of travel time and time to clear hurdles) for that attacker.
4. Calculate the available response time as the smallest of all the response times for each attacker.

Step 1 is calculated from inputs provided by the sensors and physical access control mechanisms providing locations of all individuals in the data center. Step 2 is calculated based on the result of Step 1 and the pre-calculated physical layout of the data center. We define Step 3 as follows. For a given VM vm running on Server s, and an attacker a, let $P(a,s)$ represent the set of all the paths from the position of a to the position of server s. The response time for VM vm from threat a while being hosted on server s is:

$$T_r(vm, s, a) = min_{p \in P(a,s)}\{T_w(a, s, p) + T_h(a, vm, p)\} \quad (1)$$

where $T_w(a,s,p)$ is the amount of time required by the attacker a to cover the distance between himself and the victim server s on a given path p and $T_h(a, vm, p)$ is the amount of time required by the *attacker* to clear all the hurdles between himself and the victim server s on path p. The value for $T_w(a,s,p)$ can be calculated by the length of path p divided by the average running time for a human. In order to calculate $T_h(a,vm,p)$ we need to know what type of hurdles are present on path p, and how much time attacker a would take to clear those hurdles. Whether or not an individual (intruder, maintenance personnel, etc.) is an attacker or not is determined by the $vm's$ security policy.

Step 4 calculates the nearest threat as follows. Let A be the set of all the potential attackers detected in the data center. The available response time for a given VM vm hosted on server s is the minimum of all the response times calculated for each potential attacker, calculated as follows:

$$T_r(vm, s) = min_{a \in A}\{T_r(vm, s, a)\} \quad (2)$$

The type of defensive action chosen must fit this T_r.

5. RELATED WORK

Numerous physical measures are used in data centers to ensure the security of the data center infrastructure from physical attacks [11]. Barriers, alarms, entry control, contraband detection, CCTV (closed-circuit television) surveillance, and other means have been used for protecting data centers [8]. Many physical security measures mainly focus on environmental, not human, factors such as fire security or the failure of supporting utilities (e.g., power) [27].

Preventing outsiders from gaining access to data centers typically includes measures like security locks, biometric authentication, isolation of secure areas, sign-in books, two-factor authentication, etc. These mechanisms are often complemented with mechanisms for detecting physical intrusions such as cameras, sensors, surveillance guards, etc. These physical defense measures provide time constraints on any potential attackers. Each measure slows down the attackers, although it does not necessarily stop them.

An example of a "moving target defense" [14] strategy is one where VMs are pro-actively moved from one server to another. Past work, however, has not looked at using physical triggers as a means of influencing moving target defenses.

6. CONCLUSION

We presented details of a cyber-physical security framework for cloud computing data centers that combines the security mechanisms in cyber and physical spaces, and exploits the power of virtualization to provide dynamic security against physical attackers. The framework protects against *human* attackers who can use physical access (illegitimate or legitimate as in the case of insider attacks) to extract applications or data from the compute infrastructure inside the data centers. We secure applications and data through the use of cyber defenses based on the strategies of migration, encryption, deletion and cloning. While the first three are reactive defenses triggered by the detection of a potential human attacker, the last one, cloning, is a preemptive strategy that can be used for the most security-sensitive applications. We leverage physical intrusion detection systems to warn of an impending physical attack to trigger the first three defenses: migration, encryption and deletion. When there are enough resources for pre-emptive cloning, it can provide faster response when an attack actually happens. We hope our work will simulate more research into the use of cyber defenses for protecting against physical attacks.

7. REFERENCES

[1] Amazon EC2 Instance Types. http://aws.amazon.com/ec2/instance-types/.

[2] The Apache HTTP Server Project. http://httpd.apache.org/.

[3] D. Champagne and R. B. Lee. Scalable architectural support for trusted software. In *Proceedings of the International Symposium on High Performance Computer Architecture*, HPCA, pages 1 -12, January 2010.

[4] W. Dawoud, I. Takouna, and C. Meinel. Infrastructure as a Service Security: Challenges and Solutions. In *Proceedings of the International Conference on Informatics and Systems*, INFOS, March 2010.

[5] Dbench filesystem benchmark. http://dbench.samba.org/.

[6] J. S. Dwoskin and R. B. Lee. Hardware-rooted trust for secure key management and transient trust. In *Proceedings of the ACM Conference on Computer and Communications Security*, CCS, pages 389–400, October 2007.

[7] Faban Harness and Benchmark Framework. http://java.net/projects/faban/.

[8] L. J. Fennelly. *Effective Physical Security.* Butterworth-Heinemann, 3rd edition, 2003.

[9] GlassFish - Open Source Application Server. http://glassfish.java.net/.

[10] J. A. Halderman, S. D. Schoen, N. Heninger, W. Clarkson, W. Paul, J. A. Calandrino, A. J. Feldman, J. Appelbaum, and E. W. Felten. Lest we remember: cold-boot attacks on encryption keys. *Communications of ACM*, 52(5):91–98, May 2009.

[11] S. Heare. Data Center Physical Security Checklist. Technical report, SANS Institute, December 2001. http://www.sans.org/.

[12] K. J. Higgins. The 10 Most Overlooked Aspects of Security, November 2006. http://www.darkreading.com/security/application-security/208808177/the-10-most-overlooked-aspects-of-security.html.

[13] D. Huang, D. Ye, Q. He, J. Chen, and K. Ye. Virt-lm: a benchmark for live migration of virtual machine. In *Proceedings of the International Conference on Performance Engineering*, ICPE, pages 307–316, March 2011.

[14] S. Jajodia, A. K. Ghosh, V. Swarup, C. Wang, and X. S. Wang, editors. *Moving Target Defense: Creating Asymmetric Uncertainty for Cyber Threats.* Springer, 2011.

[15] R. B. Lee, P. Kwan, J. P. McGregor, J. Dwoskin, and Z. Wang. Architecture for protecting critical secrets in microprocessors. In *Proceedings of the International Symposium on Computer Architecture*, ISCA, pages 2–13, June 2005.

[16] mstone multi-protocol testing system. http://sourceforge.net/projects/mstone/.

[17] OpenStack. *OpenStack Compute: An Overview.*

[18] D. Perez-Botero. *Pwnetizer: Improving Availability in Cloud Computing Through Fast Cloning and I/O Randomization.* Master's Thesis, Princeton University, Princeton, NJ, 2013.

[19] S. D. Scalet. 19 Ways to Build Physical Security into a Data Center. http://www.csoonline.com/.

[20] J. S. Schultz. Should you trust mint.com? From New York Times http://bucks.blogs.nytimes.com/2010/07/06/should-you-trust-mint-com/?_r=0.

[21] smtp-sink(1) - Linux man page. http://linux.die.net/man/1/smtp-sink.

[22] G. E. Suh, D. Clarke, B. Gassend, M. van Dijk, and S. Devadas. Aegis: architecture for tamper-evident and tamper-resistant processing. In *Proceedings of the Annual International Conference on Supercomputing*, ICS, pages 160–171, June 2003.

[23] SysBench: a system performance benchmark. http://sysbench.sourceforge.net/.

[24] J. Szefer, P. Jamkhedkar, Y.-Y. Chen, and R. B. Lee. Physical Attack Protection with Human-Secure Virtualization in Data Centers. In *Workshop on Open Resilient human-aware Cyber-physical Systems*, WORCS, June 2012.

[25] TrueCrypt - Free Open-Source On-The-Fly Disk Encryption Software. http://www.truecrypt.org/.

[26] VLC media player. http://www.videolan.org.

[27] M. E. Whitman and H. J. Mattord. *Principles of Information Security.* Cengage Learning, 2011.

[28] Wireshark: the world's foremost network protocol analyzer. http://www.wireshark.org/.

APPENDIX

Table 9: Local server resources used by different Amazon EC2 VM instance types.

Resource	micro	m1.small	m1.medium	m1.large
VM's RAM	613MB	1741MB	3840MB	15370MB
VM config	$\leq$ 10MB	$\leq$ 10MB	$\leq$ 10MB	$\leq$ 10MB
Total RAM	623MB	1751MB	3850MB	15380MB
Local Swap for VM	$\leq$ 613MB	n/a	n/a	n/a
VM config	$\leq$ 10MB	$\leq$ 10MB	$\leq$ 10MB	$\leq$ 10MB
Total Disk	623MB	10MB	10MB	10MB

Monkey-in-the-browser: Malware and Vulnerabilities in Augmented Browsing Script Markets

Steven Van Acker, Nick Nikiforakis, Lieven Desmet, Frank Piessens, Wouter Joosen
{firstname.lastname}@cs.kuleuven.be
iMinds-DistriNet, KU Leuven, 3001 Leuven, Belgium

ABSTRACT

With the constant migration of applications from the desktop to the web, power users have found ways of enhancing web applications, at the client-side, according to their needs.

In this paper, we investigate this phenomenon by focusing on the popular Greasemonkey extension which enables users to write scripts that arbitrarily change the content of any page, allowing them to remove unwanted features from web applications, or add additional, desired features to them. The creation of script markets, on which these scripts are often shared, extends the standard web security model with two new actors, introducing novel vulnerabilities.

We describe the architecture of Greasemonkey and perform a large-scale analysis of the most popular, community-driven, script market for Greasemonkey. Through our analysis, we discover not only dozens of malicious scripts waiting to be installed by users, but thousands of benign scripts with vulnerabilities that could be abused by attackers. In 58 cases, the vulnerabilities are so severe, that they can be used to bypass the Same-Origin Policy of the user's browser and steal sensitive user-data from all sites. We verify the practicality of our attacks, by developing a proof-of-concept exploit against a vulnerable user script with an installation base of 1.2 million users, equivalent to a "Man-in-the-browser" attack.

Keywords

Augmented browsing; browser extension; Greasemonkey; script market; userscripts.org; malware; vulnerabilities; DOM-based XSS; large-scale analysis

Categories and Subject Descriptors

K.6.5 [**Management of Computing and Information Systems**]: Security and Protection; H.3.5 [**Information Storage and Retrieval**]: Web-based services

ASIA CCS'14, June 4–6, 2014, Kyoto, Japan.
Copyright 2014 ACM 978-1-4503-2800-5/14/06 ...$15.00.
http://dx.doi.org/10.1145/2590296.2590311.

1. INTRODUCTION

The web has evolved from a collection of purely static pages to entire web applications, making the browser the medium of choice for delivering new software and services. With this migration, many power users who used to customize their operating system and install their applications of choice, now feel the desire to customize the applications inside their browser, in a way that fits their needs. These customizations usually result in an enhanced form of browsing the web, which is called "augmented browsing".

Probably the most well-known instance of augmented browsing software is the *Greasemonkey* [8] browser extension, which, at the time of this writing, ranks fifth in the list of most popular Firefox extensions [20]. Greasemonkey users can write *user scripts*, i.e., small JavaScript programs, that manipulate loaded webpages on the client-side in any way desired. User scripts can, among others, hide ads, change the content layout of a page, and make cross-origin HTTP requests to create client-side mashups. In contrast with typical browser extensions, user scripts are comprised of a single JavaScript file and are not packaged in any way, making them easy to inspect and modify.

Due to the popularity of Greasemonkey and the large number of user scripts created for it, the Greasemonkey developers created `userscripts.org` [21], a community-driven script market, on which members can exchange user scripts.

The creation of a script market brings along some unique security issues, because it extends the standard web attacker model with new actors. In the regular model, a website is visited by a client and an attacker can either attack the website by exploiting server-side vulnerabilities, or the visitor through client-side vulnerabilities, like XSS or CSRF. In the augmented browsing scenario, however, the model is extended with the inclusion of a user script in the visitor's browser, a script market, and a script author creating and sharing user scripts through the script market.

In this paper, we perform an in-depth analysis of this extended script ecosystem. First, we consider the script author as a malicious actor, having the ability to create user scripts with malicious functionality, and upload them to the script market where they may be downloaded and installed by victim users. We report on the prevalence of malicious scripts, the discovered malice, and whether this malice was identified by the `userscripts.org` community.

Second, we shift our focus to the possibility of conducting attacks on poorly coded user scripts. We find many instances of benign scripts whose authors, even though they had no bad intentions, unwillingly introduced vulnerabilities which could be used to attack websites that are otherwise secure. Using straightforward static-analysis techniques, we identify more than 100 user scripts, with millions of installations, vulnerable to DOM-based XSS [12]. We also show that a certain type of user script vulnerability can be abused to launch attacks even against the Greasemonkey engine itself, leading to powerful global XSS attacks, where an attacker can steal a user's data from all sites.

Our main contributions are:

1. We evaluate the Greasemonkey browser extension, focusing on the functionality with negative security consequences.
2. We analyze the most popular, community-driven script market for Greasemonkey and describe the difficulties of relying on the community to define and identify maliciousness.
3. We demonstrate novel attacks that take advantage of benign Greasemonkey scripts to attack, otherwise secure, websites.

2. GREASEMONKEY

In this section, we describe the Greasemonkey engine, its uses, and the structure of Greasemonkey scripts. Finally we examine how Greasemonkey affects the security and isolation of scripts in the browser.

2.1 Greasemonkey engine

Greasemonkey is a popular browser add-on for augmented browsing. Using Greasemonkey, users can, on the client side, modify the appearance and functionality of any webpage. This is done by JavaScript programs that are injected in arbitrary webpages and have access to privileged functionality, not available to normal JavaScript programs. Through these Greasemonkey scripts and with the help of the browser's DOM, users can arbitrarily edit a webpage, including the removal of content, e.g., ads, or the addition of new content, e.g., adding missing functionality to a web application, or creating mashups using content from multiple domains.

While Greasemonkey was originally a Firefox-specific extension, there are also ports of the extension to other browsers, like Tampermonkey for Google Chrome. According to the extension markets of Mozilla Firefox and Google Chrome, at the time of this writing, there are almost three million users who have the Greasemonkey and Tampermonkey extensions installed. Moreover, due to the popularity of the extension, a subset of the Greasemonkey functionality is, by default, supported in many modern browsers, where Greasemonkey scripts are treated as a special case of browser extensions.

In general, Greasemonkey scripts can be considered lightweight browser extensions. Users can write their own scripts, or find scripts written by other users, either dispersed on the web, or concentrated on community-driven script markets, much like the aforementioned popular extension stores. As further explained in the next section, Greasemonkey scripts are single-file JavaScript programs, without Manifest files and directory structures, which users can inspect and edit from within the Greasemonkey extension.

2.2 Greasemonkey scripts

In this section, we demonstrate the basic structure and syntax of Greasemonkey user scripts, and the necessary concepts for the comprehension of the rest of the paper.

Listing 1 Example of a Greasemonkey user script

```
// ==UserScript==
// @name          Hello World
// @description   Description of this script
// @namespace     http://author.com/gmscripts
// @include       http://example.com/*
// @include       http://*.example.com/*
// @exclude       http://login.example.com/*
// @grant         GM_xmlhttpRequest
// ==/UserScript==

alert("Hello World");
GM_xmlhttpRequest({
  method: "GET",
  url: "http://www.shopping.com/",
  onload: function(response) {
    alert(response.responseText);
  }
});
```

2.2.1 *Structure of scripts*

Listing 1 shows a simple example of a user script. Notice that before the actual functionality of the script, there is script-specific meta-data in the form of comments enclosed by `// ==UserScript==` and `// ==/UserScript==`

The Greasemonkey engine will recognize the comments containing `@` signs and read-in the appropriate values. The `@name` and `@description` directives specify the title of a script and a user-readable description of what the script does. The `@include` and `@exclude` directives allow the script authors to specify the domains and webpages that their script should execute on. The `@grant` directive specifies that the listed function should be added to the Greasemonkey sandbox.

The actual code of the user script starts where the meta-data comment block ends. In our example, the first call is to the standard `alert` function provided to JavaScript from the Browser Object Model and used to display message boxes to the user. The second function call, however, is towards a special Greasemonkey-specific function. *Greasemonkey API* functions have the `GM_` prefix and are typically able to do operations not allowed by standard JavaScript code. In this case, the script performs a cross-domain HTTP request to `http://www.shopping.com`, an operation that is otherwise forbidden by the *Same Origin Policy* (SOP), the browser's default security policy, for security and privacy reasons. Other Greasemonkey functions allow a user script to store and retrieve persistent data, access script-specific resources, and register menu commands in the browser.

Figure 1 shows the Greasemonkey dialog that is displayed to the user trying to install our example user script. Notice that at the bottom of the dialog, the user is warned that the scripts can violate the user's security and privacy, and that the user is supposed to install scripts only from trusted sources.

2.2.2 *Important meta-data*

In this section, we expand upon some of the aforementioned Greasemonkey directives with security and privacy consequences.

`@include`. As described earlier, Greasemonkey consults the `@include` directive to determine which pages a user script

Figure 1: Greasemonkey Script Installation Dialog

should be injected in. Greasemonkey uses regular expressions to match the `@include` header against the entire URL, allowing a lot of flexibility. The script author might for instance add `@include http*://*.example.com` to allow the script to run on both HTTP and HTTPS versions of the example.com sub-domains, and the script author is even allowed to specify `@include *` to run the script on any website. If no `@include` directive is present, Greasemonkey will default to `@include *` for that user script.

`@grant`. Recognizing the merits of the least-privilege principle, Greasemonkey allows script authors to specify which functions of the Greasemonkey API should be added to the Greasemonkey sandbox, using the `@grant` header.

Consider again the user script listed in Listing 1, displaying the usage of this `@grant` header to request access to the `GM_xmlhttpRequest` function. The special directive `@grant none` is used to indicate that the script uses no Greasemonkey API functions at all, and thus none should be added to the sandbox. In the absence of `@grant` headers, Greasemonkey will attempt to infer the necessary API functions by analyzing the user script.

2.3 Attack surface

At this point, it should be evident that the extra functionality of user scripts, unfortunately comes with room for extra vulnerabilities. We consider three different attack scenarios: a) malicious user scripts abusing the pages in which they are injected, b) attackers abusing benign but vulnerable user scripts to attack webpages and, c) malicious pages trying to abuse the Greasemonkey engine and gain access to privileged functions.

In the first scenario, a victim installs a user script that advertises some functionality, e.g., automatically hiding ads on all webpages. This script may be a trojan horse which, next to hiding ads, steals private data from pages, the user's cookies, or even capture all of the user's keystrokes.

In the second scenario, an attacker can take advantage of vulnerabilities introduced by user scripts on pages that otherwise would have no exploitable vulnerabilities, e.g., the exploitation of a DOM-based XSS vulnerability on a webmail application introduced by the added functionality of a Greasemonkey user script.

In the third scenario, an attacker can take advantage of user script vulnerabilities, not just to inject code in a benign page, but to inject code in Greasemonkey's sandbox. Greasemonkey makes use of sandboxing to protect the privileged `GM_` functions from possibly malicious scripts running on a website. Despite this sandbox and additional stack-inspecting mechanisms of Greasemonkey, a poorly-written user script can still introduce unsafe code in the sandboxed environment, e.g., by `eval`-ing a string from a malicious page without performing the proper sanity checks. When this happens, a malicious script can get access to the powerful Greasemonkey API and circumvent the SOP.

3. COMMUNITY-DRIVEN SCRIPT MARKETS

Script markets facilitate the sharing of Greasemonkey scripts by providing script authors with a disseminating platform and a feedback mechanism, and consumers of scripts with comments and ratings about the quality and utility of a particular script.

We retrieved a total of 86,358 user scripts together with their accompanying meta-data, from `userscripts.org`. This meta-data includes how many times a user script has been installed, and whether or not the user script was flagged as "Harmful" by the community.

More information about the dataset can be found in [23].

4. MALWARE ASSESSMENT

Greasemonkey scripts are more powerful than traditional JavaScript programs, because they can manipulate and retrieve private data in a user's browser without SOP restrictions. Consequently, such scripts can be an attractive infection vector for malware authors, who can create malicious user scripts and trick users into installing them.

In this section, we discuss malware in Greasemonkey user scripts and how the `userscripts.org` community is currently attempting to deal with malicious scripts.

4.1 Userscripts.org issue reporting

The `userscripts.org` community website has a community-based, manual reviewing process to detect malicious user scripts. When a malicious user script is detected, the user can flag it as "harmful" and, optionally, explain her vote in the comment section.

In our dataset of 86,358 scripts, 626 (0.7%) are marked as "harmful" by at least one user of the `userscripts.org` community. Of those 626 scripts, 592 have at least as many votes in favor of "harmful" as votes against it.

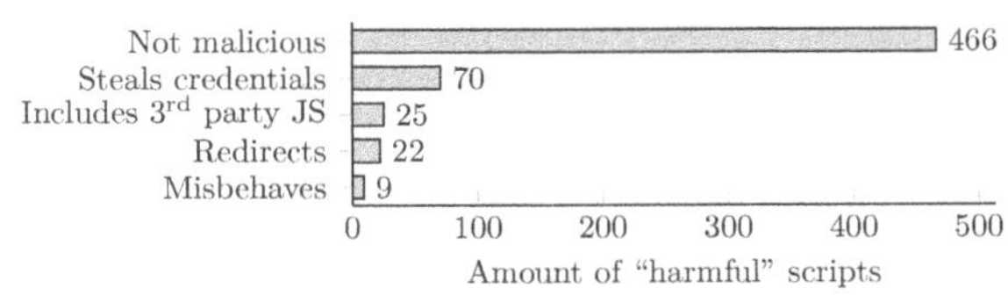

Figure 2: Categories of malware found in the 592 scripts labelled as "harmful" in the `userscripts.org` dataset. Almost 80% is harmless.

To determine the quality of this manual review process, we performed a manual analysis of these scripts to determine what users regard as "harmful". From the 592 "harmful" scripts, we could not find any trace of malice in 466 (78.7%) of them. For our purposes, we defined malice as the attempt to steal private data from a user, or trick the user into performing an action with potential monetary benefits for the attacker. We will refer to the remaining 126 scripts that do contain malware, as the *verified harmful dataset*.

A breakdown of the entire harmful dataset according to the reason the scripts were flagged, is shown in Figure 2. The largest fraction with verified maliciousness is comprised by 70 scripts containing malware designed to steal credentials in some form, from the user. The next largest fraction of scripts (25) includes third party JavaScript into a loaded page [16]. Twenty-two scripts simply redirect the user to another website, with the possible intent to lure the user into a drive-by-download scenario and install malware that way. Only five of these "redirect" scripts were reported by users to be the cause of a drive-by-download attack. Finally, there remain nine scripts which "misbehave", and do not fit in the previous categories.

Shifting our attention to the 466 benign scripts that were mislabeled as malicious, the given reasons indicate that the concept of "harmful" is not always clear to the members of the community, and that there should be a clearer definition.

A more detailed breakdown of the reported malware, as well as observations that can help in the detection of malware, can be found in [23].

5. ATTACKING WEAK SCRIPTS

In the previous section, we discussed scripts that are malicious by design, giving their authors the ability to harm those scripts' users. Because Greasemonkey injects user scripts into visited webpages, these user scripts unfortunately increase the attack surface of the user.

In this section, we discuss two vulnerabilities that occur in user scripts: DOM-based XSS and overly generic `@include` directives. Through these vulnerabilities, an attacker can trick a victim's browser into executing code on webpages onto which a user script acts, or even any webpage he wants, and potentially even gain access to powerful Greasemonkey API functions.

5.1 DOM-Based XSS

DOM XSS vulnerabilities present in user scripts are more dangerous than regular DOM XSS vulnerabilities because the vulnerability will be injected into any page on which the user script code is included. Attackers can then exploit these vulnerabilities and gain access to the Greasemonkey API, which is not bound by the SOP.

DOM-based XSS analysis setup. To determine whether any DOM-based XSS vulnerabilities occur in our user scripts dataset, we screen all scripts using a lightweight static-analysis method. Using SpiderMonkey [19], we parsed all scripts in our dataset and obtained a simplified AST for each one of them. Using a list of sources and sinks [7], we searched for sources used directly in the argument list of sinks. As such, all the results reported in the next sections are lower bounds of vulnerabilities.

Results. The results of our DOM-based XSS analysis on the full dataset retrieved from `userscripts.org`, are shown in Table 1. From the 86,358 scripts in our dataset, our analysis revealed 1,736 that contain a DOM-based XSS. The majority of scripts are vulnerable through the `e.innerHTML` sink (1,654 or 95.3%) and the various sources originating from the `document` object (99.7%).

	`document` `.body`	`.location`	*other*	`window` *.name*	Total
`doc.write(x)`	0	1	2	0	3
`eval(x)`	3	0	76	0	79
`innerHTML`	721	83	846	5	1,654 (*)
Total	724	84	924	5	1,736 (*)

Table 1: Scripts with detected DOM-based XSS vulnerabilities according to the used sources and sinks. (*) Total reflects the amount of unique scripts for the given sink, not the row sum.

Note that some sources might require the ability of an attacker to place persistent data onto a website. From the dataset, 101 scripts are vulnerable to DOM-based XSS with sources not bound by this requirement.

The most prominent, vulnerable to DOM-based XSS, user script that we discovered is the fourth most popular script on the `userscripts.org` script market, with almost 40 million installations.

5.2 Overly generic `@include`

As explained in Section 2.2, the `@include` directive specifies which webpages a user script is injected in. The `@include` directive allows wildcards, and uses regular expression to test the entire URL of the webpage being visited.

If the `@include` wildcard is used in a too generic way, this can lead to a security problem. For instance, reconsider the introductory example in Listing 1. In this script, the directive `@include http://*.example.com/*` is used. An attacker can construct the URL `http://www.mybank.com/#x.example.com/abc` and trick a user of this script to visit it. Greasemonkey's regular expression will then match the `@include` directive against this crafted URL and falsely assume that the author of the script wants the script to be executed on `http://www.mybank.com/`. The attacker has caused the script to run on a webpage for which it was not intended, by abusing the `@include` wildcard.

`@match`. The developers of Google Chrome, in their adaptation of the Greasemonkey engine, recognized that the wildcard `*` in the `@include` directive, was not strict enough and could lead to insecure situations. For this reason, they created the `@match` [4] directive which provides the same functionality as `@include`, but in a safer way.

Google Chrome's `@match` wildcard is context-sensitive and is applied by splitting a URL into three parts: a scheme, a host and a path. A `*` wildcard can occur within each part, but cannot match anything that violates the borders between the parts.

To be compatible with user scripts for Google Chrome, Greasemonkey adopted the `@match` directive alongside its `@include` directive. In cases where both `@include` and `@match` directives are used, the `@include` directive is handled first.

	@match	No @match	Total
@include securely	670	33,775	34,445
@include insecurely	770	39,955	40,725
No @include	884	10,304	11,188
Total	2,324	84,034	86,358

Table 2: `@include` and `@match` directive usage, "insecurely" means an overly generic `@include`

Usage of the `@include` *and* `@match` *directives.* Table 2 divides the scripts in our dataset with regard to `@include` and `@match` directives. From the 86,358 scripts in our dataset, 75,170 (87.0%) contain a `@include` directive, of which 40,725 insecurely with a too generic wildcard. Since scripts without an explicit `@include` directive automatically obtain a `@include *` directive, this means that 51,913 scripts or 60.1% of the full dataset can be tricked into executing on a different domain than the one they were designed for.

Only 2,324 specify a `@match` directive, of which 1,440 also specify an `@include` directive. Of those 1,440, 770 have insecure `@include` directives, meaning the `@match` directive's security advantage over a `@include`, is completely negated.

The most popular script with an unsafe `@include` directive is, at the same time, the most popular script on `userscripts.org`, a social networking script with more than 250 million downloads. It uses an overly generic wildcard `@include` directive of the form `@include http://*website.com/*`.

5.3 Resulting malicious capabilities

Global XSS. The combination of a DOM-based XSS vulnerability, and an overly generic `@include` directive, results in a critical vulnerability. Scripts which contain this combination of vulnerabilities allow attackers to execute malicious code on any webpage of choice, by having victims visit appropriately constructed URLs.

From the 1,736 vulnerable scripts revealed from our analysis to be vulnerable to DOM-based XSS vulnerabilities, 944 (54.3%) also use overly generic `@include` directives and can thus be used to perform global XSS attacks.

Privileged XSS. The case of a DOM-based XSS where attacker-controlled data find its way into an `eval(x)` sink reveals an extra security issue because it allows malicious code to execute inside the Greasemonkey sandbox and gain access to the Greasemonkey API.

Consider for instance the example in Listing 1. The example script uses `GM_xmlhttpRequest` to get access to cross-origin resources from `http://www.shopping.com/`. This API function will be present in the sandbox where the user script executes, because `@grant GM_xmlhttpRequest` is used to request it. If this example script also contained a DOM-based XSS vulnerability with an `eval(x)` sink, then a malicious website could trigger this vulnerability, executing code inside the Greasemonkey sandbox and get access to the powerful `GM_xmlhttpRequest` function.

From the 79 scripts that contain a DOM-based XSS with an `eval(x)` sink, 60 execute in a sandboxed environment with access to the Greasemonkey API and can thus leak that API to a malicious website which may abuse it.

Privileged, global XSS. To aggravate the problem further, it is possible to combine all three vulnerabilities: a script with an overly generic `@include` directive, vulnerable to a DOM-based XSS attack where attacker-controlled data flow into `eval(x)`, thereby exposing the Greasemonkey API.

A script such as this can be abused by an attacker by luring victims to a specially crafted URL, causing attacker-controlled code to be executed, with access to the powerful Greasemonkey API. Since the Greasemonkey API functions are not bound by the Same Origin Policy, an attacker could then abuse them to steal private data from the victim's browser, across all sites. From the 60 scripts we identified as being vulnerable to a DOM-based XSS with an `eval(x)` sink and which also expose the Greasemonkey API, 58 use an overly generic `@include` directive.

The most prominent example is a script installed by 1.2 million users, which can be forced to run on any website, due to its overly generic use of wildcards. Moreover, the script makes insecure use of `eval` allowing an attacker to execute arbitrary code in the Greasemonkey sandbox. We created a proof-of-concept exploit which amounts to a Man-in-the-Browser attacker, i.e., we can conduct requests towards all websites (together with the user's cookies), read the responses, and inject malicious JavaScript on any domain.

We are in the process of disclosing the vulnerabilities to the involved parties.

6. RELATED WORK

To the best of our knowledge, this paper is the first one that tries to shed light on alternative, community-driven, JavaScript markets. Closely related, however, is research done in identifying malicious and vulnerable browser extensions from the official extension markets of Mozilla Firefox [3] and Google Chrome [9], showing that extensions often request more privileges than needed. VEX [2] analyzes Firefox extensions, such as Greasemonkey, for privilege escalation vulnerabilities, but does not analyze the user scripts used by Greasemonkey itself.

While malicious browser extensions are typically written in JavaScript, malicious JavaScript, today, has a different connotation, that of code which exploits some vulnerability in the browser or in one of the browser plugins to eventually lead to drive-by downloads. Due to the great magnitude of the problem, there has been a significant body of research in detecting malicious JavaScript, using honeypots [15], dynamic analysis of JavaScript code [5, 11, 13, 17], and hybrid systems [6, 18] which utilize both static and dynamic techniques to analyze JavaScript code.

The main difference of this type of malicious JavaScript with the types of malicious Greasemonkey scripts analyzed in this paper, is that in our case, maliciousness is context-specific. That is, it may only be discoverable when the user is on a specific page of a specific website, making dynamic detection of context-specific maliciousness significantly harder to define, as well as detect.

Typical JavaScript sandboxing techniques [1, 10, 14, 22] attempt to isolate malicious code in a controlled environment and prevent references to powerful functionality from leaking inside the sandbox. In contrast, Greasemonkey creates a sandbox with its powerful API inside and attempts to prevent the leakage of references to this API to the outside.

7. CONCLUSION

In this paper, we analyzed the Greasemonkey browser extension and the `userscripts.org` script market, searching for evidence of malware and vulnerabilities, as well as documenting the ways with which community-driven script markets deal with malicious scripts. Through this process, we find that the review process of `userscripts.org` is ineffective in 78% of the cases.

Moreover, we identify and analyze two types of vulnerabilities found in user scripts, which could allow an attacker to use the restricted and powerful Greasemonkey functions to, among others, bypass the Same Origin Policy, and force a user script to run on any website.

We found that DOM-based XSS vulnerabilities are present in 2% of user scripts and that 60.1% of user scripts can be forced to run on any webpage. Finally, we show how an attacker can combine many vulnerabilities to launch powerful privileged, global XSS attacks and discover 58 scripts that are susceptible to this attack. We verify this attack through a proof-of-concept exploit for one of these user scripts, installed by over a million users, allowing an attacker to steal user data across all sites.

Acknowledgements

This research was performed with the financial support from the Prevention of and Fight against Crime Programme of the European Union (B-CCENTRE), the Research Fund KU Leuven, the FP7 projects STREWS, NESSoS and WebSand, and the IWT project SPION.

8. REFERENCES

[1] P. Agten, S. Van Acker, Y. Brondsema, P. H. Phung, L. Desmet, and F. Piessens. JSand: Complete client-side sandboxing of third-party javascript without browser modifications. In *Proceedings of the 28th Annual Computer Security Applications Conference*, pages 1–10. ACM, 2012.

[2] S. Bandhakavi, S. T. King, P. Madhusudan, and M. Winslett. Vex: Vetting browser extensions for security vulnerabilities. In *USENIX Security Symposium*, pages 339–354. USENIX Association, 2010.

[3] A. Barth, A. P. Felt, P. Saxena, and A. Boodman. Protecting browsers from extension vulnerabilities. In *NDSS*. The Internet Society, 2010.

[4] Match Patterns - Google Chrome. `https://developer.chrome.com/extensions/match_patterns.html`.

[5] M. Cova, C. Kruegel, and G. Vigna. Detection and Analysis of Drive-by-Download Attacks and Malicious JavaScript Code. In *Proceedings of the World Wide Web Conference (WWW)*, 2010.

[6] C. Curtsinger, B. Livshits, B. Zorn, and C. Seifert. Zozzle: Fast and precise in-browser javascript malware detection. In *Proceedings of the 20th USENIX Conference on Security*, SEC'11, pages 3–3, Berkeley, CA, USA, 2011. USENIX Association.

[7] DOM XSS Test Cases Wiki Cheatsheet Project. `https://code.google.com/p/domxsswiki/`.

[8] Greasemonkey. `https://addons.mozilla.org/en-US/firefox/addon/greasemonkey/`.

[9] A. Guha, M. Fredrikson, B. Livshits, and N. Swamy. Verified security for browser extensions. In *Proceedings of the 2011 IEEE Symposium on Security and Privacy*, SP '11, pages 115–130, Washington, DC, USA, 2011. IEEE Computer Society.

[10] L. Ingram and M. Walfish. Treehouse: JavaScript sandboxes to help web developers help themselves. In *Proceedings of the USENIX annual technical conference*, 2012.

[11] A. Kapravelos, Y. Shoshitaishvili, M. Cova, C. Kruegel, and G. Vigna. Revolver: An Automated Approach to the Detection of Evasive Web-based Malware. In *Proceedings of USENIX Security*, 2013.

[12] A. Klein. DOM Based Cross Site Scripting or XSS of the Third Kind. `http://www.webappsec.org/projects/articles/071105.shtml`, April 2005.

[13] C. Kolbitsch, B. Livshits, B. Zorn, and C. Seifert. Rozzle: De-cloaking internet malware. In *Proceedings of the 2012 IEEE Symposium on Security and Privacy*, SP '12, pages 443–457, Washington, DC, USA, 2012. IEEE Computer Society.

[14] J. Magazinius, P. Phung, and D. Sands. Safe wrappers and sane policies for self protecting javascript. In *15th Nordic Conference on Secure IT Systems*, 2010.

[15] Y. min Wang, D. Beck, X. Jiang, R. Roussev, C. Verbowski, S. Chen, and S. King. Automated web patrol with strider honeymonkeys: Finding web sites that exploit browser vulnerabilities. In *Proceedings of 13th Network and Distributed Systems Security Symposium (NDSS '06)*, 2006.

[16] N. Nikiforakis, L. Invernizzi, A. Kapravelos, S. Van Acker, W. Joosen, C. Kruegel, F. Piessens, and G. Vigna. You are what you include: Large-scale evaluation of remote JavaScript inclusions. In *Proceedings of ACM Conference on Computer and Communications Security (CCS)*, 2012.

[17] P. Ratanaworabhan, B. Livshits, and B. Zorn. Nozzle: A defense against heap-spraying code injection attacks. In *Proceedings of the 18th Conference on USENIX Security Symposium*, SSYM'09, pages 169–186, Berkeley, CA, USA, 2009. USENIX Association.

[18] K. Rieck, T. Krueger, and A. Dewald. Cujo: Efficient detection and prevention of drive-by-download attacks. In *Proceedings of the 26th Annual Computer Security Applications Conference*, ACSAC '10, pages 31–39, New York, NY, USA, 2010. ACM.

[19] Mozilla SpiderMonkey. `https://developer.mozilla.org/en-US/docs/Mozilla/Projects/SpiderMonkey`.

[20] Mozilla add-ons - featured extensions. `https://addons.mozilla.org/en-US/firefox/extensions/`.

[21] Userscripts.org. `http://userscripts.org/`.

[22] S. Van Acker, P. De Ryck, L. Desmet, F. Piessens, and W. Joosen. WebJail: least-privilege integration of third-party components in web mashups. ACSAC '11, pages 307–316, New York, NY, USA, 2011. ACM.

[23] S. Van Acker, N. Nikiforakis, L. Desmet, F. Piessens, and W. Joosen. Monkey-in-the-browser: Malware and vulnerabilities in augmented browsing script markets – extended version. Technical report, Mar. 2014.

IntentFuzzer: Detecting Capability Leaks of Android Applications

Kun Yang[1,3], Jianwei Zhuge[2,3], Yongke Wang[4], Lujue Zhou[2], and Haixin Duan[2,3]
[1]Department of Computer Science and Technology, Tsinghua University
[2]Institute for Network Science and Cyberspace, Tsinghua University
[3]Tsinghua National Laboratory for Information Science and Technology
[4]Institute of Information Engineering, Chinese Academy of Sciences

ABSTRACT

Capability leak is a vulnerability in Android applications, which violates the enforcement of permission model and threatens the secure usage of Android phone users. Malicious applications can launch permission escalation attacks with this vulnerability. In this paper, we propose a dynamic Intent fuzzing mechanism to uncover vulnerable applications in both Android markets and closed source ROMs. We built a prototype called IntentFuzzer. With it, we analyzed more than 2000 Android applications in Google Play and hundreds of in-rom applications inside two closed source ROMs. We found that 161 applications in Google Play have at least one permission leak, and 26 permissions in Xiaomi Hongmi phone and 19 permissions in Lenovo K860i stock phone are leaked. Finally, we give several cases of exploitation to verify our analysis result.

Categories and Subject Descriptors

D.2.4 [**Software Engineering**]: Software/Program Verification; D.2.5 [**Software Engineering**]: Testing and Debugging

General Terms

Security, Design, Experimentation

Keywords

Smartphone Security, Intent Fuzzing, Capability Leak

1. INTRODUCTION

Android smartphones market share has exploded in recent years. Compared with traditional PC, smartphones are much closer to users. Considering the sensors such as cameras and voice recorder integrated into mobile devices, it's necessary to protect these usage of the sensors. Moreover, smartphones have become the main way to store and handle private data, including SMS messages, call logs, contact information and photos, which are imperative to be protected.

ASIA CCS'14, June 4–6, 2014, Kyoto, Japan.

ACM 978-1-4503-2800-5/14/06 ...$15.00.
http://dx.doi.org/10.1145/2590296.2590316 .

Permission model is essential in the design of Android security. In this model, sensitive resources are protected by permissions that other applications don't have. However, because of the existence of vulnerable applications, it is possible for attackers to break through such permission model. Capability leak is such a vulnerability that an application exposes some permissions, by which other applications without these permissions can access protected resources.

Several static analysis systems have already been built to detect capability leaks in applications [7, 6, 10, 5]. DroidChecker [5] has found 6 vulnerable apps including Adobe Photoshop Express 1.3.1. Woodpecker[10] detected 11 permissions are leaked in 8 stock phones from world's leading manufacturers. These tools are effective, but they may all have false positive, and should manually verify how to trigger permission leaks.

To precisely uncover capability leaks in millions of applications automatically, we used an old technique - fuzzing in this new situation. By sending testing Intents to various exposed interfaces, we can detect if any capability leaks happen. Compared with static methods, our method has an advantage in precision. While static analysis only sees the possible calling connections between function calls, dynamic fuzzing can detect permission leaks that really happen, which can be recorded and used to reconstruct all the scenes.

We developed a prototype called IntentFuzzer, and used it to analyze over 2,000 popular applications in Google Play. Our result shows that 161 applications have at least one permission leak. We also apply IntentFuzzer to closed source ROMs that customized by various vendors, and found that 26 permissions in Xiaomi Hongmi phone and 19 permissions in Lenovo K860i are leaked.

The rest of paper is organized as follows: Section 2 briefly introduces background knowledge of Android permission model and Inter Component Communication mechanism. Section 3 and Section 4 describe our system design and implementation respectively. Section 5 presents the detailed evaluation results from our study. Section 6 discusses limitations and future work. Section 7 describes related work and Section 8 summarizes our conclusions.

2. BACKGROUND

2.1 Permission Model

To mitigate security threat related to personal privacy, Google has designed a permission-based model. Android application is prohibited from accessing dangerous permis-

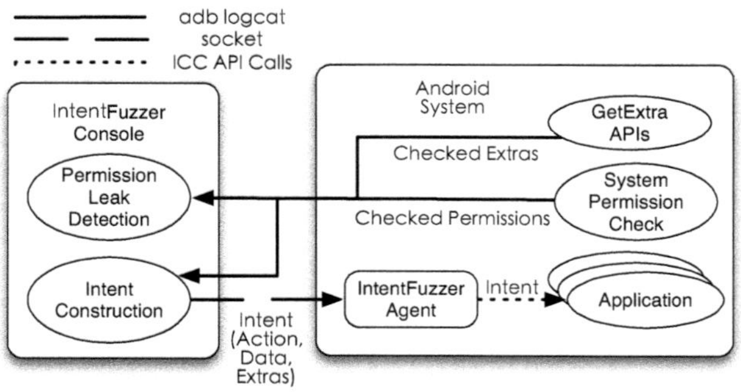

Figure 1: Architecture of IntentFuzzer

sions by default. Users should authorize the privileges that apps request at install-time.

2.2 Inter Component Communication

ICC(Inter Component Communication) is a mechanism to help apps interact with each other. Each app is made up of several components, or logical building blocks. There are 3 types of components that use ICC: *Activity*, *Service*, and *Broadcast Receiver*. They can communicate with each other using *Intent* objects[3]. Intent is a data structure for carrying messages from one component to another.

Developers could set the "exported" attribute of the application components as "true" to accept Intent from other components, or "false" to deny. If the attribute is not set, it's also possible that system marks it as "exported" by default. We focus on the exported components to detect capability leaks.

2.3 Capability Leaks

`Capability Leak`, also known as Permission Re-Delegation [7], occurs when a vulnerable application performs a privileged action on behalf of a malicious application without that permission. For example, a benign application has been authorized with permission P. If one of its exposed component C fails to check the caller's permission, a malicious application may perform unprivileged actions by constructing and sending Intent to component C.

To avoid capability leaks, a component can specify that an Intent sender must have a certain permission by either adding a permission requirement to component's manifest file, or by calling checkPermission API.

However, many developers don't fully understand the potential risks in Android application components. They either expose the components unintentionally, or expose them intentionally but failed to check the component caller's permissions.

3. SYSTEM DESIGN

We aim at detecting capability leaks in Android applications using fuzzing technique. We dynamically generate appropriate Intents and send them to the components to see if any capability leak indeed happens.

Figure 1 depicts IntentFuzzer's architecture. IntentFuzzer Console is a fuzzing control center and responsible for constructing Intents and processing feedbacks from IntentFuzzer Agent. IntentFuzzer Agent is an Android application running in Android system, taking charge of sending real Intents to the application components to be diagnosed. Several modules in Android system are modified in order to generate feedbacks for the Console. With these feedbacks, Console will amend the Intent for deeper execution path of the receiving components, and decide if any potential permission leak has actually happened.

We will discuss the details in the rest of this section.

3.1 Fuzzing Strategy

There are three types of components that can receive Intents: Activities, Services, and Broadcast Receivers. Activities will always provide a screen for users to interact with. So we need to automatically generate correct interaction with the user interface when fuzzing Activities, which is not a well-studied topic[9]. Although malicious applications have some possibilities to perform an escalation attack stealthily, expecting users to make right interaction to trigger harmful action, users may notice such kinds of attacks and close the activity interface to avoid attacks. So, this kind of threat is not very serious.

In terms of Services and Broadcast Receivers, they both run in the background. Permission escalation attack can be performed without any awareness of users. Capability leaks of Services and Broadcast Receivers are principal threats. So we focus on fuzzing Services and Broadcast Receivers.

There are two forms of services: Started service and Bound Service. Started services receive Intents, while Bound Services don't. The exposed interface of Bound Service is defined by a Messenger, or AIDL(Android Interface Definition Language), which is not as simple as Intent delivery. Arguments transferred between callers and callees are not like Intents that have some construction rules to follow, they can be various types and numbers[4]. Our motivation is to heuristically generate Intents to audit Android components for capability leaks. So we further narrow down the fuzzing targets to Started Service and Broadcast Receivers.

Intents can be divided into two groups: explicit Intent and implicit Intent[3]. Explicit Intents designate the target component by its name while implicit Intents do not name a target. Implicit Intents will be resolved to proper component by system according to the Intent filters defined by each component.

There are two possible situations for permission leaks. Components intend to receive all the Intents including implicit Intents, but failed to check caller's permission; Components intend only to receive intra-application Intents which mean explicit Intents, but are exported to the public. So in both situations, vulnerable components will receive explicit Intents. We use explicit intents to do fuzzing.

3.2 Permission Leak Detection

IntentFuzzer Agent is the application that sends Intents. We request no permissions for IntentFuzzer Agent. If a privileged action is triggered by the Agent, a permission leak happens.

Although the permissions of Android applications are authorized during the installation time. Permission checking is enforced during runtime. To detect if any permissions related actions are performed after sending intents, we modified the permission checking module in Android System. The inserted code will inform Console of what permissions are passed in the checking process at runtime. Details of system modification will be clarified in Section 4.

3.3 Intent Construction

On receiving explicit Intents, components will execute from their entries. For Started Services, entry method is onStartCommand(); for Broadcast Receivers, entry method is onReceive(). We don't consider Bound Services as mentioned above.

To detect more permission leaks, we should expand the execution path coverage as much as possible. So it's important to deliver appropriate Intent to the components.

An Intent object contains a bundle of information:

- *Action* is a string naming the action to be performed. There are predefined constants of generic actions. Developers can also define their own action strings for activating their components. Self-defined Action string should include the application package as a prefix to avoid naming conflict.
- *Data* is represented by the URI, which also implies the MIME type.
- *Category* is a string containing additional information about the kind of component that should handle the intent. So Category is just for implicit Intent resolution which we don't construct Intent with.
- *Extras* are key-value pairs for additional information that should be delivered to the component handling the Intent.
- *Flags* are predefined values for instructing the Android System how to launch an Activity. It's not related to Broadcast Receivers and Services. We don't construct Intents with Flags.

How to construct an Intent with Action, Data, and Extras? Details are explained in the subsections as below.

3.3.1 Action Construction

To generate Action of Intents for fuzzing, we consider two aforementioned situations of vulnerable applications separately.

For the components that intend to be exported to receive implicit Intent, they will define *Intent Filters* in their manifest file. Intent Filters are used to inform the system which implicit Intents they can handle. So proper intents attributes can be inferred using Intent Filters. By sending appropriate Intents that meet the Intent resolution rule, components can handle it well and execute into deep path. Each Intent Filter may consists of three types of rules: Action, Category, and Data. An Intent Filter may specify more than one Action, but an Intent object names just a single Action. So we construct Intents with each Action in each Intent Filter. We call the Action inferred from Intent Filter as *explicit Action.*

For the exported components that do not intend to be exported, they will not contain Intent Filters, because these components are developed only for intra-application usage and accept explicit Intents. They may compare the Action in the Intent with some predefined Actions to perform different tasks, which may lead to potential capability leaks if the attacker can specify a correct Action. Below is a code example of a Broadcast Receiver entry method.

```
public void onReceive(Context context, Intent intent) {
    SmsManager smsManager = SmsManager.getDefault();
    String action = "com.example.test.action.SEND_SMS";
    if (action.equals(intent.getAction())) {
            smsManager.sendTextMessage("10086", null, "test",
                null, null); }
}
```

The mistakenly exported Broadcast Receiver above will not specify any Intent Filter in the manifest file, because it's only for self-use. To get our fuzzer deep into the code line of the API sendTextMessage, we must construct the correct Action. We assume that all the Action strings will be defined by const string rather than be generated by runtime code, which is just how the most programers do. Then we use a conservative static method. We first get all the strings from the string pool of dex or odex file of the app[1]. Among such strings, we choose the ones including a prefix of the application package as potential Actions since Google recommends developers to use the package name as a prefix to ensure uniqueness, and we also include the strings that are standard Actions defined by Android(e.g. android.intent.action.DELETE). Thus we get a list of potential appropriate Actions. We call the Action extracted from bytecode as *implicit Action.*

Thus we can generate Intents with both explicit Actions and implicit Actions.

3.3.2 Data Construction

For the occasion of explicit Action, each component will have Intent Filter defined in the manifest file. As Intent Filters may contain rules for Data, we can infer corresponding data type that the component is able to handle. Data rule can be specified by scheme, host, port, and path for each part of the URI scheme://host:port/path. So we prepare common data types as common form of URI before fuzzing. For example, we store pictures of common type in both websites and system content providers, providing possible URIs such as http://example.com/a.jpg and content://media/external/images/media/1. If any URI we prepared fits the rule of Data in the Intent Filter, we construct an Intent with it. If no rule of Data is specified in Intent Filters, we don't construct any Data URI in Intents.

For the occasion of implicit Action, there is no corresponding Intent Filter, so we also don't construct Data URI in Intents.

3.3.3 Extras Construction

Extras are key-value pair information in Intents. Extra keys are strings while values can be any Java primitive type or Class. They are not specified in Intent Filters. Intent recipient may check the Extra data for later use in performing privileged actions. There is a code example of a Service entry point method.

```
public int onStartCommand(Intent intent, int flags, int
      startId) {
    SmsManager smsManager = SmsManager.getDefault();
    String smsContent = intent.getStringExtra("sms");
    if (smsContent != null && smsContent != "") {
       smsManager.sendTextMessage("10086", null, smsContent,
           null, null); }
    ...
}
```

The Android API getStringExtra() will extract the string value mapped by key "sms" from the Intent. If Extra is not included in the Intent, the Service above will not trigger sendTextMessage method, and the permission leak of android.permission.SEND_SMS could not be detected. In this situation, false negative will be produced.

To decrease this kind of false negative, we built a runtime feedback system to construct Extra data with appropriate key and type that components can handle. Console will keep a set of the requested Extra keys and value types. Components that receive Intents must call APIs(e.g. getStringExtra) to get Extra data. We instrumented these APIs and the inserted code will inform Console of what key and value type is requested. Console will add this Extra key and type of value to the list. So in the next round of fuzzing, the detected new Extra data with detected key and type will be randomly generated and feed to the component. By using such a feedback based iteration method of Extras construction, execution can go deeper.

We only construct Extra data of Java primitive types and don't consider types of Java Class, because it's non-trivial to deal with various Classes defined in various libraries or by app developers.

3.4 General Fuzzing Steps

We define the component to be fuzzed as C. IntentFuzzer first checks if there exists any Intent Filter in C. If so, C is exported on purpose and we do fuzzing in steps as follows:

1. For each explicit Action defined in each Intent Filter, do the step 2 to 5;
2. Construct Data only when the Intent Filter contains Data tag;
3. Initialize an empty Extras data set E;
4. Send an Intent with constructed Action, Data, and all the Extras in E;
5. Wait for several seconds. Scan for permission leak logs and getExtra API logs. If new Extra data requests are found, add them to E, and goto step 4; If not, then exit the iteration.

If no Intent Filter is specified for C, IntentFuzzer takes it as a mistaken exported component and do fuzzing in the following steps:

1. Construct implicit Actions, and for each implicit Action, do the steps 2 to 4;
2. Initialize an empty Extras data set E;
3. Send an Intent with constructed Action, and all the Extras in E;
4. Wait for several seconds. Scan for permission leak logs and getExtra API logs. If new Extra data requests are found, add them to E, and goto step 3; If not, then exit the iteration.

We record all the permission leak results and their corresponding Intents that trigger the them for post-analysis.

4. IMPLEMENTATION

To accelerate prototype development, we reused existing excellent open source tools.

4.1 Architecture

We built our prototype IntentFuzzer on top of Drozer[2] - an open source security assessment framework for the Android platform. Drozer prompts users a console to dynamically interact with the ICC endpoints exported on a device. Drozer employs the similar architecture as IntentFuzzer, which consists of an agent installed in Android system and an server-side console on PC. All modules in the server-side console are written in Python.

IntentFuzzer benefits a lot from Drozer's modular design. We implemented our IntentFuzzer Console by inserting a single module in it.

4.2 System Modification

Android's permission system is enforced by both Android system services and Linux kernel[11]. Most permissions are checked by Android system services and finally handled by *checkPermission(String permission, int pid, int uid)* in *ActivityManagerService*. File system and network related permissions are enforced by the GID isolation mechanism in Linux kernel, such as android.permission.INTERNET and android.permission.WRITE_EXTERNAL_STORAGE. Combining manual analysis of Android sources and some tests, such kernel enforced permissions are also passed to ActivityManagerService in Android 4.2, which is not the case in old version of Android[8]. So we only need to instrument the method checkPermission to record what UID of Android application is checked, and what permission is checked. Console can use the UID in the log to look up leaked permissions.

We also modify Extras getting APIs to catch components' requests for extra data. There are a bunch of Extras getting APIs for different data types, such as getStringExtra(String name), getIntExtra(String name, int defaultValue). We outputted type and key of each Extra request. Leveraging logcat logs, IntentFuzzer Console will generate corresponding new Extras in the next round of Intent fuzzing until the iteration ends.

5. EVALUATION

5.1 Experiment Design

To evaluate IntentFuzzer, we use it to detect capability leaks of applications in both Google Play and closed source ROMs. We downloaded 2183 free applications from Google Play, all of which are among top 200 most popular apps in each category in www.appbrain.com. We install them and do fuzzing one by one in our modified Android 4.2.2 Samsung Galaxy Nexus phone. Galaxy Nexus phone is a device supported by Android Open Source Project, which we can build ROM from source and directly flash the device.

In terms of closed source ROMs, it's not easy to migrate all in-rom applications to other environment due to dependency problems. So we choose to directly modify closed source ROMs by rewriting framework bytecode and do fuzzing inside themselves. We selected Xiaomi Hongmi phone and Lenovo K860i phone for our evaluation. Xiaomi Hongmi phone runs Android 4.2.2, and Lenovo K860i runs Android 4.2.1. Both phones use updated system version from their vendors.

After analyzing an application package, a report will be produced recording leaked permissions and Intent attributes that trigger the corresponding permission leak.

5.2 Results

It took 2240 minutes to fuzz all 2183 apps from Google Play, 90 minutes for 104 packages in Xiaomi Hongmi phone, and 95 minutes for 105 packages in Lenovo K860i phone.

From analysis reports, we detected 161 application packages that have at least one permission leak, and found 26

Table 1: **Leaked Permissions in Google Play Applications**

Permissions	Packages	Components
ACCESS_NETWORK_STATE	91	86
READ_PHONE_STATE	42	39
WAKE_LOCK	22	30
INTERNET	11	14
ACCESS_FINE_LOCATION	9	8
ACCESS_WIFI_STATE	8	8
GET_ACCOUNTS	6	9
VIBRATE	4	4
SYSTEM_ALERT_WINDOW	3	5
CHANGE_WIFI_STATE	3	3
ACCESS_COARSE_LOCATION	2	2
GET_PACKAGE_SIZE	2	2
READ_CONTACTS	2	2
READ_SMS	2	2
READ_EXTERNAL_STORAGE	1	1
WRITE_SMS	1	1
WRITE_CALL_LOG	1	1
GET_TASKS	1	4
RESTART_PACKAGES	1	1
CLEAR_APP_CACHE	1	1
BLUETOOTH_ADMIN	1	1

permissions in Xiaomi Hongmi phone and 19 permissions in Lenovo K860i phone are leaked. We organized reports into three tables. In each table, leaked permissions are listed. For each permission, we counted the total numbers of packages and components that have the corresponding permission leakage. We can see results of 2183 Google Play applications in Table 1, results of Xiaomi Hongmi phone in Table 2, and results of Lenovo K860i in Table 3. Permissions' standard package prefix is omitted in the tables.

Except for capability leaks, we also detect the runtime exceptions occurred during fuzzing via default logcat information. There are 11 components from 9 packages in Xiaomi Hongmi phone, 13 components from 12 packages in Lenovo K860i, and 141 components from 123 apps in Google Play crashed during fuzzing. This information may also help developers to diagnose the robustness of their apps.

5.3 Exploitation Analysis and Case Study

Capability leaks don't mean that attackers can do every action authorized by the leaked permission. Exploitation depends on how vulnerable components deal with the Intents.

Both ICC of Broadcast Receivers and Started Services do not return results. So the leaks of permissions that are related to accessing some data are not easy to exploit. Attackers cannot find a channel to receive sensitive data protected by the leaked permission. Maybe attacks should combine other permission leaks, or other vulnerabilities.

For the leaks of permissions that are related to changing some status, they are easy to exploit and often result in great harm, e.g. sending messages, changing system settings. Some detailed exploitation cases are given below.

Clean Master is an app that pre-installed in the Xiaomi Hongmi phone. It can help user to kill all background processes and get memory freed. However, the permission android.permission.RESTART_PACKAGES is leaked and all other apps could invoke the exposed component to kill background processes. The vulnerable component is com.cleanmaster.appwidget.WidgetService. Exploiting method is just starting the service using an Intent with Action com.cleanmaster.appwidget.ACTION_FASTCLEAN. This case is similar to another app called Smart RAM Booster. Sending

Table 2: **Leaked Permissions in Xiaomi Hongmi Phone**

Permissions	Packages	Components
CHANGE_COMPONENT_ENABLED_STATE	9	11
ACCESS_NETWORK_STATE	8	9
READ_PHONE_STATE	8	9
WAKE_LOCK	6	7
INTERNET	5	7
GET_ACCOUNTS	4	5
DEVICE_POWER	3	4
STATUS_BAR	3	4
ACCESS_ALL_DOWNLOADS	2	4
READ_CONTACTS	2	2
READ_DREAM_STATE	1	1
READ_CALENDAR	1	3
UPDATE_DEVICE_STATS	1	1
WRITE_CALENDAR	1	1
RESTART_PACKAGES	1	1
DELETE_PACKAGES	1	1
READ_CALL_LOG	1	1
READ_SMS	1	1
GET_PACKAGE_SIZE	1	1
MODIFY_PHONE_STATE	1	1
INSTALL_PACKAGES	1	2
com.android.email.permission.ACCESS_PROVIDER	1	1
WRITE_SECURE_SETTINGS	1	1
VIBRATE	1	1
ACCESS_WIFI_STATE	1	2
DELETE_CACHE_FILES	1	1

an intent with Action com.anttek.rambooster.action.BOOST to the Service com.anttek.rambooster.service.BoostService will also get background processes killed.

Package com.popularapp.fakecall is an application called Fake Call & SMS, which can help user to fake coming calls and messages. WRITE_SMS and WRITE_CALL_LOG permissions are leaked in receivers com.popularapp.fakecall.incall.MessageAlarm and com.popularapp.fakecall.incall.CallAlarm respectively. Attacker with no permission can reproduce any messages and calls which is preset in this application at any time, by sending Intents with an "id" Extra.

We detected 4 apps that leak android.permission.VIBRATE Permission. Package cn.etouch.ecalendar2 is a calendar application. Sending an Intent with Action ACTION_SUISENT_ECALENDAR_ShowNotice to the receiver cn.etouch.ecalendar.service.NoticesReceiver will vibrate the phone. Package com.azumio.android.sleeptime is an alarm app. If one of its component com.azumio.android.sleeptime.alarm.AlarmReceiver receives an Intent with Action value of com.azumio.android.sleeptime.WAKEUP will make the phone vibrate and beep. Package br.com.gerenciadorfinanceiro.controller is a personal finance manager app. Any empty Intent sending to the component br.com.third.utils.GerarNotificacao will also make the phone vibrate. The last one is the app in Xiaomi Hongmi phone that is similar with Apple Siri, which targets at assisting users via voice recognition. The exposed component is com.miui.voiceassist.SiriReceiver. Broadcasting an Intent to with Action com.miui.voiceassist.alarm and an string Extra, will read out the string and vibrate the phone.

Stk(Sim Toolkit Application) app in both Xiaomi and Lenovo phone leaks MODIFY_PHONE_STATE permission. Attackers without this permission can send an Intent with Action android.intent.action.stk.command to the com.android.stk.StkCmdReceiver component in the package com.andro-

Table 3: Leaked Permissions in Lenovo K860i Phone

Permissions	Packages	Components
ACCESS_NETWORK_STATE	11	11
CHANGE_COMPON-ENT_ENABLED_STATE	8	11
WAKE_LOCK	6	7
READ_PHONE_STATE	5	5
GET_ACCOUNTS	3	4
READ_EXTERNAL_STORAGE	2	2
INTERNET	2	2
READ_CALL_LOG	2	2
READ_DREAM_STATE	1	2
READ_CALENDAR	1	3
DEVICE_POWER	1	1
ACCESS_WIFI_STATE	1	1
ACCESS_ALL_DOWNLOADS	1	1
STATUS_BAR	1	1
BLUETOOTH	1	1
DELETE_PACKAGES	1	1
MODIFY_PHONE_STATE	1	1
BLUETOOTH_ADMIN	1	6
READ_CONTACTS	1	1

id.stk. This intent will kill the current application running on the phone interface. An exploitation case is that attackers can hang up the phone when any call is coming.

6. DISCUSSION

There are some limitations in our work. IntentFuzzer cannot search for capability leaks in Bound Services. IntentFuzzer also cannot handle Broadcast Receivers which are registered at runtime. IntentFuzzer only detects permission leaks when a component performs a privileged operation immediately after receiving a Intent. If a component that receives an Intent internally changes the state of the target app and lead to a capability leak in the future, IntentFuzzer will produce false negative.

We used a heuristic method to construct Intents. To achieve smarter fuzzing and higher path coverage, symbolic execution techniques should be applied to generate correct Intents for each execution path in the future.

7. RELATED WORK

In recent years, much work has been devoted to detecting capability leaks. ComDroid [6] is a tool for developers to analyze their own applications before release. Warnings of security risks in inter-application communication will be raised. Felt et al. [7] created a static path-finding tool to find potential attack path in application components. Woodpecker [10] can detect capability leaks in stock Android smartphones. With consideration of object inheritance and callbacks, Woodpecker has a better accuracy. DroidChecker[5] applies inter-procedural control flow graph analysis and static taint checking to search for capability leaks. All tools above use static method and may contain false positives, and their detection results must be verified manually. To the best of our knowledge, we are the first to apply dynamic fuzzing technique in detecting capability leaks. All the leaks we detected are all real occurrences of permission leaks, without false positives.

8. CONCLUSIONS

We propose a novel fuzzing approach to detect capability leak vulnerabilities of Android applications. We invent a Intent construction strategy to achieve higher execution coverage. With our prototype IntentFuzzer, we analyze more than 2,000 applications in Google Play and find 161 applications with at least one permission leak. We also tested IntentFuzzer in Xiaomi Hongmi phone and Lenovo K860i phone, and find 26 and 19 permission leaks respectively.

Acknowledgements

This work is partially supported by China Core Electronic Devices, High-end Generic Chips and Basic Software Award 2012ZX01039-004, NSFC No.61161140454, The National Key Technology R&D Program under Grant No.2012BAH38B03, and China InformationTechnology Security Evaluation Center under Grant No.CSTC2011AC2143.

9. REFERENCES

[1] Dalvik Executable Format. `http://source.android.com/devices/tech/dalvik/dex-format.html`.

[2] drozer. `https://labs.mwrinfosecurity.com/tools/drozer/`.

[3] Intents and Intent Filters. `http://developer.android.com/guide/components/intents-filters.html`.

[4] Services. `http://developer.android.com/guide/components/services.html`.

[5] P. P. Chan, L. C. Hui, and S. Yiu. Droidchecker: analyzing android applications for capability leak. In *Proceedings of the fifth ACM conference on Security and Privacy in Wireless and Mobile Networks*, pages 125–136. ACM, 2012.

[6] E. Chin, A. P. Felt, K. Greenwood, and D. Wagner. Analyzing inter-application communication in android. In *Proceedings of the 9th international conference on Mobile systems, applications, and services*, pages 239–252. ACM, 2011.

[7] A. P. Felt, H. J. Wang, A. Moshchuk, S. Hanna, and E. Chin. Permission re-delegation: Attacks and defenses. In *Proceedings of the 20th USENIX Security Symposium*, volume 18, pages 19–31, 2011.

[8] C. Gibler, J. Crussell, J. Erickson, and H. Chen. Androidleaks: Automatically detecting potential privacy leaks in android applications on a large scale. In *Trust and Trustworthy Computing*, pages 291–307. Springer, 2012.

[9] P. Gilbert, B.-G. Chun, L. P. Cox, and J. Jung. Vision: automated security validation of mobile apps at app markets. In *Proceedings of the second international workshop on Mobile cloud computing and services*, pages 21–26. ACM, 2011.

[10] M. Grace, Y. Zhou, Z. Wang, and X. Jiang. Systematic detection of capability leaks in stock android smartphones. In *Proceedings of the 19th Annual Symposium on Network and Distributed System Security*, 2012.

[11] Y. Zhang, M. Yang, B. Xu, Z. Yang, G. Gu, P. Ning, X. S. Wang, and B. Zang. Vetting undesirable behaviors in android apps with permission use analysis. In *Proceedings of the 2013 ACM SIGSAC conference on Computer & communications security*, pages 611–622. ACM, 2013.

Remotely Wiping Sensitive Data on Stolen Smartphones

Xingjie Yu[†,‡,♮] Zhan Wang[†,‡,*] Kun Sun[♯]
Wen Tao Zhu[‡,†] Neng Gao[‡,†] Jiwu Jing[†,‡]

† State Key Laboratory of Information Security, Institute of Information Engineering, Chinese Academy of Sciences, CHINA
‡ Data Assurance and Communication Security Research Center, Chinese Academy of Sciences, CHINA
♮ University of Chinese Academy of Sciences, CHINA
♯ Center for Secure Information System, George Mason University, USA
Email: xjyu@is.ac.cn, zwang@is.ac.cn, ksun3@gmu.edu, wtzhu@ieee.org, gaoneng@is.ac.cn, jing@is.ac.cn

ABSTRACT

Smartphones are playing an increasingly important role in personal life and carrying massive private data. Unfortunately, once the smartphones are stolen, all the sensitive information, such as contacts, messages, photos, credit card information and passwords, may fall into the hands of malicious people. In order to protect the private data, remote deletion mechanism is required to allow owners to wipe the sensitive data on the stolen phone remotely. Existing remote deletion techniques rely on the availability of either WiFi for Internet connection or SIM card for cellular network connection; however, these requirements may not be satisfied when the phones are stolen by some sophisticated adversaries. In this paper, we propose a new remote deletion mechanism that allows the phone owner to delete the private data remotely even if the WiFi is disabled and the SIM card is unplugged. The basic idea is to use emergency call mechanisms to establish a communication connection with a service provider to verify the state of the phone and perform remote deletion. We present a case study of our mechanism with the Universal Mobile Telecommunications System (UMTS) network.

Categories and Subject Descriptors

K.6.5 [**Management of Computing and Information Systems**]: Security and Protection

General Terms

Security

*This author is the corresponding author.

ASIA CCS'14, June 4–6, 2014, Kyoto, Japan.

http://dx.doi.org/10.1145/2590296.2590318.

Keywords

Mobile Device Security, Remote Deletion, Emergency Call

1. INTRODUCTION

Smartphones are playing an increasingly important role in our daily life to access personal and corporate email, prepare tax returns, and review customer documents, etc [6]. US military also announced that it will equip soldiers with Android devices for accessing classified documents [10]. Smart phones provide massive non-volatile memory to store private and sensitive data such as SMS (Short Message Service) messages, photos, credit card information and social security numbers, user names and passwords [15]. The popularity of mobile devices raises serious and yet unsolved concerns, particularly with respect to data security on stolen or lost devices. From the mid-1990s many crimes have declined significantly, but the theft of mobile phones has become an increasingly serious problem - 49% New Yorkers have experienced mobile loss/theft [11]. Once a smartphone is lost, its sensitive data may be compromised through directly breaking into the phone system or connecting the phone to a PC as an external USB storage.

A number of smartphone wipe-out mechanisms have been developed to delete the sensitive data from lost smartphones. One solution is to automatically delete the sensitive data after a number of failed authentication attempts [12]. However, it may cause accidental data deletion when the owner forgets the password or someone plays with another's phone. Moreover, an adversary still may access the sensitive data by connecting the smartphone to a PC. Remote wipe-out mechanisms allow owners to remotely delete the sensitive data by sending a wipe-out command to the lost devices through the Internet or SMS. For example, iCloud remote wipe-out system [4] can initiate the deletion of all user data by sending "kill" messages to lost mobile devices through the Internet. All existing solutions have to rely on the Internet or cellular network to send specific commands to the smartphone.

Unfortunately, sophisticated adversaries can defeat all existing remote wipe-out mechanisms by removing the SIM (Subscriber Identity Module) card and turning off the WiFi. Once a smartphone is stolen, since the adversary can physically access the device, he/she can remove the SIM card to disrupt normal communication through cellular network and disable or jam all the WiFi connections to the Internet. Thus, without receiving a wipe-out command, the smartphone has no chances to be remotely wiped out.

In this paper, we develop a remote wipe-out mechanism that allow owners to remotely wipe out a smartphone even if WiFi is unavailable and the SIM card has been unplugged. The basic idea is allow the smartphone use emergency call channel of the cellular network to receive remote commands. When the SIM card is unplugged, no normal calls can be made since the service carrier requires the SIM card for authentication and billing. However, the smartphone still can make emergency calls such as 911 in the US. In our solution, when the smartphone detects the removal of the SIM card, it will initiate a stealthy emergency call to the wipe-out service provider, who will send back a wipe-out command after confirming that the phone has been lost or stolen. The adversary will be blind to the undergoing emergency call. To the best of our knowledge, our solution is the first to enable remote data erasure without relying on the availability of SIM card or the WiFi connection. Our system guarantees that only the real owner can activate the remote wipe-out service through user authentication. Moreover, we can prevent the service provider from accidentally deleting user's data. We choose strong data deletion mechanisms to prevent adversaries from recovering the deleted data after the remote wipe-out process. The whole wipe-out process is unobservable to the adversary.

To demonstrate the feasibility, we provide an example of such a remote wipe-out service in the Universal Mobile Telecommunications System (UMTS) cellular network. Our system only requires a small extension to the current emergency call mechanism, and there is no change on current network structure.

In summary, we make the following contributions:

- We propose a remote wipe-out framework that enables the owner to remotely wipe the data on a smartphone even if the adversary removes the SIM card and disables the WiFi connection.
- We evaluate the feasibility of our design by providing a prototype in the UMTS network.

The next section discusses related work. Section 3 describes the threat model and assumptions. In Section 4, we describe the design of our remote wipe-out mechanism. In Section 5, we take UMTS network environment as a study case. Section 6 discusses the integration of our proposed mechanism with current existing remote data erasure mechanisms. Section 7 concludes this paper.

2. RELATED WORK

To protect sensitive data on stolen smartphones, several anti-theft schemes have been proposed. Tang et al. [14] presented an Android-based scheme called CleanOS, which identifies and tracks sensitive data in RAM and on stable storage, encrypts them with a key, and evicts that key to the cloud when the data is not in active use on the device. However, CleanOS requires network connectivity with the cloud all the time. In addition, Ion et al. [7] found that most users do not trust the cloud provider. As a home-based scheme, Avinash et al. [12] proposed a PIN-based extended security mechanism for iOS devices that can be wiped out automatically after a certain number of attempt failures. Unfortunately, this may cause accidental deletion.

Kuppusamy et al. [9] proposed a model to control a stolen smartphone remotely via SMS. However, it is subject to the removal of the SIM card. Another remote control system, proposed by Joe et al. [8], communicates with remote devices through the Internet. However, none of these solutions can communicate with a smartphone with neither the SIM card nor the WiFi connection.

To improve the privacy and security of lost and stolen smartphones, various anti-theft applications exist and help increase post-theft data control, such as Find My iPhone of iCloud [4], Avast Free Mobile Security [5], Norton Mobile Security [13]. All these apps support remotely wiping the data on an on-line stolen or lost smartphone. However, they all rely on the Internet connection based on the WiFi or the data service from cellular network. Some apps also allow the user to wipe confidential files by sending a special SMS, such as Avast Free Mobile Security [5] and Norton Mobile Security [13]. All SMS-based solutions only work on a smartphone with the SIM card plugged; however, since most devices or data thieves tend to immediately disable the WiFi and remove the SIM card, these solutions cannot guarantee to wipe out the sensitive data remotely.

3. THREAT MODEL AND ASSUMPTIONS

In our threat model, we allow the adversary to remove the SIM card from a stolen smartphone and turn off the WiFi. We assume that the adversary is interested in obtaining its locally stored data, but has not extract the storage chips or transferred the user data before removing the SIM card. We do not consider the sophisticated adversaries who keep a stolen smartphone switched off or position the phone in an electromagnetic shielding environment or keep the battery unplugged all the time. For example, if the attacker performs the attack inside a cage or underground chamber without any signal from the cellular network, our wipe-out mechanism cannot work correctly.

IMSI (International Mobile Subscriber Identity) is used to identify and authenticate a subscriber and is a unique identification associated with all cellular networks. For a GSM (Global System for Mobile Communication) phone, this number is provisioned in the SIM card. The R-UIM (Removable User Identity Module) card used by the CDMA2000 (Code Division Multiple Access 2000) phone is analogous to the SIM card for a GSM phone. In this paper, we use the SIM card to represent all similar components which have the same functionality in different networks.

We perform remote control through emergency call channel. However, not all the cellular networks support using the IMEI (International Mobile Equipment Identity) instead of the IMSI as identification in the emergency call establishment. We assume that the operator accepts the emergency call that uses the IMEI as the identification.

Although the IMEI is usually a unique number to identify mobile phones, sophisticated attackers may be able to tamper with this number. However, this number is still used to uniquely identify a stolen smartphone in most countries. For example, Australia first implemented IMEI blocking across all GSM networks, in 2003 [1]. We assume that the IMEI is unique for a stolen smartphone.

Some smartphones use an internal SIM card instead of a removable SIM card. In addition, some mobile phones have an IMSI written by special software module. For those devices, the adversary cannot remove the SIM card easily, so we can remotely wipe the device through the SMS or the Internet-based solutions as [13, 5, 4] do.

4. WIPE-OUT SYSTEM DESIGN

4.1 Overview

To provide sensitive data protection for a stolen smartphone without the SIM card and the WiFi connection, we put forward a remote wipe-out mechanism, as shown in Figure 1. Our proposed mechanism allows users to remote control their stolen phones through the emergency call channel, which in our opinion is the only communication channel between such a smartphone and the outside.

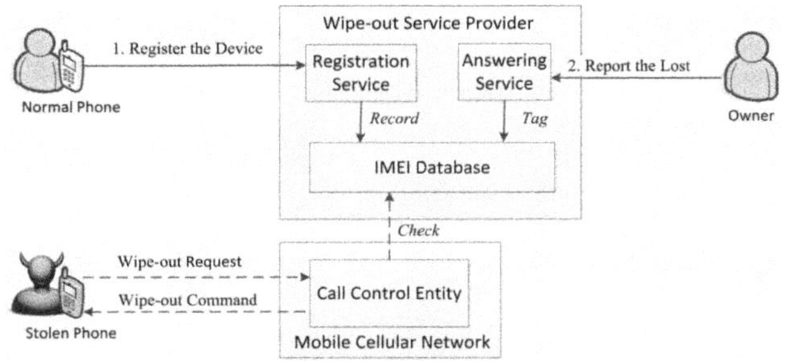

Figure 1: Remote Wipe-out Framework

To remotely wipe sensitive data on a stolen smartphone, the owner interacts with the service provider as follows:

1 The owner subscribes to the remote wipe-out service from the service provider and registers his/her phone before it is stolen. After a successful registration, the service provider records the IMEI number of the phone in the IMEI database and marks its state as normal.

2 The owner reports the loss and asks for erasing the data on the device, as soon as he realizes the lost of the smartphone. After authenticating the user, the service provider tags the associated item of the reported phone as stolen in the IMEI database.

To enable the remote wipe-out service, a backstage application is required to be installed on the phone. Once the SIM card is removed from a smartphone, it may imply that the phone is stolen. In this circumstance, the backstage application starts to ask for data erasure through making a customized emergency call automatically and stealthily. The backstage application will be triggered to make a customized emergency call by either of the following two events: the SIM card is removed from a switched-on smartphone or the smartphone is powered on with the SIM card unplugged. Stealthy operation means that the procedure runs in the backstage: the screen neither lights up nor shows any related information, and any other relevant reminder program could not be activated, for the purpose of preventing the adversary from being conscious of the running procedure.

Once the call control entity of the network receives a wipe-out request from the smartphone, it will check the state of this phone in the IMEI database of the service provider. Here we detail this procedure:

1 The smartphone attaches a deletion indicator to an emergency call, and makes this customized emergency call attempt on the mobile cellular network. The IMEI is used as the equipment identification.

2 The call control entity checks the state of the smartphone in the IMEI database of the service provider, after receiving the request for setting up a customized emergency call.

3 If the smartphone is tagged as stolen in the database, the call control entity sends the wipe-out command to the smartphone. Otherwise, the call control entity responds with a call accepted message which is the same as the access permission for a normal legal emergency call.

The smartphone performs stealthy data erasure after receiving the wipe-out command. If the smartphone receives the call accepted message (case 3), it ends the ongoing emergency call. The customized emergency call can be dialed only once, which consumes little power. But in this case, if the adversary removes the SIM card before the owner realizes and reports the theft, the stolen phone will have no chance to receive the wipe-out command, as the service provider/owner has already missed the only call. To provide higher security, the smartphone can make customized emergency calls periodically until the reception of the wipe-out command. The higher frequency of making such emergency calls, the higher possibility of wiping the data before the adversary peeks at or transfers the user data. However, high frequency results in high power consumption and heavy burden on network as well.

In case there is a normal emergency call dialed on the screen, the backstage application stops making customized emergency call attempts and the ongoing customized emergency call is cancelled instantly. Moreover, the backstage application keeps monitoring the state change of the SIM card. If a SIM card is plugged in after the backstage application has detected the absence of the SIM card, the device stops making the customized emergency call and the data on the device can be remotely wiped out through other current existing mechanisms.

4.2 Device Registration

To remotely wipe sensitive data on a stolen phone without the SIM card and the WiFi connection, a user needs to subscribe to the remote wipe-out service before the smartphone gets lost. The owner registers the service with identification information (e.g., ID card information) that can uniquely identify himself to the service provider and installs our application on the smartphone. The application may be downloaded from a specified web site or obtained through any other way following the specification of the service provider. The identity information can be submitted online or through any other specified way. The service provider records the IMEI number of the registered smartphone and marks its state as normal in the IMEI database.

4.3 Report of Lost Smartphone

If the smartphone is stolen, the owner could request for remotely wiping out the device through a service call or web interface, or even the SMS. The specific way to report the theft is dependent on the specification of the service provider. But the service provider must authenticate the user before recording the report and perform follow-up procedure, in case that the data erasure is initiated by malicious people. So the user needs to provide identity information for authentication. When the user reports the theft and the identity is verified successfully, the service provider updates the record of the stolen device in the IMEI database by tagging its state as stolen.

4.4 Remote Wipe-Out

When the SIM card is removed from a smartphone, any service that uses the IMSI as the subscriber identification cannot be requested by this phone, such as the basic call service and SMS. However, a smartphone without the SIM card still could camp on an available network to make an emergency call, using IMEI as equipment identification. So we use the emergency channel to remotely control a stolen smartphone.

4.4.1 Deletion Indicator

Once the smartphone detects the absence of the SIM card, it asks for data erasure through making a customized emergency call with a deletion indicator attached. It will receive a wipe-out command after the call control entity of the network confirms that the phone has been stolen. The deletion indicator is attached to an emergency call on the premise that the signaling procedure of the customized emergency call is consistent with the normal emergency call originated by a smartphone as defined in standard protocols. So the network carriers can support our mechanism without any change to the current network structure. The deletion indicator is attached based on minimal modification of the implementation of current protocols. For example, the deletion indicator could be attached by using reserved bits in certain data fields to assign customized values.

4.4.2 Phone State Confirmation

Our mechanism guarantees that the data on the phone will be erased only if the device is indeed stolen. If the call control entity receives a request for setting up a customized emergency call, it checks the state of the smartphone by querying the IMEI number and its state in the IMEI database of the service provider.

The usage of the IMEI database is similar to the blacklist of IMEI numbers which is used during the normal call establishment procedures. The blacklist is an IMEI database deployed in the mobile cellular network. This list records the IMEI numbers of the phones reported stolen or whose operation will adversely affect the network. During any procedure of establishing a call, the call control entity could check the IMEI of the phone in the blacklist and determine whether the device needs to be blocked. Similarly, for a customized emergency call, the call control entity checks the IMEI number in the IMEI database of the service provider confirming the state of the phone, and then decides whether the device needs to be wiped out.

4.4.3 Wipe-out Command

If the returned state is stolen in the IMEI database, the call control entity sends a wipe-out command to the device. The wipe-out command could be formatted through assigning a specific value for a special data field of the call reject message defined in the current call control protocol. Upon receiving the wipe-out command, the smartphone initiates the data erasure.

On the other hand, if the state of the phone is normal, the network will send a call accepted message to the smartphone consistent with the access permission for a legal ongoing emergency call originated by a smartphone without the SIM card. This design aims at keeping the consistency with current protocol. The smartphone hangs up the customized emergency call releasing all occupied resources after receiving this message.

4.5 Security Analysis

Since the service provider verifies the reporter's identity when a smartphone is reported stolen, we can prevent a malicious attacker from misusing our system to falsely wipe another user's smartphone. When a user registers the remote wipe-out service, he submits certain identification information that can uniquely identify himself to the service provider. Furthermore, the service provider may enhance the authentication process by challenging the reporter who wants to activate the wipe-out service with certain specific questions, such as providing one phone number with the most frequent communication.

We can also prevent the service provider or the network carrier from accidentally or maliciously wiping out a smartphone. The user specifies the PIN code for further authentication when installing the wipe-out application on his phone. The user only needs to disclose the PIN code to the service provider when he wants to activate the wipe-out service. The service provider should send the PIN code to the call control entity, if the state of the queried IMEI is stolen. The smartphone should verify the PIN code when receiving a wipe-out command from the call control entity. The PIN code will be deleted during the wipe-out procedure. Users should choose different PIN codes for different mobile devices due to the disclosure of one PIN code to the operator when one device is stolen.

Most anti-theft mobile apps provide two options for users to remotely wipe out a mobile device, *factory reset* and *security deletion*. We test five popular data recovery apps to recover the data deleted by resetting. Though those apps cannot recovery all data, they may recover some data in user partitions. Since resetting can be easily defeated by adversaries, we demand secure deletion instead. Our framework is flexible to accommodate various secure deletion solutions. To ensure a completed deletion, secure deletion should not be interrupted by adversaries, except for power off or being out of battery. Even in this case, an unfinished secure deletion procedure will automatically resume at the next boot until all sensitive data are totally wiped out. Since the execution of secure deletion is transparent to the user, the adversary will not be alerted.

5. CASE STUDY

5.1 UMTS Network

UMTS is a third generation mobile cellular system standard. Smartphone is known as MS (Mobile Station) in UMTS. The MSC (Mobile Switching Center) is the primary call control entity in UMTS network, responsible for setting up and releasing the end-to-end connection, handling mobility and hand-over requirements during the call.

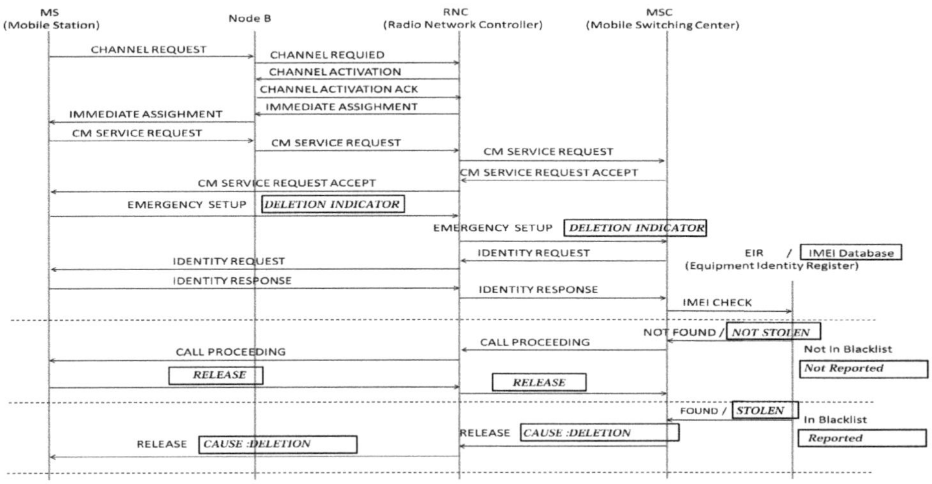

Figure 2: Emergency Call Establishment Procedure in UMTS Network

The core network of UMTS can be accessed through either UTRAN (Universal Terrestrial Radio Access Network) or GERAN (GSM EDGE Radio Access Network). Here we describe the radio access network of UMTS using Radio Network Controllers (RNC) and Node B in UTRAN, which could be substituted by Base Station Control (BSC) and Base Transceiver Station (BTS) in the GERAN.

Equipment Identity Register (EIR) deployed in the UMTS network contains the blacklist of the IMEI numbers associated with banned devices. For a normal call, the MSC could check the IMEI number of the MS in the EIR to decide whether the call needs to be terminated. If the IMEI of the MS is in the blacklist, the MSC will release all active connections for this call.

5.2 Emergency Call

The procedure of establishing an emergency call in UMTS network is shown in Figure 2, and the bordered words indicate our customizations. The "CM service request" message specifies the requested CM (Connection Management) service type as an emergency call and the equipment identification as the IMEI. If the network supports using IMEI as identification, the request will be accepted and the mobile station will send an "emergency setup" message to the MSC asking for the establishment of a call control connection for the emergency call.

5.3 Deletion Indicator

As stipulated in UMTS specification, the information element "emergency category" of the "emergency setup" message indicates the emergency service requested by the MS [3]. Each emergency number stored on the MS is associated with a specific emergency service. The call control entity routes the emergency call to a related emergency center, according to the emergency service category. To customize an emergency call for our remote wipe-out service, we attach a deletion indicator to the "emergency setup" message by assigning a special emergency service category value, indicating the emergency service for data erasure.

The emergency category field is defined in UMTS specification [3], each bit of this field stands for one emergency case, including police, ambulance, fire brigade etc. Specially, bit 8 is reserved and set to 0. Mobile station may set one or more bits to 1 to specify an emergency service category.

8	7 6 5 4 3 2 1
	Service Category IEI
Length of Service Category	
0	Normal Emergency Service Category Value
1	Customized Emergency Service Category Value

Table 1: Emergency Category

To distinguish data erasure from any other emergency service, we set the reserved bit of emergency service category value to 1 as shown in Table 1 and specify this value as "10000000" indicating emergency service for data erasure. This value can be specified to any other value with the bit 8 set to 1.

5.4 Wipe-out Command

For a normal emergency call attempt, the MSC sends a "release" message to the MS with a specific cause value if the IMEI of the MS is in the blacklist. The cause information element in the "release" message is used to indicate the reason for the abortion. We customize a cause "Deletion" through assigning a special cause value.

Upon receipt of the customized "emergency setup" message, the MSC initiates the identification procedure asking for equipment identity, and then it queries the responded IMEI and its state in the IMEI database of the service provider. If the state of the phone is stolen, the MSC sends a "release" message with the cause "Deletion" to the MS as a wipe-out command. We define the cause "Deletion" as 01100111 which is distinguished from all existing cause values, so as to avoid accidental deletion from misunderstanding of a "release" message.

6. DISCUSSION

We design a remote deletion mechanism for smartphones, which will be enabled even though the SIM cards are unplugged and the WiFi is disconnected. However, an adversary may keep the smartphone in different conditions.

Communication Channel	SIM Card Plugged	WiFi Availability
SMS Channel/Internet	√	√
SMS Channel/Internet	√	×
Internet	×	√
Emergency Call Channel	×	×

Table 2: Remote Deletion Mechanism

To provide a full-fledged remote wipe-out mechanism, we suggest implementing several developed remote data erasure methods together with our framework as shown in Table 2. For a stolen smartphone with the original SIM card plugged or replaced by another SIM card, the owner can send a specific wipe-out SMS message to the device. Moreover, if the data service from cellular network or the WiFi connection is available, the owner can remotely wipe out an online device through the Internet. In addition, our proposed mechanism enables remote data erasure on a stolen smartphone when the SIM card is removed and the WiFi connection is not available.

The implementation of our prototype on Android platform is our future work. To support our wipe-out mechanism, we need to make some modifications on current procedure of making an emergency call, involving both the application processor and the modem, so that our remote wipe-out application could make the customized emergency calls and perform the stealthy dialing automatically. Although our mechanism needs the support from cellular network carriers, the carriers only need to make some extensions on their software modules rather than changing their infrastructures. Some carriers in US have already promised that they would support a free and secure anti-theft application for Android devices if and when a manufacturer provides an appropriate solution [2].

7. CONCLUSION

Smartphones are increasingly used for processing and carrying sensitive data, meanwhile become the main targets for thieves, which poses serious security risk on personal data. We propose a novel remote data destruction mechanism for a stolen smartphone when whose SIM card is unplugged and the WiFi is disabled. The network operators can integrate our proposed mechanism to provide remote wipe-put service for the user without any modification on current network structure. Once a smartphone is stolen, its owner can report the theft and ask for wipe-out. If the SIM card is removed by the adversary, the stolen smartphone starts to request user permission for wipe-out through making customized emergency call. We utilize the only communication channel for remote control in such connection constrained environment. We present the remote wipe-out mechanism here to encourage further investigation of implementing remote data deletion on a stolen smartphone.

8. ACKNOWLEDGMENTS

Xingjie Yu, Zhan Wang and Jiwu Jing were partially supported by the National 973 Program of China under Grant 2014CB340603. Wen Tao Zhu and Neng Gao were partially supported by the National 973 Program of China under Grant 2013CB338001. The authors were partially supported by the Strategy Pilot Project of Chinese Academy of Sciences under Grant XDA06010702 and the National Natural Science Foundation of China under Grant 61272479. Dr. Kun Sun's work was supported by U.S. Army Research Office under Grant W911NF-12-1-0060.

9. REFERENCES

[1] AMTA. FAQs on mobile security. `http://www.amta.org.au/pages/amta/FAQs.on.mobile.security`.

[2] Brian X. Chen. New York Asks Cellphone Carriers to Explain Why They Rejected Antitheft Switch. `http://www.nytimes.com/2013/12/11/technology/new-york-asks-cellphone-carriers-to-explain-why-they-rejected-antitheft-switch.html`.

[3] ETSI. TS24.008 Mobile Radio Interface Layer 3 Specification. `www.etsi.org/deliver/etsi_ts/124000_124099/124008/08.06.00_60/ts_124008v080600p.pdf`.

[4] Apple Inc. Find my iPhone, iPad, iPod touch, or Mac. `www.apple.com/support/icloud/find-my-device/`.

[5] AVAST Inc. Avast Free Mobile Security. `http://www.avast.com/en-us/free-mobile-security`.

[6] McAfee Inc. The lost smartphone problem. `http://www.mcafee.com/us/resources/reports/rp-ponemon-lost-smartphone-problem.pdf`.

[7] Iulia Ion, Niharika Sachdeva, Ponnurangam Kumaraguru, and Srdjan Čapkun. Home is safer than the cloud! : privacy concerns for consumer cloud storage. In *Proceedings of the Seventh Symposium on Usable Privacy and Security*, page 13. ACM, 2011.

[8] Inwhee Joe and Yoonsang Lee. Design of remote control system for data protection and backup in mobile devices. In *Interaction Sciences (ICIS), 2011 4th International Conference on*, pages 189–193. IEEE, 2011.

[9] Senthilraja .R G. Aghila Kuppusamy. A model for remote access and protection of smartphones using short message service. *International Journal of Computer Science, Engineering and Information Technology (IJCSEIT), Vol.2, No.1, February 2012.*

[10] M Milian. Military to get secure Android phones. `http://edition.cnn.com/2012/02/03/tech/mobile/government-android-phones/`.

[11] Lookout Mobile Security. Lost and Found: The challenges of finding your lost or stolen phone. `https://blog.lookout.com/blog/2011/07/12/lost-and-found-the-challenges-of-finding-your-lost-or-stolen-phone/`.

[12] Avinash Srinivasan and Jie Wu. SafeCode–Safeguarding Security and Privacy of User Data on Stolen iOS Devices. In *Cyberspace Safety and Security*, pages 11–20. Springer, 2012.

[13] Symantec Inc. Norton Mobile Security. `https://antitheft.norton.com/`.

[14] Yang Tang, Phillip Ames, Sravan Bhamidipati, Ashish Bijlani, Roxana Geambasu, and Nikhil Sarda. CleanOS: Limiting mobile data exposure with idle eviction. In *Proceedings of the USENIX Conference on Operating Systems Design and Implementation, Berkeley, CA, USA*, 2012.

[15] Joe Wilcox. Two stories of smartphones stolen. `http://www.oddlytogether.com/post/485601927/two-stories-of-smartphones-stolen`.

Author Index

www.ingramcontent.com/pod-product-compliance
Ingram Content Group UK Ltd.
Pitfield, Milton Keynes, MK11 3LW, UK
UKHW051416290926
15471UKWH00009B/1631

9 781450 330817